COMPARATIVE EDUCATION

ASHE Reader Series

Edited by
Ken Kempner, University of Oregon
Marcela Mollis, University of Buenos Aires
William G. Tierney, University of Southern California

Bruce Anthony Jones, Series Editor

SIMON & SCHUSTER
CUSTOM PUBLISHING

Cover art: "Color Conscience III," by Christina Lanzl.

Printed in the United States of America

10 9 8 7 6 5 4 3 2 1

Please visit our website at www.sscp.com

ISBN 0–536–01215–6

BA 98123

SIMON & SCHUSTER CUSTOM PUBLISHING
160 Gould Street/Needham Heights, MA 02194
Simon & Schuster Education Group

Copyright Acknowledgments

Grateful acknowledgment is made to the following sources for permission to reprint material copyrighted or controlled by them:

"Patterns in Higher Education Development: Towards the Year 2000," by Philip G. Altbach, reprinted from *Prospects,* Vol. 21, 2, 1991, Unipub Publishers.

"The Political Economy of Education," by Martin Carnoy, reprinted from *International Social Science Journal,* Vol. 37, 1985, UNESCO.

"The Problematic Meaning of 'Comparison' in Comparative Education," by Erwin H. Epstein, reprinted from *Theories and Methods in Comparative Education,* 1988, Lang Communications.

"Comparing Higher Education Systems," by Maurice Kogan, reprinted by permission from *Higher Education,* Vol. 32, 1996. Copyright © 1996 by Kluwer Academic Publishers.

"The Use and Abuse of Comparative Education," by Harold J. Noah, reprinted by permission from *Comparative Education Review,* Vol. 28, No. 4, 1984. Copyright © 1984 by University of Chicago.

"New Perspectives on an Old Problem: The Position of Women Academics in British Higher Education," by Sandra Acker, reprinted by permission from *Higher Education,* Vol. 24, 1992. Copyright © 1992 by Kluwer Academic Publishers.

"The Academic Profession in International Perspective," by Philip G. Altbach and Lionel S. Lewis, reprinted by permission from *The International Academic Profession: Potraits from 14 Countries,* 1996. Copyright © 1996 by the Carnegie Foundation for the Advancement of Teaching.

"The Market Oriented University and the Changing Role of Knowledge," by Howard Buchbinder, reprinted by permission from *Higher Education,* Vol. 26, 1993. Copyright © 1993 by Kluwer Academic Publishers.

"Work," by Burton R. Clark, reprinted by permission from *The Higher Education System: Academic Organization Cross-National Perspective,* 1983. Copyright © 1984 by the Regents of the University of California.

"Places of Inquiry," by Burton R. Clark, reprinted by permission from *Places of Inquiry: Research and Advanced Education in Modern Universities,* 1995, University of California Press. Copyright © 1995 by the Regents of the University of California.

"The University in a Democracy - Democratization of the University," by Jurgen Habermas, reprinted by permission from *Toward a Rational Society*, 1970. Copyright © 1970 by Beacon Press.

"Producing Knowledge in Africa Today: The Second Bashorun M.K.O. Abiola Distinguished Lecture," by Paulin J. Hountondji, reprinted from *African Studies Review*, December, Vol. 38, No. 3, 1995, University of South Carolina.

"Cultural Influences on the Construction of Knowledge in Japanese Higher Education," by Ken Kempner and Misao Makino, reprinted by permission from *Comparative Education*, Vol. 29, No. 2, 1993. Copyright © 1993 by the University of Chicago.

"Culture and the Role of Women in a Latin American University: The Case of the University of Costa Rica," by Susan Twombly, reprinted from *The Social Role of Higher Education: Comparative Perspectives,* 1996, Ken Kempner and W.G. Tierney, eds. Copyright © 1996 by Garland Publishing.

"Universities and Academic Systems in Modern Societies," by Joseph Ben-David and Awraham Zloczower, reprinted by permission from *European Journal of Sociology,* Vol. 3, 1962. Copyright © 1962 by Cambridge University Press. Previously published in the European Journal of Sociology, Vol. 3, 1965.

"The Dilemma of Change in Indian Higher Education," by Philip G. Altbach, reprinted by permission from *Higher Education*, Vol. 26, 1993, Higher Education Research Institute. Copyright © 1993 by Philip G. Altbach and Suma Chitnis.

"Public and Private Sectors in Higher Education: A Comparison of International Patterns," by Roger L. Geiger, reprinted by permission from *Higher Education*, Vol. 17, 1988. Copyright © 1988 by Kluwer Academic Publishers.

"The Decline of Latin American Student Activism," by Daniel C. Levy, reprinted by permission from *Higher Education*, Vol. 22, 1991. Copyright © 1991 by Kluwer Academic Publishers.

"The Paradox of the Autonomy of Argentine Universities: From Liberalism to Regulation," by Marcela Mollis, reprinted by permission from *Latin American Education: Comparative Education*, 1997, eds. Carlos Albertos Torres and Adriana Puiggros. Copyright © 1997 by Westview Press.

"Latin America: Higher Education in a Lost Decade," by Simon Schwartzman, reprinted from *Prospects*, Vol. 21, No. 2, 1991, Unipub Publishers.

"Cultural Politics in a Latin American University: A Case Study of the University of Panama," by William G. Tierney, reprinted from *La Educacion*, Vol. 118, No. 2, 1994, UNESCO.

"Higher Education in Advanced Developing Countries," by Philip G. Altbach, reprinted from *Prospects*, Vol. 12, No. 3, 1982, Unipub Publishers.

"The Policy Perspective," by Ladislav Cerych, reprinted by permission from *Perspectives on Higher Education: Eight Disciplinary and Comparative Views,* 1984, ed. Burton R. Clark, University of California Press. Copyright © 1984 by the Regents of the University of California.

"What is Changing in Mexican Public Universities in the Face of Recent Policy Initiatives for Higher Education," by Rollin Kent, Presented at the 18th Annual Conference of the Association for the Study of Higher Education, 1993.

"Conceptualizing the Role of Education in the Economy," by Peter Easton and Steven Klees, reprinted from *Emergent Issues in Education in Education,* 1995, State University of New York Press.

"Universities and National Development: Issues and Problems in Developing Countries," by Lawrence J. Saha, reprinted from *Prospects,* Vol. 21, No. 2, 1991, Unipub Publishers.

"The Privatization of Higher Education," by Jandhyala B.G. Tilak, reprinted from *Prospects,* Vol. 21, No. 2, 1991, Unipub Publishers.

"The Capitalist State and Public Policy Formation: Framework for a Political Sociology of Educational Policy Making," by Carlos Alberto Torres, reprinted from *British Journal of Sociology of Education,* Vol. 10, 1989 Cambridge University Press.

"Equality of Higher Education in Post-Communist Hungary and Poland: Challenges and Prospects," by Kassie Freeman, reprinted by permission from *Reform and Change in Higher Education: International Perspectives,* 1995, eds. J.E. Mauch and P. Sabloff. Copyright © 1995 by Garland Publishing.

"A Subnational Perspective for Comparative Research: Education and Development in Northeast Brazil and Northeast Thailand," by Gerald Fry and Ken Kempner, reprinted by permission from *Comparative Education,* Vol. 32, No. 3, 1996. Copyright © 1996 by University of Chicago.

"Latin America's Private Universities," by Daniel C. Levy, reprinted by permission from *Comparative Education,* Vol. 29, No. 4, 1985. Copyright © 1985 by University of Chicago.

"Independence and Choice: Western Impacts on Japanese Higher Education," by Shigeru Nakayama, reprinted by permission from *Higher Education,* 1989, Vol. 18. Copyright © 1989 by Kluwer Academic Publishers.

"The Academic Estate in Western Europe," by Guy Neave and Gary Rhoades, reprinted from *The Academic Profession: National, Disciplinary, and Institutional Settings,* 1987, Burton .R. Clark, ed., University of California Press.

"The Crisis in Higher Education in Africa," by Samuel O. Atteh, reprinted from *The Journal of Opinion,* Vol 24, No. 1, 1996.

"Reform at Mexico's National Autonomous University: Hegemony or Bureaucracy," by Imanol Ordorika, reprinted by permission from *Higher Education,* Vol. 31,1996. Copyright © 1996 by Kluwer Academic Publishers.

"Higher Education in Developing Countries: The Scenario of the Future," by George Psacharopoulos, reprinted by permission from *Higher Education,* Vol. 21, 1991. Copyright © 1991 by Kluwer Academic Publishers.

Contents

Acknowledgments

Advisory Board

The editors wish to thank Iain Johnston, University of Oregon, for his assistance in assembling the manuscripts.

Introduction

Rather than merely provide a travelogue that describes higher education in one country or another, the purpose of this Reader is to present works that consider *why* particular national systems operate as they do and the interrelated effects these systems have on one another, on national and global development, and on the production of knowledge. The works included in this Reader address not merely the assessment of inputs and outputs of institutions, but the meaning these inputs and outputs have in relation to the larger cultural context that defines a nation's location in the international knowledge networks.

Constructing this Reader on Comparative Higher Education has not been an easy task because of the diversity that characterizes the field. This diversity and plurality of perspectives, however, provides the meaning of the Reader. Our intention has been to include the hegemonic vision produced by a small group of western intellectuals who dominate the field, as well as disempowered male and female voices who express nondominant theories and methodologies within the core and on the periphery. We have emphasized the cultural perspectives of higher education by editing a selection of articles that represent a diverse vision of theory and methodology in comparative education. For this reason we include readings that engage the paradigmatic debate between modernist and postmodernist perspectives and between structuralist and poststructuralist models. We adhere to Morrow and Torres's (1995) assertion that any attempt at a sense of certainty and analytical precision in a world which is increasingly imprecise and diverse is pretentious and, perhaps, naive.

In the last decade the use of comparison in social sciences has attempted a rather unusual task: to explore the question of comparisons across disciplines using an interdisciplinary perspective and epistemology. This perspective applied to comparative higher education is situated at the crossroad between history and the sociology of education. It also explores a methodological approach which challenges traditional positivist assumptions. Comparison in the discipline of history, for example, has been understood conventionally as satisfying the need to ascertain the differences or similarities of a particular phenomenon. In general, the strategy of comparison is reduced to a method that fulfills two types of goals: to unveil the deficiencies of a given process (i.e., a comparable one), or to understand the similarities of an object of study in terms of a similar one. Hence, the issue of similarities or differences strikes at the heart of the process of comparison. This approach to comparisons, however, excludes the "other" and the possibility of discovering "otherness."

From an interdisciplinary perspective, the method of comparison acquires a new meaning: it is oriented towards the interpretation of differences as well as to the recognition of the "other" (Giddens, 1991, Harvey, 1989; Liebman & Paulston, 1994). Hence the use of comparison refers more to a problem of theory than to one of method (Mollis, 1996; Pereyra, 1994). Rejecting traditional methods of comparative education that homogenize systems, the new perspectives in comparative higher education downplay the normative distinction between value judgments and empirical judgments. These new perspectives attempt greater flexibility in their approach, even employing a more playful notion of science, empirical events, and theoretical analysis. The new emerging perspectives employ more open-ended scientific models which search less for patterns of regularity and universal results. Likewise, newer perspectives seek a greater inclusiveness that attempt to avoid, or at least recognize, the dominance of Western thought and solutions.

In our attempt to be inclusive in the Reader we adhere to Kelly and Altbach's (1986) suggestion that comparative education must be guided by a larger, more integrative understanding or "world systems analysis." Such an analysis enables a greater recognition of the dependent relationships among nations in economics, politics, and education in the creation and exchange of knowledge. To enable this recognition our intent for the Reader was to address the broader conceptions of thought in the postmodern age of higher education and development. In particular with the Advisory Board members (listed in the front of the Reader) we sought to highlight, as much as possible, works from developing countries, cross-national studies, and multicultural and cross-cultural scholarship in an attempt to be culturally comparative, political, and critical, not merely international.

This text is an attempt to engage readers in a debate about modernity and postmodernity by sampling the field and presenting what the Advisory Board and ourselves believe captures the spirit of comparative education. Therefore, this reader is not an archival text saved for future generations about how one defines comparative higher education at the end of the 20th century but, rather, a compendium of what the Advisory Board and ourselves view as representative of the existing literature. Herein, we offer our disclaimer that we too have been held captive by existing literature. We have not found the depth and breadth of culturally comparative studies that we hoped. We have not found an abundance of disempowered voices of scholars on the periphery and in the core who have previously been published in the field.

To mediate the existing dominance of the core in comparative education we sought an Advisory Board composed of a cross-selection of scholars who represented geographic, racial, gender, sexual preference, and ideological differences in how they view comparative education. As the editors, we selectively chose scholars who represented and challenged traditional modernist assumptions and development theories of the role higher education plays in the national, regional, and global marketplace. Our perspective is that the flow of knowledge and culture is not only from the developed to the developing nations. Not to accept this assumption denies the agency of other cultures and enables only "first world" solutions to "third world" problems; thus we selected Advisory Board members who represented a cross-cultural perspective of comparative educational scholars who would seek out manuscripts that engage the debate over the political economy of higher education.

How the political economy affects higher education policy is among the critical issues argued in the Reader, especially how economic globalization affects higher education in developing countries. Foremost in this discussion is the identification of the contested effects of neo-liberal economic policies of international agencies, such as the World Bank, as well as the redefinition of the historical relationships between the State and public universities—as is the case in Europe. In the context of current higher education policies in developing countries in particular, there are some relevant commonalties in shaping reforms argued throughout the Reader. The core issues include:

1. the shift from the "Benefactor State" of the 1970s to the "Evaluating State" of the 1990's according to the neo-liberal precept of a minimum state with a maximum market in a context of structural adjustment and a regulatory framework;

2. the reduction of public subsidy for higher education jointly with institutional expansion (in the private sector mainly)

3. renewed demands for public accountability and the associated influence on accreditation systems.

Within this debate many of the European and Latin American authors included in the Reader observe that central evaluation practices have resulted in an increase in the influence of government, a paradox at a time when the ideas of decentralization and financial autonomy of universities have become fashionable (Neave and Van Vught 1995; Mollis, 1997). This paradox is produced by new economic conditions of developing countries in a globalized world market, which lead to a severe retrenchment of the public sphere's traditional entrepreneurial functions and to smaller state apparatus. The capacity of civilian elites to impose restrictions on organized labor strengthened the public and governmental authority significantly. Though many different reasons are given to support the "Modernizing Agenda for Higher Education in Latin America and Africa" (Psacharopoulos, 1991; Schwartzman, 1991,1993), there are a few which are currently cited as justifications for change:

- the scarcity of financial resources to invest in high levels of education for the general population;
- the increase in demand for higher education associated with "open access" strategies of many Latin American universities
- the signs of declining quality within higher education systems; and
- challenges in the regions for transition to technologically-based globalized market economies, requiring an improvement in the quality of national production and human resources.

In our attempt to engage the international debate over these issues of modernization for higher education policy and to include the perspectives of those participating in this debate, we asked our Advisory Board members first to nominate existing works they believed best represented the cultural perspective of the Reader within several general categories. From this initial list we then asked the Advisory Board to vote for the articles and chapters they believed exemplified the best examples of comparative work from a cross-cultural perspective. After several rounds of voting the list was pared down to the articles appearing in this Reader.

Three distinct issues emerged in the preparation of this reader for us. The first was our discomfort at not finding as many readings as we hoped that focused specifically on culture. We found more holes than we expected in the literature. These holes created a greater disjuncture in the readings than we had expected, but the missing literature should give scholars many ideas for future work.

Second, the majority of the readings are single-country studies, not really comparative at all. As Epstein (1988) explains in the following Introduction section, the comparison of Comparative Education is problematic for the field in general. Not surprisingly, this Reader mirrors the difficulty in conducting truly comparative studies. As with the literature in general, it is too often the task of the individual reader to compare country to country, article by article to draw the comparative meaning from the research. We were not able to select a significant number of cross-cultural, cross-country studies because such truly comparative work is not readily found in the literature, for reasons Epstein, among others in the Reader, explains.

Third, we were somewhat surprised at the contested nature of some of the readings. Selecting the final readings among our Advisory Board members was, at times, an argumentative process. The contested nature over some of the choices for the readings yielded an interesting scholarly debate among several of the Advisory Board members. Some of the Advisory Board members protested the selection of certain articles because history has shown the premise or actual facts of the article to be false. For example, the article by Psacharopoulos (1991), "Higher Education in Developing Countries," was criticized by several Advisory Board members who are from developing countries. Among their criticisms included concerns over the effect of the US-Russian cold war on higher education in periphery countries. In particular, the "Sputnik effect" was seen as inappropriately applied as a consequence for the expansion of higher education in these Board member's developing countries. Similarly, the premise that civil servants were preferably educated "locally" was seen as incorrect in those developing countries that invested heavily in sending individuals to be educated in prestigious universities of the core countries. Levy's article (1991) on the decline of student activism in Latin America, for example, was criticized by several Advisory Board members as not representative of the spectrum of issues affecting many Latin American countries, notably

Mexico. While these Board members took issue with the analysis, the article does capture Levy's perspective in 1991 that is countered by newer interpretations and reassessment of historical events in the 1980s.

Certainly, contemporary research loses its currency in the face of new historical circumstances and reassessments of past events. In general, the articles should not be assumed to be historical fact, but, instead, should be read as studies of comparative education, some contested, some now historically wrong, some controversial, but all culturally-biased works presenting an author's theoretical and intellectual perspective at a particular moment in time. Unfortunately, because the cultural perspective of every author is not always evident, it is then incumbent upon each reader to understand and identify, if possible, the conceptual and cultural bias that guides each author's work, interpretation, and meaning.

Although certain articles were contested by some of the Advisory Board members, we chose, as the editors, to keep those articles that a majority of the Advisory Board selected to be representative of the field of comparative education. These articles present the contested nature of comparative work. If not their veracity, the perspective and substance of all these articles has shown to make a valuable contribution to our understanding of comparative higher education.

We have organized the Reader into five sections: Introduction, Faculty Work and The Production of Knowledge, Organizational Contexts, The State, and The Social Context of Higher Education. The construction of these sections is by no means sacred, but provided for us a purposefully broad organizational scheme to group articles along basic dimensions of comparative education. For example, most of the pieces included in the sections titled "The State," "Social Context of Higher Education," and "Organizational Context," might be included under the more encompassing subject of "Political Economy of Higher Education," given the core issues focused on in the articles. Understanding, however, that many of the articles could be placed in one or more categories, our point is that residence in a particular category does not situate or isolate a work, its ideas, or author into one dimensional way of addressing comparative education. To understand the effect a country's social, cultural, economic, and political systems have on higher education necessitates a complex way of understanding such effects. We do not propose that these five organizational sections offer the definitive way to capture such complexity. We do, however, find these five sections enabled us to incorporate the range of dimensions affecting the participants, agencies, and contexts of higher education.

Introduction. This section of the Reader presents selections that offer a basic overview of "being comparative" and the methods used to understand and compare higher education across borders and boundaries. The articles presented in this introductory section help clarify the perspective that the problems and controversies of comparative work are not merely methodological arguments over the primacy of instrumental positivism. For example, Epstein's article explores the inherent theoretical problems with the concept of "comparison," whereas Noah enjoins the debate over uses and abuses of comparative education. Whether or not one finds Psacharopoulos's future scenarios for higher education to be problematic, the value of his article is the comparative approach he has taken to develop such a scenario and the model it affords other researchers to also peer into the future.

Faculty Work and the Production of Knowledge. The role the faculty plays as autonomous or dependent intellectuals in the production of knowledge and intellectual property, their work as academics, their contribution to social and technological development, and their place in the administration of institutions serves as the focus for this section. The differing quality, prestige, autonomy, remuneration, and overall role faculty play as teachers, researchers, social and political leaders is introduced and explored in this section. The function of faculty work in relation to students and administration and as members of the local, national, and global academy is considered by Clark, for example. Cultural differences across international boundaries are addressed by Kempner and Makino in their consideration of Japan and Hountondji provides an assessment of producing knowledge in Africa. Other considerations of the faculty task of producing knowledge in this section include Altbach and Lewis's broad overview of the academic professions and Acker's perspective on the "old problem" of women in the academy.

Organizational Contexts. This section addresses higher education organizations by considering, among other issues, institutional culture and the role the organization plays in intellectual, aesthetic, and scientific development currently and in the future. In this cultural analysis of higher education the authors highlight issues at the organizational level of quality, change, leadership, development, and internal reform, as presented in the articles by Tierney, Mollis, and Schwartzman. How institutions operate and manage their development within the larger state, nation, and global context is addressed in several of the articles, including Ben-David and Zlockzower. The role students play within these organizations, their access to governance and their role in the organization's development is considered as well by Levy and other authors in this section.

The State. The effect the state has on institutional autonomy and the role higher education plays within national development serves as the focus for this section. In general, the social contract between the state and higher education is considered in this section and the regulatory framework used to administer this contract. Torres's article, in particular, considers the effect of the capitalist state on educational policy. Issues of control, privatization, financing, technological change, political influences, role of international agencies, regional cooperation, and reform are all considerations throughout the articles in this section. The role the state plays in centralizing or decentralizing higher education for purposes of student access, equity, social and financial investment, and market orientation are further examples of the issues addressed by the authors. Saha, for example, considers these issues as they affect directly higher education in developing countries. How the state determines its support of students and the policies for tuition, scholarship, and overall access are also among the issues addressed in this section as well.

Social Context of Higher Education. How the political economy and the social and cultural context affect higher education provides the focus for this final section. The articles in this section explore at the local, state, regional, and global level the contextual effects on individual institutions, as well as on national systems. The differential effects of developed and developing national systems, capitalistic and socialistic, are explored along with region-specific issues, such as those affecting Latin America, as presented by Levy, Schwartzman, and Ordorika. The perspectives of this section are decidedly cultural by addressing how comparative differences in ideology affect higher education systems, students, faculty, and administration, as considered by Singh and Nakayama. The articles in this section pay particular attention to the global marketplace of ideas, the politics of technology and the international exchange of knowledge.

As discussed above, each section in the Reader is not discrete but is relational to other sections. Because, as noted, most articles fit in more than one section, the consideration should not be where any particular article fits but, rather, how it relates comparatively to the other articles. Furthermore, because most selections are not comparative in themselves, each reader bears the responsibility for drawing comparisons among the works. The meaning of any particular work is made from its comparative position theoretically, geographically, culturally, and economically with the works included here and the larger field in general. Likewise, the works presented in this Reader are not the definitive explanation of any particular country or issue.

Rather, this Reader is but an introduction to the vast field of comparative higher education and the issues that affect the role higher education plays in any country's cultural and economic development. Because the field of comparative education is constantly changing and evolving this Reader attains its value not only from cross-country and cross-cultural comparisons but from comparisons across time boundaries as well. This reader takes its place and value as a contribution to the evolving nature of higher education as we perceive it today and as we theorize its future.

KK, MM, WGT

References

Epstein, Erwin H. 1988. The Problematic Meaning of "Comparison" In J. Schriewer and B. Holmes, eds. *Theories and Methods in Comparative Education.* New York: Lang.

Giddens, Anthony. 1991. *Modernity and Self-Identity: Self and Society in the Late Modern Age.* Stanford: Stanford University Press.

Harvey, David. 1990. *The Condition of Postmodernity.* Cambridge, Ma. & Oxford, UK: Blackwell.

Kelly Gail, and Philip Altbach 1986. "Comparative Education: Challenge and Response," In P. Altbach and G. Kelly, Eds., *New Approaches to Comparative Education.* Chicago: University of Chicago.

Liebman M. and R. Paulston. 1994. "Social Cartography: A New Methodology for Comparative Studies," *Compare,* 24, 3:233–245.

Mollis, Marcela. 1996. "El uso de la comparación en la Historia de la Educación," in Ruben Cucuzza, ed., *Historia de la Educacion en Debate,* Buenos Aires: Mino y Dávila Editores, Instituto de Investigaciones en Ciencias de la Educacion de la Universidad de Buenos Aires.

Mollis, Marcela 1997. The Paradox of the Autonomy of Argentina's Universities: from Liberalism to Regulation. In Carlos Alberto Torres and Adriana Puiggros, eds., *Latin American education: Comparative perspectives.* Boulder: Westview.

Morrow, R. and Carlos A. Torres 1995. *Social Theory and Education: A Critique of Theories of Social and Cultural Reproduction.* Albany: SUNY Press.

Neave, Guy & Frans Van Vught. 1994. *Prometeo Encadenado.* Barcelona: Gedisa.

Pereyra, Miguel. 1990 "La comparación, una empresa razonada de analisis. Por otros usos de la comparacion," In Revista de Educación, Numero Extraordinario, Madrid: Ministerio de Educacion y Ciencia.

Psacharopoulos, G. 1991. Higher education in developing countries: The scenario for the future, *Higher Education* 21, 3–10.

Schwartzman, Simon 1991. Latin America: Higher education in a lost decade. *Prospects* 21 (2) 463–473.

Schwartzman, Simon. 1993. Policies for higher education in Latin America: The context. *Higher Education* 25, 9–20.

PART I

INTRODUCTION

Patterns in Higher Education Development: Towards the Year 2000*

PHILIP G. ALTBACH

Universities are singular institutions. They have common historical roots yet are deeply embedded in their societies. Traditionally élite institutions, modern universities have provided social mobility to previously disenfranchised groups. Established in the medieval period to transmit established knowledge and provide training for a few key professions, universities over the centuries have become the most important creators of new knowledge through basic research.[1] The contemporary university stands at the centre of its society, an institution which is crucial to every modern society. It is the most important institution in the complex process of knowledge creation and distribution, not only serving as home to most basic science but also to the increasingly complex system of journals, books and data bases which communicate knowledge worldwide.[2]

Universities are the key to providing training in an ever-increasing number of specializations that are important for modern societies. Universities have also taken on a political function in society—they often serve as centres of political thought, and sometimes of action, and they train those who become members of the political elite. This article is concerned with discussing the patterns of higher-education development evident in the post-Second World War period throughout the world and in analysing some of the reasons for these trends and will point to likely directions for universities in the coming decades. Questions such as autonomy and accountability, the role of research and teaching, reform and the curriculum and the implications of the massive expansion that has characterized universities in most countries are of primary concern here. Universities are simultaneously international institutions, with common historical roots, and are also embedded in national cultures and circumstances. It is worth while to examine the contemporary challenges to higher education in both a historical and comparative perspective.

A Common Heritage

There is only one common academic model worldwide. The basic European university model, which was established first in France in the thirteenth century, has been significantly modified but remains the universal pattern of higher education. The Paris model placed the professor at the centre of the institution and enshrined autonomy as an important part of the academic ethos. It is significant that the major competing idea of the period, the student-dominated University of Bologna in Italy, did not gain a major foothold in Europe, although it had some impact in Spain and later in Latin America.[3] The university rapidly expanded to other parts of Europe—Oxford and Cambridge in England, Salamanca in Spain, Prague and Krakow in the Slavic areas and a variety of institutions in Germany were established in the following century.

Much later, European imperialist nations brought universities to their colonies. The British, for example, exported academic models first to the American colonies and later to India, Africa and South-East Asia;[4] the French in Viet Nam and West Africa; the Spanish and Portuguese throughout Latin America; the Dutch in Indonesia. Other colonial powers also

*The author is indebted to Robert Arnove, Gail P. Kelly and Lionel Lewis for their comments on this article and to Lalita Subramanyan for her assistance with editing.

exported academic institutions. Colonial universities were patterned directly on institutions in the mother country, but often without the traditions of autonomy and academic freedom that the latter enjoyed.[5]

The university was by no means a static institution. It changed and adapted to new circumstances. With the rise of nationalism and the Protestant Reformation in Europe, the universal language of higher education, Latin, was replaced by national languages. Academic institutions became less international and more local in their student bodies and orientations. Universities were significantly affected by their national circumstances. Protestant Amsterdam differed from Catholic Salamanca. Fledgling Harvard, although patterned on British models slowly developed its own traditions and orientations. Academic institutions have had their ups and downs. Oxford and Cambridge, strongly linked to the Church of England and the aristocracy, played only a minor role in the development of the Industrial Revolution and the tremendous scientific expansion of the late eighteenth and nineteenth centuries.[6] In France, universities were abolished after the Revolution in 1793. They were gradually reestablished and the Napoleonic model became a powerful force not only in France but also in Latin America.[7] German universities were severely damaged during the Nazi period by the destruction of autonomy and the departure of many of their professors, permanently losing their scientific pre-eminence.[8]

For our purposes, two more recent modifications of the Western academic model are relevant. In the mid-nineteenth century, a newly united Germany harnessed the university for nation-building. Under the leadership of Wilhelm von Humboldt, German higher education was given significant resources by the state, took on the responsibility for research aimed at national development and industrialization, and played a key role in defining the ideology of the new German nation.[9] The reformed German universities also established graduate education and the doctoral degree as a major focus of the institution. Research became for the first time an integral function of the university. The university was reorganized as a hierarchy based on the newly emerging scientific disciplines. American reformers took these German innovations and transformed higher education even more by further stressing the links between the university and society through the concept of service and direct relationships with industry and agriculture, democratized the German chair system[10] through the establishment of academic departments and the development of the 'land grant' concept for both high-level research and expanded access to higher education.[11] Institutions which seem deeply embedded in the national soil have in fact been significantly influenced by international ideas and models.

The world's universities follow institutional patterns which are basically derivative of these Western models. There are virtually no exceptions. The one remaining fully non-Western institution, the Al-Azhar University in Cairo, focuses mainly on traditional Islamic law and theology. Significantly, its science faculties are now organized along European lines.[12] There are many variations, including post-secondary polytechnic institutions in the United Kingdom, the Soviet Union and other countries, Open Universities in the United Kingdom, Israel, Thailand and elsewhere and even the two-year community colleges in the United States and similar institutions, often following the American model, in other countries.[13] While the functions of these institutions may differ from those of traditional universities, their basic organization, patterns of governance and ethos remain remarkably linked to the basic Western academic ideal.

Networks of Knowledge and Higher Education

There are many explanations for the domination of the Western academic model and the lack of alternatives in the modern world. The fact that the Western university institutionalized the study of science and later its production is a key factor. The link between universities and the dominant world economic systems no doubt is a particularly important reason for Western domination. For significant parts of the world, academic institutions were imposed by colonizers. There were few possibilities to develop independent alternatives. In many cases, traditional indigenous institutional forms were destroyed by the colonizers, as in India when in the nineteenth century the

British imposed European patterns and no longer recognized existing traditional institutions.[14]

It is significant that none of the formerly colonized nations have shifted from their basically European academic models. The contemporary Indian university resembles its pre-Independence predecessor. Japan, never colonized, recognized after 1868 that it had to develop scientific and industrial capacity and jettisoned its traditional academic institutions in favour of Western university ideas. It imported ideas and models from Germany, the United States and other countries in the development of its universities.[15] Other non-colonized nations, such as China and Thailand, also imported Western models and adapted them to local needs and conditions.[16]

Western universities were seen to be successful in providing advanced education, in fostering research and scientific development and in assisting their societies in the increasingly complex task of development. Universities in both the United States and Germany were active in fostering industrial and agricultural development in the nineteenth century. The harnessing of higher education to the broader needs of national economic and social development was perhaps the most important innovation of the nineteenth century. The idea that higher education should be generously supported from public funds, that the university should participate in the creation as well as the transmission of knowledge and that academic institutions should at the same time be permitted a significant degree of autonomy was behind much of the growth of universities in this century.

Further, Western universities were at the centre of a knowledge network that includes research institutions, the means of knowledge dissemination such as journals and scientific publishers, and an 'invisible college' of scientists. It is worth noting that the bulk of the world's scientific literature now appears in the English language. Even scholars in such industrialized nations as Sweden and the Netherlands often find it necessary to communicate their research findings in English. The large Dutch multinational publishers, Elsevier and Kluwer, publish virtually all of their scholarly and scientific books and journals in English.

The circulation of scholars and students worldwide, and in a sense even the 'brain drain' is an element of the international knowledge system, helping to circulate ideas and also maintaining the impact of the major 'host' countries and their research hegemony. There are more than one million students studying outside their home countries. The large majority of these students are from Third World nations and they are studying in the industrialized nations, with the United States, the United Kingdom, Germany and the Soviet Union among the major 'host' countries.[17] They gain expertise in their studies, but they also learn the norms and values of the academic system in which they are located, often returning home with a zeal to reform their universities in a Western direction. Frequently, foreign graduates have difficulty readjusting to their home countries, in part because the advanced training they learned abroad may not be easily assimilated into less well-developed economies. Such frustrations, along with the blandishments of significantly better remuneration, leads to the brain drain. However, in the contemporary world, the brain drain is often not permanent. For one thing, members of the Third World scientific diaspora often maintain contact with their colleagues at home, contributing advanced knowledge and ideas. They frequently return home for periods of time and work with local academics. And in an increasing number of instances, they return home permanently when academic—and sometimes political—conditions are favourable. They bring with them considerable expertise and often assume leadership positions in the local scientific and academic communities. Without question, the massive circulation of highly educated personnel has a great influence on the transfer of knowledge. With few exceptions, the knowledge and institutional patterns that are transferred are from the major industrialized nations to the Third World—or even to other more peripheral industrial countries—with very little traffic in the other direction.[18]

The knowledge network is complex and multifaceted, and there is evidence that while its centres remain extraordinarily powerful, there is a movement towards greater equalization of research production and use. Japan, for example, already has a powerful and increasingly research-oriented university system and some of the newly industrialized countries of East and South-East Asia are building up research capacity in their universities.[19] While hegemony may be slowly dissipating, inequality will remain endemic to the world knowledge system.

Expansion: Hallmark of the Post-War Era

Post-secondary education has dramatically expanded since the Second World War. Expansion has taken place in virtually every country in the world to differing extents. The growth of post-secondary education has in fact been, in proportional terms, more dramatic than that of primary and secondary education. Writing in 1975, Trow spoke of the transition from élite to mass and then to universal higher education in the context of the industrialized nations.[20] While the United States enrolled some 30 per cent of the relevant age cohort in higher education in the immediate post-war period, European nations generally maintained an elite higher education system with fewer than 5 per cent attending post-secondary institutions. By the 1960s, many European nations educated 15 per cent or more of the age-group: Sweden, for example, enrolled 24 per cent in 1970, and France 17 per cent. At the same time, the United States increased its proportion to around 50 per cent, approaching universal access.

In the Third World, expansion was even more dramatic. Building on tiny and extraordinarily élitist universities, Third World higher education expanded rapidly in the immediate post-independence period. In India, enrollments grew from approximately 100,000 at the time of Independence in 1947 to over 3.5 million in 1986. Expansion in Africa has also been dramatic, with the post-secondary student population growing from 21,000 in 1960 to 437,000 in 1983.[21] Recent economic difficulties in much of sub-Saharan Africa have meant that per-student expenditure has dropped significantly, contributing to a marked deterioration in academic standards.

Similar trends can be seen elsewhere in the Third World. In a few instances, such as the Philippines, where more than one-third of the age cohort enters post-secondary education, Third World enrollment ratios have reached the levels of many of the industrialized nations, although in general the Third World lags far behind in terms of proportions of the population attending higher education institutions. For example, despite China's student population of more than 2 million, only about 1 per cent of the age cohort attends post-secondary institutions—about 4 per cent of those graduating high school. Expansion in the Third World has, in general, exceeded that in the industrialized nations, at least in proportional terms, although there are significant variations among Third World nations—some countries maintain small and relatively élitist university systems while others have expanded more rapidly.

Regardless of political system, level of economic development, or educational ideology, the expansion of higher education has been the most important single post-war trend worldwide: about 7 per cent of the relevant age cohort (20 to 24 years) attend post-secondary educational institutions—a statistic that has shown an increase each decade since the Second World War. Higher education expanded dramatically first in the United States, then in Europe; currently the main focus of expansion is in the Third World. There are, of course, significant variations in enrollment statistics and ratios. Women, in general attend university less frequently than men although they now constitute approximately 40 per cent of enrollments—with considerable variations by country. The industrialized nations with a few exceptions, have a higher proportion of the age cohort in post-secondary education than Third World countries. Generalized statistics concerning enrollments in post-secondary education mask many key differences. For example, many industrialized nations have a higher proportion of students in technological and scientific fields than in the traditional liberal arts, which tend to predominate in the non-socialist developing nations.

There are many reasons for the expansion of higher education. A key factor has been the increasing complexity of modern societies and economies, which have demanded more highly trained personnel. Post-secondary institutions have, almost without exception, been called on to provide the needed training. Indeed, training in many fields that had once been imparted 'on the job' have become formalized in institutions of higher education. Entirely new fields, such as computer science, have come into existence and rely on universities as a key source of research and training. Nations now developing scientific and industrial capacity, such as the Republic of Korea and Taiwan, have depended on academic institutions to provide high-level training as well as research expertise to a greater extent than was the case during the first Industrial Revolution in Europe.[22]

Not only do academic institutions provide training, they also test and provide certification for many roles and occupations in contemporary society. These roles have been central to universities from their origins in the medieval period but have been vastly expanded in recent years. A university degree is a prerequisite for an increasing number of occupations in most societies. Indeed, it is fair to say that academic certification is necessary for most positions of power, authority and prestige in modern societies. This places immense power in the hands of universities. Tests to gain admission to higher education are key *rites de passage* in many societies and are major determinants of future success.[23] Competition within academe varies from country to country, but in most cases there is also much stress on high academic performance and tests in the universities. There are often further examinations to permit entry into specific professions.

The role of the university as an examining body has grown for a number of reasons. As expansion has taken place, it has been necessary to provide increasingly competitive sorting mechanisms to control access to high-prestige occupations. The universities are also seen as meritocratic institutions which can be trusted to provide fair and impartial tests that will honestly measure accomplishment and therefore access. When such mechanisms break down, as in China during the Cultural Revolution, or where they are perceived to be subject to corrupt influences, as in India, the universities are significantly weakened. The older, more informal and often more ascriptive means of controlling access to prestigious occupations, are no longer able to provide the controls needed nor are they perceived as fair. Entirely new fields have developed where no sorting mechanisms existed and academic institutions have frequently been called upon not only to provide training but also examination and certification.

Expansion has also occurred because growing segments of the population of modern societies have demanded it. The middle classes, seeing that academic qualifications were increasingly necessary for success, demanded access to higher education. Governments generally responded by providing access.[24] When governments did not move quickly enough, private initiative frequently established academic institutions in order to meet the demand. In countries like India, the Philippines and Bangladesh, a majority of the students are educated in private colleges and universities.[25] At present, there are worldwide trends towards imposing user fees, increasing the stress on private higher education, and raising tuition fees in public institutions. These changes are intended to reduce the cost of post-secondary education for governments while maintaining access, although the long-term implications for quality, access and control of higher education are unclear.

In most societies, higher education is heavily subsidized by the government and most, if not all, academic institutions are in the public sector. While there is a growing trend towards private initiative and management sharing responsibility with public institutions, there is little doubt that the government will continue to be the main source of funding for post-secondary education.[26] The dramatic expansion of academic institutions in the post-war period has proved very expensive for governments worldwide.[27] None the less, the demand for access has proved to be an extraordinarily powerful one.[28]

There have been significant variations in higher education expansion. For example, many analysts writing in the 1960s assumed that the world, and particularly the Western industrialized nations, would move from élite to mass and finally to universal access to higher education, generally following the American pattern.[29] This has not occurred. In much of Western Europe, the expansion that characterized the 1960s slowed and in some countries came to a complete halt, although there are now signs of renewed expansion. The causes for this situation were in part economic, with a slowdown of the Western economies following the 'oil shocks' of the 1970s; in part the causes were demographic, resulting from a significant drop in the birth rate and a smaller cohort of young people; and in part philosophical, as countries were less sympathetic to further growth of public institutions, including universities.

Generally, the proportion of the age cohort going on to higher education in Western Europe stabilized at under 20 per cent.[30] With the exception of the Soviet Union, most Eastern European countries also enroll under 20 per cent of the relevant age-group in higher education, thus maintaining relatively élitist academic systems. Similar trends are also evident in the United States, where access is considered to be 'universal' and enrollments have stabilized at around 50 per cent of the age-group.

In sharp contrast to the Western industrialized countries, Third World universities have, in general, continued to expand without stopping, despite the fact that, at least in Africa and Latin America, there have been serious economic problems in the past two decades. While with only a very few exceptions, such as the Philippines, Third World enrollment ratios remain significantly lower than those in the industrialized nations, there continues to be a strong commitment to continued expansion and access. This is the case even in countries like India where there is severe unemployment of graduates and where there is a significant brain drain of university graduates abroad. In sub-Saharan Africa, there has been a slowing of expansion, not so much because demand for higher education has decreased but due to severe economic problems which have limited the ability of governments to pay the costs of continued growth. In many Third World countries, it remains impossible for local universities to absorb all of those qualified to attend, thus creating an exodus of students abroad. This is the case in Malaysia, where about half of the country's enrollments are abroad.[31]

It is necessary to analyse the prospects for continued expansion of higher education from several perspectives. While there are common worldwide trends, such as the increasingly important role of technology, there are also important differences among countries and in different parts of the world. The Third World presents a specific set of circumstances. While it is likely that its pace in some Third World countries will slow in the coming decade, expansion will continue to be a key factor in higher education. Regional variations will be important, with economic factors dominating. Universities will very likely grow more slowly in less-successful economies. Rapidly expanding economies, such as those of the newly industrializing countries in East Asia, will have resources to expand higher education and at the same time there will be a demand for graduates. Taiwan and the Republic of Korea, for example, can easily absorb university graduates as well as the expenditures needed for large and better-equipped universities. Yet, even where there is evidence that higher educational growth should slow or even stop, it is unlikely that this will take place since popular demand for post-secondary education will remain high and political authorities will find it easier to provide access than to limit it.

The situation in the Western industrialized nations is more difficult to predict. A variety of factors argues for a resumption of growth, although probably not at the levels of the 1960s. There is evidence of a modest upturn in population in some age categories in some Western nations although demographers predict that this will be relatively short-lived. The large number of graduates trained in the 1960s and now occupying positions in schools and universities as well as in government and in industrial enterprises will be retiring in large numbers in the coming years, triggering a significant demand for university-trained personnel. There is also a recognition that university-based research is an important ingredient for scientific and technological strength in an increasingly competitive world economy. Much, however, will depend on broader economic trends. It is also difficult to predict whether resistance to governmental spending in general and for education in particular will continue to be an important political factor in many Western countries.

Despite imponderables, it is likely that in general there will be increased support for higher education spurred by demographic and market factors and continued demand for access by an ever-widening segment of the population. Whether there will be a resumption of the growth of access to wider segments of the population—both of the traditional age-group and of 'non-traditional' students—remains to be seen.[32]

Change and Reform: The Legacy of the 1960s

The demands placed on institutions of higher education to accommodate larger numbers of students and expanding functions resulted in significant reforms in higher education in many countries. There was much debate concerning higher education reform in the 1960s—and a significant amount of change did take place.[33] It is possible to identify several important factors which contributed both to the debate and to the changes that took place. Without question, the unprecedented student unrest of the period contributed to a sense of disarray in higher education. Further, the unrest was in part precipitated by deteriorating academic conditions which resulted from rapid expansion. In a few instances, students demanded far-reaching reforms in higher education although, generally, they did not propose specific changes.[34] Students frequently demanded an end to the rigidly hierarchical organization of the traditional European university, and significant changes were made in this respect. The 'chair' system was weakened and the responsibility for academic decision-making, formerly a monopoly of the full professors, was significantly expanded—in some countries to include students. At the same time, the walls of the traditional academic disciplines were broken by various plans for interdisciplinary teaching and research.

Reform was most dramatic in several very traditional Western European academic systems. Sweden's universities were completely transformed in the most far-reaching of the reform movements. Some of the changes effected in Sweden resulted in democratizing decision-making, decentralizing the universities, expanding higher education to previously under-served parts of the country, providing for interdisciplinary teaching and research and vocationalizing the curriculum.[35] Significant changes also took place in France and in the Netherlands. Reformers in both these countries stressed interdisciplinarity and a democratization of academic decision-making. In Germany, the universities in areas dominated by the Social Democratic Party were also significantly altered, with the traditional structures of the university giving way to more democratic governance patterns.

But in many industrialized nations, structural change was not dramatic, and in many instances very limited. In the United States, for example, despite considerable debate during the 1960s, there was very limited change in higher education.[36] Japan, the site of significant unrest and a large number of reports on university reform, saw virtually no basic change in its higher education system although several 'new model' interdisciplinary institutions were established, such as the science-oriented Tsukuba University near Tokyo. The United Kingdom, less affected by student protest and with an established plan for expansion in operation, also experienced few reforms during the 1960s.[37] It is also the case that some of the changes implemented in the 1960s were criticized or abandoned. In Germany, for example, reforms in governance that gave students and junior staff a dominant position in some university functions were ruled unconstitutional by the German courts.[38]

Vocationalization has been an important trend in changes in higher education in the past two decades. Throughout the world, there has been a conviction that the university curriculum should provide relevant training for a variety of increasingly complex jobs. The traditional notions that higher education should consist of liberal, non-vocational studies for élites or that it should provide a broad but unfocused curriculum, have been widely criticized for lacking 'relevance' to the needs of contemporary students. Students, worried about obtaining remunerative employment, have pressed the universities to be more focused. Employers have also demanded that the curriculum be more directly relevant to their needs. Enrollments in the social sciences and humanities, at least in the industrialized nations, have declined because these fields are not considered vocationally relevant.

Curricular vocationalism is linked to another major worldwide trend in higher education: the increasingly close relationship between universities and industry.[39] This relationship has implications for the curriculum, as industrial firms have sought to ensure that the skills that they need are incorporated into the curriculum. It also has significant implications for academic research, since many university-industry relationships are focused largely on research. Industries have established formal linkages and research partnerships with universities in order to obtain help with research that they find important. In some countries, such as Sweden, representatives of industry have been added to the governing councils of higher education institutions. In the United States, formal contractual arrangements have been made between universities and major corporations to share research results. In many industrialized nations, corporations are increasingly providing focused educational programs for their employees, sometimes with the assistance of universities.

University-industry relations have significant implications for higher education. Technical arrangements with regard to patents, confidentiality of research findings and other fiscal matters have assumed importance. Critics also have pointed out that the nature of research in higher education may be altered by these new relationships as industrial firms are not generally interested in basic research. University-based research, which has traditionally been significantly oriented toward basic research, may be increasingly skewed to applied and profit-making topics. There has also been some discussion of the orientation of research, for example in fields like biotechnology, where broader public policy matters may conflict with the needs of corporations. Specific funding arrangements have also been questioned. Pressure on universities to serve the immediate needs of society and particularly the training and research requirements of industry is currently a key concern for universities and one which has implications for the organization of the curriculum, the nature and scope of research and the traditional relationship between the university and society.[40] Debates concerning the appropriate relationship between higher education and industry are likely to continue, as pressures grow even stronger on universities to provide direct service to the economy.

Universities have traditionally claimed significant autonomy for themselves. The traditional idea of academic governance stresses autonomy and universities have tried to insulate themselves from direct control by external agencies. However, with the increase in the size, scope, importance and cost of universities, there has been immense pressure by those providing funds for higher education—mainly governments—to expect accountability from universities. The conflict between autonomy and accountability is one of the flashpoints of controversy in recent years, with the result that there has been an increase in accountability from academic institutions, again with significant implications for them.[41] The issue takes on different implications in different parts of the world. In the Third World, traditions of autonomy have not been strong and demands for accountability, which include both political and economic elements, are especially troublesome.[42] In the industrialized nations, accountability pressures are more fiscal in nature.

Despite the varied pressures on higher educational institutions for change and the significant reforms that have taken place in the past two decades, basic institutional patterns have remained and there have been few structural alterations in universities. One of the few has been in Sweden as part of the dramatic reform that has taken place there. Elsewhere, curricula have been altered, expansion has taken place, and there have been continuing debates concerning accountability and autonomy, but universities as institutions have not changed significantly. As Edward Shils has argued, the 'academic ethic' has been under considerable strain, and in some ways it has been weakened, but it has survived.[43]

Towards the 1990s

The university as an institution in modern society has shown considerable durability. It has maintained key elements of the historical models from which it evolved over many centuries. At the same time, it has successfully evolved to serve the needs of societies.[44] There has been a significant convergence of both ideas and institutional patterns and practices in world higher education. This has been due in part to the implantation of European-style universities in the developing areas during and after the colonial era and because universities have been crucial in the development and then the internationalization of science and of research.

Despite remarkable institutional stability over time, universities have significantly changed and have been subjected to immense pressures in the post-Second World War period. Many of the changes which have been chronicled here have come as the result of great external pressure and despite considerable opposition from within the institution. Some have argued that the university has lost it soul.[45] Others have claimed that the university is irresponsible because it uses public funds and does not always conform to the direct needs of industry and government. Pressure from governmental authorities, militant students or external constituencies have all placed great strains on academic institutions.

The period since the Second World War has been one of unprecedented growth—and of the increasingly central role of higher education in virtually all modern societies. While growth may continue, the dramatic expansion of recent decades is at an end. It is unlikely that the place of the university as the most important institution for training personnel for virtually all of the top-level occupations in modern society will be weakened. The role of the university in research will also continue, although as has been noted, there are significant pressures concerning the nature and focus of university-based research and perhaps a weakening of the commitment to basic research.[46]

Internationally, there may well be some further convergence as science becomes even more international and as the circulation of academic élites continues through foreign study. While significant national variations will remain, universities have increasingly similar roles throughout the world and research is increasingly communicated to an international audience.

The challenges are, none the less, significant. The issues discussed below, no doubt among others, will be of concern in the present decade and beyond.

Access and Adaptation

Although in a few countries, access to post-secondary education has been provided to virtually all segments of the population, there is in most countries a continuing demand for higher education. Progress towards broadening the social class base of higher education has slowed and in many industrialized countries stopped in the 1970s. With the emergence of democratic governments in Eastern Europe, the possible re-emergence of demand in Western Europe and continuing pressure for expansion in the Third World, it is likely that there will be heightened demand for access and thus expansion of enrollments in many countries. Limited funds and a desire for 'efficient' allocation of scarce post-secondary resources will come into direct conflict with demands for access. These demands for access by previously disenfranchised groups will continue to place great pressure on higher education. In many countries, racial, ethnic or religious minorities play a role in shaping higher education policy. Issues of access will be among the most controversial in debates concerning higher education. This topic may be especially volatile since there is a widespread assumption that all segments of the population should be able to obtain a university education—yet, the realities of higher education in most countries do not permit this level of enrollment.

Administration, Accountability and Governance

As academic institutions become larger and more complex institutions, there will be increasing pressure for a greater degree of professional administration. At the same time, the traditional forms of academic governance will be under increasing pressure not only because they are unwieldy but because in large and bureaucratic institutions they are inefficient. The administration of higher education will increasingly become a profession, much as it is in the United States. This means that there will be the growth of an 'administrative estate' in many countries where it does not now exist. The demands for accountability will increase and will cause academic institutions considerable difficulty. As academic budgets increase, there will be inevitable demands to monitor and control expenditures. There is, at present, no general agreement concerning the appropriate level of governmental involvement in higher education. The challenge will be to ensure that the traditional—and valuable—patterns of faculty control of governance and the basic academic decisions of universities are maintained in an increasingly complex and bureaucratic environment.

Knowledge-Creation and Dissemination

Research is an increasingly important part of the mission of many universities and of the academic system generally. Key decisions concerning the control and funding of research, the relationship of research to broader curricular and teaching issues, the uses made of university-based research and related issues will increasingly be in contention. Further, the system of knowledge dissemination, including journals and books and increasingly computer-based data systems, is rapidly changing and hotly debated. Who should control the new data networks? How will traditional means of communication, such as the journals, survive in this new climate? How will the scientific system avoid being overwhelmed by the proliferation of data?[47] The needs of peripheral scientific systems, including both the Third World and smaller academic systems in the industrialized world, are increasingly important.[48]

While the technological means for rapid knowledge dissemination are available, issues of control and ownership, the appropriate use of data bases, problems of maintaining quality standards in data bases, and related questions are very important. It is possible that the new technologies will lead to increased centralization rather than wider access. It is also possible that libraries and other users of knowledge will be overwhelmed by both the cost of obtaining new material and the flow of knowledge. At present, academic institutions in the United States and other English-speaking nations, along with publishers and the owners of the communications networks stand to gain. The major Western knowledge producers currently constitute a kind of OPEC of information, dominating not only the creation of knowledge but also most of the major channels of distribution. Simply increasing the amount of research and creating new data bases will not ensure a more equal and accessible knowledge system. Academic institutions are at the centre but publishers, copyright authorities, funders of research and others are also necessarily involved.

The Academic Profession

The professorate has found itself under increasing strain in recent years in most countries. Demands for accountability, increased bureaucratization of institutions, fiscal constraints in many countries, and an increasingly diverse student body have all challenged the professorate. In most industrialized nations, a combination of fiscal problems and demographic factors led to a stagnating profession. Now, demographic factors and a modest upturn in enrollments are beginning to turn surpluses into shortages.[49] In the Newly Industrialized Countries (NICs), the professorate has significantly improved its status, remuneration and working conditions in recent years. In the poorer nations, however, the situation has, if anything, become more difficult with decreasing resources and ever-increasing enrollments. Overall, the professorate will face severe problems as academic institutions change in the coming period. Maintaining autonomy, academic freedom and a commitment to the traditional goals of the university will prove a challenge.

In the West, there will be difficulties in luring the 'best and brightest' into academe in a period when positions will again be relatively plentiful: in many fields, academic salaries have not kept pace and there has been a deterioration in the traditional academic life-style. The pressure on the professorate not only to teach and do research but also to attract external grants, do consulting and the like is significant. In the United Kingdom and Australia, for example, universities have become 'cost centres', and accountability has been pushed to its logical extreme. British academics entering the profession after 1989 will no longer have tenure, but will be periodically evaluated. In the NICs, the challenge will be to create a fully autonomous academic profession where traditions of research and academic freedom are only now developing. The difficulties faced by the poorer Third World countries are perhaps the greatest: to maintain a viable academic culture in deteriorating conditions.

Private Resources and Public Responsibility

In almost every country, there has been a growing emphasis on increasing the role of the private sector in higher education. One of the most direct manifestations of this trend is the growing role of the private sector in funding and, in many cases, directing university research. In many countries, there has been an expansion of private academic institutions. And there has been an emphasis on students paying an increasing share of the cost of their education, often through loan programs. Governments have tried to limit their expenditures on post-secondary education while at the same time recognizing that the functions of universities are important. Privatization has been the means of achieving this broad policy goal.[50] There are, of course, important implications of these trends. Decisions concerning academic developments may move increasingly to the private sector, with the possibility that broader public goals may be ignored. Whether private interests will support the traditional functions of universities, including academic freedom, fundamental research and a pattern of governance which leaves the professorate in control is unclear. Some of the most interesting developments in private higher education can be found in such countries as Viet Nam, China and Hungary, where private institutions. have recently been established. Inevitably, private initiative in higher education will bring with it a change in values and orientations. It is not clear that these values will, in the long term, be in the best interests of the university.

Diversification and Stratification

While diversification—the establishing of new post-secondary institutions to meet new needs—is by no means an entirely new phenomenon, is a trend that has been of primary importance in recent years and will continue to reshape the academic system. In recent years, the establishment of research institutions, community colleges, polytechnics and other academic institutions designed to meet specialized needs and serve specific populations has been a primary characteristic of growth. At the same time, the academic system has become more stratified: once individuals are within a segment of the system, it is difficult to move to a different segment. And there is often a high correlation of social class and other variables with selection to a particular segment of the system. To some extent, the reluctance of the traditional universities to change is responsible for some of the diversification. Perhaps more important has been the belief that it is efficient and probably less expensive to establish new limited-function institutions. An element of diversification is the expansion of the student population to include larger numbers of women and other previously disenfranchised segments of the population. Women now constitute 40 per cent of the student population worldwide and more than half in fifteen countries.[51] In many countries, students from lower socioeconomic groups and racial and ethnic minorities are entering post-secondary institutions in significant numbers. This diversification will also be an important challenge for the coming decades.

Economic Disparities

There are substantial inequalities among the world's universities and it is likely that these inequalities will grow. The major universities in the industrialized nations generally have adequate resources to play a leading role in scientific research—in a context where it is increasingly expensive to keep up with the expansion of knowledge.[52] At the same time, universities in much of the Third World simply cannot cope with the combined challenges of continuing pressure for increased enrollments and budgetary constraints and in some cases fiscal disasters. For example, universities in much of sub-Saharan Africa have seen dramatic budget cuts and find it difficult to function, let alone improve quality and compete in the international knowledge system.[53] In the middle are academic institutions in the Asian NICs, where there has been significant academic progress and it is likely that these institutions will continue to improve. Thus, the economic prospects for post-secondary education worldwide are mixed, with considerable challenges ahead.

Universities worldwide share a common culture and reality. In many basic ways, there is a convergence of institutional models and norms.

The key issues identified here are experienced worldwide. At the same time, there are significant national differences which will continue to be felt. There is little chance that the basic structures of academic institutions will significantly change, although some of the traditional academic ideologies and practices are threatened and alterations are likely, for example concerning the continuing growth of an administrative cadre in universities. Unanticipated developments are also possible. For example, while conditions for the emergence of significant student movements, at least in the industrialized nations, do not seem likely at the present time, circumstances may change.[54] In the Third World, student movements continue to be an important political and academic force.

This article has pointed to some key factors that have affected academic institutions worldwide. The past decade has not been an especially favorable one for higher education, yet academic institutions continue to be very important institutions, if anything expanding their impact on both science and society. The future presents significant challenges but the very centrality of the university in modern society creates a degree of optimism.

Notes

1. For a historical perspective, see C. Haskins, *The Rise of Universities*, Ithaca, N.Y., Cornell University Press, 1957.
2. P. G. Altbach, *The Knowledge Context: Comparative Perspectives on the Distribution of Knowledge*, Albany, N.Y., State University of New York Press, 1987.
3. For further discussion of this point, see A. B. Cobban. *The Medieval Universities: Their Development and Organization*, London, Methuen, 1975.
4. The history of British higher education expansion in India and Africa is described in E. Ashby, *Universities: British, Indian, African*, Cambridge, Mass., Harvard University Press, 1966.
5. I. Gilbert, "The Indian Academic Profession: The Origins of a Tradition of Subordination," *Minerva*, No. 10, July 1972, pp. 384–411.
6. For a broader consideration of these themes, see L. Stone (ed.), *The University in Society*, Princeton, N.J., Princeton University Press, 1974, 2 vols.
7. J. Ben-David, *Centers of Learning: Britain, France, Germany, the United States*, pp. 16–17, New York, McGraw Hill, 1977.
8. F. Lilge, *The Abuse of Learning: The Failure of the German University*, New York, Macmillan, 1948.
9. C. E. McClelland, *State, Society and University in Germany, 1700–1914*, Cambridge, Cambridge University Press, 1980. See also J. Ben-David and A. Zloczower, 'Universities and Academic Systems in Modern Societies,' *European Journal of Sociology*, Vol. 3, No. 1, 1962, pp. 45–84.
10. In the German-originated chair system, a single full professor was appointed in each discipline. All other academic staff served under the direction of the chair-holder, who held a permanent appointment to the position. Many other countries, including Japan, Russia and most of Eastern Europe, adopted this system. In time, it was criticized as too rigid and hierarchical.
11. L. Veysey, *The Emergence of the American University*, Chicago, University of Chicago Press, 1965. For a somewhat different analysis, see E. T. Silva and S. A. Slaughter, *Serving Power: The Making of the Academic Social Science Expert*, Westport, Conn., Greenwood, 1984.
12. In Egypt, the Al-Azhar University still offers Islamic higher education in the traditional manner. There are virtually no other universities which fundamentally diverge from the Western model. For a discussion of the contemporary Islamic university, see H. H. Bilgrami and S. A. Ashraf, *The Concept of an Islamic University*, London, Hodder & Stoughton, 1985.
13. P. G. Altbach, 'The American Academic Model in Comparative Perspective,' in: P. G. Altbach (ed.), *The Relevance of American Higher Education to Southeast Asia*, pp. 15–36, Singapore, Regional Institute for Higher Education and Development, 1985.
14. For a case study of British higher education policy in India, see D. Lelyveld, *Aligarh's First Generation: Muslim Solidarity in British India*, Princeton, N.J., Princeton University Press, 1978.
15. M. Nagai, *Higher Education in Japan: Its Take-off and Crash*, Tokyo, University of Tokyo Press, 1971.
16. For case-studies of a variety of Asian universities, see P. G. Altbach and V. Selvaratnam (eds.), *From Dependence to Autonomy: The Development of Asian Universities*, Dordrecht (Netherlands), Kluwer, 1989.
17. For a full discussion of the issues relating to foreign study, see P. G. Altbach. D. Kelly and Y. Lulat. *Research on Foreign Students and International Study: Bibliography and Analysis*, New York, Praeger, 1985.
18. A telling example in this respect is that the number of American students going abroad is only a small proportion of foreigners coming to the United States—and the large majority of Americans who do study in other

countries go to Canada and Western Europe and not to the Third World. See also R. Arnove, "Foundations and the Transfer of Knowledge," in: R. Arnove (ed.), *Philanthropy and Cultural Imperialism*. pp. 305–30, Boston, Mass., G. K. Hall, 1980.

19. For a discussion of higher education development in the NICs, see P. G. Altbach et al., *Scientific Development and Higher Education: The Case of Newly Industrializing Countries*, New York, Praeger, 1989.
20. M. Trow, "Problems in the Transition from Elite to Mass Higher Education." Paper prepared for a conference on mass higher education held by the organisation for Economic Co-operation and Development (OECD), Paris, 1975.
21. For documentation concerning African higher education, see World Bank, *Education in Sub-Saharan Africa: Policies for Adjustment, Revitalization and Expansion,* Washington, D.C., World Bank, 1988, particularly Chapter 6.
22. Altbach et al., *Scientific Development and Higher Education . . .*, op. cit.
23. M. A. Echstein and H. J. Noah. "Forms and Functions of Secondary School Leaving Examinations," Comparative Education Review, No. 33, August 1989, pp. 295–316.
24. It is also the case that academic institutions serve as important 'sorting' institutions in modern society, sometimes diverting students from highly competitive fields. See, for example, S. Brint and J. Karabel, *The Diverted Dream: Community Colleges and the Promise of Educational Opportunity in America, 1900–1985*, New York, Oxford University Press, 1989.
25. R. L. Geiger, *Private Sectors in Higher Education: Structure, Function and Change in Eight Countries*, Ann Arbor, Mich., University of Michigan Press, 1986. For a focus on Latin America, see D. C. Levy, *Higher Education and the State in Latin America*, Chicago, University of Chicago Press, 1986.
26. It is significant that private higher education institutions are being established in Viet Nam and in China. At the same time, Malaysia has rejected proposals for the establishment of private universities.
27. D. B. Johnstone, *Sharing the Costs of Higher Education: Student Financial Assistance in the United Kingdom, the Federal Republic of Germany, France, Sweden and the United States*, Washington, D.C., The College Board, 1986.
28. It is worth noting that agencies such as the World Bank have strongly argued against continued expansion of higher education, feeling that scarce educational expenditures could be much more effectively spent on primary and secondary education. See *Education in Sub-Saharan Africa: Policies for Adjustment, Revitalization, and Expansion*, Washington, D.C., The World Bank, 1988.
29. Trow, op. cit.
30. See L. Cerych and P. Sabatier, *Great Expectations and Mixed Performance: The Implementation of Higher Education Reforms in Europe*, Trentham (United Kingdom), Trentham Books, 1986. See, in particular, Part 2 for a consideration of access to higher education in Western Europe.
31. J. S. Singh, "Malaysia," in P. G. Altbach (ed.), *International Encyclopedia of Comparative Higher Education*, New York, Garland, 1990.
32. There will also be some significant national variations. For example, the United Kingdom, under Margaret Thatcher's leadership, consistently reduced expenditures for post-secondary education, with significant negative consequences for higher education. See, for example, Sir Claus Moser, "The Robbins Report 25 Years After: and the Future of the Universities," *Oxford Journal of Education*, Vol. 14, No. 1, 1988, pp. 5–20.
33. For broader considerations of the reforms of the 1960s, see L. Cerych and P. Sabatier, *Great Patterns of the Higher Education System*, London, J. Kingsley, 1989; P. G. Altbach (ed.), *University Reform: Comparative Perspectives for the Seventies*, Cambridge, Mass., Schenkman, 1974; and P. G. Altbach, *Perspectives on Comparative Higher Education: Essays on Faculty, Students and Reform*, Buffalo, N.Y., Comparative Education Center, SUNY Buffalo, 1989.
34. For an example of an influential student proposal for higher education reform, see W. Nitsch et al., *Hochschule in der Demokratie*, Berlin, Luchterhand, 1965.
35. J. E. Lane and M. Murray, "The Significance of Decentralization in Swedish Education," *European Journal of Education*, Vol. 20, No. 2/3, 1985, pp. 163–72.
36. See A. Astin et al., *The Power of Protest* (San Francisco, Jossey-Bass, 1975) for an overview of the results of the ferment of the 1960s on American higher education.
37. "The Legacy of Robbins," *European Journal of Education*, Vol. 14, No. 1, 1988, pp. 3–112.
38. For a critical viewpoint, see H. Daalder and E. Shils (eds.). *Universities, Politicians and Bureaucrats: Europe and the United States*, Cambridge, Cambridge University Press, 1982.
39. See, for example, "Universities and Industry," *European Journal of Education*, Vol. 20, No. 1, 1985, pp. 5–66.
40. Of course, this is not a new concern for higher education. See T. Veblen, *The Higher Learning in America: A Memorandum on the Conduct of Universities by Business Men*, New York, Viking Press, 1918.
41. See K. Hufner, "Accountability," in P. G. Altbach (ed.), *International Encyclopedia of Comparative Higher Education*, op. cit.
42. P. G. Altbach, "Academic Freedom in Asia: Learning the Limitations," *Far Eastern Economic Review*, 26 June 1988, pp. 45–84.

43. E. Shils, *The Academic Ethic*, Chicago, University of Chicago Press, 1983.
44. A classic discussion of the development of the modern university is Ben-David and Zloczower, op. cit.
45. See, for example, R. Nisbet, *The Degradation of the Academic Dogma: The University in America, 1945–1970*, New York, Basic Books, 1971. A. Bloom, in his *The Closing of the American Mind* (New York, Simon & Schuster, 1987) echoes many of Nisbet's sentiments.
46. It is significant to note that in those countries that have located much of their research in non-university institutions, such as the Academies of Sciences in the Soviet Union and some Eastern European nations, there has been some rethinking of this organizational model, as well as a feeling that universities may be more effective locations for the major research enterprise. See A. Vucinich, *Empire of Knowledge: The Academy of Sciences of the USSR (1917–1970).*
47. See T. W. Shaugnessy et al., "Scholarly Communication: The Need for Action—A Symposium," *Journal of Academic Librarianship*, Vol. 15, No. 2, 1989, pp. 68–78. See also *Scholarly Communication: The Report of the National Commission*, Baltimore, Johns Hopkins University Press, 1979.
48. These issues are discussed in P. G. Altbach, *The Knowledge Context . . .* , op. cit. See I. L. Horowitz, *Communicating Ideas: The Crisis of Publishing in a Post-Industrial Society* (New York, Oxford University Press, 1986) for a different perspective.
49. For an American perspective, see H. Bowen and J. Schuster, *American Professors: A National Resource Imperiled*, New York, Oxford University Press, 1986.
50. D. C. Levy, *Higher Education and the State in Latin America: Private Challenges to Public Dominance*, Chicago, University of Chicago Press, 1986. See also R. L. Geiger, *Private Sectors in Higher Education: Structure, Function and Change in Eight Countries*, Ann Arbor, Mich., University of Michigan Press, 1986.
51. G. P. Kelly, "Women in Higher Education," in: P. G. Altbach (ed.), *International Encyclopedia of Comparative Higher Education*, op. cit.
52. A possible exception to this situation are the universities in the United Kingdom, where a decade of financial cuts by the Thatcher government has sapped the morale of the universities and has made it difficult for even such distinguished institutions as Oxford and Cambridge to continue top-quality research. See G. Walford, "The Privatization of British Higher Education," *European Journal of Education*, Vol. 23, No. 1/2, 1988, pp. 47–64.
53. *Education in Sub-Saharan Africa . . .*, op. cit., pp. 68–81.
54. For a survey of student movements, see P. G. Altbach (ed.), *Student Political Activism: An International Reference Handbook*, Westport, Conn., Greenwood Press, 1989.

Philip G. Altbach (United States of America), Professor, Director of the Comparative Education Center, State University of New York at Buffalo. He has written widely on higher education, and is most recently Editor of *International Encyclopedia of Comparative Higher Education* (1990). Former Editor of *Comparative Education Review*.

The Political Economy of Education

MARTIN CARNOY

Traditional economics of education emphasizes the role that education plays in altering individual characteristics, altering the position of the individual in the labour market, and increasing the economy's capacity to produce. The focus of such views is to estimate the 'universal' relations between competitively determined wage rates, individual decisions about schooling, and the effects of these decisions on the economy as a whole.

The political economy of education, on the other hand, treats education as a factor shaped by the power relations between different economic, political and social groups. How much education an individual gets, what education is obtained and the role of education in economic growth and income distribution are part and parcel of these power relations. For political economists, no study of the educational system can be separated from some explicit or implicit analysis of the purpose and functioning of the government sector. Since power is expressed at least in part through a society's political system, any political economy model of educational change has behind it a carefully thought out theory of the functioning of government—what we shall refer to as a 'theory of the state'.

The state is and has been for a long time intimately involved in trying to develop, expand, and control formal schooling in most countries. What is the relation between the state, the private production sectors, and education in capitalist societies? And that between the state and various social class groups? And that between the state and the educational bureaucracy it created? And that between state economic planning and the educational bureaucracy in socialist societies? The way in which the state provides education may have a lot to do with intergenerational mobility and changes in the distribution of income over time. Thus, understanding the process of public investment in education is necessary to any political economy theory of education and economic change.

Political economists (Carnoy, 1974; Bowles and Gintis, 1976; Carnoy, 1980; Carnoy and Levin, 1985), political sociologists (Offe, 1980; Lenhardt, 1979; Weiler, 1980) and even philosophers (Althusser, 1971) have made the state a primary focus of analysing education-economy relations. In that discussion, the state in capitalist economies is seen, in one form or another, as mediating between the needs of employers to increase profits and workers who want to increase wages and be employed in better jobs. In order for the democratic state to be legitimate, it must give in to the demands of the mass of voting workers; but to maintain its revenue base and the basis of its social function, the state must also reproduce the dominance of the capital owners and managers over the investment and production process. In this context, education plays a variety of roles: it supplies skills for production and makes possible the allocation of skills to various kinds of jobs; it socializes youth to work in particular ways and to accept the work system; and it also inculcates a general ideology in the population which promotes the existing production

Martin Carnoy is Professor at the School of Education Stanford University, Stanford, California 94305-2384, United States. He has published widely on economics, political economy and sociology of education, including *Education as Cultural Imperialism* (1984) and, together with H. M. Levin, *Schooling and Work in the Democratic State* (1985).

system and the political process as fair and rational. Yet, as Carnoy and Levin (1985) suggest, this reproductive role can also be the source of contradiction for the economic and political process; for example, young people may become 'overeducated' for existing jobs (Rumberger, 1981) or school idealizations of an equitable and just society may be taken seriously by youth and translated into demands on the workplace and on politicians.

The political economy of education, therefore, explains the education-economy relation in the context of conflicting power relations and the playing out of these conflicts in the state. It is not unusual, then, that political economists are similarly concerned with the issue of education's role in economic and social inequality. In our survey of specific topics, we emphasize political economic writings that deal with education, social mobility, earnings distribution, and discrimination. But before turning to these specific topics, we can better illustrate the political economy approaches to education by analysing the several general models that have appeared recently in the subject literature.

General Approaches to the Political Economy of Education

For the French institutional functionalists, Pierre Bourdieu and Jean-Claude Passeron (1977), the principal function of schooling is to reproduce the hierarchical relations between different groups or classes in the society and to legitimize those relations. The *raison d'être* of formal education is to reproduce the existing power relations—the domination of one group over others—from generation to generation without having to use violence. The principal means to achieve this reproduction is through the system of teaching, and the language used as the basis of communication in the schools is the dominant group's 'cultural arbitrary': a system of values, norms and languages.

Bourdieu and Passeron's analysis provides a number of important insights into the educational system and the process of teaching and selection, especially with regard to the 'class' nature of that process. They suggest a different kind of understanding of the relation between an idealized, meritocratic school and the reality of who gets to higher levels of schooling and into higher-paying jobs. Yet, from the standpoint of the development of a general political economy model there are a number of difficulties with this analysis.

First, there is no discussion of the source of power relations. We learn that the 'dominant group' is able to use the school system to reproduce its power. But where did the dominant group get its power in the first place? The implication of the analysis is that the source of power is power itself: being dominant allows you to reproduce your dominance through the institutions of society that you control because you are dominant. It gives you control over knowledge, learning, attitudes and values. Neither does resistance to power by the subordinate classes have any base but resistance itself. Resistance is implicit only, appearing solely in the fact that the schools are accepted by the working class against its own 'interest'. This theory of relations between groups has repercussions for Bourdieu and Passeron's characterization of education; school is seen as part of increased domination with a reduction of physical violence—the internalization of repression and the substitution of symbolic for real violence. Working class consent to domination is assumed and explained by the pedagogical authority and autonomy of the schools. Nowhere is evidence presented that the working class has in fact accepted a class-based schooling or a dominant class. Nor are other forms of repression—openly violent forms which complement the more ideological nature of the schools—discussed.

This difficulty leads to a second problem: this analysis has no dynamic. We are left without an understanding of how the system changes. Reform occurs, but the operation of the school system is fundamentally the same. Why did the reform occur in the first place? Why the necessity to mystify the real power relations in society and the function of the schools? Is this necessity simply a function of the dominant group need to reduce physical violence?

The assumption of power expressed through institutions, fundamental to the institutionalist-functionalist view, makes schooling itself a definer of the class structure. A Marxian analysis rejects this assumption. Schools are not a 'subject' of power; institutions themselves are not considered the 'creator' of class hierarchical relations. The power structure is defined by the system of production, outside the school system; education then reflects class relations inherent in the way commodities are produced.

A structuralist Marxian alternative to Bourdieu and Passeron is found in the work of Baudelot and Establet (1972). While agreeing with much of what Bourdieu and Passeron say about education as a reproductive institution, Baudelot and Establet's interpretation differs on two essential points:

> They describe French power relations in terms of their material base. Thus, they consider that one class dominates others and uses the school system to reproduce this relation of dominating-dominated, but the group or class which does this is not an abstraction in capitalist society, it is the bourgeoisie which dominates other groups and the bourgeoisie's power is rooted in their economic position as the owners of capital and controllers of investment. In this view, the school—which is outside the production system—is fundamental to the reproduction of capitalists' dominant position, primarily through the inculcation of dominant ideology.
>
> Baudelot and Establet suggest, however, that working class pupils do not fully accept this attempt by the dominant class to impose its ideology; that is, the working class does resist in the schools. This provides the beginning of a dynamic which is absent from Bourdieu and Passeron's work.

Rather than speaking of institutional-functionalist inequalities in the school system, Baudelot and Establet argue that these are contradictions in the schools: 'inevitable contradictions in the functioning of the school apparatus in which the existence of two types of schooling, camouflaged as the single school, is the evident proof' (1972, p. 312).

My own work (Carnoy, 1974) was the first attempt to understand the spread of Western educational systems into the Third World within the context of a critical political economy analysis. Using a structuralist framework, I showed that Western education developed in India, Africa, and Latin America as an extension of colonial and neo-colonial relations between the metropolitan country and the periphery. As part of direct colonialism in India and West Africa, British and French education for their colonial subjects was limited by the prescribed role of colonial economies in the international division of labour and the prescribed role of the subjects in administering that division.

In free trade colonialism in nineteenth century Latin America, the new economic relationship between the periphery and the metropolitan country allowed for more flexibility, but educational expansion was still determined by that relationship.

This 'determinism' is an important defect of the analysis. In practice, I now believe that there was and is more autonomy of local actors (missionaries, local educators and, later, independent peripheral states) than my analysis allowed for. Yet the analysis was correct in arguing that actors in the periphery and metropolitan country are bounded by the structure of their relationships and the international division of labour. Some may want to change that structure through education, but there has to be a conscious knowledge of and attack on the structure to do so.

Bowles and Gintis' work on education in the United States (1976), is the best example to date of political economy of education applied to a national educational system. They present a model which analyses educational reform as a function of capitalist development—of changes in the production sector. Such changes in production, themselves a result of class conflict, determine the subsequent changes in the way schooling is called upon to reproduce the relations of production. Bowles and Gintis explicitly reject non-Marxist explanations of education's economic role in terms of 'the mental skills it supplies students and for which employers pay in the labor market' (1976, p. 9). Rather, they argue that the relation between the economy and education must be traced through schooling's effect on 'consciousness, interpersonal behavior, and personality it fosters and reinforces in students' (ibid., p. 9); therefore, any explanation of what schooling does depends on understanding the economy. In the United States understanding the economy means grasping the essential elements of capitalism. And this understanding means dealing with the social process of extracting surplus from workers, a process which is 'inherently antagonistic and always potentially explosive'.

There are three principal implications of their interpretation. First, the all-important point that the dominant group in the ruling class turns to the superstructure to attenuate conflict in the base structure, but that the class conflict in the superstructure is not particularly successful in influencing the shape of the educational system—neither its organization nor its content.

Second, Bowles and Gintis put primary emphasis on the reproductive function of schools in all the different stages of capitalist development in the United States. Reproduction is defined as the reproduction of labour power—the allocation of skilled labour to different parts of the hierarchy based on pupil workers' social class background—and the reproduction of the relations of production. Thus, the reproduction of economic inequality and the legitimation of that inequality, as well as the legitimation of capitalist relations in production, receive top billing in the role played by education.

Third, Bowles and Gintis are more convincing when analysing the correspondence of the economic sector (structure) and the educational system (superstructure) than when analysing contradictions in the superstructure and its implications for the base. The principal purpose of their work, indeed, is to show the close connection between changes in the economy and changes in education, to focus on the close links between changes in capitalist relations in production and educational reform.

But if the contradictions in superstructure are essential to understanding capitalist crises—that is, if the state and its apparatuses are also subject to class struggle—then struggle in the schools can serve directly the process of change, and it is even conceivable that schools in a capitalist society could become largely dysfunctional to capitalist reproduction. Bowles and Gintis' analysis does not discuss this possibility, even though in theory their model allows for it. Because of their emphasis on the close ties between capitalist production relations and school reform, they lose sight of the possibility that superstructure may gain in the process an autonomy that allows it to become a focus of struggle which challenges the structure itself. This could have implications for production, or at least for the nature of the labour-capital conflict in the production sector.

Specific Topics in the Political Economy of Education

We can now turn from these general approaches in the political economy of education to more specific topics. Political economy has paid particular attention to the relation between education and economic output and to the inequality of educational opportunity. In pursuing these concerns, it has made its more important contribution in analysing education in relation to its economic value, its allocation of economic roles, its links with social class, income distribution, and discrimination. Let us consider each of these in turn.

The Economic Value of Education

In the mid-1950s, the interest in expenditures on education as a possible source of increasing output grew out of the failure of traditional theories of development—in which inputs were defined as homogeneous labour and capital—to explain more than about half of the total increase in economic output during a given growth period. Early works on education and economic development, therefore, concentrated on establishing education as an input into the growth process—a form of increasing the productive quality of labour. In the earliest work by Robert Solow (1957), the 'residual' of unexplained growth was ascribed to technological change, but later this general term was broken down to include improvements in the quality of capital (Denison, 1962; Griliches and Jorgenson, 1966) and the investment in human beings (Schultz, 1959, 1961). In a series of pioneering studies, Schultz developed the idea that expenditures on education were not primarily consumption but rather an investment in the increased capacity of labour to produce material goods. Hence formal schooling was at least in part an investment in human capital, an investment with economic yield in terms of higher product per worker, holding physical capital constant.

Human capital theory ultimately provided a rationale for a massive expansion of schooling in the developing countries: if expenditures on such schooling contributed to economic growth, educational planners argued, governments could satisfy the demands for schooling while contributing to the overall material growth of the economy.

In the second wave of empirical work on education as human capital, the cost of investment in education was related to the increase in income (used as a proxy for productivity) realized on average by individuals in the labour force. This rate of return on educational spending showed how much education was worth economically compared with other possible public and private investments in a particular economy. As a subproduct of these studies, some analysts such as myself (Carnoy, 1967) for Mexico, and Hanoch (1967) for the United States, measured functions that relate individual earnings to years of schooling, age, and other variables. Such functions, unlike the earlier rate-of-return studies, enabled analysts to isolate the part of earnings differences that could be attributed directly to schooling differences, correcting for on-the-job training and parents' social class background.

Psacharopoulos' work (1973) summarized most of the rate-of-return studies done in the 1960s and early 1970s. All these studies indicated that the payoff to formal schooling as it exists in developing countries is positive and even large, implying an important contribution to economic growth. Was this research correct? Many political economists thought that it was not. The concept that the correlation of schooling with earnings reflects a causal relation between schooling as an investment good and the higher productivity of labour was not universally agreed upon.

It is possible that the principal function of schooling in economic growth lies in its legitimation of the existing or emerging social order. The acceptance by the masses of a particular social structure could have a positive effect on economic output. However, if the accepted economic organization (accepted in part because schools have helped to make it legitimate) is maximizing not the total output but only the income of certain groups, schooling could have a negative effect on economic growth.

Schooling probably does all of these things, but the main discussion centres on which of these functions best characterizes schooling's role (Blaug, 1972). The question is not so much whether schooling contributes to growth, but how much it contributes. It is clear that when dealing with measures, such as rate of return, based on individual observations, we are picking up relationships between individual characteristics and income, which are rather independent of schooling (social class, ambition, culture) in the sense of preceding it, yet which may be correlated with it. Although there is little doubt that productivity can rise with increases of physical capital per worker, holding human capital constant, does productivity of labour rise over time if human capital is increased but physical capital per worker is held constant?

A possible argument based on the legitimation hypothesis is that as human capital in the labour force is increased in a society that economically and politically favours those with higher incomes, no matter what happens to physical capital per person employed, better-educated workers are able to keep their wages higher relative to their productivity than less-educated workers, because the better educated are closer to members of economically powerful groups than are those with less education. The fact that as education expands secularly relative to physical capital growth, rates of return to education fall first for lower levels of schooling, then for progressively higher levels, lends support to this argument (Carnoy 1972; Carnoy and Marenbach, 1975). Eventually, of course, even rates to university education fall if physical capital per employed person is expanding slowly relative to investment in education, but within university education divisions appear which still ensure high returns to certain kinds of training and the groups that receive it (Carnoy, 1978; Psacharopoulos, 1980).

Education as an Allocator of Economic Roles

The human capital approach is based on the concept that the correlation of schooling with earnings reflects a causal relation between schooling as an investment good and the higher productivity of labour. Sophisticated statistical analysis—Blau and Duncan (1967), Duncan,

Featherman and Duncan (1972), for example—indicated that even when the parents' education and occupation (highly correlated with family income) were accounted for, an individual's schooling still provided a significant explanation of occupational position and earnings. This implies that additional schooling is a factor in additional earnings even when an adjustment is made for a possible correlation between the socio-economic family position and children's schooling. Although this did not prove that schooling was not primarily a consumption good, it strengthened the argument that there was a direct relation between schooling and earnings (more schooling leading to higher earnings) that had to be explained in some way.

But, even if more schooling leads to higher earnings for the individual, does this mean that increasing schooling produces higher productivity? Do earnings equal productivity? Vaizey (1961) and others were willing to concede that the individual saw schooling as an investment, i.e. that he or she correctly expected to earn more by going further in school, but that this did not necessarily imply that schooling actually produced more aggregate output. Education could be an allocator of the share of output going to labour, assigning more earnings to those with more schooling, and less earnings to those with less, even though the marginal product of both groups could be approximately equal. In that model, higher investment by society in schooling would not necessarily produce more goods for distribution among the labour force, but the pattern of investment among individuals and groups would be important in determining who received the share of output going to labour.

Lester Thurow and Robert Lucas (1972) contended that education and training are not important factors in determining potential productivity of workers because productivity is an attribute of jobs, not of people. Jobs associated with modern capital equipment are high productivity jobs, and workers queue up for them. Once a worker is hired, the cognitive skills necessary to raise his or her productivity to the productivity of the job are learned through formal and informal training programmes. The chief criterion which employers use in selecting workers for jobs is 'trainability', in that those who possess background characteristics which employers feel reduce costs for training go to the head of the queue and receive the best work.

The 'queue' concept of education in the labour market sees the correlation between schooling and earnings as unrelated to any specific knowledge that schooling imparts to workers which makes them more productive; schooling rather provides a convenient device for employers to identify those workers who can be trained more easily, based it seems primarily on non-cognitive values and norms acquired by students as they progress in school. Is this a contribution to worker productivity? Or is it a subsidy to employers to make it easier for them to select workers for various jobs—a transfer of resources from the public sector to owners of capital?

Similarly, Arrow (1972) suggested that schooling may act as a mechanism to filter 'desirable' from 'less desirable' employees. The screening hypothesis and the queue concept both implied that education did not contribute directly to economic growth but served as a means to sort people for jobs, higher and lower productivity jobs paying higher and lower wages. Although some economists argued that screening did in fact contribute to higher output because it made employers' labour search costs lower, Arrow showed that such a transfer to employers made the economy no better off. This took the discussion back to the level of determining whether there were persuasive reasons to believe that education contributed directly to higher worker productivity or whether it was primarily a sorter of individuals for differentially paying jobs.

The argument for schooling contributing to growth lay in the productivity-raising skills that schooling allegedly provides to students as potential workers. Unlike the queue theory, in which more schooling made students more trainable as workers, the screening argument rested on the certificates awarded to students as they went further in school. For the screen to function, some type of criteria have to be used, but these need not be cognitive, productivity-raising, or even based on trainability.

Segmentation theory goes further: in its most technical version, it reinforces queue theory, arguing that wages are a function of the kind of technology used in particular industries, and that there are barriers to entry into the high-pay, high-technology jobs. This is the dual labour market theory (Doeringer and Piore, 1971). Labour markets in the high-technology industries have different promotion rules, different payoffs to schooling, different rules, etc., to the low-pay, low-technology industries. In the Marxian version of the theory, segmentation is the product of capitalist development and the class struggle between labour and capital; segmentation of the labour force is a structure of the labour market which develops as part of capital's attempts to extract increased surplus through a more sophisticated division of labour (Reich, Gordon and Edwards, 1973, 1982; Carter and Carnoy, 1974; Rumberger and Carnoy, 1980; Rosenberg, 1975). In both versions, wages are structured by the nature of jobs and job differentiation, on the type of capital associated with each job, not by the human capital characteristics of workers in the jobs. Indeed, there is a subset of studies within segmentation analysis which estimates the low increase in employment probability and wages of those in 'secondary' (menial, repetitive, low-wage) jobs as a result of education and training programs (Harrison, 1972; Rumberger and Carnoy, 1980; Levin, 1979). These studies suggest that the 1960s War on Poverty programmes in the United States were not successful because they incorrectly assumed that poverty could be reduced by marginal increases in the skills of the poor, when in fact the job market itself is much more crucial in explaining wage structure.

Bowles (1975) and Gintis (1971) complemented this perspective; they suggested that young people were allocated different occupations and earnings largely on the basis of their parents' social class (income, occupation, education) and that the principal function of schooling was to legitimize the reproduction of the unequal class structure through a façade of meritocracy. Thus, the Bowles-Gintis view contended that schooling was more than a screening device for labour as an input to production (a benefit to employers as entrepreneurs); it was an institution which served employers' class interest in perpetuating the capitalist social hierarchy. In this view, the growth function of schooling is not rejected; Bowles and Gintis argue that there is a cognitive component to schooling, but that this cognitive component is overshadowed by the importance of class values and norms in school output and in assigning groups of individuals to various economic roles. But as I have pointed out (Carnoy, 1974), the function of schooling as an ideological arm of the state, reinforcing and reproducing the social structure, may have a negative effect on economic growth, since it places priority on distribution of power (profit) and on hierarchical rules rather than on maximization of output.

Education and Social Class

The literature on screening, queue theory, and labour market segmentation indicates that schooling may designate who gets the high- and low-paying jobs in an economy. But the variation of income among jobs in that concept of the role of schooling would not be affected by the distribution of schooling in a society; income distribution is a function of the types of jobs available and the incomes attached to those jobs. Bowles and Gintis' (1976) reproduction of the class structure argument also implies a distribution role for schooling, primarily in maintaining groups of people in the same relative income position from generation to generation.

In order to clarify these relationships and our knowledge of them, the discussion should be divided into two parts: (a) the effect of education on inter-generational changes in relative income position (mobility), and (b) education's relation to intragenerational changes in income distribution.

The first of these issues has been the object of many studies, particularly by sociologists (Floud, Halsey and Martin, 1957; Havighurst and Gouveia, 1969; Jencks et al., 1972; Sewell and Hauser, 1974). In the United States, Sewell and Hauser found that the educational and occupational status of parents is highly correlated with children's educational attainment, but that while the overall effect of parents' status and income is the most important single variable explaining the child's current income, the child's educational attainment is almost as important, and the overall explainability of earnings variation by parents' socio-economic status, and child's IQ and educational attainment is very low (less than 10 per cent). This argument was also presented in Jencks' study. On the other hand, a person's occupational status seems to be largely explained by educational attainment, not by parents' social status. If these results are correct, schooling appears to increase mobility, even when parents' social class background is accounted for, both in explaining how much schooling is received and in the income equation.

Samuel Bowles (1972) argued that such studies generally underestimate the effect of social class on present earnings and occupational status relative to the effect of schooling on those variables, for two reasons:

1. There is a bias in remembering parents' education and occupation relative to the amount of schooling a person received. People with high education tend to remember their parents as having less education and lower-status occupations than they actually had, and those with less schooling tend to remember their parents as having higher education and status than they actually had, thus reducing the variance in social class relative to the variance of the education of the person interviewed.
2. The parents' education and occupation is only a proxy for their class position; parents' income and wealth are better predictors of the effect of social class and child's earnings than parents' education or occupation. The work of William H. Sewell and Robert M. Hauser (1974) on Wisconsin data bear out this contention.

In low income countries, the effect of schooling on earnings appears to be greater than in the United States (Psacharopoulos, 1973; Carnoy et al., 1979), but very few of the low income country studies carry out an analysis where the effect of parents' social class background is related to both child's school attainment and child's income. In cases where this is done, the results indicate that the effect of schooling on earnings is much greater than in the United States. Also, schooling and social class variables together explain a higher fraction of variance in low income countries. In the studies where the social class of parents variable does not enter, schooling alone as an explainer of earnings is more important than in American estimates.

These results lead us to believe that, much more than in high income countries, schooling and socio-economic background variables in developing economies are together highly related to earnings and occupational position. In other words, there appears to be less of a chance factor in a person attaining his or her economic position in the low income situation.

Although there is not very much information on whether the parents' social class in low income countries is important in explaining the amount of schooling received by children, recent work in Brazil indicates that the parents' social class explains about 30 per cent of the variance in individual educational attainment (Belloni and Vasquez, 1975). Other work in Kenya also shows a high correlation between paternal income and the amount and kind of schooling taken (Mwaniki, 1973). As far as intergenerational mobility is concerned, therefore, schooling undoubtedly contributes in developing societies to such mobility, but parents' social class seems to be very influential in determining how much schooling a person gets. Schooling to an important degree appears to reflect the social class of a person's parents, and legitimizes the passing of that social position from one generation to the next. The relation varies from country to country; we tend to believe that this role of schooling is more pronounced in Latin America, for example, than in Africa, where multiple social structures still exist (tribal versus colonial). But even in Africa, as Mwaniki's work indicates, new social structures based on European-type peasant/worker/urban/bourgeois divisions are developing rapidly.

Education and Income Distribution

The role of schooling in intragenerational variation in income is much more complex. As early as the mid-1950s Kuznets argued in his 1955 Presidential Address to the American Economic Association that he felt that the distribution of income became more equalized as an economy reached higher levels of income per capita (see also Kuznets, 1959; Mincer, 1958). One of the main reasons for this equalization, in Kuznet's view, was the higher education of the labour force in higher-income economies. In other words, an increased level of schooling in the labour force contributes to a more equal distribution of earnings.

In part, Kuznets came to this conclusion because he felt that a more educated labour force is more likely to agitate politically for a more equal wage structure, but there are also good economic reasons in the neo-classical framework for believing that a higher average level of schooling will contribute to a lower variance in earnings. If there is a direct connection between education and productivity, and between productivity and earnings, raising the average level of schooling could eventually reduce the variance of years in schooling in the labour force. There probably is an upper limit on how much schooling people would be willing to take, since there are fewer and fewer years in which to collect increased earnings from such additional schooling, and since governments seem increasingly committed to providing a minimum level of schooling to its young population, with that minimum rising as the average level of schooling in the labour force rises. These two effects reduce the variance of schooling in the labour force over time and should, if the connection between education, productivity and earnings holds, also reduce the variance in productivity and hence earnings. The reduction in the variance of schooling in the labour force can be affected directly by concentrating investment in lower levels of schooling (Fishlow, 1973). In any case, varying the distribution of schooling in the labour force should have a direct effect on the distribution of earnings if the causal connection between these two variables really exists.

In his study of the drastic decrease in income equality in Brazil between 1960 and 1970, Langoni (1973) explains the change in precisely this way: the distribution became more unequal in part because the distribution of schooling became more unequal—Brazilian university education expanded much more rapidly than primary school education. Indeed, Langoni goes along with Kuznets on another implicit assumption, made explicit in Langoni's work; not only was the change in distribution of schooling partly responsible for the change in earnings distribution, but the pattern of the expansion of education was a 'natural' phenomenon in the economic growth process. So, just as Kuznet uses natural phenomena in the economic growth process to predict an evolution to more equal income distribution, Langoni uses them to explain an increasingly unequal income distribution.

But if productivity is primarily a function of jobs, not a characteristic of workers, as in the queue and segmentation theories, the effect on income distribution of changing the distribution of schooling in the labour force should be negligible. It would be the job or income structure itself which would have to be changed in order to influence income distribution. Education would serve to allocate people to jobs with various earnings attached to them. In cases where their distribution was highly unequal, the value of additional schooling would be high, and in cases where their distribution was more equal, the value of additional schooling would be correspondingly lower. Again in a Brazilian study, Malan and Wells (1973) present evidence that the increased inequality of Brazilian incomes did not occur during the rapid growth period of the late 1960s, but rather in a single year (1965/66) when the Brazilian Government intervened directly in the wage structure by holding wages fixed during an inflationary period, and allowing salaries of higher paid workers to rise more rapidly than prices. Although no other country has had an empirical debate of this sort, data for Chile (Johnston, 1973; Frank, 1975) also indicate that changes in the distribution of schooling during the 1960s apparently had a negligible effect on income distribution, while direct government wage policy during three successive regimes significantly increased inequality from 1966 to 1970, reduced inequality from 1970 to 1973, and drastically increased inequality from 1973 to 1975.

United States data, furthermore, point to unemployment as a key factor in income distribution, apparently more important than either the level of education or its distribution (Chiswick and Mincer, 1972). The fact that employment (number of days worked annually) is a function of policies (business cycles, the direct intervention of the state in fiscal and monetary policy, even direct controls over investment and employment) which have little to do with schooling, again suggests that the distribution of income, while possibly related to the distribution of education in the labour force, is more closely related to government macroeconomic strategy with regard to income policies. If a government is dedicated to ensuring full employment and reducing the variance of earnings in the labour force as part of its development policy, as in Israel and Sweden, for example, the income distribution will be more equal than in economies where the government is primarily concerned with shifting income to professionals and administrators, as in Brazil and Mexico, among others. It is likely that, in both cases, educational investment will be oriented to the overall incomes policy (although in Chile between 1964 and 1973 it was not), so it may not be possible to separate the effect of education from the direct intervention of the state. Nevertheless in the studies we have cited education seems to play a rather limited role.

It is important to note that in most of the literature on both intergenerational and intragenerational education in relation to earnings, the dependent variable being discussed is wages and salaries (earnings), not income. But wages and salaries represent only a fraction of the total product of the economy, 65 to 75 per cent in the United States (Kuznets, 1959; Machlup, 1963); 70 to 75 per cent in Western Europe (Denison and Poullier, 1967); and perhaps as low as 50 per cent or less in Latin America. Even if changing the distribution of wages and salaries through an educational policy could work, therefore, it would affect less than three-fifths of the total income distribution in low income countries unless other measures were taken to equalize wealth. Similarly, making the access to wages and salaries less dependent on paternal education and earnings—through making access to education more equal for various groups, for example—would probably have little effect on the access to non-wage and salary income derived from capital wealth (land and physical capital). While there are large variations in wage and salary income in every non-socialist country, these variations are considerably smaller than the distribution of all income (which includes income from physical wealth).

Education and Discrimination

In the United States, income distribution and mobility issues are closely tied to racial and sexual discrimination. The political economy of education has considered discrimination an important area of study, particularly in assessing the degree of discrimination itself; changes in the relative incomes of blacks and whites or women and men, and the role that education plays in those changes; and estimating the relation between education and female participation in the labour force.

Discussion of these issues has run closely parallel to the discussion of the relation between education and productivity. The race discrimination discussion has been summarized by Marshall (1974), Levin (1979) and Reich (1981); while a summary of women's labour force participation and wage discrimination discussion can be found in Standing (1978) and Amsden (1980). Those analysts who assume that productivity is a function of human capital characteristics have also stressed that race and sex discrimination can be explained largely by a combination of employer profit-maximizing behaviour and human capital differences between blacks and whites or women and men (Becker, 1957; Smith and Welch, 1977, 1978; Freeman, 1974; Mincer and Polachek, 1974; Fuchs, 1974).

According to Becker, racism is fundamentally a problem of race and attitudes. Whites are defined as having a 'taste for discrimination' if they are willing to forfeit income in order to be associated with other whites instead of blacks. Since white employees and employers prefer not to associate with blacks, they require a monetary compensation for the psychic cost of such an association. Becker tries to show that white employers lose financially from discrimination while white workers gain. Smith and Welch, on the other hand, explain converging incomes of blacks and whites in the post-war period (particularly since 1964) by converging quantity and quality of the black educational experience. Thus, discrimination is not discrimination at all, but the logical result of differences in human capital. As human capital converges, productivity and hence earning equalize. They disagree with Freeman's findings that the main influence on the increasing black/white earnings ratio since 1964 was reduced discrimination. Levin (1979) supports Freeman and questions the human capital interpretation on three grounds:

1. Convergence in educational patterns between the races has taken place for at least the last fifty years, yet convergence

in income is a relatively recent phenomenon.

2. Returns to college education have risen for blacks relative to whites in the post-1964 period, but the opposite has happened for returns to elementary and secondary education, which seriously questions the human capital hypothesis.
3. The black/white income ratio rose for older as well as younger workers, indicating that even those whose schooling experience did not change were affected by the general trend of the 1960s and early 1970s. 'Rather, the improvements in the black/white earnings ratio were pervasive and the shift appears to have been an abrupt one coinciding with the intense civil rights activity and passage of major civil rights legislation in the early and middle sixties' (Levin, 1979, p. 107).

If the issue is discrimination and not human capital, does this mean that Becker's 'taste for discrimination' has been reduced? Reich (1981) contends, as does Levin, that it is not 'taste' (an exogenous factor) which has been changed, but that increased struggle by blacks changed the political possibilities for exploiting black workers more than whites. He sees racism (discrimination) rooted in the economic system and not in 'exogenously-determined attitudes'. Reich shows, in his exhaustive study, that the economic consequences of racism are not only lower incomes for blacks, but also higher incomes for employers coupled with lower incomes for white workers—exactly the opposite of Becker's findings.

Wage discrimination against women is the subject of a similar debate. Mincer and Polachek (1974) argue that much of the difference in wages between men and women can be explained by differences in work histories and by differences in job investment and depreciation. Thus, years of work experience differ significantly among the men and women of 30 to 44 years old in their sample (19.4 years for men, 15.6 years for single women, and 9.6 years for married women).

However, other analysts see the program from a segmented labour market, or occupational segregation, point of view (Bergmann, 1974; Chiplin and Sloane, 1974). In these analyses, women are limited in their occupational choice by employers and by male workers and wages are 'customarily' lower in 'women's occupations'. Thus it is not human capital differences but labour market conditions which set lower wages. This position corresponds to the queue and segmentation view of education and labour markets.

Educational Expansion and Political Legitimacy

Where does all this leave us? The political economy of education presents a perspective that places education in the context of economic power relations played out through the economy and the state. Thus, the allocation of economic roles is not primarily a function of the individual acquisition of education or training, but rather primarily a function of the structure of jobs in the labour market. The structure of jobs, under capitalism, is a function of the power conflict between capital and labour. Similarly, social mobility is not a function of individual decisions, but of the social class structure and the job structure, again a function of social and political conflicts. Income distribution does not depend primarily on the distribution of individual characteristics, but on the division of labour, the minimum wage, and the wage structure, all subject to conflict between capital and labour in the economy and the state. Finally, discrimination is explained in capitalism as part of the labour-capital conflict, but overlaid by non-class power relations—in this case, racial and patriarchal relationships. Thus, the analysis of discrimination rests on an understanding of class conflict combined with other power relations that pre-date capitalist classes but are shared by them.

Education's role in these conflicts is inescapably shaped by them as they are manifested in the organization of the state. This is where political economy most differs from traditional human capital theory; for it is the assumption that the state and education are inseparable from inequitable power relations in the 'private' economy that directly opposes the human capital assumptions of education's neutrality in the context of a 'neutral' state.

We are fairly certain therefore that increased schooling in the labour force contributes to productivity and that reducing the variance of school investment in the labour force reduces income inequality, but both of these important economic/social considerations may be rather irrelevant to actual educational spending decisions in a given society. Education is part of the public sector—the state—and reflects state policies. These policies, in turn, are influenced by political/social power conflicts. Education as such has become important as a symbol of progress and of individual success. It is prestigious to be more schooled, as well as materially rewarding. If there is enough widely observable evidence in a society that those who are more schooled and have attended more prestigious educational institutions are more materially and socially successful, the value of schooling as such increases at all levels. To reach higher levels of schooling requires attending lower levels first, and so even these lower levels acquire high value, more in terms of what they can lead to than for their intrinsic worth.

The unceasing and probably increasing demand for education in developing countries is a fact of political life in such societies. Education has become a form of social right for populations whose material standard of living increased slowly in the 1970s. As unemployment has risen in the 1970s and 1980s the demand for education has increased, because unemployment is generally higher for those with less schooling, particularly in urban areas. Thus, more than the rate-of-return or equity arguments put forth as educational spending rationales by international agencies, political reality dictates educational expansion in response to education as a public right. As Alan Wolfe (1979) suggests, such public spending is necessary for a government to maintain 'political legitimacy'.

Why public education expansion has become so central to the legitimacy issue in most societies is a complex issue. Western education has been associated with progress and 'civilization' for at least two centuries, but the incorporation of mass education into this concept in the developing countries is generally a postwar phenomenon, with some notable exceptions such as Argentina, India, and the Philippines (Carnoy, 1974). Governments in developing countries focused on educational spending as a means of developing their societies, and their commitment to education was spurred by the industrial economies' assistance agencies in the 1960s. In addition, the fundamental role of planned educational expansion in the Soviet development process had an important influence on lower income countries trying to gear up for growth.

But no matter how it began, once the process of featuring education as the means to individual and national success was under way, expanding the educational system and making schooling more accessible to the population became a crucial element of political legitimacy for any government. To a very large extent, education as a symbol of development has been incorporated into the view that society has of itself and its 'mission'; the future of developing societies is inextricably tied to their plans for the expansion and improvement of schooling. At the very least, all of these countries have an objective of economic growth that will keep pace and hopefully outrun the growth in population to provide a rising standard of living.

That objective, in turn, is associated with educated labour being available in appropriate quantities to attract the necessary investment for growth. Education is also associated with increasing the potential productivity of workers so they can move from traditional to modern occupations. Moreover, the reduction of substantial inequalities between regions and between families is also associated with educational intervention as a way of more nearly equalizing investments in skills and human capital. So most developing societies, as societies, view education as an important instrument for economic growth and democratization of opportunities. Education is viewed by the state as having substantial political value in itself for meeting aspirations of populations for literacy, skills, credentials, and status. As a public service, education may be a cheap way to secure such political value or legitimacy, compared to making structural changes in the economy that would redistribute income and wealth. Spending on education is on the one hand a way to provide a consumption good (children's education) to low income populations, and on the other hand it places responsibility for material gains resulting from such educational opportunities squarely on the shoulders of parents and children themselves. Such spending also probably makes labour more 'trainable' and hence subsidizes investment in physical capital, even though the social return to educational investment may be relatively low.

References

Althusser, L., 1971. *Lenin and Philosophy and Other Essays*, New York, Monthly Review Press.

Amsden, A. H., 1980. *The Economics of Women and Work*, New York. St Martin's Press.

Arrow, K., 1972. *Higher Education as a Filter*, Stanford, Calif., Institute for Mathematical Studies in the Social Sciences, Stanford University. (Technical Report, 71.)

Baudelot, C., Establet, R., 1972. *L'école capitaliste*. Paris, Maspero.

Becker, G., 1957. *The Economics of Discrimination*, Chicago, University of Chicago Press.

Belloni, I., Vasquez de Miranda, G., 1975. *The Determinants of Educational Attainment in Minas Gerais, Brazil*, Paper presented at ECIEL Conference. Lima, Peru.

Bergmann, G., 1974. Occupational Segregation, Wages and Profits when Employers Discriminate by Sex, *Eastern Economics Journal*, Vol. 1, No. 2–3, pp. 103–10.

Blau. P., Duncan, O. D., 1967. *The American Occupational Structure*, New York, Wiley & Sons.

Blaug, Mark, 1972. The Correlation between Education and Earnings. What Does it Signify? *Higher Education*, Vol. 1, No. 1, pp. 53–76.

Bourdieu, Pierre; Passeron, Jean-Claude, 1977. *Reproduction*, Beverly Hills, Sage Publications.

Bowles, Samuel, 1972. Schooling and Inequality from Generation to Generation, *Journal of Political Economy*, Vol. 80, No. 3, Part II, pp. 219–51.

_____. 1975. Unequal Education and the Reproduction of the Social Division of Labor, In: M. Carnoy (ed.), *Schooling in a Corporate Society*, 2nd ed. New York. David McKay.

Bowles, Samuel; Gintis, Herbert, 1976. *Schooling in Capitalist America*, New York, Basic Books.

Carnoy, Martin. 1967. Rates of Return to Schooling in Latin America. *Journal of Human Resources*, Vol. 2, Summer, pp, 359–74.

_____. 1972. The Political Economy of Education, In: Thomas LaBelle (ed.), *Education and Development in Latin America and the Caribbean*, Los Angeles, UCLA Latin American Center.

_____. 1974. *Education as Cultural Imperialism*, New York, David McKay.

_____. 1978. La educacion universitaria en el desarrollo economico del Peru, *Revista del Centro de Estudios Educativos*, Vol. 8, No. 1.

_____. 1980. *Marxian Approaches to Education*. Stanford, Calif., Institute for Research on Educational Finance and Governance, Stanford University. (Program Report 80–B13, July.)

Carnoy, Martin et al., 1979. *Can Educational Policy Equalize Income Distribution in Latin America?* Geneva, International Labour Organization.

Carnoy, Martin; Levin, Henry M., 1985. *Schooling and Work in the Democratic State*, Stanford, Calif., Stanford University Press.

Carnoy, M., Marenbach, D., 1975. The Return to Schooling in the United States. *Journal of Human Resources*, Vol. 10, No. 3, pp. 312–31.

Carter, M., Carnoy, M., 1974. *Theories of Labor Markets and Worker Productivity*, Palo Alto, California, Center for Economic Studies, (Mimeo.)

Chiplin, B., Sloane, P. J., 1974. Sexual Discrimination in the Labour Market, *British Journal of Industrial Relations*, Vol 12. No. 3, pp. 371–402.

Chiswick, B., Mincer, J., 1972. Time Series Change in Personal Income Inequality in the United States from 1939, with Projections to 1985, *Journal of Political Economy*, Vol. 80, No. 3, Part 2, pp. 34–66.

Denison, E. F., 1962. *The Sources of Economic Growth in the United States and the Alternatives Before Us*, New York, Committee for Economic Development.

Denison, E., Poulier, J. P., 1967. *Why Growth Rates Differ*, Washington, D.C., The Brookings Institution.

Doeringer, P., Piore, M., 1971. *Internal Labor Markets and Manpower Training*, Lexington, Mass., Heath Lexington Books.

Duncan, O. D., Featherman, D. L. Duncan, B., 1972. *Socioeconomic Background and Achievements*, New York, Seminar Press.

Fishlow, A., 1973. *Brazilian Income Size Distribution: Another Look*, Berkeley, Calif., University of California, (Mimeo.)

Floud, J. E., Halsey, A. H., Martin, F. M., 1957. *Social Class and Educational Opportunity*. London, Heinemann.

Frank, A. G., 1975. An Open Letter about Chile to Arnold Harberger and Milton Friedman. *Radical Review of Political Economics*, Autumn, pp. 61–76.

Freeman, R., 1974. Changes in the Labor Market for Black Americans, 1948–72. *Brookings Papers on Economic Activity, I, 1973*, pp. 67–120, Washington, D.C.

Fuchs, V., 1974. Recent Trends and Long-Run Prospects for Female Earnings. *American Economic Review*, Vol. 64, No. 2.

Gintis, Herbert, 1971. Education, Technology and Worker Productivity. *American Economic Association Proceedings*, Vol. 61, No. 2, pp. 266–71.

Griliches, Z., Jorgenson, D., 1966. Sources of Measured Productivity Change: Capital Input, *American Economic Review*, Vol. 61, May, pp. 50–61.

Hanoch, G., 1967. An Economic Analysis of Earnings and Schooling, *Journal of Human Resources*, Vol. 2, Summer.

Harrison, B., 1972. Education and Underemployment in the Urban Ghetto. *American Economic Review*, December, pp. 796–812.

Havighurst, R., Gouveia, A., 1969. *Brazilian Secondary Education and Socioeconomic Development*, New York, Praeger.

Jencks, C., et al., 1972. *Inequality*. New York, Basic Books.

Johnston, C., 1973. *Educacion y distribucion del ingreso*. Thesis presented to the Faculty of Economics, University of Chile, December.

Kuznets, S., 1959. Quantitative Aspects of Economic Growth of Nations. IV: Distribution of National Income by Factor Shares, *Economic Development and Cultural Change*. April, Part II.

Langoni, C., 1973. *A distribucao da renda e deservolvimento economica da Brasil*, Rio de Janeiro, Editora Expressao e Cultura.

Lenhardt, G., 1979. *On Legal Authority, Crisis of Legitimacy and Schooling in the Writings of Max Weber*, Stanford, Calif., Institute for Research on Educational Finance and Governance, Stanford University. (Program Report 79–B13, October.)

Levin, Henry M., 1979. *Education and the Earnings of Blacks and the* Brown *Decision*, Stanford. Calif., Institute for Finance and Governance, Stanford University. Project Report 79–B13, October.

Machlup, F., 1963. Micro and Macro-economics. *Essays in Economic Semantics*, Englewood Cliffs, N.J., Prentice Hall.

Malan, P., Wells, J., 1973. Distribucao da renda e desersolvimento economics da Brasil. *Pesquisa e planijamento economic*, December.

Marshall, R., 1974. The Economics of Racial Discrimination: A Survey. *Journal of Economic Literature*, Vol. 12. September, pp. 849–71.

Mincer, J., 1958. Investment in Human Capital and Personal Distribution of Income, *Journal of Political Economy*, Vol. 66, August, pp. 281–301.

Mincer, J., Polachek, S., 1974. Family Investment in Human Capital. *Journal of Political Economy*, Vol. 82, No. 2, Part 2, pp. 76–108.

Mwaniki, D., 1973. *Education and Socio-Economic Development in Kenya: A Study of the Distribution of Resources for Education*. Unpublished Ph.D. dissertation, Stanford University, Calif.

Offe, Claus., 1980. *Notes on the 'Laws of Motion' of Reformist State Policies*, Bielefeld University, Federal Republic of Germany (Mimeo.)

Psacharopoulos, G., 1973. *Returns to Education: An International Comparison*, The Hague, Elsevier.

_____. 1980. *Higher Education in Developing Countries: A Cost-Benefit Analysis*. Washington, D.C., World Bank. (World Bank Staff Working Paper No. 440.)

Reich, M., 1981. *Racial Inequality: A Political Economic Analysis*, Princeton, N.J., Princeton University Press.

Reich, M., Gordon, D., Edwards, E., 1973. A Theory of Labor Market Segmentation. *American Economic Review*, Vol. 63, May, pp. 359–65.

_____. 1982. *Segmented Work, Divided Worker*, New York, Cambridge University Press.

Rosenberg, S., 1975. *The Dual Labor Market: Its Existence and Consequences*, Unpublished Ph.D. dissertation, University of California, Berkeley.

Rumberger, Russell, 1981. *Overeducation in the U.S. Labor Market*, New York, Praeger Special Studies.

Rumberger, Russell, Carnoy, Martin, 1980. Segmentation in the U.S. Labor Market: Its Effects on the Mobility and Earnings of Whites and Blacks, *Cambridge Journal of Economics*, Vol. 4, pp. 117–32.

Schultz, T. W., 1959. Investment in Man: An Economist's View. *Social Service Review*, Vol. 33, June, pp. 110–17.

_____. 1961. Investment in Human Capital, *American Economic Review*, Vol. 5, March, pp. 1–17.

Sewell, W. H., Hauser, R. M., 1974. *Education, Occupation and Earnings: Achievement in the Early Career*, Department of Sociology, University of Wisconsin.

Smith, J., Welch, P., 1977. Black-White Male Wage Ratios: 1960–1970. *American Economic Review*, Vol. 67, June, pp. 323–31.

_____. 1978. *Race Difference in Earnings: A Survey and New Evidence*, Santa Monica, Calif., Rand Corporation.

Solow, Robert., 1957. Technical Change and the Aggregate Production Function, *Review of Economics and Statistics*, Vol. 39. August, pp. 312–20.

Standing, G., 1978. *Labour Force Participation and Development*, Geneva, International Labour Organization.

Thurow, Lester, Lucas, Robert, 1972. *The American Distribution of Income: A Structural Problem*. Hearings before the Joint Economic Committee, Washington, D.C.

Vaizey, J., 1961. *The Economics of Education*, London, Faber & Faber.

Weiller, Hans N., 1980. *Legalization, Expertise, and Participation: Strategies of Compensatory Legitimation in Educational Policy*, Paper prepared for delivery at the Conference of Europeanists, Council for European Studies, Washington, D.C., 23–25 October.

Wolfe, Alan, 1979. *The Limits of Legitimacy*, New York, The Free Press.

The Problematic Meaning of "Comparison" in Comparative Education

ERWIN H. EPSTEIN

To Marc-Antoine Jullien, generally considered the "father of Comparative Education,"[1] nothing could be clearer than the meaning of comparison. It refers to the act of contrasting the features and methods of education in different countries. In his now famous *Esquisse,* Jullien went so far as to specify concretely an appropriate methodology for comparison, involving the use of standard questionnaires to collect information and arranging the findings into comprehensive tables so that differences in education among countries could be appreciated at a glance. These tables would show the elements that could profitably be transplanted from one country to another, taking into account local particularities and especially "differences in mentality". His ultimate aim was as clear as his method: "to deduce true principles and determined rules so that education be transformed into an almost positive science."[2]

Jullien set the stage 170 years ago for positivism as the field's mainstream tradition. Among all comparativists none have staked out a more unambiguous position for Comparative Education than those who have displayed an epistemological affinity with his perspective. Indeed, some modern positivists have gone so far as to claim that only through comparison can human behavior be studied truly scientifically, and that the essential nature of education cannot ultimately be understood without cross-national examination. For Noah and Eckstein, "Comparative Education . . . emerges as the attempt to use cross-national data to test propositions about the relationship between education and society and between teaching practices and learning outcomes."[3] For Farrell, *"there can be no generalizing scientific study of education which is not the comparative study of education."*[4] For Merritt and Coombs, "without . . . systematic cross-system comparisons, we won't develop the theories we need; without these theories we won't explain much of anything, even within a single (national) system (of education)."[5] And for Le Thành Khoi:

> "A truly general theory of education would be based on an in-depth study of reciprocal relations between education and society in different types of historical civilizations . . . The goal of such an undertaking would be to arrive possibly at a formulation of *laws*: laws that would not have the validity of those generated in experimental sciences but that would express relatively constant relationships in space and time.
>
> Comparative Education is indispensable to developing such 'laws.' Comparative Education is more than a discipline: it is a field of study that covers all the disciplines that serve to understand and explain education . . . Comparison permits us to classify and develop typologies and, under given conditions, to make 'indirect experiments'."[6]

All of these formulations are clear about what comparison is: the cross-national method of discovering invariant relationships between education and aspects of society to, in Anderson's words, "throw light on processes abstracted from time and even apart from conceptions of (evolutionary) stages."[7] They are also clear about its importance: no understanding of education can be complete without it, and Comparative Education must ultimately be the capstone to the study of schools. Finally, they are clear about how education must be studied: only empirical statements about education are scientific and only scientific statements are meaningful. That is, for a proposition to be meaningful it must be testable or verifiable in principle, and for it to be regarded as true it must be subjected to an experiential test.

There have been, however, serious challenges within Comparative Education to the positivist position. This in itself is not remarkable, since thriving fields often display dissension. In physics, for example, an irreconcilable difference in assumptions about the existence of neutrinos was the result not of experimental evidence—neutral currents cannot be detected—but of different theoretical traditions that provide vastly different interpretive contexts.[8] And, of course, different interpretive contexts provided by different disciplines have produced disparate explanations of the same phenomena. To explain the extinction of dinosaurs, Benton notes that,

> "astronomers and geophysicists go for asteroids or comets; atmospheric scientists go for acid rain; ophthalmologists for cataract blindness; botanists for alkaloid poisoning; and dieticians for a reduction in fiber and natural oils leading to rampant dinosaurian constipation."[9]

Yet unlike these differences, certain dissenting positions in Comparative Education represent not simply alternative interpretations of phenomena, but challenges to the field's viability. One comparativist recently said,

> "my own reading of the substantial body of literature on the nature and methods of Comparative Education leads me to the inescapable conclusion that *there is no such thing as Comparative Education*, that is, Comparative Education as a field of study does not exist."[10]

In my presidential address before the Comparative and International Education Society I suggested that certain rival orientations constitute a threat to Comparative Education because they were in essence epistemologically, and even ideologically, irreconcilable.[11] In this essay I wish to further that argument by focusing on the challenge of relativism not only to positivism but to Comparative Education as a field. I also wish to clarify some of my earlier ideas, and in particular show how some comparative approaches do not fall as neatly into the positivist or relativist traditions as I may have earlier implied.

The Relativist Impulse

I believe that there are two discernible relativist strands in Comparative Education. The first has existed almost as long as positivism, and has achieved considerable acceptance especially in Europe. I refer here to cultural relativism, which in Comparative Education is usually displayed by an adherence to some variation of the concept 'national character'. Although cultural relativism is incompatible with positivism, it furnishes a viable alternative approach in the field. The second, much more recent strand is not only contrary to the positivist orientation, but is inherently uncongenial to any meaningful conception of comparison. I make reference to the remarkable introduction of phenomenological (or ethnomethodological)[12] additions to the literature. I shall consider each of these orientations in order.

Cultural Relativism

In direct contrast to the nomothetic explanations—the discovery of underlying trends and patterns that account for whole classes of actions or events—of positivist science stand the idiographic explanations, which examine the special circumstances that differentiate particular events from others, of cultural relativism. Normally associated with the anthropologists Franz Boas, Ruth Benedict and Melville Herskovits, cultural relativism is essentially the position that "all assessments are assessments relative to some standard or other, and standards derive from cultures."[13] Herskovits, who coined the term 'cultural relativism', had a fundamental antipathy toward generalizing about cultures and a vigorous skepticism regarding purported behavioral universals. Only the constraining and shaping character of culture was universal, and even perception of color, shape, time and space, the physiology of taste, and responses to pain were absolutes molded by culture or particular social relations.[14] Benedict contended that universal behavioral abnormalities did not exist;

there are cultures for which behaviors that are considered abnormal are perfectly normal:

> "It does not matter what kind of 'abnormality' we choose for illustration, those who indicate extreme instability, or those which are more in the nature of character traits like sadism or delusions of grandeur or of persecution, there are well-described cultures in which these abnormals function at ease and with honor, and apparently without danger or difficulty to the society."[15]

The anthropologist's purpose was to record the particularities of individual cultures and show the variability among them.

It is evident that from a positivist viewpoint one who embraces cultural relativism cannot be a comparativist. The relativist denies the existence of nomological principles and, in fact, has as a guiding purpose to expose the uniqueness of all cultures. For the relativist 'comparison' is not a generalizing process but a method to discover cultural absolutes, in marked contrast to the 'comparative method' used by positivists. Relativists eschew that method as a futile exercise which ignores the relativity of norms and values to cultural contexts. For positivists the very purpose of comparison is to generalize across the boundaries of cultures. 'Comparison' thus has very different meanings for positivists and relativists. Even so it is interesting that the positivist and relativist orientations have been the strongest and most persistent in Comparative Education.

Cultural Relativism in Comparative Education

If cultural relativists eschew nomological principles, what then is the purpose of research? Why 'compare' societies if findings are culturally unique and therefore ungeneralizable? For Herskovits the purpose of comparison was to discover the different ways human beings have devised to fulfill their needs, and thus to gain an appreciation of human variability. "The very core of cultural relativism", he said, "is the social discipline that comes of the respect for difference—of mutual respect."[16] Such discipline is important because ethnocentrism is unavoidable; although we cannot escape it we can guard against its militant form and make it 'benevolent'. A benevolent ethnocentrism consists of a strong ego-identification with one's own group but not so extreme as to degenerate into behavior detrimental to the well-being of other groups. It thus becomes an important stabilizing force in social life without giving rise to deprecation of others' values.[17]

Cultural relativism in Comparative Education takes a similar form. For Vernon Mallinson the comparative study of education is a process of gaining knowledge about foreign schools in order to gain a better understanding of one's own system. Only by seeing the uniqueness in the way others carry on education can one genuinely appreciate the distinctiveness of education at home. But our focus must not be simply on schools but the particular cultural contexts that account for their distinctiveness. In other words, schools must be seen as 'fitted' to a cultural environment. Mallinson makes frequent reference to a "fixed mental constitution", "relatively permanent attitudes . . . common to a nation", "semi-permanent dispositions", and "modal personality structure"[18] to show that individuals and schools are linked by "national character." People's search for personal identity tends to find expression through available cultural patterns, permitting the suppression of individual desires in the service or common values which undergird a nation. These patterns are *sui generis*, shaped by particular social, geographic, economic, historical, religious and political factors. Hence, the cultural boundaries of a nation severely circumscribe the extent to which scholars can validly generalize from one school system to another.

Although cultural relativism is most clearly displayed in Mallinson's concept of national character, it found expression in the works of even early comparativists and informs much current scholarship as well. Jullien's contemporary, Victor Cousin, acknowledged the "indestructible unity of our (French) national character" when 'comparing' schools, and Michael Sadler contended that "all good and true education is an expression of national life and character (and) is rooted in the history of the nation and fitted to its needs."[19] More recently, Edmund King examined schools in view of their particular cultural environments. For example, he analyzed French education as rooted in "the country of rationalism and intellectualism" and as displaying the "academic purism" and "rationalist secularism contending with traditional piety" so characteristic of "the land of truly gracious living." By contrast, American schools are shaped by "technological distinction and commercial pre-eminence." His view is "that a proper study of Comparative Education must be grounded on a sympathetic description-with-analysis of all that adds up to 'education' in each human workshop—that is, in one cultural whole."[20]

We see, then, that positivism and cultural relativism manifest wholly disparate ideas about comparison and the proper study of education. Positivist scholars examine invariant relationships that transcend the boundaries of particular societies. Relativists focus on the partlcularities of cultures as these are linked to the idiosyncracies of national systems of education. One uses 'comparison' to generalize about schools across cultures; the other employs it to grasp the unique character of a nation's schools. These perspectives are not simply different but mutually exclusive.

However much these orientations clash, I will show that there have been attempts to formulate methods that draw on both.

First, however, I wish to examine another anti-positivist position: one that challenges positivism even more forcefully than does cultural relativism. I refer here to the phenomenological impulse.

Phenomenology

When anthropologists refer to cultural relativism as "the opposite of ethnocentrism,"[21] they usually mean simply that the relativist has nothing to say about intra-cultural value systems other than to report the pervasiveness and prevalence of certain norms and values; relativism thus avoids casting judgment on what is observed, including the practices and conduct of people who do not share the observer's values. Positivism, although it violates the integrity of cultural boundaries and leads to overly facile conclusions, is not necessarily ethnocentric, insofar as it is limited to merely observing general relationships among phenomena. Phenomenology, however, does claim that positivist inquiry *is* by nature unavoidably biased and judgmental, and therefore represents a more extreme repudiation of positivism.

Phenomenologists object to the positivist view of social facts as 'things', embodied in the form of prior hypotheses, operational definitions of variables and statistical tests of significance. Positivist inquiry ignores the 'internal logic' of conditions under study—the rules used by the participants themselves, including the observer, to generate 'facts' or 'variables'. Unlike physical objects social phenomena are 'real' only insofar as we organize our activities in such a way as to routinely confirm their real existence; they have no innate 'real' properties, no real parts, experience no real changes and no causality. For Husserl,

> "to attribute a nature to phenomena, to investigate their real component parts, their causal connections—that is pure absurdity, no better than if one wanted to ask about the causal properties, connections etc. of numbers."[22]

Phenomenology thus rejects the positivist assumption of an empirical social world constructed essentially of a preconstituted field of objects awaiting explication and whose existence is independent of the processes through which it is studied and understood. Rather, it views as problematic the very availability of the world for analysis. For the phenomenologist, positivist analysis consists of nothing more than the investigator's common-sense reasoning, and the use of operational definitions, rather than provide an objective description of the real world, produce no more than self-validating results that confirm a preconceived view of it.

Like cultural relativists, phenomenologists view the cultural state of the researcher as a potentially binding influence on observations. But the cultural relativist seeks to escape that influence by scrupulously avoiding judgment over the observed reality. By contrast, such avoidance—as well as all devices aimed at achieving objectivity that are external to the interaction observed—is itself a part of a construct that the phenomenologist insists must be taken into account. Whereas the social world as observed by the researcher is constructed by the individuals who comprise it, a process that may be described as first-order construction, that world is not susceptible to detached analysis because the interpretational relevance of particular facts and events cannot be determined from the outside. Unfortunately, positivists must rely on second-order constructs — i.e., constructs of constructs—which they form based on their common-sense interpretations of the social world, a world that can only be meaningfully understood in terms of its existential subjectivity.[23] Suffice it to say that no technique that objectifies observations can stand up to the test of phenomenology.

For my purpose it is important to note that 'comparison'—however disparately defined by positivists and cultural relativists—seems necessarily to violate phenomenological strictures. Whether as a method of generalizing across cultures or as a means of identifying unique cultural configurations, comparison is a device external to the interaction of the observed subjects. Yet, surprisingly, phenomenologically oriented scholars are counted among the ranks of comparativists, and their works have appeared in Comparative Education journals.

Phenomenology in Comparative Education

Probably the earliest, and perhaps the most significant, phenomenologically-inspired anti-positivist critique in the literature on Comparative Education is by Benjamin Barber. He claims that positivists commonly misconstrue methodology as science, and thus "presume that reliability, precision, and certitude can be attained by the dutiful application of specified methods and techniques—irrespective of the nature of the subject under study."[24] Indeed, he contends that generalization based on observed contingency among events is unwarranted, that the inductive process

> "by which we get from isolated instance in the perceptual world to the general, law-like ('causal') propositions of the theoretical world . . . is itself an *a priori* principle whose legitimacy can never be demonstrated in empirical (*a posteriori*) terms."[25]

And, further:

> "A datum is a carefully selected facet of sensory experience answering to specific mental categories and reflecting what can only be called a theory of the world; it is not a *Ding an sich*, a self-defining, unambivalent thing. Stones, electrons, trees and men, no less than states, ideals, curricula and bigots are artificial categories imposed by man through language on an otherwise inchoate, unknowable world. Social scientists often recognize, in selecting among data, that values and purposes are likely to play a crucial pre-empirical role, but what they fail to perceive is that data in themselves are mere products of mind."[26]

It would seem to follow from this that all comparison, at least as positivistically defined and based on cross-societal generalization, is futile, and, indeed, Barber accepts the positivist definition: "Now in comparative studies, the aim is to find salient questions around which comparison can be undertaken, ideally a set of 'invariant points of reference' that would serve as universal categories."[27] Yet, inexplicably, he argues—perhaps as a sop to the public for which he is writing—that "comparison remains an invaluable research technique" (if it is not abused by comparativists who fail to recognize that their observations are a function of their own interests, values and intentions).[28] Despite this last gesture, it is clear that comparison fails to stand up to Barber's ineluctable logic: comparison is positivistic, positivism as an empiricist and generalizing approach does not provide a sound basis for understanding social reality, therefore comparison is unsound. Significantly, not even positivists have recognized how fundamentally incompatible the phenomenological critique is to the 'comparative method'.[29]

This is not to say that phenomenology furnishes merely a critique of positivism, without having anything to say about proper procedure. Several phenomenologically-oriented 'comparativists' have attempted to show how comparison should be done. Clearly for them it should be microanalytical (or 'interactionist' or 'interpretative'). Heyman contends that it should "concentrate on the detailed analysis of social interaction as the most obvious source of the social reality of education."[30] Clignet has probably gone the farthest to sketch out an approach that "distinguishes the perspectives of each individual organism and differentiates its modes of adaptation to the environment."[31] By focusing on the problems of teaching pupils how to read, he tries to show "that the natural history of the coordination between the patterns of adaptation used by each educational actor varies with the normative and socio-psychological profile of each classroom situation."[32] And Masemann believes that "in comparative studies, one would need to examine the cultural context of studies of classroom interaction and language use."[33]

What is remarkable about the phenomenological position is that it renders the idea or 'comparison' *meaningless*. To her credit, Masemann recognizes that

> ". . . from a non-interpretive standpoint all (interpretive) studies are inherently limited by their lack of generalizability, their lack of connection to a wider theoretical framework, and their essentially (suppressed) functionalist analysis of social relations. While they give insights into the workings of an educational reality, the sum of all such realities does not add up to a study of Comparative Education which would satisfy those interested in a more general theory of school/society relationships."[34]

Thus phenomenologists may acknowledge that since general theory is the objective of positivism, interpretive studies are inconsequential to positivists. Yet it is not simply that they are inconsequential to some scholars; it is also patently evident that the findings of all interpretive studies are inherently *incomparable*.

Generalization across societal boundaries defines, as I have noted, the comparative method for positivists. For cultural relativists, comparison is a process of observing the distinctiveness of individual cultures to gain an understanding of the unique attributes of each. These positions are, to be sure, incompatible, but they both rest on a procedure that requires multicultural analysis, and therefore can be said to employ some reasonable concept of 'comparison'. This is not so for phenomenological approaches, which carry relativism to a nihilistic extreme that allows only for interpretation of highly idiosyncratic interactions within severely limited contextual boundaries. Within such parameters not even *culture* is sufficiently contextually delineated to constitute a basis for analysis. In brief, phenomenological assumptions about the nature of reality and its susceptibility to understanding vitiates comparison.

Attempts at Synthesis

The few comparativists who have acknowledged epistemological incongruities in Comparative Education have generally called for a synthesis that would build on the special contributions that each approach could make to an overall analysis of schools.[35] Regrettably, as I have also noted earlier,[36] epistemologies are less amenable to such accommodating impulses than proponents would have us believe. To illustrate this point, some attempts at synthesis are worth examining.

The Case Study Approach

Some exponents of case study research have a misconception of positivism, contending that the latter orientation is perforce contrary to idiographic methods. This applies to Crossley and Vulliamy, who, following Stenhouse,[37] believe that the "case study research paradigm" offers "opportunities for further challenges to the epistemological and ideological dominance of the positivist."[38] They argue that positivism undervalues observation and description and overvalues written sources, statistical manipulation and the accounts educational systems give of themselves. Comparative Education, they maintain, should display greater balance by the infusion of micro-level, case study approaches.

Unfortunately, Crossley and Vulliamy confuse method with epistemology, the means to achieve knowledge with theory about how knowledge is to be achieved. This is a common mistake that has been addressed by several scholars. Mann, for example, argues that different epistemologies do not lead to different research practices, and that, in fact, even relativists tend to use methods common to positivists, since relativism does not provide a firm research agenda.[39] Bryman shows that there is no clear correspondence between epistemological position and technique in decisions to use quantitative or qualitative approaches.[40] Snizek contends that the logical implication theoretical paradigms make of methodological choices is negligible.[41] In her study of the coincidence between functionalism and the survey method, Platt concludes that

> "the tendency to see theory and method as intimately related has in it, both in this case and more generally, more of ideology about what the relation between them ought to be than it has of close historical observation of what actually happened."[42]

In fact, the case study approach is not inimical to positivism if the ultimate objective is to employ findings about particular instances to explicate larger patterns of social relations. In this respect it is meaningless to contend, as Crossley and Vulliamy do, that "given the epistemological foundations of case study . . . no attempt (in case study research) is made to extrapolate general laws or universally applicable recommendations in a positivistic sense,"[43] since the case study technique *per se has no particular epistemological foundation*. The case study method can only be used in a manner adverse to positivism if it is employed in the service of an incompatible epistemology such as cultural relativism. Indeed, Crossley and Vulliamy advocate case study as a *complement* to positivist approaches, to be used "to enhance the potential generalizability of research findings." What they fail to understand is that such use of case study becomes itself the instrument of a positivist framework.

The Morphogenetic Approach

A second, rather recent approach responds to the issue of positivists' tendency to view educational growth as dependent on particular changes in other sociocultural systems. This is not, of course, a view shared exclusively by positivists; Marxists, relativists and, indeed, the great majority of Comparative Education scholars have heeded Sadler's dictum that events outside the school matter as much as what occurs inside. Now, however, a small group of macrosociologists have emerged to challenge the idea that education responds invariably to discrete external pressures generated by such events as evolving industrial needs or systemic political changes. Archer in particular has inspired a growing belief that educational systems are expanding largely independently of particular external economic and political structures, that, indeed, education has a life of its own.[44]

It is interesting that Archer uses criticism of positivist theories of education development—including human capital theory, consumption theory, social control theory, and ideological diffusion theory—to establish the relative merit of morphogenecism, which is itself based on positivist principles. Her fundamental premise is that educational systems possess considerable autonomy and display "unintended consequences, unexpected aggregate properties, and unsought emergent features."[45] Although educational systems originate from and are sustained by their interaction with other sociocultural systems, no general explanation can correctly advance some particular social variable or process as universally responsible for change. Instead, only a morphogenetic paradigm—one that takes account of the intricate combination of social interaction and structural factors that generate systemic elaboration over time—can yield an adequate explanation of the development of educational systems.

Why is Archer uncomfortable with the approaches of most other positivists? After all, in common with them she accepts the Comtian view that all knowledge is derivable from observable phenomena, and opposes both the Marxian notion that growth is a matter of structural necessity induced by the economic system and the historicism and holism of relativists. Her argument with other positivists resides in their tendency to be unidimensional, to establish universal, law-like generalizations based on a particular independent variable. Indeed, while she rejects historical specificity, her morphogenecism—with its emphasis on contextuality and microscopic analyses of corporate structure-primary actor interaction—is as close to relativism as a positivist would dare embrace.

What most establishes Archer as a positivist is her belief that if only the right independent variables to explain systemic growth could be discovered and identified we would have a complete understanding of educational expansion. Her quarrel with other positivists, however, is that they fail to account for the subtleties and intricacies of the independent variables, that they are too quick to propose unidimensional factors that can explain only a small amount of the variance in educational growth. To them, I suspect, Archer's reductionism would appear excessive; to subject interactions to minute contextual scrutiny is to preclude the formulation of meaningful explanation. Moreover, despite her reductionism, Archer posits the existence of three crucial phases of systemic development—associated with an emergent system, a developing system, and a contemporary system—a contention that seems contrary to her aversion to general theories.

The Problem Solving Approach

Brian Holmes's problem solving approach is the most genuinely eclectic in the Comparative Education literature, and it is perhaps an exaggeration to label it relativistic, as I had done earlier.[46] Indeed, that approach acknowledges the role of "sociological laws" as fundamental, but always as "hypothetical, contingent, and refutable under given circumstances."[47]

Holmes contends that social scientists have been slow to recognize the cogent meaning of relativity in the natural sciences for social theory and research and for the need of a paradigmatic revolution. Just as relativity gave reason to question the logical validity of the absolutist traditional concepts of mass, force, and the like in the physical world, so should it challenge the idea that fundamental eternal laws underlie all behavior and social development, an idea that forms the basis for most contemporary social research. Rather than by a search for eternal or infallible laws, social theory should be informed by a search for contextual generalizations in which behavior is seen as governed by specific spatiotemporal, linguistic, and socio-psychological conditions within varying circumstances. Since the pursuit of absolute laws is fruitless, 'pure' research is unwarranted and represents a waste of time and resources. Instead, the social sciences, and Comparative Education in particular, should be responsive to practical problems and the need for application. Piecemeal social engineering oriented to policy and emphasizing modest objectives within the context of specific initial conditions and unique national circumstances should guide comparative research. Investigation should begin not with the collection of data but from a careful identification and analysis of a discrete practical problem.[48]

Holmes's method represents a refutation of the positivist view that if all factors giving rise to a particular social behavior were known, then a multivariate statement would explain that behavior wherever and whenever it occurs. Rather than a search for universal regularities in nature and history, Holmes believes that comparative social research should be guided by ideal-typical normative constructs as models with which to examine particular structures and social relationships. Such constructs, insofar as they give coherence to the multiplicity of beliefs that exist in society and provide clues to collective mental states and social action, are appropriate starting points for investigation. The proposed use of such models is not an abrupt departure from earlier theory in Comparative Education. Rather, it is somewhat analogous to Mallinson's use of national character. Ideal-typical models focus more, however, on general aims and theories regarding man, society, and knowledge than on intangible, immanent forces. Holmes argues that aims, theories and mental states are relevant constituents of the initial specific conditions associated with the 'problem' to which the attention of the researcher is to be directed.

Despite its apparent complexity, the problem solving approach can be reduced essentially to two basic elements: the construction and use of ideal-typical models to describe particular 'real' worlds, and the establishment of 'sociological laws' that relate the operation of educational, socioeconomic and political institutions with one another. The use of ideal-typical models attempts to satisfy the relativist impulse without being relativistic. It requires the use of "constitutions, legislation, and psychological, sociological, and epistemological theories" to infer normative orientations about the nature of man, society and knowledge in particular settings. But Holmes also maintains that such models alone would make for an incomplete analysis. Similarly, the use of sociological laws tends to satisfy the positivist impulse without being positivistic. It permits the necessary preparation of taxonomies of educational and societal institutions but, as with ideal-typical constructs, such laws are not themselves the objective of research.

Unfortunately, in trying to avoid the disabilities of positivism *and* relativism the problem approach may satisfy no one. On the one hand, by admitting that sociological laws are viable, even if inadequate by themselves to address practical issues, Holmes leaves himself open to the argument that positivism has simply not had sufficient time to develop into an effective epistemology in Comparative Education, that with increased (positivistic) knowledge and more (positivistically trained) scholars, we will eventually be able to address difficult problems. On the other hand, by claiming that the examination of interaction and contextuality is vital for proper analysis, he is vulnerable to the relativist claim that general laws are irrelevant. Both relativists and positivists can argue that the problem approach attempts to mesh irreconcilable epistemological assumptions, and is so unwieldy as to be impractical. Indeed, despite Holmes's claim that "a great many doctoral students have stated explicitly that their research was informed by the 'Holmes problem-solving approach',"[49] the published literature contains few samples. To illustrate his approach Holmes tends to refer back to the 1954 Year Book of Education,[50] hardly an expression of widespread acceptance.

Conclusion

Comparativists have generally failed to notice how fundamentally incompatible have been certain rival epistemological orientations in Comparative Education. Indeed, without acknowledging it positivists and cultural relativists differ on the very meaning of 'comparison', and phenomenologically-oriented scholars approach the field in a way that vitiates any reasonable interpretation of that term.

This is not to say that all comparativists fail to recognize epistemological disparities. A few have sought a synthesis of varying orientations, but they have not yet succeeded. For one thing, there is a tendency to misconstrue method and theory, leading to the employment of a technique often associated with one epistemology unwittingly in the service of another. Some investigations explicitly employ both contextual, interpretive analysis and cross-national generalization, but these tend also to serve the purpose of a particular epistemology. The viability of the most genuinely eclectic effort, Holmes's problem-solving approach, has yet to be demonstrated, but the prospect of it becoming an alternative to prevailing epistemologies is dubious. Until a synthesis can be developed that satisfies the requirements of both positivism and relativism, and is sufficiently operationalizable to be commonly employed, we should accept more than one meaning of 'comparison' as governing Comparative Education.

Notes

1. Stewart E. Fraser, *Jullien's Plan for Comparative Education, 1816–1817* (New York: Teachers College, Columbia University, 1964).
2. Marc-Antoine Jullien, *Esquisse et Vues Préliminaires d'un Ouvrage sur l'Education Comparée* (1817); cited in Alexandre Vexliard, *Pedagogia Comparada: Métodos y Problemas* (Buenos Aires: Editorial Kapelusz, 1970), pp. 32–3.
3. Harold J. Noah & Max A. Eckstein, *Toward a Science of Comparative Education* (New York: Macmillan, 1969), p. 114.
4. Joseph P. Farrell, "The Necessity of Comparisons and the Study of Education: The Salience of Science and the Problem of Comparability," in: *Comparative Education Review* 23 (February, 1979), no. 1, p. 10 (emphasis in the original).
5. Richard L. Merritt & Fred S. Coombs. "Politics and Educational Reform", in: *Comparative Education Review* 21 (June–October, 1977), nos. 2–3, p. 252.
6. Le Thành Khoi, "Toward a General Theory of Education," in; *Comparative Education Review* 30 (February, 1986). no. 1. pp. 14–5.
7. Charles Arnold Anderson, "Methodology of Comparative Education", in: *International Review of Education* 7 (1961), p. 29.
8. See Andrew Pickering, *Constructing Quarks: A Sociological History of Particle Physics* (Chicago: University of Chicago Press, 1984).
9. Michael J. Benton. "Theories Getting Out of Hand?" in: *Natural History* 96 (June, 1984), no. 6, pp. 54–9.
10. Edward R. Beauchamp, "Some Reflections on Comparative Education," In: *East West Education* 6 (Fall, 1985), no. 2, p. 12 (emphasis in the original).
11. Erwin H. Epstein, "Currents Left and Right: Ideology in Comparative Education", in: *Comparative Education Review* 27 (February, 1983), no. 1, pp. 3–29.
12. Although ethnomethodology does not necessarily employ phenomenological methods, the two approaches have the same antecedents and are sufficiently similar for my purposes to warrant using the term 'phenomenology' to refer to both. See Lewis A. Coser, "Presidential Address: Two Methods in Search of a Substance," in: *American Sociological Review* 40 (1975), pp. 691–700; James L. Heap & Phillip A. Roth, "On Phenomeno-

logical Sociology", in: *American Sociological Review* 38 (1973), pp. 354–67; and Don H. Zimmerman. "Ethnomethodology", in: *American Sociologist* 13 (February, 1978). pp. 6–15.

13. I. C. Jarvie, "Rationalism and Relativism", in: *British Journal of Sociology* 34 (1983), p. 45.
14. Marshall H. Segall, Donald T. Campbell, & Melville J. Herskovits, *The Influence of Culture on Visual Perception* (Indianapolis: Bobbs-Merrill, 1966).
15. Ruth Benedict, "Anthropology and the Abnormal", in: *Journal of General Psychology* 10 (1934), p. 60.
16. Melville J. Herskovits, *Man and His Works* (New York: Knopf, 1948), p. 77.
17. Melville J. Herskovits, "Some Further Comments on Cultural Relativism," in: *American Anthropologist* 60 (1958), pp. 266–73.
18. Vernon Mallinson, *An Introduction to the Study of Comparative Education* (London: Heinemann, 1975), pp. 12–4 and 271.
19. Quoted in Noah & Eckstein, *op. cit.*, pp. 22 and 46.
20. Edmund J. King, *Other Schools and Ours: A Comparative Study for Today* (New York: Holt, Rinehart & Winston, 1967), pp. 3, 4 and 8.
21. See, for example, Conrad P. Kottak, *Anthropology: The Exploration of Human Diversity* (New York: Random House, 1987). p. 209.
22. Edmund Husserl, *Phenomenology and the Crisis of Philosophy* (New York: Harper Torchbooks, 1965), pp. 106–7.
23. See Alfred Schütz, *Reflections on the Problem of Relevance* (New Haven: Yale University Press, 1970); and David Walsh, "Sociology and the Social World," in: Paul Filmer et al., *New Directions In Sociological Theory* (London: Collier Macmillan, 1972), pp. 15–35.
24. Benjamin R. Barber, "Science, Salience and Comparative Education: Some Reflections on Social Scientific Inquiry", in: *Comparative Education Review* 16 (October, 1972), no. 3, p. 425.
25. *Ibid.*, p. 426.
26. *Ibid.*, p. 427.
27. *Ibid.*, p. 432.
28. *Ibid.*, p. 433.
29. Farrell goes so far as to describe Barber's work as an "excellent critique of methodologism masquerading as science." Farrell, *op. cit.*, p. 8,
30. Richard Heyman, "Comparative Education from an Ethnomethodological Perspective," in: *Comparative Education* 15 (1979), p. 248.
31. Remi Clignet, "The Double Natural History of Educational Interactions: Implications for Educational Reforms," In: *Comparative Education Review* 25 (October, 1981), no. 3, p. 334.
32. *Ibid.*
33. Vandra L. Masemann, "Critical Ethnography in the Study of Comparative Education," in: *Comparative Education Review* 26 (February, 1982), no. 1, p. 7.
34. *Ibid.*, p. 8.
35. See, for example, W. D. Halls, *Culture and Education*, and Reginald Edwards, "Between the Micrometer and the Divining Rod," in: R. Edwards, B. Holmes & J. Van de Graaff (eds.), *Relevant Methods in Comparative Education* (Hamburg: UNESCO Institute for Education, 1973); and Rolland G. Paulston, "Social and Educational Change: Conceptual Frameworks," in: *Comparative Education Review* 21 (June/October, 1977), nos. 2–3, p. 395.
36. Epstein, *loc. cit.*
37. Lawrence Stenhouse, "Case Study in Comparative Education: Particularity and Generalization," in: *Comparative Education* 15 (1979), no. 1, pp. 5–10.
38. Michael Crossley & Graham Vulliamy, "Case Study Research Methods and Comparative Education," in: *Comparative Education* 20 (1984), no. 2.
39. Michael Mann, "Socio-logic," in: *Sociology* 14 (November, 1981), no. 4, pp. 544–50.
40. A. Bryman, "The Debate about Quantitative and Qualitative Research: A Question of Method or Epistemology," in: *British Journal of Sociology* 35 (March, 1984), no. 1, pp. 75–92.
41. W. E. Snizek. "An Empirical Assessment of 'Sociology: A Multiple Paradigm Science'," in: *The American Sociologist* 11 (November, 1976), no. 4, pp. 217–9.
42. Jennifer Platt, "Functionalism and the Survey: The Relation of Theory and Method," in: *The Sociological Review* 34 (August, 1986), no. 3. pp. 501–36.
43. Crossley & Vulliamy, *loc. cit.*
44. Margaret S. Archer (ed.), *The Sociology of Educational Expansion: Take-Off, Growth and Inflation in Educational Systems* (Beverly Hills, Calif.: Sage, 1982).
45. *Ibid.*, p. 6.
46. Epstein, *op. cit.*, pp. 22–3.
47. Brian Holmes, "Paradigm Shifts in Comparative Education," in: *Comparative Education Review* 28 (November, 1984), no. 4, p. 593.
48. Brian Holmes, *Comparative Education: Some Considerations of Method* (London: Allen & Unwin, 1981).
49. Holmes, Paradigm Shifts, *op. cit.*, p. 585.
50. Brian Holmes, *A Comparative Approach to Education* (London: Comparative Education Department, University of London Institute of Education, n.d.), p. 91.

Comparing Higher Education Systems

MAURICE KOGAN

At the 1994 CHER conference, we were warned somewhat sternly about the need to avoid opportunistic opportunities for making comparisons between systems and instead to base our work upon the articulation, testing and accumulation of generalisable hypotheses. This is a noble ambition. but as yet we lack an Isaac Newton in our field of studies.

Comparative studies are always being attacked for, or are self-defensive about, their inadequacies. There are several reviews of comparative public administration which have concluded that there is not much real comparison going on in the study of public administration. That may be because the comparativists are attempting exercises which are not feasible with the issues with which they work. There is, however, a lot of room for good conceptualisation and the search for common themes is a worthwhile exercise. The comparative study of public administration is, as Heady (1990) argues, struggling to accommodate two seemingly inconsistent tendencies. One tendency is to try to 'generalise by making comparisons that are as inclusive as possible and by searching for administrative knowledge that transcends national regional boundaries' (Heady 1990, p. 3). The other tendency is towards case-specific or idiosyncratic analyses) with only scant attention, or none at all, to foreign experience' (ibid.). Clearly public administration has never experienced the same significant orientation towards comparative, cross-national analysis which characterises most other fields of political science' (Pierre, 1995, p. 5).

Types of Comparative Studies

Page (1995) helpfully divides comparative studies under four headings: single country studies; juxtapositions; thematic comparisons and causal explanations.

Single country studies account for nearly three quarters of all empirically based articles published in leading English language public administration journals. They can be classed as comparative inasmuch as they add to knowledge in specifying what it is that marks off one set of administrative arrangements from another. The comparison need not be undertaken by those offering a particular study. The fact that one-offs are available in the literature, however, makes it possible for comparisons to be made somewhere within the universe of scholars. The many edited collections of essays on a range of countries that are published are obviously examples of these.

Juxtapositions bring together single country studies and, at minimum, allow a relatively rapid impression of the range of experiences to be secured.

It is with thematic comparisons that we have our best hope of finding a systematic presentation of evidence which allows common questions about different political systems to be asked. At the most ambitious level, facts can

This paper discusses the range of comparative studies which might legitimately be attempted. It considers the separate issue of whether they must necessarily be directed towards the testing of pre-constructed hypotheses. It describes how the Brunel-Gothenburg-Bergen international team is attempting to compare their three national systems and academic working within them.

be used reiteratively as explanatory factors when the institutions are examined one by one (Finer, 1956). Thematic comparisons might include specified objectives of the comparison, and gather common data in order to generalise on the basis of those data. They attempt to establish regularities in different patterns of administration and deviation from this pattern. Finer hopes that the process might lead to causes. I fear that such a quest often leads to banality rather than illumination. But even if one might be able to determine causal relationships, data collection does not of itself produce fruitful theorising.

The Current State

Where do current higher education comparisons stand in this? I take Ulrich Teichler's analysis of higher education systems (1988) to be an exemplary case of thematic comparisons. He created a conceptual framework enabling evidence to be organised so that comparisons between different higher education systems could be made.

We have the work produced by the CHEPS scholars. In two books (Goedegebuure et al., 1994; Goedegebuure and van Vught, 1994) a helpful framework of themes is offered and is discussed within an international perspective. They are, however, somewhat aggressive about 'individual hobbyhorses' which they think will be 'curbed' by providing an overarching framework to 'maximise comparability of outcomes of the constituent parts.' This sounds like a worthwhile objective, but in fact in their own work they offer thematic blocks against which they organise national characteristics. They do this with intelligence and relevant knowledge but it is difficult to see how these constitute any kind of integrated framework of paradigms, hypotheses or theories.

Goedegebuure and van Vught (1994) follow Ragin (1987) in his claim that comparative method in the social sciences is distinguished by its use of attributes of macro-social units in explanatory statements. They also follow Lane in sponsoring the thick definition of comparative research which involves the analysis of properties of various kinds of spatial units.

An example from van Vught and Goedegebuure is that the extent to which steering mechanisms are facilitatory or controlling affects the propensity of curriculum reforms to go through. But how macro- or thick is the necessary level of analysis there? Without very fine grained analyses of curriculum change, some of them unique, that kind of generalisation will not be true for one country, let alone in comparison across countries. As Teichler (1993) rightly complains, 'higher education research does not seem to move to any balance regarding theories, disciplines and themes, but rather research linked management and policy issues seem to take over the scene.' In my submission, policy and management issues not only take over the scene but their pursuit fails to have much force if they do not take account of the true criteria variables, namely changes in research, scholarship and teaching, in which particularity rather than commonality is likely to be the rule.

The work of our CHEPS colleagues on regulation, steering and control in higher education is important. My point is that it would be valuable even if they did not try to emulate physics and economics in hypothesis forming.

Do We Need Hypotheses?

Page (quoting Sartori, 1970) notes that the whole of political science is a trade-off between configurative or detailed discussion of one case or a few cases and broader and more abstract theoretically based generalisations which 'are best seen as a continuum rather than as categories of comparison'.

Archer (1979), too, has noted that it has proved virtually impossible to make an adequate match between micro analysis, in which the verities of close grained empirical studies can be demonstrated, and macro analysis, in which more generally applicable propositions can be announced and interrogated. Has not the world of knowledge increasingly accepted that more than one incommensurate or apparently inconsistent proposition can be advanced simultaneously? In the social domain, in particular, reality does not pile up in well connected hierarchies of paradigm and theorems.

If stating hypotheses from previous accumulated knowledge and testing, verifying and adding to them were to be our dominant intellectual and research procedure, we would be subscribing to a major hypothesis which is dubious in its own right. The presumption would be that there are sufficient regularities in social experience for them to be capable of being incorporated into 'overarching' frameworks and hypotheses. Such an intellectual procedure is both possible and necessary in the physical world, although some natural phenomena, such as those to be found in metallurgy, and, indeed, in biology and biochemistry, are not capable of subordination to assumptions of rigid regularity. The data emerge in topological rather than progressive arrangements. And uncertainty is the name of much of modern physics as well. Whilst we can certainly look for juxtapositions and thematic comparisons, and attempt to find causal explanations, we will be tying ourselves into an unnecessary bed of nails if we try to direct our research on the basis of pre-structured hypotheses. Where there are usable hypotheses let us enjoy them. Otherwise there is plenty of good work done at the third level, of thematic comparisons, as Frans van Vught's own work amply demonstrates.

It is wrong to assume that without hypothecating there is no theorising. Page, again, says: 'The quest for theoretical focus or purpose for the comparative public administration is . . . misplaced. Certainly there is plenty of room for much more sophisticated, broad and falsifiable theorising in the field. . . . To expect comparative public administration to generate as its focus a particular set of questions or theories makes almost as little sense as expecting multiple regression of content analysis to do the same.' Causal explanations 'should remain as a major objective but at best they can only deal in establishing the strength of the evidence supporting plausible hypotheses rather than offer more direct tests of causality associated with statistical technique. The way forward in comparative research is not to be found in a search for an overall theory, or the institutionalisation of administrative data gathering. Intellectually interesting questions are more likely to provoke data collection than the other way round.'

Some Hypotheses

There are, however, some hypotheses which are already available and workable: Clark's triangle (Clark, 1983), as adumbrated by Becher and Kogan (1992), refers to the way in which higher education policy and the systems resulting from it are the resultant of a triangle of forces—professional-collegial; governmental-managerial and market. Becher and Kogan, adapting Premfors, added a welfare state force. This could now be expressed as a civil society force which might accommodate community, distributive and other welfare functions of higher education. An important subset of this hypothesis is that academics have a dual accountability to their invisible colleges of fellow academics and to their institution.

On these hypotheses it is indeed possible to compare systems and, at any one time, to denote the extent to which one force eg managerial as against collegial, or civil society as opposed to market criteria, is driving the system.

A second hypothesis, invented for the purpose of this paper, is that there is an irreducible quantum of authority to be found in any system. If central authorities yield power to the institutions, a new line of authority, usually at the level of the rector or vice-chancellor, emerges within the institutions. The reason for this is plain. Complex systems need authority at some level or the other to hold them together.

A third hypothesis derives from a functionalist theory of organisations, namely, the concept of socio-technology. Joan Woodward (1965) developed the theme that social relationships develop in response to the underlying technology that an institution performs. Thus the traditional view of collegial academic governance was based on the assumption that the process was based on diverse and individualistic work. It followed that the main production unit was the free academic who required freedom to generate good research and teaching. It followed from this that the structures of higher education would be collegial rather than managerial. By contrast, if the civil society functions of higher education predominate, academic freedom is tempered by social concern and that requires a somewhat more hierarchical channel of authority to secure it.

A fourth set of hypotheses concerns the relationships between the types of knowledge being generated and disseminated and the higher education organisation required to sustain them.

This point taken from work by Tony Becher (1989) and Basil Bernstein (1963) relates to the extent to which forms of knowledge, hard and soft, the collected and integrated curriculum, affect and are affected by its social or organisational forms. It follows that higher education organisation, such as decentralisation, binary systems, more power to rectors, are/should be determined in part by the extent to which they are applicable to the component knowledge structures in teaching and research. A fifth hypothesis, taken from Geertz (1983) and Archer (1979), is that forms of knowledge, feeling or value become shaped and structurated into procedures, processes and structures. It thus refers to a basic generative process in higher education development.

These are stated here as hypotheses. But do they explain causes? Some might—for example, the relationships of structuring to forms of knowledge, or the growth of authority at institutional level, are 'explained' by reasonably universal laws. Any such statements might be worthwhile playing against empirical data to see. For the most part, however, they seem to me to allow most of all for thematic comparisons rather than for the highest level of theory building.

Our Own Approach

Our own approach, as elaborated by Susan Marton (1994), follows that of Castles who, by using methods of comparison, attempts 'to comprehend the purposes for which and the strategies by which policy is elaborated' (Castles, 1989, p8). One method he suggests is the use of comparative case studies of two or more countries, the distinctiveness or similarity of whose policy outcomes is highlighted by the similarities or differences in other respects.

Our British-Norwegian-Swedish project has given a lot of thought to methods of study, including its capacity to yield comparisons, The zones in which we will be making comparisons are as follows:

- changes in the theories of the state in the three countries
- changes in the mechanisms of government in the three countries
- policy formation and the place of elites, interest groups and networks
- the nature of the reforms created by government
- the impacts of the reforms in terms of the epistemic identities and working practices of academics in a range of seven disciplines, and in a range of institutions in the three countries
- case studies in the generation, application and impacts of quality assurance policies in the three countries
- other case studies relevant to the particular countries such as graduate education and the enterprise initiative in the UK.

Our study involves empirical work in which the relationships of policies to the impacts on academics is the principal conceptual and empirical focus. This involves, we have no doubt, going in very deeply into the working life of academics in the three countries. As work goes on, we are deriving propositions which are exchanged at regular meetings and through the circulation of papers among the three teams. Ultimately we expect to have competent statements of the nature of policy movements and structures, and of more general political systems, in the three countries and the extent to which each of them has had effects on academic working and values and identities. We do of course begin with a sequence of propositions which guide the questions we ask at interviews and our reading of primary and secondary material.

It is already clear that comparisons can be made across the three countries by working strongly from inductive methodologies which are essentially bottom up and starting from the analysed experiences and not the other way round. But this does not mean that we start with atheoretical perceptions. The kind of hypotheses stated in the paragraphs above are among those which are in our minds as we analyse our work. We have as well, for example, good immersion into the theory of elites, interest groups and pressure groups against which to analyse the extent to which these are important in the three countries, and the extent to which the differences in their operation and power reflect differences in the national political culture or expectations of the higher education systems.

In conclusion, it has been the aim of this paper to demonstrate that the comparative method does not only consist of testing pre-established hyptheses. In addition, the comparative method can be used as 'a mode of locating and exploring a phenomenon as yet insufficiently understood' (Castles, 1989, p. 9). The Brunel-Gothenburg-Bergsen research team hopes that the use of the selective comparative case studies will yield comparative research results that will contribute to the field, rather than being attacked for its inadequacies.

References

Archer, M. S. (1979). *The Social Origins of Educational Systems*, Sage.

Becher, T. (1989). *Academic Tribes and Territories: Intellectual Enquiry and the Cultures of the Disciplines*, SRHE and Open University Press.

Becher, T. and Kogan, M. (1992). *Process and Structure in Higher Education.* (2nd edition) Routledge.

Bernstein, B. (1963). *Class, Codes and Control: Vol 3, Towards a Theory of Educational Transmission*, Routledge & Kegan Paul.

Castles, F. (ed.) (1989). *The Comparative History of Public Policy*, Polity Press.

Clark, B. R. (1983). *The Higher Education System: Academic Organisation in Cross-National Perspective*, University of California Press, Berkeley.

Finer, F. (1956). *Governments of the Greater European Powers*, Methuen.

Geertz, C. (1983) *Local Knowledge*, Basic Books.

Goedegebuure, L., Kaiser, F., Maassen, P. and de Weert, E. (1994). 'Higher education policy in international perspective: an overview' in Goedegebuure, L., Kaiser, F., Maasen, P., Meek, L., van Vught, F. and de Weert, E (eds), *Higher Education Policy: An International Comparative Perspective*, Pergamon Press.

Goedegebuure, L., Kaiser, F., Maassen, P., Meek, L., van Vught, F. and de Weert, E. (1994). 'International perspectives on trends and issues in higher education policy' in Goedegebuure, L., Kaiser, F., Maasen, P., Meek, L., van Vught, F. and de Weert, E (eds), *Higher Education Policy: An International Comparative Perspective*, Pergamon Press.

Goedegebuure, L. and van Vught, F. (1994). 'Comparative higher education policy studies' in Goedegebuure, L. and van Vught, F. (eds), *Comparative Policy Studies in Higher Education*, CHEPS.

Heady, F. (1990). 'Introduction' in Dwivedi, O. P. and Henderson, K. M. (eds), *Public Administration in World Perspective*, Iowa State University Press.

Marton, S. (1994). 'Issues in comparative methodology', Annex to Bauer, M., Henkel, M., Kogan, M. and Marton, S. *The Impacts of Reform on Higher Education: An Anglo-Swedish Comparative Study*, Paper given at Conference of Consortium of Higher Education Researchers, Enschede, October 5–7, 1994.

Page, E. C. (1995). 'Comparative public adminstration in Britain', *Public Administration*, Spring 1995, Vol. 73 No. 1.

Pierre, J. (1995). 'Comparative public adminstration: the state of the art' in Pierre, J. (ed.), *Bureaucracy in the Modern State, An Introduction to Comparative Public Administration*, Edward Elger.

Ragin, R. (1987). *The Comparative Method, moving beyond qualitative and quantitative strategies*, University of California Press.

Satori, G. (1970). 'Concept misinformation in comparative politics' *American Political Science Review*, 64.

Teichler, U. (1988). *Changing Patterns of the Higher Education System: The Experience of Three Decades*, Jessica Kingsley Publishers.

Teichler, U. (1993). 'Research on higher education in Europe: Some aspects of recent developments' in Frackmann, E. and Maasen, P. (eds), *Towards Excellence in European Higher Education in the 90s*, Proceedings of 11th European AIR Forum, University of Trier, 27–30 August 1989, EAIR.

Woodward, J (1965). *Industrial Theory and Practice*, Oxford University Press.

The Use and Abuse of Comparative Education

HAROLD J. NOAH

My favorite anecdote in comparative study is from the field of comparative philology. One day, the story goes, a Spanish-speaking student of Russian language went to her professor and asked him: "Professor, do you have in Russian any equivalent of our Spanish word 'mañana'?" After brief reflection, the professor said to her: "Why, yes. In Russian we have 27 equivalents for 'mañana', but none of them I think conveys the same sense of urgency!"

The more urgent and intractable our educational problems seem to be, the more tempting becomes the notion of a "quick fix." Reports of success in foreign lands are all that is needed to release a flood of what I call "*My Fair Lady* prescriptions"—you remember:

> Why can't the English teach their children
> how to speak?
> Norwegians learn Norwegian, the Greeks are
> taught their Greek . . .
> Arabians learn Arabian with the speed of
> summer lightning,
> And the Hebrews learn it backward, which
> is absolutely frightening . . .

We have all surely noted the fanfare of attention given just at present to the (alleged) merits of the Japanese education system and the calls for us to learn from Japanese successes and to imitate what we can. A far cry indeed from the years of postwar occupation of Japan, when the shoe was precisely on the other foot! There may indeed be some truth to the adage that if you live long enough you will see everything at least twice, the second time the opposite of the first.

Recall, too, the exhibitions of intense interest in the Soviet school system after *Sputnik* was sent aloft. *What Ivan Knows That Johnny Doesn't* was the apt title that summed up the mood of the times.[1] Later in the 1960s the search for an educational model shifted to Britain and the well-publicized attractions of Open Education in the early school grades. Now it is Japan's turn. Perhaps we should be grateful for small mercies. After all, only a relatively small group here in the United States during China's Cultural Revolution urged us to follow that splendid example by sending our teachers out to the countryside for political reeducation, with specific attention to be paid to improvement of their latrine-cleaning skills.

So, there are clearly some problems, if not abuses, to contemplate in the comparative study of education—especially so when the object of the exercise is to find an easy solution abroad for complex problems at home. But comparative education does have its valued and legitimate uses, as well.

The Uses of Comparative Education

Properly done, comparative education can deepen understanding of our own education and society; it can be of assistance to policymakers and administrators; and it can form a most valuable part of the education of teachers.[2] Expressed another way, comparative education can help us understand better our own past, locate ourselves more exactly in the

This is a slightly altered version of the original paper, delivered as an inaugural lecture for the Gardner Cowles Chair, Teachers College, Columbia University, New York, on November 1, 1983.

present, and discern a little more clearly what our educational future may be. These contributions can be made via work that is primarily descriptive as well as through work that seeks to be analytic or explanatory; through work that is limited to just one, or a very few, nations, as well as through work that embraces a wider scope; through work that relies on nonquantitative as well as quantitative data and methods; and through work that proceeds with explicitly formulated social science paradigms in mind as well as in a less formalized manner.

Description

Let us look first at the uses of description. Accurate description is a kind of "mapping" of what other countries are doing or not doing, planning, abandoning, or changing in their educational enterprises. A great deal of this used to go on in departments and ministries of education. Recall the work of the United States Bureau of Education under William Torrey Harris and of the Board of Education in England. Michael Sadler's series of Special Reports on foreign educational developments are a model of this genre. I have always been in special debt to one volume in the series, entitled simply *Education in Russia* and published in 1909, by one of His Majesty's Inspectors of Schools, Thomas Darlington. It is a work that reveals quite terrifying powers of observation, assimilation, and reporting.[3]

Help in Decision Making

It would be wrong to typify these efforts as "mere description." First of all, there is nothing "mere" about the tremendous amount of effort that has to be exerted simply to acquire systematic, parallel data on educational systems that differ in the particulars of their structure.

Second, accurate, reliable description will often show us that our own problems are not unique, and such knowledge can be most useful. It directs us to search out and try to understand forces and factors at work that transcend the boundaries of our own society. Exercises in mapping the experiences of other countries can feed directly into policymaking and decision taking. Indeed, as Edmund King has pointed out, comparative studies of education are legitimated and energized precisely to the extent that they originate from the need to make decisions about the conduct of education.[4]

Thus, we worry a great deal about youth unemployment, and we question whether our schools are preparing young people properly for the labor market. This is by no means a uniquely American concern; the British, for example, are struggling with similar problems, as are the French. In such cases, it is not only knowledge of parallel phenomena that is useful but also knowledge of other countries' attempted solutions and of the problems that those solutions are encountering.

These considerations are particularly to be borne in mind at present, as we try to deal with the flood of recent reports on the condition of American education and what we should be doing about it. If we have a tendency to flagellate ourselves for our shortcomings a little too enthusiastically, it may be because we do not recognize that other nations are also experiencing severe problems in defining what makes for an education of excellence in the modern world. From Britain to the Soviet Union to Australia and on around the globe, there are currently going on most vigorous discussions of proposals to change profoundly the content and structure of secondary education. Knowledge of what is being proposed and tried in cognate situations abroad is indispensable for reasoned judgment about what we need to do at home.

Comparative Standards

Another important use of descriptive studies lies in the opportunity they provide to estimate the standing of the United States relative to other countries along dimensions of education that are of interest. This was a major preoccupation in the early years of the nineteenth century; it remains a significant and viable contribution of comparative education. How do our arrangements for the education of the handicapped, the gifted, the very young, and the not so young stack up against those of other countries that we consider our peers? The studies of the International Association for the Evaluation of Education Achievement (IEA) are built on a painstaking mapping of what school children in dozens of countries know in their own and foreign languages, mathematics, science, civics, and the like. Used properly (and, as we shall see, that is not always the case), the resultant intercountry rankings can be powerful pointers toward special problems and needed improvements.

Remedying Misperceptions

Even single-nation studies can be immensely useful, especially those dealing with countries that are important to us but to which access is difficult. The Soviet Union is a case in point. When I was working on aspects of the financing of Soviet education, the accepted view was that vocational education and higher education were the favored sectors of the Soviet system and that general secondary education took second place to other sectors that promised a more direct contribution to economic growth. My research led me to a quite opposite conclusion: as far as ruble allocations were concerned, the Soviet authorities had treated general secondary education far more generously than vocational and higher education.[5] Other single-nation studies in comparative education have shown equally unexpected results. Just one example is Foster's demonstration that Ghanaian vocational secondary schools did not so much provide the economy with a pool of young people ready to enter manual trades as serve as a vehicle for furthering the academic aspirations of Ghanaian youth.[6]

Education as Touchstone

Only cynics believe that nations get the governments they deserve, but it may well be that nations get the educational institutions they merit. As the recent report on secondary education from the Carnegie Foundation for the Advancement of Teaching put it: "A report card on public education is a report card on the nation. Schools can rise no higher than the communities that support them."[7] If this is true, then the state of the schools may be an indicator of more than just educational conditions. For example, indifference in the schools to the value of intellectual activity may betoken a more general anti-intellectualism in society; authoritarian classrooms may reflect authoritarian political arrangements; and inefficient use of resources devoted to education may simply be an extension of inability to use resources effectively in industry, agriculture, and commerce.[8] If these things are so, and there is a good deal of evidence that they are, comparative education can be a fruitful approach to understanding the values, culture, and achievements of other societies—certainly not in their entirety but, nonetheless, a significant portion of what we need to know about our neighbors on this globe.[9]

As I found when I was engaged in a study of school policies in Austria, the processes of educational policymaking told a good deal about Austrian society in general. I was a member of an international team reviewing Austrian education for the OECD. Two aspects impressed us deeply. One was the emphasis placed on what the Austrians termed *Betreuung,* which can be translated as "trust," or "stewardship." Teachers and school administrators, politicians and parents, employers and trade unionists all used the word, meaning by it their sense that the schools bore what I understand lawyers term "a duty of care" for the students. The second was the careful attention to collaborative decision making—joining government, employers, and trade unions—when figuring out arrangements for the final years of school and entry into the labor market. Both of these approaches were characteristic of contemporary Austrian attitudes in the wider arena. The concept of stewardship enunciated by Aquinas in medieval Catholic thought is alive and well today and living in Austria.[10]

Obviously, too, there are instances where the schools do *not* complement political aspirations or social processes of a given society. Take, say, the shah's Iran. Like so many of the oil-rich nations, it was a society with two distinct facets, the modern and the traditional. The shah's schools served the sectors of society that he most wished to develop: business, the army, the towns. But "modernized" schools flew in the face of the aspirations and world outlook of the more traditionally orientated segment of the nation. Hence, to look at the shah's schools was to have regard for official Iran only. Meanwhile, traditional Iran lived on, as strong as ever, and nursed its resentments to the point of revolution. Parallel disjunctions were evident in many of the colonial territories before independence as the schools and universities established by the colonizers produced an elite no longer subservient to imperial interests. Such disjunctions between school and society are keys to understanding the pressures that can build up toward sudden, and often discontinuous, political change.

Origins and Influences

Although comparative education characteristically tends to emphasize differences, the basic similarities of formal education across countries are also of interest. With increasing speed, beginning about 1860, the nations of the world have made available the facilities for formal schooling to ever-larger fractions of their population. The institutional frameworks, the preparation of teachers, the equipment used, the systems of grading and examinations, the issuing of certificates and diplomas—all contribute to the basic commonality of school systems, wherever they are located. Two main factors have been at work to create this standardization: diffusion of educational practices across national boundaries, and ever-greater sharing of common objectives for expanding resources for formal education.[11]

Contemporary European practices in education cannot be understood without reference to models developed in the United States. For example, secondary education all over Europe has been powerfully influenced by the American model of the neighborhood comprehensive high school. Sweden was the leader in the European movement to establish secondary schools that were no longer differentiated according to the social class origins of their students. The Swedish planners and bureaucrats who effected the reform were well acquainted with the American experience and took it into account when formulating their plans (even though the American philosophy of decentralized control and predominantly local financing did not appeal to them at all).[12] From Sweden, the comprehensive school movement radiated to influence developments in England, France, the other Scandinavian countries, and recently even Spain and Portugal. In West Germany, some states (particularly those with Social Democratic governments) moved toward the comprehensive pattern (it is, e.g., the basic mode of secondary school provision in West Berlin), while the Christian Democratic Länder largely resisted what had become a European trend.[13] In each of these countries, there were local differences and adaptations, but the twin elements of comprehensive secondary education (massive expansion of enrollments and reduction in institutional differentiation) were everywhere in evidence, as they diffused either directly or indirectly from the American example.

Sometimes the diffusion was more forceful and took on the character of deliberate implantation or imposition. European and American colonial activities have spread a model of schooling that shows every sign of possessing tremendous survivability. For this reason, it is impossible to understand education in, say, contemporary Nigeria, Tunisia, or the Philippines without taking into account the models planted in those places by the British, the French, and the Americans, respectively.

Cross-cultural study of education, then, can identify the potentials and the limits of international borrowing and adaptation. Although nobody has yet tried to do a complete accounting, my impression is that international borrowing of educational ideas and practices has more failures to record than success. Transplantation is a difficult art, and those who wish to benefit from the experience of other nations will find in comparative studies a most useful set of cautions, as well as some modest encouragement.

From the Particular to the General

I now come to that use of comparative study which I believe to be its most exciting, though perhaps also its most difficult, that is, its potential for establishing the generalizability of what we think we know about education. Of course, results based on research conducted within a single country can be most valuable, and I am aware of the increasing trend among social scientists to emphasize the merits of particularist approaches and to express a distrust of generalization. This may simply be another swing of the pendulum of fashion in research, or it may have more substantial bases. But comparative education is caught inextricably in what Isaiah Berlin has described as the classic dilemma of those who wish to know about the world and to act on it.[14] Do we want to be "hedgehogs," who know one big thing, or do we want to be "foxes," who know many things—none of them presumably very big? Clifford Geertz, in his recent book *Local Knowledge,* wants us to settle for lots of little things; one big thing, he believes, is simply not attainable.[15] The debate will not be settled quickly—in comparative education or in any of our other intellectual enterprises. Those enterprises are characteristically partly a matter of science and partly a matter of art. Scientists take the very complex, even the mysterious, and by their work make it ordinary, lawlike, explicable. Artists take the ordinary and the humdrum and impart to it wider meaning, even mystery at times. In this manner, some in comparative study systematically try to move from the particular to the more general; others are concerned with enriching our understanding of a greater number of particulars. While I enjoy the richness of the particular, I am committed to the enterprise of trying to make sense out of (which I take to mean "bring order to") the bewildering variety of educational phenomena we observe. One way that we do this is to take the propositions that arise out of the work done in single countries and test the extent to which they can be said to hold in other situations.

For example, research in the United States has shown that a child's family birth order has some relation (though not a large one) to the child's scholastic achievement. This finding lends support to theoretical models that emphasize the importance for children's school achievement of the time and other resources that parents spend on their children and the tendency for firstborn children to get more of their parents' (undivided) attention and purchasable resources than do subsequent children. Cross-national studies have shown, however, that the simple relation between birth order and school achievement does not always obtain, for example, in Scotland and France. Subsequent research has shown that, rather than birth order, it may be the spacing of births and family size that are of prime significance, and that the effect of birth order on achievement is mediated through family size and the birthrate.[16] In this way, cross-national work has not only pointed toward improved theoretical models but has also, in fact, prevented overgeneralization on the basis of results derived from a single country.

Let me take just one further example. What if we find that rates of return on investments in higher education are falling in the United States? The comparative approach primes us immediately to ask, Where else in the world is this happening? Are there countries that show rising rates of return? Which are they? What are the country characteristics that are related to declining or rising rates of return to education, respectively?[17] Is it true that rates of return to education are inversely related to rates of enrollment expansion in the recent past? Such a hypothesis is not unreasonable: as the number of young people graduated increases, we might expect a more abundant supply of labor to drive entry-level wages down and vice versa. If a relationship of this kind can be observed in a number of countries, we can be somewhat more confident that we are not observing just a chance phenomenon. There is also potential insight to be gained from examining more closely those countries where rates of return are not being driven down, despite a sizable increase in the number of young entrants into the labor market. We can try to answer the question, Under what conditions do rates of return to education hold up?

A comparative approach enlarges the framework within which we can view the results obtained in a single country: by providing counterinstances, it challenges us to refine our theories and test their validity against the reality of different societies; and, by providing parallel results, it can yield important confirmation of results obtained elsewhere.[18]

The Abuse of Comparative Education

After all this sweetness and light, let me now turn to the more problematic side—though I am happy that I can report much less in the way of abuse of comparative education than there seems to be legitimate use.

As I have pointed out, comparative education is an applied field of study that finds particular justification in the service of evaluation, management, administration, and policymaking. Like all applied fields, it is open to potential abuse by those who wish to use its results to support (or oppose) a specific program of change.

Making a Case

As I also noted when I began, we have special reason to be cautious in the United States when advocates of change rely heavily on reports of a successful program abroad. Diane Ravitch, in her recent book, *The Troubled Crusade,* provides a splendid recounting of the substantial misuse of reports of those English practices in infant education that became known as Open Education. She describes how Joseph Featherstone's original quite balanced account was soon superseded by exaggerated and distorted reports of what had been going on in a relatively few exemplary schools. American readers were given the impression that teachers in England had found a magic solution to the most fundamental problems of early education: sustaining the children's active interest in inquiry and learning while building a firm base for future scholastic progress.[19] Without a doubt there were some admirable aspects of some of the things some teachers in England were doing in some classrooms and schools. But of which nation is this not true? The Open Education message became the basis for an overenthusiastic movement, supported by considerable public funds and extending far beyond the early years of schooling (for which it was developed in England), even into the high school. Of such stuff are present fads and future disasters made. The authentic use of comparative study resides not in wholesale appropriation and propagation of foreign practices but in careful analysis of the conditions under which certain foreign practices deliver desirable results, followed by consideration of ways to adapt those practices to conditions found at home.

A cautious approach to reports of foreign successes is particularly in order for the United States. Education in the United States is characteristically more open to experimentation and new ideas than is the case in most other countries—indeed, too open, in the opinion of many observers abroad. In such a climate, the job of the comparative educator often consists in tempering enthusiasm with a dash of realistic reporting. Not so in other, more conservative countries (e.g., the Federal Republic of Germany), where resistance to external ideas is much, much greater.

Misinterpreting Results

Scholars in general are used to seeing their results misinterpreted by reason of carelessness, ignorance, or intention. And scholars in comparative education are no exception. In the behavioral and social sciences and in historical and philosophical inquiry, responsible scholarship more often than not requires tentativeness in advancing conclusions. Explanatory models are not overly strong, data are often defective, and criteria for confidence in making inferences are subject to dispute. We do the best we can, and, when it comes time to announce our results, they are in effect offered up as hostages to those who can make use of them. Sometimes the use that is made surprises us.

A recent example of misinterpretation of results is probably known to many of my readers today, but let me cite it all the same. Barbara Lerner, in the fall 1982 issue of *Public Interest,* sought to answer the question, How are we doing in American schooling, and, in particular, how much have American youngsters achieved in the various school subjects, compared with their counterparts in other countries? Using data from the publications of the IEA, she concluded, "Relatively little."[20]

As my colleague Richard Wolf pointed out in an incisive critique of the various adjustments Lerner chose to make in the IEA data and the inferences she drew on the basis of those adjusted data, the original findings simply do not support her sweeping conclusion. The achievement picture is much more mixed than she would have us believe: relative to youngsters in other economically advanced countries, American school-children performed quite well in some school subjects at some age levels; they did only moderately well in others and really quite poorly in still other subjects.[21] All of us, no doubt, will agree with Lerner that there is room for substantial improvement in American school achievement levels: we should not be satisfied with the pattern of results that was revealed (especially among blacks and students in the South). But the vital enterprise of raising school achievement levels in the United States is not assisted by misinterpretation of results of cross-national scholarship.

Ethnocentrism

One of the most difficult problems of the comparative method is ethnocentrism. This is the fault of looking at the world *primarily* from the point of view of the observer's own culture and values. Ethnocentrism has potential for bedeviling comparative education at every stage—

from choice of topic to study, through choice of procedures to apply, to judgment concerning the meaning of the results of inquiry.

When we choose to define as a "problem" some phenomenon that is really a problem only from *our* point of view and given our set of values but is by no means a problem from the point of view of people in other societies, we have fallen into something of an ethnocentric trap. An oft-cited example of such inappropriate projection of problems has to do with the term "modernization." A great deal of work has been done in comparative education to trace the process and correlates of the so-called modernization process.[22] Special attention has been paid to the contribution that schooling has made to those changes that mark the transformation from a "traditional" to a "modernized" society. Patterns of change that describe well what happened to European and North American societies are assumed to be generalizable to other societies at a later date. Perhaps they are generalizable; perhaps they are not. Although this is a matter for empirical inquiry, the tendency has been to take their generalizability for granted and to go on from there. This lends a spurious color of definiteness to a process that may proceed very differently from one society to the next.

Projecting our own problems often entails exporting our own concepts and using them in situations where their fit with reality may not be very good. Thus, despite the efforts of scholars (notably among them, Lawrence Cremin) to broaden our view of education, it remains true that our concept of education is still typically limited to what goes on inside schools. If that broadened view is desirable in the United States, how much more necessary it is for work in societies that have not developed the elaborate systems of formal schooling that we have here.

Elsewhere, I have made this point in the following terms:

> . . . modernization and education in India [are typically] examined on [some such] basis as the number of technical school places opened and filled. This procedure simply reflects the role of formal technical education in Western societies. Yet the most important means of modernization in Indian society may be the increasing availability of automobiles, bicycles, water pumps, and so forth—all the Western-type machines that impose on their operators disciplines of use, maintenance, and repair. Insofar as the comparative educator is interested in examining the relationship between education and development, he would be utterly misled by giving attention just to the formal system of education and neglecting the informal educational effects of introducing Western machinery.[23]

Conclusion

Enough then of abuses, actual and potential. Let me conclude by underlining my belief that, with all its problems, comparative study is a most desirable way of approaching an understanding of education. The challenge is to do it in ways that are valid, persuasive, practically usable, and, above all, enlightening. But, beyond this, I assert that we need comparative scholarship in general, and comparative education in particular, for a reason that transcends workaday considerations of usefulness.

Our generation, and all those since August 6, 1945, live in a world fundamentally different from that which existed before the bombing of Hiroshima. Before that date man's inhumanity to man, most violently expressed in war, could be (and was) startling in its destructive effects; but the damage to people, institutions, and things was relatively localized, and recovery in at most a generation or two was the norm. Ours is a different prospect, so that unless we are exceedingly careful, lucky, and, above all, wise, we may be the last generation to inhabit a planet that we would recognize as our Earth.

The special wisdom that we and our heirs must cultivate is the wisdom to get along with our neighbors on this planet, in the company of weapons of overwhelming destructive capacity. However much we may wish that these weapons would simply go away, even the smallest dash of realism must tell us that this will not happen. In a sense that is profoundly Faustian, we have paid for our gifts of intelligence in the coin of permanent fear of global annihilation.

I am sufficiently Aristotelian to believe that knowledge is part of wisdom, though I am a long way from believing that it is the whole of that precious commodity. The knowledge we need more urgently than ever before is knowledge of our own society and of others'. And these two species of knowledge are separable only for purposes of cataloging them. For the fundamental assertion of comparative study is that we can truly comprehend ourselves only in the context of a secure knowledge of other societies: knowledge that is parochial is partial, in both senses of that word, and therefore potentially dangerous. It is knowledge without completeness, and it is knowledge without appreciation of the rest of the world's experience.

It may be that even our best efforts to negotiate the perils ahead will come to naught, and that humankind will indeed destroy itself in a tantrum of nationalistic and ideological rage. But, by cultivating throughout our society a tradition of rich understanding and knowledge of the other societies with which we share the planet, we shall at least have given the business of species survival our "best shot." Ultimately, I suppose, that is the real test of how well we have used the comparative approach.

Reprinted from *Comparative Education Review,* vol. 28, no. 4 (November 1984).

Notes

1. Arther S. Trace, *What Ivan Knows That Johnny Doesn't* (New York: Random, 1961).
2. I do not discuss the uses of comparative education in the education of schoolteachers in this paper. See Merle L. Borrowman, "Comparative Education in Teacher Education Programs," and three commentary papers by Andreas M. Kazamias, Harold J. Noah, and Cole Brembeck, in *Comparative Education Review,* vol. 19 (October 1975), for presentation of a variety of viewpoints.
3. Board of Education, *Education in Russia,* Special Reports on Educational Subjects, vol. 23 (London: His Majesty's Stationery Office, 1909).
4. Edmund J. King, *Comparative Studies and Educational Decision* (London: Methuen; Indianapolis: Bobbs-Merrill, 1967).
5. Harold J. Noah, *Financing Soviet Schools* (New York: Teachers College Press, 1966), pp. 109–13.
6. Philip Foster, *Education and Social Change in Ghana* (Chicago: University of Chicago Press, 1965).
7. Ernest L. Boyer for the Carnegie Foundation for the Advancement of Teaching, *High School: A Report on Secondary Education in America* (New York: Harper & Row, 1983), p. 6.
8. A. Harry Passow, Harold J. Noah, Max A. Eckstein, and John R. Mallea, *The National Case Study: An Empirical Comparative Study of Twenty-One Educational Systems* (New York: Wiley, 1976). See esp. chap. 3.
9. Max A. Eckstein and Harold J. Noah, *Scientific Investigations in Comparative Education* (New York: Macmillan, 1969) presents many examples of the approach under discussion.
10. Organization for Economic Cooperation and Development, *Reviews of National Policies for Education: Austria—School Policy* (Paris: OECD, 1979).
11. See particularly works published by Francisco O. Ramirez and John W. Meyer, e.g., "Comparative Education: The Social Construction of the Modern World System," *Annual Review of Sociology,* vol. 6 (1980).
12. Rolland G. Paulston, *Educational Change in Sweden: Planning and Accepting the Comprehensive Reforms* (New York: Teachers College Press, 1968), pp. 30, 100–101, 109, 124, identifies individuals in Sweden who were influential in spreading the American comprehensive gospel. However, Paulston concludes that the U.S. experience was too remote for clear Swedish emulation and that probably the English progressives had a greater impact on Swedish developments. Of course, English educational reformers who were promoting comprehensive secondary schools between 1930 and 1950 were strongly influenced by American models. See W. H. G. Armytage, *The American Influence on British Education* (New York: Humanities, 1967), pp. 72–76.
13. Max-Planck-Institut für Bildungsforschung, *Bildung in der Bundesrepublik Deutschland: Daten und Analysen,* 2 vols. (Stuttgart: Ernst Klett/Rowohlt, 1980), is an indispensable source for contemporary developments in West German education.
14. Isaiah Berlin, *The Hedgehog and the Fox: An Essay an Tolstoy's View of History* (New York: Simon & Schuster, 1953).
15. Clifford Geertz, *Local Knowledge: Further Essays in Interpretive Anthropology* (New York: Basic, 1983).
16. R. B. Zajonc, "Family Configuration and Intelligence," *Science* 192 (April 16, 1976): 227–36.
17. George Psacharopoulos, *Rates of Return: An International Comparison* (San Francisco: Jossey-Bass, 1973) examines 53 case studies in 32 countries to establish relationships between measured return to education and basic characteristics of the countries.
18. The World Bank has an extensive program of inquiry concerning factors affecting rates of return to education around the world. For a description, see George Psacharopoulos, "Educational Research at the World Bank," *Research News* 4 (Spring 1983): 5–8.

19. Diane Ravitch, *The Troubled Crusade: American Education, 1945–1980* (New York: Basic, 1983), pp. 239–51.
20. Barbara Lerner, "American Education: How Are We Doing?" *Public Interest* (Fall 1982), pp. 59–82.
21. Richard M. Wolf, "American Education: The Record Is Mixed," *Public Interest* (summer 1983), pp. 124–28.
22. See, e.g., Don Adams, *Education and Modernization in Asia* (Reading, Mass.: Addison-Wesley, 1970).
23. Harold J. Noah and Max A. Eckstein, *Toward a Science of Comparative Education* (New York: Macmillan, 1969), p. 116.

Higher Education in Developing Countries: The Scenario of the Future*

GEORGE PSACHAROPOULOS

Introduction

The papers in this issue are representative of the challenge facing most university systems in today's developing world. Higher education systems have multiple and various tasks, including nation building, training of high level manpower, satisfying the social demand for education, conducting research and being centers of excellence. As shown by experience, the above batch of laudable objectives is seldom, if ever, achieved. Why?

In this introduction I attempt to explain briefly why the dynamics underpinning the development of university systems in low income countries might have changed drastically relative to, say, 30 years ago, and offer a vision of the inevitable directions higher education might be heading.

The Changed Scenario

Until the middle of this century, only a small fraction of the eligible population attended universities. Higher education systems were able to accommodate the demand for education at the tertiary level based mainly on public funding. As shown in Table 1 and Figure 1, higher education enrollments increased dramatically during the second half of this century to a multiple of what they were in the 1950s. In Latin America, for example, the higher education enrollment ratio increased 10 times between 1950 and 1987.

But as shown in Tables 2, 3 and 4 the public resources for education in general, and higher education in particular, have not increased *pari passu* with enrollments. For example, the share of the public budget devoted to education has remained constant, if not declined, throughout the period under consideration in all parts of the world.

There are explanations for both trends described above.

Enrollment growth. Industrialized countries first took the lead in increasing enrollments in the early sixties. The main reason for the sharp rise in enrollment in the developed world, I believe, was the Sputnik effect. The United States first, followed by European countries, felt that they were lagging behind in technology relative to the Soviet Union. Hence universities (along with the accompanied R & D) were given a great boost. Developing countries followed as a demonstration effect (or to catch up with the metropolis) and also because of the rise of the indigenous civil service in these countries. As the expatriates went home, the country had to produce its own high-level manpower. The thinking was that civil servants should preferably be educated locally, rather than be exposed to a 'foreign model'.

A secondary effect boosting higher education enrollments in both developed and developing countries was the rise in real incomes. As per capita income increased, so did the demand for luxury goods that could not be afforded before. University attendance, regardless of career plans after graduation, increased, along with demand for cars and refrigerators. Also, the rise in the public sector in general

* The views expressed here are those of the author and should not be attributed to the World Bank.

TABLE 1
Higher education enrollment ratio (percent of age group)

Region	*1950*	*1960*	*1970*	*1980*	*Latest 1987*
Africa	0.8	0.7	1.5	3.5	4.3
Asia	1.5	2.6	3.5	5.6	7.3
Latin America	1.6	3.0	6.3	13.5	16.9
Europe	2.2	10.3	17.3	22.1	25.2
Northern America	7.2	28.9	45.4	54.3	63.8
Developing Countries	—	2.1	3.0	5.7	7.4
Developed Countries	—	13.5	23.4	30.3	34.1
World	2.8	5.3	8.5	11.5	12.6

Source: UNESCO, Statistical Yearbook, 1980, 1989.
. . . Data not available.

fueled the demand for higher education—a university degree became the *sine qua non* qualification for entering the public sector.

A third reason for university expansion, especially in developing countries, lies in the development model used in the post World-War II period, which is known as manpower forecasting. For a country to grow economically it should have a given number of engineers, architects and other high level manpower that only a university could produce. (For a review of this model and the reasons it has been discredited, see Psacharopoulos (1984).) Much of university expansion in Africa, for example, was based on this rationale.

It should be noted at the outset that the numbers in Figure 1 refer to actual enrollments and not to the demand for higher education. Demand for university studies vastly exceeds enrollment because many systems cannot offer as many university places as demanded by students and their families.

Finance trends. The main reason why public funds for higher education, and education in general, have not increased *pari passu* with enrollments is that there are many other sectors competing for scarce resources. Food and shelter might be more important than education. Often education ministries are in a weak position relative to other ministries in persuading

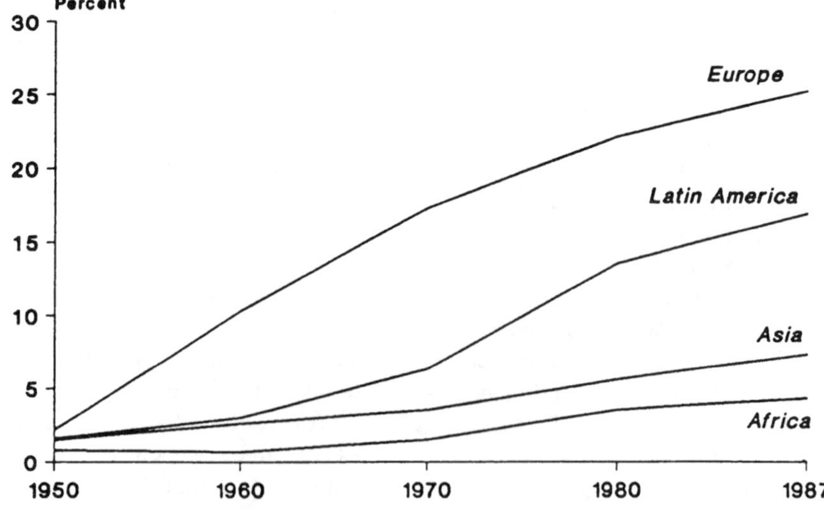

***Fig. 1.* Higher education enrollment ratio by region**
Source: From Table 1.

TABLE 2
Public expenditure on education as percentage of the GNP

Region	*1975*	*1980*	*Latest 1987*
Africa	4.5	5.0	6.6
Asia	4.3	4.5	4.5
Latin America	3.4	3.8	4.1
Europe	5.7	5.5	5.5
Northern America	6.4	6.7	6.9
Developing Countries	3.5	3.8	4.1
Developed Countries	6.0	6.0	5.9
World	5.5	5.5	5.6

Source: UNESCO, Statistical Yearbook, 1989.

the ministry of finance to allocate more resources to education in general. Another reason is that there are limits to the generation of public funds through taxation.

In fact, regarding the split of public funds allocated to education, there has been a shift towards higher education (see Table 4). The reason is that the incidence of university attendance is higher among the wealthier parts of the population whose families are more articulate than those of the farmer. Hence richer groups appropriate more public funds for the education of their offspring.

The Present Response

Different higher education systems have responded in different ways to increased demand for university entry in the presence of financing constraints. Some have accommodated more students at a reduced unit cost, flagging 'mass education', but tacitly sacrificing quality. Others have reduced the number of years required for graduation or changed the mix of subjects offered towards the cheaper social sciences. Of course other systems have shifted towards more reliance on private, rather than public, funds for university financing.

Among the various responses, perhaps the one that relies on greater private sector participation is the most sustainable one, leading to higher efficiency and equity in a given society. In order to understand why this is so, let us briefly analyze the current state of affairs in a typical developing country university system.

Fact No. 1: There is more demand to enter public universities than the state budget can respond to—what economists call 'excess demand'.

Fact No. 2: The demand for university entry is fuelled by the following factors:

—the low cost of entry (no fees, or token fees being charged);

—the high benefit of being a university graduate (higher lifetime earnings, better working conditions);

—the requirement of a university degree for entering the civil service.

Fact. No. 3: The incidence of university attendance is higher among wealthier groups in the population. There are not as many students per 100,000 population whose father is a farmer relative to those whose father is a white collar employee.

The combination of the above facts leads to a series of economic inefficiencies and social inequities.

Inefficiencies. In the first place, anything that is free of charge can be abused. If I have to pay for the electricity I am using, I am more likely to turn off the lights before I leave home. If I do not have to pay, the lights may stay on. The university analog is that many may wish to enroll as 'students' and stay in the university nearly for ever in order to appropriate secondary benefits associated with university attendance (e.g., reduced bus fares, subsidized lunches). If someone has to somehow contribute to the cost of his/her study, it is more likely that this person will think twice before enrolling. And it is less likely that he/she will become an eternal student.

The pressure for university entry by the most articulate, often wealthiest, groups in the population may result in the country misallocating resources devoted to education. If (a) the education budget is more or less fixed, as is the case in most countries, (b) the country has a high incidence of illiteracy, and (c) the most articulate classes divert resources to higher rather than primary education, the country might be underinvesting in what it needs most: primary education to create a literate population and labor force.

TABLE 3
Public spending on education as a share of public budget, major world regions, 1965–80 (percent)

Region	*1965*	*1970*	*1975*	*1980*
Africa	16.0	16.4	15.7	16.4
Asia	14.2	13.1	12.2	12.7
Latin America and Caribbean	18.7	18.9	16.5	15.3
Europe, Middle East, and North Africa	12.4	12.5	11.5	12.2
Developing Countries	16.1	15.8	14.5	14.7
Developed Countries	16.0	15.5	14.1	13.7

Source: Based on World Bank (1986), p. 7.

TABLE 4
The share of higher education in public recurrent expenditure, 1965–80 (percent)

Region	*1965*	*1970*	*1975*	*1980*
Africa	10.8	11.7	21.2	22.1
Asia	16.0	17.0	17.8	20.2
Latin America and Caribbean	14.3	15.9	23.4	23.5
Europe, Middle East, and North Africa	10.4	18.3	21.8	21.7
Developed Countries	13.9	18.6	19.4	19.1

Source: Based on World Bank (1986), p. 54.

Inequities. Who are those most likely to be excluded from the present higher education financing system? Certainly, it is not the offspring of high income families. These will either enroll free of charge at the public university (perhaps because better coaching or attendance at a private secondary school gave them more chances to compete successfully at the national university entrance examinations). Or, if they fail to enter the domestic public higher education system, they will enroll in a private university or go abroad for their studies.

Of course it is those who come from the lower income classes that are most likely to be excluded from 'free higher education' because, although they will also pay no enrollment fees, the foregone income while studying deters them from even applying for entrance. Or, if they compete at the national university entrance examinations, they might be at a disadvantage relative to those from wealthier families because they did not receive equivalent coaching.

Also, if (a) universities are supposed to select the most able among the pool of candidates, (b) the distribution of abilities is the same among the two socioeconomic groups described above, and (c) selection is made principally by social class rather than ability, this adds a further inefficiency in the system. (See Pinera and Selowsky 1981.)

The Alternatives

Now compare the above situation to one in which the financing of higher education relies to a greater extent on private resources and contributions from users. What would be the efficiency and equity implications of this change?

First, excess demand for university education would be reduced. This reduced pressure for university entry may translate into more public resources being used for primary education, which is still investment priority number one in developing countries.

Second, tapping private finance sources means more resources for universities as a whole. Whether it is by means of the establishment of private universities, or the paying of fees at public universities, the great unsatisfied demand for university places will translate, although not automatically, to better quality education.

But I think the ultimate efficiency effect of the introduction of a system of even partial cost-recovery in higher education lies in the accountability it brings with it. If universities charge fees, the consumers must see a value to what they are getting in return. If not, such universities will not survive and give way to better ones. At the individual student level, the charging of fees means greater accountability to themselves, in the sense of being motivated to study hard and complete courses on time.

Charging of fees also provides a more efficient student selection mechanism, as it will be only those who are likely to succeed who would be willing to pay the fees. One should note that cost-recovery does not automatically mean privatization. Fees could be charged at public universities so that accountability is introduced at both the university and student level.

It may sound paradoxical that the introduction of student fees is equitable. Yet if one compares a cost-recovery scenario to the present one, (where both rich and poor do not pay any fees at all, and where the poor might be deterred from entering university because of the foregone earnings involved), things become clearer. Selective cost-recovery (directly related to some measure of parental wealth), can redress inequities in the financing of higher education. In addition, students from low income families cannot only continue to study free of charge, but also receive a scholarship in order to compensate for their foregone earnings.

When combined with the availability of student loans, cost-recovery in higher education is associated with further equity gains. Anybody, whether poor or rich, could then borrow to finance his or her university studies. The equity effect comes from the fact that those who later in life will have higher earnings (due to their university education) relative to the rest of the population (who are not university graduates), will finance their studies themselves—not the general taxpayer. (For an elaboration and empirical evidence on this theme, see World Bank (1986).)

Political Feasibility

The above propositions might be considered theoretical, given the tremendous political cost in introducing cost-recovery in education. Yet several countries have done it. It is my prediction that selective cost-recovery *cum* student loans will be the higher education financing scenario of the future. This will not happen overnight given the political costs. However, higher education systems around the World are inevitably heading in that direction. The simple contrast of the private demand for higher education and the available public resources does not permit any other sustainable financing system in the long run.

References

Pinera, S. and Selowsky, M. (1981). 'The optimal ability-education mix and the misallocation of resources within education magnitude for developing countries', *Journal of Development Economics* 8, 111–131.

Psacharopoulos, G. (1984). 'Assessing training priorities in developing countries: current practice and possible alternatives', *International Labor Review* 123 (5), 569–583.

Financing Education in Developing Countries: An Exploration of Policy Options (1986). The World Bank.

PART II

Faculty Work and the Production of Knowledge

New Perspectives on an Old Problem: The Position of Women Academics in British Higher Education

SANDRA ACKER

Abstract. Women academics in Britain are an elite group among women. Nevertheless, there is abundant evidence that they are disproportionately in lower grades and less secure posts than their male counterparts. These are longstanding inequities which appear to have been met with complacency rather than commitments to bring about change. This paper draws upon feminist theory to outline a range of perspectives which can be used to analyze this situation. Different approaches define the problem differently: it can be located in sex-typed socialization; family-career role conflicts; under-investment in women's education; sex discrimination; or the working of capitalism and patriarchy. The strategies which follow from each approach are discussed and evaluated. Certain features of the British university system may operate to the detriment of women, and there is no network of powerful liberal feminist organizations that can act as a watchdog to safeguard their interests. The unsettled situation of higher education in Britain would seem to make this an inauspicious time to initiate reform, but there are contradictions which might be a basis for feminist action. Socialist and radical feminist frameworks go further than liberal ones in making sense of the entrenched inequalities and resistance to change. Yet there is a case for pursuing liberal feminist strategies, at least in the short run.

Introduction: What is the problem?

This paper returns to the theme of a book I co-edited in 1984, *Is Higher Education Fair to Women?* (Acker and Warren Piper 1984). My chapter was called 'Women in higher education: what is the problem?'. Seven years later, I still ask the same question: how can we best conceptualize the situation of women in higher education in order to understand factors which impact upon it and in order to change it.

There is, of course, the view that there is no real problem, a position which I hope to counter in this introductory section. Otherwise, the 'problem' can be variously located: in sex-typed socialization; family-career conflicts; under-investment in women's education; sex discrimination and career structures; the workings of capitalism and patriarchy. In the main body of the paper I review these approaches, drawing upon feminist theory—that is, ways of understanding gender relations and the structural subordination of women—to help group the 'explanations' and to extend our thinking. The familiar divisions of liberal, socialist and radical feminism are useful here, despite their shortcomings. I also consider strategies for change which follow from these perspectives.

My focus will be mainly on British higher education and on women academics, mostly those in universities and to a lesser extent in polytechnics. To concentrate on women academics is not to suggest that they exist in splendid isolation; on the contrary, like the men, they are part of a complex containing students and support staff, many of whom are also women providing the services which enable academics to get on with their research and teaching.

I write about British universities because I have worked in one for the past nineteen years. I also want to argue that an appreciation of the situation of women in British universities provides a challenge to a tendency in North American writing to give insufficient attention to developments elsewhere. Middleton (1991) takes up this point, commenting that in her experience of teaching university courses on women and education in New Zealand, feminist grand theory developed in the 'wrong' cultural and historical setting can lead to anger and alienation among students who do not recognize the discourse as reflecting their own lives. The focus on differences among women emerging in American writing needs to be extended beyond the boundaries of the United States or even North America as a whole.

What little comparative evidence we have on women academics in a range of countries suggests certain commonalities. Moore (1987) gives figures for 23 countries. She writes that 'it is the rare country that reports a faculty percentage [of women] greater than 25' (p. 28). The representation of women declines at each upward step of the education system virtually everywhere (p. 24). Women tend to be in traditional women's subjects, in subjects of lower status or in the lower status sectors of other subjects. 'Tenured positions, power and prestige continue to elude most women in most countries' (p. 28).

But there are differences, too. Moore's figures are from the early 1980s and it is not clear what assumptions they contain or how they were collected (reflecting typical difficulties in cross cultural statistical comparisons). Yet they show a variation in the proportion of faculty who are women from 2.3% (Switzerland) to 53% (The Philippines). Factors in each country's history, traditions and politics shape the opportunities for women in complex ways. An interesting example is provided by Acar (1990) who suggests that in Turkish universities, a preference for higher class women over lower class men, plus the ready availability of cheap household help and support from the extended family, have encouraged a relatively high proportion of women among academics (32%) despite the country's patriarchal Islamic heritage.

Even if we narrow our range of interests and consider only similar, advanced industrial countries, we get variations in proportions of women in universities, the extent of women's studies, the prevalence of committees on the status of women, and so forth, which call for explanation. For example, legal obligations such as federal contract compliance legislation in the United States and Canada buttress attempts to recruit and promote women in universities, whereas in Britain, any institution can call itself an 'equal opportunity employer' and most do, without any signs of machinery for instituting or monitoring evidence of such an achievement (Johnson 1990).

In Britain, feminist groups have relatively little input into the political process (Gelb 1989). There is little public concern about the situation of women academics, and hardly any literature on the topic. Even among feminists, the plight of women academics—seen as a relatively privileged elite—has remained a low priority item. For nonfeminists, the strong emphasis on merit as a central ideal of the modern university often makes charges of discrimination simply unbelievable (Williams *et al.* 1990; Thomas 1990). McAuley (1987) suggests that there is a 'male commonsense view' which leaves many academics bemused wondering what all the fuss is about. The Cambridge Women's Action Group (1988) notes that many people believe inequality to be a thing of the past and thus equal opportunities policies can only tell 'us to obey laws which . . . we obey already' (p. 1).

The Commission for Racial Equality sent a questionnaire asking about the existence of equal opportunities policies to Academic Registrars in all 44 universities and 30 polytechnics in England and Wales listed in the Education Yearbook (Williams *et al.* 1989). Of the 42 universities which replied, 3 regarded the exercise as irrelevant, and 20 claimed that their original charters were sufficient evidence of their commitment to non-discrimination. Only 5 had both a policy and a means of implementing it and all of these were limited to employment issues, usually regarding women. The authors conclude that 'the majority of institutions of higher education have barely begun to consider the issues seriously' (p. 14).

Yet all the evidence suggests women academics are at a serious disadvantage vis-a-vis men. In Table 1, Section A shows all full time university academic staff (faculty in American terminology) as a group. Women are about 19% of all academics. Sections B and C are subsets of A. Section B includes the academics following a 'normal' career of teaching with expectations of doing research as well, while C, 'research only', comprises persons hired specifically to work on research projects. Women are a much higher proportion (31.1%) of group C than of group B (13.4%).

The people in Group C are on contracts, which means that they are usually paid from funds from bodies outside the universities and have little security. In the past, these jobs were a way station, where someone could get experience and prove their worth, before moving on to a lectureship. In recent years the numbers of contract researchers have shot up, from about 5,000 researchers in 1972 to over 14,000 in the late 1980s (Rees 1989; UFC 1990). One commentator (Aziz 1990) calls this 'creeping casualization', and comments that no other profession has such highly qualified people in such lowly positions. Moreover, while of all academic staff, about a *quarter* of the men are 'research only', *half* of all the women hold these precarious posts.

Among the 'traditional' academics (B in the table), women are far more likely to be in the bottom grades, which contain about 80% of the women and 56% of the men. Only 3% of the women (compared to 15% of the men) are in the highest grade, which is called professor. (In the British university system, the lecturer is the so-called career grade, equivalent to a combination of assistant and associate professor in North America. Readerships and senior lectureships are usually internal appointments, a restricted number available each year in each institution and competed for on a university-wide basis. Professorships are sometimes internal promotions, but are more often advertised nationally. There are rarely more than one or two in a department, and more can be hired only when a position is vacant.) Over time there has been some but relatively little improvement in women's promotion chances.

TABLE 1
Percentage distribution of each sex across the grades for full-time academic staff in universities, Great Britain, 1988–89

	A. academic staff	
	Men	*Women*
Professor	11.3	1.6
Reader/Sr. Lecturer	22.3	8.7
Lecturer	58.1	65.6
Other	8.2	24.1
Total %	99.9	100.0
N	(37,490)	(8,792)

	B. teaching and research staff		*C. research only*	
	Men	*Women*	*Men*	*Women*
P	15.2	3.2	0.8	0.1
R/SL	29.3	16.4	3.3	1.6
L	54.9	76.2	67.0	55.8
O	0.6	4.2	29.0	42.6
Total %	100.0	100.0	100.1	100.1
N	(27,371)	(4,231)	(10,119)	(4,561)

Source: UFC University Statistics 1988–89, Vol. 1 (USR 1990).

Note: 27.0% of men and 51.9% of women are 'research only'.

In 1972 there were 61 women professors (Rendel 1984); in 1988–89 there were 140 (UFC 1990). But if women had the same distribution as men across the grades there would be *993*.

A few figures are available for other categories of university workers and for polytechnics. In 1984 women were 47% of library staff; 30% of administrators; 30% of research and analogous staff; 22% of 'other related' (a category which includes computer staff) in universities. In all cases, women were disproportionately at the lower levels and very scarce at the top ones. Age band comparisons suggested women were 10 to 15 years behind men of the same age in promotion terms (Donoghue 1984). Women were 15% of academics in polytechnics in 1985. Roughly equal proportions of men and women were in senior lectureships (the 'career grade'), but 28.5% of the men and 12.2% of the women were in higher-ranked posts than senior lectureships, while 8.1% of men and 22% of the women were in lower ones (DES, 1987).

These figures suggest that although women academics are privileged in comparison with 'most women' and certainly in comparison with women working in higher education as secretaries, cleaners and so forth, if the comparison group is male academics, women are clearly at a disadvantage. They are better represented than they were thirty years ago but the increase has been at such a slow rate that progress is hard to claim (Sutherland 1985). This type of discrepancy should be of concern, if only as a case of injustice. Moreover, it means that women have little input into decision-making about higher education policy, student admissions, promotion criteria and the like. The next generation sees men firmly in charge. How do we explain these patterns? Feminist theory gives us some possible answers.

Liberal Feminism

Most accounts of women in higher education draw at least loosely on liberal feminist perspectives. The aim of liberal feminism is to alter women's status and opportunities within the existing economic and political frameworks. It concentrates on removing barriers that prevent girls and women from attaining their full potential; that is, on the creation of equal opportunities for the sexes. Key concepts include equal opportunities, sex stereotyping, socialization, role conflict and sex discrimination (Acker 1987).

In Britain, the liberal feminist discourse of 'equal opportunities' is the most widely acceptable analysis (Acker 1986; Weiner 1986). With respect to higher education, there are a number of strands. Liberal feminists consider the impact of socialization; conflicting roles; inadequate social investment in women's education; and sex discrimination.

Socialization

A common explanation for women's 'failure' to achieve high status places responsibility on parents, schools and other socialization agencies which have encouraged women from early childhood to develop a constellation of characteristics not easily compatible with achievement, especially in certain fields. Women are said to display lack of confidence, low aspirations and ambition, concern with people and nurturance, need for approval, desires for dependency, motives to avoid success. Feminist researchers have moved away from simplistic versions of such conceptualizations, recognizing their potential for 'blaming the victim' and taking the 'male-as-norm'. Government publications still carry the rhetoric, however.

Researchers, too, sometimes fall back on this perspective uncritically. An example is A. H. Halsey's short newspaper article based on his study of British academics. Women's lesser likelihood of being in senior positions, and their uneven distribution in different subject fields, are attributed partly to slightly poorer publication records and partly to 'differential gender socialization . . . experiences of girls in their families and schools' (Halsey 1990, p. 17). A reply by Ramazanoglu (1990) began 'Can Professor Halsey be serious?', pointing to the effects of working in hostile institutions and the multiple mechanisms through which men maintain women in subordinate positions, as identified by feminist research. The tabulations presented in the article also failed to compare like with like, for example by asking whether men and women of similar age and experience, in the same subject fields, publish equally and have the same chances for promotion.

Conflicting Roles

A similar argument adduces that women put family first ('domestic responsibilities') and thus are unable to compete effectively. In this view they are held back by overload and time problems; by guilt; by the demands of a husband's career; by anticipation of the demands of a husband's career; by their consequent inability to plan a career for themselves which is compatible with the age norms of high status occupations. It is necessary to look carefully at these arguments. Many studies report that women academics are less likely than male colleagues to be married or have children, although the gap may be culturally and historically variable (Sutherland 1985). Researchers in various countries have tried to calculate the effects of marriage or parenthood on publishing productivity, with contradictory results (Lie 1990).

It seems there are so many variables interacting here—age, experience, subject, ages of children, rank and others—that it is difficult to come to any firm conclusions. Accounts which invoke family-career role conflicts as explanation too often simply blame the victim for not achieving a successful resolution of competing commitments or suggest that women are powerless in the face of social expectations. These are inadequate conceptualizations. Yet marriage and parenthood are facts of women's (and men's) lives.

A more convincing approach considers the role of marriage and parenthood in conjunction with institutional factors which make these statuses more or less compatible with academic life. For example, a report from Cambridge University (Spurling 1990) finds that women academics experience strains caused by conflicts between family and work. These are analyzed, however, in an institutional context specific to Cambridge University and King's College, a formerly all-male constituent college within it. The university offers no part-time posts and no assistance with childcare, holds meetings in late afternoon or evening, and operates age restrictions affecting access to jobs or funding for those whose careers have been interrupted. At a subtler level, there is a pervasive male model of what a professional academic *is*, including a preference for combative, aggressive, competitive modes of operation.

Investment in 'womanpower'

Another view of the problem is that society fails to invest sufficiently in 'womanpower'. This approach can be pursued with or without feminist input. In the 1950s and 1960s a frequently encountered argument was that individuals benefit from investment in education and so does the country. With women there was too much 'wastage' (movement out of the labour force; failure to practice after training; failure to train up to capacity). Writings, especially about graduate women, claimed 'the country needs them' (Arregger 1966). These arguments are often elitist as it is 'talented' or 'able' women who are needed, not the others (except perhaps to look after the children of the talented?).

In recent years there have been attempts in Britain to get women 'back' from the so-called PIT (pool of inactive teachers) to combat teacher shortage in primary and secondary schools, especially in mathematics and scientific subjects. Some Local Education Authorities suffering shortages are offering all sorts of incentives, including salary increments for time spent at home. Similar calls are made for mature women to become students in higher education, although the way is not always made easy. What is ahead is the so-called demographic time bomb in the mid-1990s where young skilled and professional workers will be in short supply; it has been argued that mature women will be needed to make up the shortfall. Might these arguments apply to the academic workforce as well as others?

Discrimination

Can we explain the position of women in higher education in terms of sex discrimination? This is a common argument, made both by feminists and others concerned with equality and justice.

What is sex discrimination? Legally speaking, discrimination consists of less favourable treatment of a member of one sex than would be accorded to a person of the other sex whose relevant circumstances are the same or not materially different. There is parallel legislation for race relations. Built into the UK legislation is a greater concern for the fate of individuals than for the welfare of groups. In most cases discrimination has to be established by means of comparisons between individuals rather than by demonstrating statistical patterns. Discrimination may be *direct* (unequal treatment because of one's sex) or *indirect* (unequal treatment using some other criterion that puts one sex at a disadvantage and is not otherwise justified). In contrast to the United States, one cannot take an action on behalf of a larger group; the use of statistics to show a pattern of underrepresentation is not adequate to win a case; 'positive action' is strictly limited and positive discrimination illegal; financial or other penalties for noncompliance are minimal.

Some institutions of higher education have set up working parties to develop policies and consider discrimination. There is no documentation of these, as far as I know. Professional bodies and lecturers' unions have made similar studies. As mentioned earlier, many universities and polytechnics have taken to calling themselves 'equal opportunities employers', a label which at best is often wishful thinking, at worst justifies complacency and blocks correction. Top-level enquiries (for example, anything comparable to the Swann Report on ethnic minorities and education) are conspicuously absent, as is substantial research funding on gender in higher education or Chairs in Women's Studies.

What can we say about sex discrimination among employees of the academy? There are many occupational careers within higher education, running the gamut from manual work to mental labour. Think of catering, cleaning, portering, clerical, labouring, technical, computer, library, administration, research and teaching occupations. They tend to be sex-segregated, along familiar lines. It is unusual to move between them, apart from an occasional secretary who becomes an administrator, or researcher who moves into a lectureship. Figures presented earlier showed that among academics, men are far more likely than women to be professors, readers or senior lecturers.

Figures collated by the Association of University Teachers (AUT) demonstrate women's poor chances for promotion (Aziz 1990).[1] For example, in 1986, 536 people were promoted from lecturer to senior lecturer or reader. Only 53 of these were women. From 1984 to 1986 the figures hardly varied: 'the proportion of women promoted is consistently smaller than the proportion of women in the pool of lecturers from which the promotions are made' (Aziz 1990, p. 36).

But are these figures proof of discrimination? Not according to the law, which requires direct comparisons between named individuals. In a recent example, four women lecturers from Newcastle Polytechnic took their case under the Sex Discrimination Act to an industrial tribunal, with support from the Equal Opportunities Commission. (Buswell vs. Newcastle City Council 1989).[2] They claimed they had been directly discriminated against for promotion. A principal lectureship [a senior position] had been advertised within the department and four women and two men applied. One of the men was appointed. The women felt he was junior to them in seniority and experience, and less qualified than some of them in other respects. Various witnesses appeared for each side before a tribunal made up of two men and one woman. The women *lost.*

The official report shows, first, the enormous difficulty of proving discrimination in cases where 'academic judgements' are involved. It is clear the tribunal was unable to understand in depth the politics of academic institutions; 'this was a foreign world' the chairman admitted (p. 10). Second, it shows how a tribunal is itself likely to rely on stereotypes about the sexes. The tribunal was impressed by the coolness and rationality of the polytechnic management; it declared itself unimpressed by the 'obsessive, emotional involvement' of the women (p. 12).

What about indirect discrimination? Several interesting legal cases have concerned part-time work in universities. The figures in table 1 were for full-time academics only. Part-time workers are more likely to be female. In one successful case involving a woman scientific researcher at the University of Dundee, a tribunal ruled that making part-time workers as a group redundant would affect women more heavily than men, thus constituting indirect discrimination. Also successful in establishing indirect discrimination have been several cases challenging age requirements, using the argument that women are more likely to be older when they reach certain points of their occupational careers, especially if they have taken time out of work to look after children.

Indirect discrimination may take more subtle forms. Simply working in a mostly-male environment imposes different pressures on women. The career structure is designed on a 'male norm'—career breaks or part-time work do damage to promotion chances. Time out from full-time work may be more damaging still in areas where knowledge is proceeding rapidly and where there is little provision for catching up (Jackson 1989). Women may also be at a disadvantage in the informal socializing that aids promotion chances.

Strategies

What strategies follow from the liberal feminist perspectives reviewed above? If the problem lies in women's attitudes or personalities, as formed through socialization, the solution appears simply for the individual to make the best of a bad situation. One can simply try harder. I have a post-it note pad from the United States which sums it up as the 'career woman's checklist for success: look like a lady, act like a man, work like a dog'. Women are to 'dress for success', learn career-planning strategies from mentors and develop assertiveness through training.

The path is full of pitfalls, for double standards make such strategies difficult. Women academics who are highly successful at publishing or obtaining research funding, or who try to be 'one of the boys', risk disapproval for breaking norms for feminine women. Meanwhile feminist women criticize them for their lack of concern about other women's progress. Those who do take a feminist stance are regarded as eccentric if not actually strident and uncongenial. Whatever one does seems only to reinforce the male-as-norm definitions.

For family-career conflicts, a helpful partner, clever manoeuvring, luck and money might provide a nanny or other solution. But again, these are *individual* solutions, and not open to all. One woman finds a way, but the same problem is there for the next.

The womanpower and discrimination arguments shift the analysis somewhat, still staying within the liberal framework, but examining structures rather than individuals. We become more sociological, understanding women's actions within the frameworks that constrain them. But there are still difficulties. The demand for womanpower is bound to fluctuate over time and some groups are not perceived as being in shortage. For example, there has not yet been a call for women to come into university teaching comparable to the one for school teaching, although a 'womanpower' argument has been made in a project which recruited highly-qualified women returners to university fellowships in science and engineering (Jackson 1988). There have also been rumours that contract researchers in universities are becoming more difficult to recruit, perhaps because of their poor remuneration and prospects. The university academic population in Britain is aging, a result of expansion in the 1960s and early 1970s followed by contraction since the 1980s. At some point, mass retirements from the 'bulge' will require replacement. But recent government policies have squeezed the universities and starved them of funds, hardly auspicious circumstances for extending equal opportunities to women or minorities. Arts and humanities, and certain social sciences, have experienced particularly severe cutbacks. It is difficult to defend a 'womanpower' argument that supplies talent only to fields designated by the government of the day as in the national interest.

If discrimination is seen to be the problem, use may be made of the law, the Equal Opportunities Commission, union procedures. Steady pressure can be put on colleagues. The situation can be brought to the notice of the wider public. Generally strategies rely on persuasion, rational argument, the assumption of good will and distaste for injustice. Using the law and publicizing successful outcomes, as the Equal Opportunities Commission does, may raise the level of consciousness but there is little evidence of fundamental change. The number of successful cases is small and there are few effective sanctions to stop the same discriminatory treatment occurring again elsewhere.

Extending the Analysis: Socialist and Radical Feminism

The approaches discussed thus far give us an idea how social arrangements operate to the detriment of women but not why they have developed this way. We can deepen our understanding of women in higher education if we go beyond the various varieties of liberal feminist thought outlined above. Both socialist feminist and radical feminist theories are concerned with underlying causes.

Socialist Feminism

The long-term aim here is to end oppression under capitalism but the immediate task is to elucidate the processes involved. Most socialist feminist theoreticians have focused on women's position within the economy and the family. For those concerned with education, the key question is 'how is education related to the reproduction of gender divisions within capitalism?' (Arnot and Weiner 1987).

The labour market is looked at from a different perspective from those we have considered so far. Rather than being a consequence of lots of individual decisions, systematic patterns, such as the way in which particular groups are found in 'segments' of the labour market, are highlighted. Dual labour market theory, for example, posits a primary sector and a secondary sector. Many women hold jobs in the secondary sector—that is, jobs with low levels of skills, low security, low wages and poor career prospects. For jobs where rapid turnover helps employers adjust to swings in demand for their product, casual labour is preferred, and women who have major domestic responsibilities fill such positions.

Divisions in the labour market are perpetuated over time, or 'reproduced'. How is it that the sexual division of labour in the labour market and the domestic sphere endures? How are public and private spheres articulated? Why is it that women are concentrated in certain marginal manual occupations; or in lower white collar (secretarial) work; or in the caring professions—in lower grades and lower status specialities? If education is about increasing social mobility, how is it that these patterns are so persistent? Why does the same amount of education bring a lower rate of return for women and minorities than for white men?

Like school education, higher education can be seen to reinforce divisions, keeping the segregated labour market and its domestic support system going. Higher education is a scarce prize which sections off an elite, dividing the credentialed from the remainder.

Even including all forms of education and training (apprentices, schemes for the young unemployed, etc.), the rate of participation of 16–18 year olds in 'education' in the UK (69%) is below that of most European countries and below Canada (75%) or the US (80%) (DES 1990b). With a more restrictive definition that excludes some of the forms of training, the participation percentage comes down to 55%. But most of these young people are either still at secondary school or in 'further' rather than 'higher' education, the latter being the sector which gives bachelor's or equivalent and higher degrees. Only 16% of men and 13% of women aged 19–20 are in higher education (DES 1990a).

Williams et al. (1989, p. 8) point out that in 1984 only 8.6% of male school-leavers and 6.3% of female school-leavers entered degree courses (the overall participation rates are higher because some go first to further education or tertiary colleges to get the requisite qualifications for entry to university or polytechnics). New procedures for ethnic monitoring suggest only about 1% of university students and 4% of polytechnic students are black (Utley 1991). Although institutions increasingly provide access courses to facilitate entry into higher education for nontraditional groups, the channel is still narrow. Courses are almost all full-time.

Thus, from a socialist feminist perspective, education is involved in the reproduction of both social and sexual divisions of labour. The patterns I have identified—differentiated career structures; family-work role conflict; sex discrimination; socialization into sex stereotyped subjects and feminine dispositions—all can be seen as being reinforced by an education system in service of a capitalist economy.

In particular, the enormous growth in temporary contract research staff can be regarded as an instance of the process called proletarianization. Ozga and Lawn (1988) argue that white collar occupations, including schoolteaching, suffer from this phenomenon. Increasingly, execution is separated from control and the pace of work is intensified. Some workers are reskilled to manage others who are deskilled. There is vigorous debate over the extent to which teachers are experiencing proletarianization and the role gender plays. The abolition of tenure in universities by the government's Education Reform Act of 1988 would seem to suggest academics are vulnerable, too.

Radical Feminism

In radical feminism, the operation of patriarchy is the fundamental reason for observed social patterns. There are different definitions of patriarchy, but the usual ones depict a system whereby men as a group (not necessarily every individual man) are dominant. Radical feminists want to eliminate patriarchal structures and put girls and women at the centre of concern. Several themes stand out, such as male dominance; the sexual politics of everyday life; the critique of 'knowledge' as 'manmade'; and the possibilities of finding space for a 'women's culture' in higher education.

Male dominance. The figures in table 1 can be rearranged to support the argument of male dominance in universities. We can take each grade and consider the relative representation of men and women within it (the distinction between representation and distribution is developed by Rendel, 1984). Table 2 shows that jobs in the higher categories, i.e. the professorships, senior lectureships and readerships, are nearly all held by men. For all academic staff, women hold 3.1% of the professorships and 8.4% of the other senior posts. They are just under 21% of the main grade, the lecturer or equivalent level. This last percentage drops to 17.7% if we exclude the researchers. In the 'research only' category, women make up just over a quarter of the lecturer-equivalent category and 39.9% of the 'others', those on salary scales lower than lectureships.

Looking at the figures this way tells us what picture of universities is presented to the outside world. It also tells us who runs universities. Professors in UK universities are the people who head departments, represent the university to the government, serve on working parties, act as external examiners, make appointments, hire and promote others. At the university in England where I worked until recently, all professors, plus a small number of elected representatives of non-professorial

TABLE 2
Percentages of men and women in each grade, full-time academic staff in universities, Great Britain, 1988–89

	Prof.	*Reader/. Sr. Lect.*	*Lecturer*	*Others*	*All*
	A. All academic staff				
Men	96.9	91.7	79.1	59.3	81.0
Women	3.1	8.4	20.9	40.7	19.0
Total %	100.0	100.1	100.0	100.0	100.0
N	(4,389)	(9,122)	(27,560)	(5,211)	(46,282)
	B. Teaching and research				
Men	96.9	92.1	82.3	46.9	86.7
Women	3.1	7.9	17.7	53.1	13.4
Total	100.0	100.0	100.0	100.0	100.1
N	(4,307)	(8,720)	(18,233)	(337)	(31,602)
	C. Research only				
Men	96.3	82.1	72.7	60.1	68.9
Women	3.7	17.9	27.3	39.9	31.1
Total %	100.0	100.0	100.0	100.0	100.0
N	(82)	(402)	(9,322)	(4,874)	(14,680)

Source: UFC *University Statistics 1988–89*, Vol. 1 (USR 1990).

Note: 'B' and 'C' are subsets of 'A'.

staff, were members of the Senate. There were only two women professors in the university. Not all men will 'make it' to the professorship level—in fact, most will not—but those people who do are almost always men.

Sexual politics. Another concern is with power men hold over women, at an extreme becoming sexual harassment. This means unwanted sexual attentions or advances—which may be looks, gestures, pictures, physical advances, threats, etc. In the United States many institutions have developed policies and there have been widely publicized court cases. A Harvard survey found 32% of tenured women faculty, 49% of those without tenure, 41% of women graduate students and 34% of women undergraduates reported experiencing at least one incident of harassment by a person in authority while at the University (Simeone 1987, p. 115).

Little is known about the extent of sexual harassment in British universities. An article in *The Observer* (Watts 1990) shocked readers by suggesting it was widespread in Oxford colleges and that several cases of rape had been hushed up. We do not know whether female academics suffer similar threats. There is a sense, however, in which being a woman academic in a male dominated institution brings milder forms of 'sexual politics'—dilemmas of power, visibility, relationships—into everyday life (Acker 1980).

Knowledge and the curriculum. There has been a thoroughgoing critique of scholarship in many fields by feminist critics (not all radical feminist). Are women forced to use a language not their own, as Dale Spender (1980) claims? Jeri Wine (1989) identifies stages feminist criticism goes through, starting with correcting the record and finally attempting to construct woman-centred alternatives. Writers in Britain like Stanley and Wise (1983) try to develop a specifically feminist research methodology.

Feminist scholarship is exciting. An accolade comes from a male professor in Australia:

> . . . the redressers of sexual oppression are currently producing a critical and analytical literature of an intellectual liveliness and practical relevance unmatched in any other field of social science . . . (Connell 1985, p. 260).

Nevertheless, there are numerous examples of important ways in which feminist work is outside the mainstream. For example, Sara Delamont (1989) shows that the Winfield report on submission rates for social science theses among graduate students ignored all the research on *women* graduate students. Specializing in feminist scholarship may harm one's promotion chances (Gumport 1990).

A women's culture within the academy. How much scope is there for finding an alternative way to organize pedagogy, curriculum and management so as to prioritize traditionally female values? Women's studies are gaining ground quietly in Britain but the field is subdued in comparison with developments in the United States where a different organization of higher education permits new courses to flourish provided they attract students. Women's studies aim to do more than add observations on women to existing scholarship; in some versions, it will transcend the disciplines (Klein 1984). Attempts to create new ways of working within the relatively rigid world of British higher education can be painful, as high expectations held by the students clash with university conventions.

The question of whether the university or polytechnic must inevitably embody 'men's culture' and what a feminist alternative would look like is a challenging one (Smith 1975). Women who do become heads of department or professors find themselves allowed in (as individuals) to a culture which is shaped by men. They are always highly visible. Trying to help other women or change the climate itself in feminist directions is not easily accomplished (David 1989).

Strategies

The goals of socialist and radical feminism are unrealizable in the immediate future; one cannot devise strategies for ending capitalism and patriarchy in the same way as, for example, introducing an equal opportunities policy or encouraging women to apply for promotion. Consistent with socialist feminist analysis would be efforts to develop further a class-gender-race analysis of the university's social role; to encourage alliances of workers, especially women workers, across occupational segments and across social divisions; to raise consciousness of oppression among these groups; to increase awareness of and commitment to gender issues in the more left-leaning political parties and trade unions; to increase access to universities for groups traditionally deprived of it such as black and working-class people, the disabled, older people and women of all groups.

Feminists in academic life work in a situation of uncomfortable contradiction. We are part of a social system which, through its everyday processes (admissions, marking), labels a small number of individuals as talented and excludes or downgrades the rest. Universities are deeply marked by hierarchy and stratification. Different groups of workers; students and faculty; administration and others;—all take their place in a complicated system of differential power and reward. We need more scholarship and research from a socialist feminist perspective on higher education; that there is so little (especially when British socialist feminist work is so strong in other areas) is itself a 'problem' for analysis. Thomas (1990, p. 177) develops the argument that 'intellectual workers' receive their relatively high status, remuneration and security in exchange for conformity. Perhaps this explains the scarcity of critical scholarship from socialist feminists and others which takes higher education as its target, a kind of 'NIMBY' (Not In My Back Yard) syndrome. It is simply safer to analyze other sites; other people; other practices.

Radical feminist strategies focus on putting women at the centre of concern: developing woman-centred knowledge; making institutions safe for women; finding space for women within (or outside) the academy. This may mean encouraging women-only courses and groups. The difficulty here is that the territory is still controlled by men, as the figures show. Women's studies courses in Britain—as, indeed, is any input on 'gender' to any course—are usually marginal, poorly resourced, dependent on the energies of a few committed individuals doing the work 'on top' of their responsibilities in traditional departments. They exist because enough students like them and because tradition supports the individual academic's autonomy, even eccentricity. Attempts to inject a feminist way of working into traditional departments meet with greater resistance, as Miriam David's (1989) account of her experiences as Head of Social Sciences in a polytechnic demonstrates.

Conclusion

This paper has taken a tour of theories and perspectives on women's position in higher education. I have looked at analyses which feature socialization, family role conflicts, investment in 'womanpower', sex discrimination, socially reproductive aspects of higher education and patriarchal underpinnings of power relations and conceptions of knowledge. There is some 'truth' in all of these, and the problem is clearly much more complex than first impressions would have it.

Although the representation of women as *students* has increased considerably, and many institutions have made gestures in the direction of equal opportunities, women academics are relatively disadvantaged, and the universities and polytechnics remain firmly dominated by men. Feminist scholarship has been superb, but some disciplines and some individuals have barely heard of it.

The feminist theories discussed in this paper advance reasons for the structural subordination of women. Those considered under the liberal feminist umbrella tend to identify processes and answer the question of how women become disadvantaged, i.e. through socialization, conflicting role expectations, inadequate investment in 'womanpower' and discrimination. The socialist and radical feminist approaches aim for a deeper, more fundamental understanding, addressing the question of *why* such disadvantage occurs (Acker 1984). As it is impossible to ascertain 'why' with any certainty, we are left with competing but untestable hypotheses. Moreover, behind every 'how' question, a 'why' is lurking, untestable as it may be; for example, if we believe socialization to be the cause of women's subordination, we still must question why socialization operates in this particular fashion.

Socialist or radical feminist approaches help us understand that change will be slow and resistance substantial, for there are vested interests with a stake in the status quo. I have tried to suggest that these perspectives are necessary if one wishes to understand the enduring nature of gender inequality. But when we come to consider strategies for change, we confront something of a paradox. Either strategies are long term (working towards the end of capitalist or patriarchal oppression) or provocative and likely to arouse opposition or even ridicule (transcending boundaries of the established disciplines by introducing women's studies; constructing feminist methodology). Liberal feminist strategies, on the other hand, tend either to put too much onus on the individual to make changes, often in herself, or to rely on arts of persuasion and assumptions of good will and justice. Nevertheless, it may be that even those with radical or socialist sympathies need to pursue liberal strategies in the short run, accepting that they will have mixed results.

A case in point is the introduction, withdrawal and re-introduction of the Committee of Vice Chancellors and Principals' draft code on equal opportunities. The CVCP is an association of the heads of universities in the UK. In the summer of 1990 it released the draft code. The *Times Higher Education Supplement* commented dryly that 'by British standards the simple fact that vice chancellors now believe equal opportunities are an issue that should be policed by national guidelines is evidence of progress' (*THES*, August 3, 1990, no. 926). But by November, the *THES* reported 'Equality code dropped' (November 23, 1990, p. 1). A spokesman for the CVCP commented that 'the view taken was that the CVCP should give advice, not impose rules'. Another Vice Chancellor added that the stringent financial climate was not conducive to forcing institutions to commit scarce resources. But vigorous protests came, especially from the lecturer's union, the Association of University Teachers (AUT), and eventually the code was reinstated. A final version was released in February 1991, with sixteen specific recommendations and fairly extensive discussion of legislation and arrangements universities might make to advance equal opportunities (CVP 1991). The story attests both the limited success of liberal strategies and to the resistance that even they evoke.

Whilst feminist theory gives broad reasons for inequalities of gender, focused studies in specific countries and educational systems are necessary to fill in the detail. Britain appears to lag behind other, similar, countries in its commitment to improving the status of women in general and women academics in particular (Johnson 1990). Reasons might be sought in its particular historical and political traditions (Gelb 1989). Gelb argues that in comparison with the United States and Sweden, British feminist groups are more radical, ideological and decentralized. Like other grassroots groups, they lack input into the policy-making process. Britain has no active and effective liberal feminist network of committees and pressure groups pushing for implementation of feminist priorities. Feminism remains a fringe pursuit, outside the dominant discourse. The years of Conservative government have enshrined this principle; a few women, like Mrs Thatcher, could 'make it', but only by their own efforts, not by virtue of socially progressive policies.

Other features of the British higher education system itself indirectly reinforce the disadvantage of academic women. There is a strong belief that merit is the only differentiator; institutions seem complacent, confident in their meritocratic liberalism (Williams *et al.* 1989; Thomas 1990). Thomas points out that many primary and secondary schools are far ahead of higher education in their awareness of antiracist and antisexist initiatives. Universities prefer 'gender blindness' (Wormald 1985; Coffey and Acker, 1991); to make positive efforts on the part of a specific group strikes many as discriminatory rather than restitutive.

The conventions of the promotion system may be working against able women. Unlike the American practice of allowing individuals to compete against a standard to attain higher ranks, judged by one's peers, the typical British university makes its candidates for internal promotion (senior lectureships and readerships) compete against one another, usually judged by senior personnel (professors). Only a certain number of promotions will be available in a given institution each year. The academic profession is aging and there are large numbers at the top of the 'lecturer scale' (which is reached at about age 40) competing for promotion. The system discourages geographic mobility (why start over again in a lectureship somewhere else?) except at the professorial level and is open to micropolitical manoeuvring as professors struggle to get 'their' candidate promoted. The professors and deans making these judgements, as we have seen, are almost all men. Few will be familiar with research on gender, thus placing women doing research and scholarship in that area at a possible disadvantage. Because women are concentrated in relatively few subject fields, they also in effect compete against one another to the extent promotions are such a scarce resource, and many candidates are of equal merit, that male preference will operate, however unconsciously.

A further, ironic, consequence of the small numbers of women in the system is that opportunities for organizing to improve matters are thereby limited. Women academics are too scattered to provide a critical mass, nor do they hold many positions of influence. Johnson (1990) makes this clear using the example of music, a subject with a majority female undergraduate enrolment. As of 1988, two thirds of university music departments had no women academic staff. There were no readers or professors. Wales had no women lecturers. One of the limitations of women's studies is that it will make few inroads where there are few women already present.

Finally, the economic situation has been perilous for some time in Britain. Universities have been experiencing cuts and retrenchment since the early 1980s (Reynolds 1990). It would not seem an auspicious time to institute feminist reform, as the vice chancellor quoted above suggested. But there are always contradictions and points of intervention. For example, the increasing impact of market forces means that student demand should be a factor in shaping provision. The massive increase in temporary staff unsettles old certainties about the meaning of the university as a workplace. The very business of education carries contradictions in its simultaneous reproductive and liberating potential. The institution is reproducing the divisions of the labour market while at the same time providing the chance for challenge and critique.

Feminist strategies will need to be adapted to their context: universities complacent towards certain issues but in flux and crisis. Working through academic unions may provide a 'respectable' base. Feminist academics can use their skills as scholars to look at their own institutions. We need to recognize the historical and cultural specificity of our case, and within it actively take up the position and the identity which feels most compelling as a political point of departure (Alcoff 1988; Nicholson 1990). Feminist theories help us understand how serious the situation is, and why change is so frustratingly slow. But we have no choice other than to try to make things better.

Notes

1. Promotion procedures vary from one institution to another. However, generally readerships and senior lectureships are internal promotions. Readerships require demonstration of contributions in the research area, while senior lectureships are usually some combination of research, teaching, administration or other contributions to the department and university. Professorships are usually advertised and may be either internal or external appointments. Until a few years ago, there was a quota (40%) on senior posts.
2. Carol Buswell kindly provided transcripts and other materials from the tribunal proceedings.

References

Acar, F. (1990). 'Role priorities and career patterns: a cross-cultural study of Turkish and Jordanian university teachers', in Lie, S. and O'Leary, V. (eds.), *Storming the Tower: Women in the Academic World.* London: Kogan Page.

Acker, S. (1980). 'Women, the other academics', *British Journal of Sociology of Education* 1, 81–91.

Acker, S. (1984). 'Sociology, gender and education', in Acker, S., Megarry, J., Nisbet, S. and Hoyle, E. (eds.), *World Yearbook of Education 1984: Women and Education.* London: Kogan Page.

Acker, S. (1986). 'What feminists want from education', in Hartnett, A. and Naish, M. (eds.), *Education and Society Today.* Lewes: Falmer.

Acker, S. (1987). 'Feminist theory and the study of gender and education', *International Review of Education* 33, 419–435.

Acker, S. & Warren Piper, D. (eds.) (1984). *Is Higher Education Fair to Women?* Guildford: SRHE; Milton Keynes: Open University Press.

Alcoff, L. (1988). 'Cultural feminism vs post-structuralism,' in Minnich, E., O'Barr, J. and Rosenfeld, R. (eds.), *Reconstructing the Academy.* Chicago: University of Chicago Press.

Arnot, M. & Weiner, G. (1987). *Gender and Education Study Guide.* Milton Keynes: Open University Press.

Arregger, C. (1966). *Graduate Women at Work.* Newcastle upon Tyne: Oriel.

Aziz, A. (1990). 'Women in UK universities: the road to casualization?', in Lie, S. and O'Leary, V. (eds.), *Storming the Tower: Women in the Academic World.* London: Kogan Page.

Buswell, C. vs. Newcastle City Council (1989). *Decision Document Folio Ref: 9/213/179. 6 Feb. 1989.* (Available from Regional Office of Industrial Tribunals, Newcastle upon Tyne NE1 6NT.)

Cambridge University Women's Action Group (1988). *Forty Years On . . . Cambridge: CUWAG.*

Coffey, A. and Acker, S. (1991). '"Girlies on the warpath": addressing gender in initial teacher education', *Gender and Education* 3, 249–261.

Committee of Vice Chancellors and Principals (1991). *Equal Opportunities in Employment in Universities.* London: CVCP.

Connell, R. (1985). 'Theorizing gender', *Sociology* 19, 250–272.

David, M. (1989). 'Prima donna inter pares? Women in academic management', in Acker, S. (ed.), *Teachers, Gender and Careers.* Lewes: Falmer.

Delamont, S. (1989). 'Gender and British postgraduate funding policy: a critique of the Winfield Report', *Gender and Education* 1, 51–57.

Department of Education and Science (1987). *Statistics of Education: Teachers in Service, England and Wales 1985.* London: HMSO.

Department of Education and Science (1990a). *Education Statistics for the United Kingdom 1989 Edition*, Statistical Bulletin 4/90, March. London: DES.

Department of Education and Science (1990b). *International Statistical Comparison of the Education and Training of 16 to 18 Year Olds,* Statistical Bulletin 1/90, January. London: DES.

Donoghue, H. (1988). 'Vital statistics 2: age patterns', *AUT Woman,* No. 13: 2.

Gelb, J. (1989). *Feminism and Politics.* Berkeley: University of California Press.

Gumport, P. (1990). 'Feminist scholarship as a vocation', *Higher Education* 20, 231–43.

Halsey, A. H. (1990). 'Long, open road to equality', *Times Higher Education Supplement*, 9 February, 17.

Jackson, D. (1988). *Fellowship Scheme for Women Returners to Science and Engineering: Personal Experiences of the Returners.* Guildford: University of Surrey.

Jackson, D. (1989). 'Women returners'. Paper presented at the conference on Women and Higher Education, King's College, Cambridge, 29 April.

Johnson, J. (1990). 'Behind the bastion', *Times Higher Education Supplement,* 20 April, 14.

Klein, R. D. (1984). 'The intellectual necessity for women's studies', in Acker, S. and Warren Piper, D. (eds.), *Is Higher Education Fair to Women?* Guildford: SHRE; Milton Keynes: Open University Press.

Lie, S. (1990). 'The juggling act: work and family in Norway', in Lie, S. and O'Leary, V. (eds.), *Storming the Tower: Women in the Academic World.* London: Kogan Page.

McAuley, J. (1987). 'Women academics: a case study in inequality', in Spencer, A. and Podmore, D. (eds.), *In a Man's World.* London: Tavistock.

Middleton, S. (1991). 'Towards a feminist pedagogy for the sociology of women's education in Aotearoa/New Zealand: a life-history approach'. Paper presented at the Annual Meeting of the American Educational Research Association, Chicago, April.

Moore, K. (1987). 'Women's access and opportunity in higher education towards the twenty-first century', *Comparative Education* 23, 23–34.

Nicholson, L. (1990). 'Introduction', in Nicholson, L. (ed.), *Feminism/Postmodernism.* London: Routledge.

Ozga, J. and Lawn, M. (1988). 'Schoolwork: interpreting the labour process of teaching', *British Journal of Sociology of Education* 9, 323–336.

Ramazanoglu, C. (1990). 'Letter to the editor' *Times Higher Education Supplement,* 16 February, 12.

Rees, T. (1989). 'Contract research: a new career structure?' *AUT Woman,* No. 16: 1,4.

Rendel, M. (1984). 'Women academics in the seventies', in Acker, S. and Warren Piper, D. (eds), *Is Higher Education Fair to Women?* Guildford: SHRE; Milton Keynes: Open University Press.

Reynolds, P. A. (1990). 'How long is a piece of string: reflections on British higher education since 1945', *Higher Education* 20, 211–221.

Simeone, A. (1987). *Academic Women: Working Towards Equality.* South Hadley, Mass.: Bergin & Garvey.

Smith, D. (1975). 'An analysis of ideological structures and how women are excluded: considerations for academic women', *Canadian Review of Sociology and Anthropology* 12, 353–369.

Spender, D. (1980). *Man Made Language.* London: Routledge & Kegan Paul.

Spurling, A. (1990). *Report of the Women in Higher Education Research Project.* Cambridge: King's College.

Stanley, L. and Wise, S. (1983). *Breaking Out.* London: Routledge & Kegan Paul.

Sutherland, M. (1985). *Women Who Teach in Universities.* Stoke-on-Trent: Trentham.

Thomas, K. (1990). *Gender and Subject in Higher Education.* Milton Keynes: Open University Press.

Universities Funding Council (1990). *University Statistics 1988–89,* vol. 1. Cheltenham: Universities' Statistical Record.

Utley, A. (1991). 'Blacks fare badly in entry stakes', *Times Higher Education Supplement,* 21 June, 1.

Watts, J. (1990). 'Rape in the Quad', *The Observer,* 25 November, 49–50.

Weiner, G. (1986). 'Feminist education and equal opportunities: unity or discord?' *British Journal of Sociology of Education* 7, 265–274.

Williams, J., Cocking, J. and Davies, L. (1989). *Words or Deeds: A Review of Equal Opportunities Policies in Higher Education*. London: Commission for Racial Equality.

Wine, J. (1989). 'Gynocentric values and feminist psychology', in Miles, A. and Finn, G. (eds.), *Feminism: From Pressure to Politics*. Montreal: Black Rose Books.

Wormald, E. (1985). 'Teacher training and gender blindness', *British Journal of Sociology of Education* 6(1), 112–116.

The Academic Profession in International Perspective

Philip G. Altbach and Lionel S. Lewis

For nearly three decades, The Carnegie Foundation for the Advancement of Teaching has been surveying the academic profession in the United States, analyzing the attitudes, values, and professional orientations of the professoriate, as well as chronicling its changing demographic profile. Since the first survey in 1969, the number of U.S. faculty has increased greatly and the faculty has become more diverse, a reflection of changing social conditions apparent in the academy not only in the United States but in other countries as well. Recognizing both the common challenges facing the academy worldwide and the increasing international connections of the professoriate, the Foundation coordinated the first international study of the academic profession.

The work of higher learning has always crossed national boundaries. In fact, since the establishment of the Western university model in the medieval period, there has been an international community of scholars, with professors frequently teaching abroad, usually in Latin, the international language of academe in the medieval period. (In this century, English has become the international language of research and scholarship, with ramifications that will be touched on later.) In the modern period, with the evolution of the international academic labor market and scientific community, along with more efficient travel and communications, the international community of scholars and scientists has become much stronger and more professionally connected.

With the advent of the research university in the late nineteenth century, the internationalism of scientific study in particular expanded through ever-increasing collaborative efforts around the globe. International intellectual exchanges have also occurred with increasing regularity in the social sciences and humanities. Like the fine arts, scholarship travels well, and more academics than ever before now benefit from exchanges with colleagues in countries far from home. These relationships have undoubtedly contributed richly to the work of the academy and have expanded the world's reservoir of knowledge.

In the International Survey of the Academic Profession, 1991–1993, academics in fourteen countries were surveyed in order to gather information on the demographic facts of the profession, on attitudes toward teaching and learning, on the governance of academic institutions, on morale, and on the involvement of scholars and scientists at the national and international levels. In addition, information was gathered on how academics spend their time, and about their participation in research. As a result of this survey we now for the first time have comparable data about the attitudes and activities of the academic profession in fourteen countries. This study can provide—and in fact already is providing—the basis for similar research in other countries as well.

The fourteen countries included are all middle-income or wealthy, and all have rather well-developed, well-supported higher education systems. The nations participating in the survey are Australia; the Asian countries of South Korea, Japan, and Hong Kong; the Latin American countries of Brazil, Chile, and Mexico; the United States; the European countries of England, Germany, the Netherlands, Sweden, and Russia; and Israel in the Middle East.

The survey was carried out at a particularly important time for the academic profession. For a number of years, the professoriate has been undergoing change and has been under strain almost everywhere. Fiscal problems for higher education are now evident in all of these fourteen countries, with the crises especially severe in Russia, Israel, and England. In most of the nations, the somewhat unprecedented phenomenon of increasing enrollments has been allowed to supersede allocated resources. Reassessment by policymakers and opinion leaders of the role of the academic profession in teaching and research is also widespread. At the same time, professors in a number of countries are being asked to be more entrepreneurial—for example, in bringing research grants and contracts to their institutions. The insulated world of academe is clearly undergoing significant change, and this presents unprecedented challenges for the academic profession. There is little doubt that insight concerning how academics in these fourteen countries are coping with the strain of fiscal difficulties and other factors has broad policy implications.

The relevance, then, of this survey is considerable. It is now possible to study in greater depth the similarities and contrasts among academics in different countries, to examine how the organization of academic systems, specific crises, or distinctive emphases may affect the attitudes and the roles of the academic profession. As indicated, colleges and universities throughout the world have common historical roots—academic institutions in Japan, Germany, the United States, Brazil, and, indeed, all other countries look to a common European heritage. Yet each university operates in a particular country as well, and the realities of the academic profession are very much affected by national policies and even by local situations.

It cannot be overemphasized that the greatest value of this study is that it enables us to examine both the national and the international aspects of the academic profession. The survey explores just how scholars see international links and what use they make of research from other countries. Looked at as a whole, these chapters reveal that, while the separate countries have sharply contrasting higher education histories and governance arrangements, a community of interest is emerging. The study indicates areas that academics around the world have in common.

This study is also unique in that it was designed and implemented by researchers in the participating countries. While the questionnaire is loosely based on The Carnegie Foundation's original format, it has been modified to be relevant to the international context and to focus on the topics that were identified as particularly salient by the members of the research group. The very process of designing the questionnaire was itself a revealing exercise, as differences in priorities of the professoriate, and even in the meaning of basic concepts, were discussed, debated, and ultimately resolved. The questionnaire was carefully translated into the languages of the countries involved (Dutch, German, Hebrew, Japanese, Korean, Portuguese, Russian, and Spanish, with the English version used in Australia, England, Hong Kong, Sweden, and the United States).

A common methodology was used to select institutions and individuals to ensure a random sample from each country. The number of respondents ranged from more than thirty-five hundred to somewhat fewer than one thousand. Response rates varied among the countries, but fell within what is considered appropriate for surveys of this kind. Altogether, the total sample was close to twenty thousand. The twelve-page questionnaire included more than two hundred questions, some of which had country-specific variations to reflect national circumstances. One can expect such variations in any large-scale international survey, especially when the survey explores a completely new subject. We are convinced, however, that the results are reliable and valid, and indeed various statistical tests conducted support this belief. This chapter is based on an analysis of the basic descriptive tables designed to reflect the international responses to the questionnaire. Our goal is to present a profile of the professoriate from an international perspective and, in the process, to define priorities that might focus the discourse of scholars.

The Importance of Context

While the professoriate is part of an increasingly international profession, and universities worldwide stem from a common European heritage, there are important national variations. Moreover, as Burton Clark has pointed out, academics are also divided by discipline and field, and these identities are powerful in shaping attitudes and values. This chapter, by focusing on broad themes and comparisons, necessarily ignores many specific details pertaining to strictly national contexts, as well as other particular variations within the academic profession, such as department of teaching appointment. In the chapters that follow, contributing authors focus on those circumstances in each country affecting the nature of the overall findings of this survey.

In some of the countries, dramatic changes in the structure and function of the higher education system have affected the nature of academic work. In others, economic problems have had a profound impact on the profession. While it is not possible to quantify how these challenges have shaped survey responses, it is clear that respondents have been affected by a decade largely unfavorable to the academic profession in virtually all of the countries included here. The following discussion focuses on some of the major circumstances that have affected higher education systems and the scholars and scientists working in them.

One nearly common denominator of circumstance internationally has been fiscal constraint, often as a corollary of greatly expanded enrollments. Of all the survey countries, only Hong Kong enjoyed generally favorable economic circumstances in higher education during the past decade. All of the rest have had problems ranging from modest to severe. The Asian countries have been least affected by economic crisis, although Japan's recession has had a modest impact on academe. Western Europe has also been spared significant cuts, despite economic recession in Germany, Sweden, and elsewhere. Even in these countries, however, governmental policy has increased enrollments without adding necessary resources. While the Latin American countries in the survey have not experienced major cuts in funding for public higher education—indeed, there has even been some growth—enrollments have increased significantly, thereby having an overall negative effect on academic systems.

In Russia the impact of economic crisis and enormous political and social change on the academics who responded to our questionnaire must have been significant, but it was impossible to gauge the effects. The response rate for Russia is quite low, perhaps one reflection of the unstable situation. The greatest difficulties have additionally been experienced by the English-speaking nations and Israel, where economic downturns have been accompanied by growing enrollments and fiscal difficulties for higher education. The impact in the United States has varied by state and region, with the Northeast and California suffering most. Israel experienced severe cuts in higher education funding, so much so that the professors engaged in a lengthy strike, shutting down academic institutions, which happened to take place during the administration of our questionnaire. In the end the professoriate won only modest gains.

England and Australia are among the most interesting cases, since economic downturns were accompanied by significant reforms in higher education policy. These reforms were bitterly opposed by the academic profession and have led to major changes within academe. Both countries sought to improve productivity in post-secondary education by combining separate sectors of the system and downgrading the elite sector of higher education. The changes were especially contentious in England, where the Thatcher government dismantled the binary system, the division between the traditional universities and the more vocationally oriented polytechnics. All were combined into one system in which the polytechnics and other post-secondary colleges became universities. Controversial performance measures were implemented. At the same time, enrollments were increased to provide greater access, and an effort was made to rank the institutions so that research funds could be awarded to those at the top of the rankings.

Another common denominator is the issue of tenure. While academics worldwide share many similarities in their employment arrangements, and secure appointments remain the rule, we found significant variations from country to country. We found, also, an increasing contrast between academics who have tenure, or at least are in a career-grade position, and those who have appointments that are nonpermanent. Nonpermanent appointments are common in Germany and are increasing in

Sweden and the Netherlands, although the guarantees of academic job security in all three countries remain significantly stronger than in the United States. In perhaps one of the most drastic changes ever implemented in an established academic system, England, at the time of our survey, actually abolished the tenure system for new entrants to the profession, replacing it with renewable contracts. Korea has just instituted a formal tenure system, although most academics have had virtually lifetime employment. Japan, too, with its tradition of lifetime employment throughout society, has less mobility among its academics than is the case elsewhere.

It is fair to say that in most of the countries included in our survey major change was occurring in higher education at the time of the administration of the survey—and continues to this day. In every case, change was opposed by academics, sometimes vociferously and sometimes with resignation. Given the depth of the changes in some of these countries, we were somewhat surprised that our respondents were not less sanguine about their careers and about the future than we found them to be.

Other factors influencing the attitudes we report here, such as gender, age, rank, or full-time versus part-time status and departmental differences are noteworthy and extremely relevant as well. We found significant variations among these categories. The Latin American nations, for example, have significantly higher proportions of part-time faculty, as well as more women in their academic professions. An aging academic profession is evident in virtually all of the countries in the survey, and quite pronounced in a few. On some topics, the views of professors more oriented to research differ noticeably from those of professors who focus on teaching. Some demographic highlights are included in other chapters. Here we give a quick overview.

A Demographic Profile of the Profession

Our demographic profile of each country includes the factors of gender, age, and income—the most important indicators of the status of the academic profession—as well as data on academic training, typical career patterns, disciplinary backgrounds, and the current employment situation (full-time or part-time). Our brief overview compares the first three aspects, career patterns, and current employment arrangement.

We learned that the majority of academics are men—in Japan and Korea, nine out of ten academics are male, while in Brazil, at the other end of the spectrum, the figure is six out of ten. Males are more likely than females to hold the highest degrees in their disciplines and generally can be found in the higher academic ranks.

The academic profession is middle-aged—in most of the countries the large majority of professors are between forty and fifty years of age. There is considerable variation among countries, with Mexico having the youngest faculty and Israel, Russia, and Japan having the oldest. Very few in our sample are older than sixty-five years of age.

In all countries, most academics are employed full-time, although the proportion of part-time professors seems to be increasing worldwide, and some countries, especially in Latin America, have traditionally had a proportionately large part-time faculty.

While variations in such things as exchange rates, cost of living, and inflation make it difficult to draw definitive conclusions about the data concerning the income of the academic profession from country to country, it seems that most academics are clearly in the middle class in their respective countries. Nevertheless, few scholars and scientists report their salaries to be good or excellent—indeed, there is considerable dissatisfaction about earnings and quite a bit of pessimism about future prospects for improvement in this area (Table 1). In only two places, Hong Kong and the Netherlands, do more than half of the faculty rate their own salary as good or excellent. By contrast, in six countries, fewer than one-fifth of the faculty report this degree of satisfaction. In some countries, a number of faculty have turned to paid consulting projects and other extramural work to make ends meet. This is especially true in Russia, where more than 80 percent agree that an outside income is essential to augment their salary, no doubt reflecting the difficult economic situation in Russia today. In Japan, too, a number of faculty hold outside academic appointments, and there it is a

TABLE 1
How Would You Rate Your Own Academic Salary?
(Percentages)

	Excellent	*Good*	*Fair*	*Poor*
Australia	3	31	44	22
Brazil	3	22	27	48
Chile	0	5	28	67
England	2	22	47	29
Germany	7	41	39	13
Hong Kong	25	46	23	5
Israel	1	6	30	64
Japan	1	10	45	44
Korea	1	12	36	51
Mexico	1	14	32	54
The Netherlands	9	50	31	10
Russia	1	7	16	76
Sweden	2	20	41	38
United States	9	37	35	20

Source: Ernest L. Boyer, Philip G. Altbach, and Mary Jean Whitelaw, *The Academic Profession: An International Perspective* (Princeton, NJ: The Carnegie Foundation for the Advancement of Teaching, 1994), 87.

common occurrence for professors in prestigious universities to also teach courses in less-renowned institutions.

Job mobility is not generally pronounced in academe—most academics have been employed at their institutions for fairly long periods of time. About half of the respondents have held an appointment at only one institution, and another quarter at two schools. Over one-fourth of the faculty in these countries (Australia, Brazil, and Israel), however, have worked at three or more institutions during the course of their careers. Those faculty who had had previous appointments spent from one to four years at institutions other than the one where they received our questionnaire (Table 2). Older faculty, of course, have moved more times than have their younger colleagues. Mobility is lowest in Korea, Russia, and Japan. The principal explanations given by respondents for why they might leave their current institutions are related to income and resources for research. Less important are the school's academic reputation, their relationships with colleagues (which are generally good), and geographical location. There are a few instances of significant variation according to disciplinary field and among a few countries, but overall there is considerable similarity in the responses to these questions in the profession internationally.

Regardless of the level of satisfaction that academics feel vis-à-vis their salary, the majority receive the largest proportion of their incomes from their college or university, with consulting and teaching away from their home institutions comprising a relatively minor part of their earnings. There are some exceptions: in Brazil, for example, almost a third and in

TABLE 2
At How Many Different Institutions of Higher Education Have You Ever Held a Regular Academic Appointment?
(Percentages)

	One or Two	*Three or More*
Australia	68	32
Brazil	70	30
Chile	80	20
England	78	22
Germany	80	20
Hong Kong	75	25
Israel	74	26
Japan	89	11
Korea	95	5
Mexico	88	12
The Netherlands	88	12
Russia	91	9
Sweden	79	21
United States	75	25

Source: Ernest L. Boyer, Philip G. Altbach, and Mary Jean Whitelaw, *The Academic Profession: An International Perspective* (Princeton, NJ: The Carnegie Foundation for the Advancement of Teaching, 1994), 74.

Mexico about 15 percent of full-time faculty hold paid, full-time nonacademic positions. On the other hand, in Australia, Germany, Hong Kong, and England, fewer than 1 percent hold other paid, full-time nonacademic positions. The other extreme is evident in the small minority in the research cadre at the top of the profession that earns significant income from external sources and functions in the cosmopolitan atmosphere of international research.

Working Conditions

The conditions under which the professoriate works help to determine not only productivity but also morale. Not surprisingly, working conditions of the professoriate differ considerably from country to country, but we found that most academics have a positive sense about the most overreaching and essential issue of intellectual atmosphere, including the courses they teach. The relationships professors have with administrators, with each other and with students vary according to several factors, as do their attitudes about future prospects (Table 3). Regarding a third level of working conditions—the physical facilities and such things as libraries and computers—we found a wide range of dissatisfaction. Overall, while being asked by academic administrators and policy makers to do more with fewer resources, faculty are being told that they should not expect to be rewarded—financially or otherwise—for meeting ever-increasing demands. Yet, while obviously frustrated by day-to-day working conditions and by poor prospects for increased rewards, when asked about their overall morale, most respond that it is relatively high. Many report finding intellectual pleasure in their work, and that this in large part sustains them.

TABLE 3
Based on Your Experience at This Institution, How Would You Assess Relationships Between Faculty and Administration? (Percentages)

	Excellent	*Good*	*Fair*	*Poor*
Australia	3	28	39	30
Brazil	6	46	35	12
Chile	3	25	48	24
Hong Kong	3	28	47	22
Israel	9	40	31	20
Japan	3	22	58	18
Korea	1	15	47	38
Mexico	6	43	37	15
The Netherlands	3	29	47	22
Russia	3	47	42	8
Sweden	4	34	41	21
United States	7	36	36	21

Source: Ernest L. Boyer, Philip G. Altbach, and Mary Jean Whitelaw, *The Academic Profession: An International Perspective* (Princeton, NJ: The Carnegie Foundation for the Advancement of Teaching, 1994), 95.

Faculty express general dissatisfaction with their classrooms, laboratories, research equipment, libraries, and with the technologies available for teaching, although they are more satisfied with existing computer facilities. In almost all of these areas, the faculty of five countries—Hong Kong, the Netherlands, the United States, Sweden, and Germany—are generally less critical. Faculty most involved in research also have fewer complaints about facilities than do those most involved in teaching.

Regarding opinions about students, in five countries, over half of the faculty describe their students as excellent or good, although a look at language and math separately reveals some dissatisfaction. In nine of ten countries, less than one-third of the respondents report that their students are adequately prepared in writing and communication skills; in four countries, the figure is 20 percent or less. In most countries, faculty also feel that students lack adequate training in mathematics, with faculty in the United States being the least satisfied, and faculty in Hong Kong being the most satisfied. In most of the countries, the largest proportion of faculty report that the quality of students is about the same as it was five years ago. In two countries, faculty feel that students were better prepared five years ago; in Korea, the largest proportion of faculty find that students are better now. Female faculty have more favorable attitudes about students than do males. There is widespread agreement that too many students, except students majoring in the respondents' own fields (an exception that probably deserves further scrutiny), are inadequately prepared to fully benefit from higher education.

Bridging issues of intellectual concerns and physical facilities are the courses professors teach and other aspects of their jobs, such as prospects for promotion and job security.

Academics (especially in the humanities) seem relatively satisfied with what they teach (Table 4), but have mixed feelings about the resources given to them to carry out their work. Females and junior faculty are less likely to be satisfied with their circumstances than are males and senior professors. Clearly, the latter enjoy greater benefits, encounter fewer hurdles, and can expect fewer surprises as their careers continue to unfold. Males and senior professors also teach fewer courses.

Generally, however, the demands for teaching are greater as enrollments continue to climb, and a large number of respondents report that this is occurring at a time when fewer resources are available. Many report a general unease about this situation, along with considerable pressure to be more productive as scholars and scientists.

In light of all of the above, it is hardly surprising that in half of the countries, two-thirds of the respondents report that relationships between faculty and administration are only fair or poor; in no country did even 10 percent judge these to be excellent.

The professoriate, especially female faculty, is not entirely satisfied with the overall situation of higher education. Many are uneasy about their lack of control over the contemporary situation, and a number are unsure of what the future holds. In addition, many respondents, with Japanese, Korean, and British scholars and scientists scoring especially high, report their careers to be a source of considerable personal strain. On the other hand, slightly less than a fifth of the faculty in Israel report experiencing this sort of tension, a finding that seems surprising given recent difficulties faced by the Israeli academic system. Finally, a majority of respondents in every country except the Netherlands believe that a sense of community is lacking on campus. Still, despite widespread dissatisfaction about many aspects of their day-to-day life, most academics indicate that they would again choose the academic profession if they were starting their careers over.

In sum, one could not readily conclude that faculty morale is either good or bad. The picture that emerges is quite blurred. The professoriate around the world may express considerable discontent, but it has not lost sight of the positive aspects of academic life.

TABLE 4
To What Extent Are You Satisfied With the Courses You Teach? (Percentages)

	Satisfied	*Neutral*	*Dissatisfied*
Australia	77	16	7
Brazil	64	31	5
Chile	78	18	4
England	76	17	7
Germany	59	27	14
Hong Kong	72	23	5
Israel	81	17	2
Japan	54	35	11
Korea	82	15	3
Mexico	79	16	6
Russia	60	36	4
Sweden	74	21	5
United States	86	11	4

Source: Ernest L. Boyer, Philip G. Altbach, and Mary Jean Whitelaw, *The Academic Profession: An International Perspective* (Princeton, NJ: The Carnegie Foundation for the Advancement of Teaching, 1994), 91.

There is ample evidence that professorial working conditions are deteriorating in most of the countries included in this study. In the countries of East Asia and Latin America objective circumstances seem to be fairly stable in terms of workload, salary, and the overall situation on campus. Elsewhere we find that classes are getting larger, faculty are under pressure to teach more, research funds are declining, and salaries are not keeping abreast of inflation. In a few countries, the significant systemic reorganization has created stress for academics, while in others, including the United States, retrenchment threatens some faculty. Indeed, we were surprised that the academic profession is as optimistic as our data indicate (Table 5).

Professional Activities: Teaching, Research, and Service

There has been considerable concern about how the professoriate spends its time and about the level of productivity in higher education. How are teaching, research, and service organized in this broad range of countries? Are there significant variations? At the heart of such questions is the intensity of the

TABLE 5
If I Had It to Do Over Again, I Would Not Become an Academic (Percentages)

	Agree	*Neutral*	*Disagree*
Australia	16	18	66
Brazil	15	7	78
Chile	16	12	72
England	20	17	63
Germany	17	15	69
Hong Kong	17	15	69
Israel	9	6	85
Japan	16	30	54
Korea	10	14	76
The Netherlands	13	18	69
Russia	11	17	72
Sweden	8	8	84
United States	11	10	79

Source: Ernest L. Boyer, Philip G. Altbach, and Mary Jean Whitelaw, *The Academic Profession: An International Perspective* (Princeton, NJ: The Carnegie Foundation for the Advancement of Teaching, 1994), 94.

commitment faculty feel to the students they teach, to the scholarship of their discipline, and to the institution in which they work.

While it is difficult to make broad generalizations not only among countries, but also among different academic ranks, disciplines, and institutional types, the data about professors' attitudes and investment of time with

TABLE 6
Please Indicate the Degree to Which Your Affiliation With Your Academic Discipline Is Important to You (Percentages)

	Very Important	*Fairly Important*	*Not Too Important*	*Not At All Important*
Australia	67	27	5	2
Brazil	95	4	1	0
Chile	87	13	0	0
England	64	29	6	1
Germany	62	29	6	3
Hong Kong	68	27	3	2
Israel	75	23	2	0
Japan	69	28	3	0
Korea	80	19	1	0
Mexico	71	26	1	0
Russia	66	30	3	1
Sweden	55	34	9	2
United States	77	21	3	0

Source: Ernest L. Boyer, Philip G. Altbach, and Mary Jean Whitelaw, *The Academic Profession: An International Perspective* (Princeton, NJ: The Carnegie Foundation for the Advancement of Teaching, 1994), 80.

TABLE 7
Please Indicate the Degree to Which Your Affiliation With This Institution Is Important to You (Percentages)

	Very Important	*Fairly Important*	*Not Too Important*	*Not At All Important*
Australia	22	51	21	6
Brazil	76	19	5	1
Chile	65	30	5	1
England	18	46	28	8
Germany	8	26	35	31
Hong Kong	28	50	18	4
Israel	42	46	10	2
Japan	31	48	19	2
Korea	37	51	11	1
Mexico	56	38	6	0
Russia	45	45	10	1
Sweden	19	47	29	5
United States	36	46	15	3

Source: Ernest L. Boyer, Philip G. Altbach, and Mary Jean Whitelaw, *The Academic Profession: An International Perspective* (Princeton, NJ: The Carnegie Foundation for the Advancement of Teaching, 1994), 80.

regard to teaching, research, and service furthers our understanding of academic work in contemporary higher education.

Before exploring academics' professional activities, it is of interest to note the importance of their affiliation to their disciplines, departments, and institutions (Tables 6 and 7). (Perhaps the results reflect the professionalism of the academy, despite the fact that in some countries professors are civil servants or the role of unions makes some of them reject the idea of their belonging to a profession.) In every country, the largest proportion ranks in order of importance their disciplines first, their departments second, and their institutions third. Academics obviously value relationships with colleagues—whether on campus or far away. In only three countries, paradoxically all in Latin America (where, it will be recalled, high proportions of faculty have work commitments off-campus), do significant numbers of faculty believe their institutions are very important. In the other countries, the majority of the respondents rank the institution where they hold an appointment as only moderately important. This finding may be surprising given the modest level of mobility for faculty among institutions in most countries.

Teaching is a primary activity of the professoriate in most of the countries in the survey,

TABLE 8
Regarding Your Own Preferences, Do Your Interests Lie Primarily in Teaching or in Research? (Percentages)

	Primarily In Teaching	*Leaning To Teaching*	*Leaning To Research*	*Primarily In Research*
Australia	13	35	43	9
Brazil	20	42	36	3
Chile	18	49	28	5
England	12	32	40	15
Germany	8	27	47	19
Hong Kong	11	35	46	8
Israel	11	27	48	14
Japan	4	24	55	17
Korea	5	40	50	6
Mexico	22	43	31	4
The Netherlands	7	18	46	30
Russia	18	50	29	3
Sweden	12	21	44	23
United States	27	36	30	7

Source: Ernest L. Boyer, Philip G. Altbach, and Mary Jean Whitelaw, *The Academic Profession: An International Perspective* (Princeton, NJ: The Carnegie Foundation for the Advancement of Teaching, 1994), 81.

but a significant proportion of academics in a large number of the countries express, both in word and deed, a real commitment to research (Tables 8 and 9). It is significant that in the United States, where there has been so much criticism recently of an overemphasis on research by American academics, the majority indicate that their primary interest and commitment is to teaching. The U.S. is joined by Brazil, Chile, and Russia in this preference. The majority of faculty in the other countries lean toward or have primary interest in research. In Japan, Sweden, the Netherlands, Germany, and Israel, a strong proportion of scholars and scientists express a primary commitment to research. The other countries hover closer to half and half, but interest in research remains on top. More males have an orientation to research, while more females are primarily interested in or lean toward teaching.

On average, respondents spend close to twenty hours a week in teaching activities when classes are in session. This ranges from more than twenty-two hours a week in Australia and Korea to fewer than seventeen hours a week in Mexico or Sweden, and includes time for tutorials, lab sessions, and preparation. At the same time, in Australia and Chile, faculty spend considerably more time on teaching than on research. Senior faculty are more likely than junior faculty to favor research over teaching, although the former are not necessarily more involved nor more productive as researchers. A sizable proportion of respondents in most countries report no hours at all spent on service, but a notable contrast is that in Brazil and Mexico, faculty spend on average more than ten hours in a typical week on service activities.

Service activity—defined as paid and unpaid work with a professional organization or with clients or patients, at the university or off-campus, and committee work at the institution—is also an academic responsibility. Many report that they are paid for a portion of their service and consulting work. As indicated in a few countries, they note that this income is necessary for economic survival.

Regardless of whether school is in session, those who prefer teaching over research spend somewhat more time on local or campus-related activities (teaching, service, and administration) than do those who prefer research over teaching. But faculty who prefer research spend a few more hours per week on their total professional work when classes are in session and several more per week during breaks. This is accounted for by the much larger portion of hours they spend on their research than those whose preference is for teaching. But

TABLE 9
Mean Hours Per Week of Professional Work, by Teaching or Research Preference

	Teaching Preference	*Research Preference*
Classes in Session		
Teaching	22.2	17.1
Research	10.3	20.3
Service	6.5	5.2
Administration	7.7	7.2
Other	3.1	3.4
Total	49.8	53.2
Classes Not in Session		
Teaching	9.0	6.4
Research	16.8	28.6
Service	6.7	5.2
Administration	7.1	6.0
Other	3.7	3.9
Total	43.3	50.1

Source: The Carnegie Foundation for the Advancement of Teaching, The International Survey of the Academic Profession, 1991–1993, Princeton, NJ.

regardless of preferences, their involvement in research increases when classes are not scheduled.

It is also the case that the academic profession is largely a *teaching* profession, in which people spend most of their time, when classes are in session, on teaching and university service activities. This is true for the majority of countries in the survey.

As far as types of classes are concerned, most respondents teach a combination of undergraduate and graduate/professional students. The majority also report that the traditional lecture is the primary means of communicating knowledge, although class discussions are prominent in all of the countries surveyed except Japan.

Despite their putative interest in it, scholars in most countries publish remarkably little research, at least as expressed by a simple count of number of publications, including books and articles. It is worth noting, however, that in many disciplines (e.g., in the sciences) books are not the conventional mode of reporting research. Just fewer than half of the sample responded to a question asking whether they had authored or edited scholarly books in the previous three years; half of the respondents had not published a book, and for the minority who had published, the mean number of books was 1.1. Fewer than one in five had edited a book—the mean number of edited books was 0.74. In sum, at the very most, a quarter of the respondents report publishing a book in the previous three years. The actual figure, of course, could be considerably smaller.

A significantly larger proportion of the sample responded to a question asking for the number of scholarly articles they had published in the previous three years. Of those who responded, the mean number is just under six, or about two articles a year. Ten percent report publishing no articles. The average number of papers presented at a scholarly conference over the previous three years is slightly below five. On the whole, male faculty are more involved in research and publication than are female faculty. Consistent with expressed interests, academics in the Netherlands, Israel, Germany, Japan, and Sweden generally publish more articles than those in other countries.

Rates of publication may relate to funds available for research, to the nature and emphasis of the system of evaluation for academic promotion, and to the academic culture in the country. For example, scholars and scientists who indicate that their primary commitment is to research publish more and obtain more research funds than do those who stress teaching. It is clear that research is easier to assess than teaching, and this may also contribute to the research culture that is emphasized by many of the academics in this study.

Only a small minority of the academic profession in the fourteen countries does most of the publishing and obtains most of the research funds. There is a clearly identifiable "research cadre," usually located at the top universities, that accounts for a very significant proportion of research production. The four factors that characterize a clear research commitment (and subsequent productivity) are, first, whether individuals were more interested in research than in teaching; second, whether on average they spent more time on research and less time on teaching than others; third, whether they published scholarly books and articles; and fourth, whether they received funding for their research. The professoriate in four countries (Brazil, Chile, Mexico, and Russia) stood out as having the lowest research commitment, while those in five countries (Germany, Israel, Japan, the Netherlands, and Sweden) could be characterized as having a relatively high commitment.

It is unclear why academics as a whole express a commitment to the idea of research while actual productivity is in fact limited to a minority of the profession. More than three-quarters of those faculty members who indicate that their academic positions require them to be involved in research report that they actually are (the figure is more than 90 percent in the United States, Australia, Israel, Hong Kong, and Sweden). Only a small number report significant publications, i.e., more than two articles and two presentations or papers in a year and more than one book in three years. Why more academics do not produce more publications from their research more often may have to do with time rather than with money, as about half of the respondents in most countries report that they had received some funding for their research (less than half in Russia, Brazil, and Mexico). In most cases, however, the amounts of money were relatively small. Members of the research cadre, numbering less

TABLE 10
In My Department It Is Difficult for a Person to Achieve Tenure if He or She Does Not Publish (Percentages)

	Agree	*Neutral*	*Disagree*
Australia	64	15	21
Brazil	25	21	55
Chile	33	35	32
Germany	78	8	14
Hong Kong	60	16	24
Israel	81	4	15
Japan	48	23	29
Korea	38	15	48
Mexico	28	24	48
Russia	32	41	27
Sweden	58	18	24
United States	75	8	17

Source: Ernest L. Boyer, Philip G. Altbach, and Mary Jean Whitelaw, *The Academic Profession: An International Perspective* (Princeton, NJ: The Carnegie Foundation for the Advancement of Teaching, 1994), 84.

than 5 percent of those who report receiving any funding, indicate that they received significant financial support. Many scholars feel—probably quite accurately—that research funding is more difficult to obtain now than five years ago. This perception was most acute in Israel, England, Germany, Russia, and the United States.

Faculty express some ambivalent attitudes concerning research. More than three-quarters in all countries, excepting Brazil, Russia, and Korea, note that a strong record of successful research activity is important in faculty evaluations, and in six countries a majority agree that it is difficult for a person to achieve tenure if he or she does not publish (Table 10). Many feel that they are under pressure to do more research than they would like to—more than 30 percent in six of the countries (Table 11).

At the same time, those who write more articles and books are, sometimes by great margins and sometimes by narrow margins, more satisfied with their work life and less likely to feel vulnerable to acute and chronic pressures they encounter on campus than those who write fewer articles and books. There is a relationship between research productivity and a sense of empowerment and overall satisfaction.

Nonetheless, faculty worldwide do not endorse the view that teaching and research necessarily work at cross-purposes. Indeed, more faculty than not are convinced that their research has a positive influence on their teaching, and the majority of faculty in all countries except Hong Kong are of the opinion that the pressure to publish does not reduce the quality of teaching. However, such a conflict is noted by a significant minority in Chile, England, Israel, the Netherlands, Germany, the United States, and Australia. Administrative assignments are seen as having a more negative influence on research than on teaching.

Regarding expectations of students, instructors in most countries establish a variety of requirements, including regular class attendance, written work, oral presentations, and examinations. Considerable disagreement was found on whether teaching effectiveness should be the primary criterion for promotion. Academics in every country feel that students should have a role in evaluating teaching, but in general, senior faculty were more likely than junior faculty to express reservations about the merits of a more active student role in academic affairs.

In common with respondents in Carnegie surveys of the U.S. academic profession, international respondents report that they devote many hours to teaching, research, service, and administrative activities. There are some variations according to country and further differ-

TABLE 11
I Frequently Feel Under Pressure to Do More Research Than I Actually Would Like to Do (Percentages)

	Agree	*Neutral*	*Disagree*
Australia	31	23	46
Brazil	13	17	71
Chile	38	27	36
England	34	24	42
Germany	28	17	55
Hong Kong	36	21	43
Israel	13	12	76
Japan	37	31	32
Korea	36	18	45
Mexico	20	25	55
The Netherlands	22	26	52
Russia	12	47	41
Sweden	25	21	54
United Stares	30	20	50

Source: Ernest L. Boyer, Philip G. Altbach, and Mary Jean Whitelaw, *The Academic Profession: An International Perspective* (Princeton, NJ: The Carnegie Foundation for the Advancement of Teaching, 1994), 84.

ences according to institutional affiliation and to gender and rank. Most of those surveyed express a significant commitment to all of the standard faculty roles but are most impatient with their administrative responsibilities. At the same time, they are also critical of administrators who have taken over these tasks.

Governance

It is well known that there are striking variations in governance arrangements from one country to another; in some countries colleges and universities are government controlled, while in others committees composed of a mix of academics and officials set policy, and in yet others there is a tradition of institutional independence. Funding sources for institutions range from total government support to only private support. In a small majority of the countries included in our survey, most academic institutions are government-sponsored, although in Japan, Korea, and the three Latin American countries, a majority of students study in private colleges and universities. Yet academics everywhere have a significant degree of autonomy, and the ideology of internal governance in colleges and universities is strong.

Our survey asked scholars and scientists to reflect on issues of governance, and some common concerns emerged. Respondents, when asked about institutional centralization and decentralization, generally report that there is a mixture when it comes to most of the major elements of decision making. Since World War II, as higher education rapidly expanded, the sense of academic community has been weakened. Many of our respondents are aware of this and are also concerned about the trend toward centralized power in higher education. They are unhappy and unsure about how to cope with the more hierarchical, more rigid governance structure. As a result, faculty dissatisfaction with current administrative and governance arrangements is high, and a cause for concern. Senior faculty were more sympathetic to administrators than were junior faculty who had more questions about the competence and goodwill of those who manage institutions of higher learning. Not surprisingly, many believe that they have most influence on decision making in their academic department or similar unit, with majorities in almost all countries feeling that they were either very influential or somewhat influential at this level. Respondents in Germany and Mexico are least likely to express this view.

At the same time, fewer than 10 percent in almost all of the countries feel that they play a key role in governance at the institutional level (Table 12). Obviously, scholars and scientists around the world feel considerable alienation from the higher echelons of administration at their institutions. An unusually large number express dissatisfaction with and doubts about the quality of the leadership provided by top-level administrators at their colleges and universities—Japan is the only country in which a majority of the respondents agree that top administrators are providing competent leadership (Table 13). The distrust is pervasive. Less than half feel that they are informed about what is going on, and close to half characterize communication between the faculty and the administration as poor.

In eight countries, the majority of faculty report that academic administrators are autocratic (Table 14), and in six countries, a majority agree that a lack of faculty involvement in governance is a problem. Only in Brazil, Israel, the

TABLE 12
How Influential Are You, Personally, in Helping to Shape Key Academic Policies at the Institutional Level? (Percentages)

	Very Influential	*Somewhat Influential*	*A Little Influential*	*Not At All Influential*
Australia	2	6	14	78
Brazil	3	18	36	43
Chile	3	14	20	64
England	2	8	16	74
Germany	1	5	14	80
Hong Kong	1	6	13	81
Israel	5	7	31	57
Japan	5	24	40	31
Korea	3	8	33	57
Mexico	3	13	23	61
Russia	3	19	25	53
Sweden	5	13	18	64
United States	3	11	22	64

Source: Ernest L. Boyer, Philip G. Altbach, and Mary Jean Whitelaw, *The Academic Profession: An International Perspective* (Princeton, NJ: The Carnegie Foundation for the Advancement of Teaching, 1994), 94.

TABLE 13
Top-Level Administrators Are Providing Competent Leadership (Percentages)

	Agree	*Neutral*	*Disagree*
Australia	29	26	46
Brazil	46	27	27
Chile	28	31	42
England	26	25	49
Germany	24	27	49
Hong Kong	23	29	48
Israel	28	31	41
Japan	60	22	18
Korea	24	31	45
Mexico	33	23	44
The Netherlands	32	42	26
Russia	30	53	17
Sweden	30	38	32
United States	39	22	38

Source: Ernest L. Boyer, Philip G. Altbach, and Mary Jean Whitelaw, *The Academic Profession: An International Perspective* (Princeton, NJ: The Carnegie Foundation for the Advancement of Teaching, 1994), 97.

United States, and Japan do more than half of the faculty feel that administrators even support academic freedom. Other questions elicit a general dissatisfaction on the part of faculty. Granted, the financial setbacks higher education has faced in recent years have contributed to faculty unrest. Yet, there is clearly a need to create new mechanisms to bring faculty and administrators together to resolve problems, reestablish communications, and renew collegiality so that in the end mutual trust and respect are fostered.

TABLE 14
The Administration Is Often Autocratic (Percentages)

	Agree	*Neutral*	*Disagree*
Australia	63	23	14
Brazil	44	20	36
Chile	58	23	19
England	64	21	16
Germany	67	21	13
Hong Kong	64	23	13
Israel	57	24	19
Japan	40	34	26
Korea	46	30	24
Mexico	54	20	27
The Netherlands	37	38	25
Russia	43	41	16
Sweden	43	36	21
United States	58	22	20

Source: Ernest L. Boyer, Philip G. Altbach, and Mary Jean Whitelaw, *The Academic Profession: An International Perspective* (Princeton, NJ: The Carnegie Foundation for the Advancement of Teaching, 1994), 96.

Academic freedom is one of the core values of higher education. Our respondents, in general, have reasonable confidence that they are protected by this principle (Table 15). Large majorities in every country (except Russia and Brazil) note that they are free to determine the content of the courses they teach, and similarly large numbers feel free to do research on any topic of interest. Since intellectual freedom is indeed at the heart of academia, the widespread sense of security about its strength may be a key factor contributing to academics' overall satisfaction with their chosen careers despite problems with marginal conditions.

When it comes to perceptions of restrictions on what a scholar or scientist can teach or publish, additional variations were noted, some of which seem to conflict with the notion of academic freedom (Tables 16 and 17). While a strong majority of the respondents feel free to determine course content, significant numbers do feel constraints: one-third in the United States, for example, and more than 40 percent in Korea. Current debate in the United States concerning "political correctness" may cause some in the social sciences and humanities to feel that there are limits on expression. The responses of Korean academics can be

TABLE 15
Is Academic Freedom Strongly Protected in This Country? (Percentages)

	Yes	*No*
Australia	77	23
Brazil	38	62
Chile	71	29
Hong Kong	71	30
Israel	92	8
Japan	79	21
Korea	74	26
Mexico	69	31
The Netherlands	74	26
Russia	16	84
Sweden	83	17
United States	81	19

Source: Ernest L. Boyer, Philip G. Altbach, and Mary Jean Whitelaw, *The Academic Profession: An International Perspective* (Princeton, NJ: The Carnegie Foundation for the Advancement of Teaching, 1994), 99.

TABLE 16
At This Institution, I Am Fully Free to Determine the Content of the Courses I Teach (Percentages)

	Agree	*Neutral*	*Disagree*
Australia	67	9	24
Brazil	69	9	22
Chile	70	14	17
England	62	14	25
Germany	61	15	24
Hong Kong	61	9	29
Japan	80	13	7
Korea	90	7	3
Mexico	65	14	21
Russia	45	27	28
Sweden	64	13	24
United States	78	8	14

Source: Ernest L. Boyer, Philip G. Altbach, and Mary Jean Whitelaw, *The Academic Profession: An International Perspective* (Princeton, NJ: The Carnegie Foundation for the Advancement of Teaching, 1994), 100.

explained by the fact that, although the campuses have been hotbeds of activism (and of repression) in previous regimes, democracy is a recent phenomenon in Korea and activism continues on a more sporadic basis.

The issue of the evaluation of academic work is currently of considerable interest to scholars around the world. A significant proportion of faculty in all countries except Korea and Russia report that a strong research record is important in faculty evaluation. Understandably, those who feel the least need to publish also feel little pressure about doing research (again, this is most true for Brazil, Mexico, Israel, and Russia). Israel presents an interesting case, though, since 81 percent of the faculty believe that they must publish, but only 13 percent feel that they are asked to do more than they would like.

TABLE 17
I Can Focus My Research on Any Topic of Special Interest to Me (Percentages)

	Agree	*Neutral*	*Disagree*
Australia	81	7	12
Brazil	72	12	16
Chile	76	14	11
England	79	10	11
Germany	63	14	23
Hong Kong	83	8	9
Japan	87	8	5
Korea	85	10	5
Mexico	66	14	20
Russia	65	19	16
Sweden	79	8	13
United States	89	5	6

Source: Ernest L. Boyer, Philip G. Altbach, and Mary Jean Whitelaw, *The Academic Profession: An International Perspective* (Princeton, NJ: The Carnegie Foundation for the Advancement of Teaching, 1994), 100.

Scholars and scientists in most of the countries said that their work is regularly evaluated (Table 18). Only in Germany and Russia do up to a third report that this is not so. (Here, the United States, with more than 85 percent of the faculty reporting regular evaluation, ranked highest.) Respondents in all countries note that teaching is evaluated most often, with research coming second; service activities are seldom assessed. In Brazil, England, Hong Kong, Mexico, and the United States, more than 90 percent report regular evaluation of teaching. Only in the Netherlands is research evaluated more frequently than teaching. Students are most likely to evaluate teaching—96 percent and 91 percent of faculty in Sweden and the United States, respectively, report that students regularly evaluate their teaching (Table 19). And only in Korea is the percentage less than half (12 percent). In Korea, however, senior administrators, rather than students, evaluate teaching. In most countries, in addition to evaluation by

TABLE 18
Which of These Activities Are Appraised or Evaluated Regularly? (Percentages)

	Teaching	*Research*	*Service*
Australia	89	78	42
Brazil	93	71	38
Chile	88	85	0
England	94	91	33
Germany	42	83	25
Hong Kong	92	73	38
Israel	87	54	8
Japan	45	95	17
Korea	65	97	11
Mexico	92	53	25
The Netherlands	69	87	17
Russia	86	57	8
Sweden	77	65	12
United States	97	77	68

Source: Ernest L. Boyer, Philip G. Altbach, and Mary Jean Whitelaw, *The Academic Profession: An International Perspective* (Princeton, NJ: The Carnegie Foundation for the Advancement of Teaching, 1994), 85.

Note: More than one response could be selected.

TABLE 19
By Whom Is Your Teaching Regularly Evaluated?
(Percentages)

	Your Peers in Your Department	*The Head of Your Department*	*Members of Other Departments at This Institution*	*Senior Administrative Staff at This Institution*	*Your Students*	*External Reviewers*
Australia	28	64	6	11	74	6
Brazil	53	51	15	28	54	5
Chile	30	61	26	23	51	4
Germany	30	44	6	8	59	2
Hong Kong	23	70	7	23	76	24
Israel	24	45	7	7	85	7
Japan	42	43	10	41	37	5
Korea	18	29	9	70	12	8
Mexico	37	62	23	55	57	10
The Netherlands	49	29	7	7	79	17
Russia	32	76	14	21	62	6
Sweden	20	26	11	7	96	9
United Kingdom	16	67	7	13	67	21
United States	49	78	16	34	91	7

Source: Ernest L. Boyer, Philip G. Altbach, and Mary Jean Whitelaw, *The Academic Profession: An International Perspective* (Princeton, NJ: The Carnegie Foundation for the Advancement of Teaching, 1994), 85.

Note: More than one response could be selected.

students, respondents report that heads of department regularly evaluate teaching. Despite the general commitment to evaluation, we found widespread dissatisfaction with the way teaching is assessed. Most faculty in all countries agree that better methods are necessary to make the process more meaningful.

Research seems often to be less rigorously evaluated, at least formally. A surprising percentage of respondents say that at their institutions publications are just "counted," not qualitatively evaluated (Table 20). For most countries, heads of department are the main evaluators of research, but on occasion external reviewers, departmental peers, and senior administrative staff also play a role.

International Dimensions of Academic Life

We are convinced that as the world has become increasingly interdependent and national academic boundaries have been blurred, science and scholarship are becoming increasingly international. Indeed, we found that while international consciousness in all of the countries in the survey, except the United States, is quite high in certain ways, actual international involvement is somewhat limited. Among the relatively small minority who are heavily involved in research, five countries—Sweden,

TABLE 20
At This Institution Publications Used for Promotion Decisions Are Just "Counted," Not Qualitatively Evaluated
(Percentages)

	Agree	*Neutral*	*Disagree*
Australia	52	27	20
Brazil	45	22	34
Chile	54	24	22
Hong Kong	59	24	18
Israel	34	20	45
Japan	46	28	27
Korea	52	17	31
Mexico	55	21	24
The Netherlands	48	18	34
Russia	61	25	14
Sweden	27	28	45
United States	45	17	38

Source: Ernest L. Boyer, Philip G. Altbach, and Mary Jean Whitelaw, *The Academic Profession: An International Perspective* (Princeton, NJ: The Carnegie Foundation for the Advancement of Teaching, 1994), 85.

TABLE 21
International Activities of Faculty for the Last Three Years, by Teaching or Research Preference

	Teaching (Mean Number of Times)	Research (Mean Number of Times)
Published in another country	1.3	4.0
Article or book written in another language	1.2	4.2
Organized classes for foreign students	1.1	1.2
	Teaching (Mean Number of Months)	*Research (Mean Number of of Months)*
Worked on research with academics from abroad	1.8	5.2
Traveled abroad for study or research	1.5	2.6
Served as faculty in another country	0.5	1.1
Spent sabbatical abroad	0.4	0.8

Source: The Carnegie Foundation for the Advancement of Teaching, The International Survey of the Academic Profession, 1991–1993, Princeton, NJ.

Note: Only between 45 and 60 percent of respondents answered these questions.

Germany, Hong Kong, the Netherlands, and Israel—had significantly more international publications than the rest, and four of the five (not Germany) plus Japan reported writing more frequently in a language other than their own.

On all but two of the fourteen measures of international activity (teaching classes for foreign students within the last three years and within the last ten years), those more committed to research than teaching had a greater likelihood of international involvement. That is, professors oriented to research are, not surprisingly, the professors who more often write for an international audience, travel and work abroad, and have relationships with academics in other countries (Table 21). The ease of spreading ideas through improved technology and the synergistic aspects of academics' research has contributed to increased internationalism, particularly in the natural sciences.

A relatively high proportion of scholars and scientists report that foreign faculty have taught at their institutions or that foreign students have come to study there—with the United States, Australia, Japan, and Russia scoring especially high in these activities. In all countries except Korea, 50 percent or more of faculty report that foreign students have been enrolled at their institutions, at least occasionally; the number of faculty reporting that students from their institutions study overseas was also impressive.

Faculty worldwide are convinced that the curriculum should be more international in scope (Table 22). (In Israel, where less than one-third of the respondents supported this idea, the curriculum is already international in scope.) Next lowest were the United States and Australia, where not quite half of the faculty were in favor of this idea.

Overall, the academic profession expresses a high degree of commitment to internationalism. There is considerable support for international exchange. In the past three years, over

TABLE 22
The Curriculum at This Institution Should Be More International in Focus (Percentages)

	Agree	Neutral	Disagree
Australia	47	40	13
Brazil	61	22	17
Chile	79	12	9
Germany	57	31	12
Hong Kong	66	27	7
Israel	29	32	39
Japan	67	31	2
Korea	76	20	4
Mexico	75	17	8
Russia	59	39	3
Sweden	59	34	7
United States	45	37	18

Source: Ernest L. Boyer, Philip G. Altbach, and Mary Jean Whitelaw, *The Academic Profession: An International Perspective* (Princeton, NJ: The Carnegie Foundation for the Advancement of Teaching, 1994), 104.

TABLE 23
For How Many Months During the Past Three Years Have You Traveled Abroad to Study or Do Research? (Percentages)

	None	*One or More*
Australia	38	62
Brazil	63	37
Chile	39	61
England	47	53
Germany	35	65
Hong Kong	28	72
Israel	7	93
Japan	45	55
Korea	38	62
Mexico	57	43
The Netherlands	30	70
Russia	64	36
Sweden	25	75
United States	65	35

Source: Ernest L. Boyer, Philip G. Altbach, and Mary Jean Whitelaw, *The Academic Profession: An International Perspective* (Princeton, NJ: The Carnegie Foundation for the Advancement of Teaching, 1994), 104.

half of the professoriate in ten countries made at least one trip abroad for study or research (Table 23). The range is quite wide. Israel leads the way, with more than 90 percent of the respondents studying abroad. At the other extreme, Brazil, Russia, and the United States trail well behind, with only about one-third reporting such activity. Fewer faculty spend time teaching in other countries. Again, Israeli faculty are the most active—more than 65 percent say that they had taught abroad in the past three years—followed by faculty from the Netherlands and Hong Kong. On the other hand, fewer than 10 percent of the professoriate from Brazil, Korea, Japan, Russia, and the United States—countries with larger systems of higher education—have recently taught overseas.

More than three-quarters of respondents in most countries indicate that contacts with scholars in other countries are important for their professional work (Table 24). Notably, only the United States and England scored lower. In all countries except the United States, more than 90 percent of faculty indicate that a scholar or scientist must read books and journals published abroad to keep up with his or her discipline (Table 25). Similarly, faculty overall agree that colleges and universities should do more to promote student and faculty mobility from one country to another, with the United States scoring well below the average on this item, too.

English is increasingly the language of research, perhaps contributing to the feeling by American and British scholars that they need

TABLE 24
Connections With Scholars in Other Countries Are Very Important to My Professional Work (Percentages)

	Agree	*Neutral*	*Disagree*
Australia	81	15	4
Brazil	85	11	4
Chile	95	3	2
England	63	26	11
Germany	78	14	8
Hong Kong	85	12	4
Israel	86	8	6
Japan	88	11	2
Korea	91	8	1
Mexico	79	15	6
The Netherlands	81	11	8
Russia	89	11	1
Sweden	87	11	2
United States	55	26	19

Source: Ernest L. Boyer, Philip G. Altbach, and Mary Jean Whitelaw, *The Academic Profession: An International Perspective* (Princeton, NJ: The Carnegie Foundation for the Advancement of Teaching, 1994), 106.

TABLE 25
In Order to Keep Up with Developments in My Discipline, a Scholar Must Read Books and Journals Published Abroad (Percentages)

	Agree	*Neutral*	*Disagree*
Australia	98	2	1
Brazil	92	3	4
Chile	98	1	1
Germany	91	5	4
Hong Kong	98	1	1
Israel	98	2	0
Japan	93	5	2
Korea	96	4	1
Mexico	91	6	3
The Netherlands	95	3	3
Russia	99	1	0
Sweden	96	3	1
United States	62	17	22

Source: Ernest L. Boyer, Philip G. Altbach, and Mary Jean Whitelaw, *The Academic Profession: An International Perspective* (Princeton, NJ: The Carnegie Foundation for the Advancement of Teaching, 1994), 105.

not be so concerned about academic contacts with the rest of the world. Faculty and students are increasingly peripatetic, with more than one million students studying outside their home countries. The United States and Britain are major host nations and account for approximately half of the world's total. They also host a highly disproportionate percentage of visiting scholars and scientists. Events have fostered a more professionally connected, international community of scholars and scientists, and there is a deep conviction both that higher education is an international enterprise and that the academic profession is becoming a more global community. Internationalism in all aspects of academic life will inevitably increase in the coming years.

Attitudes Regarding Higher Education and Society

As the academy moves toward the twenty-first century, some important questions must be addressed—issues relating to access, equity, and expansion. Following World War II, student enrollment policies began to shift in many countries, so that today even the most elitist systems have increased the access to higher education. All of the academic systems included in this survey have dramatically increased enrollments in recent years and, with the exception of the United States, enrollment growth continues. Yet, little effort has been made to determine what faculty think about this fundamental change, one that affects the climate of the campus and the work of the professoriate so profoundly.

Overall, faculty in most countries believe that a majority of young people can complete secondary education. Moreover, two-thirds of the scholars and scientists sampled support the idea that any student who can meet minimum entrance requirements for post-secondary education should be permitted to pursue at least a bachelor's degree, which leaves a third holding reservations about expanded educational opportunity. On the other hand, faculty in Germany, where admittance to one institution means a student can attend or transfer to any of the others, overwhelmingly support open access.

In the United States, more than half of the relevant age group currently pursues post-secondary education; this is the greatest number among the fourteen countries, yet academics elsewhere seem to be supportive of the continuing expansion of higher education in their countries. At the same time, with the exception of Australia, where half of the respondents were in favor, few respondents believe that admission standards should be lowered to permit disadvantaged students to enroll. In the other countries, the proportion ranged from 7 percent in Japan to 38 percent in Chile, with the United States in the middle at somewhat under 20 percent. Clearly, while the academic profession favors continuing expansion of higher education, they are not at this point in time broadly committed to such programs as special admission criteria or affirmative action for disadvantaged students.

Additional responses further indicate that the academic profession supports the ideas that higher education should prepare students for work, that research and scholarship should continue to be a key part of the mission of the university, that intellectual inquiry should be protected, and that higher education should help to solve basic social problems. The

TABLE 26
Faculty in My Discipline Have a Professional Obligation to Apply Their Knowledge to Problems in Society
(Percentages)

	Yes	*No*
Australia	86	14
Brazil	78	22
Chile	74	26
England	79	21
Germany	93	7
Hong Kong	84	16
Israel	76	24
Japan	81	19
Korea	86	14
Mexico	86	14
The Netherlands	87	13
Russia	61	39
Sweden	68	32
United States	82	18

Source: Ernest L. Boyer, Philip G. Altbach, and Mary Jean Whitelaw, *The Academic Profession: An International Perspective* (Princeton, NJ: The Carnegie Foundation for the Advancement of Teaching, 1994), 102.

response to this final question was overwhelmingly affirmative—except in Russia and Sweden (Table 26). We believe that these figures reflect the faculty's confidence in the practical value of their knowledge.

Despite their optimism about what they might accomplish, academics do not generally believe that they wield much influence in their countries. The most optimistic professors were in Korea, where they feel that they have relatively high levels of influence; those in England and Israel do not. With regard to England, one wonders what the responses would have been a decade or two ago, before the Conservative government's restructuring of the higher education system. In any case, despite the importance of colleges and universities in modern society, academics do not feel that they are among the most influential opinion leaders (Table 27). Another measure of public support for higher education is the respect academics feel they receive in their own country (Table 28). While responses vary, the general pattern is, again, not encouraging: about 60 percent of faculty feel that overall respect for academics is declining in their country—ranging from a high of nearly 80 percent in Brazil to a low of 40 percent in the Netherlands and Sweden. Scholars and scientists in a number of countries feel that institutions of higher learning are increasingly subject to interference from special interest groups. This is particularly true for respondents from the United States, England, Mexico, Brazil, and Australia.

When asked whether government should define the overall purposes and policies for higher education, faculty responses ranged from a high of 90 percent in Russia to a low of 10 percent in the United States, with other countries clustering between 20 percent and 50

TABLE 28
Respect For Academics Is Declining
(Percentages)

	Agree	*Neutral*	*Disagree*
Australia	57	32	11
Brazil	78	10	12
Chile	51	28	21
England	73	20	7
Germany	50	29	20
Hong Kong	49	33	18
Israel	60	23	18
Japan	65	30	6
Korea	69	22	9
Mexico	56	20	24
The Netherlands	44	41	15
Russia	64	26	10
Sweden	43	36	21
United States	64	23	13

Source: Ernest L. Boyer, Philip G. Altbach, and Mary Jean Whitelaw, *The Academic Profession: An International Perspective* (Princeton, NJ: The Carnegie Foundation for the Advancement of Teaching, 1994), 101.

TABLE 27
Academics Are Among the Most Influential Opinion Leaders in My Country
(Percentages)

	Agree	*Neutral*	*Disagree*
Australia	19	27	54
Brazil	39	17	44
Chile	16	30	54
England	11	25	63
Germany	15	29	56
Hong Kong	26	36	38
Israel	12	26	62
Japan	40	46	15
Korea	63	29	8
Mexico	30	28	42
Russia	24	33	43
Sweden	30	29	41
United States	21	27	52

Source: Ernest L. Boyer, Philip G. Altbach, and Mary Jean Whitelaw, *The Academic Profession: An International Perspective* (Princeton, NJ: The Carnegie Foundation for the Advancement of Teaching, 1994), 102.

TABLE 29
In This Country, There Is Far Too Much Governmental Interference in Important Academic Policies
(Percentages)

	Agree	*Neutral*	*Disagree*
Australia	57	26	17
Brazil	42	23	35
Chile	17	32	51
Hong Kong	43	32	25
Israel	31	22	48
Japan	48	41	11
Korea	89	8	3
Mexico	55	22	23
The Netherlands	46	32	22
Russia	33	39	27
Sweden	25	36	39
United States	34	33	33

Source: Ernest L. Boyer, Philip G. Altbach, and Mary Jean Whitelaw, *The Academic Profession: An International Perspective* (Princeton, NJ: The Carnegie Foundation for the Advancement of Teaching, 1994), 99.

percent. When asked if government interferes too much in important academic policies, responses varied from 90 percent in Korea to less than 20 percent in Chile (Table 29). In Russia and the United States, about one-third of the faculty feel that there is too much government interference. It is striking that Russian faculty favor governmental policy making but believe there is too much interference.

Generally, scholars and scientists are supportive of a significant societal mission for higher education and support expansion so that qualified young people can obtain access to post-secondary education. Yet they would, for the most part, like to distance themselves and their institutions from government edicts and officials.

Conclusion

This portrait of the academic profession in fourteen countries shows a complex web of attitudes and values. One cannot but be struck by the many similarities among the scholars and scientists in these diverse countries. It is with regard to those working conditions most affected by local political and cultural customs and policies that international differences are most apparent.

The professoriate worldwide is committed to teaching and research, and in varying degrees to service. While there is a feeling that higher education faces many difficulties and that conditions have deteriorated in recent years, most academics are committed to the profession and to its traditional values of autonomy, academic freedom, and the importance of scholarship, both for its own sake and for societal advancement. Academics are not especially supportive of senior administrators, yet they express remarkable loyalty to the profession and to other academics. They seem prepared to respond to the call that higher education contribute more tangibly to economic development and social well-being. They believe that they have an obligation to apply their knowledge to society's problems.

Specific national circumstances have no doubt shaped the responses to the questionnaire. Dramatic societal transformation and stresses in Russia, the structural changes in higher education of the past decade in the United Kingdom, and continuing tension between academics and the government over salary issues in Israel, to name just a few examples, are factors that have obviously influenced the responses reported here. Continuing expansion and diminishing resources have characterized the academic landscape in virtually all countries. To be sure, if there were more money and resources available and if academic administrators did not have to say no so often, there would be fewer criticisms of how institutions of higher education were managed.

Resiliency, determination, and a focus on the core functions of higher education characterize the academic profession in these fourteen countries. While the vicissitudes experienced by the profession in recent years have been considerable, the professoriate is by no means demoralized. In all but three countries, 60 percent or more agree that this is an especially creative and productive time in their fields. Professors are generally satisfied with the courses they teach, and with few exceptions are pleased with the opportunities they have to pursue their own ideas. The intellectual atmosphere is good; faculty do not regret their career choices and are generally happy with their relationships with colleagues.

This portrait of the professoriate depicts a strong, but somewhat unsettled profession. Academics around the world are inspired by the intellectual ferment of the times. The intrinsic pleasures of academic life obviously endure. Academe is facing the future with concern but with surprising optimism.

The Market Oriented University and the Changing Role of Knowledge

HOWARD BUCHBINDER

Abstract. The development of corporate-university linkages occurs within the orbit of two major influences, the information society and the globalization of capital. The presence of the information society builds great pressure towards the production and transfer of knowledge. The economic contraction of recent years is juxtaposed against the globalization of capital which demands that productive enterprises compete on a world wide scale. Universities are not exempt from this dynamic as they too are propelled toward a market orientation. This process leads to a series of conflicts within our universities which define the parameters of the transformation.

The first part of this paper discusses these areas of development and conflict within the market university: 1) autonomy and collegiality, 2) the market and the university, 3) ideology, 4) globalization and privatization, 5) pluralism. The second part focuses on the role of knowledge within market university and the change from social knowledge to market knowledge. The focus here includes: 1) the social context of knowledge, 2) science, research of knowledge, 3) knowledge as property, 4) the transfer of knowledge. It is in this context that a new public policy for universities must be charted.

Introduction

The development of corporate-university linkages has led to a debate over the possible outcomes. Business has looked to university research to provide them a "window" on scientific research and development. University research laboratories are seen as potential innovators in the development and production of marketable products. Underfunded universities and university researchers struggling to fund their research from inadequate research funding have turned to the private sector. This process has been encouraged by government, as well as non-governmental agencies such as the Canadian Corporate–Higher Education Forum, who see a "marriage" between private industry and university research as a more efficient way to survive in a political economy characterized by severe recession. "Efficiency" is articulated in terms of market processes and products and the streamlining of university institutions which are seen as too cumbersome and unwieldy to survive in a political economy characterized by recession, contraction and global competition. This contraction is juxtaposed against this globalization of capital which demands that productive enterprises compete on a world-wide scale. At the same time the development of the information society builds great pressure towards the production and transfer of knowledge. The ownership and marketing of information and knowledge has become a critical concern. The outcome is a turbulent situation which transforms the university as it struggles to reconcile the pushes and pulls of the information society, on the one hand, and the globalization of capital on the other. This process leads to a series of conflicts within our universities which define the parameters of the transformation. At one level the overall conflict is between the demands of the information society and the effects of the globalization of capital. At another level the conflict can be described as between collective well being and personal gain.

The integration, at low cost, of rapid computation with the instantaneous transmission of information is the major technical advance which has facilitated this global information network. The ownership and marketing of information and knowledge has become a critical concern (Buchbinder and Newson 1991, p. 18; Menzies).

How will these events influence the university which has been a repository of social knowledge preserved and developed in the public interest? How will it be affected by the globalization of production and markets on a wide ranging international scale? "The analysis of globalization must begin with the internationalization of production" (Cox 1991, p. 336). Along with the internationalization of production is the internationalization of the state. During the past half century the priority of the state (within its support of the domestic accumulation process) was domestic welfare. "In the past couple of decades the priority has shifted to one of adapting domestic economies to the perceived exigencies of the world economy" (Cox 1991, p. 337).

The social context in which university developed knowledge lived and grew over the past twenty years can be described as a contracting economy in which policy is driven, in the main, by budget considerations and rooted in neo-conservative ideology and economics. Universities are seen as having to be like business and "learn to pay twice as much to half as many people" (Hague 1991, p. 13). This view can be illustrated from a British neo-conservative perspective as represented by "Thatcherism."

> . . . British universities represent a sheltered system, shielded from competitive pressure by two types of monopoly: natural monopolies of brain power and certain physical resources, like libraries or laboratories; and man made (sic) monopolies, bestowed by government, first through restrictions on the power to confer degrees and, second, through the university cartel. Over time, the growth of the knowledge industries will give organizations outside the universities the power to erode these monopolies (Hague 1991, p. 31–32).

The response of universities to the underfunding by governments, the pressure of reduced research resources, the ascendancy of the neo-conservative free market ideology and the impact of knowledge industries has led university administrations to seek solutions in corporate linkages.

Within this broad context the combination of underfunded universities, high tech developments, corporate needs, and prevailing ideology lead to a basic transformation in the university; a transformation to a university oriented to the market-place. This change affects the production and transmission of knowledge, which is the central function of the university and is stimulated by the demands of the information society. It also alters patterns of governance. These changes in turn affect academic autonomy and collegiality. In addition, there is a qualitative change in the form and transfer of knowledge. There are a series of conflicts which define this process and lay the groundwork for a consideration of the role of knowledge.

Part I: Aspects of the Market University

1. Autonomy and Collegiality in the Academic Workplace

The university as we know it is a very unusual sort of workplace. The academic staff, charged with the production and transmission of knowledge are the core of the university along with the students who are the recipients of that knowledge and often engage in its production as well. Without the academic staff there would be no academic enterprise. Hence the structure of the academic workplace needs to support the centrality of academic workers. It would therefore be essential to assess the organization of the institution at any point in time in terms of how well it provided that support.

A key ingredient in the production and transmission of social knowledge is autonomy; autonomy of the academic worker and autonomy of the academic institution. Autonomy can be defined in terms of control over academic work.

> Thinking about the autonomy of the university tends to proceed on two assumptions that are rarely questioned. First, the autonomy of institutions devoted to

> research and teaching is highly desirable and should be defended if threatened. Second: autonomous universities constitute an essential element of democracy, that is, university autonomy does not merely fit reasonably well into the constitutional framework of democracy, but rather university autonomy is an integral feature of democracy because it is a way of institutionalizing freedom of research and teaching. Both these assumptions must be scrutinized in the light of recent experience and present trends in western society (Kielmansegg 1983, p. 46).

Thus, the achievement of autonomy is tied to both internal and external forces, the influence of the political economy and the internal structures and dynamics of governance within the university. These forces and influences have varied over time. In fact the above quoted passage ends with a suggestion that autonomy be scrutinized and evaluated in relation to present trends. These trends are producing a shift of university towards a market orientation, a shift with many implications for academic autonomy[1] within this context of globalizing tendencies along with the centrality of information systems.

One thread which has been woven into the historical fabric of the university and which has been linked to the academic enterprise has been that of collegial decision making. The autonomy involved in the production and transmission of social knowledge is linked to the ability of the collegium to make decisions. The structure and authority of the collegium to make decisions has varied over time and has been dependent on the form of university governance. Collegiality is the interactive expression, the linkage of autonomous units. Collegiality is the way in which autonomy is organized. It represents a sharing in the governance of the academic institution. Peer review and organizational expressions such as the academic senate and the faculty associations within an academic institution are examples of collegial process and organization. When either autonomy or collegiality is threatened responses are forthcoming. Unionization is one such response, a response which introduces a more adversarial dynamic in attempting to secure a more autonomous base for collegial decision making. The changes in university management have influenced the relationships between autonomy and its collegial expression. Autonomy and collegiality define the structure and politics of participation in the academic enterprise. Together they provide a way of conceptualizing democratic process in institutions of higher education.

In Canada the post World War II years represent the period of development which lays the foundations for the contemporary university of the 1960s and beyond. As an example, in Ontario, the pre-World War II university system was composed of 5 universities. Toronto, Ottawa and Queens had roots deep in the 19th century, while McMaster and Western were products of the 20th century. In the post World War II period the Ontario system increased from 5 to 15 universities. (Bissell 1972). This expansion was tied to growth in the economy, infrastructure development, new immigration, the post-war "baby boom" as well as the influence of the Cold War and Sputnik. This set the basis for change in a university system which was narrowly focused, elitist and class bound:

> For a period of at least forty years before 1960, the undergraduate curricular requirements of nondenominational Canadian universities were, with some exceptions, uniform and unchanging. Higher education was distinctly and unapologetically elitist, serving no more than 6% of university aged youth . . . The academic atmosphere was intense, paternalistic and hierarchical . . . (Axelrod 1982, p. 101).

The struggles of the 1960s over forms of participation in university management were in response to this paternalistic, patriarchal and hierarchical past. In the 1980s and 90s, the move is again back to greater hierarchy and less participation.

2. The Market and the University

We are still near the beginning of the 1990s decade. However, it is possible to see the consolidation of processes developed during the 1980s. More and more university policy (and broader national social policy) is budget driven. The symbol of the times is "attend to the deficit." The slogan and mission for public sector activity seems to be to do more with less. Canadian universities during the last 15 years have suffered through a long period of underfunding accompanied by significant increases in enrollment. From the early 1980s there has been a concerted effort to link universities with private sector enterprises. (Newson and Buchbinder 1988). The roots of these linkages are the combination of underfunding in a climate of globalization where efficiency and competitiveness are the slogans underlying the practice.

The development of these linkages has occurred within the ethos of the marketplace; the goals of research and the development of knowledge are more and more linked to the production of marketable products rather than social knowledge.

> The recently announced $85 million corporate sponsored research agreement between Shiseido Company and Massachusetts General Hospital, a Harvard teaching hospital reminds us that universities and their affiliates are among the hottest commodities in the international market-place . . . The corporation will be entitled to exclusive marketing rights over patents resulting from work done at the M.G.H. laboratory, which is largely funded by taxpayers (Bourke 1989, p. 495).

There are more and more examples of this market orientation in North American universities. In this type of university it is the market which will determine the direction of research, not the academic enterprise.

> To compete successfully with industrial as well as academic institutions, a university must recruit and equip the most commercially promising researchers—most of whom will do very little undergraduate teaching—and it must provide them with the most advanced equipment and laboratories (Minsky and Noble 1989, p. 477).

The emergence of the market-driven university in Canada is accompanied by a centralization of management, which reduces the possibilities for collegial democracy. This drive towards the market is seen by Neave to be "the principal element underlying European Higher Education policy." He formulates three phrases which characterize the development of this process. There is a reduction of spending. The resulting demand for greater "efficiency" and the withdrawal of the state leaves the action to civil society and the market[2]. Neave argues that the consequences of the process have led to strategic planning, centralization of management and what he refers to as "heterogeneity" in autonomy and standards (Neave 1990). Both unions and senates are more and more by-passed, not by conspiracy but rather by the effects of these institutional changes. Policy appears to derive almost solely from budget conditions[3] and the university as an institution must rationalize itself in accord with those constraints. The objectives of higher education which are expressed as the production and transmission of knowledge as a social good are replaced by an emphasis on the production of knowledge as a market good, a saleable commodity. Simultaneously, the development of a market-oriented university supersedes academic decision making. This can result in an "efficient," well managed institution in which academics are marginalized, academic institutions are by-passed and social knowledge is diminished as market knowledge achieves greater prominence. The academic peer system which has served to critique academic work is displaced by corporate proprietary rights under which secrecy is maintained and the collegium is thereby by-passed by managerial prerogatives. More and more, the market oriented university characterizes the Canadian university in the 1990s. The same would seem to hold for Europe as well. Neave's analysis, from a European perspective, poses a tension between civil society and the market on the one hand which acts to counterbalance the state and academic oligarchy on the other (Neave 1990, p. 112). This occurs in a context of growing financial exigency, shifts in policy orientation, and the influence of the projected European Community. Both the European and North American experiences would seem to have some similar characteristics.

The development of a higher education sector which is increasingly oriented towards the production of knowledge in the service of the private sector leads to the commodification of said knowledge, the development of knowledge (research) as a marketable product. In Canada universities are public institutions and it is within the framework of a public institution that these processes are occurring. This is not to say that the viability of public sector institutions are not under threat.

Clearly, the role of the state and the public sector is not disappearing even as the call for markets increases. "The search for a new institutional order between the state and the market is now at the centre of the policy agenda of governments." (Drache and Gertler 1991, p. xiv). The market is touted as producing efficiency and democracy. The university is inserted into this debate with the creation of the "service university" agenda and the development of corporate-university linkages which move in the direction of what is referred to here as the market oriented university (Buchbinder and Newson 1991). Yet there is a mythology about the so-called free market which was clearly identified by Karl Polanyi many years ago:

> The road to the free market was opened and kept open by an enormous increase in continuous, centrally organized and controlled interventionism . . . Lassez faire was planned; planning was not (Polanyi 1957, p. 140, quoted by Drache and Gertler).

Nevertheless,

> today, the market is once again the primary institution shaping history from East to West, and it is assumed that market freedom can be reconciled with individual choice and political pluralism (Drache and Gertier 1991, p. xv).

The growth of these corporate-university linkages has had many effects on university governance which are now becoming quite evident. The development of entrepreneurial professors with equity in private companies and large outside funding tends to relocate power away from the departmental level to the centre and to the entrepreneurial professor who often has control over large sums of money. These developments can make the faculty union/association into a more peripheral body. Unions have been primarily concerned with terms and conditions of employment. Now we have a situation where activities related to corporate-university linkages are not terms and conditions of employment and so by-pass union authority. It is also the case that in many instances the senate is by-passed as well. So collegial democracy, such as it was, disappears to an even greater extent.

Research funding is altered as well and some of its alterations would seem to affect democratic process and equal access. We refer to the changes in funding rules which now designate "track record" as the most important criterion for all but young, beginning academics. The intrinsic value of a research proposal is now overshadowed by prior success in securing research funding. In addition it appears that funding councils such as NSERC will begin to determine what areas will receive higher funding priority so that academics will be channeled into those areas if they wish to receive funding.

3. Ideology

The shift to a neo-conservative ideology from one of welfare liberalism informed by Keynsian theories has encouraged policies which aim towards dismantling the public sector and deifying the "free market." This view is most clearly reflected in Sir Douglas Hague's monograph on higher education (Hague 1991). This is one of the *Hobart Papers*, published by the Institute of Economic Affairs in England. The central theme of these papers is identified as "the optimum use of scarce resources in a market economy, within an appropriate legal framework" (Hague 1991, p. 5). In the Foreword to this little book Walter Allen writes:

> The major period of growth of the "Red Brick" universities occurred during the early 1960s, when economic wisdom consisted of interventionism, paternalism, corporatism and Keynesianism. It was against this background that the Robbin's Report advocated the expansion of higher education in Britain (Hague 1991, p. 5).

This sort of "economic wisdom" is written off as is the resultant policy of accessibility heralded by the Robbin's Report. It is argued that the four "isms" of welfare liberalism need to be replaced by universities that can "organize and operate in ways more like those of the knowledge businesses themselves . . . (Hague 1991, p. 9). This will not be simple writes Hague since

> most British universities are in the public sector and most knowledge business is in the private sector (and) this will be a battle in which the private sector will threaten some of the public sector's most entrenched monopolies.
>
> To avoid being driven out of activities which they have imagined their own by right, the universities will have to make

> substantial changes in what they do and how they do it. Where they find that difficult, one solution will be to form alliances with the interlopers. Increasingly, the choice will be alliance or annihilation (Hague 1991, p. 13).

The university is thereby "put on notice" that it will need to make an alliance with business or be annihilated. In fact, in order to become efficient, universities will have to be like businesses; the public form will disappear. Thus if the university does collaborate with this agenda, if it does make the alliance it will, in its present form and function be annihilated—indeed a "Catch 22." This challenge is paralleled by the creation of the "service university" in Canada; a university to serve the corporate sector (Buchbinder and Newson 1991a).

The ideological emphases in these developments appear to either grasp firmly the neo-conservative agenda or nostalgically dream of a return to welfare liberalism.

> Unfortunately the left has either remained mired in its Keynsian position of the 1960s . . . or else (as in the case of some social democrats) has seemingly accepted the neo-conservative rationale of globalization without being very clear about how this is to be reconciled with socialism's commitment to social equity. There is an intellectual vacuum to be filled . . . (Cox 1991, p. 336).

4. Globalization and Privatization

It is important to consider these new politics of higher education within the broader political economic context of the times and the prevailing ideological base which determines policy. One outcome follows which has been referred to as a "two sector model," the private sector and the public sector. Cameron describes the private sector as operating on the basis of the profit principle with an economic goal of efficiency. The method of achieving this goal is via the price system. Much "that is external to the market (for example, government, environment, labour and social relations) is taken to be non-economic by definition and is therefore not valued in market terms." (Cameron 1991, p. 435) The second sector in this model is the public sector which operates on a principle of service. The public sector serves as the scapegoat when there is economic crisis. It is the public debt rather than the private debt which concerns the public. The university can be seen as an institution which emerges from the public sector. It is more and more pressured to operate according to the terms of the private sector. In fact the two sector model is "incomplete, inaccurate and misleading." The public sector is involved in supporting the private sector process of accumulation. Nevertheless, the popular mythology is otherwise.

> . . . Such policies as privatization and deregulation are based both on the supposed superiority of the private sector and the presumed burden of the public sector on society (Cameron 1991, p. 436).

Along with the notion of market comes the notion of private. When we think of a market in the terms presented here it describes transactions which occur in the private sphere. The effects and process of making things private is best described by use of a very cumbersome term, privatization. The results of privatization can take any one of three forms. The first form is one in which government sells off its assets to the private sector. This has been happening in the eastern European "bloc" with the abandonment of state or public ownership. In Canada, the federal government has been selling off crown corporations to the private sector. A second form of privatization is one which the government allows private companies to buy or build public structures, like roads, and then operate them by government's rules. In Toronto a new terminal at Pearson International Airport (a federal government facility) has been built and is managed by a private development company. In the third form of privatization the government hires private companies to provide public services or just generally do its bidding. In Scottsdale, Arizona, there is a private fire department. In Denver, Colorado, private bus companies provide public transit (Landsberg 1991).

The trend to privatization began with the election of the Thatcher government in 1979. The policy of that government was "to reduce the extent of state ownership and increase competition by providing offers of sale" (Laux 1991, p. 290). This state ownership was seen as the vehicle for the intrusion of the state into the working of civil society. Privatization was the antidote. The market place was seen as a source of vitality and discipline while government ownership was seen as "suffocating." (Laux 1991, p. 291).

An example closer to home is that of a Canadian firm, Rockcliffe Research and Technology Inc. The president of this private corporation is Dr. Stuart Smith, former president of the Science Council of Canada, former leader of the Liberal party in the Canadian province of Ontario, and more recently the appointed commissioner in a one person commission to study the state of universities in Canada. This private firm of Dr. Smith's tries to "marry science, politics and business and turn a profit for himself and a small group of investors who are backing him" (McCarthy 1991). This is an attempt to commercialize government research. Individual researchers will be encouraged to start up their own companies to market their innovations. Patents will be held by the government, with the researcher as licensee and the centre as minority shareholder. Rockcliffe will provide management, venture capital and marketing (McCarthy 1991). So, much of what might be publicly funded university research slips into the hands (if successful) of such private sector corporations. Universities are therefore challenged to compete on the market for their share of research dollars. At the same time the search for more dollars continues in other areas.

Shortfalls in capital requirements can be ameliorated by using university land as a marketable product. My university sold 22 acres to a developer in order to secure funds for new construction. Once realized, some institutional services were privatized. The university terminated the existence of a university health service in favour of a private clinic now located at the university in a "mall" which was built on the campus. It is not that new services are unnecessary; it is rather that they are privatized in use if not in form.

The development of market relationships between universities and private business corporations is characterized by the presence of academic secrecy and proprietary rights. The production of research for private corporations abandons social knowledge for market knowledge. Responsibility to one's peers, which has been at the heart of producing social knowledge is abandoned for responsibility to the organization/corporation funding the project. Research contracts, offices for technology transfer, control of spin-off corporations, centres of excellence and other marketing tools and relationships are handled by the central administration of the university, not by the department, the faculty association, or even the academic senate. The reliance on strategic planning (Keller 1984) and centralization, often in the office of the president, are two of the consequences cited by Neave (1990).

5. Pluralism

Another effect of this market orientation with its various consequences is the erosion of the pluralist dynamic. The various contending and/or co-operating forces and bodies within the university are diminished in their force and activity; bodies such as departments, faculty associations, student organizations and academic senates. The pluralist model begins to dissolve as the contending bodies get integrated within the market structure and lose the capability to contend. Although the university continues to operate within a corporate form a new model emerges[4]. This is the structure we see emerging in the 1990s.

Thus, in summary, over the past four decades the university has operated within a corporate form of organization. There has been a pluralist dynamic operating within this form which is now disintegrating as the market university emerges. Contention between administration, faculty and students is replaced by a managerial hegemony in which the student and faculty groupings are marginalized and market strategies predominate[5]. The presence of a democratic collegium is much less possible in this emerging organizational form. This process involves privatization of institutional structures and functions. It reflects the process of privatization occurring throughout the public sector. It is in this context that we must evaluate the presence or absence of collegial democracy and academic autonomy. Contraction and budget driven policy will lead to a repeat of the cost-cutting, rationalizing initiatives characteristic of the late 1970s. Except this time there will be some significant differences. Now management will have much more power to effect these changes by fiat. There will be less possibility for faculty via its unions, associations and senates to fight back. In addition, the emergence of the market university will change the ground rules. Cost will be the criterion. The market university will be characterized by less democracy, less collegiality, more privatization, more centralization. However, this scenario does not begin and end with the university.

On a broader scale there is a growing articulation between democracy and the market. Events in the USSR and eastern Europe have shattered the hold of "democratic centralist" regimes. This process has been encouraged by the bankruptcy of command economies. The alternative, being offered by the capitalist world and sought after by the emerging post-communist regimes is the market. It is seen as the way to achieve democracy and meet consumer demands. With the demise of communism the range of political options narrows. We seem to have a "choice" between capitalism and social democracy, both of which operate within a market framework. Socialism appears to have disappeared as a strategy for change or a vision of the future. The political left does not appear to have formulated a response in the face of these momentous events. The ascendancy of the market as a possible panacea is reflected in many of our institutions, among them the university. The results of this direction towards the market may not prove to be a panacea either in society at large or within the universities. In fact, they may herald less democracy for the collegium.

Part II: The Social Context of Knowledge

The first part of the paper develops the parameters of change in the university as it moves to a market orientation. This orientation focuses on efficiency, cost-cutting, centralization with a much stronger managerial focus. This impacts on the centrality of academic autonomy and collegial participation in governance. The move to the "free market" produces a more rigid, top heavy institution in which control has been taken away from academic workers. Thus, free is not free, nor is it democratic. Perhaps the most critical development in this process is what happens to the production and transmission of knowledge in the market oriented university. It is an issue since it is the major raison d'être of the university.

The social context of knowledge refers to the political economy and the institutional response from which the form and process of producing and transmitting knowledge emerges. There are two forms of knowledge that emerge, social and market. The shift is from social knowledge to market knowledge.

> Knowledge that was free, open and for the benefit of society is now proprietary, confidential and for the benefit of private companies (Harris 1991).

Science, Research and Knowledge

The Royal Society of Canada produced a 1989 study on university research in Canada which is useful in terms of identifying the extent of research (i.e., the production of knowledge) in Canada. The Royal Society defines research as "the systematic testing of ideas against the available evidence and experience, with the objective of gaining new insights" (Royal Society 1989, p. 3). The terrain on which this takes place is a Canadian university system of 35,000 university faculty members with average salaries of $58,000 per year and with a "total annual expenditure approaching $1 billion in sponsored research funding." (ibid). Roughly half of this funding is from the national granting councils. The other half comes from provincial governments, private foundations, federal government departments and agencies and industry. Of the 82 universities in Canada, 62 receive less than 20% of the total sponsored research funding, while 20 universities receive over 80% of the total research funding (ibid, p. 8). While this provides us with a quantitative measure of the amount of research which is funded it doesn't deal with either its quality or for whom it is done.

The definition of research articulated by the Royal Society refers to an objective of gaining new insights. Sklar, in considering the purposes of science identifies three objectives. The first relates to the seeking of knowledge for its own sake. In this instance the researcher "gives no thought to the consequences of his (sic) work outside the solution to particular sets of cognitive problems." The second purpose is more altruistic or socially motivated. In this instance research is accomplished for others' benefit, for humanity or for the sake of the scientific community. The third purpose identified by Sklar is expressed as follows: "Knowledge may be sought for financial gain, as a job, in the form of wages or profits or both." (Sklar 1973, p. 103).

It is this third purpose which has come to characterize the production of knowledge in the past decade. It is the shift in emphasis from the production of social knowledge, (knowledge to work out questions or cognitive problems; knowledge to resolve specific social problems or needs) to market oriented knowledge, (knowledge for profit, knowledge for sale). This scares many scientists. However, the shift towards the production of knowledge for the market is not characterized only by short term, applied considerations. It also generates secrecy in order to protect against competition and to insure proprietary rights. This process has been fairly well developed in other work (Buchbinder and Newson 1991, 1991a; Newson and Buchbinder 1988). This process

> threatens to transform the university from an open, inquiring and relatively free institution committed to the widespread dissemination of knowledge to a closed, secretive institution preoccupied with the commercial and security concerns of its private and public sector partners (Langford 1991, p. 156)[6]

Yet, it is argued that this traditional, social form of the university is a cumbersome institution slow to respond to the new knowledge industries that are "characterized by new cultures, often young, dynamic, flexible and highly innovative" (Jacques 1991).

Knowledge is the central function of the university; knowledge transmitted to students, to the intellectual community and to the community at large; knowledge as a social good. The structure of the academic workplace would need to support the centrality of academic workers, knowledge workers, knowledge producers, knowledge transmitters. The academic workplace, the university for our purposes, gains its force from the outcome of the intellectual endeavour. As we have seen, this force is directed in accordance with the way in which knowledge is characterized which itself is determined by the form and commitment of the university itself.

Knowledge as Property

Information becomes a form of property and the "ownership of economically exploitable information slips from the hands of individual faculty members and researchers into those of the university and its corporate and governmental partners" (Jacques 1991, p. 166). The comparison of a model based on social knowledge to one based on market knowledge allows us to identify the formulation of knowledge with an organization form. Langford uses the concept of the "traditional model" and the "partnership model" as a way of identifying the organizational aspects of each. The traditional model includes the pursuit of knowledge for its own sake with free transmission of information and ideas. The market (partnership) model involves partnerships with industry and/or government with the focus on short-term applied research geared towards the development of marketable products in an atmosphere of secrecy in which the free transmission of information and ideas is blocked by proprietary rights and industrial security. These two forms do not exist in a benign atmosphere. They contradict each other. In its older form the university was a repository of social knowledge that was developed and preserved in the public interest. The newer institutional form focused on attracting and securing markets, cultivating entrepreneurial professors, attracting corporate clients and securing intellectual property rights. It is this concept of intellectual property rights which is most important of consideration.

In the market oriented university knowledge becomes a form of property, intellectual property. It is traded in the market like any other form of property. As property, it is owned by its owner. It is private. Ownership may be transferred but is usually subject to some form of exchange. Where the production of knowledge is social it is available to all. It is transmitted via academic journals or within the pedagogical process. Certainly the producer of the knowledge receives credit for the findings but it is not a marketable product. As I have indicated earlier in this paper, it is social, not private property. This means there is a qualitative difference between the two forms of knowledge. Social knowledge is an ongoing social process and is socially "owned" whereas commodified knowledge is reified as a "thing," privately owned, often secret and evaluated in terms of saleability.[7]

This is most interesting within the context of the present major focus in Canada on reforming the constitution. The government of Canada is engaged in attempting to foster a national dialogue. One of the proposals being put forth by the government is the guarantee of property rights.

> The Government of Canada reaffirms unequivocally its support for rights guaranteed in the Charter[8]. However, the Charter does not guarantee a right to property. It is, therefore, the view of the Government of Canada that the Canadian Charter of Rights and Freedoms should be amended to guarantee property rights (Shaping Canada's Future 1991, p. 3).

Such a proposal, it can be argued, provides market ideology with constitutional status (CCPA 1991)[9].

> The right to property . . . means that the law will establish and protect a right to ownership of "things." A "thing" can be almost anything—personal items, real estate, money, information, stocks and bonds, to name a few. The important point is that if you have a property right in a thing, you may use that thing pretty well as you wish and be protected by the law in doing so (CCPA 1991, p 6).

Note that among the "things" mentioned in the above critique of the proposal is "information." What I have referred to as intellectual property, would be a part of the entrenchment of property rights in the Canadian Constitution. Those who are concerned about and critical of this proposal see it as an obstacle to the free transmission of knowledge. It would entrench the hold on knowledge in a legal sense. The market university would have a legal base for marketing and owning knowledge produced within the institution.

Transfer of Knowledge

Along with the production of knowledge is the form and politics of its transmission. Open publication of research findings, communication with peers, work with graduate students and teaching are all ways of transferring knowledge in a social manner. It is given, it is announced, it is criticized by peers in the context of an open social endeavour. Once knowledge is treated as a commodity, market knowledge, its transfer follows market procedures. It is priced, there are terms of sale and often these terms violate the social character of such a transfer. Secrecy, proprietary rights, ownership now become characteristic of market knowledge transfer. Yet the mythology of market activities is articulated in terms of freedom, the free market. Karl Polanyi, in his seminal work (see above), indicated that the "free" market required centralized organization and control to function.

It is an irony that as the traditional model of social knowledge is submerged beneath the expanding market model and intellectual property is privatized, the resultant academic atmosphere will suffer from the same problems as the former Soviet influenced model of centralized, controlled use of knowledge in the service of the state and its productive apparatus; only now it is market forms that will dictate this. It is impossible to set out a demarcation line between academic and political questions. Hayhoe, commenting on Chinese sources, concludes that "academic debates of the type which could advance knowledge are only possible through authentic political democratization." (Hayhoe 1988, p. 129). Although this has to do specifically with transfer of knowledge between nation states, is there not a similarity regarding the transfer of knowledge between a university and its constituent society? Market knowledge, intellectual property, the market model, lead away from "radical intellectual freedom and open-ended research." (Hayhoe 1988, p. 129).

Knowledge also represents power. The transfer of knowledge between countries is not generally symmetrical but rather represents patterns of domination and control. Yet one would hope and expect that there would be a mutuality in the transfer of knowledge among countries. The ideal type model might be characterized as follows:

> Equity suggests project aims and forms of organization that are reached through full mutual agreement. Autonomy suggests a respect for the theoretical perspectives rooted in peripheral culture that would require centre participants to gain a thor-

> ough knowledge of this culture. Solidarity suggests forms of organization that encourage maximum interaction among peripheral participants and growing links between them and their fellow researchers. Participation intimates an approach to knowledge that does not stratify in a hierarchical way but assumes the possibility of a creative peripheral contribution from the very beginning. (Hayhoe 1989, p. 134)[10].

Yet, claims Hayhoe: "There can be little doubt that contemporary co-operative educational projects are expressions of political or economic penetration on the part of OECD countries." (Hayhoe 1989, p. 139). The transfer of knowledge then, in international circles relates to the development of international markets with the forms of knowledge transfer reflecting these forms of domination.

Summary and Conclusions

The production of knowledge has been undergoing a process of change characterized by what might be called privatization of the social context in which market mechanisms begin to predominate. Knowledge produced within such a context becomes a commodity. It can be bought and sold. It is intellectual property, private intellectual property.

Not only is knowledge produced, it is also transferred. It may be transferred via a collegial process, as a social product or as a saleable, marketable product; or, as an artefact of power. The transfer of knowledge may occur between universities in one or more than one country, between universities and industry. In all instances the transfer occurs within the relationships determined by the social context. It affects the formulation of knowledge, the transfer of knowledge and the character of knowledge.

In examining changes in the university, in trying to understand its meanings and influences, the role of knowledge is key. The social context within which knowledge is produced and the form and relationships are essential indicators to understanding. In this case the shift to a market oriented university alters the form of knowledge. The struggle towards a market university mirrors the struggle on the world political scene. Democracy is identified with the market yet, at the same time, the balance between efficiency and equity is affected by market forces which emphasize efficiency. The alternatives of centralist authoritarianism, command economies, democratic centralism and five year plans have been seen and shown to be bankrupt. Since the proposed alternative, the market is seen as perpetuating inequity where does the choice lie? Public ownership appears "out of synch" with present political agendas. If we oppose the market oriented university what options confront us? The social university we talk about is itself a class bound liberal university which in periods of growth and expansion allowed for a broadening of constituencies. What then can be our strategic position? Clearly the political horizons have narrowed. Can we appropriate market structures in the service of equitable social ends? Can we appropriate public planning structures to provide a situation which is both equitable and efficient? Thus far there does not seem to be a clear answer.

However, it is clear that a market base to the production and transmission of knowledge requires a centralized, authoritarian infrastructure to support the more "flexible" academic entrepreneurialism which develops. The convergence of the struggle within the university and the struggle outside the university suggests that there is no strategy unique only to the university. In this case the ideological and the political economic roots are the same for both.

The present form of university governance mitigates against active participation, reduces academic autonomy and participation in governance. The role of collective bargaining, which in the past has served as a locus for action appears less certain as events by-pass union activity. The social context of the market university encourages entrepreneurialism and a more individualistic, private ethos. The dismantling of the public sector, reductions in social programmes and privatization of public programmes and public corporations all serve to reinforce developments within the university.

Yet, to make this criticism is to be confronted with the question of alternatives. There is an old adage of community organizers which states that to do nothing is to support existing arrangements. It is clear that the preference expressed here is for the production and transmission of social knowledge within an institutional context that supports said knowledge. But here one must express a warning. What appears to be the preferred model also falls short. The context of social knowledge is defined by the ruling ideas. It remains ideologically defined. To add further to this difficulty there does not appear to be an alternative to the market which has widespread currency. Producing a utopian vision may not help, producing a change strategy may. Perhaps the best we can do is define the struggle.

> The search for a new institutional order between the state and the market is now at the centre of the policy agenda of governments . . . Liberal society has no way to redress the fundamental inequality in the transfer of power and wealth that results when private property is made sovereign. Thus at the centre of even a reborn, postmodern liberal society there remains a chronic, deeply rooted instability. Market rights work to suppress the democratic and libertarian possibilities inherent in liberalism (Drache and Gertler 1991, p. xv–xvi).

It is in this context that a new public policy for universities must be charted; a policy which addresses the impact of globalization in an information society and recognizes the shortcomings of a market oriented panacea.

Notes

1. Proprietary rights, managerial control, market determinations all affect academic autonomy.
2. The Canadian state has played a more indirect role in what is a public education system, in its use of buffer bodies and the particular nature of federal-provincial relations.
3. For example, the undermining of universal social programmes is presented as a necessary response to financial (budget) difficulties rather than a shift in the ideology which underlies the formulation of such policies.
4. The corporate form refers to a board-senate structure which operates as a corporation, in this case a corporation created via a legislative authority.
5. It would appear from this that academics are silent, non-complaining and even compliant in the face of these developments which appear to marginalize them. There are indeed strong intra-mural struggles that take place within university faculties (see Newson and Buchbinder 1988). However, this means that faculties are divided. This was true over unionization and it is apparently true over the market university. The difficulties in getting any sort of dialogue among academics on these issues is one indication of apathy but also may be seen as an indicator of marginality.
6. This is not to imply that before the contraction of the 1980s the university was only involved with social knowledge. In fact, corporate interests, military interests (especially in the US), skewed the academic endeavour. The difference was that the terrain was broader, the funding more expansive—but the university was primarily a class institution and social knowledge needs to be seen within a class framework. Social knowledge was primarily ruling class knowledge.
7. I am indebted to Professor Norman Feltes for his clarity of thought and his help in thinking about social and market knowledge.
8. This refers to the Charter of Rights and Freedoms.
9. This paper was completed prior to the Charlottetown Accords and the referendum debate. It does not draw on the language of the constitutional proposals. In fact at this writing the definitive language is not yet available.
10. The use of the terms centre and periphery already suggests an unequal relationship.

References

Altbach, P. G. (1987). *The Knowledge Context, Comparative Perspectives on the Distribution of Knowledge.* Albany, NY: State University of New York Press.

Axelrod, P. (1982). *Scholar and Dollars*, University of Toronto Press, Toronto.

Bourke, J. (1989). 'Mergermania', *The Nation*, October 30, 495.

Buchbinder, H., and Newson, J. (1991). 'Social knowledge and market knowledge: universities in the information age', *Gannett Center Journal*, Spring–Summer 5(2–3), 17–29.

Buchbinder, H. and Newson, J. (1991a). 'The policy brokers: advancing toward the "Service University"', paper presented to a joint session of the Canadian Sociology Anthropology Association and the Canadian Society for the Study of Higher Education, Kingston, Ontario, June 1991.

Bueckert, D. (1991). 'Scientific freedom threatened, laureate warns', *The Globe and Mail,* December 27, 1991.

Cameron, D. (1991). 'Beyond the market and the state: how can we do better?', Drache and Gertler, *op. cit.*, pp. 435–447.

(CCPA) Canadian Centre for Policy Alternatives, 'Briefing notes on the Tory constitutional proposals', Ottawa, September 30, 1991.

Cox, R. W. (1991). 'The global political economy and social choice', Drache and Gertler, *op. cit.*

Drache, D. and Gertler, M. (1991). *The New Era of Global Competition: State Policy and Market Power.* London: McGill-Queens University Press.

Hague, Sir D. (1991). *Beyond Universities.* Institute of Economic Affairs: London.

Hayhoe, R. (1988). 'China's intellectuals in the world community', *Higher Education,* 17, 121–138.

Hayhoe, R. (1989). *China's Universities and the Open Door.* Toronto: OISE Press.

Hoffman, S. (1984). 'Universities and human rights', *Human Rights Quarterly,* 6(1), 5–20.

Jacques, M. (1991). 'For red brick or Oxbridge, the way is high-tech', *London Times,* May 1, 1991.

Keller, G. (1983). *Academic Strategy: The Management Revolution in Higher Education.* Baltimore: Johns Hopkins Press.

Kielmansegg, P. G. (1983). 'The university and democracy', Chapman (ed.) *The Western University on Trial,* University of California Press.

Landsberg, M. (1991). 'Public? Private? The line blurs', *The Stuart News* (Florida), July 1, 1991.

Langford, J. W. (1991). 'Secrecy, partnership and the ownership of knowledge in the university', *Intellectual Property Journal,* June, 155–169.

Laux, J. K. (1991). 'Shaping or serving markets? Public ownership after privatization', Drache and Gertler, *op. cit.,* pp. 288–315.

McCarthy, S. (1991). 'Partners for profit', *Toronto Star,* August 18, 1991.

Menzies, H. (1990). *Fast Forward and Out of Control.* James Lorimor, Toronto.

Minsky, L., and Noble, D., 'Privatizing academe, corporate takeover on campus', *The Nation,* October 30, 9.477.

Myles, J. (1991). 'Post industrialism and the service economy', Drache and Gertler, *op. cit.* pp. 350–366.

Neave, G. (1990). 'On preparing for markets: trends in higher education in Western Europe, 1988–1990', *European Journal of Education,* 25(2), 195–222.

Royal Society of Canada (1989). 'A study of university research in Canada: the issues', August.

Schank. R. C. (1984). *The Cognitive Computer. On Language, Learning and Artificial Intelligence.* Don Mills, Ontario: Addison-Wesley Publishing Co.

Shaping Canada's Future Together (1991). Proposal, Minister of Supply and Services, Canada.

Sklar, L. (1973). *Organized Knowledge: A Sociological View of Science and Technology.* Great Britain: Paladin.

(THES) (1991). 'Beyond universities?', *The Times Higher Education Supplement,* May 3, 1991.

Weiler, H. N. (1991). 'The international politics of knowledge production and the future of higher education', paper prepared for an international meeting on 'the new roles of higher education at a world level'. UNESCO-CRESALC, Caracas, Venezuela, May 2, 1991.

Work

BURTON R. CLARK

In the beginning there is work, for if we reduce a knowledge-bearing system to its primordial elements we find first a division of labor, a structure of organized effort within which many people individually and collectively take different actions. The division of labor is a definition and delegation of tasks. It puts people in special roles and assigns particular duties to them. It thereby generates many different commitments, turning the whole into a plurality of well-rooted interests.

How then is the work divided? We first turn to the primary modes.

The Discipline and the Enterprise

Academic activities are divided and grouped in two basic ways: by discipline and by enterprise. The enterprise, or individual institution, is commonly a comprehensive grouping, in that it links together such disparate specialists as chemists, psychologists, and historians, specialists and nonspecialists, professors and students and administrators. Its wide coverage typically expands as it grows older. Occasionally, its scope is limited to a small set of fields, as in technological universities. Another variant, seen in Italy, are such abbreviated odd-lot groupings as law and teaching, or science and pharmacy, that happen to accumulate in a particular locale or are allocated to a city or region as part of the division of a formal national system. Notably, nearly all enterprises specialize by locality, normally existing in whole or in large part in one geographic place rather than in many, and hence dividing a larger system into geographic blocs. With this comes a set of buildings, contiguous or locally scattered, which make the individual university or college a definite and sizable physical entity, something that can be seen and touched, even if we have to wander around a city (as in Europe and Latin America) to find it all. As a way of organizing knowledge groups, the enterprise catches everyone's eye and is well known. A state, provincial, or national system is commonly "seen" as a set of such institutions. Basic data about the system are gathered primarily on this basis, with national reports and international data books listing the enterprises and summing their students, faculties, and resources. Enterprise is the organizing mode that preempts attention.

The discipline is clearly a specialized form of organization in that it knits together chemists and chemists, psychologists and psychologists, historians and historians. It specializes by subject, that is, by knowledge domain. The profession follows a similar principle, putting together similar specialists. But the discipline (or profession) is also comprehensive in that it does not specialize by locality but rather pulls together a craftlike community of interest that reaches across large territories. Notably, it cuts across enterprises, linking parts of one with similar parts in another. Thus, a national system of higher education is also a set of disciplines and professions, even though we do not normally perceive larger systems in these terms. In addition, the reach of the discipline need not stop at the boundaries of the national system. Academic scientists, in particular, find it natural to practice world community. Their disciplinary perspectives and interests readily extend across nations, much as people in specialized lines of industry, commerce, and banking find more in common with counterpart specialists abroad who "speak the language" than with others outside the specialty at home. Faculty members also specialize within disciplines, teaching specific subjects not shared with many, if any, local colleagues but rather with scholars elsewhere at home and abroad. This point was less true in the past than it is in the present, less true in underdeveloped than in developed countries. But it is the discipline mode of organization that has rendered higher education, over time and space, basically metanational and international, much more than elementary or secondary education. Lacking work commitments that so strongly cut across institutions and systems, the lower levels are more bounded by local and national structures and cultures.

Despite the common tendency to overlook the importance of the discipline, it can readily be seen as the primary mode. A simple test suggests its power: give the academic worker the choice of leaving the discipline or the institution and he or she will typically leave the institution. It is more costly to leave one's field of expertise than to leave one's university or college, since the higher the level of one's advanced education, the greater the import of one's specialty in determining commitment. Not only are most academics trained to the highest levels available but they also serve as the trainers of all others in their respective specialties, including those who will replace them. To be sure, as seen in chapter 3, institutions can sometimes provide an imposing counterweight in the form of attachment to the enterprise as a whole. And differentiated systems of higher education contain segments in which the bonds of specialty are weakened, as when a U.S. community college instructor teaches sociology *and* anthropology *and* psychology. Then, too, in times of personnel stagnation, some enterprises may even attempt to retrain surplus professors and shift them within the organization to another field. But such possibilities are marginal in importance compared to the commitment to specialized fields that academics acquire as they go through advanced training and the stages of a working career.

For example, a "faculty development" movement that received much attention in the U.S. system during the 1970s focused on instructional skills and job shifting across specialties, to the exclusion of content specialization. But research at the end of the decade on the results found that within every segment of the system, faculty overwhelmingly asserted the importance of knowing their discipline. Of all the ways to improve themselves—workshops, courses, consultants, etc.—the clear favorites were sabbatical leaves and study or research grants. Faculty expressed concern about their teaching but saw the problem as one of keeping abreast of one's discipline rather than of pedagogy. Having a field and knowing a discipline remained central.

In short, the discipline rather than the institution tends to become the dominant force in the working lives of academics. To stress the primacy of the discipline is to change our perception of enterprises and systems: we see the university or college as a collection of local chapters of national and international disciplines, chapters that import and implant the orientations to knowledge, the norms, and the customs of the larger fields. The control of work shifts toward the internal controls of the disciplines, whatever their nature. And their nature, according to Norton Long, is clearest in the case of the more scientific fields:

> The organization of a science is interesting for a student of administration because it suggests a basis of cooperation in which the problem and the subject matter, rather than the caprice of individual or collective will, control the behavior of those embarked in the enterprise. Thus physics and chemistry are disciplines, but they are not organized to carry out the will of legitimate superiors. They are going concerns with problems and procedures that have taken form through generations of effort and have emerged into highly conscious goal-oriented activities.

If these "going concerns" crosscut enterprises, then what becomes of the distinction between organization and environment when applied to higher education? The disciplinary mode of organization tears it to shreds, since a large array of occupationally specified slices of the "environment" have basic representation and location within the "organization." Crucial parts of the so-called environment run right through the enterprises. It then helps little to speak of aspects of the environment that have internal location. It is more helpful to recognize the great extent of crosshatching in academic systems. Such systems are first-class examples, written large, of "matrix structures," arrangements that provide two or more crosscutting bases of groupings way organizationally to "have your cake and eat it, too." In international business firms, for example, managers of worldwide product lines have responsibility for operations that crisscross those of managers of geographical regions. Similarly, in the academic world, the disciplines are "product lines," and the enterprises are geographically centered. The representatives of the first crisscross the representatives of the second—professors paid to push physics come face to face with administrators responsible for developing a university or a set of universities. The large and permanent matrix structures of academic systems are not planned for the most part but evolve spontaneously, so compelling "in the nature of things" that there does not seem to be an alternative. In fact, there is none. Higher education must be centered in disciplines, but it must simultaneously be pulled together in enterprises.

The differing foci of interest of disciplines and enterprises are reflected in a split in the scholarly literature. Most of those who write about "higher education" write of enterprises and their students. But other scholars focus on disciplines. Foremost among the latter are historians and sociologists of science, searching for the conditions of scientific creativity within given fields, isolating the reward structures of particular disciplines, and of science as a whole, and devising such concepts as "invisible college" to point to informal and quasiformal linkages of researchers across institutions. Secondary have been those who have studied the academic profession as a whole in various countries, pursuing the roles, orientations, and careers of "the academic man." And then a small effort has been made to study the national academic associations that represent and help organize the basic fields and the profession as a whole. Those who do research on science and scholarship focus on disciplines, which link personnel within the limits of specialties, for the simple reason that they are fundamentally so committed. In contrast, universities and colleges as entities reflect particularly the teaching and service commitments of academic systems. They are preeminently places for linking specialists and students; in countries where general education is practiced, they also introduce different specialists to one another. Disciplines pressure institutions to be scholarly, and sometimes to be interested in research. Institutions pressure disciplines to be student-centered, and sometimes to be cognizant of other fields of study.

The discipline and the enterprise together determine academic organization in a special way. To the extent that systems concentrate on their knowledge tasks, the most important single fact about their operation is that the discipline and the enterprise modes of linkage converge in the basic operating units, the primary working groups of the academic world. The department or the chair or the institute is simultaneously a part of the discipline and a part of the enterprise, melding the two and drawing strength from the combination. The combination makes the operating parts unusually strong and central. Naturally, organizational parts are important everywhere in the sense that the larger entities depend on their functioning. But organizations in different sectors of society vary greatly in how much their constituent parts are central, each in its own way and one from the other. As academic parts import the disciplinary connection, their centrality is enormously enhanced and even made qualitatively different from that found in nearly all other parts of society.

The argument can be summarized in three points:

(1) *The core membership unit in academic systems is discipline-centered.* As observed in Sweden, even after much modern reform,

> the most important membership group consists of teachers and researchers. They are organized in subsystems according to disciplines (departments, etc.), and their main competency as well as their professional identity is chiefly connected with the discipline. The discipline also determines their national and international contacts outside of their own departments.

The disciplines in effect determine much of the division of labor within the enterprises, and give content to the divisions. Each has something approaching a monopoly of specialized knowledge, on the local scene, for a specific operation. And increasingly so, since as disciplines become more thoroughly professionalized, they strengthen their autonomy by emphasizing credentials, qualifications, and jurisdictions in order to delineate boundaries more clearly. In a sense, they become more narcissistic. They are also capable of generating highly intense motivations and competitiveness. Burkart Holzner and John H. Marx were not far off the mark in stating flatly that "few contemporary institutions have insistently and successfully demanded such uncompromising loyalties and continuous efforts from their members as academic disciplines."

(2) *Each disciplinary unit within the enterprise has self-evident and acclaimed primacy in a front-line task.* As two English observers noted: "Underlying the status of the department [in Britain] is its crucial characteristic of being authoritative in its own field of learning." Individual and group authoritativeness holds across the great range of knowledge areas, each of which has a front-line role in teaching, research, and the other activities of managing knowledge. The academic members of a department of physics have such a role, and no other cluster of people in the institution or the system at large can claim to know as much physics, and to know as much about its operation as a field, as the physicists. This is equally true in all the other fields.

(3) *The characteristics of core membership groups affect everything else of importance in the organization.* The special qualities of core groups preeminently render universities and colleges something other than unitary organizations; make collegial control not an accident; and require an unusual vocabulary of crafts and guilds, federations and conglomerations, to tease out the realities of academic organization that remain hidden when approached by the standard terminology of organizational life. The radiated effects will be dealt with throughout the analysis in this and later chapters.

The Fragmented Profession

The centrality of the discipline affects the academic profession as much as the academic organization. The profession has long been a holding company of sorts, a secondary framework composed of persons who are objectively located in diverse fields, and who develop beliefs accordingly. Professors belong to one or more regional, national, and international associations in their own fields. Then, if they have enough money left for a second set of dues, they may join an encompassing association, such as the American Association of University Professors (AAUP), or a professional union, for collective representation, particularly on economic issues. The emergence of new specialties is generally marked by the formation of associations. In the United States, approximately 300 "discipline-oriented" associations existed in the late 1960s, organized around not only such major disciplines as physics, economics, and English but also the specialties indicated by such special titles as American Association of Teacher Education in Agriculture, American Folklore Society, Psychometric Society, and Society for Italian Historical Studies. These associations constituted a class of organizations entirely separate from such institutional ones as the Association of American Universities, the Association of American Colleges, and the American Council on Education.

The large number of disciplinary associations found in the United States is hardly typical of the world, since the United States has a strong tradition of voluntary association and the American higher education system is now the most advanced in academic specialization. But to a lesser degree, academics elsewhere similarly come together within specialties by forging associational bonds. No developed or semideveloped country is without organized academic disciplines, reflected nationally in such a common form as the learned society.

The situation of "the academic profession" is thus fundamentally different from that of every other profession. Medicine, law, engineering, and architecture, for example, are relatively singular. Despite their internal specialties, which continue to proliferate, they can be loosely, or even tightly, unified by a body of values, norms, and attitudes developed over time within the profession itself and considered an intrinsic part of it. Then an organization loaded with members of a profession, as a hospital is by doctors, can be integrated in part by professional norms as well as by bureaucratic rules. Larger sets of organizations, such as those of a "health system" of a state, region, or nation may be similarly integrated. There is a dominant occupational type.

In academic institutions and systems, however, this pattern does not hold. Here, under the general label of "professor," there are medical doctors on the medical faculty, lawyers on the law faculty, architects on the architecture faculty, and other quite distinct clusters within professional units that may number up to fifteen or twenty. Then, of course, the number of specialized clusters is much larger when we turn to the physical sciences, social sciences, and humanities. And, in turn, the major disciplines are extensively subdivided. For example, physics is broken down into such major subdisciplines as optics, mechanics, fluids, nuclear physics, and elementary particle physics—the latter dividing still further into cosmic ray physicists, who study natural particles, and high-energy physicists, who use accelerators. These major subfields, in turn, contain more specialties. Within high-energy physics alone, as Jerry Gaston has observed in Great Britain, there is a highly specialized division of labor, a community of researchers located in about twenty universities and several independent laboratories, which "is divided into theoretical and experimental roles that are further divided into types of experimentalists and theorists." The division of labor accounts for large differences in originality and type and degree of competition, more than does social and educational background and institutional characteristics.

Hence, the distinct quality of academic institutions and systems is a high degree of fragmented professionalism. In the past it was possible for a faculty of law or philosophy to dominate a university. Such subject-centered imperialism may still obtain occasionally in the higher education system of a less-developed society. But in modern systems, no single discipline on a campus or in a system at large is in a position to dominate the others. Rather than a closely knit group of professionals who see the world from one perspective, academic systems are loose connections of many professional types.

Thus, we have another important principle: when professional influence is high within a system and there is one dominant professional group, the system may be integrated by the imposition of professional standards. But where professional influence is high and there are a number of professional groups coexisting side by side, the system will be split by professionalism. Academic systems are increasingly fractured by expertise, rather than unified by it.

In short, colleges and universities are indeed professionalized organizations, and academic systems are professionalized systems, with control and coordination highly influenced by the presence of professionals, but the professionalism is heavily fragmented. And it is this characteristic of fragmentation that sets the stage for our discussions of multiple authority and diverse means of integration in chapters 4 and 5.

The Division of Academic Enterprises

In focusing on enterprises as constituent units of national systems, a four-way analysis helps clarify the division of labor. Differentiation occurs horizontally and vertically, within institutions and among them. Within institutions, we refer to the horizontally aligned units as *sections;* the vertical arrangement as *tiers*. Among institutions, the lateral separations are called *sectors;* the vertical, *hierarchies*. Sections, tiers, sectors, and hierarchies appear in various forms and combinations in different countries, affecting a host of crucial matters. We here examine the two internal axes of alignment.

Sections

Horizontal differentiation within the individual university or college is the primary form of division by fields of knowledge. Such division has occurred typically at two levels of organization, although complex universities may exhibit as many as four, since each of the main levels develop substructures to help carry out their tasks. The broadest groupings, known by such terms as *faculty, school*, and *college*, encompass preparation for a certain type of occupation, e.g., law, business, or a set of "basic disciplines" like the humanities or the natural sciences. Each country arrives at a definition of these major clusterings of knowledge, which number from as low as three or four to more than fifteen, with a clear trend over time for the number to increase. For example, the French university system of the nineteenth and twentieth centuries (until 1968) had a standard set of major subdivisions throughout the country, consisting of the four faculties of law, medicine, letters, and science, with theology at one time and pharmacy at another also having faculty standing. German universities during the same period stayed largely with their four classical faculties of law, medicine, theology, and philosophy, with the latter eventually encompassing a wide range of academic disciplines. Italian universities of the mid-twentieth century found their logic in a dozen possible faculties, nine of them essentially professional, such as engineering and agriculture, and three in letters, science, and political science, with individual universities possessing anywhere from one to twelve of the faculties. Alongside a major faculty of arts and sciences that typically encompasses all the basic disciplines, American state universities often have fifteen or more professional schools for such fields as business, education, forestry, journalism, music, and social work.

The narrower groupings, which are the basic building blocks or operating units, known generally as *chair, institute*, or *department*, encompass a specialty within a profession (e.g., constitutional law, internal medicine) or an entire basic discipline (e.g., physics, history). For example, in the traditional French and Italian universities, departments as such have not existed, and the loci of control and organization within the faculties have been the professors occupying chairs in specialties, with the chair having a domain of teaching and research that sometimes spanned a discipline as large as political science or physics. Hence, in a chair system, the different types of chairs are at least as numerous as the disciplines covered, and they become more numerous as they are used to organize subfields within disciplines. A major university might have 50, 100, 200, or more chairs. In contrast, in the United States, departments, not chairs, have been the basic building blocks, numbering a dozen or two in a small college and 50, 100, or more in modern multiversities, usually in the form of subunits within professional schools and within the arts and sciences.

What are the crucial fixed and varying characteristics of these two levels of sectioning within universities (and colleges)? How do national systems vary in these substructures? The sections of universities have two significant features that are common among national systems: they have decidedly different contents with which to work, and they have a low degree of interdependence. The sections vary most sharply across nations in their internal organization.

Knowledge Content. The sections of universities and colleges vary in the qualities of the bodies of ideas and skills with which they work. Certain chairs and departments, faculties and schools, encompass fields that have well-developed and relatively clear structures of knowledge, as in the natural sciences, engineering, and medicine; but counterpart units labor with poorly integrated and ambiguous bodies of thought, as in the "softer" social sciences, the humanities, and such semiprofessions as education and social work. The variation, in short, is by type of discipline, and hence cuts across enterprises and systems. Everywhere physics, operating with a dependable corpus of theory and method, is a more structured and coherent field than sociology. Everywhere chemists can depend on elaborate sets of well-tested and interlocked propositions and formulas, but professors of education cannot. Nothing is more basic than these varying compositions of knowledge materials in accounting for differences within universities that appear as common patterns among nations.

The consequences of knowledge contents are immediately observable. Consider the effects on student access. Access became publicly defined in the late 1960s and early 1970s as the most important problem of the many problems brought about by the expansion of national systems into mass higher education. Research, ideology, and policy alike have treated this problem largely in global terms, as an issue of general entry into large systems. But access has long varied greatly and systematically within individual enterprises themselves, not to mention within the system at large, on the de facto grounds of the difficulty of fields. It is decided considerably by the relative need for students to move through closely regulated sequences of courses in order to master a complex body of knowledge.

Highly structured disciplines such as mathematics have been relatively difficult to enter and to remain in. Mathematicians arrange their courses in specific sequences and distinguish clearly between beginning, intermediate, and advanced students. They establish barriers all along the way, guarding the door to the classroom with "prerequisites." The barriers form a tapering funnel: the overwhelming majority of students cannot gain access to the higher levels, even if they desired. Since students perceive the difficulties, they "self-select" away from such fields: "It is really not right for me; it is too hard." Similarly elaborate course sequences are found throughout the physical and biological sciences and in engineering. Among the major professional fields, particularly medicine (in most countries) has learned how to limit access through claimed difficulty of knowledge content, and with such additional criteria as "effective clinical training," "number of laboratory spaces," and "high per-student costs."

In contrast, other disciplines and professional schools are characterized by lack of agreement on what knowledge content is basic and how it ought to be taught. Courses are only weakly stacked in sequences, if at all, since they do not necessarily precede and follow one another logically. Hence, in many of the humanities, the more qualitative of the social sciences, and such semiprofessions as education, social work, and business, it is not only easier for students to enter but also to negotiate their way, muddling through the ambiguities of the field as best they can, toward at least the first major degree. The advent of mass higher education has widened these internal differentials, with medicine, the natural sciences, and sometimes engineering protecting their standards through limited access, but with other units in the less well-structured fields taking all comers. In short, through both formal and informal means, access is differentiated across the many fields of knowledge and their supporting organizational sections, and this form of selection does not receive much argument. For the most part, it occurs quietly, student by student, classroom by classroom, course by course, specialty by specialty, and it appears legitimate.

Consider the effects on administration. Departments that operate with well-developed bodies of knowledge can arrive at a consensus more readily than those confused by ambiguous and conflicting perspectives. Decisions on the selection and retention of faculty are more easily made when all members of the department, or a major specialty within it, perceive quality in similar terms of theoretical grasp and methodological competence. In contrast, in departments where the knowledge base is vague, dissensus is more likely to reign, as otherwise "rational" people, with different understandings of the field, fight over courses and appointments.

Organizational analysts have picked up effectively on this point. Working from Thomas Kuhn's concept of paradigm, they have treated ideas as the technology of higher education and suggested that academic disciplines can be viewed as technologies involving different degrees of task predictability. Janice B. Lodahl and Gerald Gordon write: "Since the structure of knowledge determines what is taught as well as what is investigated, the degree of paradigm development and accompanying predictability in a given field should affect both teaching and research." This is a sensible notion and one tested in research on differences in behavior and attitudes in American departments. The results led to conclusions at two levels of organization. At the department level, "university professors in a given scientific field must operate at the level of predictability permitted by the structure of knowledge within the field. Social scientists operate in a much less predictable and therefore more anxious environment than physical scientists." Social scientists have more difficulty agreeing on course and degree requirements; they have in general a higher degree of conflict, both within and among individuals.

For the enterprise level, Lodahl and Gordon argue strongly "against some current tendencies to view university structure and university problems in terms that are too simple to match the demands of technology and the associated realities of activities and attitudes found within scientific disciplines." It is not true that a department is a department is a department, with all treated by administration and planners as a single kind. Rather, "any attempt to change the university must take into account the intimate relations between the structure of knowledge in different fields and the vastly different styles with which university departments operate."

Thus, across the fields of the arts and sciences, across the professional schools, *and* across such major types of institutions as universities, teachers' colleges, and technological schools, the styles of operation will vary greatly depending on the respective structures of knowledge. Hence, "any attempt at universal standards for academia will impose a uniformity of activity and output which is inconsistent with the particular subject matter requirements of specific areas." One can read for a long time in the literature of educational planning and reform in the United States, Great Britain, and elsewhere without encountering this simple idea—additional evidence, if more is needed, that analysis and policy need to take seriously the ways in which universities and colleges are internally differentiated around knowledge.

Knowledge contents do have important integrating effects, however, since there are organic uniformities in higher education that follow from the reach of disciplines. Each major subject matter promotes, even forces, some common contents within and among national systems. Whatever organized enterprises and formal systems do by way of grouping higher education differently, the disciplines have the crosshatching effect of carrying common bundles of knowledge and related styles of work.

Interdependence. Compared to other types of organizations, universities and colleges do not have strongly interdependent parts. The sections have distinct materials in their subject matters. If necessary, and generally by choice, they can put out their own products—new knowledge, graduates, and services in law or medicine or the natural sciences or philosophy. Hence, as remarked earlier, ties among the sections are strongly centrifugal, since the discovery, storing, and transmitting of knowledge can take place within the units in relatively self-contained ways. Law does not need archeology; English literature does not need physics. There is not the need for close interdependence that obtains within business firms organized around the production and distribution of a set of products. In the language of organizational analysis, there is not a long-linked technology involving interdependence among units, but rather an intensive technology that, in the academic case, can take place in separate compartments. The fragmentation is typically so great that "technology" is more usefully thought of as "technologies."

However, *among* types of universities and colleges, and especially among national academic systems, the degree of interdependence varies considerably. One source of variation is degree of commitment to specialized or general education; a second is the primacy of research or teaching.

Specialized training is highly fragmenting organizationally, whereas any type of general or liberal education requires various sections to take one another into account, fitting their work together as integrated parts of a larger "product," such as the liberally educated person. Reflecting this source of variation, the basic fault line among the more inclusive operating units in national systems is between relatively specialized faculties and schools and comprehensive counterparts. The prototypic specialized unit concentrates on a profession: law, medicine, architecture, pharmacy, engineering, agriculture, teaching, commerce. All teachers and students therein have a common occupational commitment and identity, providing an important internal source of collegiality and cohesion but, at the same time, distancing the unit from others within the university. Students are there to specialize in one field of work, with little or no possibility of transferring laterally to other units within the institution.

Such units have loomed large and often dominated in Europe and in Latin America. The French and Italian arrangements, identified earlier, are examples. The European faculties have had mutually exclusive personnel, clientele, and resources, despite their formal locations within regional and national public systems that ostensibly would bring them into close relationship. These faculties have been so self-contained that there has been little need to group them physically. Hence, they could scatter around a city, blocks and kilometers apart, in a generalized version of the geographical dispersion found occasionally in the American university when the medical school or school of business or school of agriculture is located across the river, or miles away in the nearest big city. Some faculty in the arts and sciences would maintain that that is not far enough! Faculty autonomy tends to be very high in universities composed mainly of professionally specialized units, a feature of most Continental universities and those around the world modeled after them. We will frequently note this characteristic in analyzing authority and integration. In the United States, the one-occupation specialized school or faculty can also be highly autonomous. Indeed, such units often take care of themselves: in private universities they may be told to raise their own income, each to become "a tub that stands on its own bottom"; in state universities they become major fixed and protected line items in governmental allocations; and, in both private and public universities, they may even become de facto arms of a national bureau, as in the case of the heavy dependency of medical schools at leading universities on the U.S. Public Health Service, one of the principal operational bases for the term "federal grant university."

The prototypic comprehensive unit has been the American faculty of arts and sciences, embracing dozens of fields and their carrying departments, extending across the humanities, the social sciences, and the natural sciences. The arts and sciences faculty is typically the core personnel unit in the American university, predominating in importance over the faculties of the professional schools. In the American liberal arts college concentrating on undergraduate education, it is the entire faculty. So heterogeneous is this unit in the modern American university that it becomes difficult to hold it together by sheer collegiality. This core American unit typically has one or more dean's offices set above the departments, staffed with full-time administrators and linked hierarchically to such central campus administrative offices as president and provost. The comprehensive nature of this basic faculty has helped make campus bureaucracy characteristic of American universities and colleges.

The degree of interdependence in the structure of faculties heavily determines the possibilities of curricular reform. The university composed of specialized faculties is an unnatural setting for general education. Historically predicated on the completion of the student's broad education in the secondary school, with entry to higher education tantamount to a commitment to specialize, the specialized faculties of European and Latin American systems, and most other countries, became deeply institutionalized, connected on this basis to secondary education and job markets. Thus, what Joseph Ben-David has referred to as the abandonment of liberal education in such universities became fixed in their structures. Any reform in the direction of general education is exceedingly difficult, at times virtually impossible. It becomes a matter of attempting to develop, within areas of specialization, a somewhat more general "first cycle" of courses, to be taken by students before going on to the more specific courses in the specialties.

In contrast, in the United States, general or liberal education, even while in decline, has had two key organizational supports. One has been the existence, in great numbers, of the private four-year college, where the total organization of the institution provides the framework and the authority for creating and coordinating a general-education curriculum. The other key has been the central faculty of arts and sciences within the university, public and private, which can work to foster some cooperation among its constituent departments and divisions and is driven in that direction by involvement in the general preparation of undergraduates. The consensus across disciplines that is required to effect general education can there be organizationally mustered, at least to a degree that gives plausibility to the institutional claims of providing a broad education. The arts and sciences faculty, or such units as the "undergraduate college" within the university, offers a large collegial body as a counterweight to atomistic inclinations among the departments. The faculty members of the departments come together in an inclusive faculty, or all-college faculty, that controls "*the* curriculum" and, as a body, monitors the many general and specific requirements set for students.

Thus, it is possible to speak of whole classes of universities and colleges in which it is possible to have, or not to have, general education. This is true because these institutions possess, or lack, the required internal organization, specifically in the form of specialized and comprehensive faculties and schools. Here is another instance of a general rule that holds strongly in academic systems: organization determines the fate of ideas and reforms.

The degree of interdependence among constituent units and the strength of centrifugal forces among them depend also on relative commitment to discovery and transmission of knowledge. Discovery requires an exceedingly high level of autonomous action on the part of individuals and groups, since it takes place at the leading edge of specialization within each discipline and involves venturing into the unknown. Discovery is difficult to plan and program, since higher authorities, if involved, are limited to setting general directions. In contrast, transmission involves some routine handling of what is already known and classified. It can be somewhat coordinated by a group of peers within the disciplinary unit, and secondarily by higher-level generalists and nonpeers. Hence, members of a department in an English or Swedish or Danish university, if they are to have an adequate curriculum, will more readily dictate to one another what must be taught and how it should be organized than what is to be researched. In short, "freedom of research" is more organizationally fragmenting than "freedom of teaching." Problems of coordination and control are then set accordingly, with centrifugal forces stronger in research settings than in teaching settings.

Finally, the sections of universities are rendered interdependent in varying degrees by the forms of authority, analyzed in chapter 4, that predominate in and around them. The high autonomy and low interdependence of faculties in European and Latin American universities reflect the weakness of institutional bureaucracy; the much stronger administration of the U.S. campus aids the integration of its departments and faculties.

In this regard, a notable case of extremely high faculty independence is found in contemporary Yugoslavia. There the faculties, not the universities as wholes, are very much the main units of local organization. Their strength has been increased by the deliberate decentralization of power in virtually all societal sectors, which has made Yugoslavia so unlike other Communist countries. For what does "worker self-management" mean when applied to higher education? As Geoffrey Giles has shown, it means that power flows to disciplinary clusters. Individual units can set themselves up and govern themselves in whatever form they wish, with the higher levels of government even constitutionally barred, after 1974, from powers of supervision. The units of Yugoslavia in the best position to seize the opportunity of self-management were the faculties, which, numbering twenty at the University of Belgrade in 1970, have more of the disciplinary focus of U.S. departments than the wider clustering nature of the faculties in Western Europe. Thus, we have the ironic situation in which the extreme case of minimal interdependence of units within a university comes not from age-old doctrines and practices of the medieval collegium carried into the modern period, but from one of the latest and most noted socialist experiments. To the specialization of work and commitment that has caused European faculties to have quite low interdependence, there has now been added new doctrines and practices of authority that encourage the disciplines to go their own way. In the Yugoslav model, the university as a whole lies somewhere between a voluntary association and a confederation.

Thus, academic enterprises do vary within and across national systems in the interdependence of their parts. But they have in common, compared with other types of organization, a relatively low degree of interconnectedness. The metaphors of "holding company" and "conglomerate" are to be taken seriously.

Group Organization. Now we come to the most important difference in the way that enterprises in different national systems organize their lowest operating units: chair versus department organization. The chair concentrates the responsibilities of the primary unit in one person, the chair holder. He or she is in charge of academic activities in a work domain, with other staff serving in subordinate capacities. If research in the domain is organized by means of an institute, the chair holder also becomes the director of the institute or shares authority with several other chair holders. In chair systems, research institutes tend to be fused to the chairs, since the latter are the primary positions in the university structure below the faculty level of organization. In contrast, the department spreads responsibilities and powers among a number of professors of similar senior rank and more readily allows for some participation by associates and assistants. It thereby becomes a basis for collegial as well as bureaucratic order at the operating level.

Chair organization is very old. It has been the traditional form of operational control in most European and Latin American universities, with its roots in the original organization of medieval universities as guilds and guild federations of master professors who took unto themselves a few journeyman assistants and a small batch of student apprentices. The internal hierarchy came from the guild model:

> At the bottom were the ordinary students, equivalent to the guild apprentices who were learning the elements of the trade and were under the full authority of the master craftsmen. Next came the bachelors, who were advanced students and were allowed to lecture and dispute under supervision. They correspond to and derived their names from the journeymen or bachelors, who worked for a daily wage and had not sufficient maturity to establish themselves in the trade. (Hence they were still unmarried.) At the top of the profession was the master, a rank common to both universities and guilds. He was a man who had demonstrated both his skill and maturity to the satisfaction of his fellow masters. Entrance to this stage was gained after elaborate examinations, exercises in the techniques of teaching, and ceremonial investiture. . . . The three titles, master, doctor, professor, were in the Middle Ages absolutely synonymous.

It is fairly certain, despite large gaps in the written record, that this key aspect of academic guilds was effectively carried forward in Europe down through the centuries. When the title of "chair" emerged is unclear, but the position was there all along. What is abundantly clear is that the chair form of organization was reinvigorated and given modern trappings in the German research university, which became the most important worldwide academic institutional model of the nineteenth and early twentieth century. Centered on "the research imperative," this modern prototype "integrated research and teaching in the full professor, reinforcing his dominance as director of his research institute and as part-time policy maker at other levels of university administration."

Chair organization has had some influence in Great Britain, where, more than on the Continent, it has been blended with department and all-college bodies. Where chairs and departments coexist, the chair holder is likely to be the department head, probably a permanent one, but the department will still be the basic unit for organizing work. The chair has also been tempered in the British system by the college tradition of Oxford and Cambridge, within which work is organized primarily by multidisciplinary faculty clusters in colleges rather than departments of the university. Most important, chair organization has spread throughout the world wherever German, French, Italian, Spanish, Portuguese, and English modes of academic organization have been implanted by colonial regimes or voluntarily adopted, and it has persisted as the normal way of structuring and manning the university. Thus, it has been much more important than departmental organization—a point generally overlooked by Americans—throughout Asia, Africa, and Latin America. In Japan, where public and private sectors are organized somewhat differently, the dominant sector of national universities is a striking case. There, by set formulas that vary by field, each chair is apportioned several positions for assistants, with, as the joke goes, the chair thereby becoming a sofa.

Departmentalism is relatively new, a deviant form that has developed most strongly in the United States, where it arose in the context of trustee and administrative control over growing individual colleges and emerging universities in the nineteenth century. Within such frameworks, bureaucratic models of subdivision could and did predominate over guild models. When the all-inclusive faculty had to subdivide in order to organize growing and disparate specialties, especially after the common classical curriculum gave way to the elective system—with free choice for students *and* more room for faculty experts to pursue their specialties—there was not already in place at the operating levels the guildlike presumptions and forms that had come down from the medieval universities in Europe.

The existence of chair organization as opposed to department organization has had major effects in national systems, and those outcomes will be pursued in greater detail in later chapters. In brief, chair organization is a persistent source of personal dominance, as against collegial as well as bureaucratic control. In contrast, the department is a less personal form. Thus, the chair scores high in concentrating authority and in creating local monopolies. Chair organization is also the more potent source of faculty control over higher levels of organization, strengthening the thrust of senatorial politics. And, as academic enterprises and systems have grown, the chair, compared to the department, has been an increasingly inappropriate unit for swollen disciplines. Systems that have both kept the chair as primary unit and have grown much larger have exhibited overload and extreme fragmentation. Most important, the chair system has a weak capacity to correct errors, particularly in the crucial area of faculty appointments. When a mistake is made in selecting a mediocre person to fill a chair, the effect is long-lasting, through the rest of the academic life of the incumbent and beyond. Hence, an important step in serious reform, a topic we return to in chapter 6, has been to replace chairs with departments or to absorb them somehow in departmentlike units. Considered a hopelessly old-fashioned unit by American reformers, the department is one of the primary means of reform elsewhere. It is capable of supporting and integrating modern disciplines to an extent not normally possible under the hegemony of chairs.

Tiers

Vertical differentiation in organizations is normally viewed as a matter of ascending administrative levels, a topic taken up in a later discussion of authority. But in the organization of academic *work*, there is the prior and more basic consideration of organizing on the basis of what Thomas F. Green has called "the principle of sequence," the notion that activities will be arranged above and below one another according to defined difficulty. From the elementary school years onward, some aspects of teaching and learning are more advanced than others. Within higher education, even in the softer fields, there is beginning work, intermediate work and advanced work for students; hence, there are such curricular levels as lower division and upper division, first cycle and second cycle. The question becomes: How are the levels of training and related certification organizationally handled? Then, too, where is research placed in relation to the levels of training? Every system must develop some vertical placement of its work activities.

The differences among countries in tier construction are fascinating. Historically, most have had only one major tier; a few have had two or more. A single tier has predominated in the European and Latin American mode of organization, in which the professional school within the university is entered directly after completion of secondary education. With general education completed at the secondary level, higher education has been defined primarily as a place to prepare for the learned professions and the high civil service. Hence, the student enrolls immediately in medicine or law or another professional faculty, with law serving as the main road to the civil service. If the student enters a faculty based on one or more of the fields of the natural sciences, social sciences, or humanities, it is understood that he or she is also there to specialize.

The first major degrees, taken after some three to six years of course work, then certifies professional or disciplinary competence—the *licence* in France, the *laurea* in Italy, the *diplom* in Germany, the *licenciado* in Latin America. This degree has been and remains the first step in, and often the sole basis of, the extremely rigorous state certification requirements in Continental systems for employment in the professions and the civil service, the latter including school teaching and the academic profession itself. In some single-tier university systems, such as Italy, there has been virtually only the one degree; in some others, such as Germany and France, there have been higher degrees, historically available to only a few, but in any event not handled by a separate higher unit. Distinct units of organization for work above the first degree have been nonexistent or only weakly developed. The higher degrees have been handled by the same faculty units that concentrate their energies in the first tier.

Two distinct tiers have predominated in the American mode of university organization. The first tier, the undergraduate realm of four years, is devoted primarily to general education, with limited specialization available as students choose a major subject on which to concentrate in the last two years. The first major degree, the bachelor's, does not in most cases certify any particular professional competence, giving most of its holders a general and ambiguous connection to the job market. Specialization has found its home in a second major tier composed of the two distinct forms known as the graduate school and the professional school, units that can be entered only after completion (or at least several years) of first-tier course work. Hence, one gains entry to the top professions only after taking a second degree offered solely by units located at this higher level. And one enters employment in one of the disciplines with maximum scholastic qualifications only after taking a second *and* a third degree monopolized by this level.

The American vertical differentiation was created only a century ago, at a time when "the university" was added to a domain that had been occupied for over 200 years by "the college." The university model of the last quarter of the nineteenth century, German-inspired, meant a place for research and advanced training. And if the German model had been borrowed wholesale, there would have been no need at the time for a distinct graduate school. But the college form was deeply institutionalized, in power and in public understanding, and was not to be blown away, particularly since there was not enough state control to enforce a sweeping reform. Most colleges existing at the time remained pure colleges (e.g., Amherst and Oberlin), a first tier committed to broad education; some colleges became both college and university (e.g., Yale and Harvard); and newly created universities found viability in being colleges as well as universities (e.g., Johns Hopkins, Chicago, and Stanford). The emergent solution was a distinct graduate and professional level with its own organization, placed in the educational sequence on top of the now "undergraduate" level, which was so well rooted in a college of its own.

The differences in tier structure are enormously consequential. For one, they markedly affect access. The problems of access in modern higher education are most severe in the systems whose primary enterprises have only one tier. Broadened entry, then, means the right of much larger numbers of students who complete the secondary level to enter into the one meaningful level, specialize in it, and graduate with a certified job-related competence. In Europe, selectivity for any of the fields, including the professional ones, became a major political issue in the 1960s and 1970s—the question of *numerus clausus*—since to introduce selection appeared to deny greater access, *and* at a time when more middle-class and lower-class students were graduating from the secondary level. In the dual or multitier arrangement, in contrast, the lower levels can even offer open-door access, and the upper levels operate selectively. No one finds it strange in the United States that graduate schools, law schools, and architecture schools can be highly selective. The lower levels screen for the upper levels, just as the secondary levels traditionally have screened for higher education. The internal vertical differentiation of levels *within* given programs of instruction, as well as within the system as a whole, allows the work of screening to move up the educational ladder another level or two. It combines open and limited access.

A second set of effects rests in job placement and the connections of higher education to the job market. The one-tier system historically had the advantage of linking higher education specifically and closely to job placement. The graduates of the first tier had a high probability of placement in the top administrative stratum of the national civil service, of entry directly into practice in one of the leading professions, or of entry into secondary-school teaching, which was under the civil service, prestigious, and so closely linked to higher education as to operate as a waiting room for openings in the universities. (Professors in the selective classical or scientific secondary school could hope to become university professors.) As long as higher education was elite in number—under five percent of the age group—this arrangement had a clarity of connection that was not possible in the multitier structure, where the terminating graduates of the first level have a more generalized connection to the job market (as in the case of B.A.-level graduates in the humanities and most of the social sciences in the United States). Here, confusion has reigned, contributing to the anxiety of that troubled age group in modern society, the fifteen-to-twenty-five-year olds.

But the development of more accessible higher education in nations with single-tier systems has overloaded that type of structure, and nowhere more so than in connection to jobs. The historic promise of precise, elite placement can no longer be honored: there are simply too many persons. Often five or ten times too many enter the pipeline of training, expecting the high rewards of old, only to exit to saturated traditional markets. No more secondary-school teachers are needed after expansion has swelled those ranks with a generation or two of new teachers fixed in the permanent civil service; the administrative civil service cannot be indefinitely expanded to accommodate the flood tide of new graduates, even though countries like Italy or Mexico can push this form of conflict abatement a long way, soaking up discontent by expansion of the government's payrolls; and certain of the professions are also threatened with unemployment of the qualified and dilution of rewards as the supply of professionals expands enormously. Such systems experience a great gap between student expectations, shaped by a long history of elite placement, and the realities of limited placement at the higher levels for the much larger supply of recruits. Hence, again, as in the case of access, the problem of job placement pushes such systems toward greater vertical differentiation, *within* institutions, to sieve and to funnel and to provide a number of exit points at varying levels of preparation.

A third class of effects are to be found in the support of such elite functions as research. Research is plainly in trouble where increasingly swollen, comprehensive universities still place it in the hands of faculties loaded with the burdens of mass teaching and advising. Those whose primary commitment is to research then find their energies wrongly used and seek to escape to external research settings, encouraging governments to separate research from teaching in the form of a separate structure of research institutes. The dual- or multiple-tier structures are able to protect research in something like the graduate school, legitimating it with involvement in the training of the most advanced specialists and separating it from the needs of the undergraduate college, but still keeping it within the institution.

Joseph Ben-David has suggested that a fruitful coupling of two tiers, with different functions, is the key to the possible maintenance of general or liberal education in universities. If there is not a dependable home for research and highly specialized training at second and third levels, then those operations have to be serviced at the first and only level, thereby compromising and most likely subordinating general education. When the one and only tier is deeply rooted in specialization, the revitalization or reintroduction of general education is made all the more difficult.

The Division of Academic Systems

Academic systems, in varying degrees, have their activities separated into different types of institutions. Those institutions, deliberately or otherwise, are arranged in hierarchies. As systems become loaded with more activities, these larger forms of differentiation become increasingly important, perhaps obtaining an even greater role than the internal divisions in determining the nature and capabilities of academic systems. If there is a single structural key in the negotiating of effective modern systems, it appears to lie in sectoral differentiation.

Sectors

Horizontal differentiation among institutions takes four general forms in the national systems of higher education of the twentieth century. From simple to complex, they are: a single sector of institutions within a single public system; several sectors within one governmental system; several sectors in more than one formal public subsystem; and several sectors under private support as well as public-system allocation.

Single Public System: Single Sector. This pattern expresses a double monopoly, one of system and one of institutional type. The whole of higher education falls almost completely under a unified national system, topped by a national ministry of education, and the system contains essentially only one form, the state university, with eighty percent or more of enrollment in that one type of institution. During the nineteenth century, virtually all of Latin America conformed to this pattern. The clearest example of this form in Western Europe in the twentieth century has been Italy, with its nationalized system of public universities, complemented by a few "free" institutions that have had to attach themselves to the national system, and with as many as ninety-eight percent of all higher-education students attending places called universities. The university, then, includes not only preparation for public administration and the professions, as elsewhere, but also teacher training, engineering, and some technological fields, which in many countries are located in separate sectors. Other Mediterranean countries, such as Spain,

Portugal, and Greece, have traditionally adopted this form. Sweden also had this type of institutional pattern traditionally, with a handful of universities within a unified national system absorbing eighty to ninety percent of the students.

Single Public System: Multiple Sectors. In this pattern, higher education remains under the hegemony of one level of government, but the system is substantially differentiated into two or more types of institutions. This is the most common pattern around the world, the dominant arrangement in Communist societies, Western democracies, and Third World nations alike. Typically, the main sector is a set of universities, with one or more "nonuniversity" sectors organized around technological-technical-vocational instruction or teacher training, or both, but occasionally organized around esoteric functions prized by one or more departments of the central government. All sectors are financed primarily by the national government, sometimes through a single ministry but often along several ministerial avenues.

France has been and still is a striking example of this pattern, with its historical differentiation of universities and *grandes écoles*, specialized schools that for the most part rank above the universities in prestige. The university sector, containing the largest share of students, has successively fallen under the Ministry of Education, the Office of the Secretary of State for Universities (1974), the Ministry of Universities (1978), and, again, the Education Ministry (1981). Some institutions in the *grandes écoles* sector also report to the Education Ministry but have "special status"; others in this elite group answer to other ministries, e.g., the *école polytechnique* to the Ministry of Defense. Then there are additional small sectors of University Institutes of Technology (IUTS) and other enterprises devoted to technical education and teacher training.

Countries as different as Thailand, Iran, and Poland have fallen within this pattern of nationalized diversity. In Thailand, nearly all institutions are governmental, with only about five percent of the students in nominally "private" institutions, which are mainly in business training, and even these colleges are "under the supervision" of a national government department. The governmental institutions divide into two major types—universities, with about fifty-five percent of the enrollment, and more specialized colleges, with approximately thirty-five percent—with a third miscellaneous category making up the rest. As in France, different types of institutions come under different central bureaus: the universities under the Office of University Affairs; teacher training and vocational colleges under the Ministry of Education; and seven nursing colleges under the Ministry of Public Health. This nationalized system is an excellent example of one spawned in the twentieth century by different governmental ministries: "Originally, none of the higher institutions possessed autonomy; they were only service units in various ministries." Various institutions are considered to be not only under government departments but within them: "In actual fact these colleges [agricultural, commercial, vocational, and technical] are suborgans of a larger department which is considered the juristic person."

In prerevolutionary Iran, as in Thailand, educational institutions were basically governmental: as of 1975, all were supported by government funds. Approximately twenty universities and fifty colleges, all founded in the twentieth century, varied widely in type, from the relatively huge University of Tehran, which had thirty percent of all the students in the mid-1970s, to specialized colleges, schools, and institutes in accounting, hospital management, forestry, sports, and telecommunications. In this patchwork of enterprises, most fell under the Ministry of Science and Higher Education, but they did so in various ways. This was a system full of "special statuses," such as being "directly under the trust" of some members of the royal family, and thereby "less subject to the control of the governmental bureaucracy." And such ministries as Labor and Agriculture had direct control over some institutions.

In postwar Poland, the private sector has consisted of only one institution, the imposing Roman Catholic University in Lublin, which since 1945 has been the only Catholic university in all of Eastern Europe. All others are governmental, run by the national government alone. But the governmental realm is heterogeneous in institutional type and bureau sponsorship. A polytechnic or technological sector of eighteen institutions (1977) had about a third of the enrollment, as did a university sector consisting of nine institutions, leaving another third of the students in teachers' colleges, agricultural academies, economic academies, medical academies, and on down an extensive list to arts colleges and sports colleges. While most of the institutions are subordinate to one national office, the Ministry of Science, Higher Education, and Technology, others come under such diverse bureaus as the Ministry of Health and Social Welfare, the Ministry of Arts and Culture, and the State Committee for Sports and Tourism.

Finally, the most important system of all among Communist countries, that of the USSR, is extensively divided between a small university sector of some 50 institutions that has only about ten percent of the enrollment and a huge, variegated nonuniversity sector of some 750 institutes with all the rest of the enrollment. All the enterprises are public, controlled directly by a national bureau or a ministry at the republic level, which is in turn heavily influenced by national policy and administration. The universities are relatively comprehensive, covering the physical sciences, social sciences, and humanities. But the numerous institutes are highly specialized, focusing on such distinct areas as agriculture, engineering, medicine, "physical culture," and teacher training. Notably, only about half of all the enterprises come under the jurisdiction of a higher education ministry. The others come under, for example, ministries of culture, health, agriculture, and transportation, linking them to the tasks of many government departments that attend, in the main, to practical needs of an economy run by the national state. A man-power approach is thereby thoroughly institutionalized.

Since this type of sectoral differentiation commonly entails supervision by a number of central bureaus, it brings with it the problem of how these agencies relate to one another. "Coordination," as seen in chapter 5, is then something quite different from what is normally depicted as integrated governmental control.

Multiple Public Systems: Multiple Sectors. This pattern occurs primarily in nations that have a federal structure of government, with higher education falling within a number of state or provincial systems, influenced in varying degrees by national government. Theoretically, multiple public systems could have only one type of institution within them, but in reality they seem always to coexist with multiple sectors, apparently for the simple reason that two or more authorities will generate more variety than a simple all-embracing one. When the formal organization of higher education takes place primarily at the subgovernment level, it will more likely reflect provincial differences in the need and preference for types of universities and colleges. In these systems, we can note a dual trend in the postwar period, especially after 1960: on the one hand, greater influence by national government; on the other, a reduction of the private sector, if it existed at all, to a small part—ten to fifteen percent or less—of student enrollment.

With considerable variation, Australia, Canada, Great Britain, West Germany, and Mexico all fall into this pattern. Australia has three distinguishable sectors: universities, colleges of advanced education, and colleges of technical and further education, with the sectors organized in the six systems of the Australian states. These systems vary somewhat in character. For example, the one in Victoria, which includes the University of Melbourne, is considerably older, larger, and more advanced than the one in Western Australia.

Canada has multiple types of universities and colleges, including an important sector of two-year units similar in general form to U.S. community colleges. The sectors are organized within provincial systems, eleven all together, with those systems varying considerably in type and mixture of institutions (for example, the Atlantic provinces versus those of western Canada, and especially Quebec, with its French-Canadian traditions, versus all the other provinces). Within this set of public systems, Quebec is loaded with unique features (e.g., a de facto division of postsecondary education into French-language and English-language subsystems, a heavy clerical tradition, a particular style of strict state supervision, and a sector of about thirty-seven public colleges of general and vocational education *[Collége d'enseignement général et professionel]*, which contain a two-year track for transferring to universities and a three-year terminal vocational track). Canada clearly has a higher education system where differences among institutional sectors are extended by differences among provincial subsystems.

Great Britain has developed a variety of institutional types. First, there are several kinds of universities: Oxford and Cambridge as a class in themselves; the University of London as a class in itself; the nineteenth-century-spawned civic universities; and the set of new universities built essentially in the 1960s. Second, there is a host of technical and technological enterprises, some bracketed under university status and others constituting a polytechnic sector. These are the nonuniversity institutions that most aggressively challenge the privileges of the universities. Third, there are teacher-training colleges and a diffuse set of institutions of "further education." Furthermore, even though the nation is not generally considered to have a federal structure of government, there are the distinctive regions of England, Wales, Northern Ireland, and Scotland, which operate in nonuniversity higher education as public authorities. The Scottish subsystem overall has long been so rooted in its own distinctive set of characteristics that "the Scottish universities" are considered to be a different type from "the English universities," even to the point of having played a separate role as a model for higher education in the United States and other countries. Then, too, many of the technical colleges, teacher training colleges, and other "nonuniversity" enterprises have been sponsored by local educational authorities (LEAs), encouraging them to take on local identity and unique character.

As a fourth case, West Germany's system of the mid-1970s had about two-thirds of its students in a university sector, which subdivided into classical-type universities and technical universities; another twenty percent of the students in a vocational sector *(Fachhochschulen)* composed largely of merged units of engineering and commerce upgraded from the secondary level; another eight percent in a third sector of teachers' colleges; and six percent in a sector of new comprehensive institutions that are combinations of the other types. The 200 institutions of these four sectors are grouped in eleven subsystems, following the traditional allocation of responsibility for education in Germany to the *Land* level of government, a pattern interrupted by the Nazi regime but restored after World War II. Hence, there is a fundamental structural similarity in the way public control is divided among provinces and states in Australia, Canada, and the United States—so-called federal systems—with West Germany an imposing exception to the general rule on the European continent that public control is national.

Lastly Mexico is an important instance of this federal pattern among the Latin American systems. A federal republic since the mid-nineteenth century, the country has spawned institutions of higher education under national, state, and private auspices. In the 1970s, there were over 200 enterprises distributed among thirty states, including a central federal district around Mexico City, the capital. The university has been the dominant institutional type, with the technological or technical institution the most prevalent nonuniversity form. The private universities and colleges, comprising some ten to fifteen percent of enrollment, have various antecedents in early church sponsorship and post-1960 private initiatives. But amid the scatter there has also been considerable concentration. Two-thirds of the enrollment is located in the federal district and the two states of Jalisco (containing Guadalajára) and Nuevo León (around Monterrey). Over forty of the institutions and forty percent of the enrollment are in the federal district alone, with that enrollment heavily concentrated in the huge Autonomous National University of Mexico in the capital city. The system simultaneously is much divided into national and state components and tilted toward the predominance and influence of a central institution in the magnet-like area of the country, drawing and concentrating resources and thereby contributing to a gross imbalance between the center and the periphery.

Private and Public Systems: Multiple Sectors. The fourth national arrangement exhibits multiple institutional types under private as well as public sponsorship, at least to the point where fifteen to twenty percent of the students are in institutions that receive most of their financing from nongovernmental sources and have boards of control selected through private channels. The existence of one or more private sectors increases considerably the division of forms, first by providing a private-public cleavage and second by multiplying subtypes and unique institutions as the search for competitive advantage among the private universities and colleges leads some to different postures.

Japanese higher education is an impressive case, since that populous country of over 100 million people moved rapidly into mass higher education in the 1950s and 1960s by allowing the burdens of expansion to be picked up by private institutions, to the point where some seventy-five to eighty percent of the students came to be located in the private sector, a share much greater than in the United States, where the proportions of private and public enrollment are the reverse. This huge system of over 1,000 institutions and 2 million students (as of 1975) has numerous major sectors: a small set of national, formerly "imperial," universities; other national universities; universities supported by the municipal level of government; private universities and colleges, numbering in excess of 300 and varying widely in type and quality; and over 500 junior colleges, public and private, but mainly private. As in the United States, each private institution is under its own board of control and governs itself. The great heterogeneity of institutions entails vast differences in selection, from exceedingly tight, as at the universities of Tokyo and Kyoto, to exceedingly loose, as in some private colleges that became virtual degree mills. Enormous differences in job placement are also the rule, from guaranteed placement to top administrative ranks in government to unspecified entry into a broad band of the total job market, including some blue-collar work, clerical positions, and sales occupations.

The United States is the second great example of this pattern, with 3,000 institutions divided into about 1,500 private colleges and universities and a similar number of public ones, the latter divided into the 50 subsystems of the states. Hence, in international comparison, both the public sector and the private sector are extensively fragmented. Each of the state systems has its own mixture of the three basic institutional types: the state university, the state college, and the community college. The latter in many states are supported considerably by local funds and are under the control of local educational authorities. The private universities vary from the well-known "research universities" to lesser-known "service universities" that have little endowment and have learned to survive on tuition and fees, much like the majority of Japanese private universities and colleges. The hundreds of private colleges, representatives of the type most deeply rooted in American history, run the whole gamut of selectivity and quality and, indeed, the full range of secular and religious differences in American life. The worst are a soft underbelly, indeed.

The differentiation of this system of over 11 million students (as of 1980) has been so extensive that the best efforts in the 1970s to classify institutions developed at least ten categories of types of institutions, and about twenty when the public-private distinction is made. The division of labor that is thereby revealed has been largely overlooked by American as well as foreign observers. For example, on simple parameters, about one-half of all students entering higher education enter the community colleges, which number more than a thousand; about a third of all enrollment at a given time is in the community colleges, another third is in four- and five-year colleges, and the remaining third is in doctoral-granting institutions. The traditionally heterogeneous university category has become ever more so as various state colleges have developed advanced programs and some research capacities and have acquired the formal title of university. Adding such places to the many private universities that have long had the character of service rather than research universities means that the images of "the American university" long formed by the Ivy League and such leading state universities as California, Michigan, and Wisconsin are poor guides to reality. The expansion of enrollment has been greatest in the enterprises that have heavy teaching loads of nine, twelve, and fifteen classroom hours a week, with large class enrollments, essentially precluding research and tilting the reward system away from research productivity and toward teaching performance and service to the institution. Less than a fifth of American students *and* faculty are in the research universities that couple teaching and research to a major degree, following the traditional model of the university idealized in the three major systems of Germany, Britain, and the United States since the last quarter of the nineteenth century.

The higher education systems of Latin America have been moving toward this pattern since 1960 and are now well rooted in it, despite a heritage of public monopoly and a widespread impression that these systems are entirely public. Private-sector enrollments doubled in the fifteen-year period between 1960 and 1975, from seventeen to thirty-five percent. Chile and Peru had become about thirty percent private, Columbia fifty percent, and the large system of Brazil sixty to seventy percent." The private institutions provide various kinds of alternatives to the public realm. In some cases, they are more vocationally oriented and directly responsive to job markets; in others, they are more selective and "elitist"; in still others, they offer more open access. In each case, the buildup of the private alongside the public has meant greater institutional heterogeneity.

The division of higher education systems into institutional sectors thus has many forms, which range along a continuum from simple to complex. The divisions also vary in whether they were imposed by the central government or emerged as the products of local and regional action. Then, too, sectors vary between isolated and articulated. In most systems, isolated sectors have predominated, with a particularly sharp line between "university" and "nonuniversity." Articulation is indexed by the ability of students to move from one to another, receiving credit for courses already completed. Sector boundaries are permeable when students can cross them with transferable course credits. U.S. sectors overall are highly permeable, since there are course credits and certificates common across them, and the division of labor among sectors within the state systems is premised on a common medium of exchange. Sometimes the coin of one institution is partially discounted in the next, giving students only partial credit; but a high degree of articulation in the U.S. system generally helps weld together what would otherwise be a large number of discrete tunnels. Such linkage is partly a matter of state administration and partly a product of market-type interaction among discrete enterprises, a distinction in national integration pursued in chapter 5. But such permeability is unusual: the more common arrangement internationally has been the reverse, that is, few, if any, common units across sectors, and little or no sector transferring. Typically, a national "system" consists of national or regional authorities sponsoring a division of labor among segments that do not interact on the basis of a course-and-credit medium of exchange.

Hierarchies

Vertical arrangements of institutions and sectors are of two sorts: high and low placement based on level of task, a hierarchy of sequence; and ranking based on prestige, a hierarchy of status, which is often but not always closely related to the first. The first form of hierarchy comes from sectors having tasks that cover rungs in the educational ladder, with the sectors themselves then taking up location at lower and higher rungs, lower ones feeding higher ones. For example, in the United States, the typical tripartite differentiation of state systems has a basic vertical component: the community college is coterminous with the first two years in the basic structure of grades; the state college overlaps those years and extends upward to take in another two or four years, through the bachelor's and master's degrees; and the state university overlaps both of the first two institutions and extends upward another several years to the doctoral degree and postdoctoral training. For transferring students, the feeder sequences run strongly from the first to the second and third, and from the second to the third, as students move upward through levels of training that are assigned differentially to sectors. This is a quite objective matter. Even if the three sectors had a parity of esteem, there would still be a noticeable vertical differentiation based on place in the ladder of education. With each place there are predictable associated activities: research is likely to locate at the uppermost levels; general education is likely to appear in the lower steps; specialized education in the higher steps.

But parity of esteem among types of institutions rarely if ever obtains. The search for such parity has been as illusory as the search for a classless society: sectors do not remain innocent of status differences. Occupational and social positions are ranked by the public as well as by incumbents; and institutions that place their graduates differentially are assigned different levels of prestige. What in comparative higher education is referred to as "institutional hierarchy" is a prestige ranking of institutions and sectors based primarily on perceived social value of graduation. Where are graduates placed in the labor force, and otherwise in social circles, that might shape life chances? The U.S. structure and others like it involve graduates stepping out into the labor force at different levels of occupational prestige, with a virtually automatic parallel assignment of prestige by the public back to the training institutions (e.g., the prestige of doctors, teachers, and secretaries assigned, respectively, to universities, four-year colleges, and two-year colleges). And sectors are even more likely to be ranked sharply by prestige when lower ones are unable to feed higher ones, but exist instead as airtight compartments that clearly place graduates at different occupational levels. When sectors designed for technical training and teacher training do not have the potential for transferring their students into the university sector, status rankings become more clear-cut and severe.

National systems vary extensively in the extent of status hierarchy, from sharply peaked to relatively flat structures, and we may note three types that range along a continuum. In the first type, several institutions have a monopoly, or near-monopoly, of elite placement that helps to give them much higher prestige than all others. Japan is an outstanding example. A small set of imperial universities were fathered and given superior resources by the central government as instruments of rapid modernization in the late nineteenth and early twentieth centuries. Within the cluster of seven institutions, the universities of Tokyo and Kyoto were given, and seized, an even more special place. They became a class unto themselves, to the point where certain high positions in government could be entered only by graduation from certain faculties, particularly the faculty of law at Tokyo. As precise connections were institutionalized, a small elite sector became fixed as highly superior to all other institutions, a sharply tapered hierarchy that has persisted and conditioned the rest of the system even as the system swelled greatly in size and as diverse sectors emerged.

A high degree of institutional hierarchy has been found also in France and Great Britain. The French case is particularly clear-cut: a few institutions in the *grandes écoles* sector have had a lock on top governmental positions, and increasingly on placement in top executive ranks in industry, selecting vigorously to recruit the crème de la crème for those positions and acquiring a superior standing that has kept them well apart from the problems of university expansion. This institutional elite has been so untouchable that it never even became an issue in the great 1968 French educational crisis or in the host of attempted and effected reforms of the following decade. In a less explicit but still highly effective fashion, Oxford and Cambridge have constituted an institutional elite in Great Britain, still showing in the 1970s the historic capacity to stock the top political and bureaucratic offices of the government, even if, at the same time, they failed to provide industrial leaders and thereby contributed to "the British disease" of lagging economic progress.

The middle ground of status hierarchy is occupied by such systems as the Canadian and the American, in which pronounced differences exist in the social standing of institutions and sectors, without a few institutions monopolizing elite placement. Institutions and sectors are definitely ranked—Canadian universities above Canadian community colleges, U.S. Ivy League universities above state colleges—but placement to high office in public as well as private spheres is institutionally diversified and overlaps sectors. No one or two institutions have a lock on sponsorship of top offices, political or administrative. American presidents are about as likely to be graduates of small unheard-of colleges as graduates of leading universities. For example, Lyndon Johnson graduated from Southwest Texas State Teachers College, Richard Nixon from Whittier College, and the recruits to the central administrative agencies come from a variety of public and private colleges throughout the fifty states.

A third type is characterized by little status ranking. In Italy, there is virtually no nonuniversity sector that could be second best, and all the universities can send graduates to elite positions in government and the professions. A *laurea* in law serves as a general passport to the top administrative stratum in the national civil service, and it can be obtained at any one of several dozen law faculties scattered throughout the country. The system of the Federal Republic of Germany is somewhat more hierarchical than the Italian, since its nonuniversity components devoted to technical and teacher training have a lesser standing than the universities. But there are few status differences among the universities, with no one or two places serving in the manner of Tokyo-Kyoto or Oxford-Cambridge, nor, as in the United States, are there universities competing for the status advantages of attracting the best students. As the best study of the German system has put it: "In general, universities are considered to be of equal standing. There are no major differences in status among the universities of the Federal Republic as there are in Anglo-Saxon countries." And, going on: "This is the reason why there is no competition among the universities to get the best students by way of entrance examinations, a fact that often amazes foreign observers."

These important national cases make it clear that institutional sectors tend not to remain merely that, but instead become segments of hierarchies that vary in steepness and rigidity. Hierarchy is seemingly most strongly restrained by minimizing sectors and subtypes within them. If a national system works for decades to equate its institutions in resources and personnel, *and* establishes a single national degree in each field of study instead of institutional degrees, *and* elaborates a public doctrine that the state-awarded degree has the same value for employment no matter where one studies, then the hierarchical tendency is considerably restrained. If a system has multiple sectors that handle different forms and levels of training, those sectors will vary in esteem, and a steeper hierarchy is thereby produced. Beyond task differentials, higher-ranked institutions or sectors, through governmental policy or self-aggrandizement, acquire and institutionalize greater financial resources with which to attract well-regarded faculty and students, and this perpetuates and enhances their privileged position. There is a snowballing effect that is basic to the inertia of institutional hierarchies in higher education.

The pros and cons of the division of sectors and the development of hierarchies are fundamental issues in public policy in higher education and will reappear in later discussions of change and values (chapters 6 and 7). To anticipate, the issues involve trade-offs among such values as equity, competence, and liberty. Minimizing sectors, and hence hierarchies, allows for more uniformity in practices and rewards. The single formal system composed of one type of institution gives greater strength to "coercive comparisons," in which "have-nots" exercise strong leverage for equity against the "haves," the less-noble against the noble. But the limited-sector system, with little hierarchy, also seems particularly vulnerable to overload in activities and to conflict among tasks. It is susceptible to structural insufficiency in completing work, as activities multiply and more people seek to be served. New functions crowd in upon old functions, as when the burdens of mass teaching and counseling in comprehensive universities absorb time and resources formerly allotted to research and advanced training. Also, what should and should not be done becomes institutionalized in the expectations and powers of the established interests in the single type of institution, with certain activities then unserved. Hence, the limited-sector systems have difficulty in accommodating an increasingly wide and diverse range of activities.

Multisector systems seem more capable of handling heavy loads of activity and reducing conflict among contradictory operations. New clusters of activities are given to a separate type of institution, as in the creation of community colleges in the United States, University Institutes of Technology (IUTS) in France, The Open University in Great Britain, and regional technological institutes in Mexico. The norms of the old sectors are then not as coercive upon the new as they would be if the new cluster of activities were placed within the old. Hence, choice is increased and adaptability of the system enhanced. But as the extensive-sector system develops institutional hierarchy, it will thereby create certain inequalities in rewards. Competitive advantages and disadvantages become institutionalized. Hence, equity tends not to be well served, at least in the short run, and those who are primarily interested in the promotion of equality are offended.

The bearing of status hierarchies upon the competence of national systems is complicated indeed. As we will note again later, extreme hierarchy has had the great advantage of guaranteeing talent to the top public and private offices. It is hardly a bad thing to have competent civil servants, but such hierarchy usually leads to some "hardening of the arteries," with major unanticipated difficulties. Japanese researchers have shown that a monopoly of top status at the universities of Tokyo and Kyoto has led to serious problems of nepotism. While producing a small output of top-quality people for government and industry, the system developed closed circles within itself that restricted a larger production of both trained people and quality research. Academic inbreeding became characteristic, as high as 100 percent at times in key faculties at the University of Tokyo. The small, closed subsystems virtually froze the life chances of university graduates and future academics at about the age of eighteen, the time of entry to the universities, with achievement criteria that had replaced ascriptive criteria in Japanese society ironically replaced at that point by precise ascription: "Achievement came to transform itself into ascription after the eighteen-plus [examinations]. After that time one's evaluation depends on the name of institutions to which he belongs or from which he graduates rather than achievement or merit," a phenomena referred to as "achieved ascription."

These aspects of the top of the Japanese hierarchy contribute heavily to two basic features of student life in that country: for aspiring young people, it is critical to get into the top subsystems, and hence the preuniversity years have become a long period of intense study capped by an "examination hell"; at the same time, the university years are relatively relaxed academically, since entry is what counts, and student energies are thereby freed to flow into political and other extracurricular activities.

Hidden Sectors. In a fourfold scheme of differentiation, we have located two forms within institutions and two within the system at large. But such analytical lines should not obscure the ways in which one form shades into another, nor the simple fact that national systems may appear in different categories and as different types, with minor changes in definition. For example, private sectors take several forms, with some completely under private finance and control; others are supported mainly by governments but maintain private boards of trustees and the appearance of being private.

A national system such as Mexico's, with only about ten percent of its enrollment in private institutions, appears in the classification above as an instance of the third type; Brazil, counting a much larger proportion in the private sector, is clearly in the fourth category. But the Mexican private sector is much more completely private, on its own; the mammoth Brazilian private sector actually is quasi governmental. Hence, the two systems could be oppositely classified. Then, too, one major form of differentiation may serve as a substitute for another, particularly in the case of divisions within enterprises acting like sectors of the overall system. Sections of universities, as in the highly autonomous faculties in continental European universities, may function much like institutional sectors. For example, faculties of pedagogy operate with much autonomy inside Italian universities. When more teachers were needed in the 1960s, these faculties could swell considerably in size autonomously, much as if they constituted a separate teacher-training sector. In a sense, there are as many sectors as there are autonomous faculties operating with virtually direct budget allocations from central offices. When the university is but a holding company for faculties, considerable sector differentiation is hidden within its nominal unity.

This point comes up later in analyzing academic change, since one tendency in recent reform has been to compose "comprehensive universities" in which virtually all fields of study are brought under the umbrella of the university designation, but, at the same time, major parts have different subgroupings of subjects and different sublabels. The German *Gesamthochschulen* of the 1970s have constituted one such effort. A second and more thoroughgoing one has been the changes enacted in Sweden in the late 1970s to incorporate its small nonuniversity sector with universities—"comprehensivization" all the way, in line with the basic principle that all postsecondary education in the same location should form a single integrated institution. Even in American universities, which as a general class are relatively integrated, the college of agriculture or the school of medicine may be organizationally distant from the core arts and sciences faculty, with distinct financial arrangements. When countries lump much of higher education together in omnibus organizations, "sectors" will be hidden as sections.

The Loose Web of Academic Organization

The work of higher education is carried out in every country in a structure that decomposes tasks within and among institutions. Some elemental features of differentiation, preeminently those centered in disciplines, have wide currency. They flow across national boundaries and thereby become similar, to a considerable degree, across national systems. Systems "break out" the natural sciences, and within that large aggregate of tasks, they break out physics and chemistry and biology and major specialties thereof. But other features of differentiation, those centered on institutions, vary widely among nations, subject to particulars of origin and context. National systems thereby make the disciplines operational in such different forms as the chair and the department, the one-tier and the two-tier university, the single-sector and the multisector national system. Whatever the combination of sections and tiers within institutions, and sectors and hierarchies among them, the prevailing structure sets many of the problems of control and conditions all important issues of continuity and reform. Hence, an understanding of the basic structure becomes the necessary footing for better comprehension of a wide range of problems and issues. To study academic differentiation is not only to determine the academic division of labor in its specific operational settings but also to pursue the expression of academic values and the foundations of academic power.

As major social units, academic systems fall between "organization" and "society." They have a complexity of tasks that is more than we expect of organizations. Their institutional parts have an uncommon primacy, always allowed in some serious measure to wander organizationally in different directions, driven by the dynamics of individual fields. The parts have limited mutual influence. Hence, even at the institutional level, academic complexes are not well understood by means of models of integrated organizations that have been fixed in the public mind by long acquaintance with business firms and public bureaus. When those models depict a division of labor, they tell of a differentiation of tasks within an hierarchical complex under a single authority. The center holds; the top manages to dominate. But universities and colleges have become entities too diverse and fragmented to be thus comprehended; and the state, regional, and national entities that are the larger organized composites, quite loosely coupled when judged by any traditional idea of organization, vary even more from standard models. Such systems, formally organized or not, are loosely webbed sectors of the larger society, to be likened as much to the way societies are organized as they are to the means of integration in unitary organizations. In societal organization, the division of labor has long been viewed by leading thinkers as a specialization of autonomous social units. Further differentiation grows out of the dynamics of the individual segments and interaction among them as much as from top-down command or from simple bargaining among a few groups. Linking mechanisms operate that are overlooked or underutilized in explanations of how organizations perform as social actors: unplanned change looms large.

Because of the growing complexity of bodies of knowledge and related tasks, the division of academic labor is increasingly characterized by fragmentation within and among universities, colleges, and institutes. But this is not to say that national systems are falling apart, for there is much else that fragments and integrates. For one, as we shall now see, the beliefs of academic groups must be brought into the equations that determine an academic system, providing, as they do, a second primary dimension of organization.

Places of Inquiry

Burton R. Clark

Near the end of the twentieth century, little doubt remains that advanced nations move into a stage of development in which for individuals and organizations alike highly specialized and rapidly changing knowledge serves as a primary source of competence, intellectual energy, power, and wealth. Acquired mainly by means of organized study, this productive resource is rooted in training that develops problem-solving capabilities. Such schooling requires sustained investment in knowledge-creating capital: one or more sectors of society must develop substantial capacity to generate new knowledge and rapidly disseminate it. Only nations willing to serve as saving remnants for received wisdom and past virtue, and that alone, can ignore the modern need for a widening base of activities organized around inquiry, a base within which, in many forms, training for research continually expands.

As societies seek to develop an inquiring base, higher education is generally called to the fore. While much research is increasingly carried out in industry and other societal institutions, universities generally possess the best foundations and most effective methods for both long-run augmentation of the fund of knowledge and its distribution. Organized to develop and maintain operational communities of inquiry across many subjects, they are best positioned to train generations of inquiring minds in tandem with production of research results. Research universities constitute an important institutional pipeline to the future.

Centrality of Inquiry in the University Complex

Universities are uncommonly organized around ongoing flows of knowledge that are encapsulated in disciplines, professions, and interdisciplinary fields.[1] Caught up in those flows and the interest of their supporting groups, modern universities are also uncommonly dominated by a research outlook. Esteemed contributions to knowledge become the highest achievements for faculty; research-based degrees, notably the doctorate, become high attainments for students. Universities make a particular wager with knowledge within which a scientific or rational pursuit of truth develops its own morality, one that leads some participants and constituent groups to a particular sense of responsibility embedded in the scientific ethic and the academic calling.[2] While subject to intensifying political and bureaucratic controls and confronted with deepening demands for mass instruction and occupational relevance, these enterprises place at their core a sphere of intellect in which theoretical knowledge is highly valued.

The location of universities on a foundation of knowledge and inquiry remains a poorly understood phenomenon. The subject has been avoided in perspectives that locate universities' center of gravity in the realm of student development in first-degree (undergraduate) programs. Such perspectives have dominated popular and academic thought in the United States and increasingly come to the fore in other countries as concern has risen about the quality and cost of mass higher education.[3] When observers and researchers concentrate on the admission, retention, and attainment of first-degree students, research activities typically are either ignored or viewed negatively as a distraction from teaching and learning. Teaching is seen as the central activity of academic staff, despite the clear evidence that in leading universities, and in other emulating universities and colleges caught in the tides of academic drift, research comes first in the reward systems of professors, basic units, and entire institutions—and, we can add, the academic profession generally. In the American case, the student-centered approach has fixated not only on undergraduates but also on the issue of liberal or general education, thereby overlooking the extensive work of the universities in advanced degree programs in letters and science fields and graduate professional schools, which together, as we have seen, account in major U. S. universities for over half of faculty time, *and* of total expenditures, *and*, in many leading private universities, even of students. Thus limited, the student perspective has been unable to grasp the diversity of tasks and complexity of organization that inhere in modern universities. Largely ignoring the central role of research activity and research training, analyses of student development have not sought to explain the three-way relationship between research, teaching, and learning.

A knowledge perspective stands in sharp contrast. It starts with the centrality of knowledge production, hence the primacy of inquiry, and pursues teaching and learning from that base. The institutional footholds of discovery are seen as foundation for virtually all else that goes on at advanced levels of university work in the basic disciplines and an increasing array of professional fields. At the same time, of course, a vast body of accumulated knowledge is at hand, available for instruction by teachers untouched by research activity. But even among those who purport to proffer the wisdom of the ages, and that alone, a restless spirit of critical analysis and revision typifies the academy. Embroiled in controversial interpretation, humanities professors treat revision of received doctrine as a scholarly form of discovery. In one form or another, social scientists become discovery oriented. Virtually without exception, academic fields seek to roll forward their modes of thinking and their bundles of knowledge. With inquiry as their focus, research universities increasingly look forward, not backward.

A perspective that emphasizes the development of knowledge must accommodate what at first glance is a contrary phenomenon: as a widening gamut of professions and semiprofessions develop specialized expertise, their recruits require more preparation and their established members more periodic retraining. More people then go on beyond the first major degree to take advanced vocational training that does not find its footing in intensive research activity. Graduate education in the United States, for example, as formulated by Geiger, has "two different faces. Study for the master's degree is largely oriented toward providing limited advanced knowledge of mostly practical fields. Business and education in fact account for half of all degrees. Doctoral study . . . is distinguished by the eventual production of an original piece of scholarship."[4] In the United States or elsewhere, as we have seen, it can hardly be otherwise. Research-based doctoral work does not remain the only advanced activity, or even numerically the predominant one. Just as mass involvement in undergraduate (preadvanced) programs followed historically the development of mass secondary education, mass graduate education in time follows in train. Vocationally oriented graduate programs flower in bewildering complexity as new programs seek to mix the training needs of numerous outside occupational specialties with relevant disciplinary knowledge. As a common trend among advanced national systems, the directly vocational side of advanced work expands in size and proportion; the great expansion of business studies and management training in Britain and on the European continent is a strong case in point. In the American system, as noted, master's degrees and professional degrees together, by a ratio of ten to one, numerically dominate the research-based Ph.D.

With this growth in vocational advanced education, research and research training are seemingly pushed aside. But only in part. The attitude of critical inquiry, broadly construed, steadily infiltrates the vocational programs that seem tailored entirely for teaching. A taught master's, as in Britain, has the public face of a program that with little or no regard to research transmits the codified knowledge of a professional specialty: only formalisms of the lecture and the book are apparently needed. But teaching that is innocent of the research attitude does not wear well in advanced professional training and does not long endure. Themselves educated in universities, the teaching staffs are aware of the power and prestige of research. They may well have encountered the subtle ingredients of tangible knowledge and tacit attitude characteristic of programs based on strong research foundations. They will at least have become aware of the instructional value of gathering students in seminars and laboratory-like settings, places where students can grasp in a first approximation what inquiry is about and how knowledge percolates back from the frontiers of relevant specialties. Proof of this virtually inescapable infiltration is not hard to find: the research attitude spread a long time ago into medicine, law, engineering, and agriculture; it is also now thoroughly embedded in schools of management, education, architecture, social work, nursing, and librarianship.

In short, the inquiring attitude cannot be bottled up in certain areas of advanced education and kept entirely out of others. Barriers can be erected against its wholesale diffusion and adoption by such means as heavy teaching loads, research-absent funding, and low unit-cost support. But in advanced university education, the genie of inquiry is everywhere out of the bottle. While preparation for research work is research centered, preparation for professional practice is increasingly research informed. In one profession after another, we find a deepening need for research-sensitive practitioners: if you cannot understand and effectively evaluate "the literature," you cannot keep up. Such leavening by the research attitude, while concentrated on tangible doctrine and technique, may suggest to vocational students that the research process contains a realm of tacit learning. Minimally, professional-field students introduced to modes of inquiry are less likely to accept uncritically and passively the "truth" as propounded and handed down in lecture and book by the professional expert claiming closed mastery of an established body of thought and technique.

At the end of the twentieth century, it is not unreasonable for systems of higher education to attempt to educate a third or more of the traditional university age group as far as the first major degree. Among an increasing share of those who reach that level, there then emerges in most countries a competitive advantage to be gained by pursuing higher studies or returning for advanced degrees after some time at work. And, along the line, beginning in the upper years of first-degree programs, if not sooner, there is advantage in knowing what researchers are about, to grasp at least in a general way their thought processes and methods and to be able to communicate with those fully invested in research. Students in strong research environments gain access to special bodies of knowledge, including, as this study has emphasized, tacit as well as tangible elements. If other advanced students are kept entirely away from research environments, they are denied access not only to powerful bundles of knowledge but also to styles of thought and practices of inquiry that are valuable tools of problem solving.

Hence, in seeking to absorb a research attitude into their own midsts, it is not irrational or simply a matter of narrow self-interest that professional school faculties in effect ape the sciences or the social sciences or even certain scholarly approaches found in history, philosophy, and linguistics. From the standpoint of widening access to knowledge, it is not irrational that nonuniversities should drift toward the research mentality of universities, even if their movement brings them only part of the way. As specialized knowledge becomes increasingly rarefied, continua of small differences in degree of research engagement, extending from research cores to practical peripheries, may serve to preserve contact among experts and between remote specialists and mainstream participants. Such linking contact is substantially weakened when sharp lines are drawn between types of institutions in an effort to keep research entirely out of vocational or undergraduate programs and to thereby confine half or more of postsecondary institutions to a posture of "teaching only." The struggle for access of the general citizenry to the knowledge of experts is aided by limited access in higher education of advanced students in professional fields, as well as preadvanced students who will go no further than the first major degree, to the thought styles of the academic tribes that most firmly possess the tools of the inquiring trade.

The Inevitability of Complexity and Contradiction

From amid the many conditions of fragmentation and integration of the research-teaching-study nexus set forth in chapters 6 and 7, several trends that dominate, in turn, the research system, the higher education system, and the funding system come together to create a swell of complex and contradictory relations in the joined world of science and university. Foremost is the enormous driving force of the specialization imperative that characterizes the research system internationally and virtually all academic disciplines individually. The steady decomposing of disciplines into specialties, and then of specialties into still more specialties, operates across universities as an uncontrollable self-amplifying phenomenon. Disciplinary subdivision is a powerful pressure for departmental substructuring. Even when existing specialties are recombined in a new interdisciplinary field, as in cognitive science and environmental studies, the ironic result is a new specialty that in the bloom of success becomes a program, a type of degree, and a unit of organization. Departments, faculty, and students come under unrelenting pressure to attend to ever more specific specialties, with advanced levels of instruction specifically in the line of fire. Disciplinary steerage is widespread and intense, a penetrating mode of influence whose magnitude and depth distinguishes universities from other types of organizations such as business firms and governmental bureaucracies. A relentless sophistication of the university's primary commodity is inescapable.

Second, the university complex is inescapably elaborated and diversified. Planners, administrators, and faculty in many countries, as we have seen, often seek to define and then to fund universities as similar and equal. Formal categories are even used to declare all higher education institutions to be universities and part of a single unified system: in the 1970s and 1980s, such nominal equality has been newly evident in systems that stretch from Sweden to Australia. But no matter how fervent the desire, similarity and parity are not the long-lasting result. Instead institutional dissimilarity and inequality grow as systems struggle to differentiate large clienteles, contain the insatiable appetite of research budgets, and control overall costs. Central to the division of labor that emerges is the extent of research investment in different institutions and the consequent balance of effort between research-based advanced education, on the one side, and preadvanced instruction and codified vocational programs, on the other. Institutions then increasingly range widely along continua that stretch from extremely research dominated to fully teaching devoted, from top- to bottom-heavy in the weight of program and degree levels that range from postdoctoral work to the two-year degree.

In short, diversity, not uniformity, is the master trend. The need to concentrate and hence to differentially distribute financial resources *and* personnel *and* equipment *and* students grows ever stronger as higher education systems grow in population size and in coverage of cognitive territories. The institutional division of labor can no more be stopped, let alone reversed, than the division of labor in society. Hence the thought that all institutions of higher education can be equal becomes a species of utopianism. If differentiation is not effected among institutions, it will take place within them, producing ever more polyglot universities that call for heroic internal management to simply maintain peaceful relations among disparate factions and somehow insert a capacity for spontaneous change.

Third, the funding system moves in the direction of a diversity of sources for the individual university, with single-source support replaced by multiple governmental and nongovernmental channels. Central and provincial (state) governments everywhere have made clear that they will not offer full institutional support for ever-expandable mass higher education and especially for an increasingly intensified research enterprise. Greater pluralism in funding sources and channels is then inescapable: more central mission agencies, research councils, provincial and local public agencies, business firms, private foundations, professional associations, and individual benefactors and contributors. Such diversification has replaced lump-sum funding as the best guarantor of university autonomy; many partial dependencies offer better protection than full dependency on a single patron. University self-steerage comes to depend on fund-raising capabilities that stretch from lobbying numerous central ministries to manipulating student tuition and fees to competing for research grants to recovering costs on hospital services to convincing wealthy supporters that they should specify the university as a beneficiary in their wills. Funding diversification elaborates the business side of university affairs, encouraging the deployment of midmanagement staff in the form of development officers, public relations experts, and administrators in charge of auxiliary services.

The trends of knowledge specialization, university differentiation, and diversified funding lead inexorably to greater complexity and contradiction in the operation of individual universities and the university complex as a whole. Modern academic knowledge itself cannot be other than confused and confusing: in Peter Scott's terms, the academy's chief commodity "has become diffuse, opaque, incoherent, centrifugal."[5] Mass systems, quasi-universal in tendency, move in the direction of any person, any study, any research, any service. Despite widespread effort among officials, administrators, and academics to simplify and clarify, purposes multiply and become more ambiguous. Pushed and pulled in many directions, universities are less and less likely to be characterized by the tight linkage of unitary organization and more by the loose coupling characteristic of federations. Inherently centrifugal along its base of operations, the comprehensive university is a very complicated and generally loosely joined organism. The thrust of complexity is to turn universities into multiversities and then into conglomerates.

With deepening complexity, universities become unhappily more problematic. The institution that has three, five, or ten times the funds, staff, and students that it had a quarter- or a half-century ago is not simply the old institution written large. Transactions seemingly grow geometrically, along with much greater internal division and many more external ties. Operations become an impenetrable maze; bureaucracy grows, collegial clusters diverge. Critically, university operations become much more difficult for outsiders to perceive and understand. Old images of unifying central values and institutional simplicity no longer apply to the fast-changing reality of opaque complexity. Embedded incoherence promotes a sense of ongoing "crisis."

Much strain in modern research universities necessarily follows from the contradictory and confusing thrusts of the three primary efforts frequently noted in this study: education for the professions, or specialized vocational training more broadly; general or liberal higher education, where learning may be seen as an end in itself; and research and research training, the area of university operation on which this study has concentrated.[6] As we have seen, the university complex of each nation tends to tilt in one direction or another among these efforts, exhibiting strengths that beget weaknesses. Critically, each task becomes more varied with the passage of time. Research and professional education clearly become more diversified. As Ben-David has argued persuasively, general education must also take many forms: "Since general education has to cater to the largest variety of students, it can be successful only if there are different programs and constant change and experimentations."[7] Variety within and among universities is needed which is adaptive to the particular needs of different student publics; in particular, introductory levels of higher education are pulled in opposite directions. Clienteles coming from other than strict secondary schools, with attendant need for "remediation" or at least new approaches in teaching, pull the early years of university work toward a helping or developmental orientation that has long been more characteristic of secondary education, while the need to align preadvanced with advanced programs together with the specialized inclinations of academic staff pull teaching toward the focused study characteristic of the advanced levels. Indeed, in line with the latter bent, a liberal education arguably should incorporate an attitude of critical inquiry best acquired in specialized study, a strength of the British commitment to the specialized undergraduate degree.

If the main commodity of higher education—knowledge—becomes more diffuse, opaque, incoherent, and centrifugal and basic educational tasks more complicated and contradictory, then the struggle of various interest groups within universities and between them and external groups is bound to widen and intensify. As overarching values recede as the basis for trust and integration, the political struggle of faction against faction for resources and rewards is emboldened. In response, to contain conflict and provide some minimal clarity of purpose, the coordination of organizational structures and cultures takes on heightened importance. It is no simple matter in the mass university to commit effort in three or more major directions that are not mutually supportive; to fashion acceptable channels that constrain the interest group struggle; to provide accountability among basic units strongly impelled to self-steer; and to assert symbolic ties that bind the many parts into a whole.

The problem of responding to inevitable complexity and contradiction is not one of philosophical reconciliation of ideas. It is overwhelmingly a problem of organization, of structuring and restructuring of the university and the university complex within which the relationship of research activities to teaching and learning is always in issue. In one fashion or another, deliberately or unconsciously, the nexus highlighted in this study is organizationally sorted out.

The Essential Compatibility of Research and Teaching

The way that universities have been transformed into places of inquiry during the last century and a half has shown that Humboldt's perceptions were acute: research and teaching can be integrated and made to serve each other. Research itself can be a highly efficient and effective form of teaching; when it also becomes a mode of learning, it can serve as the integrative vehicle for an intimate fusing of teaching and study. The resulting three-way nexus is the great operational secret of the well-ordered university laboratory in a scientific field and of the teaching-research seminar in the humanities and social sciences in which professors and students pursue a similar approach to research or a common set of research problems.

Once the possibilities and outcomes of a fruitful connection between research activities and the activities of advanced teaching and learning are grasped, the core strain in modern universities takes on a different light. In the standard view, the main conflict in faculty tasks lies between teaching and research. But the critical fault line actually runs between preadvanced instruction that presents codified knowledge and may operate at some distance from research and advanced teaching and advanced teaching closely linked to research. In American terms, the fault line is between undergraduate teaching, especially that devoted to the first two years of study, and graduate teaching, especially that found in doctoral programs. The first is not far from secondary school teaching; in contrast, the second often contains elements of at-the-bench interaction between expert and neophyte and a form of learning by doing that is found in research institutes inside and outside the university.

As systems of higher education both shift from elite to mass participation and incorporate ever more sophisticated knowledge, an incompatibility thesis seemingly acquires greater public acceptance and stronger voice in the academy. In the American system, it has for some time been voiced frequently and with much vigor. When professors in universities are not in the undergraduate classroom, they are viewed as having run off somewhere to do research, not recognizing that they also teach graduate students and do research in their company. The time devoted to individual advanced students, especially on doctoral dissertations, is not counted as teaching time. The escape-from-teaching belief was also strengthened in American circles during the 1980s by especially contentious battles over the curricular content of general education, fixated on the "canon" located primarily in a few literature and history courses, that managed to radically downplay the importance of the sciences in modern general education as well as to ignore advanced programs. The call for more attention to teaching and less to research that periodically enlivens the American scene has become in effect a call for diversion of commitment and energy from advanced to preadvanced levels of instruction. Research is viewed as a wrongheaded and dysfunctional distraction. The motto for reform becomes less research, more attention to undergraduate teaching and general education.

As higher education systems differentiate into a range of research-oriented and teaching-centered institutions, the incompatibility thesis also finds comfort in aggregate statistics about what most faculty do and think. Summary numbers lump together diverse settings and become a sum of opposite stories. For example, during the 1980s, conclusions from national surveys in the diverse American setting were drawn that relatively few faculty members actively engage in research, that those who do publish research results are coerced to do so by institutional pressures—"publish or perish"—and that most faculty members prefer to concentrate their energies on teaching rather than on research. But when the global figures are disaggregated, the appropriate conclusion about whether American academics find teaching and research to be compatible or incompatible is that outside of institutional settings where they are expected to teach only undergraduates and to be in the classroom twelve or fifteen or eighteen hours a week, they combine teaching and research in the apportioning of their time and do so by personal preference. How much and how they do so is heavily conditioned by institutional locale. Notably, faculty in the best undergraduate-centered liberal arts colleges in the United States reported research involvement, viewing it as necessary for effective undergraduate teaching in both the short run and the long run and essential for their personal development, standing, and identity as productive academics.[8] Such academics know something that outsiders rarely see: research and teaching are compatible, even in undergraduate programs and even when defined in terms that largely leave out the close fusing of the two in graduate forms of research-based teaching and study.

The zest for research widely found in both universities and liberal arts colleges in the American system is in many ways even more widespread in other leading national systems of higher education that, coming later to mass higher education, have not gone as far in separating teaching-dominated institutions. From Finland to Australia, and across the other major university systems reviewed here, the assumption has remained strong within and outside the national system that a large share of professors, if not all, should be engaged in research as much as a third or a half of the time. The research commitment is viewed as normal, rational, and preferable. But official preferences change when costs get in the way and greatly expanded instruction of beginning and intermediate students comes to the fore. Then the views of normalcy and rationality shift somewhat from research activity for all staff to its concentration in certain institutions and virtual elimination in others. The view that research and teaching are incompatible and ought to be separated then serves two practical and pressing demands: it helps to legitimate cost-cutting measures in line with the edict that "we cannot afford to support research in all universities and colleges"; it is also used to protect preadvanced programs—"we need to have more academics spend more of their time teaching the beginning students"—which also serves to contain costs.

But the case remains strong that even for preadvanced programs, from the entry year onward, student participation in a research environment can be a highly appropriate form of teaching and learning. Regardless of its specific nature, a research project involves a process of framing questions, developing reliable methods to find answers, and then weighing the relevance of the answers and the significance of the questions. Not only is student research activity a scholarly process for defining questions and finding answers but it is clearly also a way of inducing critical thinking and developing inquiring minds. Notably, it can be an active mode of learning in which the instructor provides a frame and an attitude but does not offer answers to be written down, memorized, and given back. Even when resources and setting do not permit an actual plunging of preadvanced students into projects, small or large, instructors who bring a research attitude into their teaching are likely to exhibit key features of the processes of inquiry. Good pedagogical reasons abound why academics, when told they must only teach, resist a flight from research.

The commandment to do research most fully takes over at advanced levels of university instruction in the basic disciplines. The nexus on which we have concentrated then becomes central. Our inquiry has identified essential conditions for its strong expression, for a full integration of advanced teaching and study with research perspectives and methods and with the learning that is bottled up within the working knowledge of academic disciplines. As concluded in chapter 7, what is finally most critical is the particular construction of on-the-ground local contexts in which faculty and students interact. The optimal setting can be likened to a double helix; it is composed of intertwined strands of teaching and research, institutionally expressed as a teaching group and a research group. The setting for students then takes the shape of a binary group. In a blended arrangement, their life of study extends simultaneously, or in a defined sequence of course work and dissertation, into a teaching setting that is intensively research oriented and into a research setting that is infused with instruction. The binary group is an anchor to the wind that holds the university against the tides of research drift and teaching drift. It counters the specific interests of government and industry that would otherwise place research in one isolated setting and teaching in another—and leave students to find their way to these different locations and to somehow bring them together.

When disciplines were new and simply composed, as was the case in many fields during the nineteenth century, the research group alone could possibly encompass all necessary teaching. Even a single mentor could hold in his or her mind and impart directly and indirectly to research apprentices the existing small sum of tangible disciplinary knowledge, along with the tacit knowledge that the research group unconsciously conveys. But when disciplines have become epistemologically complex, as in most fields in the late twentieth century, the single strand is not enough to flesh out the research-teaching-study nexus. In response, universities tend to develop the capacity to sustain a teaching strand and interweave it with the operational modes of research groups. That is the core of the graduate school phenomenon.

As the teaching group and the research group combine into a binary group, they become the chartered molecule in the university organism for a modern fusion of teaching and learning with intensified research. When well interrelated, these twin strands serve as a focal point of paired bases whereby science is strongly expressed in the educational work of higher education and, in turn, higher education is operationally expressed in the work of science. The binary group is the centerpiece of the infrastructure by which modern universities are best made into places of inquiry.

Notes

1. An earlier formulation of the perspective developed here, stressing knowledge as the common commodity of higher education, may be found in Clark, *Higher Education System*, chap. 1, "Knowledge," and passim.
2. For an illuminating discussion of actual and possible moral effects of the scientific calling and its "wager with knowledge," see Scaff, *Fleeing the Iron Cage*, 112–120.
3. The student development line of research became a veritable academic industry in the United States, apace diffuse public and academic concerns about the many confusing effects of undergraduate programs. A review and synthesis of the American literature on student development in the undergraduate years published in 1970 identified 1,500 studies carried out up to that time. A second encompassing review published in 1991 found an additional 2,600 studies. At the same time, graduate programs and their effects on students have gone virtually unobserved and unreported. See Feldman and Newcomb, *Impact of College on Students*, and Pascarella and Terenzini, *How College Affects Students*.
4. Geiger, "Introduction, Section II: The Institutional Fabric," 1034.
5. Scott, "Knowledge's Outer Shape, Inner Life," *THES*, August 16, 1991, 12.
6. See particularly, Ben-David, *Centers of Learning*.
7. Ibid., 91.
8. See Clark, *Academic Life*, 73–89.

Bibliography

Allen, G. C. *The Japanese Economy*. New York: St. Martin's Press, 1981.

Amano, Ikuo. "Continuity and Change in the Structure of Japanese Higher Education." In *Changes in the Japanese University: A Comparative Perspective*, edited by William K. Cummings, Ikuo Amano, and Kazuyuki Kitamura, 10–39. New York: Praeger, 1979.

_____. *Education and Examination in Modern Japan* (Shiken no Shakai-shi). Translated by William K. Cummings and Fumiko Cummings. Tokyo: University of Tokyo Press, 1990.

Ashford, Douglas E. *Policy and Politics in France: Living with Uncertainty*. Philadelphia: Temple University Press, 1982.

Ball, Christopher, "The Merging of the PCFC and the UFC: Probable, Desirable, or Inevitable?" *Higher Education Quarterly* 45, no. 2 (1991); 117–124.

Bartholomew, James R. *The Formation of Science in Japan: Building a Research Tradition*. New Haven: Yale University Press, 1989.

Beauchamp, Edward R., and Richard Rubinger. *Education in Japan: A Source Book*. New York: Garland Publishing, 1989.

Becher, Tony. *Academic Tribes and Territories: Intellectual Enquiry and the Cultures of Disciplines*. Milton Keynes, U.K.: Society for Research into Higher Education and Open University Press, 1989.

_____. "Graduate Education in Britain: The View from the Ground." In *The Research Foundations of Graduate Education: Germany, Britain, France, United States, Japan*, edited by Burton R. Clark, 115–153. Berkeley, Los Angeles, and Oxford: University of California Press, 1993.

_____(ed.). *British Higher Education*. London: Allen and Unwin, 1987.

Becher, Tony, Jack Embling, and Maurice Kogan. *Systems of Higher Education: United Kingdom*. New York: International Council for Educational Development, 1977.

Becher, Tony, and Maurice Kogan. *Process and Structure in Higher Education*. London: Heinemann, 1980.

Ben-David, Joseph. "The Universities and the Growth of Science in Germany and the United States." *Minerva* 7 (1968): 1–35.

_____. *The Scientist's Role in Society: A Comparative Study*. Englewood Cliffs, N.J.: Prentice-Hall, 1971.

_____. *Centers of Learning: Britain, France, Germany, United States*. New York: McGraw-Hill, 1977.

Ben-David, Joseph, and Abraham Zloczower. "Universities and Academic Systems in Modern Societies." *European Journal of Sociology* 3 (1962): 45–84.

Bendix, Reinhard. *Max Weber: An Intellectual Portrait*. Garden City, N. Y.: Doubleday, 1960.

Benjamin, T. Brooke. "Overladen with Honours." *Times Higher Education Supplement*, January 17, 1992, 18.

Berdahl, Robert. "Coordinating Structures: The UGC and US State Co-ordinating Agencies." In *The Structure of Governance of Higher Education*, edited by Michael Shattock, 68–106. At the University, Guildford, Surrey: Society for Research into Higher Education, 1983.

Berelson, Bernard. *Graduate Education in the United States*. New York: McGraw-Hill, 1960.

Bernstein, Richard. *Fragile Glory: A Portrait of France and the French*. New York: Alfred A. Knopf, 1990.

Bertilsson, Margareta. "From University to Comprehensive Higher Education: On the Widening Gap between '*Lehre und Leben*.'" Stockholm: Studies of Higher Education and Research, Council for Studies of Higher Education, no. 1, 1991.

Beyerchen, Alan. "On the Stimulation of Excellence in Wilhelmian Science." In *Another Germany: A Reconsideration of the Imperial Era*, edited by Jack R. Dukes and Joachim Remak, 139–168. Boulder, Colo.: Westview Press, 1988.

Bienaymé, Alain. *Systems of Higher Education: France*. New York: International Council for Educational Development, 1978.

Block, Hans-Jürgen. "Higher Education in the Federal Republic of Germany: Facts, Trends, and Policies." Unpublished paper, 1989.

_____. "The University System in Transition: Possibilities and Limitations of Universities in the 'Steady-State.'" In *The Research System in Transition*, edited by S. E. Cozzens et al, 35–50. Dordrecht: Kluwer Academic Publishers, 1990.

Bowen, William G., and Neil L. Rudenstine. *In Pursuit of the Ph.D.* Princeton: Princeton University Press, 1992.

Brubacher, John S., and Willis Rudy. *Higher Education in Transition: A History of American Colleges and Universities, 1636–1968*. New York: Harper and Row, 1968.

Campbell, Donald T. "A Tribal Model of the Social System Vehicle Carrying Scientific Knowledge." *Knowledge* 1, no. 2 (1979): 181–201.

Campbell, John Creighton. "Japanese Budget *Baransu*." In *Modern Japanese Organization and Decision-Making*, edited by Ezra F. Vogel, 71–100. Berkeley, Los Angeles, and London: University of California Press, 1975.

Carnegie Foundation for the Advancement of Teaching. *A Classification of Institutions of Higher Education: 1987 Edition*. Princeton: Princeton University Press, 1987.

Carrier, Denis, and Frans A. van Vught. "Government and Curriculum Innovation in France." In *Governmental Strategies and Innovation in Higher Education*, edited by Frans A. van Vught, 143–167. London: Jessica Kingsley Publishers, 1989.

Carswell, John. *Government and the Universities in Britain: Programme and Performance 1960–1980*. Cambridge: Cambridge University Press, 1985.

Cazenave, P. "Financing of Institutions." In *The Encyclopedia of Higher Education*, edited by Burton R. Clark and Guy Neave. Vol. 2, *Analytical Perspectives*, 1367–1376. Oxford: Pergamon Press, 1992.

Cheit, Earl F., and Theodore E. Lobman. *Foundations and Higher Education: Grant Making from Golden Years through Steady State*. Berkeley: Carnegie Council on Policy Studies in Higher Education, 1979.

Clark, Burton R. *The Higher Education System: Academic Organization in Cross-National Perspective*. Berkeley, Los Angeles, and London: University of California Press, 1983.

_____. *The Academic Life: Small Worlds, Different Worlds.* Princeton: Carnegie Foundation for the Advancement of Teaching and Princeton University Press, 1987.

_____. "Is California the Model for OECD Futures?" In *The OECD, the Master Plan, and the California Dream,* edited by Sheldon Rothblatt, 61–77. Berkeley: Center for Studies in Higher Education, University of California, Berkeley, 1992.

_____, ed. *The Research Foundation of Graduate Education: German, Britain, France, United States, Japan.* Berkeley, Los Angeles, and London: University of California Press, 1993.

Clark, Terry Nichols. *Prophets and Patrons: The French University and the Emergence of the Social Sciences.* Cambridge: Harvard University Press, 1973.

Cole, Jonathan R. *Fair Science: Women in the Scientific Community.* New York: Free Press, 1979.

Committee of Vice-Chancellors and Principals (CVCP). *The State of the Universities.* London: CVCP, 1991.

Committee on Higher Education Report (Robbins Report). Cmnd. 2154, H.M.S.O. 1963.

Conrad, Clifton F., Jennifer Grant Haworth, and Susan Bolyard Millar. *A Silent Success: Master's Education in the United States.* Baltimore: Johns Hopkins University Press, 1993.

Coser, Lewis A. *Refugee Scholars in America: Their Impact and Their Experiences.* New Haven: Yale University Press, 1984.

Crane, Diana. *Invisible Colleges: Diffusion of Knowledge in Scientific Communities.* Chicago: University of Chicago Press, 1972.

Crosland, Anthony. In Edward Boyle and Anthony Crosland, *The Politics of Education,* edited by Maurice Kogan. Harmondsworth, Middlesex, England: Penguin Books, 1971.

Crozier, Michel. *The Bureaucratic Phenomenon.* Chicago: University of Chicago Press, 1964.

_____. *The Stalled Society.* New York: Viking Press, 1973.

_____. *Strategies for Change: The Future of French Society.* Cambridge: MIT Press, 1982.

Crozier, Michel, and Erhard Friedberg. *Actors and Systems: The Politics of Collective Action.* Chicago: University of Chicago Press, 1980.

DiMaggio, Paul J., and Walter W. Powell. "The Iron Cage Revisited: Institutional Isomorphism and Collective Rationality in Organizational Fields." *American Sociological Review* 48 (April 1985): 147–160.

Dore, Ronald P., and Mari Sako. *How the Japanese Learn to Work.* London: Routledge, 1989.

Durand-Prinborgne, C. "France." In *The Encyclopedia of Higher Education,* edited by Burton R. Clark and Guy Neave. Vol. 1. *National Systems of Higher Education,* 217–224. Oxford: Pergamon Press, 1992.

Elzinga, Aant. "Research, Bureaucracy, and the Drift of Epistemic Criteria." In *The University Research System: The Public Policies of the Home of Scientists,* edited by Björn Wirtrock and Aant Elzinga, 191–220. Stockholm: Almquist & Wiksell International, 1985.

Eustace, Rowland. "United Kingdom." In *The Encyclopedia of Higher Education,* edited by Burton R. Clark and Guy Neave. Vol. 1. *National Systems of Higher Education,* 760–777. Oxford: Pergamon Press, 1992.

Eustace, Rowland, and Graeme C. Moodie. "CNAA: Case for the Preservation." *Times Higher Education Supplement,* March 6, 1992.

Farant, John H. "Central Control of the University Sector." In *British Higher Education,* edited by Tony Becher, 29–52. London: Allen & Unwin, 1987.

Feldman, Kenneth A., and Theodore M. Newcomb. *The Impact of College on Students.* Vol. 1. *An Analysis of Four Decades of Research.* San Francisco: Jossey-Bass, 1970.

Fermi, Laura. *Illustrious Immigrants.* 2d ed. Chicago: University of Chicago Press, 1971.

Fleck, Ludwik. *Genesis and Development of a Scientific Fact.* Chicago: University of Chicago Press, 1979. (Originally published in German, 1935.)

Frackmann, Edgar. "Resistance to Change or No Need for Change? The Survival of German Higher Education in the 1990s." *European Journal of Education* 25, no. 2 (1990): 187–202.

Freeland, Richard M. *Academia's Golden Age: Universities in Massachusetts 1945–1990.* New York: Oxford University Press, 1992.

Friedberg, Erhard, and Christine Musselin. "The Academic Profession in France." In *The Academic Profession: National, Disciplinary, and Institutional Settings,* edited by Burton R. Clark, 93–122. Berkeley, Los Angeles, and London: University of California Press, 1987.

Fruton, Joseph S. *Contrasts in Scientific Style: Research Groups in the Chemical and Biochemical Sciences.* Philadelphia: American Philosophical Society, 1990.

Garvin, David A. *The Economics of University Behavior.* New York: Academic Press, 1980.

Geiger, Roger L. "Reform and Restraint in Higher Education: The French Experience, 1865–1914." Working Paper no. 2, Higher Education Research Group, Yale University, October 1975.

_____. *Private Sectors in Higher Education: Structure, Function, and Change in Eight Countries.* Ann Arbor: University of Michigan Press, 1986.

_____. *To Advance Knowledge: The Growth of American Research Universities, 1900–1940.* New York: Oxford University Press, 1986.

_____. "Historical Development of the American Research University." Paper presented at the annual meeting of the American Association for the

Advancement of Science, San Francisco, January 16, 1989.

_____. "Introduction, Section II: The Institutional Fabric of the Higher Education System." In *The Encyclopedia of Higher Education,* edited by Burton R. Clark and Guy Neave. Vol. 2. *Analytical Perspectives,* 1031–1047. Oxford: Pergamon Press, 1992.

_____. *Research and Relevant Knowledge: American Research Universities Since World War II.* Oxford: Oxford University Press, 1993.

Gellert, Claudius. "The German Model of Research and Advanced Education." In *The Research Foundations of Graduate Education: Germany, France, Britain, United States, Japan,* edited by Burton R. Clark, 5–44. Berkeley, Los Angeles, and London: University of California Press, 1993.

_____. "The Conditions of Research Training in Contemporary German Universities." In *The Research Foundations of Graduate Education: Germany, France, Britain, United States, Japan,* edited by Burton R. Clark, 45–66. Berkeley, Los Angeles, and London: University of California Press, 1993.

"German Universities Bursting at the Seams." *Science,* vol. 243, March 17, 1989, 1427.

Gerth, H. H., and C. Wright Mills, eds. *From Max Weber: Essays in Sociology.* New York: Oxford University Press, 1946.

Gilpin, Robert. *France in the Age of the Scientific State.* Princeton: Princeton University Press, 1968.

Glazer, Judith S. *The Master's Degree: Tradition, Diversity, Innovation.* ASHE-ERIC Higher Education Research Report no. 6, 1986. Washington, D. C.: Association for the Study of Higher Education, 1986.

Goldberg, Pierre. "The University System in France." In *Funding Higher Education: A Six-Nation Analysis,* edited by Lyman A. Glenny, 25–51. New York: Praeger, 1979.

Guin, Jacques. "The Reawakening of Higher Education in France." *European Journal of Education* 25, no. 2 (1990): 123–145.

Gumport, Patricia J. "Graduate Education and Organized Research in the United States." In *The Research Foundations of Graduate Education: Germany, Britain, France, United States, Japan,* edited by Burton R. Clark, 225–259. Berkeley, Los Angeles, and London: University of California Press, 1993.

_____. "Graduate Education and Research Imperatives: Views from American Campuses." In *The Research Foundations of Graduate Education: Germany, Britain, France, United States, Japan,* edited by Burton R. Clark, 261–293. Berkeley, Los Angeles, and London: University of California Press, 1993.

Hackett, Edward J. "Science as a Vocation in the 1990s." *Journal of Higher Education* 61, no. 3 (1990): 241–279.

Hackman, Judith Dozier. "Power and Centrality in the Allocation of Resources in Colleges and Universities." *Administrative Science Quarterly* 30 (1985): 61, 77.

Hagstrom, Warren. *The Scientific Community.* New York: Basic Books, 1965.

Halsey, A. H. *Decline of Donnish Dominion: The British Academic Professions in the Twentieth Century.* Oxford: Clarendon Press, 1992.

Halsey, A. H. and M. A. Trow. *The British Academics.* Cambridge: Harvard University Press, 1971.

Harrold, R. "Resource Allocation." In *The Encyclopedia of Higher Education,* edited by Burton R. Clark and Guy Neave. 2: 1464–1476. Oxford: Pergamon Press, 1992.

Hearnden, Arthur. *Education in the Two Germanies.* Boulder, Colo.: Westview Press, 1976.

Henkel, Mary, and Maurice Kogan. "Research Training and Graduate Education: The British Macro Structure." In *The Research Foundations of Graduate Education: Germany, Britain, France, United States, Japan,* edited by Burton R. Clark, 71–114. Berkeley, Los Angeles, and London: University of California Press, 1993.

Heyck, Thomas William. "The Idea of a University in Britain, 1870–1970." *History of European Ideas* 8, no. 2 (1987): 205–219.

Hirsh, Wendy. "Postgraduate Training of Researchers." In *The Future of Research,* edited by Geoffrey Oldham, 190–209. At the University, Guildford, Surrey: Society for Research into Higher Education, 1982.

Hoch, Paul K. "The Reception of Central European Refugee Physicists of the 1930s: U.S.S.R., U.K., U. S. A." *Annals of Science,* vol. 40, 1983, 217–246.

Hoffman, Stanley. "Paradoxes of the French Political Community." In *In Search of France,* edited by Stanley Hoffman, 1–117. Cambridge: Harvard University Press, 1963.

Hofstadter, Richard, and Walter P. Metzger. *The Development of Academic Freedom in the United States.* New York: Columbia University Press, 1955.

Hogan, J. V. "Graduate Schools: The Organisation of Graduate Education." ESRC Policy Document. Warwick: Center for Educational Development Appraisal and Research, University of Warwick, 1993. Occasional Paper.

Holmes, Frederic L. "The Complementarity of Teaching and Research in Liebig's Laboratory." In *Science in Germany: The Intersection of Institutional and Intellectual Issues,* edited by Kathryn M. Olesko, 121–164. Philadelphia: History of Science Society, 1989. *Osiris,* vol. 3.

Hough, J. R. "Finance." In *The Encyclopedia of Higher Education,* edited by Burton R. Clark and Guy Neave. 2: 1353–1358. Oxford: Pergamon Press, 1992.

Huber, Ludwig. "A Field of Uncertainty: Postgraduate Studies in the Federal Republic of Germany."

European Journal of Education 21, no. 3 (1986): 287–305.

Hüfner, Klaus. "Differentiation and Competition in Higher Education: Recent Trends in the Federal Republic of Germany." *European Journal of Education* 22, no. 22 (1987): 133–143.

Hughes, H. Stuart. *The Sea Change: The Migration of Social Thought, 1930–65.* New York: Harper & Row, 1975.

Humboldt, Wilhelm von. "On the Spirit and the Organizational Framework of Intellectual Institutions in Berlin." Translated by Edward Shils. *Minerva* 8 (1970): 242–250.

Ince, Martin. "Science Mandarins Back Elite Schools," *Times Higher Education Supplement,* 1992.

Institute for Scientific Information (ISI). "The Electrical Engineering Nifty 50: Top 25 Universities and Top 25 Industrial Firms Ranked by Citation Impact." *Science Watch* 2, no. 9 (October 1991): 1–8.

_____. "Chemistry That Counts: The Frontrunners in Four Fields." *Science Watch* 3, no. 3 (April 1992): 1–8.

_____. "Latest Citation Statistics Show U.S. Science Still Strong." *Science Watch* 3, no. 7 (Sept. 1992): 1–8.

International Consultative Committee on New Organizational Forms of Graduate Research Training. "Postgraduate Research Training Today: Emerging Structures for a Changing Europe." Ministry of Education and Science, The Netherlands, 1992.

Irvine, John, and Ben R. Martin. *Foresight in Science: Picking the Winners.* London: Frances Pinter, 1984.

_____. "International Comparisons of Scientific Performance Revisited." *Scientometrics* 15, nos. 5/6 (1989): 369–392.

Irvine, John, Ben R. Martin, and Phoebe A. Isard. *Investing in the Future: An International Comparison of Government Funding of Academic and Related Research.* Aldershot, Hants., England: Edward Elgar, 1990.

James, Estelle. "Cross-Subsidization in Higher Education: Does It Pervert Private Choice and Public Policy?" In *Private Education: Studies in Choice and Public Policy,* edited by Daniel C. Levy, 237–257. New York: Oxford, 1986.

_____. "Decision Processes and Priorities in Higher Education." In *The Economics of American Universities,* edited by Stephen A. Holmack and Eileen L. Collins, 77–106. Albany: State University of New York Press, 1990.

James, William, "The Ph.D. Octopus." In James, *Memoirs and Studies.* London: Longmans, Green, 1912.

Jencks, Christopher, and David Riesman. *The Academic Revolution.* Garden City, N. Y.: Doubleday, 1968.

Jensen, Jens-Jorgen. "Research and Teaching in the Universities of Denmark: Does Such an Interplay Really Exist?" *Higher Education* 17 (1988): 17–26.

Joas, Hans. "The Federal Republic of Germany: University and Career Opportunities for Young Scientists." *Higher Education Policy* 3, no. 1 (1990): 41–45.

Johnson, Harry G. "National Styles in Economic Research: The United States, The United Kingdom, Canada and Various European Countries." *Daedalus* (Spring 1973): 65–74.

Johnson, Jeffrey Allan. *The Kaiser's Chemists: Science and Modernization in Imperial Germany.* Chapel Hill: University of North Carolina Press, 1990.

Jones, David R. *The Origins of Civic Universities: Manchester, Leeds, & Liverpool.* London: Routledge, 1988.

Jungnickel, Christa, and Russell McCormmach. *Intellectual Mastery of Nature: Theoretical Physics from Ohm to Einstein.* Vol. 1. *The Torch of Mathematics 1800–1870.* Chicago: University of Chicago Press, 1986.

Kanigel, Robert. *Apprentice to Genius: The Making of a Scientific Dynasty.* New York: Macmillan, 1986.

Karl, Barry D., and Stanley N. Katz. "The American Private Philanthropic Foundation and the Public Sphere 1890–1930." *Minerva* 19 (1981): 236–270.

Kawashima, Tatsuo, and Fumihiro Maruyama. "The Education of Advanced Students in Japan: Engineering, Physics, Economics, and History." In *The Research Foundations of Graduate Education: Germany, Britain, France, United States, Japan,* edited by Burton R. Clark, 326–353. Berkeley, Los Angeles, and London: University of California Press, 1993.

Kehm, B., and U. Teichler. "Federal Republic of Germany." In *Encyclopedia of Higher Education,* edited by Burton R. Clark and Guy Neave. Vol. 1. *National Systems of Higher Education,* 240–260. Oxford: Pergamon, 1992.

Kerr, Clark. "A Critical Age in the University World: Accumulated Heritage versus Modern Imperatives." *European Journal of Education* 22, no. 2 (1987): 183–193.

_____. "The New Race to be Harvard or Berkeley or Stanford." *Change* (May/June 1991): 8–15.

Kimball, Bruce A. "Japanese Liberal Education: A Case Study in Its National Context." *Teachers College Record* 83, no. 2 (1981): 245–261.

Kitamura, Kazuyuki. "Mass Higher Education." In *Changes in the Japanese University: A Comparative Perspective,* edited by William K. Cummings, Ikuo Amano, and Kazuyaki Kitamura, 64–82. New York: Praeger, 1979.

Kogan, Maurice. "Implementing Expenditure Cuts in British Higher Education." Paper presented at the International Conference on Studies of Higher Education and Research Organisation, Dalerö, Sweden, 1983.

Kogan, Maurice, with E. Boyle and A. Crosland. *The Politics of Education.* Harmondsworth (U.K.): Penguin, 1971.

Koh, B. C. *Japan's Administrative Elite.* Berkeley, Los Angeles, and London: University of California Press, 1989.

Kubota, Akira. *Higher Civil Servants in Postwar Japan: Their Social Origins, Educational Backgrounds, and Career Patterns.* Princeton: Princeton University Press, 1969.

Latour, Bruno, and Steve Woolgar. *Laboratory Life: The Social Construction of Scientific Facts.* Beverly Hills, Calif.: Sage Publications, 1979.

Levy, Daniel C. *Higher Education and the State in Latin America: Private Challenges to Public Dominance.* Chicago: University of Chicago Press, 1986.

Lindsay, Alan W., and Ruth T. Neumann. *The Challenge for Research in Higher Education: Harmonizing Excellence and Utility.* ASHE-ERIC Higher Education Report no. 8. Washington, D. C.: Association for the Study of Higher Education, 1988.

Lundgren, Peter. "Differentiation in German Higher Education." In *The Transformation of Higher Learning 1860–1930: Expansion, Differentiation, Social Opening, and Professionalization in England, Germany, Russia, and the United States,* edited by Konrad H. Jarausch, 149–179. Chicago: University of Chicago Press, 1983.

McClelland, Charles E. *State, Society, and University in Germany 1700–1914.* Cambridge: Cambridge University Press, 1980.

Massow, Valentin V. *Organization and Promotion of Science in the Federal Republic of Germany.* Bonn: Inter Nationes, 1986.

Merton, Robert K. "The Matthew Effect in Science." In Robert K. Merton, *The Sociology of Science,* 439–459. Chicago: University of Chicago Press, 1972.

Metzger, Walter P. "The Academic Profession in the United States." In *The Academic Profession: National, Disciplinary, and Institutional Settings,* edited by Burton R. Clark, 123–208. Berkeley, Los Angeles, and London: University of California Press, 1987.

Ministry of Education, Science and Culture (Japan). *Statistical Abstract of Education, Science and Culture.* 1988 ed. Tokyo, 1988.

_____. *Statistical Abstract of Education, Science and Culture.* 1989 ed. Tokyo, 1989.

Mommsen, Wolfgang J. "The Academic Profession in the Federal Republic of Germany." In *The Academic Profession: National, Disciplinary, and Institutional Settings,* edited by Burton R. Clark, 60–92. Berkeley, Los Angeles, and London: University of California Press, 1987.

Morrell, J. B. "Science in the Universities: Some Reconsiderations." In *Solomon's House Revisited: The Organization and Institutionalization of Science,* edited by Tore Frängsmyr, 51–64. Canton, Mass.: Watson Publishing International, 1990. (Science History Publications, U.S.A.)

Moses, Ingrid. "Teaching, Research and Scholarship in Different Disciplines." *Higher Education* 19 (1990): 351–375.

Muir, William R. "The Historical Development of the Teacher-Researcher Ideal in Germany and the U.S.A." Paper presented at the Annual Meeting of the Association for the Study of Higher Education, San Diego, Calif. February 1987.

Nagai, Michio. *Higher Education in Japan: Its Take-Off and Crash.* Translated by Jerry Dusenbury. Tokyo: University of Tokyo Press, 1971.

Narin, Francis, and J. Davidson Frame. "The Growth of Japanese Science and Technology." *Science* 245 (August 11, 1989): 600–604.

National Research Council (U. S.). *Learning the R&D System: University Research in Japan and the United States.* Washington, D. C.: National Academy Press, 1989.

_____. *The Working Environment for Research in U. S. and Japanese Universities: Contrasts and Commanalities.* Washington, D. C.: National Academy Press, 1989.

National Science Board (U.S.). *Science and Engineering Indicators—1991.* Washington, D.C.: U.S. Government Printing Office, 1991. (NSB 91-1.)

National Science Foundation (U.S.). *Science and Engineering Education for the 1980s and Beyond.* Washington, D.C.: NSF, 1981.

_____. "Science Resources Studies Highlights." August 25, 1989. Washington, D.C.: NSF, 1989.

Nature. "Opinion: Tokyo's Brave Reform." Vol. 338, March 9, 1989, 100.

Neave, Guy. "Elite and Mass Higher Education in Britain: A Regressive Model?" *Comparative Education Review* 29, no. 3 (1985): 347–361.

_____. "France." In *The School and the University: An International Perspective,* edited by Burton R. Clark, 10–44. Berkeley, Los Angeles, and London: University of California Press, 1985.

_____. "On Preparing for Markets." *European Journal of Education* 25, no. 2 (1990): 114–116.

_____. "On Visions of the Market Place." *Higher Education Quarterly* 45, no. 1 (1991): 25–40.

_____. "Séparation de Corps: The Training of Advanced Students and the Organization of Research in France." In *The Research Foundations of Graduate Education: Germany, Britain, France, United States, Japan,* edited by Burton R. Clark, 159–191. Berkeley, Los Angeles, and London: University of California Press, 1993.

_____. "On Meat and Poissons: Exceptionalism and Similarity in the French Research Training System." Unpublished paper, 1992.

_____. "Utilitarianism by Increment: Disciplinary Differences and Higher Education Reform in France." Unpublished paper.

Neave, Guy, and Richard Edelstein. "The Research Training System in France: A Microstudy of Three Academic Disciplines." In *The Research*

Foundations of Graduate Education: Germany, Britain, France, United States, Japan, edited by Burton R. Clark, 192–220. Berkeley, Los Angeles, and London: University of California Press, 1993.

Neave, Guy, and Gary Rhoades. "The Academic Estate in Western Europe." In *The Academic Profession: National, Disciplinary and Institutional Settings,* edited by Burton R. Clark, 211–270. Berkeley, Los Angeles, and London: University of California Press, 1987.

Neumann, Ruth Theresia Rosa. "A Study of the Research Role within Academic Work." Ph.D. dissertation, Marquarie University, 1990.

Olesko, Kathryn M. *Physics as a Calling: Discipline and Practice in the Königsberg Seminar for Physics.* Ithaca: Cornell University Press, 1991.

Oleson, Alexandra, and John Voss, eds. *The Organization of Knowledge in Modern America, 1860–1920.* Baltimore: Johns Hopkins University Press, 1979.

Organisation for Economic Co-operation and Development (OECD). *The Future of University Research.* Paris: OECD, 1981.

_____. *Post-Graduate Education in the 1980s.* Paris: OECD, 1987.

_____. *Universities Under Scrutiny.* Paris: OECD, 1987.

_____. *Financing Higher Education.* Paris: OECD, 1990.

_____. *Main Science and Technology Indicators: 1992 (2).* Paris: OECD, 1992.

Palmer, R. R. "The University Idea in the Revolutionary Era." In *The Consortium on Revolutionary Europe, 1750–1850.* 1972 Proceedings, edited by Lee Kennett, 1–17. Gainesville: University of Florida Press, 1972.

_____. *The School of the French Revolution.* Princeton: Princeton University Press, 1975.

_____. *The Improvement of Humanity: Education and the French Revolution.* Princeton: Princeton University Press, 1985.

Pascarella, Ernest T., and Patrick T. Terenzini. *How College Affects Students: Findings and Insights from Twenty Years of Research.* San Francisco: Jossey-Bass, 1991.

Peisert, Hansgert, and Gerhild Framhein. *Systems of Higher Education: Federal Republic of Germany.* New York: International Council for Educational Development, 1978.

Perkin, Harold. "The Historical Perspective." In *Perspectives on Higher Education: Eight Disciplinary and Comparative Views,* edited by Burton R. Clark, 17–55. Berkeley, Los Angeles, and London: University of California Press, 1984.

_____. "The Academic Profession in the United Kingdom." In *The Academic Profession: National, Disciplinary, & Institutional Settings,* edited by Burton R. Clark, 13–59. Berkeley, Los Angeles, and London: University of California Press, 1987.

Portes, Richard. "Economics in Europe." *European Economic Review* 31 (1987): 1329–1340.

Pratt, John, and Tyrell Burgess. *Polytechnics: A Report.* London: Pitman, 1974.

Ringer, Fritz K. *Education and Society in Modern Europe.* Bloomington: Indiana University Press, 1979.

Rohlen, Thomas P. *Japan's High Schools.* Berkeley, Los Angeles, and London: University of California Press, 1983.

Rontopoulou, Jeanne Lamoure, and Jean Lamoure. "French University Education: A Brief Overview, 1984–1987." *European Journal of Education* 23, nos. 1/2 (1988): 37–45.

Rosenzweig, Robert M. "Graduate Education and Its Patrons." Keynote Address, 28th Annual Meeting, and Occasional Paper. Washington, D.C.: Council of Graduate Schools, 1988.

_____. "Grant Financing: PI Salaries." *Science* 247 (March 23, 1990): "Letters."

Rosovsky, Henry. *The University: An Owner's Manual.* New York: W. W. Norton, 1990.

Rothblatt, Sheldon. *The Revolution of the Dons: Cambridge and Society in Victorian England.* Cambridge: Cambridge University Press, 1981. (First published by Faber & Faber and Basic Books, 1968.)

_____. "The Idea of the Idea of a University and Its Antithesis." Bundoora, Australia: Seminar on the Sociology of Culture, La Trobe University, 1989.

Rowland, Henry A. "A Plea for Pure Science" (an 1883 address to the American Association for the Advancement of Science). In *The Physical Papers of Henry Augustus Rowland,* 593–619. Baltimore: Johns Hopkins University Press, 1902.

Rudd, E. *The Highest Education.* London: Routledge and Kegan Paul, 1975.

Saline, George H. "The Two Democratic Traditions." *Philosophical Review* 61 (October 1952): 451–474.

Scaff, Lawrence A. *Fleeing the Iron Cage: Culture, Politics, and Modernity in the Thought of Max Weber.* Berkeley, Los Angeles, and London: University of California Press, 1989.

Science. "News and Comment: Japan Faces Big Task in Improving Basic Science," vol. 243, March 10, 1989, 1285–1287.

Scott, Peter. *The Crisis of the University.* London: Croom Helm, 1984.

_____. "Knowledge's Outer Shape, Inner Life." *Times Higher Education Supplement* (August 16, 1991): 12.

_____. "Anachronistic Elites." *Times Higher Education Supplement,* 1992.

Seibold, E. "Funding of Research in Germany." *Science and Public Affairs* 4 (1989): 21–30.

Selvaratnam, Viswanathan. *Innovations in Higher Education: Singapore at the Competitive Edge.* Washington, D.C.: World Bank, March 10, 1992. (Background paper, Education and Employment Division, Population and Human Resources Department.)

Shattock, M. L. "The UGC and Standards," In *Standards and Criteria in Higher Education*, edited by Graeme Moodie, 46–64. At the University, Guildford, Surrey: Society for Research into Higher Education, 1986.

Shinn, T. "How French Universities Became What They Are." *Minerva* XXIII, no. 1. (Spring 1985), 159–165.

_____. "Specialized Institutions: *Grandes Ecoles.*" In *The Encyclopedia of Higher Education*, edited by Burton R. Clark and Guy Neave. Vol. 2, *Analytical Perspectives*, 1225–1229. Oxford: Pergamon Press, 1992.

Simpson, Renate. *How the Ph.D. Came to Britain: A Century of Struggle for Postgraduate Education.* At the University, Guildford, Surrey: Society for Research into Higher Education, 1983.

Smith, Bruce L. R., ed. *The State of Graduate Education.* Washington, D.C.: Brookings Institution, 1985.

Smith, Bruce L. R., and Joseph J. Karlesky. *The State of Academic Science: The Universities in the Nation's Research Effort.* New York: Change Magazine Press, 1977.

Smith, Robert J. *The École Normale Supérieure and the Third Republic.* Albany: State University of New York Press, 1982.

Spurr, Stephen H. *Academic Degree Structures: Innovative Approaches.* New York: McGraw-Hill, 1970.

Squires, Geoffrey. *First Degree: The Undergraduate Curriculum.* Buckingham: Society for Research into Higher Education, 1990.

Stewart, W. A. C. *Higher Education in Postwar Britain.* London: Macmillan, 1989.

Storr, Richard J. *The Beginning of the Future: A Historical Approach to Graduate Education in the Arts and Science.* New York: McGraw-Hill, 1973.

Suleiman, Ezra N. *Elites in French Society: The Politics of Survival.* Princeton: Princeton University Press, 1978.

Taxell, Christoffer. "Higher Education System and Higher Education Policy in Finland." Paper presented at conference "Policy Change in Higher Education," University of Turku, Turku, Finland, June 1990.

Teichler, Ulrich. "The Federal Republic of Germany." In *The School and the University: An International Perspective*, edited by Burton R. Clark, 45–76. Berkeley, Los Angeles, and London: University of California Press, 1985.

_____. *Changing Patterns of the Higher Education System: The Experience of Three Decades.* London: Jessica Kingsley Publishers, 1988.

_____. *The First Years of Study at Fachhochschulen and Universities in the Federal Republic of Germany.* Kassel: Wissenschaftliches Zentrum für Berufs- und Hochschulforschung der Gesamthochschule, 1990.

Times Higher Education Supplement, July 29, 1988.

Thulstrup, Eric W. *Improving the Quality of Research in Developing Country Universities.* Washington, D.C.: World Bank, January 11, 1992. (Background paper, Education and Employment Division, Population and Human Resources Department.)

Trow, Martin A. "Problems in the Transition from Elite to Mass Higher Education." In *Policies for Higher Education*, 51–101. Paris: OECD, 1974.

_____. "The Analysis of Status." In *Perspectives on Higher Education: Eight Disciplinary and Comparative Views*, edited by Burton R. Clark, 132–164. Berkeley, Los Angeles, and London: University of California Press, 1984.

_____. "Academic Standards and Mass Higher Education." *Higher Education Quarterly* 41, no. 3 (1987): 268–291.

Turner, Henry Ashby, Jr. *The Two Germanies Since 1945.* New Haven: Yale University Press, 1987.

Turner, R. Steven. "The Growth of Professorial Research in Prussia, 1818 to 1848—Causes and Consequences." *Historical Studies in the Physical Sciences.* 3 (1971): 137–182.

_____. "University Reformers and Professorial Scholarship in Germany 1760–1806." In *The University in Society.* Vol. 2. *Europe, Scotland, and the United States from the 16th to the 20th Century*, edited by Lawrence Stone, 495–531. Princeton: Princeton University Press, 1974.

Umakoshi, Toru. "Korean Higher Education from a Japanese Perspective." In *Development of Higher Education in Korea and Japan*, 63–73. Seoul: Korean Council for University Education, 1985.

U.S. Congress, Office of Technology Assessment (OTA). *Educating Scientists and Engineers: Grade School to Grad School.* OTA-SET-377. Washington, D.C.: U.S. Government Printing Office, 1988.

Ushiogi, Morikazu. "Graduate Education and Research Organization in Japan." In *The Research Foundations of Graduate Education: Germany, Britain, France, United States, Japan*, edited by Burton R. Clark, 299–325. Berkeley, Los Angeles, and London: University of California Press, 1993.

Van de Graaff, John H. "Federal Republic of Germany." In *Academic Power: Patterns of Authority in Seven National Systems of Higher Education*, edited by John H. Van de Graaff, Burton R. Clark, Dorotea Furth, Dietrich Goldschmidt, and Donald F. Wheeler, 15–36. New York: Praeger, 1978.

Van de Graaff, John H. and Dorotea Furth. "France." In *Academic Power: Patterns of Authority in Seven National Systems of Higher Education*, edited by John H. Van de Graaff, Burton R. Clark, Dorotea Furth, Dietrich Goldschmidt, and Donald F. Wheeler, 49–66. New York: Praeger, 1978.

Veysey, Laurence R. *The Emergence of the American University.* Chicago: University of Chicago Press, 1965.

Weber, Max. *From Max Weber: Essays in Sociology.* Translated by H. H. Gerth and C. Wright Mills. New York: Oxford University Press, 1946.

Weick, Karl E. "Contradictions in a Community of Scholars: The Cohesion-Accuracy Tradeoff." *Review of Higher Education* 6, no. 4 (1983): 253–267.

Weisz, George. *The Emergence of Modern Universities in France, 1863–1914*. Princeton: Princeton University Press, 1982.

Williams, Bruce. *University Responses to Research Selectivity*. London: Center for Higher Education Studies, Institute of Education, University of London, 1991.

Williams, Gareth, and Tessa Blackstone. *Response to Adversity: Higher Education in a Harsh Climate*. SRHE Leverhulme 10. At the University, Guildford, Surrey: Society for Research into Higher Education, 1983.

Wolfle, Dael. *The Home of Science: The Role of the University*. New York: McGraw-Hill, 1972.

Zuckerman, Harriet. *Scientific Elite: Nobel Laureates in the United States*. New York: Free Press, 1977.

The University in a Democracy—Democratization of the University*

JURGEN HABERMAS

In the vicinity of Sde Boker in the Negev, Israel's large desert, Ben-Gurion wants to found a university town to serve the exploitation of this desert area. The new town is being planned for ten thousand students and the corresponding number of faculty and is to bring Israeli youth into contact with the development of the desert through the acquisition of the necessary knowledge of the natural sciences and technology. It is intended primarily to develop the trained personnel who will be necessary for future industry in the desert. In particular, the development of such industry will involve enterprises that require much scientific knowledge and little raw material.

This news item appeared in the *Frankfurter Allgemeine Zeitung* of January 11, 1967. If, without additional knowledge, we read it correctly, a university is to serve as an instrument for the industrial development of an almost inaccessible region. From the very beginning industrial production will be initiated at the level of the most advanced technology. For the future of Israel this is probably a vital project. For us, however, the idea of a university as the starting point for the industrialization of a strip of desert is unusual. Yet the Israeli example is not so out of the way. Our educational institutions also have tasks to fulfill in the system of social labor.

Universities must transmit technically exploitable knowledge. That is, they must meet an industrial society's need for qualified new generations and at the same time be concerned with the expanded reproduction of education itself. In addition, universities must not only transmit technically exploitable knowledge, but also produce it. This includes both information flowing from research into the channels of industrial utilization, armament, and social welfare, and advisory knowledge that enters into strategies of administration, government, and other decision-making powers, such as private enterprises. Thus, through instruction and research the university is immediately connected with functions of the economic process. In addition, however, it assumes at least three further responsibilities.

First, the university has the responsibility of ensuring that its graduates are equipped, no matter how indirectly, with a minimum of qualifications in the area of extra-functional abilities. In this connection extra-functional refers to all those attributes and attitudes relevant to the pursuit of a professional career that are not contained per se in professional knowledge and skills. The classified advertisements provide weekly information about the catalog of leadership characteristics and loyalties supposed to be possessed by employees in managerial positions. Analogously, judges are expected to be capable of an institutionally adequate exercise of official authority, and doctors of quick action in situations of uncertainty. Of course, the university certainly does not produce the virtues of these unwritten professional standards, but the pattern of its socialization processes must at least be in harmony with them. When this does not happen, conflicts arise. One need only think, for example, of the protests of Protestant congregations against ministers of the younger generation from the Bultmann school. We can be sure that

*This essay was originally a lecture given at the Free University of Berlin in January 1967 at the University Conference.

these ministers are not worse exegetes than their predecessors. In short, the problem is not their functional abilities.

Second, it belongs to the tasks of the university to transmit, interpret, and develop the cultural tradition of the society. The influence of interpretations provided by the social sciences and humanities on the self-understanding of the general public can be seen easily. Today the hermeneutic sciences, no matter how positivistically disciplined in their methods, cannot in studying active traditions completely escape the constraint of either continuously reproducing them, or developing them or critically transforming them. We need only recall the recent discussion among German historians about the origins of World War I. Or imagine how future schoolteachers' picture of German classicism would be altered if for one generation the radical authors published by Suhrkamp Verlag occupied the chairs in modern German literature at the universities.

Third, the university has always fulfilled a task that is not easy to define; today we would say that it forms the political consciousness of its students. For too long, the consciousness that took shape at German universities was apolitical. It was a singular mixture of inwardness, deriving from the culture of humanism, and of loyalty to state authority. This consciousness was less a source of immediate political attitudes, than of a mentality that had significant political consequences. Without planned actions, without the organized study of political science and without political education, without the student body's political mandate in questions of current politics, without student political organizations—indeed under the aegis of an apparently apolitical institution—generations of students were educated in the disciplines of knowledge and simultaneously were educated in a politically effective manner. This process reproduced the mentality of a university-trained professional stratum for which society still intended a relatively uniform status. Transcending differences of faculty and profession, this mentality assured the homogeneity of the university-trained elite to the extent that in some leadership groups academic training even sufficed to preserve continuity through the German defeat in 1945. Nevertheless, at the universities themselves this tradition has not survived fascism. As we know, the academic stratum, shaped by a uniform mentality, has dissolved in connection with long-term structural changes in society. Does this mean, however, that today's universities no longer meet the task of providing political education, or, insofar as they take care of this function in another way, no longer need to meet it?

The example of the desert university planned as a center of industrial development suggests the peculiar idea that research and instruction today have to do only with the production and transmission of technologically exploitable knowledge. Can and should the university today restrict itself to what appears to be the only socially necessary function and at best institutionalize what remains of the traditional cultivation of personality as a separate educational subject divorced from the enterprise of knowledge? I should like to argue against this suggestive illusion and advance the thesis that under no circumstances can the universities dispense with the three tasks I have mentioned that go beyond the production and transmission of technologically exploitable knowledge. In every conceivable case, the enterprise of knowledge at the university level influences the action-orienting self-understanding of students and the public. It cannot define itself with regard to society exclusively in relation to technology, that is, to systems of purposive-rational action. It inevitably relates also to practice, that is, it influences communicative action. Nevertheless it is conceivable that a university rationalized as a factory would exert an influence on cultural self-understanding and on the norms of social actors indirectly and without being conscious of its own role in doing so. If the university were exclusively adapted to the needs of industrial society and had eradicated the remains of beneficent but archaic freedoms, then behind the back of its efficient efforts, it could be just as ideologically effective as the traditional university used to be. It could pay for its unreflected relation to practice by stabilizing implicit professional standards, cultural traditions, and forms of political consciousness, whose power expands in an uncontrolled manner precisely when they are not chosen but result instead from the ongoing character of existing institutions.

After 1945 the primary aim of university education in West Germany was to use the dimension of general education, mediated by neohumanism and strongly anchored in institutions, with the goal of educating the citizens of the university to become reliable citizens of the new democratic order. The general-education programs that appeared everywhere were easily connected with political education. The administrators of culture were not petty in establishing chairs in political science and sociology. Student governments were occupied with current political issues and student political organizations were welcomed and promoted. Whether it was interpreted as a formal commitment to political education or not, the political enlightenment of students seemed desirable, especially in the period of the Cold War. If I may generalize, at that time the university was inserted into democratic society with a certain political extension of its traditional self-understanding, *but otherwise just as it was*. Unchanged was the university's crisis-proof foundation of self-governing autonomy. A by-product of the latter, of course, was a certain immobilism, for it turned out to be an impediment to self-motivated university reform. That is why today, two decades after the first post-war reform program, a discontented society has presented the cumbersome university corporation with a bill for which it is admittedly not solely responsible.

In this situation *those* professors who would like to preserve the traditions of the German university are confronted with an alternative. They can read the latest recommendations of the Council on Education and Culture (*Wissenschaftsrat*, a government council on long-term changes in the educational system) as a technologically conceived strategy for adaptation and adopt it. Then they would be sacrificing sanctified foundations of tradition, putting up with regulation, and, above all, saving their own position in a university run by full professors. Or they can interpret it, after discounting the bureaucratically pressured reduction of the length of the course of study, in accordance with the so-called progressives. Then they can keep the university open to that dimension that we associate since the days of German Idealism with the concept of self-reflection. But this, it seems to me, would require the price of a transformation of internal structures.

The link between our postwar democracy and the traditional university—a link that seems almost attractive—is coming to an end. Two tendencies are competing with each other. *Either* increasing productivity is the sole basis of a reform that smoothly integrates the depoliticized university into the system of social labor and at the same time inconspicuously cuts its ties to the political, public realm. *Or* the university asserts itself *within* the democratic system. Today, however, this seems possible in only one way: although it has misleading implications, it can be called *democratization of the university*. I should like to substantiate my vote for this second possibility by trying to demonstrate the affinity and inner relation of the enterprise of knowledge on the university level to the democratic form of decision-making.

The argument with which I begin is borrowed from the philosophy of science, since the traditional self-understanding of scientific inquiry that goes back to Hume argues for the existence of a fundamental *separation* of practice from science and for the coordination of science and technology. Hume demonstrated that normative statements cannot be derived from descriptive statements. Hence it seems advisable not to confuse decisions about the choice of norms, that is, about moral or political problems, with problems of the empirical sciences. From theoretical knowledge we can at best, given specific goals, derive rules for instrumental action. Practical knowledge, on the contrary, is a matter of rules of communicative action and these standards cannot be grounded in a scientifically binding manner. This logical separation thus suggests an institutional separation: Politics does not belong at the university except as the object of a science that itself proceeds according to an unpolitical method.

Now the argument propounded by Hume is not false. But I believe that it does *not* imply the strategy for which Hume's positivistic successors have invoked it. We do not need to judge scientific inquiry only under the logical conditions of the theories that it generates. For another picture emerges if we examine not the results of the process of inquiry but its movement. Thus metatheoretical discussions are the medium of scientific progress—I mean methodological discussions of the utility of an analytic framework, the expedience of research strategies, the fruitfulness of hypotheses, the choice of methods of investigation, the interpretation of the results of measurement, and the implicit assumptions of operational definitions not to mention discussions of theoretical foundations of the fruitfulness of different methodological approaches.

Interestingly enough, however, from the logical point of view, discussions of this kind do not follow rules different from those of any critical discussion of practical questions. This sort of *critical* argumentation is distinguished from straight deductions or empirical controls in that it rationalizes attitudes by means of the justification of a choice of standards. True, the relation between attitudes and statements cannot possibly be one of implication. Yet the approval of a procedure or the acceptance of a norm can be supported or weakened by arguments: it can at least be rationally assessed. And this is precisely the task of critical thought, both for metatheoretical and practical decisions.

Of course it makes a difference whether we are discussing standards that, as in science, establish the framework for descriptive statements or standards that are rules of communicative action. But both are cases of the rationalization of a choice in the medium of unconstrained discussion. In very rare cases practical questions are decided in this rational form. But there is one form of political decision-making according to which all decisions are supposed to be made equally dependent on a consensus arrived at in discussion free from domination—the democratic form. Here the principle of public discourse is supposed to eliminate all force other than that of the better argument, and majority decisions are held to be only a substitute for the uncompelled consensus that would finally result if discussion did not always have to be broken off owing to the need for a decision. This principle, that—expressed in the Kantian manner—only reason should have force, links the democratic form of political decision-making with the type of discussion to which the sciences owe their progress. For we must not overlook the element of decision-making in scientific progress.

Here we see evidence of a subterranean unity of theoretical and practical reason. Today we can only formally take note of this unity; we have no philosophy that could explicate its content. In relation to the sciences, philosophy today can no longer claim an institutionally secured position of privilege, but philosophizing retains its universal power in the form of the self-reflection of the sciences themselves. In this dimension, occupied by philosophy, the unity of theoretical and practical reason that does not hold for scientific theories themselves is preserved. Philosophy, having become circumscribed as a specific discipline, can legitimately go beyond the area reserved to it by assuming the role of interpreter between one specialized narrow-mindedness and another. Thus, I consider it philosophical enlightenment when doctors learn from sociological and psychoanalytic studies to appreciate the influence of the family environment in the genesis of psychoses and thereby also learn to reflect on certain biologistic assumptions of the tradition of their discipline. I consider it philosophical enlightenment when sociologists, directed by professional historians, apply some of their general hypotheses to historical material and thereby become aware of the inevitably forced character of their generalizations. They thus learn to reflect on the methodologically suppressed relation of the universal and the individual. I consider it philosophical enlightenment when philosophers learn from recent psycholinguistic investigations of the learning of grammatical rules to comprehend the causal connection of speech and language with external conditions and in this way learn to reflect on the methodological limits to the mere understanding of meaning. These are not examples of interdisciplinary research. Rather, they illustrate a self-reflection of the sciences in which the latter become critically aware of their own presuppositions.

Such immanent philosophizing also confirms its validity with regard to the transposition of scientific results into the life-world. The translation of scientific material into the educational processes of students requires the very form of reflection that once was associated with philosophical consciousness. The developers of new pedagogical methods for curricula in college-oriented schools should go back to the philosophical presuppositions of the different fields of study themselves. Thus, for example, the transmission of basic grammatical structures in a language class at the primary school level, where the bases of several languages are taught simultaneously and comparatively, cannot be meaningfully discussed without confronting the problems of the philosophy of language as they have developed from Humboldt through Saussure to Chomsky. Similarly pedagogical problems of history instruction on the junior high school level lead to the problems connected with the emergence of the historical consciousness that has developed since the end of the seventeenth century with the tradition of the philosophy of history. Equally important is the demand for self-reflection that such pedagogical questions create for the natural sciences and mathematics. It would be easy to show in the cases of other disciplines the crossover points between theory and practice where self-reflection arises: in jurisprudence the practice of the application of laws leads to problems of hermeneutics, and in the social sciences it is the practical need for aid in decisions and planning which has called forth discussions about basic methodological questions.

All of these examples characterize a dimension in which the sciences practice reflection. In this dimension they critically account to themselves, in forms originally employed by philosophy, both for the most general implications of their presuppositions for ways of viewing the world and for their relation to practice. This dimension must not be closed off. For only in it is it possible to fulfill in a rational fashion those three functions which the university must in some way deal with over and above the production and transmission of technically exploitable knowledge. Only in this dimension can we promote the replacement of traditional professional ethics by a reflected relation of university graduates to their professional practice. Only in it can we bring to consciousness, through reflection, the relation of living generations to active cultural traditions, which otherwise operate dogmatically. Only in it, finally, can we subject to critical discussion both attitudes of political consequence and motives that form the university as a scientific institution and a social organization. Students' participation in research processes essentially includes participation in this self-reflection of the sciences. But if critical discussions of this type occur in the area of comprehensive rationality, in which theoretical and practical reason are not yet separated by methodological prohibitions that are necessary on another level, then there is a continuity between *these* discussions and the critical discussion of practical questions: critical argument serves in the end only to disclose the commingling of basic methodological assumptions and action-orienting self-understanding. If this is so, then no matter how much the self-reflection of the sciences and the rational discussion of political decisions differ and must be carefully distinguished, they are still connected by the common form of critical inquiry.

Therefore, so long as we do not want to arbitrarily put a halt to rationalization, we do not need to accept the existence of an opposition between a university aiming at professional specialization and one aiming at external politicization. For the same reason, however, we must not be satisfied with a depoliticized university. Current politics must be able to become part of the internal university community. I say this even though a National Democratic Club (a right-wing group associated with neo-Nazism) has been founded at the University of Frankfurt. And I believe it possible to advocate this thesis because the only principle by which political discussions at the universities can be legitimated is the same principle that defines the *democratic form* of decision-making, namely: rationalizing decisions in such a way that they can be made dependent on a consensus arrived at through discussion free from domination.

This is, as noted, a principle. It is binding but not real. That is why when considering the process of democratic decision-making we must distinguish, at least for analytical purposes, between (a) the discussion of proposals and justifications and (b) the demonstration of a decision with appeal to the preceding arguments. With regard to matters other than conflicts between parts of the corporation about questions of university politics, the university is not the place for the demonstration of political decisions. But it is, I believe, an ideally suited place for the discussion of political issues, if and to the extent that this discussion is fundamentally governed by the same rules of rationality within which scientific reflection takes place. This structural connection also renders comprehensible the fact that students make extensive use of their civil and political rights in order to demonstrate their will outside the university as well. Inversely, however, it is then just as understandable that members of the university are expected, in their role as citizens, to make clear the connection between demonstrations and the argumentation that preceded them.

This thesis seems to be supported by my attempt to demonstrate an immanent relation between the enterprise of knowledge at the university and the critical enterprise. But this relation can also be defended pragmatically by the need for political self-protection. In a democracy that is not firmly established, we must expect masked states of emergency that are *not* interpreted and recognized by the authorities as violations of legality. Often in such cases the only thing that works is the mechanism of self-defense, based on solidarity, undertaken by the whole institution under attack. The particular interest then seems to draw strength from beyond its own limits through an acute convergence with the general interest. The Spiegel affair was an example. In rare unity of spirit the entire press took up arms against this violation of the freedom of the press. A violation of wage autonomy would surely set off a no less united protest by the unions. And so, too, if the constitutional norm that guarantees freedom of instruction and research should ever be violated again, the first resistance should come from the universities themselves, with professors and students side by side. An act of self-defense of this sort could no longer be expected from a depoliticized university.

If for this pragmatic reason we not only permit but promote the critical discussion of practical questions at the university, then students naturally have an even greater right to take part in discussions in which the university itself is a political issue. They have a legitimate role in determining local and national policies about the university and higher education. Now for years an active and logically persuasive minority of students has demanded a democratization of the university. The university run by professors, which simulates a community of teachers and students, would be replaced by a corporation in whose administration all three parties would take part with the opportunity of asserting their own interests: students, junior faculty, and professors. Also, the dualism of academic hierachy and the administration of institutes would be overcome. Again, students and junior faculty, in accordance with their actual functions, would participate in administering the resources of the institutes. These proposals have been subject to misunderstandings, partly because they are based on false models, for example, workers' co-determination in industrial enterprises.

I cannot discuss this further here. But I am of the opinion that we as professors have no reason to abstain from such discussion. If, for example, the present conflict at the Free University—whose open character, contrary to the lament of part of the press, cannot hurt the universities standing or freedom—can still lead to a politically meaningful result, then it might be the following: the formation at the universities of Berlin and the Federal Republic of joint commissions in which professors confer unrestrictedly with instructors and students about all demands regarding university policy, including the most aggravating ones. And the public should be immediately informed of the results.

Producing Knowledge in Africa Today: The Second Bashorun M. K. O. Abiola Distinguished Lecture

PAULIN J. HOUNTONDJI

I wish first to thank the National Panels Committee and the Board of Directors of the African Studies Association for extending this kind invitation to me.

Allow me to pay homage to the man after whom this series of lectures was named. Bashorun M.K.O. Abiola has been in detention for 134 days, that is more than four months, since June 24, 1994. I had the opportunity and honor to meet him about two years ago, when I headed the Department of Culture and Communications in Benin and was in charge of a project known as "The Slave Route Project," which was similar to Bashorun Abiola's campaign for reparations. Mr. Abiola visited Benin and had long talks with President Soglo.

Without interfering with the domestic affairs of any particular country, but also without seeking to pour oil on the fire, let me mention that it is a shame for Africa and for human civilization at the end of the twentieth century that a man should be arrested for winning elections. Every additional day Bashorun Abiola spends in detention makes the crisis more serious and more intolerable.

Whatever difficulties they face, however complex the national situation, present rulers in Chief Abiola's country should realize that they are making a martyr at their own expense and that their interest is to release, as early as possible, a man whose innocence is evident to all. What in the eyes of non-Nigerians still makes Nigeria a great country and a model to all Africa is certainly not a reign of sheer force but the tenacity and courage of Nigerian democrats in their continuing struggle for human rights and the rule of law. The ultimate judge remains History. I am sure I express the feelings of a vast majority of scholars and intellectuals inside and outside Africa.

Let Nigeria be Nigeria again! Let Africa be Africa again!

In examining knowledge production, we should look in two different and complementary directions. First, we should pay attention to a specific aspect of underdevelopment. I tried to do this five years ago, in a lecture delivered at Cornell University and then at Ohio State University in November 1989 on "Scientific Dependence in Africa Today."

Secondly, we should pay attention to what is going well. We should acknowledge achievements and work in progress and seek how to cope with present difficulties and develop new strategies for overcoming dependence. We should promote scientific and technological innovation and self-reliance as means to meet, first and foremost, Africa's own needs.

Let me first look in the first direction. I will start from where I stood five years ago, in the aforementioned lecture published in the Fall 1990 issue of *Research in African Literatures.*

I argued that scientific and technological activity, as practiced in Africa today, is just as "extroverted," or externally oriented, as economic activity. Most of the shortcomings that can be identified should not be perceived, therefore, as natural and inevitable. They should be traced back, on the contrary, to the history of the integration and subordination of our traditional knowledge to the world system of knowledge, just as underdevelopment as a whole results, primarily, not from any original backwardness, but from the integration of our subsistence economies into the world capitalist market. My argument went through a number of steps which I would like to recall briefly.

First, with respect to modern science, the heart of the process is neither the stage of data collection nor that of the application of theoretical findings to practical issues. Rather, it lies between the two, in the stages of theory building, interpretation of raw information and the theoretical processing of the data collected. These stages lead to more or less complex experimental methods and machinery. Based on these procedures, statements are produced.

Second, the one essential shortcoming of scientific activity in colonial Africa was the lack of these specific theory-building procedures and infrastructures. Only the initial and final stages of the whole process were developed. No facilities for basic research, no laboratories and no universities existed in colonial Africa. We only had centers for so-called applied research that allowed, first, the feverish gathering of all supposedly useful information, aimed for immediate exportation to the so-called mother country and secondly, an occasional, hasty and limited application of metropolitan research findings to some local issues.

Third, this theoretical vacuum was substantially the same as the industrial vacuum that characterized economic activity in the colonies. Laboratories were missing, just as industrial plants were. In the field of knowledge, dependencies were reduced to immense data banks, storehouses of bare facts and information reserved for exportation to the ruling country. There is a global parallelism, a striking analogy between the two sorts of activity.

Fourth, beyond mere parallelism, I argued that both activities could be seen, in the last analysis, as identical. Scientific activity is but a specific mode of economic activity in the wider sense of the word, that is, the overall process of the human transformation of nature including production, consumption and exchange of goods. In the usual and narrower sense, economics is concerned only with material goods and therefore with such activities as agriculture, industry and commerce. But, in the wider sense, it is concerned with both material and non-material goods. Science, as we said, is the production of a specific kind of statements: non-material goods. It is, therefore, part and parcel of economy in the wider sense.

Fifth, economics in the narrower sense remains basic and plays a paradigmatic role vis-á-vis all other aspects or levels of human productive activity. In other terms, the mode of production of material goods determines, in the last instance (to use Marx's words) or becomes a model for the other form of production, that of immaterial goods.

Sixth, theories of underdevelopment based on evolutionist assumptions, as propounded by Rostow, Leibenstein and some others, do not allow real understanding of the so-called economic backwardness of Africa and the Third World. The historical approach to underdevelopment, as propounded by authors like Immanuel Wallerstein, André Gunder Frank, Samir Amin and others, is much more enlightening. It views underdevelopment as an effect of domination, the result of accumulation on a world scale, entailing forced integration of subsistence economies into the world capitalist market. In these conditions, at the level of surface description, the main feature of an underdeveloped economy appears to be extroversion, i.e., production of luxury goods aimed at satisfying, first and foremost, the needs of consumers in industrial metropoles, instead of local mass consumption (Rostow, 1960; Leibenstein, 1957; Wallerstein, 1974; Frank, 1970; Amin, 1970).

Seventh, the same approach can be applied, by analogy, to what might at first sight appear as scientific and technological backwardness. Instead of interpreting the facts from an evolutionist standpoint, it would be enlightening to replace the present state of affairs in Africa into its historical context and view present-day shortcomings and weaknesses in the field of knowledge as a result of peripherization, that is, forced integration into the world market of concepts, a market managed and controlled by the North, just as the other world market, that of material goods. On a descriptive level, underdevelopment in the field of science and technology should also be characterized, as in the field of economics in the narrower sense, as an extroverted activity.

This is approximately where I stood five years ago in my attempt to define the historical background and design a conceptual framework for the analysis of what I considered scientific underdevelopment or, more exactly put, scientific dependence. I went further than forging out concepts. I tested these concepts by trying to identify in present-day Africa as many indices as possible of scientific extroversion, of which I found thirteen.

First, almost all our research equipment, from the most sophisticated down to the simplest instruments, are made in the North. *Second,* despite the growth of libraries and publishing houses in our countries, we are still dependent on an international scientific information system based in and largely controlled by the North. *Third,* as a consequence of this, no African scholar can claim to be doing top-level research without traveling back and forth from South to North, resulting in a type of institutional nomadism. *Fourth,* the much talked about brain-drain should not be perceived as an evil per se or an independent phenomenon, but as a borderline case of this institutional nomadism. *Fifth,* the theoretical work now developing in the South is still mainly bound to a kind of insularity, in the sense that research programs, units and facilities are still not aimed at answering the needs and concerns of the societies that host them, and behave like artificial islands floating on the surface of a sea without any roots in the soil at the bottom. *Sixth,* the international division of scientific labor is still reinforced by a widely spread prejudice, even among scholars and political leaders in the South, against basic research.

Seventh, the need to secure an audience or readership, a legitimate need, often leads Southern scholars to a type of mental extroversion. They are preoriented in choosing their research topics and methods by the expectations of their potential public. *Eighth,* as a consequence of both this mental extroversion and prejudice against theory, African scholars are often tempted, especially in the social sciences, to lock themselves up into an empirical description of the most peculiar features of their societies, without any consistent effort to interpret, elaborate on, or theorize about these features. In so doing, they implicitly agree to act as informants, though learned informants, for Western science and scientists.

Ninth, scientific research is often directly put in the service of economic extroversion, as was the case, till recently, of agronomic research. *Tenth,* the development, within Western science, of a discipline or group of disciplines known as ethnoscience, including ethnobotany, ethnozoology, ethnomathematics and the like, shows the only kind of relationship that could exist in the context of domination, between so-called modern science and so-called traditional knowledge, where the latter is either marginalized or, better still, *eaten* by the former. We have been experiencing for almost a hundred years (the word *ethnobotany* was coined in 1895 and the word *ethnoscience* not earlier than 1950) a sort of scientific cannibalism.

Eleventh, mastering foreign languages is still an absolute prerequisite for access to any research activity in most African countries. This, too, is a sign of continuing dependence. *Twelfth,* scientists from Africa and the Third World are much busier getting involved in a vertical exchange and dialogue with scientists from the North than in any horizontal exchange with their fellow scholars from the South. The lack, or poor development of internal scientific discussions and debates within and between our scientific communities, the general stampede of our scholars for individual acknowledgment by the North—which, of course, is not really their fault—is also a sign of continuing dependence.

Thirteenth, most professors or heads of our universities and research centers, acquired their degrees from Western universities. When they happen to be good scholars, they can play an exceptional role in pulling the whole institution upwards, both through their own example as first class scholars and their efforts to organize the local scientific community. Conversely, when they happen to be bad scholars, they can become national disasters and unintentionally foster what I termed a system for the reproduction of mediocrity, and therefore, the continuation of dependence.

Among the conclusions I drew from this analysis, at least two points deserve being recalled. First, having noted that the study of the relationship between science and society is the specific object of a fairly new discipline, known as the sociology of science, I observed that this relationship has only been examined for some sixty years, within industrial societies, and that better attention should be paid to the particular conditions of the production of knowledge in developing countries as well as the scientific and technological relations of production on a world scale. Second, I recalled some of the misunderstandings that developed around the critique of ethnophilosophy and called for its deepening into a wider critique of ethnoscience as a whole and, more generally, a critique of the entire process of marginalization.

Almost each point in this Ithaca-Columbus paper calls for further elaboration and discussion. I have, through other essays, brought about some of the revisions and new evidence required to support these basic views (Hountondji 1988a, 1988b, 1992, 1994). I have also come across publications that look in the same direction, for instance the excellent paper by Olufemi Taiwo, "Colonialism and Its Aftermath: The Crisis of Knowledge Production," published in *Callaloo* (1993). I remain convinced that a good analysis and description of scientific dependence or, more generally, of the state of modern scholarship in Africa and its relationship both to Northern scholarship and to traditional knowledge procedures in Africa, needs to be developed to allow a correct diagnosis and adequate definition of new objectives and tasks.

Let us make it clear that, if this were our last word, if we do not go further than this diagnosis, we would be feeding that discourse of recrimination so familiar to Africa, by which we constantly tend to reject onto others the responsibility for all our misfortunes and misdeeds. Yesterday it was imperialism, colonialism and neo-colonialism, today it is the World Bank and the IMF, tomorrow it will probably be new incarnations of the same demon. We would be feeding, on the other hand, the discourse of afro-pessimism, so fashionable today within larger and larger circles in the West, among people who, first, overlook the history and ongoing problems of their own societies and, secondly, fail to replace Africa within the context of her history and complex relationship with the rest of the world.

The real question, once a diagnosis has been made, is: What to do? How far did the dependence machine succeed in crushing all initiative and stifling all indigenous activity? Which islets of such creativity, which skills, which domains of knowledge, have remained untouched, and can they be not only safeguarded, but developed, improved, updated and actively reappropriated? In the field of so-called modern science and technology, what is occurring in Africa? What are the research programs, what are the findings, what important results have been achieved during the past years? Given the fact that we have not cared, until now, to set up a strategy that could allow us to utilize our research findings for our own sake, what can be done to correct this state of affairs and start at last capitalizing, managing, mastering and occasionally applying our own as well as other people's findings to improve the quality of life in our countries?

If I could answer all these questions, I would not be far from a demigod. Instead, I would like to say a few words on the issue of traditional knowledge.

I initiated a research program on the subject with the support of the Council for the Development of Economic and Social Research in Africa (CODESRIA) in Dakar. The outcome was a collective book published under the title, *Les savoirs endogènes: pistes pour une recherche* (1994). I am not going to summarize it here. I do not think it says the last word on the subject. But I do believe we need a renewed, systematic reflection on the status, the mode of existence, the scope and limits and the perspectives of development of so-called traditional knowledge.

My colleagues and I felt that the word "traditional" would incline the reader to perceive this kind of knowledge as something fixed, immutable and reluctant to change over the centuries. We preferred the word "endogenous" to dwell on the origin of a cultural product or value that comes from, or at least is perceived by people as coming from inside their own society, as opposed to imported or "exogenous" products or values—though we should admit, in a sense, that there is no absolute origin at all, and the concept of endogeneity itself should therefore be relativized.

The logic of marginalization, as developed through centuries of forced integration, including the slave trade, colonization and neo-colonization, has not succeeded in blowing out our age-old heritage of knowledge, both practical and theoretical. If this had been the case, we should no longer have any handicraft, any weaving, any pottery, any basket-making, any cooking, any metallurgy, any rainmaking technique, any "traditional" medicine and pharmacopoeia, any divination system, any counting system, any botanical and zoological taxonomy or any original teaching methods and procedures. All of these and much more still exists and needs to be discovered or rediscovered (Ichitchi 1994; Zaslavsky, 1973). My colleague Goudjinou P. Mètinhoué, an historian and contributor to *Endogenous Knowledge,* rightly speaks of "the immense field of traditional techniques," and he is running in collaboration with another historian, Franqois de Medeiros, and an archaeologist, Alexis Adandé, a research program on "material civilisation" in the Gulf of Benin (Mètinhoué 1994).

That such material civilization should have survived clearly indicates the failure of attempts at cultural cannibalism or ethnocide at which I previously hinted. It also calls for an effort to look deeper into the past than the last five centuries, and consider the tragedy of the slave trade as well as subsequent events, as accidents happening to an age-old civilization or, in other terms, experiences by Africa herself.

Cheikh Anta Diop appealed for such a view of African history (1954, 1967, 1973, 1981). It entails a complete reversal of the usual perspective. It leads once more to the relativization of the phenomenon of underdevelopment, not only by viewing it as the result of an historical process as seen before, but by replacing the process itself into a wider, deeper long-term history that makes it appear, finally, as an episode limited in time and therefore, due to be overcome.

Among the innumerable techniques and skills developed in the past, quite a number have now been forgotten. Alexis Adandé humorously recalls, in *Endogenous Knowledge,* a saying that became widely spread throughout French colonies in Africa during the campaign before General de Gaulle's referendum of 28 September 1958. Opponents to self-determination used to say: You don't even know how to make a needle, how can you want independence? The outcome of this referendum showed how efficiently this kind of propaganda worked, except in Sékou Touré's Guinea. People, as well as their political leaders, had simply forgotten that they themselves had developed, for thousands of years before colonization, a strong and wealthy iron industry. The iron industry included not only secondary metallurgy, consisting of transformation of the metal as blacksmiths do, but also primary metallurgy, or the extraction of iron from iron ore. Scientists have now localized very precisely quite a number of sites, for instance in Ghana, Niger, Nigeria, Burkina Faso, Togo, Benin and Mali, where this extraction took place (Adandd 1994).

That such an active industry should have fallen into oblivion shows how much human civilizations are constantly threatened by the risk of historical regression. It also shows how urgent it is to set up devices and procedures for retrieving, recollecting and critically reappropriating all that can be useful and relevant to present-day problems in our age-old heritage. It shows how urgent it is to help Africans recover self-confidence after centuries of inferiorization and racism. This is an important task for African and Africanist scholars.

Another problem exists. Why is positive knowledge in Africa so often mingled with mythical beliefs and practices? Why does the "traditional" healer always begin this cure by an invocation to gods, spirits and the ancestors and by all sorts of less intelligible incantations? Why does he prescribe specific rituals to his patient just as he prescribes leaves, roots, decoctions or other ingredients? Why is the Ifa diviner so convinced that, when he throws his kola nuts or his cowries, or his rope, his hand is secretly guided by deities which preside over human's fates? Why, if this form of geomancy, as my colleague Victor Houndonougbo puts it, is in the last analysis the vehicle of a complex mathematical knowledge, why not develop this knowledge for its own sake and rid the horizon of all these gods and goddesses (1994)?

In connection with this, why, instead of giving simple, clear and straightforward answers to questions, do some practitioners tend to blame people who dare to ask questions, and threaten them with all sorts of evils and misfortunes? In other terms, why is knowledge reserved for initiates—why try, by all means, including intimidation, to exclude non-initiates?

These facts should not be interpreted as Lévy-Bruhl did, by reference to a so-called primitive mentality, supposedly unable to distinguish between the natural and the supernatural (1910, 1931). My hypothesis is that, first, in oral civilizations, there are quite a number of mnemotechnic means to ease and facilitate memory. Personification of basic categories, including the mythical projection of configurations of the divination material into deities, might be one of these mnemotechnic devices. Secondly, the esoteric, initiatic form of specialized knowledge and the many devices of intimidation and exclusion used to keep it secret may be perceived as a form of protection of intellectual property and copyright in civilizations where, despite the lack of legal and social protection of invention, inventors needed, as in any other country, to earn a living from their specific competence.

The degree of optimism or pessimism about Africa's future depends on how far one looks behind and recalls historical achievements and experience. As Aimé Césaire declared at the First International Congress of Black Writers and Artists, "La voie la plus courte vers l'avenir est celle qui passe par l'approfondissement du passé." The deeper you look into the past, the shorter your way to the future (1956).

Considering only the present state of affairs in Africa, whether in the fields of knowledge or economic, political, social and cultural life, may lead to fatalism and despair. One has questioned, however, the origin of this situation and discovered the hidden dynamics behind it, the slow process that led to where we are, once the whole ugliness is inserted into its overall context, it begins to lose its appearance of being eternal and inevitable. It can be realized at last that all that has begun at a given time is also likely to have an end.

The historical, neo-marxist approach to underdevelopment allows such an enlightening of the present by the past (Amin 1970; Frank 1979). What I tried to do is to extend it beyond the restricted area of economics where it originally developed to another important though long-neglected field, that of knowledge.

Nevertheless, this kind of approach, if not taken with care, can lead to mistaking the part for the whole. I had to take into account, therefore, forms of knowledge—much more informal and in many respects, much older and more deeply rooted than the institutional, so-called modern form of knowledge, that is, science and technology as recently extended to our countries through centuries of integration. This wider perspective allows further relativization of present-day incoherences. It reinforces self-confidence and trust in Africa's capabilities and future.

In short, we are faced today in the field of knowledge with a twofold task. First we have to appropriate, assimilate and make entirely ours, with lucidity and critical mind, all the international heritage now available including the very process of scientific and technological innovation. Secondly, after critically assessing, testing and updating, reappropriate our own ancestral heritage and the creativity, adaptability and ability to innovate that made our ancestors what they were. This is not traditionalism, but the exact opposite.

I am not sure whether the way out of dependence lies, as was recently said, in delinkage or disconnection as an antidote to world capitalist integration (Amin 1985). But I do believe that, at least in the field of knowledge, a sort of reconnection might prove necessary and urgent with both old traditions of creativity and, beyond the scraps of knowledge now imported from the North, the overall strategy of research and innovation that made them possible.

References

Adandé, Alexis. 1994. "La Métallurgie 'traditionnelle' du fer en Afrique occidentale," in Paulin J. Hountondji (ed.) *Les savoirs endogènes: pistes pour une recherche.* Dakar: CODESRIA, pp. 57–75.

Amin, Samir, 1970 *L'accumulation à l'échelle mondiale.* Paris: Anthropos.

_____. 1985. *La déconnexion.* Paris: La Découverte.

Césaire, Aimé. 1956. "Culture et colonisation," *Présence Africaine* special issue (June–Nov).

Diop, Cheikh Anta. 1954. *Nations nègres et culture.* Paris: Présence Africaine.

_____. 1967. *Antériorité des civilisations nègres.* Paris: Présence Africaine.

_____. 1973. "La métallurgie du fer sous l'ancien empire Égyptien," *Bulletin de l'IFAN* 35/3:532–47.

_____. 1981. *Civilisation ou barbarie.* Paris: Présence Africaine.

Frank, André Gunder. 1970. *Le développement du sous-développement: l'Amérique latine.* Paris: F. Maspero.

Gosselin, Gabriel (ed.) 1988. *Les nouveaux enjeux de l'anthropologue—Autour de Georges Balandier.* Bruxelles: *Revue de l'Institut de Sociologie* 3–4.

Houndonougbo, Victor. 1994. "Processus stochastique du Fâ: une approche mathématique de la géomancie des côtes du Bénin," in Paulin J. Hountondji (ed.) *Les savoirs endogénes: pistes pour une recherche.* Dakar: CODESRIA.

Hountondji, Paulin J. 1988a. "L'appropriation collective du savoir: tâches nouvelles pour une politique scientifique," *Genève-Afrique* 27/1:49–66.

_____. 1988b. "Situation de l'anthropologue africain: note critique sur une forme d'extraversion scientifique," in Gabriel Gosselin (ed.) *Les nouveaux enjeux de l'anthropologue—Autour de Georges Balandier.* Bruxelles: *Revue de l'Institut de sociologie,* pp. 98–108.

_____. 1990. "Scientific Dependence in Africa Today," *Research in African Literatures* 21/3:5–15.

_____. 1992. "Recapturing," in V. Y. Mudimbe (ed.) *The Surrepitious Speech. "Présence Africaine" and the Politics of Otherness: 1947–1987.* Chicago and London: University of Chicago Press, pp. 238–44.

_____. (ed.) 1994. *Les savoirs endogènes: pistes pour une recherche.* Dakar: CODESRIA.

Leibenstein, H. 1957. *Economic Backwardness and Economic Growth.* New York: Wiley.

Lévy-Bruhl, Lucien. 1910. *Les fonctions mentales dans les sociétés inférieures.* Paris: Alcan.

_____. 1931. *Le surnaturel et la nature dans la mentalité primitive.* Paris: New edition, Presses universitaires de France, 1963.

Métinhoué, Goudjinou P. 1994. "L'étude des techniques et des savoir-faire: questions de méthode," in Paulin J. Hountondji (ed.) *Les savoirs endogènes: pistes pour une recherche.* Dakar: CODESRIA, pp. 37–56.

Mudimbe, V. Y. (ed.) 1992. *The Surreptitious Speech. "Présence Africaine" and the Politics of Otherness: 1947–1987.* Chicago and London: University of Chicago Press.

Rostow, Walt Witman. 1960. *The Stages of Economic Growth: A Non-Communist Manifesto.* Cambridge: Cambridge University Press.

Taiwo, Olufemi. 1993. "Colonialism and Its Aftermath: The Crisis of Knowledge Production," *Callaloo* 16/3:891–908.

Tchichi, Toussaint Yaovi. 1994. "Numérations traditionnelles et arithmétique moderne," in Paulin J. Hountondji (ed.) *Les savoirs endogènes: pistes pour une recherche.* Dakar: CODESRIA, pp. 109–38.

Wallerstein, Immanuel. 1974. *The Modern World System.* New York: Academic Press.

Zaslavsky, Claudia. 1973. *Africa Counts: Number and Pattern in African Culture.* Boston: Prindle, Weber, Schmidt.

Cultural Influences on the Construction of Knowledge in Japanese Higher Education

KEN KEMPNER AND MISAO MAKINO

Introduction

Japan's economic influence is pervasive throughout the world, yet its role as an academic, political, and diplomatic leader is more problematic. Many individuals concerned about Japan's future role as a world leader focus initially on the problems with its educational system. As Fukunaga (1992) explains:

> [T]he collapse of education, for example, serves as eloquent proof that society has run aground. Japanese education was designed to produce good *kigyo senshi*, or corporate soldiers for Japan, Inc. This made sense only when the nation was relatively poor and struggling to rebuild. Not anymore. School children today are sick of outdated educational policies, and many either drop out or become delinquent. Ironically, Japan may be unable to produce even good corporate soldiers. (p. 5)

Higher education, in particular, is often singled out as an impediment to Japan's future development (Amano, 1986). Competition for entry into *élite* institutions of higher education has caused Japan's elementary and secondary system to be structured around achieving success on college entrance examinations. Meanwhile, however, the deficiencies of the higher education system itself have largely been ignored (see Amano, 1986; OERI Japan Study team, 1987).

Foremost in understanding higher education in Japan is the significance education has within the larger social and political infrastructure of the country. Because the entrance examination provides a sorting function, the actual educational process of higher education is almost secondary. As Reischauer (1986, p. xviii) observed: "the squandering of four years at the college level on poor teaching and very little study seems an incredible waste of time for a nation so passionately devoted to efficiency".

The focus for higher education in Japan is more upon the certification of individuals most able to run the instruments of the state and industry. The former imperial universities (now the National) have traditionally been the training school for government *élites*. At these institutions teaching future bureaucrats has been the major focus. Increasing economic pressure on the Japanese economy from world markets has caused Japan's leaders to reassess the role and function of higher education and research at the national levels. Faced with the burst of the bubble economy, federal bureaucrats are cutting the budgets of the national universities owing to increasing criticism of the failure of universities to contribute to national development. The higher education system is criticised for its lack of creativity, parochialism, rigour and for its low quality of instruction. However true this criticism may be, Kitamura (1991, p. 315) explains that little systematic evaluation has been conducted of the higher education system "in terms of its quality of its efficiency".

How quality and efficiency issues are defined in Japanese higher education provides the impetus for our inquiry. Because Japanese higher education resides within the larger Japanese culture, it is a product both of its own culture and its membership in the international knowledge networks, dominated by the other industrialised countries (see Altbach *et al.*, 1989, Altbach, 1993). The science and knowledge that institutions of higher education produce are human activities that reside within national and international cultures that guide scientists' ways of thinking and the language they use to interpret their findings. How this larger cultural context defines what is efficient, what is quality, what is knowledge and how it is produced are the basic questions guiding our study. Specifically, in this study we consider the effect cultural issues have on what is accepted as knowledge in Japanese universities and the influence this larger culture has on scientific communities' ways of thinking and producing knowledge. First, we discuss the larger conceptual issues regarding how knowledge is constructed and the role culture plays in defining this construction. Secondly, we address the method we used to gather and interpret the information collected. Thirdly, we present our findings and, finally, we conclude by discussing the cultural, political-historical and economic issues that affect the construction of knowledge in Japanese universities.

Constructing Knowledge

What scientists and the societies in which they live accept as knowledge depends not only upon how knowledge is produced, but also upon the social and cultural context in which this knowledge is constructed. Language, for example, provides scientists the method of expression to interpret and present their findings. The theories they derive from their observations of the physical and social world are human interpretations of phenomena, not objective reality. It is the context or larger culture in which scientists operate that defines how they understand the world and what is accepted as appropriate behaviour and knowledge. Kuhn (1970) uses the example of the Copernican revolution to explain how the larger society defines what is considered appropriate knowledge. What makes Copernicus so notable was that he interpreted a physical reality that was contrary to the dictates of his culture, i.e. the earth was not the centre of the universe. According to Geertz (1973, p. 5), we can think of the larger culture within which individuals operate as "webs of significance humans spin about themselves". These webs of significance define how we understand social, political and even scientific reality. The ways in which scientists, in particular, develop their theories and interpret their findings is termed by Kuhn (1970, p. 182) a "disciplinary matrix". This matrix defines what is accepted as appropriate knowledge, language, and behaviour for a community of scientists. The matrix is the cultural 'web' scientists spin about themselves. Because scientists are also members of larger social and political cultures they are never quite free from the influences and perspectives of the larger social and political cultures within which they find themselves. For this reason Keller (1985, p. 7) reminds us: "The laws of nature are more than simple expressions of objective reality". These laws are manifestations of how scientists interpret their findings in their own language and cultural terms.

What is accepted as scientific knowledge is defined not only by cultural issues, but by how knowledge fits within the international knowledge networks (Altbach *et al.*, 1989). Our study here of research in Japanese universities attempts to understand how the construction of knowledge is affected both by the Japanese culture and by the external, scientific culture of Western countries. Foremost in understanding how the Japanese culture affects the production of knowledge is the place institutions of higher education have within the larger social, political and educational infrastructure of the country. For example, high school students' attendance at *jukus* (cram schools) in order to pass university entrance exams is a well-known feature of Japanese culture. Reischauer (1988, p. 195) explained, however, that higher education in Japan "probably fills less of a role in society than the pressures over entrance examinations would suggest". The most difficult aspect of higher education for students is, simply, getting in. Because the entrance examination provides a sorting function, the actual educational process of higher education is almost secondary. Similarly, as Reischauer (1988, p. 195) noted: "The role of the university in research activities, once very important, is also shrinking in comparison with research conducted directly by business or government". Herein lies the focus of our study: What role does research play in the Japanese university and how is this role affected by the larger Japanese culture?

Methodology

To understand the influence of culture on the production of research in higher education we relied on published and unpublished literature and documents (in Japanese and English), a survey of National University professors by the Committee for the Financial Base of National Universities, and interviews we conducted with faculty members, administrators, students and parents. We interviewed faculty members and administrators from the University of Tokyo and Waseda University, students from these universities and from Keio University, and parents whose children are at several different institutions (approximately 35 people in total.)

The intent of our study is 'revelatory' (Yin, 1989, p. 49), in that we sought to illustrate the manner in which cultural issues influence the work that Japanese scholars do. The lens we use to interpret the data we reviewed and gathered is a cultural one. Such a frame enables us to consider the nature of social reality in ways traditional, and rationalistic approaches do not (see Fay, 1987). Rather than accepting social data as truths waiting to be collected, we presume social information is always interpretive. Furthermore, this interpretive process is influenced by the culture within which the individual gathering the data resides. Similarly, by assuming this perspective in our investigation, we propose the effects of culture are central to understanding what knowledge is valued and what research is 'appropriate' in Japanese universities.

In our study we sought theoretical categories that would help to explain how research is defined, produced and disseminated. Rather than presuming pre-ordinate explanations by testing hypotheses, we sought explanations and interpretations to understand how scientists' disciplinary matrices mix and conflict with the larger social culture of Japan and the West. Similar to Wolcott's (1990) argument, in this study we are not trying to 'convince' anyone of the certainty of our findings, but rather to reveal and seek to understand the influence of culture on the construction of knowledge.

We also are guided in our study by the four strategies for qualitative analysis proposed by Goetz & LeCompte (1981). We employ inductive logic rather than deductive logic, we seek propositions and constructs from the data rather than verification, we seek to generate propositions in a constructive process rather than an enumerative one and we follow a subjective process of interpretation rather than an objective one. As Goetz & LeCompte (1981, p. 54) explain: "the goal is to reconstruct the categories used by subjects to conceptualize their own experiences and world view."

In our attempt to present this 'world view', we divide our findings into three major sections. First, we address the function of higher education in Japan by considering findings from the literature and from our interviews and discussions with faculty, students, administrators and parents. Secondly, we review the nature of the Japanese higher education system and, thirdly, we address the role of research in Japanese higher education by presenting additional findings from our interviews and a report of National University professors on their research activities.

The Function of Higher Education in Japanese Society

Foremost in understanding higher education in Japan is recognising the significance education has within the larger social and political infrastructure of the country. Thomas & Postlethwaite (1983, p. 57) address this issue by quoting from the Japanese Fundamental Education Law of 1947:

> Education shall aim at the full development of personality, at rearing a people, sound in mind and body, who love truth and justice, esteem individual values, respect labor, have a deep sense of responsibility, and are imbued with an independent spirit as builders of a peaceful state and society.

How best to produce such "builders of a peaceful" state would appear to be at the core of Japanese social, economic and educational policy. The ruling structure of Japanese society responsible for developing and implementing such policy is best illustrated by a triangle with statesmen at one corner, businessmen at another and bureaucrats, at the third corner. Comparatively, the bureaucrats and businessmen (and it is almost exclusively men) hold the balance of control. Members of these two groups often attended the same schools and universities and have been grooming for these positions since childhood. As one professor explained to us, higher education is central in this attainment process, because, other than 'marrying up', it offers the only other 'chance' for social mobility. He explained further that as opposed to the United States, where individuals can also advance themselves by being entrepreneurs, "Japan society is more closed. Japanese are not so adventuresome as Americans, they have to get into the union". The union being, of course, *élite* higher education institutions. For example, graduates of the University of Tokyo comprise a significant number of the highest-level bureaucrats, while many top business leaders are graduates of the *élite* private universities, such as Waseda and Keio.

The 'bureaucratic focus' of the national universities, according to one professor, is simply to "raise very able bureaucrats for governing the country". The former imperial universities (now the national) were the traditional "training school for government *élites*". Teaching at these institutions was and is the focus because, as this professor explained, "teaching is important to raise bureaucrats". He explained further that the purpose of the national universities is, therefore, to provide "people useful for running Japan Inc.".

Because education provides the 'source of national power', as one professor explained, it is of such national importance that public higher education is heavily affected by the role bureaucrats in the Ministry of Education, Science and Culture (*Monbusho)* play. With the increasing economic pressure on the Japanese economy from world markets, bureaucrats are busily reassessing the role of public higher education in the national infrastructure. Federal bureaucrats are presently cutting the budgets of the national universities because they do not see the universities as 'efficient'. As one professor explained, the government has "lost patience" with the universities and is more and more inclined for efficiently organised education". In general, the Japanese government is "increasingly embarrassed that Japanese universities are not contributing to the country's power . . . they see them as not contributing to national goals".

For many professors, the functionalist view of education by the federal bureaucrats is disturbing, especially in times of shrinking budgets. Whereas the national system of higher education was designed to recruit students of the highest ability from all over Japan, this meritocratic ideal is impeded because of urbanisation and testing. Because Tokyo is so central to Japanese society, the most successful individuals are educated and employed there. As a professor said, you must go to Tokyo to be 'really educated'. To gain admittance to the best Tokyo public and private universities students must have the best preparatory schooling possible. Students from cities outside of Tokyo are at a disadvantage because of location. Any student enrolled in an inferior preparatory school is unlikely to pass the entrance examination to an *élite* university. Because only the wealthiest students can afford the best schools, these students are those most likely to get into the best universities. Even among those less wealthy students who do pass the entrance examinations, many have great difficulty affording life in Tokyo, since there is virtually no financial assistance for them.

This dual bind of urbanisation and 'testing hell' mediates the meritocratic ideals of the federal educational system. Furthermore, the emphasis on testing compromises the underlying goals of Japanese education. By teaching to the test, preparatory schools and *jukus* treat knowledge as a commodity to be bargained for employment (see Wexler, 1987, p. 71). Within this system, knowledge is a utilitarian commodity or package constructed for the purpose of passing entrance examinations not for the "full development of personality" (Thomas & Postlethwaite, 1983, p. 57). "Indeed", as one professor observed, the system is "not accomplishing" its educational purpose. This professor explained that testing "is like the nuclear arms race. We need disarmament".

While Japan's modern educational development continues to assure the traditional high esteem of the educated person, what constitutes education is being compromised by the construction of pre-packaged knowledge for the purpose of passing examinations. The competition for having this package of definable knowledge continues to escalate, as evidenced by the number and prominence of *jukus* that high school students attend to pass the university entrance examinations. *Jukus* have become such an indispensable part of a student's college preparation that those who can afford it attend. The most successful *jukus* (measured by the number who pass the *élite* universities' exams) have become so profitable that they are able to hire the best teachers, and use the newest technology to evaluate and monitor their teachers' performance. Teachers who do not turn out successful students are quickly replaced. *Jukus*, and the form of specific, packaged education they provide are so essential to Japanese preparatory education that some politicians propose ending public support of education at the elementary and secondary levels, allowing the *juku*-type education to replace public schools. Privatisation of schools would create a system for the sole purpose of passing college entrance examinations. According to several professors we interviewed, however, more and more parents are choosing *not* to send their children to *jukus* and abandoning the idea of entry into the *élite* universities. Because the odds are so low for a student to gain admittance to the University of Tokyo, for example, some parents are seeking alternatives for their children, such as high quality private institutions that do not require entrance examinations or universities in other countries, notably the US.

The Higher Education System

As noted, the most difficult aspect of higher education for students is gaining admittance to their college of choice. Once accepted, however, students are freed from the rote learning they underwent in the secondary schools and *jukus*. The entrance examination provides a sorting function that is of such importance that the academic process of higher education is of secondary concern for many institutions (Amano, 1986).

National and local public universities and colleges account for 28% of the total institutions of higher education in Japan (US Department of Education, 1985). In 1990, the total enrollment in all public universities and colleges was 685,675 with 100,898 full-time faculty for a student teacher ratio of 7 to 1. In comparison, 2,017,230 students enrolled in private institutions with 97,635 full-time teachers for a student ratio of 21 to 1. Education at the exceptional public universities, such as the University of Tokyo and Kyoto University, and at the top private universities, such as Waseda and Keio, is of the highest quality. Classes at these institutions are generally smaller and the professors are limited to the amount of outside teaching they can do. For most students, even in the high prestige universities, the goal is to gain the highest possible position in the workplace, not to participate in research or the production of knowledge for the social good. In fact, the orientation toward gaining a good position in business among Japanese students is so pervasive that little evaluation or consideration of the academic role of higher education has been conducted (Kitmaura, 1991).

In contrast to the public universities are the overwhelming majority of private institutions. The governance and funding structure of these private institutions is somewhat unique to Japan. Control of private institutions is often exercised through a president by a Board of Directors, who often own the university. The Board chair, who has the most discretion in allocating resources, is often not an educator and lacks academic credentials. Although the Board may select an educator to be president, more often presidents are chosen on the basis of their family ties, their loyalty to the institution or their ability to raise money. Although private universities are self-supporting, educational reforms in Japan have allocated an increasing amount of public funds to these institutions (Schoppa, 1991).

Among the many private Japanese universities, control by a single family or person is common. The criteria for hiring faculty in such institutions does not rest solely on academic merit or considerations. For example, a typical procedure at many private institutions is to increase their status by filling faculty positions with retired professors of public universities. Many of these faculty members have already completed the years of their most active teaching, research and writing at their primary institutions. The least active among these retired faculty help contribute to an educational culture where students do little work compared to their peers in Western institutions.

Whereas institutions of higher education may presume to serve an altruistic public service, many private institutions merely increase the status, prestige, power or profit of a particular family. Even though these institutions may be dedicated to academic excellence, they do so in terms of Japanese social values, not in terms of institutional academic practices common in the West. The motives for private ownership are often simply for the accrual of personal benefits to a small family or group of owners and not for the production of knowledge or cultural enrichment.

The conflict between private interests and public service is particularly problematic for the older generation of private university leaders and owners in Japan. This conflict creates an academic climate for the production of knowledge and research in Japanese universities much different from those in the West. Considering the US, in particular, Baldridge (1971, pp. 9–11) identifies two characteristics of US universities that differentiate them from Japanese higher education institutions: (1) 'competence' as the criterion for appointment and (2) the exclusivity of the career—'no other work is done'. In Japan, although hiring and promotion require publications and research, loyalty and deference are important criteria in university success. Although university professors in the United States may hold other jobs, the criterion for exclusivity is much stricter, both formally and informally, than in Japanese universities, where some professors may teach at several institutions at once.

These differences between the US and the Japanese professorates have important consequences for the relationships between faculty and students and between the faculty and the university. Many Japanese professors teach as many as 500 students in five lecture classes that meet 2 days a week. Some of these professors will then teach another 200 students at a different institution. Often, mid-term and final exams are not returned to students after grading and students receive grade reports only at the end of the year-long term. Obviously, the quality of interaction and communication between students and professors is impeded by this situation. Faculty members' ability to conduct research is greatly compromised by multiple teaching positions and by personnel evaluation based on competence defined in social rather than academic terms.

Research in Higher Education

The history of the development of modern research in Japan began at the turn of the century with a pivotal event being the establishment of the Rikagaku Kenkyujo (Institute for Physics and Chemistry) in 1917. This institute was founded by Nakamura Seiji, a professor at Tokyo Imperial University and Takamine Jokichi, the discoverer of adrenalin in 1900. Riken, as the institute is known, "has done more to advance creative research than any other single organisation in modern Japanese history" (Nagai, 1971, p. 69). Under the eventual direction of Okochi Masatoshi and the appointment of the renown physicist Nishina Yoshio, as section chief in 1928, Riken was at the forefront of physics research in modern Japan. Unfortunately, the contributions of Riken and its stature in research has largely been overlooked in the development of Japanese higher education.

Although Riken offers an excellent example of the capacity of Japan's research in higher education, many existing universities and colleges have no research facilities, centres, or institutes. A recent survey by the Ministry of Education Science and Culture (*Monbusho*, 1990) indicates that of the total research institutes in Japan, 14,761 are owned and operated by private businesses or corporations, 1396 research institutes are free-standing without company or university affiliations, and 2146 are associated with universities and colleges. This information reflects the long-range trend in post-war development that research is not primarily done in universities, which focus instead on the sorting and selecting of the new generation of Japanese *élites*.

Because higher education serves predominantly a selection process, faculty research inherently conflicts with this traditional goal. As one professor observed: there is a "permanent friction between the teaching function and research function". He explained further that the view of the bureaucrats is that "Japan should be armed with efficient education—forget the search for truth". For this reason Government bureaucrats question those aspects of higher education that do not directly and substantially contribute to the national goals of Japan, as defined in economic terms. Accordingly, as this professor explained, the federal bureaucrats are asking: "Is funding for social science necessary for Japan? What good has it been? . . . There is no pressing need to continue to support these professors".

Faculty do receive support for research, but it is by no means a uniform distribution of funding. Research money comes from three major sources: automatic funds from *Monbusho*, grants from private companies and grants directly from federal agencies. *Monbusho* distributes funds to universities on a formula based on number of faculty, number of students, and a fixed amount dependent on the national importance and prestige of the institution. In general, faculty do not find this 'automatic' amount sufficient to support their research and related activities. As one faculty member explained: *Monbusho* "is interested more and more in the American system. *Monbusho*'s idea is to make them [the faculty] more dependent on private companies for grants". Preference in national support, as in the US, is for research in high technology areas that yield immediate economic pay-offs (see Slaughter, 1990). Because of the limited nature of *Monbusho*'s funding and the priorities on high technology research, many faculty seek funds from outside sources. Grants from private companies are awarded to professors, but even these grants must be approved by the full departmental faculty. As one professor explained, social science faculty are especially resistant to outside money. A variety of federal agencies do offer grant awards directly to faculty, but as the overall federal budget declines so do opportunities for such grants.

To understand better the present state of research in Japanese universities we present the findings from a recent study conducted by the Survey and Study Committee for the Financial Base of National Universities (1991). Questionnaires were mailed to every level of university professor, lecturer and research associate. A total of 34,325 completed questionnaires were returned (a response rate of 65%). Not surprisingly, the faculties of science, engineering and agriculture had the highest response rate, "reflecting their grave concern and interest in E&R [education and research] funding problems" (Survey and Study Committee, 1991, p. 1).

Overall, the faculty surveyed were quite positive about the contribution of the national universities to the public good (see Fig. 1). Over 90% of the faculty believed the national universities contribute 'greatly' to the advancement of academic research. This confidence is mediated by concerns over the current situation for funding of the research environment, as presented in Fig. 2. As Fig. 2 indicates, a high percentage of the faculty believe their research equipment (60%), buildings (42%) and salary (88%) are currently worse than those in private institutes and universities. Perhaps, even more

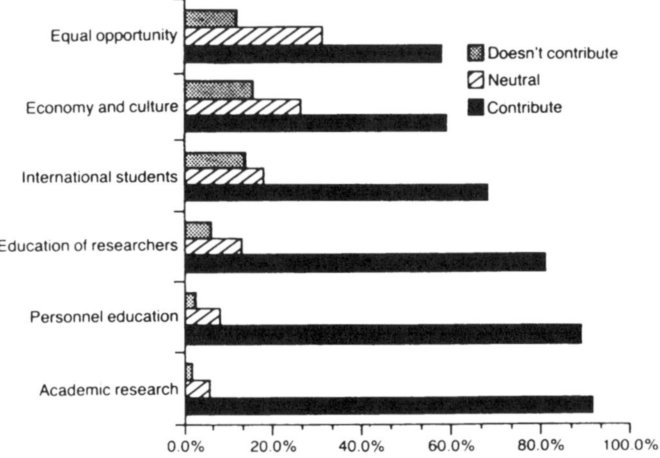

***Fig. 1:* Roles played by National Universities in Japan.**

Source: Survey and Study Committee for the Financial Base of National Universities, 1991.

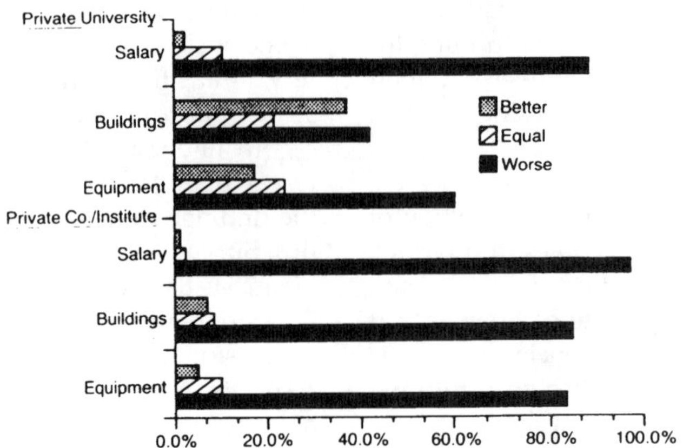

***Fig. 2:* Present research environment in Japan.**
Source: National Universities Survey, 1991.

significant is the concern of faculty over the deterioration of their research environment in the next 10 years. While 65% of the faculty believe the national universities are currently superior to private universities, in 10 years 30% fear the private universities will be superior in research (Survey and Study Committee, 1991, p. 8). Faculty also expressed concern over how the deteriorating financial situation affects the recruitment of quality researchers, students and the promotion of academic exchanges.

When asked to compare the current level of departmental expenses to actual needs, all faculty found great discrepancies. Most faculty believed their departments were funded at less than 50% of actual need, with faculty in the Health Sciences facing the worst situation (see Fig. 3). Faculty in all areas felt increases in the budgets for salary and travel were most important, followed by increases in allocation for equipment (see Fig. 4). The priority of salary increases over equipment did vary by academic area. For example, 85% of the Science and Humanities faculty expressed the greatest preference for reform in the allocation of salaries, with only 8% choosing increases in equipment as most important. In contrast, 50% of the Health Sciences faculty selected salaries as most important with 34% preferring increases in budget allocations for equipment.

Because all faculty find support of research to be declining, many report having to buy professional books and equipment from their own personal funds. This trend of supplementing a university's expenses with personal funds has direct impact on the faculty's ability to participate in the larger, international knowledge networks. A substantial number of faculty researchers in the Health Sciences (20%) and in the Science and Engineering (30%) fields report spending between 300,000 and 500,000 yen ($2500–4000) per year to attend academic conferences and to conduct research outside of Japan.

Inadequacy of research funds from the 'Grant-in-Aid for Scientific Research' (GASR) programme through *Monbusho* is a critical concern for the faculty. Because GASR is the primary source of research funding for faculty in the national universities, the programme is criticised as being inadequate. Even though the national universities are among the most prestigious in Japan, only 53% of the faculty report having received a GASR only once in 5 years, with 33% of the faculty never having received a grant. This finding is even worse for the national universities in smaller cities where 40% of the faculty have never received a grant.

Whereas GASR funds, theoretically, are given to enable and foster new research, faculty report needing GASR money to support expenses for research that are not covered by grants apportioned by the unversities. Although the GASR is a significant source for research funding outside of the university, it alone is 'far from satisfactory' to fill the need for Educational and Research funds at the individual university level (Survey and Study

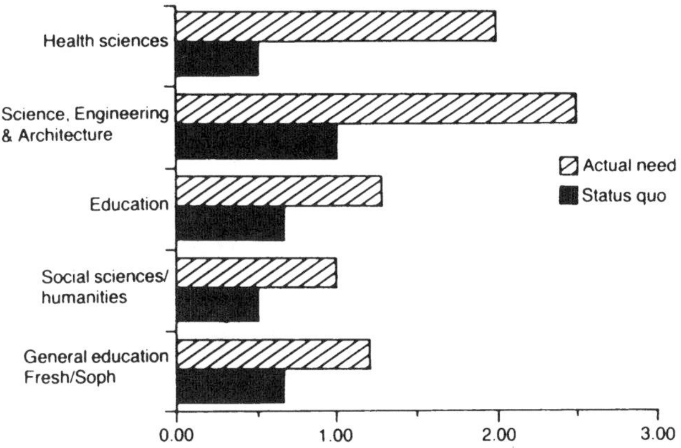

Fig. 3: **University Expenditures.**

Note: Scale is in Million Yen, a weighted calculation of funding per student FTE.

Source: National Universities, 1991, Japan.

Committee, 1991, p. 6). Approximately 70% of the faculty, therefore, support further expansion of GASR support along with similar increases in funding from municipal governments and private foundations. Fewer faculty (approximately 50%) favour the acceptability of research funds from private companies, however.

Because advanced measurement and analytic instruments are such a vital part of high technology research, faculty members express, as well, grave concern over the adequacy of their equipment. Approximately 80% of the faculty rate their current equipment as inadequate or very inadequate and 85% express the need for new equipment.

On how to renew national universities, the majority of faculty selected 'openness' and a policy of 'publicity', particularly regarding achievements in academics and research from the choices presented in the questionnaire (see Fig. 5). A large number of faculty also favoured instructional innovations, such as student ratings and self-assessment, but an equally large number are neutral on such ideas. Similarly, faculty were diverse in their opinions regarding third-party evaluation or accreditation.

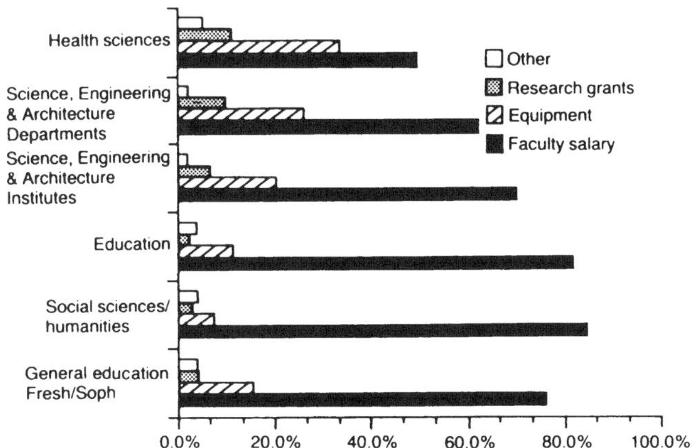

Fig. 4: **Priority of faculty budget needs.**

Note: Percentage is proportion of Faculty preference for budget reform.

Source: National Universities Survey, 1991, Japan.

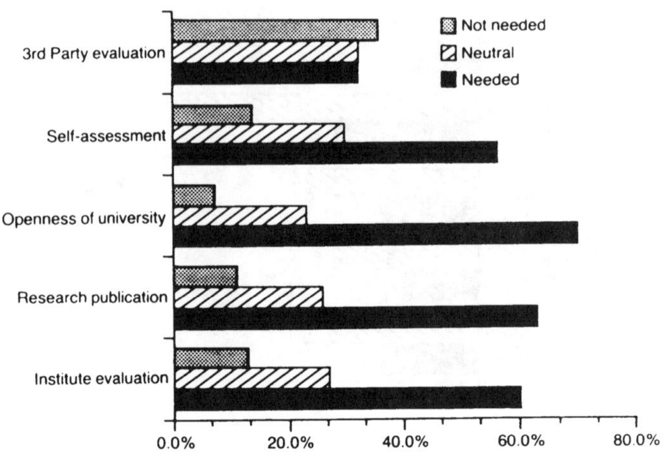

Fig. 5: **How to renovate the university.**
Source: National Universities Survey, 1991.

Discussion

Carnoy & Samoff (1990, p. 8) suggest that the key to understanding the role of education in modern societies lies in the development of "a coherent theory of the relations among the economy, ideology, and political system (the state) and, in turn, a theory of the relationship between the state and the educational system". Our purpose in this study is not so ambitious as to develop a completed, coherent theory. Rather, our intent is to illustrate the effect cultural issues have on what is accepted as knowledge in Japanese universities and the influence culture has on scientific communities' ways of thinking and producing knowledge. We believe the actions of three inter-related cultural groups are central to understanding this construction process in Japan: the state, corporate or business interests and scientists themselves.

The State

Because Japan's government, business and education is so centralised, the federal and prefecture 'state' apparatus in Tokyo exerts tight control over the modern cultural webs spun in Japan. The worry expressed by professors over the state's irritation with their inefficiency and inability to contribute to national development is indicative of the state's interests in protecting its bureaucrats through educational and economic policy. Because higher education serves predominantly a selection process, there is little incentive for state bureaucrats to foster research that does not directly contribute to their functionalist notions of the 'national goals'. There appears little interest among bureaucrats, therefore, in the 'disarmament' of the culture of testing, since the present system does indeed offer the appearance of a meritocracy. Failure to succeed in the university examination is accepted as individual misfortune, not a larger social one. That there are differences by gender and class does not seem problematic to the state (see Kitmura, 1991).

Within the educational and cultural webs the state spins and supports there is obvious conflict between the selection and research functions of higher education. Higher education's role in supporting a democracy is not a major issue of concern, but how higher education contributes to national economic development is. We found the concept of educational policy to be decidedly utilitarian among many of the educational administrators with whom we talked. Some were openly confused by the concept of educational policy and others did not understand the argument that knowledge is a social construction. Most administrators simply accepted uncritically the form and function of Japanese higher education.

The Corporatist Culture

The second influence we found critical to understanding research in higher education was that of the corporatist or business culture—'Japan Inc.' as many people refer to it. This corporatist culture exerts a pervasive influence over the place of higher education in Japanese society. We found, as Slaughter (1990, p. 29) noted in the US: "Indeed, basic research in graduate universities is in the process of being redefined as entrepreneurial science". Educational 'efficiency' is determined by its contribution directly to corporate welfare. Unlike the US, however, the lines between public and private interests are not as well defined in Japan. Nonetheless, the questions Slaughter (1990, p. 36) poses for higher education in the US are equally problematic for Japan: "What kinds of social priorities order research and whom do they benefit? What kinds of expertise are being provided to which sectors of society? What is the social utility of teaching, research, and service?".

The Scientists

Finally, the scientists themselves and the disciplinary matrices within which they operate are critical to understanding how knowledge is constructed in Japanese universities. As we have found, the conflict among the social, economic and cultural interests in Japan creates a climate that confines appropriate avenues of inquiry to utilitarian conceptions of knowledge. The structure of higher education itself greatly limits professors' ability in the pursuit of knowledge in realms not deemed useful by state or corporatist interests. Scientists do mediate somewhat the effects of state and corporatist interests by their membership in the international knowledge networks. As intellectuals, scientists also are free to exercise their individual volition of 'human agency' in choosing what they wish to study and write (Fay, 1987). Unfortunately, the pessimism in the national survey reported above does not augur well for the evolution of an open system for scientific inquiry.

The ability of Japanese professors, especially in the social sciences, to produce knowledge, is severely restricted by the utilitarian conceptions of higher education. As quoted above, one professor explained that state bureaucrats are questioning why funding for social science is even necessary for Japan. If higher education's function is simply as a selection device and its research is only to serve short-term corporatist interests, then social science may indeed be peripheral. If, however, higher education is to be central to the long-term continuation of a democratic society then construction of new forms of knowledge should be fostered. Utilitarian self-interests in higher education may actually be counterproductive to the long-term national interests of Japan. Ironically, social science research may be far more utilitarian than state bureaucrats realise, if Japan is to become both an economic and political world leader.

Conclusion

Our purpose, as stated above, is not to convince anyone of the correctness of our findings, but rather to illustrate how Japan's modern culture influences the construction of knowledge in its universities. We propose here that understanding the interactions among the state, corporatist interests, and the scientists reveals insights into how the larger culture influences educational policy and the knowledge that is produced in universities.

In seeking to understand the role of higher education in Japan we found the relationship between the state and the educational system to be primarily a functional one. The state defines the role of the university in terms of its level of efficiency in promoting economic development for Japan Inc. Effectiveness, therefore, is judged by the state in terms of the efficiency of the university in its contribution to 'national goals'. Because of the highly centralised system in Japan, the state exerts tight control over what is considered appropriate knowledge production and who has access to the national universities. State control over higher education is both supported and enabled by the corporatist or business community.

Because the state bureacracy functions in such close concordance with private business interests in Japan, policy concerns for education are highly dependent upon the 'efficiency' concerns for economic development. Higher education is judged on its ability to support corporatist interests, not on its ability to distribute expertise throughout all sectors of society for the public good. For example, in discussions with higher education administrators we learned presidents of many smaller private universities spend a considerable amount of time visiting officials of major corporations to encourage them to hire the university's graduates. Because the prestige of universities is tied directly to which businesses hire their graduates, university presidents lobby corporate executives to hire their students in hopes of increasing the university's status. New students are then attracted to the private universities whose graduates are employed by the most prestigious corporations, which then increases the competition for entry into these universities.

Because higher education functions primarily as a filter to certify students for entry into corporations or government, the actual education process of universities is secondary. Students are hired by corporations principally on the basis of which university they attended. Because, as noted, the most rigorous part of higher education is getting in—passing the entrance examination—academic performance while at the university is a subsidiary concern. Each university secures its place in the market through the examination process of students. The very best students are those who pass the examinations for the University of Tokyo, and so on down the status hierarchy of the national and private universities. High schools secure their places in the educational market by which universities their students attend and middle schools by which high schools their graduates attend. Even grade schools and nursery schools have their place in this status hierarchy. We were told by one parent that her child was denied admission to nursery school because she did not have the 'proper credentials'. Within this educational structure knowledge is a commodity only to improve one's chances to gain entrance to the next level.

Even within this strict hierarchical system, we found many professors do mediate the functional nature of university education. Because many professors are linked to the larger, international knowledge networks, they do practice their science and are educating the next generation of scientists. Although we consider the effect of state policy to be quite pervasive in the national universities, individual scientists, many of whom were educated in the West, continue to pursue avenues of research not supported or only marginally supported by the state. The role scientists' individual volition or 'human agency' plays in the production of knowledge is an important consideration along with the interactive effects of the larger culture and the scientists' disciplinary matrices. Certainly, the human agency of individual scientists is remarkably strong, especially among those scientists who are connected to the international knowledge networks through colleagues in other countries. Notably, many Japanese social scientists are pursuing critical avenues of cultural and social inquiry with international colleagues. Our investigation here is an example of such collaborative research that bridges national cultures in the production and construction of knowledge.

Finally, our investigation demonstrates the necessity that scientists understand how their research supports and contests state and business interests. We encourage not only the scientists, but state bureaucrats and members of the business community, as well, to understand the role culture plays in influencing the knowledge scientists produce. Ultimately, to further both social and economic development for Japan these three cultural groups should promote higher education policy that truly aims "at the full development of personality" and helps create "builders of a peaceful state and society".

Acknowledgements

Funding for this research was provided by the Yamada Foundation. The authors also thank Nozumo Matsubara for his assistance, without which this research could not have been conducted. Initial findings from this study were presented at the AERA Annual Meeting, San Francisco, California, April 1992.

References

Altbach, Philip G. (1993) International knowledge networks, in: B. Clark & G. Neave (Eds.) *International Encyclopedia of Higher Education* (Oxford, Pergamon).

Altbach, Philip G. *et al.* (1989) *Scientific Development and Higher Education: The Case of Newly Industrializing Nations* (New York, Praeger).

Amano, Ikuo (1986) Educational crisis in Japan, in: W. K. Cummings *et al.* (Ed.) *Educational Policies in Crisis: Japanese and American Perspectives* (New York, Praeger).

Baldridge, J. Victor (1971) *Power and Conflict in the University: Research in the Sociology of Complex Organizations* (New York, John Wiley & Sons).

Carnoy, Martin & Samoff, Joel (1990) *Education and Social Transition in the Third World* (Princeton, NJ, Princeton University Press).

Fay, Brian (1987) *Critical Social Science* (Ithaca, NY, Cornell).

Fukunaga, Hiroshi (1992) Japan at a dead end, *Tokyo Business Today*, 60(9), p. 5.

Geertz, Clifford (1973) *The Interpretation of Cultures* (New York, Basic Books).

Goetz, Judith P. & LeCompte, Margaret D. (1981) Ethnographic research and the problem of data reduction, *Anthropology and Education Quarterly*, 12, pp. 51–70.

Keller, Evelyn Fox (1985) *Reflections on Gender and Science* (New Haven, Yale Press).

Kitamura, Kazuyuki (1991) The future of Japanese higher education, in: E. Beauchamp (Ed.) *Windows on Japanese Education* (New York, Greenwood Press).

Kuhn, Thomas (1970) *The Structure of Scientific Revolutions*, 2nd edn. (Chicago, University of Chicago).

Ministry of Education, Science, and Culture [*Monbusho*] (1990) *Waga Kuni no Bunkyo Shisaku [White Paper on Japan's Educational Policies]* (Tokyo, *Monbusho*).

Nagai, Michio (1971) *Higher Education in Japan: Its take-off and crash,* Jerry Dusenbury (trans.) (Tokyo, University of Tokyo).

OERI Japan Study Team (1987) *Japanese Education Today: A Report from the US Study of Education in Japan* (Washington, DC, US Department of Education).

Reischauer, Edwin O. (1988) *The Japanese Today: Change and continuity* (Tokyo, Tuttle).

Schoppa, Leonard James (1991) *Education Reform in Japan: a case of immobilist politics* (New York, Routledge).

Slaughter, Sheila (1990) *The Higher Learning and High Technology: Dynamics of higher education policy formation* (Albany, SUNY Press).

Survey and Study Committee for the Financial Base of National Universities (March 1991) Interim status report: National university scholars now face the fund problem of Education and research, Unpublished document (Tokyo, University of Tokyo).

Thomas, R. Murray & Postlewaite, T. Neville (1983) *Schooling in East Asia: Forces of change* (New York, Pergamon Press).

US Department of Education (1985) *Japanese Education Today* (Washington, DC, US Government Printing Office).

Wexler, Philip (1987) *Social Analysis of Education: After the new sociology of education* (New York, Routledge, Kegan Paul).

Wolcott, Harry (1990) On seeking—and rejecting—validity in qualitative research, in: E. Eisner & A. Peshkin (Eds) *Qualitative Inquiry in Education: The continuing debate* (New York, Teachers College).

Yin, Robert K. (1989) *Case Study Research: Design and methods,* revised edn (Newbury Park, California, Sage).

Culture and the Role of Women in a Latin American University

SUSAN B. TWOMBLY

In 1993 the University of Costa Rica (UCR), one of the premier Central American public universities, had what seemed like an extraordinary number of women in positions of authority. Most of these women were directors of their respective *escuelas*, or departments; four were deans; and three occupied positions in the highest ranks of the university. That four deanships should be held by women—including the dean of the School of Engineering—was surprising. That each of these women had to survive a potentially politically charged electoral process made the numbers seem almost unimaginable. In several cases these were not the first women to have held deanships of their respective schools. The School of Education has had a long history of prominent women deans.

From my perspective as a female North American academic, the number of women administrators holding prominent positions was a surprise for two reasons. First, in my own U.S. university there are few women in such high positions. Although women are increasingly gaining department chair positions, only the third female dean in the university, the first ever in the School of Education, assumed the position on July 1, 1994. My university is hardly unique. Women students outnumber men in North American colleges and universities, and yet women's struggle to gain faculty and administrative positions, and thus access to sites of influence, in these culturally powerful institutions has been less than totally successful (see for example, Aisenberg and Harrington 1988; Tack and Paritu 1992).

Second, North American writers tend to view Latin American countries as machista and Latin American women as leading constrained lives while portraying themselves to be more advanced (Behar 1993). Perhaps this is because the majority of research on Latin American women has focused on lower-class women. (Stromquist 1992 is an exception.) We know much less about the potentially powerful class of professional women in these countries: how the larger society and institutional culture shape their professional choices and lives and how they, through their work, seek to maintain or make changes in those cultures. This chapter explores how culture shapes roles and possibilities for academic women in one university.

As major sites where knowledge is produced, culture mediated, and future generations of professionals trained, universities are sites of power. They have their own cultures that reinforce certain norms, attitudes, and behaviours, including how power is exercised and who has access to positions of influence (Kuh and Whitt 1988; Tierney and Rhoads 1994). Participants not only contribute to the development of institutional culture; their activity within the organization is shaped by that culture. If we accept the proposition that access to the professions is critical to improvement of women's status, it is important to examine how the university, as gatekeeper to professions, shapes women's roles. In this case we are concerned with how a particular group of people—women in positions of influence—participated in the life of a major university; how they perceived their roles to be defined by the culture and how they, in turn, shaped the culture. During the spring of 1993, there were approximately twenty-five women in positions of authority at UCR. How did the university culture shape the possibilities for women?

What factors helped them and hindered them in their professional development? Did these women perceive they had equal power to men within the university? How did they view the role and status of women in the university and society and their role in either maintaining or changing that status? In the process of answering these questions, a picture of the university culture and how it did or did not create possibilities for women emerges.

In an attempt to answer these questions, I interviewed eighteen of the approximately twenty-five women who held elected positions of authority in April 1993. My Costa Rican colleagues helped me develop the interview protocol. All interviews were conducted in Spanish. The reader is reminded that in most cases these women were speaking from relatively elite positions; however, they also tried to speak for women more generally.

Women in Costa Rica: A Brief Overview

Girls and women fare relatively well in this small country the size of West Virginia in which the extremes of wealth and poverty so characteristic of much of Latin America are unfamiliar. In 1991, women comprised 49.5% of the total population of approximately 3,100,000 persons (*Market Data* 1992). Two of the factors that work in favor of women are a low birthrate and a relatively high level of education (García and Gomáriz 1989). Between 1960 and 1988, the percentage of women in the workforce increased from 17% to 28% (excluding domestic labor) (García and Gomáriz 1989).

It is the area of education that distinguishes Costa Rica most from its neighbors. In 1990 Costa Rica had one of the lowest illiteracy rates in Latin America, the second lowest illiteracy rate among rural women, and, with Argentina, the lowest gap between illiteracy rates of men and women (Stromquist 1992, 26). Only 6.9% of the female population was classified as illiterate in 1984 (García and Gomáriz 1989). Furthermore, in Costa Rica, women comprise 50% or more of the students at every level of education except that of higher education, in which their participation lags behind that of men by only 1% point or less (Blanco, Delgadillo, and Méndez 1989; García and Gomáriz 1989). In 1990, 37% of the University of Costa Rica faculty were women (Universidad de Costa Rica 1992). The university has a dynamic gender studies program. A virtual alphabet soup of activist women's organizations exists in the country; and Margarita Penón, former "Primera Dama" of the country and a credible presidential precandidate in Costa Rica's recent national election, worked openly for women's rights while first lady. Married professional women seldom use their husbands' last names, and other very visible symbols of women's rights activities such as posters and marches are common.

Some reservation is warranted, however. Educational equality does not necessarily mean social equality, and Costa Rican women face many obstacles. (See Bonder 1992 and Mendiola 1992 for related discussions.) In fact, despite this picture of relative equality, the women interviewed described the society in which they live as machista and traditional, in which women face a number of problems, especially violence. They were optimistic that traditional gender role expectations were changing in the younger generation.

Social Class and Education

These women had grown up in a culture of social mobility in which it was possible for women to enter university and even to attain advanced degrees. Among this group of women, some clearly grew up in wealthy and/or socially prestigious families. For example, "I come from a family with a long academic tradition," said the dean of letters. "My grandfather, uncle, and father were all academics." They had been influential leaders in the founding and subsequent reform of the university. The vice rector for academic affairs had completed all of her higher education (bachelor's through doctorate) in the United States. However, some of the women came from poor homes. The director of the University Council described her family as "very poor." One dean used the term "culturally limited" to describe the fact that her parents had little formal education. Finding themselves forced to work due to illness or death of a family member, several dropped out of school for a period or changed career plans.

By far the majority described themselves as middle class.

With few exceptions, families placed a premium on education, even for women. "There wasn't any exclusion," said the director of the Department of Sociology and Anthropology. "The perspective of our parents was to study and keep studying." The dean of education said that her good grades "motivated my parents because they had plans that all of us were going to study and today we are all professionals." She confirmed what several others said: "We all studied and found that education was the mechanism to mobility. This stimulated us further." Regardless, then, of social class origins, the majority of these women received much support to study. And study they did. Six of these women held doctorates, ten master's degrees, and only two the licenciatura. Some of the younger women will earn doctoral degrees. They ranged in age from late twenties to mid-fifties. The majority were in their forties.

University Culture and the Role of Women

University Organizational Structure

The present University of Costa Rica was founded in 1940 and enrolls 30,000 students in five faculties. The university is governed by the University Assembly (consisting of all tenured faculty); the University Council, a representative group elected to make policy; the rector (president); and five appointed *vicerrectores*: academic affairs, research, community outreach, administrative affairs, and student affairs. The institution is divided into *facultades* (colleges), *escuelas* (departments), sections, agricultural stations, research centers, and institutes and has four regional centers located throughout the country.

Each school is headed by an elected dean and a college assembly; each department, by an elected director. Terms for all elected positions are four years with the possibility of reelection for one additional term. In schools divided into departments, directors or department chairpersons hold more direct power than deans. See Table 1 for a listing of areas, schools, and departments.

Because all deans and director positions, excepting the vice rector positions, are elected positions, aspirations for careers in academic administration are constrained by the electoral process and, more generally, by the boundaries of the university. Most of the women in this study said that they ran for their current position because colleagues asked them to and because they believed they could make a difference. Most said they planned to return to full-time teaching after their four-year term ended; however, several clearly aspired to other administrative postions.

Women in the University of Costa Rica: A Statistical Picture

The official list of university administrators issued in January 1992, modified to bring it up to date, included the following women: vice rector of academic affairs, vice rector of community outreach, director of the University Council, a member of the University Council, the dean of engineering, dean of education, dean of fine arts, dean of letters, and five vice deans including the graduate division. Ten women held positions as directors of schools (departments) out of forty-one departments while eleven served as subdirectors. Two women directed interdisciplinary careers (majors) and women directed the law and education research institutes (two out of ten total). Assistant directors of three of these were women. Out of seventeen research centers, four were headed by women: history, hemoglobin research, electron microscopy, and training and research in public administration (*La Gaceta* 1992).

The data on the representation of women faculty reported in Table 1 indicate that women were more highly represented in some areas and departments than in others. Overall, women tended to be concentrated in the areas of arts and letters, social sciences, and health. Each area, however, represents a wide range of academic schools and departments, and women's participation must be analyzed carefully. From a comparative perspective, the most interesting figures are those in the sciences. Even within the area of engineering and architecture, where the percentage of women was low, 21% of the faculty in industrial engineering, 27% in architecture, and 38% in computer science were women. Women were also well represented in the schools of pharmacy and microbiology and the Department of Nursing.

TABLE 1
Women Faculty by Academic Unit, July 1990

Academic Unit	*Percent*	*Number*	*Academic Unit*	*Percent*	*Number*
Total	*36.5*	*854*	Faculty of Education	61.3	98
			Administration	27.3	6
General Studies	*45.5*	*45*	Teacher Education	67.2	41
			Counseling and Spec. Ed.	80.0	32
Area of Arts and Letters	*48.4*	*104*	Physical Education	41.7	10
Faculty of Fine Arts	32.6	30	Library Science	75.0	9
Theater	33.3	4	Faculty of Law	14.1	11
Music	34.0	17			
Art	31.0	9	*Area of Engineering*	*14.5*	*42*
Faculty of Letters	60.2	74	*and Architecture*		
Philology/Linguistics	60.7	17	Faculty of Agriculture	13.0	10
Philosophy	33.3	8	Ag. Economics	14.3	2
Modern Languages	68.6	48	Fitotechnology	9.1	3
			Animal Science	14.3	4
Area of Basic Sciences	*24.1*	*49*	Food Technology		
Faculty of Sciences	24.1	49	Faculty of Engineering	15.1	32
Biology	50.0	14	Agricultural Engineering	18.2	2
Physics	16.3	8	Civil Engineering		
Geology	10.0	2	Electrical		
Mathematics	22.1	17	Industrial	20.7	6
Chemistry	28.6	8	Mechanical	9.5	2
			Chemical	15.8	3
Area of Social Sciences	*43.2*	*260*	Architecture	26.7	4
Faculty of Economics	26.1	42	Topography	9.55	2
Business Administration	18.5	12	Computer Science	38.2	13
Public Administration	44.0	11			
Economics	20.5	9	*Area of Health*	*33.3*	*154*
Statistics	37.0	10	Faculty of Pharmacy	52.4	11
Faculty of Social Sciences	52.6	120	Faculty of Medicine	32.8	107
Anthropology and Sociology	49.2	29	Nursing	96.2	50
Communication	39.3	11	Medicine	17.4	39
Political Science	40.0	4	Faculty of Microbiology	44.0	22
History and Geography	42.4	25	Faculty of Dentistry	21.2	14
Psychology	63.3	31			
Social Work	87.0	20			

Source: UCR, Oficina de Planificación Universitaria, Perfil del Funcionario Docente, 1992.

Obtaining a faculty position is one thing, but promotion to the highest academic ranks is quite another. An individual who is hired for a position *propiedad* (with tenure) moves through a series of ranks beginning with instructor, adjunct, and associate, to the highest rank of *catedrático*. At the time of this study, there was no time limit for moving from one rank to another. Criteria for promotion from one rank to the next highest included publications, teaching experience, degrees attained, and mastery of foreign languages.

Available data revealed that women were more highly represented in the lower ranks (Blanco, Delgadillo, and Méndez 1989). In 1987, 47% of women faculty were at the rank of instructor compared to 40% of the men. At the other end of the spectrum, 26% of the men held the rank of associate and 21% that of *catedrático* compared to 24.3% and 11.9% of the women, respectively. However, 11.9% is approximately double the percentage of women holding full professorships in major U.S. research universities in the same time period (Moore and Sagaria 1993). These last percentages are important because one must hold at least the rank of associate to stand for election to positions of authority. Although the percentage of women who held the rank of *catedrático* had increased since 1982, from 6.2% to 11.9%, it still lagged behind that of men. Therefore, women were not as well represented in the rank that has the most influence within the university (González, personal communication 1993).

The Role of Women

How does the university culture define, facilitate, or constrain the role of women within it? This section will focus around three central aspects of women's role in the university: (a) their location, (b) factors that helped or hindered their success, and (c) their perceptions of their own power and influence. The interviewees described a larger societal culture that disadvantages women and a university culture that is more or less favorable to them. But their words also revealed many ambiguities.

Location in the University

With several notable exceptions, the women in positions of power in the University of Costa Rica were in departments or schools in which women constituted the majority or near majority. This was true in fact as well as in perception. "In the university the majority of women are in positions identified especially for women. There are a few exceptions, and in these cases, women have achieved the positions with a base of support," said the director of the University Council. She went on to say:

> *Although in UCR there are many women in positions of power, there are certain careers which are considered women's fields.... Engineering and medicine are masculine. The culture of the country is masculine. If we talk of women in positions of power in this University, we are talking about women who are luchadoras, very strong women with a very strong trajectory of struggle, and they are outstanding from an academic point of view.*

The vice rector for academic affairs explained further, "The educational system is discriminatory at the level of training of students.... When students select majors, self-discriminating factors enter, perhaps cultural and universal factors. Women tend to choose certain types of careers."

The university system facilitates women's access to positions of authority in fields in which there are more women to vote. A department director explained: "The assembly in the School of Medicine is 80% men. Men are going to win any election for this reason." However, it did not always follow, said some, that women would win elections just because there were more women in a school or department. The system of electing administrators did seem to have facilitated women's chances of attaining positions in certain areas.

This apparent success was qualified by one dean:

> *We are women deans in schools divided in departments. Why? Because the power in these schools is held by the departments. The dean is more or less a coordinator. Some would say a figurehead, but I don't agree with that. Deanships in schools not divided in departments, such as law and pharmacy, do not have women deans. [A woman had recently held the deanship of the School of Law.] Who are the deans then: in Letters—school divided in departments, in Engineering—also divided in departments. She is very important. There should not be a woman dean in Engineering.*

The dean of letters provided additional insight into why there were more women in some fields than in others:

> *We have always said that Letters is one of the most matriarchial of the schools in the entire university. Traditionally, teaching has been viewed as women's work. Here, above all, primary, and later secondary education, was in hands of women. It was supposed that women were mothers and therefore good teachers. Above all, primary education was seen as an extension of the home, and education was directed by women. The School of Letters was a school that primarily trained for teaching. However, this has changed some recently. There has been greater specialization, and now we have postgraduate studies and emphasis on research has increased. But fortunately this happened when we already had the territory clearly controlled [she laughed]. The concern in the School of Letters has been that the department of philosophy had been very patriarchial as a result of the stereotypical idea that thinking is masculine and feeling feminine. Recently women have begun to invade this territory [she chuckled], demonstrating that philosophy is not just men's territory. When there is a male dean, he comes from philosophy.*

At the time the interviews were conducted, the School of Education was also dominated by women with only the Department of Educational Administration headed by a man. The only other male in the assembly was the student representative.

Several of the women noted that the position of vice rector for academic affairs was also a position for women. "The vice rectorship of academic affairs is always in women's hands, because of its relationship to teaching. This is also a stereotype, but there have been extraordinary women in this position," said one woman. Another woman suggested that this was only compensation for the rector always being a man.

Factors that Enhanced or Inhibited Success

When asked how success was defined in the university, these women provided a broad answer of which promotion in academic rank was only part. They included factors such as recognition as a good teacher and as an expert in one's field. Election to positions of authority was one indication of this recognition.

With few exceptions, these women believed that it was more difficult for them than their male colleagues to achieve success. "I can't speak of equality," said the director of the University Council. "We have to be two times better to succeed in the university. If one is equal in qualifications, the man has more opportunities; but if one stands out and excels, she can achieve success more easily than a man. . . . For the Consejo, one has to be an outstanding woman in order to win. Men get points just for being men."

In commenting on success in the university, one dean laughed as she said,

> *Success? Officially or unofficially? Officially by ability, curriculum vitae and academic area. Unofficially, to be male carries more weight. . . . In practice one observes very subtle obstacles. For example, stereotypes function as rationality for men. . . . Recognition of scientific publications is very easy. However, recognition of literary works is much more complicated, and art is even more difficult. One has to demonstrate doubly that literary work and art have value because traditionally women are associated with emotion and men with science.*

"Stereotypes still put women in subordinate positions. We aren't good administrators. We are good secretaries," said one woman. Moreover, "it costs women more to hold an administrative position." This was largely due to family responsibilities. All but four of the women interviewed were married or divorced. Only these four and two of the younger, recently married women did not have children. The three women in the highest positions were single, as predicted by one of the department directors. The status of being "single, never married" is still somewhat uncommon in Costa Rica. Although these women were viewed as being able to take on top positions because they did not have husbands and children, they were clearly exceptions.

Most agreed with the dean who said: "The university system does not disadvantage the woman. It is the real time available that limits one." She asked, "Does the woman have time to write? time for professional development? time to learn another language? Can she make the decision to go to another country to study if her husband is not an academic? These are the limitations." The system of academic ranks was described as being sex blind and nondiscriminatory. "Success doesn't have anything to do with sex," added one department director. "It is a matter of will, intention, ability, and free time."

However, one director's description of her efforts to produce scholarship shows how their time was limited. "In spite of a good family situation, it is hard to do research. One has to achieve a balance between family and work. One can't dedicate much more time to one area or the other. I am a housewife, nurse, wife, mother. This affects my ability and time to commit myself to research, thinking, and conceptualizing." For those who had children, it was clear that their primary responsibility was to the children, especially when they were young.

Although the university was quite flexible in allowing women with full-time appointments to work part time when necessary, there were no time limits for promotions; and one could teach in *interino* (instructor) status for as long as one wished, these advantages had potentially negative consequences for women as a young, recently married department director explained:

> *Five of us entered university careers in the same year. We all have the same number of years working in the university and we are all at different ranks. One has a child. She is low on the scale. One does not do research. The third has children also, but now they are older. I am an associate and am preparing my papers for the* catedrática. *I don't have any children. For me*

> *this is a factor which has weighed heavily on the women in this school: their condition as mothers and women, women who do not want to neglect their role as mother.*

It was true that some of these women had full-time housekeepers to care for the children; however, full-time help was too expensive for some. One of the deans remarked that even though she did have help in her home, she still bore the majority of the responsibility for transporting the children, helping them with their homework, and managing the home. She described her day:

> *Yesterday I worked here [at the university] until two in the afternoon. I went home [about fifteen miles from the university]. I worked at home with the children a little. I left them at school and returned to a meeting of the Consejo Superior of the School of Education. In the meantime I ran to buy some things for the children. On the way home I went to buy some groceries and returned to my house at 7:30. Then, for the next two hours I helped the children. . . . We have something that most North American families don't have: domestic help. However, the maid is more likely to attend to the man of the house. I can arrive very late and very tired, but she never asks me if I would like a cup of tea or if she can help me with anything. She shines my husband's shoes, puts out his clothes, asks him if he wants tea, etc. This is the structure I would change.*

Women frequently complained about the lack of quality day care centers.

When asked specifically about the role of the family, the women generally agreed that societal expectations of women were the single most important limitation for women in general even if not for themselves. Even so, few labeled family as an obstacle. One woman who worked in a highly technical, typically masculine field in which men were suspicious of her competence made the following comment:

> *It is difficult to obtain positions of responsibility. Independent of whether there is open discrimination or not, of whether there are children or* empleadas, *the woman has to do the housework. It is an unequal situation, very bothersome. One supposes also that if the woman accepts work outside of the home, she is a bad mother. People are going to ask why you aren't attending to your children. All my life I have been called a bad mother, even by some of my colleagues. The former director of my department used to ask me what I was doing at the university, why wasn't I home with the children? It is a catch-22 [her word]. There is no way to come out well because if you are a mother, you can't be a good worker.*

Postgraduate degrees and knowledge of foreign languages are important criteria for moving through the ranks (although not necessary to obtain positions). Until recently, the only option for men and women to earn doctoral degrees was to travel outside the country. The interviewees described how this affected women:

> *When I applied for a scholarship to study in Canada, a federal scholarship, in an absolutely competitive situation, I didn't feel any limitations. I had to pass through many filters. I did this with the benefit of having many women in positions of leadership, including —— the Vice Rector for Academic Affairs. . . . There was never a question that my being a mother or woman affected my getting the scholarship.*

The catch is that women are less likely than men to apply for scholarships. While several women told about husbands who took leaves from their positions to accompany them abroad, most agreed with the woman who said: "The opportunities are greater for men to leave to get a graduate degree than for women because of their commitment as mothers." This woman also offered the opinion that people still believed that education for a man was a better investment than for a woman. In addition, embassy sexism and the university's narrow family reimbursement policy were cited as factors that discourage women from seeking study opportunities outside of the country. In general, these women believed that they lived in a place and time in which, in the words of one, "Men can rise in the ranks more easily because it is easier for them to travel outside of the country."

Not all agreed the university presented more obstacles for women than for men. Several women echoed the sentiments of one research center director: "The obstacles are not very great. . . . They are surmountable. . . . It costs to assimilate. . . . It depends in part on personality. There are men too who have been affected because their personality is weak. It almost doesn't matter whether one is male or female, but rather the personality counts more and what one wants in life." Another woman noted that she had

> *personally not experienced any difficulty. It is a cultural problem, the limitations that one faces. It is also a problem of defining priorities. . . . For me, at a certain time my first priority was to be a mother, second was a professor, and third was to be a researcher. The limitation that one has is to define priorities. Obstacles one defines oneself.*

"I haven't faced any obstacles," said the vice rector. "At the level of society, that is where women face obstacles."

While societal and cultural factors were identified as inhibiting women, they largely credited themselves for their success. The director of the University Council is an example:

> *I had to excel not only in my studies for the licenciatura but in the studies for the doctorate in Belgium also. . . . I worked harder than men. . . . My case is a special case. I am a very tenacious woman. If one has equal professional qualifications to a man, the man has more opportunities. If a woman stands out and excels she can achieve success more easily than a man.*

A director of a scientific research institute attributed her success to her character: "I have never been one to stay behind." One department director became pregnant out of wedlock before having finished her education. She made the very difficult decision not to marry the father:

> *If I had married, I would not have worked, would not have earned my master's degree. . . . I would have run into a wall. The father of the child had told me that I could not work. Because I had my undergraduate degree and an established job, I couldn't become the housewife he wanted me to be.*

This decision required an extreme amount of courage and foresight on this woman's part. She later left the child with her parents for two years in order to earn a master's degree in Chile.

"To be the only woman in a major had certain advantages," said another. "While I felt alone, it gave me pleasure to belong to this elite." It's all "personal attitude," said one dean. "I speak the language without losing my femininity. They respect me and I have always played within the men's rules even though they represent a handicap for me."

These academic women cited other factors that helped them. God was credited with having given one woman ability and forcefulness. "Because where did I get this strength?" she asked. "From my husband? No. He always has been against my working. Until now. Now I am attending to *my* needs." This woman, who had raised five children before entering the university herself, told the story of how she finally gained confidence in herself. She was teaching a course in special education:

> *There were thirty students from rural areas. . . . One of the students had serious health problems and couldn't attend classes. He had to have kidney dialysis. But he worked very hard. He was poor and shy. . . . One day he came to my office and told me that he needed a new kidney but there was no donor. . . . The story is that I gave him my kidney. This marked a very important situation for me. It was a tremendously important decision. My husband did not even want me to give blood. When I had the courage to tell him that I was going to donate my kidney, I did not even ask him. I told him and waited for what was going to happen. It was the most important decision that I have made in my life, and it has made a great difference in my whole life. From then on I lost the fear of making decisions.*

It was clear that on a personal level, these women had worked hard to succeed, by their own accounts at least twice as hard as their male colleagues, and their ability to do so was a result of personal characteristics and having survived many battles.

However, the university was also described as being a good place for women to work—better than private industry. Two aspects of the university were particularly helpful to women: its flexibility and its growth during the 1970s and 1980s when most of these women began their careers. In the words of one director:

> *The advantages of UCR facilitate the entrance of women. . . . In one sense machismo favors this. The norm has been to enter the university as an* interino *[nontenure, part-time faculty] and stay in this level for a while. Because women are married, it is not their responsibility to guarantee work stability. I can be* interino *and if they need me, fine; and if they do not, I don't have the same pressure that men have. Above all, the university woman does not have to maintain the family economically. The uni-*

versity also permits us to work part time when we have to. In a private company, one can't work part time.

These particular women also benefitted from being in the right place at the right time. They began their careers during a period in which the university was growing rapidly and needed faculty. However, one department director noted that this boom period was now over and that it was not as easy to obtain a tenured position. The effect this will have on the number and percentage of women in the university is not known.

Several of the younger women credited their helpful husbands for making their ability to hold these positions possible. What was missing was any reference to mentors. While one or two women noted the importance of role models to their professional development, such as former deans, ministers of education, and a woman who had run for rector recently, mentors were apparently not a factor. Even when asked specifically, women did not identify influential mentors.

Elections, Power, and Administrative Work

There were mixed opinions about whether women faced more obstacles than men in the election process or had equal power. A very prominent woman had run for, and narrowly lost, the election for rector in the late 1980s. She, and others, described the nature of the campaign politics. "Women have to be purer than men," observed one woman. The recently elected member of the University Council explained how the election process worked against her:

> *All of the other candidates from my area were men, men who had followed traditional university careers. I had been coordinator of the master's program in the School of Education. The men had held ministry positions. There is also a political career. There were very subtle things. In one round table discussion they wanted me to speak first. I said "No señores," because it is a disadvantage to go first, and we drew straws. There is a tendency to attack one's personal life. There is more interest in elections for high positions, and more weapons are used. In the case of the married woman, they invent a lover. If one has one, it becomes public. If one doesn't have a lover, they invent one. It isn't the same for a man. In my case they attacked me on, let's say, a professional issue.*

A number of women reinforced the fact that a double standard operates with respect to personal life. Women, they said, are expected to be more perfect. In two cases, the candidates' husbands were also a member of the same unit. These women had to convince their units that the husbands were not really going to run things. As one woman said, "No one has ever asked any of the previous directors about the influence their spouses had over them." Perhaps because most women held positions in areas where women were well represented, they did not generally feel that the election process worked unduly against them. The stakes were higher for positions of higher rank, and elections potentially more volatile.

The interviewees disagreed about whether women and men in equivalent positions had equal power and how their status as women affected administrative work. Men and women have ". . . completely equal power. Here in the unversity there is no difference," said one woman director. This sentiment was shared by another director: "There is much sexual harrassment and more discrimination in the administrative area among the secretaries; however, in the higher level positions, there are fewer problems." Yet another woman added, "In the university in general, there is no difference, but some schools, such as medicine, are exceptions." Some women firmly believed that women's participation and power were significantly different in units in which women were the majority and those in which they were the minority.

One of the institute directors believed she had gained power: "When they elected me, they might not have had any confidence. That's why I said before that it is indespensable to demonstrate that one can act and that one knows how to make decisions."

These women generally considered themselves to be more dedicated, equally able to solve problems, and in some cases more effective at certain types of activities than men and therefore they had equal power: "Women are more dedicated to the university. Because men have to maintain a house and family, many have to work outside the university. When women sign to do full time, they do it." This was true in part because in a machista society, men are expected to support the family economically, thus forcing many academic men to hold more than one job to earn a sufficient living. Women, on the other hand, when not the main economic support for a family, can survive on the university's salary and not have to take on additional jobs.

Once again these women attributed their equal power to themselves as well as to policies. "Women have equal capacity to resolve problems [therefore equal power]," said one woman. Another added, "Women have more ability to visualize solutions to problems." "Women are more organized despite the fact that they are not in decision-making positions. If women had more access to positions of power, these countries would be better organized," offered another.

When a difference in power was noted, it was largely attributed to the fact that "power is determined by number of votes." According to this theory, the larger areas and larger departments and schools have more power. "If one controls size, it doesn't matter if it is men's or women's field," argued one director. Another observed that "In general terms, when resources are distributed, the School of Social Sciences is the school that receives fewer resources, for example, materials and building, compared to the others. It is not because of gender," she said. However, it was also true that overall the social sciences had high numbers of women and students compared to medicine and engineering. One of the deans reported that the one woman director in her school had more power than male directors because she had more resources, including an entire building under her responsibility; but her success was totally up to her, said the dean.

There were others who provided a somewhat different picture. "By law, yes. Within the position, yes [men and women have equal power], but when it comes to work, the vice rector of administration (a man), for example, can work with other men—*majae*—the old boys' network. Women don't understand the informal language.... Women have to fight like men." Moreover, if a woman makes a decision, "[she is] a loudmouth, a castrating woman," reported one. "If I'm not forceful, I am incapable of making decisions. They don't want to recognize my technical knowledge," added another. One of the research institute directors spoke of a meeting she had just come from in which several male administrators had tried to convince her to give up her space and build a new building with less than sufficient resources:

> *Today I realized that the assistant to the rector thought I was a mere imbecile, an idiot who did not understand what was going on and that they could easily get what they wanted by pressuring me with the university administration and leave us with little. They pressured me in meetings with all sorts of important people sitting around a table.... One person by herself is not as strong as two. I brought the dean. They thought they were going to impress me with important surnames and all that.... These games are not professional.... I realized that most women are naive in this sense and we do not play these games. They had to listen when both of us came to the meeting.*

Not more than ten to fifteen minutes later, this same director said emphatically "No, women do not face obstacles in the university."

One of the deans in a largely female-dominated school offered the opinion that the number of women in positions indicated that sexism and discrimination within the university had been conquered. "We haven't had a rector yet. We have had very good vice rectors in the last few years. I don't know how many. For more than ten years the major vice rector has been a woman." This woman went on to say, "The university system doesn't disadvantage women at all. It is the free time women don't have that limits them.... But from a legal point of view, we have real equality."

Conclusion

How, then, did the university culture shape women's participation, and how, in turn, did these women who held significant administrative positions support or subvert this culture?

For many of these women, the university was perceived to be an oasis in an otherwise machista society, and university culture itself, they believed, did not limit their participation. In fact the presence of a relatively high percentage of women was itself an artifact, suggesting that women's participation in the university is acceptable. Rather, they shared the belief that larger societal values regarding women's role were responsible for difficulties faced by academic women. Time and time again women said that the university was a good place to work. Laws and university policy, they believed, established a more or less equal situation for men and women, while societal expectations and stereotypes inhibited women's ability to achieve by restricting the time they had to devote to activities such as publishing, their ability to study abroad, and the way women were viewed. In this respect, the university itself played the role of a subculture that countered values of a larger society at least for women in positions of power. Although some women talked specifically about discrimination, about having to work twice as hard and be twice as competent as men, the old boys' network, and other ways in which they were disadvantaged, they largely described the rules as gender blind. The exact reasons for UCR's seeming receptivity to women are unclear but may be related to a variety of factors, such as the coincidence of UCR's growth with the availability of women to assume positions, relatively low professorial salaries, the university's emphasis during critical formative years on preparing secondary teachers, and the belief that this was an acceptable role for women.

In other ways the university reproduced societal views of women. The most overt way in which the university limited women faculty and administrators was by "restricting" their participation to predominantly women's fields—areas that may have less influence within the university. Even so there were several exceptional women included in this study, namely the dean of engineering and the director of the University Council, who did not conform to the pattern. Women revealed ambivalent attitudes toward gender segmentation in the university. They expressed concern about ghettos of powerlessness and agreed that women should be able to pursue any field of study, but many also spoke very positively about why they were in a "woman's field." One dean even spoke defiantly about women having her area under control.

There are several ways to think about women being "restricted" to women's fields. On the one hand, women working in traditional women's fields such as nutrition, education, and health have an opportunity to affect services essential to the well-being of women and of a developing society. From a comparative perspective, although women historically dominated some fields such as home economics and nursing, women have not dominated such traditionally "women's fields" as education or social welfare in U.S. universities. Moreover, some social science fields that were considered "women's fields" in Costa Rica are not so in the United States. So even though women attained powerful positions in women's fields, at least they gained positions of power in these fields. However, while these traditionally female professions may have influence over individuals, they have not had as much political influence as medicine and law. In fact, statistics reveal relatively high percentages of women students in the schools of law, medicine, and dentistry (Blanco, Delgadillo, and Méndez 1989). Whether these women graduate and actually practice their chosen profession and if not, why not, are significant questions that should be addressed.

The important question is whether and, if so, how women academics in positions of influence used their power to bring about changes in the culture for women. Two questions about the definition of feminism and necessary changes in the university provided insight into how these women viewed their own situation and whether they worked to maintain the status quo or for change.

These women fell into three groups with respect to activism on behalf of women: The traditionalists essentially said that women experienced no problems except those imposed by society and identified nothing within the university in need of change. Reluctant activists, clearly recognizing obstacles, spoke in a more feminist way about their own lives, even while rejecting the term feminist as a self-descriptor. These women did not believe much change was necessary in the university and did little to change it. The quiet subversives recognized inequalities in the university and engaged in activities to change the status quo, but often in very subtle ways. These activities included gender inclusive language, and their recommendations for changes in the university included paying attention to how committees were constituted, hiring more women, and electing a woman rector.

Academic women in Costa Rica did not embrace the term "feminist" as typically defined from a Western perspective (see Perreault 1993 for a discussion of such definitions). Although most defined the term as equality between the sexes, most agreed that to adopt the label would make change more difficult for women because of the hostility it engenders. "I am not a militant feminist," said the member of the Consejo Universitario, "but I fight very hard." Others prided themselves on the same behavior—practicing gender equality, even being very proactive in their own lives and for others—while rejecting the term feminist. Most acknowledged the important work of the gender studies program and recognized a need to work together. "Men always support other men, but women don't necessarily support other women. I have recently become aware of this and will now vote for women," noted one of the directors. But even the gender studies program, while offering courses, focused on working with community women's groups outside of the university. Actively confronting women's status within the university occupied a seemingly small part of their agenda. In fact, women in positions of power generally took the long view, arguing that gradual change would result in a better life for the next generation of women.

When asked if they included gender issues in their classes, many said no, even though they placed their faith in new values in the younger generation. Some, including the director of the Consejo Universitario, were strong supporters of the gender studies program. The reluctant activists often said that to treat everyone equally was their contribution. One of the quietly subversive directors said she did address women's issues, but more than that she discouraged her mostly women students from marrying too young and encouraged them to stay in school. The director of the computer science department directly dealt with gender issues in her math classes and in seminars for engineering students. The dean of letters taught courses on feminist theory and literature. The gender studies program has recently implemented a master's degree. Negative responses to sexist language was a common form of resistance.

Because the causes of gender inequality were externalized to the society at large and women were typically located in units with high percentages of women, it should not be a surprise that these women had few suggestions for changing the university to make it a better place for women. These women were sufficiently divided in their views of the university that they did not constitute a conscious subculture and certainly not a subculture bent on revolutionizing the university. In fact, paralleling the close relationship of the Latin American university to the state, there was in some ways a blurring of lines between the external and institutional levels of culture with respect to women. Women did not leave their private lives at the door when they donned their professional hats.

Already viewing their lives as better than those of the majority of working women, it was difficult for them to envision improvement in the university. Rather than defining themselves as victims of a machista society in which the *doble jornada*, or double workload, weighed heavily on them, they described themselves as strong, capable women who had succeeded in that society. They agreed that changes in the university organization without concomitant changes in societal attitudes would be useless. Sociologist Lynne Phillips's conclusion about her own struggle to interpret Latin American women's responses to their situations seems valid here: "Looking for evidence of women's resistance only in articulated protests . . . I ignored the possibility that their resistance was to be found precisely in their self-constructions" (1991, 100). The response these women forged to their circumstances was to be successful themselves and, by doing so, to improve the lives of the women around them.

Notes

An earlier version of this chapter was presented at the Annual Meeting of the American Educational Research Association, New Orleans, Louisiana, April 8, 1994.

Agradezco muchisimo a Mirta González Suárez, Irma González y Dunnia Morales por haber hecho posible este estudio y también a las profesoras que participaron y compartieron sus vidas conmigo.

References

Aisenberg, N. and M. Harrington. 1988. *Women of academe: Outsiders in the sacred grove.* Amherst: University of Massachusetts Press.

Behar, R. 1993. *Translated woman: Crossing the boarder with Esperanza's story.* Boston: Beacon Press.

Blanco, G. L. Delgadillo, and Z. Méndez. 1989. *Análisis cuantitativo y cualitativo de la participación de la mujer en la Universidad de Costa Rica.* Cuidad Universitaria Rodrigo Facio: Universidad de Costa Rica.

Bonder, G. 1992. Altering sexual stereotypes through teacher training. In *Women and education in Latin America,* ed., N. Stromquist. Boulder, Colo.: Lynne Rienner Publishers.

La Gaceta Universitaria. 1992. University of Costa Rica.

Garcia, A., and E. Gomáriz. 1989. *Mujeres centroamericanas. Tomo 1.* Facultad Latinoamericana de Ciencias Sociales. Consejo Superior Universitario de Centroamérica, Universidad para la Paz.

González, M. March 1993. Personal communication.

Kuh, G., and E. Whitt. 1988. *The invisible tapestry: Culture in American colleges and universities.* ASHE-ERIC Higher Education Report No. 1. Washington, D.C.: Association for the Study of Higher Education.

Market Data. Costa Rica. 1992.

Méndez, Z., V. E. Davis, and S. L. Delgadillo. 1989. *Informe regional projecto de investigación análisis cuantitativo y cualitativo de la participación de la mujer en las universidades estatales centroamericanas confederadas al CSUCA: Fases cuantitativas.* San José: Universidad de Costa Rica.

Mendiola, H. 1992. Gender inequalities and the expansion of higher education in Costa Rica. In *Women and education in Latin America,* ed., N. Stromquist. Boulder, Colo.: Lynne Rienner Publishers.

Moore, K. M., and M. A. D. Sagaria. 1993. The situation of women in research universities in the United States. Reprinted in *Women in higher education,* eds., J. Glazer, E. Bensimon, and B. Townsend. Needham Heights, Mass.: Ginn Press.

Perreault, G. 1993. Contemporary feminist perspectives on women and higher education. Reprinted in *Women in higher education,* eds., J. Glazer, E. Bensimon, and B. Townsend. Needham Heights, Mass.: Ginn Press.

Phillips, L. 1991. Rural women in Latin America: Directions for future research. *Latin American Research Review* 25:101.

Stromquist, N. (ed.) 1992. *Women and education in Latin America: Knowledge, power, and change.* Boulder, Colo.: Lynne Rienner Publishers.

Tack, M., and C. Patitu. 1992. *Faculty job satisfaction: Women and minorities in peril.* ASHE-ERIC Higher Education Report Nol. 4. Washington, D.C.: The George Washington University School of Education and Human Development.

Tierney, W., and R. Rhoads. 1994. *Faculty socialization as cultural process: A mirror of institutional commitment.* ASHE-ERIC Higher Education Report No. 93–6. Washington, D.C.: The George Washington University, School of Education and Human Development.

Universidad de Costa Rica. 1992. Oficina de planificación universitaria. *Perfil del funcionario docente.*

Vicerrectoría de Docencia. 1990. *Universidad de Costa Rica.* Ciudad Universitaria Rodrigo Facio: Universidad de Costa Rica.

PART III

ORGANIZATIONAL CONTEXTS

Universities and Academic Systems in Modern Societies

JOSEPH BEN-DAVID AND AWRAHAM ZLOCZOWER

Universities engage in teaching and research. They prepare students to become men of action in practical politics, the civil service, the practice of law, medicine, surgery etc. Others studying at universities want to become scholars and scientists whose style of work is far removed from the on-the-spot decision-making which is so important among the former category. The professions and disciplines taught and developed at universities require a great variety of manpower and organization of entirely different kinds. Universities nevertheless insist on comprising all of them, in the name of an idea stemming from a time when one person was really able to master all the arts and sciences. They, furthermore, attempt to perform all these complex tasks within the framework of corporate self-government reminiscent of medieval guilds. Indeed there have been serious doubts about the efficiency of the university since the 18th century. Reformers of the "Enlightenment" advocated the abolition of the universities as useless remnants of past tradition and establish in their stead specialized schools for the training of professional people and academies for the advancement of science and learning. This program was actually put into effect by the Revolution and the subsequent reorganization of higher education by Napoleon in France. The present day organization of higher education in the Soviet Union still reflects the belief in the efficiency of specialized professional schools as well as specialized academic research institutions.

Even in countries where universities are the typical institutions of higher education and research there are constant doubts about the ways universities are actually going about their tasks.[1] Some accuse them of undue traditionalism and advocate the setting up of technological universities, training for a much larger variety of practical callings than most universities (at least in Europe) actually do. Others, on the other hand, accuse some of the universities (mainly in America) of having abandoned the true standards of science and scholarship by the introduction of courses of study which are really vocational in their nature. Universities are often criticized for their inefficient methods of teaching, resulting from the overwhelming interest of their staff in research. At the same time it is deplored that some universities pay too much attention to teaching, neglecting research which should be the principal task of the university. There is general agreement that teaching and research should be complementary rather than competing with each other, although it is well known that the two functions are not always compatible. The ability for teaching does not always go together with the ability for doing research, and research requires a different organization than teaching.

There is, finally, the question of the "unity of science" which the university is supposed to represent. The more successful universities are in promoting research, the greater becomes the gap in communication between the various branches of learning. There has been a constant demand for bridging this gap by means of some sort of general studies. The gap however does not seem to have diminished. Increased specialization also seems to counteract another cherished purpose of the university, namely, the formation of moral character. It becomes more and more difficult to see how and which part of university studies are suited for the accomplishment of this purpose. Finally, there seem to be great inefficiencies in university self-government. The autonomy of the academic body is defended by all. But professors constantly complain that their administrative duties encroach upon their time.

Yet, in spite of all these inconsistencies and contradictions, the university has been a successful institution. Everywhere in the world universities have expanded rapidly. New countries, which had not possessed universities before, regard the establishment of a university as one of their first priorities. Universities have also been markedly successful in research. The overwhelming majority of Nobel prizes and other scientific distinctions have gone to university professors, and their output of scholarly work has not been less impressive.[2] Universities, therefore, present a baffling problem for the sociologist. They have apparently chronic and irremediable problems of internal organization, yet they manage to be in some important ways extremely efficient in accomplishing their tasks; and in spite the constant flow of criticism directed against them, there is a general belief in their necessity even among their critics.

It is not the purpose of this essay to take a stand for or against this widespread belief in the idea of the university or to suggest a solution for its problems. We shall rather ask the question how and why universities became what they are today. Instead of trying to arrive at some concept about the essence or the idea of the university, we shall try to find out under what conditions universities assumed their great variety of functions, and to what extent have they been able to cope with them.

1. German Universities and the Idea of the Modern University

For about a hundred years, between the early nineteenth century and the advent of Nazism, German universities served as model academic institutions. The education of an American or British scientist was not considered complete until he had spent some time in Germany, studying with one of the renowned professors, far more of whom had won acclaim and scientific distinction than the scientists of any other country.[3] The still prevalent conception or 'idea' of the university, as well as the definition of the professor's role, originated in Germany during the 19th century. It was, furthermore, in the German universities, more than anywhere else, that the main fields of scientific enquiry developed into 'disciplines' possessing specialized methodologies and systematically determined contents.[4] Students who wanted to know what a discipline really was had to read German textbooks and those who wanted to keep abreast of scientific research had to read German journals.

The outside world, which became aware of the excellence of German achievements, connected these achievements with the internal structure and organization of the German universities. It came to be widely believed that what a university should be and how a university should be run was discovered in Germany. The discovery was—and still is—often attributed to the ideas of German philosophers from Kant to Hegel who conceived of the university as a seat of original secular learning pursued as an end in itself, and who imparted to it supreme dignity.[5] During the 19th century reforms were introduced following the German example in Britain, France and the U.S., leading invariably to a rising standard of scientific work and a growing volume of production.[6] This confirmed the belief that the peculiar ideas and arrangements of German universities accounted for their excellence.

We shall attempt to show that these ideas and arrangements were not the cause but rather the result of the circumstances which had historically shaped the German university; that it was not the idea of the university which explains the success of the German university system, nor the diffusion of this idea abroad which explains the impetus to science in those countries introducing organizational reforms under its impact. In order to do this we shall have to examine the circumstances which determined the strength as well as the weaknesses of the German university system.

The pioneering period of the German universities, marked by the rapid development of the different academic fields and their differentiation into systematic and specific disciplines lasted until about the end of the 19th century. By about 1860 the original four faculties of theology, philosophy, law and medicine, comprising just about all higher knowledge existing at the beginning of the century had been transformed beyond all recognition. A host of new disciplines had found their place within the loose frame of the faculties, none of which—with the exception of theology—seems to have been averse to incorporating new fields. Commencing with the third quarter of the century this process of expansion and differentiation slowed down. Neither the emerging social sciences nor the various fields of engineering attained proper academic status at the universities. The latter was banished to the *Technische Hochschulen*, which only over the strenuous opposition of the universities attained the right of confering the title "doctor".[7] The universities not only began to offer increasing resistance to the introduction of new sciences which had mushroomed outside their walls, they also placed often insurmountable obstacles on the path of disciplines which had begun to develop organically within the established disciplines. Where previously it had been relatively easy to carve out new disciplines from the broad fields and gain recognition through the establishment of separate chairs for them, new specialities were increasingly condemned to permanent subordinate status under the pretext of being too narrow or shallow, and, therefore, '*nicht ordinierbar*'. The division of labor which arose in the *Instituten* (research laboratories usually attached to a university chair but not properly integrated within the university) raced far ahead of the increasingly out-of-date academic division of labor. The unity of teaching and research broke down when the academic scientist was forced to specialize in the *Institut* in research that threatened to isolate him from the main discipline which he had to teach if he wanted to become a full professor. The usual rule that each discipline was represented by only one professor contributed much in the previous decades to the establishment of new chairs, because the expansion of the academic staff could take place only in this manner. After the development of the institutes, however, the same rule became a veritable strangling-noose: research could be conducted only in the *Institut* but only one person, the director, could be professor.[8]

Thus gradually a fence was drawn around the existing academic fields, excluding an increasing part of scientific and scholarly enquiry from the universities. Originally the university was meant to embrace all intellectual enquiry.[9] It absorbed all existing disciplines, theoretical and practical. Even its philosophical founding fathers, like Fichte, Schleiermacher, and Schelling, were as much publicists as 'academic' philosophers. In the middle of the century the university became more strictly academic, but it created new disciplines and enlarged its scope, so that practically all the important scientific activity of that time originated at the university. Towards the end of the century both processes of extending the scope of the university came to a standstill.

This growing resistance to differentiation within, and to intellectual (or practical) influence from without, was accompanied by inflexibility of the organizational structure. The professorial role, and the career pattern *Privatdozent-Professor*, so well suited to the needs of research and teaching at the beginning and in the middle of the nineteenth century, when techniques and organization of research were simple, became unable to carry any more the whole burden of research and teaching. *Privatdozentur* in particular became an anomaly in fields where the most necessary research facilities were open only to assistants in the *Institut*, so that a *Privatdozent* without a position in an *Institut* had no opportunity for doing scientific work. The main career-line became, therefore, the assistantship. Yet the constitution of the university and its official structure of roles has hardly taken note of the change. Officially, even today the institutes are only appendages facilitating the professor's research.[10] Even if in some cases this arrangement works well (depending on the personality of the professors and the nature of the discipline) it shows extreme traditionalism and ritualistic clinging to organizational forms which no longer reflect the changed functions of the university.

The explanation of this contradiction between the innovative vitality of the early years of the German university and its subsequent rigidity lies mainly in two circumstances":[11] the fact that the German cultural area extending over the major part of Central Europe has always exceeded the limits of any German state, and the position of the university in Germany's class system.[12] Due to the first factor there did not arise in Germany central national universities, like Paris in France, or Oxford-Cambridge in England. The university system was decentralized and competitive. Universities tried to outdo each other, or, at any rate, had to keep pace with each other. As a result innovations were introduced in Germany more easily and accepted more widely than elsewhere. The second factor, namely the position of the university in the class system, accounts for the inflexibility of its organizational structure which became manifest late in the 19th century. As it will be shown later, the status and the freedom of the university, seemingly so well established and secure, were as a matter of fact precarious, engendering fear of and resistance to any organizational change.

This interpretation of the developments is not in accordance with the usually accepted view which relates the rise of the German universities to the reforms introduced early in the century under the influence of the then current philosophical ideas, especially the establishment of the University of Berlin. We have to see, therefore, what was the share of ideas, and of competition and class structure, in the process. Indeed, Berlin was the first university in which the philosophical faculty (including arts and sciences) obtained a status formally equivalent, but in influence superior, to the old faculties of law, medicine and theology. There is no doubt that the granting of academic status to the new arts and sciences was a decisive step, and that philosophers had a great part in this innovation. There was a growing class of intellectuals in Germany towards the end of the 18th century who would not enter any more into the clergy as people like them had done before, and who interested themselves in the broad field of learning and methodical thinking which was called at that time philosophy. They were seeking social recognition and economic security, but these were unattainable for them under the existing circumstances: the bourgeoisie was relatively poor and backward, most of the aristocracy had no tradition of education, and the minority who had such interests, preferred French to German education. The only career open to young German intellectuals was a university appointment which, in the philosophical faculty, carried little prestige and did not allow real freedom of thought and speech, since universities were subject to the double control of the state and the church.[13] Partly as a result of this control, universities were also intellectually poor institutions. They were harshly criticized, as French universities had been prior to the Revolution, and there was a tendency among enlightened circles to replace them with specialized professional schools. As a matter of fact, quite a few universities were closed down and some professional schools were established during this period.[14]

The Napoleonic wars gave a new chance to the philosopher-intellectuals as well as to the universities. Their advocacy of German instead of French culture, unheeded before, became now the popular ideology affecting even the French-educated upper class. There was a feeling that the real strength of the nation was in the realm of spirit and culture. Indeed, after their subjugation by Napoleon, Germans had little else left to fight with but spiritual strength. This seemed all the more so because political and military defeat coincided with an unprecedented flowering of German philosophy and literature. Philosophers now became national figures, and education was given high priority. Under these circumstances the philosophical faculty was given its full university status.[15] Since at the same time, and for the same reasons, secondary education was also reformed (through the introduction of the *Abitur*), the new faculty had plenty of students preparing for teaching in the *Gymnasium*.[16]

Undoubtedly these reforms, which grew up in response to this constellation of circumstances, gave an important impetus to academic work, especially in philosophy and the humanities, the subjects most in fashion at that time in Germany. But only this initial impetus can be attributed to the philosophical ideas attending the birth of this new type of university. All the upsurge of the various *Fachwissenschaften*, especially of the natural sciences, occurred not as a result, but rather in spite of these ideas. The intentions of the founders and the ideologists of Berlin University would only have made it into a unique showpiece radiating light to all corners of Germany and attracting students and scholars to the somewhat provincial Prussian capital.[17] The decisive thing, however, in the transformation of higher education and research in Germany was the fact that exactly the opposite happened. Berlin never became a unique center but rather the archaic little universities which had been hovering for decades on the verge of dissolution became transformed within a short period of time into institutions modelled on the example of Berlin. In addition a number of new universities were founded.[18] This quite unintended success was the result of the decentralization of the German academic life. The universities, competing with each other, had to follow the successful example established in one university.

Instead of asserting, therefore, that philosophy created the new German university, we propose that the German university system provided the basis for the great development of philosophy as a systematic discipline. But contrary to the intention of the philosophers, the university system made philosophy into just one of the academic disciplines, and added to it a great many new ones. The competitive system worked according to a logic of its own. The establishment of new universities, the raising of the status of the philosophical faculties and the firm establishment of the new type of philosophy in them, created a widespread demand for philosophers in a system comprising more than twenty universities. The student of 'philosophy' in Berlin who habilitated himself could take his choice: Bonn, Greifswald, Königsberg, Göttingen, Iena were all in the market for the bright young scholar, offering professorships in the new philosophical faculties of the reorganized university system. By 1840 the philosophical faculty—fifty years previously a mere preparatory part of the theological faculty—was by far the largest in its number of teachers comprising nearly half of all the professors, *extraordinarii* and *Privatdozenten* (270 out of 633; 124 out of 253 and 142 out of 326 resp.). In addition, there was a demand for the philosophically trained person in the theological, legal and even the medical faculties which, in the latter case, prevented the development of empirical approach for quite a while.[19]

During the first twenty to thirty years after the reform of the universities, the general intellectual approach which hardly distinguished between philosophy, history, literature and even natural sciences was broken down into specialized disciplines: history, linguistics, philology etc. All these were closely connected with the ideological bias of German philosophy which identified culture mainly with the humanities.[20] But the breaking down of 'philosophy' into specialized disciplines was in itself a departure from the ideological bias, and it occurred as the result of a simple mechanism; whenever the demand for professors in a certain field was saturated, there was a tendency among the more enterprising students to enter new fields regarded until then as mere sub-specialities of an established discipline, and to develop the speciality into a new discipline. Thus when the humanities were saturated around 1830–40, there occurred a shift of interest towards empirical natural sciences, and the interest in speculative philosophy at the universities abated.

This process has been traced in the development of physiology.[21] Lectures in the subject were held already during the first decades of the 19th century at German universities, but work was sporadic and haphazard. In 1828 physiology as an experimental discipline was represented in only six German universities by seven lecturers.[22] It was a side-line of anatomy which was beginning to separate from surgery, staking out the entire field of theoretical medicine as its domain. This process took place during the 30's and 40's and by the end of that period anatomy had become the main discipline of scientific medicine, the nucleus from which medicine was turned into a natural science. This new anatomy was taught at almost all German universities in connection with physiology. Competence in physiology, rather than in surgery, became a necessary qualification for attaining the chairs for anatomy. It was however not always possible to implement this requirement. Vacant chairs for anatomy could be staffed with scholars familiar with and competent in both fields, but what was one to do with the anatomists of the old school whose privilege to teach anatomy could not be revoked, who yet would not, and could not, teach the new subject? To establish separate chairs for physiology was easier than the creation of a second chair, part of whose function would be to duplicate work entrusted already to the incumbent of a recognized discipline.[23] The forties and fifties were thus periods when specialization in physiology was encouraged and scientific activity in this sphere stimulated. Scholars who hoped for calls to chairs in anatomy were encouraged to focus their research on physiological problems, since most universities still hoped to entrust the teaching of both physiology and anatomy to a single professor, while here and there separate chairs for physiology had already established the complete independence of the new discipline. The prospect of separate chairs stimulated those scientists with special aptitude to devote themselves entirely to the new discipline. Their concentrated work partly, no doubt (in response to the prospect of rapid advancement), soon disqualified the non-specialists from effective competition, and universities had to grant the demand of physiologists for the establishment of separate chairs.[24] The separation of physiology from anatomy, which had been a temporary 'emergency solution' to cope with obstacles to the modification of the role of 'anatomists', thus became inevitable. This separation was implemented during the fifties and sixties of the 19th century. When in 1858 Johannes Müller died, and his chair was split into one for anatomy and one for physiology, this was not a pioneer innovation, but the rectification of an anachronism. Although the final separation in Giessen did not take place till 1891 the process of separation had been accomplished at almost all universities by 1870.[25]

Between 1855 and 1874 twenty-six scientists were given their first appointment to chairs of physiology (sometimes still combined with anatomy). Ten of these were appointed between 1855–59 alone. But therewith the discipline reached the limit of its expansion in the German university system (the number of chairs for physiology in German universities—excluding Austria and Switzerland—had reached 15 by 1864, 19 in 1873 and remained at 20 in 1880, 1890 and 1900).[26] Between 1875 and 1894 only nine scholars received appointments to chairs in physiology, stepping into chairs vacated by their incumbents.

That aspiration to a professorship in physiology during the seventies and eighties was all but hopeless, is shown by the tenure of chairs at various universities throughout that period by first-generation physiologists, the generation which had in a cohort-like manner conquered the chairs which the university system was capable of providing. Du Bois-Reymond monopolized the chair in Berlin from 1858–96; Brücke reigned in Vienna for four decades 1849–90; Eckhard held the chair in Giessen from 1855–91. Karl Ludwig, after more than fifteen years in the Josefinum in Vienna, Zürich and Marburg, managed to put in a further thirty (fruitful) years in Leipzig between 1865–95; Karl Vierordt remained in Tübingen from 1855 till his death in 1884; Göttingen, Breslau, Bonn and Munich were held during 1860–1905, 1859–97, 1859–1910 and 1863–1908 by Meissner, Heidenhain, Pflüger and Voit respectively, while Ecker and Rollett kept the chairs in Freiburg 1850–87 and Graz 1863–1903 out of circulation. Large and small universities alike had not a single vacancy in physiology for decades, and no prospect of such an occurrence was in sight during the seventies and eighties.[27] The result was that research in physiology lost momentum. A count of discoveries relevant to physiology in Germany shows that 321 such discoveries were made during the twenty years period of rapid expansion between 1855–1874 compared with 232 during the subsequent (and 168 during the preceding) twenty years.[28] Scientific idealism notwithstanding, young scholars sought greener pastures. The number of *Privatdozenten* and extraordinary professors which had been 12 in 1864 declined to 4 in 1873, 6 in 1880 and rose again only in 1890 to 13. There were better ways of becoming a professor than through the study of physiology: hygiene for instance had only one chair in 1873 and grew to 19 by 1900. Psychiatry grew from one chair to 16 and ophthalmology from 6 to 21 during the same period, while pathology, which had only 7 chairs in 1864 had reached 18 by 1880.[29] The enthusiasm for physiology cooled considerably.

This was the characteristic manner in which the German universities operated *as a system*, determining the life cycles of academic disciplines. It was the decentralized nature of the system and the competition among the individual units which brought about the rapid diffusion of innovations and not the internal structure of each unit, or the dominant philosophy of education. More than twenty first-rate full-time research positions in any one discipline was a huge market for early and mid-nineteenth century conditions, and an emerging discipline could attract considerable talent competing for those positions.

The same twenty positions, however, fell dismally short of the requirements of sustained scientific research under modern conditions. But the internal structure of the individual universities, bolstered by the idea of the university, allowed the perpetuation of this archaic arrangement in the face of changing conditions, and obstructed the growth of research roles capable of meeting the demands of modern science. The structural limitations of the German university remained latent so long as role-differentiation permitted the continued expansion of the academic profession, but once the *Institut* blocked this path toward professorial chairs, the inadequacy of the structure became manifest.

The reason why at that stage the structure of the university was not modified lies, as pointed out, in the class structure of Germany. In order to understand the way this affected the universities, we have to go back again to the origins. Prussia's rulers, even when, heeding the propaganda of intellectuals, they established the University of Berlin, were no intellectuals themselves. For them the professional training of lawyers, civil servants, doctors and teachers was the main function of higher education. By inclination they would have preferred the Napoleonic type of separate professional schools, and indeed had established such schools themselves earlier. They were converted to the idea of the university, since, as shown above, under the circumstances philosophy served the political interests of the nation and because this was also a reasonable decision from the point of view of their absolutistic principles. By granting corporate freedom to the universities they not only showed themselves as enlightened rulers, sympathetic to the intellectual mood of the time, but also vindicated the principle of legitimacy; the corporate rights of the university had been, after all, a medieval tradition destroyed by the French Revolution.[30]

As a result, the newly founded University of Berlin, as well as the other universities following its example, have never been the institutions of which the philosophers had dreamt. The freedoms effectively granted to them were limited and the functions assigned to them were much more practical and trivial than desired.

First of all the influence of the state was always decisive, even where not visible. One of the simple ways through which state interference worked was the existence of government examinations for various professional titles. Formally, these examinations did not infringe the freedom of the universities to confer their own degrees, or establish their own courses of study. Since, however, the overwhelming majority of the students learnt for practical purposes, the curricula were greatly influenced by the wishes of the government. The influence was all the stronger, since the establishment of new chairs also depended on the government.[31]

The curricula and in consequence the chairs and the faculties were, therefore, so constituted that the university was overwhelmingly a professional school. The freedom of the academic staff could only manifest itself within the framework established by the interest of the state. It manifested itself in the emphasis on basic subjects rather than practical training, and on theory rather than knowledge. This was the case even in the faculties of medicine and law, not to speak of the humanities and natural sciences.[32] In these latter, the fact that the overwhelming majority of students prepared for secondary school teaching was only recognized in the usual combinations of disciplines studied, but not at all in the contents of the teaching. This aimed only at imparting the systematic knowledge of the disciplines, but took no account of teaching methodology, educational psychology etc., all of great importance to the future teacher.

Academic freedom furthermore manifested itself in the criteria used for appointments or promotions. Achievements in original research were considered—at least in principle—the most important criteria, even in such supposedly practical fields as e.g. clinical medicine, and the expert judgement of the academic staff, supposedly the most competent to judge people according to this criterion, was always one of the important bases of appointments (made actually by the state).[33]

These circumstances then determined what was studied at the university and how it was studied. The philosophical or, later, the systematically scientific aspects were emphasized in courses, the contents of which were determined largely by professional requirements. And the dual role of the professor, officially paid for teaching a subject to would-be professionals, but actually appointed for outstanding research (not necessarily central to his subject of teaching), arose as a result of similar compromise. The idea of the university, according to which both arrangements were considered as the best ways of promoting university study as well as research, was but an ideological justification of this practical compromise. Like all ideologies, it was used in defense of a constantly threatened position. Universities had to be on their guard, lest by being used openly for practical purposes—for which they were used as a matter of fact under the guises and compromises here described—they lose their precarious freedom of engaging in pure research. Hence the resistance to the dilution of the charismatic role of the professor chosen from the ranks of free *Privatdozenten,* by fully institutionalizing the new research and training roles growing up in the institutes. These latter looked 'dangerously' like mere bureaucratic-technical careers. For similar reasons the granting of academic standing to technology and new practical subjects was usually opposed. In brief, the freedom and the prestige of the German universities seemed to be safest when the university was kept isolated from the different classes and practical activities of society; it pursued, therefore, a policy aimed at the preservation of an esoteric and sacred image of itself.

Another important limitation of academic freedom was the fact that University professors were civil servants, and considered it a privilege to be part of this important corps. They were, therefore, expected to be loyal to the state, which under absolutist rule implied a great deal. As long as one genuinely agreed with the purposes of the rulers, this problem was not apparent. There was, therefore, a semblance of real freedom at the universities during the nationalist struggle and shortly thereafter, when on the one hand intellectuals often identified with Prussian politics, and on the other hand state-power was not very efficient. But after the middle of the century, when social problems and imperialism became the main political issues and the state increasingly efficient and powerful, the potential restraints on freedom became felt. Identification with the politics of the state often meant fanatical nationalism and obscurantism, a famous example of which was Treitschke, while opposition to it might have provoked interference by the state, as it happened in the case of social-democrats seeking academic appointments.[34]

Thus, again, freedom had to be sought within these given limits. It was clear that under the prevailing conditions the introduction of actualities, whether in the form of philosophical publicism, or in the form of politically relevant social science, would not have led to detached discussion and the emergence of objective criteria, but to the flooding of universities by antidemocratic demagogues and the suppression of the limited amount of liberalism which existed in them. Thoughtful liberals, such as Max Weber for example, chose, therefore, the doctrine of *Wertfreiheit* of scientific enquiry.[35] Declaring value judgements to be incompatible with true scientific enquiry and academic teaching seemed the most efficient way of ensuring freedom of discussion at the university. It was a morally respectable and logically justifiable principle which could be defended without recourse to the actual situation. But it was the actual situation which made this approach more or less the accepted doctrine of the university. It was the doctrine best suited to the maintenance of the delicate balance in a situation where free, non-utilitarian enquiry was supported and given high status by an absolutist state; and where free-thinking intellectuals taught students usually sharing the autocratic views of the rulers of the state, and preparing for government careers as civil servants, judges, prosecutors and teachers.[36]

This doctrine of *Wertfreiheit,* most clearly formulated by Weber after the First World War, had been as a matter of fact an important guiding principle of academic thinking and action in the second half of the 19th century, i.e. as soon as the possible conflict between academic freedom and absolutism became acute.[37] It explains the extreme caution and wariness towards intellectual influences coming from outside the universities, especially if these influences had some ideological implications.[38]

The observed inflexibilities of the German university were, therefore, the results of its precarious position in the German class structure. Intellectual enquiry in Germany did not thrive as part and parcel of the way of life in a 'middle class' of well-to-do people, whose position was based not on privilege but on achievement in various fields. It started thriving as a hot-house flower mainly on the whimsical support of a few members of the ruling class, and desperately attempted to establish wider roots in society. The universities created under the—from the point of view of the intellectuals—particularly favourable conditions of the struggle against Napoleon, were the only secure institutionalized framework for free intellectual activity in the country. The status and the privileges of the universities were granted to them by the military-aristocratic ruling class, and were not achieved as part of the growth of free human enterprise. It was, therefore, a precarious status based on a compromise whereby the rulers regarded the universities and their personnel as means for the training of certain types of professionals, but allowed them to do this in their own way and use their position for the pursuit of pure scholarship and science (which the rulers did not understand, but were usually willing to respect). The universities had to be, therefore, constantly on the defensive, lest by becoming suspected of subversion, they lose the élite position which ensured their freedom.

The idea of the German university evolved as a result of these conditions. It stressed the pursuit of pure science and scholarship as the principal function of the university, divided learning into disciplines with specialized methodologies, extolled *Wertfreiheit* in scholarly teaching and writing, and wary of applied subjects, as well as non-academic influence (including non-academic intellectual influence), and refused to grant institutional recognition to any teaching or research roles besides those of the *Privatdozent* and Professor. As it has been shown here, these ideas were not originally conceived as a means to an end. They were rather the description made into an ideology of the tactics actually employed by the universities in their struggle for maintaining their freedom and privileges.

It is true that the German universities had been highly successful in the development of the so-called pure scientific and scholarly fields. This success, however, was not due to any deliberate design or purpose on their part (according to the original idea there should have been a single German university devoted mainly to speculations in idealist philosophy), but to the unintended mechanism of competition which exploited rapidly all the possibilities for intellectual development open to the universities. That this development was largely limited to the basic fields was the result of the factors here described, as were the other aspects of growing inflexibility; the slowing down of the differentiation of existing disciplines into their unfolding specialties, as well as the ossification of university organisation refusing to take proper notice of the transformation of scientific work.

2. The English Universities: Higher Education for the "Classes"

If Germany was the first country to develop a system of modern universities, England was the first major country to be influenced by it. From the 1830s to World War I German universities were held up as a challenge, and/or a model to the English ones, and all the numerous new foundations and reforms of higher education and research were influenced by the German example.[39] Nevertheless, there never developed in England a German type of university. What emerged was something rather baffling to observers accustomed to use the German "idea of the university" as a yardstick for measuring academic accomplishment.

They admired English universities for the quality of their graduates; criticized them for their mediocre performance in many fields and their seeming indifference toward the active promotion of research; and were mystified by the nevertheless brilliant work of some English scientists.

This lack of success of the English universities in matching the German—or more recently the American—ones in the systematic development of research as well as their success as institutions of higher training and education has been the result of the social conditions of their growth. The same conditions used in the explanation of the German case, namely the extent of centralization and the relationship of the universities to the different classes of society, seem to have been also the main determinants of university development in England. But the English university system has been centralized to a much greater extent than the

German, while the class structure of England was much more open than that of Germany.

The influence of these two factors has been apparent from the very beginning. The emergence of modern German universities can be closely linked to the foundation of the University of Berlin, an action of the Prussian government marking the adoption of a policy of higher education which—due to competition—had to be followed all over Germany. There is no such single event marking the beginnings of the modern English university. As the product of an open class system, its origins were in a variety of institutions created by various groups of people pursuing different interests.

The core of the English university system has always been Oxford and Cambridge. Until the middle of the last century they had educated the sons of the nobility, and future clergymen.[40] They were educational institutions of the élite. Their scholarly standards were low, according to some even extremely low, but scholarship or science were irrelevant for the majority of élite positions. The few students who subsequently became physicians, surgeons or lawyers, could comfortably learn their professions as apprentices in their respective professional corporations, and all the erudition required by a clergyman could be acquired by private study. Intimate knowledge of the ways of the gentry was certainly more important for the ecclesiastical career than theological sophistication.

While Oxford and Cambridge served the gentry and the clergy, a new type of intellectual, interested in science and secular philosophy, grew up in the cities. Under their influence, and with the support of a liberal upper middle class, there arose different institutions, such as the Royal Institution, mechanics institutes, philosophical societies, colleges etc., providing some facilities for research and a platform for the dissemination of modern science. University College, London was the first university to emerge from these various popular efforts. It was meant to be a utilitarian institution designed for the acquisition of knowledge useful in practical life (about half of the students prepared for medicine).[41] This utilitarian tendency was enhanced in the University of London, chartered in 1836, which became an examining body, granting recognized degrees to students of an increasing variety of London colleges, provincial and colonial institutions, and later even to students preparing for the examination privately. This arrangement had incidentally introduced a great deal of uniformity to a great variety of provincial institutions.[42]

The modern English university arose, therefore, out of two traditions: aristocratic élite education designed to mould the character and impart a peculiar way of life on the one hand, and utilitarian training and teaching for professional and industrial middle class careers on the other hand. Universities were not—as in Germany—preserves of privileged intellectuals, isolated from the various classes of society, granted the monopoly of teaching for middle class careers, and enjoying the freedom of doing, as a matter of fact, a great many other things (especially research). They were educational institutions providing training for the diffuse positions of the élite, or for specific middle-class careers, in both instances for a practical purpose.

Until the middle of the nineteenth century the two kinds of universities existed side by side without the one affecting the other. The reform of Oxford and Cambridge after 1850 was not the result of these universities attempting to change their function of élite education, but of apprehensions about the loss of their élite function. The new scientific and professional class acquired an increasingly important position in society and exercised a growing influence on the conduct of public affairs. Some of them were rising into the élite, others became the "new clerisy" replacing the influence of the clergy on the minds of men as writers, philosophers, advisers, experts and last but not least teachers.[43] Had Oxford and Cambridge not accepted the new learning, then inevitably they would have lost their central place in the so-called Establishment.

The reforms starting about 1850, with the establishment of degrees with a serious intellectual content in the arts as well as the sciences, and culminating in the establishment of up-to-date research laboratories in the 1870s, turned Oxford and Cambridge into something deceptively like German universities, or, more correctly, like the ideal which its ideologists would have liked the German university to be. They were teaching academies where a creative intellectual élite informally taught the cream of the youth. Students did not study for some particular bread and butter profession, but in order to become a creative élite themselves in the arts and the sciences, or in politics and the service of the state. The subjects taught at the university, and the contents of the majority of its degrees were not determined by the needs of some professional practice, but by the internal logic of scholarship and science. The arts and sciences were really the core of the studies, and there were few professional degrees conferred by the universities. They taught law as part of the humanities, claiming no university monopoly of training lawyers, and taught the basic medical sciences, leaving clinical training to the hospital medical schools. In addition these were extremely wealthy and prestigeful institutions which payed their teachers relatively better and conferred on them higher status than German universities ever did.[44] For these reasons they could easily attract the best teachers as well as the best students.

Seemingly there existed, therefore, in Oxford and Cambridge after 1870 all the conditions for their becoming the most important centers of scientific and scholarly research in the world. As a matter of fact, however, they have remained, as they had been before their reform, mainly undergraduate institutions. In some fields they have attained high distinction, but by no means in all. Even in fields where most outstanding work was done, research was often hampered and limited because of the lack of facilities which poorer universities than Oxford or Cambridge did not find impossible to procure.[45] Neither the adoption of modern ideas of scientific and scholarly excellence, nor the availability of exceptional resources of talent and wealth have been enough to turn the two leading English universities into research centers comparable to the German universities of the past, or the American ones at present.

The fact that this did not happen was due to lack of competition. Research—apart from very limited fields—had not been a much sought after commodity until the Second World War. It was highly respected and, if successful, sometimes even paid for, like poetry. But sustained demand for research in all fields of science and scholarship could only develop where a competitive system of universities created a special market for it. The question then is why did not such a market arise in England in spite of the existence of a relatively large number of universities. In order to answer this question we have to turn again to the development of provincial universities (including London).

All through the 19th century these institutions had been in flux, and it was not clear which way they would develop. There were suggestions of developing them into institutes of technology following the model of the *Eidgenössisches Polytechnikum* in Zürich and similar German institutions. At the turn of the century there were suggestions of following American models by turning the new universities into "community service stations".[46] This latter idea indeed left its mark on the provincial universities of Britain, each of which (with the exception of Durham which as a church foundation does not properly belong to this category) established subjects of study in commerce, technology or agriculture peculiarly adapted to the needs of the region.

Thus all through the 19th century it seemed that there would emerge in England universities of different type than Oxford and Cambridge, challenging the leadership of these two universities, and changing the character of British higher education and research. It seemed that these universities would develop into advanced and pioneering institutions of professional training, and applied research.

This, however, happened to only a very limited extent. The pioneering diversity of these institutions has been increasingly reduced. From the beginning of this century, when the provincial universities were given their charters they have grown increasingly like each other concerning the types of study pursued in them, and the way these studies are pursued.[47] The great variety of degree courses offered by the different universities including such things as commerce, household, social sciences, journalism, fine arts, public administration, etc. do not prove the contrary, since the large majority of the graduates in all universities studied the traditional arts and science courses, or medicine and engineering. The innovations made in provincial universities were not adopted elsewhere. They remained isolated, and tended to become little different from more traditional and generally accepted courses.[48]

The process seemed to have worked somewhat like this. The two ancient universities possessing superior privileges and incomparably larger means had usually the best teachers and the best students. As a result subjects adopted at these two universities after their reform automatically attracted relatively more first rate minds than those taught only at a provincial university. Thus in these subjects there arose an impressive group of graduates whose prestige was enhanced by their Oxford and Cambridge background. They were readily given chairs at the provincial universities where they became the most prestigeful and influential members of the staff.[49] The difference in quality—real or imagined—between graduates of Oxford and Cambridge and those of other universities has been so great that vacancies in subjects not existing at the two ancient universities were preferably filled by their own graduates trained in related fields, rather than graduates of other universities possessing specialized training. This of course did not add to the prestige of these "provincial" subjects, so that there was little interest to introduce them elsewhere, and a great deal of interest to turn them as much as possible into something respectably, though humbly, like a related, higher prestige discipline. One outstanding person at Oxford or Cambridge might have been enough to create a "school" in a certain field strongly represented in the next generation at all British universities whereas the chances of the same thing happening to a subject with one outstanding representative elsewhere were much less (except if he so impressed the two leading universities that one of his students was invited to them). The strong development of physiology, physics, economics, and social anthropology compared with the much slower development of clinical medicine, many branches of psychology, sociology, business administration, education etc., illustrate the working of this mechanism.[50]

The English university system has, therefore, never become competitive. Universities, like so much else in that society, arranged themselves in a relatively neat hierarchy. Authority in academic matters has been centrally wielded by groups of people, most of whom were related one way or another to the two ancient universities. There has been no incentive for academic innovations: the two leading universities did not need it, and the rest had limited chances of competing with them through the introduction of novelties. The way to academic prestige has been through imitation of the accepted disciplines, of the 'solidly established standards' and the habits of thinking of the most prestigeful universities rather than through innovation and experimentation.

This explains the way the English system has worked. The universities, unlike those in Germany, or as will be seen later, in America, did not create new disciplines, or professions, and did not develop research systematically. At the same time, however, they were much more open to outside influences than were the German universities. Both parts of the system served certain classes of the society: Oxford and Cambridge the élite, and the provincial universities the middle classes. They have responded with relative flexibility to demands arising in these classes. Thus the two old universities introduced, in addition to arts, empirical science and a limited amount of professional studies, while provincial universities admitted a much greater variety of professional subjects. Research was also introduced as a result of specific outside demands (e.g. in agriculture), or as a requirement of teaching certain subjects, mainly experimental natural sciences, at a university level. This is why its development has seemed haphazard; it followed the emergence of this variety of demands, rather than its own internal logic.

The hierarchic structure of the system of universities has also in the end somewhat reduced its flexibility to satisfy outside demands. The case of engineering illustrates this point. English universities introduced engineering studies to their curricula quite early, overcoming with relative ease the qualms about the academic respectability of this subject which were so evident in Germany. But having admitted them they never developed them to a very large extent. The field, peripheral in Oxford and Cambridge, remained somehow peripheral in the system as a whole. Institutions like Imperial College, or some of the provincial universities, originally established mainly as technological universities, became isolated parts of the system. The bulk of technological education was relegated to technical colleges lacking university status, and applied research in technology developed—so far as it did—largely in specialized government establishments.[51] Only quite recently have Colleges of Advanced Technology been established.

It is interesting to compare this development with that of higher technological education in Germany. Universities there were less flexible than in England. They did not admit engineering into the universities and were opposed to the granting of full academic status to them. Only through direct intervention of the government were these institutions granted academic standing. But then they became veritable technological universities. Inflexibility broken down by direct government intervention in academic affairs produced better results than flexibility limited by the working of an academic hierarchy.

This flexibility, limited by lack of competitiveness, also explains the development of academic roles in England. English universities managed to institutionalize a greater variety of roles than the German ones. Concrete—even sustained—achievements in research, such as publications and discoveries, are not the only criteria for university appointments and promotions. In mathematics and the natural sciences where there are few acceptable criteria apart from outstanding achievement in research, the definition of the professor's role is not much different from that which developed in Germany. But in the humanities, social sciences, and the professions, intellectual excellence may be manifested in other ways than research. Essayists, writers, brilliant public speakers and administrators have found their way to universities to a greater extent than in Germany. The differentiation between teaching and research careers is manifested to some extent in differently defined positions, such as tutors, senior lecturers etc., on the one hand, and readers on the other, though usually the differences are not formalized.

This relatively greater willingness to face the fact that universities perform a variety of functions on a variety of levels has prevented the development of such rigidly hierarchical relationships as developed in German institutes. The question of some specializations being broad or profound enough, or of some new discipline academic enough, did not have to be decided in each case as a matter of principle. Permanent university appointments in the lower ranks could be made relatively easily and a more complex division of labor could arise without much difficulty.

But the amount of flexibility in the adaptation of the academic roles to the changing functions of the university has also been limited—like the introduction of new disciplines—by the lack of innovativeness of the system. The different criteria for appointment are not clearly differentiated. Rather a more generally—at times one feels rather subjectively—defined excellence seems to be accepted as the principal criterion, with research achievements, teaching ability and all the rest as subsidiary criteria. Such a loose conception of excellence allows a fair amount of leeway for all kinds of practical considerations, since excellence can manifest itself in different ways. Besides, it makes possible to consider from time-to-time new kinds of excellence without entanglement in ideological arguments. This approach has produced in English university departments a greater diversity of intellectual orientations, and skills, than in the German ones.[52] But as long as the criteria are not made explicit, and the different functions of teaching, training, research and education more consciously considered, the results are bound to remain partial and unpredictable.

In this case too, the hierarchic structure of the universities seems to have limited their adaptability to their varied functions. Loosely defined excellence is well suited to the needs of institutions designed to educate a national leadership with relatively diffuse functions, such as higher civil servants, politicians and heads of large corporations. But through the peculiar working of this hierarchic system the criterion has seeped down, preventing the emergence of a clear differentiation of roles and functions in the whole system.

3. The American University: The Large-Scale Academic Enterprise

The transformation of the modern university into a system serving a variety of purposes and adjusting itself to the needs of different classes of society began, as we have seen, in England. The transformation, however, was limited and with the passing of time lost momentum, due to the centralized hierarchic system of universities which turned the middle-class provincial universities into intellectual colonies of Oxford and Cambridge. The potentialities of the English beginnings were only realized in the United States. American universities grew out of the British tradition, and American class structure was even more open than the British: there was constant interchange and movement between the classes, and, in addition, there was no central hierarchy regulating these movements. The mobility of individuals, classes, and universities did not have to assume, therefore, the form of a gradual approach to the central model, but took place through competition, each unit exploiting its relative advantages.

During the first half of the 19th century the American academic scene was very similar to that of Britain. On the one hand there were the colleges, similar in their organization and scope of studies to the English or the Scottish universities, but their numbers were much greater, and none of them possessed a relative standing similar to Oxford and Cambridge. These were at that time institutions of modest intellectual calibre, usually of religious character. On the other hand there was a bewildering variety of professional schools in medicine, law and technology. There existed also numerous societies and colleges which advocated the cause of science but did very little about it. The reasons for this backwardness were the same as those which retarded academic development in England: scientific knowledge and research had few practical uses, and America was an even more utilitarian and pragmatic society than England. There were groups and individuals interested in science and scholarship as a hobby and quite a few who believed in its ultimate usefulness: but a great deal of conviction was needed to believe that one would go further by extending the frontiers of knowledge than by pushing back the frontier in the West.[53]

The transformation starting about 1860 was due to similar circumstances as in Britain, namely increasing conviction of the practical usefulness of science and higher education on the one hand, and the growth of scientific interest among a few rich and/or influential people on the other. As in England the first, utilitarian influence led to the establishment of vocationally oriented institutions, such as the M.I.T., the land-grant colleges, state universities etc., while the second led to the reform of Harvard and other older institutions, and the establishment of Johns Hopkins University aimed at fostering pure scholarship and science. In the U.S.A., therefore, as in England, the introduction of modern science and up-to-date specialized scholarship into existing universities, as well as the foundation of new types of colleges and universities, followed rather than created the emergence of social demand for such activity. Both were in these respects "open" educational systems, readily influenced by pressures arising at the same time in various classes of society.[54]

Here, however, the parallel ends. As indicated above, the U.S. has never possessed a representative university situated in the capital or near to it, with the intellectual élite of the country residing in the vicinity. This created the conditions necessary for competition, such as existed in Germany during most of the 19th century, but not in Britain. The old established universities could not, therefore, be content in the U.S. to stay out of the race for innovation, and even less could they inhibit by their example and the all-pervasive influence of their alumni the innovations made in the newer universities. They were rather compelled to follow suit, and to engage in innovations themselves, trying to preserve their pre-eminence through executing those innovations better than the others, or through different innovations of their own.

Thus when Gilman, the president of the newly founded university of Johns Hopkins, refused to follow the example of Harvard, and established a research university such as did not exist anywhere, Harvard and eventually all the important universities had to follow suit. A similar mechanism brought about the growth and diffusion of the practical professional training developed in the land-grant colleges.[55] As a result old colleges developed graduate departments and professional schools, technological institutes and state colleges introduced humanistic studies and social sciences, and all types of schools—though not all individual schools—developed research in a variety of basic and applied fields.

Thus have arisen the very large American universities within which there is a clear differentiation of functions. Undergraduate teaching is separated from the research-oriented graduate school, and in addition there are professional schools and often research institutions of one kind or another.

Another result of competition in this equalitarian system is the tendency towards specialization. In spite of the constant addition of functions, universities may decide to do without certain departments or faculties altogether and concentrate their resources in fields where they have the greatest chances of success. A good university may exist without a medical school, or may deliberately neglect some of its basic science or humanities departments; some tend to concentrate on their graduate schools, others on undergraduate teaching. These are of course things which occur in England as well. But (*a*) some of the differentiations hardly exist there at all (e.g. undergraduate/graduate schools); and (*b*) the smaller universities specializing in certain selected fields never attain real excellence through specialization. In the U.S. there are specialized undergraduate colleges of very high prestige, and first-rate law and medical schools in mediocre universities; and small generally unimportant institutions may attain fame in a short time through concentrating on one or two subjects. This possibility of establishing the high standing of a university through developing a field neglected by others has introduced into American universities departments of creative writing, dramatic arts, music etc., i.e. cultural traditions—and such less "cultural" ones as football and sports—which remained in Europe largely outside the universities.

Thus in spite of the unprecedented comprehensiveness of the large American university, there does not exist in America the conception that a university has to consist of so many faculties and that each faculty has to contain a certain well defined series of departments as a minimum. A number of relatively large universities would be considered by European standards as only part institutions. The conception of the university has obviously changed: it does not pretend to refer to some assumed organic whole of all humanistic and scientific knowledge. The fact that the different faculties and professional schools have entirely different requirements is more clearly faced than in Europe. The question, therefore, of which faculties and schools should exist in a given university is not considered as a matter of principle but rather as one of expediency.

The same applies to the internal structure of the faculties. Here too the fiction that a faculty consists of professors, i.e. individuals rather than departments, has disappeared. The units within the faculty are departments which are not a one-man show, but an institution deliberately designed to provide an efficient and well rounded unit where experts in the different specialties complement each other. This is an entirely different organization from the German institute which exists to foster the research of its head, and where the representatives of other specialities than that of the head of the institute are invariably in a subordinate position. In an American department there may be, and in a good one there always are, several professors of equal rank, there is often a strong spirit of colleagueship, and the division of labor is functional rather than hierarchic.[56]

This provides a basis for teamwork and graduate training such as exists nowhere in Europe. Even in England where, as we have seen, there arose more differentiated departments than in Germany, the 'chairs' are severely limited and there are many invidious distinctions of status and power which prevent the development of an atmosphere of independence and self-confidence necessary for genuine co-operation.[57] It has to be repeated that the development of the departments into such self-contained and efficient units has been the result of competition. The distribution between universities of Ph.D. degrees in different subjects shows that only a relatively small number of institutions confer such degrees at all, and that the list of universities conferring Ph.D. degrees in each subject is constantly changing.[58] This shows that only efficient departments can compete at this level, so that universities have to concentrate constantly on building up their individual departments (and, as shown, quite often to make their choice among them). The existence of a growing number of industrial and governmental research units in a great many fields only enhances this tendency towards building up the departmental organization.

This variety of schools and departments each with its specialized function is reflected in the differentiation of academic roles which goes much further even than that existing in England. There are specialized academic educators and administrators; academic researchers who are hardly teaching at all, as well as advanced practitioners of professions and arts.

This peculiar working of the system explains the often stated fact that the research function evolved in German universities and grafted on to both the English and the American ones took much better hold on the latter than on the former. But it is a mistake to assume simply that American universities took over and developed what they learnt from Germany. Research in America has developed in the departments which, as we have seen, are quite different organizations from German university institutes. It has thus become a regular university operation which, at times, may be of equal or superior importance to teaching. Universities, furthermore, fostered applied research of a kind which never developed in Germany.[59] One cannot, therefore, attribute these developments to beneficial European influence. They were rather the result of the same inherent characteristics of the American system which brought forth the much less admired proliferation of professional schools. This has been a system which placed a premium on innovations, and has been open to a great variety of social pressures. It adopted and developed, therefore, an ever increasing variety of functions in research, as well as professional and other types of education. Innovation became a pervasive tendency of the American university system, as in the similarly competitive German one during the 19th century, but in contrast to the German case this innovativeness has not been limited to pure non-utilitarian science and scholarship but has been extended to applied and professional fields too.

Comparing the three systems so far surveyed it can be said that while German universities were bent upon creating new science, and English universities intended to teach it to those using it (provided that they proved themselves 'respectable' enough for higher education), American universities have tried not only to teach and create new science but also new applications and professions catering for the élite as well as the masses. Thus universities assumed an important function in the growing professionalization of occupational life, and in making research an increasingly permanent aspect of business, industry, and administration.

For better or worse, the American university system, with its constantly expanding and heterogeneous functions, is now the most influential system of higher education and research. Most of the discussions about higher education and of the changes introduced in it since the end of the Second World War all over the world have been the result of American influence. This influence spreads partly through the increasing international contacts of academic workers which converge nowadays on America as they used to converge in the past on Germany, and partly through the emergence of new demands among development-minded government administrators, industrialists and businessmen for American-type professional training.

4. France and the U.S.S.R.: A Note

Before summarizing our conclusions in detail a few remarks have to be made about the French and Soviet systems of higher education. Neither of these fits precisely into the tradition here dealt with. They too have their universities, but specialized institutions for higher education and research play a more important role in these countries than in Germany, Britain or the United States.

France is the only country which did as a matter of fact abolish universities as institutions combining within one structure several faculties engaged in teaching as well as research.[60] She was without such institutions for about a century (1793–1896). Like all radical reforms in the organization of higher learning and research treated in this paper, the abolition of the universities in France ushered in a period of great scientific productivity. The first decades of the 19th century mark the high tide of French predominance in the natural sciences. The French organization of higher education and research, as developed after the Revolution and under Napoléon, was perhaps the most farsighted, taking account of all the needs and uses of higher education and scientific research as far as these could be perceived at that time. There was a clear differentiation of functions between the "university" faculties (which were in fact separate professional schools), and other institutions of higher education such as the École polytechnique, the École normale supérieure etc., on the one hand, and organizations designed as centres for original research and intellectual endeavour on the highest levels, such as the Collège de France, the Muséum national d'histoire naturelle, the École pratique des Hautes Études, and even to some extent the "Institut" on the other. This system has been extensively criticized and blamed for the decline of French science. It appears that this criticism was not entirely justified, since the decline set in only about 40 years after the reforms (around 1840), and was due to the centralization of the system rather than its organisational features usually criticised.[61] As a result of this criticism a series of reforms were undertaken, culminating in the re-establishment of the universities in 1896. But even after this reform the peculiar characteristics of the French academic system have remained. The "Grandes Écoles" and other specialized institutions have not changed their structure. In addition, some of the provincial universities did not have all the customary university faculties and remained in fact specialized professional schools. The Academy has also retained some of its importance as the dispenser of high intellectual prestige, and the separation of research from teaching has been preserved to a considerable degree. The research facilities of the universities are limited, but there exist separate organizations with considerable funds, most notably the Centre national de la recherche scientifique designed to promote research. However, unlike most research foundations in Western Europe and America which mainly allocate grants for research carried out at universities, the C.N.R.S. provides regular employment in its own premises for research workers, the most senior ones of whom are usually also employed by universities.[62]

The separation of functions between universities, specialized professional schools, and separate research institutions is even more pronounced in the U.S.S.R. than in France.[63] The fact that the organization and financing of research in the Soviet Union is done mainly by the Academy, and not by a separate organization like the C.N.R.S. does not alter the essential similarity. There is also a parallel between the allocation of universities: in France there has to be a university in each territorial "académie" though some of these, as mentioned before, do not possess all the faculties. In the U.S.S.R. there is a university in every republic, and similarly, not all of them possess all the usual faculties. Finally, in both countries high academic prestige lies in membership of the Academy or Academies and *not* in university appointments (with this qualification that, in France, professorship at the Collège de France is the appointment which commands the most prestige of all).

The main difference between the academic organization of the two countries is the extensive development of specialized professional schools in the Soviet Union. The pioneering specialized schools in France, such as the Polytechnique, the École normale, the Conservatoire national des Arts et Métiers etc., have all remained unique institutions, guarding their traditions rather than trying to expand and innovate. Those among them which were élite institutions (e.g. the École polytechnique and the École normale) even managed to eliminate altogether the specialized professional aspects of their early days and became general educational institutions for the technological/managerial élite of the civil service, on the one hand, and the professorial élite of the lycées and—as a matter of fact—of the universities as well, on the other hand. In the Soviet Union specialized education for the professions has become the most widespread form of higher education. It has developed in practical directions, often reminiscent of higher professional education in the U.S.A.[64]

This has been a relatively decentralized branch of the Soviet system of higher education, since the various schools are financed by different ministries, both at the national and local level, with a good deal of overlapping. Engineers, for instance, are trained in a variety of schools, some under the aegis of particular industries, others belonging to various branches of the armed forces and still others financed directly by the Ministry of Education.

It appears that there is a parallel between the development of French and Soviet systems of higher education and research on the one hand and that of the English and American systems on the other. All four seem to have been relatively flexible systems which adapt themselves to the carrying out of a great diversity of functions; in France and the U.S.S.R. through division of labor between different types of organizations, and in England and America through division of labor within the universities. This division of labor remained rudimentary in France and England, but developed very highly in the Soviet Union and America. Thus the formal organization of the French academic system is like that of the Soviet Union, but its functioning and evolution is similar to that of England; while the Soviet Union resembles the U.S. in this latter respect.

France and the U.S.S.R. eliminated the hold of aristocratic and corporate traditions on their government and intellectual life through revolutions. This led to the conscious use of higher education for the training of highly skilled personnel necessary for the efficient performance of certain functions of the state (civil service, secondary school teaching, law medicine, and later engineering) without regard to academic tradition. This was the educational program of enlightened absolutism initiated in both places before the Revolution, but put into full effect by the autocratic régimes following the revolutions which were unhampered by respect for traditions and established rights.

The function of higher education was conceived in both countries as training for practical purposes and teaching in the right spirit. In addition there was in both countries "enlightened" recognition of the importance of research, for which purpose separate institutions were established. These were conceived in both places as restricted élite institutions. Thus there was created in both countries an academic system conceived as a whole, purposively adapted to a variety of purposes, and considered as integral part of the machinery of the state. The formal organization of these systems, then, is the result of the working of an open class system where—as in England and America—academic structure is open to provide for the needs of different classes of society. But while in the first two countries those needs have been communicated to the universities by groups and organizations directly representing the interested elements of the population (though in England this is now increasingly less the case), in France and the U.S.S.R. they were communicated to it through the government.

The second parallel, concerning the extent of the division of academic labor, is particularly clear in the cases of England and France. In both countries there is great centralization of academic life, in France even more than in England. The most important academic institutions being all concentrated in Paris, differentiation of functions between them becomes to a large extent illusory. The same intellectual and scientific—and very often the same individuals—circles hold the chairs at the universities, are in control of research at the C.N.R.S., and later in life are elected to the vacant chairs of the Collège de France and the various Academies of the Institut. Thus, in spite of the existence in France, like in Britain, of considerable outside pressure from the educated middle-classes and the government to diversify the framework of higher education as well as research, in the end all are assimilated to the conservative traditions of Paris academic circles who, having no competition, can easily afford to remain conservative. The limited development of specialized institutions and the unsystematic development of research (in spite of very rationally conceived plans) is, therefore, the result of similar factors as in England: the whole academic system has constantly adjusted itself to the tastes and traditions of an intellectual "establishment" concentrated in a few élite institutions, monopolizing influence, and colonizing provincial universities.[65]

The situation in the Soviet Union, so far as the present authors can judge from secondary sources available to them, is still in flux. The much greater dimensions of the country and the determined efforts of the government at diversification and decentralization of the academic framework might well serve to check the tendencies inherent in hierarchic centralization. It is certain that there does exist in the Soviet Union a problem of overlapping positions, as a result of which a relatively small number of individuals, located in Moscow, have a decisive influence over a vast field of research. Government sponsored decentralization, does not necessarily assure the sensitivity of these central agencies to innovations at the periphery.[66] This is a situation very similar to England and France.

Thus the Soviet system of higher education and research, in spite of its spectacular achievements, has structural features impeding organizational innovations and their diffusion. Its successes, though on a much vaster scale, may be comparable to those which occurred in France during the decades following the reforms of the Revolution and Napoléon, those in England following the university reform, in the U.S. after the Civil War and in Germany after the introduction of empirical science into her universities. A great deal of academic deadwood was cleared away and a new, imaginative and broad framework was created, providing unprecedented new opportunities for a relatively large number of scientists and scholars. Such a situation must bring about an upsurge of scientific creation. The question, however, is whether the new system which thus emerged will be able to differentiate and expand further out of its own initiative, or whether there is no such built-in dynamism in the system, so that changes will have to be forced upon it from the outside, as usually happens in England and France.

5. Conclusion

Universities only a hundred years ago were exclusive academies of scholars pursuing privately their learned interests and instructing a small number of highly selected students who prepared to enter the civil service or one of the traditional professions, and in exceptional cases became scholars themselves. Today universities educate—in some countries—as much as a fourth to a third of all the young people in the appropriate age groups, and conduct research of vital importance for the survival or destruction of human society.

This change of functions has been to a large extent the result of the work of the universities, though not everywhere and not at every time were universities equally active in creating new functions for themselves. As shown in this paper their eagerness to recognize and develop innovations into new disciplines depended on the existence of a decentralized competitive market for academic achievements; while their willingness to try and develop bits and pieces of practical insight and professional tradition into systematic theory depended on their direct, or government-mediated relationship to the different classes of society.

For reasons connected with their social structure the large countries of Western and Central Europe—England, France and Germany—have not kept pace with this evolution of the functions of higher education and research. They adhered to a conception of the university of a hundred years ago. This conception stems from an age when science had few practical uses, its fields seemed clearly mapped out, and significant research could be conducted in private librairies and laboratories. Today there seems to be no end to the potential uses of systematic research and knowledge; research in every field has become a co-operative enterprise where the lone worker becomes an increasingly rare phenomenon; specialization is so complex that most of the disciplines which about a hundred years ago still seemed narrow specializations are nowadays considered too broad fields for any one person to comprehend; and few people would dare to predict any more what will be the legitimate scope of science to-morrow. The European conception of the university is, therefore, woefully out-of-date. Incomparably more differentiated organization is needed to carry out all the greatly increased and increasingly varied functions of higher education and research.

Such complex academic organization has arisen in the United States and in the Soviet Union. In spite of the vast difference in the formal organization of their higher education and research, both countries have developed clearly differentiated functions of pure as well as applied research and purely scientific and scholarly education alongside highly practical professional training. And both countries managed to create a much greater variety of higher educational and research institutions—whether called universities or not—and, correspondingly, to institutionalize a greater variety of academic roles than the European countries.

European systems of higher education have, as a result, found themselves under pressure from a variety of sources urging them to adopt American academic forms and practices (the influence of the Soviet example is perhaps more felt in America than in Europe). These have resulted in considerable expansion of university education and research facilities and, to a more limited extent, in the establishment of new types of institutions (such as the establishment of technological universities in Britain). These reforms and the expansion which they involve will probably be beneficial to scientific work as such things always are. If, however, the present analysis is correct, the long term success of university reform in Europe will be dependent on the establishment of much less hierarchic and much more decentralized systems of higher education and research than those existing in England and France, and a much less authoritarian and much more flexible university structure than that existing in Germany.

This involves, besides concrete changes of organization, an important modification of the thinking about universities. It is feared that by consciously adapting to new functions academic systems may neglect the one function which, so far, no other organization has managed to foster efficiently: free research, unhampered by any practical consideration, aiming only at original and scientifically significant discovery. There is no doubt that in this respect American and Soviet work often fell below acceptable standards. The criticism levelled against their providing room for courses of doubtful academic standards, or research of no significance, may be justified; but not the conclusion drawn from it that these failures prove the correctness of the European approach, where academic institutions safeguard their standards by strict adherence to established academic forms placing the preservation of established standards before innovation and emphasizing the exclusive esoteric nature of scientific work. Such a conclusion is based on the same kind of fallacy which at the time of the industrial revolution led people to believe in the superiority of the old handicraft system over the new industries since the latter produced at times rather shoddy goods. It is simply not true that the expansion of scientific work lowered standards. The élite group of pure scientists working freely on their own problems has not disappeared in America and the Soviet Union, but has rather developed much beyond whatever exists in Europe. The exodus of European scientists and scholars to the United States has not only been motivated by higher income but often by better conditions for and greater freedom of research.[67] It is clear, therefore, that the irreverent uses made of higher education and research have not estranged science from its immanent standards and values. They have presented to it such dangers, but academic institutions are in a position to safeguard their own ideas where they form a huge and powerful system vitally involved in the affairs of society. There is, however, very little which is worth safeguarding where excessive fear of lowering established standards has led academic institutions to prefer the function of the critic to that of the active initiator of scientific and professional advance.*

*The authors are indebted to Éric de Dampierre for his very useful suggestions and kind help in obtaining source material.

Notes

1. Most of the discussion about the subject has been influenced by Abraham Flexner, *Universities: American, English, German* (New York, Oxford University Press, 1930). For some of the more recent discussion of the problems of universities, cf. Logan Wilson, *The Academic Man* (New York, Oxford University Press, 1942); H. E. Geurlac, "Science and French National Strength, in E. M. Earle ed., *Modern France* (Princeton, Princeton University Press, 1951), pp. 81–105; Helmuth Plessner ed., *Untersuchungen zur Lage der deutschen Hochschullehrer* (Göttingen, Vandenhœck and Ruprecht, 1953), 3 vols.; Jacques Barzun, *Teacher in America* (New York, Doubleday, 1954); Dael Wolfle, *America's Resources of Specialized Talent* (New York, Harper, 1954); W. H. G. Armytage, *Civic Universities* (London, Ernest Benn, 1955); George F. Kneller, *Higher Learning in Britain* (London, Cambridge University Press, 1955); Theodore Caplow and Reece J. McGee, *The Academic Marketplace* (New York, Basic Books, 1958); David Riesman, *Constraint and Variety in American Education* (New York, Doubleday, 1958); John J. Corson, *Governance of Colleges and Universities* (New York, McGraw Hill, 1960); Hans Anger, *Probleme der deutschen Universität* (Tübingen, Mohr, 1960).
2. Cf. Bernard Barber, *Science and the Social Order* (Glencoe, the Free Press, 1952), pp. 139–169.
3. Cf. D. S. L. Cardwell, *The Organisation of Science in England* (London, Heinemann, 1957).
4. Cf. F. Paulsen, *The German Universities* (New York, Longmans Green, 1906), p. 56; Plessner, *op. cit.* vol. I., pp. 23–24.
5. The main protagonist of this idea was Flexner, *op. cit.* p. 326; cf. also Paul Farmer, Nineteenth Century Ideas of the University, in Margaret Clapp ed., *The Modern University*

(Ithaca, Cornell University Press, 1950), pp. 16–17.

6. Cf. about England Élie Halévy, *History of the English People*, Epilogue: 1895–1905, Book 2 (London, Penguin Books, 1939), p. 24; about France, Guerlac, *op. cit.*, and about the U.S.A., Abraham Flexner, *I Remember* (New York, Simon and Schuster, 1940), pp. 63–64. About the fluctuations of scientific productivity in different countries, cf. T. J. Rainoff, Wave-like Fluctuations in Creative Productivity in the Development of West European Physics in the 18th and 19th centuries, *Isis*, XII (1922), 287–319; and Joseph Ben-David, Scientific Productivity and Academic Organisation in Nineteenth Century Medicine, *American Sociological Review*, XXV (1960), 828–843.
7. Cardwell, *op. cit.* pp. 184–185; Flexner, *Universities, op. cit.* pp. 331–332. There were however some who were sympathetic to the introduction of engineering studies at universities, cf. Paulsen, *op. cit.* pp. 112–113.
8. Christian v. Ferber, *Die Entwicklung des Lehrkörpers der deutschen Hochschulen 1864–1954,* vol III of Plessner, *op. cit.* pp. 67–71; for particular cases, cf. e. g. F. v. Müller, *Lebenserinnerungen* (München 1953), pp. 150–151; H. Friedenwald, *A Chronique Scandaleuse* in the Vienna School, in Emmanuel Berghoff, *Festschrift zum 80. Geburtstag Max Neuburgers* (Wien 1948).
9. Cf. René König, *Vom Wesen der deutschen Universität* (Berlin, Verlag Die Runde, 1935), pp. 134 sqq.
10. Plessner, *op. cit.* vol. I., pp. 37–49, 192, 223; von Ferber, *op. cit.* pp. 87–88; Flexner, *Universities, op. cit.* p. 332.
11. This *Erstarrung* of the German university was observed by Troeltsch; cf. Samuel and Thomas, *Education and Society in Modern Germany* (London, Routledge and Kegan Paul, 1949), p. 123.
12. The importance of these circumstances in the development of scientific research has been treated in Joseph Ben-David, *op. cit.*, and in "Roles and Innovations in Medicine", *American Journal of Sociology*, LXV (1960), 557–568.
13. About the situation of German intellectuals at the end of the 18th century, cf. Henri Brunschwig, *La crise de l'État prussien à la fin du XVIIIe siècle et la genèse de la mentalité romantique* (Paris, Presses Universitaires, 1947), pp. 161–186.
14. König, *op. cit.*, pp. 20ff, 49–53; Paulsen, *op. cit.* p. 443. The closing down of some of the universities was connected with French occupation.
15. Alongside a number of other reforms designed to create a popular identification with the state, cf. Koppel S. Pinson, *Modern Germany* (New York, Macmillan 1955), pp. 33–49.
16. Paulsen, *op. cit.* p. 63.
17. Fichte certainly thought of one central university; cf. König, *op. cit.* p. 82.
18. Bonn 1818; München 1826; Zürich 1833.
19. About the predominance of *Naturphilosophie* in medicine, cf. Richard H. Shryock, *The Development of Modern Medicine* (New York, Knopf, 1947), pp. 192–201, and Paul Diepgen, *Geschichte der Medizin* (Berlin, Gruyter, 1955), vol. II–1, pp. 23–28.
20. Cf. Paulsen, *op. cit.* pp. 55–63.
21. Awraham Zloczower, *Career Opportunities and the Growth of Scientific Discovery in 19th Century Germany, with special reference to physiology*, M.A. Thesis, Hebrew University, Jerusalem 1960 (unpublished).
22. K. E. Rothschuh, *Geschichte der Physiologie* (Berlin, Springer, 1953), p. 93.
23. Bruno Kisch, *Forgotten Leaders in Modern Medicine* (Philadelphia, American Philosophical Society, 1954), p. 174. On the refusal of physiologists to accept chairs obliging them to teach anatomy as well, cf. E. Gagliardi *et al., Die Universität Zürich 1833–1933 und ihre Vorläufer* (Zürich, Erziehungsdirektion, 1938), pp. 539–548.
24. Zloczower, *op. cit.*
25. Rothschuh, *op. cit.* p. 108.
26. v. Ferber, *op. cit.* pp. 204–205.
27. Zloczower, *op. cit.*
28. Tabulated from K. E. Rothschuh, *Entwicklungsgeschichte physiologischer Probleme in Tabellenform* (München und Berlin 1952).
29. v. Ferber, *loc. cit.*
30. Paulsen, *op. cit.* p. 51.
31. Samuel and Thomas, *op. cit.* pp. 114–115.
32. Cf. Diepgen, *op. cit.* vol. II–1, pp. 152–153; Theodor Billroth, *The Medical Sciences in the German Universities* (New York, Macmillan 1924), p. 27.
33. Paulsen, *op. cit.* pp. 83–86.
34. Samuel and Thomas, *op. cit.* pp. 116–118; Paulsen, *op. cit.* pp. 105, 246–247; C. D. Darlington, Freedom and Responsibility in Academic Life, *Bulletin of the Atomic Scientists*, XIII (1957), 131–134.
35. Max Weber, "Science as a Vocation", *in* H. H. Gerth and C. Wright Mills, *From Max Weber: Essays in Sociology* (New York, Oxford University Press, 1947), pp. 129 sqq.; cf. Samuel and Thomas, *op. cit.* pp. 121–123.
36. *Ibid.* pp. 116–121, 128, about the delicate balance of the status of the *Gelehrtenstand,* and the spirit prevailing among students.
37. *Ibid.* p. 118 about the reaction in the spirit of *Wertfreiheit* of the first Congress of German Historians in 1893 to the imperial decree of 1889, directing education to the task of combating revolutionary political doctrines.
38. E.g. the social sciences; about their limited development, only somewhat modified after the first world war, cf. Flexner, *Universities, op. cit.* pp. 328, 332–333.
39. Cardwell, *op. cit.*

40. Cf. C. Arnold Anderson and Miriam Schnaper, *School and Society in England; Social Background of Oxford and Cambridge Students* (Washington, Public Affairs Press, 1952).
41. Armytage, *op. cit.* pp. 173–174.
42. *Ibid.* p. 216; Cardwell, *op. cit.* pp. 36–37, 72.
43. Cf. Armytage, *op. cit.* pp. 178, 206.
44. Flexner, *Universities, op. cit.* pp. 300–301.
45. *Ibid.* pp. 280–287; Darlington, *op. cit.* (for the description of the state of experimental physics in Oxford at the end of the last century. The present authors do not agree with Darlington's interpretation).
46. Armytage, *op. cit.* pp. 224–225.
47. The typical pattern of the development of the provincial universities was: "Foundation, through the generosity of one or more private benefactors, of a college designed to teach chiefly scientific and technical subjects to the people of a great industrial town; the expansion of this into a university college by the addition of 'faculties' in the humane subjects and a department for the training of teachers and, finally, the securing of a Royal Charter". H. C. Dent, *British Education* (London, 1949), p. 28.
48. Cf. Kneller, *op. cit.* pp. 96–99.
49. Flexner, *op. cit.* p. 256; Armytage, *op. cit.* p. 231.
50. Cf. for instance Flexner's (approving) remarks about the difference between the Department of Commerce at Birmingham University and American Business Schools, *ibid.* pp. 257–258. About the influence of Oxford and Cambridge, cf. also E. A. Shils, The Intellectuals, I: Great Britain, *Encounter,* April 1955; A. H. Halsey, British Universities and Intellectual Life", *Universities Quarterly,* XII (1958), pp. 141–152.
51. Cf. Sir Eric Ashby, *Technology and the Academies* (London, Macmillan, 1959); George Louis Payne, *Britain's Scientific and Technological Manpower* (Stanford, Stanford University Press, 1960), pp. 172–173.
52. The authoritarian homogeneity of German departments was, however, mitigated somewhat, though insufficiently, by the custom of students transferring from one university to another, in order to have an opportunity for study under different teachers; cf. Flexner, *Universities, op. cit.* p. 326; Plessner, *op. cit.* p. 196.
53. Cf. Richard Hofstadter and C. DeWitt Hardy, *The Development and Scope of Higher Education in the United States* (New York, Columbia University Press, 1952), p. 21; Richard J. Storr, *The Beginnings of Graduate Education in America* (Chicago, University of Chicago Press, 1953), pp. 1–6, 24, 52, 63, 79–80, 102, 107; Richard H. Shryock, *Medicine and Society in America 1660–1860* (New York, New York University Press, 1960), pp. 138–143.
54. Donald H. Fleming, *William Welch and the Rise of Modern Medicine* (Boston, Little Brown, 1954), pp. 173 sqq., Hofstadter and Hardy, *op. cit.* pp. 26–28, 38, 60 sq.; Abraham Flexner, *Daniel Coit Gilman* (New York, Harcourt, Brace and Company, 1946), pp. 38 sq.
55. Flexner, *ibid.* p. 108; Richard Hofstadter and Walter P. Metzger, *The Development of Academic Freedom in the United States* (New York, Columbia University Press, 1955), pp. 378–383.
56. Logan Wilson, *op. cit.* pp. 53–93; Caplow and McGee, *op. cit.*
57. Cf. J. M. Ziman, The American Scientist, *New Statesman*, LXII [No. 1591] (1961), 300–302.
58. Cf. Office of Scientific Personnel, *The Baccalaureate Origins of the Science Doctorates Awarded in the United States* (Washington, National Academy of Sciences/National Research Council, Publication No. 382, 1955), p. 19.
59. Hofstadter and Metzger, *op. cit.* pp. 380–383.
60. About the development of the French academic system, cf. *Œuvres de Monsieur Victor Cousin* (Paris, Pagnerre, 1850), 5-e série « Instruction publique », vol. I and II; Stephen d'Irsay, *Histoire des universités françaises et étrangères* (Paris, Auguste Picard, 1935), vol. II; Guerlac, *op. cit.*; Abraham Flexner, *Medical Education in Europe* (New York, The Carnegie Foundation for the Advancement of Teaching, 1912), pp. 221–223.
61. Cf. Ben-David, *op. cit., Am. Sociol. Review:* Cousin, *op. cit.*, I, p. 44.
62. About the present-day organisation cf. J. B. Piobetta, *Les institutions universitaires en France* (Paris, Presses universitaires, 1951); Étienne Gilson, La maison à l'envers, *Le Monde,* 21 mars 1947; Avons-nous des universités?, *ibid.,* 17 juin 1947; and the article by Raymond Aron, *infra.*
63. For descriptions of the Soviet academic system, cf. Nicholas DeWitt, *Soviet Professional Manpower* (Washington, National Science Foundation, 1955); Alexander G. Korol, *Soviet Education for Science and Technology* (New York, John Wiley, 1957); Vyacheslav Yelyutin, *Higher Education in the U.S.S.R.* (New York, International Arts and Sciences Press, 1959).
64. The growth of professional education in the U.S.S.R. has, however, been limited largely to technological, medical and pedagogical fields. Education in the broader sense, management, social work and other human relations fields have been much less developed, perhaps because of the schooling in these spheres received by professional Communists in various courses organized by the party.
65. Cousin, *op. cit.*, II, pp. 400–470; Gilbert Gadoffre, Facultés ou instituts, *Le Monde,* 17 avril 1947.
66. For tendencies of centralization and conservatism, cf. Eric Ashby, *Scientist in Russia* (Harmondsworth, Penguin Books, 1947), pp. 19–23; for recent attempts at decentralization, cf. Korol, *op. cit.* pp. 145–152.

67. Cf. the interesting accounts of André Weil, "Science française", in *La Nouvelle Revue Française*, III (1955), 97–109; Ziman, *op. cit.*, and for a French testimony about conditions at the beginning of the century, René Leriche, *Am Ende meines Lebens* (Bern/Stuttgart, Huber, 1957), p. 34.

The Dilemma of Change in Indian Higher Education

PHILIP G. ALTBACH

Abstract. India has been trying to reform its higher education system for more than a half-century but the results in terms of systemic change have been minimal. The universities have expanded dramatically to meet the demands of an increasingly powerful middle class although resources have not been adequate to ensure the maintenance of standards. In India's bureaucratic environment, political will to change the universities has been inadequate. For these and other reasons, the mainstream of Indian higher education, now including 7,000 colleges and 150 universities serving more than 4 million students, suffers from deteriorating standards, occasional unrest and inadequate resources. However, at the margins of this seemingly unmovable system have been a variety of significant changes and reforms. The Indian Institutes of Technology, for example, provide high quality post-secondary education. Even within the traditional universities and colleges, some interesting reforms in curriculum have been successful in limited areas. This analysis points to the factors inhibiting reform and change as well as some examples of limited successes.

The planning and reform of higher education is a difficult process in any country. The fact that India has been notably unsuccessful in its efforts to control its burgeoning higher education system is, in comparative terms, not especially unusual. This essay focuses on the patterns of growth and change in higher education in India and with providing a comparative dimension to Indian developments. India is a particularly important Third World case because it began earlier to develop universities and colleges and because it now has the largest academic system in the Third World. It can provide lessons to other Third World countries—and the same time an international dimension may shed light on India's own experience with growth, change and reform in higher education.

It is worthwhile to place India in a comparative context, not only because India's situation is not unique but because other countries may learn from India's experience. India is, after all, the largest academic system in the Third World—indeed, it is the second largest in the world with four million students enrolled in close to 7,000 colleges and 150 universities. India is also the Third World's research superpower, spending about 8% of the Third World's funds for R and D and producing a significantly larger proportion of Third World scientific output in terms of books and journal articles (Chauhan 1990; Gupta 1990). India has one of the oldest higher education systems in the Third World, with universities dating to 1857 and collegiate institutions older than that. Even though, as Eric Ashby has pointed out, India's higher education institutions are patterned on Western models and are not truly indigenous institutions, they have nonetheless become integral to contemporary India (Ashby 1966, pp. 54–166). India, because of its academic history and the size of its academic system, can yield some useful lessons for other Third World countries.

Indian higher education has grown dramatically in the past four decades but this expansion has been largely unaffected by the many plans and proposals to guide it (Kaul 1974). India, more than any other Third World country, has attempted to plan its post-secondary development and there are at least a dozen major reform proposals which have failed (Narain 1985). At the same time that the macroplanning for higher education has failed, important limited but quite specific reforms have been successfully implemented. These changes have taken place, however, in the broader context of uncontrolled expansion and a broad deterioration of standards in higher education. There is data and there are detailed proposals—the problem is that implementation of the major reform proposals have failed. One theme in the higher education policy literature is that unplanned expansion must be halted. It is significant that overexpansion has been criticized at least since the Calcutta University Commission of 1917–1919 and is part of every document dealing with higher education (National Policy on Education 1986). Yet, expansion has continued and growth in enrollments has averaged close to 9% per annum for a thirty year period (Raza 1991, p. 40).

Indian higher education seems like an enigma enveloped in contradiction. Pockets of excellent teaching and research are surrounded by a sea of substandard colleges. The best graduates compete successfully in the world job market, but unemployment at home is reality for many. Scholarship is often superseded by politics and, in many institutions, crisis is the norm. A system which was at one time highly selective has opened its doors to large numbers, yet at the same time there is conflict and sometimes violence over access to what remains a scarce commodity. By world standards, India is providing post-secondary education to a relatively small proportion of its young people—about 4.8% of the relevant age group, while the United States educates half and Europe about one-fifth. Resources are at the heart of the higher education dilemma. While student numbers have increased at a rate of more than nine percent per year for close to a half-century, government expenditures increased by two percent per annum and expenditures per student have actually declined by 2.9% when measured against inflation (Swamy and Raina 1984, p. 37). It is not surprising that standards have declined under these circumstances.

At the same time that expansion has been the hallmark of higher education and systemic reforms have largely failed, there has been much change in Indian higher education. Many analysts have pointed out that much of this change has been negative—deteriorating standards for much of the system, student political activism, the growth of corruption and the like and there is little doubt that these characterizations are correct (Singh 1985; Srivastava 1979). There is also evidence that a good deal of positive change has occurred in the system, often at the margins. For example, the Indian Institutes of Technology were established more than two decades ago with the aim of providing top quality education in engineering and related fields. The IITs have succeeded in this task and while they have not transformed the universities, they have had a significant impact in terms of proving that high quality higher education in engineering, computer science and related fields is possible in the Indian context (Indiresan and Nigam 1992). The IITs, as well as some of the other small-scale innovations have proved that change can be successful. Within the traditional system, several curricular improvement schemes in science and in the social sciences and humanities have been widely praised. These innovations, the COSIP in the sciences and the COSHIP in the social sciences, were initiated and largely funded by the University Grants Commission. In addition, there are many examples of local initiatives that have, often against great odds and without funding, improved higher education.

The Indian academic system has not been significantly altered. Indeed, the system seems to proceed according to an internal logic of its own, affected by but at the same time somewhat insulated from the regulated economy and the heavy hand of the bureaucracy. Indeed, it might well be that higher education suffers from the worst of all possible circumstances—it is subject to many of the bureaucratic regulations of the central and state governments and at the same time is beyond the scope of rational planning and administration. It is my contention that a powerful combination of forces makes systemic reform in higher education virtually impossible. It is probably the case that the higher education system is beyond the control of government in terms of basic change. The system responds to market forces in society, to a variety of stimuli—including government at several levels, politicians representing a wide range of constituencies, and highly organized special interest groups (Kaul 1988). There is neither the means of controlling the higher education system because post-secondary education is a joint responsibility of the central government and the states—with close to 30% of university income coming from fees and private sources—nor seemingly the will to do so because the status quo serves the interests of many articulate segments of the population (Raza 1991, p. 134).

India in Comparative Perspective

India is not alone in encountering difficulties in implementing university reform. Many Indians have criticized their academic system for its foreign roots and its inability to become more 'indigenous' (Kaul 1988, p. 21). The fact is, however, that no Third World academic system has discarded the Western model. In many other parts of the Third World, academic institutions have changed less and are more tied to Western models and traditions than is the case in India. Expatriate professors are a common phenomenon and universities frequently remain tied to counterparts in the metropole. India, despite its problems, has built a more indigenous economic and academic infrastructure than is the case for most Third World nations. The analogy with the automobile industry may be relevant here—India's decision to rely on domestic production and technology meant that India's vehicles are not up to the World standard. Yet, they are indigenous. In higher education, the academic system, while based on Western models, has a much higher degree of 'indigenous content' in terms of books, research, journals and the like, than is the case in most Third World countries. India's academic system continues to be dependent to some extent on the world system because the bulk of world science is produced in the industrialized countries. Higher education in the Third World remains very much a part of an international knowledge system in which power and influence remains, to a significant degree, in the industrialized nations. For this reason, it is not surprising that India has found it difficult to discard the norms, values and institutional arrangements of the West.

The metropolitan languages, mostly English and French, remain entrenched in Third World universities as well. There are many reasons for this. In all Third World countries, decisions about language are political as well as educational. In multi-lingual Third World countries, choosing one language means downgrading others, with issues of regional preferences entering into the equation. In countries with a number of languages—India of course is in this category along with many African and some Asian nations—choices become even more difficult. Africa's problems are especially severe because many indigenous languages are spoken by quite small populations and some are not written. There are also technical problems involved in shifting to indigenous languages for higher education. Textbooks and other written materials often do not exist and sometimes vocabularies for advanced scientific purposes are missing. Changing the language *status quo* is a matter of considerable controversy, complexity and often expense. In those relatively few countries that have changed the medium of instruction to an indigenous language, difficulties have been encountered and standards have almost without exception declined.

The contrast between Indonesia and India with regard to language choice is an interesting one. Language was an integral part of the program of Indonesian nationalism—the movement was committed to a national language, *bahasa Indonesia*. Significantly, this language was not the mother tongue of a significant part of the population but was rather a widely known *langua franca* used for trade. At the time of independence, *bahasa Indonesia* was immediately adopted as the medium of instruction in education, including higher education. There were serious problems in providing sufficient textbooks and other written materials, but in time materials became available although there are difficulties at the advanced levels even now. Despite Gandhi's emphasis on using Hindustani as the national language, no decision was implemented concerning the language of education at the time of Independence. Having lost the initiative, later language policies became subject to controversy and sometimes social unrest. After a half-century of independence, there is still no widely accepted language policy and the higher education system improvises workable solutions. Comparative analysis provides a few examples of countries which have made conscious decisions concerning language and which have implemented them, but in a much larger number of cases, language continues to be an issue of considerable controversy. Language problems are by no means limited to Third World countries. Canada and Belgium, for example, have seen considerable debate and unrest related to language issues and the educational system is a frequent linguistic battleground. Thus, India is by no means alone in its linguistic dilemma.

The implementation of specific university reforms has also proved difficult throughout the world. Indeed, it is generally true that successful university reforms have been legislated from above by governments and that universities have seldom been willing to reform themselves (Cerych and Sabatier 1986; Altbach 1991; pp. 261–273). Where there are centralized governmental authorities with a clear educational perspective, such as in Sweden, significant reforms in higher education were legislated and implemented over the strong objections of the academic community (Ruin 1982; pp. 329–364). And even in the Swedish case, the academic community has remained rather critical of the reforms and was able to slow their implementation. In West Germany, the academic community, through legal action and other pressure, limited the impact of the reforms legislated in the aftermath of the student revolts of the 1960s. Japan is another example of a country where traditional academic structures have been widely criticized and reform plans proposed but virtually no success has been achieved in basic systemic reform (Kitamura 1986, pp. 153–170). It is perhaps significant that the most recent example of systemic higher education reform is in Britain, where the Thatcher government, over the very strong opposition of the universities and the academic community, has abolished tenure, consolidated institutions and introduced economic-based performance measures to determine budgetary allocations and got rid of the University Grants Committee as the main vehicle for funding the universities (Berdahl, Moodie and Spitzberg 1991). The Thatcher government also moved toward combining the two major education sectors—the universities and the polytechnics—into one. These changes were made through direct government initiative at a time when the Conservatives held a strong majority in the House of Commons and when there was a clear governmental consensus on education policy.

Despite their differences in wealth and economic development, India and the United States provide an interesting point of comparison in terms of higher education reform. Both academic systems are large and both serve a diverse population. Both have a large number of institutions functioning at many different academic levels. Most relevant, both have divided governmental responsibility for higher education—with the major power in the hands of the state governments but with the central government playing an important role in research and in several other selected areas and with a large and important private sector. Both countries have experienced massive expansion in higher education in the past four decades. However, neither has made any significant changes in the structure, function or orientation of the academic system. The different levels of the academic system operate quite independently and there is relatively little coordination.

In the United States, federal government policies in such fields as student loans and grants and legislation concerning affirmative action (programs for enrolling minority group students and women and special efforts for hiring minorities and women in colleges and universities) have had a significant impact on national policy. Further, the federal government has a key role in providing funding for research. Similarly, the central government in India has an impact on academic policy through the initiatives of the University Grants Commission, which has worked to increase the salaries of the academic profession, to stimulate reform in various areas and to improve quality in higher education. In both countries, the impact of central initiatives has been limited, in large part because of the diffusion of responsibility for higher education and the fact that the bulk of funding comes from the states. In India, for example, the central government provides around 23% of funding for higher education and the states and other sources 77%. It is worth noting that the central share declined significantly—from 39% to 23%—between 1971 and 1984 (Ansari 1991, p. 135).

Because of the very large amounts of money made available by the federal government in areas of national priorities, such as basic research, defense-related research, and loan guarantees for students, national policy has had a substantial impact on higher education. Further, American federal law mandates compliance with specific policies when federal funds are accepted by institutions. This means that colleges and universities which have federal funding for research or which use federal students loans must follow federal regulations concerning affirmative action, guidelines for access to loans, and a myriad of other regulations. Institutions have the option of not participating in federal programs and thus do not have to follow many of these regulations, and a few colleges do not accept these funds. The large majority, however, do take federal money and are thus liable to regulation. It should also be noted that in the past few years, national government priorities have again shifted and funding for higher education has been cut and the specific legislation dealing with guaranteed student loans has been changed, limiting access to these funds as well as significantly reducing allocations. In the American system, national higher education policy exists in a relatively limited number of areas, and in these spheres the federal government has had significant impact. But there has been a constant debate concerning where policy is best made and where power over the direction of higher education should reside (Gove and Stauffer 1986). The policies of the various states are of primary importance when it comes to higher education—and there are significant variations in policy.

The point of this comparative analysis is to indicate that the formulation of national higher education policy and, even more important, the implementation of policy, especially as it relates to reform and innovation, is highly controversial and contested in many countries. Even in Europe, which has highly centralized educational policy arrangements, the implementation of university reform has not been easy. It is, therefore, not surprising that the implementation of significant reform has been difficult in the Indian context. It might be useful for India to study the process of policy implementation both in the industrialized nations and in other Third World countries for insights.

The Politics of Indian Higher Education

Higher education in India is contested territory. Everyone has a stake in it. The public, and particularly the educated segments of the population, sees access to post-secondary education as a high priority. There has been strong opposition to limiting enrollments and there is much interest in higher education policy. Perhaps nowhere else in the world are academic issues so frequently reported in the newspapers. The political system at all levels is also very much concerned with colleges and universities—higher education claims a significant share of governmental expenditures. Education, for example, accounts for about 4.4% of expenditures of the Net Domestic Product of the states—and higher education accounts for about 15.5% of education spending by the states (Ansari 1991, p. 138). Further, academic institutions are important political institutions—the source of patronage and prestige for politicians. Those within the academic system are also very vocal and are concerned with academic developments. Student activism is frequently concerned with higher education issues and internal college and university matters, a phenomenon which is quite unusual internationally (Altbach 1989). Also somewhat unique is the intense political organization of the academic staff, which jealously guards its prerequisites and especially jobs in higher education. Everyone is concerned with the colleges and universities—so much so that these various powerful interest groups are often able to cancel each other out when it comes to academic policy.

Academic institutions confer degrees and access to at least the possibility of jobs in a highly competitive environment. They are themselves important sources of employment for members of the articulate and politically powerful middle classes. Indeed, in smaller towns and poorer parts of the country, a college may be the largest and most important institution in the area. Colleges are sources of patronage for those in charge of them. Admission to degree programs can be allocated and jobs, ranging from professorships to janitorial staff, can be awarded. Colleges are immensely powerful institutions in their own realm. They confer political power and authority. This reflects India's society of scarcity, where access to resources of all kinds engenders conflict. The fact that academic institutions are so politically charged—that they mean so much to so many people has meant, in the Indian context, that it has been extraordinarily difficult to get any consensus concerning change or reform.

Higher education is a volatile political issue in any society. In India, political factors are overwhelmingly important in higher education planning and in the everyday life of academe (Rudolph and Rudolph 1972). Political factors have entered into higher education at every level and, perhaps to an extent unprecedented internationally, affect academic decisions. Political factors affect the appointment of academic staff, sometimes the admission of students, decisions on curriculum and selection of textbooks and a variety of other matters. Because academic institutions—from colleges located in rural areas to metropolitan universities—are key organizations with scarce resources, they are subject to intense political pressures. Added to the 'normal' politics of higher education is the great weight of governmental involvement in academic decisions at all levels. The governments of the states are the most important factors since higher education is a responsibility of the states although the central government is also involved in key academic decisions. State governments have frequently intervened in academic matters on issues large and small. For example, the government of Rajasthan passed a law that replaced some elected university governing bodies with ones selected by the government. At another level, state government officials are frequently instrumental in appointing professors. In Bihar, one of the most politicized states, there is frequent interference in the appointment of academic staff. In one state, a Vice Chancellor was fired because he was involved with a book critical of the Prime Minister (Sethi 1983). Indian higher education is politicized from the lowest level to the highest and the convergence of different and often opposing political forces—in government, within academe and sometimes the public arena—has a profound impact on higher education reform. In India, the 'normal' academic politics is made more volatile by the frequent intrusion of external forces into the decision making bodies of colleges and universities.

The 'small politics' of internal governance operates everywhere and often inhibits reform because it is difficult to obtain consensus among the key groups involved in the governance process. In India, the structures of internal governance are usually complex. The internal governance of universities is not only subject to the usual complexities and consensual arrangements found in most countries, but because access to academic jobs and to admission to higher education institutions are prized, academic politics becomes more contested. J. N. Kaul argues, for example, that the lack of a tradition of autonomous internal governance has made the development of effective structures difficult in the post-independence period. He also points out that the key academic structures in Indian universities—the Senate and the Academic Council—are too large, with more than 100 members in many cases, to be effective. The Executive Council, a smaller body which is supposed to have considerable authority, is often factionalized and heterogeneous and frequently at odds with the Vice Chancellor. The academic departments, which are supposed to have considerable autonomy, have never built up their own traditions, have a weak legal basis and have maintained a system of a powerful and often permanent Head (Kaul 1988, p. 157). The complexity, weakness, and factionalism of the internal governance structures of Indian universities make decisive decision making difficult and contributes to the politicization of the campus.

Reform is a key concern of government since it will necessarily involve in allocations of resources, changes in institutional and other structures and it will impact on people within the academic system and often on the wider public as well. In the Indian system, there is relatively little insulation of higher education from governmental bodies—a tradition going back to the colonial period (Gilbert 1972). Unlike the academic systems of many industrialized nations, which claim a significant degree of autonomy, Indian higher education is directly subject to governmental involvement. The traditions, norms and legal protections of autonomy are, in general, lacking in the Indian context (Shils 1983).

Structural Sclerosis

The basic structure of the Indian academic system, as has often been pointed out, was put into place by the British, who had specific aims for higher education (Ashby 1966; Basu 1974). The concept of the affiliating university—the London model—which was imposed in India made good sense in the context of British needs, but it was not necessarily the best arrangement for a rapidly growing university system after independence. What made the situation even worse is that this system became, with a few exceptions, the standard organizational structure for Indian higher education. There was virtually no opportunity for variation. The major efforts in recent years to 'open' the organizational structure of Indian higher education have been successful at the margins in that some alternative models have been introduced—such as the agricultural universities, the institutes of technology and, most recently, autonomous colleges—but these have not affected the basic structure of the system. The weight of the historical past is a heavy burden for Indian higher education—one that the mainstream academic system has been unable to break. However, it should also be noted that the will to part from the past or even to open up the system in significant new directions has been lacking.

There are a variety of factors that have induced structural inertia in Indian higher education. Among these are: (1) the impact of the colonial model, (2) the lack of a readily available alternative, (3) the concentration of the academic system on expansion, (4) the lack of adequate funds and an orientation toward institutional survival, (5) the lack of consensus on directions for systemic change and opposition to change from a variety of constituencies, including students, academic staff and others, (6) the dispersion of responsibility for higher education among several levels of government and (7) a highly bureaucratized system that does not stress innovation.

The Domination of Expansion

The hallmark of Indian higher education since Independence has been growth. Student members have grown from 174,000 in 28 universities and 695 colleges in 1950 to 3,948,000 students in 144 universities and 6,912 colleges in 1989—a growth rate of almost 10 percent a year for a forty year period (Nair 1990, p. 3). Expansion has taken place at all levels of the academic system—from increases in numbers in postgraduate and professional education to the massive expansion of undergraduate arts and sciences colleges throughout the country, including to smaller towns and even to rural areas.

Expansion has continued despite a variety of policy statements and reports that have indicated that continued growth is not necessary and results in a misallocation of resources. Virtually every official commission has recommended against further expansion, some urging that no public funds be allocated to new institutions. It has also been recognized that many of the newer colleges lack appropriate facilities and enroll an inadequate number of students (Chalam 1986, p. 31). Yet, expansion continues with only a modest decline in the rate of growth.

The fact is that expansion serves powerful forces in Indian society. Those who aspire to social and economic mobility in India's very competitive society know that they have a significantly better chance if they hold a postsecondary degree. While research shows that someone with a bachelor's degree in an arts subject has little chance of obtaining a job soon after graduation, though jobs are eventually obtained. Further, the kind of employment available to degree holders is more prestigious even if not always more remunerative than what is open to those who have not gone on to postsecondary education. Thus, the availability of places in colleges and universities is a top priority of the aspiring middle class and to growing segments of the upwardly mobile rural and urban poor. Expansion also serves powerful political interests who see academic institutions as a base of political influence and power. These two immensely powerful forces in Indian society are not interested in increased quality of higher education. Indeed, they may well oppose more rigorous standards because this would place limitations on growth and would introduce more accountability into the academic system.

The reality of growth has meant that much of the attention of both the academic system and governmental authorities concerned with higher education has been devoted to dealing with expansion. Governmental resources have gone to providing funds to new colleges and universities. The universities, which have responsibility for awarding degrees to students in their affiliated colleges, have been reluctant to permit more autonomy fearing a further decline of standards. It is fair to say that expansion has dominated the thinking and the resources of a very large part of the academic system in India, leaving little time and few resources for more basic reform.

The mainstream academic system has simply been overwhelmed with the tasks of coping with unending growth. There is no reason to expect the basic *status quo* to change because of the political and other pressures and press for further expansion. While there has been some success in slowing the rate of growth, it seems entirely impossible to stop expansion or even to create conditions under which coping with numbers will not be the primary task of the large majority of academic institutions in India.

The Academic Profession

The Indian academic profession is a large and diverse group of 250,000, with more than 80 percent teaching exclusively at the undergraduate level. Academics everywhere are conservative when it comes to institutional change and have generally opposed reform (Altbach 1991, pp. 23–46). In almost every country and in almost every historical circumstance, the professoriate has opposed change in higher education. The Indian academic profession is no exception and as a result has been a significant stumbling block to reform. It also has other characteristics that create additional problems, such as significant differentiation according to institutions, relatively poor conditions for teaching and research, especially in the undergraduate colleges and others. As Irene Gilbert and Edward Shils have pointed out, Indian academics have few traditions of autonomy, creating a mentality of subordination (Gilbert 1972, Shils 1969). As has been noted, the Indian academic profession was created by a colonial administration interested more in loyalty and docility than in creativity and research.

Remuneration for the profession has traditionally been quite low, although recent adjustments have, especially at the senior ranks improved salaries significantly. The profession has traditionally been very much concerned with economic security even though many academics now earn salaries which place them firmly in the Indian middle class. There is nonetheless, a sense of economic insecurity, perhaps fed by weak procedural protections of job security and a tradition of powerful and often autocratic academic administration, especially in the undergraduate colleges. Like many in the Indian middle class, fear of decline in status and income is never far from the surface and this contributes to a conservatism in the academic profession.

The profession is also unionized to a significant degree, and the unions have almost always opposed major reforms, distrusting policy makers and fearing that changes in working conditions would create problems for their members. The profession, in some institutions, is also politicized. Academics often see their world in political terms because of the intense politicization of the governance structures of academic institutions and political involvement in academic appointments at all levels. Academic unions are often themselves involved in politics, both at the institutional level and in the society. Unions are frequently affiliated with political parties and movements and to some extent bring the ideological or sometimes ethnic or caste politics of the society onto the campus. Because the unions often have political allies in society, the unions are able to mobilize extra-university forces on their behalf, often within state legislatures or in the *Lok Sabha*. Academic unions, in the Indian context, are not well understood, but they are a powerful force in higher education—and one which has an impact on reform as well as on other aspects of academic decision making.

The fact that most teachers working in undergraduate colleges have virtually no role in policy making has limited their feeling of participation in the academic enterprise. Significant reform is almost always seen as a threat to the established patterns of work of the academic profession and possibly a threat to job security in a context (at least in the undergraduate colleges) where tenure is often not very safe. Thus, the sociology, psychology and institutional status of the academic profession has generally meant that they have opposed reform efforts.

Resources

Indian higher education is chronically short of money. Even when compared to the resources provided to higher education in many other Third World countries, India seems, when measured on a per capita basis, to be relatively poorly endowed. As has been noted, expansion has taken place without a commensurate increase in funding. Yet, there is widespread agreement that higher education should receive a smaller proportion of the education budget (Tilak 1990). This makes the overall situation of higher education extraordinarily difficult since it has been impossible to limit growth at the same time that resources are not provided to adequately provide for increased numbers.

The usual means for implementing innovations in higher education has been for the central government, through the University Grants Commission, to provide partial or sometimes complete funding for specific innovations, such as examination reform or curricular reform, for a limited period of time. At the end of the period of central funding, the state governments or individual institutions must take fiscal responsibility. This system has had several implications. One is that innovations end when the period of funding ends—even though commitments have been made to continue them. Another pattern is for the innovations to be inadequately funded at the state or local levels, and after a period of time fall into disrepair. Agencies at the state and local levels are simply too much concerned with the day-to-day survival of the institutions and with the pressure of ever increasing numbers to be able to maintain innovations, especially when those changes were the result of external forces rather than local ideas.

On several occasions, however, resources have been found to implement significant new initiatives in higher education. The establishment of the institutes of technology more than two decades ago is an example. The IITs have proved successful in terms of providing high quality higher education in specific fields. They have, when compared to the traditional colleges and universities, been quite expensive. In general, however, funding has not been available for significant reforms in the mainstream sector of higher education—the colleges and universities.

Directly related to the issue of resources for change in higher education is the question of 'who should pay?' for higher education. In India, as Tilak points out, fees account for under ten percent of the total cost of higher education—down from twenty percent in 1950 (Tilak 1990, p. 45). And the fees paid by Indian students, when measured in real terms, are about half of what was paid in 1950. There are few loan programs in Indian higher education. It is clear that there are a variety of complex issues related to resources for higher education in general and for significant reform in particular. While there are some reforms that can be implemented without massive infusions of money, most systemic change requires fairly significant funding, and it seems unlikely that governmental resources, either at the center or in the states, will be available. Other alternatives may be considered—such as increased fees to students, more significantly differentiated tuition based on the cost of instruction, loan schemes and other ways of raising the income of higher education institutions. The question of resources for reform is both crucial and daunting.

The Examination System

The system of lockstep examinations that has been common in Indian higher education for more than a century has been identified as a key problem for reform (Singh 1974, pp. 291–311). Examinations shape the curriculum and determine the nature of instruction. They reduce the autonomy of the instructor in the classroom and severely limit the possibility of innovation. And there has been widespread criticism that examinations do not adequately measure what has been learned (Gupta 1975). The problems of administering the examination system have also been widely discussed—the inefficiency, occasional dishonesty and disruptions of the system have brought considerable disrepute to the academic system as a whole.

At the same time, they are said to maintain a 'floor' of quality in a mass higher education system in which standards are difficult to maintain. While every official commission that has examined higher education for the last forty years has attacked the examination system and efforts by agencies such as the University Grants Commission and the Association of Indian Universities have attempted to improve or modify the system, virtually nothing has been done. Many in the system are unwilling to take the risk of reform, fearing that anarchy will result. The examination system is one of the few common elements that maintains some uniformity. The examination system is symptomatic of the broader problems of reform in Indian higher education. There is an unwillingness to take risks that may produce problems in an academic system that is frequently on the brink of breakdown.

Over the past two decades, reforms have seized on the examination system as a key element of what is wrong with Indian higher education and have tried to change it. Some have attempted to tinker with the existing system by proposing 'question banks,' better national supervision and other improvements in efficiency. Another popular proposal has been to permit more internal assessment, thereby bringing the instructor into the process of assessment and reducing the reliance on the centralized examination structures. A few have urged scrapping the system altogether, arguing that the examination system lies at the root of all bureaucracy and corruption in Indian higher education and that 'market forces' should be permitted to decide which academic degrees are valued in the market-place.

What is significant is that none of these proposals has yielded results. The fact that this one element of the traditional system, seemingly relatively easy to change, has proved not only difficult but impossible to significantly improve or reform tells us quite a bit about the problems of broader systemic reform. It is not difficult to understand why the system should be so difficult to alter. It is very much a part of the traditional academic balance in India. Students know what to expect and means have been evolved to help students pass the traditional examinations. The ubiquity of profit-making coaching institutions, the widespread (but mostly formally forbidden) offering of private classes by many teachers as a means of earning additional remuneration, and even institutionalized cheating in some parts of India have all built up patterns of behaviour and expectations regarding the examination system. The system benefits the teachers because they can not only earn money through coaching but also from grading the examinations. The system itself, with its supposed incorruptibility because the tests are designed and graded centrally, also offers some protection against favoritism and corruption. The fact that many fail the exams and as a result do not obtain their degrees does not seem to make much of a difference. It is estimated that between 20 percent (in many science and technology fields) and 60 percent (in some arts and social sciences areas) fail the university examinations each year (Gupta 1990, p. 13). The examination system, established by the British colonial authorities, is deeply ingrained not only in the educational system but throughout Indian society. Changing it requires not only altering the approach to the award of academic degrees but, in a sense, a shift in the psychological approach to meritocracy. Many do not trust the existing system, assuming that some corruption and favoritism has crept in, but few are willing to trust an entirely new and untried arrangement.

Society and the Universities

Higher education in India plays many roles. It is of extraordinary importance to many and reforms are often seen as significant threats to specific social arrangements that provide benefits to powerful groups. As has been seen in this analysis, the checks and balances of societal forces as well as entrenched groups on the campus have inhibited—indeed prevented—significant reforms. The politics of the society is often played out in the universities, escalating campus conflicts and further politicizing higher education. Social unrest is the result and most often the changes are not implemented.

An example of an effort to help solve a significant societal problem through a reform in higher education is the highly volatile issue of the reservation of university places for students from scheduled castes and tribes and, more recently, to students from other disadvantaged sectors in the society who have not been specifically identified in the Indian constitution as being disadvantaged. The issue of 'reservations' has been a volatile one in many parts of India for many years. The efforts by the governments of Gujarat to expand the number of groups for which reservations would apply led to major social unrest, riots and eventually the collapse of the state government over the issue. Other states also began to implement more wide ranging reservations policies. Andhra Pradesh, for example, identified 44 percent of the places in colleges and universities (as well as in the government bureaucracy) which would be subject to reservations—14 percent of the seats reserved for scheduled castes, 4 percent for scheduled tribes, and 25 percent for other listed backward castes (Chalam 1986, p. 143). In the past several years, when former Prime Minister V. P. Singh moved to implement the recommendations of the Mandal Commission, which recommended that the central government provide far-reaching reservations, similar to those in Andhra Pradesh, the issue took on national prominence. Not surprisingly, the most dramatic protest against the implementation of the Mandal recommendations came from the campuses (Ilaiah 1990, pp. 2307–2310; Agarwal and Aggarwal 1991). Reservations are unpopular among the academic community as well as among students. Violent demonstrations took place, especially in north India, and a number of students immolated themselves in protest. After considerable unrest, widespread unfavorable commentary and political maneuvering in the Lok Sabha, V. P. Singh's Janata Dal government fell—further indicating the political importance of issues that directly affect higher education. The point of this discussion is to indicate that it has not been unusual for governments to seek to solve broad societal issues by looking to higher education. Nor has it been unusual for the academic community to react vigorously and sometimes violently.

Language has been a similar issue in which government attempted to solve a difficult social and political problem through policy relating to higher education. As N. Jayaram (1993, p. 93) points out, despite considerable conflict and controversy and quite a few proposals for reform over several decades, there is still no solution to the issue of medium of instruction in Indian higher education.

> Different states have varying approaches to the medium of instruction in higher education, reflecting regional political and cultural factors and there are significant variations even among the universities within states. English, after almost a half-century of independence, remains an important language in Indian higher education. It continues to dominate the sciences and technological fields and is considered the 'prestige language' in most fields. While Hindi has made considerable inroads in the 'Hindi heartland' of the north, it has little importance elsewhere.
>
> Controversies concerning the medium of instruction in schools and especially in higher education have, from time to time, erupted into violence. Students have generally been at the forefront of militant protest. The issues are complex and emotional. On some occasions, regional cultures are being protected against what is seen as 'Hindi imperialism.' In other cases, the English-medium status quo is being defended against regional demands. In still others, local rights are considered paramount. The complex language situation in higher education not only reflects another failure to use the universities as an instrument of national social policy but also complicates any effort to implement major reforms at the national level. It further indicates how deeply felt and often emotional elements resist change.

The point of these examples is that the use of higher education to implement broader social policy inevitably creates controversy and has, in general, not been successful. It also detracts from more purely educational issues and debates. India, of course, is not alone in using education as a lever for social change. Schools and universities are relatively powerless institutions—and they are in any case dependent on public funding. As a result they are logical targets for manipulation. The implications are always serious and sometimes unanticipated.

There is little question that systemic reform in higher education engenders similar controversy. Virtually any meaningful reform has implications for articulate segments of the public and is also of concern to political leaders at various levels. Given the politicization of Indian higher education, it is hard to see how such reforms could be implemented. Unrest from various segments of society and extended debate in the press and in government would, if the past is any indication, either severely compromise the proposed reforms or scuttle them.

Because higher education is such an important social institution in almost all societies, it is subject to considerable scrutiny. As can be seen from this discussion, the factors that impinge on higher education policy and development are complex and powerful. Higher education serves many, often conflicting, interests and needs. In India, for example, higher education serves as an avenue for social mobility, as a means of providing the skills needed for a modernizing society, as a 'parking lot' for people who would otherwise be unemployed, as a source of political power, and sometimes even as a business enterprise. While it is the case that India did not choose its academic model, it has had ample time since Independence to make changes—and changes have in fact been made. The Indian university system has evolved in line with political, demographic and societal pressures. In this sense, the system as it now stands serves some important societal needs. It reflects the realities of Indian society.

What Does It All Mean?

Is meaningful systemic reform possible in Indian higher education under the circumstances discussed here? Probably not. The complexity of the social context in which higher education exists very likely makes systemic reform impossible. It is certainly the case that the proposals for reform, the political will for implementation and the economic resources required would have to be extraordinarily powerful. The thoughtful and articulate proposals of the Radhakrishnan Commission and the 1964–66 Education Commission were not fully implemented, although these proposals, and others in recent years, yielded some results, none of which could be considered systemic. The establishment of the University Grants Commission (UGC), for example, stemmed from proposals in the Radhakrishnan report. It took from 1949 to 1956 for the UGC to be fully established, and it has never fulfilled its mission completely (Chaturvedi 1989). The point here is that it may be possible to implement relatively small but meaningful reforms in the higher education system even if systemic change is beyond reach.

The development of Indian higher education since Independence has, in many respects, been impressive. Despite the criticism of the overexpansion of higher education, the provision of post-secondary education to more than three million students and the expansion of post-secondary education from the cities to a much wider geographical area in a developing society is a significant achievement—and one which has had considerable societal support over the years. There are also accomplishments in terms of quality and new higher education initiatives. The establishment of the institutes of technology and the expansion of high quality education in engineering and related fields, the growth of postgraduate teaching and research in the universities through Centres of Advanced Study, the painfully slow progress of the autonomous college movement and a variety of other innovations show that there has been progress.

The great monolith of the Indian academic system has steadily grown for a half century and shows no sign of major reform. Yet, at the margins there has been significant change and development. Perhaps this is the model for future reform. The central core of the academic system, however inadequate it is perceived in terms of quality and its direct relationship to technological development and employment, is seemingly a permanent fixture of Indian society. Change can, however, occur around the edges of this monolith. And it seems possible to make modest improvements in the academic system itself rather than to focus entirely on the non-university sector. Indeed, the seeds of reform planted in the universities may yield results which will have wider implications than establishing entirely new institutions (such as the institutes of technology).

Is this analysis optimistic or pessimistic? Perhaps it can be best characterized as realistic. Post-secondary education in India is an extraordinarily important part of modern Indian society and it is intertwined in the political and social systems of the society. It is in need of change, development and improvement. In order to effectively plan for reform and improvement, it is necessary to have a realistic perception of what is possible and what is not.

References

Agarwal, S. P., and Aggarwal, J. C. (1991). *Education and Social Uplift of Backward Classes: Mandal Commission and After.* New Delhi: Concept.

Altbach, P. (ed.) (1989). *Student Political Activism: An International Reference Handbook.* Westport, Ct.: Greenwood.

Altbach, P. (1991). 'The Academic Profession', in Altbach, P. (ed.) *International Higher Education: An Encyclopedia.* New York: Garland. pp. 23–46.

Altbach, P. (1991). 'University Reform,' in Altbach, P. (ed.) *International Higher Education: An Encyclopedia.* New York: Garland, pp. 261–273.

Ansari, M. M. (1991). 'University Finances: Determinants and Implicatons,' in Raza, M. (ed.), *Higher Education in India.* New Delhi: Association of Indian Universities, p. 135.

Ashby, E. (1966). *Universities, British, Indian, African.* Cambridge, Mass.: Harvard University Press.

Basu, A. (1974). *The Growth of Education and Political Development in India, 1898–1920.* New Delhi: Oxford University Press.

Berdahl, R., Moodie, G., and Spitzberg, I. (1991). *Quality and Access in Higher Education: Comparing Britain and the United States.* Buckingham, England: Open University Press.

Cerych, L., and Sabatier, P. (1986). *Great Expectations and Mixed Performance: The Implementation of Higher Education Reforms in Europe.* Stoke on Trent, England: Trentham.

Chalam, K. S. (1986). *Costs and Productivity of Higher Education.* New Delhi: Inter-India Publications.

Chaturvedi, R. N. (1989). *The Administration of Higher Education in India.* Jaipur: Printwell.

Chauhan, C. P. S. (1990). *Higher Education in India: Achievements, Failures and Strategies.* New Delhi: Ashish.

Gilbert, I. (1972). 'The Indian Academic Profession: The Origins of a Tradition of Subordination,' *Minerva* 10, 384–411.

Gove, S., and Stauffer, T. M. (1986). *Policy Controversies in Higher Education.* Westport, Ct.: Greenwood.

Gupta, A. K. (ed.) (1975). *Examination Reforms: Directions, Research and Implications.* New Delhi: Sterling.

Gupta, S. P. (1990). *Indian Science in the Eighties and After.* Delhi: Ajanta.

Ilaiah, K. (1990). 'Reservations: Experiences as Framework of Debate', *Economic and Political Weekly* October 13, pp. 2307–2310.

Indiresan, P. V., and Nigam, N. C. (1993). 'The Institute of Technology: An Experience in Excellence,' in Chitnis, S., and Altbach, P., (eds.) *Higher Education Reform in India: Experience and Perspectives.* New Delhi: Sage.

Jayaram, N. (1993). 'The Language Issue in Higher Education: Trends and Issues,' *Higher Education,* this issue.

Kaul, J. N. (1974). *Higher Education in India, 1951–1971: Two Decades of Planned Drift.* Simla: Indian Institute of Advanced Studies.

Kaul, J. N. (1988). *Governance of Universities: Autonomy of the University Community.* New Delhi: Abhinav.

Kitamura, K. (1986) 'The Decline and Reform of Education in Japan: A Comparative Perspective,' in Cummings, W. K. et al., (eds.) *Educational Policies in Crisis* New York: Praeger, pp. 153–170.

Nair, P. V. B. (1990). *Costs and Returns of University Education.* Trivandrum: CBH Publications.

Narain, I. (1985). 'Reforming Educational Administration in India: Some Observations Specifically in the Context of Higher Education', *Indian Journal of Public Administration* 31.

'National Policy on Education: Program for Action' (1986). *New Frontiers in Education* 16, 34–116.

Raza, M. (ed.) (1991). *Higher Education in India: Retrospect and Prospect.* New Delhi: Association of Indian Universities.

Rudolph, S., and Rudolph, L. (eds.) (1972). *Education and Politics in India.* Cambridge, Mass.: Harvard University Press.

Ruin, O. (1982). 'Sweden: External Control and International Participation—Trends in Swedish Higher Education', in Daalder, H., and Shils, E. (eds.) *Universities, Politicians and Bureaucrats.* Cambridge, England: Cambridge University Press, pp. 329–364.

Sethi, J. D. (1983). *The Crisis and Collapse of Higher Education in India.* New Delhi: Vikas.

Shils, E. (1983). *The Academic Ethic.* Chicago: University of Chicago Press.

Shils, E. (1969). 'The Academic Profession in India', *Minerva* 8, pp. 345–372.

Singh, A. (1974). 'Examinations: The Strategy of Change', in Singh, A., and Altbach, P. (eds.), *The Higher Learning in India.* New Delhi: Vikas, pp. 291–311.

Singh, A. (1985). *Redeeming Higher Education: Essays in Educational Policy.* Delhi: Ajanta.

Srivastava, A. P. (1979). *Pathology of Higher Education.* Kanpur: Reprint.

Swamy, D. S. and Raina, B. N. (1984). 'Subversion of Universities' *Seminar* No. 296.

Tilak, J. B. G. (1990). *The Political Economy of Education in India.* Buffalo, NY: Comparative Education Center, State University of New York at Buffalo.

Public and Private Sectors in Higher Education: A Comparison of International Patterns

ROGER L. GEIGER

Abstract. This paper seeks to extend understanding of the varying nature and varying forms of private higher education. Three basic structural divisions between private and public sectors of higher education are compared: mass private and restricted public sectors; parallel public and private sectors; and, comprehensive public and peripheral private sectors. The private sectors are then contrasted in terms of such functional characteristics as state authority, financial constraints and dominant orientation toward either academic goals, the student marketplace or external patrons. The highly diverse American private sector is viewed in this context. A consideration of mass private sectors then suggests that parameters of public policy are set by structurally derived characteristics of higher education systems.

Mixed systems of higher education can be analysed on three different levels: 1) how national systems of higher education are differentiated between public and private sectors; 2) how these different patterns give rise to different consequences or characteristics; or, 3) how these characteristics relate to possible alternatives for public policies for the development of higher education. The first of these levels is focused on structure and function, the second on operating characteristics, and the third on change over time. The principal aim of this paper is to examine relationships between the first and second levels in different types of systems. In the first section three basic structural types of higher education systems are described. The middle section seeks to establish that certain behavioral characteristics are inherently associated with each of these types and why this is the case. Explaining the existence of private sectors in these mixed systems tends to illuminate the most salient differences between structural types, and that is the approach that will be followed here. Finally, partly for illustrative purposes, some observations are offered on the policy issues facing mass private sectors today.

1. Structural Types of Higher Education Systems

The dichotomy between publicly and privately controlled institutions is commonly employed for purposes of record keeping, general discourse, and occasionally scholarly analysis. As conventionally applied to higher education systems, however, this simple dichotomy obscures a profoundly important aspect of the subject: while public sectors can be regarded, directly or indirectly, as creatures of the state, the state also to a considerable extent molds the conditions of existence for privately controlled institutions. The state is thus a powerful factor on both sides of the divide. To some extent this has always been the case, but in the last half of the twentieth century the modern state has played an undoubted role in structuring, regulating, and ultimately helping to finance private sectors. In some countries, notably Canada and Sweden, the expansion of state authority over higher education has virtually extinguished private institutions. But in most nations private colleges and universities have endured, and in some cases (e.g. Belgium, Japan, Brazil) even enlarged their share of total enrollments. The development of public sectors can to a considerable extent be analysed in terms of responses, mediated through the political process, to perceived social demands. Private sectors, however, are the result of more diverse factors; and their persistence testifies to the fulfillment of vital educational functions.

There are three basic structural patterns of public-private differentiation (Geiger, 1986):

1. *Mass private and restricted public sectors.* This pattern is exemplified best by Japan, but also found in the Philippines, South Korea, Brazil, Columbia, and to some extent Indonesia (RIHE, 1985). These systems are inherently hierarchical, with the state sponsoring, among others, high cost, academically elite universities. The private sector too is hierarchical, with the highest status usually accorded to old and established institutions. Much of the private sector, however, is left with the task of accommodating the considerable excess social demand for higher education. During the course of the last generation, when the demand for higher education escalated greatly, these elements of mass private sectors have expanded to accommodate these students. This has produced a majority of higher education enrollments in private institutions.

2. *Parallel public and private sectors.* This pattern results from the need to guarantee a significant degree of cultural pluralism within a nonhierarchical system. The existence of national degrees requires that each university provide education of equivalent value. But in order to achieve meaningful equality, and to satisfy different cultural groups, private institutions have to possess resources comparable to public ones. Under welfare-state conditions, such as exist in Belgium and the Netherlands, this has ultimately meant full state funding for private universities. Geographically and culturally far removed, Chile and Hong Kong have evolved along quite similar lines.

3. *Comprehensive public & peripheral private sectors.* In this situation the public sector is basically designed to fulfill all of society's higher educational needs; but invariably certain tasks are neglected, thus leaving opportunities (if permitted by law) for private initiatives. A peripheral private sector might consist of only one, "singular" institution, such as Sweden's Stockholm School of Economics, which performs its chosen mission so effectively that there is no practical reason to transform or supplant it. On the other hand, where serious deficiencies exist and persist in a comprehensive state sector, the private sector may have an opportunity to grow to significant size. Such "public-sector failure" has occurred in Mexico, for example, where over-crowding and politicization in government universities have been factors encouraging approximately fifteen per cent of students to enroll in what constitutes essentially a peripheral private sector.

Definite patterns of institutional orientation and behavior correspond with each of these three basic types. These patterns stem from the two ubiquitous conditions in the existence of private universities: state authority and financial constraint. The first of these represents an authority outside of the institution, while the second is a variable under some institutional control. Coming to terms with financial constraint, given the nature of higher education, requires that an institution make fateful decisions about what tasks to fulfill and what groups to serve. Basically, it is possible to discern three general orientations that a private university might adopt.

The first would be toward research and academic attainment. Such aspirations correspond with the incentives for faculty members that are inherent in the disciplinary reward structure—the recognition and prestige associated with advancing knowledge that are conferred by the national and international scientific-scholarly communities. Academic orientations carry the highest prestige—and the highest costs—within higher education.

The second possible orientation would be toward the marketplace, or more specifically, the labor markets in which graduates are rewarded directly for the investments that they have made in schooling. Market-oriented institutions are sensitive to the career considerations of their clientele, who in turn are generally willing to pay for the schooling and credential that they receive (Cf. Clark, 1983).

The third orientation would be toward patronage—principally voluntary support, but also encompassing ongoing advantageous service relationships with external parties that help to sustain the institution. Thus, patronage can orient a university toward wealthy individuals, particular social groups, private industry, or any benefactor with sufficient discretionary resources to provide assistance on a significant scale (Cf. Lee, 1987).

These orientations are not necessarily mutually exclusive. The Stockholm School of Economics presents an example of an institution that simultaneously manages academic distinction, a sustaining relationship with an economic elite, and close ties to business education. More commonly, however, these goals conflict. A vocational orientation, especially toward non-elite occupations, is not conducive to patronage; obsequiousness toward privileged social groups threatens academic commitments to meritocratic procedures; and dedication to academic attainment precludes certain vocational or service roles. Before these intricacies are explored further, however, it is necessary to specify the roles of the state and the nature of the financial constraints facing private universities.

2. Relative Characteristics of Structural Types

In the typology just described the state tends to appear as the proactive force—the actor that chooses its preferred tasks, leaving the remainder for private hands. In truth, however, public-private differentiation is more usually a reciprocal process. Universities are among the most venerable of social institutions, and new entrants to higher education, whether public or private, have almost invariably adapted to what has already existed. Beyond the role of sponsoring and maintaining the public sector, though, the state plays an important and variable role in the private sector.

In mass private sectors, the state tends to assume the negative role of the enforcer of minimal standards in private institutions. The most direct way in which this is done is through state regulation. Since one aim is to establish a floor of supposed pedagogical effectiveness, ministries of education often resort to detailed and specific requirements for curricula, degrees, and even classroom conduct. Because some parts of the private sector are often distrusted, bureaucratic regulation is sometimes extended to financial matters as well under the pretext of consumer protection. Finally, because the "mass" features of mass private sectors—rapid and seemingly uncontrolled growth—tend to alarm public authorities, some form of control is at some point often extended to student enrollments. Mass private sectors, in fact, would seem to present an unusual example of state-imposed enrollment restrictions on private schools. Extensive state regulation, then, is a concomitant to mass private sectors, with the result that a great number of private institutions does not produce a particularly high degree of diversity.

The state is also deeply involved with parallel private sectors, but there the aim is to guarantee a high intellectual standard, generally that set by a system of national degrees. Another difference in this type of system is that financial support precedes, and eventually causes, greater regulatory presence. Historically, in order for cultural minorities to have university education on an equal basis, it became necessary first to provide a state subsidy in lieu of private tuition. Then, in order for the privates to grow with the expansion of higher education enrollments, it became necessary to subsidize their capital needs. Finally, in order for them to maintain the academic standards required for national degrees it was necessary extensively to subsidize their operations. In Belgium and the Netherlands near total state support for private institutions, based upon rigid formulae, also brought in its wake close government regulation to assure conformance with legal requirements. Here too, then, large private sectors contain a limited degree of diversity—only in fact along the single axis of cultural beliefs.

State regulation and oversight of peripheral private sectors tends to be low, but at the same time legal barriers are often erected that restrict the operation of private institutions. For example, the decision taken in France more than a century ago to preclude Catholic universities from granting national degrees condemned those institutions to peripheral roles. A similar process produced peripheral Catholic universities in the Napoleonic systems of Spain and Italy. Thus excluded from the sphere of state responsibility (i.e. guaranteeing the validity of degrees) they were also spared from state scrutiny. Sometimes official state recognition may be required in the form of a license or a charter, but even where such documents imply conformity to government regulations, these provisions tend not to be rigorously enforced (e.g. Mexico). The logic of a comprehensive public sector weighs against close regulation of private alternatives, except where political motives are involved. When the state accepts total responsibility for the social provision of higher education through a comprehensive public system, in theory it need pay scant attention to those eccentrics who choose not to accept what the state has supplied. In practice, however, political antagonisms, such as those in the past between Catholic universities and secular governments or more recently between institutions with close links to private industry and left-oriented state universities, can cause the state to be prejudicial toward peripheral private sectors.

With respect to finances, private universities face just two problems: capital and income! Proprietary educational institutions may be common in highly vocational subjects, but academic higher education is seldom offered on a profit-making basis, although the Philippines and Thailand provide exceptions. Private colleges and universities are generally nonprofit organizations [NPOs] (Powell, 1987). Capital formation is a basic weakness of NPOs, and for that reason they tend to be found in service industries rather than capital-intensive ones. The rationales for the non-profit form of organization in general have centered upon the intentions of optimizing the satisfaction of producers and/or consumers. For this reason NPOs favor utilizing their discretionary resources to extend and improve the services they provide. Generating a return on capital is at odds with this fundamental orientation, and for that reason NPOs ordinarily avoid entering the capital markets, at least on normal terms. They prefer by far to rely on donated capital; failing that, they sometimes turn to the government; and at worst they make special arrangements to borrow at below-market rates.

In the past the capital needs of higher education were quite modest. Some land and a few buildings would generally suffice for the founding of a private college. Physical capital was usually accumulated slowly through sporadic gifts, and church affiliation often provided the contacts and organization for modest fund-raising efforts. Conditions changed in the mid-twentieth century with the vast expansion of higher education. Universities were compelled to grow and were consequently faced with substantial capital needs. Often it was necessary to purchase and construct entire new campuses. The ability to raise capital became a limiting condition for private colleges and universities throughout the world.

In most developed countries with significant private sectors government involvement was at some point required to meet capital needs. In Sweden and Canada government provision of large amounts of capital to facilitate expansion was the precipitating factor that brought private institutions under government control. Essentially the same process occurred in the United States when several urban private institutions became the nuclei of new state universities. In these public-service oriented institutions there was no compelling justification for preserving private control. In Belgium and the Netherlands, however, where private universities were sponsored by major subcultural populations, independence from the state was considered inherent to their mission. In both countries the government provided the capital for expansion, sometimes at exceedingly low rates of interest, without calling into question private control. In the United States too, the federal government provided capital to the private sector, but only for specified purposes, like dormitories, classrooms and laboratories, that were consistent with the public interest.

Events in Japan illustrate the pitfalls awaiting private institutions that were forced to raise capital on their own. Japan's private colleges responded to a feverish rate of enrollment growth in the 1960s by resorting to bank loans to finance campus expansion. Faced with mounting student militancy at the end of the decade, it became impossible to pass the mounting interest charges through to students by raising fees. A team of OECD examiners that reviewed the system at this juncture found the private sector to be essentially bankrupt, i.e. the private colleges could not expect to repay their debts with foreseeable revenues (OECD, 1971). This situation was an important factor in the government's 1970 decision to begin direct subsidization of private colleges. Thus, in Japan too government intervention was ultimately required, although indirectly, to meet the capital needs created by the expansion of private higher education.

TABLE 1
Dominant tendencies of different structural-functional types of private sectors

	Mass private	*Parallel private*	*Peripheral private*	*U.S. private*
State authority	high [min. standards]	high [high standard]	low	low [indirect]
Financial constraint	tuition dependent	publicly supported	private resources	pluralistic support
Orientation toward:				
Academic attainment	low	high	low	highest for research university
Marketplace	high	low	high/low	highest for urban service university
Patronage	low	low	low/high	highest for liberal arts colleges

The American private sector has been most successful in raising capital privately through philanthropy, although it has not been unique in this respect. Both the Stockholm School of Economics and the Free University of Brussels have benefited from the patronage of important industrial families. Still, aside perhaps from the Oxbridge colleges, no other private sector has been shaped to a greater extent by the action of private philanthropy. But the fact remains that for most private universities in the world philanthropy is not a realistic source of significant financial assistance.

With respect to income, perhaps the fundamental problem of private university finance is raising funds to cover the difference between what students pay for their education and what it actually costs. Higher education now receives state subsidization in every developed nation for both its value to society and to uphold some degree of social equity in access. It is widely accepted that the social rate of return to higher education exceeds the private rate, and that imperfections in capital markets preclude students from financing their studies by borrowing against future income. Most advanced nations also share the concern that education should not be rationed on the basis of price. These concerns apply to both public and private higher education, and for that reason some form of state subsidy to private institutions has become the rule as well.

The issues underlying such policies are, first, how much of the cost of their education should students in private institutions be made to bear, and second, how do these charges affect the relationship between state and private instruction. The resolution of these issues in different national systems has depended upon structural type. Only in the United States does the mechanism of tuition pricing have a major bearing on the relationship between the public and private sectors.

Welfare states such as Belgium, Sweden and the Netherlands have opted to have private university students pay little or none of the direct costs of their education. Each country has chosen to make higher education available at nominal cost and to eliminate price differentials between alternatives. The result in Belgium and the Netherlands has been that private universities are financed in much the same way as state ones. In fact, in financial matters these institutions have little independence. In Sweden, however, the state negotiates a long-term contract with the Stockholm School of Economics to determine the amount of its annual subsidy and the conditions for receiving it. These payments represent only about a third of the School's income. Thus, it has the independence of a private income, but also the obligation to raise additional funds through voluntary support and by providing services to private industry.

Private institutions in mass private sectors are most heavily dependent upon student tuition. They are primarily engaged in instruction, and for the most part spend little on amenities or overheads. Students have consequently been expected to pay something close to the full cost of their education (one indication of this: student fees vary by faculty within the university, thereby better reflecting true costs). The advent of government subsidies in Japan altered this to some extent, but without fundamentally changing the situation. Student tuition is much higher in the Japanese private sector than the public, but this is not necessarily the case in less-developed countries with mass private sectors. Nevertheless, with the public sector being highly selective, the majority of students have little recourse other than seeking a place in the private sector.

From the perspective of these two different types of private sectors it becomes evident that the American private sector provides education that is functionally equivalent to that offered in the public sector to students who have considerable freedom to choose where they will attend; yet private colleges and universities charge considerably more than their state counterparts. American private colleges and universities thus have a tacit obligation to provide advantages of academic quality, services, or cultural/pedagogical style that are not readily available in state institutions. This underlying competition consequently motivates private schools to sustain the quality and the variety of their programs. This in itself places upward pressure on costs. But increased costs cannot be readily passed along to students, both because of competition from the public sector and because the costs of education are not fully reflected in tuition. The tuition pricing of private higher education is thus a complicated matter that is vital to the existence of the American private sector.

With these patterns of state authority and financial constraint in mind, it is possible to elaborate the dominant tendencies of private sectors in each different structural pattern. To assist the reader, these consequences are presented in schematic form in Table 1. Of course, these "dominant" characteristics do not preclude the existence of exceptions.

Mass private sectors. Since the driving force behind mass private sectors is private demand for higher education, private universities operate in a kind of seller's market. They thus have the opportunity to charge something close to the full cost of the educational services that they provide. During particularly rapid periods of expansion, they might even be able to charge more than their marginal costs, thus raising some small amounts of capital. The histories of private higher education in Japan, the Philippines, and Turkey, however, suggest that this is a temporary phenomenon. Consistent capital generation would require raising tuition to levels that stimulate consumer opposition. Moreover, this opposition tends to be manifested in political terms (state regulation) rather than economic terms (decreased demand). Thus, with a few possible exceptions, like some recently founded private medical and dental schools in Japan, the level of tuition that can be charged is constrained by the capacity to pay of the mass of student/consumers, the effects of competition between institutions, and the intrusion of the state.

Tuition dependence is thus an inherent limitation on the quality of the educational services that private universities can provide. In particular, it allows for a comparatively limited amount of the kind of amenities associated with academic attainments. Private universities thus leave the pursuit of research and scientific recognition chiefly to the universities of the state. This lack of integration with national and international research communities produces a weakness and fragmentation of the academic profession in mass private sectors.

Since the resource bases of private universities are, largely for historical reasons, quite unequal, the private sector as a whole is markedly hierarchical. Prestige, however, results less from academic attainment than it does from success in the marketplace. The capacity to place graduates in good jobs is the principal mark of success—and a lure for future high-quality students. This type of vocationalism is not conducive to patronage. The private universities appear to be producing private benefits that accrue to their students (and perhaps more through screening than through creation of human capital); there would thus seem to be little justification for donating funds to expand or improve these services.

Parallel private sectors. The logic of parallel private sectors springs from a system of national degrees that are meant to guarantee a fairly high level of academic attainment. This virtually requires the integration of private university faculty members with national and international scientific/scholarly communities; the attendant high costs can only be met through government subidization. The greater the extent of direct government support, the more extensive in the long run government regulation is likely to be. This tends to produce a rather rigid academic curriculum that is little influenced by the marketplace for university graduates. Vocational subjects, in fact, are usually segregated in a non-university stratum, of postsecondary education. The greater the extent of government support, the fewer private resources likely to be directed toward the private sector. Private universities as a result are unresponsive towards external constituencies other than their actual sponsors.

Peripheral private sectors. As adjuncts to comprehensive public systems, peripheral private sectors must have an important *private* reason for existing. Concomitantly, they will be predominantly dependent upon private resources for their sustenance. In theory, the state should have little concern about their operations; but in fact there is often a political antagonism, tacit (Stockholm School of Economics, Mexican Business Schools) or overt (Catholic Universities in France), that encourages the state to circumscribe their activities. Academic integration is a luxury that some peripheral institutions may be able to afford, but for most the dominant orientation will be toward those external groups upon whom they depend. This can have two quite different results. In some cases concern for attracting a student clientele produces an overt orientation toward the marketplace, and this carries with it a corresponding low likelihood for a significant contribution from private patronage. Where significant patronage is available from supporting groups, however, peripheral institutions may be able to distance themselves from the production of useful skills and salable credentials, and pursue a more academic mission.

The United States private sector. The American private sector deserves separate consideration because of its size and because it offers several different kinds of alternatives to the numerically dominant public sector. The private sector as a whole shows a high degree of pluralism in its funding, receiving significant amounts from student tuition, indirect government support (to purchase student instruction or research), and private patronage. But aggregate statistics conceal distinctive orientations for different types of institutions. Private research universities consider academic distinction to be the most important institutional mission. They are able to excel academically in part because of past and current patronage, but particularly due to large-scale government funding of scientific research. Urban service universities tend to be tuition dependent, and consequently are exceedingly sensitive to the marketplace. The wealthy liberal arts colleges are the most purely dependent upon patronage, which has allowed them to maintain the margin of quality in undergraduate education by which they justify their existence. The indirect nature of federal government support, as well as the federal political structure, make government authority only one of many influences upon American private higher education.

3. Policy and Change

In the light of the foregoing analysis, it would seem that policies aimed at maximizing the advantages, or minimizing the disadvantages, of private sectors should be designed to complement the inherent characteristics of the particular structural type present in a given country. Expressed so baldly, this may appear to be no more than common sense. But sensibleness has not always been common in public discussions of private sectors. The recent debate in Western Europe, for example, has been highly unrealistic in both claims for and objections against private institutions (Geiger, 1985). And in the United States the virtues of private higher education are almost ritualistically invoked in defense of vested interests without regard to the differing orientations of the private subsectors.

Private higher education does indeed potentially possess qualities that might be of value to most societies. One set of such qualities is associated with diversity. The existence of diversity in a system enhances individual choice and thus the optimization of individual welfare. Diversity is also produced as organized groups within society pursue their collective ends, the result in this case being the enhancement of pluralism. In both cases, the responsiveness of private institutions to stimuli external to the higher education system helps to adapt higher education to society's needs. An additional potential benefit of private sectors is the mobilization of private resources for higher education that would not otherwise be available. In part these resources come from students as fees for service, but occasionally they can be derived from external groups as patronage. The challenge of higher education policy, then, is to influence the characteristics of given types of private sectors in order to realize such advantages as are feasible, while also seeking to minimize the effects of inherent weaknesses. In practical terms, this could be illustrated by applying the framework to some of the policy alternatives facing mass private sectors.

Mass private sectors possess the important social advantage of accommodating a large private demand for higher education and for university credentials, and in doing so chiefly through the mobilization of private resources. Their inherent drawbacks include a weak resource base, low academic standards in many institutions, and a consequent state effort to compensate for low standards through extensive regulation. The combination of credentialism and regulation produces a fairly low level of diversity. Thus, one desirable direction for future change would be to lessen government regulation and encourage the stronger private universities, in particular, to develop distinctive areas of strength. The Philippines has been contemplating just such a policy, which would rely upon accreditation through established private agencies. Institutions that meet accrediting standards might be exempted from certain types of government regulations, and the thrust of regulation could then focus on maintaining minimal standards in the weaker institutions (Gonzalez, 1987).

Japan is alone among mass private sectors in being able to boost the resource base of private colleges and universities through the infusion of significant amounts of public funds. Moreover, this has been done in an imaginative way that established financial incentives for private institutions to increase those inputs that would strengthen them academically. In terms of the typology suggested above, one could say that Japan, by attempting to raise the floor of minimal standards, has endeavored to move in the direction of parallel public and private sectors. Two features of mass private sectors, however, would seem to create obstacles to the translation of additional resources into improvements in academic quality. First would be the problem of increasing the incentives for academic achievements among students who are chiefly motivated to obtain credentials for the labor market. South Korea has attacked this problem by attempting to motivate students in a particularly heavy-handed manner. It has been proposed that private universities fail 30 per cent of each entering class in order, as Voltaire put it, "to encourage the others". Such a policy would seem to be harmful to precisely the strongest private universities—those capable of attracting a well-qualified student body. A more constructive approach might aim at the creation of positive inducements to student achievement, such as offering greater recognition and reward for high grades or enhancing the content of academic programs (a notorious deficiency in credential-oriented mass private sectors).

Probably one of the most difficult and pervasive problems of mass private sectors would be the weakness of the academic profession, and hence the low motivation among private sector faculty for research, publication, or even general intellectual involvement with their fields. In Japan government subsidies have increased salary levels for faculty in private universities—an important prerequisite for improving quality in the long run—but it has not yet become apparent that this in itself has improved the academic performance of private sector faculty. Perhaps it would be appropriate to consider more focused policies. One possibility might be a program of faculty fellowships for sabbatical leaves. Greater availability of external research funds might also encourage private universities to place a higher value on the academic involvement of their faculty. The further development of graduate education, as well, would have positive effects.

Such observations are offered, not as prescription for future policies, but rather to illustrate how comprehension of the principal patterns of public/private differentation, and their distinctive consequences, can identify problem areas or policy concerns that are common to given structural types.

Note

An earlier version of this paper was delivered to the Third International Seminar on Higher Education in Asia, sponsored by the Research Institute for Higher Education, Hiroshima University, Hiroshima, January 28–29, 1987. This version has benefited from the comments of the Conference participants, as well as those of Paul DiMaggio.

References

Clark, Burton R. (1983). *The Higher Education System: Academic Organization in Cross-National Perspective.* Los Angeles: University of California Press.

Geiger, Robert L. (1985). "The Private Alternative in Higher Education," *European Journal of Education* 20: 385–97.

Geiger, Roger L. (1986). *Private Sectors in Higher Education: Structure, Function and Change in Eight Countries.* Ann Arbor: University of Michigan Press.

Gonzalez, Andrew B. (1987). "Public and Private Sectors in Philippine Higher Education". In RIHE, 1987: 35–48.

Lee, Kwan (1987). "Past, Present and Future Trends in the Public and Private Sectors of the Korean Higher Education System". In RIHE, 1987: 49–70.

Levy, Daniel C. (1986). *Higher Education and the State in Latin America: Private Challenges to Public Dominance.* Chicago: University of Chicago Press.

OECD (1971). Organization of Economic Cooperation and Development, *Review of National Policies for Education: Japan.* Paris: OECD: 153–62.

Powell, Walter W. (ed.) (1987). *The Non-Profit Handbook.* New Haven: Yale University Press.

RIHE (1985). Research Institute for Higher Education, Hiroshima University, *Higher Education Expansion in Asia.* Hiroshima: RIHE.

RIHE (1987). Research Institute for Higher Education, Hiroshima University, *Public and Private Sectors in Asian Higher Education Systems: Issues and Prospects.* Hiroshima: RIHE.

The Decline of Latin American Student Activism

DANIEL C. LEVY

Abstract. If Latin America once represented a worldwide reference point for potent student activism, the region now stands out for the decline of activism. While other regions experience new forms and impacts of activism, Latin America's decline should be understood within two broad contexts: macropolitical and higher educational.

The macropolitical context subsumes at least three major causal factors. One is the role of authoritarian rule, especially powerful in the 1970s but leaving a legacy that itself works against activism. Second, we must consider the more complex and mixed impacts of the redemocratization that has swept the region. The third factor is the general decline of the left both domestically and internationally.

On the higher education side, decades of unprecedented growth in student numbers have fragmented the student body, especially as growth is accompanied by extraordinary institutional proliferation. Many of the newer institutions are inhospitable for student activism. Privatization has had an especially strong demobilizing effect. The institutional changes are accompanied by a changing profile of fields of study, away from some most associated with student politics. Finally, the concentration of top social scientists in research centers apart from the universities—and from the students—is also crucial.

Introduction

As other regions witness increased student activism in the closing years of the century, Latin America—long seen as the extreme in such activism—witnesses a notable decrease. This article explains the decrease in terms of two clusters of factors. The first is the macropolitical context. The second, surer in its limiting effects, is the higher education context. Both clusters will show how diversification is crucial in understanding the decline.

Perception of decline stems partly from images of extraordinary activism that were formed when most of the literature on Latin American students was written, in the 1960s and early 1970s. The literature was itself a response to what can now be interpreted as a temporary peak in student politics. Since that time, however, very little has been written, so that extant literature would leave readers with either false impressions or, at best, a lack of explanation for the changes.[1] And these changes involve not just a fall from the peak but a longer-term transformation that requires attention.

Macropolitical Context

Too often works on student activism consider the macropolitical context only insofar as it is the object of protest; yet the context also largely determines propensities, orientations, and, crucially, permissible bounds of activism.

Authoritarian Rule

The point about bounds was made painfully clear in recent times, particularly in the 1970s. It has already been analyzed (Levy 1981) but must be summarized here, despite the fact that democracies have subsequently swept the region, because extended military rule was so crucial to the decline of activism in the 1970s and also the 1980s and because the legacy of that rule still has a telling effect.

Historically, authoritarian rule in Latin America usually allowed for pockets of autonomy, of which the university was a leading example. Starting with Brazil in 1964, however, militaries assumed power with intentions not just to save the status quo and quickly turn government back to trustworthy civilians but to remake society through extended rule. Repression and exclusion were central characteristics of their policy toward the university and beyond. So on the one hand student activism on campus was prohibited while, on the other, related structures in which students had participated beyond the campus (e.g., political parties) were also outlawed. Violations of prohibitions were often dealt with brutally. The impact on student activism was especially profound because repression came in precisely those nations where activism had gone furthest in the years just before the coups and because these nations (Brazil, Argentina 1966 and 1976, Chile and Uruguay 1973) accounted for well over half the higher education enrollments; and the figures would expand if we include aggressive military rule in Central America and, at times, certain other South American nations in the 1970s.

As to the chilling legacy of repressive military rule, I would emphasize a few points consistent with a wider literature on political culture. Many youth see politics as dirty, and are apathetic. Accordingly, fewer than half those eligible voted in renewed Argentine student elections (1984), and surveys show distrust of student political leaders (Mollis 1989, pp. 344–345). Then too, long military rule showed many the ultimate weakness of student activists, particularly as most of the latter's goals were diametrically opposed to the military's policies within and beyond the university. Additionally, the military's brutality taught many that leftist activism carries great risks, and that things could indeed be much worse than they are under centrist or even rightist civilian regimes. Finally, extended military rule helped the development, of some rightist student groups: juxtaposed to groups of decidedly different tendencies, these contribute to fragmenting diversification.

Democratization

To be sure, democratization has allowed renewed student activism. To deny that would be to deny the obvious in pursuit of an unqualified thesis about decline. Even in the opening up process, while militaries still governed, student activity increased. Regime power and legitimacy to repress was waning; dynamics were underway in which 'softliners' and realists (about transition) were ascendant within the regimes themselves (O'Donnell, Schmitter, and Whitehead 1986). The process was especially long in Brazil; students were demonstrating fairly freely and voting in their universities for a decade before the nation directly elected its president (1989). In fact, Brazil shows how student activists could assume important leadership roles, and set examples, in the wider struggle for redemocratization. Something similar happened in Chile from 1983 to 1990, even though most student goals were of limited institutional scope. (With qualifications we could even cite the role of Mexican student activists since the mid-1980s in demanding unprecedented democratization of their nation's civilian authoritarian regime.) As in Eastern Europe, students in Latin America were spurred by the realization that an impact was possible when regimes were on the ropes.

Once democracies are established, authoritarian restrictions are naturally replaced by ample freedom to be active. Students typically regain some representation within their institutions and a credible power of protest beyond as well. Meanwhile, the re-establishment of other organizations in civil society reopens multiple routes for activism long characteristic of civil regimes (e.g., activism associated with youth wings of political parties, sometimes en route to recruitment to government positions). Additionally, the center-right economic policies of most of the post-military democracies in South America (Brazil, Chile, and Argentina) and, especially by 1990, Central America, are logical targets for criticism by student leftists, a point that applies well also to the rightward flow of the Mexican regime. In Guatemala, national university students protested President Cerezo's austerity policies. In Nicaragua, where a center-right coalition replaced the Sandinistas (1990), student activists formed even during the transition to demand demobilization of the contras, huge pay increases for faculty, and other measures that suggested an active future.[2]

Granted all this, the new democratic context also carries factors, admittedly more subtle, that cut against student activism.

First, most of the democracies are brittle. Consequently, the authoritarian legacy is especially vivid. Even such relatively developed nations as Argentina and Brazil have had precious little experience with democracy; the former has suffered through repeated periods of military rule, as have many smaller nations. Furthermore, all the new and renewed democracies, with the partial exception of Chile, have assumed power amid terrible economic crisis. While the striking movement toward neoliberal economic policy provokes some student protest, it is also a humiliating illustration of the impotence of student politics on the national scale, as activists have lobbied for quite opposite policies; credibility declines. Then too, the crisis has pushed student groups to focus on corporate self-protection, such as protesting increased prices in the cafeteria, medical services, and public transportation. That may be activism, but hardly the romantic or inspired kind that builds great movements. Beyond that, the crisis leads many to regard activism as a luxury or an irrelevance; many become but part-time students as they work off campus.

Second, democracies have replaced not just modern authoritarian military rule but also oligarchies, at least if we compare 1990 to 1970 and 1960 as well as to 1980. It was under such oligarchies that students often achieved their greatest impact due to the narrowness of the regime alongside the absence of other strong actors in civil society (Silvert 1967). More to the point here, such potential impact, including the heralded cases related to toppling personalistic dictators, encouraged activism. By contrast, students are at best one group among many in today's democracies. Student activity now often flows through other organizations, weakening student movements per se. Albornoz (1989, p. 412) shows how much all Venezuelan groups, including students, are coopted by the main political parties. Silva Michelena (1986) likewise finds that the student movement no longer serves as the voice of national identity, as multiple mass media grow, and he accurately generalizes about the decline of activism in the 'old democracies' (which, for the inclusion of Mexico alongside Venezuela, Colombia, and Costa Rica, I have called 'reconciliation' (Levy 1981) or 'civil' regimes). Thus, activism will not necessarily increase as new democracies institutionalize themselves.

A third factor is how the moderation of the democracies fragments student politics. Widespread revulsion, common for student bodies facing tottering oligarchies and modern militaries, does not materialize here. For example, disagreement with policies that do not vigorously pursue former human rights violators is not nearly so intense as that over the violations themselves.

Moving the analysis beyond the form of government to the general political climate, we see further reason for declining activism. After all, it is the general population that is electing centrist to conservative governments. A salient political fact is this: the left itself has been weakening.

Events in Eastern Europe and the Soviet Union have reduced the attraction of leftist groups, putting them on the defensive. So have Chinese reforms followed by brutal repression. Closer to home, Cuba appears an embarrassing anachronism more than an inspiration, and the Sandinista defeat is another shock. Additionally, I would emphasize: the discrediting of the left during its reign preceding (or, arguably, even partly precipitating) military rule (e.g., Chile, Brazil, Argentina); the relatively conservative drift of West European democracies; and an increasingly favorable view of the United States.

The decline of the left contributes to the decline of student activism as that activism has generally been leftist. The less leftist, the less distinctive. Moreover, the decline of leftism is tied to a decline of beliefs in certainties and in optimistic views about the likelihood of change.[3]

Of course, some students remain on the activist left. But as others do not, movements diversify politically or are marginalizted. Indeed, this marginalization is increasingly accompanied by outright rejection by the bulk of the student body. This is something different from the mix of sympathy and apathy with which many students historically viewed activists. Moncada (1986, p. 366) contrasts the heyday of activist popularity in Ecuador with a contemporary reality of a movement that is 'dispersed, incoherent, confused, weakened and often stuck in violent electoral disputes.' (Silié 1988, p. 179) echoes the idea for the Dominican Republic, where most youth see student organizations as alien, not for them. Albornoz (1989, pp. 407–409) argues that Venezuela's once powerful left is almost gone, as former activists are in the system, and surveys show high school students favoring the status quo, distrusting politics, and disliking student activists. Bernales (1986, pp. 400–401) reports that the terror of Sendero Luminoso (the guerrilla group) has had a discrediting effect in Peru. More generally, Silva Michelena (1986, pp. 293–298) finds moderation breeding hostility to student radicalism. In Chile, it is striking that only the Communist Party has pushed co-government (which involves strong student representation) for universities, and most leftist parties have joined with the center in keeping that party out of the ruling democratic coalition. Finally, in Mexico, students did successfully mobilize to beat back academic reforms at the National University but activists failed in attempts to seize the opportunity to build an ongoing movement and press for co-government and other demands.

Higher Education Context

A complete division between the macropolitical and higher education context would be artificial as the former has affected the latter. Examples include the ways military repression of public higher education has spurred multiple types of privatization. But none of the higher education changes has been caused solely by macropolitical changes, and some have occurred rather independently. In any event, shifts in the higher education context have been more secular, less uncertain, than the macropolitical ones. Moreover, they have more consistently undermined student activism.

System Growth

Tremendous growth in student enrollments from the 1950s at least into the 1970s, depending upon nation, driving the regional cohort percentages from 3% in 1960 to 12% by 1975, has transformed the higher education system. Though military rule sometimes thwarted growth, other regimes and macropolitical forces (e.g., the ideology of development) as well as broad socioeconomic forces promoted it.

Initially, surging numbers may have contributed to activisim and a new sense of power. But the stronger secular effect seems to have been divisive diversification. Students increasingly come from different backgrounds from one another. Commonality, objectively defined and subjectively perceived, has declined. So has the aura of national leadership, and the claim of serving as a national voice. Such settings are more natural for elite systems—and may well explain sharp differences with the African cases discussed elsewhere in this issue. Indeed, Brunner (1986, pp. 279–283) depicts such fragmentation, with the decline of student leadership and unified student culture, as central for explaining diminished activism in Latin America.[4]

Furthermore, admission of nonelite groups has meant that an increased percentage of students must work outside the university. This obviously undermines any sense of unified community, as it emphasizes the immediate practical needs of many students. The weakening effect on student activism has been powerful in such systems as the Brazilian and the Dominican. And the effect is exacerbated as other university actors have increasingly become full time. For one thing, the core of full-time professors tends to look askance at excessively nonacademic student activities, as seen in their reaction to student demonstrations at Mexico's National University in the last few years. For another, full-time professors have their own concerns and weight within the university, marginalizing students; in these same recent years Venezuelan universities have been closed more from the professoriate's demands regarding salary and benefits than from student activism (Albornoz 1989, p. 407), quite a turn around from the 1960s. Moreover, in these two nations and many others, activist university workers have become the most disruptive dissident political force on campus. Finally, however, Brunner (1986, p. 284) keenly notes how so much of the affairs of large academic institutions are now handled by professional bureaucrats, in routinized and technocratic ways that help make student activism remote.

Growth has also undermined unity in terms of fields of study. The traditional 'big three' of medicine, law, and engineering, now account for only about one-third of total enrollments (Levy 1986, pp. 268–271). Moreover, the literature has always found activism linked with only certain fields (Lipset and Altbach 1967), and a huge proportional decline has occurred in the fields most associated with student activism. Law, with less than one-tenth of contemporary enrollments, is a key example. Likewise, the 'academic' social sciences (e.g., sociology) are now outdistanced three to one by business-related studies. Such diversification is mostly related to broad differentiation processes that help define development. Also relevant is the increasing technification and even conservative drift of government, along with privatization of the economy.

Additionally, field diversification relates strongly to another form of diversification spurred by student growth: institutional proliferation. Though large universities have gotten larger, most growth has eventually channeled itself into different institutions. Crucially, national universities have lost their role, sometimes held for a century and a half, as either monopolies or at least undisputed center and leader of higher education systems. A country like Venezuela has alongside its national university the following official categories of institutions: other public autonomous universities, public experimental universities, private universities, an open university, pedagogical institutes, polytechnical institutes, both public and private university institutes of technology, and both public and private colleges (CNU 1982, pp. 17–46). Such proliferation has made unified student movements much harder to achieve. Not only do students at different institutions have different backgrounds, aspirations, living conditions, and socializations, they are physically separated. And many find themselves at institutions, such as technical institutes, with no tradition, interest or tolerance for student activism. Even the newer university institutions, however, are somewhat less prone to activism than are their more venerable counterparts, as Argentina shows (Cano 1985, p. 94).

Privatization

The most striking aspect of institutional proliferation affecting student activism has been privatization. A detailed account of how privatization weakens student activism (Levy 1981, pp. 366–374) is updated, summarized, and augmented in the ensuing paragraphs.

Whereas in 1960 still only 15% of total enrollments were in private institutions, by 1975 it was 34% and has held relatively steady since. Every nation except Cuba has a private sector, and three (Brazil, Colombia, and the Dominican Republic) have the majority of their enrollments there. The numbers are significant as private institutions typically allow no or minimal student representation on decision-making bodies. More importantly, they boast a general lack of activism (and certainly disorder) through protest.

Explanations for the lack of activism stem from the reasons actors have created, supported, and chosen private institutions. Many governments have directly or indirectly promoted privatization, partly because of the antigovernment bent of student activism in the publics. But, paradoxically, governments promoting public growth have often exacerbated factors that lead others to see the publics as failures, and seek private alternatives. Many families have chosen privates precisely because they promise a lack of disorder. In turn, the private institutions are conservative and themselves would allow little activism. Even in the exceptional cases where private institutions allow student representation and voting, as by law in Peru, no flavor of activism resembles the public sector.

The private sector's political orientations combine with socioeconomic ones. Private students come disproportionately from privileged families disinclined toward leftist politics, and seeking institutions that offer the best routes to the best jobs. Many of these become the most selective institutions, and they specialize in job-oriented fields such as business administration, not normally linked to activism. Again a mutually reinforcing dynamic develops between institutional selection and student self-selection. Then, as privates hold an edge in terms of privileged clientele, job prospects, academic prestige, etc., public institutions—and the student politics at them—become more marginalized. To choose the region's three oldest universities, the national universities of Peru, Mexico and the Dominican Republic is to choose three telling examples. Unlike their predecessors, public student activists there and elsewhere do not speak from the pinnacle. Furthermore, each time activists block academic reform at their public universities, they contribute to the lag behind leading privates. No wonder activists usually fought hard against the creation of growth of private sectors. But today's battle in Costa Rica is but a faint echo of the great battles of recent decades. The activists have lost.

Two trends further bolster the depoliticizing effect. One concerns democratization. The private-public difference had a less decisive impact when authoritarian regimes blocked activism across-the-board. Inter-sectoral differences have been much more decisive in civil systems, such as Venezuela's and Mexico's, and so could well assume increased significance in the new democracies. The other trend concerns subsectors on the private side. In fact, some Catholic universities of the 'first wave' of privatization have seen, over time, a degree of activism, though rarely has it approached public sector dimensions. And this Catholic phenomenon may be more than counterbalanced by the fact that the private weight has passed increasingly into secular institutions. The elite ones, which some prestigious Catholic institutions increasingly resemble as they lose distinctive religious identity, have been famously incompatible with activism. But the main private growth especially in the 1980s has come in nonelite secular institutions. These do not conform to all the traits elaborated above but they are typically based on commercial fields, are populated by part-time students, and are small and multitudinous—all of which aggravates the fragmentation.

Research Centers

A further major fracturing of the system that has hurt student activism is the startling ascendancy of research centers. Many of these, including most that are freestanding outside the universities, are private research centers (prcs), overwhelmingly concentrated in the social sciences (Brunner and Barrios 1987). Others exist within the universities (urcs) themselves, especially the public ones; they cover principally the natural and social sciences.

Prcs have surged largely as responses to authoritarian regimes, which made critical work impossible in most universities. Funding would come overwhelmingly from international sources, with added protection sometimes afforded by church connections. Prcs have dominated the social sciences, except economics, in Argentina and Chile; in Brazil, they would share the scene with universities. But the prcs are not disappearing with redemocratization. And they are increasingly sharing the scene or dominating it in a wide range of other nations including Peru, the Dominican Republic, and most in Central America. The main reason is clear: prcs are a response largely to the difficulties of the main universities, whether or not those difficulties stem from regime repression. Most private universities do not do much academic social science and most public ones suffer from the problems elaborated above, including disorder. On the other hand, urcs (also 'institutes' within universities) reinforce the point about how research centers now exist in nations throughout the region, and about how they grow largely because of the 'micropolitical' and other problems of the universities. They are often at least partial sanctuaries from the difficulties plaguing the mainstream faculties.

Research centers work against student activism in several significant ways. First, overlaying everything else, they lack students. Depending on one's definition of prcs and urcs, they have either no students or few students, or students in but peripheral status. Teaching either does not exist, is limited to nondegree courses, or, even where most prevalent, subordinated to research. No students, no activism. Few students, little activism, especially as these are almost always graduate students, often carefully selected and much more academically oriented than 'undergraduates.' (Indeed, graduate education represents a further fracturing of the student body.) Again we see a mutual selection process that rules out much student activism. Furthermore, the research centers tend to be very serious about academic work, typically emphasizing objective and/or practical or theoretical over pointedly ideological research; prc dependence on performance for its soft money income in fact denies much margin for tolerating disorder. Moderation and professionalism have also been promoted decisively by study in the U.S. and Western Europe, a common experience for those at research centers. Finally, the lack of student activism fits what are actually quite hierarchical organizations. Urcs typically have much less participation by students or even junior professionals than do faculties within the same universities. And prcs, rather ironically given the progressive ideologies of many of the researchers forced out of the public universities, are run in even more markedly top-down fashion; elections, for example, are rare. Overall, most prcs are rather consensual organizations, to which one affiliates by choice, and within which little dissidence emerges.

The College of Mexico, the Corporation of Economic Research for Latin America in Chile (CIEPLAN), the Center for the Study of State and Society in Argentina (CEDES), the Institute for Peruvian Studies (IEP), the University Research Institute of Rio de Janeiro (IUPERJ), and other prcs do not have student activists. Nor do the urcs of the natural sciences, or apparently even the social sciences, at national universities in Costa Rica, Mexico, and elsewhere.

But it is not just that those at the research centers eschew activism. It is that they hold such a weight within the system. Unquestionably, Latin America's best research and ideas in the social sciences (in terms of both scholarship and policy relevance), and a vastly disproportionate share of the good professors, students, and physical resources are at the prcs. A parallel exists, though less strongly, regarding the urcs versus mainstream teaching faculties. Consequently, student activists at the public university faculties are once again marginalized.

Conclusion

One way to summarize is to speculate very sketchily in a comparative mode. The decline of Latin American student activism surely has much to do with development. On the macropolitical side there is the diversity of participatory vehicles in civil society. On the higher education development side there is the enormous differentiation stemming from growth and other factors. From both sides we see not only diminished disposition toward activism but, crucially, diminished political weight for potential activists at the public universities. In a very general way, therefore, Latin America may suggest something about the long-run future of Africa (and less-developed nations in Asia), where civil society is much less developed and higher education remains much smaller, elitist, and undifferentiated than in Latin America. On the other hand, changes within Latin America may make it fit somewhat more than before with the experiences of the First World in terms of lower levels of activism.

But such speculations must remain very loose for now, and very tentative. Experience breeds wariness about even hints of developmental determinism. No clear linear progression exists. Furthermore, the macropolitical side analyzed in this article is still in considerable flux, with many consequences for activism still uncertain. Democratization obviously promotes some activism, and austerity may provoke more; so could threats or realities of authoritarian comebacks, or, conceivably, opportunities to dump the remaining dictatorship in Cuba. In Central America and elsewhere not only is formal democracy weak but civil society is fragile. Even on the higher education side, particular features such as the dilution of conservative vigor at some now venerable private universities, while public universities hang onto the clear majority of enrollments, could cut against basic tendencies toward declining activism. And then there are all the factors that are presently unforseen. All the while, student activism is not dead.[5]

Nonetheless, I conclude by emphasizing that diminished student activism has been a sure fact in Latin American politics over the last two decades. The macropolitical context provides some important explanations for that, even while its effects are mixed. The higher education context, itself shaped by broader political and socioeconomic tendencies, provides another set of explanations and these are overwhelmingly related to diminished student activism.

Notes

1. The only recent sources I know that thematically treat decline in more than one nation are Brunner (1986) and Silva Michelana (1986), both of which make pioneering contributions, especially on fragmentation within higher education; nonetheless, my work attempts a contribution particularly regarding macropolitics and the role of privatization and

research centers. The next most recent piece would be Levy (1981), but it is weak on the higher education context beyond privatization, and its macropolitical analysis was based on the 1970s, with but a sketchy update in Levy (1989). One review article covering earlier work is Peterson (1970); even then, students were not as active as stereotypes had it. Unfortunately, the present contribution can give but the scantest attention to several related matters including: the evolving forms lingering activism assumes; details on individual nations and enormous variation across nations; comparisons to other regions.

2. In Panama students have also demonstrated for such measures as increased wages for professors, but the most notable point so far has been a low profile both during and immediately after the U.S. invasion, whereas anti-U.S. protests were visible while Noriega was in power.
3. On the other hand, a new belief in certainty has arisen with neoliberal student movements. Argentina's, lacking precedent in the nation's history, blossomed by the mid-1980s and assumed a key role in seeking popular support for the new right. Argentina's conservative parties had previously denounced student politicization, but then welcomed the anti-state ideology and its explanations for public university failures (Gibson 1990).
4. I do not want to exaggerate prior unity. Even among activists, bitter splits (e.g., along national political lines) were common in nations such as Chile by the 1960s. Mexico had hundreds of student unions at one time (Mabry 1982, pp. 289–290).
5. Although this article has not attempted to document where activism persists, even so it has made passing reference to roles in ending recent military regimes and pressing for democratization, and to effective efforts to block policies (ranging from increased fees for student services to academic reform) that would directly affect individual and corporate interests.

References

Albornoz, O. (1989). 'Venezuela', in Altbach, P. (ed.), *Student Political Activism: An International Reference Handbook.* New York: Greenwood Press, pp. 405–416.

Altbach, P. (ed.) (1989). *Student Political Activism: An International Reference Handbook.* New York: Greenwood Press.

Bernales, E. (1986). 'Los problemas de la juventud universitaria en el Perú, in Tedesco, J. C. and Blumental, H. (eds.), *La juventud en América Latina.* Caracas: CRESALC, pp. 383–401.

Brunner, J. J. (1986). 'El movimiento estudiantil ha muerto. Nacen los movimientos estudiantiles', in Tedesco, J. C. and Blumental, H. (eds.) *La juventud en América Latina.* Caracas: CRESALC, pp. 279–390.

Brunner, J. J. and Barrios, A. (1987). *Inquisicion, mercado y filantro pía.* Santiago: FLACSO.

Cano, D. (1985). *La educación superior en la Argentina.* Buenos Aires: FLACSO/CRESALC.

CNU (Consejo Nacional de universidades) (1982). *Boletín estadístico no. 8.* Caracas: Oficina de Planificación del sector universitario.

Gibson, E. (1990). 'Democracy and the new electoral right in Argentina', working paper no. 12 of Columbia University's Institute of Latin American and Iberian Studies.

Levy, D. (1986). *Higher Education and the State in Latin America.* Chicago: University of Chicago Press.

Levy, D. (1989). 'Latin American student politics: beyond the 1960s', in Altbach, P. (ed.), *Student Political Activism: An International Reference Handbook.* New York: Greenwood Press, pp. 315–338.

Levy, D. (1981). 'Student politics in contemporary Latin America', *Canadian Journal of Political Science* 14(2), 353–376.

Lipset, S. M. and Altbach, P. (eds.) (1967). *Students in Revolt.* Boston: Houghton, Mifflin.

Mabry, D. (1982). *The Mexican University and the State: Student Conflicts 1910–1971.* College Station: Texas A & M.

Mollis, M. (1989). 'Argentina', in Altbach, P. (ed.), *Student Political Activism: An International Reference Handbook.* New York: Greenwood Press, pp. 339–350.

Moncada, J. (1986). 'Experiencias nacionales de políticas universitarias: el caso ecuatoriano', in Tedesco, J. C. and Blumenthal, H. (eds.), *La juventud en América Latina.* Caracas: CRESALC, pp. 359–368.

O'Donnell, G., Schmitter, P., and Whitehead, L. (eds.) (1986). *Transitions from Authoritarian Rule.* Baltimore: Johns Hopkins University Press.

Peterson, J. (1970). 'Recent research on Latin American university students', *Latin American Research Review* 5(1), 37–56.

Silié, R. (1988). 'Educación superior dominicana: situación y perspectiva', Santo Domingo. Unpublished manuscript.

Silva Michelena, J. A. (1986). 'La participación estudiantil en las actividades políticas', in Tedesco, J. C. and Blumenthal, H. (eds.), *La juventud en América Latina.* Caracas: CRESALC, pp. 291–302.

Silvert, K. (1967). 'The university student', in Snow, P. (ed.), *Government and Politics in Latin America.* New York: Holt Rinehart and Winston.

Tedesco, J. C. and Blumenthal, H. (eds.) (1986). *La juventud en América Latina.* Caracas: CRESALC.

The Paradox of the Autonomy of Argentine Universities: From Liberalism to Regulation

MARCELA MOLLIS

University autonomy refers to the capacity of university institutions to self-govern. However, this definition does describe the complexity of the political, normative and organizational, and its practical consequences for the Argentine institutions. Part of that complexity remains because "autonomy" is not a self-explanatory concept. It arises from multiple interpretations of actors with divergent interests, which enrich the concept with multiple historical meanings.

This chapter will intend to show the incidence of diverse historical meanings in the Argentine university autonomy through the process of building its organizational identity. To achieve this purpose, the dynamic interaction between actors and interests (individuals and public) shaping the present state of the university autonomy in Argentina, will be introduced. The inner changes produced from the liberal conceptualization of university autonomy to the regulated concept of autonomy recently prescribed in the promulgated Law of Higher Education in Argentina will also be discussed.

The University Autonomy: A History of Dependence of the Medieval Powers

Universities, traditionally, like churches, have usually had a degree of autonomy from political and economic control that is quite remarkable, partly because they have been protected by the upper classes, however, constituted, at nearly all times in almost every society. They have on occasion, through what has gone on within them, helped to change the world but have themselves been much less changed than most of the rest of the world (Kerr, C. 1994:45).

University autonomy was not only provided as a constitutive characteristic of medieval institutions of higher learning but it helped in shaping its ecumenical and universalistic tradition as well. Based on an analysis of the relationship between autonomy and public powers (empires, principalities, communes, etc.), it is necessary to go back to the birth of universities in the Twelfth Century. The creation of the University of Bologna (the university of students) it is particularly relevant to understand the organizational model of the Argentine University Reform movement in 1918, basically because it gave students so much influence and power that dominated faculty organization.

In medieval times intellectuals organized themselves, as members of any other medieval guild, and identified with a forum that provided them with corporative privileges to act with certain independence. The University whether of masters or of students, was only a particular kind of guild (Rashdall, 1936:97 in Clark, B. 1977:8).

In the case of the University of Bologna, given its imperial origin, it gained independence from the power of the Church and other local powers. That is how some universities began to develop a "constitutive autonomy," that is to say, an autonomy that was intrinsic to, a precondition for the development of their medieval nature as corporations of higher learning. They gained autonomy with respect to certain powers enjoying a set of corporative privileges, and also depending exclusively from the public power that allowed them those same privileges. There were historical tensions, however.

As Burton Clark describes in the case of old Italian universities:

> The towns, no longer to be intimidated by threats of secession, took over basic control from without, while the masters, now permanently employed by the state, were no longer dependent of students and student approval for their income. What had been an essentially commercial relationship between buyers and sellers of service was replaced by a more hierarchical one, based on state support of the professor, in which the consuming student was now subordinate (Cobban, 1971:35, in Clark, B, 1977:10).

Historically considered, university autonomy does not mean total independence from all power. On the contrary, it does imply a relationship of searching for legitimacy between actors with a determined "vocation including scholars, students, and representatives of the public power" (Le Goff, 1983).

Universities institutionally considered, emerged by the hand of the public powers as corporations, sought to achieve a monopoly of schooling, and particularly a monopoly in granting degrees, that put them against the authorities of the Church but not in conflict with the public power. As a consequence of the control they had on the school trade, the public power found advantages in generating a dependent relationship with universities, both in terms of their professional skills and in terms of the regulation of public social order in general. Though, these academic guilds, sought juridical autonomy whose recognition was obtained from the public power according to the tradition set by Federico Barbarroja for Bologna, the Authentica Habitat, was considered to be the legitimate source for all academic freedom.

Usually, members of the majority of corporations were independent from the public power due to the fact that they lived off the income of their trades. In the case of scholars guilds, even though they enjoyed sufficient legitimacy for students to pay for their salaries, such collectae was not enough.

It is today relevant to acknowledge that historical payment to the academics, emerged together from the ecclesiastical benefits, from the salaries and rents given by the cities, princes and sovereigns. In exchange, the public powers demanded the right of presentation together with patronage. This particularity, since the moment it was founded, prevented the university corporation from enjoying one of the essential privileges of the corporations: self-recruitment of their membership. However it is evident that they accepted the limitation of their independence in exchange for the material benefits of the financial underwriting of the "chair" by the public power.

The relationship between universities and public power was not defined only by antagonisms, struggles and crises. On the contrary, they have also been defined by reciprocal services, mutual respect and a system of privileges in exchange for the prestige gained by the university intellectuals financed by public powers.

One can conclude that universities were centers for professional training, as well as institutions which concentrated a particular socio-demographic group such as "intellectuals." They provided a degree of prestige to the public powers in exchange for receiving all sorts of privileges, which in turn, guaranteed their independence from other powerful individuals (Le Goff, 1983:193–205; Mollis, 1994:179–210).

Considering this tradition, what mutual services do Latin American higher education and the State provide each other today? What type of State do they need to produce "intelligence," and what type of university does the State need to be more capable, fair and equitable? (Hilderbrand, M. and Grindle, M., 1994).

Dependence of the State and Independence of the Central Government

> While governments may centralize control and rule from the center, they ought not to attempt to administer from the center. (Alexis de Tocqueville: 1954, in: Clark, B., 1977:36)

Alexis de Tocqueville, admirer of American federalism, established early in 1830, the before-mentioned strategic principle in what administration concerns. Administrating from the center means to concentrate authority in the central bureaus of national agencies, instead of expanding it among several local centers and offices. Following Robert Fried's interpretation of the Italian historical tradition in this matter (an appropriate approach to understand the Argentine situation) "to rule from the center is to centralize political control, moving authority from local and provincial government to the national level. To administer from the center is to concentrate authority in the central offices of the national agencies. . . . The tendency to do both has run deep in Italy" (Fried, R., 1963, in Clark, 1977:37).

The text of the first Argentine University Law (1597 Law) recognized as Avellaneda's Law, has been influenced by a model inspired by the French Napoleonic university, as in the Italian case. This organizational type results from the organization of a confederation of schools or colleges, headed by a Rector who has in practice merely honorific functions. The so called Avellaneda's Law shows that Tocquevillian spirit, which justifies the liberal tradition of our institutional autonomy. It reads as follows:

First Article: The Executive Power will decree that the superior councils of the Universities of Cordoba and Buenos Aires will dictate statutes in each of these universities, subject to the following rules:

1. The University will be composed by a Rector, elected by the University Assembly, which will have a duration of at least four years in his post, and could be re-elected;
2. By a Superior Council and by the departments that function now or are to be created by laws to be enacted later on. The University Assembly is formed by all the members of all the departments.
3. The Rector is the representative of the university. He presides over the sessions of the Assembly and the Council and executes its resolutions. It will correspond to the Rector to enjoy the position of honor in all those solemn acts that the schools celebrate (UBA, 1959, 75). The key item to understand the liberal spirit of the decentralized administration, is one that refers to the designation of professors, the initiative remained in the hands of the schools.
4. Each school will exert the police function and disciplinary jurisdiction within their respective institutions, project the study plans, grant the certificates to authorize academic examinations, and according to the results in the examinations, to exclusively award the diplomas of each scientific profession, approve or reform the study program presented by the professors, dispose of the university funds assigned for their expenses giving account of these to the Superior Council every year, and set the conditions of admission for students that enter their classrooms.
5. In the composition of each school government there will be at least a third of the professors that head their classes, corresponding to each department nominated by all the active members. All schools will have the same number of members which must not exceed 15.
6. The vacant chairs will be filled in the following way: the faculty will vote a slate of candidates which will be presented to the Superior Council, and if this Council approves it will be taken up to Executive Power who will design which professor will be in charge of the chair.
7. The university rights (that is, the resources appropriated for the functioning of each chair position) will constitute the "university fund," with exception of the part that the Superior Council assigns, with approval of the Ministry of education, for its expenses and for those of the schools and colleges. Every year, the Congress will be informed of the existence and investment of these funds (UBA, 1959:76).

Since then, Argentine public universities, and particularly those of large size, embody the idea of a university as a "confederation of schools or faculties." President Julio Argentino Roca, during his second presidency (1898–1904) and the Minister of Public Instruction Osvaldo Magnasco, were representatives of a liberal thought which conceived the Argentine state as the "political representative of society," and as such, the only one responsible for public instruction at the three educational levels: elementary, intermediate and higher education. The liberal conception of that Executive Power in 1899, described the University as the institution that was responsible for two essential functions: professional training on one hand, and scientific training, on the other. According to each one of these, the State had different responsibilities and attributes. As to the first, it had to supervise and control, and as to the second, it had to respect the unconditional liberty and the necessary autonomy to carry out scientific investigation. As it is expressed in the Message and law project on the general and university instruction plan:

> To the Honorable National Congress: (. . .) The State cannot consent in that respect: public education must respond not to private ambitions, but to the highest requirements of national interest, and in such a way, break away from the old empiricism and conform to the healthy rules of the natural science of education, particularly in the first school years. Now well, isn't it true that the university should lose the promiscuous character that it routinely holds among us? The natural rule prescribes another order, . . . higher education must also be successively characterized by a double and clear tendency. The first is the professional or immediately economic; the other, the merely scientific or speculative. The former ends up in the individual trade . . . , the latter is of pure investigation and its economic role would be of auxiliary contribution towards the encouragement and progress of the applied sciences or just the delight of the spirit. That's why the double role of the university work; the one that conducts towards professional exercise and the one that transports intelligence to the higher studies, to the greatest perfection of mental discipline, to the most subtle investigation of the methods, to the discovery of the great principles, thus, to the refinements of the application. (. . .) The State cannot, either theoretically, legally or economically, renounce to its immediate intervention in whatever concerns studies or careers of this type, if not the political precept that enables the Congress to prepare the university plans and confers the Executive certain absolute attributions in this respect and which they can't decline. If the State is the political representation of the society it cannot be indifferent to professional production. (. . .) It is logical to think that only the State must elaborate those plans, give them character and tendency, and organize the teaching of this class in accordance to the social goals. (. . .) The tasks of scientific investigation, in as much as they constitute not a factory of professionals but a high intellectual culture, are tasks which are alien to the functions of the government and, on such grounds, it could not, without injustice and danger sometimes, deny the erudite which sustain autonomy, the truth of their demands and the need for emancipation. The university must have, in this aspect, ample faculties and such complete independence as the nature and the objectives of this last higher discipline requires: organize and distribute the studies, select the methods, establish their regimen, designate the teaching staff, set conditions, grant certificates and patents, without more restrictions than the natural and constitutional restriction of any liberty, the discreet observance of the State just to defend and ensure social order and public interests that the workers and scientific doctrines may on occasions affect or compromise (. . .) Julio A. Roca, Osvaldo Magnasco (Diario de Sesiones, 1899:107–122).

This message has the virtue of showing the type of liberal Nineteenth Century speech, foundering of the Argentine public universities, whose notable difference in respect to the actual neoliberal doctrines, is the valuation of "scientific activity and high intellectual culture," and the recognition of its independence from all governmental control. The University as a "source of producing culture and scientific thinking" must respond to the liberty of the discipline itself. It was with this emancipating spirit that the disciplines that "encourage the progress of the sciences, of applied sciences or just the delight of the spirit" historically enjoyed a real autonomy only interrupted by the coups d'état and the authoritarian governments. Together with culture and science, the public universities also had as objective, to form "professionals" who will be looked after by the State.

Luis Scherz (1968) characterized the "professional university" by using three dominant adjectives: secular, pragmatic and state. Consequently, he undertook the task of forming citizens, professionals and administrators. This model would have surged together with the Napoleonic idea of the university. It adapted to relatively static social systems, it maintained a close relationship with the State, which acknowledges forums and rights and finances them. That way, the post-colonial universities went consolidating themselves, particularly the two most traditional Argentine universities: the National University of Cordoba and the National University of Buenos Aires. These turned into public national institutions towards the end of the nineteenth century, subject to the "teacher state," which, as such, was the administrator and inspector of all the educational system: exclusive sovereign of all educational matters (Scherz, 1968:107; Martinez Paz, 1980). These were elite universities which opened their doors to a minimum percentage of youngsters with the corresponding age.

On the other hand, Law and Medicine were the most popular and most prestigious careers because of the professional development they offered. Hence, the possibility of introducing careers linked to a scientific and/or technological production was restricted.

Another aspect that identifies them, refers to its "professorial" conformation and its organization in chairs of a more teaching rather than scientific orientation. This feature had its influence hindering the development of innovations coming from disciplinary fields, or in the development of the scientific knowledge of the specialty (Mollis, 1990). The lawyers who graduated from these institutions were professionally or ideologically related to the agrarian property, and as statement or public employees they created the instruments for political control within the State institutions such as the courts, prosecutor offices and police departments. Through the schools and the press, they managed other activities that allowed them to broaden the expression of the class hegemonies as writers, poets or educators.

> This group generated a bureaucratic elite and a political class with a formalist and flamboyant style that adequated itself perfectly to the interests of the dominating class (Canton, 1966:37–49; Allub, 1989:130).

One of the constitutive characteristics of this type of university is the academic and administrative autonomy to organize its institutional offers. What appears as the main task of the "university for lawyers" is its professional preparation. For this reason it attends to the demands of a political and cultural social class which shares or controls the political power, exerts a significant influence in the field of ideas and has a growing weight in the system of cultural institutions (Brunner, 1990:55).

When the Intervention of the Central Government Guaranteed Autonomy

Among the multiple paradoxes that condition the historical concept of autonomy is that at times the intervention of the Executive Power guaranteed and promoted university autonomy. That was the time of the University Reform, the time of the outbreak of a movement that recuperated the feudal corporative tradition of Bologna as well as giving birth to the new history of Latin American universities. The academic autonomy became a fundamental principle for the reformist institutions, since it was its purpose to break the vicious circle of the mediocre personnel (i.e., academic members for life) of the traditional government in charge of education, and it was projected in the university culture through the participation of the three collegiate bodies (professors, students and graduates) in the pedagogical, academic and scientific decision making. This meant that the selection and appointment of professors via public contest—curriculum and public class—the freedom of teaching and research of the professorship, the elaboration of syllabi, the conditions for admission and promotion, remained in the hands of the Executive Councils of each school and the Superior Councils of each university, represented by the three collegiate bodies. This movement organized the pedagogical and academic government around the university actors, just as the University of Bologna had done seven centuries before. The academic autonomy was achieved through the intervention of the Executive Power (Decreto del PE, 1919:81), the successive statutory reforms of the universities and the financial dependence of the State. The faculty searches through public contest, the alternative teaching (also called parallel courses), promoted by the renewed statutes could be implemented by a "partner"—like those public feudal powers in the past—who would finance those procedures. What better partner than the State, politically representing the middle classes, which, thanks to the "universal suffrage law," had conquered the central power?

The Autonomies, in Plural

It has been mentioned, so far, that the concept of "autonomy" presents multiple dimensions: on the one hand the academic dimension, on the other the financial dimension (legally known as autarchy). Even though both dimensions are interwoven in the concept of autonomy, they must not be confused. Another dimension connected to these two is the administrative. Since the '70s when enrollment skyrocketed, and important tension between two logics coexisting within public universities developed.

On the one hand, there is a bureaucratic—administrative logic—that is the pyramidal bureaucratic logic linked to the concept of the university as a state organism or public institution, whose administration reminds us more of a Ministry of Education than a center for intellectual activity. On the other hand, there is a corporative academic logic of the "academics" (professors, intellectuals, researchers) that intimately relates to the history of the medieval universities and even to the Humboldtian model of German university. To understand the concept of institutional autonomy it is easy to recognise that there are fields for confrontation within universities. For example, in relation to the diversity of functions and interests one can describe some antinomics pairs who embody antagonic logics: faculty members (the academic logic) versus administrative staff (the bureaucratic logic); full-time professors versus a majority of part-time professors (unionized or not); scholars versus academic officials (academic administration); student movement versus academic officials.

Each of these actors has a different institutional identity that submit him or her to the power of the State under different formulas: civil servant (part-time professors), ad honorem civil servants (university bureacracy), professionals corporation (professors, researchers), students corporation (student union groups). What intervention implies for some, may mean control for others, supervision to a few, subjugation of professorial liberty to the rest, etc. Finally, a set of truths conditioned to the practice of the different functions and the development of the institutional identities (also different) is produced around institutional autonomy, which adds more complexity to the description we have been developing.

The Policies of Higher Education of the 1990s: From State to Central Government

> The course of historic events has proved they emancicipated the classes whose special interests they represented, rather than human beings impartially. . . . Fortunately it is not necessary to attempt the citation of relevant facts. Practically everyone admits there is a new social problem . . . and that these problems have an economic basis (Dewey, J., 1960:271).

Argentina, like Mexico and Brazil, has been influenced and conditioned by an international agenda of the modernization of the higher education systems (Brunner: 1993b) that implies the reduction of state subsidies, the expansion of private institutions and enrollment, the promulgation of a Higher Education Law with consequences on systems of evaluation and accreditation and the traditional concept of institutional autonomy, a selective control for the distribution of financial resources, etc. From the point of view of the relation between State and university, modernization is organized mainly around the transformation of a political actor: from the liberal State of the final stages of the nineteenth century to the central government of the twentieth century. Any component of this formula is also present in other Latin American cases "modernized" before the process put in motion by the Menem administration (for instances Chile and Mexico). In Argentina, an important paradox has taken place instead. One of the disadvantages of centralization in respect to university government being in the hands of an omnipresent State, is the control that the latter has over the institutions hindering an independent and pluralist academic and scientific development (Levy, D., 1993b). However, and as a consequence of a reformist government, the academic control remained in hands of the collegiate bodies of each university, whereupon institutional autonomy is as powerful as the American models compared to the continental European model. This characteristic of the Argentine universities leads us to ask ourselves about the apparent contradiction between the proposals that claim for more control against more autonomy which "self-regulation" promotes.

The Argentine Higher Education Law: Control or Self-Regulation?

The Argentine Higher Education Law No 24.521, was promulgated the 7th of August, 1995, and includes all institutions of higher formation, be them universities or non-universities, national, provincial or municipal, state-owned or private, all form part of the National Educational System regulated by Law No. 24.195. It comprises IV titles, subdivided into Chapters and Sections with 89 articles in all. The topics which head each part express the matters it legislates on: About Higher Education: Aims and Objectives, Structure and Articulation, Rights and Duties; about Non-University Higher Education: jurisdictional responsibility of the institutions, degrees and syllabuses, institutional evaluation, about University Higher Education: university institutions and its functions, autonomy: its reach and guarantees, conditions for its functioning—general requisites—degrees, evaluation and accreditation, about National University Institutions: creation and organizational basis, governing bodies, support, economic and financial regimes, about private university institutions about Provincial Institutions (there are no subheadings) about the Government and coordination of the University system Complementary Dispositions.

The aforementioned Law introduces substantial changes in what has to do with the historical concepts of autonomy, financing and university governing. As an example, it authorizes university institutions to establish their own system of admissions, permanence and graduation of their students in an autonomous way in universities with more than 50.000 students the conditions for entry, permanence and promotion may be defined by each school or school; it authorizes each university to set its own scheme for scholars salaries and administration of personnel, assuring them the decentralized management of the funds they themselves generate; they can foster the constitution of societies, foundations, or any other form of civic associations destined to support the financial action and facilitate relations of the universities and/or schools with the environment; the collegiate bodies will have the task of defining policies and methods of control while the unipersonal bodies will have executive functions; it modifies the integration of the faculty of professors authorizing them (even auxiliary staff) to be elected to represent their faculty; it increases the number of bodies represented on the collegiate bodies integrating the non-teaching staff representatives and establishes as a requisite for the students representatives the attendance and approval of at least two chairs per year. Apart from introducing changes that affect traditional university methods, it also sets new evaluating processes through the establishing of organisms and actors dedicated exclusively to such thing.

The institutional evaluation is promoted at both levels, internal and external. Apart from introducing changes that affect traditional university methods, it also sets new evaluating processes through the establishing of organisms and actors dedicated exclusively to such thing. The institutional evaluation is promoted at both levels, internal and external. The internal evaluation—in the hands of the universities themselves—has the objective to analyze the achievements and difficulties in the observance of the university functions, as well as to suggest measures for its operation. The external evaluation takes place every six years, and it is made by the National Commission for University Evaluation and Accreditation. Together with this body there may also be private entities recognized for such task. In both cases, with the participation of peers of accepted competence. The National Commission for University Evaluation and Accreditation is an decentralized organ and it operates under the Ministry of Culture and Education. It is formed by 12 members designated by the National Executive Power (PEN) and proposed by the National Inter-university Council (CIN) (five members), the Private Universities Rectors' Council (CRUP) (three members), the National Academy of Education (1 member). They shall last in their posts for four years. Through accreditation any of these organisms award public recognition to the institutions, guaranteeing to society that they meet pre-established standards. The recommendations that arise from the evaluation will be made public. That "frame" spirit of the so called Avellaneda Law with its four articles (Mignone, F., 1979), is today replaced by a law with 89 articles (one referred to the universities with more than 50.000 students), that remits by comparison to a more disciplinarian spirit.

One can detect certain tensions between a type of neo-liberal view that aspires to steered by the freedom of the markets and the new type of selective financing of the central Government, and so then to institutional self-regulation, and other conservative expressions that seek control of the university institutions that rush into the described autonomies. Four public universities (University of Buenos Aires, University of Rosario, University of Mar del Plata and the University of La Plata) have interposed an appeal in court because they consider Law 24.521 to be anti-constitutional in what concerns autarchy and autonomy. The universities—as it has been endorsed by a federal judge—cannot be considered as a dependency, delegation or decentralization of the national Executive Power, as they have institutional hierarchy demarcated by the same Constitution (*La Nación*, 1995:13).

The International Scenario of the Autonomies

> Institutions of higher education have been in existence now for nearly twenty-five hundred years—for the first two thousand years in the wandering scholar model under the sponsorship of students and scholars and in some places also of the church—and now for nearly five hundred years increasingly under the sponsorship and then control of the nation-states (Kerr, Clark 1994:25).

Burton Clark (1977) recognizes that, even though autonomy can be manipulated from the financial point of view, from the point of view of those dimensions that are often cast aside by the central administrators (intangible aspects of power), it is really difficult to control. When significant changes and innovations for the institutions are intended, it is indispensable to identify the organizational tradition that underlies the institutional methods. It is not enough to know the "lean facts of institutional history," it is also necessary to recognize "the organizational legend" (Brunner, J. J., 1990:53).

The universities of continental Europe—German, Dutch or Italian—characterize themselves for a type of centralized organizational tradition, dependent of the State and the government that controls and supervises the universities. In the '70s, it was the State who planned the academic activity of the universities (the designation and appointing of professors), it took part in curricular matters, in the conditions for entry and graduation, etc. (Neave, G and Van Vught, F. 1994:388–389). This idea of a planning State in the '70s conditioned European university autonomy, opposing the concept of state planning to that of institutional autonomy. The said model tends to homogenize the products and propose homogeneous policies that apply to a reality that is supposedly undifferentiated.

Today, Holland, Belgium and Sweden show the need to change the tendency of a "controlling State" for an "Evaluating State," which implies that the State ceases to intervene in the academic affairs of the university to advance towards self-regulation. In this sense, the university gains more freedom and can organize its own administration better, which was, in fact, the preoccupation since the last years of the '80s. However, the experts show certain apprehension (Van Vught, F, 1989) in respect to the strategies used by the central governments: ". . . Behind a facade of amply proclaimed autonomy, the traditional strategy for planning and control is perhaps as active as never before . . . the renouncement of the governments to develop an interventionist policy is, in the best of cases, only partial since at the same time those governments are engaged in projecting procedures and instruments equally coercive for higher education" (Van Vught and Guy Neave, 1994:392). The preoccupation arises in the same way that Latin America by the hand of criteria that link autonomy with financing. These European universities have developed strategies to free themselves from the weight and control of the State, but at the same time the State has developed strategies that imply the reduction of funds for university financing. This way, the process of reinforcing the European academic liberty was accompanied by policies of budget reduction. The European specialists acknowledge the paradoxical situation that is generated by the need of greater autonomy together with State financing reduction.

Higher Education at the Turning Century: The Challenge of Integrating Autonomies

> The fate of an epoch that has eaten of the tree of knowledge is that it must . . . recognize that general views of life and the universe can never be products of increasing empirical knowledge, and that the highest ideals, which move us most forcefully, are always formed only in the struggle with other ideals which are just sacred to others as ours are to us (Max Weber, in: Harvey, D. 1995:1).
>
> [We alumni and alumnae of the colleges] . . . our motto too is noblesse oblige and unlike them [the aristocrats] we stand for ideal interests only, for we have no corporate selfishness and wield no powers of corruption . . ." Les Intellectuals"! What prouder club-name could there be that this one which refers to those who still retained some critical sense and judgment (William James [1907] 1995).

It has been shown how the concept of autonomy historically, became more complex to the point of making it dependent of the public powers, of associating it to the intervention of the Central Government and to the interests of a certain political class, to the game of a variety of institutional actors and, so, to the necessary reference in plural to the autonomies. The charm of autonomy is found prisoner of the "charmer" that promotes it.

New conditions of the Latin America of the 1990s, such as market-oriented restructuring, lead to a severe retrenchment of the public sphere's traditional "entrepreneurial" functions and to a smaller state apparatus, on the one hand. On the other hand, the capacity of civilian elites to impose restrictions on organized labor, strengthened the public and governmental authority significantly (O'Donnell, G., 1994; Torres, C. 1994; 1996). These new tendences applied to the institutions of higher learning, make the autonomies play on a stage, as complex as paradoxical: control and self-regulation, liberalization and supervision, globalization and regionalization, external conditionalities and institutional self-evaluation, systematic policies and institutional cultures.

The traditional social contract between public universities and the State, has been broken in the name of a "minimum State" with maximum market and, at the same time, in a context of structural adjustment and regulatory framework. The neoliberal reform may be characterized by both images of the State: stronger and weaker. The universities' autonomies are being constituted in a process of globalization (McGinn, N., 1995; Torres, C., 1995) that affects the institutional culture.

> Changes in the composition and strength of the State are already affecting especially public universities in Latin America. State support for higher education is declining in some countries and in all threatened. The new doctrine of the World Bank urges a shift of public funds away from traditional forms of universities toward new kinds of post-secondary institutions, away from public institutions toward private institutions. The national State has been affected by the ascendance of supranational organizations that reduce the ability of a state to be the major influence on everything that takes place within its borders. In effect, supranational organizations contribute to reduced national sovereignty (McGinn, N. 1994:7).

The reduction of sovereignty and the notion that to govern is to manage the economy effectively are two of the most powerful regulatory policies of the plural autonomies of today. Anyway, in order to change the undesirable effects of the status-quo oriented tradition of the universities, it is necessary to find responses to:

- who will be in charge of controlling quality in higher education: experts, technicians, academics or politicians?;
- what must the market finance and what must the State?;
- How do the external conditionalities of globalization relate with the intrinsic

"faculty" liberties of teaching and learning?

The tensions that crop up about the problem of autonomy can be summarized in two models: a) the model of governmental control or interventionist State; and b) the model of State supervision or evaluating State (Neave, G. 1994). The former conceives higher education as a homogeneous enterprise with the governmental intention of regulating and controlling all the elements of the system dynamics: admission, curriculum, requirements for awarding diplomas, personnel recruitment, quality of the offerings, etc., It does not recognize the organizational culture of higher education as "loosely coordinated" and "multidimensional." The latter recognizes the need for the State to establish basic parameters for functioning but leaves in the hands of the institutions the fundamental academic decisions, shown in model 1. Clark Kerr looking into the twenty-first century claims a new meaning for the concept of autonomy given by the convergence and the construction of institutional consensus (Kerr, C. 1994). The challenges of the twentieth century for the Argentine universities—and probably for Latin American universities in general—lies in the impossibility of combining both models without affecting the different autonomies. The new role of the State minimized in the neoliberal context, expresses its new contract deals of the good citizen for the economic subject, global and rational consumer, indoctrinated by the new market religion, leaving no room for the scientific labors and the high intellectual culture which Roca spoke of at the beginning of the century. Our proposal is to reconstruct the subtle enchantment of the autonomies, on the basis of the integration of the institutional powers, the public-social powers, the political powers and the economic powers in a framework of negotiation, consensus and construction of institutional capabilities for the better of the university culture.

References

Debate Parlamentario sobre la Ley Avellaneda. 1959. Universidad de Buenos Aires, Departamento Editorial, Imprenta de la U.B.A.

Roca, Julio Argentino y Magnasco, Osvaldo. 1899. iMensaje y proyecto de ley sobre el plan de instruccion general y universitariai, en: Diario de Sesiones, Sesiones Ordinarias, Cmara de Diputados de la Nacion Canton, Daro (1966) El Parlamento Argentino en Epocas de Cambio: 1816–1916–1946, Editorial Instituto, Buenos Aires. Decreto del Poder Ejecutivo interviniendo la universidad y designando Comisionado Nacional (1919), en: La Reforma Universitaria en la Universidad de Cordoba, en la Universidad de Buenos Aires, Buenos Aires, Penitenciara Nacional.

Allub, Leopoldo. 1989. iEstado y Sociedad Civil: Patron de Emergencia y Desarrollo del Estado Argentino (1810–1930i, en: Ansaldi, W y Moreno, J. L. (1989) Estado y Sociedad en el Pensamiento Nacional, Editorial Cantaro, Buenos Aires, Boletin Oficial de las Republica Argentina (1995) Ley de Educaci, Superior 24.521, Jueves 10 de Agosto, Buenos Aires.

Brunner, J. 1990. *Educación Superior en América Latina, Cambios y Desafios,* FCE, Santiago de Chile.

Clark, Burton. 1977. *Academic Power in Italy. Bureaucracy and Oligarchy in a National University System,* The University of Chicago Press, Chicago and London.

Cunha, Luiz A. 1988. *A Universidade Reformanda,* Francisco Alves, Rio de Janeiro.

Dewey, John. 1960. *On Experience, Nature and Freedom: Representative Selections,* Ed. R. Bernstein, Bobbs-Merrill, Indianapolis.

Harvey, David. 1990. *The Condition of Postmodernity,* Blackwell Publishers, Oxford.

Hilderbrand, M. and Grindle, M. 1994. *Building Sustainable Capacity. Challenges for the Public Sector,* Harvard Institute for the International Development, Harvard University, Massachusetts.

James, Williams. 1907. "The Social Value of the College Bred Man," 21; in: Lerner R. and Nagai, A. and Rothman, S. (editors) (1995) *Molding The Good Citizen,* Prager, USA.

Kerr, Clark. 1994. *Higher Education Cannot Escape History. Issues for the Twenty-first Century,* State University of New York Press, New York.

Le Goff, Jacques. 1983. Tiempo Trabajo y Cultura en el Occidente Medieval, Taurus, Barcelona.

Levy, Daniel. 1993. "El Gobierno de los Sistemas de Educación Superior," en: Pensamiento Univeristario, No. 1, Buenos Aires.

Levy, Daniel. 1993. "The New Pluralist Agenda for Latin American Higher Education," Documento presentado en el Seminario sobre Educación Superior en América Latina, Universidad de los Andes, IDEE/World Bank, Colombia.

Levy, Daniel. 1993b. "Formas de Gobierno en la Educación Superior," en: *Pensamiento Universitario,* No. 1, Buenos Aires.

McGinn, Noel. 1994. *Options for Higher Education as Latin America Joins the World Economy,* Harvard University, December (unpublished).

McGinn, Noel. 1995. "The Implications of Globalisation for Higher Education," in: *Learning from Experience: Policy and Practice in Aid to Higher Education,* CESO Paparback, The Hague, No 24, 77–93.

Mignone, Fermón. 1979. Universidad y Poder Político en Argentina: 1613–1978, FLACSO, Buenos Aires.

Mollis, Marcela. 1990. *Universidades y Estado Nacional,* Biblios, Buenos Aires.

Mollis, Marcela. 1994. Estilos Institucionales y Saberes en: *Revista de Educación,* No 303, Ministerio de Educacion y Ciencias, Madrid.

Neave, Guy and Van Vught, Frans. 1994. *Prometeo Encadenado,* Gedisa, Barcelona.

O'Donnell, G. 1994. "The State, Democratization and Some Conceptual Problems (A Latin American View with Glances at Some Post-Communist Countries)," in: *Latin American Political Economy in the Age of Neoliberal Reform,* Smith, Acuña and Gamara (editors) North South Center, University of Miami, 157–181.

Van Vught, Frans. 1989. *Governmental Strategies and Innovation in Higher Education,* Jessica Kingsley, London.

Scherz, Luis. 1968. *El Camino de la Revolución,* Universitaria, Editorial del Pacifico, Santiago de Chile.

Torres, Carlos A. 1994. Estado, Privatización y Politica Educativa. Elementos para un critica del Neoliberalismo, Ponencia presentada al Coloquio Internacional sobre Relaciones entre el Gobierno, Justica y Cultura, Embajada de Francia, Mexico, Oct 4–6 (unpublished).

Torres, Carlos A. 1995. "State and Education Revisited: Why Educational Researchers Should Think Politically about Education" in: *Review of Research in Education* 21, 255–331.

Latin America: Higher Education in a Lost Decade

SIMON SCHWARTZMAN

The Lost Decade

The 1980s will be remembered in Latin America as the lost decade. Almost without exception, all countries faced political deterioration, economic stagnation, worsening living conditions, and cultural perplexity. The feeling in the early 1990s is that all roads have been travelled, all possibilities tested, and nothing really worked. In the 1950s and 1960s it was still possible to put the blame on the local oligarchies and their international allies, and hope that a new era could be produced through increasing political mobilization and participation. In many countries, populism led to military regimes, which begot revolutionary guerrillas, which in turn begot military repression and widespread violence. As the military regimes exhausted their cycles, they were replaced by shaky and unconvincing democracies, unable to control their budgets, check corruption and face the mounting problems of economic obsolescence and urban decay.

Economic stagnation shook a central tenet of past decades, that progress would inevitably follow social and economic modernization. No region modernized so rapidly in the last twenty years as Latin America. Almost everywhere, traditional agriculture was replaced by mechanized agro-industries, and the rural population flocked to the cities. Mass communications reached every corner, spreading the language, consumption patterns and values of urban life. Improvement of basic health conditions led to a dramatic fall in infant mortality and a large increase in life expectancy, resulting in a population explosion that is only now slowing down through generalized access to birth-control devices. Education, even if still not universal, reaches more people, proportionally, than it ever did, from basic to graduate levels. Latin America is very unequal, and many countries and regions still face the traditional problems of rural poverty, illiteracy and lack of access to basic health and sanitary services. But the problems of the 1990s are very modern: urban overcrowding, environmental pollution, poor education, mass culture, youth unemployment, organized crime, urban violence, drug and alcohol abuse, alienation, swollen public bureaucracies and the growing inability of established governments to deal with these problems.

The key question is whether the lost decade was just a transitional period or will remain as a permanent fixture of Latin American societies. The current crisis affects some countries and regions more than others, and some authors are beginning to distinguish between 'viable' and 'non-viable' countries, believing that the latter are facing the same processes of economic, social and political degradation that affect so many sub-Saharan African countries. This may prove true in some extreme cases, but it is in an unacceptable simplification. To replace the old, naïve belief in

Simon Schwartzman (Brazil). Professor of political science, Faculdade de Filosofia, Letras e Ciências Humanas, University of São Paulo; Scientific Director, Nucleo de Pesquisas sobre Educação Superior (NUPES, University of São Paulo); President, from 1989 to 1991 of the Brazilian Sociological Association. Author or co-author of numerous articles and publications, among them: *Universidade Brasileira: organização e problemas; A pesquisa universitaria em questão* and *The Development of the Scientific Community in Brazil.*

economic development and progress with wholesale pessimism and gloom will not lead very far. A much closer look at past and present experiences is needed, to find out not only why so many hopes and projects have failed, but also why others seem to work better, and to point toward more positive roads.

Higher education is just one element of this broad picture, and its recent changes and current dilemmas cannot be understood without the full picture of the lost decade in our minds. There would be no point in looking at higher education in detail, however, if we took it as just another instance of a picture of global pessimism. Our assumption is the opposite. In spite of its obvious difficulties, higher education is one among other areas in which there are still opportunities to be explored, and hopes to be found for a broad, positive role in the region's predicaments.

The Origins

Latin American higher education, as it exists today, was organized during the period of independence, in the early nineteenth century, grew slowly for about 150 years, went through a period of explosive growth in the 1960s and 1970s, and levelled off again in the 1980s. Before independence, where they existed, higher education institutions were run by the Catholic Church of the Counter Reformation, as part of the Spanish colonizing enterprise. The struggle for political independence was coloured by the ideals of secularism, the appreciation for technical knowledge, and a general attack on the traditional university institutions.

Throughout, the rhetoric was about tradition and present times, scholastic and practical knowledge, general and professional education, the colonial tradition and the building of modern nation-states. Universities were a natural place for these confrontations to take place. Conservative and liberals, Catholics and positivists fought each other through the following century, creating new public institutions, closing down Catholic universities, opening them up again, supporting them with public money or cutting off their lifelines. In Mexico the Catholic universities disappeared, in Chile the two coexisted, in Brazil the Catholic institutions appeared only in the 1940s, in Argentina still later.

Political independence did not mean much in terms of social and economic transformations. Enlightened Latin American élites spoke French, travelled to Europe and handled French concepts, including their democratic and rationalist ideals; yet, their societies remained restricted to the limits of their economies, based on a few export products, large pockets of traditional or decadent settlements, one or two major administrative and export centres, and, in Brazil, a slavery system that lasted almost to the end of the nineteenth century. There were not many jobs requiring specialized knowledge and skills, except for handling the tangled legal systems inherited from Iberian baroque legislation, for military work and health care. Law, military engineering and medicine were main fields of study, none of them demanding enough to put special premium on innovation and achievement.

To the prevalence of rhetoric, feeble intellectual and technical competence and reduced social impact, should be added centralization and bureaucratic control. There was a matter of symmetry, new states organizing their educational institutions against the centralizing traditions of the past; then, most of the education business dealt with bestowing honours, titles and privileges, rather than with knowledge as such, formal goods that can only exist if regulated from above. More generally, the whole colonial enterprise, both in Portuguese and Spanish America, was carried on through centralized authority and control, and the local élites did not know otherwise.

Centralization did not go unchecked. The landmark of the reaction was the student rebellion at the University of Córdoba, Argentina, in 1918, which led to joint academic governance by faculty, students and alumni. The Córdoba movement—the Reforma—soon spread its word throughout the continent, leading to the adoption of similar governance rules in national universities in most countries. The Reforma movement was incendiary in its rhetoric against the university establishment but conservative in its accomplishments. Where it succeeded universities became less subject to daily interferences from central government, but did not incorporate new social groups nor improve the quality of teaching.

Self-governance meant that decisions had to be taken by vote, and no place could exist for institutional leadership. It is not a coincidence that the Reforma started in Córdoba, an Argentine province that was declining in face of the intense economic and political growth of Buenos Aires. Even where economic development did not occur, cities were growing, populations increased, and traditional power arrangements were difficult to maintain. The Latin American reformed universities became the place where the children of the traditional élites expressed their frustrations against the decadence of their elders, and their hopes for the future.

In the early 1960s, the contrasts between the modernization drives of Latin American societies and the narrowness of their political regimes led to intensified political activism, followed by unprecedented levels of repression. Political repression came from the confrontation of student, and sometimes teacher, activism against the military regimes that emerged more or less at that time in many countries: Argentina after 1966; Brazil at first in 1964, but intensifying in 1969; Chile in 1973; not forgetting the massacre of students in Mexico City of 1968. For the military, at the beginning, the problems of higher education were a matter of police and discipline. With different emphasis in one place or another, elected rectors were replaced by colonels, teachers were dismissed, students arrested, the social sciences were banned, mandatory civic education was introduced. Large sectors of the universities were destroyed and demoralized, while hundreds of students took up guerrilla warfare. The cycles of expansion, repression and insurrection came together to their end in the late 1970s and early 1980s. It was then time to pick up the pieces, see what remained of higher education from the past years and decide what could be done about it. By then political mobilization of students had lost its virulence, to be replaced by the unionization of teachers and employees. In most public institutions the traditional part-time professor had been replaced by a new professional, the full-time teacher (who had been very often the militant student of ten years before) and sometimes by the academically oriented researcher, educated abroad and expecting his institution to become like the research university where he received his degree. Most military regimes had by then disappeared, but a new scourge was already looming—economic stagnation.

The Uncertain Future

Published in 1983, Juan Carlos Tedesco's study of the tendencies and perspectives of development of higher education in Latin America and the Caribbean is an unsurpassed gathering and organization of the available information, and a reasoned and scholarly reflection on why higher education reached the problems and difficulties it faced. Following Tedesco's study, it is possible to travel in time from the traditional élitist Latin American universities to the current mass education systems, and see how the traditional interpretation of Latin American universities as training grounds for political élites gave way, after the 1950s to the human-capital approach, which was replaced, in turn, by a much more sceptical view of its role in socio-economic development and modernization. We can trace the evolution from the times when reformed and expanded universities were expected to become landmarks of democratization, to a time when education came to be perceived as little else than the reproduction and consolidation of old patterns of social stratification and social inequality; the transition from a period of optimism about the academic communities' ability to find their own ways on the road of competence and social relevance, if given enough freedom and resources, to a reluctant return to the need of governmental planning and oversight.

Expansion

Tedesco (1983) starts by showing the extraordinary expansion of higher education in Latin America since the 1960s, coinciding with the growth of urban centres and the replacement of the old oligarchic political regimes with different systems of mass politics, in alternation with periods of authoritarian rule. Writing on the same subject a few years later, Winkler (1990, p. xii) noted that

> higher education enrolments in Latin America increased tenfold between 1960 and 1985, resulting in levels of access approaching those found in many industri-

Table 1
Enrolment in higher education in Latin America, 1985

Country	*Enrolment*	*Women (%)*	*Rate*[1]
Argentina	846,141	53	36.4
Bolivia	95,052	—	19.0
Brazil	1,479,397	48	11.3
Colombia	391,490	49	13.0
Costa Rica	63,771	58	23.0
Cuba	235,224	54	21.4
Chile	197,437	43	15.9
Dominican Republic	123,748	—	19.3
Ecuador	277,799	39	33.1
El Salvador	70,499	44	13.8
Guatemala	48,283	—	8.4
Haiti	6,289	—	1.1
Honduras	30,632	42	9.6
Mexico	1,207,779	36	15.7
Nicaragua	29,001	56	9.8
Panama	55,303	56	25.9
Paraguay	33,203	—	9.7
Peru	443,640	35	23.8
Uruguay	87,707	—	35.8
Venezuela	347,618	—	26.4

1. Higher education enrolment as percentage of the population in the 20–24 age bracket, for 1985 or the closest available year.

Source: Brunner, 1990; based on UNESCO, 1988.

alized countries. Private institutions absorbed more than their share of this growth and now represent one-third of total enrolments in the region.

The expansion is to be explained by broad social and political trends, and was stimulated by the huge wage differentials that still exist in Latin America across educational levels. In 1950, only Uruguay, Argentina and Cuba had around 5 per cent of the age group enrolled in universities; in 1980 only Honduras, Guatemala and Haiti had less than 10 per cent. Table 1 gives the picture for the whole region in the middle of the 1980s.

In no country was this growth the product of government planning or decision. In all regions, expansion was related to the massive incorporation of women in higher education, and led to the prevalence of 'soft' fields of knowledge, like the social sciences and humanities, over the traditional careers of law, medicine and engineering. It came also from older people hoping to improve their educational credentials and gain access to, or promotion in, public jobs in the region's expanding public bureaucracies. For the first time, most of the students came from families with no previous experience of higher education.

In their drive for higher education, students got into the careers they could, rather than to those they preferred. The predominance of the social sciences and humanities stems from their lower costs and less demanding academic requirements, not by a sudden preference of young Latin Americans for such topics. But it was compatible with large increases in tertiary occupations that were occurring at the time, typical of Latin American modernization. While the countries' economies supported it, expansion of higher education was largely financed from taxation, and university-level employment was provided by an expanding public sector and by the creation of professional privileges for the holders of educational credentials.

Economic stagnation in the 1980s caught educational expansion at full speed, constraining the job market, limiting the universities' budget and causing widespread perplexity and frustration (see Table 2). The problem was aggravated by the time it took for the education sector to react to economic expectations. Data from Brazil show that the creation of new courses peaked in the early and mid 1970s, reflecting the economic expansion of those years, and was still going strong in the 1980s, when the signs of crisis were already visible (Fig. 1).

Table 2
World expenditure on education, 1975–85

Year	*Total ($ millions)*	*% of GNP*	*Per capita ($)*
World total			
1975	330,117	5.5	84
1980	618,195	5.5	144
1985	681,195	5.6	144
Developing countries			
1975	40,433	3.6	14
1980	93,384	3.9	29
1985	95,846	4.1	27
Latin America and the Caribbean			
1975	13,477	3.5	43
1980	31,397	3.9	88
1985	25,392	3.8	63

Source: Brunner, 1990, based on UNESCO, 1988.

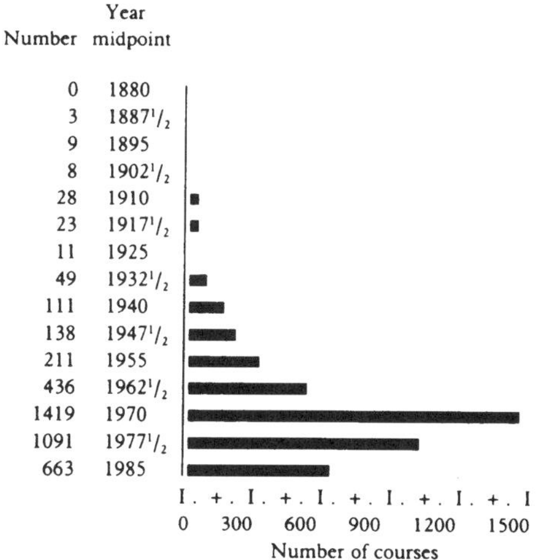

Valid cases: 4.2000
Without information: 100

Fig. 1: **Number of higher-education courses created by year in Brazil (by 7.5-year intervals). After: ME/SEEC, 1988.**

Differentiation

One effect of expansion was the development of a large private sector, which in some countries, such as Brazil and Colombia, accounts now for more than half of current enrolments, and reaches about a third of the enrolments in the region. The growth of private higher education is the subject of a book by Daniel Levy, for whom private institutions have 'remolded the relationship between higher education and society's multiple classes, groups, interests, and they have remolded the relationship between higher education and the State' (Levy, 1986, p. 334). This is the more visible, but by no means the only differentiation that took place in recent years: universities have become internally stratified, non-university sectors have grown in many countries, and significant regional decentralization occurred everywhere.

The issue of public versus private education has its roots in colonial times, when the only universities in the continent were those organized by the Catholic Church, in close alliance with the Spanish Crown. Political independence, in the early nineteenth century, led to the establishment of secular higher-education institutions, usually based on the Napoleonic model of state-controlled professional 'faculties' or schools. Levy gives the details of this transformation. By the end of the colonial period, Spanish America had about twenty-five universities (the Portuguese, however, always refused to establish higher-education institutions in Brazil). A century later, only Colombia and Chile had private Catholic universities (Levy, 1986, pp. 28–32). In the 1930s the Church moved to recover its role in higher education, trying in some cases to re-establish its association with the state, as in Colombia and Brazil (see Levine, 1981; Schwartzman et al., 1984) or, more frequently, creating their independent institutions. Catholic universities were to provide the students with the traditional religious, moral and humanistic education they thought the public universities neglected, and in their defence of educational freedom they joined hands, unwillingly, with the liberal students who, starting with the Córdoba movement, unfolded the banner of university autonomy from the state.

The second wave of privatization, following Levy's chronology, was a backlash from sectors of Latin American élites against the deterioration of public education. As the public universities absorbed the growing demand for higher education in the 1960s and 1970s, they changed from an élite to a predominantly middle-class constituency, their academic standards deteriorated and they became the focus of permanent political agitation. In many countries the élites decided to move away to their exclusive institutions, a role taken up by Catholic institutions, newly created private universities or special élite institutions established with government support.

The third wave happened mostly in response to situations where the public sector did not open widely enough to absorb the demand for large quantity, low-quality mass education. Brazil, Costa Rica, Colombia, the Dominican Republic and Peru are the major examples. The new institutions kept their costs down by paying their teachers by the hour, teaching in the 'soft' fields where no special equipment and technical support was needed, opening evening classes for working students, and packing them into large classrooms.

With expansion and privatization, higher education remained homogeneous horizontally but became increasingly stratified vertically. Expansion could be expected to lead to different institutions doing different things, responding to the varying needs of different people. However, this tendency tended to be checked by strong pressures for equal rights and status to all educated persons, which resulted at the end in increased, if barely disguised, forms of discrimination. Horizontal homogeneity came from a blurring of the frontiers between religious and lay, public and private, technical and professional institutions, careers and courses. Today in Latin America few students go to Catholic universities through religious conviction, and few Catholic institutions manage, or even try, to infuse their students with the religious and moral teachings that led to their organization as independent entities. Direct and indirect public subsidies to private institutions, on one hand, and the administrative autonomy, the ability to raise money and even to charge tuition in public universities, on the other, make the distinction between public and private less straightforward than in the past. A final convergence is among what could be considered 'university proper' institutions and those like teachers' colleges, technical institutes and vocational schools. In the past, as in Europe, higher education was the privilege of the few, with a narrow access path provided by education in the liberal arts or in basic sciences, to be obtained at secondary school. Now, in most countries, any secondary-school diploma can lead to university, and no course programme taught at the tertiary level, from medicine to nutrition, from economics to hotel management, from physics to production engineering, can be denied 'university' status.

Horizontal homogeneity has not led to more equality, but to increased stratification: there is little incentive for less prestigious careers like teaching and technical work, and extremely high rates of failure and frustration in the competition for the most prestigious degrees, now supposedly accessible to all. Where, in the past, a secondary-school diploma was an achievement, today anything less than a four-year university degree is a failure. Careers and institutions are strongly stratified and socially selective, whether it be in Brazil, where difficult entrance exams screen out the less qualified students from the more prestigious careers, or in Argentina, where there is a policy of open admission, but the less qualified students are screened out after one or two years of schooling.

Efficiency, Equity and Costs

Latin American higher education is in obvious need of improvement, and evaluations and proposals abound. The issues of efficiency, equity and costs are the central concerns of the discussion paper prepared by Donald R. Winkler (1990) for the World Bank, another trove of useful data.

Efficiency in Latin American universities, that is, the ratio between input and output within an educational institution, is low by almost any indicators one wishes to take: students per faculty, administrators and staff; percentage of funds allocated to non-personal categories of expenditure; faculty salaries; teaching loads; scientific output. The reasons pointed out by Winkler for this situation include: (a) the prevalence of political over performance criteria in academic governance; (b) the emphasis on university autonomy, which rejects policy directives from government; (c) the lack of a tradition of careers in university administration; and (d) a lack of norms on efficiency measures.

A deeper problem is that nobody knows what social benefits higher education can really bring, beyond the private gains of graduates. Winkler approaches this problem with the concept of 'external efficiency'. If it were possible to know how many medical doctors, engineers, sociologists and managers a society needs, it would be possible to compare the figures with what the education institutions produce, evaluate their efficiency in meeting the needs, and steer them in the proper direction. Manpower forecasts, however, are now in disrepute, and economists prefer to resort to estimations of 'rates of return', which is a comparison of earnings of degree holders with the costs of their education. If society is willing to pay a given amount for a professional's work, this could be taken as an estimate of how useful this work is. Educational efficiency could then be measured and improved by comparing the rates of return of higher with those of lower education, or the returns of one profession with those of another. Exercises of this kind show that returns of higher education in Latin America are higher than in other countries, but still lower than those of other levels, and seem to have been coming down in recent years, and that some professions pay substantially higher salaries and have more employment opportunities than others.

Is it possible to use this information to derive policy recommendations such as to redirect public investment from higher to lower educational levels, and from ill-paying to better paying fields and specialities? Besides its technical difficulties (Leslie, 1990), the problems with policies based on social rates of return are not very different from those coming from the now out-of-fashion manpower planning approach. Except under near pure market conditions, which are very far from what exists in Latin America, earnings obtained by different professional groups depend on a combination of professional privileges, market monopolies, legal benefits, corporatist arrangements and social biases that have little connection with the skills supplied by the specialist.

The thrust of the World Bank recommendations is to shift investments from higher to basic education, to charge tuition and to reduce the public sector's investments in higher education. Winkler's suggestions for improvement are more topical. They include: (a) the introduction of modern information management systems, to allow for the assessment of costs and productivity; (b) the introduction of performance criteria in allocation of resources among units within the universities; (c) the establishment of evaluation mechanisms; and (d) the training of university administrators in the use of these tools. Winkler does not discuss the reasons why these management tools have not been adopted more extensively. It is not a question of ignorance; most universities have courses in administration and economics where these issues are taught. The answer lies in the contrast between Winkler's diagnosis, which is political and institutional, and the recommendations, which are technical and managerial. Is it possible to improve administrative efficiency without tackling the political and institutional issues?

Public universities are autonomous regarding governments; departments and schools are autonomous within the universities, and their priorities are seldom those of improving efficiency and performance. There are no incentives to improve internal efficiency in public or government financed institutions, and universities are no exception. Budgetary allocations are usually based on past expenditure, if not on political patronage, and money saved this year can mean a lower budget next time. Beyond some very gross indicators like students per faculty or articles published, there are no consensual indicators of what good performance really is. Does it mean teaching more students with a little less quality, fewer students with more quality, reducing the teaching load to allow time for research, or investing in useful technical assistance at the expense of academic publications? There are advocates and vested interests for each of these and many other alternatives. The establishment of evaluation procedures and the introduction of performance criteria in the internal allocation of resources would require to take sides on these issues, and could lead to painful conflicts between departments, teachers, researchers and students. Instead of in-fighting, why not try to come together and pressurize the government for more money? While it was possible to keep expanding the public budget, this strategy worked well. Now that the money is drying up, for many institutions it is still better to cut expenditure across the board than to make painful decisions on priorities and preferences.

Would a professional body of university administrators change the situation? Latin American public universities are typically governed by professors elected or appointed to administrative offices, and controlled by all kinds of collective bodies formed by delegates from professors of all ranks, students and employees. They hold very different and often contradictory notions of the role of universities, what goals are worth pursuing and how priorities should be established. They go from small groups of research-minded scholars, who can only think of universities as places for scholarship, to many ill-trained and unionized full-time teachers, who see themselves as just another branch of the civil service; from students eager to get their degrees in prestigious fields and move on to high-paying careers, to those in the 'soft' and less prestigious fields, lacking the qualifications and professional perspectives of the former, and expressing their frustrations through collective agitation or anomic behaviour. They lack a common academic culture and ethos, which would accept what the goals of higher-education institutions should be. Good managers could hardly tip the power from these networks of widely contradictory interest groups towards the administration, and could not provide their institutions with the cultural traditions they lack.

The professional privileges and salary differentials granted to degree holders, discussed neither by Winkler nor Tedesco, are in themselves an important dimension of inequity in Latin American higher education. Winkler shows that access to higher education is socially biased—children from lower-income families are less likely to be admitted—and government subsidies benefit high income more than lower-income groups. This situation is particularly serious in Brazil, where private secondary schools function as filters selecting middle- and high-income students who later gain admission to wholly subsidized public universities. The inherent inequity of higher-education access was not perceived as a problem when social mobility was high and educational opportunities were increasing for everybody, but it has become evident now that the economy is stagnating, and that those who go up do so at the expense of others going down.

Now, as Tedesco says, it is impossible to continue to pretend that higher education is an unqualified boon to everybody. The income differentials obtained by university degree holders came to be perceived as the product of social transfers, rather than the consequence of increased productivity. Public expenditure in higher education, which used to be considered good and self-evident investments in human capital, started to be seen as subsidies to private consumption and personal privilege. The issues of financing of higher education ought to be seen as political questions, linked to the social dispute over the appropriation of economic surplus, rather than as purely technical matters. Political considerations should not preclude efforts to devise financing mechanisms able to achieve the requisites of social equity, efficiency and reduction of public expenditure, and the educational usefulness of the money spent, but those considerations cannot be set aside (Tedesco, 1983, p. 19).

Modernization and Reform

Contemporary attempts and proposals to improve the condition of Latin American universities have usually come from outside, whether piecemeal or comprehensive, through incentives or forceful imposition, and have seldom produced the expected results.

Incentives were typical of gentler times, when it was believed that better trained scholars, technical assistance and exchange programmes could do wonders. For many years, in the 1960s, the Universidad de Chile developed a comprehensive co-operative programme with the University of California, with support from the Ford Foundation. Large projects like this were rare, but thousands of students from Venezuela, Brazil and other countries went to get their advanced degrees in the United States and Europe, with money provided by national and foreign agencies. Most of these co-operation projects hoped to train students in the modern sciences and bring scientific research to Latin American universities. In Brazil, in the 1970s, millions of dollars were poured into the organization of a new tier of graduation education in public universities. In the 1960s and 1970s, research councils were created in most countries, and their money went usually to researchers in universities, allowing them to rise above the limitations of their institutions.

Thanks in part to these efforts, it was possible to form a sophisticated and modern scientific élite in many countries, and to develop a series of research institutions that strive to keep Latin America abreast with what is happening in the world of modern science with what is happening in the world of modern science and technology (Schwartzman, 1991). This was not enough, however, to affect higher education more profoundly, because Latin American universities were going through two contradictory modernization tendencies. One was in the direction of making them more scientific, more competent and internationally more up-to-date, and, in this sense, more élitist; the other was pulled by the expansion of enrolments, which would require a set of education and pedagogic skills and priorities which were not in the minds of this élite. The better educated found it increasingly difficult to deal with their universities, and took refuge in their laboratories, research institutes, international networks, and even whole new institutions, leaving the broader problems of their universities untouched. To this relative failure should be added another, which was the inability of most scientific and technological research to contribute more effectively to the countries' social and economic needs. In consequence, there is today a feeling in some circles that Latin American countries should not really try to develop scientific competence, but put their resources to the service of more humble and pressing problems (Vessuri, 1990).

Comprehensive reforms have been unusual and often traumatic. The Brazilian reform of 1968 was carried out under a military government, which made it difficult to distinguish its political from its truly academic intentions. Its inspiration was the American research university. The old chair system was replaced by the department structure, together with American entities such as the credit system, the central institutes and the graduate programmes. In practice, the new system was superimposed on the traditional one, and there was no provision to account for the expansion of demand which was already on its way. In 1985, with the military out of power, a national commission was created to reorganize the whole system. It was to be a democratic commission, representative of all political parties and interest groups. Incredibly, it managed to produced a coherent blueprint for reform, based on the recognition of institutional differentiation, the introduction of evaluation procedures and autonomy and increased accountability for results. None of it, however, was implemented (Schwartzman, 1988).

The Chilean reform of the 1980s was very different from anything ever tried in the region. Between 1973 to 1980 the Chilean universities were kept under military control, which led to the dismissal of about a quarter of its faculty and the closing of many departments in the social sciences and the humanities (Cox, 1989). In 1981 the military government started to implement a policy which was the opposite of that of Brazil in the 1960s. Instead of a single university model, differentiation; instead of trying to improve quality through graduate education and research, the introduction of market mechanisms; instead of the reliance on the traditional, public universities to set the pattern, the creation of new private, universities. Tuition was introduced in all institutions, government subsidies were given to a limited number of institutions, private or public, and competitive mechanisms were introduced to stimulate quality and efficiency.

The reform did not produce the expected results, but it would be naïve to dismiss it as just another nasty attack by the military against the academy. In 1991 the new civilian government in Chile established a national commission to set a policy for its higher-education sector, and, in its proposal, several innovations from the 1981 reforms were retained, among them the demarcation lines between universities, professional institutes and technical schools, mechanisms for competition and accountability, including indirect subsidies, and the principle that students who can should pay for their studies. The new project introduces a National University Council responsible for supervising the whole system and to establish mechanisms for evaluation, accreditation and budget allocation, and there is a clear commitment to improving quality, assuring equity and stimulating the development of research and graduate education.

It is still too early to know what will happen with this project, which, as of this writing, is being submitted for approval to the Chilean Congress. If it succeeds, it can become an inspiration for other countries, showing that there is still hope for higher education in Latin America, and that the lost decade was not completely wasted, if it left the region with some lessons for the future.

The first lesson should be that no single model of higher-education institutions can account for the complexity of current needs and demands. The traditional Napoleonic model geared to certification for the liberal professions left little room for research, technical education, distance learning, continuous education, short-term vocational courses and liberal arts programmes. The indiscriminate adoption of the university research model may have helped to solve the first of these problems in some places, but made the others still more intractable. Whenever a single model is adopted, very often in the name of egalitarianism, a few institutions set the pace while the rest become just a series of fading shadows of a vanishing ideal. Differentiation is unavoidable, and it cannot be understood as just a series of strata in a ladder of social prestige.

The second lesson is that governments will be increasingly less able to maintain, supervise and care for the quality of higher education. There are many reasons for this, from budgetary restrictions to the impossibility of central bureaucracies to lead institutions driven by the spirit of initiative, involvement and enthusiasm of their members to set its goals and work for their fulfilment. Academic autonomy and decentralization are unavoidable, and they are likely to blur still further the dividing lines between private and public institutions, leading to a continuum going from proprietary, profit-making operations to publicly funded, national universities, with all gradations in between. A corollary for content and institutional differentiation is the gradual development of a competitive market for higher education, both through actual competition for students and resources and the establishment of reliable and public mechanisms of evaluation and institutional accreditation.

The third lesson is that it would be naïve to expect Latin American higher-education institutions to make these changes on their own, but it would be still worse to pretend that these changes could be introduced through government imposition or management patches. With all its problems and limitations, higher-education institutions are still a repository of competent and motivated people, and no reform that begins by demoralizing them would have any chance of succeeding. The quandary is only apparent, since there are enough people in Latin American higher-education institutions aware of the current difficulties and needs, and willing to participate and co-operate in any well-conceived and academically legitimate reform project.

The fourth lesson is that the scientific, technological and educational competence that exists in the region's higher-education institutions is a precious asset, which should not be depleted in the name of narrow, pragmatic or egalitarian concerns. Good universities and competent scholars, scientists and technologists are essential for whatever Latin American countries hope to do in the future, in basic education, higher education and in other fields. There is not assurance, of course, that they will do what should be done, or succeed in their undertakings, and it is certain that they can do little alone by themselves. But the fifth, and probably more important lesson of the lost decade should be to reject the anti-intellectual, 'no-nonsense' attitude that have accompanied so many of the frustrated reforms and reform proposals of those years.

References

Brunner, J. J. 1990. *Educación superior on América Latina: cambios y desafios.* Santiago de Chile, Fondo de Cultura Económica.

Clark, B. C. 1986. *The Higher Education System—Academic Organization in Cross-National Perspective.* Berkeley/Los Angeles/London, University of California Press.

Cox, C. C. 1989. Autoritarismo, mercados y conocimiento: evolución de las políticas de educación superior en Chile en los años '80'. *Educaçao e Sociedade,* Vol. 32, April, pp. 27–50.

Levine, D. 1981. *Religion and Politics in Latin America: The Catholic Church in Venezuela and Colombia.* Princeton, N. J., Princeton University Press.

Leslie, L. L. 1990. Rates of Return as Informer of Public Policy: with Special Reference to the World Bank and Third World Countries. *Higher Education,* Vol. 20, No. 3, pp. 287–300.

Levy, D. C. 1986. *Higher Education and the State in Latin America—Private Challenges to Public Dominance.* London/Chicago, University of Chicago Press, 1986.

Tedesco, J. C. 1983. *Tendencias y perspectivas en el desarrolo de la educación superior en América Latina.* Paris, UNESCO. 43 pp.

Schwartzman, S. 1988. Brazil: Opportunity and Crisis in Higher Education. *Higher Education,* Vol. 17, No. 1, pp. 99–119.

_____. 1991. *A Space for Science—The Development of the Scientific Community in Brazil.* University Park, Pa., The Penn State Press.

Schwartzman, S.; Bomeny, H.; Costa, V. 1984. *Tempos de Capanema.* Rio de Janeiro/São Paulo, Paz e Terra/Editora da Universidade de São Paulo.

UNESCO. 1988. *Statistical Yearbook.* Paris, UNESCO.

Vessuri, H. M. C. 1990. O Inventamos o Erramos: The Power of Science in Latin America. *World Development,* Vol. 18, No. 11, pp. 1543–53.

Winkler, D. R. 1990. Higher Education in Latin America—Issues of Efficiency and Equity. Washington, D. C., World Bank. 147 pp. (Discussion Paper, 77.)

Cultural Politics in a Latin American University: A Case Study of the University of Panama

William G. Tierney*

Summary

This text employs a cultural framework and qualitative methodology to investigate and analyze the problems and challenges that confront one Latin American university. The intent of the article is twofold. The author first explicates how one might use a cultural framework and methodology of organizations to interpret postsecondary institutions in Latin America. The second goal is to suggest the implications of such a framework with regard to decision-making and strategy.

Accordingly, the paper has three parts. In part one the author explicates the terms of organizational culture and applies them to Latin American postsecondary institutions. A cultural framework relates to how an organization's participants interpret five cultural components: (a) mission and ideology; (b) knowledge and power; (c) communication and language; (d) leadership and strategy; and (e) environment and constituencies. The author then discusses the strengths and weaknesses of a qualitative methodology and underscores the researcher's role in the development of the data. Part two is a case study of one institution to highlight how one might analyze the activities of such an organization by using a cultural framework. The data for the text derives from interviews at the University of Panama during 1992. The article concludes in part three with a discussion of the implications of the framework. In particular, the text considers three challenges that confront postsecondary institutions—existential, intellectual and political—and relates these challenges to the cultural framework outlined in the article.

Virtually all texts that pertain to Latin American higher education work from quite similar initial premises. The lack of funding, the relatively low number of full-time faculty, the massification of the student body, the dilemmas of research, and a host of other "social facts" form a base with which authors begin their analyses. As with social science research in general, these analyses derive from a mixture of methodologies—historical, quantitative, and economic, to name a few—and diverse theoretical frameworks.

In a helpful article, Paulston (1992) has argued that researchers have used four overarching theoretical frameworks to discuss Latin American education. He labels these frameworks, "structural-functionalist," "radical functionalist," "interpretive," and "radical interpretive." With regard to interpretive views Paulston comments, "Interpretive representations of Latin American education, although they lack a strong research tradition, definitely constitute an idea whose time has come" (193). If we were to use an interpretive framework and methodology to analyze Latin American higher education, what kinds of questions would be asked, how would they be asked, and perhaps most importantly, how would they be analyzed?

In this text I use an interpretive, or what I shall call a cultural, framework to answer those questions and to analyze the problems and challenges that currently confront one Latin American university. My purpose is twofold. I first explicate how we might use a cultural

*William G. Tierney is Professor and Senior Scientist of the Center for the Study of Higher Education at Pennsylvania State University.

framework and methodology of organizations to interpret postsecondary institutions in Latin America. I then suggest the implications for such a framework with regard to decision making and strategy.

Accordingly, in the first part of the paper I define the terms pertaining to organizational culture and apply them to Latin American postsecondary organizations. I then offer a case study of one institution to highlight how we might analyze the activities of such an organization by using an interpretive framework. The implications follow, and I conclude with suggestions for further research.

Studying Organizational Culture

The study of organizational culture has taken hold in the United States and Europe over the last two decades. Studies of the culture of businesses, governmental agencies, and, in particular, educational organizations have abounded (Deal and Kennedy 1982; Schein 1985; Chaffee and Tierney 1988). Three principles have undergirded these investigations. The work (a) has been interpretive, (b) has employed a social constructionist framework, and (c) has used qualitative methods. Interpretive social science works from the assumption that the researcher uses himself/herself to make sense of the object under study. Hence, the social world is seen as constructed both by the organization's participants and, in a sense, reconstructed by the researcher. The most appropriate manner to study culture is thus through interviews, observations, and the full host of qualitative techniques that enable the researcher to come to terms with the "reality" of the organizational participants. As with any qualitative work, the point is not to generalize across all sites and situations but rather to gain an understanding of the complexity of a particular situation. At the same time, those of us involved in the study of organizational culture have struggled to develop a general schema which we might use to interpret colleges and universities (Tierney 1988). That is, the attempt is to develop an organizing framework with which to analyze a university whether the institution is in France, Chile, or Peru. The manner in which the participants interpret and enact the framework will differ from institution to institution depending on the unique culture in which it exists.

Obviously, each principle has exacted a degree of reformulation and disagreement. Some individuals, for example, stress the interpretive role of the researcher more than others; some researchers subscribe to postmodernist notions of a fractured and cacophonous organizational world; others believe that a unitary interpretation of organizational life is possible. I have simplified the principles for clarity while recognizing that each point merits more discussion than is possible here.

Similarly, although debate and disagreement still exist with regard to an exact definition of organizational culture, I focus on five key themes that are helpful in the interpretation of the culture of a postsecondary organization. Again, because of the paucity of research pertaining to Latin America in this area, these themes have derived from analyses of colleges and universities in the United States and Europe. Accordingly, another objective of this paper is to see whether they fit Latin American institutions. I suggest that each cultural theme occurs in postsecondary settings. Yet the way a theme gets defined, and its importance, differs from setting to setting.

Mission and Ideology

Over half a century ago José Ortega y Gassett commented:

> An institution is a machine in that its whole structure and functioning must be devised in view of the service it is expected to perform. The root of university reform is a complete formulation of its purpose. Any alteration or adjustment of this house of ours unless it starts by reviewing the problem of its mission—clearly, decisively, truthfully—will be love labour's lost. (1944, 28)

Ortega y Gassett's comment is helpful for it highlights the importance of organizational definition. The mission of the university defines and gives meaning to organizational actions and participants. As the overarching ideological apparatus of an organization's culture, the mission also underscores the social relations at work in an institution. Mission statements are historical in that they evolve from specific documents and goals; they are current in that they get redefined by the needs of the internal and external constituencies; and they are future-oriented in that they help define where the institution wants to go. The University of Guatemala at San Carlos, for example, has historical roots as the first university in Central America. It is defined by the current context of Guatemalan society, and it changes with an eye to not simply what they are, but what they want to become. In this light the mission is a temporal artifact embedded in societal understanding of the role and nature of the university.

I have purposefully linked the idea of ideology with mission so that we realize that a mission is more than simply a formulaic goal of an institution. Goertz has noted how ideologies are symbolic systems that enable incomprehensible situations to become meaningful (1973, 220). Ideology, then, involves understanding the taken-for-granted assumptions of the organization's participants about the mission and the culture.

Knowledge and Power

Two key precepts concerning knowledge from a cultural viewpoint are that (1) it is socially constructed and that (2) it is linked to formations of power. Rather than the positivist conception of knowledge as something that exists independent of the knower and which can be discovered, a cultural view of knowledge is one where the participants, embedded in social and historical events, create knowledge. And since knowledge is created, it is neither objective nor value-neutral. Instead, it is a power-laden object that helps control discourse and organizational activity.

A cultural view of knowledge forces the researcher to come to terms with contextual definitions. Questions such as how the participants define knowledge, how definitions of knowledge have changed over time, and how knowledge is transmitted, take on importance. Such questions, we discover, vary from institution to institution based on factors, such as institutional mission and ideology, institutional country, and the specific idea being studied. These questions, although important in any organizational setting, gain particular importance in postsecondary institutions where supposedly one of the key roles of the professorate is to set the terms for knowledge production and dissemination. And too, questions of knowledge production are of equal importance with regard to Latin America. If a cultural view of knowledge assumes that knowledge is produced in contextual surroundings, then how might Latin American institutions foment culturally specific forms of thought?

Communication and Symbols

The manner in which work gets done, the signals employed to display particular meanings, and the communicative framework for the organization all highlight aspects of culture. Ortega y Gassett, for example, characterized the institution as a "machine"; presumably the interactions of individuals who work on a machine will be different from those who characterize their work as a "symphony." An institution that exhorts individuals to work as a "team" may well be different from an organization that has an individualistic culture in both words and deeds.

The assumption, of course, is that an organization's language and symbols help define and are defined by the organization's culture. Indeed, as with each theme discussed here, the organization's culture shapes and is shaped by how the actors utilize the theme. As we shall see, a rector who places signs around the campus attesting to the progress of his administration is trying to communicate to the university community a variety of symbolic messages. Since communication presupposes shared symbols, the rector employs the symbolic language of his or her organization subordinates. In Latin America, for example, governance is the product of political negotiation and the participants use the communicative symbols of the political arena. Thus, we would not see a college president in the United States call upon the same communicative strategies a rector uses in Latin America because of the unique culture in which he or she operates.

Environment and Constituency

All organizations exist within a specific context and serve specific constituencies. A cultural view of these themes emphasizes the interpretive and dynamic nature of an organization's environment and constituency. Private and public universities in the United States learned in the economic downturn of the 1970s that they needed to redefine their "markets" and attract students whom they had not considered as part of their constituencies before, such as part-time students, or students who could only take classes on the weekend. Similarly, Latin American public universities, to varying degrees, have had to reconsider how they defined and worked with their environment as they faced increased competition from private universities.

The institutional environment often provides rationales for change. The government faces economic difficulty and fewer resources are available for the public university. Students—the central constituency—demand courses that are shorter in length or more career oriented, and an institution needs to shift its internal focus or risk losing its clientele. If the economy takes a downturn, unemployment rises and students flock to the university in search of retraining. Although each of these facts—unemployment, rapid inflation, and the like—may occur in several countries, the actors within the organization may react and interpret the events in quite different manners depending on the organization's culture.

Leadership and Strategy

Decision making is unique to the culture in which it resides. The structure of the organization, the style of the particular leader—indeed, who is deemed a leader and who is not—and the avenues employed to create plans and to reach decisions all highlight the culture of the organization. Again, the organization's culture both structures and is structured by particular facets of the theme. A new leader arrives whose style differs dramatically from one's predecessor and the decision-making process suddenly becomes more fluid and less formal. The governing body of higher education for a country is overhauled and new structures are put in place with regard to who is involved in setting policy and planning.

All of these themes highlight specific cultural attributes that will be found in any institution; however, how the actors come to define these themes may differ significantly. One obvious difference is found when we compare institutional cultures across regions and countries. The mission and ideology of public universities in Central America varies significantly from public universities in the United States. Indeed, how knowledge gets defined and how research is attempted differs at the public universities in the neighboring countries of Panama and Costa Rica. Even within a country as small as Costa Rica, we find significant differences with the actors' interpretation of what is good leadership and what is an adequate structure for decision making between two public universities.

The Qualitative Method

To illustrate the meaning of each theme, I provide examples drawn from a case study of the University of Panama. The data are drawn from a series of on-site visits and interviews undertaken during the academic year 1992–93. I interviewed 32 individuals connected with the institution; as is standard and required in qualitative research, they are presented by their roles rather than by their proper names to ensure anonymity. Individuals ranged from faculty in a variety of disciplines to deans and administrators in the Rector's office.

In all of the interviews I worked from a standard research protocol. Interviews in general lasted for one hour. As with any research, the researcher's own biases and frameworks enter into the study. Indeed, the object of the study itself in part frames what we are to find. A feminist who conducts research will have different entry points for analysis than would an economist who subscribes to neoliberal notions of society. In particular to this study, one needs to be aware of the comparative and cross-cultural borders that are crossed when a North American researcher such as myself becomes involved in a project in Latin America. The point here is not so much to invalidate any study because of the position of the author—as if only like minded researchers ought to study a specific project—but to engage the text in a manner that forces the reader to reflect on his or her own experience and consider how one's perceptions of a given situation differ, or are similar with, the project presented in the text. The following examples underscore the culture of the University of Panama and provide insight into decision making and strategy.

The Culture of the University of Panama

Background

Although there are historical precedents of other postsecondary institutions, the modern University of Panama (UP) was founded in 1935 and in some respects has followed similar patterns of other Latin American universities. In 1970, 8,000 students attended the University primarily at one campus and in 1990 there were over 40,000 students taking classes in educational centers throughout the country. There are almost twice as many women students as there are men students, and over half of the students take classes in the evening. UP has 2,100 teachers distributed in 14 faculties; over half of the faculty is tenured (Granásequi 1992, 545). The main campus is in the nation's capital, Panama City. Master's degree programs have been created in many fields, but doctorates exist only in Medicine and Law. For the first thirty years of its existence, the University was without significant competition whereas in the 1990s there has arisen a plethora of private, public, and international institutions that offer postsecondary degrees in Panama. Furthermore, many wealthy students study abroad.

Panama's literacy rate is over 85 percent. Primary education is compulsory and there are 350,000 students currently enrolled in grades one through six. Enrollment in secondary grades is 200,000. About 60,000 students attend postsecondary institutions in Panama and abroad. Thus, about 94 percent of Panamanian youth attend primary school, 48 percent go to high school, and 3 percent attend postsecondary institutions (Ramos, Avila, and Cordero 1991, 15). After UP, the second largest institution in the country is the Technological University, which enrolls about 10,000 students who study engineering and allied fields. About 5,000 students are enrolled in the University of Santa Maria la Antigua, a private Roman Catholic institution.

Panama is 90 percent Catholic. The overall population is roughly two and a half million; the vast majority is Mestizo and Spanish speaking. The indigenous population (Cuna, Ngobe or Guaymí, Emberá or Chocó, Bokotá, and Teribe) is 5 percent of the total citizenry. In 1821 the land that was to become Panama received independence from Spain, and in 1903 Panama separated from Colombia. The United States began to have a dominating influence as work was started on the Panama Canal. Throughout the 1960s and 1970s there was increased pressure from various forces within Panama such as the University of Panama, for the United States to return the Canal to Panama, which resulted in the treaty of 1977.

The recent political history of Panama began in 1968 with a military takeover that led to the establishment of a government by General Torrijos in 1969. Torrijos was a charismatic leader whose populist domestic programs and nationalist foreign policy appealed to many in the country. The death of Torrijos in 1981 gradually led to the control of the government by General Manuel Noriega. Widespread corruption and the regime's crackdown on civil liberties created problems within the country. Outside Panama, the Bush administration created the perception that General Noriega was a security risk to the United States. The United States cut off foreign aid to Panama, which increased unemployment and economic instability. When a United States soldier was stopped by Panamanian security forces in 1989, President Bush used the incident as a pretense to invade the country. The massive invasion led to Noriega's downfall and arrest, and the United States installed Guillermo Endara as president. Panamanian sentiment about the invasion has ranged from criticism about continued U.S. interference in the internal affairs of Panama, to support for the overthrow of a dictator. The result of the invasion has been increased unemployment, poverty, and health care problems. The civilian areas of Panama City that were bombed have yet to be rebuilt. The citizenry has, however, gradually moved toward democracy and stabilization. Presidential elections are scheduled for 1994, and the completion of the transfer of the Canal to Panama will take place in 1999.

Mission and Ideology

The development of the University began with heavy input from European intellectuals resulting in the institution being founded with a quasi-European philosophy. During the takeover of the government by Torrijos in 1968 the University was closed; it reopened seven months later. Perhaps this event more than anything else led to a redirection in the basic ideology of the institution away from elite training and toward massification. Regional centers were started. Open admissions became the norm. An ideology of higher education as a basic right available to every citizen became the overriding mission of the institution. Of consequence, there was a 400 percent student increase in a relatively short period (Cresalc 1985, 8). This dramatic and abrupt change in institutional philosophy affected not only the number of students in the University but also virtually every aspect of the institution—from teacher salaries to how one defines research. The relationship between the state and the university was perceived in a different manner from before.

Historically, the modern mission of the University has been to act as the nation's critical conscience (Universidad de Panamá 1993). In this light, the institution's role has been to aid in the development of national independence. At the same time, as discussed above, how one interprets a mission changes over time due to social and historical contexts and the ideas of the organizational actors. Clearly, the example of massification highlights how the institution's participants interpreted and enacted its mission in the late 1960s and 1970s. Morales (1992) has pointed out that there have been at least three different interpretations of the mission: an oligarchic model from 1935–1960; a developmental or democratic model from 1960–1980; and a neoliberal model during the 1980s.

At present, many of the interviewees noted that the greatest problem lies in the basic tension of what the mission of the university is and how it relates to societal advancement. "Our problems are not fiscal, but cultural," commented one individual. "We have yet to define our role in society." "What is the role of faculty?" asked another individual. "We do not know." "The invasion has caused Panamanians to think about what a new Panama should be;" said another, "but to do that we must also consider what our role [the university] is in a new Panama. We have not done this." Indeed, from the interviews one discovers that the organization's participants believe an institutional mission has not been defined other than that the University exists with open doors. "Academic quality, what it means to be a professor, and what an academic career means are examples of things we have not defined," explained another person. "Research is either by individuals at the University, or in Institutes outside the University. We have no mind set about what research is, what is needed," added another individual.

Knowledge and Power

Coupled with the lack of understanding of what kind of research, if any, should be attempted at the University is the inability to see how the institution defines knowledge. My point here is that, as Ortega y Gassett noted, an institution's mission ought to explicitly affect all areas of institutional life. Camargo and Miranda, for example, have argued that research and teaching should be developed that utilizes Panamanian culture and history, but at present no such work is being done (1992). In the interviews at the University everyone noted massification as a key component of institutional life, but no one articulated how the mission affected, for example, pedagogy or research.

Many individuals pointed out that the research function of the institution was virtually nonexistent: "Most faculty are part-time," explained one person, "so they do not have time to do research." A second person added, "The bureaucracy is too great. It's easier to do your work outside of the University." "Politics plays into everything," added a third. "If you don't get involved you'll find yourself without a lab, even a desk. If you do get involved you end up with no time to do your research." And a fourth individual commented, "We have no research tradition other than when someone is trained abroad. But they come back here and the conditions are so different that it becomes impossible." A fifth person observed, "We do research. We have a National Congress where people present their work, but it is not a central part of our consciousness as faculty."

Relatedly, no one discussed the relationship between the academic curriculum and pedagogy; that is, some people commented on the curriculum as being that which pertains to knowledge, but how knowledge gets transmitted to the learner was not a point of concern. One wonders how it is possible to create culturally specific forms of Panamanian thought within the University if knowledge production does not take place and discussions about the relationship between teaching and learning is absent. To be sure, many institutes, centers, and "think tanks" exist in Panama, but they have increasingly been started outside the University because, as the interviewees noted, of the politicization of the academy or the bureaucratic structures that further hindered research.

Consequently, knowledge gets defined in quite traditional ways and the transmission of knowledge to the students occurs in the most formal of mechanisms—the lecture. Any sense that a mission of a public university defined as helping the working class should have a unique curricular or pedagogic structure is virtually absent. Similarly, the idea that power is somehow linked to academic forms of knowledge only occurs as abstract arguments rather than in concrete analyses of the relations between academe and society.

The participants pointed out that power, in general, is wielded traditionally so that coalitions form and grow or fall according to political elections. As one person noted, "The unions have a voice, and we constantly think of elections—for the dean, the rector." Another person added, "People are declaring themselves candidates now, even though the election [for Rector] is not for two years." "A rector appoints who he wants," said another individual, "and they are debts for supporting him. It's all political."

Because of his structural position, then, the Rector had power. Once a rector was elected he appointed vice rectors who needed to be confirmed by the academic assembly, which almost always happened. Further, the relationship among individuals within the University who belong to political parties outside the University is remarkably close so that governmental and university relations are very often defined in terms of political relationships. "Political parties in society determine relations in the University," commented an individual. "A rector must get along with the government. It doesn't matter who, Noriega, Endara, or whoever. The rector must work within the political framework of society." Thus, any sense that the mission of a public university is to be a conduit for alternative forms of knowledge or the empowerment of the masses (rather than the government) has been consumed by the conflicting relations of power between government and university, and political strife amongst vying factions within the university. As one person summarized:

We are contained by the system. You always work in a political environment. The system is centralized. It is democratic because of the assemblies and the ability of faculty to speak. But the organic structure must change. Now everything is bureaucratic. We do not think about the future. We think of how to defeat one group and help our group.

> "We are so centralized," continued another individual, "that the controller general of the country is the one whom you must see when you want to buy something." Thus, although autonomy from the government may exist in other public universities such as in Mexico (Levy 1980), virtually all of the participants interviewed at UP felt that at present the University existed in light of governmental actions. Such an assumption highlights an institution where the participants define power contextually as the ability to control resources and positions. Knowledge is constructed implicitly along these lines rather than argued and fought over in explicit terms.

Communication and Language

When one sets foot on campus, the most obvious signs that exist in numerous locations are large billboards highlighting that a particular building is being renovated during the administration of the current rector. As with any symbol, the interpretation of such a sign is manifold. Presumably the administration has placed these signs throughout the campus to convey a sense of change and optimism about the future as well as to highlight how institutional funds are being spent. As I noted in the previous section, the rector also calls upon quite common political symbols in large part because he exists within a political framework.

However, the overwhelming sentiment of the interviewees was one of pessimism and/or cynicism. "This administration is lamentable," said one person. "He will be remembered for painting the university," said another. "We have serious problems," added a third person, "and all we see is more centralization and more signs."

More than any other cultural theme pertaining to UP, an analysis of communication and language highlights an institution that is bereft of identity and in a general sense of depression about the present and future. One question asked during the interviews was open-ended: "Is this a good university?" The intent of the question was to provoke respondents' categories for how they defined quality or excellence. When asked at other institutions in Central America the responses enabled categories to be developed about quality such as with whom the interviewees compared themselves (e.g., other Central American institutions, the United States, etc.), or what categories the respondents used to think about quality (e.g., teaching, research, public service). However, at the University of Panama over 90 percent of the respondents answered in the negative; they felt the institution was not good. "The university should be cleaned," said one person, "close it. Get students who are serious and faculty who are serious. Then reopen it." "I am sad for the University," said another person, "I received my degree here. We are no longer good." "People only come here because they have to," said a third person. A fourth person added, "We don't think like that. We don't think about quality. It's a political institution, so we haven't experienced a concern for excellence." A fifth person summarized, "I don't know what we will be in the future. We can't wait for five years. We must work at changing the structure and become important."

Their responses existed primarily in two domains. Either they felt there had been a complete breakdown of institutional communication because of politicization, or that the centralized structure made organic change impossible—and for the institution to be good, dramatic change was needed.

Other reasons pertained to points one hears quite commonly in Latin America—lack of adequate supplies, insufficient classroom space, lack of student preparation, and the like. The respondents' pessimism about the University is interesting not only as a cultural comment but also as a comparative one, for participants at institutions with similar problems in funding or resources commonly responded that their institution was good. What, then, has caused the construction of a culture turned against itself?

Leadership and Strategy

Individuals highlighted three areas of concern with regard to decision making at the University. As the individual most in the spotlight, the Rector came in for a great deal of criticism as someone "too political" or "too concerned with his welfare" or "too centralized." Centralization came up with virtually every discussion about the problems of the institution. "The central problem is centralization," explained one individual; and a second said, "The Rector is centralized, but it is the system that makes us centralized. He just hasn't changed it." A third person elaborated:

> If you want anything you must go to the Rector. Some people think even he doesn't make decisions, that he goes to the controller of the country. But it means no one has authority. We're too bureaucratic.

One of the additional dilemmas for the current administration was that the Rector's vice rectors were not seen as independent of him. In other words, "the Rector doesn't have a team. Everyone finds out what to do from him." "The vice rectors," added another, "do what the Rector says. He got rid of the one person who didn't do what he said." Many people also felt that a climate of fear existed where there was little academic debate and the Rector tried to rule by fiat. Most people also noted that the Rector acted within the parameters of how individuals expected a Rector to act; the position is a political role, for example, and the Rector acted as a politician. At the same time, individuals seemed to feel it was time to break the mold.

The second concern was the inability to articulate a shared vision of the University in any meaningful manner. The point here was that the structure of the institution did not allow for meaningful dialogue but instead was oriented toward politicization. As noted, although the institution always has had the role of being the critical conscience of the country, most individuals could not articulate how they felt the University enacted that role.

Along with the Rector, faculty unions carried a considerable amount of authority, and the academic assemblies thus were able to consider proposals put before them. Yet the interviewees felt in general that the unions and assemblies did not stimulate concrete ideas about the direction and nature of the institution in the 21st century.

The third related point addressed the difficulty UP had in breaking free from the government and generating enough income to prosper. More than Costa Rican universities, such as the University of Costa Rica or National University, UP's budget was almost entirely driven by governmental subsidies. Further, the income from the government was insufficient. In 1990 the government provided a 40 million dollar budget which was 10 million dollars less than in 1986. The conflict with the United States and resulting unemployment were the primary reasons for the drop in funding. Tuition at $26/semester, coupled with a national scholarship system, generated no income.

Little sponsored research existed. Brunner has estimated that less than 15 percent of Latin America's professorate are active researchers (1992, 13). When I asked respondents about the percent of research at UP, they uniformly responded that the percent would be much lower. The result is that indirect costs or finance from outside sources for buildings and laboratories was virtually nonexistent.

Individuals felt that the fortunes of the economy and the direction of the government would largely determine the institution's future. Although authors such as Candanedo, González, and Avila (1991) have argued that the university should protect its autonomy, virtually no one in the interviews felt that the institution was free from government interference. Again, the point to be learned from these comments was that the participants existed within a culture where they felt that they were neither making attempts to control their destiny, nor were they able to do so.

Consequently, when asked "what will this institution be like in five years," few individuals could respond in any meaningful manner. As with the previous open-ended question one expects responses that will locate the culture in a particular manner. To say that research will be more important, for example, indicates that research has become an area of discussion. To say that students will be better prepared suggests that discussions about academic quality are a point of concern. But in general the respondents at UP could not envision what their institution would be like. "We can't wait five years," said one person, "We need to figure out what we will be tomorrow." Another person commented, "We need dramatic change and it is not possible now. I do not know what I should do."

Environment and Constituencies

If faculty lamented the poor communicative climate within the university, they pointed to the environment as the single greatest factor for determining how the institutional culture became fractured. To be sure, any institution is influenced by its environment; however, the respondents' comments pertained more to the tight relationship between the government and the institution than to the simple facts of currency and change.

I noted how cultural themes are capable of action and reaction. The organization's participants at UP defined constituencies in two ways. The government was a constituency because they provided funding; students were constituencies because it attended the universities. Other than those two groups, however, the respondents did not seem to have actively considered alternative definitions. Relationships with other Panamanian postsecondary institutions were formal and distant, and with other Latin American institutions they were virtually nonexistent. The business sector, private foundations, or agencies that might be able to provide income were not aggressively sought. Students were defined narrowly as those from the working class, so that middle-class students now attended the Catholic university in Panama, and wealthy students went abroad. And most importantly, relationships with the external environment in terms of the citizenry seemed to be absent. Obviously, some foundations provided money, some middle-class students attended the University, and some faculty were critically involved in their communities as faculty members. But, in general, the institutional culture did not support alternative definitions of constituency partly because the larger environment had placed the institution in a specific context with which the University had not aggressively responded. That is, massification created an influx of working class students, and the concomitant changes in society made it harder for the institution's participants to redefine themselves and their culture to more adequately meet the needs of these students.

Analysis and Implications

The term "cultural politics" has gained currency over the last decade in large part because the phrase highlights the relationship between culture and ideology and the political system (Tierney 1993). From this perspective, overarching definitions of terms such as "knowledge" or "power" are rejected in favor of particularistic analyses that emphasize cultural production based on social and historical forces that are both constructed and inherited. Culture operates within a political terrain that constrains and inhibits action, but at the same time, individuals and constituencies are able to create change. Individuals are both objects and subjects in the organization's culture. I have offered a cultural framework that is useful in determining how an organization's participants view different aspects of the culture. What remains to be done, however, is to use this framework in a manner to create dynamic change. In Panama, Juana Camargo and Virginia Miranda (1992) have analyzed the entire educational system and have suggested areas that demand change pertaining to what I have called cultural politics. Candanedo, González, and Avila (1991) have located specific practices that need to be initiated in order to enhance institutional autonomy in Panama. De León and Chang de Méndez have considered what needs to occur to improve academic conditions in the university (1992). On a more general scale, Cornel West has argued that three challenges confront proponents of cultural politics: intellectual, existential, and political (1990, 94). I will use these points to analyze the findings pertaining to the University of Panama's culture.

The Intellectual Challenge

The changes begun with the reopening of UP after Torrijos came to power offer an initial portrait of the intellectual struggle over cultural politics. European or North American forms of organizational life were rejected in favor of a Latin American concept—massification. Yet this initial movement toward self-definition of what constitutes Panamanian public higher education has not moved beyond the first step, but it must (Camargo 1991).

Olmedo Garcia has effectively argued that foreign intervention in the University has not moved intellectual activity toward culturally specific actions in concert with Panamanian ideals but instead it has moved UP in the opposite direction—toward the homogenization of teaching, research, and service. Garcia labels loans from the World Bank or agreements on technical assistance as examples of "sociological espionage" (1989, 20) insofar as such activities provide massive ideological influences on the nature of activity at the University. To be sure, neither all loans nor all offers of technical assistance are examples of conscious attempts at "espionage." Yet in the absence of clear mission statements that have direct linkages with the daily activities of an institution, the logic of Garcia's idea takes on credence.

In this light Garcia's argument is an extension of Ortega y Gassett's call for an institution's participants to come to terms with the mission of their institution so that activities can be defined and acted on that are in support of the organization's culture. The organizational participants at the University of Panama have neither actively redefined the environment nor the constituencies for 25 years. The curriculum and its transmission remain locked in European modes of thought. Research in general is absent, and research within the University that struggles to articulate Panamanian concepts or needs is rare. The intellectual challenge, then, revolves on the ability of individuals to define specific cultural practices that relate to each of the cultural themes discussed.

The Existential Challenge

West helps define this challenge with a question: "How does one acquire the resources to survive and the cultural capital to thrive" (1990,

106). "Cultural capital" refers to those critical and social practices that enable individuals to succeed in the larger world order. Thus, how does an institution acquire fiscal and cultural resources that enable independent thought and action and do not necessitate an over reliance on the whims of governments or foundations. Such a question is a structural concern that demands the creation of unique forms of leadership, decision making, and strategy.

A variety of possible responses exists. One answer is to suggest that increased levels of training will raise the quality of the institution. In this light, for example, more professors who hold doctorates will change the institution. Although one cannot deny that to undertake research, institutions need individuals with technical and intellectual skills, we should not fool ourselves into thinking that advanced training is an end in itself. Indeed, such training is one form of cultural imperialism that Garcia warns against. Merely to mirror the status quo does not move an institution closer to concerted action around institutional purpose.

A second possible solution is xenophobic in nature and suggests that the academic institution should be insular, self-contained and sever ties with its environment to the extent possible. Relations with other institutions are cut to a minimum. Intellectual interchange is seen as unimportant and little effort is made to understand the needs of the constituencies. The problem with this response is twofold. First, such a suggestion is antithetical for an institution whose central organizing concept is that it must be public space where ideas are to be debated and argued. Second, as West notes, "If it becomes a permanent option it is self-defeating in that it usually reinforces the very inferiority complexes promoted by the racist mainstream. Hence, it tends to revel in parochialism" (1990, 108). The strength of this approach is that it encourages independent thinking; but, ultimately, for academic thought to be sustained and advanced, the community's members need dialogue.

I suggest a third alternative. As long as an institution has a clearly thought out mission that gets articulated throughout the institution's components then the concerns of hegemonic thought or involvement with outside constituencies are capable of being understood for what they are and of being used according to the needs of the institution. That is, in a curious sense, to develop institutional autonomy, the University of Panama needs to develop short-and long-range plans that offer new funding mechanisms, more involvement with outside financial agencies, and new formulations of how they work with their environment and who their constituencies are. This suggestion follows the comment of the individual above who argued that the institution's problems were "cultural and not fiscal." Autonomy is not simply a fiscal relationship determining who gives an institution funding and who does not. Institutional autonomy, and in this case specific cultural practices, precedes fiscal decisions. To be sure, funding, structures and decision making play a central role in how an institution is to present itself publicly and to one another; the argument here, however, is that essentially these concepts are intimately tied to the underlying ideology of institutional life.

The Political Challenge

Responses to the intellectual and existential topics enable an organization's participants to deal with the political challenge. This theme pertains not only with how to interact with external forums such as governmental agencies, but also is action-driven and goal-oriented with regard to all institutional activities. If the intellectual challenge is philosophical and the existential challenge is strategic, the political challenge is where cultural themes get articulated and enacted.

It would be ironic, not to say mistaken, to outline specific actions that an institution such as the University of Panama should take, for the basic premise of cultural action is that the organization's members need to come together to decide those actions. To impose ideas from the outside, especially by way of a North American researcher, would only retard collective thought and concerted action on the part of the organization's members. Instead, I return briefly to each cultural theme and ask a series of questions specific to the University of Panama that might provoke dialogue.

Mission and Ideology

- How is the mission unique to Panamanian culture?

- How does it enable the participants to define themselves differently from other postsecondary institutions in Panama, the region, and world?
- How does the mission foment culturally specific action in all arenas, and especially in teaching, research, and extension?

Knowledge and Power

- How is knowledge linked to power?
- How does knowledge get transmitted to students in a manner that accentuates Panamanian culture?
- How is research undertaken that foments praxis and advances Panamanian thought?

Communication and Language

- What culturally specific forms of communication need to be created that enable dialogue?
- Whose voices are silenced in academic decision making?
- What are the symbols and discursive strategies that UP uses to convey its message to external constituencies and how might they be changed?

Leadership and Strategy

- How might a form of Panamanian intellectual leadership be enacted that foments action?
- What strategies need to be developed that link the intellectual and existential challenges with the political challenge?
- What basic changes must be done to the organization's structure to encourage, rather than retard, culturally specific dialogue and debate?

Environment and Constituencies

- How might a more interpretive analysis and relationship be developed with one's environment?
- How might the institution's participants redefine their constituencies in light of the needs of the 21st century?
- What does the University need to do to create explicit linkages between the needs of the local citizenry and the capabilities of the institution?

These questions are interrelated and action-oriented. A mission that takes into account the needs of the Panamanian citizenry will of necessity redirect how individuals think about knowledge production, teaching, and pedagogy. A reanalysis of constituencies could conceivably create dialogues about the need for doctorates in particular areas. A reassessment of the organization's structure might induce a movement away from the overt politicization of decisions and toward different forms of communication. My point is neither to set the terms of the debate nor to advocate for particular responses; I am attempting to highlight how an interpretive analysis of an organization's culture might be used to construct dialogue and action.

Conclusion

Carlos Tunnermann has pointed out that "we are not able to offer the democratization of teaching in a society where there is no democracy" (1980, 5). Yet curiously, education also has been one of the main avenues to empower people and create societal change. The University of Panama is at a crossroads where the society around it is changing, and the institution must change as well (Ramos, Avila and Cordero 1991). What kinds of academic careers should be offered? What forms of leadership are needed, and what will be the relationship of the institution to the government and to society? These kinds of questions remain to be answered in the waning days of the 20th century.

I have suggested that an interpretive framework of an organization's culture is one way for researchers and an organization's participants to come to terms with the situation in which an organization exists. Because qualitative researchers are not in search of generalizations, and in particular because such little interpretive research exists about Latin American postsecondary education, a wealth of possible research remains to be undertaken so that we may better understand the social and cultural dynamics on postsecondary education in Latin America. Research on differing forms of leadership and structural responses to massification, for example, will enable greater understanding from a comparative perspective of what is meant by leadership and strategy in Latin American higher education. Investigations into knowledge production and teaching and learning may also help create a better understanding of the situatedness of knowledge. And with further research one hopes that an organization's participants will be better able to deal with the multitude of problems that confront academe as we approach the 21st century. Such problems are as great in the United States and Europe as they are in Latin America, for issues such as institutional autonomy or the freedom of academic thought transcend national borders.

To be sure, budgets must be balanced and courses must be offered. Yet how we interpret how that budget should be balanced or what courses should be offered are cultural questions that demand interpretation. If we are able to analyze an institution from a cultural perspective, we might be better equipped to consider how change occurs. Thus, I have suggested here that individuals will gain particular insights when they interpret postsecondary organizations as unique cultures in dynamic environments and think of themselves as cultural leaders rather than bureaucratic managers.

Resumen

Este texto emplea un esquema conceptual cultural y una metodología cualitativa para investigar y analizar los problemas y desafíos que enfrenta una universidad latinoamericana. El artículo persigue dos fines. En primer lugar, el autor explica cómo se puede utilizar un esquema conceptual cultural y una metodología de organizaciones para interpretar las instituciones de estudios postsecundarios en América Latina. La segunda meta consiste en sug erir los efectos de este esquema conceptual con respecto al proceso de adopción de decisiones y estrategias.

En consecuencia, el artículo tiene tres partes. En la primera, el autor explica los términos de la estructuración de la cultura y los aplica a las instituciones de estudios postsecundarios de América Latina. Un esquema conceptual cultural analiza la forma en que los participantes de una organización interpretan los cinco componentes culturales: a) misión e ideología; b) conocimiento y poder; c) comunicación y lenguaje; d) liderazgo y estrategia, y e) medio ambiente y grupos de apoyo. Luego el autor analiza las ventajas y desventajas de una metodología cualitativa y destaca el papel que desempeña el investigador en el desarrollo de datos. La parte dos presenta un caso de una institución para destacar cómo se pueden analizar las actividades de una organización de ese tipo mediante el uso de un esquema conceptual cultural. Los datos utilizados en este texto se basan en entrevistas realizadas en 1992 en la Universidad de Panamá. El artículo concluye en la parte tres con un análisis sobre las consecuencias del uso del esquema conceptual. Específicamente, el texto considera tres desafíos que enfrentan las instituciones postsecundarias: el existencial, el intelectual y el político, y los relaciona con el esquema conceptual cultural que se bosqueja en el artículo.

Résumé

Ce texte emploie un encadrement culturel et une méthodologie qualitative pour examiner et analyser les problèmes et les défis auxquels est confrontée une université latino-américaine. Le but de cet article est double. L'auteur explique d'abord comment il est possible d'employer l'encadrement culturel et la méthodologie des organisations pour interpréter les institutions post-secondaires en Amérique latine. Le deuxième but est de suggérer les consérer les conséquences qu'un tel encadrement peut avoir sur la prise de décisions et les stratégies.

Le document se divise ainsi en trois parties. Dans la première partie l'auteur définit les termes de la culture organisationnelle et les applique aux instituions post-secondaires latino-américaines. Un encadrement culturel se rapport à la façon dont les participants d'une organisation interprètent les cinq composantes culturelles: a) la mission et l'idéologie; b) la connaissance et le pouvoir; c) la communication et le langage; d) le leadership et la stratégie; et e) l'environnement et les localités. L'auteur examine ensuite les points forts et les points faibles d'une méthodologie qualitative et souligne le rôle du chercheur dans l'élaboration des données. La deuxième partie est une étude de cas d'une institution visant à mettre en exergue la façon dont il est possible d'examiner les activités d'une telle organisation en employant un cadre culturel. Les données reprises dans le texte découlent d'interviews menées à l'Université du Panama au cours de l'année 1992. Dans la troisième partie l'article se termine par une discussion concernant les conséquences d'un encadrement. Ce texte examine, en particulier, trois défis auxquels sont confrontées les institutions post-secondaires—existentiel, intellectuel et politique—et établit un rapport entre ces défis et l'encadrement culturel décrit en grandes lignes dans cet article.

Resumo

Este texto usa um quadro de referência cultural e uma metodologia qualitativa para investigar e analisar os problemas e desafios enfrentados por uma universidade latinoamericana. O propósito do artigo é duplo. Primeiramente, explica o autor como se pode usar um esquema cultural e metodologia de estudo organizacional para interpretar instituições pos-secundárias na América Latina. Em segundo lugar, sugere as implicações desse esquema com respeito a tomada de decisões e estratégia.

O trabalho divide-se em três partes. Na primeira, o autor explica os termos da cultura organizacional e os aplica às instituições pos-secundárias latinoamericanas. Um quadro de referência cultural relaciona-se com o modo pelo qual os que participam de uma organização interpretam cinco componentes culturais; (a) missão e ideologia; (b) conhecimento e poder; (c) comunicação e linguagem; (d) liderança e estratégia; e finalmente (e) ambiente e grupos representados. Ainda nesta parte discute as forças e fraquezas de uma metodologia qualitativa e sublinha o papel do pesquisador no desenvolvimento dos dados. A segunda parte é um estudo de caso de uma instituição, para exemplificar como se pode analisar-lhe as atividades usando um quadro de referência cultural. Os dados provêm de entrevistas na Universidade do Panamá. Na parte final, discute as implicações do quadro de referência. O texto considera em particular três desafios às instituições pos-secundárias—existencial, intelectual e político—e os relaciona com o quadro conceitual esboçado.

Bibliography

Brunner, J. 1992. *Educación superior, sociedad y estado en América Latina.* Santiago, Chile: Facultad Americana de Ciencias Sociales.

Camargo, Juana. 1991. "Educación e invasión: Algunos elementos para el análisis de la educación panameña". *Revista Panameña de Sociología* 7: 73–82.

Camargo, Juana, and Virginia Miranda. 1992. *Lineamientos generales para el análisis de la educación nacional.* Universidad de Panamá: Instituto de Estudios Nacionales.

Candanedo, Miguel, R. González, and V. Avila. *Autonomía Universitaria Y Universidad Democrática.* Universidad de Panamá: Dirección General de Planificación Universitaria.

Chaffee, E., and W. Tierney. 1988. *Collegiate Culture and Leadership Strategy.* New York: MacMillan.

Cresalc. 1985. *La educación superior en Panamá.* Caracas, Venezuela: UNESCO.

Gandásegui, M. 1992. "Panamá." *The Encyclopedia of Higher Education.* Eds. B. Clark and Gu. Neave. New York: Pergamon.

Deal, T., and A. Kennedy. 1982. *Corporate Cultures.* Reading, MA: Addison-Wesley.

De León, E., and Chang de Méndez. 1992. "La educación panameña en el contexto de la crisis: Problemas y alternativas". *Acción y Reflexión Educativa* 18: 13–47.

García, O. 1989. *La educación superior ante la crisis nacional.* Panamá: APUDEP.

Geertz, C. 1973. *The Interpretation of Cultures.* New York: Basic Books.

Levy, D. 1980. *University and Government in Mexico: Autonomy in an Authoritarian System.* New York: Praeger.

Morales, F. 1992. "Papel de la universidad de Panamá en el momento actual". *Acción y Reflexión Educativa* 18: 3–12.

Ortega y Gassett, J. 1944. *The Mission of the University.* New York: Norton.

Paulston, R. 1992. "Ways of Seeing Education and Social Change in Latin America." *Latin American Research Review* 27.3: 177–202.

Ramos, P., V. Avila, and A. Cordero. 1991. *Integración de la educación.* Universidad de Panamá: Dirección General de Planificación Universitaria.

Schein, E. 1985. *Organizational Culture and Leadership.* San Francisco: Jossey Bass.

Tierney, W. G. 1988. "Organizational Culture in Higher Education." *Journal of Higher Education* 59.1: 2–21.

_____. 1993. *Building Communities of Difference: Higher Education in the Twenty-First Century.* Westport, CT: Bergin and Garvey.

Tunnermann, C. 1980. *Pensamiento universitario centroamericano.* San José, Costa Rica: EDUCA.

Universidad de Panamá. 1993. *Ante proyecto de la comisión especial designada por el congreso universitario.* Panama: Universidad de Panamá.

West, C. 1990. "The New Cultural Politics of Difference." *October* 53: 93–109.

PART IV

The State

Higher Education in Advanced Developing Countries*

PHILIP G. ALTBACH

Discussions of higher education in the Third World are often predicated on assumptions of low literacy rates, fiscal problems, lack of needed infrastructures, and in general a low efficiency level of the educational system. Problems of graduate unemployment, the brain drain and shortages of trained academic personnel are held to be common realities. This article focuses on the growing number of developing countries that are now building their academic systems based on a fairly firm educational and economic situation. These countries face quite different realities than have been commonly understood in much of the literature and have the possibility of building impressive academic structures fairly quickly. Due in part to changing fashions in development policies, less attention is currently being paid to university development by scholars and by international agencies although in fact Third World nations remain committed to higher education as an important part of the process of modernization.[1] University development is seen as an important priority in virtually every Third World nation regardless of ideological persuasion or economic status. It is therefore important to consider the problems and prospects of academic development in the Third World.

The Advanced Developing Countries

This discussion focuses on the growing number of Third World nations that are now devoting substantial attention and resources to higher education development, that have a high rate of economic growth, relatively substantial financial resources and in general have been successfully involved in the modernization process. Such countries as Singapore and Malaysia in South-East Asia, Taiwan and the Republic of Korea in East Asia, Zimbabwe and several of the smaller states in southern Africa, and the oil-rich nations of the Middle East are all in this category. Their populations tend to be relatively small, rates of economic growth have been high and in general there has been a degree of economic and political stability and government efficiency that has permitted development plans to achieve a measure of success. These countries, and a number of others, have different ideological perspectives and certainly have their share of socioeconomic problems, but they are none the less in a relatively favoured position in terms of the development of an academic system.

The advanced developing countries also have some distinct advantages in educational

Philip G. Altbach (United States of America). Director of the Comparative Education Center and Professor of Higher Education and Foundations of Education at the State University of New York at Buffalo, he is editor of the *Comparative Education Review*. Among his books are *University Reform: An International Perspective, Student Politics in America, Higher Education in American Society*, and *Comparative Higher Education*.

*I am indebted to S. Gopinathan for comments on an earlier draft of this article.

terms. Their relative economic prosperity has permitted them to provide funds sufficient to build and to maintain educational institutions at all levels. Their well-developed societal infrastructures have given needed support for the growth of educational institutions. Where established structures did not exist, it was possible to import appropriate technology or personnel. For example, most of the advanced developing countries have access to computer-based technologies for use in education as well as in government or commerce. The growth of educational institutions has been relatively slow and this has permitted those responsible for educational development to ensure that quality was maintained, although of course expansion inevitably causes strains. Planning has been deliberate and the relationship between the process of planning and the implementation of educational programmes has been reasonably close.

The advanced developing countries constitute a successful example of educational development at the post-secondary level. This discussion focuses both on some of the achievements and on the challenges that face universities in this new category of Third World nation. The process of academic development is complex and relates to the internal realities of a country, to the international knowledge network, and to historical traditions. The 'advanced' Third World nations constitute a special category of country and face special problems—but they have achieved a good measure of success and have the potential for especially impressive development. It may be possible, in these countries, for academic institutions to move rapidly into the ranks of internationally recognized academic institutions.

On many dimensions, the universities in the advanced Third World nations compare favourably on international standards. While detailed statistics are difficult to obtain, student-teacher ratios, library facilities, the basic amenities, teaching loads and in some countries even salaries are very much in accord with international standards. In a sense, as universities in such countries as the United Kingdom, Canada, the United States and Australia experience severe fiscal and other problems, some of the academic institutions discussed in this article may provide the best models for advancement in the contemporary world. Because the major research facilities are in the Western universities and the major journal and book publishers are located in North America and Europe, research productivity and dissemination remains centred in the West. But as Third World universities are able to build up capabilities in these areas and as they make a commitment to research as part of their academic systems, the level of research productivity will also increase.

Academic institutions in the advanced Third World nations are all based on Western, often colonial, institutional models and tend to be small and to serve a limited urban clientele (often less than 1 per cent of the relevant age cohort). The colonial bias in favour of the liberal arts and legal education dominates the established institutions and this orientation also reflects economic realities that are now changing. Western languages play a very important role, in many institutions serving as the key medium of instruction. But even where indigenous languages are used (such as in Malaysia and Taiwan), books in European languages dominate at least the advanced curriculum and most students must be bilingual. There is generally a high demand for university graduates in all fields, with a special need for skilled manpower in technological areas. There are strong pressures from the educated and growing middle classes and from government to ensure the expansion of post-secondary education.

It is my hypothesis that universities in the more prosperous Third World nations have some important decisions to make in order to ensure continued progress in higher education. The experience, both positive and negative, of other Third World nations is useful as a background. The policies and practices of the industrialized nations will also have a considerable influence on future developments. But the realities of this new category of nation are sufficiently unique that new and original patterns may develop.

Lessons of the Past

Higher education development has suffered from shifting expectations. It was first considered the key to socio-economic development and more recently has been as irrelevant and perhaps even harmful. Dore (1976), for example, has argued that the stress on university education and particularly on academic credentials does not contribute to progress and only exacerbates class and ethnic divisions, Earlier expectations were unreasonably high, were impossible to fulfill and disillusionment soon followed. However, higher education did achieve some notable results in the Third World. It succeeded in fairly quickly training a basic cadre with the expertise to administer the newly emerging states. It expanded to provide some education in scientific and technical fields. It provided a means of social mobility for the urban middle classes and in some countries for lower economic strata as well. With some tension and lowering of academic standards, universities expanded rapidly to meet the manifold demands placed on them.

In many countries, however, universities overexpanded (Kaul, 1974). Governments found it easier to build up educational institutions to meet some of the needs of newly articulate segments of the population than to rapidly develop the economy. The emphasis of higher education remained on the humanities and law, in part because of academic traditions, in part because it was less expensive to expand enrollments in these areas and in part because the economy at that early stage did not require highly qualified scientists or technologists. As a result, infrastructures in the sciences were not built and the employment opportunities made available by independence in government and in commerce were quickly filled. The social sciences were expanded, and these subjects were useful in coping with some of the problems of modernization. As a result of a combination of economic factors, overexpansion and an inability to alter both resource allocation and student flows into the social sciences and emerging scientific fields as opposed to the traditional fields, problems of graduate unemployment grew.

Virtually no formerly colonial academic system has diverged from the basic administrative and curricular structure that was implanted by the colonial power (Ashby, 1966). Further, none of the many efforts at higher education reform have dislodged those basically external models (Altbach, 1980). Even those countries that attempted to radically alter aspects of higher education to keep in tune with radical political change have not succeeded in developing successful indigenous patterns of curriculum, administration or function (Shirk, 1979). It is clear that the reform of higher education is a very complex and difficult process and it is thus not surprising that few academic systems have managed to break significantly with the past or to serve entirely new functions in the Third World.

There has been an over-reliance on higher education as a means—some would say a panacea—to assist in rapid social and economic development. Certainly, universities can and indeed must play an important role in the development process (Thompson and Fogel, 1977). But they are not the key to rapid growth nor to political stability. Many countries, and a large number of scholars and policy-makers in the industrialized nations, stressed the importance of university development as a key to broader progress in the 1950s and 1960s. As a result, massive investments were made in higher education, by newly independent Third World nations and by aid agencies. This investment was effective in stimulating the rapid growth of higher education, but it did not pay off in socioeconomic development. Basic literacy grew only modestly and some societal dislocations were caused by the overly rapid expansion of higher education. Because higher education is so costly, it consumed large proportions of education budgets, skewing priorities in countries with limited resources. Further, higher education served only a small part of populations that are largely rural and without access to post-secondary institutions. But this small minority proved to be highly articulate and politically powerful and once expansion was undertaken and access provided to a small but growing group, it was difficult, if not impossible, to halt expansion.

While most Third World nations began university development programmes with a clearly articulated plan, growth took place without regard to careful planning in many instances (*Comparative Education Review*, 1972). In a few countries, private interests started educational institutions, while in others different levels of government competed in the education arena. Generally, projections for expansion were exceeded and expenditures grew out of proportion.

Much has been written about the interrelationships of higher education and particularly about how Third World and industrialized nations interact (Altbach, 1977, 1981; Mazrui, 1975). The basic reality is that virtually all Third World universities are at the periphery of an international knowledge system that is dominated by the major industrialized nations (Shils, 1972; Spitzberg, 1980). The domination of the world's research system, of publishing houses, the use of the major metropolitan languages, and the sheer size and wealth of the academic systems in the industrialized nations have contributed to their continuing domination of the knowledge system. Many have argued that foreign assistance programmes, with some exceptions, have contributed to the continuing peripheral status of the Third World (Mende, 1973). The realities of the international relationships of universities are complex and must be recognized as higher education systems plan for the future. Among these realities is a basic element of inequality that has placed Third World universities at continuing disadvantage.

The above characterizations and limitations are not valid for all Third World nations nor is the post-independence picture completely bleak. Indeed, academic institutions have often helped to define newly emerging nations, have provided training for skilled manpower, and faculty have advised governments. Most colonial powers spent little on education, and the building of new universities and the expansion of access was a necessary step. The point of these comments is to indicate that the experiences, positive and negative, of a decade or more of academic development in the Third World can help to guide the planning and implementation of higher education in nations that are still in a pattern of growth. Many of these nations are in the fortunate position not only of being able to avoid the errors of others but also of having the financial resources necessary to build high quality higher education.

The Elements of Growth

The advanced Third World nations have academic traditions that do not differ dramatically from those described above. But they differ sharply in their contemporary socioeconomic circumstances, and as a result they have the opportunity to develop complex academic systems on a much firmer base. The following issues, which are by no means exhaustive, indicate some of the challenges that face this new category of developing nation.

Government-university relations. The appropriate relationship between government, which most often provides funding for education, and academic institutions is a matter of controversy in almost all Third World nations. In the United States and other industrialized nations, similar debates concerning 'accountability', the desire of government to have information about all aspects of academic institutions and programmes and to exercise significant control over them, and 'autonomy', the traditional concept of institutional self-government and the ideal that universities should set their own goals, is a hotly debated issue (McConnell, 1981). In the Third World, where higher education is often one of the most costly items in the national budget and where academic institutions are expected to perform direct service to society, a significant portion of government involvement is accepted. Further, the academic tradition of colonialism in some countries and the relative newness of institutions all make the development of autonomy difficult.

Yet, even if academic institutions have become virtual departments of government, the issue of university autonomy remains an important one. The basic elements of academic autonomy at the level of the individual teacher are important to preserve, for it is under conditions of relative autonomy and academic freedom that the best teaching and research occurs. The best universities in the world have preserved a substantial degree of autonomy, both for the institution and for the individual. While many of the traditions of universities are archaic, they have protected academic institutions from too rapid change. Further, academic communities seem to function most effectively when they have a degree of self-respect and autonomy.

There is no easy formula to provide for all countries a guide to the appropriate relationship between higher education and government. Clearly, government must exercise some control over the direction of an institution which provides manpower, expertise and which has considerable cultural influence. There must be accountability for the very substantial budgets provided to higher education. At the same time, academic institutions must have a degree of autonomy in order to function with the maximum of creativity. Morale, an elusive commodity, is very important. Autonomy is difficult to quantify and more difficult to maintain with all of the pressures inevitably buffeting academic institutions—political, economic and demographic. Institutional autonomy also requires a degree of self-restraint and responsibility in the Third World. Universities are inevitably politically important institutions and are often centres for dissent and intellectual ferment. While the right of individual academic staff to express opinions should be protected, academic institutions have a responsibility to remain neutral on political matters in most contexts. The internal balance between self-expression and academic freedom on the one hand and responsibility and sensitivity to the often sensitive role of the university in the Third World is often difficult to determine.

What may be an appropriate level of autonomy in Switzerland may not be relevant in Singapore because of different social and educational conditions. The point of this discussion is to indicate that the common tendency to virtually eliminate institutional and in some cases individual autonomy is probably a mistake and a constructive dialogue between academic institutions and government is very much needed.

Language. The medium of instruction, research and academic discourse is often a matter of considerable controversy within universities as well as in society (Noss, 1967). The choice of the language of instruction is a matter of great sensitivity and also of immense consequence for the university. It is inevitably involved in broader issues of politics, public policy and cultural contestation. Typically, academic institutions in the Third World functioned in a European language under colonialism, and most academic systems have been slow to shift to indigenous languages. Some academic systems continue to function in European languages and have no plans to change. This is the case in countries with no clearly dominant indigenous language or in which a European language has been deeply entrenched.

Nigeria, with its multiplicity of languages, has been content to continue its university system in English although there has been considerable debate concerning the language issue. India long ago made a commitment to function in the various regional languages of the country and some universities have shifted to instruction in these languages. Many, however, continue to teach in English, particularly in the more prestigious sector of the system. Singapore, which until recently had instruction in both Chinese and English, has shifted to English as the sole medium of higher education. Malaysia, on the other hand, has moved its entire academic system to Bahasa Malaysia. While all of the Arab countries are committed to Arabic as the medium of instruction, a number use English in part of their academic systems. Kuwait, for example, has English in its science faculties and in medical education while Arabic serves the rest of the university (Al-Ebraheem and Stevens, 1980).

Language choices have many ramifications. The continued use of a European language in higher education typically eliminates a significant part of the population from access to higher education. It is often said that the use of a European language insulates a university from its society. Privileged strata of the population, largely in the cities, who have had access to education in the metropolitan language, will dominate the higher education system and thereby the upper reaches of the society. The use of indigenous languages will broaden the influence of higher education and of the research and analysis done in universities by communicating in a widely understood medium. Access will be much wider and ethnic and economic integration will have the opportunity of taking place in higher education. Modern ideas will be more readily communicated to the society and the indigenous culture. The intellectuals in the universities will, at least, speak the same language. Nation building may be enhanced through the use of indigenous languages throughout the education system.

On the other hand, use of an indigenous medium cuts an academic system off from the international knowledge network to some extent. Academic staff in many countries are not immediately prepared to teach in an indigenous language and, more important, textbooks and other instructional materials are often unavailable and are expensive and difficult to produce. It is a common complaint in countries that use an indigenous language that they still depend on books in European languages and thus, students must learn a foreign language in any case. Advanced training at the post-baccalaureate level is almost inevitably linked to the international academic system and hence to a European language. Even in countries that have shifted undergraduate education to indigenous languages, post-baccalaureate education has often remained in a European language.

Despite these problems, much progress has been made in using non-European languages in higher education. Japan pioneered the use of an indigenous language as the sole means of higher education at the end of the last century and Japanese has been successfully adapted for use as a scientific medium. Although Japan still depends on translations from European languages and there is considerable stress in Japanese schools on learning foreign languages, Japanese is the medium of higher education at all levels. Taiwan, and of course the People's Republic of China, successfully use Chinese as the sole medium of instruction. Indonesia changed from the use of Dutch to Bahasa Indonesia immediately after independence, and, although there are still problems of the availability of textbooks and curricular materials, there has been overall success. Malaysia is now in the process of change, and although there is a lack of text materials, agencies like the Dewan Bahasa dan Pustaka are producing translations and original materials for use in higher education.

Other countries have moved more slowly with language change and many have chosen, for a variety of reasons, to retain a European language as the main medium of higher education. Zimbabwe, like many African nations, has difficulty in choosing among several indigenous languages, none of which have ever been used for academic or research purposes. As a result, English continues as the sole medium in higher education. It should also be noted that in many Third World nations, most students are effectively bilingual in any case and the combination of instruction in an indigenous language combined with the use of books and text materials in a European language is by no means impossible.

The point of this discussion is to indicate that there are difficult choices to be made and whatever the choice, there are inevitable consequences, many of them unanticipated. In addition, when choices are made, mechanisms must be set up to ensure as much success as possible. For example, when Malaysia decided to shift to Bahasa Malaysia, it enlarged its textbook production and translation facilities. The wealthier Third World nations have the capability to develop the infrastructures, including journal and book publishing in indigenous languages, if they decide to change the medium of instruction.

In the past, emerging academic systems often did not confront the language situation and simply continued to use the colonial language. Recently, academic planners have considered the ramifications of language use and have made more rational decisions. Whatever the choice, however, consequences follow and countries need to consider all of the ramifications and provide the needed infrastructure for language development.

Curriculum and the organization of study. Most Third World academic systems inherited a curriculum heavily weighted toward the humanities and organized in a classical European manner. Students were assumed to come from a highly educated élite and were propelled toward prestigious positions in the civil service, religion or the independent professions. Realities in the Third World made many of the basic assumptions of higher education false. The clientele for higher education did not have a Western cultural background. The need for educated manpower was quite different—as Third World universities were providing personnel for emerging technological societies. The other educational infrastructures (such as polytechnics and apprenticeship programmes) were missing and thus the universities were given added burdens. The traditional curriculum, based on humanistic studies and a few professional specializations, was not entirely relevant. And the traditional management of studies, with infrequent examinations, was not appropriate for a student body that was, on average, younger and certainly less experienced with higher education.

Despite widely recognized deficiencies in the traditional curriculum and organization of study, change has been slow. Third World nations felt the pressure to offer university studies to a growing population and the pressure to expand proved stronger than the necessity for reform. As a result, universities continued to offer a traditional European curriculum and to organize programmes of study in a traditional manner. This produced alienation, contributed to an oversupply of graduates in the humanities in some countries and contributed to the decline in academic standards. Since the traditional models were entrenched and did not change with the coming of independence, they became even more difficult to dislodge later.

In order to avoid the conservatism of the traditional universities, many developing countries, at great expense, established entirely new institutions of higher education to provide different curricular and organizational models. In some countries, private institutions were founded to reflect the demands of the marketplace for professional training. In others, non-university research and training institutes, such as the institutes of technology in India, provided high quality academic work in areas of national need. In still other places, new universities based on different organizational patterns were set up, often with the assistance of the aid programmes of industrialized nations and with foreign technical help. The experience of these efforts is important in planning for academic development in the advanced Third World nations (Thompson and Fogel, 1977).

A number of trends can be seen in the Third World, however, which have redirected the focus of higher education. While dramatic changes in academic organization has been rare and the basic curriculum remains similar to what is offered in the industrialized nations, there have been some important shifts in emphasis. The traditional concentration on the humanities has gradually been lessened, first by a stress on the social sciences and later on natural scientific fields and applied technology. Fields such as engineering, management studies and others have become prominent. In some countries, it has been difficult to build up high-quality laboratory and research facilities but significant experiments in medical education (in China) and in rethinking agricultural technology have been attempted with some success. Third World academic institutions have been thinking about the appropriate levels of training and technology relevant for particular needs. Further, there is much more variety in academic specialities and programmes than was the case a decade ago. Tropical agriculture is now widely studied in colleges of agriculture and management studies is a popular field. Malaysian higher education has specializations that focus on the local economy, for example, and this is increasingly common in Third World higher education. There needs to be closer links between industrial and agricultural producers and higher education and perhaps financial support from these concerns, but there has been considerable progress in making higher education more responsive to the direct needs of local economies.

In most fields, including the newly established applied specialities, the curriculum remains closely tied to Western models. Textbooks tend to be imported or adapted from those used in the industrialized nations. Those teaching are very often trained in Europe or North America and often do not adapt their academic experiences to suit local circumstances. In some countries, expatriates constitute a significant part of the teaching staff, especially in the newer applied and scientific fields. The proportion of expatriates varies by country, and a number of the advanced Third World nations have substantially indigenized their teaching staffs. Curricula in fields of economics, sociology, education and other specialities have been partly adapted to indigenous needs, but significantly more thought needs to be given to the details of curriculum reform. Concern not only for broader curricular innovations but also for the less dramatic but quite crucial smaller supporting elements is also required.

There have been widespread efforts to modify the classical organization of studies. In general, academic systems have moved from the European to the American pattern of organization. 'Continuous assessment' of academic work has been substituted for widely spaced examinations. Courses are shorter and specific marks are assigned frequently so that students are monitored more closely. This arrangement permits the teaching staff to be in more direct touch with the learning process and provides 'feedback' for students. Some universities, such as the University of Kuwait, implemented a major shift from a British model to an American-style 'course-credit' system. Other institutions have been less dramatic in the nature of their changes. Many academic systems, such as the bulk of India's universities, have retained the traditional system despite widespread recognition that it is not well suited for Indian realities.

There is no single model for the nature or the organization of the curriculum that will work well in all developing countries. Indeed, what may be effective for a faculty of management may not be well suited for a school of agriculture within the same university. What is very clear is that the traditional European curricular and organizational pattern inherited from colonialism or copied without serious consideration is not well suited to the Third World. Neither the needs of a developing economy nor the realities of larger and more heterogenous universities are suited to the European élitist curriculum. Many of the alterations attempted have been pioneered in the United States, largely because American higher education moved from an élitist to a mass base many years ago and the university system has long allowed a wider range of applied fields.

Coping with expansion. While the major higher education systems in Europe and North America have ceased to expand in the 1970s and 1980s, Third World higher education is still growing at a rapid rate. There is a particular need for academic growth in those countries with a high rate of economic expansion and which have a small university system. For example, many developing countries send as many students out of the country for higher education as study within the nation, always at great expense (Spaulding and Flack, 1976). There are, of course, many strategies for coping with expansion. In the United States, the trend in public higher education has been to build university systems that have a centralized administration and many campuses. In addition, many American university campuses have grown quite large, with as many as 40,000 students. India has continued to use the British 'affiliating' university model, with a single university-based administration and examining body for a large number of semi-independent colleges in a defined geographical area. Most nations do not have academic systems as large as those of the United States or India, and so the problems of scale are not so great. The British, during the period of expansion engendered by the Robbins report in 1963, chose to build new universities very much along traditional lines and with small enrollments rather than to expand existing institutions. The French, prior to the 1968 reforms, permitted existing institutions to expand until the University of Paris had more than 100,000 students. In many countries expansion took place without a clearly planned agenda and university systems simply dealt with increased numbers as best they could. This ad hoc policy in most cases created many difficulties and contributed to the student unrest of the 1960s in many nations.

A growing number of countries have decided that clear limits have to be placed on the expansion of higher education. The experience of India in permitting virtually unbridled expansion and the negative consequences of this expansion have become clear to many nations (Kaul, 1974). In general, a more balanced view of educational development has been evident, stimulated in part by the criticisms of over-expansion and too great expenditures on higher education in the past. But expansion is nevertheless very much part of higher education policy, since most of the wealthier Third World nations have critical needs for highly trained personnel and currently are educating only a tiny proportion of the relevant age-groups.

A number of strategies have been used to plan for and implement expansion. Recognizing past failures, it seems that growth is taking place more slowly than in the past and there has been considerable concern for maintaining quality. But the problems are substantial. Smaller nations have a distinct advantage in dealing with expansion since it is possible to provide effective centralized control over the nature of expansion. The links between planning and implementation seem to be closer where very large numbers of institutions are not involved. In general, the new institutions that are being created do not differ dramatically from those that already exist. It is not clear whether quality can be maintained while enrollments are doubled in a few years. Some countries, such as Singapore, have been very careful to maintain academic quality and to provide for adequate facilities while expanding enrollments. Others, such as Zimbabwe, have greater pressures for expansion and fewer resources.

While there is no common model for expansion, most countries rely on centralized planning to determine the nature and scope of the growth of academic institutions. Since funding is crucial, and virtually all money comes from central government authorities, ministerial control of planning is not surprising. Too often, however, the universities have been left out of the process. There is little doubt that in the immediate agenda of Third World higher-education development management and control of expansion ranks at the top of key issues.

External influences. That universities everywhere are part of an international intellectual network is clear. Historical origins are common and the various academic disciplines are linked by common research paradigms, journals and organizations. It is also clear that this network is dominated by major universities in the large industrialized nations. These institutions are at the centre of the system, while academic institutions elsewhere are to some extent peripheral (Altbach, 1981). The problem for Third World universities is to come to grips with elements of peripherality and to devise policies aimed at maximizing independence. Language policies are important in this regard and, as pointed out earlier, have many implications. The use of an indigenous language can create a more accessible university but can also cut off the intellectual community from the international network. Even the Japanese, who have developed an efficient translation system, often feel cut off from the mainstream of international intellectual and scholarly life because of the limitations of language.

A number of newly emerging universities have tried to instill a concern for research as part of the development of the academic system. Further, scholarly journals and in a few cases publishing enterprises have been established to help with the dissemination of local scholarship. Such emphases and the creation of the infrastructures of knowledge distribution can help to build a self-conscious academic community able to participate on more equal terms in the international system.

The role of expatriates and of foreign advisers is, of course, a key part of academic policy. A number of the newly emerging Third World universities have relied heavily on expatriate staff during the colonial era and into the present. It may be necessary to hire expatriates in order to staff rapidly growing universities and to provide training in fields in which local scholars are not available. Yet, the cost of expatriate talent goes beyond their often rather high monetary salaries. Expatriates almost inevitably reflect the academic values and training of another academic system and most represent the metropolitan values of the major Western European or North American universities. Instilling these values, and also the methodological and substantive academic orientations may be useful to some extent in new universities. But an orientation toward foreign norms and values can also be a dangerous precedent. Expatriate staff seldom have deep institutional loyalties nor an overwhelming concern for national development. They often find themselves in positions of considerable academic power, as senior professors or even administrators and thus often help to shape institutional values at the crucial early stage of development.

Foreign advisers are often an integral part of the academic planning process. Such advisers are often necessary to provide expertise in many areas. In addition, where academic development is part of a foreign assistance scheme, advisers are often an integral part of the aid process. Advisers necessarily reflect the values and norms of their own academic systems (Adams, 1969). This is not an argument against the use of expatriate staff or advisers as parts of an academic development scheme, but it is important for Third World countries to consider carefully the implications of the use of different staffing arrangements.

An often ignored element of the external impact on Third World higher education is the foreign-educated student who returns to assume an important role in the academic hierarchy. The 'brain drain' is not a serious problem in the wealthier Third World nations as most overseas graduates return to remunerative positions. Further, a very large proportion of the most highly educated segment of the population is trained overseas without any concern about the impact of foreign training and orientations on these graduates. In many Third World nations, the top indigenous academic leadership will be foreign educated for a generation to come. Without question, the values, methodological orientations, attitudes toward the role and nature of higher education and perhaps political and social mores as well are strongly influenced by overseas training. Thus, the influence of the major academic systems of the United States, the United Kingdom, France and to a lesser extent the Federal Republic of Germany, where the bulk of Third World academics who are trained abroad have obtained their advanced degrees, will continue to be strong.

Policies concerning overseas study and concern about the impact of foreign study need to be an integral part of academic planning in the Third World. This is a particularly important issue in countries where close to half of those pursuing post-secondary education are studying outside the country. For example, more than half of the Malaysian students in post-secondary education study outside Malaysia. Statistics are similar for Hong Kong. Taiwan and the Republic of Korea send large numbers abroad for training, as does Zimbabwe, Nigeria and most of the countries of the Arabian Gulf. Even where the proportion of students abroad is not as high, the choice of countries to which to send students and the academic specializations of these students remains an issue of significance.

Finally, the importance of regional collaboration as an aspect of the international relationships of universities in the Third World needs to be stressed. Agencies like the Regional Institute for Higher Education and Development in South-East Asia, Unesco's Regional Center for Higher Education in Latin America and the Caribbean and the Association of African Universities can all play a more active role in providing links among universities, centralizing some aspects of academic planning and research and in other areas. Regional co-operation is already pursued in some areas. For example, a significant proportion of the students at the University of Singapore are from other countries in South-East Asia and large numbers of Third World students obtain degrees in Indian universities. It would seem that further pooling of resources, differential specialization and other aspects of regional co-operation can assist in building a sense of academic interdependence among countries with similar problems.

Conclusion

The gross generalizations applied to universities in the Third World do not reflect a complex reality. A significant number of Third World nations now in the process of expanding their higher education systems do not fit into the usual stereotypes of poverty and lack of resources. Further, these countries have the benefit of carefully examining the experience of other Third World nations which earlier made efforts to build their academic systems. Countries that have benefited from the recent changes in, for example, the price of oil also have the opportunity to rethink and perhaps reform their universities.

While higher education has received less emphasis from experts in the industrialized nations in recent years, universities continue to be established and to grow in the Third World. The choices being made about the nature of this expansion is of crucial importance to the countries involved and in the long run to the international knowledge network throughout the world. Issues of accountability and autonomy, specialities and of the adaptation and development of new institutional models remain matters of importance and debate.

Post-secondary education in the advanced developing nations not only has the potential for impressive achievement, but it has already accomplished a great deal. Recognition of these accomplishments and careful analysis of future directions will yield impressive results. A first step is to recognize the new analytic category of Third World nations that are at a high level of economic development and of education. Without doubt, these nations face a myriad of problems, but they have the considerable advantage for the development of post-secondary education.

Note

1. Stress on non-formal education, on the importance of building up basic literacy and critiques of the role of universities in

development have all contributed to decreasing emphasis on higher education by planners and analysts. The current criticisms of higher education in the industrial nations (including questioning the economic benefits of higher education) combined with declining enrollments in a number of countries have further diminished concern about higher education.

References

Adams, R. N. (ed.). 1969. *Responsibilities of the Foreign Scholar to the Local Scholarly Community.* New York, Education and World Affairs.

Al-Ebraheem, H. A.; Stevens, R. S. 1980. Organization, Management and Academic Problems of an Arab University: The Kuwait University Experience. *Higher Education,* Vol. 9, No. 2, pp. 203–18.

Altbach, P. G. 1977. Servitude of the Mind?: Education, Dependency and Neocolonialism. *Teachers College Record,* Vol. 79, No. 2, pp. 188–204.

_____. 1980. *University Reform: An International Perspective.* Washington, D.C., American Association for Higher Education.

_____. 1981. The University as Center and Periphery. *Teachers College Record,* Vol. 82, No. 4, pp. 601–21.

Ashby, E. 1966. *Universities: British, Indian, African.* Cambridge, Mass., Harvard University Press.

Comparative Education Review. 1972. Vol. 16, No. 2, pp. 229–351. (Special issue on 'University Reform'.)

Dore, R. P. 1976. *The Diploma Disease: Education, Qualification and Development.* Berkeley, University of California Press.

Kaul, J. N. 1974. *Higher Education in India, 1951–1971: Two Decades of Planned Drift.* Simla, India, Indian Institute of Advanced Study.

McConnell, T. R. 1981. Autonomy and Accountability: Some Fundamental Issues. In: P. Altbach and R. Berdahl (eds.), *Higher Education in American Society,* pp. 35–53. Buffalo, N. Y., Prometheus.

Mazrui, A. A. 1975. The African University as a Multinational Corporation: Problems of Penetration and Dependency. *Harvard Educational Review,* Vol. 45, No. 2, pp. 191–210.

Mende, T. 1973. *From Aid to Recolonization: Lessons of a Failure.* New York, Pentheon.

Montefiore, A. (ed.). 1975. *Neutrality and Impartiality: The University and Political*

Noss, R. 1967. *Higher Education and Development in Southeast Asia: Language Policy,* Vol. 3, Part 2. Paris, Unesco and International Association of Universities.

Shils, E. 1972. Metropolis and Province in the Intellectual Community. In: E. Shils (ed.), *The Intellectuals and the Powers and Other Essays,* pp. 355–71. Chicago, Ill., University of Chicago Press.

Shirk, S. 1979. Educational Reform and Political Backlash: Recent Changes in Chinese Educational Policy, *Comparative Education Review,* Vol. 23, No. 2, pp. 183–217.

Spaulding, S.; Flack, M. 1976. *The World's Students in the United States—A Review and Evaluation of Research on Foreign Students.* New York, Praeger.

Spitzberg, I. (ed.). 1980 *Universities and the International Distribution of Knowledge.* New York, Praeger.

Thompson, K.; Fogel, B. 1977. *Higher Education and Social Change.* New York, Praeger. 2 vols.

The Policy Perspective

LADISLAV CERYCH

The development of higher education in the past ten to twenty years has been marked by an exceptionally large number of new policies and reforms,[1] but most of these have resulted in much less change than was originally envisaged. Examples abound in virtually all European countries and elsewhere as well.[2] A large number of the universities founded in Germany in the 1960s—Konstanz, Bochum, and Bielefeld, for example—are now part of the university establishment instead of having become models for the organization, content, and methods of the country's higher education. The nine new universities founded at the same time in the United Kingdom have similarly converged upon traditional forms, procedures, norms, and values. Furthermore, new institutional sectors set up to provide alternatives to traditional higher education, such as the polytechnics in Great Britain, the Norwegian regional colleges, and the French *Instituts universitaires de technologie* (IUTs), either have tended increasingly to resemble the traditional university model or to fall short of their projected size and place in the national system.

At the global level, the situation is much the same. The German *Gesamthochschule* (comprehensive university), once expected to serve as the new general organizing principle for the whole of German higher education, has only partly materialized in two of the eleven *Länder.* Meanwhile, in France, the three goals of the well-known *loi d'orientation* of 1968—multidisciplinary teaching, student participation, and institutional autonomy—have been achieved only to a very limited degree or, some might say, not at all. Policies concerning specific aspects of higher education have not fared much better. New admissions policies designed to widen university access for students from underprivileged social strata have rarely resulted in a significant increase in their proportion of total enrollments, and even less so for those in regular full-degree programs. This applies to eastern European countries, to the relatively radical Swedish 25/5 admissions scheme (later called "25/4"), and, in part, to the British Open University.

These partial achievements or limited outcomes are often explained in a rather simple way: universities are conservative institutions; academics resist change; higher education can develop only gradually; the reform goals were over-ambitious. There is certainly some truth in these statements but, without saying (for the moment) that they are not necessarily true, they do not, in fact, constitute any explanation at all. Why are universities conservative (if they are so) and why does higher education usually change by accretion and only very slowly?

In this paper I attempt to show that policy analysis can provide some meaningful answers to these and similar questions, thereby throwing light on the nature and functioning of higher education. I first discuss the nature of policy analysis and its relations with other social science perspectives, and I then turn to a comparison of a number of case studies of specific reforms which were developed in a major study of policy implementation in European systems of higher education.

The Field of Policy Analysis

Most of the disciplinary views presented in this volume stress the interconnections and the overlap with other disciplines. To some extent, specialists in any one of them might even be justified in thinking that their own discipline underlies, cuts horizontally across, or constitutes a common denominator for the others. This idea applies to policy analysis as much as to history, sociology, economics, and so on, but here an additional problem arises. The content and specific nature of policy sciences are indeed very imprecise, particularly in the way they relate to or differ from political science. In this respect, it is perhaps significant that many languages have no distinct term for "politics" and "policy." In French, for example, the word *politique* means both, as does the German *Politik* or *politika* in most Slavic languages. Moreover, even in English-speaking countries, many of those who pursue policy studies are political scientists by academic background and affiliation.

Yet policy studies or policy sciences are by no means the exclusive domain of political scientists.[3] Since they are primarily concerned with causes, content, and consequences of public policies, and since such policies have or might have almost any dimension—for example, economic, sociological, organizational—any tool or any perspective on social inquiry may be useful or even indispensable. And policy studies may, I suggest, make an important contribution to the understanding of higher education, particularly to the process of its change (or resistance to change). To do so, a relatively recent offspring of policy studies, implementation analysis, has to be taken into consideration and perhaps even emphasized. In concrete terms, such analysis means essentially an assessment of the extent to which policy objectives have been achieved, the reasons explaining their achievement, nonachievement, or distortion of original goals, as well as an assessment of the unintended effects of a given policy.[4]

Above all, implementation analysis is concerned with processes, rather than with the mere measurement of policy impacts, which is the proper concern of policy evaluation. Even if the boundary between implementation and evaluation analysis is often blurred, there is a major difference or emphasis with significant methodological and conceptual implications.

Policy and political sciences have, of course, always been concerned with implementation. In a sense, that is what the field of public administration is about and what philosophers, writers, and scientists from antiquity to modern times have dealt with. Along with the discussion of moral and other principles of government went also the means and conditions for carrying them through. The new interest in implementation analysis and its development into a more or less self-contained field of study, with its own methodology and vocabulary, is a response to at least three main factors. One is a consciousness of the growing complexity of almost any public policy implementation. This is the gist of what may be regarded as the classic starting point of all recent implementation analysis literature, and it is the subject of the book by Pressman and Wildavsky.[5] Second is the realization that implementation processes are essentially dominated by bureaucrats and that conflicts between bureaucrats and local implementers are always influenced by outside forces and clients. Third is the finding (or feeling) that the major cause of program failures may be found in the complexity and politicized nature of implementation processes. Again, the Pressman and Wildavsky classic or, more exactly, its subtitle illustrates this point: "Implementation: How Great Expectations in Washington Are Dashed in Oakland; Or, Why It's Amazing that Federal Programs Work at All, This Being a Saga of the Economic Development Administration as Told by Two Sympathetic Observers Who Seek to Build Morals on a Foundation of Ruined Hopes."[6]

By trying to evaluate the degree of achievement of policy objectives and to explain the frequent gaps between original aims and outcomes, implementation analysis has a twofold function. On one hand it provides information that should be practical for decision makers because it illuminates the factors and forces that favor or inhibit the success of particular policies and reforms. In this sense it constitutes an essential element of organizational learning as well as a tool for formulation of more effective implementation strategies and, if necessary, for reformulation of policy goals.[7]

From a more general theoretical point of view implementation analysis, by identifying factors of achievement and failure,[8] offers a particular insight into the functioning of a specific social subsystem (here, higher education) and into the interrelation among its various components and between them and forces external to the system.

Implementation analysis aims, therefore, both at better comprehension and more effective control. Its connections with other disciplines are obvious; the factors promoting goal achievement and the constraints inhibiting it indeed belong to a multiplicity of areas: economic, sociological, historical, legal, and administrative. Implementation analysis then is in itself an interdisciplinary approach; selecting elements of knowledge and information provided by a variety of fields, it orders or connects them within its own conceptual framework.

A particular and rather complex relation exists between implementation analysis and the stage preceding it, policy formulation. Earlier I pointed out the difficulty of distinguishing between political science and policy studies or sciences. For the purposes of the present paper I emphasize that policy implementation is part of the design and definition of a policy (including the motivations leading to policy formulation), its adoption and its subsequent reformulation, and its conversion into routine practice or its rejection. Whether and to what extent the policy implementation process can be analytically separated from the policy formulation process is a matter for discussion which cannot be pursued here. In any event the close relation between the two has to be kept constantly in mind.

The existence of a particularly close relation between implementation analysis and history should also be stressed. On the one hand, many of the factors in the implementation of a policy are determined by historical development and can probably be fully understood only in this perspective. Attitudes toward central authorities, the status of particular social groups, the interplay between the center and the periphery, the concept of local autonomy—all are more or less inherited from the past. On the other hand, since the implementation of a policy constitutes a process, its analysis automatically poses methodological problems with which history is particularly familiar. The implementation analyst certainly has much to learn from the historian, even if he usually deals with relatively short recent periods.

Two Analytic Questions

Two questions should be raised at this point, the discussion of which will complete the general treatment of policy analysis and implementation. First, is the implementation of policies of higher education fundamentally different from the implementation of any other public policy? Second, what particular contribution can implementation analysis of higher education reforms make to implementation analysis in general?

Any analysis of a particular social subsystem pursued in sufficient depth will reveal unique aspects as well as characteristics held in common with some or all other areas. Thus, while there may be some fundamental similarities to policies in other fields, we may at the same time argue that implementation of higher education reforms poses several special problems. The problems are set primarily by the inordinate complexity of the system: in particular, the large number of relatively autonomous actors and the diffusion of authority throughout the structure and in the various forms or types. Even in a centralized state, higher education as a system or organization is, to use Burton R. Clark's words, "bottom-heavy," more so than other social subsystems and certainly more than lower education levels. Policy implementation then becomes interactive, and implementation analysis becomes a study of the respective interactions. Of course, all this is not unique; a health system, for example, involves considerable multiplicity of actors and authorities, partly independent. But the range of differences and the diffusion of authority are not so wide. In higher education, within one system, there are autonomy-seeking clusters of professionals in law, architecture, education, business administration, physics, sociology, classics, and on and on, as well as in medicine.

In addition, the ambiguity of the goals and functions of higher education complicates policy implementation. Although higher education deals primarily with knowledge, it has been called upon, especially since the 1960s, to assume many new functions which are only indirectly related to its responsibility, as traditionally perceived, for extending and transmitting knowledge. It is supposed now to be an active agent in social equalization, to provide more vocationally oriented training, to serve as a pole for regional development, to cater increasingly to adults, and so on. There is no general consensus regarding these new functions and, if and when they become specific policy objectives, the latter are immediately questioned and are more or less openly contested. Implementation analysis may as its starting point consider policy goals as those formally adopted by an act of parliament or a governmental decree and thus disregard their justification. In that sense, it is neutral and the terms "success" and "failure" may be used in their relative meaning only, that is, in relation to the given goals without any implied judgment as to their desirability or intrinsic merits. The questioning of the goals or their divergent interpretations, however, almost always become an important factor in the implementation process and, as such, have to be taken into account by implementation analysis.

I would therefore argue that the study of higher education can draw as much benefit from policy and implementation analysis as the latter can derive from the study of higher education policies and the way they unfold. If my assumption is correct, policy analysis also provides a basis for an answer to the second question. Implementation analysis in general can probably benefit from the specific case of higher education, in that the latter pushes, almost to an extreme, the evidence of complexity of policy implementation in a situation with a multitude of actors. All these different related points should become clearer when specific recent higher education policies and their implementation are considered.

Comparative Case Studies

Implementation analysis has not often been applied to higher education policies, but several recent books and articles about this topic are directly relevant to it.[9] No less relevant are the numerous works of political scientists and of organizational theorists or sociologists who do not speak explicitly of implementation analysis but who deal extensively with various aspects of "carrying through a policy," that is, with policy implementation.[10]

Implementation analysis was applied specifically to higher education in a series of case studies conducted by the European Institute of Education and Social Policy in Paris.[11] Information and findings from these studies constitute the main empirical basis of the present paper. I investigated the following specific reforms along with their implementation and often refer to them in the course of my discussion:

1. Creation and development of the University of Tromsø in the far north of Norway. This institution was expected to differ in several respects from existing Norwegian universities: it was supposed to play a direct and important role in the economic and social development of its surrounding region and thereby help redress the imbalances between the south and the north; teaching and research were expected to be more interdisciplinary than in traditional universities; new fields of study not existing in other establishments of Norwegian higher education were to be introduced; the proposed system of university government presupposed participation of groups much less represented in traditional universities (students, nonscientific staff, etc.).
2. Creation and development of a network of regional colleges in Norway. These institutions represented a new type of "short-cycle higher education" with vocational courses as well as those leading to further university studies. Moreover, the colleges were expected to be directly relevant to their respective regions and play an important role in continuing adult education.
3. Creation and development of the University of Umea in the north of Sweden. The main objective of this university was similar to that of Tromsø: to help overcome imbalances between the southern and northern parts of the country. Its main contribution however, was to provide higher education opportunities in an area that had none. Teaching and research at this university were also to pay attention to specific regional needs and conditions, but they were not expected to be radically

different from those in existing Swedish universities.

4. The introduction of the 25/5 admission rule in Swedish higher education. This rule implied that individuals twenty-five years or older, with at least five years of occupational experience, should be allowed to enter some of the liberal arts faculties, irrespective of their formal education background. (At a later stage the rule was changed to 25/4 and was applied to the whole system.) Equalization of educational opportunities, bridging the generation gap, and providing new vocational and professional training facilities were among the explicit goals of the scheme.
5. Creation and development of the British Open University. The main goals and features of this institution are well known: admission on a "first come, first served" basis; distance teaching through a combination of correspondence, radio, and television courses; special efforts in curriculum development; respect for established academic standards.
6. Creation and development of the university institutes of technology (*instituts universitaires de technologie*) in France. These institutes, constituting a new type of short-cycle (two years) higher education with vocational orientation, were expected to enroll, within six years of their launching, about a fourth to a third of the entire French student population.
7. Creation and development of the University of Calabria in Cosenza, Italy. This university, like those of Tromsø and Umea in Scandinavia, was expected to play an active role in the economic and social development of its region. Moreover, it was the first Italian university based on a departmental structure, the preferential admission of students of modest social and southern Italian origin, a full-time teaching staff, and a campus arrangement with the majority of students residing on campus.
8. The development of the German *Gesamthochschule* ("comprehensive university"). Originally this concept was envisaged as a model for a new organization of all West German higher education. It aimed at an integration of hitherto separated parts of the system, namely, universities and less prestigious technical colleges; at an equalization of the status of teachers and students in these two sectors; and at curriculum reform emphasizing a close relation between higher education and practical life. Ultimately, only six institutions were established with these formal objectives in two of the eleven German states.
9. The introduction of a "preferential point system" in admissions to universities in Poland. This system aimed at the facilitation of access to Polish higher education for students from workers' and peasants' families, thereby increasing their percentage and representation in total enrollments.

Clearly, the differences among these reforms are considerable: some concern single institutions, others deal with groups of institutions, and still others with the system as a whole either in one of its aspects (e.g., admission) or in a multiplicity of its features. They represent different political, administrative, and historical contexts, and they aim at different policy objectives, from social equalization to regional, economic, and structural goals. But all these differences are precisely of interest. They enable us to look at the implementation process with a more general perspective and thereby to formulate broader, more valid, conclusions than those reached by studying only one country or one policy.

I now consider such conclusions by examining five aspects of higher education policy implementation which resulted from a comparative view of the cases cited above. The discussion of a sixth and more general issue—the problem of change in higher education in the light of implementation analysis—serves as an overall conclusion to my analysis.

The Impact of Goals

Setting aside policies that represent mere legitimation of what exists or of what is expected to happen, most of the recent reforms in European higher education confirm a previously stated point: it is difficult to separate implementation from the process of policy design. Moreover, in many instances, the formulation of objectives has taken place in several stages, with priorities often changing from one stage to the next. For example, although the Swedish 25/5 scheme was initially based on economic considerations, including education as an investment and the demand for qualified manpower, the need to bridge the generation gap later became the prime objective, only to be displaced subsequently by social equalization. Also, the officially stated objectives are frequently ambiguous. Such ambiguity may be deliberate, either because more precise definition would have precluded the agreement of all interested parties (thus lack of precision is the price paid for essential political consensus), or because the legislature preferred to leave the detailed determination of goals to various types of planning or steering committees set up as a first step in implementation.

A single precise goal, however, does not guarantee better implementation. The Polish preferential point system had a clear single aim: to increase the proportion of students from working-class and peasant families in University enrollments. Yet it failed to a large extent.

Then, too, many higher educational reforms incorporated several seemingly conflicting goals. This point is well illustrated by the Norwegian regional colleges set up in 1969, for which two declared aims were regional relevance and the provision of a new type of higher education which would be of shorter duration and more vocationally oriented. Almost simultaneously, other virtually contradictory objectives were also implicitly or explicitly adopted. The regional colleges were supposed to lessen pressure on the universities while providing an education qualifying some students for subsequent university study, and also to respond to national needs, recruiting students and teachers from throughout the country. Unavoidably, the implementation process was strongly influenced by conflicts inherent in this goal structure, as well as by shifts of emphasis among differing and inconsistent aims. Yet conflicting aims were inevitable for the same reason as ambiguity was, in that it would have otherwise been difficult or impossible to reach a consensus on the proposed policy.

Finally, in many instances the implementation of reforms resulted in the achievement of unexpected and unintended goals. The Swedish 25/5 scheme, for instance, did not increase substantially the proportion of regular full-degree students from the lower socioeconomic classes, but it did contribute to increasing the number of students entering universities with a view to taking no more than a single course, thereby imparting to Swedish higher education an extension function of a kind generally associated with British and American universities.

In short, ambiguity and conflict in goals are, in most instances, unavoidable. Thus, also unavoidably, the door is left open to alternative developments in the implementation process, and often it is impossible to speak of a straightforward success or failure of a reform. Of vital importance is the question, "Which goals and whose?" since in view of the multiple objectives generated around every reform, both before and after its formal adoption, what is successful in one respect might be undesirable in another.

Moreover, success and failure obviously depend on expectations. As pointed out by Burton R. Clark, "the higher the expectations, the more likely the judgment of failure."[12] For example, the hopes for the German *Gesamthochschule* were so broad and so high that the outcome was almost bound to be disappointing, even if implementation had been much smoother than it actually was.

The Role of Assumptions and Evaluation

It is surprising how many of the reforms were based on assumptions that simply did not meet any criteria of already existing knowledge. Reforms aiming at social equalization fall into this category. Several of them have merely offered favorable conditions of access to higher education to under-privileged groups, without providing any special support measures. Yet it has been known for many years that merely widening formal access has limited effects and does not, in any event, lead to equality on the output side. Another example is that new types of higher education degrees and new contents of higher education programs do not help graduates obtain employment, for potential employers are not stirred to change their recruitment procedures. Of course, it can almost always be said after the fact that the nonachievement of a particular reform goal is owing to erroneous assumptions and thus to a wrong theory. Clearly, not everything can be foreseen in advance. Constraints emerge which could not have been predicted and individual and group behavior changes, often on nonrational grounds.

In theory, it is always stressed that evaluation should be an integral part of the implementation of reforms. In practice, even when it exists, evaluation is rarely used as a means toward correcting errors, identifying unforeseen constraints, or reformulating implementation strategies or, if necessary, even goals.[13] Evaluation has not been so used even in countries like Sweden, where "evaluation consciousness" is relatively developed. Yet many of the shortcomings and their reasons could have been relatively early and easily identified if the first outcomes of a reform had been analyzed and assessed. The fact that equalization policies primarily benefited the already relatively privileged groups instead of the main target population, that certain incentives were insufficient, that new behavior emerged after socioeconomic conditions had changed, could have been grasped early on and corrective measures possibly taken. The interesting question then becomes: Why was evaluation so little used? Aaron Wildavsky offers a simple answer: "Organizations do not want to rock the boat. . . . resistance to evaluation is part of self-protection. . . . scepticism clashes with dogma in organizations as well as in thought."[14] My analysis of the implementation of many recent reforms in European higher education confirms this interpretation.

Group Support and Resistance

In a sense, we may look at the whole policy implementation process in a perspective that focuses almost exclusively on group actors and on the power they can bring to bear on this process. As put by Burton R. Clark, "Innovations 'fail' because the innovators cannot acquire enough power to protect their new ways. They are allowed to start but unless they attach the interests of various groups to their own, persuading potential opponents at least to be moderate in their opposition, they can be tightly bounded—resocialized or terminated—as others raise their own level of concern, clarify their own self-interests, and increase the bearing of their own weight."[15] This general finding, which draws on Arthur Levine's analysis of the effort of the New York state system to turn the University of Buffalo into "a Berkeley of the East,"[16] is largely confirmed by the different case studies mentioned above. The implementation is affected not only by groups directly concerned by the policy in question, but also by groups in those parts of the higher education system which this policy does not involve. Their perception of it as a potential advantage or threat to their established positions is often decisive in determining the behavior of those who are directly concerned. The misfortunes of the *Gesamthochschule* have been largely due to such relatively external reactions.

Also significant is the role of certain groups situated completely outside the higher education system and, in particular, that of the employers (or potential employers) of graduates produced by new institutions or different educational patterns. The improved image of the French IUTs, and of certain courses at the University of Tromsø, resulted in part from a favorable attitude on the part of employers.

Of interest are also the "compensatory strategies" adopted by groups that feel threatened by a particular reform if, for one reason or another, it apparently cannot be resisted or blocked, like the Polish preferential point system in favor of working-class and peasant children. One of the explanations for the limited increase in the proportion of students from less privileged strata, a few years after the introduction of the scheme, was the special effort made by the children and families of the intelligentsia to overcome the relative disadvantage to which they were exposed. Special courses, private lessons, and similar forms of study became, for many, a means of improving examination marks and thereby compensating for the preferential points awarded to those from working-class and peasant families.

It is trite merely to say that a reform succeeds when there is enough support for it and vice versa. But this truism only poses the question: How should support be mobilized and resistance overcome? Obviously, the answer is, most frequently, by an adequate system of rewards and sanctions. These do not need to be, and often cannot be, financial in nature. Promotion, recognition, and similar rewards might be equally important. It is surprising how often this rather simple principle has been disregarded.

A good example is the goal of interdisciplinary teaching and research pursued by several of the new universities and, in particular, by Tromsø. This goal could almost never be fully implemented because the existing system of academic rewards was based largely on recognition provided by peers in established disciplines, and it so remained. Thus, even those most enthusiastic about an interdisciplinary structure at the outset, in order to safeguard their academic status and their career opportunities, eventually had to moderate their support of the new goal. Conversely, higher education institutions that hoped to develop consultant services for their surrounding regions were in general successful in doing so when such activities generated additional income for the individuals and departments involved.

It has also been noted, in certain instances, that absence of support or even latent opposition does not prevent compliance. Usually this is so when all those concerned believe that the new policy will be implemented anyway, and when they believe that there is a strong political will behind the reform which will make resistance useless. It is for this reason that for a long time there was no open resistance (even by very conservative groups) to the German *Gesamthochschule*. To again use Burton R. Clark's formulation, "potential opponents were persuaded at least to be moderate in their opposition."

In this context the role of leaders or strong personalities committed to the reform should also be mentioned. In general this role, as all implementation literature and common sense or practical experience shows, is crucial.[17] Such individuals participated in most of the reforms concerned with the establishment of new universities, but much less in reforms related to the system as a whole. Usually their role was limited to policy formulation and adoption and to the very early phase of implementation. We might even wonder whether a number of difficulties, distortions, and conflicts that arose later could not have been overcome had real "fixers" been there long enough. Their absence might be explained by a certain climate surrounding European higher education after the early 1970s which did not attract strong personalities.

Environmental Changes

All the reforms mentioned here were adopted in the second half of the 1960s or the early 1970s, during the so-called "golden age of higher education," when new policies were not infrequently fueled by "the spirit of May 1968." However, much of the implementation of the policies took place under considerably different economic, political, and social conditions. The impact of the changed environment was not always detrimental to the achievement of initial goals. Indeed, in some cases, the apparent worsening of a situation has encouraged a policy that, in the years of euphoria, would not have gotten off the ground. For example, the French IUTs gained noticeably in prestige and popularity in the second half of the 1970s when the weakness of the labor market made vocationally oriented higher education more attractive. Similarly, the Swedish 25/5 scheme had the effect of compensating for a decline in traditional enrollments, thereby enabling many university departments to maintain an unchanged course capacity and teaching staff and causing them to look more favorably upon the reform.

Then, too, a lack of financial resources, compared with the larger supply in the 1960s, has not appeared to be a decisive factor in the failure to achieve or implement certain objectives. Similarly, inadequate or totally erroneous forecasts of policy costs have not necessarily inhibited implementation. When, in 1968, the Norwegian parliament decided to create the University of Tromsø, it approved an estimated investment cost for the project of some 200 million Kroner (at constant prices) for the pre-1980 period and, although the real cost has in fact amounted to some 500 million, the enormous overspending has never threatened the university's future.

At the same time, many of the policies I have reviewed were subject to some financial difficulties: the range of courses offered could not be sufficiently enlarged, as in Tromsø; the buildings of a new institution could not be completed according to the agreed schedule, as in Calabria; and the number of classes opened stayed well below the envisaged target, as in the French IUTs.

The most significant effects of a change in the socioeconomic climate seem to have shown up as differences in the priority given to one or another of several objectives in a given policy. Sometimes this choice was deliberate, but more often it resulted from quasi-spontaneous pressures and led to stronger emphasis on more traditional goals, as in the German *Gesamthochschule*, where academic recognition and respectability became more important than curricular innovation. In short, there was no clear direction in which the worsened socioeconomic environment influenced implementation of higher education reforms. In some instances the impact was negative; in others it was not; and in still others it facilitated implementation. Even when it was negative, it was not the decisive factor in a failure of implementation.

Centralized versus Decentralized Control

Can implementation analysis add anything to the vast existing literature on this subject? Viewing comparatively the numerous higher education reforms adopted in Europe in the past twenty years, we certainly cannot say that specific reform goals were better achieved in countries with centralized systems than in those with decentralized ones. But neither can we say the contrary.

In centralized France, the *instituts universitaires de technologie*, created as a new type of short-cycle, vocationally oriented higher education in the middle of the 1960s, got off the ground and achieved several of their original goals, albeit with smaller enrollments than had been anticipated. But so did the regional colleges in more decentralized Norway. The University of Tromsø in Norway seems to be more innovative than the University of Umea in centralized Sweden; but the technical University of Lulea in Sweden differs from established patterns as much as Tromsø does. Central control did not ensure significant progress in the distribution of students by social origin, either in the Polish preferential point scheme or in the Swedish 25/5. But the British Open University, part of a more decentralized system, was, in this respect, much the same. Both centralized and decentralized systems were relatively successful in achieving "regional relevance" objectives, although both have encountered, and have not always overcome, conflicts between these objectives and general national and international norms.

In sum, what counts in implementation processes, and what influences the relative ease or difficulty of implementation, is not just the centralized or decentralized nature of a higher education system, but also the nature of the goals to be implemented along with numerous other factors. A few other examples are worth mentioning here.

One example is the reforms aimed at amalgamating new types and newly created institutions with existing ones. Neither in centralized nor in decentralized systems was this goal ever achieved. Thus, the French IUTs were expected to integrate and to replace the STSs (*sections de techniciens supérieurs*), which were extensions of secondary schools with a strictly vocational orientation but much more specialized than the IUTs. In fact, the STSs grew as rapidly as the IUTs and no amalgamation took place. Almost the same happened in decentralized Norway. The initiators of the regional colleges strongly intended to make them umbrella organizations for all nonuniversity higher education. This objective had to be given up even before the colleges were formally created. Similarly, in Germany, neither the weak control at the federal level nor the much stronger powers of the *Länder* governments allowed the setting up of new institutions (*Gesamthochschulen*) which would integrate existing universities with other higher education establishments.

The *Gesamthochschulen* (GHS) point to another reason that the existence of central control might be unable to push through a particular reform. Even when speaking of centralized systems, we are facing not one but several sources of control and power, not just a ministry of education but also other ministries and authorities that may have different if not conflicting strategies. Thus, in Germany, the key prerequisite of the GHS—an integrated teaching staff—could not be implemented because the status of different categories of teachers as civil servants—their salaries and terms of promotion which were to be unified—was subject to rules established by a special section of the Ministry of the Interior. The policy of this particular ministry remained, for a long time, inconsistent with the GHS policy of the federal and several *Länder* ministries of education.

In brief, centralization of decentralization in itself does not often seem to be a decisive factor in implementation. Linked to other forces, however, it can be of strategic importance in amplifying either favorable circumstances or obstacles. In the case of the German GHS, as long as this reform was backed in the government by a strong political will, at both federal and state levels, all potential and natural opponents of the reform—in particular, the academic community—were ready to yield. As soon as this will disappeared the opponents won the battle. The development of the University of Tromsø in Norway was carried through, in spite of its very high cost and a certain "economic irrationality" in the project, because it corresponded to a strong central political will to establish a better balance between the north and the south of the country.

We may conclude that strong central control facilitates implementation of higher education reforms provided that other conditions are met: the achievement of reform objectives must not depend too heavily upon forces beyond the control of the central authorities; and the political will to pursue the policy must remain strong. But for many objectives of reforms there are forces beyond central control and a political will that is undependable. Then decentralized systems, more attuned to marketlike adjustments, may be equally or more successful. Finally, as put by Burton R. Clark, "the effect of each major form of order upon change will vary over time, facilitating in one period and constraining in another."[18] All forms of control, including the market, are subject to the accumulation of rigidities when they have long dominated a system. Alternative forms are then, for a time, facilitating.

Three Dimensions of Change

Implementation analysis can throw light on the central problems of change in higher education. Can change be only gradual? At what level of organization does change occur most easily? What are the conditions under which policies implying radical departures from existing patterns have a chance of being carried through successfully? In what aspects of higher education—for example, admission, curriculum, teaching methods, internal structures, management—is change most difficult? Such questions may be set within a framework of three dimensions of change which I call depth, breadth, and level. The three aspects are different meanings of the term "scope of change."

Depth of change indicates the degree to which a particular new policy goal implies a departure from existing values and rules of higher education. How congruent or incongruent with traditional patterns is this goal? For example, a policy that changes admission criteria by requiring three instead of two A levels, or further knowledge of foreign languages, implies a change of rather limited depth, whereas a policy postulating that the rule "first come, first served" be applied, irrespective of secondary school qualification, is a major one. We might also use the term "moderate" or "gradual" for the first and "radical" for the second of these policies. Breadth of change refers to the number of areas in which a given policy is expected to introduce more or less profound modifications, as in admissions, teachers' qualifications, or internal structures. Narrow breadth means that one or a very limited number of areas are to be directly affected by the new policy (possibly implying a change of great depth), whereas wide breadth means change in several or many areas. Level of change indicates the target of the reform: the system as a whole, a particular sector or segment of institutions, a single institution, or an institutional subunit. Any reform involves a combination of the three dimensions, and all kinds of combinations occur in practice: these might include a reform of great depth, narrow breadth, and affecting one institution, for example, the British Open University; or a reform that scores high in all three dimensions, such as the French 1968 reform; or the German *Gesamthochschule* policy in its original nationwide formulation.

I now deal briefly with empirical evidence about each of the three dimensions and their impact on the chances of implementation. As for depth of change, it is clear that implementing higher education reforms depends largely on the degree of consistency (congruence) or inconsistency of a given reform with rules and values already prevailing in the system. The strong continuous emphasis by the British Open University on following traditional university standards unquestionably facilitated the acceptance of this institution within the national academic community.

Similarly, the Swedish 25/5 scheme, although considered a radical deviation from established rules outside Sweden, was received by Swedish higher education and society at large without significant resistance because it was perceived as a continuation, if not an additional legitimation, of the country's long tradition of adult education. In Norway, too, the regional colleges were in general received very favorably and, in their development, encountered few problems common to other countries in the creation of nonuniversity higher education institutions. The prestige of such institutions in Norway, in contrast with other countries, was always high.

Conversely, the implementation of new policies that did not refer to a traditional base in their respective national contexts, or were even clearly inconsistent with "the rules of the game" in these contexts, was often extremely difficult if not impossible. The typical example here is the French higher education reform of 1968 which aimed, among other things, at making universities more autonomous in a system accustomed to a high degree of centralization and lacking any tradition of local autonomy. Another example is the German *Gesamthochschule* which aimed at integrating what had been, traditionally, quite distinct types of higher education institutions, the university and the technical college (*Fachhochschule*). The reform materialized to only a limited extent. None of this is surprising: an innovation is more easily carried through when it falls on fertile ground, when it is in tune with the system.

But the congruence argument cannot be pushed too far; congruence does not guarantee effective implementation. The Polish preferential point scheme was definitely not a radical innovation and even less a policy inconsistent with the prevailing rules of the Polish educational system which, since 1945, had pursued the goal of widening access to all forms of education for students of working-class background. Yet the scheme failed almost completely. And the specific contents of reforms, seemingly equally congruent, made a difference. As to the *Gesamthochschule*, policymakers proposed two alternatives in bringing under one roof hitherto separated and different types of German higher education. The alternatives were the integration of these different types (curriculum, staff, student body), or simply closer cooperation between them. The first formula was the one adopted, and that in a limited number of cases; the second alternative was not carried through at all, presumably because it was not considered worthwhile.

Another important limitation of the congruence argument arises from the interconnection between depth and breadth of change. It is not true that policies that postulate a radical departure from existing rules cannot be effectively carried through. Using the evidence of the British Open University, we may argue that such radical departures can be implemented provided that they are limited to one or very few areas of the higher education system and that most of the other prevailing traditions and standards are rigorously respected. Such reforms entail a great depth but a narrow breadth of change. The Open University brought a radical change in admissions conditions ("first come, first served" instead of a minimum of two A levels) and in the delivery system (distance teaching instead of daily student-teacher contact). Most of the other key aspects of the university's functioning, however, corresponded to established patterns, including degree standards and teacher qualifications. The Open University could innovate radically in certain fields by maintaining the status quo in others. In contrast, such broad reforms as the German *Gesamthochschule* or the French 1968 law aimed at radical changes in too many areas at once.

If my conclusion is correct, it calls for a revised formulation of the proposition that higher education can change only incrementally. Policies implying far-reaching changes can be successful if they aim at strictly selective parts of the domain of institutions and operational components.

The third dimension, level of change, has now been well specified in the research literature in two books by John H. Van de Graaff and associates[19] and by Burton R. Clark.[20] These two studies distinguish six levels of authority and decision making: (1) the department or the chair-institute combination; (2) the faculty or other subinstitutional aggregates of the units belonging to the first category; (3) the individual institution (university, college); (4) multicampus or regional groupings of institutions (alternatively, one might speak of sets of institutions of a particular type and academic level, such as all community colleges, *grandes écoles*, etc.); (5) local or regional authorities, essentially the main political subdivisions of a federation (states, *Länder*, etc.); and (6) the national government. To simplify and adapt this typology for my purposes, I refer to two levels only: (1) the individual institution as well as sets of institutions either within a particular geographic unit or nationwide, such as institutions of a particular type and orientation; and (2) the national system as a whole (or a major part of it, such as all French universities).

It is commonly assumed that a reform will succeed more easily if it concerns the institutional level rather than the system as a whole. On the same assumption it is said that a radically new pattern of university education can be developed through a single (preferably newly created) institution or through a limited group of establishments, rather than by changing all the existing ones. This theory seems logical, since the higher the level, the larger the number of implementers concerned. In the terminology of implementation analysis, a larger number of participants means an increasing number of "veto points,"[21] places where persons can block or delay implementation.

Much relatively successful reform in Europe and America has been in line with these assumptions. The Open University is certainly an example, as are, to some extent, the University of Tromsø and the regional colleges in Norway, as well as a number of other newly created or extensively reformed institutions on both sides of the Atlantic.

There are also, however, many examples of the reverse trend, such as the new German and British universities created in the 1960s. All of them have more or less (sometimes completely) yielded to the pressure of the global system to become, eventually, universities like any other. In Arthur Levine's terms, they have been "resocialized" or, at best, "enclaved."[22] A closer look at the implementation process clearly shows how this pressure operates. Members of the university, whether old or new, and particularly its academic staff, are subject to the same promotion rules. They must be loyal not only to their institutions but also to their national academic guilds. Students have to be aware of employment prospects, which are largely determined by the requirements and criteria of the national labor market. Such circumstances constitute a powerful force that makes the development of a completely different institution difficult and sometimes almost impossible, even if it is only a single establishment. In certain centralized countries such as France, this problem has occasionally been used as an argument in favor of a systemwide change and against a mere institutional reform.[23]

There is, therefore, no simple relation between the difficulty of change and the level at which it is envisaged, initiated, and implemented. Much depends on the two other dimensions of change, depth and breadth. An institution that is to be different in all or many of its functioning areas might face even more pressing problems than would the entire system in carrying through an even more radical reform which, however, is limited to a single area.

The relation among level, depth, and breadth of change may serve as a basis for a typology of the main categories of higher education reforms. In a simplified form, such a typology may be represented by a pair of identical two-by-two matrices: the first for policies implying a relatively limited depth of change, that is, those that are relatively congruent with established rules and traditions; and the second for policies requiring a great depth of change, a radical departure from prevailing patterns or criteria.[24]

Each square of the two matrices in the accompanying diagram corresponds to a policy implying change of a particular scope considered in its three dimensions. For example, the development of the Open University would fall in category five; the French 1968 reform, or the German *Gesamthochschule* in its original nationwide conception, in category eight; and the Polish preferential point system, in category two. The numbers are not a score for difficulty in implementing reforms or for

TYPOLOGY OF CHANGE

Policies implying a small depth of change

		Level of change	
		Institution	System
Breadth of change	Narrow	1	2
	Wide	3	4

Policies implying a great depth of change

		Level of change	
		Institution	System
Breadth of change	Narrow	5	6
	Wide	7	8

chances that most of the policy goals will be achieved. But a few important relationships stand out. Reforms in category eight are extremely difficult and often impossible to implement fully. Almost the same is true of reforms in category seven (an institution wanting to be totally, and in too many respects, different, compared with the rest of the system). Surprisingly, policies in the second category, those with too limited a breadth and depth of change, are not necessarily easy to implement, whereas those in category five, such as the Open University, may often be successful.

The scope of change as measured by the 1-to-8 scale of the matrices in the diagram does not correlate closely with the degree of difficulty or the changes of successful implementation and can be easily explained: too many other factors besides the scope of change play a role in the implementation process. Several of them have been discussed under the preceding five subheadings. An additional one is the time dimension of the process: the difficulties of implementation of a particular policy vary, as we have seen, from one period to another. What looks like a failure or a relative failure after the first few years may appear as a success some years later (for example, the French IUTs), or vice versa. This, by itself, is another reason that it is almost pointless to speak of the success or the failure of a particular higher education policy. Reforms are usually a mixture of achieved, partly achieved, and unachieved goals, of intended and unintended effects, and of positive and negative results.

In conclusion, I want to stress again two points. In higher education, the difficulties of policy implementation are exacerbated by the natural complexity and "bottom-heaviness" of the system. Second, we do not explain the dynamics of academic change and, in particular, the limited successes of reforms when we turn to such simple answers as "universities are conservative," "academics resist change," "adequate financial resources are the primary condition of success," and "only gradual and slow change of higher education is possible." Rather, complex systems require varied and complex answers. Toward those answers, it helps to cultivate a policy perspective and to explore the interaction of various dimensions of reform and change.

Bibliography

Argyris, Chris, and Donald A. Schön. *Organizational Learning: A Theory of Action Perspective.* Reading, Mass.: Addison-Wesley, 1978.

Bardach, Eugene. *The Implementation Game.* Cambridge: MIT Press, 1977.

Berman, Paul. "The Study of Macro- and Micro-Implementation. " *Public Policy* 26 (Spring 1978): 172–179.

Bie, K. *Creating a New University: The Establishment and Development of the University of Tromsø.* Oslo: Institute for Studies in Research and Higher Education, 1981.

Cerych, Ladislav, et al. *The German Gesamthochschule.* Paris: Institute of Education, 1981.

Clark, Burton R. *The Higher Education System: Academic Organization in Cross-National Perspective.* Berkeley, Los Angeles, London: University of California Press, 1983.

_____. "Implementation of Higher Education Reforms in the USA: A Comparison with European Experiences." In volume edited by Ladislav Cerych and Paul Sabatier. Forthcoming.

Crozier, Michel. *On Ne Change Pas la Société par Décret.* Paris: Grasset, 1979.

Crozier, Michel, and Erhard Friedberg. *L'Acteur et le Systéme.* Paris: Seuil, 1977.

Elmore, Richard. "Organizational Models of Social Program Implementation." *Public Policy* 26 (Spring 1978):199–216.

Ingram, H. M., and D. E. Mann, eds. *Why Policies Succeed or Fail.* Beverly Hills, Calif.: Sage, 1980.

Kim, L. *Widened Admission to Higher Education in Sweden: The 25/5 Scheme.* Stockholm: National Board of Universities and Colleges, 1982.

Kogan, Maurice. *Educational Policy-Making.* London: Allen and Unwin, 1975.

Kyvik, S. *The Norwegian Regional Colleges.* Oslo: Institute for Studies in Research and Higher Education, 1981.

Lamoure, J. *Les Instituts Universitaires de Technologie en France.* Paris: Institut d'Education, 1981.

Levine, Arthur. *Why Innovation Fails.* Albany: State University of New York Press, 1980.

Majone, Giandomenico, and Aaron Wildavsky. "Implementation as Evolution." In *Policy Studies Review Annual,* 1978, ed. Howard Freeman. Beverly Hills, Calif.: Sage, 1978.

Mayntz, Renate. "Environmental Policy Conflicts." *Policy Analysis* 2 (Fall 1976):577–588.

Mazmanian, Daniel, and Paul Sabatier. *The Conditions of Effective Implementation.* Lexington, Mass.: D.C. Heath, 1980.

Murphy, Jerome. "Title I of ESEA: The Politics of Implementing Federal Educational Reform." *Harvard Educational Review* 41 (1971):35–63.

Premfors, Rune. *The Politics of Higher Education in a Comparative Perspective: France, Sweden, United Kingdom.* Studies in Politics, 15. Stockholm: University of Stockholm, 1980.

Pressman, Jeffrey, and Aaron Wildavsky. *Implementation.* Berkeley, Los Angeles, London: University of California Press, 1973.

Ripley, R. B., and G. A. Franklin. *Bureaucracy and Policy Implementation.* Georgetown, Ontario: Dorsey Press, 1982.

Rodgers, Harrell, and Charles Bullock. *Coercion to Compliance.* Lexington, Mass.: D. C. Heath, 1976.

Van de Graaff, John H., Burton R. Clark, Dorotea Furth, Dietrich Goldschmidt, and Donald F. Wheeler. *Academic Power: Patterns of Authority in Seven National Systems of Higher Education.* New York: Praeger, 1978.

Van Meter, Donald, and Carl Van Horn. "The Policy Implementation Process." *Administration and Society* 6 (Feb. 1975):445–488.

Wildavsky, Aaron. *Speaking Truth to Power.* Boston: Little, Brown, 1979.

Williams, Walter. *The Implementation Perspective: A Guide for Managing Social Service Delivery Programs.* Berkeley, Los Angeles, London: University of California Press, 1980.

Woodley, A. *The Open University of the United Kingdom.* Paris: Institute of Education, 1981.

Notes

1. Conceptually the terms "policy" and "reform" have different meanings but I use them here interchangeably because I assume that every higher education reform implies or reflects a policy (while the reverse is not necessarily true).
2. Although my discussion here centers on European experiences, I believe it has a much broader validity.
3. I am indebted to Rune Premfors for several points made in this section.
4. Among the major works specifically dealing with policy implementation are Bardach, *Implementation Game;* Berman, "Study of Macro- and Micro-Implementation"; Elmore, "Organizational Models of Social Program Implementation"; Majone and Wildavsky, "Implementation as Evolution"; Mayntz, "Environmental Policy Conflicts"; Murphy, "Title I of ESEA"; Pressman and Wildavsky, *Implementation;* Rodgers and Bullock, *Coercion to Compliance;* Mazmanian and Sabatier, *Conditions of Effective Implementation;* Van Meter and Van Horn, "Policy Implementation Process"; Williams, *Implementation Perspective;* Ripley and Franklin, *Bureaucracy and Policy Implementation;* Ingram and Mann, eds., *Why Policies Succeed or Fail.* (The major part of this selective bibliography was prepared by Paul Sabatier.)
5. Pressman and Wildavsky, *Implementation.*
6. Ibid.
7. Using the terms of Argyris and Schön, *Organizational Learning,* one might speak of "double-loop learning," implying the resolutions of incompatible norms not merely by correcting errors in implementation (called "single-loop learning"), but also "by setting new priorities and weighing of norms or by restructuring the norms themselves together with associated strategies and assumptions" (p. 24).
8. We shall see later in this paper that the term "failure" (as well as the term "success") should be used with great caution, if at all.
9. For example, Premfors, *Politics of Higher Education in a Comparative Perspective;* Kogan, *Educational Policy-Making;* Clark, *Higher Education System;* Levine, *Why Innovation Fails.*
10. Of the many works that might be listed, reference is made here to just a few of the more recent ones: Crozier and Friedberg, *L'Acteur et le Système;* Crozier, *On Ne Change Pas la Société Par Décret;* Wildavsky, *Speaking Truth to Power.*
11. Case studies published within the framework of this project are, as of October 1982, Woodley, *Open University of the United Kingdom;* Lamoure, *Instituts Universitaires de Technologie en France;* Kyvik, *Norwegian Regional Colleges;* Bie, *Creating a New University;* Cerych et al., *German Gesamthochschule;* Kim, *Widened Admission to Higher Education in Sweden.* A volume comprising summaries of all the case studies and a comparative analysis of their findings will be published in 1983. It was

prepared and the project as a whole was conducted jointly by Paul Sabatier, University of California, Davis, and myself. Sabatier's extensive knowledge of the literature on policy implementation and his own research and writings in this area helped me greatly in my interpretation of the different findings of the project and in my work on the present paper. He did not, however, have the opportunity to comment on any of its drafts and is, therefore, in no way responsible for my formulations and conclusions.

12. Clark, "Implementation of Higher Education Reforms in the USA."
13. See Argyris and Schön, *Organizational Learning*.
14. Wildavsky, *Speaking Truth to Power*, pp. 5–6.
15. Clark, "Implementation of Higher Education Reforms in the USA."
16. Levine, *Why Innovation Fails.*
17. Eugene Bardach uses the term "fixer," meaning thereby a person who monitors the implementation process, intervenes whenever necessary with authorities and agencies which might block or advance this process, and helps to "iron out" major difficulties (*Implementation Game*).
18. Clark, *Higher Education System*, p. 204.
19. Van de Graaff et al., *Academic Power.*
20. Clark, *Higher Education System.*
21. For a further discussion of the notion of "veto points," i.e., points of decision and clearance necessary for completion of a program, see Pressman and Wildavsky, *Implementation.*
22. Levine, *Why Innovation Fails.*
23. This flexibility, incidentally, calls for a reformulation of the popular assumption that universities change very slowly because their key protagonists, the professors, are conservative and resist change. Many certainly do, but many do not, or at least they do not resist change per se. If an innovation is adopted only at the level of their institution, they may find themselves in a conflictual situation which they often resolve by yielding to the norms of the system, rather than to the originally subscribed-to, or supported, institutional reform.
24. Ideally, of course, a three-dimensional matrix would be preferable. Moreover, none of the three dimensions is in practice dichotomous and at least three-by-three matrices would better correspond to reality. But that configuration would lead to twenty-seven categories instead of eight, a situation that is obviously too complex for the purpose of this discussion.

What Is Changing in Mexican Public Universities in the Face of Recent Policy Initiatives for Higher Education?

ROLLIN KENT

This paper examines the changes that are emerging in Mexican higher education, focusing especially on the shifting nature of government-university relationships and some of the consequences for management and governance at the establishment level. It provides a brief outline of trends in the recent past, discusses the changes that have developed in government policy toward higher education in the 1990s, and explores how the universities are responding. The most important policies are listed and discussed in reference to the following basic issues pertaining to regulatory relationships: (1) diversification/homogenization of higher education institutions; (2) academic roles and values—teaching and research; (3) institutional autonomy; (4) selection and assessment of students; (5) institutional governance; (6) funding; and (7) evaluation. The report also lists the changes in the dominant relationships and values among basic actors in higher education from the 1970s into the 1990s, including how different types or institutional leadership structures and strengths respond to government policy. (Contains 21 references.) (GLR)

1. Introduction

Governmental policy toward higher education in Mexico has gone through important changes over the past four years. During the crisis years of the 1980's the much heard lament was low salaries, restricted governmental funding, and loss of prestige of public universities. Nowadays one hears government officials, university rectors and department heads picking up on the optimistic chant of modernization which stresses raising quality, improving efficiency and above all making education more *relevant* to economic development.

In this paper, I shall look at some of the changes that are emerging in higher education, and I shall focus especially on the shifting nature of government-university relationships and some of its consequences for management and governance at the establishment level. This is a progress report on ongoing research by a group of Mexican sociologists who are monitoring changes in higher education. Rather than a finished product, it is a discussion of some initial findings from several case studies that are currently underway (Kent, Moreno & De Vries 1993; Hernández 1993; Ibarra 1993; Rodríguez 1993; Ruiz 1993). These studies are based on interviews, documentation and institutional statistics, and they are thought of as preparation in the development a more precise framework we need for looking at how academic cultures and relationships change in the face of new governmental policies.

2. A Brief Outline of Trends in the Recent Past

The basic processes at work in the higher education system in Mexico today must be understood against the backdrop of the changes that

This paper was presented at the annual meeting of the Association for the Study of Higher Education held at the Pittsburgh Hilton and Towers, Pittsburgh, Pennsylvania, November 4–7, 1993. This paper was reviewed by ASHE and was judged to be of high quality and of interest to others concerned with the research of higher education. It has therefore been selected to be included in the ERIC collection of ASHE conference papers.

took place over the past two decades. We realize now that many of our fairly serious current problems grew out of rapid, unplanned expansion in the 1970s, when enrollment swelled from 200,000 students in 1970 to about one million in 1985. At present a national average of about 15% of the 20 to 24 year age group is enrolled in higher education, albeit in a context of great regional differences within the country itself. In the prosperous 1970s, when the economy was stoked by high world prices for Mexico's petroleum, numerous public and private institutions were created: in 1970 there were 100 institutions, whereas today there are more than 370 institutions in operation. About 75% of enrollment expansion was absorbed by the public universities, some of which grew to unmanageable proportions and became centers of political conflict. This development affected their public image, undoubtedly contributing to the growth of the private sector in recent years (Kent, 1992; 1993). One important corollary of this growth was the improvised hiring of young academics needed to teach the growing numbers of students enrolled: national figures for academic posts went from under 20,000 in 1970 to about 100,000 in the mid-1980s. Since the postgraduate level was very small at that time, many of the people hired as university teachers lacked high level training. Another crucial element to be considered here is that as university organizations were subjected to extreme pressures of rapid growth and politicization, they mostly reacted with the traditionally unprofessional administrative cultures at their disposal, resulting in top-heavy, inefficient and politically fragmented bureaucratic structures and a low capacity to follow coherent development strategies (Brunner, 1991; Kent, 1990; Schwartzman, 1993).

The crisis years of the 1980s—the so-called *lost decade* in Latin American economic development—brought to the surface some of the contradictions inherent in this process of unregulated expansion. The economic crisis and the government policies aimed at opening the economy and restricting the role of the public sector meant that funding for universities between 1983 and 1989 was severely restricted. Additionally, high inflation in the 1980s whittled away at academic salaries, reducing their real purchasing power by about 40% on the average. Although universities were not as hard hit as other areas of the public sector, which were actually closed down or sold off, this severe retrenchment had drastic effects on institutional and academic morale: whereas some leading scientists and academics left for greener pastures abroad, the majority of Mexican professors were forced into finding additional employment, and several institutions went into downward spirals of factionalist struggle over decreasing resources. This, evidently, did nothing to offset growing criticism of public universities and to stem the increasing flow of students toward private institutions.

Socially and culturally, the 1980s brought other transformations. First, the growth of student demand for higher education has slowed down (from 10% yearly in the 1970s to about 1% yearly since 1986), and it has become more specific, more employment-oriented, and more diversified by social strata. The inertial quality of student demand in the expansive 1970s, when higher education was seen as an *entitlement*, has given way to the sense of education as an *investment*.

Criticism of massive public universities became common in the 1980s, and enrollments in the private sector expanded accordingly, at about 5% annually since the mid-1980s. This growing preference for private institutions, especially on the part of the upper social strata, has resulted in the privatization of the educational trajectories of economic and political elites: leaders in politics and business today have gone basically to private elementary and secondary schools, to elite private universities and from there perhaps to a US graduate school. With some exceptions, public universities have been pushed off center stage of national public life.

3. Changes in Government Policy toward Higher Education in the 1990s

The Salinas administration reached the presidency in 1988 armed with a distinct modernization discourse: continue to diminish import tariffs, reduce government presence in the economy, dismantle traditional corporativist relationships within the ruling party and the state apparatus, develop infrastructure, and increase foreign investment. This government has also focused strongly on education at all levels, both by increasing funding in real terms and also by replacing the traditional *incrementalist* stance in educational finance for a *more selective and competitive* outlook. Thus, perhaps the most important element here is the government's intention to restructure its relationship with the educational system, apparently seeking to move from a *demand-led* to an *expenditure-led* approach.

Many measures have been effected in the higher education sector over the past four years. In order to give an orderly presentation of the most important policies, I shall list them in reference to the following basic issues that pertain to changes in the regulatory relationships between government and higher education institutions (Meek, Goedegebuure, Kivinen and Rinne, 1991; Becher and Kogan, 1992):

a. Diversification/ homogenization of higher education institutions.
b. Academic roles and values: teaching and research.
c. Institutional autonomy.
d. Selection and assessment of students.
e. Institutional governance.
f. Funding.
g. Evaluation.

a. Diversification: The government has made it clear that it considers institutional diversification desirable:

— Eighteen new *Technological Institutes* have been created, some of which offer two year post-secondary training closely linked to regional job markets and in close coordination with local business leaders. The community college experience in the United States seems to have inspired policymakers in this effort.

b. Academic roles and values

— Development of the teaching function is emphasized through the following programs: productivity grants to individual teachers based on evaluation scores from students and peers; curriculum evaluation and restructuring is being emphasized as a result of on site visits by external peer review committees that were set up in 1991; and a teacher retraining program through the promotion of graduate studies is currently being designed.

— Research has received far greater attention than teaching: funding has increased substantially; there is a lot of rhetoric about developing applied research linked to industry (something that neither Mexican scientists nor businessmen are used to); funding criteria have become increasingly selective with a focus on internationally competitive research projects (Alzati, 1991).

c. Institutional autonomy

Since autonomy is a jealously guarded value in public universities and is protected by the constitution, federal policy makers have been careful not to talk about reducing autonomy. But officials have been quick to point out that they have been able to implement radical top-down curricular reforms in the Technological Institutes, which are directly linked to the federal Secretary of Education (Zedillo, 1933), whereas at times they have expressed impatience with the slow response of autonomous universities. In fact, governments at the state level have in some cases adopted an active interventionist posture toward autonomous universities, by pushing the local legislature to change the university statutes even in the face of opposition by professors and students. It would seem then that autonomy is disregarded in certain cases where activist politicians feel strongly about their plans for modernization and where institutional leadership cannot or will not deflect outside intervention.

d. Student selection and assessment

— Discarding the traditional "open-door" admissions policy in most universities, the government has insisted that entrance examinations be applied at all institutions. The College Entrance Examination Board has been hired by several universities to develop these instruments, whereas other institutions have developed their own examinations.

— A series of tests for assessing minimum professional competence in graduates is being studied for certain disciplines and professions (health professions, engineering, and law, for example) (ANUIES 1993).

e. Governance

Policy makers are using selective funding as an incentive for universities to develop more efficient management and strategic decision making systems based on the use of systematic information. Greater public accountability of the use of funds is also being stressed.

f. Funding

— Government money for higher education has increased considerably over the past three years, but the *incrementalist* and *benevolent* funding formula was dropped in the mid-1980s and has been replaced by selective and competitive mechanisms to finance research, innovative programs and individual productivity grants for teachers and researchers (Gago, 1992).

— Additionally, public institutions have been urged to expand their income from non-governmental sources by raising their traditionally nominal student fees, selling services and establishing contracts with local industry (Arredondo, 1992).

g. Evaluation

The government has set up a National Evaluation Commission for Higher Education in order to develop evaluation at the following levels:

— Institutional self-evaluation, which is performed by each establishment according to pre-designed government criteria and is supposed to lead to a mission statement and a development strategy, which in turn is a prerequisite for applying for additional government funds applicable to specific innovations.

— External review of academic programs, which is carried out by several Peer Committees set up by the government. Their mission is to recommend changes to academic departments.

— Individual evaluation of professors and researchers: this is conducted at the department and establishment level and the results are used to administer individual performance grants.

— Evaluation of graduate programs is being performed by the National Council for Science and Technology, a federal agency run by government officials in close consultation with leading scientists. This process is based on performance indicators centered on the research productivity of the department's academics, which are analyzed by peer committees. The results are used to formulate a list of so-called *programs of excellence* which are then eligible for research grants, scholarships and other financial assistance.

4. How Are Universities Responding?

For a higher education system that evolved under a lax regime of political regulation underpinned by a welfare ideology, this series of policies represents a profound change in several respects. They certainly point to a change in the *culture* of the system at the government level. Whether or not cultural changes are actually occurring at the department and the individual operating level of each institution is a question that goes beyond the scope of this paper. Now I would like to point to a number of changes that are emerging in the relationships between establishments and the government and in institutional governance. The following diagram shows a global map of some of these changes.

There are new actors and new values on stage whose interaction with some of the actors and cultures of the previous period is not always smooth. Most active in this new context is the government, which has made it clear what direction it wants higher education to move toward. Power shifts at the national level and decreasing legitimacy of universities in the wake of the 1980s crisis have enabled the government to move toward closer regulation of

Changes in the Dominant Relationships and Values Among Basic Actors in Higher Education

1970s to 1980s	***1990s***
Rectors as coalition chieftains & power-brokers.	*Rectors* as managers, aided by expert staff, interested in stability, competition for funds & public respect.
Unions mobilized for wage raises & influence.	*Leading scientists and academics:* participating in evaluations, funding decisions & development strategies.
Student groups demanding free access & influence.	*Individual students* as clients & investors, interested in jobs.
Political parties mobilized within universities, the only politically liberal zones of an authoritarian political system.	*Businessman & donors:* interested in making decisions & developing projects with universities.
Government as "benevolent" funder & seeker of political stability.	*Federal & state governments:* selective funders & guardians of quality and efficiency.
Association of Rectors as political buffer for resolving major conflicts & as formal vehicle for legitimizing government plans.	*Association of Rectors:* pushing for participation in designing evaluation policies, trying not to lose political influence.
Demand-led expansion: regulation by political relationship and entitlement pressures.	**Expenditure-led & evaluation-led policies: regulation by incentives and demonstration of results.**

the basic variables of the higher education system. The Undersecretary for Higher Education has asserted that the government has abandoned its old role as a mere *funding agency* and wants to operate now as a *guardian of quality* and *relevance* (Gago, 1992). The old focus on growth and political stability have given way to a new interest in efficiency and evaluation of outcomes. This is not strictly a shift from a political to a market form of regulation, since the federal government is still the major source of funds for higher education. But it is a shift in the direction of increasing government concern with *steering* the system and with the use of various specific policy instruments aimed at meeting particular goals.

It is surprising to some observers of the higher education scene that this change in outlook and government strategy has occupied center stage fairly quickly. The emergence of a new set of issues and policies occurred with the government taking the initiative from the beginning of the 1990s and using financial incentives to soften the establishment of a new form of discourse.

From our study, it would seem that rectors have adopted the ideology of modernization partly because it was costly not to do so and partly because the traditional institutional coalitions—who express opposition to this new policy—have lost ground over the recent years. In some cases, this process has endowed the role of rector with newfound powers and forms of influence within his or her own establishment. The figure of *manager* or *entrepreneur* is emerging, as rectors don the clothing of the modernizer. The case studies of four universities mentioned above have shown clearly that institutional leadership has played an important part in the manner in which different universities have responded to the new policies. The institutions being studied[1] have been especially quick to adopt and implement government programs, although each one of them has focussed on different priorities and has followed different routes. The following table shows some of the measures that have been adopted by some universities that stand out as examples of early and—according to the government—"successful implementation" of federal programs. Some of them also exemplify important shifts in institutional leadership and ideology, and all of them have received financial assistance from the government in response to the measures they have carried out. They are by no means the only institutions that

How Different Types of Institutional Leadership Respond to Government Policy

Strong Internal Academic Leadership with Government Backing	*Strong Internal Political Leadership with Government Backing*	*External Coalition of Government & Business Leaders vs. Weak Internal Leadership*
– Smooth transition to new policies – Clear move towards research university; – Pay increases for high performing academics; – Close links with local business; – Participatory evaluation.	– Conflict: successful confrontation with internal coalition; – Rigorous entrance exam to reduce student numbers; – Increase in student fees – Top-down managerial style – Support for research	– Conflict: local government intervenes to restructure university – More power to administrators – Creates a Board of Trustees – Transforms Faculties into Departments – Reduces union prerogatives, defeats student opposition

have experienced this type of changes and are used here only to point to the importance of the role of institutional leadership in policy change. Something else that should be pointed out is that the focus here is on the *most visible* initial products of policy change.

One conclusion, then, is that the type of prevailing institutional leadership plays an important role in the way each university is responding to current policies. Unsurprisingly, initiative by the rectors seems to be an important factor. But different directions are taken depending on various ingredients:

— The existence of an organized internal coalition of union officials, student leaders and university politicians may mean strong opposition to these policies, and they do not go away without a fight. A probable outcome of a successful struggle against such opposition is strong managerialist style of governance with feeble collegial elements.

— The existence of a strong and organized academic community within the establishment will mean pressure to moderate managerialism and to develop new policies along collegial lines.

— The absence of a strong academic and/or political community within the university may (or may not) lead external coalitions of business people and politicians to intervene to restructure the university if it is sufficiently important for them. A managerial style is bound to emerge.

Universities whose rectors take the initiative in adopting government policies meet with a positive response in the government and in the local political and business communities, but they may face internal strife. Thus, it is important to see the higher education system in Mexico as a complex political system whose actors, values and rules of operation are going through important changes. University politics today seems to center more on figures such as rectors, department heads, policy consultants, researchers, businessmen and government officials. Being pushed off to the sidelines are union leaders, student activists, and the *lower clergy* of Mexican academia. In this changing arena, rectors are discovering that the so-called modernization of higher education brings power shifts that enhance their positions. Whether these developments will lead to bettering the quality and the effectiveness of higher education is a question that must be answered by further research on the consequences of these processes for the private domains of the department and the classroom.

References

Alzati, Fausto (1991) "Una política científica y tecnológica" *Examen*, Mexico, Vol. 3, No. 31, Dec., 5–9.

ANUIES (1993), "Propuesta del Cuerpo Consultivo sobre el Examen Nacional Indicativo previo a la Licenciatura y el Examen General de Calidad Profesional", México.

ANUIES (1992), *Anuario Estadístico*, México.

Arredondo, Victor (1992) "La estrategia general de la Comisión Nacional de Evaluación de la

Educación superior: resultados preliminares", S.E.P., *Evaluación, promoción de la calidad y financiamiento de la educacion superior: experiencias en distintos países*, México, 157–170.

Becher, Tony, and Kogan, Maurice (1992) *Process and Structure in Higher Education*, Routledge, 2nd. ed.

Brunner, José Joaquin (1991) *Educación Superior en América Latina: Cambios Y Desafios*, Mexico: Fondo de Cultura Económica.

Fuentes, Olac (1991), "Las cuestiones critícas: una propuesta de agenda", *Universidad Futura*, Vol. 3, No. 8–9, 5–12.

Gago, Antonio (1992) "Ejes de la reforma: calidad y pertinencia," report by the Undersecretary of Higher Education to the Chamber of Deputies, *Universidad Futura*, Vol. 4, No. 10, 14–33.

Hernández, Lorena (1993) "La política de la evaluación institucional: el caso de la Universidad de Guadalajara", Discussion Paper, Centro de Investigación Educativa, Universidad de Guadalajara, Mexico.

Ibarra, Eduardo (ed.) (1993) *La Universidad ante el Espejo de la Excelencia: Enjuegos Organizacionales*, México: Universidad Autónoma Metropolitana—Iztapapalapa.

Kent, Rollin (1993), "Higher Education in Mexico: from Unregulated Expansion to Evaluation", *Higher Education*, vol. 25, No. 1, January: Special Issue on Higher Education in Latin America, 73–84.

Kent, Rollin (1992) "Expansión y diferenciación del sistema de educación superior en México, 1960–1990", Cuaderno de Investigación Educativa, No. 21, Depto. de Investigaciones Educativas, CINVESTAV.

Kent, Rollin (1990) *Modernización Conservadora y Crisis Academica en la UNAM*, México: Ed. Nueva Imagen.

Kent, Rollin, Ricardo Moreno and Wietse de Vries (1993), "The Higher Education System in Mexico: Structures, Growth and Current Policies", Discussion Paper, Centro de Estudios Universitarios, Universidad Autónoma de Puebla, Mexico.

Meek, L., L. Goedegebuure, O. Kivinen & R. Rinne (1991) "Policy change in higher education: Intended and unintended consequences", *Higher Education*, Vol. 21, No. 4, June, 415–60.

Mendoza, Javier (1992) "El proyecto de modernización universitaria: continuidades e innovaciones," *Revista de la Educación Superior*, Vol. XXI, No. 4, 7–40.

Rodríguez, Raúl (1993) "La instrumentación de politicas de educación superior en la Universidad de Sonora", Discussion Paper, Universidad de Sonora, Mexico.

Ruiz, Estela (1993a) "Las universidades tecnológicas en la politica federal", *Universidad Futura*, Vol. 4, No. 11, 28–38.

Ruiz, Estela (1993b) "Las politicas de vinculacion entre universidades e industrias", Discussion Paper, Centro de Investigación y Servicios Educativos, UNAM.

Schwartzman, Simon (1993) "Policies for higher education in Latin America: the context", *Higher Education*, Vol. 25, No. 1, 9–20.

Zedillo, Ernesto (1993), Newspaper interview with the Secretary of Education, *La Jornada*, 12 September.

Note

1. The studies cover the following institutions: the Autonomous Metropolitan University in Mexico City, the University of Puebla, the University of Guadalajara and the University of Sonora. They include two of the largest and one of the leading public universities.

Conceptualizing the Role of Education in the Economy

PETER EASTON AND STEVEN KLEES

Throughout the post–World War II era, and particularly since the sixties, thinking about educational policy and practice has been heavily influenced, if not dominated, by ideas about education's role in the economy. Issues of economic growth, better job opportunities, international competitiveness, education-labor market mismatch, or even fairness in the allocation of jobs, income, and other social rewards all depend critically on how one conceives of relationships between education and the economy. Moreover, if one takes a broad view of what is meant by the term "economy," including in it all organizations that produce goods and services, from the family to the government, then how we think about education and the economy critically influences discussion of major social issues that surround democracy, the environment, the community, and the family, to name just a few.

It is our contention that, despite useful ideas, we have at present no adequate way of conceptualizing the role of education in the economy, none sufficient to deal with the myriad issues suggested above. Worse yet, the view of education-economy linkages that has dominated the discussion of such issues has turned out to be a dead end. It has offered little useful guidance to policy, channeling discussion toward providing bad answers to bad questions.

For the last thirty years in the Western world, in much of the South, and, even, to some extent, in the East, the dominant view of the role of education in the economy has come from a few particular, and rather narrow, interpretations of human capital theory and its underlying framework, neoclassical economics. In this paper we will examine the views of education that come out of these interpretations and explain why we find them to be dead ends or worse yet, ideological biases masked as technical knowledge.

We also include a brief examination of the perspectives on education and the economy developed by other schools of economic thought, both historically and currently, plus a concluding assessment of some of the changes in direction required to "reconceptualize" the role of education in the economy. The critical question is, "What are the alternatives?" and, in conclusion, we explore some initial thoughts about this topic. The field of economics, of course, is not the only place to look for alternative ways to connect education and the economy, and it may not be the best one. In the future we need to pay much more attention to a number of other fields from anthropology to literature to religion, or "even" to education, for illumination on actual *and* desirable education-economy interrelationships.

In what follows, we begin with a brief historical look at the evolution of economic thought, both to give a sense of its range and diversity in the relatively recent past, and to better understand the current dominance of neoclassical theory in the West. Section three focuses on neoclassicism and its embodiment in the economics of education—namely, human capital theory. In section four we turn to a brief assessment of institutional and radical political economy approaches to education and the economy as alternative frameworks for conceptualizing their relationship. We conclude in section five with some thoughts about directions to take in reconceptualizing the education-labor market linkage.

Economic Perspectives on Education: An Historical Overview

Though the rapid development of work on the economics of education in the 1960s has been rather extravagantly termed the "human investment revolution in economic thought," in fact economists since Adam Smith have concerned themselves with education and recognized its investment value. Moreover, economic views of manpower, training, and education issues have varied considerably over the years in tenor and approach. In the eighteenth and nineteenth centuries, this interest was more implicit than explicit—Thurow lists a number of reasons why economists of the period studiously avoided adopting the notion of "human capital"—but questions regarding labor and its training were never very far from the surface. Problems in accounting for the human factor in production were one of the principal factors in the break-up of classical economics, just as they were later to prove the Achilles' heel of neoclassicism. An understanding of the history of economic thought helps greatly to illuminate the stated and unstated differences in economic views of education but is more than can be attempted at any length here. A few notes will nonetheless help to provide a critical backdrop for our discussion of the role of education in the economy.

The discipline of "political economy," as it was originally termed, took shape in the Western world in the late eighteenth and early nineteenth centuries as Europe was emerging from an era of nation-building and State mercantilism and glimpsing the beginnings of the industrial revolution. Commercial wealth had grown considerably since the European conquests in Africa, Asia, and the Americas, and business interests—particularly in England—were chafing under State regulation of commerce and sensing new potentials for expansion and development in the operation of free capital markets. The Classical economists (most prominently Smith, Bentham, Malthus, Ricardo and J. S. Mill) all focused their attention on explaining societal processes of production and distribution and on identifying the factors that contributed to assuring "the wealth of nations." The free operation of markets and the uninhibited movement of capital were principal among those they identified.

As codified by the last in the line, John Stuart Mill, the Classical view of the economy had, however, a number of shortcomings. For one thing, it was entirely static: though concerned at the outset with growth, the theory included no principle to explain advances in technology, industrial development or the evolution of the economic system over time. Furthermore, classical economics remained unable to resolve the quandary of "distributive shares" that had so divided its principal architects: that is, to explain how and why the economy determined the proportion of the profits of production to be attributed to each of the factors involved—labor, capital and land. Yet these were precisely the questions that the history of Western Europe in the nineteenth century was throwing into sharper and sharper relief.

The attempt to deal with such questions—and with the social reality underlying them—split the economics field into opposing schools of thought in the late nineteenth century. At least two tendencies and four main approaches can be identified. On the one hand were those, principally Marxists and proponents of the German Historical school, who maintained the classical focus on production and on the macro-institutional structure of the economy but sought to better describe the historical evolution of economic life and so to devise a dynamic model. On the other hand lay the marginalists and the Austrian economists, who shifted the focus to the micro-level of consumption and exchange and sought to understand the nature of markets and the conditions of their optimal operation. Marginalists devoted themselves to the development of mathematically precise models of market equilibrium; whereas Austrians focused instead on human behavior in markets and the dynamics of entrepreneurial activity. These theoretical trends were at the same time intimately tied to real world events. To a considerable if varying degree, Marxists and German historicists were reacting to perceived excesses of capitalism, and marginalists and Austrians to perceived threats of socialism.

The American Economic Association (AEA), founded in 1886 by disciples of the German Historical School who became known in the United States as "institutionalists," initially reflected much of this tension and debate. Its first president, Richard Ely, oriented the association and the economic profession toward active involvement in the solution of social problems. This sort of partisan commitment, however, was increasingly perceived as threatening by a discipline with scientific pretensions and growing professional ambitions. A new basis for unity on the right was forged at the end of the century by the English economist Alfred Marshall, who blended the mathematical approaches of the marginalists and the cost and production concerns of the classicists into a distinctive method of economic analysis thereafter termed the "neoclassical synthesis." Within a few years of the publication of Marshall's *Principles of Economics* in 1892, disciples of his work, or "neoclassical economists," had taken control of the American Economic Association and occupied key positions in academic and policymaking circles. Neoclassicism has been the dominant economic theory in the United States since that time.

The ascendancy of neoclassicism has not been without its problems, however. The microeconomic "perfect competition" model underlying neoclassical theory offered little help in explaining the negative consequences of capitalism that were increasingly evident or in understanding the macroeconomic shocks—recessions, boom and bust phenomena—that the United States experienced in the early twentieth century. The neoclassical school essentially split into a number of factions over the question of how best to address such issues of "market failure"—in short, how to deal with recognition that truly competitive conditions did not exist in the real world and that capitalist markets were not producing general social welfare. Those on the liberal side favored government intervention to restore competitive conditions or redress socioeconomic inequities, an approach that gave birth to the whole tradition of welfare economics and Keynesian countercyclical fiscal policy. Those on the conservative side—who in effect espoused many of the theses of Austrian economics—condemned government intervention and favored fuller reversion to laissez-faire policies.

It is significant to note that the most recalcitrant domain—both in the capitalist economy and in the discipline of economics—remained labor. The question of how to treat the human factor in production continued to prove as ticklish theoretically as it did for business and industrial practice. In both classical and neoclassical economics, workers were considered standard and uniform inputs to the production process; only their numbers entered into the mathematical formulations of the neoclassicists. However, these assumptions plus the "marginal productivity" theory of wages did not yield a very good explanation of why levels of remuneration in the real world should differ as markedly as they did and no explanation whatsoever of the phenomena of strikes, labor unions, closed and open shops, and so on.

The practical consequence of these theoretical shortcomings of neoclassicism was that institutional economists, with their descriptive, sociological and meliorative bent, moved into the forefront of debate and policy-making about labor and human resources in the United States around World War I, a situation which persisted for most of the first half of the twentieth century. Students of Mitchell and Commons and economists like John Dunlop and J. M. Clark filled positions of importance in American academic and government circles and focused attention on industrial relations, labor unions, wage differences, and a host of structural phenomena in the labor market, with the result that this branch of economics became further and further divorced from the neoclassical mainstream of the discipline.

This anomaly in a sea of increasingly abstract economic thought was effectively brought into the neoclassical fold with the advent of human capital theory, whose advocates believed they had finally solved the analytical problem of treating labor like any other commodity determined by supply and demand. Economists had long admitted, but never formally recognized, that one person's work was not identical to another's, and that "labor" was therefore not an entirely homogeneous factor of production that could be measured in simple hourly units. The idea of varying quantities of "capital" embodied in human beings gave a name to these differences, yielded theories about why they exist, and led to new explanations of a variety of social phenomena in areas as diverse as economic growth, health, migration, education, and training.

In the next section, we look more closely at the current status of human capital theory and of the neoclassical paradigm that underlies it. Here it is important simply to stress two points often overlooked but of major importance to any effort to rethink the role of education in the economy. First, there is in fact a full spectrum of economic perspectives on questions of labor, human resource development, and education. Second, this variety of views did not arise overnight, but is the fruit of a rich history of economic thought—a "history," moreover, of which we are a part and which continues to unfold in sometimes unexpected ways. In the United States and Canada, the relative influence of different schools of thought has changed several times over the last century; and the current state of economics in, for example, Brazil or France is not the same as it is in the North America.

The Current Orthodoxy: Neoclassical Economics and Human Capital Theory

Since the 1960s, neoclassical economics has furnished the dominant paradigm for the economic analysis of education as well as the dominant template for the application of economics to issues of educational research, policy, and planning. In this section, we wish to review briefly the status of the current economic orthodoxy and its embodiment in the field of education: human capital theory.

The development of the notion of human capital in the early sixties provided the medium for applying the neoclassical model to the domain of education and human resource development. It also furnished a lens through which activities that lead to human capital formation could be seen as productive investments, at both individual and societal levels. Human capital theory thus gave neoclassical economists a rationale for involving government in educational investments and some tools for measuring their yield. It is this investment connection between education and the labor market that has dominated thinking about the role of education and the economy over the last thirty years. The dominance is at times so strong that education seems to have become no more than a conceptual appendage to the labor market and is automatically blamed for the recurrently perceived "mismatch" between the two.

The ascendancy of the economic rationale was somewhat moderated in the sixties and seventies by the attention given to issues of fairness and equity. Because of the assumed connection between education, jobs, and earnings, education and training programs were considered potentially effective means for improving the circumstances of the poor. For a while, in the 1970s, there was even a remarkable level of agreement among neoclassical economists that providing more resources to educational programs was an efficient and equitable use of public monies.

The consensus was thin, however, and the model on which it was based proved to have fundamental weaknesses. When you import neoclassical theory into the labor and education field, it should be no surprise to discover that you have also imported most of the paradigm's shortcomings and dissensions. In the following pages, we highlight some of the critical debates within the dominant paradigm over the application of economics to education, and the underlying weaknesses of neoclassical theory that this debate reveals.

Debates Over Orthodoxy

The consensus in the seventies that education could be both an efficient and an equitable social investment was undercut by the long-standing liberal vs. conservative split among neoclassical economists, and it dissolved completely in the eighties as an even more conservative view became predominant. The liberal/conservative disagreement grew sharpest over the role of the government in the economy. The key to understanding the debate lies in understanding how neoclassical economics views the public sector as a whole.

Neoclassical economics provides a very precise theoretical rationale for public sector action: government intervention is justified in cases of "market failure," that is, where the private market proves inefficient, and in instances where desirable social goals—like greater social equity and growth, or lower unemployment and inflation—cannot be achieved by reliance on the private sector. Unfortunately, this theoretical precision becomes quite fuzzy in practice. For example, to the extent that education has effects beyond the individual—on the family, neighbors, community, or nation (effects that neoclassical economists call "externalities")—neoclassical logic indicates that leaving the educational system completely to the private sector would be inefficient. One example often given of externalities associated with education is its ability to contribute to a better functioning democracy by educating thoughtful, active, and responsible citizens. To the extent that this is correct, a neoclassical economist should by rights consider the contribution of education to the functioning of democratic institutions to be just as much a part of education's "social efficiency" as its contribution to the production of goods and services. The only difference is that neoclassical economists believe they can measure the latter, while the former seems impossible to capture quantitatively, at least in the monetary terms that would allow it to be included in rate of return calculations.

Consideration of the wider—though economically relevant—effects of education, or of any social intervention, obviously raises important general questions about the neoclassical analysis of the role of the public sector in the economy. To what extent are such externalities critical to the evaluation of government activities in all forms or education, and in other sectors as well? What does their presence mean the government should do? A similar aura of ambiguity surrounds neoclassicism's analysis of other instances of market failure, and there is an equivalent amount of debate over the desirability of—and means for—attaining other social goals.

This ambiguity has led to considerable divergence in the way liberal and conservative neoclassical economists interpret and operationalize their framework. Liberals tend to see myriad instances of market failure in the real world and a wide range of structural inequities which combine to justify a very strong, active, and interventionist role for government. Conservatives, on the other hand, find many fewer clear-cut cases of market failure, and many fewer instances where government intervention would help to correct such market imperfections. Moreover, they are strengthened in the conviction that less government is better by an equally strong belief that social inequities arise principally from individual differences rather than from environmental and structural causes.

Conservatives and liberals also have tended to differ on *how* the government should intervene in those cases where both camps agree it may need to. At the macroeconomic level, there has been a long-standing debate over fiscal vs. monetary policy, with the liberals favoring government spending policies and the conservatives more indirect banking system controls. At a more microeconomic level, the disagreement has often focused on how specific public sector activities could best achieve efficiency and other goals. In the seventies there were debates between those advocating more centrally controlled, technically-determined strategies to guide government social service provision and those who saw the need for more decentralized, and sometimes participative strategies.

In the domain of education, rivalry and disagreement between the two camps has manifested itself in a variety of ways. Until this past decade, both liberal and conservative neoclassical economists recognized the need for considerable government involvement in education because problems of "market failure" made major private sector provision inefficient in this domain. Moreover, both recognized that government needed to play a role in ensuring the equitable distribution of educational opportunities, since these were seen to underlie a fairer distribution of economic opportunities. Yet differences over the extent of market failure and of equity justifications for government intervention led to very divergent conclusions. Liberals generally affirmed the need for public primary and secondary schooling, as well as a strong government role at the university level. Conservatives believed that the government should be less intrusive in education. In a now classic essay on "The Role of Government in Education," noted economist Milton Friedman argued for voucher schemes for secondary schooling and greatly reduced expenditure of public monies on higher education.

While the conservatives did have some influence, a more or less liberal-dominated economics consensus prevailed throughout the seventies, justifying the expansion and improvement of public education, both in the western and developing worlds, as an appropriate and beneficial societal investment. In the eighties, the coming to power of Ronald Reagan and Margaret Thatcher in the United States and United Kingdom signaled a broad societal shift in both public and professional ideologies (see the Miriam David chapter in this text). In economics, this shift was led by a very conservative faction, the so-called "public choice" school, heirs in part of the Austrian economists. While conservative economists had recognized that market failure justified some, albeit limited, government intervention, the "neoconservatives" generally argued that experience showed "government failure" to be a more severe problem than market failure. That is, even if the market may not always be efficient, government interference inevitably results in worse outcomes than those it is designed to remedy. The conclusion of this strain of argument is that to improve "public choices"—that is, to increase the quantity and quality of options available to the citizenry—government should abandon much of what it does, returning many of these activities to the private sector.

In recent years, public education has been hard hit by a combination of conservative and neoconservative thinking. There has been a strong movement in rich and poor countries alike to reduce the amount of government tax revenues devoted to education and to increase the share of education supplied or managed by the private sector. The World Bank now routinely recommends that Third World countries improve their educational systems through charging "user fees" and increasing privatizations whereas in the seventies, similar problems of educational effectiveness and equity would have led to a call for governmental expansion and improvement of education and an increase in taxes to pay for it. If anything, this current orthodoxy strengthens the narrowest neoclassical view of the connection between education and the economy. Since, in the neoconservative view, education is principally a means for job preparation, and greater social equity is not seen as a major issue, the rationale for government involvement in education is greatly weakened.

Reflections on the Underlying Neoclassical Model

Elsewhere we have critiqued in more detail this currently dominant vision of the role of education in the economy. In theory, conservative neoclassicists do recognize that education plays a variety of roles, and that some of these may be more important to social efficiency than its labor market function; and they admit that this situation could justify greater government effort and spending on behalf of education than is now the case. Yet on ideological grounds, the neoconservatives have changed the major educational policy recommendation put forward by economists from one of government investment to one of general divestment.

Criticism of neoconservative human resource economics does not necessarily imply that the liberal variant is much less problematic, however. There have been repeated attacks on human capital orthodoxy since its inception. Some of the most telling critiques focus on issues and arguments like the following: earnings are a very inadequate measure of the social benefits of education; the framework ignores the very real institutional structures through which unequal power operates; it offers no satisfactory mechanism for understanding and dealing with problems of equity; and it cannot explain such phenomena as persistent discrimination along sex, race, and class lines.

The weaknesses of human capital theory are symptomatic of those of the neoclassical paradigm as a whole. The linchpin assumption that wages are in fact a decent measure of productivity comes directly from the neoclassical model of the economy. Like most of the underlying tenets of neoclassicism, it is true in an ideal world of perfect competition and perfect information where personal preference functions are entirely independent, all factors of production are fully monetized, the payment to each is an accurate expression of its marginal productivity, and all the social consequences or externalities of production are accurately valued on the market. The problem is that such conditions simply do not exist, and the reasons why they do not exist are in fact quite significant: not all factors of production are monetized or monetizable, personal preference schedules are in fact interdependent, myriad externalities and social consequences do not get priced, and the topography of our economy appears fundamentally shaped by institutional realities into a welter of discrete if overlapping markets . . . to name just a few.

In the real world, therefore, wages and other prices bear scant resemblance to the signals of efficiency that neoclassical economists claim they theoretically represent. In fact, within neoclassical economics itself, the "theory of second best" says that one single "imperfection" in an otherwise perfectly competitive economy (for example, just one monopoly) sets off such reverberations and distortions that market prices for goods and services cease to give any indication of social efficiency. Under these conditions, the idea of efficiency itself becomes nonoperational, and cost-benefit calculations lose their claim to social significance.

This quandary is deepened by the impossibility of separating efficiency and equity concerns in the real world. Economists cling to this theoretical distinction because it allows them to play the role of neutral "scientists" in advocating policies that they deem efficient. In practice, the groups that bear the social costs of a program are rarely the same ones that reap the majority of its benefits, and thus the real question is always "efficient for whom?" Elsewhere we have elaborated this critique in more detail. Overall, our point is that the guiding concept of neoclassicism—"social or Pareto efficiency"—breaks down completely once we leave the fantasy world of perfect competition and that it does not offer even partial guidance for resource allocation in the real world.

Another critical problem for neoclassical economists—as well as for researchers from other perspectives and disciplines—is the failure of empirical methods to yield the type of reliable information about causal relations that is essential to cost-effectiveness and cost-benefit calculations. It makes little sense to perform rate of return computations or to compare costs and outcomes unless you can determine the actual effects of an educational program and distinguish them from chance correlations and unrelated events. As argued elsewhere in greater detail, we believe, quite to the contrary of prevailing social science views, that the use of regression analysis methodologies (e.g., path analysis, probit, logit, LISREL, discriminant analysis, etc.) has proven to be a dead end and provides no valid information about causal impacts.

Our rationale is based on theoretical and empirical grounds. On the theoretical side, one can never fulfill the requirements of full and complete model specification, and the effort in the literature using regression simply leads to endless fishing expeditions through alternate specifications and no replication across studies. On the empirical side, the result is interminable debate among social scientists about the impact of any variable on any phenomenon of interest—typified, for example, by the squabbles between human capital theorists who consistently find in their regressions that structural and institutional variables have no effect on individual earnings differences, and their economist and sociologist critics who find on the contrary that they always do.

If causal linkages are impossible to determine by such quantitative means, it does not mean that data are irrelevant, but it does imply that we should adopt a much less positivistic approach to social "science" than economists (among others) have been taking. Perhaps we can not hope to answer questions about, for example, the relative impact on educational outcomes of spending additional funds on teacher training as opposed to textbooks. Perhaps, more generally, we can only rely on cross-tabulation and qualitative data as information, instead of pseudo-scientific techniques that purport to separate the effects of multiple causes. And perhaps this all implies that we must focus much more on the processes for debating our different interpretations of this evidence than on the never-ending search for some mythical scientific truth.

Overall, in its theoretical and technical dimensions, the neoclassical paradigm thus seems to be in a very sorry state. It is saddled on the theoretical side with a very rigid, yet ambiguous conceptual framework that requires a strong injection of faith and ideology in order to yield policy implications and that can be applied in very different and sometimes diametrically opposed ways. On the technical side, it deploys a set of refined mathematical methods that do not work without highly unrealistic assumptions and considerable fudging. These all seem like signs of a degenerative paradigm. Why, then, is the model not supplanted? The most frequent answer from neoclassicists who admit the paradigm's weaknesses is that there are no decent alternatives; and it is to this question that we wish to address ourselves in the following section.

Current Status of Alternative Conceptual Frameworks

Defenders of the current orthodoxy in the economics of education often claim that critics have no alternative to offer, or at least nothing as fully elaborated as neoclassical theory and technique. In this section, we wish to examine briefly the current status of the institutionalist and radical political economist schools of thought and their analysis of the role of education in the economy.

Institutionalist Approaches

Whether marginal or dominant, the institutionalist movement never really disappears from the scene. Since its proponents attach a great deal of importance to the actual phenomena of social change and economic development, for them to recede from policy prominence simply means to get involved in practical issues of human resource planning and research. Examples of institutionalist economists pursuing this path might include Sar Levitan, Georgetown professor and author of numerous studies of training; or Eli Ginzberg, venerable human resource economist who over a fifty year period, from the Depression through the human capital heyday, continued to work and publish on questions of skills formation and the education-labor market linkage, whatever the current conceptual vogue.

Institutionalist economics in general has, however, experienced something of a resurgence over the last thirty years, demonstrated by the founding of the Association for Evolutionary Economics and the creation of the *Journal of Economic Issues* in the 1960s, both currently going strong. In more specific reference to education and its role in the economy, institutionalists have been principally responsible for the development of theories and studies of labor market segmentation and internal labor markets—borne once again from careful attention to the actual contours of the economy—which highlight the barriers to free labor mobility or to the simple productivity determination of wages. At the same time, the institutionalist impulse was a predominant influence in development of the screening critique of human capital theory. Though most of the mainstream response to screening consisted of efforts to sidetrack the debate into limited technical issues amenable to neoclassical treatment, the systematic articulation of alternate explanations for the education-earnings correlation had no small effect on the field. Furthermore, many of the most trenchant sociological analyses of the relation of education to job markets are in effect institutionalist critiques of human capital theory.

Radical Economics Perspectives

Radical political economics (or, equivalently, neomarxist economics)—and analyses of education—also experienced a considerable renaissance starting in the 1960s. *The Review of Radical Political Economy,* established in 1964, and the *Monthly Review,* which preceded it by ten years, are two prominent publications among the numerous journals that view the economy from a radical perspective. Neomarxists have stressed the ways in which educational institutions reproduce existing relations of production and so the degree to which the structure of educational institutions mirrors or corresponds to the fundamental economic structure of society. During the past decade, radical political economists refined their analysis of societal superstructure—including the education system and, more broadly, the State as a whole—to bring to light the class conflicts *within* these institutions and the respect in which all such social agencies are in fact "contested terrain". While there are relatively few radical economists in the United States writing about education, those few have been both prolific and influential; moreover, many researchers from other disciplines operate from, and have made substantial contributions to, a political economy understanding of education. Worldwide there are many more economists working in this alternate arena.

Though there is not space here to go into a detailed examination of institutionalist or neomarxist analyses of education, it is at least evident that these alternative schools of thought are alive and well. The dominant paradigm provides a methodology for the evaluation of education as an investment, and neoclassicists often fault their critics for not proposing improvements on this methodology or new ways of measuring the investment value of education. However, the critics in effect frame the entire question differently. Institutionalists view education as an historically-determined response to an institutionalized and socially-created demand; they tend to investigate the ways in which organized patterns of social behavior shape supply and demand in the labor market, and how they determine the demand for education and the uses to which it is put. Radicals view education as an apparatus for the replication of social relations of production and cultural patterns of hegemony, as well as a source for the contradictions that can produce progressive social change. They examine how these roles are manifested and developed, what determines the direction the educational system will take, and how the patterns of behavior and social status acquired in school fit with, or sometimes contradict, prevailing power relations in society.

Institutionalists and radicals concur in critiquing and debunking as "myth" the neoclassical notion that the market is a naturally occurring and naturally optimizing phenomenon. As institutionalist economist William Dugger recently phrased this general point:

> The market does not just happen. It is . . . a set of instituted social relations, a set of rules determining what things can be exchanged . . . how they can be exchanged, who can exchange them, [and] who will benefit from the exchange . . . . In short, the market is not a result of Adam Smith's natural system of liberty. It is a result of the exercise of power.

"In a market economy," Dugger continues, "the market becomes a powerful enabling myth: The market (not the owner) made management close the plant."

It is clear to us that there is considerable conceptual vitality outside of the neoclassical camp. Yet, despite this vitality and the major deficiencies of the neoclassical model that we have highlighted, there has been relatively little use of alternative frameworks and even little debate. A number of social scientists have argued persuasively that cross-paradigmatic, even adversarial, analysis of policy questions offers the strongest basis for social decision-making. In fact, however, this sort of debate rarely takes place—and is almost totally unknown in the field of economics—because the paradigms in question are not just competing theories, they are also social and political institutions. It is to this "political economy" of educational policy and planning, and to the causes and consequences of paradigm dominance, that we wish now to turn.

The Political Economy of Educational Policy-Making

If the dominant paradigm is as defective as we have portrayed it to be, and if valid alternatives do in fact exist, then why aren't these alternatives more in evidence—or, to put it in the vernacular, if you're so smart, why ain't you rich?

Elements of the answer that we would propose to this question have already appeared in the foregoing pages. As many have argued, a paradigm is not just a conceptual framework. It has a technical and sociopolitical reality as well—that is, it is at the same time a body of technique and a supporting structure of political roles and social entitlements. Such an interpretation gives a clearer meaning to the notion of paradigm "dominance" and a more critical sense of what some of the causes and consequences of that dominance may be. Most particularly, given the capitalist organization of much of the Western world, it is not surprising that the reigning version of economics is one so intricately linked to the support of capitalism.

As a consequence, proponents of the dominant paradigm virtually monopolize access to funds for research and to field contexts for the development and application of methodology. Robert Kuttner has identified the same problem in the field of economics as a whole:

> The economic orthodoxy is reinforced by ideology, by the sociology of the profession, by the politics of who gets published or promoted and whose research gets funded. In the economics profession the free marketplace of ideas is one more market that doesn't work like the model.

In the arena of international educational planning, this phenomenon is clearly demonstrated by the large share of research funds regulated and dispensed by the World Bank and its affiliates. No evil intent or conspiracy to obstruct trade is required here; rather a conscious effort would be—and is—required to avoid such ideological monopoly of resources for research, planning, and policy analysis.

As one further consequence of this dominance, the neoclassical paradigm appears—at least in the eyes of its proponents—to have a virtual monopoly on applicable techniques and its competitors are seen to offer little but carping criticism. At the same time, the position of power that the neoclassical paradigm enjoys seems to incline it toward myopia and even anti-empiricism, in the sense of a lack of interest in "deviant observations" and refractory data. Neoclassical economists are notoriously disinclined to collect first-hand data or to admit the worth of anything qualitative or ethnographic, though their own basic framework is fundamentally microanalytic. Along with this myopia goes a general neglect of field work in favor of mathematical modeling. An analysis of over four hundred articles in the *American Economics Review* from March 1977 to December 1981 revealed only one piece of actual empirical research: a study of utility maximization in pigeons.

In short, the relations of alternate paradigms in economics are far from perfectly competitive. Resources are distributed in such a way that there is a considerable degree of monopoly in the marketplace of research and ideas, considerable "monopsony" in the labor market for academic and policy positions; and the whole field is undergirded by relations of power that have much to do with the general political economy of our epoch. Given what we have learned from Kuhn, and, especially, Feyerabend, about the dynamics of intellectual history and the anatomy of "scientific revolutions," the dominance of a social paradigm, irrespective of its merits, should come as no surprise. What can be done under such circumstances to reconceptualize the role of education in the economy? We now turn to this question in the last section of the paper.

Conclusions: Reconceptualizing the Economy-Education Linkage

How one conceives of relationships between education and the economy is critical to practice. What we have argued here is that, despite the existence of sensible alternatives, there has been a three decade long monopolization of debate and resources by one narrow, and, for the most part, bankrupt perspective. It is not that neoclassical economists have nothing to offer: their notion of tradeoffs and opportunity costs, and their emphasis on the need to consider the costs and benefits to all affected parties, are sensible and important. However, the baggage with which they surround such notions and collect them into one overall, integrated, and measurable idea of societal efficiency remains pure nonsense.

Clearly, this criticism has implications far beyond the education sector. Under capitalism, the "efficiency" of market solutions or of selected government actions has been an ideological bulwark and a criterion used to justify policy. If the notion is empty, current practice distorts social decision-making processes by incorrectly evaluating some alternatives and ignoring others. More broadly, we believe that this situation is part of an increasing self-delusion in our understanding of society and social policy. A technicist, rationalistic view has increasingly dominated policy debate in rich countries and poor, in capitalist countries and socialist, embodied in notions of scientific management in the early part of the nineteenth century and in cost-benefit analysis today. Yet the search for technical answers has been a rigged game: ideology chooses the dominant framework and a supposedly scientific methodology allows us to find almost any answer we choose, all done in such a way that few believe they are cheating.

In our view, there are no clear alternative perspectives that offer the same universal applicability as that (falsely) promised by neoclassical economists. Radical political economy, the most fully developed alternative, provides considerable insight in its analysis of correspondences and contradictions in the relations of education to the broader economy and within the educational system itself, but even in the eyes of its proponents, it furnishes little basis for agreement about educational practice and policy reform, especially in capitalist societies. To a neoclassical economist these radical and institutional approaches are vague and subjective. However, the only reason for the endless profusion of precise neoclassical recommendations is the erroneous belief that neoclassical economists have a technical, efficiency criterion enabling them to choose among alternatives in a manner that optimizes social outcomes. If there is in fact no overriding technical criterion to guide social choice, as implied by a conflict view of the world, then a belief in democratic values necessarily leads one to envisage a messy, participative, negotiation-oriented and collective process of defining, analyzing, and selecting among alternative policy options.

Clearly, therefore, we are confronted with a task of *re*-conceptualizing the role of education in the economy and their reciprocal relationship. At first blush, the task looks daunting and the outlook none too hopeful, given the entrenched nature of neoclassicism outlined in the foregoing section. As Amy has commented concerning the problem of supplanting or modifying the larger philosophical currents of which neoclassicism is a part, "Positivism survives because it limits, in a way that is politically convenient, the kinds of questions that analysis can investigate." From where can genuine renewal be expected to come?

One thing to note is how helpful it can be to look at the question in *comparative and historical perspective.* Economic analysis of social practice is not approached the same way in France or Brazil, in the Soviet Union or India as it is in the anglophone West. Of particular interest are the political economic perspectives being developed in different portions of the world in opposition to the prescriptions of institutions like the World Bank and the International Monetary Fund. Neoclassical economists have paid scant attention to comparative economic thought. In fact, the more dogmatic positivists among them would maintain that there is only one true standard of scientific economics, and such comparisons are therefore by nature irrelevant. But as it becomes evident how highly dependent the operationalization of economic theory is upon the assumptions made—and thus, upon the ideology and general world view informing them—it likewise becomes more and more important to look at alternate specifications of the education-economy linkage. Greater emphasis on the comparative perspective, greater attention to the "naturally occurring" variation in this domain—that is, the divergent models developed and applied by economists from various societies in radically different material and social circumstances—can provide an essential source of new understanding.

Similarly, the historical point of view helps to restore some balance to the picture and to renew confidence that paradigmatic shifts are inevitable sooner or later. It is clear in an historical framework that the evolution of economic thought has been and will continue to be characterized by competing perspectives, and that neoclassicism represents an unstable compromise of a few of these tendencies at one particular period in time. The questions posed by institutionalists and radical economists have not gone away and may again move back toward the top of the social and intellectual agenda. Since neoclassicism is increasingly beleaguered within and without—and for a host of other reasons—the last decade of the millennium may be a time for some profound and widespread changes in economic perspectives. In any case, there are some reasons to be hopeful and to continue working on the nuts and bolts of alternative frameworks.

Elsewhere we have sketched out some initial ideas that we believe suggest directions for the task of reconceptualization. They include the need to challenge neoclassical positions, particularly in their increasingly doctrinaire policy applications; to abandon completely the totem of "efficiency"; to forswear regression analysis and undertake alternate forms of economic research; and to focus research, policy, and planning on debate, not on some mythical technical search for "truth" and "optimality." It is also worthwhile taking a page from the institutionalists by continuing to work on practical educational issues at the local level (city, county, region), because no good concept of education will be developed in isolation from practice. As the environmentalists say (and the peace movement before them), "Think globally, act locally."

A central issue on the conceptual agenda concerns *reviving and rethinking the demand side in the education-labor market linkage,* and so getting beyond the supply-side fixation that has characterized human capital thought to date. We have accepted too long and too passively the notion that the mismatch between education and the labor market is an indictment of schooling to be remedied solely by educational reform or improved educational "efficiency". Certainly, part of the function of education is to make us better workers. But this idea has been embedded in a lot of quasi-religious nonsense about the sanctity of "the market" determining what employment should be, coupled with a belief that if we make education better, jobs will automatically become better.

This latter view is basically an incarnation of what economists call Say's Law, after the early nineteenth century French merchant and man of letters who first proposed the nostrum: supply creates its own demand. Economists have long since rejected Say's Law as an adequate description of market dynamics, and the market for labor is no exception. Yet most human capital thought betrays at its root this same oversimplification. Human capital proponents implicitly assume that the relationship between education and earnings is a causal one—a rate of return to education is based on little else—and that educated workers will automatically get jobs which match (and reveal) their potential productivity. In fact, while the supply of educated labor will surely influence the type of technologies that producers of goods and services use, and, therefore, the amount and nature of jobs created, the demand for labor depends on a host of other interrelated factors that are determined in far from perfectly competitive local, national, and global economies. To believe that by increasing the supply of educated and skilled workers, one automatically insures their employment and the productive utilization of their skills is purely wishful thinking. Worse, it is profoundly irresponsible thinking, since proponents of these views simply abandon to the market the onus of creating a world of plentiful, good jobs.

Such supply-side educational strategies are also fundamentally unworkable. How children survive and succeed through our school systems will depend largely on what they and their families see ahead for themselves, in work and in life. At present, in the United States as in many other countries, the bulk of students and their parents quite accurately perceive a lack of interesting, challenging, and remunerative employment opportunities. Nor, contrary to popular mythology, do jobs seem to be getting better, either in their nature or in their pay. Even in wealthy industrialized nations like the United States, the deskilling and automation of work seems to be increasing. Under such circumstances, there are no strong incentives to study, to learn, or to think, and all the well-intentioned reforms to teach better basic or higher order skills will, at best, have very limited success.

Our point is that we have to work on *both* the supply and demand sides of the educational equation. Leaving the creation of jobs to the competitive marketplace, as much of neoclassical economic ideology argues, is not a solution, but the source of the problem. It has been the nonsensical idea of efficiency that has left the nature of work outside the public policy arena, as a derivative question for the market to determine based on available production technologies and our relative preferences for toothpaste, shoes, health care, and so forth. There is no reason to continue such neglect of one of the most basic features of our social environment.

It is not enough to seek educational policies that can yield better educated people. For such policies to work, we *must* also be thoughtful about social and economic policies that can yield better quality work opportunities. We can no more leave the latter task to economists than we can leave the formation of sensible nuclear power policies to engineers and physicists. Those concerned with making educational policy must also concern themselves with policies that ensure that better education is utilized and rewarded.

Our argument implies a need to reverse the tables on the sort of mindset implicit in the title of this paper itself and of many similar reflections on the economics of education: "Conceptualizing the Role of Education in the Economy." Attention needs to be given as well to the *role of the economy in education*—that is, to the learning consequences of different patterns of social and economic organization, at the micro- as well as at the macro-level. Practicing educators have long been aware that how much and how well people learn, how much they change and grow, is highly dependent on the possibilities for application of new skills in their environment and the potential for mastering new functions and resources with the knowledge acquired. There lies at this juncture a whole field for critical research and experimentation in what might be termed—with tongue only half in cheek—"macro-instructional design," where education (both learning on the job and in school) is the dependent variable and patterns of social and economic organization constitute the independent ones. What are the implications of alternate choices about social organization for the way in which people learn and grow and the way in which schools function?

In the long run, of course, it is no more adequate to say that demand creates its own supply than it is to maintain the reverse. Demand for educated manpower and labor supply arise and interact in complex and institutionally-mediated ways which can only be understood in cross-disciplinary perspective. Social, cultural, and political factors play a critical role in shaping these forces and their interaction in the labor market. The task of reconceptualizing the relationship of education and the economy is thus necessarily an interdisciplinary one.

It is therefore also a task that can only be accomplished if a host of people who have not been considered economists—or have not considered themselves that way—enter into the fray and help put the economics of education on new tracks. This means learning some unaccustomed language and opening debates to some unaccustomed participants. But the game is certainly worth the candle, as the French say. The economics of education is too important to be left to the economists.

Universities and National Development: Issues and Problems in Developing Countries

LAWRENCE J. SAHA

If the relationship between education and national development is complex, the contribution of various levels of education to development, that is, primary, secondary and tertiary, is even more perplexing. Each level has to be seen in the context of the target population relevant to its function, the curriculum, the expectations of its products, the recruitment and training of its teachers, and the costs and funding of its operations. During the past decade, there has been disagreement among planners and researchers about the appropriate priorities for the educational strategies of countries wishing to promote development. The difficulty increases when questions about development are addressed, such as: What kind of development? For whom? For what purpose? How?

This article will not attempt to discuss these questions for all levels of education, but will focus specifically on one, the tertiary level and, to be more precise, on universities. The relationship between universities and national development will be addressed in the context of a multidimensional concept of national development. Although the term "development" is often used with a taken-for-granted meaning (most often as economic development), Fägerlind and Saha (1989) argue that greater precision is needed to isolate the various paths of development, paths which are often contradictory, each with its own determinants and consequences. These three dimensions are the economic, the socio-cultural and the political. Following this distinction, it can be shown that universities play distinct roles for each dimension of national development. Furthermore, as will become clear, it is possible that in given country contexts, it will be impossible for all three dimensions to be pursued simultaneously.

Thus in the following pages we will examine the relevance and contribution of universities for national development for each of the three dimensions. Within each of these dimensions specific issues will be addressed as appropriate—for example, rates of return, employment and unemployment, vocational and academic curricula, equality and ideology.

Universities and Economic Development

In so far as the economic growth model has tended to dominate most research and debate about development, much of the assessment of the contribution of universities to development has been in this context. Thus ultimately the contribution of universities has been evaluated in the context of increases in per capita income, shifts in the base and structure of economic systems (for example, from agricultural to industrial and service-based economies), and rates of return to society and to individuals. Although these indicators of economic growth are generally accepted by all countries, their relevance and character will differ between the developed and less developed countries. They will also differ between regions such as Africa,

Lawrence J. Saha (United States). Reader in the Department of Sociology, the Australian National University, Canberra. Co-author with Ingemar Fägerlind of *Education and National Development: A Comparative Perspective* (2nd ed., 1989), and co-editor with John P. Keeves of *Schooling and Society in Australia: Sociological Perspectives* (1990).

South-East Asia and Latin America (Hallak, 1990).

The disparity between countries in primary, secondary and tertiary enrollments is taken for granted: in all countries, primary enrollments are highest while tertiary enrollments are lowest. Furthermore, these enrollments (at all levels) are lowest for the least developed countries and highest for the most highly developed countries. For example, in 1985 the average enrollments for low-income economies at the primary level was 67 per cent, at secondary level 22 percent and at the tertiary level 5 percent. Conversely, in the industrial market economies, there was 100 percent enrolment at the primary level, 93 percent at the secondary level, and 39 percent at the tertiary level (World Bank, 1988*b*).

The increase in enrollments at all levels from 1965 to 1985 is also revealing (see Table 1). Low-income countries increased primary enrollments by 52 percent, secondary by 144 percent and tertiary by 400 percent. For the industrial market economies, the increases were 0 percent (100 percent primary enrollments had already been reached by 1965), 48 percent and 86 percent, respectively. For countries at all levels of development, the increases at the tertiary level were the highest.

Although it stands to reason that expansion will be the greatest where there is room for it, there are other considerations which are equally relevant. First, in the less developed countries, expansion at the tertiary level has increased rapidly, and well before universal primary and secondary education have been attained. This would suggest that tertiary-level education is both highly valued and much in demand in the less developed countries, and that the rapid expansion might be indicative of attempts to emulate the prestige of universities in the industrial societies. At the same time it has been argued that tertiary education, at least in sub-Saharan Africa, might be over-expanded (World Bank, 1988*a*). One interpretation of this "higher-education paradox" is that the expansion has lowered the quality of output, with the result that there has been an actual increase in the shortage of highly skilled graduates.

TABLE 1
Percentage increase of enrolments by levels of education and of development, 1965–85

Country classification	*Level of Education*		
	Primary	*Secondary*	*Higher*
Low income	52	144	400
Lower middle income	37	163	225
Upper middle income	8	97	128
Industrial	0	48	86

Source: World Bank, 1988b.

A second, and much more important, consequence of rapid growth in the tertiary sector is cost. Of the three levels of education, the unit cost of higher education exceeds by many times the unit cost of primary and secondary education. For example, in 1981 the unit cost of secondary education for African countries was seven times that of primary education, while the unit cost of higher education was fifty-seven times higher (Cocco and Nascimento, 1986, p. 257). In French-speaking Africa the unit cost of universities in 1983 was nine times the cost of a secondary pupil and forty times that of a primary pupil (Diambomba, 1989).

Furthermore, the relative cost of higher education for the less developed countries is higher than for the industrialized countries. In the early 1970s the percent GNP per capita for a unit cost of higher education in less developed countries was 1,405, compared with 55 for the OECD countries (Fägerlind and Saha, 1989).

These relatively high costs of higher education pose serious problems for the less developed countries of the world, particularly during times of diminishing revenue and declining economies. In setting priorities regarding the maintenance of these education systems, one consideration must be the social and individual returns to investment in education for each of these levels.

The individual costs of education include fees, books and, most importantly, foregone earnings. For society the costs include "the costs of teachers and other staff, books, other goods and services such as heating and lighting, and the value of buildings and equipment" (Psacharopoulos and Woodhall, 1985). The benefits to the individual are almost exclusively calculated in terms of higher income as a result of educational attainment, whereas for society the benefits are in terms of the increase in productivity due to education credentials. Although the calculations of rates of return are complex and subject to a number of

TABLE 2
Returns to education for selected countries: rates of return by educational level

Country	*Survey Year*	*Private Returns*			*Social Returns*		
		Primary	*Secondary*	*Higher*	*Primary*	*Secondary*	*Higher*
Ethiopia	1972	35.0	22.8	27.4	20.3	18.7	9.7
Kenya	1971	28.0	33.0	31.0	21.7	19.2	8.8
Nigeria	1966	30.0	14.0	34.0	23.0	12.8	17.0
Mexico	1963	32.0	23.0	29.0	25.0	17.0	23.0
Greece	1977	20.0	6.0	5.5	16.5	5.5	4.5
Yugoslavia	1969	7.6	15.3	2.6	9.3	15.4	2.8
Canada	1961	—[1]	16.3	19.7	—	11.7	14.0
Sweden	1967	—	—	10.3	—	10.5	9.2
United Kingdom	1977	—	11.7	9.6	—	3.6	8.2
United States	1969	—	18.8	15.4	—	10.9	10.9

1. Figures not available.

Source: Psacharopoulos and Woodhall, 1985, pp. 56–7.

assumptions (see Psacharopoulos, 1985), the general patterns appear clear. A selection of rates of individual and social rates of return for the less developed and advanced countries are given in Table 2.

On the basis of these figures, Psacharopoulos and Woodhall (1985, p. 58) conclude that the private rates of return are higher than the social rates of return, that both social and private rates of return are higher for primary education, and that the rate of return is higher in the developing countries than the developed countries. Furthermore, in the developing countries the social rates of return to higher education are lower than the returns to primary and secondary education (27, 16 and 13 percent, respectively).

These figures clearly indicate that the social rates of return to education are the lowest for the most expensive level of education, at least for the developing countries. Therefore, at least in terms of economic development, it would appear that universities and other forms of higher education should have the lowest priority for educational planning and expansion. Furthermore, because the private rates of return for higher education are greater than the returns to society, the financing of higher education becomes problematic. For example, why should a government subsidize universities and other forms of higher education when the main beneficiaries are the individuals and not the rest of society? This is precisely why recent policy recommendations have argued that the consumers of higher education should be the ones who pay rather than the government.

The consequences of reverting to user-pays or cost-recovery policies are not completely known, and in any event are highly complex. For example, would universities and other forms of higher education be underfunded (and under-invested)? Would the demand for universities decline? Would universities become accessible only to the wealthy and the élite?

Ultimately, these questions bear directly on issues of equality and efficiency. If governments continue to fund universities at a level needed to maintain quality and meet the social demand, will the main beneficiaries be those who are already advantaged, or will those from less privileged backgrounds also gain access? Although the wealthy usually choose to send their children to private primary and secondary schools (Schiefelbein, 1983), this is less likely to be the case for universities, even if private universities were available alternatives, which in many countries they are not. As Diambomba (1989) observes, entry to universities, in Africa at least, has served only to produce graduates who later receive high salaries, therefore not only reproducing privilege in society, but also imposing extremely high costs on society as a whole.

Although a number of mechanisms have been suggested to equalize opportunities for university and higher education attendance (for example, vouchers and loan systems), none that would equitably transfer the high costs of universities to the user has been adopted.

Efficiency and National Development

Carnoy et al. (1982) note that one explanation for the apparent decline in relative spending per student in higher education has been economies of scale and the ability to increase enrollments at less cost per student. For those countries that have reduced their costs per student, increases in enrollments have been possible. Although the reduction in government expenditure on universities and higher education might be seen as more equitable because the user and main beneficiaries carry most of the cost, the "privatization" of universities may turn out to be inefficient. In this respect efficiency is evaluated in terms of the provision and delivery of higher education in those areas, in those fields, and for a wide range of able students who are seen as beneficial for society as a whole. A privatized university system is more likely to respond to market forces rather than the benefit of society (unless the two are defined as the same). This could mean that universities will be found mainly in urban areas, in pleasing climates, and will recruit from the affluent and able students (Schiefelbein, 1983, p. 15).

Diambomba (1989) suggests that the key factors for the inefficiency of higher education in Africa have been the inadequate links between universities and job markets, the imbalance between enrollments in specific disciplines, and finally the lack of appropriate training for the skills needed in the labour market. In other words, by following too closely the demands of students, the African universities have not produced the kinds of graduates needed by society. In particular, the aspirations of university graduates are not only inordinately high, a pattern consistent with findings related to the education systems in less developed countries as a whole (Saha, 1991), but graduates' attitudes toward work make them unable to seek out, or take on other kinds of occupation, such as entrepreneurial activities.

Overall, then, because of the high cost of universities, their inequity and inefficiency, and low rate of return compared with primary- and secondary-level education, it could be said that higher education in general and universities in particular are obstacles rather than agents for economic development. Unless universities and other forms of higher education can be made less costly to society (as compared with costs to individuals), and unless they can be better integrated to the needs of their countries, at the risk of becoming more marginal to the international university community, and unless the social rate of return can be increased through a combination of reduced costs and cost-recovery mechanisms, then universities in developing countries will have a lower priority in educational planning policies.

As stated at the outset, economic development is only one dimension according to which we can assess issues related to universities and national development. While economic considerations are certainly essential, particularly in the context of diminishing economic resources, there are other dimensions which may be less tangible and less amenable to quantitative analysis, but nevertheless provide alternative bases for the evaluation of the contribution of universities to the national development of society. One of these is the social and cultural dimension.

Universities and Social Aspects of National Development

Although it would be erroneous to suggest that concerns with economic aspects of development are motivated only by investment in human capital considerations, it has been said that since Schultz's 1960 address there has occurred a "human investment revolution in economic thought" (Sobel, 1978). Yet a preoccupation with economic development runs the risk of overlooking and neglecting other important dimensions in the development process. Furthermore, there are limits to the economic development perspective with respect to education (Klees, 1986), and it would seem that this is particularly true with respect to universities.

Therefore, following the three dimensions outlined above, it is appropriate to consider the extent to which universities are related to the social and cultural development of a society, and thus to national development and nation-building. In other words, the contribution of universities to national development must be evaluated according to criteria in addition to cost-benefits, rates of return or increases in productivity, all of which regard education as a form of investment in human capital.

A focus on higher education and the social and cultural dimensions of national development include, first, an examination of the modernizing effects of universities, that is, changes in values, attitudes and life-styles. Second, we will examine the extent to which universities in developing countries represent the interests of their own country, or conversely represent colonial or international interests, which are mostly Western in tradition.

Universities, Values, Attitudes and Life-styles

One of the best documented research findings is that, compared with those with no higher education, persons who have attended some form of higher education tend to be less traditional, less family-oriented, more secular and more change-oriented in attitudes, values and behaviour. Although it is debated whether or not attendance at university "causes" these modernizing effects, or whether a self-selection is the cause, the association is nevertheless clear.

The modernizing impact of universities on students, in some respects, is nothing more than an extension of the effects of education generally. Higher education in general, and universities in particular, exercise impacts on society as well as on individuals. With respect to society, the impact affects the mobilization and the use of human resources, and also the way that society is stratified (Bergendal, 1985). Although the mobilization of human resources is more closely linked to questions of economic development and work productivity, there is also an impact on the values, attitudes and life-styles of individuals in society.

Because those persons who attend universities are more likely to come from higher-status and higher-income family backgrounds, the graduates of universities are more likely to attain social and occupational levels comparable to their origins. To this extent, universities serve to reproduce social structures, not only in the sense that the occupational and income distribution in a given society is likely to remain the same, but because the inequalities will be inherited from one generation to the next. However, this effect of universities is likely to be greater in countries where a larger proportion of an age cohort, such as 25 or 30 percent, attends university, as compared with countries where only 5 percent do (Bergendal, 1985). Thus this particular impact is likely to be greater in Western advanced countries rather than the developing countries, which have small proportions of age cohorts attending university.

A further way that universities have an effect on values, attitudes and life-styles is through the inculcation of a body of legitimate knowledge to students. The cognitive impact of university attendance on students has been well documented; students who take courses in certain subjects, at least in a factual sense, know more about those subjects compared with those who have not taken them (Dahlgren, 1985, p. 2224). However, the long-term effects of these cognitive gains suggests that over time, the deterioration of this factual knowledge is 'dramatic'.

An additional problem with respect to the acquisition of knowledge by university students is the question of what knowledge is learned. Although there has been considerable concern about the legitimation of knowledge by school and university curricula in all societies, both developed and the less developed, the legitimation of knowledge poses more serious issues for the developing countries.

Much of what is valued and taught in the universities of developing countries is imported from the developed countries. This is particularly the case with science and technological knowledge, 95 percent of which is produced in the industrial countries (Ahmed, 1985). A major difficulty of most developing countries is that while science and technological knowledge is seen as important for solving a country's problems, such as poverty, disease and illiteracy, its importation from the industrial countries poses difficulties of adaptation and use. The reason is that this knowledge is not neutral but Western in value-orientation and application. As Ahmed (1985) notes, the Western version of science and technology has been largely irrelevant for solving the problems of developing countries, and Third World universities that use books, curricula and materials from the industrial countries succeed only in producing graduates suited for employment in those industrial countries.

The type of inappropriate science and technology education in developing countries results in experts who do not understand, do not appreciate or are not committed to the solution of problems in their own countries. Because they look to scientists and technologists in the developed countries as their reference group, they choose inappropriate research topics, publish in overseas journals, and where possible, take higher paid and possibly more prestigious jobs overseas. Their own countries lose the very talent that it has inappropriately educated and trained. Ahmed (1985, p. 4476) argues that universities in developing countries can counter this tendency by introducing courses 'where the learner is engaged in tasks of creative and divergent thinking as well as in constructive actions to implement scientific and technological ideas in the surrounding society'. Research opportunities and facilities in the universities of developing countries must be improved, and research productivity rewarded. Only then will universities in developing countries produce graduates who are committed to the solution of their own countries' problems and not join the brain drain which has been so characteristic of many graduates of Third World universities.

Altbach (1990) develops these same observations further, and perhaps more optimistically, in his analysis of universities and scientific development in four countries: Malaysia, Singapore, Republic of Korea and Taiwan. Because science represents an 'international' knowledge system, Altbach shows how the dominance of English and the frequency and prestige of overseas university training and degrees serve as important links between Third World scientists and 'mainstream' science in the industrialized world. There are both advantages and disadvantages in these pressures on the universities and scientists in the developing countries to emulate and keep up with the mainstream. Nevertheless, with respect to the four countries under consideration, a sufficiently indigenous scientific base was developed so that science and technology as taught and researched in local universities have made important contributions to the national development of these four countries.

How did this indigenous scientific base come about? First, by sacrificing the desire to have the national language dominate throughout the education system and in science teaching and research, these countries to a greater or lesser extent allowed English to dominate. Thus the commitment to the international scientific community has meant the development of a strong international scientific community, but at the cost of furthering the decline in the importance of indigenous languages and cultures. As Altbach notes, Singapore has taken the most extreme commitment to the internationalization of local science by using English throughout the educational and professional scientific community. On the other hand, while supporting an indigenous scientific community, the Republic of Korea nevertheless has used English as the medium for the most advanced work. In other words, although population size and the entrenchment of local and national cultures make possible a commitment to an indigenous science, the most advanced scientific teaching and research is invariably done in English. This is a hard fact that cannot be ignored in decisions about science and technology teaching and research in the universities of the developing countries.

A further issue in this context concerns both the proportion of academics who have received their training in overseas universities in the industrialized countries, and also the number who migrate to the industrialized countries to pursue their professional careers, that is, the brain drain. Although the brain drain from the developing to the developed countries is often interpreted in a negative way, Altbach takes a more optimistic perspective and identifies several dimensions whereby the process may in fact be beneficial for the home country. For example, many emigrants do maintain contact with their home country and serve as a source of contact for indigenous scientists. Furthermore, many of those who have allegedly migrated, do in fact return to make an important contribution to their home country.

The brain drain, however, should not be seen as a concern only for the developing countries. There is considerable movement between universities in all countries of the world, both developing and developed. The academic profession is, more than any other, an international profession. Apart from political and language considerations, it is often thought that academics should be free to pursue their careers in whatever locale they think appropriate and possible. Thus the brain drain occurs between the developed countries and between the developed and the developing countries. Although the presence of large numbers of expatriate academics are seen as detrimental to Third World universities, the pattern exists in some of the countries of the developed world as well. For example, a study of Australian universities between 1961 and 1974 found that a steady rate of about 40 percent of academics were appointed from overseas, although about half of them were returning Australians (Saha and Klovdahl, 1979). Similar patterns occurred in Canada during the same period. Thus the presence of expatriate academics, and the brain drain itself, are not phenomena unique to the developing countries. Nevertheless the departure of trained academics from the developing countries to the developed represents a loss of human resources which could impede the maintenance of a relevant local university system and the attainment of national development objectives.

Aspirations and Expectations

It has been argued that the process of modernization has brought about an individualistic orientation as compared with the collectivist orientation commonly found in traditional cultures. In so far as universities represent an end point in the educational process, they are also responsible for modernizing and individualizing the orientations of students such that individual ambitions take priority over collective ones. There is considerable empirical evidence to support the notion that higher levels of educational attainment in the less developed countries result in inordinately high levels of both educational and occupational aspirations and expectations. For example, Biraimah (1987, p. 575) found in her study of 500 students at the University of Ife, Nigeria, that 57 per cent of the males and 33 per cent of the females expected to obtain doctorates, expectations which she regarded as 'inflated and unrealistic.'

This tendency, which has been observed in many Third World countries, has been even more dramatically shown in an analysis of the study of science knowledge in eighteen countries conducted by the International Association for the Study of Academic Achievement (IEA). Using a pooled sample from all eighteen countries, Saha (1991) found an inverse relationship between the level of socio-economic development of country and the level of educational and occupational aspirations of students. In other words, with home background and science knowledge controlled, students from the less developed countries had higher levels of educational and occupational aspirations than those from the developed countries.

There are a number of persuasive explanations for this pattern, for example the 'revolution of rising expectations' or the existence of strong links between educational credentials and occupational positions. Nevertheless the implications for universities in the developing countries, as agents for the promotion of national development, is important. In so far as inflated and blocked ambitions can be a source of frustration, political discontent and emigration (see Saha, 1991), the contribution of universities to national development in any country, but particularly the developing countries, has to be seen as problematic. Whether the solution lies in the dampening of inflated ambitions, the tolerance of the negative consequences, or the conscious loosening of the links between educational credentials and occupations, is a matter for educational and political policy-makers to consider.

Universities and National Political Development

One of the neglected areas of research on education generally has been its relationship to the political development of a country. By political development, Coleman (1965) means the institutionalization of political integration and participation. To the extent that an education system produces citizens who are politically aware, and who have a strong sense of national identity, and who are interested and participate in the political processes of their country, education can be said to contribute to its political development.

The processes of political integration and participation can take many forms, ranging from saluting the flag to voting, from a psychological sense of 'we-ness' to reading newspapers. From the point of view of education, however, these processes of integration and participation are reflected in the tasks of political socialization, the training of political élites and the promotion of a national political consciousness (Fägerlind and Saha, 1989).

Although universities clearly contribute to these processes of political development, with the exception of student political activism, little research attention has been directed to their unique political impact. This may in part be due to the smaller proportions of students in universities in the developing countries. However the role of universities in developing countries for political development, in many respects, is unique and crucial for a number of reasons.

First, the political systems in many developing countries are fragile and often not well established. Universities, because they expose students to a wider range of ideas and knowledge, are often seen as potential threats to the official political ideology of the government. The potential for university-based political activity is reflected in the frequency with which universities are closed by governments when their political security is threatened. It takes a secure regime to tolerate the articulate and sophisticated levels of criticism which often emanate from universities.

Because of the small proportions of the population enrolled in Third World universities, and the way that they are selected for entry, the students are already by definition members of an élite. Often they become members of a political élite as well, but it can happen that the university-educated élite can clash with the traditional élite, as in Papua New Guinea (Latukefu, 1988), resulting in tensions and conflict.

Therefore, rather than promote political integration, universities in some Third World countries may appear to threaten it. Third World universities, particularly those removed and detached from the indigenous culture of their societies, can therefore be divisive. However, it is important to keep in mind that in the case of totalitarian regimes, the role of dissent played by universities and their students may represent a contribution to national political development, if the dissent results in a move towards a more democratic and politically stable government.

Finally, the contribution of universities to the development of national political consciousness in Third World countries is equally problematic. On the one hand universities might be expected to inculcate political consciousness simply as an extension of political socialization generally. However, if universities in developing countries represent cultural outposts of the industrial societies, then it could happen that the opposite effect might occur. Universities would, in these circumstances, produce graduates whose orientations and political loyalties lie outside their own countries. The brain drain of graduates becomes, in part, the result of a displaced national political consciousness.

Thus the contribution of universities to national political development is problematic for all countries, but particularly for the developing countries. The latters' universities, by trying to emulate and compete with universities in the industrialized countries often become out of step with their own culture and insensitive to their own society's needs. In these circumstances the contribution to political development may be counter-productive. Furthermore, because many universities adopt a critical stance toward their own societies, conflicts occur between universities and governments, particularly when those governments are totalitarian, insecure and intolerant of dissent. This political dimension of universities with respect to national development is clearly one of the most sensitive, problematic and perhaps the most important of the three dimensions considered in this article.

The relationship between universities and the national development of societies is multidimensional and complex. However, irrespective of which dimension of national development one considers, the ambivalence of universities stems largely from the fact that in structure and history, they are both international and national institutions. Universities and their members have their feet in two worlds—that of their own country and that of the international university community. This dual membership does not pose the same problems for the universities of the industrial societies as it does for the universities of developing countries. There is greater divergence between the two in the developing-country context, and the contribution of these universities to the national development of their own countries must be balanced by their simultaneous participation in an international university community. Herein lies the major source of the issues and problems which they must continuously confront.

References

Ahmed, R. 1985. Scientific and Technological Education in Developing Countries. In: T. Husén and T. N. Postlethwaite (eds.), *The International Encyclopedia of Education*, Vol. 8. Oxford, Pergamon Press.

Altbach, P. G. 1990. Higher Education and Scientific Development. *New Education*, Vol. XII, No. 1.

Bergendal, G. 1985. Higher Education: Impact on Society. In: T. Husén and T. N. Postlethwaite (eds.), *The International Encyclopedia of Education*, Vol. 4, Oxford, Pergamon Press.

Biraimah, K. L. 1987. Class, Gender and Life Chances: A Nigerian University Case Study. *Comparative Education Review,* Vol. 31, No. 4.

Carnoy, M., Levin, H., Nugent, R., Sumra, S., Torres, C., Unsiker, J. 1982. The Political Economy of Financing Education in Developing Countries. *Financing Educational Development*. Ottawa, International Development Research Council.

Cocco, I., Nascimento, G. 1986. Trends in Public Expenditure on Education, 1975–83. *Prospects*, Vol. XVI, No. 2, pp. 253–8.

Coleman, J. S. 1965. *Education and Political Development*. Princeton, N.J., Princeton University Press.

Dahlgren, L. O. 1985. Higher Education: Impact on Students. In: T. Husén and T. N. Postlethwaite (eds.), *The International Encyclopedia of Education*, Vol. 4, Oxford, Pergamon Press.

Diambomba, M. 1989. Universities and Development in Africa: Problems and Challenges for Planning. In: F. Caillods (ed.), *The Prospects for Educational Planning*. Paris, UNESCO/International Institute for Educational Planning.

Fägerlind, I., Saha, L. J. 1989. *Education and National Development: A Comparative Perspective*. 2nd ed. Oxford, Pergamon Press.

Hallak, J. 1990. *Investing in the Future*. Paris, UNESCO/ International Institute for Educational Planning.

Klees, S. 1986. Planning and Policy Analysis in Education: What Can Economics Tell Us? *Comparative Education Review*, Vol. 28, No. 3.

Latukefu, S. 1988. The Modern Elite in Papua New Guinea. In: M. Bray and P. Smith (eds.), *Education and Social Stratification in Papua New Guinea*. Melbourne, Longman Cheshire.

Psacharopoulos, G. 1985. Cost-Benefit Analysis in Education. In: T. Husén and T. N. Postlethwaite. *The International Encyclopedia of Education*, Vol. 2, Oxford, Pergamon Press.

Psacharopoulos, G., Woodhall, M. 1985. *Education for Development: An Analysis of Investment Choices*. New York, Oxford University Press.

Saha, L. J. 1991. The Effects of Socio-Economic Development on Student Academic Performance and Life Plans: A Cross-National Analysis. (Unpublished MS.)

Saha, L. J., Klovdahl, A. S. 1979. International Networks and Flows of Academic Talent: Overseas Recruitment in Australian Universities. *Higher Education*, Vol. 8.

Schiefelbein, E. 1983. *Educational Financing in Developing Countries*. Ottawa, International Development Research Centre.

Sobel, I. 1978. The Human Capital Revolution in Economic Development: Its Current History and Status. *Comparative Education Review*, Vol. 22, No. 2.

World Bank, 1988*a*. *Education in Sub-Sahara Africa: Policies for Adjustment, Revitalization and Expansion*. Washington, D.C., World Bank.

____. 1988*b*. *World Development Report 1988*. Oxford, Oxford University Press.

The Privatization of Higher Education

JANDHYALA B. G. TILAK

The Context

Privatization of higher education is not a new phenomenon in the world economy. In many countries of the world, the private sector has come to play either a limited or predominant role in higher education. In some countries, the origin of privatization can be traced back a few centuries. But privatization has assumed greater significance as a policy strategy of the development of education in recent times, essentially, but not wholly, due to stagnating—and in some countries declining—public budgets for education, on the one hand, and on the other, increasing social demand for higher education, manifested in slogans like 'higher education for all' (Roderick and Stephens, 1979).

There has been remarkable growth in privatization during the last two to three decades in several countries of the world, as shown in Table 1. The number of private colleges and universities has increased, and enrollments in private institutions increased at a much faster rate than in public institutions. Enrollments in private institutions increased by several times in many countries—for example, in Colombia, by 1.7 times the rate of growth of public education and 2.03 times in Peru from the mid-1960s to the mid-1970s (Brodersohn, 1978, p. 176). In a good number of countries the share of enrollments in private education and the number of private institutions as a proportion of the total

TABLE 1
Privatization Trends in Selected Countries (percentage of enrollments in private higher education)

Country	*Earlier Year*		*Latest Year*		*Change*
Colombia	1953	33.6	1983	60.4	+26.8
Japan	1950	57.0	1980	81.3	+24.3
Republic of Korea	1955	55.2	1986	76.9	+21.7
Latin America	1955	14.2	1975	33.7	+19.5
Thailand	1967–71	1.9	1977–81	5.5	+3.6
Argentina	1970	14.6	1987	9.8	–4.8
United States	1950	49.7	1988	24.7	–25.0

Sources: Colombia: Patrinos, 1990, p. 163; Japan and United States: Kaneko, 1987, p. 27, Cohn and Geske, 1990, p. 73; Republic of Korea: Lee, 1987, p. 56; Latin America: Levy, 1985; Thailand: Malakul, 1985. p.56; Argentina: Balan, 1990, p. 14.

number of institutions are more than half of the total (see Tables 2 and 3).[1]

Private education has grown for several reasons, which can be summed up in two categories: excess demand and differentiated demand for higher education (James, 1987). First, the social demand for higher education exceeds the public supply, and the private market seeks to meet the unsatisfied demand.[2] Secondly, demand for different quality (presumably high quality) and content in education (such as, for example, religious education)

Jandhyala B. G. Tilak (India). Professor and Head of the Educational and Finance Unit at the National Institute of Educational Planning and Administration (New Delhi); previously with the World Bank. He has also taught at the University of Delhi, the Indian Institute of Education and the University of Virginia. His publications include: *Economics of Inequality in Education; Educational Finances in South Asia; Education and Regional Development; Education, and Its Relation to Economic Growth; Poverty and Income Distribution;* and *Political Economy of Education in India.*

TABLE 2
Enrollments in public and private higher education (percentages)

Country	Year	Public	Private	Total[1]
Philippines	1984/85	15.3	84.7	1504
Republic of Korea	1986	23.1	76.9	1262
Japan	1989	24.4	72.6	2067
Indonesia	1985/86	33.3	66.7	900
Colombia	1983	39.6	60.4	356
Cyprus	1986/87	41.9	58.1	3.5
Burma	mid-1980s	42.0	58.0	—[2]
Bangladesh	mid-1980s	42.0	58.0	—
India	mid-1980s	43.0	57.0	—
Pakistan	1968	49.0	51.0	151
Chile	1986/87	54.5	45.5	233
Brazil	1983	64.8	35.2	693
Malaysia	mid-1980s	76.0	24.0	—
United States	1988	75.3	24.7	8500
Argentina	1987	91.2	9.8	7531
Papua New Guinea	mid-1980s	94.0	6.0	—
Thailand	mid-1980s	94.0	6.0	—
Spain	1981/82	97.0	3.0	—
China	mid-1980s	100.0	0.0	—
Sri Lanka	mid-1980s	100.0	0.0	—

1. In thousands.
2. Not available.

Sources: Philippines: Elequin, 1990, p. 312; Republic of Korea: Lee, 1987, p. 56; Japan: Nishihara, 1990, p. 26; Indonesia: Toisuta, 1987, p. 73; Colombia: Patrinos, 1990, p. 163; Cypres: Koyzis, 1989; Pakistan: Jiménez and Tan, 1987*b*, p. 178; Chile: Schiefelbein, 1990; Brazil: Schwartzman, 1988, p. 100; United States: Cohn and Geske, 1990, p. 73; Argentina: Balan, 1990; Spain: McKenna, 1985, p. 461; other (Asian) countries: Tan and Mingat, 1989, p. 202.

TABLE 3
Percentages of public and private sectors in higher education: Institutions

Country	Year	Public	Private	Total[1]
Republic of Korea	1986	19.6	80.4	256
Philippines	1985/86	27.6	72.4	1158
Japan	1985	28.8	71.2	1103
Brazil	1983	83.9	16.1	124
United States	1980	84.5	15.5	—[2]
Pakistan	1976/77	96.1	3.9	433

1. Actual numbers.
2. Not available.

Sources: Republic of Korea: Lee, 1987, p. 56; Philippines: Elequin, 1990, p. 340; Japan and United States: Kaneko, 1987, p. 23; Brazil: Schwartzman, 1988, p. 100; Pakistan: Jimenez and Tan, 1987*a*, p. 178.

also contributes to the growth of privatization. On the supply side, private entrepreneurs are ready to provide higher education either for philanthropic or other altruistic motives, or for profit. The dividends could be social and political gains, or quick economic profits.

Diversities in Privatization

Higher-education systems in the world present enormous diversity. Two major categories of higher education can be found in this context; predominantly public higher-education systems, where higher education is provided and funded by the state (as it is in socialist countries, for example), and mixed higher-education systems with varying roles by both public and private sectors (as found in the rest of the world). Again under the latter category, there is significant diversity from country to country. Some systems are dominated by the private sector, which can be termed as 'mass private and restricted public sectors' as in several market economies (e.g. Japan, Republic of Korea, Philippines, and Latin American countries such as Colombia). Then there are mixed systems dominated by the state sector, as in several developing countries of South Asia (including India), Africa, and Western Europe. These systems can be aptly described as 'parallel public and private sectors.' In some welfare states such as the Netherlands and Belgium, both coexist under state funding. Systems where the private sector has a very limited role, as in Sweden, the United Kingdom, France, Spain, Thailand, etc., can be described as 'peripheral private sector' (Geiger, 1987*a*).

In practice, the public/private distinction of a higher-education institution is not very clear. If the criterion used to define it is its source of funding, a private university may be receiving substantial financial resources from the government; and a public university may generate large amounts of resources from private sources. On the other hand, if it is to be defined on the basis of management, a private institution may be effectively controlled by the state, and may be administered according to government regulations. Alternatively we may prefer to define institutions in terms of their character, that is, whether they be 'profit-making' or 'non-profit making'. All this shows how ambiguous the term 'privatization' can be.

Several forms of 'privatization' of higher education may be noted and classified into four categories (Tilak, 1991).

First, an extreme version of privatization implying total privatization of higher education, colleges and universities being managed and funded by the private sector, with little government intervention. These pure or 'unaided' private institutions do provide financial relief to the government in providing higher education, but at huge long-term economic and non-economic cost to the society.

Second, there is 'strong' privatization, which means recovery of full costs of public higher education from users—students, their employers or both. Due to the externalities associated with higher education, privatization of this type may not be desirable, and of course not empirically feasible.

Third, there is a moderate form of privatization implying public provision of higher education but with a reasonable level of financing from non-governmental sources. Since higher education is a quasi-public good, 100 percent public financing of education can be seen as economically unjustified. Since private individuals also benefit, it is reasonable that they share a proportion of the costs. So the state, students/families and the general public pay for higher education. This will be discussed in more detail below.

Lastly, there is what can be termed 'pseudo-privatization', which cannot be really called privatization. Higher education institutions under this category are private but government-'aided'. They were originally created by private bodies, but receive nearly the whole of their expenditure from governments. Thus these institutions are privately managed but publicly funded. A substantial number of private higher-education institutions in several countries belong to this category, and they receive government aid to meet almost all their recurrent expenditure. Hence strictly from the financial point of view, such private colleges do not play any significant role.[3]

Despite these diversities, a broad generalized analysis of the role of the private sector in higher education can be made. However, the generalizations made below refer mostly to the first and the fourth categories of privatization, as described above. Some of the following general features may also fail to take account of certain particularities of some private institutions which are exceptions to the rule.[4]

Myths and Facts About Privatization

The case for privatization of higher education exists mostly on the basis of financial considerations. Public budgets for higher education are at best stagnant, and are indeed declining in real terms, more particularly in relation to other sectors of the economy. Privatization is also favored on the grounds that it would provide enhanced levels of internal and external efficiency of higher education, and higher quality of education; and as the private sector would have to compete with the public sector, the competition would result in improvement in quality and efficiency not only of private education but also even public higher education. In the long run, due to economies of scale, private institutions provide better quality education at lower cost than public institutions, as in Japan. Furthermore, by reducing public subsidies to higher education, the 'perverse effects' of public subsidization of higher education on income distribution could be reduced, and, through privatization, inequities in funding education would be substantially reduced (see Psacharopoulos, 1986; Psacharopoulos and Woodhall, 1985; Roth, 1987; James, 1987).

On the other hand, privatization is opposed on at least three sets of grounds. The existing market system does not ensure optimum social investment in higher education, as externalities exist in the case of higher education, which is a 'quasi-public good' (Tilak, 1991). The market system also fails to keep consumers well informed of the costs and benefits of higher education. It is likely that the costs of private education are much higher than public education as in the United States and the Republic of Korea. Finally, a private system of higher education is also insensitive to distributional considerations and in fact contributes to socio-economic inequalities. Accordingly, public education is not only superior to private education, but private institutions cannot even survive without state support.

All these arguments for and against privatization, by its defenders as well as its opponents, are open to empirical verification, without which they may be brushed aside by the opposing side as merely politico-ideological arguments. Sophisticated arguments based on hard core evidence are rarely made in favor of privatization (Breneman and Finn, 1978, p. 6). Without empirical evidence, all the arguments, however well-formulated and articulated, remain as 'myths'. With this in mind, a few of these myths are empirically examined below, by examining the scanty evidence available, with examples drawn from diverse countries.

The First Myth

There is huge demand for private higher education, as private education is qualitatively superior to public education.

The Facts

The evidence shows that the higher quality of private education compared with public higher education is exaggerated. In Japan, public higher education provides better facilities, which are significantly related to quality, than private universities and colleges. The number of pupils per teacher in public universities is only eight, compared with twenty-six in private universities (James and Benjamin, 1988). While more than 75 per cent of students enrolled in higher education in the country are in the private sector, teachers in this sector constitute less than half the total. The pupil/teacher ratio in private institutions is three times the ratio in state institutions in Indonesia and the Philippines, and more than double in Thailand. The difference is not as high in Brazil, but the ratio clearly favors public higher education, the ratios being fourteen and ten respectively in private and public universities. Private universities are found to employ more retired, part-time, and underqualified teachers in Japan, Colombia, Brazil, Argentina, Indonesia and in several other countries. The teachers are also paid less. Only government subsidies could raise the salary levels of teachers in private universities in Japan. On the whole, teachers in private institutions have less academic prestige.

Even the availability of space per student and other facilities are reasonably higher in public universities than in private universities in Japan. In all, private universities spend less than half of what public universities spend per student (see Table 4). For example, in Japan, in 1980, expenditure per student was 1,982,000 yen in public universities, compared with 848,000 yen in private universities (Kaneko, 1987). It is only in the United States that the difference is in favor of private universities.[5] All this should indicate that quality differences are indeed more favorable to public than to private universities.

Yet private universities may sometimes show better results in final examinations, as essentially they admit only the best prepared students. However, 'graduation of the "best" graduates is not by itself proof of the "best" education' (Levy, 1985, p. 454).

Even if the quality of output is taken into consideration, that is, internal efficiency, measured in terms of academic achievement, success rates, drop-out rates, failure rates, etc., private education does not compare favorably with public education. The large body of evidence available on this issue refers to the school sector, and not to higher education. Even with respect to the school sector, recent studies (Willms, 1987) have found that the advantage of private schooling with respect to academic achievement for an average student is not significant, as reported earlier (Coleman et al., 1981). The limited information available on higher education leads us to question the beliefs regarding the superiority of private education. Drop-out rates are higher in private colleges than in government colleges in Thailand (NEC, 1989, p. 287), and in the Philippines (Arcelo and Sanyal, 1987, p. 154), and the rates of failure are high in Colombia (Patrinos, 1990). The productivity of private universities in Indonesia is found to be much

TABLE 4
Expenditure per student in higher education (private/public)

Country	*Year*	*Ratio*
Thailand	1977–81	0:25
Republic of Korea	1985	0:71
Japan	1980	0:72
United States	1988	1:60

Sources: Thailand: Malakul, 1985, p. 59; Republic of Korea: Kim, 1990, p. 240; Japan: Kaneko, 1987, p. 29; United States: Cohn and Geske, 1990, p. 73.

lower than public universities (Pramoetadi, 1985, p. 33).

In the Philippines, while the private sector increased accessibility to education to the people, it was found to have contributed to a deterioration in the quality and standards of higher education to such an extent that many people argued for a halt of the public laissez-faire policy in the growth of higher education and for the expansion of state supported institutions (Tan and Alonzo, 1987, p. 159). In Brazil and Peru, the quality of private higher education was described as 'disgraceful' (Levy, 1985, p. 453).

In India, except for those institutions recognized by the public sector, private colleges, which receive no aid from the government, have been increasing in number essentially due to the existence of excess demand for higher education, particularly from the upper classes and those who fail to gain admission to government colleges. Rarely is the quality of these institutions regarded as superior. Their growth also has to do with the fact that people tend to equate high fees with a high quality of education (Breneman, 1988). Above all, many non-élite private universities and colleges were created, as is the case in some Latin American countries, to provide job-related training, rather than higher education *per se.*

It is also argued that as the private sector has to compete with the public sector, the efficiency of the former and, equally important, the efficiency of all higher education, including public, improve significantly. But in countries where mass private sectors prevail, or in countries where private sectors play a peripheral role, there is little scope for competition, and as a result, the private sector may turn out to be very inefficient, and even economically corrupt.[6] Thus the arguments on efficiency and quality of private higher education do not withstand close scrutiny.

The Second Myth

It is widely believed that graduates from private universities receive higher rewards on the labor market in the form of lower unemployment rates, better paid jobs and consequently higher earnings (Jimenex and Tan, 1987*b*; Patrinos, 1990). In short, the external efficiency of private higher education is argued to be greater than public higher education, which would explain the growth of privatization.

The Facts

The empirical evidence does not support these assumptions. Unemployment rates among graduates from private universities are about 2.8 times higher than those from public universities in the Philippines (Arcelo and Sanyal, 1987, p. 190). This is also the case in Thailand where 27 percent of graduates from private universities are unemployed during the first year after graduation, compared with 13.3 per cent of the graduates from national universities (Setapanich et al., 1990, p. 420). Private universities in Cyprus are found to be fuelling the diploma-inflation problem, leading to a serious problem of graduate unemployment (Koyzis, 1989. p. 18).

Estimated rates of return, a summary statistic of the external or labor-market efficiency of education (presented in Table 5), show that public higher education pays better than private higher education, particularly from the point of view of individuals in several countries, including Japan, the Philippines, and Thailand. Social rates of return for public and

TABLE 5
Percentage rates of return to private versus public higher education

	Private	*Public*
United States		
Private rates of return	15.0	18.0
Thailand		
Private rates of return	10.46	19.51
Social rates of return	9.75	9.48
Philippines	8.75	12.55
Japan		
Private rates of return		
Social sciences	7.5	9.0
Engineering	7.0	9.0
All higher[1]	6.7	7.1
Social rates of return		
Social sciences	7.8	7.6
Engineering	7.1	6.6
All higher[1]	6.9	5.4

1. Yano and Maruyama, 1985, p. 80.

Sources: United States: Leslie and Brinkman, 1988, p. 64; Thailand: National Education Commission, 1989, p. 169; Philippines: Arcelo and Sanyal, 1987, p. 169; Japan: James and Benjamin, 1988, pp. 77, 106.

private university education are close in Thailand, showing little significant advantage for private higher education, even from the point of view of the society.[7]

The Third Myth

Private institutions provide considerable relief from financial burden to the governments, as they are self-financing.

The Facts

States such as Malaysia allocate huge investments—more every year—to prop up dubious private institutions, while growth and expansion of public institutions are frozen. In Thailand, while 30 per cent of students attend private institutions, the ratio of government expenditure to private expenditure on higher education is 97:3 (Malakul, 1985). Explicit appropriations may not be very high; but implicit subsidies or indirect government support to the students to purchase higher education is an important source of funding for private universities in the United States. State scholarships have exposed the myth of the pure privateness of universities like Harvard, Columbia, Yale, etc. (Levy, 1986*b*, p. 171).[8] Around 85 to 90 per cent of scholarship money in California goes to students in private universities, while private enrollments form only 10–12 per cent of the state's total (Levy, 1986*b*, p. 174). In Japan, 21.5 per cent of private higher-education expenditure is covered by state subsidies (this figure was nil in 1951). State subsidization of private institutions in Japan originated due to the bankruptcy of private higher education. The resources of the private institutions are boosted 'through infusion of significant amounts of public funds' in several countries (Geiger, 1987*b*, p. 18). In many countries, state subsidies cover more than 90 per cent of the recurrent expenditure of private institutions. In Sweden and Canada, the government provided the capital needs of the private institutions. More than 77 per cent of the government budget on higher education in Uttar Pradesh in India goes as aid to private colleges (Muzamil, 1989, p. 247). Whatever the reasons, private and public universities in Belgium and the Netherlands receive equal funding from the state (Geiger, 1988). All this leads us to conclude that most private institutions are not totally private, at least from a financial standpoint.

The Fourth Myth

The private sector responds to the economic needs of the individual and society, and provides relevant types of education. 'The major advantage of private universities has been in responding more quickly or efficiently to market demands' (Balan, 1990, p. 17).

The Facts

In most countries, private higher-education institutions offer mainly low capital-intense disciplines of study. It is true that not only are there few private universities involved in research activities, but they are also involved in providing cheap commercial and vocational training as in the case of several Latin American countries, or in the case of 'parallel' colleges in Kerala in India (Nair and Ajit, 1984). As can be seen in Table 6, no private institutions in Bolivia offer higher education in law, medicine, exact sciences, engineering; 58 per cent specialize in 'commercial' courses, and 12 per cent in the humanities. In Peru, Colombia and Ecuador, a negligible proportion of private institutions offer courses in medicine and exact sciences. However, when the potential for economic profit is high, the private sector entered into professional fields and opened engineering and medical colleges, as in India (Kothari, 1986). On the whole, research and broad educational needs of the economy are barely served by the private sector. Private institutions tend to provide more personal and fewer social benefits to students. The private sector responds to market demands, but only in the short term, while 'improvement of schools requires long-term planning—not the quick alteration of a commodity to meet changing fashions' (Ping, 1987, p. 21).

The Fifth Myth

It is generally believed that private enterprise has genuine philanthropic motives in opening private colleges and universities, which are by definition pant of the 'non-profit

TABLE 6
Percentage of specialization of private and public sectors in higher education in Latin America

	Bolivia	*Columbia*	*Ecuador*	*Mexico*	*Peru*	*Argentina*[1]
Commercial						
Private	58	37	23	35	47	—[2]
Public	10	10	18	20	23	—
Humanities						
Private	12	5	9	1	7	9
Public	2	7	6	2	0	—
Law						
Private	0	16	6	6	5	2
Public	8	4	6	9	4	—
Medicine						
Private	0	4	1	20	1	7
Public	21	9	11	20	7	—
Exact Sciences						
Private	0	4	3	1	6	—
Public	15	12	5	4	4	—
Engineering						
Private	0	17	8	17	8	—
Public	23	26	17	24	29	—

1. Balan, 1990, p. 16.
2. Not available.

Source: Levy, 1985, p. 456.

sector'. They also make huge investments in higher education.

The Facts

Private institutions are largely funded either from students' tuition fees and charges or from public subsidies. Very few private institutions make any investment from their own resources. These institutions are in fact operated in a kind of seller's market, recovering the full costs plus profits from some source or other. For instance, in Japan 70 percent of the costs of higher education in private institutions are met from tuition fees, while the corresponding proportion is 82 percent in the Republic of Korea. The role of private finances other than fees, such as donations, endowments etc., is not at all significant. In the United States, however, tuition charges account for only slightly more than one-third of the total costs. Private institutions are involved in disguised profit-making operations in almost all countries, including Brazil and India.

The private colleges that receive little public support in India expect huge donations and capitation fees, and charge abnormally high fees, ten to twenty times higher than those charged by government colleges. While universities and colleges are, by definition, non-profit institutions, these private institutions do not merely cover their costs, they also make huge 'quick profits', which are not necessarily reinvested in education. Educational considerations hardly figure in this context (Tilak, 1990). As a result, higher education is subject to vulgar commercialization.

The Sixth Myth

It is generally noted that private education is élitist, and caters to the needs of the wealthy. For example, I have hypothesized earlier (Tilak 1986), largely based on evidence on the school sector, that the benefits of education in private institutions—costly and presumably of high quality—accrue largely to the élite (as the private sector caters mainly to the needs of the élites), while the benefits of education in public schools—which are generally compelled to choose quantity rather than quality and, accordingly, provide inexpensive education—mostly for the masses.

The Facts

Private universities generally serve a privileged clientele. In Colombia private universities are dominated by high-income groups. Barely 2 percent of the students are from the bottom quintile and 13 percent from the bottom 40 percent of the income group population. The picture is similar in Japan. In Thailand, students in private universities have parents with, on average, one and a half times the income of those of students in public universities. The democratization of public higher education has reduced considerably the élitist character of higher education. The social élitism attached to private higher education was found to be one of the most important factors in the growth of an élite private sector in higher education in Latin American countries (Levy, 1985). The private institutions lent an élitist or secular-élitist character to higher education.

In countries characterized by 'mass private and restricted public sectors' such as Japan, the Philippines and Brazil, the evidence is not clear cut, as there are significant diversities within private universities. Some private universities are highly élitist and selective, while others are not. In these countries, there are a few élite private universities, and a large number of low-quality, low-cost private universities and colleges—for example, in Colombia and Brazil.

On the whole, however, as fees in private universities are very high compared with public universities, only the relatively well-to-do opt for private higher education. In the United States and Thailand, for example, fees per student in private universities are five times those in public institutions; the corresponding ratio in Japan is 2.5:1. But as access to public higher education is restricted, students from the upper and professional classes are more or less forced to go to private universities. However, 'public universities continue to be the first choice for many' for educational and financial reasons (Levy, 1985, p. 454).

The Seventh Myth

Most public higher-educational institutions are politicized. Only private institutions are apolitical.

The Facts

Basically the inadequacy of public policies results in the growth of the private sector. In some Latin American countries, as public policies favored leftist political activism in public universities, private universities have grown to counter these forces. But to argue that private institutions are free of political forces is not true. Private education has been found to strengthen a given political ideology and to help in reproduction of class structure (Salter and Tapper, 1985). In several countries, state support to private universities is based on political and ideological factors, which can be called 'political-economic' factors. In India, for example, more than half the private engineering colleges in Maharashtra are owned by politicians, and used for political purposes. Motives of profit, influence and political power explain the growth of these private colleges (Rudolph and Rudolph, 1987, p. 296; Kothari, 1986).

The Eighth Myth

Privatization of higher education improves income distribution, as public funding of higher education, with all its 'perverse effects' is generally found to be regressive (Psacharopoulos, 1977; Blaug, 1982).

The Facts

As evidence from Japan—one of the few countries to have carried out elaborate investigations on this issue—shows, public universities seem to have slightly higher redistributive effects than private universities in transferring resources from the top income quintile to the others. The advantage enjoyed by public institutions is greater in the school sector (James and Benjamin, 1988, p. 127). In the case of India, it has been found that the private education system contained forces that contribute to disparities, and that the state sector was not adequate enough to counteract these forces. As a result, the whole education system was found to be a contributing factor towards accentuating income inequalities (Dasgupta, 1979).

An Assessment of Pros and Cons

Previously, I classified privatization into four categories: (a) extreme privatization (total or pure private institutions); (b) strong privatization (full cost recovery); (c) moderate privatization (partial cost recovery); and (d) pseudo-privatization (government-aided private sector). The above analysis largely refers to the first and last forms of privatization only. Based on available evidence on a few major countries of the world, this analysis has exploded some of the myths.

In many countries, the growth of privatization can be attributed largely to the failure of public universities, while private universities have certainly made positive contributions. Private universities in some countries, such as the United States, have contributed in important and unique ways to diversity, independence, quality, efficiency and innovation (Breneman and Finn, 1978, p. 6). In countries like Japan, each private university has its own identity, tradition, culture, etc. In contrast, public universities hardly offer any diversity or individual choice. In this sense, privatization increases the possibilities for individual choice in the type and quality of higher education. But 'the stress upon individualism—upon individual preference—at the expense of social responsibility and cohesiveness must be a matter of concern' (Ping, 1987, p. 291).

In many countries private higher education eases the impending financial burden faced by the public authorities. One noteworthy example is Chile, where total public expenditure on higher education was reduced from \$171 million in 1981 to \$115 million 1988 (Schiefelbein, 1990) as private education grew. Without this, governments would either have to suppress the huge demand for higher education, or find themselves in deeper financial deficit. In fact, political and economic stability would have been threatened in some Latin American countries, if it were not for the role of private sector (Levy, 1985, p. 451). In most cases, however, resources come from students, not from other private sources. Private institutions supplied manpower not only to the private but to the public sector of the economy as well. Private universities are also believed to reduce the number of students going to foreign universities, as in the case of Greece (Psacharopoulos, 1988).

But the goals and strategies of the private sector in higher education are on the whole highly injurious to the public interest. First, the private sector has turned the 'non-profit sector' into a high-profit-making sector not only in terms of social and political power, but also in terms of financial returns, and as profits are not allowed in educational enterprises in several countries, private educational enterprises have resorted to illegal activities in education. When governments attempted to regulate profits by allowing state subsidies and restricting fee levels, all the private institutions found they had one thing in common—a demand for subsidies. In the first instance, state subsidies eased the financial crisis of the private universities, as in Brazil, and in the long run contributed to 'private enrichment at public expense'. As a result of all this, many countries today have 'bastard' private-sector colleges, either illegally set up to do legal business, or legally created to do illegal work (Singh, 1983).

Secondly, by concentrating on profit-yielding, cheap, career-related commercial studies, the market-oriented private universities provide vocational training under the name of 'higher education' and ignore 'broader higher education'. Private universities also totally ignore research, which is essential for sustained development of higher education.

Thirdly, by charging high fees, private institutions create irreparable socio-economic inequities between the poor and rich income groups of the population. As a World Bank study noted, private education turns out to be 'socially and economically divisive' (Psacharopoulos and Woodhall, 1985, p. 144). Access to higher education by lower income groups is negatively affected by the rapid growth of privatization.

It is generally felt that 'even if one assumes that the private sector is generally superior to the public sector, it does not logically follow that proportional expansion of the private sector would make for a better system' (Levy, 1985, p. 458). In short, private education is not found to be economically efficient, qualitatively superior, and socially equitable. Accordingly, it is feared that increased privatization of higher education would present more problems than solutions, as in case of Colombia (Patrinos, 1990, p. 169). Thus the inappropriateness of the market metaphor in higher education is abundantly clear.

Towards a Desirable Pattern of Privatization

Privatization of the second and third categories mentioned above may not be characterized by so many problems. As higher education is a quasi-public good, 100 percent cost recovery may not be desirable. In other words, the second type is neither desirable nor practically feasible. At the same time, since individuals do benefit from higher education, it is natural that they are required to pay for their education (Tilak, 1991). The dwindling economic abilities of governments also make it necessary. Hence the notion of choice relates only to the third category.

Under this category, privatization implies provision of public education, but with reasonable levels of costs recovered from the users. In other words, it means private purchase of public education at less than full cost. In this context, there are a few major proposals being discussed in several countries, such as increase in fees, student loans, graduate tax, etc. (World Bank, 1986). Some of these are being tried out in a few countries. The experience of those countries makes it clear that each of these alternatives has its own strengths and weaknesses (see, for example, Tilak and Varghese, 1991). A tax on graduates would be efficient if there were a strong relationship between education, occupation and productivity, and a low degree of substitution between different layers and types of higher education, so that those with higher education do not find themselves unemployed. Student loans transfer the burden from the present to the future, and for the loan schemes to work effectively, well spread credit markets to float educational loans are required, without which the recovery of loans would be a serious problem. Of these three measures, fees seem to be the most effective. The experience of the Republic of Korea is encouraging in this regard: nearly half the costs of public higher education are met by students in the form of fees (Table 7). However, instead of a uniform increase in fees, selective pricing (Tilak and Varghese, 1985; Jimenez, 1987; Tilak, 1990) may be more efficient and equitable.

TABLE 7
Fees as percentage of total expenditure on higher education

Country	*Year*	*Public*	*Private*	*Total*
Colombia	mid-1980s	5.0	85.0	—
Republic of Korea	1985	49.6	82.3	73.4
Japan	1980	13.3	70.4	54.0
United States	1986/87	14.5	38.7	22.4

Source: Colombia: Jimenez and Tan, 1987*b*, p. 134; Republic of Korea: Lee, 1987, p. 61; Japan: Kaneko, 1987, p. 24; United States: Williams, 1990, p. 9.

Under selective pricing, students belonging to different socio-economic groups would be required to pay different rates of fees, which would be related to the ability of the students to pay and the costs of courses. Privatization of this type would be more efficient, generating additional private resources for higher education, and also more equitable, as it would not create dual structures of higher education, as do the other forms described above—one for the élite and another for the masses. As Ping (1987, p. 291) noted, 'All children matter, not just those whose parents have learnt to play the market effectively.' In fact, privatization of this form will be free from most of the evils of other forms discussed above, and may assimilate the diverse strengths of privatization.

Notes

1. However, even though the private market mechanism is, in general, strong, the share of the private sector in higher education in enrollments, in the United States decreased from about half in 1950 to a quarter in 1988.
2. For example, in 1988 the rapid growth of demand, including overseas demand, for higher education in Australia, led to privatization of hitherto public higher education (Stone, 1990).
3. Other types of classification have been proposed. (See, for example, Khadira, 1900).
4. Universities, colleges and other higher education institutions, either public or private, vary in size and other characteristics. Here they are referred to as if they were homogeneous.
5. The private higher-education system in the United States seems to be distinct from others, with respect to several other characteristics.

6. While Latin American countries may present an excellent example of the first kind, countries like India provide examples for the second category.
7. In Kenya, government schools are found to yield returns 50 percent higher than private (*harambee*) schools, both to the individual and to society (Knight and Sabot, 1990, p. 291). See also Psacharopoulos (1987) for similar data on Colombia and Tanzania.
8. Voucher schemes also come under the same category.

References

Arcelo, A. A., Sanyal, B. C. 1987. *Employment and Career Opportunities after Graduation. The Philippine Experience*. Manila, Fund for Assistance to Private Education, for IIEP.

Balán, J. 1990. Private Universities within the Argentine Higher Educational System, Trends and Prospects. *Higher Education Policy*, Vol. 3, No. 2, pp. 13–17.

Blaug, M. 1982. The Distributional Effects of Higher Education Subsidies, *Economics of Education Review*, Vol. 2, No. 3, pp. 209–31.

Boyd, W. L., Cibukala, J. G. 1989. *Private Schools and Public Policy, International Perspective*. London, Falmer.

Breneman, D. W. 1988. *College Cost and Tuition, What Are the Issues? Proceedings from a National Conference*. Washington, D.C., National Center for Post-secondary Governance and Finance.

Breneman, D. W., Finn Jr., C. E. 1978. An Uncertain Future. In: D. W. Breneman and C. E. Finn, Jr. (eds.), *Public Policy and Private Higher Education*, pp. 1–61. Washington, D.C., Brookings.

Brodersohn, M. S. 1978. Public and Private Financing of Education in Latin America. A Review of Its Principal Sources. *The Financing of Education in Latin America*, pp. 146–76. Washington, D.C., Inter-American Development Bank.

Cohn, E., Geske, T. G. 1990. *Economics of Education*, 3rd ed. Oxford, Pergamon Press.

Coleman, J. S., Hopper, T., Kilgore, S. 1981. *Public and Private Schools*. Chicago, National Opinion Research Center.

Dasgupta, A. 1979. Income Distribution, Education and Capital Accumulation. Washington, D.C., World Bank. (Draft.)

Elequin, E. T. 1990. Survey Report—Philippines. In H. Muta (ed.), *Educated Unemployment in Asia*, pp. 305–72. Tokyo, Asian Productivity Organization.

Geiger, R. L. 1987*a*. *Private Sectors in Higher Education, Structure, Function and Change in Eight Countries*. Ann Arbor, University of Michigan Press.

_____. 1987*b*. Pattern of Public-Private Differentiation in Higher Education, An International Comparison. In: RIHE, *Public and Private Sectors in Asian Higher Education Systems: Issues and Prospects*, pp. 7–20. Hiroshima, Hiroshima University.

_____. 1988. Public and Private Sectors in Higher Education, A Comparison of International Patterns. *Higher Education*, Vol. 17, No. 6, pp. 699–711.

_____. 1990. The Dynamics of Private Higher Education in the United States, Mission, Finance and Public Policy, *Higher Education Policy*, Vol. 3, No. 2, pp. 9–12.

Haertel, E. H., James T., Levin, H. M. (eds.). 1987. *Comparing Public and Private Schools*. Vol. 2: *School Achievement*, New York, Falmer.

James, E. 1987. The Public/Private Division of Responsibility for Education, An International Comparison, *Economics of Education Review*, Vol. 6, No. 1, pp. 1–14.

James, E., Benjamin, G. 1988. *Public Policy and Private Education in Japan*. London, Macmillan.

Jiménez, E. 1987. *Pricing Policy in Social Sectors*. Baltimore, Johns Hopkins/World Bank.

Jiménez, E., Tan, J.-P. 1987*a*. Decentralized and Private Education. The Case of Pakistan. *Comparative Education*, Vol. 23, No. 2, pp. 173–90.

_____. 1987*b*. Selecting the Brightest for Post Secondary Education in Colombia: The Impact of Equity. *Economics of Education Review*, Vol. 6, No. 2, pp. 128–35.

Kaneko, M. 1987. Public and Private Sectors in Japanese Higher Education. In: RIHE, *Public and Private Sectors in Asian Higher Education Systems, Issues and Prospects*, pp. 21–34. Hiroshima, Hiroshima University.

Khadira, B. 1990. Privatization of Higher Education, *Mainstream*, Vol. 28, 24–25, 7–14, April, 25–26, Vol. 35, and 24–28.

Kim, T. C. 1990. Survey Report—Republic of Korea. In: H. Muta (ed.), *Educated Unemployment in Asia*, pp. 223–304. Tokyo, Asian Productivity Organization.

Knight, J. B., Sabot, R. H. 1990. *Education, Productivity and Inequality, The East African Natural Experiment*. New York, Oxford/World Bank.

Kothari, V. N. 1986. Private Unaided Engineering and Medical Colleges: Consequences of Misguided Policy. *Economic and Political Weekly*, Vol. 21, No. 14, pp. 593–96.

Koyzis, A. A. 1989. Private Higher Education in Cyprus: In Search of Legitimacy, *Higher Education Policy*, Vol. 2, No. 2, pp. 13–19.

Lee, K. 1987. Past, Present and Future Trends in Public and Private Sectors of Korean Higher Education. In: RIHE, *Public and Private Sectors in Asian Higher Education Systems, Issues and Prospects*, pp. 49–70. Hiroshima, Hiroshima University.

Leslie, L. L., Brinkman, P. T. 1988. *The Economic Value of Higher Education*. New York, Macmillan/American Council on Education.

Levy, D. C. 1985. Latin America's Private Universities, How Successful Are They? *Comparative Education Review*, Vol. 29, No. 4, pp. 440–59.

_____. 1986*a*. *Higher Education and the State in Latin America—Private Challenges to Public Dominance*. Chicago, University of Chicago Press.

_____. 1986*b*. 'Private' and 'Public', Analysis Amid Ambiguity in Higher Education. *Private Education: Studies in Choice and Public Policy*, pp. 170–92. New York, Oxford.

_____. 1986*c*. Alternative Private-Public Blends in Higher Education, International Patterns. In: D. C. Levy, (ed). *Private Education: Studies in Choice and Public Policy*, pp. 195–213. New York, Oxford.

_____. (ed.). 1986*d*. *Private Education: Studies in Choice and Public Policy*, New York, Oxford.

Malakul, P. 1985. Prospects and Problems in Higher Education Expansion in Thailand. In: RIHE, *Higher Education Expansion in Asia*, pp. 52–65. Hiroshima, Hiroshima University.

McKenna, J. B. 1985. University Reforms in Spain, *Comparative Education Review*, Vol 29, No. 4, pp. 460–70.

Muta, H. (ed.). 1990. *Educated Unemployment in Asia*. Tokyo, Asian Productivity Organization.

Muzamil, M. 1989. *Financing of Education*. New Delhi, Ashish.

Nair, R. G., Ajit, D. 1984. Parallel Colleges in Kerala. *Economic and Political Weekly*, Vol. 19, No. 42/43, pp. 1840–7.

NEC (National Education Commission). 1989. *Costs and Contributions of Higher Education in Thailand*, Bangkok, NEC.

Nelson, S. C. 1978. Financial Trends and Issues. In: D. W. Breneman and C. E. Finn, Jr. (eds.), *Public Policy and Private Higher Education*, pp. 63–142. Washington, D. C., Brookings.

Nishihara, H. 1990. Private Colleges and Universities in Japan, Glittering Prizes. *Higher Education Policy*, Vol. 2, No. 2, pp. 26–30.

Patrinos, H. A. 1990. The Privatization of Higher Education in Colombia, Effects on Quality and Equity. *Higher Education*, Vol. 20, No. 2, pp. 161–73.

Ping, R. 1987. Privatization in Education, *Journal of Education Policy*, Vol. 2, No. 4, pp. 289–99.

Pramoetadi, I. S. 1985. Higher Education Development in Indonesia. In: RIHE, *Higher Education Expansion in Asia*, pp. 13–35. Hiroshima, Hiroshima University.

Psacharopoulos, G. 1977. Perverse Effects of Public Subsidization of Education or How EquitableIis Free Education? *Comparative Education Review*, Vol. 21, No. 1, pp. 69–90.

_____. 1986. Welfare Effects of Government Intervention in Education, *Contemporary Policy Issues*, Vol. 4, No. 3, pp. 51–62.

_____. 1987. Public versus Private Schools in Developing Countries: Evidence from Colombia and Tanzania, *International Journal of Educational Development*, Vol. 7, No. 1, pp. 59–67.

_____. 1988. Efficiency and Equity in Greek Higher Education, *Minerva*, Vol. 26, No. 2, pp. 119–37.

Psacharopoulos, G., Woodhall, M. 1985. *Education for Development*. New York, Oxford/World Bank.

RIHE (Research Institute for Higher Education). 1985. *Higher Education Expansion in Asia*. Hiroshima, Hiroshima University.

_____. 1987. *Public and Private Sectors in Asian Higher Education Systems, Issues and Prospects*. Hiroshima, Hiroshima University.

Roderick, G., Stephens, M. (eds.). 1979. *Higher Education for All?* London, Falmer.

Roth, D. C. 1987. *The Private Provision of Public Services in Developing Countries*. New York, Oxford/World Bank.

Rudolph, L. I., Rudolph, S. 1987. *In Pursuit of Lakshmi: The Political Economy of the Indian State*. Chicago, University of Chicago Press.

Salter, B., Tapper, T. 1985. *Power and Policy in Education, The Case of Independent Schooling*. London, Falmer.

Samoff, J. 1990. The Politics and Privatization of Tanzania. *International Journal of Educational Development*, Vol. 10, No. 1, pp. 1–15.

Schiefelbein, E. 1990. Chile: Economic Incentives in Higher Education. *Higher Education Policy*, Vol. 3, No. 3, pp. 21–6.

Schwartzman, S. 1988. Brazil, Opportunity and Crisis in Higher Education. *Higher Education*, Vol. 17, No. 1, pp. 99–119.

Setapanich, N., Prasatvetayakul, V., Kohengkul, S., Chang-Jai, K. 1990. Survey Report—Thailand. In: H. Muta (ed.), *Educated Unemployment in Asia*, pp. 373–442. Tokyo, Asian Productivity Organization.

Singh, N. 1983. *Education Under Siege*. New Delhi, Concept.

Stone, D. L. 1990. Private Higher Education in Australia, *Higher Education*, Vol. 20, No. 2, pp. 143–59.

Tan, E. A., Alonzo, R. P. 1987. The Philippine Experience in Manpower Planning and Labour Market Policies. In: R. Amjad (ed.), *Human Resource Planning: The Asian Experience*. pp. 151–80. New Delhi, ARTEP/International Labour Office.

Tan, J. P., Mingat, A. 1989. Educational Development in Asia. Washington, D.C., World Bank. (Report No. IDP51.)

Tilak, J. B. G. 1986. A Comment on 'Differences in the Role of the Private Educational Sector in Modern and Developing Countries' by Estelle James. *International Conference on Economics of Education*. Dijon, IREDU.

_____. 1990. *Political Economy of Education in India*. Buffalo, State University of New York.

_____. 1991. Financing Higher Education. Research Seminar on Reform and Innovation in India Higher Education. Buffalo/Bombay, State University of New York/SNDT Women's University.

Tilak, J. B. G., Varghese, N. V. 1985. Discriminatory Pricing in Education. New Delhi, National

Institute of Educational Planning and Administration. (Occasional Paper No. 8.)

_____. 1991. Financing Higher Education in India. *Higher Education*, Vol. 21, No. 1.

Toisuta, W. 1987. Public and Private Sectors in Indonesian Higher Education. In: RIHE, *Public and Private Sectors in Asian Higher Education Systems, Issues and Prospects*, pp. 71–9. Hiroshima, Hiroshima University.

Walford, G. (ed.). 1989. *Private Schools in Ten Countries, Policy and Practice*. London, Routledge.

Williams, G. 1989/90. Changing Patterns of Finance, *OECD Observer*, No. 161.

Willms, J. D. 1987. Patterns of Academic Achievement in Public and Private Schools, Implications for Public Policy and Future Research. In: E. H. Haertel, T. James, and H. M. Levin (eds.), *Comparing Public and Private Schools*, Vol 2: *School Achievement*, pp. 113–34. New York, Falmer.

World Bank. 1986. *Financing of Education in Developing Countries, An Exploration of Policy Opinions*. Washington, D.C., World Bank.

Yano, M, Maruyama, J. 1985. Prospects and Problems in Japanese Higher Education. In: RIHE, *Higher Education Expansion in Asia*, pp. 68–84. Hiroshima, Hiroshima University.

The Capitalist State and Public Policy Formation: Framework for a Political Sociology of Educational Policy Making

CARLOS ALBERTO TORRES

Abstract. *This article argues that public policy formation cannot be understood without a consistent theory of the capitalist state and politics. This is particularly true with respect to education policies. Expanding capital accumulation and increasing the legitimation of the entire mode of production seem to be the principal roles of the capitalist state, a role that is in perpetual tension. Coming to grips with this tension constitutes a principal challenge for the state. Considering educational policies, programs and practices, to inquire into the reasons for the growth of a given educational level—how programs have been devised historically, by whom, for what purposes, and how they are related to the educational clientele that they are supposed to serve—is to ask for an explanation of the determinants of educational policy formation. In this article a framework for a political sociology of educational policy making and a set of hypotheses on the production rules of public policy are offered.*

Determinants of Education Policy Formation

In comparative research in political science and public administration, determinants of public policy have been cataloged from a vast array of contrasting perspectives. Siegel & Weinberg, for instance, have emphasized the following domestic, internal influences in policy making: (a) environmental determinants of public policy (e.g. economic factors, physical environment, and social and demographic factors), and (b) political system determinants of public policy (e.g. political community, political regimes and the authorities). Among external influences in policy making, they have distinguished the following: (a) international development forces (e.g. military and political developments), and (b) international organizational cooperation, assistance and pressures (which certainly have proven to be very relevant for some areas of educational policy making in various countries) (Siegel & Weinberg, 1977). An alternative schema has been substantiated by H. Leichter for use in analyzing public policy. He has distinguished between *situational factors* (divided into six complementary sets of factors which extend from economic circles to technological change); *structural factors* (which include the political structure and the economic structure); *cultural factors* (distinguishing between political culture and general culture); and finally *environmental factors* (distinguishing between international political environment, policy diffusion, international agreements and multinational corporations) (Leichter, 1979).

These are merely a few examples of common trends in the empirical analysis of public policy. Unfortunately, there are very few studies which address themselves to an analysis of educational policy formation in capitalist states which at the same time try to overcome the narrow and technical point of view commonly used in studies of policy making and planning.

Policy making, for instance, has been commonly analyzed as: (1) the production of interaction between political controllers and professional providers of services (Saran, 1973); (2) the focus on timing and feasibility as crucial elements in policy making (David, 1977); (3) research such as Wirt & Kirst (1982) which, by assuming that schools are miniature political systems, falls into the contradiction of accepting a pluralist power structure in the United States, but ends up portraying schools as a world of harmony and consensus; (4) research that deals with local state policy making, and the development of educational policies taxonomies, especially basic control mechanisms available to state-level policy makers, in which the independent (explanatory) variable would be the political culture and educational assumptions of policy makers (Peabody Journal of Education, 1985); or (5) an Eastonian-system analysis perspective that focuses on education units as parapolitical subsystems that include the processing of demands, the generation of support by authorities, regime and the political community, and the feedback response factor (Howell & Brown, 1983). All of these fairly conventional approaches lack an understanding of theory of the state, and a critical conceptualization of issues such as domination, power, rules and political representation in analyzing policy making. But perhaps they are especially faulty in that the methodological individualism of these studies led to an underestimation of the constraints (or restraints) on policy-makers' actions, and particularly their conspicuously naive worldviews. In short, these types of studies lack the theoretical sophistication needed to understand a very complex and rather sophisicated political process of educational decision making in capitalist societies. As Richard Bates has said, "Underlying this onslaught of criticism was a clear impatience with the value neutrality of classical public administration and its tendency to distance itself from complex and controversial issues while focusing on narrow empiricist studies of administrative processes" (Bates, 1985, p. 15). They also lack a holistic approach to determinants of policy making, i.e. an ability to link what happens in schools and nonformal education settings with what happens in terms of accumulation and legitimation processes in the overall society. Above all, they have a practical-pragmatic bias in which the guiding knowledge interest (borrowing the term from Habermas, 1968) of the research is exclusively empirical-analytical, thus oriented toward potential technical control, rather than, or in addition to, an historical-hermenueutic interest or a critical-emancipatory one.

Hence, prevailing methodological individualism in social theory, and pragmatic-empiricist epistemological assumptions in educational administration have defined the study of policy making as a political process "in which constraints and opportunities are a function of the power exercised by decision-makers in the light of ideological values" (Child, 1973 cited in Clegg & Dunkerley, 1980, p. 338).

In this article, I shall argue that a critical theory of power and the state is a necessary starting point to study educational policy making—hence, moving the analysis from the strict realm of individual choice and preference, somehow modeled by organizational behaviour, to a more historical-structural approach where individuals indeed have choices, but they are prescribed or constrained by historical circumstances, conjunctural processes, and the diverse expressions of power and authority (at the micro and macro levels) through concrete rules of policy formation. Also, I will argue that any study of education as public policy should deal with the issues of the organizational context in which power (as an expression of domination) is exercised. The relationships between power, organization and the state should be understood from a combined perspective of the political economy and a political sociology of educational policy making.

I shall argue that policy making should be studied in the context of a theory of politics. Following Clegg (1975), I assume that the concept that articulates political life is domination which has manifold expressions, from economic dominance of one class over others in the material production and reproduction of social life, to patriarchal relations and intersubjective, male to female domination in the household (Morrow & Torres, 1988). Similarly, the distinction between surface/deep structure models of rules, borrowed from structural linguistics, could be very useful as a starting point in understanding power in decision making (Clegg, 1975, p. 70). Chomsky (1968) has distinguished between 'deep structure' (a semantic interpretation of sentences) and 'surface structure' (which implies the phonetic interpretation of sentences) where they both constitute the dynamics of language structure as a vehicle of meaning.

TABLE 1
Power structures

Structure	*Concept*	*Objective processes*
Surface structure	Power	Exchanges
Deep structure	Rules	Rationality
Form of life	Domination/exploitation	Economic activity

Source: adapted from Clegg (1975, p. 78).

The deep structure is composed of a set of *restrictive* and *enabling rules,* "those which operate to modify independently existing forms of behaviour and activity, and those which create new forms of behaviour and activity" (Shwayder, in Clegg, 1975, p. 75). At the level of deep structure, a given combination of rules constitute different rationalities as, for instance, in Weber's three modes of legitimate authority or domination (e.g. traditional, charismatic and bureaucratic). At the level of surface structure, observable exchanges between individuals and institutions would constitute exchanges of power (which in turn, as Marx pointed out in Chap. 23 of Vol. I of *The Capital,* will inhibit or contribute to the simple and complex reproduction of economic exploitation/domination structures in social life). Clegg has graphically described the articulation of these categorical-analytical relationships (Table 1). In Clegg's terms: "Power is about the outcomes of issues enabled by the rule of a substantive rationality which is temporally and institutionally located. Underlying this rule is a specific form of domination. The progression is from domination → rules → power" (Clegg, 1975, p. 78).

This approach to rules, power and domination, which are essential stand-points to the study of policy making, has to be complemented with a discussion of a theory of the state in order to understand what I have called, following Claus Offe, the production rules of public policy. The next section attempts, first, to highlight the importance of a theory of the state for the study of educational policy making, and second, to introduce the notion of state authority in capitalist societies. For the sake of clarity, the theoretical, analytical and political differences between the theories and authors that are discussed below, and that inspired our framework (e.g. the state derivationists, Poulantzas, Offe, Therborn, Gramsci, etc.), will not be discussed in great detail. Similarly, illustrations and examples that may bring to life this theoretical framework will not be extensively used due to space restrictions.

Theory of the State and Education

A common thread that runs through Marxist and Marxist-influenced educational research is the analysis of education as part of the state-administered reproduction of fundamental societal relations (Broady, 1981, p. 143). It has been discussed elsewhere that, in general, the notion of social reproduction (a) presupposes theories of society as a complex totality which develops through contradictions; (b) takes relatively complex societies as the object of inquiry within which formal and specialized educational institutions play a significant role; (c) argues these educational institutions constitute strategic sites for the stability and further development of these societies; (d) studies the relations of mutual interaction between these institutions and the larger society which provides the basis for sociologies of education; (e) suggests that policy formulation within the educational sphere constitutes a crucial context of negotiation and struggle which may have decisive effects on the capacity of society to maintain or transform itself, hence, educational settings are a microscopic representation of the larger macroscopic societal dynamics; and (f) paradoxically considers education to be either a powerful (and somehow a unique) tool for socialization into a given social order or to challenge and resist a hegemonic culture or social practice. In short, theories of social reproduction in education are linked with power, race, gender, class, knowledge and the moral bases of cultural production and acquisition (Morrow & Torres, 1988).

Although the relationship between education and the State is at the core of the definition of education's reproduction function in capitalist societies, it has rarely been thoroughly analyzed in contemporary social theory. Research questions concerning the capitalist state and its class-based proceedings, state impingements on educational structures, practices, codes, and especially educational planning and policy making, still lack sound theoretical understanding and appropriate methodological procedures for their study.

For instance, the influential book *Schooling in Capitalist America* focused on the notion of capital and its intervention in the educational system, particularly in the preparation of students as future workers at the various levels in the hierarchy of capitalist production (Bowles & Gintis, 1976). Bowles & Gintis have suggested a *correspondence principle* which explains educational development. In brief, there is a perceived correspondence between the social relations of production and the social relations of education (Bowles & Gintis, 1981, p. 225). Responding to the critics, they have argued that this correspondence principle depicts five main features of capitalist schooling: (a) the surprising lack of importance of the cognitive aspects of schooling in the preparation of good workers and in the intergenerational reproduction of social status; (b) an assessment of the limits of progressive education which is social rather than biological or technological; (c) a focus on the experience of schooling, which provides a consistent analytical framework for understanding the school as an arena of structured social interaction, and the school curricula as an outcome of these interactive processes; (d) a larger framework to integrate the effects of schooling on individuals (e.g. skills, attitudes, scholastic achievement) into a broader process of structural capitalist transformation and reproduction; and finally (e) Bowles & Gintis claim their analysis shows that, in order to understand the structure of schooling, it is not the ownership but the control of the means of production that matters (Bowles & Gintis, 1981, pp. 226, 227).

The emphasis here is on the general, class-based social determination of educational policy and schooling which is expressed in the correspondence principle. In a more recent contribution, Carnoy & Levin (1985) have emphasized that this earlier analysis of education and reproduction lacks a concrete theory of the State. Similarly, although it is important to consider the process of correspondence between education and capital accumulation, it is even more important to focus on the process of state mediation of contradictions. It is argued that the major problem with the type of analyses produced by Bowles & Gintis and Boudelot & Establet is, ". . . that it does not account for the contradictory trends towards equality and democracy in education . . . Indeed, Bowles and Gintis argue that the 'laws of motion' of correspondence are so dominant that democratic or egalitarian reforms must necessarily fail or be limited in their impact" (Carnoy & Levin, 1985, p. 22).

To understand these complex relationships of correspondence and contradiction in education an explicit theory of the State and politics is necessary. I will argue that to study public policy formation, one must identify concretely the institutional apparatus of the State and who directly controls this apparatus. Similarly, it is of fundamental importance to identify the roles of the capitalist state (and education) in regard to the process of capital accumulation and social legitimation (Curtis, 1984).

Before I turn to discuss the notion of the State and policy making, I would like to assume that the capitalist state has a relative autonomy from the social classes, which seem to be recognized by Marxist and non-Marxist scholars alike (Archer & Vaughan, 1971, pp. 56–60; Offe & Ronge, 1975; Bourdieu & Passeron, 1977, p. 199; Alvater, 1979; Skocpol, 1980, pp. 155–201; Fritzel, 1987, pp. 23–35). Indeed, this relative autonomy is structural and is built into the very foundations of the capitalist mode of production (Boron, 1982, p. 47). Similarly, I will assume that state intervention in civil society has become one of the State's crucial features which takes different forms in different countries, involving such diverse issues as: (a) the articulation and/or independence of the capitalist state and the bloc-in-power, to use the expression developed in Poulantzas's writings (Poulantzas, 1969a, pp. 237–241), (b) the articulation of the State-subordinate class relationships; (c) the degree of direct and indirect state action in the regulation of capital accumulation (i.e. the State's role in the economy); (d) the State-Nation relationship in the context of the World System—as a macrocosmic condensation of broader dynamics and strains built into this structural relationship, particularly in the case of peripheral dependent states; and (e) the issue of the crisis of the capitalist states, with its implications in terms of hegemony and legitimation processes.

State Authority and Policy Formation

The concept of the State has become a fashionable term in political science. However, many authors would refer to political authority and policy making as the role of the Government or the public sector, and some may even be inclined to use a more comprehensive notion such as the 'political system' rather than the State. This is not the place to argue on behalf of the usefulness of the concept. I shall point out that I share the rationale of Daniel Levy (1986, pp. 12–25) regarding the advantages of using the concept of the State.

I use the notion of the State, first of all as a reaction against liberal-pluralist political approaches that for many decades worked within a 'stateless' theoretical framework; and second, in order to highlight particularly, the role of the state as an actor in policy making with purposeful and relatively independent action while at the same time becoming a terrain where public policy is negotiated or fought over.

I propose to consider the State, at the highest level of abstraction, *as a pact of domination and as a self-regulating administrative system.* Cardoso has suggested that the state should be considered "The basic pact of domination that exists among social classes or factions of dominant classes and the norms which guarantee their dominance over the subordinate strata" (Cardoso, 1979, p. 38). Similarly, Claus Offe (1972a, b, 1973; 1974, 1975a, 1975b, 1984) conceptualizes state-organized governance as a selective, event-generating system of rules, i.e. as a sorting process (Offe, 1974, p. 37).

Offe views the State as comprising the institutional apparatuses, bureaucratic organizations, and formal and informal norms and codes which constitute and represent the 'public' and 'private' spheres of social life. The primary focus, then, is neither the interpersonal relations of various elites nor the decision-making process *per se*. Therefore, the class character of the State[1] does not reside in the social origin of the policy-makers, state managers, bureaucracy or the ruling class, but in the internal structure of the state apparatus itself due to its necessary selectivity of public policy; a selectivity that is "built into the system of political institutions" (Offe, 1974, p. 37).

In a similar vein, Goran Therborn identifies two main sources of determination of policy formation in the capitalist states. On the one hand, those determinations which originate at the level of state power, that is, the specific historical crystallization of relations of forces condensed into a pact of domination which acquires expression in a set of policies concerning the productive process, and, on the other hand, those determinations which originate in the structure of the state apparatus and the class bias of its organizational form (Clegg & Dunkerley, 1980, pp. 433–480; Therborn, 1980, pp. 144–179).

In summary, the emphasis here is on the *dual character* of the capitalist state and its organizational forms. That is to say, while the state claims to be the official representative of the Nation as a whole[2], it is at the same time the object, product and determinant of class conflict. Through its policies directed toward the constitution and reproduction of the capitalist system, it is protected from various threats and guides its transformation: yet by acting as a factor of cohesion, the State's long-term planning synthesizes the goals of economic and social reproduction of capitalism as a system of commodity production, despite the sectoral or factional short-term needs and disputes of individual capitalist or corporative groups (Altvater, 1973; Offe, 1973; Skocpol, 1982, pp. 7–28).

Having outlined in very abstract terms the use of the notion of the State, I turn now to advance a set of working hypotheses on the production rules of public policy.

Production Rules of Public Policy: A theoretical assessment and hypothesis

Is Public Policy Formation Mainly a Response or Anticipation to Social Threats?

At the highest level of generalization, the first hypothesis advanced here will stress that any mode of state intervention is linked to a changing pattern of potential or actual threats, or to structural problems that emerge out of the process of accumulation of capital. Thus, the modes of state activity[3] (which will be identified in the next section) can be seen as responses to these social threats and problems (Offe, 1975b, pp. 137–147; O'Donnell, 1978a, b, 1982; Wright, 1978, p. 277; Curtis, 1984, p. 12).

Obviously, this pattern of perceived social threat and state response should not be taken mechanically. As Goran Therborn has so aptly argued in studying the origins of welfare state policies in Europe and the strengthening of class activism:

> What is being argued is, (1) that a threat from the working-class movement, perceived by the political rulers, was a necessary (but not sufficient) condition for welfare-state initiatives; (2) that there is a structural affinity between the first major welfare-state initiatives and the modern labour movement; and (3) that there is a chronological relationship between the emergence of the modern labour movement and the beginning of the welfare state, which makes it probable that there is a causal link between the two, the nature of which remains to be demonstrated. (Therborn, 1984, p. 12)

However, after saying that, Therborn claims that there is always a certain tension between the identified historical processes and the analytical categories used for its study. Arguing that public policy is made out of opposing social-policy perspectives, Therborn cautiously emphasizes that

> the forms and principles of public social commitments have been politically controversial. These controversies have not been merely conjunctural, and have not only pitted individual politicians or civil servants and political parties and interest groups against each other. They have also developed along class lines, and the various specific issues are to a significant degree intelligible in terms of opposite class perspectives. Classes are not decision-making bodies, which is a fundamental reason why policy making is inherently irreducible to class conflict and class power. Yet a class analysis provides an explanatory framework that can make the study of politics and policy into something more than a modernized *histoire événementielle* of strings and episodes acted out by individual policy-makers. (Therborn, 1984, p. 25)

The extent to which these changing social patterns of threats alter not only public policy formation, but also the very same form of the capitalist state, is not our immediate concern here. However, there seem to be certain affinities between the perceived pattern of threat and the pattern of state response/transformation. For example, recent political sociology argues that the emergence of a highly repressive form of political regime, e.g. the Bureaucratic-Authoritarian State in Latin America, is causally related to the internalization of the production in Latin America and the perceived threats from the subordinate social classes. Guillermo O'Donnell argues that the emergence of such regimes is linked to a particular phase or crisis of capital accumulation encountered in the maturation of dependent, industrializing economies. In short, this is the phase in which 'easy' import-substitution possibilities have been exhausted and further expansion seems to depend upon new investments in capital intensive, technologically advanced industries. Included with this 'economic framework' of the explanation, there is an increased activation of the popular sector and working classes which threatens the political stability of the capitalist regime (what Huntington has termed the "praetorianization" of the masses); finally, there is an increased importance of technocratic roles in the State. The evolution of these two major variables, namely the 'deepening of industrialization' and the so-called 'background variables', lead the societal situation to an elective affinity between advanced industrialization and bureaucratic authoritarianism (Collier, 1979, pp. 3–26, 380; O'Donnell, 1982).

Why is this issue of social threats so important, and how are they dealt with by advanced capitalist states? The so-called 'German Debate' (Holloway & Piccioto, 1979, pp. 19–31; Jessop, 1982; Carnoy, 1984) will give us some clues. A prominent participant in this debate, Eltmar Altvater, pointed out that capital is unable, as a result of its existence as many factionalized and mutually antagonistic capitalists, to produce the social preconditions of its own existence. State interventionism is derived (deduced) as a particular state form working toward shortening and overcoming those deficiencies of private capital by organizing individuals into a viable body (namely, a general capitalist interest).

Altvater derives the nature of state interventionism from the four general functions of the State which he has envisaged.

> There are essentially four areas in which the State is primarily active, namely, 1) the provision of general material conditions of production ('infrastructure'); 2) establishing and guaranteeing general legal relations, through which the relationships of legal subjects in capitalist society are performed; 3) the regulation of the conflict between wage labour and capital and, if necessary, the political repression of the working class, not only by means of law but also by the police and the army; 4) safeguarding the existence and expansion of total national capital on the capitalist world market. (Altvater, 1979, p. 42)

Claus Offe not only explicitly recognizes his agreement with Altvater (Offe, 1973a, p. 110) in their mutual criticism of the State Monopoly Capitalism Thesis (STATEMOP Thesis)[4]. Offe also adds to Altvater's formulation that state domination should be understood as a regulating system or as a system of filters with the specific selective mechanisms of: (a) extracting a general class interest from many fractionalized capital units, and (b) oppressing or suppressing any anti-capitalist interest which could arise in any capitalist social formation (Offe, 1975b, pp. 125–144).

Hence, social threats are dealt with by social policies and state institutions as part of this preventive and regulative role of the State. In regard to these state functions, Therborn's comment on the need to look at the State's everyday routines would show a fundamental activity that has not been highlighted so far, the welfare activities which seem to dominate everyday state routine (Therborn, 1984, p. 32). In support of this, Therborn shows that since education is at the core of welfare policies—and since education and also health systems are labour intensive, they employ a sizable majority of the total public servants—school employees in 1970, at the time of the Vietnam War, for the first time since the US turned into an imperial world power, became significantly more numerous than military and civilian defense personnel (Therborn, 1984, p. 35). A similar argument could be developed for a dependent society such as Mexico where slightly more than half of the total increase in federal employment between 1970 and 1976 was allocated to education (Torres, 1984, p. 156).

In societies in social transformation, recent research (Carney & Samoff, 1988) has shown that, on the one hand, a new political regime must respond to mass demands for more schooling, better health care, and the redistribution of agricultural land. On the other hand, a fundamental task of these regimes is to accumulate capital in order to expand the national material base. It seems that while, hypothetically, social demands and the accumulation of capital are complementary since healthier, more educated people will have higher productivity and therefore will increase output, to choose one to the relative exclusion of the other may mean, in the worst case, to risk failure of the political project itself. Carnoy, Samoff and co-workers have demonstrated how in all of the case studies, which included Cuba, Nicaragua, China, Tanzania and Mozambique, the expansion of public services such as education and health care also have ideological implications, and that the legitimacy of the State in both low- and high-income countries is therefore affected by its capability to deliver such services to the population at large.

Patterns of State Activity: The pursuit of abstract systemic interests or single-class-based interests? On Modes and Methods of State Intervention

Claus Offe recognizes four main guiding patterns of state action. First, *exclusion:* since the State has no authority to order production or to control it, State and accumulation are somehow divorced in such a way that production and accumulation cannot be separated. Second, *maintenance:* the State does not have the authority but rather has the mandate to create and sustain conditions of accumulation, as well as to avoid, regulate or repress social threats. Threats may come from other accumulating units (e.g. interfirm, interindustry and international competition), from non-capitalist entities (e.g. the working class, social movements), or from criminal or 'deviant' behaviour. Third, *dependency:* the power relationship of the capitalist state and its main decision-making powers depend, like any other relationships in capitalist society, upon the presence and continuity of the accumulation process. A last guiding pattern of state activity is the *legitimation* function of the capitalist state. The State can only function as a capitalist state by appealing to symbols and sources of support which conceal its true nature (Offe, 1975b, pp. 126, 127). In a more crude economic analysis of the advanced capitalist societies, Offe has suggested a structural discrepancy between abstract, surplus-value-related forms and concrete, use-value-related forms used in the implementation of state functions. Thus, this discrepancy can be maintained, if not solved, over time only by a system of legitimacy. Indeed, it is likely that as state power acquires more functions, it also requires an increase in legitimation (Offe, 1973b, p. 74).

Considering the above-mentioned fundamental parameters of state intervention, what remains to be clarified is the analytical distinction between *modes* of state intervention and *methods* of state intervention. The former refers to state action *vis-à-vis* state expected functions under the logic of commodity production, while the latter refers to a somehow abstract analytical distinction which embraces those several state alternatives (methods) to choose from in the process of public policy formation.

The principal *modes* of state intervention can be divided into allocative modes and productive modes. Offe has proposed the following schematic description of these types of activities:

1. *Allocative* a) allocation of State-owned resources, b) response to demands and laws ("politics"), c) demands which are positive and specific in regard to time, space, group, type, and amount of state resources, and d) decisions reached by politics.
2. *Productive* a) production of inputs of accumulation (organized production process required) in response to perceived threats to accumulation; b) conflicting or incompletely articulated demands that cannot be eliminated without threatening the overall process of accumulation; c) decision reached by policies based on State-generated decision rules. (Offe, 1975b, p.133)

Using allocative activities, the State creates and maintains the conditions of accumulation by means that simply require the allocation of resources which are already under state control (e.g. taxes, repressive forces, land, mass media). The productive mode represents state action which supplies a variable and a constant capital which the units of private capital are unable to produce. Beyond areas of competence or types of policies considered, what really differentiates these two modes is that the allocative mode is usually controlled and thereby reinterpreted by its inputs while the productive mode is generally controlled and thereby evaluated by its outputs (Offe, 1972a, p. 128).

The principal methods of state intervention are the following: (a) *state regulation* through a set of positive and negative sanctions connected with a certain behaviour of social categories (e.g. bureaucracy) or social classes, (b) *infrastructure investment* either as a *partial* or supplementary method to private capital activity (e.g. building roads, bridges, airports) or as a total method with which to replace private capital activity (e.g. the case of mass public compulsory education in some countries, law enforcement or the administration of justice. In these cases, the participation of private initiative is negligible in terms of the amount of investment and the probability of a high and consistent degree of control of systemic outcomes); (c) *participation* as the co-determination of policy making and policy-operation through consent building in decision-making bodies which incorporate several interest groups or corporative units.

Considering these modes and methods, it is important to propose a second hypothesis regarding the process of policy formation. Thus far, it has been suggested that the State's motivational force is the pursuit of an abstract systemic interest rather than any particular interest; however, it is equally important to distinguish between short-term, conjunctural processes and long-term, historical or organic processes in policy formation. The Gramscian dictum is in this regard very insightful and clear, and deserves to be quoted at length:

> A common error in historical-political analysis consists in an inability to find the correct relation between what is organic and what is conjunctural. This leads to presenting causes as immediately operative which in factor only operate indirectly, or to asserting that the immediate causes are the only effective ones. In the first case, there is an excess of 'economism', or doctrinary pedantry, in the second an excess of 'ideologism'. In the first case there is an overestimation of mechanical causes, in the second an exaggeration of the voluntarist and individual element. The distinction between 'organic' movement and facts, and 'conjunctural' or occasional ones must be applied to those in which a regressive development or an acute crisis takes place, but also to those in which there is a progressive development or one towards prosperity, or which the productive forces are stagnant. The dialectical nexus between the two categories of movement, and therefore research, is hard to establish precisely. (Gramsci, 1980, p. 178)

Are the 'Form' and the 'Content' of Policy Making Two Distinct Dimensions?

A third working hypothesis regards the distinction between *form* and *content* in the production rules of public policy which results from the same analytical distinction between deep/surface structure models of rules. For instance, analyzing welfare state politics, Therborn has argued that: "One important reason for the intricate complexity of welfare-state history is the fact that public social-policy commitments can take a number of different forms, and questions of form have often aroused more controversy and conflict than the principle of public social responsibility *per se*" (Therborn, 1984, p. 16).

First of all, at a lower level of abstraction, it is not to be expected that a situation in which a stated intention of a policy and its actual outcome faithfully coincide could ever be found. Even though at first glance this point seems to be a trivial one, nonetheless it prevents a formal comparison—so common in educational studies—between the State's alleged goals and the practical results. In general, such comparisons are too formal and generic to be worthwhile. Therefore, there will always be a gap between what is declared, what is implemented, and what is the actual policy outcome.

Second, at a higher level of abstraction, if the rationality behind a policy decision is treated as an analysis of language-in-use, any conversation will have a basic grammar, but the linguistic rules will not have entire control over the quality, intensity and meaning of the message. Similarly, "The organization structure can be conceived in terms of the selectivity rules which can be analytically constructed as an explanation of its social action and practice (its surface detail, what it does). The rules collected together, may be conceived of as a mode of rationality" (Clegg, 1979, p. 122). This mode of rationality, that is expressing selectivity rules, could be of different origins. Clegg has distinguished four types of rules: *technical rules* (know-how to carry out a particular administrative task), *social regulative rules* (any intervention to repair social solidarity in an organization, such as the implementation of human relations), *extra-organizational rules* (e.g. discriminatory practices based in racism, sexism, etc.) and *strategic rules* (social contracts, and wages and income policies).

It should be mentioned in passing that an example of a related type of analysis, although applied to education discourses (which influence and inform educational policies), can be found in Giroux when he compares different views of cultural production, pedagogical analysis and political action in the teacher-student experiences. Giroux distinguishes different pedagogical discourses (or logics-in-use in education), namely the discourse of management and control, the discourse of relevance and integration (progressivism), and the discourse of cultural politics—critical affirmative language; hence, using Giroux's terminology, a discourse that moves from a language of criticism to a language of possibilities (Giroux, 1985, pp. 22–41).

In short, the distinction between form and content of public policy is similar and related to the distinctions between rationality and social action, and between deep/surface structures. In fact, if we take into account all the possible combinations of different selectivity rules (and the fact that all of them may be co-existent at some point, or conversely, given a particular historical and organizational setting, one may predominate over the rest) with inputs (including rationalities), processes of transformation, and outputs (including social action) of policy, a simple distinction of form and content will vanish in front of our eyes; every policy form may or may not have a particular policy content if we take into account selectivity rules.

Is the State a Problem-solving Agent?

As a result of these theoretical explorations, the fourth hypothesis rejects the notion of the State as simply a *problem-solving agent*, an approach that in general places too much emphasis on the analysis of policy content and on the predominance of 'technical rules' among selectivity rules. The main assumptions of this common approach to policy making are the following: (i) the State seems to be analyzing those processes which occur in the political arena, and through a diagnosis of the chief problems, organizes its political agenda for action; (ii) from this standpoint, it is important for researchers to focus mainly upon which interests are involved in the determination of policy making; and (iii) as soon as this identification has been done, the corollary of the analysis will be to check those interests against the material outcomes and the distribution of tangible benefits which result from policies and implementation (Lindblom, 1968, pp. 12, 13). In general, these shared assumptions are used in the basic approaches to policy planning in education, including such areas as the estimation of social demand, needs analysis, manpower planning, cost-effectiveness analysis or rate-of-return analysis (Russel, 1980, pp. 1–15; Simmons, 1980, pp. 15–33; Weiler, 1980).

Is Social Control Built into the Selectivity Rules?

A fifth hypothesis suggests that any organizational structure has controls which are built into the system of political institutions. Following Clegg, an organization-structure is a set of sedimented (i.e. historically laid down and superimposed) selection rules: "The organization-structure can be conceptualized as a structure of sedimented selection rules. Those prescribe the limits within which the organization-structure might vary" (Clegg, 1979, p. 97). Furthermore, those rules of policy formation depend upon the main guiding patterns of state action, the main state resources to carry out its functions, and the principal modes of state intervention.

The central guiding patterns of state activity have been identified as (a) exclusion, (b) maintenance, (c) dependency, and (d) legitimacy. The political puzzle, then, for the capitalist state is how to reconcile those patterns in the production of public policy. I have maintained, following Offe, that the motivational and structural force underlying policy making is the attempt to reconcile these four elements. To carry on its functions, the State resorts to four principal means: fiscal policies, administrative rationality, law enforcement and repression (which should not be considered only as a special case of administrative rationality and mass loyalty. In the case of the dependent state,[5] perhaps the most significant feature is that the exercise of coercion and organized repression overlaps (and sometimes will have more prominence than) the other three standard means.

These main resources enable the capitalist state to perform its principal roles of executing preventive crisis management, determining priorities embodied in social needs, social threats and civil society problem-areas (for example in Canada, a typical case of a problem-area is the native question), and devising a long-term avoidance strategy for further threats and conflicts. In this regard, contradictions can no longer be plausibly interpreted simply as class antagonism. They must, as Offe insists, at least be regarded as necessary by-products of an integral political system of control (Offe, 1975a, pp. 4, 5). To this extent, the fiscal crisis of the State,[6] which appears to be the inevitable consequence of the structural gap between state expenditure and revenues, is at the same time a lively testimony and expression of systemic constraints.

Can Functional Interaction and Interdependency Be Differentiated According to Different Political Regimes?

A last hypothesis will stress that the different forms of functional interaction and interdependency within a bureaucratic organization can be analytically differentiated; and similarly, the form that this interaction assumes will vary according to the type of political regime considered.

For instance, Oscar Oszlak in analyzing political regimes in Latin America has identified three main types: *bureaucratic-authoritarian, democratic-liberal* and *patrimonialist;* similarly, Oszlak identifies three main types of bureaucratic interdependency: *hierarchical, functional* and *material* or *budgetary* (Oszlak, 1980).

Before exploring determinants of policy formation, it will be necessary to identify and carefully characterize the type of political regime and capitalist state, and which dominant form of bureaucratic interdependency comes into the discussion.

Production Rules of Policy Formation: A Summary

(1) The capitalist state has been defined as an arena, a product and a determinant of class and social conflict. Hence, any mode of state intervention is linked to a changing pattern of threats, potential or actual, or to structural problems that emerge out of the process of capital accumulation and political domination. Particularly in dependent states but also in industrial advanced social formations, class struggle and the political practice of social movements give shape to the state structure at the same time that an institutionalized set of selectivity rules alter the intensity, degree and level (character) of class and social conflict. Two implications can be drawn. On the one hand, the form and content of state policies give shape to the forms and content of the class and social struggles, while, conversely, class and social struggles are shaping the form and content of state policies (Sardei-Bierman *et al.*, 1973, pp. 60–69). On the other hand, there is a practical tension between consensus-oriented practices and coercion-oriented practices in the planning and implementation of state policies.

(2) There are modes and methods of state intervention which deal with those patterns and threats raised in the class and social struggles; the former (divided into allocative and productive modes) refers to a wide range of probable activities regarding the use of state resources while the latter (distinguishing between state regulations, infrastructure investment and participation) refers to the range of probable courses of action undertaken by the State. Both, methods and modes of state intervention, gives substance to the process of public policy formation.

(3) At the most abstract level, the main determinant of public policy formation is not the pursuit of any particular interest, but of an abstract systemic interest. Nonetheless, two different kinds of historical processes underpin public policy. On the one hand, there are structural determinants which have a historical-organic origin; on the other hand, there are conjunctural determinants which do represent, at a particular point in time, the short-term crystallization of a peculiar constellation of forces in class and social struggles.

(4) Particularly in liberal-democratic societies, the State always will try to reconcile its contradictory guiding patterns of activity within a concrete corpus of state policies. Then, the process of policy formation will never reach a steady-state situation nor will it be completely coherent; it will always express conflicts, imbalances, contradictions and a fragile stability in policy formation.

(5) In this regard, there always will be a gap between the publicly stated goals and targets of state policies and the actual outcomes, as well as there will be a practical and analytical difference between rationalities (as selectivity rules) and social action. Then, to consider the State (and state policies) as *only* a problem-solving agent would be grossly misleading. However, this seems to be the dominant approach in educational policy planning. This framework of the State as a problem-solving agent (needless to say, an argument usually advanced by technocratic-minded and not historically-minded scholars and administrators) fails to recognize the internally-produced and the externally-originated determinants of policies—especially those with the most causal weight in non-statistical terms. Secondly, this framework omits the display of the basic regularities, what Offe has termed the basic 'laws' of public policy formation.

(6) By combining the modes and methods of state intervention, three main laws of motion of public policy can be suggested here. These are the law of motion of bureaucracy, the purposive-action law of motion, and the participatory-consensus building law of motion. In order to study these policy laws of motion, it

would be necessary to consider not only a political framework and a theory of the State, but also an organizational approach to policy making. In this regard, any public policy, in its form and content, is bounded by a system of inputs, processes of transformation, and outputs, all of them related to deep/surface structures (rationales) expressing not only social action but domination and power.

(7) Looking particularly at the dependent state, a decisive landmark is the State's bureaucratic encapsulation of policy making. In this sense, there are different forms of functional interaction within a bureaucratic organization; those forms of interaction can be analytically differentiated; and the form this interaction assumes will vary according to the type of political regime considered. This point leads us to recognize several common traits in the historical evolution of state apparatuses, for example in Latin America (Oszlak, 1981, pp. 3–32); traits that are of paramount importance in the study of educational policy formation in a corporatist state such as the Mexican State, with the complex interaction between a ruling party in power for more than 40 years, the forceful action of corporative trade unions and capitalist associations, and the ideology of efficiency held by the organic bureaucracy of the state (Pescador & Torres, 1985).

(8) Since capitalism did develop differentially in each country, the configuration of the State will sharply differ across countries. I have assumed here that it is crucial to characterize the type of state, its historical traits and main features as a mode of political control and political organization, and the balance of power established in the society by the ongoing confrontation between social and political forces, prior to undertaking an empirical analysis of educational policy making. Without such a historical and political background, it would be difficult to understand the particular rationale of resource assignment and the underlying motives for the creation (or elimination) of institutions, services, plans or policies. Finally, turning now to education in greater detail, it is necessary to clarify theoretically education's particular role in capital accumulation and political domination. By considering a theory of the State and education, it will be possible to assess in detailed fashion the politics of educational policy making, and policy making as politics.

Conclusion: A theoretical approach to public policy-formation in education

It has been suggested here that the inquiry about policy formation must be in light of the following dimensions: (1) *the main actors of policy formation,* including the bureaucracy, administrative agents and social constituencies and clienteles; (2) in terms of organizational studies, there are *the main systemic elements* which can be found within a given educational setting—I will name them inputs, processes of transformation and outputs; (3) *the main institutional phases, stages and/or units of policy formation* (the levels of policy planning, policy making, policy operation and even the policy outcome)—these distinctions are useful in analytical terms for undertaking case studies; finally (4), the intellectual, institutional and ideological atmosphere where those decisions are made (the policy framework). Additionally, I shall argue that those dimensions are offset or shaped by *the general framework of organizational rules,* historically embedded within a particular organization. At a second, but nonetheless determinant, level of generalization in the analysis, it may be said that the production rules of public policy identified above would offer a theoretical bridge with which to understand educational relationships between the political society and the civil society at a particular point of time.

Henry Levin (1980) has offered a concise and highly stimulating analytical framework with which to study educational policy planning. Figure 1 constitutes a good synthesis of his model of analysis which needs no further explanation.

Combining Levin's analytical dimensions, although modified, and the theoretical framework devised in this article, Figure 2 gives a graphic representation of the main analytical dimensions to be taken into account in analyzing educational policy formation.

By and large, in an analysis of educational policy making, the following concerns could be highlighted: (1) as regards *inputs mechanisms,* I

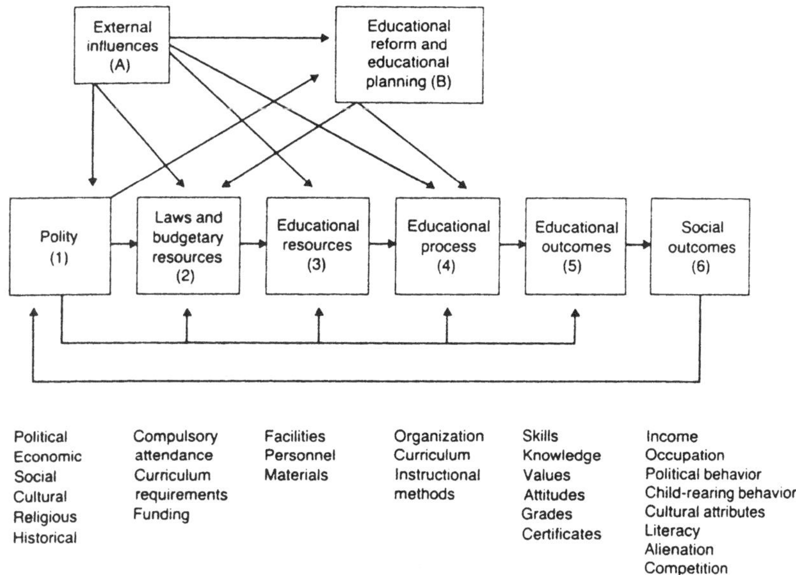

Fig. 1: **Henry Levin's policy-planning analytical framework**

will suggest the need to emphasize specially those principles regulating the type of task dealt with by the State, which is related to bureaucratic ideology and the state self-producing values and ideologies; (2) regarding *processes of transformation,* the emphasis will be placed on modes of decision making rather than on the handling of tasks. In addition, other important analytical dimensions for this study are: patterns of organizational positions and of relations among their incumbents, and the competing models of resource allocation; (3) regarding *output mechanisms,* those that should be explored and analyzed are as follows: (a) patterning of decisions and practices of the state toward the civil society (especially the educational clientele), and (b) modes of outflow of material and non-material resources from the State, understood as concrete processes of transformation of the social relations addressed generally toward particular social classes (Therborn, 1980, pp. 37–48).

While the study of policy formation should take into account the form and content of rule production and the predominant laws of motion of educational policy formation, any empirical research should confine itself, in its initial stages, to analyze specific levels and modalities in order to avoid simplistic generalizations not based on deep observation and analysis of empirical (quantitative and qualitative) data. Similarly, the production rules of public policy identified should be checked against concrete policy content and policy output in order to substantiate the main hypotheses regarding processes of transformation oriented toward the civil society.

In summary, if the main concern is to study policy formation, a preliminary attempt to do so should offset such distinct analytical dimensions as: (a) the State's goals and policy targets—the social history of state apparatus and the ebb and flow of class and social struggle; (b) modes and methods of operation in educational policy formation in dealing with social threats or problems that arise out of capital accumulation problems and/or political legitimation practices, policies and outputs; (c) the extent and type of bureaucratic organization; (d) the educational bureaucracy's ideologies contained in policy planning—as internal determinants of policy making; (e) material and non-material policy outcomes; perhaps a fundamental issue that ought to be discussed from a post-Marxist perspective is education's (and welfare activities in general) role in the production and reproduction of productive and unproductive labor, and education's contribution to production and realization of surplus-values; (f) capitalist and non-capitalist units of policy formation (Clegg & Dunkerley, 1980, pp. 486–492), which brings to light the

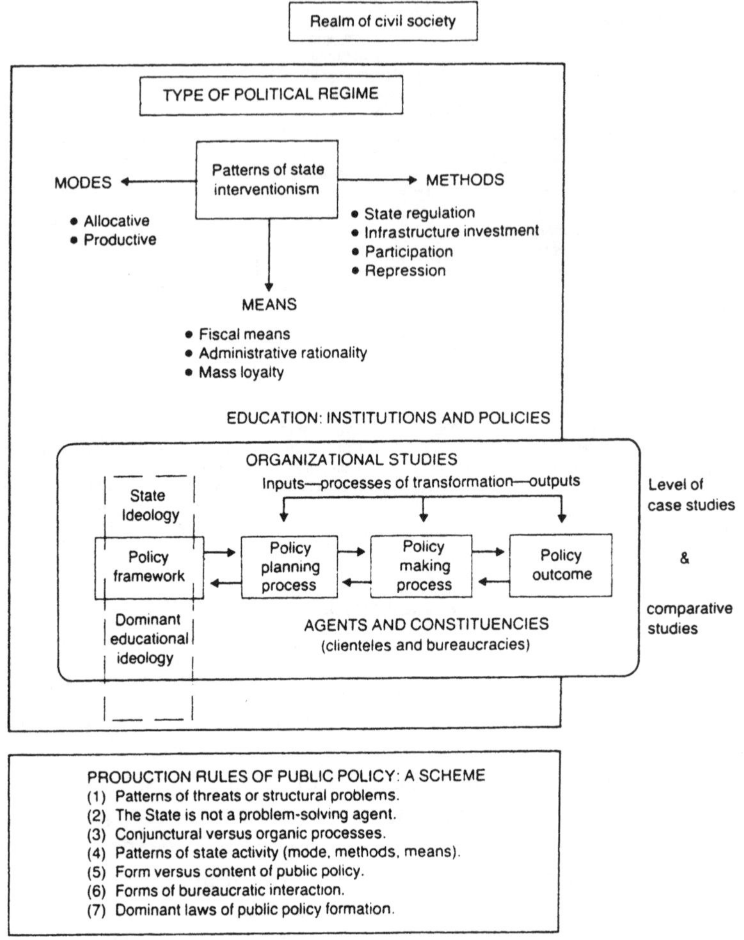

Fig. 2: **A theoretical approach to public policy formation**

important distinction between use-value and exchange-value as distinct goals of policy making in education (and other welfare activities and institutions); (g) the role of the educational policy within the overall state public policy, particularly (although not exclusively) at the level of legitimation practices. For instance, Miller (1986, p. 244) classifies within accumulation expenditures for social investment the levels and modalities of higher education and other non-elementary or secondary school education. Elementary and secondary education's expenditures are classified under accumulation expenditures for social consumptions. Perhaps adult and non-formal education expenditures, always neglected by the analysts, can also be classified, following the original O'Connor's taxonomy as social expenses; (h) and the struggles by groups and social classes to resist the hegemonic practices of the capitalist state. However, if resistance groups have some visible presence and are somehow inserted within the state apparatus, the task will then be to study how they have tried to consolidate or enlarge their position, and to promote specific policies, in the presence of restricting and enabling rules.

Correspondence: Carlos Alberto Torres, 5–109 Education North, University of Alberta, Edmonton, Alberta, Canada T6G 2G5.

Notes

1. As a pact of domination and as a corporate actor who assumes the representation of popular sovereignty and as the political authority that enforces the democratic rule, the State becomes also a terrain for struggle of national and socio-political (class) projects. These contradictory functions summarize the contradictory unity and inherent complexity of

capitalist states. Also, it highlights a crucial problem for Marxist analysis: the class character of the State—a question addressed by the neo-Marxist analysis which tries to overcome the impasse that resulted from the instrumentalist-structuralist debate and was exemplified in the exchanges between Poulantzas and Miliband almost two decades ago (Poulantzas, 1969a, pp. 237–241, 1969b, pp. 67–78; Miliband, 1970a, b).

2. The foremost penetrating pieces of research on state policies, have in one way or another pointed out this essential feature. For instance, Weber views the State as not only instrumental but immanent, that is, the State as the monopoly of force and site for exchange of services and community benefits (Weber, 1969, Vol. 1, pp. 210–215).
3. Eric Olin Wright (1978, p. 15) has suggested a schema of structural causality distinguishing diverse *modes of determination* and organizing them into several *models of determination.* Modes of determination are considered to be distinct relationships of determination among the structural categories of Marxist theory and between these categories and the appearances of empirical investigation. Models of causal determination are schematic representations of the complex interconnections of the various modes of determination involved in a given structural process. Wright has outlined six main modes of causal determination: (a) structural limitation, (b) selection, (c) reproduction/non-reproduction, (d) limits of functional compatibility, (e) transformation, and (f) mediation.
4. The STATEMOP thesis advocates that Marx's political economy was dealing with competitive capitalism. However, the development of productive forces has progressed and large monopolies have thwarted competition in such a way that the State and 'monopoly capital' has become intertwined. This new phase of 'monopoly capitalism' is seen to invalidate the general laws advanced by Marx, particularly the laws of commodity exchange, capital accumulation and the falling rate of profit. Therefore, as in this theory, the analysis of modern capitalism must build on Lenin's analysis of the State and imperialism rather than on orthodox applications of Marx's methodology. The STATEMOP main thesis and critiques are thoroughly discussed in Holloway & Piccioto's book. A very good piece of criticism is Margaret Wirth's article (1977).
5. Since the early formulation of dependency theory, there has been a challenge to the notion that international dependency relies on a set of countries which constitute a central core (industrial advanced countries) and a set of countries which constitute a periphery. Certain countries that have been identified as 'Newly Industrialized Countries' (NIC) have assumed new functions in the world division of labour by constituting industrial platforms of development through their labour-cost advantages (e.g. India, Singapore, Korea, Hong Kong, Pakistan, Brazil and perhaps Mexico). In spite of these changes, the notion of the 'dependent state' could be analytically useful if we assume that it refers to states where (i) the majority or a sizeable proportion of the labour force still remains linked with agriculture production: (ii) in many cases, most of the country's exports are essentially non-manufactured goods, (iii) there is not a political structure resembling the welfare state; (iv) and this state is subject to important constraints for future autarchic economic and political development due to a raising external debt, a continuous outflow of domestic capital and labour, and a huge 'underground' informal, non-taxable, economical exchanges; (v) in this political structure, the role of the Armed Forces is usually prominent in national politics, and it is the ultimate resort for conducting repression activities; (vi), and finally, this state is further constrained by its operation in a given orbit of geopolitical power and the presence of an imperial ruling country—in spite of the global exchangeability of commodities and the international division of labour due to the World System.
6. The first premise of James O'Connor's analysis of the fiscal crisis of the State is that the State must try to fulfill two main functions: the accumulation and the legitimation functions. Therefore, at the same time that the State involves itself in the process of capital accumulation, it also tries to win the support of the economically exploited and socially oppressed classes for its programs and policies (O'Connor, 1973b, pp. 64–96). What is initially stressed in O'Connor's claim is that these two functions are mutually contradictory inasmuch as the growth of the state sector and state spending is increasingly the basis for the growth of the monopoly sector of the economy and the total production. Reciprocally, the growth of state spending and state programs is also the result of the growth of the monopoly industries, and "the greater the growth of the monopoly sector, the greater the State's expenditures on social expenses of production" (O'Connor, 1973b, pp. 13–39, 1973a, pp. 81–82). This, for many years the standard neo-Marxist explanation, is now being critically assessed. As an example of new financial estimates and theoretical developments in radical political economy, see Miller's extension of O'Connor's analysis. Miller (1986, pp. 237–260) argues that although it seems clear that the state fulfills an accumulation and legitimation function, they should be better formulated to explain, the

state's ability to promote accumulation in the 1970s and 1980s.

References

Altvater, Elmar (1979) Some problems of state interventionism, in: J. Holloway & S. Piccioto (Eds) *State and Capital. A Marxist Debate* (Austin, Tex., University of Texas Press).

Altvater, Elmar (1973) Notes on some problems of state interventionism, *Working Papers on the Kapitalistate,* 1, pp. 96–108, pp. 76–83.

Archer, Margaret & Vaughan Michalina (1971) Domination and assertion in educational systems, in: E. Hooper (Ed.) *Readings in the Theory of Educational Systems* (London, Hutchinson).

Bates, Richard (1985) *Public Administration and the Crisis of the State* (Victoria, Deakin University).

Boron Atilio (1982) *The Capitalist State and Its Relative Autonomy: Arguments regarding limits and dimensions* (Mexico, CIDE, mimeograph).

Bourdieu, P. & Passeron, J.-C. (1977) *Reproduction in Education, Society and Culture* (London, Sage).

Bowles, Samuel & Gintis, Herbert (1976) *Schooling in Capitalist America* (New York, Basic Books).

Bowles, Samuel & Gintis, Herbert (1981) Education as a site of contradictions in the reproduction of the capital-labor relationship: second thoughts on the 'correspondence principle', *Economic and Industrial Democracy,* 2, pp. 223–242.

Broady, Donald (1981) Critique of the political economy of education: the prokla approach. Apropos of a tenth anniversary, *Economic and Industrial Democracy,* 2, pp. 141–189.

Cardoso, F. H. (1979) On the characterization of authoritarian regimes in Latin America, in: D. Collier (Ed.) *The New Authoritarianism in Latin America* (Princeton, N.J., Princeton University Press).

Carnoy, Martin (1984) *The State and Political Theory* (Princeton, N.J., Princeton University Press).

Carnoy, Martin & Levin, Hank (1985) *Education and Work in the Democratic State* (Stanford, Stanford University Press).

Carnoy, Martin & Samoff, Joel (Eds) (1988) *Education and Social Transformation in the Third World* (unpublished manuscript).

Chomsky, Norman (1968) *Language and Mind* (New York, Harcourt, Brace & World).

Clegg, Stewart (1975) *Power, Rule and Domination* (London, Routledge & Kegan Paul).

Clegg, Stewart (1979) *The Theory of Power and Organization* (London, Routledge & Kegan Paul).

Clegg, Stewart & Dunkerley, David (1980) *Organization, Class and Control* (London, Routledge & Kegan Paul).

Collier, David (1979) Overview of the bureaucratic-authoritarian model, in: D. Collier (ed.) *The New Authoritarianism in Latin America* (Princeton, N.J., Princeton University Press).

Curtis, Bruce (1984) Capitalist development and educational reform, *Theory and Society,* 13, pp. 41–68.

David, M. E. (1977) *Reform, Reaction and Resources, the three Rs of Educational Planning* (Windsor, NFER).

Fritzell, Christer (1987) On the concept of relative autonomy in educational theory, *British Journal of Sociology of Education,* 8, pp. 23–35.

Giroux, Henry (1985) Critical pedagogy, cultural politics and the discourse of experience, *Boston University Journal of Education,* 167(2), pp. 22–41.

Gramsci, Antonio (1980) *Selections from the Prison Notebooks* (edited and translated by Quintin Hoare & Geoffrey Nowell Smitt; New York, International Publishers).

Habermas, Jurgen (1968) *Knowledge and Human Interests* (edited and translated by Jermy J. Shapiro; Boston, Mass., Beacon).

Holloway, John & Picciotto, Sol (Eds) (1979) *State and Capital. A Marxist Debate* (Austin, Tex., University of Texas Press).

Howell, D. A. & Brown, Roger (1983) *Educational Policy Making. An Analysis* (London, Heinemann).

Jessop, Bob (1982) *The Capitalist State* (New York, Academic Press).

Leichter, Howard M. (1979) *A Comparative Approach to Policy Analysis: health care policies in four nations* (Cambridge, Cambridge University Press).

Levin, Henry (1980) The limits of educational planning, in: Hans N. Weiler (Ed.) *Educational Planning and Social Change* (Paris, IIEP-UNESCO).

Levy, Daniel C. (1986) *Higher Education and the State in Latin America. Private Challenges to Public Dominance* (Chicago, Ill., University of Chicago Press).

Lindblom, Charles E. (1968) *The Policy-Making Process* (Englewood Cliffs, N.J., Prentice-Hall).

Miliband, Ralph (1970a) The capitalist state—reply to Nicos Poulantzas, *New Left Review,* 59, pp. 53–60.

Miliband, Ralph (1970b) Poulantzas and the Capitalist State, *New Left Review,* 82, pp. 93–92.

Miller, John A. (1986) The fiscal crisis of the State reconsidered: two views of the State and the accumulation of capital in the postwar economy, *Review of Radical Political Economics,* 18, pp. 236–260.

Morrow, Raymond & Torres, Carlos Alberto (1988) *Social theory, social reproduction, and education's everyday life: a framework for analysis,* paper prepared for the Western Association of Sociology and Anthropology (WASA) Annual Meeting, University of Alberta, 17–20 February.

O'Connor, James (1973a) Summary of the theory of the fiscal crisis, *Working Papers on the Kapitalistate,* pp. 79–83.

O'Connor, James (1973b) *The Fiscal Crisis of the State* (New York, St Martin Press).

O'Donnell, Guillermo (1978a) Reflections on the pattern of change in the bureaucratic-authoritarian state, *Latin American Research Review,* 12, pp. 3–38.

O'Donnell, Guillermo (1978b) Apuntes para una teoria del estado, *Revista Mexicana de Sociologia,* 40, pp. 1157–1199.

O'Donnell, Guillermo (1982) *El Estado Burocrático-Autoritario: Argentina 1966–1973* (Buenos Aires, Editorial de Belgrano).

Offe, Claus (1972a) Political authority and class structures—an analysis of late capitalist societies, *International Journal of Sociology,* 2, pp. 73–108.

Offe, Claus (1972b) Advanced capitalism and the welfare state, *Politics and Society,* 2, pp. 488–497.

Offe, Claus (1973) The abolition of market control and the problem of legitimacy, *Working Papers on the Kapitalistate,* (a) 1, pp. 109–116; (b) 2, pp. 73–75.

Offe, Claus (1974) Structural problems of the capitalist state: class rule and the political system. On the selectiveness of political institutions, in: Von Beyme (Ed.) *German Political Studies* (Beverley Hills, Calif., Sage).

Offe, Claus (1975a) *Notes on the laws of motion of reformist state policies* (mimeograph).

Offe, Claus (1975b) The theory of the capitalist state and the problem of policy formation, in: Lindberg *et al.* (Eds) *Stress and Contradiction in Modern Capitalism* (Toronto, Lexington Books).

Offe, Claus (1984) *Contradictions of the Welfare State* (London, Hutchinson).

Offe, Claus & Ronge, V. (1975) Theses on the theory of the State, *New German Critique,* Fall, pp. 137–147.

Oszlak, Oscar (1980) *Politicas Públicas y Regimenes Políticos: reflexiones a partir de algunas experiencias latinoamericanas* (Buenos Aires, Estudios Cedes).

Oszlak, Oscar (1981) The historical formation of the State in Latin America: some theoretical and methodological guidelines for its study, *Latin American Research Review,* 16(2), pp. 3–32.

Peabody Journal of Education (1985) State politics of education, 62, 4.

Pescador, J. A. & Torres, C. A. (1985) *Poder Político y Educación en Mexico* (Mexico, Uthea).

Poulantzas, Nicos (1969a) *Poder Politico y Clases Sociales en el Estado Capitalista* (Mexico, Siglo XXI Editores).

Poulantzas, Nicos (1969b) The problem of the capitalist state, *New Left Review,* 58, pp. 67–78.

Russell, David G. (1980) *Planning Education for Development* (Cambridge, Harvard University Press—CRED).

Saran, R. (1973) *Policy Making in Secondary Education* (Oxford, Oxford University Press).

Sardei-Bierman, Christiansen, Jens & Dohse, Knuth (1973) Class domination and the political system. A critical interpretation of recent contribution by Claus Offe, *Working Paper on the Kapitalistate,* 2, pp. 60–69.

Siegel, R. & Weinberg, Leonard B. (1977) *Comparing Public Policies: United States, Soviet Union and Europe* (Homewood, Ill., Dorsey Press).

Simmons, John (1980) *The Educational Dilemma* (Oxford, Pergamon Press).

Skocpol, Theda (1980) Political responses to capitalist crisis: Neo-Marxist theories of the state and the case of the New Deal, *Politics and Society,* 10(2), pp. 155–201.

Skocpol, Theda (1982) *Bringing the State back in. False leads and promising starts in current theories and research,* a working paper prepared for discussion at a Conference on States and Social Structures, Seven Springs Conference Center, Mount Kisco, New York, 25–27 February.

Therborn, Goran (1980) *What Does the Ruling Class Do when It Rules?* (London, Verso).

Therborn, Goran (1984) Classes and states. Welfare state developments, 1881–1981, *Studies in Political Economy,* pp. 7–41.

Torres, Carlos Alberto (1984) *Public Policy Formation and the Mexican Corporatist State: a study of adult education policy making and policy planning in Mexico, 1970–1982,* Ph.D. dissertation, Stanford University.

Weber, Max (1969) *Economía y Sociedad* (Mexico, Fondo de Cultura Económica).

Weiler, Hans H. (Ed.) (1980) *Educational Planning and Social Change: report on an IIEP seminar* (Paris, UNESCO-IIEP).

Wirt, F. & Kirst, M. W. (1972) *The Political Web of American Schools* (Boston, Mass., Little, Brown & Company).

Wirt, F. & Kirst, M. W. (1982) *Schools in Conflict: the policies of education* (Berkeley, McCutchan).

Wirth, Margaret (1977) Towards a critique of the theory of the state monopoly capitalism, *Economy and Society,* 6, pp. 284–313.

Wright, Erik Olin (1978) *Class, Crisis and the State* (London, NLB).

PART V

Social Context of Higher Education

Equality of Higher Education in Post-Communist Hungary and Poland: Challenges and Prospects*

KASSIE FREEMAN

Introduction

Regardless of the culture, the word *equality* invariably evokes discomfort. No matter the context of discussion—whether it is education, employment or politics—it is one of those subjects that causes people to feel the need to defend their views and classify their position. Somehow, people tend to think that the word *equality* means that they have to choose between status in society (rich or poor), ethnicity or gender. In other words, the very idea of equality leads people to believe that something is being taken away from one group and given to another. Yet, education is one commodity that benefits everyone. It is through equal educational opportunities that everyone benefits. As Thurow says, "I can't afford to live with my neighbors' children ignorant because if they are ignorant my income is going to be lower than it otherwise would be."

Countless Western economists and educators have demonstrated the benefits of education to individuals and societies (Becker, 1975; Blaug, Preston & Ziderman, 1967; Bowles & Gintis, 1976; Carnoy & Levin, 1985; Cohn, 1979; R. B. Freeman, 1976; Lynton, 1984; Psacharopoulos, 1985; Schultz, 1961; Solomon, 1980; Thurow, 1972). These human capital (economics of education) theorists have concluded that individuals and society benefit directly from education, either monetarily or nonmonetarily. Direct monetary benefits to individuals are usually measured by increased earning potential after completion of an educational program. Society benefits directly from increases in taxes paid by individuals and indirectly from increased productivity of future generations of children of educated individuals.

In the U.S., the average layperson tends to think of equality of higher education in terms of color (black or white), whereas in former Communist countries, the issue of equality relates more to class in society (professional, semiskilled or manual worker). Regardless of the basis of inequality in higher education, the effects are devastating for individuals and society. The groups that are not privileged to participate in higher education are often relegated to lower status in society, holding less prestigious, dead-end jobs, participating less in the political process, and becoming victims of a permanent underclass (which tends to mean crime, drugs and other social problems). Obviously, the more people participate in the labor market, the more individuals have disposable income and the more society reaps in increased taxes. That means that countries have to spend less on social services.

As conflicts over territories shift to economic competition, higher education in former socialist countries will play a major role in how competitive these countries will become in the global marketplace. The Center for Educational Competitiveness (1992) states, "A strong human resource development is essential to the economic growth of every country." The new economies (those which compete successfully in a global marketplace) will be information- or knowledge-based, where people will be working in professions involving processing and distribution of information. While

*The Hungarian Institute for Educational Research (HIER) provided the support for the writing of this chapter.

technological advancement is forming the basis for the information age, higher education will provide the quality training and education needed.

Among higher education planners and economists, it is widely accepted that it will be necessary for post-Communist countries to gear the relevance, efficiency and capacity of their educational programs to meet the demands of a market economy (Sadlak, 1990; Kozma, 1990; World Bank, 1991). In Hungary and Poland, higher education officials have indicated the need to radically transform higher education establishments (Hungarian Draft Concept for the Legal Regulation of Higher Education, 1992; Kwiatkowski, 1990). Kwiatkowski (1990) has indicated that increasing higher education participation is particularly important in newly democratic countries for three reasons:

1. Forming values and ideas needed for sustainable democracy.
2. Fostering inter- and intra-national links, since it creates an elite needed for sustainable cultural and economic development.
3. Providing service functions needed for economic and educational development.

Both Hungary and Poland recognize the importance of ensuring equality of educational opportunities in order not to create a social drain on their fragile economies. It would further strain their economies to create a permanent underclass, people who are uneducated or undereducated for a market economy and need unemployment benefits (a system only recently created in these countries) and other social services. The Preamble of the draft of the proposed Hungarian act for higher education (1992) states their commitment to equality:

> In accordance with the principles of the Constitution and the international agreements sanctioned by Hungary, the Act wishes to guarantee to every qualified applicant the admission to institutions of higher education, irrespective of their social, linguistic-cultural, or regional ties. The institutions of higher education should at the same time pay special attention to the realization of the principle of equal opportunities, to the positive discrimination of the socially disadvantaged, and to the careful guidance of the outstanding talents.

The issue of equality of higher education is not new in Hungary or Poland. In fact, Poland and Hungary have experimented with "positive discrimination" (providing extra points for students of semiskilled and peasant origin) long before the change in their economic systems. Why has equality of higher education been a problem to achieve in Hungary and Poland in the past? What will be the prospects for achieving equity in higher education in the future?

Equality of Higher Education under Communist Rule

There are at least three reasons why it is important to understand how Hungary and Poland attempted to achieve equality of higher education under Communist rule. First, it is important to understand the rationale for admission and selection for higher education participation under the Communist regime. Under Communist rule, admission and selection criteria in higher education were controlled for political, economic and social reasons. Lukacs (1989) said that the rationale for this was twofold: first, manpower was one of the fundamental resources of the national economy, and second, reproduction of the manpower structure also represented a reproduction of the social structure (i.e., the system of social positions and the relationship between the particular classes, strata and groups).

For political reasons, according to Kozma (1990), "a strongly selective higher education system helped to control the recruitment and limit the 'production' of intellectuals" (p. 383). In other words, the State attempted to control education as a means of reshaping the social structure. Policies to ensure youths from worker and peasant classes access to higher education were implemented to break the "ruling classes" (Dobson, 1977). By controlling the qualification system and the school system, the government sought to keep the market free from spontaneous influences (Lukacs, 1989). As Lukacs said, the idea was to maintain the existing social structure and to prevent those unfit from becoming members of the ruling elite class. Therefore, access to higher education institutions in these countries is still difficult because they are traditionally classic, i.e., very academic, elitist and closed. There is no community college system, for example, which in the U.S. serves as a division between the classes.

Manpower forecasting was one of the most powerful arguments against increasing the participation in higher education. The idea was to prevent unemployment. Therefore, manpower planners developed mid-term and long-range plans (5-year and 15-year) in an attempt to determine the exact number of professionals needed in each occupation (i.e., engineers, teachers, doctors, etc.). In addition to determining the number of individuals needed in each profession, the political authorities determined the social background and what social group these individuals should represent. The availability for higher education, then, was based on projected socioeconomic demands. It is for these reasons that entrance to higher education has been highly selective and competitive. In Hungary, for example, Kozma estimates the ratio of applicants to admissions to be 3:1, and the ratio is roughly the same in Poland.

Second, an understanding of the "flow" of graduates from secondary to higher education, their perception and attitudes about higher education versus the needs of the State under Communist rule, is important for reformulating strategies for equal access to higher education. Admission to higher education in these countries is a three-step process. Applicants complete secondary schooling, have good marks in secondary school and pass an entrance examination. Noteworthy is the fact that students must determine after eight years of schooling (ages 6–14) whether to continue in a track of schooling that will enable them to be eligible for access to higher education. Should students choose apprenticeship training, for example, they would not be prepared to take the entrance examination.

The flow of students from secondary schooling to higher education was hampered by entrance examinations, manpower planning objectives and students' perception of the value of schooling. In a 20-year (from 1965 to 1985) Polish experiment to increase the tertiary participation of students of worker and peasant classes, Wnuk-Lipinska (1985) indicated that not only did the percentage of working class students not increase, but the proportion of peasant students participating in higher education actually declined from 17% to 5%. Her findings were confirmed in an earlier study by Najduchowska (1978). Lukacs (1989) reported similar findings in Hungary, i.e., the number of students from homes of manual workers increased from 1972 to 1978 but declined after then.

Students' and parents' perceptions of the value of higher education played an even greater role in students' decisions to attend higher education. The perception of the worth of schooling is typically class-based, i.e., the higher is the parents' level of schooling, the higher their aspirations for schooling for their child.

Finally, it is important to review equality of higher education under Communist rule to understand the obstacles Hungary and Poland will encounter in trying to equalize access to higher education in the future. Although under Communist rule attempts were made to equalize access to higher education, participation by students from lower classes was greatly

TABLE 1
The Social Background of Students Accepted for Higher Education in Poland in 1974

	Total Number	*Percentage of Social Background*		
		Workers	*Peasant*	*Intelligentsia*
Entered for examination	145,587 (100%)	32.0	11.3	55.0
Accepted for studies	65,987 (100%)	31.1	10.8	56.4

Source: Najduchowska, H. (1978). Higher education and professional careers: Students' perception. In B. C. Sanyal & A. Josefowicz (Eds.), *Graduate employment and planning of higher education in Poland* (p. 156). Paris: International Institute for Educational Planning.

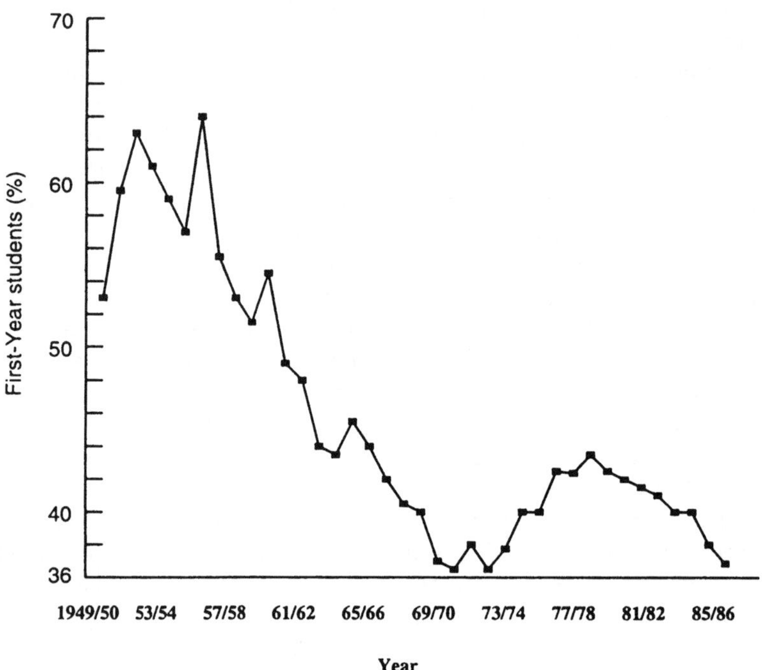

Fig. 1: **The Percentage of Children of Manual Workers among First-Year Students Attending Regular Courses at Institutions of Higher Education in Hungary**

Source: Lukacs, P. (1989). Changes in selection policy in Hungary: The case of the admission system in higher education. *Comparative Education, 25*(2), 219–28.

limited. For example, in Poland in the early 1980s, working class and peasants comprised approximately 65% of the population while less than half of the students in higher education came from these two classes (Table 1). Students of working class origin comprised 31.1% of the students accepted to higher education while 10.8% students of peasant origin were accepted. Sadlak (1991) listed similar figures for the social composition of higher education participation in Poland: 32% from working class, 9.3% from peasant families and 55% from intelligentsia. Hungary faces similar circumstances (Figure 1). In Hungary, the percentage of children of manual workers attending regular courses at higher education institutions in 1985/86 was approximately 37%. Najduchowska (1978) lists the following as reasons for the discrepancy in applications to higher education between the different social classes:

1. Inequalities resulting from hereditary and contemporary differences in the economic and social position of the various groups and classes.
2. Unequal upbringing and cultural levels acquired at home in different social and occupational groups and regions.
3. Uneven opportunities of admission to secondary and high schools, due to disparities in the geographical availability of secondary education.
4. Difference in patterns of career expectations predominant in various social classes. (pp. 154–55)

How to overcome these inequities will pose great challenges to these two countries as they make the transition to a market economy. Despite attempts of Communist countries (all countries for that matter) to equalize access to higher education, inequities still exist. How they overcome these challenges can be instructive for other countries (such as Western Europe and the U.S.) that are grappling with the same problem.

Challenges Confronting Hungary and Poland in Achieving Equality of Higher Education

By all accounts (Sadlak, 1990; Lukacs, 1989; World Bank, 1991; and Wnuk-Lipinska, 1985), post-Communist countries face at least five major obstacles in equalizing access to higher education: selectivity, tracking, motivation and aspiration, market value of education, and lack of resources. Sadlak and Lukacs raise the question, what should be the criteria for selectivity? Should higher education admission be collective- or individual-based, i.e., preferential or meritocratic, or both?

Selectivity Criteria

The first problem, then, is defining an inclusive basis of selectivity for higher education participation. Defining admission criteria and solutions to equalize access to higher education is extraordinarily difficult, since positive discrimination, tuition-free education has not increased the participation of underrepresented groups. As Sadlak (1991) has indicated, additional points for social background have apparently had marginal effect on applicants from underrepresented groups gaining admission to higher education, especially the more prestigious institutions. However, if, as Sadlak also suggests, admission to higher education were based purely on meritocracy, that would raise doubts about the sincerity of Hungary and Poland to achieve equal access to higher education. Equality and meritocracy are contradictory by definition. By meritocracy, it is assumed that all conditions are equal throughout life (e.g., socioeconomic status, environmental conditions, etc.) and, therefore, all students have an equal chance to be selected for higher education. There can never be a pure meritocracy because parents in the upper class pass on their influence to their children, thereby, in effect, continuing the creation of classes for each generation (Bell, 1977).

In Hungary, where the political mood can be described as conservative, there are two lines of thinking about the criteria for selectivity for higher education admission. One idea is that no immediate steps will be taken to develop or define a policy for equal access. The individuals who hold this view favor a policy based on meritocracy. They believe that the Communist policy of positive discrimination should be abandoned. Their views towards positive discrimination can be described as similar to conservative views in America toward affirmative action. They believe to add extra points for students from underrepresented groups would mean taking away opportunities from "much better prepared" individuals. The other line of thinking is that the conservative view will be short-lived. Their thinking is that the higher education system must be made broad enough to create real opportunity and give way to a more social democratic policy. They predict that one selection criterion that Hungary's equality of higher education policy might incorporate will resemble that of the Swedish model, where a number of predetermined slots will be reserved for students from underrepresented classes. In this model, students selected to fill these spaces will be judged on the usual criteria (entrance examination and academic background), plus they would be interviewed and judged on such criteria as motivation, creativity and work experience.

Poland, too, according to Sadlak (1990) favors discontinuing positive discrimination. However, several years ago, a number of Polish educators suggested a different method of testing students for entrance to higher education. For example, they proposed in the 1970s developing a biographical questionnaire to evaluate the all-around characteristics of an applicant and/or averaging the grades received in the top two years of secondary school, which would provide a much broader appraisal of an applicant's knowledge base (Najduchowska, 1978).

Without a concrete policy to increase higher education participation, it is doubtful that early progress will be made to equalize access for underrepresented groups. What is needed is a coherent policy with short- and long-term direction. Most researchers will agree that the decision about higher education participation is made long before students sit for an entrance examination.

Tracking System

It is the preselection process from lower secondary (primary) to upper secondary that poses a second challenge (and perhaps the biggest) in equalizing access to higher education in Hungary and Poland. A 1991 World Bank report on Hungary's transition to a market economy refers to the preselection process as "too early specialization." Students at too young an age (typically age 14) are required to make essentially lifelong career choices.

In Hungary and Poland, eight years of compulsory schooling (primary) are required, ages 6–14. At age 14 students select which track of schooling to continue. Students can select between basically three types of secondary schooling: (1) academic secondary schools (grammar schools) prepare students in general academic subjects; (2) technical professional or secondary professional schools provide general specialized or professional vocational training, e.g., for students interested in becoming engineers; and (3) apprenticeship or lower vocational schools provide students with training for specific occupations. Approximately 25% of Hungarian students attend academic secondary schools, 30% enter technical professional schools, and 45% attend apprenticeship training (World Bank, 1991). The percentages of students participating in each track of schooling in Poland is similar: 20% enter grammar school, 20% enter vocational secondary schools and 60% attend lower-level vocational schools (Wnuk-Lipinska, 1985).

While the smallest percentage of students attend grammar schools (these are typically the children of the elite), by far the highest percentage (70%) enter higher education institutions. Children from the upper class disproportionately have the best opportunity of attending grammar school (Table 2) and, therefore, have the best chance of passing the entrance examination. As noted in Table 2, in Poland in 1985, the higher the father's level of education, the more likely is the child to attend grammar school.

There are even differences in the prestige of the grammar schools that students attend. The upper-class students attend more prestigious grammar schools, which have the best teachers and the reputation for a higher percentage of students passing the entrance examination to universities. For example, in Pecs, Hungary, at one of the top grammar schools, where students have access to the best courses and teachers, 75% of the students came from upper-class families, while only 1% of the students came from manual workers' families (Schadt, 1992).

The ability of the upper class to hire tutors also works to the disadvantage of students from lower classes. Families pay large sums of money to have their children tutored in courses such as foreign languages, particularly English, which now provides extra credit towards points needed to gain entrance to university (ibid.). Location also has implications for who passes the entrance examination. In Table 2, note that even when the fathers' educational levels are equal, Warsaw had a higher percentage of grammar school graduates. The same is true in Hungary. According to Schadt (1992), high-quality village schools need to be reestablished in Hungary to provide better opportunities for rural children.

Although graduates from general vocational schools have the opportunity to take the national entrance examination, as Wnuk-Lipinska (1985) points out, the "generally low

TABLE 2
Secondary School Graduates in Poland According to the Type of School and Education Level of Father (Percentage)

Type of School	*Father with Elementary Education N = 439*	*Father with Higher Education N = 662*
Grammar School (Lyceum)	64[x]	31
Vocational School of Higher Level	12	33
Technical School	24	35

Note:[x] in Warsaw equals 82.

Source: Wnuk-Lipinska, E. (1985). Dilemmas of the Educational System in Poland. Unpublished paper. Warsaw, Poland.

level of teaching and poor curriculum in theoretical subjects give them almost no opportunity of being admitted" (p. 3). Approximately 30% of students from technical vocational schools are admitted to higher education. In Hungary, there are experimental schools (13), vocational secondary schools, which began operating in the fall of 1992 and were designed to blur the distinction in the quality of teaching between the grammar schools and vocational schools. The directors of these schools will have a freer hand in selecting and dismissing teachers who are not meeting the standards. The directors will have available the necessary resources for increasing the number of students capable of passing the entrance examination for higher education participation. The selected sites are throughout Hungary, not just the larger cities. One school site selected to participate will be in Komlo, a town of approximately 30,000, where the main industry has been mining.

These selected schools will emphasize general subjects such as cultural arts, active foreign language studies, computer techniques and other subjects, to enable these students to have a better chance of passing the entrance examination to higher education. The schools will also emphasize flexibility so that students will be able to make more informed career choices. The idea is to provide higher-quality vocational schools (which are similar to magnet schools in the U.S.) that will prepare students to choose between higher education or employment following secondary school (Rendeki, 1992).

In Poland, Najduchowska (1978) and Wnuk-Lipinska (1985) concluded that universal secondary schooling (where students would not select tracks after eight years of schooling) might be one of the most important factors in achieving equal access to higher education. In that way, students from different social classes would not have to determine so early which "track" of schooling to pursue. They also found that higher education participation went beyond accessibility; i.e., tuition-free and positive discrimination have not been enough to increase participation.

Motivation and Aspiration

At least three conclusions can be drawn about students' aspirations and motivation to attend higher education. First, the higher the father's educational level, the higher the child's aspiration and motivation. Children who come from a home where at least one parent is educated are more likely to aspire to attend higher education. That is because, says Najduchowska (1978), decisions concerning children's education are often made by parents. In Poland, she says, the advice of teachers and school psychologists plays only a small role in the choice of education for children. It is widely accepted that the value children place on learning is based on their social and cultural background. Therefore, to merely make higher education spaces available is not enough. Methods have to be developed that somehow generate student interest in higher education in the absence of a supportive family background.

Second, students' aspirations are associated with their academic achievement. The aspirations of culturally disadvantaged children are derived, in large part, from their ability to earn high grades (Dobson, 1977). Children who do not perform well academically are obviously more prone to drop out. Lower grades tend to be class-based across cultures. In Hungary and Poland academic performance has been linked to which track of schooling students select. Dobson (1977) described a survey which revealed that, in the former Soviet Union, students whose fathers had completed higher education were twice as likely as their classmates to get higher grades. Clearly, the students who are performing well academically in primary school are more likely to select grammar school and thereby stand a much better chance of passing the entrance examination. Thus, secondary school graduates who have high grades and come from the upper class have a better chance of attending higher education institutions.

The third conclusion that can be drawn about students' motivation and aspirations is that the more individuals of the same status (class and/or race) there are who are not participating in higher education, the more unmotivated individuals from that group become. This phenomenon seems to be the case across cultures. In the U.S., for example, the percentage of African Americans participating in higher education increased in the late 1960s to the mid-1970s; following that period, the participation rate began to decline. The same occurrence happened in Hungary and Poland during the same period. During the 1970s and 1980s, the percentage of students from lower classes participating in higher education in Hungary and Poland began to decline.

For many students from underrepresented groups, as they begin to perceive the decline of the prestige of higher education (the worth of higher education schooling), their motivation begins to decline. Minority and/or culturally disadvantaged youth necessarily need to perceive a more immediate return on their investment in higher education. More often they are investing more in resources, direct and indirect (Freeman, K., 1988 & 1989). Typically, underrepresented groups in higher education have less in resources, so it requires a higher percentage of their capital (e.g., in the U.S. minorities usually have to borrow more to attend higher education institutions). Even when students are receiving grants or when (in countries such as Hungary or Poland) the State provides tuition-free schooling, students from lower classes have a higher cost because their resource base is substantially lower. Indirect costs to underrepresented groups are also higher. If, as Davis and Morrall (1974) estimated, the major cost of education is the indirect cost (i.e., the amount of earnings students forgo while attending higher education), minority (underrepresented) groups pay a much greater cost. The earnings that minorities forgo while attending higher education are typically earnings that they would share in the total family income and are therefore a substantially greater loss for minority families (Freeman, K., 1988).

Market Value of Higher Education

It is the perceived lack of prestige and value of university degrees that pose another challenge for Hungary and Poland in equalizing access to higher education. In a market economy, labor market conditions play a much greater role in individuals' decisions to participate in higher education. In a market economy, much to the chagrin of educators, the worth of higher education is evaluated more in monetary terms. For example, Boyer (1987) reported that in the U.S. approximately 88% of the students and parents surveyed indicated that finding employment following graduation was one of their top priorities. Najduchowska (1978) found that in Poland students' interest in their value of higher education differed by social class. The children of university-educated families attached more importance to the interest and satisfaction of their future job, whereas students from lower socioeconomic backgrounds were concerned about the match between their job and qualifications, the ability to gain recognition and appreciation for their work, and assistance in finding accommodations quickly.

Even before the change to a market economy, the value and prestige of higher education degrees had begun to decline. The results from a survey in Poland (Wnuk-Lipinska, 1985) of youth from working-class and peasant backgrounds revealed that these youths did not think that it was worth studying if, after obtaining the degree, they were not going to get a well-paying job matching their skills and having high prestige. More of these students have begun to ask if there is a balance between the costs and benefits of higher education. It will be much more difficult to encourage students from these groups to participate in higher education now that even higher education graduates are unemployed. The unemployment rate for higher education graduates in 1992 has been predicted to be between 1–4% in Hungary, depending on location (the lowest rate is in Budapest, and the higher rates are in other locations, such as Debrecen). In Poland, in November 1990 Barbara Kunta, Manager of Career Centers, Ministry of Labor and Social Affairs, reported that approximately one-third of college graduates were without employment. In such a climate, it will be even more difficult to demonstrate to students from underrepresented groups that higher education is worth the cost. One way most countries have tried to increase student motivation to participate in higher education is through increased student aid. It is lack of financial resources that poses the most important challenge to increasing the participation of underrepresented groups in higher education in Hungary and Poland.

Lack of Resources

It is widely accepted that there are costs associated with increasing the participation of underrepresented groups in higher education. There are those direct costs (such as free tuition and waiver of fees) associated with attending universities, and there are also additional costs (such as stipends) which are necessary for students who have less resources. All of these costs are difficult for Hungary and Poland because of the current level of funding resources for higher education institutions. In Poland, according to Kwiatkowski (1990), universities have less power and money from the central government. Higher education in Hungary, on the other hand, has maintained good relations with the government; however, that does not mean that extra funding will soon be available for special programs. In fact, students will soon begin paying a share of the cost of attending higher education institutions. That is likely to further deteriorate the participation of underrepresented groups, although Hungary has indicated its commitment to continue funding the participation of lower classes.

Inevitably, when the issue of equality of higher education is mentioned, the question of quality is also raised. Cerych (1990) raises this question when discussing increasing the level of higher education participation in Central Europe. Increasing participation, he suggests, might lead to other social problems, such as large-scale unemployment of graduates. But, like most other educators, his main question about increased participation focuses on the issue of maintaining excellence: "Can the goal of excellence be pursued at the same time as the objective of a vigorous expansion" (p. 354). There, of course, are reasons for concern, but other questions about quality versus equality have yet to be raised: (1) Are quality and equality mutually exclusive, or is quality a rationale for maintaining elitism? (2) What are the real costs of increasing the participation of underrepresented groups? (3) Is it more feasible to increase funding for increasing participation in higher education or to spend more for attending social problems?

There are several ways to view the quality of higher education. Some educators and economists view quality of higher education in terms of the product produced (e.g., number of graduates employed and where they are employed). Others view quality in terms of the educational process itself (e.g., faculty/student ratio). In either case, it has been difficult to determine whether the quality of higher education of all deteriorates when underrepresented groups are admitted. That is, how many students would have to be admitted to a higher educational institution in order for the quality to begin deteriorating? "Educators and economists have been unable to identify dimensions of institutional quality which have consistent and persistent effects on student changes in knowledge and attitude," says Solomon (1987). There is not anyone who would argue that if all unprepared students were admitted to any higher education institution, the quality would diminish. That is a different argument from one that states that equality and quality necessarily have to be in conflict.

Economists and educators have discussed whether there is a higher economic return to individuals and society in providing higher education to the most gifted in a society. It is becoming increasingly clear, however, as some others have argued, that the social benefits would be higher if more resources were diverted to the less represented groups in society. More and more countries have begun to recognize the high cost of not including more groups in the higher education process. For example, the European Community (of which Hungary and Poland would eventually like to become members) has specifically indicated that opportunities for underrepresented groups to participate in higher education should be increased. This is necessary, they have indicated, because there will be an increased demand for highly skilled workers and higher education will have an increasingly important role to play in meeting this need. The U.S. also has recognized the importance of equalizing opportunities for minorities to participate in higher education, since minorities will play an increasingly important role in the labor market in the 21st century.

Meeting these challenges, then, leaves Hungary and Poland to ponder whether it is to their advantage to begin to increase the participation of underrepresented groups at this point in their transition to a market economy or to wait until the groups are so solidly divided that they will require even greater resources to motivate these students to participate in higher education. Nevertheless, while these are difficult issues to consider, there are lessons to be learned from the West, particularly the U.S.

Also the West can learn valuable lessons from the research conducted in Hungary and Poland over the years regarding equality of higher education.

Reciprocal Lessons

Since the U.S. and Central Europe had such different economic systems in the past, the question could be raised, What can the U.S. possibly learn from Central Europe, and vice versa, regarding equality of higher education? Dobson (1977) reported that the degree of inequality of higher education in the U.S. was closer to that of the Scandinavian countries and the former Eastern European countries than to that of West European countries. According to him, while access to higher education in the U.S. and Eastern Europe has not been without fault, it has been considerably better than access to higher education in Western Europe. Although there were differences in the economic systems, included among the similarities in the egalitarianism in higher education in the U.S. and Central Europe was—at least in principle—a belief in opportunities for achievement through the educational system and high levels of aspiration. That is, although "tracking" occurred (and still occurs) in both systems, it was thought to be to a much less degree than in Western Europe. Finally, Dobson (1977) lists similarities in percentage of cohorts completing secondary school (a necessary condition for continuing on to higher education) as an indication of commonalties of equality of access to higher education in former Eastern Europe and the U.S. There exist today similar obstacles to achieving equal access to higher education, e.g., attitudes about positive discrimination and affirmative action.

One lesson that is clear for all countries concerning increasing the participation of underrepresented groups is that the problems are much deeper than positive discrimination or affirmative action. It will require more than merely making spaces available. It is ironic that people in the mainstream of societies are so resistant to providing additional assistance to increasing the participation of underrepresented groups in higher education and, yet, so few members of these underrepresented groups are interested in taking advantage of this assistance. But when societies recognize the importance of providing access to education for all its citizens, it looks to positive discrimination first, a system that educators and economists know has failed over the last 20 years. There have to be new ideas, new research about ways to increase participation, and that research needs to focus on the return side of investment in higher education. Students have many questions about the worth of higher education: Is it worth the cost? What if I do not get a job? McMahon (1987) says very few studies of labor market expectations of racial minorities exist in most countries. Unfortunately, educators still only think of education in elitist terms, education for the sake of education, while more and more students and families are beginning to think of it in terms of prestige and income.

Inequality of higher education is a problem that requires alliances to resolve. Therefore, relationships between secondary school and higher education and between industry and higher education are necessary. As educators realize, interest in higher education does not begin, nor can it be instilled, as late as the last years of secondary schooling, particularly for students who are coming from homes where neither parent is educated. As research has shown in Poland (Najduchowska, 1978; Wnuk-Lipinska, 1985) and in the U.S. (as far back as the Coleman report, 1966), schools have to play a much greater role in cultivating students' interest in participating in higher education, especially students from homes where education is not stressed. That simply means that schools from primary to higher education have to work in partnership to devise strategies for increasing students' aspirations and motivation to, first, perform well academically and, second, to continue with schooling beyond the secondary level.

Industry is one of the primary recipients of higher education services, whether through research and development or graduate employment of graduates. Particularly since the 1980s, industry has developed major alliances with higher education throughout the West for many reasons, including developing strategies to curtail the decline in minority students' participation at all levels of education. It is only natural that they should have a stake in increasing the skill level of all groups. As the

U.S. has found, it is better to invest in the educational development of the work force incrementally than to wait and have to invest more later when the labor force skill level is not keeping pace with the technological advancement of the country. Industry can work in partnership with higher education in Central Europe to invest monetarily in increasing the participation of underrepresented groups. They can also provide much needed professional models of what various occupations entail and what is necessary to prepare for different types of positions. While to the typically educated person these ideas might seem too vocational in their orientation, it has to be remembered that higher education is not a naturally assumed process for students who do not come from educated homes.

Finally, most will agree that to increase participation of underrepresented groups requires a sincere commitment from all actors: politicians, educators, economists, industry leaders, etc. It is a complicated problem that requires resources, monetary and nonmonetary (new ideas, new solutions), to resolve. It has to be an aggressive approach and cannot simply be left to chance. It is reasonable to assume that the countries of Central Europe, at the moment, have an agenda of important items to attend to regarding higher education; equalizing access to higher education is probably—understandably—low on their list. The past decades, however, have shown across cultures that if concrete policies are not set to deal with this important agenda, it can cost economies more in the long run.

Prospects for Increasing Participation

Since the issue of increasing participation in higher education has been such a dismal failure in most countries, to be optimistic about Hungary and Poland achieving this in light of all the challenges they face is almost like denying the inevitable. In the short term, there is certainly reason for concern, almost pessimism. The generally conservative mood in these countries and the feeling that they have had enough of special arrangements for underrepresented groups make it even more doubtful that equity in higher education will have a high priority. Based on the experiences of other cultures, the conservative mood is likely to persist for some time. The financial constraints under which these countries are operating would make it appear that equalizing access to higher education will be even more difficult to accomplish.

In spite of these obstacles, however, there is reason for optimism, particularly in the long run. They are fully aware of the effects of inequality of access to higher education from the experiences of other countries, e.g., the U.S. and, increasingly, Western Europe, This is one of the reasons they are continuing with strategies to make higher education more accessible. Experimental programs such as the newly created vocational schools, as described earlier in this paper, are already underway. The stable size of the populations in these countries makes developing a strategy for increasing access to higher education a much more manageable process than it would in larger countries.

Economic necessity will be a driving reason for these countries to increase access to higher education. Mobilizing and developing efficient human resources is essential for economic development. The demand for a highly skilled work force will require that more previously underrepresented groups have the opportunity to participate in higher education.

The best reason to be optimistic, though, is the rich and excellent cadre of researchers and centers of research in Hungary and Poland. Researchers in these countries have over the years developed a body of research on this topic, so they are not starting from scratch. In fact, some of their research findings can be useful for the West. In the short span of three years, the researchers in these countries have defined the educational problems they will face in a market economy, including inequality of higher education, and have begun to devise methods for resolving these issues. It is the deliberate speed at which they are moving which gives much hope for positive results. While they have established contacts and cooperative agreements with scholars in the West, they are deliberately and carefully evaluating what is most appropriate for their own cultures. That does not mean that there is unanimous agreement on each decision regarding how to solve issues facing higher education, but it does appear that there is agreement on the importance of equalizing access to higher education.

Researchers in Central Europe have the best opportunity to see from the East and West some of the pressing issues and obstacles facing higher education administrators in their attempts to equalize access. They are in position to see what has worked and what has failed. Their continuing collaborative arrangements with educators in the East and West could enable Hungary and Poland to develop new ideas and new research for dealing with this very important topic.

References

Becker, G. S. (1975). *Human capital* (2d ed.). New York: Columbia University Press.

Bell, D. (1977). On meritocracy and equality. In J. Karabel & A. H. Halsey (Eds.), *Power and ideology in education.* New York: Oxford University Press.

Blaug, M., Preston, M. & Ziderman, A. (1967). *The utilization of educated man-power in industry.* London: Oliver and Boyd.

Bowles, S. & Gintis, H. (1976). *Schooling in capitalist America.* New York: Basic Books, Inc.

Boyer, E. L. (1987). *College: The undergraduate experience in America.* New York: Harper & Row.

Carnoy, M. & Levin, H. M. (1985). *Schooling and work in a democratic state.* Stanford, CA: Stanford University Press.

Center for Educational Competitiveness. (1992). *Knowledge for all Americans.* Arlington, VA: Knowledge Network for All Americans.

Cerych, L. (1990). Renewal of Central European higher education: Issues and challenges. *European Journal of Education,* 25(4), pp. 351–58.

Cohn, E. (1979). *The economics of education.* Cambridge, MA: Harper & Row.

Coleman, J. (1966). Equal schools or equal students. *Public Interest,* 4, pp. 70–75.

Davis, R. J. & Morrall, J. F., III. (1974). *Evaluating educational investment.* Lexington, MA: D. C. Heath.

Dobson, R. B. (1977). Social class and inequality of access to higher education in the USSR. In J. Karabel & A. H. Halsey (Eds.), *Power and ideology in education.* New York: Oxford University Press.

Freeman, K. (1988). The returns to schooling: Comparative analysis of Black-White MBA starting salaries—a pilot study. Unpublished empirical study. Atlanta: Emory University.

_____. (1989). The returns to schooling: The impact of career counseling on Black-White MBA starting salaries. Unpublished dissertation. Atlanta: Emory University.

Freeman, R. B. (1976). *The overeducated American.* New York: Academic Press, Inc.

Hungarian Ministry of Higher Education. (1992). *Draft act of Hungarian higher education.*

Kozma, T. (1990). Higher education in Hungary; Facing the political transition. *European Journal of Education,* 25(4), pp. 379–90.

Kunta, B. (1990, November). Interview with Ms. Barbara Kunta, Manager, Career Centers, Ministry of Labor and Social Affairs, Warsaw, Poland.

Kwiatkowski, S. (1990). Survival through excellence: Prospects for the Polish university. *European Journal of Education,* 25(4), pp. 391–98.

Lukacs, P. (1989). Changes in selection policy in Hungary: The case of the admission system in higher education. *Comparative Education, 25*(2), pp. 219–28.

Lynton, E. A. (1984). *The missing connection between business and the universities.* New York: Macmillan.

McMahon, W. W. (1987). Expected rates of returns to education. In G. Psacharopoulos (Ed.), *Economics of education: Research and studies.* New York: Pergamon Press.

Memorandum on Higher Education in the European Community. (1991). Higher education on the eve of the year 2000. *Education & Training, II–V.*

Najduchowska, H. (1978). Higher education and professional careers: Students' perception. In B. C. Sanyal & A. Josefowicz (Eds.), *Graduate employment and planning of higher education in Poland.* Paris: International Institute for Educational Planning.

Psacharopoulos, G. (1985). Returns to education: A further international update and implications. *The Journal of Human Resources,* 20(4), pp. 583–97.

Rendeki, A. (1992, July). Interview with Rendeki Agoston, igazogato, Kazinczy Ferenc Egeszsagugyi es Kezgazdasagi Szakkozepiskola, Komlo, Hungary.

Sadlak, J. (1990). The Eastern European challenge: Higher education for a new reality. *Educational Record,* pp. 29–37.

_____. (1991, March). *A return to the democratic society: Is there need for the redefinition of equity in higher education in East and Central Europe—Polish experience?* Paper presented at the meeting of the 35th Comparative and International Education Society, Pittsburgh, PA.

Schadt, M. (1992, July 21). Interview with Dr. M. Schadt, sociology professor, Janus Pannonious University, Pecs, Hungary.

Schultz, T. W. (1961). Investment in human capital. *American Economic Review,* 51, pp. 1–17.

Solomon, L. C. (1980). New findings on the links between college education and work. *Higher Education,* 10, pp. 615–48.

_____. (1987). The quality of education. In G. Psacharopoulos (Ed.), *Economics of education: Research and studies.* New York: Pergamon Press.

Thurow, L. C. (1972). Education and economic equality. *Public Interest,* 28, pp. 66–81.

Wnuk-Lipinska, E. (1985). Dilemmas of the educational system in Poland. Unpublished paper. Warsaw, Poland.

World Bank. (1991). *Hungary: The transition to a market economy, critical human resources issues.* Washington, D.C.

A Subnational Perspective for Comparative Research: Education and Development in Northeast Brazil and Northeast Thailand

GERALD FRY AND KEN KEMPNER

Abstract: *Guided by the growing emphasis on the importance of economic regions rather than nations, we utilize the Northeast of Brazil and the Northeast of Thailand as case studies to consider the fruitfulness of a subnational approach to comparative research. A major goal of this inquiry is to provide an overview of the complex interactions between economic, educational, demographic and environmental factors embedded in critically important political and cultural contexts. Our thesis is that subnational comparisons between countries are often more meaningful than aggregate, cross-national ones. The intent of this inquiry, therefore, is not to equate Thailand and Brazil, but rather to highlight the importance of subnational comparisons. The overall economic and educational evidence we present reveals the Northeast regions of both Brazil and Thailand to be substantially disadvantaged. Without a subnational comparison, however, we propose that the overall economic performance of each country cannot accurately be determined. Gross generalizations and conclusions based on measures of central tendencies ignore important subnational differences and disparities in development within a country.*

Key Assumptions, Perspectives and Research Questions

A key assumption of this study is that the nation-state as a unit of analysis is becoming increasingly obsolescent as we approach a twenty-first century in which forces of subnationalism and internationalism become more prominent. The flames of subnationalism are spreading rapidly in eastern Europe and the former Soviet Union. There is also growing fear of these forces in major Asian capitals such as Beijing.

In an insightful critique of comparative research, Ward (1985) stressed the current overemphasis on macronational data which often mask important regional variations. He argued 'that regions of some nations are more comparable to other nations *vis-à-vis* development processes' (Ward, 1985, p. 75). Similarly, a number of researchers have emphasized the growing importance of economic regions rather than nations. Prominent among these scholars is the social anthropologist and Sinologist, Skinner (1985), who argued that China can be best understood in terms of distinct economic regions. In the North American context, Garreau (1981) argued, as well, that there are 'nine nations' of North America.

Because there appear to be few comparative studies of regional areas of developing countries,[1] we utilize the Northeast of Brazil and the Northeast of Thailand as case studies to consider the fruitfulness of a subnational approach to comparative research and to define the role of education in national and regional development. Our research also represents a substantive, problem-oriented approach to international and area studies

Correspondence to: Gerald W. Fry, Director of International Studies and Professor of Political Science, University of Oregon, Eugene, OR 97403, USA. Ken Kempner, Associate Professor, Educational Policy and Management, University of Oregon. Eugene, OR 97403, USA.

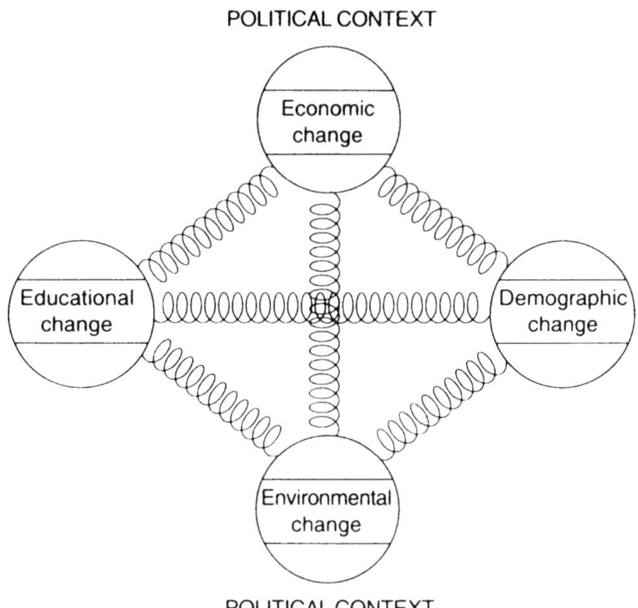

Fig. 1: **Tetrahedron model showing relations between economic, educational, demographic and environmental change.**

currently being emphasized by the Social Science Research Council (see Wakeman, 1988).

In trying to develop an in-depth understanding of a regional, subnational approach to development problems, an interdisciplinary perspective is essential. No single discipline can begin to explain the complex factors underlying the 'other Brazil' and the 'other Thailand' (see Sippanondha, 1990; Wright, 1991). The tetrahedron model indicated in Fig. 1 reflects the interdisciplinary approach emphasized in this paper. In particular, this model illustrates the interrelated role education plays in seeking solutions for national development. Educational policy alone is certainly incapable of solving developmental problems because of the myriad of economic, environmental and demographic contingencies that exist. A major goal of this paper is to provide an overview of the complex interactions between economic, educational, demographic and environmental factors embedded in critically important political and cultural contexts. It is our thesis that comparative education cannot focus only on education, but must recognize the larger political and cultural context to understand the impact of educational policy. Similarly, we propose as well that comparative education cannot operate only from a nationalistic perspective, but must recognize the subnational differences to understand the impact of educational policy.

Comparative Perspectives: Thailand and Brazil

The intent of our research is not to equate Thailand with Brazil, but, rather, to highlight the importance of an integrated and multidisciplinary approach to comparative education and of subnational comparisons and the value of such comparisons between countries. We propose further that subnational comparisons are often more meaningful than aggregate, cross-national ones. The overall economic and educational evidence from both Thailand and Brazil would place each country as newly industrialized, but our investigation reveals the Northeast region of both countries to be substantially disadvantaged. Without such subnational comparisons we might overestimate, incorrectly, the overall economic performance of each country. The 'other Brazil' and the 'other Thailand' can easily go unnoticed. Gross generalizations and conclusions based on measures of central tendencies ignore important subnational differences and disparities in development within a country.

To understand a country's social, cultural, economic and political complexity requires investigation not provided by summative generalizations of development or progress. Our contention here is that simple averages of a country's health and wealth distort subnational differences and do not account for variations at this level. Similarly, solutions for resolving these differences cannot only be educational ones or economic ones but integrated strategies that match the complexity of the country's circumstances. What we encourage here is a comparative perspective that looks beyond aggregate data and examines cultural traditions and differences to understand the meaning behind the numbers. A further concern for us in comparative education is the confusion by many scholars and politicians of equating 'development' with progress. This is a critical issue in understanding the perceptions and ideologies that guide efforts toward social, economic, educational and political change. Specifically, we do not believe aggregate economic indicators signify that a country, as a whole, is either developing or progressing. The gross national product (GNP) may be an appropriate indicator for one aspect of a country's development, but it does not show whether the country is progressing in its social reform efforts or if the lowest classes are better off now than they were under a lower GNP. Furthermore, the development of highways, energy systems, seaports and other economic manifestations of 'miracles' may offer the illusion of economic progress for a country when in reality only a small segment of the country is benefiting from such development. It is our basic contention that traditional aggregate indicators of progress can be rather misleading in portraying the reality of a country's development.

Objectives of the Study

This paper has two distinct purposes. The first objective is to provide a thick interdisciplinary comparison of Northeast Thailand and Northeast Brazil. Najita (1992), the President of the Association of Asian Studies, emphasized that contemporary studies should be rooted in historical contexts. For this reason, we present considerable cultural material reflecting the historical legacies of each subnational region being studied. Lindblom & Cohen (1979) proposed that such descriptive reporting is a valuable and useful element of professional social inquiry.

The second objective, both analytical and theoretical, is to address the following research questions.

1. Why do these two regions, which are so geographically distant and culturally diverse, share so much in common?
2. What possible factors help explain why these two regions lag behind the favored regions in their respective countries and are these explanations similar for both cases?
3. What role can education policy play in overcoming the underdevelopment of these two regions?

With respect to the second key research question, there are a number of competing theoretical perspectives to explain the relative deprivation of these two northeastern regions. These alternative perspectives can be described as follows:

1. The concept of internal colonialism explains the relative backwardness of the two northeastern regions. The Bangkok, Rio de Janeiro and São Paulo élites have exploited these regions by siphoning resources to enhance a center-dominated modernization process and by failing to invest in the development of these regions. The northeastern hinterlands in both countries have served as a source of plentiful cheap labor for the thousands of new factories associated with the Brazilian and Thai economic 'miracles'.
2. Both northeastern regions suffer distinct disadvantages because of their geographic and environmental niches, which have primarily and adversely affected their development in relation to the center within their respective countries.
3. Given the historic role of the military in the political systems of Thailand and Brazil, the subsequent 'half leaf' or

'loaded-dice' democratic systems of each country have not offered a genuine political voice for the large populations of the northeast regions. The important 'other' has not been heard politically.

4. The élites of Bangkok, Rio de Janeiro and São Paulo are 'knights in air-conditioned offices', inadequately aware of the genuine conditions in the remote northeastern regions of their countries. The media, dominated by these élites, tend to 'mask' the realities of poverty and despair.
5. The neglect of the northeastern regions is highly rational from an economic perspective. Funds invested in these areas would have far less monetary return than in areas of Brazil or Thailand with better infrastructure, communications and natural resources. Thus, the 'invisible hand' naturally directs investment and industry to the more advanced regions of each country where economic returns are highest.
6. Links of the two northeastern regions to the world economic system have led to adverse development, as explained by Evans (1979) in the case of Brazil and Eliott (1978) and Sanitsuda (1991) in Thailand.
7. The two regions have failed to develop adequately their human capital through education and, thus, they lack the pools of skilled and trained labour needed to attract external capital and investments in high value-added industries and services.

It is important to emphasize that we make no claim to have discovered 'regional economic or educational disparities' (see Foster, 1965; Clignet & Foster, 1966; Catron & Ta Ngoc Chau, 1978). These disparities, along with related regional migrations, have been an integral part of the industrial revolution for more than a century. The nature of these disparities and how nations have dealt with such inescapable tensions, however, is a critically important dimension of comparative public and educational policy. Weeramantry (1976) of Sri Lanka, in fact, saw such problems as the burning global issue of our time.

The goal of our subnational comparisons is, thus, to inform the theoretical debate about these competing alternative explanations for the relative deprivation of the northeastern regions of Thailand and Brazil. Our premise is that each of these theories in itself is reductionist and cannot alone explain the realities of the 'other Brazil' and the 'other Thailand'. The comparative analysis of these cases may lead to a syncretic, interdisciplinary theory for explaining such phenomena so directly related to the fundamental problem of basic needs and human dignity.

Brazilian Subnational Comparisons

Once there was a black El Dorado in Brazil
There it was like a shaft of sunlight that
liberty released
It was there, reflecting the divine light
from the holy fire of Olorum
And there it relieved the utopia of one for
all and all for one.

Gilberto Gil & Waly Salomão
'Quilombo, O El Dorado Negro'[2]

> Although this region [the Northeast] has accumulated through the years a great store of tradition and appreciable, unique cultural wealth, its greatest fruit has been suffering; the principal legacy of the Northeast is the wretchedness that has been handed down from generation to generation. (Castro, 1969, p. 23)

Brazil's modern economic, educational and social history was shaped by its status as a colony of Portugal. This influence of Portugal is to be found not only in the language of Brazil but also in the color of its people. With its colonies in Africa and its merchant fleet, Portugal brought ships full of slaves to Brazil and returned to Europe with sugar harvested by these slaves. The city of Salvador, Bahia was the center of this slave market and today still has the highest proportion of Black and mixed-race population. In more recent times the descendants of these slaves harvest the coffee and rubber sent to international markets. Before discussing further the unique aspects of Northeast Brazil, we examine first the present state of development of the country as a whole.

The Brazilian economy today has diversified, but agricultural products still account for a substantial part of its annual trade. The newer items of international trade include shoes and leather products, orange juice, beef, gasohol, cars and semi-precious gems. Brazil is best known, certainly, for its soccer players and music but these rich cultural traditions are not sizeable economic 'commodities' on the world market. Although Brazil is constantly trying to meet its developmental potential, it continues to suffer from an unstable economy. Estimates vary, but inflation has been approximately 200–400% a year for the past decade and has risen as high as 1500% in some years. Attempts to control inflation have typically failed. For example, during a previous round of price controls it became more expensive to buy a used car than a new car due to slow downs in the production of new cars. With the introduction of the newest currency, the 'real', inflation has slowed giving rise to cautious optimism.

Brazil emerged from a harsh military dictatorship in the 1980s in what was called the *abertura* or opening. During the *abertura* political controls were relaxed, universities and newspapers were once again relatively free and open elections were allowed at the state level, although the military hand-picked the first civilian president. Federal elections for the president were held for the first time in over 20 years in 1989. The newly elected president Collor de Mello promptly implemented a wave of economic reforms, more severe than most Brazilians thought possible. Unfortunately, although initially very popular, 2 years later Collor was impeached and then resigned in disgrace amidst indictments of corruption in his administration and personal finances. Franco, the former vice-president, assumed office, however, in an affirmation of the recently renewed democratic process for Brazil. The democratic process was reaffirmed in 1994 with the election of Juan Henrique Cardoso, but Collor was acquitted of all charges.

With a population estimated at approximately 200 million, the majority of Brazil's people live in poverty and are scattered throughout the country, which is larger in area than the continental USA. The major cities (São Paulo, Rio de Janeiro, Belo Horizonte, Recife, Porto Alegre and Salvador) account for a sizeable part of the population, but in some regions most Brazilians are predominantly rural and poor (see Table 1). Because of this rural poverty thousands migrate to the large cities and are considered urban dwellers, even though they live in shack towns or *favelas* without plumbing or electricity. The more established *favelas* have electricity, since it is easy to tap into existing power lines illegally and run cords to the shacks; plumbing is not so easily accomplished, however. Construction (for the men) and service work (primarily for women) provide the main employment opportunities for these illiterate poor (e.g. instructions on packaged cake mixes are in pictures to enable illiterate maids to bake cakes for their patrons).

Brazilians see the city of São Paulo as the engine that drives the country. It is the industrial center of Brazil, having grown primarily as the center of the coffee business (see Haynes, 1989; Wolfe, 1993). It now has a ring of international companies around the city. Brazil taxes imports heavily and encourages foreign companies to build their plants in the country, especially in the Amazon region, which has been a tax-free zone. Such economic incentives for foreign investment, the discovery of gold and the availability of cheap lumber in the Amazon region are contributing to the devastation of the rain forest. Brazil's second largest city, Rio de Janeiro, which was the capital prior to Brasilia, has always been, like Bangkok in Thailand, the cultural center, a tourist paradise and one of the largest seaports. It continues to lose economic ground to São Paulo, but remains the cultural heart of the country. The Northeast part of Brazil is primarily agricultural and poor. Its people are predominantly Black or of mixed race (Black, White and Indian) and have the lowest per capita income and highest illiteracy rates in the nation.

Even though Brazil has undergone rapid industrial growth in the past 20 years (called the Brazilian 'miracle') and is now emerging from military dictatorship, the Northeast has not shared equally in this development (Page, 1972). It remains economically the poorest region of Brazil with high infant mortality, low literacy rates and the greatest class stratification in the country. Although school enrolment is increasing throughout the country it is actually decreasing in relative terms in the Northeast (Plank, 1987). Castro (1969) summed up the plight of the Northeast:

TABLE 1
Brazil demographic statistics by region

Geography		
	km^2	% of total
Brazil	8,511,965	100.0
Northeast	1,548,672	18.2
North	3,581,180	42.07
Southeast	924,935	10.86
South	577,723	6.79
Central–West	1,879,455	22.08
Population (1990 estimate in thousands)		
	Number	%
Brazil	150,368	100.0
Northeast	42,822	28.5
North	8,893	5.9
Southeast	65,559	43.6
South	22,762	15.1
Central–West	10,332	6.9
Population density		
	Individuals per km^2	
Brazil	17.8	
Northeast	27.8	
North	2.1	
Southeast	70.9	
South	39.7	
Central–West	5.5	
Major metropolitan areas (1980)		
	Population	Region
São Paulo	12,588,725	Southeast
Rio de Janeiro	9,014,274	Southeast
Belo Horizonte	2,540,130	Southeast
Salvador	1,766,582	Northeast
Recife	2,347,005	Northeast
Porto Alegre	2,231,392	South
Fortaleza	1,580,066	Northeast
Curitiba	1,440,626	South
Brazilia	1,176,935	Central–West
Urban–rural residency (1980)		
	Urban proportion	Rural proportion
Brazil	67.59	32.41
Northeast	50.46	45.44
North	51.65	48.35
Southeast	82.81	17.19
South	62.41	37.59
Central–West	67.79	32.31

Source: Instituto Brasileirio de Geografia e Estatística (1989) *Anuário Estatistico do Brasil, 1989* (Rio de Janeiro, Fundação IBGE).

The face of the Northeast is deeply marked by suffering. For centuries both man and earth have been martyred by adverse forces—natural and cultural. The marks of suffering are so much in evidence that one has the impression the whole landscape of the Northeast is a 600,000 square-mile stage set for some high tragedy. (p. 23)

Northeast Brazil

Geographic and economic conditions. The Brazilian scholar de Andrade (1980, p. 6) noted that 'The Northeast is one of the most discussed, but least known geographic regions of Brazil'. Researchers argue over the exact boundaries of the Northeast, but, generally, this region of Brazil encompasses the states of

Fig. 2: **States and territories of Brazil. From Instituto Brasileiro de Geografia e Estatistica (IBGE) (1985).**

Maranhão, Piau, Ceará, Rio Grande do Norte, Paraíba, Pernambuco, Alagoas, Sergipe and Bahia (see Fig. 2). The Northeast itself is further subdivided into four major regions that extend from the Zona da Matta (the coastal region) through the Agreste (the coastal forests), the Serto (the arid mid-region) and the Middle-North (the savannas and palm forests). Even subnational comparisons are not precise enough to distinguish the diversity of the sub-regional differences of the Northeast. As a whole, however, scholars consider the Northeast a separate geographic, economic and cultural region within Brazil, because it is so severely underdeveloped, its people so poor and its traditions so rich compared with the rest of the country.[3]

As Table 1 indicates, the Northeast accounts for 18.2% of the land of Brazil and 29% of the people. Even with its poverty, the Northeast is not overpopulated compared with the rest of Brazil. This fact is deceptive, however, because over 40% of the land is owned by only 1% of the people with almost 50% of the remaining land owned by only another 10% of the people. (Although more current, reliable statistics are not readily available, there has not been substantial land reform to change land distribution vastly.)

The poverty of the Northeast pervades both the rural and urban areas. As indicated in Tables 1 and 2, the Northeast, along with the North, has the highest proportion of population in rural areas coupled with the lowest per capita income and the highest rate of illiteracy in the country. The harsh geography of the Northeast (especially in the Sertão), the vestiges of the slave system and the control of land ownership by the few keep this region the poorest in Brazil and among the least devel-

TABLE 2
Regional disparities of Brazil

Population percent by race				
	White	Black	Asian	*Mulato*/ mixed
Brazil	54.23	5.92	5.92	38.85
Northeast	26.80	6.73	0.13	65.82
North	20.11	2.69	0.24	76.18
Southeast	66.33	7.02	0.97	25.32
South	83.95	3.16	0.46	12.08
Central–West	49.46	4.17	0.32	45.612

Migration patterns			
	Immigration	Emigration	Difference
Northeast	2,261,697	7,853,775	–5,592,078
North	1,067,729	380,073	687,656
Southeast	9,544,860	6,490,365	3,054,495
South	2,676,107	2,740,972	–64,865
Central–West	2,652,099	737,307	1,914,792

Per capita physicians	
Brazil	1 per 1226
Northeast	1 per 2145
Rio de Janeiro	1 per 531
North	1 per 2268
Southeast	1 per 879

Mortality rates	
Brazil	87.9 per thousand births
Northeast	121.4 per thousand births

Literacy (%)		
	5 years and older	10-14 years
Brazil	68.2	77.7
Northeast	47.0	50.7
North	61.8	63.9
Southeast	78.5	88.6
South	79.2	90.7
Central–West	69.7	75.8

Per capita income by region		
	Monthly income in 1980 cruzeisos for	
	bottom 50%	top 1%
Brazil	2361	150,215
Northeast	1391	88,021
North	2914	126,341
Southeast	3075	182,305
South	2669	133,037
Central–East	2633	160,959

Source: Instituto Brasilerio de Geografia e Estatística (1980) *Anuário Estatistico do Brasil, 1980* (Rio de Janeiro, Fundação IBGE) and Instituto Brasileirio de Geografia e Estatística (1989) *Anuário Estatistico do Brasil, 1989* (Rio de Janeiro, Fundação IBGE).

oped regions in the world. The miracle of industrialization over the past two decades has not been shared equally by all Brazilians, especially the poor of the Northeast. As Castro (1969, p. 133) explained, 'for if Brazil as a whole is an underdeveloped country, the Northeast is the very nadir'.

Culture. Although the people of the Northeast are the poorest in the country, the influence of the African descendants of the region is responsible for cultural traditions that are some of the most visible in modern Brazil. As Henfrey (1981, p. 58) explained, 'The first image of Brazilian popular culture which generally comes to mind is either carnival in Rio or the famous candombles [voodoo cult houses] of Bahia'. The Northeast is rich in these musical and religious traditions. *Forró*, a country-polka music was popularized by the late Luiz Gonzaga and others in the Northeast. The world-renown *samba* music also has its roots in the African traditions of the Northeast.

The rich cultural heritage of the Northeast region is also the basis for some of the finest Brazilian literature and art, most notably Jorge Amado's novels (*Gabriella, Clove, and Cinnamon* and *Dona Flor and Her Two Husbands*), which have been made into popular films by the Brazilian director Bruno Barreto. These novels are set in Northeast Brazil and focus upon the social and political tensions between the land owners and the poor.

A number of other Brazilian authors focus upon the feudal traditions of the Northeast, Gilberto Freyre's *Casa Grande e Senzala* features the relations between the land owners in the big house (*casa grande*) and the slaves in their hovel (*senzala*). Ariano Suassuna (*Vida e Morte Severina*) and others such as Graciliano Ramos and Jose Lins do Rego also are noted Brazilian authors writing about class relations and the social injustice of the Northeast.

The culture of Brazil and particularly the Northeast, has shown a great degree of integration and adaptation of European, African and indigenous customs in food, dress, religion and social relations. The African influence in cooking is found in the regional cuisine of Bahia, which integrates local foods such as coconut milk, manioc flour, fish and a special hot sauce of palm oil, *dendê*. The Northeast cuisine is the most popular regional food in Brazil, particularly *feijoada*. Originally a slave dish composed of rice, beans and the discarded animal parts from the masters' tables, *feijoada* is the national dish of Brazil.

The slave culture has also given Brazil a rich heritage of symbols and customs that are strong reminders of the social injustice of the past and of the oppression of the present. The foremost symbol is the *figa*, a piece of jewelry in wood, silver, gold or stone worn both by women and men as a sign of good luck. The symbol originated with the African slaves. As they were being shipped off to the colonies they would raise their clenched fists with the thumb extended between the index and middle finger to each other as a sign of fertility to keep the family alive. Another slave adornment is the *balangada* or *pença*. For each good deed or act a slave performed, the master awarded an ornament for the slave to be placed on the *balangada*, a silver type belt and clasp worn around the waist. The ornaments were typically small silver pieces in the shape of fruit, fish or gourds hung on the balangada to indicate the worth of the slave. *Balangadas* are now reproduced and displayed in homes or made in silver or brass miniature as necklaces or pins.

Ethnicity and gender. As explained, the Northeast was the center of the slave trade during Brazil's colonial period and has the largest percentage of Blacks and *mulatos*, individuals of mixed races (see Table 2). Similar to the plight of Blacks in the USA, a rich ethnic tradition has emerged among blacks and the poor in the face of such utter poverty in the Northeast. An important point to note on racial prejudice in Brazil is that few people consider themselves Black. Rather, many individuals who have African ancestry are actually *mulato*, because of the intermixing with Whites and native Indians. Traditional (American and European) concepts of prejudice do not hold in Brazil. While there is severe class prejudice, different conceptions are needed to define racial prejudice (see Skidmore, 1993). For Brazilians, the Whiter one is and the more European the higher the status. For this reason, few people consider themselves 'Black', but, rather, shades of Black—each person saying he or she is 'lighter' than the next individual. Although the information by color in Table 2 includes a category for 'mixed' or *mulato*, how individuals were classified and placed in this category is somewhat unreliable.

As depicted in the novels of the Northeast, Brazilian women and in particular lower class women are objects of desire free to be used by upper class males. The Latin *machismo* continues to be strong in Brazil (Alvarez, 1990). Because of the distance between the upper and the lower classes in Brazil, most middle-class families have a live-in maid while virtually all upper class families have at least one full-time maid. This subjugation of a group of women assures a permanent underclass to serve the domestic needs of the upper classes. The maids are often illiterate *mulato* women from the rural interior of a state or are 'imported' from the poorest areas of the North and Northeast. The upper classes rationalize the keeping of full-time maids as a way of providing housing and minimal income for women who might otherwise live in abject poverty. This justification is, unfortunately, often true for the individual woman, but full-time service as a maid does not solve the problem for this class of women as a whole. As Brazil increasingly industrializes there are new employment opportunities for uneducated women and it has become more difficult to find live-in maids. Rather than full-time maids, it is becoming more common for maids to come to the homes of middle-class families on a daytime basis. These daytime maids can marry and have their own family and charge more for their services.

Migration. Because of intermittent droughts and the extreme poverty of the interior region (the Sertão), there is large and continuous migration of the poor to the coastal cities of the Zona da Matta. As Table 2 shows the migration out of the Northeast is substantially higher than the rest of the country. Not only do the poor from the Northeast migrate to the major cities of this region (Bahia, Recife and João Pessoa and the northern coastal city of Forteleza), but they also find their way to the major cities of the south in hope of work and a better life. As severe as the poverty is in the *favelas* in which the migrants find shelter, these living conditions are often better than those they left.

Religion. Just as the Brazilian cuisine is an integration of European, African and Indian influences, so too is the Brazilian form of Catholicism. Freyre (1956, p. 41) observed that 'Catholicism was in reality the cement of our unity'. Since the advent of the Portuguese in the 1500s, the Catholicism the European immigrants brought with them to Brazil has been adapted and integrated with the indigenous religions of Africa and the Indians, particularly in the Northeast. In the country as a whole, over 90% of the people consider themselves to be Catholic, but there are vast differences in religious practice throughout the Northeast from fundamentalism in the interior to voodoo or *candomble* in Bahia.

Originating with the slaves in Bahia, *candomble* (the voodoo-like cult in Brazil) is synonymous with the plight of the poor for the whole country. The syncretism of *candomble* and Catholicism is prevalent throughout Brazil and it is necessary to understand the culture and consciousness of the oppressed classes, particularly those of the Northeast. Because of the utter poverty of the slaves and their present-day descendants, *candomble* (or *macumba*) serves as the source for hope, medical care and even food. Lacking medical care the poor turn to the *orixas* or divinities for cures and remedies.

Educational philosophy. Integrally linked with liberal religious philosophy in Brazil is Freire's (1970) 'pedagogy of the oppressed'. Freire, himself from the Northeast, formed his philosophy by working with the poor from his home region. He proposed that only through education can the oppressed develop the 'critical consciousness' needed to understand the depths of their oppression. The education needed to accomplish this praxis is a 'critical pedagogy' aimed at transforming the consciousness of the poor. Freire's work in Northeast Brazil has become the basis for literacy campaigns throughout the world. Building on Freire's philosophy, the Catholic church has begun educating the poor in groups and networks in the Northeast and spreading this method throughout Brazil and the developing world. This philosophy of social justice through education has led to the development of a 'liberation theology' by the Catholic church in Northeast Brazil that integrates critical pedagogy with social justice.

Even with the emphasis on literacy campaigns in the Northeast, the population of this region remains the least schooled of Brazil. As Table 3 shows, the Northeast has the lowest overall enrollment rates, the lowest literacy rates and the lowest mean years of schooling in the country. This historical underdevelopment and undereducation of the Northeast has always assured a cheap and plentiful labor force. Rationing education has assured the continued poverty of the Northeast by supplying cheap labor for the agricultural and manufacturing industries of the Northeast and South. Because the workers from the Northeast are predominantly Black or *mulato* there has been little political incentive to alter

TABLE 3
Basic education indicators of Brazil by region, 7–14-year-old children, 1980

Region	*Enrollment ratio*	*Literacy ratio*	*Mean years of schooling*
Northeast	52.4	44.9	1.50
Urban	73.8	61.2	2.23
Rural	30.7	28.4	0.75
North	61.2	55.9	1.72
Urban	78.1	68.4	2.31
Rural	39.4	39.9	0.97
South	75.3	84.6	3.00
Urban	84.5	88.5	3.33
Rural	63.6	79.7	2.56
Southeast	80.4	83.0	2.94
Urban	86.7	87.3	3.16
Rural	57.9	68.0	2.08
Central-West	72.4	67.7	2.34
Urban	82.3	74.0	2.68
Rural	49.4	53.2	1.51
Brazil	69.2	69.3	2.38
Urban	82.7	79.5	2.91
Rural	45.9	50.9	1.51

Source: Psacharopoulos, G. & Arriagada, A. M. (1980) *School Participation, Grade Attainment, and Literacy in Brazil: 1980 census analysis*, p. 39 (Research Division, Educational and Training Department, World Bank, Washington, DC).

the situation. While the Catholic Church and a number of other groups promoting social justice work to improve the plight of the Northeasterners, the solution for the underdevelopment of the Northeast is not merely an educational one. Increasing the quality of the labour force (the input) through education would not automatically change the poverty of the Northeast, because there are no jobs (the output) in the Northeast in which to place a better educated worker. Ironically, a better educated workforce would deplete the Northeast of its talented youth, who would have to seek work in other parts of the country. Additionally, underdevelopment of the Northeast is not only a regional problem, but one for all of Brazil. As the country continues to develop and as the need for higher skilled manufacturing workers increases, the problems of education and migration from the Northeast will continue to tax the resources of the remainder of the country.

From this portrait of the Brazilian Northeast we are able to understand why Castro (1969, p. 165) believed that 'the Northeast is clearly the No. 1 national problem in Brazil'. Our intent here is not only to be informative about the Northeast of Brazil but also to illustrate how vital subnational comparisons are to understanding the internal complexity of a country. Without such internal comparisons, our generalized knowledge of a country would clearly misinform us. One cannot understand Brazil without knowing the Northeast. Similarly, Thailand cannot be understood without a knowledge of its Northeast.

Thai Subnational Comparisons

> The voices of the E-sarn people must be heard. They will be heard. Our Kingdom cannot live in peace and justice until they have. (Sanitsuda, 1987)[4]

> He who inhabits a pile house, eats sticky rice, and plays the Kaen, he is a true Laotian. The musical culture of Northeast Thailand expresses the true Lao culture though politically part of modern Thailand and separated from Laos across the Mekong River. (Miller, 1985)

> In Bangkok, the very word 'Isan' is almost a metaphor for poverty. For centuries, Isan has been baking under a merciless sun, growing steadily drier and poorer—with just enough rain, just enough good years along the way, to give its people an unshakable faith in the power of prayer, hard work and virtue to extract blessings—or, if not blessings, then pity—from the fickle spirits that control sky, earth, water, life, and death. (Kampoon, 1988)

In contrast to Brazil, Thailand was one of the very few developing countries never to have been colonized. That unique historical fact has shaped Thailand's modern economic, educational, cultural and social history. The monarchy has also been an extremely influential factor in shaping Thai polity and culture. Interestingly Brazil was the only nation in Latin America to have a post-colonial monarchy, which survived until the end of the nineteenth century (Haring, 1958). Thailand, like Brazil, had a feudal system of slavery which was abolished in 1905, 17 years later than in

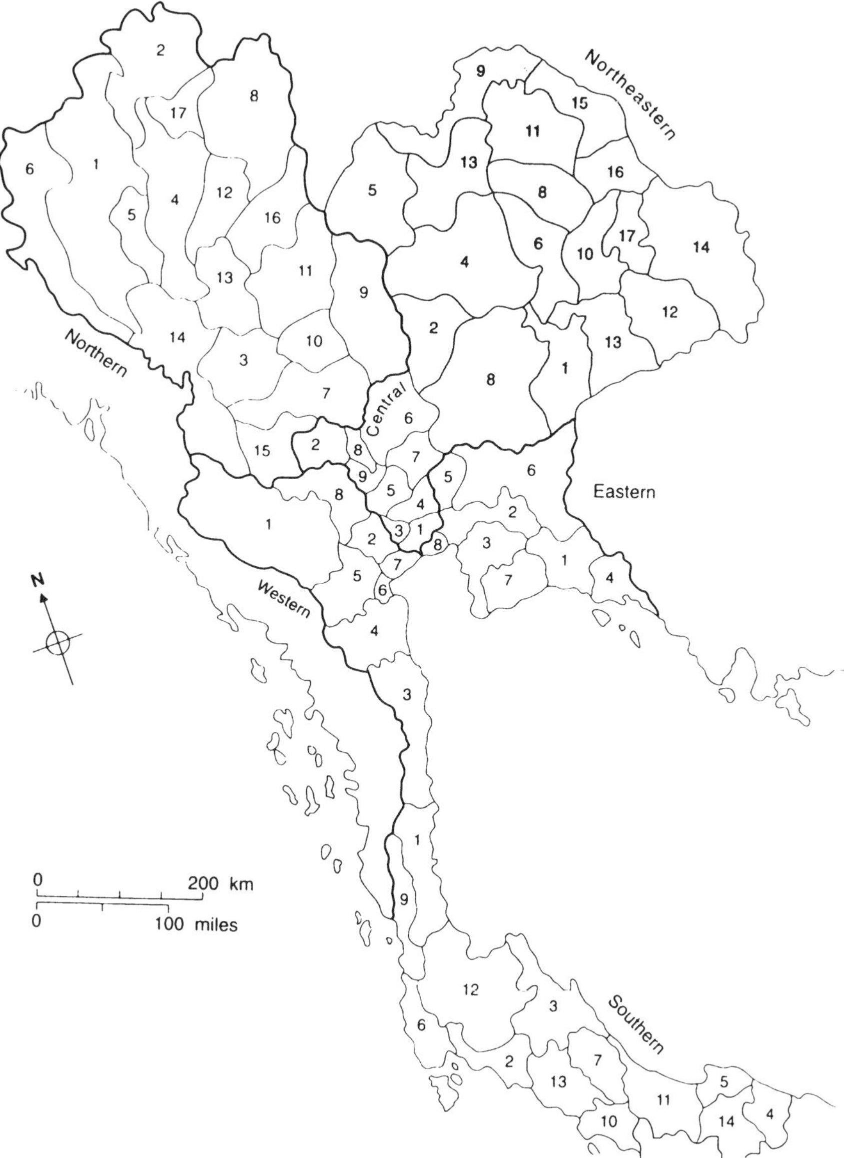

Fig. 3: **Map of Thailand showing Northeastern region.**

Brazil. Thailand's traditional economy centered on the production of rice, rubber and tin and Thailand was frequently referred to as the 'rice bowl' of Asia.

As in Brazil, the past 30 years have seen dramatic changes in the Thai economy. Successful diversification has occurred in both the manufacturing and agricultural sectors. Today, to the surprise of many, rice, rubber and tin now account for only 12% of Thailand's foreign exchange earnings (Fry, 1988). Thailand is now a major producer of hard disks for microcomputers and sent its first shipment of automobiles to the North American market in January 1988. During the past year there has been considerable debate as to whether Thailand is a newly industrialized country (NIC). Actually it is and it is not. Bangkok certainly has NIC characteristics with an income per capita comparable to that of Taiwan and higher than that of Korea. But the Northeast is definitely not an NIC. An article in the Thai language press (*Matichon Sutsapadaa,* 11 December 1988) referred to Thailand as a NIAC

TABLE 4
Regional income distribution in Thailand, 1960–1985 (per capita in current baht)

	1960	*1970*	*1980*	*1981*	*1982*	*1983*	*1984*	*1985*	*1987*
Thailand	2160	3849	14,743	16,359	17,259	18,584	19,551	20,263	23,022
Bangkok	5630	11,234	41,300	46,891	49,539	52,150	56,092	59,003	74,418
Central	2564	4662	15,646	18,508	19,448	19,554	20,861	21,133	23,638
South	2700	3858	13,745	13,496	13,419	15,058	15,200	15,358	17,832
North	1496	2699	9866	11,064	11,355	12,375	12,781	13,353	13,170
Northeast	1082	1822	6012	6581	7185	8107	8009	8124	8383
Ratio of Bangkok to Northeast	5.2	6.2	6.9	7.1	6.9	6.4	7.0	7.3	8.9
Ratio of Central to Northeast	2.4	2.6	2.6	2.8	2.7	2.4	2.6	2.6	2.8
Absolute disparity between Bangkok and Northeast	4548	9412	35,288	40,310	42,354	44,043	48.083	50,879	66,065

Source: Raw data from which this table is based are from the National Statistical Office of Thailand, from Keyes, C. F. (1967) *Thailand: Buddhist kingdom as modern nation-state*, p. 159 (Boulder and London, Westview Press) and from (1990) *Thailand Economic Information Kit*, p. 2 (Bangkok, Development Research Institute Foundation).

(newly industrialized agro-based economy). While both Brazil and Thailand have had impressively high macroeconomic growth rates, Thailand with its conservative monetary and fiscal policies has avoided Latin-style inflation and the Thai baht has been a basically stable currency for decades.

Like Brazil, Thailand's modern political history has been heavily influenced by the military (Elliot, 1978; Thak, 1979; Suchit, 1987). Though Thailand had not had a successful military *coup d'état* since 1977, a bloodless military coup on 23 February 1991 ousted the democratically elected government of Chatichai Choonhavan, confirming the impermanence of Thai politics (*Matichon Sutsapadaa*, 3 March 1991). Despite such surface 'instability', the bureaucracy and monarchy provide a core stability to Thai polity. The monarch's intervention was critical in stopping the May 1992 political violence in Thailand which forced an unelected military prime minister, who had orchestrated the 1991 coup, to resign (Fry, 1992). Having celebrated on 2 July 1988, the longest reign of any monarch in Thai history (which dates back to the thirteenth century), King Bhumipol is probably the most popular political figure of any polity in the world.

Though both Brazil and Thailand have serious levels of inequality, the overall percentage of poverty in Thailand is considerably lower (see Table 5). As in Brazil, there has been tremendous migration in Thailand from the poorer countryside to more urbanized areas, particularly Bangkok, which is now a hyper-urbanized city. Despite the rapid modernization of Bangkok during the past three decades, the number of its slums has grown to 1020 (Sopon, 1985).

As São Paulo is the engine driving Brazil, Bangkok is Thailand's premier city par excellence. Unlike Brazil, Thailand has only one large metropolitan area. Bangkok is approximately 40 times larger than the next biggest Thai city, Chiangmai. In this sense, its dominance is even more dramatic than that of São Paulo. Approximately 1200 new factories are currently being built in the Bangkok area, illustrating the dramatic industrialization of the Thai capital. Many of Thailand's best schools and universities are located in Bangkok, thus, attracting talent and youth from the rural areas

TABLE 5
Percentage of population under poverty line[1]

	1975–1976	*1980–1981*	*1985–1986*	*1988[2]*
Bangkok (city core)	6.9	3.7	3.1	2.4
Central	13.0	13.6	15.6	10.5
North	33.2	21.5	25.5	21.6
Northeast	44.9	35.9	48.2	42.5
South	30.7	20.4	27.2	23.9

[1] The poverty line is defined as those having less than 4091 baht annual income for villages and rural districts and less than 6251 baht annual income for municipal areas.

[2] Data for 1988 are based on a simulated economic model developed by researchers at the Thailand Development Research Institute.

Source: Thailand's Income Distribution and Poverty Profile and Their Current Situations (1988) p. 91 (Bangkok, Development Research Institute Foundation).

of Thailand. The famous 'bright lights' of Bangkok as a premier world center of entertainment also contribute to its magnetic qualities. In this sense and with its tremendous growth in tourism, Bangkok is a combination of São Paulo and Rio de Janeiro. Much of Thailand's 'economic miracle' has been concentrated in Bangkok, Chiangmai and the Central and Southern regions. The Northeast, however, has lagged behind significantly.

Northeast Thailand

Historical, geographic and economic conditions. The Northeast of Thailand is known as both Isan and the Khorat Plateau. It has also been called the 'Far Province' (Cripps, 1965; Donner, 1978). Isan is a Pali-Sanskrit term which can also be translated as Siva, the Hindu regent of the Northeast quadrant of the world (Kampoon, 1988). The Northeast of Thailand comprises 17 provinces which are shaded in Fig. 3. Like the Northeast of Brazil, this region of Thailand is further subdivided meteorologically into four subregions, namely, the Western mountains, the Southern Mountains, the Mackliong Valley and the Transitory zone (Donner, 1978, p. 570). The Northeast is separated from the rest of Thailand and Kampuchea by major mountain ranges to the south and west. The Maekhong River, Southeast Asia's most famous and one of the great rivers of the world, separates the Northeast physically from Laos.

The Northeast represents both approximately one-third of the land area and population of Thailand. Until 1827, the Northeast had its own political autonomy. At that time it and what is now Laos were incorporated as part of Siam. Keyes (1967) provided an excellent overview of the historical political relations between Siam and Laos. The major ethnic group of both Laos and Northeast Thailand is essentially the same (Keyes, 1967; Srisakara, 1980; Miller, 1985; Seri & Hewison, 1990). Ironically, there are approximately 10 times more ethnic Laos living in Thailand than in Laos.

Physically, the Northeast also differs significantly from the rest of Thailand. It is much drier with more irregular rainfall and it is warmer during the hot season. Its soil is much poorer than other areas of Thailand. Unfortunately the area has suffered major deforestation, much more than the Northern and Southern regions of Thailand. The province of Mahasarakham in the center of Thailand's Northeast is totally deforested.

The Northeast of Thailand: A quantitative assessment

Socioeconomic indicators. Associated with the arid conditions in the Northeast and the poor soil conditions is widespread poverty and the relative economic backwardness of the area is a major factor accounting for Thailand's serious income disparities. Table 4 shows the relative economic status of the Northeast region over time from 1960 to 1985. While economic conditions in the Northeast have definitely improved in the years since 1960, the absolute gap in income levels between the Northeast and other regions, particularly Bangkok has widened dramatically (*Bangkok Post*, 1991, p. 16). As shown in Table 5, the percentage of the Northeast's population under the poverty line actually increased between 1976 and 1986. In Roi Et, a province in the center of the Northeast, there is a doctor for every 23,681 people, a condition similar to that of the Central African Republic. In contrast, in Bangkok, there is a doctor for every 722 people (*Bangkok Post*, 1991, p. 16).

Educational indicators. The Northeast's disadvantageous position with respect to key socioeconomic indicators is mirrored in basic educational indicators as well. Studies of educational disparities in Thailand by the International Institute for Educational Planning (IIEP) and the National Education Commission (NEC) in cooperation with the International Development Research Center (IDRC) in Ottawa present detailed data on the educational status of the Northeast (Kamol *et al.*, 1978; Amrung *et al.*, 1990). The IIEP study shows that with the exception of Mahasarakham province, Northeastern provinces are distinctly disadvantaged with respect to the access of their children to upper secondary education, the key to further education and related social and occupational mobility.

The NEC-IDRC study of regional disparities uses both quantitative and qualitative data as well as longitudinal data in assessing educational disparities. The quantitative data are based on two major national Coleman-type surveys of educational achievement. Table 6 shows the basic results from the second of these surveys by region. Table 7, comparable to our economic comparisons in Table 4, shows the changes over time. The economic and educational data show remarkably parallel patterns. While educational achievement in the Northeast has certainly improved, the actual absolute gaps in cognitive achievement between the Northeast and Southern, Central, and Northern regions have actually increased. Figure 4 presents a map of Thailand with cognitive achievement shown by region. The three Northeastern educational regions, 9, 10 and 11, clearly lag behind other parts of the nation.

Table 8 presents basic primary school data by region. The Northwest lags behind on nearly every indicator.

The qualitative part of the NEC-IDRC study involved the intensive study and comparison of two Northeastern with two Central primary schools. In every category compared, the two Northeastern schools are at a disadvantage (Cummings, 1980). The following two quotations from the qualitative segment of the NEC-IDRC study (Amrung *et al.*, 1990) illustrate both the environmental and economic conditions adversely affecting the quality of schooling in the Northeast:

> Some classrooms were found to be unfit for learning: lighting was inadequate; during the rainy season, some were flooded; and many were situated by main roads, where the dust and noise were quite disturbing. (Amrung *et al.*, 1990, p. 145)
>
> One poor parent at Waat Huay Haeng School (in Northeast) bought one pencil and cut it into three so that all the three children could have a pencil to use. This pencil was in fact tied to the child's buttonhole to prevent its loss. (Amrung *et al.*, 1990, p. 292)

Differential life chances as affected by region of birth. In Thai society, education is a key factor in social and occupational mobility. This condition is reflected in both empirical studies and in literary works.[5] Given the basic educational disadvantages of the Northeast at the primary and secondary school levels demonstrated above, it is reasonable to expect that the life chances of those from the Northeast are severely limited. Based on empirical educational data, life chances have been computed for a hypothetical individual from Buriram Province, one of the poorest and most remote provinces in the Northeast (Fry, 1989). A female from this province has only 1/127 the chance of a female from Bangkok of passing the national entrance examination to enter Chulalongkorn University, Thailand's most prestigious institution of higher education (Fry, 1989). Furthermore, even though the military has provided opportunity for social mobility among some rural individuals, the individual from Buriram has only 1/35 the chance of an individual from Bangkok to become part of the military élite.

TABLE 6
Students' cognitive, non-cognitive and total achievement scores by geographic region

	Cognitive achievement		*Non-cognitive achievement*		*Total achievement*	
Geographic region	*Mean (%)*	*CV*	*Mean (%)*	*CV*	*Mean (%)*	*CV*
Bangkok	59.88	16.55	73.80	4.73	64.57	11.03
Central	54.98	14.67	74.33	6.79	61.50	10.04
North	46.08	21.90	69.33	6.31	53.92	14.50
South	49.98	15.66	70.62	4.83	56.94	10.56
Northeast	41.14	25.66	67.56	7.30	50.04	16.37

CV, coefficient of variation

Source: Chantavanich, A., Chantavanich, S. and Fry, G. (1990) *An Evaluative Policy Study of the Efficiency and Quality of Primary Schooling in Thailand*, p. 29 (Ottawa, International Development Research Center).

Demographic indicators. As early as 1956, the anthropologist Robert Textor documented the migration of Northeasterners to Bangkok to become samlor drivers during the dry season (Textor, 1961). The poverty of the Northeast pushes individuals into Bangkok and the perceived wealth and 'bright lights' of Bangkok especially pull young people from Isan (Donner, 1978, p. 587; Watanabe, 1987, p. 7). In her detailed study of Bangkok masseuses, Pasuk (1982, p. 12) found that 26% were from the Northeast, while only 2% were from the wealthier Southern provinces. Family poverty was cited as the major reason for women seeking employment as masseuses. Pasuk (1982, pp. 75–76) ended her study with the optimistic view that such migration from the Northeast may now be static or in decline as parents in the villages of the Northeast are beginning to show an aversion to their children going into such business. Recent reports in the *Bangkok Post* (1988, p. 33; 1989, p. 25) are much more

TABLE 7
Changes in students' cognitive achievement score by geographical regions

	1973 cognitive achievement			*1980 cognitive achievement*			*Changes*	
Geographic Regions	*X*	*SD*	*CV*	*X*	*SD*	*CV*	*X*[1]	*CV*[2]
Bangkok	83.74 (52.34)[3]	27.51	32.85	96.52 (60.33)	27.04	28.01	12.78 (7.99)	4.84
Central	55.74 (34.84)	22.59	40.53	88.73 (55.46)	24.13	27.19	32.99 (20.62)	13.34
Northern	50.42 (31.51)	19.66	38.99	76.53 (47.83)	25.19	32.92	26.11 (16.32)	6.07
Northeastern	42.60 (26.63)	18.60	43.66	66.55 (41.59)	26.93	40.47	23.95 (14.97)	3.19
South	55.14 (34.46)	21.32	38.67	80.68 (50.43)	24.21	30.01	25.54 (15.96)	8.66 8.66
Total	50.95 (31.84)			77.04 (48.15)				
Gini index		0.12			0.07			
Rank correlation (*p*)1.00								

[1] Increased change.
[2] Decreased change.
[3] Figures in parentheses are means in percentage.

Source: Chantavanich, A., Amrung, C., Supang, C. & Fry, G. (1990) *An Evaluative Policy Study of the Efficiency and Quality of Primary Schooling in Thailand*, p. 180 (Ottawa, International Development Research Center).

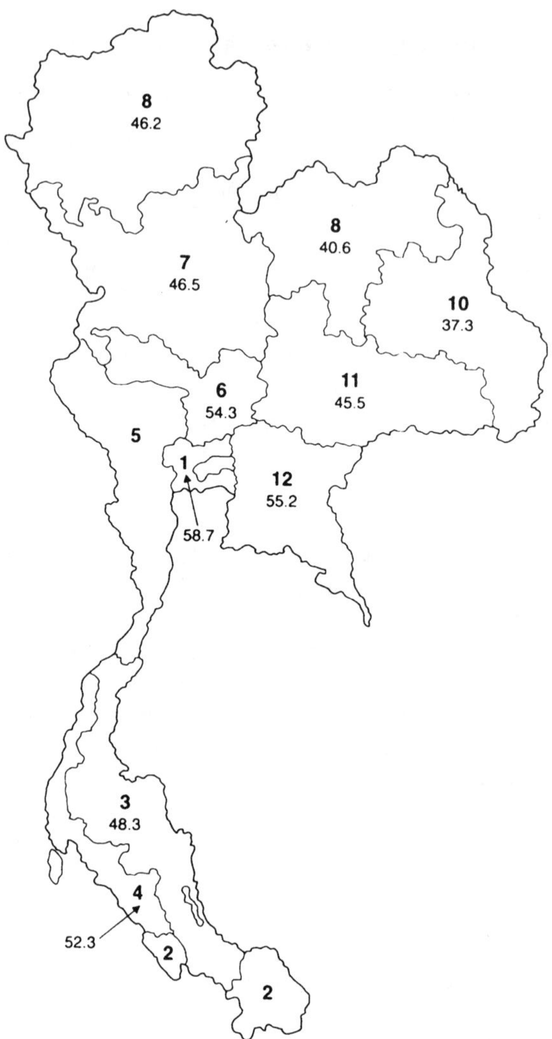

Fig. 4: **Student's cognitive achievement scores by educational region.**

pessimistic. Government figures show that there are 1–1.7 million child workers in Thailand and that many of these children are migrants from the drought-stricken Northeast. There are child brokers in the Northeast who deal exclusively in child prostitution (Hiew, 1992). Other children work as servants or in factories (see also Hiew, 1992). In a study of six major slums in Bangkok, Morell & Morell (1972, p. 27) found that 19% of family heads were from the Northeast.

Environmental indicators. Given the low agricultural yields in the Northeast, there has been tremendous pressure to expand acreage by cutting forests. There are limited opportunities for double cropping in the Northeast because of drought and the dependence on rain-fed irrigation. As a result of these agricultural pressures, there has been serious deforestation in the Northeast which was a major theme in the popular novel and film, *Khruu Baangk (Rural Schoolteacher)*, by Khammaan (1982). In 1971, 78,153 km^2 or 45.9% of the Northeast was forested (Donner, 1978, p. 610). By 1982, only 25,886 km^2 or 15% remained as forested areas (*Statistical Yearbook Thailand*, 1984, p. 269).

Culture. Despite its poverty, the Northeast has a resilient and rich culture. Its people take considerable pride in their language, music, dance, cuisine and festivals. It is common to find high

TABLE 8
Basic data on Thai rural primary education disaggregated by region, 1988

Region	X_1	X_2	X_3	X_4	X_5	X_6	X_7	X_8	X_9	X_{10}
Central	6.62	77.68	17.85	6.04	1.64	71.56	19.61	1.14	9.61	89.84
South	15.00	51.02	7.95	2.28	1.06	63.85	19.79	1.14	7.70	88.33
North	19.55	62.02	11.34	1.86	1.87	68.19	17.75	1.11	15.70	84.68
Northeast	10.08	59.55	5.84	1.29	0.90	45.57	21.49	1.07	7.60	84.80

Definition of variables: X_1 percentage of schools which are remote; X_2 percentage of schools with electricity; X_3 percentage of schools with access to public water supply; X_4 percentage of schools with telephones; X_5 percentage of schools with adult education classes; X_6 percentage of schools with libraries; X_7 student-teacher ratio; X_8 teacher-classroom ratio; X_9 percentage of small schools (those with 1–60 students); X_{10} percentage of teachers who hold a higher degree (BA or associate degree).

Source: Computed and aggregated from raw provincial data contained in (1988) *Satiti Kaanprathomsygsaa Piikaansygsaa 2531 (Primary Education Statistics for 1988)* (Bangkok, Office of the National Primary Education Commission).

ranking Northeastern bureaucrats driving modern Nissans, but listening to tapes of Isan music. The Northeasterners are also noted for their hospitality and generosity. They are considered by many to have a greater seriousness of purpose than the more care-free Central Thais blessed with much more favorable environmental and climatic conditions. Mutual self-help is also a principle in the Northeast. Kampoon (1988) pointed out that in the Northeast there has 'always been a strong belief that people are supposed to take care of each other' (p. 11). For Northeasterners, 'virtue is synonymous with honesty, kindness, hospitality, cheerfulness, industry, generosity, and courage' (p. 11). Kampoon's (1988) novel, *A Child of the Northeast*, was later made into a film. As in Brazil, the Northeast of Thailand has been a cradle for creative, politically oriented literature inspired by the culture of the region and its special problems. The most famous novel from this region, later to become a highly popular film, was a novel by Khammaan (1982) titled *The Rural School Teacher* or *The Teachers of Mad Dog Swamp*. The author, a former rural school teacher in the Northeast, provides an insightful and moving description of Northeastern culture, the educational problems of the region and the political explosiveness of environmental issues. The hero of the novel, Piya, a highly committed rural school teacher discovers the presence of major illegal logging. His intolerance of this crime against nature leads to his eventual death and martyrdom. The irony of this novel is the way in which it mirrors the recent murder of Chico Mendes, a major environmentalist, in remote Brazil. The film based on this novel won a major award for social realism at an international film festival in the former Soviet Union.

Other noteworthy Thai literature inspired by the Northeast are titles such as *Huaaak Sygsaa (Educational Empathy)*, *Baksieng Noi (Little Voices)* and *Bantyg Khong Khruu Prachaabaan (Report of a Rural School Teacher)* by Khammaan Khonkai (1978, 1980 and 1977), *Isaan Long Krung (A Northeasterner Comes Down to Bangkok)*, *Nakrian Baannook (Remote Rural Students)* and *A Child of the Northeast* by Kampoon Boontawee (1978, 1979 and 1988), *Monsoon Country* and *People of Isan* by Pira Sudham (1988 and 1987), *Little Things* by Prachuab Thirabutana (1971) and *Kamphaeng (Walls)* and *The Politician and Other Stories* by Lao Khamhom (1975 and 1973). Common themes in this rich literature are the essence of Isan culture, the neglect of the area, particularly economically and educationally and collisions between rural Northeastern and more modern urban culture.

Ethnicity and gender. Though Thailand is normally considered one of the more culturally homogeneous societies of Southeast Asia, it does have considerable cultural diversity (Fry, 1980). A major 1977 study of Mahidol University resulting in an empirically based language map of Thailand shows 75 distinct languages being spoken in Thailand. The Northeast has special richness with respect to cultural diversity. The linguist, Gerard Diffloth,

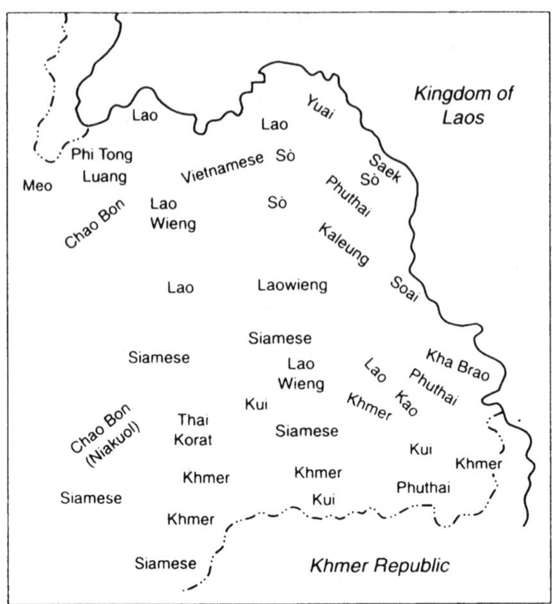

***Fig. 5:* The five faces of Thailand ethnic groups in Northeast Thailand (based on studies by W. Blanchard, E. Seidenfaden, the National Geographic Society and others).**

Source: Donner, W. (1978) *The Five Faces of Thailand*, p. 592. (New York, St. Martins Press).

for example, has found a group of 2000–3000 people in the Northeast near Korat who speak sixth century classical Mon. These individuals appear to be original descendants from the original Mon kingdom. The map in Fig. 5 shows the major ethnic groups of Thailand's Northeast, namely the Lao, Laowieng, Thai Korat, Khmer, Kui, Siamese, Phuthai, Kha Brao, Soai, Lao Kao, Chao Bon, Phi Tong Luang, Yuai, Saek, So and Vietnamese. Many of these ethnic minorities are becoming bicultural and bilingual as more and more children complete 6 years of compulsory schooling in the Central Thai language. In these national schools, students are socialized to feel part of the Thai nation and develop strong loyalty to its major institutions such as the monarchy, Buddhism and the Thai nation-state. In the early 1980s, with major support from the World Bank, Thailand also introduced a new National Educational Radio Network which covers approximately 95% of Thailand. This network reinforces the Thai national culture and values.

With respect to gender, the Northeast female, like the Thai female in general, is extremely active in the economy. Thai women have one of the highest labor force participation rates in the world (Thomlinson, 1971). Northeastern women are active in all aspects of daily life. With men often migrating to urban areas during the dry season to earn extra income, many women left behind on the farms have even greater responsibilities. Research by G. Moreno-Black (unpublished manuscript) documented their role, for example, in the gathering and marketing of wild foods. As in other countries, there are regional stereotypes about women and their values.

Migration. One out of six individuals in Bangkok is originally from the Northeast (*Statistical Yearbook of Thailand*, 1984, p. 68). Many of these individuals are found working in the informal and service sectors as well as in labour-intensive factories. In the service sector, many become engaged in prostitution. In *People of Isan*, Pira (1987) presented the paradoxical life of an Isan migrant working in the informal sector selling barbecued Isan style chicken on a busy Bangkok street:

> Meanwhile, I keep on selling charcoal grilled chicken and 'som tam' and sticky rice, and the income of about 80 or 100 baht [3 to 4 US $] a day keeps me happy. At times there are passers-by whose features bearing the peculiarities of the Esarn people remind me of home. Starving peasants

> who left their rice fields for Bangkok shuffle listlessly along the street. Some stop to beg me for something to eat, and I give them grilled chicken wings and some 'som tam' with sticky rice. (p. 67)

Religion. Thailand's Northeast is noted as an area where Buddhism flourishes. This region has long been noted for having excellent and skilled meditation masters. Vipassana or meditation masters were common among wandering monks (Seri, 1988, p. 11). In a major recent study of Buddhism, reform and community development, Seri (1988) identified eight Thai Buddhist priests noted for their charisma and commitment to helping the poor. Seven of the eight are Northeastern monks. Their activities and actions have been highly influenced by insights developed from their intimate contact with the poverty, both spiritual and material, of ordinary Isan people with whom they have contact (Seri, 1988, p. 161). A world renowned temple near Ubol in the Northeast has attracted a number of Australians who have become ordained as Buddhist monks. On the other hand, Western missionary activity has not focused on the Northeast, but instead on the North where there are large numbers of non-Buddhist hill peoples.

Educational philosophy. Interestingly, the educational philosophy of the Northeastern Brazilian educator, Paulo Freire, has significantly influenced Thailand on the opposite side of the world. The Thai educator, Dr. Vorapipatana Kowit, the father of modern Thai non-formal education, has tried to integrate Buddhist educational philosophy with that of Freire. His philosophy has been termed *Khit-Pen*, which literally means to be able to think and implies the capability of thinking independently and critically about the problems of one's life and community.

With his own charisma and his Freire-influenced Buddhist philosophy of non-formal education, Dr. Kowit has attracted some of Thailand's best and brightest young individuals to this field. By emphasizing the use of common and basic language central to the genuine conditions of the rural peasant, Kowit and his colleagues have provided an ambiance motivating an interest in literacy as a means to reduce vulnerability and to improve basic rights and opportunities. Largely as the result of such efforts by these committed individuals, Thailand can now boast a literacy rate of 91%, though literacy rates in the Northeast are still considerably lower.[6]

Similar to the plight of Northeastern Brazilians, however, the rationing of education in Northeast Thailand has assured a cheap and plentiful labor force. And, similar to Brazil, the solution for resolving this underdevelopment is not only an educational one. How educational policy can integrate with the economic and political realities of Thailand remains the critical question for comparative educators.

Conclusion

Through the richness of the case examples of Northeast Brazil and Northeast Thailand we have attempted to demonstrate how misleading typical aggregate economic and educational evidence can be. Because each of these regions is severely less developed compared to the rest of the country, gross generalizations and conclusions about the country, as a whole, would not indicate the disparities of internal development nor provide answers for successful subnational or national development (see Table 9).

It would be over simplistic and reductionist to argue that there is a single factor that accounts for the relative deprivation of these two regions. Only a syncretic approach can explain the phenomena highlighted in the comparative cases considered. We have proposed, first, that a political economy perspective is particularly helpful in understanding the causes of these regional disparities. The lack of genuine voices of the rural poor of both regions in the political process has led to economic and educational neglect. Both regions have not received their fair share of quality public goods and, thus, their economic and human capital infrastructure is inferior to more advanced regions of each country. Being weak politically, these regions are less able to attract outside capital and to resist adverse policies resulting in environmental degradation (Scott, 1985).

Second, we argued that the interaction between the international and local context represents another major explanatory factor for understanding the disparities found between the Northeast subregions and the remainder of

TABLE 9
Key statistical comparisons between Northeast Brazil and Northeast Thailand

	Brazil	*Thailand*
Geography		
Total land area in km²	8,511,965	513,115
Land area of Northeast	1,548,672	168,854
Northeast as % of total	18.2	33.0
Population (1985)		
Total	135,564,000	51,795,651
Northeast	39,145,000	18,060,945
Northeast as % of total	29.0	35.0
Population density (individuals per km²)		
Nation as a whole	14.07	100.94
Northeast	22.57	106.96
Primacy of São Paulo versus Bangkok (1980)		
Ratio of population of largest city in country so largest city in Northeast (Recife and Keon Keen, respectively)	5.36	54.82
Percentage of rural population		
Nation as a whole	32.41	82.0
Northeast	45.44	96.0
Infant mortality rate (less than 1 year) (per 1000 births)		
Nation as a whole	87.9	31.0
Northeast	121.4	54.4
Migration patterns (difference between immigration and emigration)		
Northeast	-5,592,078	-194,815
North	+687,656	-17,713
South	-64,865	-7,326
Physicians per capita		
Nation as a whole	1 per 1226	1 per 8860
Northeast	1 per 2145	1 per 35,835
Differential income per capita by region		
Ratio of income per capita of largest city to Northeast	NA	7.3
Ratio of income per capita in center/South to Northeast	3.0	2.6

Sources: (1985) *Anuário Estatístico do Brasil—1984* (Rio de Janeiro, Secretária de Planejamento da Presidêencia da Republica), (1972) *Brazil Development Series, No. 3, Amazonia, Manaus Free Zone, Northeast* (São Paulo, Telepress). (1989) *Instituto Brasileiro de Geografia e Estatistica, Anuário Estatistico do Brasil, 1989* (Rio de Janeiro, Fundação IBGE). (1987) *Statistical Handbook of Thailand 1986–1987* (Bangkok, National Statistical Office), (1984) *Statistical Yearbook Thailand 1981–1984* (Bangkok, National Statistical Office), Wantanabe, M. (1987) *Economic Development and Internal Migration in Thailand* (Tokyo, International Development Center of Japan) and Richards, P. J. (1982) *Basic Needs and Government Policies in Thailand* (Singapore, Maruzen).

the country (Huelshoff, 1992). The rapid growth of international trade and investment in areas such as Bangkok, Rio de Janeiro and São Paulo has been a magnet attracting cheap labor from the Northeastern hinterlands of both countries.

The tetrahedron model presented earlier in Fig. 1 captures the complex interactions between these economic, educational, demographic and environmental conditions resulting from the political economy and international and local nexus. These theoretical and analytical implications have significant practical implications for both educational and economic policy as well. The problems of Northeast Brazil and Northeast Thailand, for example, transcend normal disciplinary boundaries, as reflected in the tetrahedron model. Complex interactions between economic, education, demographic and environmental changes are conditioned by critically important political factors of subnational colonialism and imperialism. Awareness of such conditions has been enhanced in both Brazil and Thailand by literary creativity 'inspired' by both the cultural richness of each region and the political economy of neglect.

Awareness of the underdevelopment of the respective Northeast regions of Brazil and Thailand has not necessarily translated into assistance and support for the individuals affected most by this subnational exploitation. While awareness is certainly an initial step in improving the plight of underdeveloped regions within any country, unless an integrated public policy is instituted to mitigate such exploitation, as we propose in this paper, little is likely to change. The process of center-dominated modernization, as we have argued, is at the root of the subnational exploitation we have illustrated in Brazil and Thailand.

What then can be done? There must be a political will, either from above or from pressures below resulting from greater democratization, to enhance both the physical and educational infrastructure of these two regions. This means a far greater allocation of limited public resources to the Northeast regions away from other competing needs such as military expenditures and other urban luxury consumption. For example, Thailand has opened two new universities in its Northeast region.

Subnational comparisons, as we have conducted here, encourage us further to understand that underdevelopment in one geographic region of a country is not an isolated example of discrimination or oppression. Rather, from our analysis of Brazil and Thailand we learn that the neglect of a region and its people may be endemic to the subnational imperialism or internal colonialism of a country. For a variety of geographic, historical, racial or religious reasons one region of a country, often the most industrialized, may exploit the resources and human capital of the less developed region—just as the country itself may have been colonized and exploited by the First World. Such internal 'modernization' occurs at the expense of the exploited region, which is kept underdeveloped as a source of cheap materials and labour. The consequences of this subnational domination has important policy implications, not only for the country itself, but for its interaction in the world market-place. A critical example of this is Brazil's massive foreign debt. The money borrowed from the International Monetary Fund principally serves the interests of the industrialized South to the detriment and continued neglect of the underdeveloped Northeast and rural areas. Some programs in Brazil have focused specifically on the Northeast (SUDENE—Superintendency for Development of the Northeast), but the region remains substantially underdeveloped.

Our comparative analysis of these regions has important epistemological implications as well. Robert Ward, both a political scientist and an authority on Japan, has long been concerned about the tension between area studies and the analytical social sciences. He (Ward, 1974, p. 199) has called for 'two skills in one skull'. The research embodied in this paper involves both the area studies and functional dimensions. Our detailed descriptions of economic and educational conditions in Northeast Brazil and Northeast Thailand are *emic* (local constructs) in orientation identifying key and uniquely Northeastern Brazilian and Thai concepts and cognitive categories. But at the same time, in interpreting these distinct local phenomena, there is concern for the broader *etic* (universal) and nomothetic concepts central to nearly all developing countries facing the inescapable tension between macroeconomic growth and regional disparities. This study thus shows the fruitfulness of a regional comparative approach combined with the integration of area studies and social science functional approaches. We believe the lessons for comparative educators from this study are that much is to be learned from cross-cultural comparisons of subnational regions that share many of the same dilemmas. What can be learned from experiences in Northeast Brazil or Northeast Thailand may offer solutions that can be adapted to comparable underdeveloped regions such as Chiapas Mexico. Although comparisons can be valuable, we propose that an in-depth understanding of a country's social, political, historical and cultural circumstances is necessary before any meaningful educational policy can be developed. Educational solutions for one country carry no assurances of success in another context. In this sense, we propose that intensive case studies such as this one have theoretical, policy and epistemological implications not only for comparative education but for social policy that extends well beyond our case study of the Northeastern regions of Brazil and Thailand and their future prospects.

Acknowledgments

The initial findings from this research were presented first at the Comparative and International Education Society Annual Meeting, Cambridge, Mass, 1989. The authors wish to thank Marcos Valle for his helpful comments on an earlier version of this paper.

Notes

1. One such investigation is a comparative study of Muslim separatism by Che Mun (1990). Also see Hill (1982).
2. This passage is from a popular Brazilian song performed by Gilberto Gil and co-authored with Waly Salomão (copyright 1982 by Gege produções Artisticas Ltda., translation by Arto Lindsay). A quilombo was a settlement for runaway slaves. Palmares was one such quilombo established as a republic between 1630 and 1697 (see Freyre, 1956, p. 38). 'Olorum is the supreme divinity in the Yoruba religion' (Arto Lindsay, copyright Sire Records Company & THTI, 1989).
3. Although Brazilians typically, consider Bahia and Sergipe the 'East', these two states, for purposes of economic and cultural comparisons, are incorporated in the larger geographic designation of the 'Northeast' for our purposes here.
4. Following the cultural convention, Thai authors are listed alphabetically by first name.
5. See Evers & Silcock (1967), Blaug (1971), Likhit (1978) and Fry (1980).
6. As reposted by the Unesco Regional Office for Asia and the Pacific in Bangkok.

References

Alvarez, S. E. (1990) *Engendering Democracy in Brazil: women's movement in transition politics* (Princeton, Princeton University Press).

Amrung C., Supang C. & Fry, G. (1990) *An Evaluative Policy Study of the Efficiency and Quality of Primary Schooling in Thailand* (Ottawa, International Development Research Center).

Bangkok Post (1991) Northeast misses out on the boom, *Bangkok Post*, 4 March, p. 16.

Blaug, M. (1971) *The Rate of Return to Investment in Education in Thailand* (Bangkok, National Education Council).

Castro, J. (1969) *Death in the Northeast* (New York, Vintage Books).

Catron, G. & Ta Ngoc Chau (1978) *Reduction of Regional Disparities and Educational Planning*, working paper (Paris, International Institute for Educational Planning).

Che Mun, W. K. (1990) *Muslim Separatism: the Moros of Southern Philippines and the Malays of Southern Thailand* (Oxford, Oxford University Press).

Clignet, R. & Foster, P. (1966) *The Fortunate Few: a study of secondary schools and students in the Ivory Coast* (Evanston, Northwestern University Press).

Cripps, F. (1965) *The Far Province* (London, Hutchinson).

Cummings, W. (1980) *Education and Equality in Japan* (Princeton, Princeton University Press).

De Andrade, M. C. (1980) *The Land and People of Northeast Brazil* (Albuquerque, University of New Mexico).

Donner, W. (1978) *The Five Faces of Thailand: an economic geography* (New York, St. Martin's Press).

Eliott, D. (1978) *Thailand: origins of military rule* (London, Zed).

Evans, P. (1979) *Dependent Development: the alliance of multinational, state, and local capital in Brazil* (Princeton, Princeton University Press).

Evers, H. D. & Silcock, T. H. (1967) Elites and selection, in: H. D. Evers & T. H. Silcock (Eds.) *Thailand: social and economic studies in development*, pp. 84–104 (Canberra, Australian National University Press).

Foster, P. (1965) *Education and Social Change in Ghana* (Chicago, University of Chicago Press).

Freire, P. (1970) *Pedagogy of the Oppressed* (New York, Seabury).

Freyre, G. (1956) *The Masters and the Slaves: a study in the development of Brazilian civilization*, 2nd English edition, trans. S. Putnam (New York, Knopf).

Fry, G. (1980) Education and success: a case study of the Thai public service, *Comparative Education Review*, 24, pp. 21–34.

Fry, G. (1988) Thailand at the crossroads: a new era of political economy, paper presented at the *Annual Conference of the Northwest Regional Consortium for Southeast Asian Studies*, University of British Columbia, 3–5 November.

Fry, G. (1989) An elite production function for Thailand: a political geographic perspective, paper presented at the *Annual Conference of the Northwest Regional Consortium for Southeast Asian Studies*, University of British Columbia, 3–5 November.

Fry, G. (1992) *'Saturday Surprise', The February Coup in Thailand: Thailand's painful path to democracy* (Washington, DC, Institute for the Study of Diplomacy, PEW Case Studies Center, Georgetown University).

Garreau, J. (1981) *The Nine Nations of North America* (Boston, Houghton Mifflin).

Haring, C. H. (1958) *Empire in Brazil: experiment with monarchy* (New York, W. W. Norton).

Haynes, R. A. (1989) *The Armed Nation: the Brazilian corporate mystique* (Tempe, Center for Latin American Studies).

Henfrey, C. (1981) The hungry imagination: social formation, popular culture and ideology in Bahia, in: S. Mitchell (Ed.) *The Logic of Poverty: the case of the Brazilian northeast* (London, Routledge & Kegan Paul).

Hiew, C. C. (1992) Endangered children in Thailand: Third World families affected by socioeconomic changes, in: G. W. Albee, L. A. Bond & T. V. C. Monsey (Eds.) *Improving Children's Lives: global perspectives on prevention*, pp. 129–145 (Newbury Park, CA, Sage, 1992).

Hill, P. (1982) *Dry Grain Farming Families: Hausaland (Nigeria) and Karnataka (India) compared* (Cambridge, Cambridge University Press).

Huelshoff, M. (1992) Corporatist bargaining and international politics: regimes, multinational corporations, and adjustment policy in the Federal Republic of Germany, *Comparative Political Studies*, 25, pp. 3–25.

Kamol S., Vichai T. & Ta Ngoc Chau (1978) *Regional Disparities in the Development of Education in Thailand* (Paris, IIEP).

Kampoon, B. (1988) *A Child of the Northeast* (Bangkok, Editions Duangkamol).

Keyes, C. F. (1967) Ethnic identity and loyalty of villagers in Northeastern Thailand, in: J. T. McAlister (Ed.) *Southeast Asia: the politics of national integration*, pp. 355–365 (New York, Random House).

Khammaan K. (1982) *The Teachers of Mad Dog Swamp*, trans. Gehan Wijeywardene (St. Lucia, New York, University of Queensland Press).

Likhit, D. (1978) *The Bureaucratic Elite of Thailand: a study of the sociological attributes, educational backgrounds and career attainments* (Bangkok, Wacharin Press).

Lindblom, C. & Cohen, D. (1979) *Usable Knowledge: social science and social problem solving* (New Haven, Yale University).

Miller, T. E. (1985) *Traditional Music of the Lao: Kaen playing and Mawlum singing in Northeast Thailand* (Westport, CT, Greenwood Press).

Morell, S. & Morell, D. (1972) *Six Slums of Bangkok: problems of life and options for action* (Bangkok, UNICEF).

Moreno-Black, G. (1989) Emerging economic strategies and changes in patterns of time and labor allocation of women in Northeastern Thailand, unpublished manuscript (Eugene: Department of Anthropology, University of Oregon).

Najita, T. (1992) Opening remarks, *Theory and Asian Studies Conference*, University of Oregon, Eugene, Oregon, 15–16 May.

Page, J. A. (1972) *The Revolution that Never Was: Northeast Brazil 1955–1964* (New York, Grossman Publishers).

Pasuk P. (1982) *From Peasant Girl to Bangkok Masseuses* (Geneva, ILO).

Pira S. (1987) *People of Esarn* (Bangkok, Siam Media International Books).

Plank, D. N. (1987) The expansion of education: a Brazilian case study, *Comparative Education Review*, 13, pp. 361–375.

Sanitsuda E. (1987) *Sian Isaan* (*Voices of the Northeast*) (Bangkok, Foundation of Volunteers for society).

Sanitsuda E. (1991) *Behind the Smile: voices of Thailand* (Bangkok, Thai Development Support Committee).

Scott, J. (1985) *Weapons of the Weak: everyday forms of peasant resistance* (New Haven, Yale University Press).

Seri, P. (1988) *Buddhism, Reform and the Role of Monks in Community Development in Thailand* (Hong Kong, Arena Press).

Seri, P. & Hewison, K. (1990) *Thai Village Life: culture and transition in the northeast* (Bangkok, Mooban Press).

Sippanondha, K. (1990) *The Middle Path for the Future of Thailand: technology in harmony with culture and environment* (Honolulu, East-West Center).

Skidmore, T. E. (1993) *Black into White: race and nationality in Brazilian thought* (Durham, Duke University Press).

Skinner, W. G. (1985) Presidential address: the structure of Chinese history, *Journal of Asian Studies*, 44, pp. 271–292.

Sopon, P. (1985) *1020* (Bangkok, Center of Japanese Volunteers in Thailand).

Srisakara, V. (1980) The Lao of Thailand: Laotian settlements in Thailand, *Muang Boran Journal*, 6, pp. 67–70.

Statistical Yearbook Thailand 1981–1984 (1984) *Statistical Yearbook Thailand 1981–1984* (Bangkok, National Statistical Office).

Suchit, B. (1987) *The Military in Thai Politics* (Singapore, ISEAS)

Textor, R. B. (1961) *From Peasant to Pedicab Driver: a social study of Northeastern Thai farmers who periodically migrated to Bangkok and became pedicab drivers* (New Haven, Yale University Southeast Asia Studies Cultural Report No. 9).

Thak, C. (1979) *Thailand: the politics of despotic paternalism* (Bangkok, Thammasat University Press).

Thomlinson, R. (1971) *Thailand's Population: facts, trends, problems, and policies* (Bangkok, Thai Watana Panich).

Wakeman, F. C. (1988) Transnational and comparative research, *Items (Social Science Research Council)*, 42, p. 87.

Ward, M. D. (1985) Cargo cult social science and eight fallacies of comparative political research, *International Studies Notes*, 13, pp. 75–77.

Ward, R. (1974) Cultural and comparative study of politics, and the constipated dialectic: presidential address, *American Political Science Review*, 68, p. 199.

Watanabe, M. (1987) *Economic Development and Internal Migration in Thailand* (Tokyo International Development Center of Japan).

Weeramantry, C. G. (1976) *Equality and Freedom: some Third World perspectives* (Colombo, Hansa Publishers).

Wolfe, J. (1993) *Working Women, Working Men: São Paulo and the rise of Brazil's industrial working class, 1900–1955* (Durham, Duke University Press).

Wright, J. J. (1991) *The Balancing Act: a history of modern Thailand* (Oakland, Pacific Rim Books).

Latin America's Private Universities: How Successful Are They?

DANIEL C. LEVY

Introduction

Universities in the developing world are often maligned for not fulfilling the grand promises associated with their spectacular growth. There is profound frustration, for example, over the limited ability of universities to solidify independent national identities, promote democracy, spur economic productivity, or reduce social inequalities.

Nowhere more than in Latin America has this frustration been so long and vehemently expressed. But as most criticism has focused on traditional public universities, formidable alternatives have arisen. Significant among these are private universities. From a marginal existence a half-century ago, the private sector has come to hold fully one-third of Latin America's enrollments. Compared with the public universities, the private universities are characteristically linked to different models of development. Consequently, those interested in the role of universities in developing areas may want to consider and evaluate the performance of these private alternatives.

In comparative terms, the importance of Latin America's private models is clear. Most of the developed world, even excluding the communist world, relies almost exclusively on public institutions to perform higher education's tasks. Japan and the United States are the two major exceptions, though the U.S. private share of total enrollments has plummeted from 50 percent to just over 20 percent since 1950—markedly below the contemporary Latin American percentage. Of special relevance here, most developing nations have also pursued publicly based models. Africa, most of the Middle East, and parts of Asia basically fit this generalization—as did Latin America for most of its history. But along with contemporary Latin America, several Asian nations now rely heavily on private higher education, and many other nations, in the developing as well as developed worlds, have considered establishing private sectors. Still others have considered introducing or augmenting some characteristics of private systems (e.g., tuition) within their nominally public sectors.

To evaluate the private experience of 20 Latin American republics in one brief article is a dangerous undertaking, which should therefore begin with important qualifications. First, I must write in very general terms, either ignoring or merely hinting at what are in fact significant variations and exceptions. Although specific illustrations are included, few are fully elaborated here. From this first major qualification comes the second one. I cannot include as many examples, data, and citations as I would like to substantiate my broad assertions (much less to prove them).[1] The breadth of the subject matter also makes it difficult to develop a focused or cogent theme within such limited space. Nevertheless, I venture this: the private university has generally been successful in terms of its own goals, but these goals have been both restrictive and controversial.

I do not suggest that fulfillment of chosen goals is the single best context of evaluation, let alone the only one. It does, however, allow us to analyze both the evolution and contem-

I thank the Program on Non-Profit Organizations, Institute for Social and Policy Studies, Yale University, and the Andrew W. Mellon Foundation, respectively, for generous institutional and financial support.

porary performance of private universities within a manageable and coherent evaluative framework. Moreover, I do believe it is one very useful context of evaluation. It is important to deal with the goals—and institutional means to achieve them—of the powerful interests that are behind private (or public) growth. By contrast, works dealing with policy goals in Latin American higher education are frequently concerned with ideal-typical goals advocated by the authors themselves. Although such approaches have value, they obviously should not displace empirical investigation.[2] A central proposition guiding the analysis here is that it is worthwhile to identify how and in what senses a university has or has not been successful.

The article is divided into three major sections. First, after presenting basic data on private growth, it explores the goals behind three different "waves" of private growth, leading to distinguishable private subsectors. Thus, in the second section, we can evaluate each subsector separately in terms of the goals it fulfills and the interests and groups it serves. Finally, the third section analyzes how the subsectors' successes pose normative questions and, in any case, are limited in scope.

Goals Stimulating Private Growth

It is especially interesting to explore the goals behind the private growth when we remember that it has little precedent in Latin America and, indeed, in most of the world.[3] Why then has private higher education so dramatically emerged and grown in Latin America?

There was no private university in Latin America until the 1880s, and only Colombia and Chile deviated from the regional tradition by 1917. As late as 1930, probably less than 3 percent of total Latin American enrollments were in the private sector. Yet, by 1955, the figure had jumped to roughly 14 percent. By 1965, it reached 20 percent, growing to 30 percent in 1970, to 34 percent by 1975, and then stabilizing.[4] These private percentages can be a bit misleading because of the great weight of the unusual Brazilian case, with its massive private sector. Table 1 therefore summarizes the trends with and without Brazil.

With or without Brazil, however, the percentages reflect extraordinary private growth in proportional terms. Furthermore, this growth occurred amid unprecedented public sector expansion, especially since 1960. In fact, while Latin America's private sector grew from under 60,000 in 1955 to over 1 million in 1975, its public sector leaped from under 350,000 to over 2 million. In the 1960s, for example, public growth was greater than private growth in absolute numbers, though not in proportional terms, in all except two of the countries that had dual sectors.[5]

Some observers might argue that this emphasis on a private surge from a few percent to 34 percent of total enrollments is misleading. They might argue that private higher education is not really a new phenomenon in Latin America. The main idea is that colonial universities were church universities. Indeed, many were church universities. But they were also state universities. Considering various criteria (juridical ownership, founding authority, governance, finance, and mission), most universities were a complex mixture of private and

TABLE 1
Latin American Private and Total Enrollments, 1955–75

	1955		*1960*		*1965*		*1970*		*1975*	
	N	*%*	*N*	*%*	*N*	*%*	*N*	*%*	*N*	*%*
Latin America	57,431		83,961		171,674		429,635		1,143,395	
	403,338	14.2	546,732	15.4	859,076	20.0	1,453,596	29.6	3,396,341	33.7
Without Brazil	23,977		41,407		103,480		192,875		442,824	
	329,763	7.3	450,000	9.2	703,295	14.7	983,123	19.6	2,323,793	19.1

Source: See text, n. 4.

Note: The top row of numbers for each entry shows private enrollments; the bottom row, total enrollments (i.e., private plus public).

public. For example, Argentina's only colonial university (the University of Córdoba, 1614) was created and owned by the state but run largely by the Jesuits with papal authorization. Of course, there were also seminaries in many nations.

When the church-state partnership finally weakened, it was the public university form that strongly emerged. The Enlightenment, the French Revolution, and the European establishment of the Napoleonic university stimulated this development. But the greatest changes in Latin America came in the Independence period (after 1810). "National" universities were created from colonial ones, as with Argentina's University of Cordoba, or were created anew. Church influence greatly diminished. The state assumed fundamental authority over the university in naming officials, in fixing curriculum requirements, and in other matters of governance; at the same time, it assumed full responsibility for financing the university. The university was charged to serve society and the state, not the church. García Laguardia documents the transformations in nations such as Chile, Ecuador, Mexico, and Venezuela. Thus, for well over a century, the public sector would enjoy a near monopoly in Latin American university education. In Venezuela, for example, only three universities were created alongside the Central University in the nineteenth century, all on a similar public model.[6] The public university was the state's representative in Latin American higher education, sometimes (as in Chile) even in all of education. Such a broad generalization warrants qualification, but until the 1930s only Chile and Peru had created the kind of institution that would eventually undo the public monopoly in most of Latin America: the Catholic university.[7]

Catholic universities form the first wave of private universities. This is true of Latin America fairly inclusively and of most nations individually (Argentina, Bolivia, Brazil, Chile, Ecuador, Panama, Paraguay, Peru, and every Central American nation except Costa Rica). For what purpose, then, were the Catholic universities created? First and foremost, they were created in reaction to the secularism of the public universities. A major component in Latin American colonial higher education, religion, had been relegated or even roundly assaulted.

Politically, the creation of Catholic universities reflected the power of the Right and was meant to buttress it. Thus, conservative parties, as well as the church, were predictable promoters of the first wave, as with Venezuela's Andrés Bello University (1953). But the first wave also reflected, paradoxically, the declining power of the church. This fits the notion that Catholic universities arose to save the church and religion after they were pushed out of the existing higher education system. For example, Colombia's Javeriana University was opened shortly after the Liberal party's 1930 victory threatened the church's traditional role within the higher education system. Moreover, governments and even the Left were generally more willing to allow a special church role in part of higher education once it was clear that the church and its conservative backers no longer held the power necessary to control the bulk of the higher education system. Consider the Brazilian case (atypical in its second- and third- but not first-wave causes of growth). What the church really wanted was great influence in the existing universities. It feared that separate Catholic universities would be socially and academically marginal, preserving pockets of Christianity while abandoning most of society and politics to secular materialism. Only when their hopes of gaining prominence within the public universities faded did they campaign for their second choice: their own Catholic universities. It would be better to have pockets of Christian education than to have no Christian education. Similarly, the creation of Argentine Catholic universities in the late 1950s reflected the church's realization that it could not control the University of Buenos Aires, for example; it also reflected the state's view that Catholic universities would pose a lesser threat than they would have early in the century, when the state refused to legitimize the short-lived Catholic University in Buenos Aires.[8]

Religious goals were not the only goals that the founders of Catholic universities had in mind, however. The universities' conservative bent suggested a desire to escape the leftist political thought and action often found in the public sector. An important corollary was the desire to maintain social conservatism and class privileges. These areligious goals assumed greater significance by the 1950s and

1960s, as the public sector expanded rapidly and became increasingly identified with leftist politics. One sees the mixed goals behind the creation of, for example, Bolivia's Catholic University (1967) and the Dominican Republic's Madre y Maestra University (1962).[9] The goal of upholding church ideas amid an otherwise secular context had been more salient in the 1930s and 1940s, as reflected in the establishment of Ecuador's Pontifical University (1946).

A second wave of private universities could be called "secular elite," or "elite" for short. Here the desire for class privileges, conservatism, or just academic tranquillity and prestige comes to the fore. Religious identity is a marginal or nonexistent goal. The second wave has its main roots in the profound dissatisfaction of elite actors with the public sector. For one thing, the public sector has lost its once elite character. In Venezuela, for example, public enrollments grew from 7,000 in 1955 to 35,000 in 1965 to 175,000 in 1975—with no entrance requirements at the four traditional public universities.[10]

A key factor throughout the region was the expansion of secondary education. Consider the growth in cohort percentages, 1960–70, in five nations: Colombia from 12.5 to 25.9 percent, Costa Rica 18.4 to 32.8, Ecuador 12.6 to 28.5, Mexico 11.9 to 22.5, and Peru 16.1 to 35.6, with an overall Latin American shift from 15.0 to 28.7, moving to 42.0 percent by 1975. The higher education transformation at that time is equally impressive, with respective figures of 1.7 to 4.7 percent in Colombia, 4.8 to 10.2 in Costa Rica, 2.6 to 7.6 in Ecuador, 2.6 to 6.1 in Mexico, and 3.6 to 11.0 in Peru, with a 3.1 to 6.8 change in Latin America overall, moving to 11.7 percent by 1975.[11] Along with this opening to the middle and lower-middle class came a perceived decline in average academic quality, or at least in social prestige, leading many from the most privileged classes to seek an elite alternative. Public university degrees and credentials came to be worth less and less on the job market. Industrialists and other businessmen became increasingly disenchanted with the public universities' failure to produce trained personnel for their enterprises. Furthermore, overlapping these social and economic considerations were more purely political ones. Elites were unhappy with the increasing leftist activism of professors and even administrators but mostly of students.[12]

In short, privileged classes, employers, and conservatives in general were unhappy over what they saw as a loss of elitism, order, efficiency, and job-market relevancy. Thus, they reacted principally to perceived public sector failure. In several nations, however, they also reacted to perceived failures in the Catholic universities: too many had been either too traditional and unbusinesslike, as in Argentina or, worse yet, increasingly liberal and permissive in the aftermath of Vatican II. Therefore, the second wave was partly a reaction to the first wave. Examples include Venezuela's Metropolitan University (1965) following the Andrés Bello (1953). It was created by the nation's bourgeoisie, backed by industrialists associated with the Eugenio Mendoza Foundation. Other examples include Mexico's Anáhuac (1965) following the Iberoamericana (1943) and Guatemala's Francisco Marroquin (1971) following the Rafael Landívar (1961).

But not all the private secular growth has been directed toward elite goals. A third wave refers to nonelite secular institutions, often unselective in admissions. Some of the causes of growth are similar to those in the elite subsector. There is, for example, a preoccupation to get job-related training and to avoid leftist politicization. Fundamentally, however, the third wave represents a reaction to a different perceived public sector inadequacy: less to the excesses of social democratization than to its limits. That is, even the unprecedented public expansion has often been insufficient to meet the still more dramatic growth in student demand for higher education. The most extreme example is Brazil, where the enrollment boom occurred mostly while a conservative military held power and placed greater curbs on the public sector's ability to meet the booming demand than are generally seen in Latin America (at least until military rule transformed other South American systems in the 1970s). More typically, the third wave is not responsible for the majority of university enrollments but for either a majority of private university enrollments, as in Colombia and the Dominican Republic, or a substantial minority of private university enrollments, as in Venezuela.[13]

It is too easy to ignore the third wave because of its lack of prestige and even influence. In fact, it has surely captured the bulk of private growth in the 1970s and 1980s, as no new Catholic universities have been created and as elite universities, almost by definition, can expand only so much; meanwhile, fiscal crises in much of Latin America may place increasing restrictions on public growth.

Thus, most Latin American private sectors have really emerged from three relatively distinct waves, each with its distinct raison d'être. This is not to say that the waves are completely distinct or that there is no variation within each. Instead, these waves of growth are neither fully self-contained nor internally uniform. Nor do the universities produced in these waves always fit neatly into one category, especially as their goals and characteristics evolve. This is especially true when Catholic universities dilute or reinterpret their religious missions. Some, such as Venezuela's Andrés Bello, resemble elite universities in certain respects, whereas others, such as Peru's San Martín de Porres University, more closely resemble institutions produced by the third wave. Furthermore, there are several partial or fundamental exceptions to the three-wave rule: some nations have created no private sector (Cuba and Uruguay); others (Bolivia, Panama, Paraguay) have created only a single Catholic university, whereas Costa Rica has only a secular nonelite institution; and Chile proves exceptional in several ways. But in most nations, three waves are usefully discernible, most often with a strong though overlapping sequential flow. Consider the cases of Peru and Argentina. Lusk shows that Peru's first wave began decades before any other private institutions were created. In the early 1960s, both Catholic and elite private universities followed. Nonelite private universities did not appear until 1964, but they have dominated private growth since then. In Argentina, the Catholic universities' share of private enrollments declined from 74 to 47 percent, 1965–77, with nonelite growth particularly strong in recent years.[14]

Meeting Chosen Goals

Insofar as Catholic universities were created to promote strong religious identities, their performance might charitably be considered mixed. Few students specialize in religious study. For example, a breakdown of the fields of study in Venezuela's Andrés Bello University shows no such specialization and shows that only 0.5 percent of the students are in what may be the closest field, philosophy.[15] Nor do most Catholic universities have formidable religious course requirements for students specializing in secular fields. Meanwhile, a decreasing percentage of professors are priests. Indeed, many of the part-time teachers also teach in secular universities or work in nonreligious jobs outside academia. The picture is different for administrators, but even there the lay representation is high once we look below the top of the administrative structure. In Brazil's Catholic University of Rio, for example, priests account for 67–83 percent of the highest-ranking administrators but only 29 percent of the university council members and 14 percent of the divisional council members.[16] Furthermore, the shift of some constituents toward social activism has also diluted a traditionally distinct religious identity at several of the region's universities.

Nonetheless, the Catholic subsector has met many of its goals. Even on religious matters, its failures could easily be exaggerated. First of all, certain institutions, such as the Catholic University of Argentina, have maintained a traditionally religious flavor. Others, such as Mexico's Iberoamericana, strive for a religious identity based more on the principles of Vatican II than on traditionalism. Most Catholic universities, no matter how much they fall short of their religious goals, approximate them much more than the non-Catholic universities do, especially where there has been outright hostility toward religion in the public universities. Finally, since some of the Catholic universities created in the 1960s never intended to function fundamentally according to identifiably Catholic standards, it would, of course, be misleading to evaluate them too much by those standards.

Moreover, the major failure in terms of original goals is related to a major success. The decline of traditional Catholic missions has been accompanied by the achievement of increasing academic prestige. This is not merely a fortuitous by-product. It is a consciously pursued policy. In an obvious parallel to what Jencks and Riesman have called the "academic revolution" in the United States, the principal job of a Latin American Catholic university is increasingly to be a good university.[17] Vatican II and then subsequent Catholic university conferences have emphasized a move away from defensive dogmatic faith toward a more open pursuit of scientific truth with academic freedom.

Furthermore, academics is only one area in which many Catholic universities have performed well on the nonreligious goals that are more readily associated with the elite subsector and even more clearly achieved there. The secular elite subsector is successful with regard to each of the major sorts of goals for which it was created. Academically, it enjoys a higher prestige than does any other subsector, private or public. Socially, it tends to be the most exclusive in class terms, drawing disproportionately on those groups who are able to provide privileged opportunities—often including private secondary schooling—for their children. Economically, graduates have the best prospects, particularly with private and multinational employers.[18] Politically, these secular elite institutions sometimes explicitly promote conservative views, but they consistently avoid the conflict and disorder so characteristic of many public universities. Good examples of these elite characteristics are found at institutions such as Colombia's Los Andes University, the Dominican Republic's Technological Institute of Santo Domingo, Mexico's Institute of Technological and Advanced Studies in Monterrey, Peru's Pacific University, and Venezuela's Rafael Urdaneta University.

The third wave has also been largely successful in fulfilling its own goals. Marketplace tests may illustrate this point. New institutions are still being created at a brisk pace, while existing ones expand. Few have failed and closed. Furthermore, the students attracted are paying students. Overall, these institutions have prospered without public subsidization. Insofar as they were created to meet the demand not met elsewhere, they have made substantial contributions. For example, Costa Rica's, Colombia's, and Brazil's unprestigious private institutions have provided opportunities for working youth who could not study in the hours available in the public sector. At the same time, some of these institutions have served successfully to link other students to the job market, and almost all have provided politically tranquil atmospheres that again contrast to those often found in the public sector.

As the three private subsectors have pursued their goals, they have gratified key constituencies. The ability to please their most concerned constituencies may be taken as another measure by which to evaluate private success. We have already seen that many Catholic and especially secular elite universities serve privileged student clienteles. It is equally clear that major organizations have been served in several ways. To begin with, the church must accept that the mixed performance of Catholic universities far surpasses what the church reaps from other universities. Less equivocal gratification has been achieved by business organizations. They are confident that the elite universities, and some Catholic ones, provide efficient educations, spending donated money on relatively tranquil and job-relevant educations. Compared with the public sector, the private sector trains more students in desired fields of study. Note these illustrative contrasts of the percentage of total private versus total public enrollments (1977–78) in the fields of economics, business, administration, and communication combined: Bolivia, 57.8 versus 9.9; Colombia, 36.8 versus 10.3; Ecuador, 23.4 versus 18.2; Mexico, 35.5 versus 20.1; Peru, 47.2 versus 23.2.[19] Although the elite universities turn out highly prepared personnel, even some nonelite private institutions have trained people for applied, commercial, and management positions. Nor is the private graduate as likely as the public graduate to get involved in political activities that could interfere with work.

Less obvious, but no less important, are the ways in which the private sector has successfully served the state. The state has only sometimes made explicit its support for private growth (i.e., defined itself as a key constituency of the private sector), yet that support has been widespread—and generally rewarded. First, the private sector has satisfied socioeconomic groups that are prominent constituencies of the state. Looked at another way, the dissatisfaction of these groups could pose serious threats to the state's political and economic stability. Second, the private sector has increasingly provided personnel not just for private enterprise but also for the state. This is especially true for high-level technical and economic positions, as with those filled by graduates of the Autonomous Technical Institute of Mexico. It is also true, however, even for more strictly political positions, such as those obtained by graduates of Venezuela's Andrés Bello University and Peru's Pontifical University. All this pertains to the modernization, or "technification," of the state, favoring those trained efficiently for applied tasks. Third, the private sector has avoided the leftist political activism often characteristic of the public sector; the state enjoys a more quiescent private than public sector, without the headaches of direct administration. Fourth, the private sector is overwhelmingly self-financed, whereas the public sector continues to rely almost fully on the state. Although a few Catholic universities receive some state subsidies, these have always been significantly less than private financing (except in Chile). Tuition is the chief source, especially in the nonelite subsector, and business donations are a major addition in the elite subsector. The point is that the state is relieved of a major financial and political burden in the social-welfare field—while it benefits significantly from the fruits of private endeavors.

A Critique of the Goals

I have thus far evaluated the private sector by how well it has fulfilled its own purposes. The overall picture has been positive, with qualifications. But this obviously has been a biased and limited evaluation. It underscores the importance of the criteria one chooses or emphasizes in evaluating "success."[20]

Two fundamental kinds of negative evaluations can be made of the private sector, even by those who concede its general success in fulfilling its own goals. The first kind is normative. Observers need not approve of the goals; beyond that, some may see their fulfillment as injurious to the public interest. The second kind of criticism is empirically based. Whether the private sector's contributions are regarded as good or bad, they are limited in scope. It is not that the private sector performs tasks poorly but that it avoids many tasks. Illustratively, we would not generally regard most U.S. liberal arts colleges as failures for not doing research when they never intended to, but we may nevertheless emphasize this omission if we compare their performance with those of other universities. However, before identifying critical tasks that the private sector generally avoids, let us first consider mostly normative reservations about the private sector's pursuit of its own selected endeavors. To do so, we can again analyze privatization by subsector.

Although those Catholic universities that once fulfilled their distinctive church-oriented roles could be called successes on their own terms, detractors could argue that they did not join other universities in social or political reform; indeed they opposed such reform. By serving church interests, they served traditional conservative interests. They could also be accused of squelching academic freedom in favor of dogma and "Truth." At the same time, the business-oriented Right could find fault with the Catholic universities' traditionalism, oriented to the church rather than to capitalist development (or dependency). Then, beginning in the 1960s, the growing liberalism of many Catholic universities increasingly put them at odds with entrepreneurial and other conservative interests as the second-wave reaction followed the first wave, as suggested above. These interests denounced actions (such as demonstrations for social change) once limited to the public sector. For example, when El Salvador's Jesuit university associated itself with calls for social justice and with negotiations between guerrillas and the government, the Right was angered and the Alvaro Magaña government threatened to close the institution. (The public university had already been closed.) For another example, the intense involvement in the reform movements and political activity of the late 1960s and early 1970s of students and even top administrators from Chile's two major Catholic universities helps explain why those universities have not escaped the military backlash in effect since 1973.[21]

On the other hand, when Catholic universities have served modernizing capitalist interests, they have been targets of charges leveled principally against the secular elite universities. Naturally, the main charge against the latter is elitism, a charge sustained by data on tuitions. For example, whereas tuition is generally absent at Latin America's public universities, it is usually high (compared with average wages) in the prestigious Catholic universities but higher still in the secular elite ones. Thus, Venezuela's Metropolitana and Rafael Urdaneta universities charge roughly 50 percent more than does that nation's Andrés Bello University; Colombia's Los Andes charged an annual average of roughly US$610, whereas that nation's Javeriana charged an annual average of roughly US$350.[22] Furthermore, "intellectual elitism" may overlap with social-class elitism because the secular elite universities are so selective. The academically best-prepared students come very disproportionately from wealthier families and the most prestigious secondary schools, often private secular ones. To illustrate, even when Colombian private schools held fewer than one in five primary enrollments, they accounted for nearly nine in 10 enrollments at the two most prestigious private universities (compared with a still impressive more than six in 10 at the public National University).[23]

Often connected with this elitism is restrictive politics. Representatives of elite universities are fond of claiming to offer depoliticized alternatives to the public sector—and the claim has some validity. But virtually all universities are politicized in some significant sense; that is, they serve certain political interests more than others. This is evident in many of the elite universities tied to conservative political ideologies. Some manifest a marked intolerance for expressions of leftist views. In the name of banning politicization, they may severely limit democratic participation.[24] These limits are themselves political actions, politically motivated. The elite universities often represent the political-economic philosophies of the enterprises to which they are related; just as some Catholic universities have represented the church's political beliefs. In sum, one's evaluation of the elite universities depends largely on one's attitude toward political quiescence and the dominant order upheld by both the state and powerful private interests.

Political restrictiveness, along with accommodation to dominant economic structures, is also found in many nonelite institutions. But the principal fault with the third wave concerns the generally low academic quality that it has produced. Indeed, as in Brazil and Peru, the quality can be disgraceful.[25] Some of the institutions are unconcerned about anything except attracting students; instead, they may pursue financial rewards in ways that abuse the spirit of "nonprofit" educational status (and tax exemptions). Other institutions are at least concerned about providing their students with job-relevant skills. Even there, however, there is still room for a normative critique. That critique would also involve the elite institutions. It holds that there is a crucial difference between job-oriented "training" and broader "education," with its emphasis on reflection, independent thought, and criticism.

Thus, one chief set of reservations about the private sector's self-satisfying success is that it is accompanied by features that critics see as highly negative. Another set of reservations concerns the empirical limitations on the private sector's own success story. To begin with, the private sector's success is based in large part on the public sector's burdens. The private sector can select comparatively limited goals, whereas the public sector undertakes to fulfill many more goals, including some of the most difficult ones. Third-wave institutions are most vulnerable on this point, as most set very modest goals; for example, the "market test" of attracting students is not very challenging when demand for higher education easily outpaces the public sector's supply of openings. Yet limited undertakings also characterize the elite private universities and, though to a lesser extent, the Catholic universities. I will focus here on two concerns—admissions and fields of study—where the private sector's comparatively limited scope is quantitatively demonstrable.

Regarding admissions policy, the public sector has generally accepted the principal burden of providing higher education for secondary school graduates. As Table 1 showed, the public sector accounts for 66 percent of all enrollments. Only in Brazil (and very recently in Colombia) has the private sector absorbed more than half of the total higher education enrollments. This broad private-public contrast holds despite the existence of the nonelite private subsector and of certain exclusive public universities (such as Venezuela's Simón

Bolívar). The public sector has often taken nearly all candidates, whereas the private sector selects only those students it wants. The private sector tends to select many of the best-prepared students. Therefore, graduation of many of the "best" graduates is not by itself proof of the "best" education. The third wave is something of the exception that proves the rule. It is rarely selective—and it rarely achieves good quality.

In reality, the private success in admissions is further limited by the fact that the sector cannot attract anything approaching all the top students. The public universities continue to be the first choice for many. They do even better than that in attracting a major share of top professors. The generalized private edge is therefore an average edge based, for example, not on a near monopoly of top students but on the exclusion of most with deficient preparation. Moreover, the generalized assessment of the private sector's superiority is exaggerated to the extent that observers pay little attention to the "no-name" institutions of the third wave.[26] Yet even when one compares the elite private universities with the national public universities, the private edge must be further qualified. It rarely applies to such fields as the fine arts, exact sciences, and medicine. The last example is especially important, as it often represents the most desired option for secondary school graduates.

The public edge in certain fields is strongly evident in private-public comparisons of enrollment numbers. It becomes clear that private universities usually concentrate on those fields that are relatively inexpensive to offer. Here is an important caveat to the private sector's factually accurate claim that it basically supports itself through voluntary payments, whereas the public university relies on the state's mandatory tax system: the private universities generally steer clear of activities that require heavy financing. Some institutions within the higher education system must offer the medical sciences, exact sciences, and engineering, but if public institutions do it, the private ones can avoid it.

Several of the top Catholic universities are less vulnerable on this point than are their secular counterparts, but even they do not match the proportional enrollments (in the costly fields) found in public universities of comparable prestige. Many secular elite universities do not come close. Predictably, the nonelite institutions rarely even feign an interest in such fields.

Let us return to data from the five nations considered above with regard to the distributions of students by field of specialization. Although the private sector clearly leads in business-related fields, we now see that cost is another, powerful, basis of private-public distinction. Table 2 compares private-public data for three of the relatively least-expensive fields with probably the three most-expensive fields.

The private sector consistently and easily surpasses the public sector in proportional enrollments in the inexpensive "commercial" category. Its edge is statistically much less striking in the humanities and law, but even equal private-public percentages would suggest that cost counterbalances the weight of possibly limited job utility (humanities) and strong public sector tradition (law). More impressive, however, is the degree to which the private sector is underrepresented in the most expensive fields. This occurs in 13 of 15 cases. One of the two exceptions would follow typical patterns were it not for a single institution, the Autonomous University of Guadalajara. It has almost two-thirds of Mexico's private university medical students, but thousands of these come from north of the border.

For further evidence, consider full enrollment data for two more nations. In Argentina (1977), the private sector had 78 percent of its 82,911 enrollments in the humanities and social sciences, with only 18 percent in medicine, natural sciences, and engineering versus respective figures of 48 and 50 percent for the public sector's 453,539 students. (The remainder in each sector are located in miscellaneous fields.) In Venezuela (1978), the private sector (25,756) had it 21 to 15 percent lead in engineering and architecture combined, whereas the public sector (239,915) had a 17 to 9 percent lead in teacher education, but most differences that were hypothesized on the basis of cost emerge clearly (despite the obscuring effects of the public sector's 30 percent in a "basic cycle" vs. 7 percent for the private sector). The public sector maintains a 17 to 5 percent advantage in the medical and natural sciences, although it trails by a whopping 59 to 23 percent in the social sciences and humanities.[27]

TABLE 2
Private–Public Comparisons by Field of Specialization (%)

	Commercial		*Humanities*		*Law*		*Medicine*		*Exact Sciences*		*Engineering*	
Nation	*Private*	*Public*	*Private*	*Public*	*Private*	*Public*	*Private*	*Public*	*Private*	*Public*	*Private*	*Public*
Bolivia	58	10	12	2	0	8	0	21	0	15	0	23
Colombia	37	10	5	7	16	4	4	9	4	12	17	26
Ecuador	23	18	9	6	6	6	1	11	3	5	8	17
Mexico	35	20	1	2	6	9	20	20	1	4	17	24
Peru	47	23	7	0	5	4	1	7	6	4	8	29

Sources: See text, n. 19.

Note: Economics, business, administration, and communications are designated "commercial."

Naturally, general and definitive conclusions should ultimately be based on investigation of more concerns, such as the degree to which the private and public sectors provide regional coverage.[28] But my evidence suggests that the private sector is less constrained than the public sector to respond to diverse constituencies and to undertake diverse functions.

Conclusion

The ability of Latin America's private universities to choose desired tasks, excluding others, is one fundamental reason for their success in achieving their own goals and satisfying their own constituencies. Thus, even if they fulfill their goals better than the public universities fulfill theirs, they need not be regarded as superior. Rather, they could be considered more limited institutions, fulfilling their functions well largely because they leave other, often tougher, functions to the public sector.[29] The argument might have been probed further, with evidence that private institutions often flourish still more directly—even parasitically—off the public sector. This occurs, for example, when the private universities hire, as part-time instructors, professors who draw their principal salaries from the public universities or state bureaucracy. In other cases, and to the private sector's credit, professors purged from repressive public universities have been hired by private universities, as in Brazil in the late 1960s and early 1970s; Bolivia in the early 1970s; and Argentina in the periods following the 1966 coup, the Peronist takeover of the early 1970s, and the 1976 coup. But perhaps the clearest ongoing way in which the private sector prospers directly at the public sector's expense is by drawing away many of the nation's finest students while public universities broaden their access.

Therefore, private successes do not necessarily improve the higher education system overall. In terms of policy implications, even if one assumes that the private sector is generally superior to the public sector, it does not logically follow that proportional expansion of the private sector would make for a better system.[30]

Indeed, assessments of whether the expanding private sector has improved the higher education system to date depend greatly on one's priorities and normative perspectives. Fortunately, at least some of those priorities and perspectives can be informed by salient factual phenomena, be they adjudged favorable or unfavorable. Private universities have generally fulfilled the purposes for which they were created and grew. They have usually satisfied their chief constituencies both within the universities themselves and in society at large. They have done so largely by meeting needs or demands perceived by key actors to be unmet within a failing public sector. However, this private sector success is obviously unwelcomed by those who disapprove of the very goals of these institutions and their constituencies. Furthermore, even those who approve of what the private sector does should acknowledge that it generally undertakes tasks that are more narrowly defined, and frequently more easily attainable, than those undertaken by the public sector.

The central pursuit of this article is not to determine whether the private sector has been a success or a failure but to analyze in what ways, within what contexts, with what qualifications, and for whom the sector has been successful or not. The answers, therefore, do not amount to simple verdicts of success or failure. Instead, we are left with more complex, multiple responses. Of course, even these responses have been very general in nature, sacrificing to brevity the richness of qualifications, data, and substantiation that the central theses truly require. Still, some important outlines of the story are highlighted here and probably should be part of any overall evaluation. Thus, for example, evaluations should come to grips with enormous private-public differences. One may choose to extol or to condemn the private sector for its distinctiveness from the public sector, but it will not do to defend or downplay the private sector for pursuing the same goals as the public sector. Surely both sectors aim "to improve education" and "to serve society"; in many crucial respects, however, the private sector has chosen to define and pursue such broad goals differently from the way in which they are defined and pursued in the public sector.

Finally, our findings may have ramifications for other developing areas.[31] These are not easily determined, however. There is too much political, economic, social, and cultural variation across regions, and higher education systems differ enormously. On the other hand, there is also great variation and complexity, albeit less so, within Latin America itself and within its higher education systems.[32] Illustratively, Latin America's wave of nonelite private institutions provides insight into the performance of several Asian systems. Furthermore, some of the characteristics evaluated in this essay appear to be intrinsic to privateness; others are at least logically as well as empirically associated with it. These characteristics may therefore help us predict and understand the characteristics that private universities might assume in other developing regions. More specifically, analysis of the different types of private growth may provide special insight. For example, we might expect that elite private universities, once established, will generally be successful in terms of their own goals, with some of the accompanying negative features noted in Latin America. Such examples underscore how much is at stake in policy decisions concerning whether to permit the creation of private options in higher education.

Notes

1. See Daniel C. Levy, *Higher Education and the State in Latin America: Private-Public Dimensions* (tentative title) (Chicago: University of Chicago Press, in press [1986]), esp. parts of chaps. 2 and 7. However, many of the examples used in this article will not be found in this book, and the data and conclusions are developed in somewhat different ways. The book manuscript will include full chapter case studies on three nations (Chile, Mexico, and Brazil) but will go beyond them to consider Latin America inclusively in terms of the finance, governance, and functioning of private vs. public sectors. Readers interested in sectoral evolution might also look at comparisons drawn with the U.S. case: Daniel C. Levy, "The Rise of Private Universities in Latin America and the United States," in *The Sociology of Educational Expansion*, ed. Margaret Archer (London: Sage, 1982), pp. 93–132.
2. One work, frequently cited in Latin America, which puts forth the ideal-typical goals is José Ortega y Gasset, *Mission of the University*, trans. Howard Lee Nostrand (London: Routledge & Kegan Paul, 1963). For a recent and broadly cross-national work that dissects the true functions of higher educational systems, see Burton R. Clark, *The Higher Education System* (Berkeley and Los Angeles: University of California Press, 1983).
3. For an analysis of some non–Latin American cases, see Roger L. Geiger, *Private Sectors in Higher Education: Structure, Function and Change in Eight Nations* (tentative title) (Ann Arbor: University of Michigan Press, in press).
4. The 20 nations incorporated in the table are Argentina, Bolivia, Brazil, Chile, Colombia, Costa Rica, Cuba, Dominican Republic, Ecuador, El Salvador, Guatemala, Haiti, Honduras, Mexico, Nicaragua, Panama, Paraguay, Peru, Uruguay, and Venezuela. The figures will be documented and elaborated fully in Levy, *Higher Education and the State in Latin America.* The single major source is the Organization of American States (OAS) and its various *América en cifras.*
5. Based on OAS, *América en cifras 1972* (Washington, D.C.: OAS, 1974), pp. 201–2. The gross data in my Table 1 do not show the substantial variation across nations; at the extremes, only Cuba and Uruguay now have no private sector, whereas Brazil's accounts for two-thirds of that nation's enrollments.
6. Jorge Mario García Laguardia, *Legislación universitaria de América Latina* (Mexico City: UNAM, 1973), p. 89; Consejo Nacional de Universidades (CNU), *Matrícula estudiantil* (Caracas: CNU, 1978), p. 63.
7. Among the exceptions were Brazil and train, where no university emerged in the nineteenth century, and Colombia and Guatemala,

where *concordatos* preserved a joint government-church university presence.

8. Héctor Félix Bravo, *Las universidades privadas y el examen de habilitación para el ejercicio profesional* (Buenos Aires: Universidad de Buenos Aires, n.d.), pp. 4–6. On Venezuela's Catholic University as a second-best alternative, see Humberto Njaim, "El papel estratégio y la significación de la politica educativa en Venezuela" (paper presented at the Latin American Studies Association meeting, Pittsburgh, April 5–7, 1979), p. 15; Ecuador would provide another example.
9. Salvador Romero, former vice president of Bolivia's Catholic University (interview with author, Santiago, Chile, January 20, 1982); Eduardo Latorre, *Sobre educación superior* (Santo Domingo: Instituto Tecnológico de Santo Domingo, 1980), p. 48.
10. Various issues of OAS, *América en cifras;* CNU, *Opportunidades de estudio en las instituciones de educación superior de Venezuela* (Caracas: CNU, 1978), pp. 24–36.
11. James W. Wilkie, ed., *Statistical Abstract of Latin America* (Los Angeles: UCLA Latin American Center Publications, 1980), vol. 20, p. 123.
12. For example, the extreme Left attained majorities in student elections in Venezuela's three largest public universities six out of nine times, 1960–68, whereas it usually received less than 5 percent of the vote in elections for national office. Daniel Levine, *Conflict and Potitical Change in Venezuela* (Princeton, NJ.: Princeton University Press. 1973), pp. 170–74.
13. The two most dramatic cases of nonelite private growth are found in Brazil and Colombia, probably followed by the Dominican Republic and Peru. The restrictiveness of public sectors in the first three is suggested by the low percentage of the cohort group in higher education in 1960, against a Latin American percentage of 3.1: Brazil 1.6, Colombia 1.7, and the Dominican Republic 1.3, but 3.6 for Peru. Wilkie, p. 123.
14. Mark W. Lusk, *Peruvian Higher Education in an Environment of Development and Revolution,* Research Monograph 1 (Logan: Utah State University, Department of Sociology, 1984), pp. 91–92; and figures adapted from Consejo de Rectores de las Universidades Privadas, *20 años de universidades privadas en la República Argentina* (Buenos Aires: Editorial de Belgrano, 1978), p. 283. The fact that no more universities are created does not preclude enrollment growth in the Catholic subsector. In Venezuela, e.g., these enrollments jumped from 3,748 in 1965 to 8,284 in 1977, all within one institution. See Unión de Universidades de América Latina, *Censo universitario latinoamericano* (Mexico City: UDUAL, 1967), p. 789, as well as p. 832 of the 1980 edition.
15. CNU, *Boletin estadístico* (Caracas: CNU, 1982), vol. 1, no. 8, p. 301 (data from 1981).
16. See Pontifícia Universidade Católica-Rio, *Catálogo geral 1980* (Rio: PUC-Rio, 1980), pp. xii–xv.
17. Christopher Jencks and David Riesman, *The Academic Revolution* (Garden City, N.Y.: Doubleda,. 1968). A good introduction to some of the evolving goals of Latin America's Catholic universities is found in Consejo Episcopal Latinoamericano, *Iglesia y universtdad en América Latina* (Bogotá: CELAM, 1978).
18. See, e.g., Arthur Liebman, Kenneth N. Walker, and Myron Glazer, *Latin American University Students: A Six-Nation Study* (Cambridge, Mass.: Harvard University Press, 1972), p. 55; and Orlando Albornoz, "Higher Education and the Politics of Development in Venezuela," *Journal of Interamerican Studies and World Affairs* 19 (August 1977): 309–13. I cannot go into greater detail here about the job market or about the complex and debatable meanings of academic "quality."
19. Calculated from Unesco, *Statistical Yearbook, 1981* (Paris: Unesco, 1981), p. 388; UDUAL, 1980 edition, pp. 270–404, 428–70, 713–97; Asociación Nacional de Universidades e Institutes de Enseñanza Superior, *Anuario estadiaico 1978* (Mexico City: ANUIES, 1979), pp. 13–322; Bolivian private data from Romero (see n. 9 above).
20. Not surprisingly, two important inter-American conferences on private higher education have recently given high praise to that sector. One was "Universidades privadas: Antecedents y experiencias Latinoamericanas," Santiago, Chile, January 18–20, 1982; the other was "La educación superior particular en América Latina y el Caribe: Pasado, presente y futuro," San Juan, Puerto Rico, April 6–8, 1983.
21. See, e.g., Luis Scherz, "Reforma y contrarreforma universitaria en América Latina: Un caso significativo," working paper (Santiago: Facultad Latinoamericana de Ciencias Sociales, August 1981). However, the backlash has been even more intense in other Chilean universities.
22. CNU (see n. 10 above), pp. 34–36; Edgardo Boeninger, "Alternative Policies for Financing Higher Education," in *The Financing of Education in Latin America,* ed. Inter-American Development Bank (Washington, D.C: IDB, n.d.), p. 348.
23. Jaime Rodríguez Forero, "Universidad y estructura socio-económica," in *La universidad latinoamericana,* ed. Corporación Promoción Universitaria (Santiago: CPU, 1972), p. 225; data from mid-1960s.
24. Guillermo Malavassi, rector of Costa Rica's private university, says that students cannot have a "political vote" if they choose his uni-

versity. Interview with the author, San José, October 2, 1980.

25. See, e.g., Luís Antônio C. R. Cunha, "A expansão do ensino superior: Causas e conseqüências," *Debate e Crítica* 5 (March 1975): 38–46.
26. Examples include Peru's Ricardo Palma and de la Vega universities and the Dominican Republic's Technological University of Santiago.
27. Calculated from Ministerio de Cultura y Educación, *Estadisticas de la educación 1977* (Buenos Aires: MCE, 1977), pp. 7–8; CNU (see n. 6 above), p. 92. Even where private universities do undertake an expensive field, they tend to specialize. Thus, roughly 60 and 70 percent, respectively, of Venezuela's Rafael Urdaneta and Metropolitan universities' enrollments are in engineering, whereas the public Central University has no more than 20 percent of its enrollments in any field. Calculations from CNU (see n. 15 above), pp. 133–34, 323, 333.
28. Brazil's public sector, e.g., spreads out across the poorer regions much more than its private sector does, notwithstanding the abundance of nonelite private institutions. The prosperous Southeast is home to 75 percent of the private institutions vs. 46 percent of the public ones. Ministério da Educação e Cultura, *O ensino superior no Brasil 1974/1978* (Brasilia: MEC, 1979), p. 22.
29. However, some authoritarian regimes have felt little responsibility to sustain such broad public sectors. Daniel Levy, "Comparing Authoritarian Regimes in Latin America: Insights from Higher Education Policy." *Comparative Politics* 14 (October 1981): 31–52.
30. Similar points are crucial to the private-public debate in other settings. See, e.g.. Richard J. Murnane, "Comparing Private and Public Schools: What Can We Learn?" in *Private Education: Studies in Choice and Public Policy*, ed. Daniel C. Levy (New York: Oxford University Press, in press [1986]).
31. I have argued that many of the private-public comparisons found in Latin American higher education do find parallels in other settings, such as U.S. elementary and secondary education. The private sector often outperforms the public sector on conventional indicators of effectiveness, such as achievement levels and client satisfaction, but it does so largely because of selectivity in clientele and missions. Daniel C. Levy, "A Comparison of Private and Public Educational Organizations," in *Between the Public and the Private: The Nonprofit Sector* (tentative title), ed. Walter W. Powell (New Haven, Conn.: Yale University Press, in press).
32. For further sources on contemporary policy issues in Latin American higher education, see two recent review essays: Simon Schwartzman, "Politics and Academia in Latin American Universities," *Journal of Interamerican studies and World Affairs* 25 (August 1983): 416–23; and Iván Jaksić, "The Politics of Higher Education," *Latin American Research Review* 20 (1985): 209–21.

Independence and Choice: Western Impacts on Japanese Higher Education

Shigeru Nakayama

Abstract. Japan's universities were established in order to import Western knowledge and ideas to assist in the development of the nation beginning in the mid-19th century. Because it was never colonized and because it has successfully developed not only its academic system but also its economy, Japan is a particularly significant case study. Japan's academic development can be seen in two phases. First there was a "window shopping" period in which many Western models were explored and some partially adopted. Second, there has been an "involvement" mode in which specific Western models are adopted. This essay follows the development of Japanese higher education through its various phases, including the post World War Two impact of the United States and the growth of a mass university system. The process of internationalization of various foreign influences is examined.

Western models of higher education generally serve two purposes when they are adopted by non-Western countries. The first is the "window-shopping" mode in which complete freedom is retained on the part of non-Western recipients in selecting any one of a number of Western models. The second is the "involvement" mode in which a Western model is appropriated by a non-Western country, whether it be on a voluntary or involuntary basis.

Inherent in the window shopping mode are certain limitations in understanding and replicating Western institutions, because colleges and universities are so deeply rooted in tradition that many of the culture-specific elements are filtered out of newly created non-Western institutions. Consequently, the adopted model often exhibits indigenous traits as well as the most uptodate trends, which have not yet found their way into Western institutions. Such is the case at some Latin American universities, which have unsuccessfully attempted to introduce a radically new curriculum in the wake of political revolution.

In the involvement mode, ties are very close between Western and non-Western countries as evidenced by the exchange of faculty members and students, similar degree programs and even common employment opportunities for graduates. The recent internationalization of research has promoted a further exchange of information and personnel.

In the history of Japanese higher education, the first example of the window-shopping mode occurred in the late nineteenth century, while the involvement mode is best illustrated in the post–World War II Occupation period, in which reforms based on the American system were carried out. In contrast to other non-Western countries, where a colonial involvement mode came first, followed by a window-shopping mode in the post-war period, the Japanese experience was exactly the opposite and therefore quite unique. The following sections will present an account of both the window-shopping and the involvement modes in Japan.

Window-shopping by the Meiji Government

Absence of a Single Model

Western models of Japanese higher education used to be a favorite topic of discussion among Japanese historians of higher education. Some discussed the early American influence in structuring the entire educational system, of which higher education is a part. Others emphasized the predominant German influence in medical and later law schools. Still others appreciated British contributions in engineering education, while French law was taught in the early law schools. All in all, one can never come to any clear-cut picture of a single dominant model. This mixture of multi-country influence was an intentional one, as the Japanese government, consciously or unconsciously, preferred to strike a balance of Western power and influence not only in education but in all other fields as well. Thus, it is impossible to analyze the attempt to establish a Western-style modern university in terms of a single country model.

Governmental Initiative

Since Japan was neither colonized nor dominated by a single Western power, there was no colonial-type authority to enforce adoption of a particular existing foreign model, which contrasts sharply with the post-war Japanese experience during the American occupation period of 1945–1952. Western influence in the nineteenth century was exercised only on an individual basis by employed Western consultants rather than through a well-formulated national or corporative assistance program as is often the case in the contemporary Third World context.

Instead, a single agency was responsible for model selection: namely, the new Meiji Government established in 1868. Unlike the continuous and spontaneous development of Western universities, whose medieval origin preceded that of modern nations, the prototype of modern Japanese universities is a purely artificial product created by a Western-oriented modern government. There existed a number of schools of Western language and science supported by the Shogunate as well as the local fief governments, but these were all summarily closed. In the 1870s, the new government attempted to reorganize them with a systematic educational policy.

A product of the new government policy of the 1870s was the creation of the University of Tokyo, the prototype of modern Japanese national universities, as an indispensable sub-department of modern Japanese bureaucracy. Thus, we may be able to say that the model of modern Japanese universities is derived from bureaucratic institutions, whose ultimate origin can be traced back to ancient or medieval Chinese institutions, rather than to the medieval Western university from which all Western universities originated. All teaching and administrative staffs of the university were government employees of the Ministry of Education. Its faculty-department structure was modeled after the departmental hierarchy of bureaucratic machinery, which has been more rigidly and rationally developed in China than in the West.

One of the exemplary features of bureaucratic character in Japanese higher education is that students do not form a body independent of faculty organization but rather subordinated to the departmental structure of the faculty. A student belonged to only one particular department from his university admission to graduation or even beyond, making interdepartmental mobility extremely difficult. The merit of this system might be that it has been a very efficient and systematic way to create the strategically necessary manpower for modernization and to acquire existing bodies of Western knowledge in a short period of time.

Another feature of the Japanese university bureaucracy is that those employed by universities are all civil servants so that all members have to observe the Civil Service Regulation, which often conflicts with the free and self-generating intellectual activity of faculty members.

Model of Private Colleges

Being outside of government initiative in higher education policy, private schools had long been denied official recognition. They remained, at least in official accreditation, in academy status. Their status was raised to the collegiate level, the equivalent of national universities, only in 1919. However, they have maintained a uniquely liberal tradition, especially among the older ones.

Some of the private colleges bear a strong resemblance to American liberal arts colleges, but they are, in the final analysis, a minor sideline of the total national educational structure. And in the course of time, they have had to assimilate toward the national system by sacrificing their independent and unique characteristics and subordinating themselves to the government regulations enforced by the Ministry of Education. Especially the newer private colleges are modeled after the government universities, since most of the faculty members are graduates of old national universities who "colonized" the newly-founded private colleges.

Western missionaries, Catholic and Protestant alike, were not able to establish a stronghold in higher education, largely because the Japanese government took the initiative in nearly all areas of modern institution building. Missionary schools had a good share only in the education of females from kindergarten to the junior college, which was relatively neglected by the government up to the end of the World War II.

Guidelines for Westernalization: List of Western Models

In the draft rule for sending students for study abroad, prepared in 1870[1], the following subjects and countries were listed:

Choice of Countries to Study

Britain: machinery, geology and mining, steel making, architecture, shipbuilding, cattle farming, commerce, poor-relief;
France: zoology and botany, astronomy, mathematics, physics, chemistry, architecture, law, international relations, promotion of public welfare;
Germany: physics, astronomy, geology and mineralogy, chemistry, zoology and botany, medicine, pharmacology, educational system, political science, economics;
Holland: irrigation, architecture, shipbuilding, political science, economics, poor-relief;
U.S.A.: industrial law, agriculture, cattle farming, mining, communications, commercial law.

In view of the history of nineteenth century science, the above assessment was largely correct and objective. Presumably, the policies for science and technology, including the above recommendation, were drafted mainly on the suggestion of G. F. Verbeck and other foreign advisers to the government.

The government-sponsored students sent abroad seem to have followed the above guidelines. Parallel to this, the government hired a substantial number of foreign teachers to provide instruction in every Western discipline. As a result of these measures, Western science was successfully imported during the 1870s and 1880s. Toward the end of the 1880s, the process was nearly complete when those returning students replaced foreign teachers in the University of Tokyo faculty.

Language Prerequisites

Early in 1871, a proposal was presented to the government by Inoue Kowashi, who later played a most important role in the formulation of Japanese higher education policy. It states: "Let students master the Western languages first; then they can automatically speed up in mastering each of the specialized sciences by use of the languages".

At a time when neither native-speaking teachers of Western disciplines nor textbooks written in their native language were available in higher education, it was natural enough that the foreign teachers taught in their own language and that students were required to have excellent aural comprehension in that particular language. Thus, preparatory courses in language training were prescribed for all students. In view of the scarcity of qualified foreign teachers and the urgent needs of native personnel for administering the modernization and Westernization programs, courses were often divided into "regular" courses taught by foreign teachers and "special" courses in which instruction was provided by Japanese graduates in the Japanese language. Most of the private schools were also of this type. The latter students fulfilled the immediate needs of society, while the students in the former category played leading roles in each area of specialization throughout their careers.

In the nineteenth century, when English was not yet established as the major international language, students focused on one of three European languages: English, French or German, depending on the language of the visiting foreign professors or of the predominant scientific work in particular disciplines. This linguistic diversity soon proved unworkable and the government moved to entrench teaching in Japanese in all fields of study.

Students also found it a great burden to have to master several different European languages in order to pursue advanced studies and in 1872 the Ministry of Education decided to abolish instruction in French and German, concentrating only on English in preparatory schooling. In the process of reform, the government had to disband the polytechnic department, in which French was the language of instruction and the mining department, which was taught in German, thus giving birth to temporary departments of French physics and German chemistry in 1875. At the same time, the language instruction requirement in the preparatory stage was uniformly limited to English. Its courses of instruction followed the model of the American high school.[2]

In the University of Tokyo, founded in 1877, efforts were made to systematize language requirements in preparatory education into two languages: German for the Medical School and English for the other schools. In 1884, the Ministry of Education suggested to the University that it would be preferable to teach primarily in the Japanese language. Finally, with the establishment of a more comprehensive higher education system in 1886, language education was assigned to secondary education. English and German were taught in the Middle Schools and Higher Schools (kotogakko) respectively.

Plurality and Diversity of Western Models

Around 1870, government officials eagerly examined various Western educational literatures with the idea of adopting the best elements of each model. On the basis of these investigations, they initially formulated a crude plan for imitating Western educational systems. In early 1870, the government issued "university regulation" as well as "primary and secondary education regulations," in which students in secondary and higher level education were supposed to specialize in any one of five departments. These included theology, law, science, medicine and humanities. These arrangements are reminiscent of the faculty structure in contemporary German universities, though science and humanities (philosophy) had not yet been separated in nineteenth century Germany. The Japanese, however, failed to recognize the meaning of creating a discipline in Christian theology. Instead, some traditional scholars tried to introduce Confucian studies into the modern university curriculum. These moral and ethical subjects could not win the support of political leaders in the Meiji government, who were utilitarian materialists. Later, in the same year, the "college regulation" enumerated the disciplines of rhetoric, logic and Latin in the humanities curriculum, but in actual practice these were all neglected as the Japanese did not comprehend the content and significance of such a medievalistic course of studies. Out of the above subjects, only the discipline of logic was later recognized as a modern discipline to be studied in school.

In the early 1870s, American advisors such as Verbeck and David Murray were influential in the formation of school systems under the umbrella of the Ministry of Education. In order to meet the immediate needs of each governmental service department, such as the Army, Navy, Department of Justice, Department of Works, and the Hokkaido Development Agency, each department had to have its own system and training program in the higher education sector. For example, in the Department of Work, Scottish engineers, headed by Henry Dyer, were brought in. According to Dyer, they tried to introduce not a British but rather a Swiss system of synthesizing science and technology as practiced in the Technische Hochschule of Zurich. The Japanese Navy followed British practice, while the Army adhered to the French model. The Hokkaido Development Agency adopted the American land-grant college as the exclusive model (in particular, the University of Massachusetts).

The Ministry of Education incorporated into the *Kaiseigakko* (the preparatory school or college level predecessor of the University of Tokyo) an American liberal arts college model suggested by Verbeck, David Murray and his colleagues from Rutgers College in New Jersey. German influence also came to the Medical school, where as early as 1870 German medicine was officially adopted to the exclusion of English and other styles of medicine. In the law school, French influence was predominant in the early years, while the German model replaced it after a political event in 1881 when the government decided to switch its institutional model from other Western countries to Germany. Subsequently, more Germans were employed while the number of other foreigners gradually decreased. Traditional fields of study such as Chinese studies and Japanese studies later found their place in the Department of Literature at the University of Tokyo, giving proof of counterbalance, and self-reflection on, the process of rapid Westernization.

Amalgamation and Inclination to the German Model

The early attempt at modernization conducted by each service department following its own Western model was concluded after a decade of effort. Their teaching institutions were now unified and reorganized into the Imperial University, founded in 1886 under the jurisdiction of a single agency of the Ministry of Education. By this time, most of the faculty positions were held by natives who had studied abroad. They formed a new type of a national university, amalgamating various Western models and casting them into their own Japanese mold under governmental auspices.

The characteristic of the Japanese university which is perhaps most revealing is its school-department structure. The basic structure of six schools, including law, humanities, science, technology, medicine and agriculture, was completed in 1890. In comparison with Western universities, there are noteworthy differences in that science became independent of humanities (philosophy). In addition, traditionally vocational subjects of the modern applied disciplines, such as technology and agriculture, were elevated to university status. In spite of opposition to the university status of agricultural science among faculty members who had been trained in Europe, they were obliged to implement the government's policy.

In the initial phase of modernization in the late 1870's and early 1880's, departments of science and technology were encouraged by the government to train the manpower and develop the hardware requisite to modernization, such as building a domestic telegraph network, conducting geographical and geological surveys and so forth. Once these basic tasks were completed, the government turned its attention to the software of controlling a modern nation: it built a modern bureaucracy by inviting selected elite students to serve in the administrative offices. For that purpose the government raised the status of the hitherto relatively neglected law school by granting certain privileges to its graduates such as exemption from the Civil Service Examination, which was formulated in 1887.

For purposes of academic research, the nineteenth century German universities, particularly the philosophical faculty, provided the world's most highly regarded model. However, the Japanese government had different reasons for adopting the German model. It intended to copy the modern German bureaucracy, which was dominated by law school graduates.

At the same time, the bureaucratic character of the University was further strengthened. The founding ideology of the Imperial University was designed "to meet the urgent needs of the nation," a phrase which appeared in the beginning of the University constitution. This was not merely rhetoric for it was manifested in the career patterns of the graduates.

In spirit, it is often said that the pre–World-War II Japanese national universities were quite close to German universities. On closer inspection, the predominant German influence came after 1880s. Previous to that time, American, British and even French models were being incorporated into uniquely Japanese institutions. In retrospect, German influence was felt rather belatedly. This made it institutionally difficult to completely replace the pre-existing amalgam with a purely German ethos. For instance, uniquely German concepts such as *Abitur, Privatdozent* and mobility of students and faculty from one university of another, have never been introduced into the Japanese system of higher education. Still, the intangibly authoritarian and elitist atmosphere of the Imperial University faculty was said to be derived from German academia. The notion of academic freedom, presumably along the lines of the German model, was advocated among university faculty members at the time of its infringement by the government.

Post-War Involvement with the American Model

New Dealers in Spirit

Japan experienced a second phase of Westernization in the post-World War II period. Its intensity was certainly comparable but its impact was qualitatively different, from the first phase.

By the mid-twentieth century, Japan had firmly established a Meiji-type institutional paradigm (which spread later to new Japanese universities and colonial universities in Korea and Taiwan). Its replacement with a new American model could not be done without the application of extraordinary pressure by the Occupation Forces.

One of the initial purposes of the Occupation was the eradication of ultra-nationalistic and militaristic ideology in Japan. The Allies decided that in order to replace that ideology with "democratic" thought, it was imperative that a comprehensive educational reform should be instituted. Even though the Occupation Forces consisted of representatives of several Allied powers, the occupation of Japan, in contrast to the occupation of Germany, was administered almost exclusively by the U.S. Hence, the model for post-War reform, of not only educational but various other institutions, was purely American. In other words, for those members of the American Educational Missions who came to Japan as advisors to the Occupation Forces, it was simply inconceivable to propose any model other than the American one, with which they were the most familiar.

The American model is, however, not quite monolithic. Some Americans attempted to promote their own ideal model, which may not have existed at that time in their country. Especially in the early phase of occupation, a number of New Dealers joined the Occupation, introducing land reform and encouraging labor movements. Educational reform was also carried out, at least in the initial phase, in a similar spirit by the Civil Information and Education Section (CIE) of the Occupation Forces by way of indirect control and guidance using Japanese official and private agencies.

The reform began in the primary schools and then gradually extended to the secondary and finally to the postsecondary levels. Before the wave of reform reached the graduate schools in 1953, the Peace Treaty was concluded in 1952 and the U.S. withdrew its forces from Japan.

Educational Reform from 6.5.3.3 to 6.3.3.4

The number of years of schooling at each level of education are arbitrary and hence differ from one country to another. There was much discussion among Japanese educational planners before the suggestions of the American advisors were outlined. The Japanese preemptively resolved to move toward the American system, in which the old system of 6(primary), 5(secondary), 3(*senmongakko*, junior college level professional school or *kotogakko*, preparatory Higher School for the Imperial University) and 3(university) was abandoned in favor of 6(preparatory), 3(compulsory junior high school), 3(senior high school) and 4(college).

Higher Schools were viewed by reformers as elitist and moves were made to abolish them. They were in some ways similar to the British public school, the German *gymnasium*, and the French *grandes écoles* but quite different from the American public high schools. The emergence of these schools was regarded as a failure of educational planning during the Meiji era by the administration, but students created and enjoyed a uniquely liberal elitist culture. These schools were abolished not because they did not fit into the Japanese society and school system but because of their elitism and the fact that they did not fit into American plans for educational reform.

Democracy—From Elite to Mass Education

In pre-war Japan, college graduates comprised fewer than 7 percent of the age cohort and hence their education was naturally elitist (the prestigious Imperial Universities enrolled about 1 percent of the age cohort). The Americans strongly suggested that the Japanese expand their higher education sector to the extent that each prefecture (46 in number) would have its own university. In spite of the economic hardship that prevailed after Japan's defeat in the war, a significant expansion of expensive higher education was proposed by the Ministry of Education with pressure from the Occupation Forces, which generated numerous complaints and a great deal of confusion among the Japanese. This move certainly created a great opportunity for the *senmongakko* and normal schools to raise their status to university level. They took advantage of the opportunity and most were successful in obtaining accreditation at the university level.

These newly created colleges were very poorly equipped in terms of both teaching staff and facilities. The traditional elites criticized these new universities as being second-rate, but these new institutions prepared the way for the dramatic expansion of higher education that took place in the post-war years. One of the causes of the student revolts of the late 1960s in the Western industrial countries was interpreted as being due to overcrowding in universities. In this sense, the Japanese universities suffered less than their European counterparts because the expansion had started earlier and facilities were more adequate.

Egalitarianism—Plural Track to Single Track

Before World War II, different tracks of education were designed for those who terminated their training in the primary, secondary or *senmongakko* (junior college) levels, largely depending on students' social class origin. Hence, there were three levels of engineering, secondary, *senmongakko* and university graduates. Even in the field of medicine, practitioners were divided into two classes, university graduates and *senmongakko* graduates, despite the fact that both received the same medical license. This complicated plural track of education was changed to a single track under the egalitarian policy of the American advisors. In the same spirit, the status of private universities and women's colleges was enhanced. Normal schools were given college status.

In reality, however, in view of the short period of preparation and the lack of facilities, it was impossible for the new universities to obtain the resources necessary to rise to the standard that had existed under the old system. Thus, in spite of the creation of a new university system, the unequal pattern of resource distribution that characterized the old system remained essentially unaltered.[3]

Decentralization

Americans viewed the power of the Japanese pre-War educational system as being too centralized. They seem to have had the idea of disbanding the Ministry of Education, the hub of the power structure, but in order to maintain an indirect means of governing, they had to use the existing bureaucracy. The relationship between the American CIE and the Japanese Ministry of Education was an ambivalent one.

The creation of a national university in each prefecture, mentioned previously, was primarily aimed at the decentralization of higher education. Like the state universities in the U.S., the CIE proposed, in 1947–48, to delegate supervisory power of universities to local prefectural educational commissions.

Opposition on the part of members of the Japanese Educational Renewal Committee was so strong that the CIE gave up its original intention. The main reasons for the opposition were that local governments were not accustomed to handling matters of higher education and that they lacked resources.[4]

Lay Control

In order to avoid bureaucratic control and to promote the participation of the citizenry in higher education, the second American Educational Mission in 1950 made a recommendation to the Japanese government and the CIE followed it up by introducing the American-style "Board of Trustees" as the governing body of Japanese national universities. They also found the autonomy of and self-governance by Faculty Conferences (as practiced in major Japanese universities) too self-complacent, self-righteous and isolationist. This move was met with still stronger opposition from the Japanese. Professors simply could not conceive of allowing lay people to exercise control over academic matters. The student body, led by leftist leaders, expressed its opposition to this policy change by means of a strike. They resented the external pressure and identified it with a capitalistic, and a symbolically militaristic invasion of academia. This was persuasive especially in light of the "Red Purge" in academia carried out by the Occupation Forces during the Korean War. The debate was continued in the post-Occupation period and finally the proposal was withdrawn.

Consequently, the Japanese universities could successfully resist outside pressures from industry and remain aloof from cooperation with industrial and particularly military research, as Harry. Kelly, an advisor in science and technology in the Occupation Forces, witnessed in a comparison with American universities.[5] On the other hand, haughty Japanese national universities have turned out to be obsolete in equipment and facilities of scientific research because of their isolationist attitude.

General Education

In the pre-war period, the university curricula were all designed for the education of specialists while liberal education was conducted at lower level schools or was self-taught by students themselves. The CIE was enthusiastic in introducing the American ideal of general education. The Harvard style of general education, as advocated by J. B. Conant and illustrated in *General Education in a Free Society* (Report of the Harvard Committee, 1945), played the most important role of model, in which the trinity of course arrangement, (that is humanities, social sciences and natural sciences) was adopted.

In translating this into actual practice in new universities, courses were mostly taught to students in the first two years by teachers drawn from the Higher Schools. In the pre-war Japanese educational system, courses were divided into two classes; humanities and natural sciences. Hence, it was difficult to locate the social sciences in the new curriculum due to a scarcity of adequate teachers.

There has always been confusion between general education and preparatory or premedical courses for higher specialized courses. In the natural sciences, the demand for foundation courses was considerably higher than for general education. Later in the post-Occupation period, industry and the School of Engineering demanded more vocational education at the expense of general education.

Graduate Schools

Japanese graduate schools were founded as early as 1886. Their model might have been an American one, given the fact that such a system existed nowhere else at the time. Japanese pre-war graduate courses, however, were not structurally well-developed throughout the pre-war era. Doctoral degrees were conferred by the Faculty Conference, without having had any institutional relationship whatsoever with the graduate school.

After the war, the American Scientific Mission, rather than the Educational Mission, strongly urged that graduate schools be reformed.[6] The CIE of the Occupation Forces had formulated the model of the American graduate school system and provided guidance through a Japanese agency, the Japanese Association of University Accreditation.

There was not much resistance on the part of Japanese universities, because the old graduate school did not have any structure to conflict with the newly introduced American one. Thus, the three major aspects of the new graduate school were accepted: 1) The direct linking of the graduate school with degree programs; 2) the introduction of the three degree systems Bachelor's, Master's and Doctoral and; 3) the introduction of graduate level education.

Since the system is not the product of spontaneous growth but rather the importation of an external model, there remained a certain administrative rigidity in regulations such as the prescribed residence of two years for the master's course plus the three years doctoral program along with a *numerus clausus* for each discipline.

Graduate programs are not well funded and graduate fellow-ships and assistantships do not adequately cover living expenses. Hence, the graduate school in Japan is not as efficient as the American one. Furthermore, it may be partly a matter of culture that the Japanese graduate school has failed to create a highly competitive atmosphere, as was the case in the U.S., even after more than three decades of its existence.

Though nominally linked to degree programs, professors in the humanities and social sciences do not often confer doctoral degrees, simply because they themselves did not have the opportunity to earn a doctorate under the old system, in which doctorates were given to those older scholars who had reached the end of their research career. In the fields of science and technology, where greater internationalization has occurred, new graduate schools based on the American model are more readily accepted.

Process of Internalization

After the withdrawal of the Occupation Forces in 1952, the Ministry of Education gradually strengthened its control over higher education, However, after seven years of model change, it was utterly impossible to return to the old model that had existed before World War II. The process of internalization (in other words, domestication of the external American model) has followed.

The prototype of pre-war Japanese universities was established in the late nineteenth century and the minor changes that evolved were not enough to meet the new demands of the mid-twentieth century. Reform was desperately needed, regardless of its source. The American model was not necessarily new but the newer elements were taken up by the Japanese: one of these was mass higher education. If the elitism of the Imperial University and the Higher School still remained, it might appear to be grotesquely obsolete now.

Other elements which were incompatible with Japanese culture were, for the time being, excluded from the reform process. Hence, decentralization was discouraged in the period of internalization that followed and layman control was totally dismissed.

In higher education, academic decision-making power which resided in the Faculty Conference of each school remained intact. The efforts of reformers had been focused on the introduction of new models in general education and graduate school, new areas where old faculties had no vested interest. In the process of internalization, however, a realignment of the new arena gradually took place. For example, the University of Tokyo created a new faculty in the College of General Education where a new program of general education was designed and new experimental interdisciplinary disciplines like area studies were located. In graduate school, a new division (humanities, social, mathematics, physical, chemical and biological sciences) was introduced to promote interdisciplinary research in contrast to the old faculties of law, economics, literature, science, technology, medicine and agriculture. But because the major decision-making power still resides in the Faculty Conference of the old faculties, the structures of both the College of General Education and the Graduate School are now subordinated to the old faculties division. The ideal of general education has fallen victim to the suspicion and neglect of the old faculties. On the other hand, the Graduate School will continue to expand, since it can meet the future demands of science and technology as well as the desire of raising the status of old faculties which control degree conferring authority.

Conclusion

As stated earlier, Japanese higher education has followed a unique course of development, as far as development of an organizational structure and the adoption of a variety of foreign models. It has been seen that Japan has moved from "window-shopping" and experimenting with a number of Western models in the period prior to World War II to the direct involvement of a foreign power, the United States, following the war. In this sense, Japan has followed a bifocal approach to higher education, looking both to the American model and to earlier patterns of university development.

It is possible that another type of modeling will be more useful in explaining the contemporary situation in Japanese higher education—the transfer from a bureaucratic model to an industrial model. We have pointed out earlier that while many of the Western universities were created on a pure academic model (or ultimately on a professional guild model of the European medieval universities), the modern Japanese universities in the late nineteenth century were created by a modern bureaucratic state with specific goals in mind. In the course of time, however, the Japanese universities attained academic freedom in a limited sense and self-government through the Faculty Conferences.

Since the late 1950s, a new external pressure has been imposed on Japanese higher education as Japan has recovered her industrial capacity and has started to promote it more

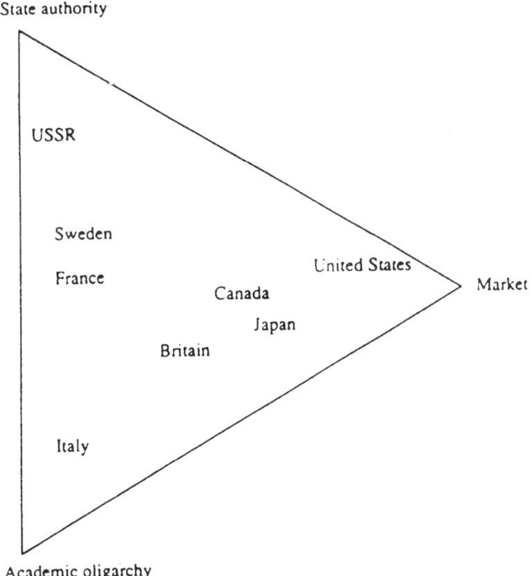

***Fig. 1.* The triangle of coordination**

Source: B. R. Clark, *The Higher Education System* (Berkeley: University of California Press, 1983), p. 143.

than at any other time in her history. The influence of the industrial community became visible at the beginning of the 1960s, as it demanded from higher education the creation of abundant scientific and technological manpower.

Around the same time, most of the major Japanese industrial laboratories were founded and have already raised the level of provision for academic research in terms of facilities and equipments, as evidenced by the fact that industrial R. & D. resources now comprise more than 80% of total national expenditure for R. & D., far outstripping those of national and academic laboratories. The impoverishment and obsolescence of university research is beginning to be scandalous. Leaders of industrial laboratories often boast, "We do not have to depend on academic science for basic science. We can make basic science by ourselves, if needed."[7]

The state of affairs of "academic coordination" is internationally compared and nicely illustrated in a triangular representation by Burton Clark.[8] We shall partially borrow it in order to show the academic decision-making power in Figure 1 and make another triangle of budgeting as an indication of research expenditure in Figure 2. While Clark's Figure 1 is based entirely on impressions without having any quantitative measure, Figure 2 has some numerical basis, as all the data come from the OECD statistics. While the location on Figure I has a close correlation with academic decision-making power, I feel that Japanese academic decision are influenced less by the market and more by faculties than the figure indicates. In Figure 2, the share of private and public sources out of the total national R. & D. expenditures is shown on the horizontal scale. The vertical scale represents the portion between governmental (largely defense) laboratories and academic research of the amount spent for R. & D.

If we superimpose Figures 1 and 2, we find a discrepancy between the location of academic decision-making power and universities' R. & D. resources. This distance is suggestive of the direction in which future higher education is heading. A comparison with the corresponding OECD data for 1965 shows that whilst both the US and Japan have during that period moved towards the right on the figure (i.e. towards private rather than public), on the vertical axis, the US has moved towards university research whilst Japanese expenditures have moved towards government laboratories. Another point which is not shown on Figure 2 is that while some public funds go to private laboratories in the U.S., some private funds go to university research in Japan.

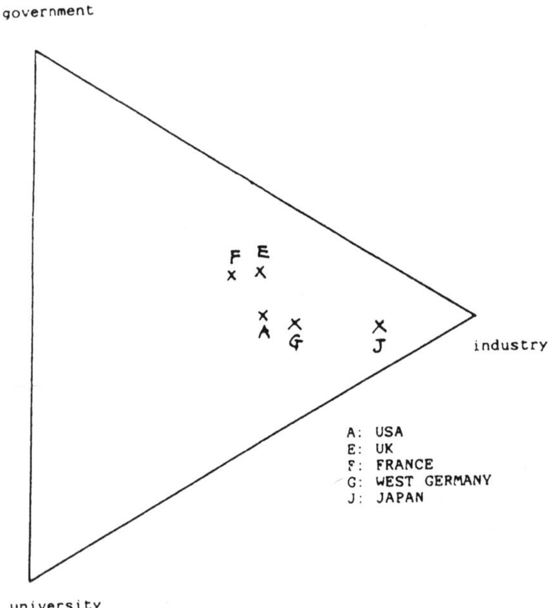

Fig. 2. **R & D Coordination triangle**

Source: Kagaku gijutu hakusho (Science and Technology White Paper, 1986).

There will be two distinctly different conceivable cases based on the dominating influence of Japanese industries:

1) Higher education will switch its model to industry, so that it organizationally assimilates towards the industrial sector and produces quality-controlled manpower and efficient research findings which the industrial community demands. Most of the science and technology faculties, as long as they remain competent in their professional performance, are inclined to the industrial model and its value system. In such a case, their academic performance in both education and research is assessed by or subordinated to the value standards of industry. Consequently, academia becomes industrialized.

2) Higher education will refuse to adopt the industrial model and preserve its autonomy and identity by keeping a respectable distance from the industrial world. While liberal and general education are maintained on campus, the outer world will no longer depend on higher education for any vocational training, for which industry will develop in-house training or some system other than existing institutions. Then higher education will turn into an enjoyable playground to spend youthful life perhaps more meaningfully or simply remain a leisure land.

Notes

1. The original Japanese text is reprinted in S. Nakayama *et al* (ed.), *Nihon kagaku gijutsushi taikei* (Source books of the history of science and technology in Japan) vol. 8 (Tokyo, Daiichi-hoki, 1967), pp. 35–36.

2. *Tokyo daigaku hyakunensi* (Hundred years of the University of Tokyo) (Tokyo: University of Tokyo Press, 1984), pp. 305–311.

3. Ikuo Amano, "Continuity and Change in the Structure of Japanese Higher Education" in *Changes in the Japanese University; A Comparative Perspective,* eds. W. K. Cummings, I. Amano & K. Kitamura (New York: Praeger, 1978) p. 38.

4. Kaigo Muneomi and Teresaki Masao, *Daigaku kyoiku (University education)* (Tokyo: University of Tokyo Press, 1969), pp. 92–96.

5. Harry C. Kelly, Interview by Charles Weiner (1975). Institute Archives and Special Collections, MIT Archives.

6. "Reorganization of Science and Technology in Japan", Report to the American Academy of Science, issued in August 28, 1947.

7. Personal communication.

8. B. R. Clark, "The Japanese System of Higher Education in Comparative Perspective" in W. Cummings *et al.* eds., *Changes in the Japanese University,* p. 237 and also B. R. Clark, *The Higher Education System* (University of California Press: Berkeley, 1983) p. 143.

The Academic Estate in Western Europe

Guy Neave and Gary Rhoades

Two features of academia in Western Europe condition change in higher education systems: its internal organization and its national nature. External forces such as governments, political parties, trade unions, and economic and demographic trends have impact. But equally important is the way academia is organized and how it interacts with those external forces bearing down on higher education. Academia helps both to structure its organizational setting and to determine the work done in it.

As elsewhere, academia in Western Europe is fragmented by disciplinary identity and specialization and by its location in different institutional sectors within the overall system of higher education. But an additional fault line characterizes it in Continental Europe, setting it apart from its fellows in the United Kingdom and the United States: the deep rift between junior and senior staff, between the largely untenured assistant class and the full professoriat. Such ranks are found in British and American academia, but they are not a basis of separate organization. They do not spawn polarized groups of academics that separately represent their interests within or outside the academy to the public central administration or legislative bodies.

This rift in Continental academia may be attributed to the chair-faculty structure predominant until the late 1960s in most Western European universities.[1] This structure is inherently hierarchical, with potential divisions of interest among academics of different ranks. It was based on a system of patronage in which members of the nonprofessorial class remained highly dependent on individual chair-holders not merely for admission into academia but also for advancement once inside.

The demographic explosion of the early 1960s coupled with the runaway demand for higher education exposed and exacerbated these underlying tensions. The rising tide of new students heightened tensions in two ways: it increased the teaching load borne by nonprofessorial staff, particularly assistants; and it unbalanced the "ecology of academia" by the rapid growth in that same staff, brought in to teach the ever-rising influx of students. If chairholders still wielded power and influence, expansion in the lower ranks placed a severe strain on their patronage networks. And, no less important in molding the expectations of younger academics, nonprofessorial positions expanded far faster than the professorial posts to which many had aspired. Expansion also profoundly changed nonprofessorial posts. In a stable academic ecology these had been a species of protracted apprenticeships that, with the fullness of time and suitable backing, would lead to professorial status. When the ecological balance was upset, however, a new subclass began to assume a permanent status, and the traditional process of socialization into academia became strained. Historically, such

This paper was written when Guy Neave was a visiting scholar at the Center for Studies in Higher Education at UC Berkeley and when Gary Rhoades was a postdoctoral research scholar in the Comparative Higher Education Research Group at UCLA. Comments and criticism from Martin Trow and Burton R. Clark have brought clarity where obscurity might have prevailed. We acknowledge their support and our gratitude. Gary Rhoades wishes to acknowledge the assistance of the National Institute of Education, whose funding enabled him to undertake the research for this paper.

socialization took place through a master-apprentice relationship. Proliferation in the lower ranks of university teachers meant either that such a process became more attenuated or that for many junior staff it was lacking.

Such tensions were deeply embedded in many of Western Europe's academic bodies. They contributed to and shaped the course of change in universities. In an attempt to secure tenure or advancement, certain sectors of non-professorial academia looked toward trade unions, reasserted their links with political parties, or formed associations inside the university directly affiliated with these institutions outside. Through them, and at times allied with students, they sought to bring pressure on external political and governmental agencies for university reform. They sought in the new world of the political process to rebalance the hierarchy of forces in the old world of academia. The rise of student activism in the late 1960s contributed in no small measure to this development.

The house of academe was divided against itself. This division brought about a remodeling of its university home and a redistribution of power within it. In many university systems the structures of internal management were either "modernized" or "democratized," depending on one's inclination. The chair-faculty structure was uprooted and replaced by new basic units of organization. Formally, nonprofessional academics were given a greater say in university affairs. These changes were not simply the product of external intervention by the legislator. They were driven by factions of nonprofessorial malcontents in academia.

But attempts by governments to introduce change in universities cannot rely on playing one group inside academia against another. In the academy, as in law, circumstances alter cases; divisions are not always prominent. A second feature of Western European academia has inhibited governmental efforts to promote certain kinds of change in higher education. In mainland Western Europe, academia is not a profession. It is an estate, whose power, privileges, and conditions of employment are protected by constitutional or administrative law. As such it is linked directly to the state and is distinctly national in orientation. The house of academe is riven with factions when the agenda involves the distribution of internal privilege and power, but on matters involving the place, privileges, purpose, and mission of academia in society—and by extension, the university—corporate solidarity very quickly replaces internecine feuding. Nonprofessorial staff in the late 1960s were not so much engaged in recasting the national purpose and place of the institution in which they worked;[2] rather their objective was to share in the power and privileges enjoyed by chairholders.

From the late 1960s, governments in Western Europe struggled to reorient and redirect the work of universities. They have attempted to "vocationalize," "industrialize," and "regionalize" university education, and generally make it "more relevant" to perceived national priorities. Academics of all ranks moved to block or impede these reforms.[3] The driving force behind their resistance to change was the desire to preserve the relatively homogeneous and national character of university education. Government proposals were perceived as detrimental to the public status of academe and the university as national institutions. Divided though it is, academia in Western Europe still conceives itself to be a national estate.

These two central characteristics of academia in mainland Europe—the junior-senior faculty rift and the close relationship to the state—are discussed in the following pages. We analyze European chair-faculty structure and contrast it with organizational patterns in British and American academia. Subsequently, we examine two variants of the ideal typical chair-faculty model. In the next section we venture more deeply into the academic estate in Western Europe, focusing on its national dimension and historical origins and on the cultural assumptions underpinning its development. In two following sections we relate these organizational characteristics to academia's role and stance in promoting and inhibiting change in university systems. Due to its fissures, academia brought about major change in the structure and governance of universities. Despite its internal divisions, it also held at bay governmental efforts at bringing about fundamental change in the work of universities.

These sections may be viewed as case studies of how academia responds to issues it regards as central. The academic body is not a monolithic entity. On the contrary, its internal schisms and alliances—quite apart from its mésalliances—are as shifting as they are kaleidoscopic. Patterns of academic organization are important in understanding the denizens of the academic world and their actions. The way the academic animal enacts a role is profoundly influenced by the internal organizational environment in which he or she evolves.

The Seats of Division

Forms of work organization, and the social relations they embody—between employer and employee, master and apprentice, or strata of professional colleagues—have embedded tensions. Academia is no exception. Generally, two patterns of organization prevail at the lowest decision-making units.[4] We focus on the chair-faculty structure, contrast it with the department-college structure, and identify its historical origins, referring to some of its variants. Special attention is drawn to inherent tensions within the chair-faculty structure which potentially can divide academics into polarized, conflicting groups.

The chair-faculty structure dominated in Western Europe through the 1960s. It was replaced in varying degrees by a department "electoral college" structure different in several ways from the department-college structure, the hallmark of American academia. One major difference is that the electoral college structure rests on the principle of constituent, corporate interests. Organized on the basis of rank in the academic career ladder, each constituency is formally represented in all university decision-making organs according to a nationally prescribed formula.[5] Unlike the American college structure, there is no collegium. British academic organization supplies still another type that combines elements from chair-faculty and department-college models.

Two Ideal Types: The Chair-Faculty and Department-College Structures

In the chair-faculty mode the salient feature is its attachment of overwhelming weight to the independence and personal authority of individual chairholders—the professors. Around this figure academic work is organized. Although a large share of work is actually done by subordinate academic staff, it is managed by the professor. Chair-holders are the "local expression" of a discipline or a field. So strong is their autonomy that Continental European universities have been described as "associations of independent practitioners."[6]

Independent though they are, chairholders are neither isolated nor freestanding. They are joined in faculties that serve diverse functions: as vehicles for coordination between professors; as units that oversee broad areas of academic work, for example, theology, law, medicine, arts, or philosophy; and as a fount of professorial self-government.[7] Nevertheless, faculties are a source of horizontal linkage, not of vertical control: they are dominated from below by the chairholders. Though they have power, faculties are not part of a vertical hierarchy above the chair. In fact, the dean of the faculty is elected by the professoriat and the deanship is largely an honorific post.[8]

Professorial power and independence derive from privileges, resources, and facilities that the state confers on the chairholder. Such resources, individually designated, are also the sinews of an authority over subordinates so absolute that professors are rulers over "private fiefdoms."[9] The medieval metaphor is apt since the origins of the chair-faculty structure are traceable directly to medieval guilds. Professors are the masters, and the subordinate academic staff serve either as their apprentices or, in a slightly less humble station, as their journeymen.[10] In either case the relationship is based on a very high degree of dependency, often for extended periods.

Commentators on chair-faculty structures have tended to emphasize its inbuilt rigidity and its lack of adaptive capacity in the face of changes and expansion in knowledge.[11] But its inflexibility extends into social relations between professorial and nonprofessorial academic staff. The institutionalization of the latter's total dependency with the former's unalloyed power had the potential to deeply divide academia into conflicting groups. Historically, social relations may have been stable. But under specific circumstances they could erupt into conflict over the distribution of academic privilege and power. They could also foster the development of academic orders whose interpretations of the academic enterprise were antithetical. If, in the realm of knowledge, the chair-faculty structure gave rise to a fragmentation and balkanization of disciplines, so too did it lead to fragmentation inside the work structure, polarizing interests along the dimensions of formal rank and official status.

The department-college structure is, by contrast, based on a group of colleagues, rather than an individual, as the basic working unit. Even in Britain, where the chair-faculty structure runs parallel to a departmental organization, chairholders possess neither the privileges nor the powers of their Continental counterparts. Academic work is organized and managed by the department, not by the individual chairholder.[12] Such an arrangement permits some measure of collegiality to be built into the basic operating unit. In the United States this is pushed further. Department heads rotate. This practice further disperses power among many academics instead of concentrating it in one permanent chairholder or head.[13]

In department-college structures nonprofessorial academics are neither powerless nor dependent on an individual chairholder. Their probationary period is not as extended as it is in Continental Europe, and they need not bank on a chairholder to be granted tenure by a department.[14] Nonprofessorial staff members participate actively in departmental life, not as complete equals nor as complete dependents. "The department spreads responsibilities and powers among a number of professors of similar senior rank and more readily allows for some participation by associates and assistants." The department-college structure provides the opportunity for more collegial interplay between academics of different ranks.[15]

Between the department and the university stands an intermediate grouping that links departments. Though terminology varies in the United States, this body is typically known as the college.[16] It has considerable power over departments, which derives from its allocation and control of resources and its involvement in decisions about academic work.

Colleges in an American university differ from faculties in Continental Europe because they have a powerful administrative framework. Heads of colleges—deans—are appointed from above, not elected from below, and colleges, unlike faculties, sit above departments as part of a vertical hierarchy.[17] The head of a department is thus accountable to the college; in Europe the chairholder is not responsible to the faculty in the same manner. If the faculty stands as a voluntary association of professors, acting only on the authority of this same group, the college in the American university occupies a separate administrative position over and above academics, and is endowed with its own powers of initiative.

The college structure engenders a sense of immediate solidarity among all ranks of academic staff, setting them apart from, sometimes in opposition to, a bureaucracy.[18] The collegium is reinforced in that it sets over against academic staff a competing non-academic, bureaucratic force. Such an organizational model stands in sharp relief to Continental European universities, where the faculty acts as the long arm of the basic unit, the chair, rather than as its potential rival.

Britain: A Midpoint

The college model in America drew considerable inspiration from the clusters of colleges in Oxford and Cambridge, striking examples of an inclusive collegium where all academics participate equally in college governance. But it tends to be an atypical form of organization, even in Britain, and is rarely emulated by other British universities. The more usual pattern brings together chair organization with departmental structure, which is overlaid by faculties, not colleges.[19]

Despite variations among universities, there are qualities common to both British faculties and their fellows in Continental Europe. If, from an organizational perspective, they stand above the department, still they do not constitute a hierarchy of vertical control. Faculties operate more as intermediary and advisory bodies, responding to initiatives coming from elsewhere in the system—mainly from professors who make up the faculty and who, through it, elect the dean.[20]

In one important respect, however, British faculties are different from those on the Continent. They are not freestanding, autonomous, exclusive academic guilds, as were the French faculties in the nineteenth century. British faculties are part of a university governmental structure that has independence and power and which, from the earliest times, has also included nonacademics who had considerable influenced—a feature serving to strengthen a common identity among academics.

The British system then stands midway between European and American structures, linking a departmental structure to a modified version of the chair-faculty system. Yet in terms of the social relations it fosters, it is closer to the American pattern. The British department has effective power over individual chairs and professors; it thus constrains how much autocratic power may be exercised by the chair-holder over nonprofessorial colleagues. Since the department provides an inclusive collegium, tensions among the ranks of academics are less pronounced. The British faculty unit further contributes to a sense of academic solidarity.

Variants of the Chair-Faculty Pattern

University systems of Western Europe and their chair-faculty patterns of work are diverse. Our discussion centers on those variations in France and in the Federal Republic of Germany. We do not pose them as basic models, although the latter did exercise no small influence over academic work organization in Dutch, Danish, Norwegian, and Swedish universities, and the former had a similar influence on Spanish and many Latin American universities.[21] Here we simply note the interplay between historical and institutional forces that give rise to these variations in the chair-faculty structure. Despite these variations, the central theme holds: embedded in the social relations of these structures are potentially divisive tensions between professorial and nonprofessorial academic staff.

French faculties were more freestanding than their German counterparts. Before implementing the Higher Education Guideline Law of 1968, M. Edgar Faure, then France's Minister of Education, suggested that before that time separate universities did not exist in France.[22] Strictly speaking, he was incorrect. In 1896 the largely self-contained faculties had been united into individual universities, thereby reviving an institution abolished by the French Revolution of 1789. But M. Faure did not entirely err because that decree remained largely unobserved. The *faculté* remained the highest organizational grouping; hence only deans of faculties existed, not university presidents. Professors alluded to themselves as *professeurs à la faculté* rather than—as Anglo-Saxon expectations might suggest—*professeur à l'université*.[23] In fact "l'université" did not mean a single establishment. It referred to the entire public secondary and higher education system and its personnel.[24] *Les amis de nos amis sont parfois de faux amis!*

By contrast, German faculties had always been part of a university structure of governance. The deanship in a German faculty was a powerless office, but the *doyen de la faculté* was not.[25] Even so, the powers of the German faculty as a corporate body were not inconsiderable. Though often subject to negotiation with central authority, it supervised the filling of vacant chairs, and also took an active part in granting the Habilitation degree. In both instances the faculty mitigated the particularistic domination of individual professors.[26]

No less important was the formal independence of German universities vis-à-vis public authorities. In France the faculty played only a part, and perhaps not the major one, in filling professorial vacancies.[27] If individual institutions lacked control over their professorial nominations, this was compounded by the presence of the *Agrégation*. Comparable in importance to the German Habilitation, the Agrégation is a centralized state examination, administered neither by a single professor nor by a single faculty. Simultaneously, it was a symbol of national excellence and institutional weakness. If faculties were autonomous in relation to individual universities in France, this autonomy was restricted by their links with centralized agencies. The German faculties, on the other hand, derived strength both from their controlling role inside universities and from the autonomy universities enjoyed in teaching and research.

Differences between the two countries are also visible within the chair structure. France and Germany are substantially different in the patterns of dependency this structure engendered. This dissimilarity reflects the diverse ways in which professorial power was developed and exercised. The two variants on the chair model have been described as the "cluster" pattern in France and the "apprenticeship" pattern in Germany.[28]

The French cluster pattern rested on the influence individual chair-holders exercised over the careers and fortunes of their students and disciplines. Clusters were composed of a dozen or so individuals, generally including *lycée* teachers, members of research institutes, and chairholders in provincial universities. These individuals were grouped as supplicants around a *patron*—an eminent chairholder more often than not based in prestigious Parisian faculties. The elements of the cluster penetrated across institutions; the cluster reflected, by its form of social grouping, the essential centralization of the higher education system and also of French political, intellectual, and cultural life.[29]

The power of patrons over their clusters was a function of linkages with elite academic institutes, research bodies, crucial agencies regulating the outer frame of higher education, and with the central administration. Particularly significant was the cluster's strength as an instrument of patronage and as a distributor of blessings for which all honor and ambition contend. Clusters acted as a substitute for national disciplinary associations or professional bodies, which in Germany, Britain, and the United States stand as key vehicles for building and advancing an academic career.

The power of the German chairholder drew on different sources: prime among them was his position as director of a research institute that, if affiliated with the university, was under the chair's sole charge. Control over a research institute also meant command of substantial research funds and other facilities furnished by the state.[30] As director of the institute, the chairholder was intellectual and administrative master of a local grouping, creating thereby a school of thought that had a particular, highly localized, spatial existence.[31] The French cluster was diffuse, dispersed across various institutions and sectors of the education system; it included other chairholders as well as select graduates. In Germany, on the other hand, the subordinates of the chairholder were local apprentices—students, and assistants.

The cluster and apprenticeship models involved different degrees and types of dependency. In France such feudal ties could often be lifelong. In Germany, however, the apprentice, when he had served out his indentures and gained the coveted Habilitation, could reasonably expect to become a professor in turn, moving to another university and setting up his own power base.[32] The relative freedom of German universities from state interference made it somewhat easier for new professors to set up power bases than, for instance, in France. The authority of the professor in Germany, then, was much more circumscribed, being limited largely to the individual university where he held his post.

These variations in the structure and operation of the chair-faculty system were differences of degree, not of kind. Both are qualitatively different from the American department-college structure. True, there were marked differences in the length and severity of dependency embedded in the French and German chair-faculty structures, but dependency there was. In both cases academics were found in separate camps, distinguished by vastly differentiated powers and privileges, and in both cases the all-powerful chairs, unfettered by the faculties, highlighted such differences.[33] Such working arrangements contained a latent conflict among different academic orders—among power holders, power seekers, and those for whom power became unattainable. If the chair was a seat of power, it was also potentially a seat of division in academia in many Continental Western European universities.

The Nation and the Academic Estate

In both Great Britain and the United States academia is assumed to be a profession. This is not the case in the majority of Western European countries. There is no sense of its being a part of one of the "liberal professions" such as medicine or law.

As a corporate entity, academia in Western Europe does not lend itself to translation into terms equivalent to the Anglo-American concept of an academic profession. In French there are two terms: one has a juridical overtone; the other has connotations of an invisible "intellectual college" that extends far beyond the university as an institution. *Les corps universitaires* (the university corporations) is a legal designation used in conjunction with the now defunct Conseil des Corps Universitaires (a national body responsible for academic appointments and promotions under the Giscardian administration). It does not link with the concept of a "profession," but rather appears to equate academia with *les corps d'état*—those technical and expert services of central government which include *le corps de mines* (engineering services) and *le corps enseignant* (the national teaching body). The second term, *le milieu universitaire et scientifique,* is more broadranging, embracing an intellectual caste both within and outside the university. It does not include the liberal professions but encompasses an invisible college whose frontiers are vague and fluctuating. Academia is deemed to be part of the intelligentsia, without presuming that all denizens of higher education are intellectuals, or that all intellectuals are to be found in higher education.

The terminology is no clearer in other European languages. In German the nearest equivalent is *Korporationen der Professoren,* a term closely aligned with the medieval guild. It does not include middle ranks of academics (*Mittelbau*) who are not formally professors. In Dutch the terminology is even more imprecise. *Wetenschappelijk Lid* merely describes individuals involved in scientific-academic activities, and might include those in upper academic secondary schools. As with the French and German terms, there is no direct and explicit identification with the liberal professions. No collective and generic term denotes academia as Anglo-Americans define it.

In part the difficulty of equivalence lies in the distance of British and American academia from the central state. In those two countries the academic profession is identified principally through its independence of the state. The control and certification of those entering it is handled not by the state but by the profession as a whole or by the individual disciplines. And academia has a professional ethic, with powers of sanction and reward for those infringing on or endorsing it.[34]

Academia in Western Europe does not share all of these characteristics. By statute, academics are civil servants, not independent professionals. Members of the state service, in their middle-to-upper ranks they are designated as such—*fonctionnaires, Beamten, Amtenaaren.* Entry to academia is regulated not by an independent profession, but by competitive, state-validated examinations.

Thus the problem of terminology goes far beyond the technicalities of translation or language. It reflects a fundamental difference in the place and status of academics in Britain and the United States as against their colleagues in Western Europe.

In the absence of a generic term for academia in the European context, and to remind ourselves of differences that exist, academia in Western Europe will be referred to as an academic estate rather than as an academic profession.[35] Academia has never held the status of an estate to the same degree as did the clergy, nobility, or burgesses in feudal times. But it did have important analogous functions within the cultural domain.

The use of the term *estate* is appropriate from another view: it defines academics by institutional position. European terminology tends to ignore this dimension.[36] European terms are not sufficiently inclusive or exclusive: they do not include all teachers in institutions of higher education. At the same time they comprise more than just that populace. By calling academia in Western Europe an estate, we place it on a footing similar to its Anglo-American counterpart; in both systems academics are defined by employment in institutions of higher education.

The notion of an academic estate, advantageously, does not imply independence from the central state. Integration with state service is a salient feature of academia in Europe, where academia has a national perspective.[37] The academic estate tends to be a national body, looking toward the center for confirmation of senior appointments and for the perceived role of the university. The commitment to serving the immediate community, though strong in public rhetoric and in debates among international organizations, is in practice ancillary, where it exists at all.[38]

Seen from this view, academia in Britain and America is unusual because it dichotomizes "cosmopolitans" and "locals"—those who are seen as operating nationwide and those whose commitments tend toward their immediate institution or locality. This split is less pronounced among British academics, who, though not part of a state service as such, nevertheless see themselves as members of a national profession.[39] Despite this cosmopolitan professional orientation, British academics tend to be highly involved in and committed to their local institutions. The United States provides the extreme case of localism. Large sections of American academia are locals in professional orientation, work, and commitment; they are not members of a national body associated with central government service. Nor, with the possible exception of those in research universities, are they members of a national profession.

Such distinctive differences in the profile of the academic estate in Western Europe are not merely contemporary in nature. They are deeply embedded in the historical development of higher education.

The Origins of the Academic Estate

The rise of the modern university in Western Europe is largely contemporaneous with the rise of the central bureaucratic state in the eighteenth and early nineteenth centuries.[40] The explicit move to identify the university with state service, legally and professionally, through the education of civil servants is part of a long process that emerged in Sweden during a thirty-year period beginning in the 1740s. A similar development took place in Austria during the reign of Josef II (1741–1790). The Humboldtian reforms of 1809–1810 together with the establishment of the Napoleonic Université Imperiale in 1811, stand as markers along this same road.[41]

The role of universities, however, was not limited to providing the pool of capable individuals from which the highest offices of the land would be filled. In such countries as France, Belgium, and Italy, the state university stood as the bulwark of secular national pluralism against the claims of religious hegemony advanced by the Catholic Church.[42] In these countries, where development of national identity was divorced from religion, the academic estate enjoyed distinct political status as the symbol of secular rationalism. This in turn derived from the broader cultural and political mission conferred on the university as a repository of scientific, rational inquiry set against the proponents of revealed knowledge. Yet even in Sweden, Prussia, and the Netherlands, where religion was incorporated into nationalism, the state possessed a firm cultural dimension reflected in the perceived standing of academia. In varying degrees, then, European universities were charged with an explicit cultural and political function. From a structural viewpoint the relationship between the state and the academic estate rested on three pillars: a monopoly in awarding certificates and degrees leading to state service; an elaborate, formal legal framework; and an explicit cultural mission.

In German, French, and Italian education systems, the state awarded certificates giving access to high honor and preferment at two levels. The first was located at the end of academic secondary schooling, in the forms of the Abitur, the Baccalauréat, and the Maturità, all state-validated, national qualifying exams. The second level, a point at the end of some period in higher education—in the Staatsexamen, in Germany, or in the various national diplomas in France and Italy—were qualifications underwritten by the state. The Staatsexamen is directly associated with public service employment and stands apart from such academic degrees as Magister, Doctor, or the Habilitation. Similarly, in France and Italy, national diplomas are distinguished from certificates awarded by individual universities. The former are validated and awarded by the state, which also accredits the individual institution teaching them. Since the state underwrites their quality, national diplomas generally are held to be superior in quality and far more prestigious than those awarded by a particular establishment. Clearly, they are considered to be so by private-sector employers.[43] Such national diplomas are the imperative prerequisite for any applicant seeking a post in public employment; hence the academic estate and the central administration are linked by these certificates that lead on to state service.

Academia is also linked to the state because academics are themselves civil servants subject to laws, decrees, ordinances, and directives that lay down both framework and detailed legislation not only in the public life of the estate but also in many areas considered by Anglo-American academics to be part of the private life of that body.[44] In addition to the usual issue of public accountability for finance and expenditure, such matters as requirements for certification, procedures for appointments, conditions of eligibility for academic posts, conditions of service and those for promotion, are all subject to formal national legislation. The academic estate employs various stratagems to operate and interpret these regulations to its advantage, but formal compliance is required. Universities in Western Europe tend to be state institutions as well as public corporations, and are subject to public and administrative law.[45]

Popular justification for this legal corset reveals the extent to which the academic estate is seen as part of the services of the nation. To European eyes the positive aspects of this legalism are threefold. First, formal bureaucratic control by central administration over selection and appointment to tenured posts is a means of upholding universalistic criteria for judging merit and advancement; the state acts as the ultimate protection against corporate reproduction and the rise of a new nobility.[46] Second, it maintains both the quality and the institutional homogeneity of establishments in a given segment of the higher education system. Third, it is a means of upholding national unity through ensuring the formal equality of provision and service among universities.[47]

The academic estate was linked to the state in another way: through its role as an instrument of cultivation and nation building. Today institutions of mass culture are located outside the university, but earlier when the formal relationship between academia and the state was being defined, the university occupied a central role in shaping national culture. Universities performed a vital role in asserting, legitimating, and perpetuating a country's claim to nationhood.[48] The concept of a *mission civilisatrice*—of culture as an assimilative agent that underpins linguistic, political, and administrative homogeneity—or of its German counterpart, the *Kulturstaat*—a common culture binding together, defining, and even transcending political boundaries—were supremely important. They not only expressed a desire for cultural normalization; they also stood as manifestations of a unity far deeper than that imposed through conquest by kings and armies. In the nineteenth century, the cultural centrality of the university was no less important than its economic centrality in the mid-twentieth.

Nineteenth-century Europe saw the imposition of national norms in the educational domain, in which values were transmitted and institutionalized away from the church and toward the school. The universities trained and nurtured the nation's political and administrative elites and supplied the elite corps of teachers. In teaching and research—and above all in the humanities—they fostered the basic values of political socialization for future citizens in a diluted form through the school curriculum. Finally, they deepened the legitimacy of the state through the writing of its history and through study of the national language.

The cultural centrality of the university not only defined the place of the professor within it but was itself reflected in his standing in public life. Individual status and organizational form were intertwined. Within the university and outside it, the professor occupied a key position in this national edifice. In the extreme case of Prussia, for example, *Kulturtrager* (the guardian of civilization) was appended to his title. But throughout Western Europe professorial stature, power, and patronage dominated. The professor's repute—especially in those countries influenced by the German model—derived from his dual role as master of his specialty inside the university, and from his position, always symbolic but at times in fact, as upholder of the nation's culture and its excellence.[49]

The professoriat enjoys a comparable standing neither in the United Kingdom nor in the United States. This can be attributed to the nature of universities and the patterns of academic organization in those countries.

A House Divided Against Itself

Within the academic estate divisions among different orders—professors, middle ranks, assistants—brought forth radical changes in internal university authority and governance.[50] Between 1968 and 1975 traditional models of authority in many university systems found themselves under severe challenge. Some crumbled. Others, such as those in Belgium and the United Kingdom, survived with minimal, if any, change.

In this period the cosmology of Europe's academic universe underwent drastic revision. The Ptolemaic notion that academia revolved around the chairholder and the faculty structure gave way to a more chaotic concept of power sharing that some have compared to Leibnitz's theory of a monadic universe.[51] The chair-faculty system of management and authority was replaced by a participant corporatist model, rooted in the collective authority of differing interest groups. These interest groups were not integrated in a collegium that previously had been embodied in the faculty system. Nor were they confined to the university. In many countries—the Netherlands, France, Italy, and the Federal Republic of Germany—such interest alignments inside academia extended outside through affiliation with trade unions and political parties—a process that fragmented authority still further.

Prior to the uproar of 1968, the chair-faculty structure was under strain, but it was not under direct challenge. Yet by 1975, with pressure from junior staff, students, and trade unions, the polity had intervened to bring about root-and-branch reform in academia's internal organization. The French Higher Education Framework Law of 1968 marked the start of this development. With the exception of medicine, which remained under the guidelines drawn up in 1958, the faculty structure was demolished and replaced by new decision-making units, each a unit for education and research (UER). Three years later, similarly wide-ranging changes in the management structure of the Dutch academic estate were enacted—though nominally on an experimental basis. Today the shocks that spread from the epicenter at Paris have not yet entirely ceased. In Greece the June 1982 law remolded both structure and function at the institutional level and within the academic body. In Spain the August 1983 University Reform Act was couched in a similar spirit. The academic estate was stratified among various ranks and power was dispersed away from the faculties.[52]

The conflict and outright hostility that accompanied these changes revealed how broad the gulf was between the party of order and the party of movement, an alignment that tended to split academia, with senior professorial staff against largely untenured junior staff. By and large, the former regarded such change as symbolizing the sleep of reason, and the measures themselves as the monster that, inevitably, such sleep must bring forth. For the lower ranks, the reforms resembled the righteous blast of the trumpet that brought the walls of academia tumbling down together with the feudal power of the professorial barons.

By forcing the intervention of the polity, junior staff successfully challenged, and in some cases brought about the demise of, the chair-faculty model. But if the tide of reform still flows strongly on the periphery of the Continent, there are signs that the center now faces an ebb. The battle over power, authority, governance, and the structures that uphold them in the academic estate is not finished. In the Federal Republic of Germany and the Netherlands, for example, the harsh economic climate and the need, once again, to protect excellence and achievement point toward a delicate and circumspect restoration of professorial power.[53]

The house of academia remains divided, and in its internal division each order continues to appeal to friends and allies in the polity. The recent petition of full professors (left and right wing) to the President of the French Republic, in a despairing effort to prevent the ravages of his Minister of Education M. Alain Savary, is a dramatic illustration of this general process.[54]

Struggles for authority within the academic estate in Europe were not rooted primarily in political disagreement among its different orders. Instead, they sprang from structural and demographic pressures that led to an "ecological imbalance" in the estate—an imbalance that not only affected the ratio between senior and junior staff but went far deeper into the process of socialization into academic values. Such a breakdown in the system of transmitting academic values posed a direct threat to the chair-faculty structure. And it led junior staff to seek a solution to their condition inside academia by calling in the polity to redress patterns of authority and governance within the university itself.

The Developing Ecological Imbalance

Academia is a repository of organizational forms and relationships that reflect "past rationalities." The rediscovery—others might say the persistence—of the guild model of academic behavior is perhaps the most obvious. Its presence has been identified and analyzed

TABLE 1
Enrollments and Growth Rates in University-Type Establishments in Western European Countries 1959–1960 to 1978–1979[a] (in thousands)

Country	*1959–1960*	*1964–1965*	*1966–1967*	*1968–1969*	*1970–1971*	*1975–1976*	*1978–1979*
Belgium	29.2	42.4	53.8	—	75.1	83.4	89.3[b]
Growth rate	100	145.2	184.2	—	257.2	285.6	305.8
France	201.1	434.0	—	—	682.6	840.0	870.7
Growth rate	100	215.8	—	—	339.4	418.1	433.0
Great Britain	104.0	138.7	—	211.5	235.3	268.7	295.9
Growth rate	100	133.4	—	203.4	226.3	258.4	284.5
Italy	243.3	354.5	449.7	—	709.8	960.2	996.2
Growth rate	100	145.3	184.8	—	291.7	394.7	409.5
Netherlands	37.7	61.8	82.5	—	103.4	120.2	137.4
Growth rate	100	163.9	218.8	—	274.3	318.8	364.5
Sweden	31.5	61.4	82.5	—	120.2	110.0	—
Growth rate	100	194.9	261.9	—	381.9	349.2	—
West Germany	189.1	246.8	266.6	—	407.1	675.3	756.9
Growth rate	100	130.5	140.9	—	215.3	357.1	400.3

Notes: a. full-time under- and postgraduate
b. 1977–1989

Sources: OECD, *The Development of Higher Education 1950–1967,* vol. 2, table 2, p. 23. Cerych, Colton, and Jallade, *Student Flows and Expenditure in Higher Education 1965–1979,* table 1, pp. 36–37.

in systems as different as Britain, Italy, and Sweden. This "inner organization" may be traced back in various ways, to the University of Paris in the fifteenth century.[55]

The incorporation of academia into state service in Western Europe did not alter this inner environment. Academia was deluged with all sorts of regulations that defined its role and responsibilities by legal and, in some cases constitutional, instruments, and at the same time strengthened faculty structure and chairholder status. This formal "exterior environment" served to protect and give expression to another relationship, key to the chair-faculty edifice. The master-pupil bond between chairholder and graduate assistant may be seen from two perspectives: first, as another enduring form of academic organization, which continued in academia long after it disappeared from other sectors of society; and second, as a system of enculturation into academic values and as an initiation into the various disciplinary cultures inside the university.[56] As a prime instrument of socialization into academia, the master-pupil relationship was crucial for reproduction of the academic estate.

The estate in Western Europe was effectively endowed with a dual nature: on the one hand, it was formally bureaucratized in such procedures as appointment, examination, and promotion; on the other, in its private life it still exercised an ethic and comportment closely aligned with the corporatist guild mentality.

The balance between the external frame and the internal environment was extremely delicate. Both professorial authority and the master-pupil model of academic socialization—the inner environment—depended on factors in the external frame. Some of these were not directly under the control of university authorities, but rested on those legal and constitutional arrangements governing the linkage between secondary and higher education. In short, stability in the inner environment of academia was dependent on the screening function of the academic upper secondary school, on its ability to limit numbers passing from school to university, or alternatively, on its ability to reorient or "cool out" all save the most brilliant and persistent.[57] Universities in Britain and the United States, by contrast, selected at the point of entry and could therefore regulate student demand in keeping with their resources, academic or financial. In France, the Federal Republic of Germany, and Italy, however, holders of the Baccalauréat, the Abitur, and the Maturità had a legal, constitutional right to a place in higher education.

Universities there could not select at the point of entry, though they did resort to an often drastic process of weeding out at various points in undergraduate study.[58]

Starting in the late 1950s, the secondary education system in Western Europe, far from limiting demand for higher education, effectively increased it, sending it onward and upward.[59] Student enrollments spiraled. Between 1959–1960 and 1970–1971, overall student numbers more than tripled in France and Sweden and reached almost the same rate of expansion in Great Britain, Italy, and the Netherlands. By the end of the following decade—1979 to 1980—student numbers were four times their level of two decades earlier in Italy, France, and the Federal Republic of Germany. They had reached three times that level in Belgium and the Netherlands and had risen by just under three times in Great Britain (Table 1).

Growth in the Academic Estate

Developments in the academic estate paralleled the path of Europe's universities away from an elite system of cultivation toward a mass system of training. Increases in student numbers brought increases in staff. Continental European universities lacked the capacity to regulate the growth of academic staff as well as student enrollment. Between 1960 and 1970, the academic estate in France, Italy, and West Germany grew by 348, 365, and 323 percent, respectively. In Britain, Belgium, and Sweden, though expansion was less substantial, it was no less marked—208 percent, 250 percent, and 206 percent (table 2)

Overall growth rates, however, hide substantial changes in the increase of the various strata within academia, particularly in the junior ranks. Table 3 illustrates the growth rate among junior staff—that group of academia that, like Louis Chevalier's nineteenth-century Parisian working class, changed from being a *classe laborieuse* to a *classe dangereuse* in the course of a decade.[60] Junior staff expanded substantially in all countries for which we have information, and particularly so in Belgium, France, and Italy.[61]

TABLE 2
Expansion of Full- and Part-Time Academic Body in Western European Countries 1960–1961 to 1979–1980

Country	*1960–1961*	*1965–1966*	*1970–1971*	*1973–1974*	*1975–1976*	*1978–1979*	*1979–1980*
Belgium	3.515[a]	4.563	7.878[b]	—	—	—	—
Growth rate	100	144.8	250.0	—	—	—	—
France	8.131	—	28.319	37.602	38.142	41.978	—
Growth rate	100	—	348.3	462.5	469.1	516.3	—
Great Britain	12.929	18.375	26.904	—	31.381[c]	—	33.300
Growth rate	100	142.1	208.1	—	242.7	—	257.6
Italy	4.980	7.804	18.215	—	30.279	—	—
Growth rate	100	156.7	365.7	—	608.0	—	—
Netherlands	—	8.429	12.953	—	14.782	—	—
Growth rate	—	100	153.6	—	175.3	—	—
Sweden	3.400	4.500	7.000	8.000[d]	—	—	—
Growth rate	100	132.4	205.9	235.3	—	—	—
West Germany	15.552	—	50.227	—	58.305	—	—
Growth rate	100	—	322.96	—	374.9	—	—

Notes: a. 1960/1961 b. 1971/1972
c. 1975/1976 d. 1973/1974

Sources:
Belgium: Verhoeven in Shils and Daalder, *Universities, Politicians, and Bureaucrats,* table 7, p. 142.
France: Salmon in Shils and Daalder, *Universities, Politicians, and Bureaucrats,* table 3, p. 77. "Evolution du Ministère de l'Education Nationale: Elèves, Etudiants Ensegnants." *Cahiers de l'Avenir de la France,* No. 1.
Great Britain: *Statistics of Education,* vol. 6, *Universities,* 1967, table 56, p. 101; 1970, p. 77; 1979, table 25, p. 53.
Italy: Giglioni, *Baroni e Burocrati,* table 1.5, p. 34.
Netherlands: Daalder in Shils and Daalder, *Universities, Politicians, and Bureaucrats,* table 2, p. 180.
West Germany: Peisert and Framhein, *Systems of Higher Education: Federal Republic of Germany,* table 6, pp. 68, 69.

TABLE 3
Junior Staff Growth Rate in Western European Countries 1959–1969 to 1979–1980[a]

Country	*1959–1960*	*1964–1965*	*1969–1970*	*1975–1976*	*1979–1980*	*Base Number*
Belgium	100	154.1	332.2	—	—	1445
France	100	—	330.8	441.2	371.4	4056
Great Britain	100	134.4	202.3	218.9	225.2	9152
Italy	100	174.8	403.2	602	—	3052
Sweden	100	127.3	225.6	288.2	—	1575
Netherlands	—	100	158.0	156.2	—	6285

Note: a. Belgium: junior staff = assistants
France: assistants and others
Great Britain: junior lecturers/lecturers, and others
Italy: assistenti di ruolo
Sweden: assistant level
Netherlands: junior staff as designated by Daalder

Sources: derived from sources cited in tables 1 and 2.

In what way did an increased junior staff affect the overall balance of the strata or the orders of the academic estate? Table 4 shows the proportion of all university staff represented by junior ranks for the period 1959–1960 to 1979–1980.

In all countries except Great Britain, the growth of academia during the 1960s involved a disproportionate increase in junior staff, even though data for individual countries show considerable variation. Though there is an element of statistical artificiality in our categories, the junior order already constituted an absolute majority in Britain, the Netherlands, and Italy, a substantial minority in Belgium and Sweden, and almost half of academia in France at the start of the decade and before the onset of expansion. By 1970 they were the majority group in academia.

Britain is odd man out. Compared to the academic estate in countries with a similar population size (France and Italy, for example) members of the British academic profesion are far more numerous. Moreover, the proportion of junior staff relative to the entire academic population fell steadily throughout this period.[62] This suggests that promotion and interrank mobility was greater in the British

TABLE 4
Proportion of Junior Staff in the University-Sector Teaching Body in Western Europe 1959–1960 to 1979–1980 (in percentages)

Country	*1959–1960*	*1964–1965*	*1969–1970*	*1975–1976*	*1979–1980*
Belgium	41.1 of 3,515	48.8 of 4,563	60.9 of 7,878	— —	— —
France	49.9 of 8,131	— —	52.9 of 25,356	46.9 of 38,242	38.03 of 39,639
Great Britain	70.8 of 12,929	67.7 of 18,375	68.8 of 26,904	63.8 of 31,381	61.8 of 33,300
Italy	61.3 of 4,986	68.4 of 7,804	67.6 of 18,125	60.8 of 30,276	— —
Sweden	46.3 of 3,400	44.6 of 4,500	50.8 of 7,000	56.7 of 8,000	— —
Netherlands	— —	74.6 of 8,429	76.7 of 12,953	76.2 of 14,782	— —

Sources: derived from sources cited in table 1.

academic profession than in the Continental European academic estate.

Britain then was successful in maintaining the ecological balance in academia, and in improving on it steadily. In part this came about because the inner environment in Britain's academic profession controlled certain dimensions in the external frame: nomination for posts, conditions of advancement, and the creation of new posts, among other factors, were not part of the formal bureaucratic overlay of national ministerial control that characterized the European academic state.

In continental Europe academia not only faced a massive influx of junior staff but had to rely on formal national and bureaucratic procedures to ensure mobility, procedures it might initiate but did not ultimately control. The academic estate was not utterly deprived of advancement and promotion—an important internal safety valve. But if one takes the growth rate of junior orders and the balance between senior and junior staff, it is arguable that a high degree of blockage in interrank mobility existed. When promotion did come, it came later and in a more panic-stricken manner. In France, for example, the growth of the middle ranks (maîtres assistants) from 1968 to 1978–1979 was as indecent as it was rapid (from 5,426 to 14,742), an astounding development, as in 1960 a mere 500 were on the rolls. A similar phenomenon prevails in Italy in relation to the *professori incaricati,* parallel figures in the academic firmament, who also rose from earth in large numbers: 2,370 in 1969–1970 and 6,668 by 1975–1976.[63]

Such promotion spurts indicate not only that the external environment of the academic estate lay under government control but also that the government appeared well aware of academia's internal tensions and sought to alleviate them by accelerating promotion for a class that, once laborious, had now become politically dangerous as well.

From a Classe Laborieuse to a Classe Dangereuse

In Western Europe the transformation of higher education from an elite to a mass institution was purchased at the price of equally massive expansion in junior staff. If such expansion altered the quantitative balance between the senior (tenured) and the junior (substantially untenured) orders of the academic estate, what impact did it have on the qualitative relationships between the two? Was the authority of the chairholder over junior staff already under attack before the onset of the "events of May"? Did the challenges posed by student unrest merely provide a heaven-sent occasion for the junior orders to throw down the gauntlet to professorial authority? Or was it, on the contrary, the final factor in a long-drawn-out drifting apart of the two orders, the origins of which lie deep within the recesses of academe? In seeking answers to these questions we need to pay attention to the ways that developments affecting the public life of academia also affected its private life.

The collegium of chairholders was the organizational heart and symbol of unity of corporate professorial authority. It existed alongside another, less visible but no less powerful collegiate linkage between senior orders of the academic estate and their aspirant junior counterparts. The "parallel collegium" operated vertically across ranks rather than horizontally among members of the full professoriat. But it was no less important in maintaining professorial authority and in simultaneously governing the expectations of the assistant class.

This vertical collegium rested on the notion—sometimes a reality at other times existing simply by force of myth—that all orders of academia were engaged in both teaching and research. Archaic though it may appear, the apprenticeship model performed two functions that were vital to the cohesion and identity of academia. It created a bond of common identity and interest between junior and senior staff, offsetting the horizontal collegium of professorial authority with an equal and no less powerful collegium of colleagues who, despite differences in age and rank, were each engaged in seeking truth. It was also the prime agency of induction and socialization into academia.

Research was not simply a matter of acquiring techniques of analysis or the accumulation of knowledge and judgment. It was also the vehicle for the passage of values—some explicit, others unspoken—from master to pupil. It was central to the perpetuation of academic cultures and to the common identity among ranks and orders of academia.[64] Research combined with teaching (or its ritual invocation) distinguished academia from schoolmastering, which was confined to the simple joys of teaching. The collegium of chairholders was bonded by the shared responsibilities and authority of coevals. The invisible collegium that underwrote a joint commitment to research held together different orders of academia—senior, middle, and junior.

In such countries as France, the Netherlands, and the Federal Republic of Germany, expansion of the academic estate did not entirely dissolve the vertical collegium, but it did weaken it. For a substantial subsection of the assistant class it had become largely irrelevant. Other agencies began to play a crucial role in the socialization of junior staff and in shaping their attitudes and perceived role in the university. These agencies primarily reflected external society, particularly then-current student ideologies. They also showed the willingness of junior staff to organize formally into bodies identified less with academia than with the trade union movement. That this weakened the internal linkage between junior staff and the professoriat reflected the fragile hold the academic estate had over its external environment.

In Britain, by contrast, if there were tensions in the "key profession" in the late 1960s, they did not take the form of younger staff seeking pro rata representation or fragmenting the guild into formal and separate electoral colleges. Two factors operating in its internal environment, plus the high degree of de facto control it exercised over its external frame, afforded greater strength to the British academic profession's maintenance of a traditional method of socialization into academic values. When expansion begin in the early 1960s, British academia was a large body relative to French and Italian counterparts. And its internal governance rested on a collegium far wider than those of professorial rank alone. By regulating student numbers, academia in Britain exercised indirect sway over its own financial underpinning.[65] And since governments were willing to maintain a student-staff ratio of approximately 9:1, the British academic profession wielded equally efficacious control over staff members as well. This was compounded by the profession's control of internal promotion without the need to apply to central administration for confirmation or nomination.

Conditions were not as favorable in most Continental European countries. There the academic estate controlled its exterior frame in a manner highly circumscribed by law and regulation. It could regulate neither student entry nor junior staff intake—this regulation was a ministry task. In addition to this were the sparse membership rolls of the academic estate before expansion. Spiraling student enrollments meant a premium was placed on recruiting graduates capable of instructing undergraduates. This made it difficult to create new academics (and maintain the supply) through the master-pupil system; socialization through research training is a protracted business. The solution was to engage a subclass within the junior staff whose responsibilities were limited to teaching, and who were usually on year-to-year contracts.

This situation in no way excluded the continued production of future academics by the time-honored method of sitting at the master's feet. But it meant that a substantial and growing number of junior staff were brought into the academic estate who had not undergone this rite of passage. The European university's path toward a mass clientele created a second route on the fringes of the academic estate, running parallel to the long-established vertical collegium. This second track differed fundamentally from the first and was only weakly associated with research training. In the minds of academia and government its sole raison d'être was the need for instructors.

This further stratification of the academic estate distinguished explicitly between those for whom the vertical collegium and eventually careers at the highest level were still viable, and those for whom neither was. By removing the research linkage, it also gave rise to a group within the instructor class that had no common interest in or formal connection to a chair-faculty system. Cut off from the privileges and rewards offered to those at the top of the estate of which they were only marginally a part, the instructor "subproletariat" recast authority in terms of naked, arbitrary power. Dependent though the apprentice academic had been on his guild master or his patron for advancement, he nevertheless could expect his training to bring him the qualifications necessary for that advancement, and with it the coveted status of civil servant—the Continental equivalent of tenure. The instructor class, by contrast, could look forward to none of these. Heavy teaching loads took up all the time needed for research that would lead to qualification. Within the formal canons of academia, instructors were not eligible for advancement and even less for tenure. Their lot was, or appeared to many to be, that of the eternal drudge who labored without reward.

In a situation reminiscent of the relation between the French nobility and the bourgeoisie on the eve of the 1789 revolution, a substantial part of the instructor class saw itself as powerless inside academia and aggrieved by the rest of the academic estate.[66] They sought to remedy their condition by appeals to more weighty interests outside. The rise of this semipermanent, untenured assistant class revealed how tenuous the estate's control was, even over its private life.

If they were isolated in the private life of the academic estate, that portion of the instructor class not part of the chairholder's patronage nexus was not segregated within the university. Against the vertical collegium that linked professors and junior staff through research, they brought to bear a countervailing linkage based on teaching.

In the social movements of the day this opposing power took various self-conscious forms. They revealed a "counter" or "alternative" culture that sought legitimacy, not merely by opposing academia's "high" culture, but from its claim to represent within the university a cultural pluralism found outside in the rapidly expanding youth culture of the 1960s.[67] This linkage was not entirely rhetorical. To be sure, it made for amusing slogans during the carnival atmosphere of May 1968: (*La jeunesse au pouvoir, Sus à la gérontocratie pédagogique,* and others less printable). Yet these appeals to age-group solidarity between younger instructor graduates and undergraduate students could not disguise certain similar interests for both parties. Together, they were affected by the deteriorating physical conditions (the most spectacular was overcrowding) accompanying the transition to mass higher education, especially in France, Italy, and the Federal Republic of Germany.[68] Both shared in the growing distance, physical and hierarchical, between the lower orders and chairholders. And both graduate instructors and undergraduate students necessarily sought redress for their grievances via political negotiation rather than through the academic process: the decision to grant civil servant status to a category of personnel depended not on academia but on national policy determined by central administration; and improvements in facilities, resources, and personnel allocation were the purlieu of the same agency. This reflected national bureaucratic power over academia's external environment, and academia's weakness in not mastering those vital frame factors that affected its physical working conditions.

By seeking redress outside the academic estate, the assistant class altered its status from a laborious to a dangerous class. Accompanied by an emerging critical ideology with which to justify its claims, it disrupted the inner environment of the academic estate. Assistants and students rose to political militancy accompanied by an ideology fundamentally hostile to the value system underlying not only the chair as symbol of academic authority but also the apprenticeship model of induction into academia. This ideology contained two major strands: first, a neo-Marxist critique of the university as a social institution; second, a concept of students as consumers of knowledge rather than as privileged members of an elite, with certain rights, not liberties.[69] Despite differences understood only by their particular adepts, these two positions agreed broadly on substantive issues. Both presumed the right of students to decide what ought to be taught—to have some say, if not the decisive one, over shaping the curriculum, determining the modes of evaluation, and, in certain instances, deciding the type of research the university should accept. For Marxists, and the German Sozialistischer Deutscher Studentenbund (SDS) in particular, such claims stemmed from the moral right of "workers" (students and junior staff) to control the means of (knowledge) production based on an industrial analogue of worker-management relations transferred to the university setting.[70] For "consumerists," the responsibilities of the "producers" (professors) was to supply knowledge deemed "relevant" or "necessary" by "consumers" (students).

These claims struck at the heart of the academic estate's private life. In so doing they also struck at the chair-faculty structure that symbolized professorial authority. In bringing into the groves of academe notions derived from labor movement history and industrial relations, which cast students and instructors as workers united against the arbitrary authority of professors as managers or intellectual capitalists, this ideology predicated a conflict model of relations. It also sought to take control over knowledge content away from those of proven excellence and achievement (the essence of the master-pupil relationship), and put it in the hands of the "counter collegium"—those who learned and those who taught. Thus the offspring of Marx, like their sire, stood Hegel, and the professorial hierarchy to boot, on their respective heads.

Academia and Unionization

The challenge to the authority of the chair-faculty structure inside academia was accompanied by attempts by junior staff to link with such outside organizations as trade unions, political parties, or both. This move, found in the Netherlands, France, Italy, and the Federal Republic of Germany, was not universal. In Britain and Sweden, for instance, the established bodies representing the interests of academia as a corporate whole remained intact. Though differing in organization, public status, and membership, both the Association of University Teachers and the Sveriges Akademikers Centralorganisation Statsjantemannens Riksforbund continued, largely unchallenged, their roles as main channels of communication with the public and the polity.[71]

In those countries where, among the junior orders of the academic estate, the drive to unionize took place, one can distinguish between those, such as the Federal Republic of Germany, where this process was also accompanied by the emergence of counterorganizations inside academia nominally independent of union organization outside, and those, such as France, where the organization of oppositional power inside was an extension of official union penetration into the university.[72]

In the Federal Republic of Germany the emergence of an organization to counter professorial power in the heartland of academia took the form of the Bundeassistentenkonferenz (BAK). Set up in 1968, the BAK, as its title implies, was a national federation supportive of the junior order. Its nomenclature alone suggested that it had been created as a deliberate counterweight to the West German Rectors Conference—one of the more powerful agencies in higher education.[73]

The political platform of the BAK included three main issues: first, the restoration of education through research; second, the establishment of an integrated system of higher education embracing universities, teacher training establishments, and high professional schools (*Fachhochschulen*); and third, the abolition of the Habilitation as the prerequisite for professorial status. The common factor was the desire to improve career security and chances of promotion, either by removing barriers to research or by large-scale systematic reorganization that would set the BAK's membership on the golden road to chair-holder status.

Organization inside academia paralleled attempts to increase political weight outside. Here the initiative was not entirely one-sided. The development of a subclass without formal research responsibilities was looked on by schoolteacher trade unions with no little rejoicing. Recruitment by teachers' unions from the instructor class not only increased membership, it presented an opportunity for them to increase credibility by tapping into the vicarious prestige of higher education. Such considerations prompted the largest teachers' union in West Germany—Gewerkschaft Erziehung und Wissenschaft—to regularly champion the assistant class during debates over reorganization of higher education around the Hochschulrahmengesetz and its aftermath.[74]

In France, Belgium, Italy, and the Netherlands, junior staff tended to avoid the creation of separate professional associations inside academia. Their approach involved the establishment of political groupings that reflected similar allegiances outside. Their goal was less to seek improvement by appeal inside the academic estate so much as to bring pressure to bear on it directly from outside through the political process.

In Belgium untenured assistants sought to pressure the government into granting them tenure through allying with the two major trade union federations, the Algemeen Christelijk Vakverbond and the socialist

Algemeen Belgisch Vakverbond.[75] A similar tactic was seen in France. French assistants tightened up their links with the left-wing Syndicat National de l'Enseignement Supérieur (SNESup). SNESup offered substantial negotiating advantages not only on its own but as one of the forty-odd organizations that comprised the Federation de l'Education Nationale, an umbrella organization that coordinated the grievances and claims of the entire corps enseignant (teaching body) and communicated them to government and Parliament. If SNESup never managed to bring together an absolute majority in French academia, its weight in the public arena was not to be underestimated. Christian Fouchet, a former minister of education, once remarked wryly that the French teaching body "was more numerous than the entire Red Army."

That the junior orders in France, like the assistant class in Germany, identified with the national teaching corps, rather than with the university, was not entirely fortuitous. The alliance sprang from both the tasks and location of the instructor class in the university. Confined to undergraduate teaching, its members saw greater similarity between their condition and that of organized primary and secondary-school teachers than they did with the corps from which it was largely excluded.

This alliance pattern is also visible in Italy.[76] It brought national trade union federations to the negotiations about structuring higher education and defining conditions of employment, and it gave the assistants a firm organizational base outside academia from which to continue to press claims on the government, to effect change in academia's private life. Demands for more posts, more guaranteed hours (many assistants in France were paid by the number of hours they taught), and more promotions from the ranks of the precarious were part of the regular academic year in France and Italy.

This affiliation increased the pressure to which governments acceded; it had other consequences as well. Since organized labor now acted as a channel of negotiation for one segment of the academic estate, it also considerably influenced how "participation" and "democracy" were defined inside academia. The formal stratification of the academic estate into electoral colleges for internal decision making and governance drew heavily from various forms of worker participation current or under discussion in industry.

The clearest examples of the application of industrial relations concepts to this domain are found in France and the Federal Republic of Germany. The concept underlying the 1968 Higher Education Framework Law in France was that of *co-gestion* (joint managerial responsibility).[77] In West Germany the notion of *Mitbestimmung* (worker coresponsibility) emerged in attenuated form in the 1976 Hochschulrahmengesetz. It gave rise to the notion of the *Gruppenuniversität* (the university of grouped interests) in contrast to the *Ordinarienuniversität* (the university governed by professors).

Pressure from junior academics and students on the polity resulted in another layer of formal bureaucratic rationality, located not in the external environment but in its heart. It replaced the organic unity of the guild by a system of stratified representation of interests—middle and junior orders of staff, students, and in certain instances, technical staff and ordinary employees. Such arrangements justified to the hilt the accuracy of W. S. Gilbert's aphorism, "When everybody's somebody, then nobody's anybody."

Reorganization of Authority in Academia

The reorganization of academic authority restrained and reduced professorial power. The chair-faculty system was replaced by other basic decision-making units—the *unités d' enseignement et de recherche* (UERS) in France, the *Fachbereiche* in Germany, and the *Vakgroepen* in the Netherlands. But pressure for change was not universally successful, nor did it have the same objectives in all instances.

The Belgian reforms of 24 March 1971 expanded the participating constituency on the board of directors (*conseil d' administration*) of a university. But professors enjoyed a built-in majority on grounds of superior knowledge. Chair and faculty structures remained intact; faculty subgroups, though present, were confined to debating the tedious issues of teaching techniques. Similar changes in participant groups on faculty councils in Italy essentially left the structure and the professorial authority system untouched. But a second phase of reform has called for a subdivision of the faculty structure into departmental decision-making units based on a system of tripartite representation—one-third students, one-third tenured and untenured assistants, and one-third senior, tenured staff.[78]

The tripartite principle of representation took root elsewhere—in Austria, West Germany, Sweden, and the Netherlands. But it was not always accompanied by changes in the faculty system, as illustrated by the Austrian University Reorganization Act of 1975. Nor was it limited to changing participation patterns inside the academic estate, as evident in the Swedish University Reform Act of 1977, which extended the participant constituency to bodies external to the university.[79]

Formally, the French Higher Education Framework Law of 1968 provided for the participation of "external personalities." But this remained, by and large, a dead letter. On paper the chair-faculty structure was replaced by a series of hierarchically arranged councils, starting from the university council and passing through the academic council (*conseil scientifique*), and down into the basic decision-making unit, the UER council. The key to the vexed issue of representation in all three bodies was a complex system of electoral colleges that determined the number of places to be assigned to each interest on a specific council. In all, French reforms identified seven specific interest groups, from which the academic estate was partitioned into three strata—full professors and readers (*maítres de conference*), lecturers (*maítres assistants*), and junior lecturers (*assistants*), together with those of indeterminant state (*autres enseignants*).[80]

But arrangements set forth by the legislator do not always remain in the form that decrees ordain. In France, for example, the establishment of UERs (now changed by the 1984 Higher Education Guideline Law to UFR-*unités de formation et de recherche*) seems little more than the chameleon of the faculty structure that changes its color to the shade of the legislative fig leaf.[81] Some have argued that the effect of the 1968 reforms was to draw power upward into the hands of university presidents; at the same time they note that neither university presidents nor UER directors had much power over the academic staff (or over teaching, research, hiring, or promotion).[82]

Legislation and change may have reduced the ostensible and in some cases the real power of the chairholder by distributing responsibility across broad-based participating constituencies. It may have satisfied junior staff and removed students from the streets. But it also transferred the conflict back inside academia. In the Netherlands, for example, junior staff continued to press home their advantage and to override those safeguards on professorial appointments and on research that the 1971 Wet op de Universitaire Bestuurleiding had set down.[83] In France and the Federal Republic of Germany, attempts to reverse the fortunes of war came from a different source—the professoriat. What could be lost on the boulevards of Paris and the streets of Länder capitals could be regained in the anterooms of the Bundesministerium für Bildung und Wissenschaft.

The press for reform by junior staff could indeed be met by technical measures, by enhanced formal representation at the institutional level, and by the occasional largesse of ministerial announcements that advanced some junior staff to middling ranks. But in higher education systems regulated by central administration, professorial power and influence is not limited to the institutional level. It is found also in individual access to highly placed key officials, parliamentarians, ministers, and important national committees, research agencies, and policy-determining bodies. There is much to suggest that professorial power, diminished at the institutional level, regrouped and consolidated itself at the commanding heights from whence the higher education system is controlled.

Two episodes in France and the Federal Republic of Germany hint at this reassertion of professorial power at the system level. First, the aptly named Loi Sauvage (the savage, or wild-man law) of 21 July 1980 restored the number of seats reserved for professors on French university councils to 50 percent of the whole, cut those set aside for students to 15 percent, and reduced those for instructors to a risible 5 percent. At the same time the qualifications for tenured status were tightened. Second, in the Federal Republic, the return of a

Christian Democrat coalition has seen moves to limit the rights of nonprofessorial staff to participate in rectorial elections and to examine Ph.D. theses, a symbolic though significant change in the 1976 Hochschulrahmengesetz.[84] If two measures do not a trend make, they suggest that the reality of professorial power is more multidimensional than its expression at the institutional level.

Operating styles of academic estate orders —the junior collectivist and public, the senior individual and private—are radically different. But each in its own way has been instrumental in shaping the house of academe. The internal division and fragmentation of the academic estate simply shows how differently each order seeks to wield it.

The National Estate and the Reform of Academic Work

Changing the internal management of universities was not the only task undertaken by governments in Western Europe. They also aimed to alter the work and role of higher education in general and the university in particular. Changes in university governance structures had arisen largely from internal rifts in the academic estate, but they in no way invalidated its self-perception as a national body. Measures that involved redirecting the work and the role of universities posed what academia regarded as an inadmissable threat to its status. Efforts by governments to assign new goals and priorities to academia as a corporate whole found themselves blocked. An estate that demonstrated spectacular disunity on one issue could, on others, give proof of an equally disconcerting obduracy. The stances of the French and West German academics are especially illuminating examples of this capacity.

Attempts to Vocationalize the University

The transition of European universities from elite to mass institutions in the 1960s paralleled a shift in their underlying paradigm. From being an institution devoted to cultivation, the university came to be perceived by governments as an instrument for economic expansion.[85] The paradigmatic shift in no way denied the centrality of the institution; it merely transferred such centrality from the task of cultural unification to that of ensuring the nation's economic growth and vitality.

In the early and middle 1960s such a change in priorities did not alter the historic role of universities in supplying qualified manpower to the state and to medicine and law. Economic expansion led to growth in the provisions of the welfare state and thus possibly increased the importance of this traditional occupational nexus.[86] Nevertheless, though vocational in the sense that they selected for occupations and granted credentials, universities in Western Europe tended neither to be geared toward the private-sector labor market nor to concern themselves with practical training.

By the mid-1960s, after the upsurge of student militancy, certain governments, including the French, West German, British, Norwegian, and Swedish, began to look at linkages with the non-public-sector labor market. Initially, efforts (especially those in France, Britain, and Norway) concentrated on the nonuniversity sector, emerging in institutional form in the university institutes of technology, the polytechnics, and the regional colleges. In part this stemmed from the same demographic pressure that had poisoned relations between senior and junior orders of the academic estate. But such policies were also driven by the feeling that, on their own, universities were not adequate to meet changes in the non-state-sector labor market.[87]

Governments also developed a sense that reform, intended to link higher education to the private-sector labor market (hitherto confined to the nonuniversity sector), perhaps ought to be extended to universities. For example, in West Germany, on the one hand the bottleneck at the transition from school to higher education, caused by growth in student numbers, resulted in the imposition of *numerus clausus*—selective entry to certain oversubscribed courses. On the other hand, the linkage between higher education and the state-sector labor market had broken down. In France massive growth in student enrollments also led to a glut of arts and science graduates and a marked decline in employment opportunities in the state sector, particularly in teaching.[88]

Thus in both the Federal Republic and in France, a more matured strategy directed at changing the university's function and long-term goals ran alongside emergency measures altering internal governance. In Germany this strategy culminated in the 1976 Framework Act for Higher Education (Hochschulrahmengesetz) and the thrust to set up new comprehensive universities (*Gesamthochschulen*). In France it took the form of the "second-cycle" (years three and four of university study) reform of the same year. Both, in their own manner, aimed at redirecting the work of universities.

One intent of the proposal to set up comprehensive universities and to publish the Hochschulrahmengesetz was to improve the "technocratic efficiency" of West Germany's higher education system.[89] Suggestions that university education ought to be more practical and more in keeping with manpower needs and skills of the private sector had been aired as early as 1967 in a report to the Baden-Württemberg Ministry of Culture by the sociologist Ralf Dahrendorf.[90] Dahrendorf recommended three-year university programs (not the more usual six or seven) with special weight on teaching rather than research. The proposal to uncouple the close relationship between universities and research was further advanced by reorganizing the university along comprehensive lines.

First presented by the federal minister of education in 1970, the Gesamthochschule policy had two consequences: it set the stage for the Hochschulrahmengesetz, and it triggered the drafting of detailed framework planning by six of the eleven Länder.[91] It called for a merger among the various types of higher education institutions, university and nonuniversity. The idea was to form establishments bringing together classical functions of universities with more practical preoccupations of higher technical colleges (Fachhochschulen), linking academic research and training to professional practice. Adaptation to economic change would be facilitated by institutional integration and curricular reform. Integration would presumably enhance mobility between academic education and vocational training tracks, provide parity of esteem among different institutions, and increase educational opportunity. Technocratic policy aims were married to democratizing plans.[92]

By contrast, French reform strategy espoused a purely technocratic approach, undiluted by considerations of educational opportunity. Changes in the second cycle in 1976 were the last phase in a policy dating from 1973 when the first cycle (years one and two) was revamped and the diplôme d'etudes universitaires générales (DEUG) was introduced as a degree leading to "practical" employment. As the DEUG developed, it turned out not to be a "terminal qualification" (in the ambiguous terminology of legislators) so much as an intermediate diploma.[93]

The main objective of second-cycle reforms was to extend the vocationalization (*professionalisation*) deeper into the university curriculum.[94] The licence was redesigned as a one-year degree after the DEUG, and was to be more practically oriented than it was as a three- or four-year purely academic program. Similarly, the maîtrise was conceived as a one-year program (consecutive to the licence) which, in certain instances, would involve scientific and technical training for a specific occupation. Both proposals contained, imprudently perhaps, provisions for selective entry. Educational efficiency was emphasized, not educational opportunity.[95]

In both the Federal Republic of Germany and in France, then, government policy toward higher education was organized around a specific form of vocationalization. Such policy aimed at linking the curriculum directly to skills in certain private-sector jobs. In officialdom vocationalization was seen as a remedy to shortcomings in university-labor market relationships. Though universities were linked to a particular "protected labor market" of state service, their training was neither specialized enough nor sufficiently based on practice. The historic role of the university had been to provide a screening and credentialing mechanism for the state sector rather than to furnish specific training for such jobs.[96]

The new vocationalism sought to alter the type of knowledge imparted by universities, emphasizing skills and shifting undergraduate attention toward the private sector. Such changes were immensely important, historically and sociologically. They uncoupled the university from its raison d'être of the past two centuries—namely, to prepare duly qualified entrants for state employment. Such a policy struck at the aspirations of many students, particularly those seeking posts in schoolteaching. By the same token, it appeared to menace both the status and identity of the academic estate, since the state labor market was associated with honor and security.[97]

The Dead Letter of Reform

For the supporters of reform the Hochschulrahmengesetz rang exceedingly hollow. Even if it stipulated that the higher education system ought to be reorganized on the comprehensive model, the six establishments worthy of the comprehensive label, already in place, antedated the legislation and enrolled no more than 10 percent of the university population.[98] The comprehensive university, like the mule, begat no offspring; and given the current economic climate, the situation probably will not change.

Even in Nordrhein-Westfalen, where five comprehensive universities were created, the state was unsuccessful in dividing the *Land* into *Gesamthochschulregionen* that would incorporate existing universities.[99] The comprehensive universities were not part of a successful comprehensive strategy; they were isolated additions to the existing university framework.

Moreover, these new additions to the ranks of German higher education have experienced "academic drift" toward traditional patterns of teaching and research, symbolized by their assumptions of "Universität" in their names. A "practical emphasis" among these comprehensive universities is really solidly established only at Kassel.[100] Evidently, attempts to reform university education in the Federal Republic show that passage into the statute book is no guarantee of success.

The reforming impulse in France fared no better. Reviewing efforts in this direction, one scholar has suggested, "It was much ado about nothing."[101] The enactment of the decrees of 1976 remained, at the institutional level, largely a dead letter. Some curriculum changes had been carried out prior to these exercises planned on paper. But confined to certain establishments mainly specializing in business studies and administration, their impact on the rest of French higher education was minimal.[102]

Just how little was achieved may be seen from the objectives set out in the new Higher Education Guideline Law of 1984. Universities were called upon to "enhance the nation's scientific and cultural development," exhorted "to help reduce social and cultural inequalities," and encouraged "to contribute to employment policy and regional development."[103] If the 1976 reforms had succeeded, there would have been no need to repeat the message.

The Academic Estate: A National Service in Resistance to Change

In both the Federal Republic of Germany and France, attempts at reform have gone little further than their formal publication. Enactment has not been accompanied by implementation. In higher education implementation depends ultimately on the will and cooperation of academia. Neither was forthcoming. Those who lose the battle at the formulation and adoption phase of reform may live to fight on at the stage of implementation, a tactic academia often efficaciously employs. A decade of research has shown just how impervious higher education systems can be to external pressure, partly because of their "bottom-heavy" nature and the consequent difficulties this presents to both political and ministerial authorities in the exercise of effective control.[104]

Reforms do not have to be killed off by strident opposition; inaction and inertia are just as effective. Success in carrying out comprehensive university reform required the compliance of the German academic estate in actively promoting, or at least agreeing to, the integration of their universities with technical colleges. This was not to be. The established universities, and even those new ones with radical reputations, were opposed to this move.[105] They did not lobby state governments to block the framework legislation; opposition was carried out privily within their own universities, and was successful in quickly undermining the implementation process.

When the comprehensive university was first broached as an idea in the earlier part of the decade, no active opposition emerged. Indeed, the authoritative West German Rectors Conference put forward its own proposals, though later it slid into tacit opposition to comprehensivization. The Gesamthochschule policy had various aims, some of which academics supported. Junior staff approved its egalitarianism—not only the intended increased access to higher education, but more important, the reduced hierarchy among academic staff.[106] The professoriat opposed it. On this score the comprehensive reform fell afoul of the battle for status and privilege within academia.

Nevertheless, both junior staff and professors were broadly united in condemning the particular stress the Gesamthochschule policy laid on the work-manpower function, the technocratic aims.[107] For instance, the BAK did not endorse the shortening of study programs or the idea that such programs ought to concentrate on instruction and practical training in place of academic education and research. That such efficiency-oriented reforms were basically unattractive to university academics as a whole is reflected in their opposition to such measures in two other contexts. The proposal to shorten study time had been aired in 1970 by the Wissenschaftsrat (Science Council) and was unearthed again in 1978. Both times strong opposition from within the universities led to its elimination.[108]

If the academic estate in the Federal Republic had little influence on policy formulation regarding the comprehensive university issue, academia's role in implementation was decisive and negative.

In January 1976 the French government presented the outlines of the second-cycle reform. Opposition was neither quiet nor slow in developing. The strikes and demonstrations that broke out lasted until the summer—far longer than the events of May 1968, to which it was inevitably compared. Students formed the mass of strikers, but protests were organized by faculty unions that, like the Duke of Plaza Torro, "led their forces from behind." As in the Federal Republic, so in France, the academic estate, senior and junior orders all, attacked the proposals mainly where closer links between the university and the economy were anticipated.[109] Opposition was no less vehement over vocationalizing courses than it was over the participation of outside representatives of industry in planning committees that would draw up the new courses.

But it was not the more spectacular acts that undermined the reform so much as the covert resistance of academia at the phase of implementation. The government placed the initiative for planning and construction of new programs at the institutional level. Submissions were subsequently to be approved by special commissions nominated by the secretary of state for higher education and by the Conseil National de l'Enseignement Supérieur et de la Recherche—a national committee with responsibility for validation and accreditation of university courses. Lack of enthusiasm among most ranks of university staff was equaled and occasioned by the lack of incentive given by central administration. Rather than setting aside additional finances, the government pushed for a redeployment of existing resources. The new programs were not supplementary to the old; they were to replace them.[110]

As in Germany, French academics had little influence on the formulation and adoption of the proposed reforms. But their massive noncompliance stymied implementation.

Resistance to Change: Its Roots in Academia

The academic estate, despite its internal divisions, has its own perception of self and status. On balance, academics regard themselves as members of a national body in the service of the nation—a view reinforced by central-government control over issues in the external environment.[111] Opposition to reform in the Federal Republic of Germany and France had this common feature, though different orders sometimes resisted from differing motives: namely, that change, as presented by the polity, boded fair to alter either their perceived standing (chairholders) or the standing they aspired to (younger staff).

The thrust of the two reforms discussed above was to assign a new mission to the university, to link it to the nation's economic well-being. Such an economic connection had justified university growth since the early 1960s. But the economic association of university and nation did not alter the national nature of the university's mission, nor did it introduce major curricular reform. On the contrary, the policy of growth in the earliest part of that decade rested on the time-honored formula of "more of the same." The economic rationale could easily fit in with the idea, retained from the nineteenth century, that the university performed a culturally unifying role in the nation.[112] When students looked to the state labor market in increasing numbers, they added a further dimension to established practice.

The collapse of the state labor market in the early 1970s altered this. From that point governments turned their attention, with varying degrees of determination, first to the private sector of the labor market and second to the linking of universities with the economic life of the region.[113] Such policies ran counter to the academic estate's self-perception as a national entity.

The regionalization of the university was profoundly antithetical to the French estate. Regional requirements of manpower and skills are not homogeneous. If universities have a regional commitment, that commitment demands differential responses, different types of courses. So regionalization threatened certain aspects of academia's prestige structure contained in the institution of "national diplomas." Teaching national diploma courses carries no small kudos, and French academics have demonstrated a continued desire to achieve this honor.[114]

Denationalization of France's academic estate also threatened to increase the administrative and social distance from the capital and central administration and also the distance from the privilege and power that come from association with that political and intellectual pole. Since the last years of the seventeenth century, Parisians have looked on the provinces with horror tinged with amusement. To be provincial is to be boorish and second rate. To be regional is not even that. In their opposition to regionalization, French academics were a faithful reflection of the prejudices of their country's elite.[115]

Academics also feared that the new policies would create differentiation and give rise to a pecking order of institutions—a major change from the formal legal situation in which, on paper at least, all were on an equal footing. With the new policies some establishments might be obliged to emphasize a particular type of research, others to stress teaching. Like their French counterparts, German academics of all orders opposed the downplaying of the research function. For it would be tantamount to reducing professorial status to something akin to a superannuated schoolmaster—as many university academics regarded their Fachhochschulen counterparts. Assistants feared that such a policy could cut them off from any hope of advancement into the prestigious realm of research. The BAK continually proposed that all institutions of higher education have a scientific orientation, and that all academics have an equal chance to pursue research as well as teaching.[116]

Given their strong academic prejudices, the vocationalism of the reform policies was distasteful to all orders of the academic estate. In their world prestige lay in both national and academic models of university education. This view derives from the early cultural and social history of European education systems at school and university levels. Traditionally, a fundamental dichotomy existed between education and instruction; the former was noble, intended to develop the whole person, to create cultivation and grace and to mature the mind. The latter was less noble: reduced in scope and intended simply to equip the bulk of the population with appropriate vocational skills. These distinctions are mirrored in the structure of Europe's education systems: the gymnasium and lycée are favored, elite establishments geared to *Allgemeinbildung* and *culture générale*, and the *Hauptschulen* and *cours complementaires* are more vocational. Similar distinctions penetrated into postsecondary education as nonuniversity institutions emerged.[117]

Antivocationalism in German and French academia was not simply a cultural holdover from the time the university's purpose was the free and unfettered pursuit of knowledge and cultivation. It was one of those deeply rooted values that served to identify academia's claims to superior status. So the notion that German university teachers ought to "instruct" was not only a derogation from the classical ideology of research and education through research passed down from the time of Alexander von Humboldt; it was also a derogation in terms of school-based hierarchies. The objection that many academics raised vis-a-vis such proposals as the "Dahrendorf plan" (it would make university studies *Schulisch*—school-like) could not have been more devastating.[118] The intensity of wide-ranging academic opposition to vocationalism showed it to be an assault on the identity and essence of academia and university work.

Regionalization and vocationalization called forth the resistance of the academic estate. This frustrated policy and set at nought the best-laid plans of bureaucrat and legislator and revealed the power of the academic estate. But such power is effective only in certain circumstances: first, when opposition is broadly consensual in all ranks, even though motives differ; second, when reform places initiative for implementation inside the inner environment of academia rather than with the exterior frame; and third, when the issues at stake are perceived by all sections of academia to call into question those fundamental values that underlie its corporate standing and identity in society as a whole, as a national body. The defense of such interests had far more priority than the internecine feuding over internal governance and structures of participation. It is one thing to rebuild one's dwelling. It is another to have the town hall forcibly order its relocation and reconstruction. To this axiom the house of academe was no exception.

Conclusion

Academia, like Proteus, has many guises. The manifold perception of its various facets, each in its various perspectives, contribute to understanding the total picture. Some observers attach importance to the unique nature of academic work. Others emphasize the concomitants of working within different institutional sectors of higher education.[119]

In this essay we have been concerned with two additional dimensions that have special significance in understanding academia in Continental Europe and in distinguishing it from its British and American counterparts: the fissures that split the orders of academia, stemming in large part from the chair-faculty structure of academic organization—fissures dividing senior tenured professors, nonprofessorial but tenured middle ranks, and the junior largely untenured assistant class; and the self-perception of European academia as a national body, an academic estate.

How these two dimensions bear on European academia and condition its role in change and reform in higher education is evident from the two cases we have explored. The first revealed the polity's accommodation to pressure from within academia to put its house in order. The second involved pressure from the polity to impose reform on academia. Measures introduced by governments to redistribute the balance of authority among various constituencies inside academia, principally along the lines of formal ranking in the academic hierarchy, corresponded to the wishes of many university teachers. On paper at least, such measures were largely successful. But the polity's bid to alter the work and role of universities and the academic estate, to regionalize and vocationalize them, were largely unsuccessful. Lacking support from academics, even the most strenuous efforts at change by German and French governments remained ineffective.

These changes were precipitated largely by developments outside the system of higher education: in burgeoning student enrollments, in corresponding prodigious growth in junior academic staff, and in a glut of under- and unemployed university graduates brought about by the inability of state labor markets to absorb the expanded supply of graduates. Such external pressures were the common lot of industrial countries in the 1960s and 1970s. But the way academia, whether profession or estate, met them was not.

In part this differential response was caused by differences in public control, accountability, and governance, which constitute regulatory mechanisms in the higher education-polity relationship. We have alluded to this as the outer frame of academia; it acts as a bureaucratic overlay, penetrating into the inner environment of that body.[120] The location and penetration of this overlay occupies a different position in the relationship between university and polity in Continental Europe than it does in either the United States or Great Britain. In the former it tends to reside with the central administration, in the ministries of education or higher education. Penetrating downward from central authority to institution, it coordinates from the top down. By contrast, in the United States and to some extent in Great Britain, the structure occupying a functionally similar position is contained within the institution and acts as an extension upward between academia and the polity.

Important though the outer frame is, it is only one aspect of the complex linkages that tie academia together. The other aspect is represented by the inner environment, which in turn is profoundly influenced by patterns of work organization and the depth of the fissures dividing academic orders in Continental Europe. If, conceptually, inner environment and outer frame appear as separate dimensions in European academia, in practice they are closely related.

In Continental Europe, reform in the authority structures of the university reflected the inability of the chair-faculty structure to take sufficient initiatives at the institutional level to prevent the accumulation of discontent. Academia in those countries had little control of, and even less latitude to maneuver within, the outer frame of bureaucratic control. Remedies for discontent were sought nationally, and issues were fought at that level.

But it is too simple to suggest that bureaucracy in Continental Europe was simply a stultifying force that prevented flexibility in academia: it also acted as a vehicle by which reform was proposed, if not disposed, and it sought to head off accumulation of discontent inside academia. Further, we do not suggest that bureaucracy in Continental Europe was a leviathan, running roughshod over a helpless academia. In focusing on the divided house of academe, we did not declare that a divided house falls because of pressure from the polity. Instead, we suggested that some members of a divided house can pressure the polity and use it as an ally to bring about change. We further demonstrated that academia is not bereft of power when the ultimate responsibility for reform lies in the heartland of the inner environment, especially when the polity attempts to impose reform that is seen as a fundamental threat to academic values and to academia as a national estate. Refusal to take on a policy designed to promote the vocational commitment of the university showed the extent to which academia is capable of exercising control over its own house.

Notes

1. Here we are concerned only with academia inside the university; in the nonuniversity sector academic organization tends to differ from the chair-faculty structure. In Great Britain, for example, academic organization in polytechnics largely rests on formal rank hierarchy. For similar divisions in the French system, see chap. 3 of this volume. Here we focus on the university *stricto sensu*. See Becher, Kogan, and Embling, *Systems of Higher Education.*
2. This generalization applies only on balance; for some of the more ideologically motivated nonprofessorial malcontents, it was not true.
3. Neave, "University and the State in Western Europe"; "Strategic Planning and Governance in French Higher Education"; and "Higher Education and Regional Development"; Premfors, "Regionalization of Swedish Higher Education"; Lane, Westlund, and Stenlund, "Bureaucratisation of a System of Higher Education"; Bladh, "Trends Towards Vocationalisation in Swedish Higher Education"; and Cerych and Sabatier, *Great Expectations and Mixed Performance.*
4. See Van de Graaff et al., *Academic Power*. Also see Burton R. Clark, *Higher Education System.*
5. However, not each stratum or ranking is formally represented as a separate interest. Some have been folded into others or combined with them. In France there are seven ranks of academics; only three are formally represented constituencies.
6. Burton R. Clark, *Academic Power in Italy*, p. 78; Ben-David, *Centers Of Learning*, p. 17.
7. This must be distinguished from academic self-government since nonprofessorial academics have no voice in faculty deliberations. Faculties tend to be exclusive collections of professors.
8. Van de Graaff et al., *Academic Power.*
9. Burton R. Clark, *Higher Education System*, p. 114.
10. Rashdall, *Universities of Europe in the Middle Ages;* Reeves, "European University from Medieval Times"; and Verger, *Histoire des Universités Françaises.* In the Middle Ages "master" and "professor" were synonymous. See Baldwin, "Introduction."
11. Burton R. Clark, *Higher Education System*, p. 186–188.
12. Van de Graaff, "Great Britain."
13. A chairholder in Britain is often a department head, a permanent position.
14. In Britain almost 90 percent of probationers are granted tenure after three to five years. See Williams, Blackstone, and Metcalf, *Academic Labour Market*, p. 108. In the United States the tenure decision usually comes after six years. A far smaller proportion of candidates achieves this status, though variations exist among disciplines, institutions, and over time. See Cartter, *Ph.D.'s and the Academic Marketplace.* See also Finkelstein, *American Academic Profession.*

15. Burton R. Clark, *Higher Education System,* p. 108. This does not occur in all departments. The spirit of collegiality between junior and senior colleagues must sometimes shine by its absence.
16. Burton R. Clark, "United States." This refers to such units as the College of Arts and Sciences or the College of Fine Arts. Professional units at this level are called schools; for example, law school, medical school, school of engineering.
17. Some universities have college-level bodies composed of and controlled by academics who work with the administration in a species of dual structure. Such bodies traditionally have been limited to full professors and are more exclusive than inclusive.
18. Inherent tensions exist in the department-college structure, but the major one tends to be between academic staff and campus or systemwide administration. This is reflected in the unionization pattern in American academia: all academics, regardless of rank, are grouped against a common foe. However, unionization does tend to differentiate academics by institutional sector. For example, academics at California state universities are unionized; academics in the University of California system are not.
19. Rudolph, *American College and University; Perkin, New Universities in the United Kingdom;* Moodie and Eustace, *Power and Authority in British Universities.* Though the new universities in Britain sought to renew the medieval legacy by remodeling the lower levels of department and faculty by boards of studies or schools, these structures tend to operate like the predominant department-faculty structure. See also Beloff, *Plateglass Universities.*
20. Van de Graaff, "Great Britain"; Moodie and Eustace, *Power and Authority in British Universities.*
21. Villanueva. "Spain."
22. Salmon, "France: the Loi d'Orientation and its Aftermath."
23. Zeldin, "Higher Education in France, 1848–1940."
24. Ringer, *Education and Society in Modern Europe.*
25. This occurred in part because a deanship in Germany was an annually rotating position, whereas the doyen may have sat in splendor for as long as a decade at a time, a practice consistent with the independence and autonomy of French faculties. See Van de Graaff, "Federal Republic of Germany"; Van de Graaff and Furth, "France."
26. For example, a departing professor had little formal influence over the choice of his successor. The Habilitation not only gives the right to lecture independently within the university, it is also the sine qua non of full professorial status. Craig, *Scholarship and Nation Building.*
27. Before 1939 perhaps the most important part in filling professorial vacancies was played by the permanent section of the Higher Council for National Education (Conseil supérieur de l'Education Nationale) in conjunction with the Consultative Committee for Public Higher Education. After 1944 this function was performed by the Consultative Committee of the Universities. See Minot, *Quinze Ans d'Histoire des Institutions Universitaires.*
28. See Terry Clark, *Prophets and Patrons.* Any dichotomous typology, such as chair-faculty versus department-college structure, obscures important variations. Within France the cluster pattern exists in law faculties but does not operate as intensely as it does in arts and science and, particularly, medical faculties.
29. Terry Clark, *Prophets and Patrons;* Van de Graaff and Furth, "France."
30. Terry Clark, *Prophets and Patrons;* Van de Graaff, "Federal Republic of Germany"; Van de Graaff and Furth, "France"; and Hennis, "Germany." Such research benefits were not automatically accorded to chairholders in France. They were obliged to get outside funds usually from centralized research organizations such as the National Center for Scientific Research (Centre national de la recherche scientifique).
31. Terry Clark, *Prophets and Patrons;* Friedberg and Musselin, "Academic Profession in France," chap. 3 of this volume. The French patron also influenced the discipline; even within this informal and dispersed structure, cluster members were expected to organize their work to test and elaborate the basic hypotheses in the patron's oeuvre.
32. Terry Clark, *Prophets and Patrons.* This comparison ought not be carried too far. Many French cluster members held posts in establishments other than those of their patron; this may have diluted the dependency level compared to the German apprentice, who relied almost totally on his master during those years spent working with and under him.
33. Since this work organization pattern persisted for centuries without incident, without an outbreak of hostilities between these two latent groups, evidently some elements of these structures cushioned and counterbalanced such disparities, for instance, the shared commitment to research.
34. In the United States a recent example of the sanctions encountered by one who is perceived to have violated this ethic is revealed in the controversy surrounding the work of a historian, David Abraham. See *Chronicle of Higher Education,* 6 February 1985.
35. This definition is similar to Smelser's in "Growth, Structural Change, and Conflict in California Higher Education," and is founded on the institutional position of academics. But Smelser distinguished among various

academic estates according to position within the system: lower division (undergraduate) students, graduate students, teaching assistants, assistant professors, deans, chancellors, members of board of trustees, full-time research staff, and other groups. The definition we use refers only to teaching staff in institutions of higher education, whether professorial or nonprofessorial, tenured or nontenured.

36. If the university professor refers to his Fachhochschule colleague using the same title he accords his coeval it is often annoying to the former and frustrating to the latter.
37. Neave, "Regional Development and Higher Education."
38. Centre for Educational Research and Innovation, *University and the Community;* Neave, "University and the Community."
39. Gouldner, "Locals and Cosmopolitans"; Halsey and Trow, *British Academics;* Perkin, "Academic Profession in the United Kingdom."
40. Craig, *Scholarship and Nation Building.* Earlier, monarchs sought to turn aside proto-universities and to link them directly with training court officials. See Kamp, "Autonomy for Servicing Societies."
41. Svensson, "State and Higher Education"; Gruber, "Higher Education and the State in Austria." Many sociologists and historians tend to see the Humboldtian and Napoleonic reforms as the beginning of the university modern bureaucratic state association. See Archer, *Social Origins of Educational Systems;* Kuenzel, "State and Higher Education in the Federal Republic of Germany." This view is tenable only as long as one looks at France and Germany. The Humboldtian and Napoleonic measures stand as the end of a process whose origins can be traced to Sweden from the 1740s to the 1770s and to the Austria of Josef II.
42. Geiger, "Universities and the State in Belgium"; Malintoppi, "Italy."
43. Malintoppi, "Italy"; Neave, "France."
44. For a discussion of the public versus the private life of universities see Trow, "Public and Private Lives of Higher Education."
45. Kuenzel, "State and Higher Education in the Federal Republic of Germany." Religious foundations are an exception. See Geiger, *Private Sectors.*
46. In certain countries, particularly Scandinavia, familial academic dynasties are not unknown. See Conference des Recteurs Européenes Bulletin d'Information, "On the Perils and Rewards of Boldness."
47. Neave and Jenkinson, *Research on Higher Education in Sweden.*
48. Ringer, *Education and Society in Modern Europe;* Craig, *Scholarship and Nation Building.* Such fields as history, classics, and to some extent, philology, were instrumental in reasserting a claim to nationhood in such countries as Italy, Belgium, and the German states, which were previously divided, occupied, or both. See Kohn, *Idea of Nationalism.*
49. For the role of the professor as a figure of "total status" see Burton R. Clark, *Academic Power in Italy.* For a less kind but illuminating view of university intellectuals as political figures, see Thibaudet, *Republique des Professeurs.*
50. French ladder ranks distinguish between *maîtres assistants* and *assistants,* roughly the equivalent in Britain to lecturer and junior lecturer and in the United States to assistant professor and instructor. The former may be tenured, the latter is rarely so; this has not prevented some individuals from being assistants for up to eleven years, on a year-by-year renewal. In 1978 the Ministry of Higher Education placed a time limit of no more than five years on the period in which assistants could hold such a post and attempt to become qualified, to reduce the servitude if not the grandeur of such appointments.
51. Lane, "Power in the University."
52. Daalder, "Netherlands"; Strathopoulos, "New Greek Law"; Villanueva, "Spain."
53. See German University Affairs, "Commission Presents Results" and "Partial Revision"; Ministrie van Onderwijs en Wetenschappen, *Beleidsvoornemens.*
54. Neave, "Strategic Planning and Governance in French Higher Education."
55. Burton R. Clark, *Academic Power in Italy;* Lane, 'Power in the University"; Becher and Kogan, *Process and Structure in Higher Education;* Verger, *Histoire des Universités Francaises.*
56. Becher, "Cultural View."
57. See Burton R. Clark, "'Cooling-Out' Function in Higher Education."
58. Burton R. Clark, ed. *School and the University.*
59. See Burton R. Clark, ed. *School and the University.* The first signs of change in the social demand for higher education emerged in the late 1950s in Sweden; by the early 1960s they began to alter quantitatively as well as qualitatively the articulation between secondary and higher education throughout Western Europe. Generally, some 5 percent of the relevant age group entered higher education at the start of the decade, a figure which, by 1970, became 12 to 13 percent. See Cerych, Colton, and Jallade, *Student Flows and Expenditure in Higher Education,* 1965–1970. The situation was made more complex in the latter 1960s and early 1970s when the Italian government (1969) and the Belgian government (1973) initiated a policy of multiple validity for school-leaving diplomas (*omnivalence des diplômes*). Essentially, this measure involved making all high school certificates, including those from technical schools, valid for a place in higher education. This had two consequences. It first

removed an important element in the school-based screening process by opening up higher education to a new group of students who previously did not have access to the university. Second, it accelerated student demand for higher education, which already was growing rapidly.

60. Chevalier, *Classes Laborieuses et Classes Dangereuses.*
61. In Sweden, Britain, and the Netherlands they increased markedly but less rapidly. The fall in numbers in France over the period 1975–1976 and 1979–1980 is the result of the government's introduction of a rapid promotion policy for this order of the academic estate. Cross-national comparison raises severe methodological difficulties. Junior staff may be defined differently in each country, or certain categories—"lecturer" in Britain, for instance—may cover both the callow and the highly qualified, the aged respectable and the unqualified. Ladder ranks are also apt to change their designation over time, a development noticeable in Britain and France. For France, see Friedberg and Musselin, "Academic Profession in France," chap. 3 in this volume.
62. Student-staff ratios in British universities are particularly favorable compared to their Continental equivalent. In 1970 the student-staff ratio in Great Britain was 8.3:1. In Belgium it was 9.5:1; in Sweden, 17.2:1. By contrast, in France and Italy it was 24.1:1 and 38.9:1 (derived from tables 5.1 and 5.2). This calculation does not include part-time staff or students, nor does it discriminate between the very different ratios of various disciplines. Probably they err on the optimistic side, particularly in such countries as France and Italy that have a significant proportion of part-time staff. Were this to be taken into account, the contrast might be even more stark.
63. Salmon, "France: the Loi d'Orientation and its Aftermath." Giglioni, *Baroni e Burocrati.*
64. See Becher, "Disciplinary Shaping of the Profession," in this volume, chap. 6; Rothblatt, "Bearers of Civilization"; and Thelander, *Forsknarsutbildning som Traditionsformedling.*
65. Neave, "Elite and Mass Higher Education in Britain"; Trow, "Defining the Issues of University Government Relations." University finance in Britain was based on student numbers, and student financing was dependent on having been selected by academia for a place.
66. In the classic Tocquevillian situation, which bred revolution in France in 1789, one estate has partial access to the activities and rewards of another or does very similar work, but it is denied access to the full rewards of the higher estate. See de Tocqueville, *Old Regime and the French Revolution;* Smelser, "Growth, Structural Change, and Conflict in California Higher Education, 1950–1970," p. 67.
67. Webler, "'Student Movement in Germany."
68. Sontheimer, "Student Opposition in West Germany."
69. Kuiper, "How Democratic Is a Dutch University?"
70. On the SDS in Germany, see Hennis, "Germany."
71. In Sweden junior academics did not organize into separate bodies because major trade union organizations already enjoyed a legitimacy in discussions about national academic policy dating from the 1950s, if not before, and because secondary-school teachers, who were hired during the higher education expansion in the early sixties, actually enjoyed an enhancement of their previous status. In Britain, though a junior faculty–trade union alignment was attempted, it was a small minority movement. The modified chair-faculty structure and the countervailing constraints on professorial power at the department level were largely instrumental in preventing the buildup of tension between junior and senior orders within the British academic profession. See Hennis, "Germany." The AUT acted as a nonpolitical, professional association of university teachers. See Perkin, *Key Profession*, and "Academic Profession in the United Kingdom," chap. 1 in this volume. The representative association for Swedish academics was a broad-bottomed union federation operating on behalf of professionals, civil servants, and people with academic degrees. See Premfors and Ostergren, *Systems of Higher Education: Sweden.*
72. The two are not mutually exclusive, as the example of the Federal Republic of Germany shows. But to draw conceptual lines between them perhaps clarifies the concept.
73. Peisert and Framhein, *Systems of Higher Education: Federal Republic of Germany.*
74. Council of Europe, "Federal Republic of Germany."
75. Verhoeven, "Belgium."
76. Malintoppi, "Italy."
77. Bourricaud, "France."
78. Verhoeven, "Belgium"; Malintoppi, "Italy"; Council of Europe, "Italie."
79. Premfors, "Regionalisation of Swedish Higher Education"; and Lindensjo, "Högskolereformen en Studie i Offentlig Reformstrategi." The Swedish situation was somewhat different. Though student unrest was present and had been instrumental in ushering in the change, basic alterations to the chair-faculty structure had been introduced in a long-drawn-out series of reforms dating from the late 1950s. See Premfors and Ostergren, *Systems of Higher Education: Sweden;* OECD, *Reviews of National Policies in Education: Sweden.* The 1977 reforms were the last step in a

coherent strategy for structural and management innovation that ended the model of university power Sweden imported from Germany—the *Ordinarienuniversität.*

80. Salmon, "France"; Minot, *Quinze Ans d'Histoire des Institutions Universitaires.*
81. For this point see Friedberg and Musselin, "Academic Profession in France," chap. 3 in this volume, and Patterson, "French University Reform."
82. Salmon, "France."
83. Daalder, "Netherlands."
84. Minot, *Quinze Ans d'Histoire des Institutions Universitaires;* Akademischer Dienst, "Hochschulverband."
85. Svensson, "State and Higher Education."
86. Zeldin, "Higher Education in France, 1848–1940." See also Ringer, *Decline of the German Mandarins;* Suleiman, *Politics, Power, and Bureaucracy in France;* Ben-David, *Centers of Learning;* and *Neave, Nouveaux Modéles d'Enseignement Supérieur et Egalité des Chances.*
87. Neave, *Patterns of Equality;* Weizsäcker, "Hochschulstruktur und Markt-system."
88. See Lohmar and Ortner, *Doppelte Flaschenhals,* for a collection of articles on the "dual bottleneck." On the German labor-market linkage see Peisert and Framhein, *Systems of Higher Education: Federal Republic of Germany.* By the end of the 1970s, only 25 percent of higher education graduates found jobs in the public sector. See Teichler, "Recent Developments in Higher Education in the Federal Republic of Germany" and *Arbeitsmarkt für Hochschulabsolventen.* On France see Geiger, "Second-Cycle Reform and the Predicament of the French University"; Levy-Garboua and Orivel, "Inefficiency in the French System of Higher Education." Arts and science faculties had the largest enrollments and had long been geared to "internal reproduction"—educating people to staff the state school and university systems as well as the state administrative apparatus. See Boudon, "French University Since 1968."
89. Kuenzel, "State of Higher Education in the Federal Republic of Germany."
90. Peisert and Framhein, *Systems of Higher Education: Federal Republic of Germany;* Cerych, Neusel, Teichler, and Winkler, *German Gesamthochschule.* But Dahrendorf's prime interest was the expansion of educational opportunity, hence the title of his book, *Bildung ist Bürgerrecht* (Education is a Civil Right). Moreover, he believed reform sprang not from economic necessity, but from the need to ensure democratic evolution. See Mushaben, "Reform in Three Phases."
91. Cerych, Neusel, Teichler, and Winkler, *German Gesamthochschule.* A ministerial, not a federal government statement, this was a nonbinding declaration.
92. Peisert and Framhein, *Systems of Higher Education: Federal Republic of Germany;* Cerych, Neusel, Teichler, and Winkler, *German Gesamthochschule;* Kuenzel, "State of Higher Education in the Federal Republic of Germany."
93. Cohen, *Elusive Reform.*
94. See the chapter on France in this volume for a discussion of the makeup of study groups to design the courses. The presence of "outsiders" (like industrialists) attests to the government's desire to ensure that practical concerns were not ignored.
95. Geiger, "Second-Cycle Reform and the Predicament of the French University" and Cohen, *Elusive Reform.* This was one basis of strong student opposition to the measures. Some faculties previously practiced de facto selection, but the reforms threatened to make selection de jure. Students feared "juridical creep" of selection across the university.
96. Crozier, *Bureaucratic Phenomenon,* p. 239. French university education was overwhelmingly theoretical, giving little attention to experience. By vocationalization the government in part meant having university students put on *stages* in private enterprises (like the British sandwich courses, *stages* in France refers to periods of practical experience through job placement, interspersed with periods of coursework at the university). Even at the summit of French higher education, the grandes écoles do not provide specialized training in the sense of narrow skills-oriented study. But many do have students serve on stages. See Suleiman, *Politics, Power, and Bureaucracy in France* and "Myth of Technical Expertise." See also Millot, "Social Differentiation and Higher Education."
97. Neave, "The Dynamic of Integration in Non-Integrated Systems of Higher Education." There is a very strong anti-industrialist ideology among wide swathes of the academic estate. See, for example, Ringer, *Decline of the German Mandarins.* But the motives as well as the form this ideology takes tend to derive from differing assumptions in junior and senior staff. Gearing university studies to the private sector devalued or downgraded university education. See Patterson, 'Governmental Policy and Equality in Higher Education," for the argument that the 1976 second-cycle reforms in France amounted to "junior collegizing" French universities.
98. Peisert and Framhein, *Systems of Higher Education: Federal Republic of Germany.* See also Cerych, Neusel, Teichler, and Winkler, *German Gesamthochschule.* According to Cerych et al., the four comprehensive establishments set up in Bavaria "in no way correspond to even the most modest definition of this new organizational form" (p. 15). One other comprehensive institution, the *Fernuniversität,* is

effectively a counterpart of the British Open University.

99. See Cerych, Neusel, Teichler, and Winkler, *German Gesamthochschule.*

100. Gesamthochschulen in Nordrhein-Westfalen are designated "Universität." Unlike the Gesamthochschule Kassel in Hessen, they have been accepted as full members of the German Research Association in recognition of the academic, discipline-oriented work they do. See Cerych, Neusel, Teichler, and Winkler, *German Gesamthochschule,* pp. 32–33.

101. Salmon, "France: the Loi d'Orientation and its Aftermath," p. 92.

102. Cohen, *Elusive Reform,* p. 122. More students are choosing professionally oriented programs of study. See Furth, "New Hierarchies in Higher Education"; Bienaymé, "New Reform in French Higher Education." But changes in student preferences bear little correspondence to those of academic staff.

103. Bienaymé, "New Reform in French Higher Education"; Neave, "Strategic Planning and Governance in French Higher Education."

104. Cerych, "Higher Education Reform"; Bladh, "Trends Towards Vocationalisation in Swedish Higher Education." See also Burton R. Clark, *Higher Education System.*

105. Cerych, Neusel, Teichler, and Winkler, *German Gesamthochschule,* pp. 40–41.

106. Ibid., pp. 45, 47. For the details of the Bundesassistentenkonferenz comprehensivization plan see Federal Conference of University Assistants, *Kreuznacher Hochschulkonzept,* and "Integrierte Wissenschaftliche Gesamthochschule." A major concern of this plan was junior staff status and their work. See also Peisert and Framhein, *Systems of Higher Education: Federal Republic of Germany,* p. 121.

107. Mushaben, "Reform in Three Phases." By 1976 various academic associations representing left to right and junior staff to professors opposed the Gesamthochschule policy. See Mushaben, "The State v. the University." The earlier support in academia was mostly very general. For instance, in the early 1970s university committee resolutions generally supported the Gesamthochschule policy. But nowhere was the policy of integrating existing universities with technical colleges supported in practice. See Cerych, Neusel, Teichler, and Winkler, *German Gesamthochschule,* p. 42.

108. The Science Council dropped the idea in 1970 when visits to forty-five universities revealed heavy opposition. See Peisert and Framhein, *Systems of Higher Education: Federal Republic of Germany,* p. 119. Similar proposals in 1978 also encountered widespread and strong opposition by university academics. See Teichler, "Recent Developments in Higher Education in the Federal Republic of Germany," p. 166.

109. Boudon, "French University Since 1968." Staff and students were hostile to the reforms from different motives. For students the main sticking point was selection for admission to these new courses. For staff an additional factor was the vocational character of the proposed programs.

110. Geiger, "The Second Cycle Reform and the Predicament of the French University"; Cohen, *Elusive Reform.* In part the government did not provide additional resources because they wished to prevent universities from devising new courses simply as add-ons.

111. Neave, "Higher Education and Regional Development," and "Regional Development and Higher Education."

112. Neave, *Patterns of Equality.* Centre for Educational Research and Innovation, *University and the Community.*

113. Neave, *Strategic Planning and Governance in French Higher Education.*

114. See our earlier discussion of national diplomas. See also Neave, "France," and "Higher Education and Regional Development"; Fomerand, "French University"; Bienaymé, *Systems of Higher Education: France.*

115. Mme. de Sevigné, *Letters of Madame de Sevigné.* It is common reading in France, and until the sixties, this was one of the classic texts in most French lower secondary schools.

116. See Peisert and Framhein, *Systems of Higher Education: Federal Republic of Germany,* p. 121. See also our earlier discussion of the BAK.

117. The noble notion of education is linked with academic education. The distinctions between academic and vocational models are so marked that the status hierarchy is dichotomous rather than continuous. Academic institutions are on a different, more prestigious, plane than vocational institutions. If a university becomes practically and vocationally oriented, it is threatened with a step down the hierarchical ladder; this loss of status could even mean falling off the edge of the world or being relegated to a lower stratum of existence.

118. See Peisert and Framhein, *Systems of Higher Education: Federal Republic of Germany,* p. 119–121. These plans generated the strongest opposition from academics. The similar intention of the French government to promote "instruction" is evident in the renaming of the UERs to UFRs: Unités d'en seignement et de recherche (education and research) are to be renamed unités de formation de recherche (training and research).

119. Burton R. Clark, *Higher Education System;* Ruscio, "Many Sectors, Many Professions," chap. 8, this volume. In the United States observer examine colleges of letters and science as opposed to professional schools. For example, see Halpern, "Professional School in the American University," chap. 7, this volume.

120. The ways it does so depend largely on its precise internal elements. We have suggested that such elements are not merely budgetary and financial, but also extend to nominations to posts, confirmation of advancement, and conditions of service.

Bibliography

Akademischer Dienst. "Hochschulverband: Forderungen zur Änderung der Hochschulrahmengesetzes. " Bonn, 10 May 1983: 15.

Archer, Margaret. *The Social Origins of Educational Systems.* Beverly Hills, Calif. Sage Publications, 1979.

Baldwin, John W. "Introduction." In *Universities in Politics: Case Studies from the Late Middle Ages and Early Modern Period,* eds. John W. Baldwin and Richard A. Goldthwaite. Baltimore: Johns Hopkins University Press, 197?

Becher, Tony. "The Cultural View." In *Perspectives on Higher Education: Eight Disciplinary and Comparative Views,* ed. Burton R. Clark. Berkeley, Los Angeles, London: University of California Press, 1984.

Becher, Tony, and Maurice Kogan. *Process and Structure in Higher Education.* London: Heinemann, 1980.

Becher, Tony, Maurice Kogan, and Jack Embling. *Systems of Higher Education: United Kingdom.* New York: International Council for Educational Development, 1977.

Beloff, Michael. *The Plateglass Universities.* Rutherford, N.J.: Fairleigh Dickinson University Press, 1970.

Ben-David, Joseph. *Centers of Learning: Britain, France, Germany, United States.* New York: McGraw-Hill, 1977.

Bienaymé, Alain. *Systems of Higher Education: France.* New York: International Council for Educational Development, 1978.

_____. "The New Reform in French Higher Education." *European Journal of Education* 19, no. 2 (1984): 151–164.

Bladh, Agneta. "Trends Towards Vocationalisation in Swedish Higher Education." Monograph 16. Group for the Study of Higher Education and Research Policy, University of Stockholm, 1982.

Boudon, Raymond. "The French University Since 1968." *Comparative Politics* 10, no. 1 (1977): 89–119.

Bourricaud, François. "France: the Prelude to the Loi d'Orientation of 1968." In *Universities, Politicians, and Bureaucrats,* ed. Hans Daalder and Edward Shils. Cambridge: Cambridge University Press, 1982.

Cahiers de l'Avenir de la France. "Evolution du Ministère de l'Education Nationale: Elèves, Etudiants et Enseignants.'No. 1. Paris, 1984.

Cartter, Allan. *Ph.D.'s and the Academic Marketplace.* New York: McGraw-Hill, 1976.

Centre for Educational Research and Innovation. *The University and the Community: The Problems of Changing Relationships.* Paris: OECD, 1982.

Cerych, Ladislav. "Higher Education Reform: the Process of Implementation." *Educational Policy Bulletin* 7, no. 1 (1979): 5–21.

Cerych, Ladislav, and Paul Sabatier. *Great Expectations and Mixed Performance: The Implementation of Higher Education Reforms.* Stoke on Trent, England: Trentham Books, 1986.

Cerych, Ladislav, Sarah Colton, and Jean-Pierre Jallade. *Student Flows and Expenditure in Higher Education 1965–1970.* Paris: European Institute of Education and Social Policy, 1981.

Cerych, Ladislav, Åyla Neusel, Ulrich Teichler, and H. Winkler. *The German Gesamthochschule.* Amsterdam: European Cultural Foundation, 1981.

Chevalier, Louis. *Classes Laborieuses et Classes Dangereuses: Le Mouvement Social à Paris Pendant la Premiere Moitie du 19 Siècle.* Paris: Plon, 1969.

Chronicle of Higher Education. "Brouhaha over Historian's Use of Sources Renews Scholars' Interest in Ethics Codes." 29 (6 February 1985): 1, 9.

Clark, Burton R. "The 'Cooling-Out' Function in Higher Education." *American Journal of Sociology* 65, no. 6 (1960): 569–576.

_____. *Academic Power in Italy: Bureaucracy and Oligarchy in a National University System.* Chicago: University of Chicago Press, 1977.

_____. *The Higher Education System: Academic Organization in Cross-National Perspective.* Berkeley, Los Angeles, London: University of California Press, 1983.

_____. "United States." In *Academic Power: Patterns of Authority in Seven National Systems,* by John H. Van de Graaff, Burton R. Clark, Dorotea Furth, Dietrich Goldschmidt, and Donald Wheeler. New York: Praeger, 1978.

Clark, Burton R., ed. *The School and University: An International Perspective.* Berkeley, Los Angeles, London: University of California Press, 1985.

Clark, Terry Nichols. *Prophets and Patrons: The French University and the Emergence of the Social Sciences.* Cambridge, Mass.: Harvard University Press, 1973.

Cohen, Habiba S. *Elusive Reform: The French Universities, 1968–1978.* Boulder, Colo.: Westview Press, 1978.

Conférence des Recteurs Européenes Bulletin d'Information. "On the Perils and Rewards of Boldness." *CRE Information* 62 (1983): 87–95.

Council of Europe. "Federal Republic of Germany: Higher Education Legislation and Student Unrest." *Council of Europe Newsletter* 5, no. 77 (1977).

_____. "Italie: Relance de la Réforme Universitaire." *Council of Europe Newsletter* 2, no. 77 (1977).

Craig, John E. *Scholarship and Nation Building: The Universities of Strasbourg and Alsatian Society, 1870–1939.* Chicago: University of Chicago Press, 1984.

Crozier, Michel. *The Bureaucratic Phenomenon.* Chicago: University of Chicago Press, 1964.

Daalder, Hans. "The Netherlands: Universities Between the 'New Democracy' and the 'New Management.'" In *Universities, Politicians, and Bureaucrats,* ed. Hans Daalder and Edward Shils. Cambridge: Cambridge University Press, 1982.

Dahrendorf, Ralf. *Bildung ist Burgerrecht.* Hamburg: Nannen, 1965.

Department of Education and Science. *Statistics of Education.* Vol. 6, *Universities.* London, 1967, 1970, 1979.

Federal Conference of University Assistants. *Kreuznacher Hochschulkonzept, Reformziele der Bundesassistentenkonferenz.* Bonn, 1968.

_____. "Integrierte Wissenschaftliche Gesamthochschule." In *Die Schule der Nation,* ed. Klaus von Dohnanyi. Düsseldorf: Econ, 1971.

Finkelstein, Martin J. *The American Academic Profession.* Columbus: Ohio State University Press, 1984.

Fomerand, Jacques. "The French University: What Happened After the Revolution?" *Higher Education* 6, no. 1 (1977): 93–116.

Furth, Dorotea. "New Hierarchies in Higher Education." *European Journal of Education* 17, no. 2 (1982): 145–152.

Geiger, Roger L. "The Second-Cycle Reform and the Predicament of the French University." *Paedagogica Europaea* 12, no. 1 (1977): 9–22.

_____. "The Universities and the State in Belgium: Past and Present Dimensions of Higher Education in a Divided Country." Higher Education Research Group Working Paper, no. 29. New Haven: Yale University, 1978.

_____. *Private Sectors in Higher Education: Structure, Function, and Change in Eight Countries.* Ann Arbor: University of Michigan Press, 1986.

German University Affairs. "The Commission Presents Results: Suggestions for a Reform of University Structures." Vol. 29, no. 2 (1984).

_____. "A Partial Revision: Federal Minister Wilms Wants Swift Measures." Vol. 29, no. 2 (1984).

Giglioli, Pier Paolo. *Baroni e Burocrati.* Bologna: Il Mulino, 1979.

Gouldner, Alvin W. "Locals and Cosmopolitans." *Administrative Science Quarterly* 1, no. 2 (1957): 281–306; 444–480.

Gruber, Karl-Heinz. "Higher Education and the State in Austria: An Historical and Institutional Approach." *European Journal of Education* 17, no. 3 (1982): 259–271.

Halsey, A. H., and Martin Trow. *The British Academics.* London: Faber, 1972.

Hennis, Wilhelm. "Germany: Legislators and the Universities." In *Universities, Politicians, and Bureaucrats,* ed. Hans Daalder and Edward Shils. Cambridge: Cambridge University Press, 1982.

Kamp, Norbert. "Autonomy for Servicing Societies." Dossier of the VIIIth General Assembly of the Standing Conference of Vice-Chancellors, Rectors, and Presidents of the European Universities. Athens: Conference des Recteurs Européenes, 1984.

Kohn, Hans. *The Idea of Nationalism: A Study of its Origins and Background.* New York: Macmillan, 1961.

Kuenzel, Klaus. "The State and Higher Education in the Federal Republic of Germany." *European Journal of Education* 17, no. 3 (1982): 243–258.

Kuiper, R. J. "How Democratic Is a Dutch University?" In *A Decade of Change,* ed. A. Armstrong. Guildford, England: Society for Research into Higher Education, 1979.

Lane, Jan-Erik. "Power in the University." *European Journal of Education* 14, no. 4 (1979): 389–402.

Lane, Jan-Erik, Anders Westlund, and Hans Stenlund. "Bureaucratisation of a System of Higher Education." Report of the Department of Political Science, University of Umea, 1981.

Levy-Garboua, L., and F. Orivel. "Inefficiency in the French System of Higher Education." *European Journal of Education* 17, no. 2 (1982): 153–160.

Lindensjo, Bo. "Hogskolereformen en Studie i Offentlig Reformstrategi." Summary in English. Stockholm Studies in Politics, no. 20. Department of Political Science, University of Stockholm, 1981.

Lohmar, Ulrich, and Gerhard E. Ortner, eds. *Der Doppelte Flaschenhals—Die Deutsche Hochschule Zwischen Numerus Clausus und Akademikerarbeitslosigkeit.* Hannover: Schroedel, 1975.

Malintoppi, Antonio. "Italy: Universities Adrift." In *Universities, Politicians, and Bureaucrats,* ed. Hans Daalder and Edward Shils. Cambridge: Cambridge University Press, 1982.

Millot, Benoit. "Social Differentiation and Higher Education: The French Case." *Comparative Education Review* 25, no. 3 (1981): 353–368.

Ministrie van Onderwijs en Wetenschappen. *Beleidsvoornemens: Taakverdeling en Concentratie Wetenschappelijk Onderwijs.* 'sGravenhage: O & W, 1983.

Minot, J. *Quinze Ans d'Histoire des Institutions Universitaires, Mai 1968–Mai 1983.* Paris: Ministrie de l'Education Nationale, 1983.

Moodie, Graeme, and Rowland Eustace. *Power and Authority in British Universities.* Montreal: McGill-Queens University Press, 1974.

Mushaben, Joyce Marie. "The State v. the University: Juridicalization and the Politics of Higher Education at the Free University of Berlin, 1969–1979." Ph.D. diss., Indiana University, 1981.

_____. "Reform in Three Phases: Judicial Action and the German Federal Framework Law for Higher Education of 1976." *Higher Education* 13 (1984): 423–438.

Neave, Guy. *Patterns of Equality,* Windsor, Berks: NFER, 1976.

_____. *Nouveaux Modèles d'Enseignment Supérieur et Egalité des Chances: Perspective Internationales.* Luxembourg: Commission des Communautes Européenes, 1978.

_____. "On Wolves and Crises." *Paedagogica Europaea* 13, no. 1 (1978): 11–33.

_____. "Higher Education and Regional Development: An Overview of a Growing Controversy." *European Journal of Education* 13, no. 1 (1979): 207–231.

_____. "Regional Development and Higher Education." *Higher Education Review* 11, no. 3 (1979): 10–26.

_____. "The Dynamic of Integration in Non-integrated Systems of Higher Education." In *The Compleat University,* ed. Ulrich Teichler, Harry Herrmanns, and Henry Wasser. New York: Schenkman, 1983.

_____. "The University and the Community: A Critique." *Studies in Higher Education* 9, no. 1 (1984): 87–90.

_____. "The University and the State in Western Europe." In *The Future of Higher Education,* ed. David Jacques and John Richardson. London: NFER-Nelson, 1985.

_____. "Strategic Planning and Governance in French Higher Education." *Studies in Higher Education* 10, no. 1 (1985): 5–18.

_____. "Elite and Mass Higher Education in Britain: a Regressive Model?" *Comparative Education Review* 28, no. 3 (1985): 347–361.

_____. "France." In *The School and the University: An International Perspective,* ed. Burton R. Clark. Berkeley, Los Angeles, London: University of California Press, 1985.

Analysis and an Evaluation. Stockholm: Almqvist and Wiksell International, 1983.

Organisation for Economic Cooperation and Development. *The Development of Higher Education, 1950–1967.* Paris, 1970.

_____. *Reviews of National Policies in Education: Sweden.* Paris, 1980.

Patterson, Michelle. "French University Reform: Renaissance or Restoration?" In *University Reform,* ed. Philip G. Altbach. Cambridge, Mass.: Schenkman, 1974.

_____. "Governmental Policy and Equality in Higher Education: The Junior Collegization of the French University." *Social Problems* 24, no. 2 (1976): 173–183.

Peisert, Hansgert, and Gerhild Framhein. *Systems of Higher Education: Federal Republic of Germany.* New York: International Council for Educational Development, 1978.

Perkin, Harold. *Key Profession: The History of the Association of University Teachers.* London: Routledge and Kegan Paul, 1969.

_____. *New Universities in the United Kingdom.* Paris: OECD, 1969.

Premfors, Rune. "The Regionalization of Swedish Higher Education." *Comparative Education Review* 28, no. 1 (1984): 85–104.

Premfors, Rune, and Bertil Ostergren. *Systems Of Higher Education: Sweden.* New York: International Council for Educational Development, 1979.

Rashdall, Hastings. *The Universities of Europe in the Middle Ages.* 2d ed. Oxford: Oxford University Press, 1936.

Reeves, Marjorie. "The European University from Medieval Times." In *Higher Education: Demand and Response,* ed. W. R. Niblett. San Francisco: Jossey-Bass, 1970.

Ringer, Fritz. *The Decline of the German Mandarins: The German Academic Community 1890–1933.* Cambridge, Mass.: Harvard University Press, 1969.

_____. *Education and Society in Modern Europe.* Bloomington and London: Indiana University Press, 1979.

Rothblatt, Sheldon. "The Bearers of Civilization." Center for Studies in Higher Education Occasional Paper, no. 28. Berkeley: University of California, 1982.

Rudolph, Frederick. *The American College and University.* New York: Knopf, 1962.

Salmon, Pierre. "France: the Loi d'Orientation and Its Aftermath." In *Universities, Politicians, and Bureaucrats,* ed. Hans Daalder and Edward Shils. Cambridge: Cambridge University Press, 1982.

Sevigné, Marie de Rabutin-Chantal. *Letters of Mme de Sevigné to Her Daughter and Her Friends.* London: Routledge, 1937.

Smelser, Neil. "Growth, Structural Change, and Conflict in California Higher Education, 1950–1970." In *Public Higher Education in California,* ed. Neil Smelser and Gabriel Almond. Berkeley, Los Angeles, London: University of California Press, 1974.

Sontheimer, Kurt. "Student Opposition in West Germany." *Government and Opposition* 3, no. 1 (1968): 49–65.

Strathapoulos, Michael. 'The New Greek Law: Structure and Function of Higher Education Institutions." *CRE Information* (September 1984).

Suleiman, Ezra. *Politics, Power and Bureaucracy in France.* Princeton, N.J.: Princeton University Press, 1974.

_____. "The Myth of Technical Expertise." *Comparative Politics* 10, no. 1 (1977): 137–158.

Svensson, Lennart. "The State and Higher Education: A Sociological Critique from Sweden." *European Journal of Education* 17, no. 3 (1982): 295–306.

Teichler, Ulrich. *Der Arbeitsmarkt fur Hochschulabsolventen,* Munich: Saur, 1981.

_____. "Recent Developments in Higher Education in the Federal Republic of Germany." *European Journal of Education* 17, no. 2 (1982): 161–176.

Thelander, Jan. *Forsknarsutbildning som Traditionsformedling*. Department of History Report, no. 3. 2d ed. Lund, Sweden: Lund University, 1980.

Thibaudet, Albert. *La Republique des Professeurs*. Geneva: Slatkine Reprints, 1979.

Tocqueville, Alexis de. *The Old Regime and the French Revolution*. Garden City, N.Y.: Doubleday Anchor Books, 1955.

Trow, Martin. "The Public and Private Lives of Higher Education." *Daedalus* 2 (1977): 113–127.

_____. "Defining the Issues in University Government Relations—an International Perspective." Center for Studies in Higher Education Occasional Paper, No. 27. Berkeley: University of California, August, 1982.

Van de Graaff, John. "Great Britain." In *Academic Power: Patterns of Authority in Seven National Systems,* by John Van de Graaff, Burton R. Clark, Dorotea Furth, Dietrich Goldschmidt, and Donald Wheeler. New York: Praeger, 1978.

_____. "Federal Republic of Germany." In *Academic Power: Patterns of Authority in Seven National Systems,* by John Van de Graaff, Burton R. Clark, Dorotea Furth, Dietrich Goldschmidt, and Donald Wheeler. New York: Praeger, 1978.

Van de Graaff, John, and Dorotea Furth. "France." In *Academic Power: Patterns of Authority in Seven National Systems* by John Van de Graaff, Burton R. Clark, Dorotea Furth, Dietrich Goldschmidt, and Donald Wheeler. New York: Praeger, 1978.

Van de Graaff, John, Burton R. Clark, Dorotea Furth, Dietrich Goldschmidt, and Donald Wheeler. *Academic Power: Patterns of Authority in Seven National Systems.* New York: Praeger, 1978.

Verger, Jacques. *Histoire des Universités Françaises.* Toulouse: Privat, 1985.

Verhoeven, Josef. "Belgium: Linguistic Communalism, Bureaucratisation and Democratisation." In *Universities, Politicians, and Bureaucrats,* ed. Hans Daalder and Edward Shils. Cambridge: Cambridge University Press, 1982.

Villanueva, Julio. "Spain: Restructuring, Reform and Research Policy." *European Journal of Education* 19, no. 2 (1984): 193–200.

Webler, Wolff-Dietrich. "The Student Movement in Germany and Its Influence on Higher Education and Research." In *A Decade of Change,* ed. A. Armstrong. Guildford, England: Society for Research into Higher Education, 1979.

Weizsäcker, C. C. von. "Hochschulstruktur und Marktsystem." In *Der Doppelte Flaschenhals—Die Deutsche Hochschule Zwischen Numerus Clausus und Akademikerarbeitslosigkeit,* ed. U. Lohmar and G. E. Ortner. Hannover: Schroedel, 1975.

Williams, Gareth, Tessa Blackstone, and David Metcalf. *The Academic Labour Market.* Amsterdam, London, New York: Elsevier Scientific, 1974.

Zeldin, Theodore. "Higher Education in France, 1848–1940." *Journal of Contemporary History* 2, no. 13 (1967): 53–80.

The Crisis in Higher Education in Africa

SAMUEL O. ATTEH*

Introduction

Africa is experiencing an educational crisis of unprecedented proportions in higher education. Having been hailed in the 1960s as agent of modernization, social mobilization, and economic growth, most African universities are now tumbling down under the pressures of diminishing financial resources. From all indications, Africa is lagging behind other developing regions in terms of public expenditures particularly on education, availability of educational facilities, equal access to education, adequate pools of qualified teachers, and sufficient numbers of professionals and skilled workers. Pertinent data show that most African governments in the 1960s and 1970s made comparable progressive accomplishments in higher education. However, these accomplishments steadily disappeared in the 1980s. What went wrong in the 1980s? Why is higher education now such a convenient target for African leaders/governments, when pressured to trim their overextended public sector? To what extent is the lack of multiparty democracies affecting the deteriorating state of higher education in Africa? Is the declining importance attached to education in sub-Saharan Africa a reflection of the lack of education among Africa's tyrannical rulers, hence the low appreciation of education? What role did the foreign financial institutions play in the African educational system? How can we turn the educational crisis around? These questions not only address African educational issues but also help us to explain the scope of this crisis. In a comparative analysis, this study describes the main African higher educational problems, identifies the root causes of the problems, and finally examines the implications for the twenty-first century.

Major Problems and Issues in African Higher Education

Higher education is in deep crisis in sub-Saharan Africa. For the purposes of this paper, crisis is defined as a catastrophic situation that requires immediate action or solution. A review of pertinent data shows that the majority of sub-Saharan African countries now face declining public expenditure on higher education, deteriorating teaching conditions, decaying educational facilities and infrastructures, perpetual student unrest, erosion of universities' autonomy, a shortage of experienced and well-trained professors, a lack of academic freedom, and an increasing rate of unemployment among university graduates.

One of the most critical problems challenging higher education in Africa is the rapid decline in public expenditure on education relative to rapid increase in enrollments at higher educational level. Pertinent data show that, the allocation of public expenditure on education in forty-nine sub-Saharan African countries fell from $10 billion in 1980 to $8.9 billion in 1983, while school enrollments increased more than 50 percent.[1] Comparatively, military expenditures in most African countries have increased at faster rates than expenditures for basic

*Samuel O. Atteh is Program Officer for the International Foundation for Education and Self-Help (IFESH), Phoenix, Arizona.

human needs such as education, health, and shelter. For instance, between 1987 and 1990 the Nigerian military government spent N6.2 billion on defense while spending about N3.7 billion on education.[2] In 1983 Malawi, Nigeria, and Somalia each spent below 10 percent of their national budgets on education.

The decrease in governmental expenditure on education has caused strained relations between the state and the public consumers of education. Unlike educational funding systems in the industrialized countries, education has traditionally been the financial responsibility of African governments. Unfortunately, due to increasing economic and demographic pressures over the last one decade, African governments are now turning aggressively to parents, private organizations, and, increasingly to foreign donors to bear the heavy burden of the costs of education. The partial shift in the responsibility of the costs of education from government to family in particular has put an additional economic burden on the already poverty-stricken parents, most of whom are already struggling economically to make ends meet. Although in most countries, accurate information on the total amount of parent and private spending is not available, existing data clearly show that parents and non-governmental organizations bear a significant and growing portion of the financial burden of education in much of sub-Saharan Africa.[3] For example, studies show that between 1975 and 1980, private expenditure accounted for 14 percent of total national spending on education in the Sudan, 23 percent in Tanzania, 31 percent in Zimbabwe, 48 percent in Sierra Leone, and 53 percent in Ghana.[4] The decline in public expenditure on education has not only failed to sustain viable educational systems but has consequently contributed to the shortage of professional and skilled manpower in Africa.

Lack of sustainable educational policies is a major factor in the shortage of manpower, especially trained teachers, in most African countries. According to a World Bank study,[5] sub-Saharan Africa is facing an acute shortage of a wide range of professionals, particularly in the areas of effective policy analysis, policy formulation, policy implementation, research and development, engineering, technology, medicine, teaching, agriculture, and many other specialized areas of development process. Some of the causes of current manpower shortage crisis could have been averted in most African states if effective educational policies had been adopted since 1960s. For example, in the 1960s, the first decade after independence, there were only 90 African university graduates in all of Ghana, 72 in Sierra Leone, and 21 in Malawi.[6] Although these figures have increased significantly today, an acute shortage of professional manpower still exists due to inadequate training facilities in Africa. Rather than providing training facilities in Africa, many African governments in the 1970s and early 1980s, sponsored thousands of African students to European and North American universities where the students were trained in highly skilled professions but at exorbitant national expense. Ironically, many of these well-trained African professionals, most of them educators, have refused to return home after receiving their training. In fact, since 1986 there has been a mass exodus of highly educated Africans from the continent of Africa to Europe, the Middle East, Australia, and North America in search of academic freedom, respect for human rights, better working conditions, higher wages, and generally wider opportunities than those available in most African countries. The United Nations Development Programme (UNDP) has noted in its Human Development Report 1992 that:

> Africa has been hit particularly hard (by the loss of skilled workers). By 1987, nearly one-third of its skilled people had moved to Europe. Sudan lost a high proportion of professional workers: 17 percent of doctors and dentists, 20 percent of university teaching staff, 30 percent of engineers and 45 percent of surveyors in 1978 . . . In Ghana, 60 percent of doctors trained in the early 1980s are now abroad—leaving critical shortages in the health service. And Africa as a whole is estimated to have lost up to 60,000 middle and high-level managers between 1985 and 1990.[7]

Moreover, researchers estimate that over 70,000 Africans who were trained in Europe and North America remained there.[8] More than 10,000 Nigerians, most of them working in educationally related areas, are now residing in the United States.[9] Over 100,000 expatriates from Europe and North America are currently working in sub-Saharan Africa, mostly for the

World Bank, the United States Agency for International Development, and Development Organizations; this number is far greater than the one at independence in the 1960s.[10] More than $4 billion is being spent annually in Africa on foreign technical assistance, primarily for policy analysis and consultation.[11] In 1979, the rapid deterioration of the standard of living coupled with a reduction of real wages caused many of Ghana's skilled professionals—e.g., teachers, doctors, engineers, and civil servants to emigrate to other West African countries such as Nigeria, leaving Ghana with a shortage of human capital. Ghana's Water and Sewage Corporation, for example, had 90 engineers in 1979; only 20 remained in 1984. During the same period, the Ghanaian Ministry of Education lost about 10,000 staff members, most of whom were teachers. Subsequently, Nigerian government expelled about one million Ghanaian migrants in 1983[12]. The international emigration of indigenous professionals, generally referred to as "brain drain," has not only contributed to educational problems such as the scarcity of trained teachers in many African countries but has also reduced the capacity of most African governments to effectively manage their economies and make corrective development policies.

In higher education, the progress that had been achieved since independence in African university systems is seemingly now at the verge of total collapse. For example, the past three decades had witnessed a tremendous increase in the number of universities and other institutions of higher learning in Africa. In 1960, there were about 21,000 students in African universities, which increased to 437,000 in 1983. Additionally, over 100,000 African students were studying abroad during this approximately twenty-five year period. The number of universities increased from 80 in 1981 to over 150 in 1992. However, universities and other higher education opportunities are unevenly distributed in sub-Saharan Africa. For example, of the 54 countries in Africa, 10 are without a university and only 14 of the remaining 41 countries have more than one university.[13] Nigeria and Egypt have the largest university systems in Africa. There are more than 50 institutions of higher education in Nigeria including over 30 universities with a total of 100,000 students enrolled.[14] In spite of this accomplishment, the status of higher education in Africa today is chaotic.

Since 1985, most African universities have been characterized by perpetual student unrest, financial crisis, deteriorating work conditions, and slow progress in science, technology, and research. The once internationally extolled higher institutions of learning such as the Universities of Ibadan, Makerere, and Legon as centers of serious research and teaching in the 1960s and 1970s, are today more or less existing on their past reputations. These once reputable universities have been almost ruined by ill-advised and misguided government policies. For financial and political reasons, even the best many African universities now lack educational facilities and infrastructures that are necessary for effective learning. For example, since 1985, the Nigerian military government took many drastic actions to undermine the Nigerian universities by cutting university budgets, abolishing student scholarships and bursary awards, and paying little attention to the impoverishment of ill-equipped research facilities such as libraries and laboratories. Some Nigerian universities have acute shortages of classrooms and student dormitories. The University of Ibadan had a population of 14,000 in 1991 which is double the figure of 1972 without any addition to the institution's infrastructures.[15] Students lack adequate furniture for studying in the classrooms. Student dormitories are overcrowded, with an average of 8 students packed in a room meant for a maximum of 2 to 3 students. Scholarships and bursary awards usually set aside to assist indigent students have been scrapped by the federal government.[16] African university professors are underpaid compared to their counterparts in developed countries. Until October 1992, faculty wages had not risen in Nigeria since 1986 despite a 95 percent devaluation of the Nigerian currency and over 100% inflation rate.[17] Lower wages further restrict the teaching profession from attracting qualified teachers from abroad. Describing the worsening conditions in the University of Kinshasa, one commentator has this to say:

> Each school day students arrive for the first class at 4 A.M. in order to reserve a seat. At 6 o'clock the 250 seat amphitheater (60 seats are already out of use) are crammed with most of the 750 students registered for

> the class which begins at 8 A.M. Sometimes the teacher does not even turn up. The classroom is an oven, the air conditioners have broken down and ventilation is poor. In the dormitories the students are five per room and there is not enough space. The University Clinic is dirty, the building is surrounded by litter heaps."[18]

The above picture is a true representative of educational crisis in most institutions of higher learning in Africa.

Paralyzing educational policies have inspired and intensified riots against the state and general student unrest on African university campuses since 1986. As a result of several confrontations between university students and law enforcement agents, more students have been killed by the police under African regimes than under the colonial governments. In Nigeria, for example, about 21 major student riots occurred between 1948 and 1979, and over 3 dozen riots have taken place since 1980. These include the Ahmadu Bello University crisis of April 1986, the national student crisis of April-June 1988, the 1989 anti-structural adjustment programs riots and several other riots that took place between 1990–1993 on university campuses across the country.[19] In May 1992, the Nigerian Military Government ordered the closure of the Nigerian universities after six months of intensifying conflicts across the country.[20] During that period, hundreds of university professors were fired, imprisoned, and ejected from their government residences partly because of their alleged sympathy with students.[21] Between 1985 and 1993, more than 100 Nigerian students were killed by riot police using live ammunition on unarmed protesters during several student confrontations with law enforcement agents. During that period, about 1,000 students were imprisoned under harsh conditions; hundreds of students were suspended and expelled without fair hearings. In 1993–1994, at least 12 Nigerian university professors were arrested, some of them exiled, and the National Association of Nigerian Students (NANS) and the Academic Staff Union of Universities (ASUU) were banned by the military government.[22] In 1989 two school Ghanaian students were shot by police as they protested the imposition of school fees. Between November 1993 and 1994, about 3,700 university lecturers at Kenya's four public universities—Kenyatta University, Moi University, Egerton College, Nairobi University—went on strike because the government refused to register their University Academic Staff Union (UASU) under the Trade Union Act.[23] In fact, the University of Nairobi has been closed down more than 17 times for varying periods of times following student disturbances.[24] One scholar summarizes these abuses:

> [S]ome of the human rights abuses documented [against academics in Africa] include: summary execution of academics and . . . arbitrary arrest and prolonged detention without charge or trial; imprisonment under conditions that are cruel and degrading; restrictions on freedom of expression, assembly, association and movement; university closures; banning of student organizations and staff unions; the prohibitions of "political activity" on campus; discrimination against students on the basis of race, ethnic or regional origin; censorship of teaching and reading materials and manipulation of curricula. Lesser forms of coercion are also used as a means of intimidation, such as denial of promotions and tenure to outspoken academics; restrictions on travel abroad for research or meetings; refusal to grant scholarships to politically active students; and the requirement that students who have been implicated in political disturbances sign pledges of "good behavior" in order to resume their studies.[25]

The above quotation represents the seriousness of human rights abuses and lack of academic freedom in most African universities. Ironically, universities have always been the main place for African governments to turn when appointing their ministers, commissioners, advisers, consultants, and those who serve on the boards of corporations and parastatals. The persistent educational crisis on university campuses in sub-Saharan Africa has contributed to the flight of university professors to Europe and North America.[26]

Factors Contributing to Educational Crisis in sub-Saharan Africa

Many factors, both domestic and international, contribute to the current educational crisis in sub-Saharan Africa. These include colonial legacy, unfavorable terms of trade, declining agricultural productivity, lack of multi-party democracy, ineffective political leadership, population explosion, foreign debt, structural adjustment program, and decline in foreign aid.

To be discussed objectively, the root causes of the current educational crisis in Africa cannot be separated from their historical and social backgrounds.[27] With few exceptions from colonial rule, sub-Saharan African countries inherited educational systems that were fundamentally inadequate to support economic and technological needs for self-reliance in post-independence Africa. According to *Phelps-Stokes Report on Education*, the colonial regimes did not seriously consider education as a solid foundation on which other elements of development could be based.[28] Due to lack of sustainable colonial educational policies, post independence African governments inherited educational systems that were essentially neocolonial, weak, fragile, and to some extent, irrelevant to African environments.[29] Most importantly, these inherited educational systems were predominantly elitist in focus rather than vocational. In Africa today, there is a disproportionate number of grammar secondary schools to vocational, technical and polytechnic schools. The colonial and post colonial educational systems overlooked the fact that the training of middle-level technical human resources is critical to Africa's growth as African economy diversifies from an agricultural economy to an industrial and service economy. This lack of balance between elite schools and vocational schools has contributed to high unemployment rates among secondary school and college graduates who cannot find gainful employment in today's modern economy. Like their colonial counterparts, African governments are still the largest employers of secondary school and university graduates, most of them working in the civil service, parastatals, schools, colleges, and universities. Any massive retrenchment of government employees could have serious adverse effects on the educational system. Furthermore, the elite school system has contributed to rural-urban migration problems, as these students have received elite type of education that has little relevance to the rural environment.

Many development analysts blame the root causes of the underdevelopment crisis in Africa on ineffective political leadership.[30] They blame the educational crisis on domestic factors for which they strongly believe African leaders are primarily responsible. Analysts assume that the fundamental causes of poverty, economic stagnation, and educational crisis in the developing countries exist within African indigenous socioeconomic structures and institutions. They point out that the consequences of political mismanagement are reflected in ineffective political leadership, the nature of economic mismanagement, massive spending on symbolic projects, widespread corruption, unproductive development schemes, total neglect of agriculture, inappropriate development policies, lax implementation policies, administrative and technical inefficiencies, ethnic politics, religious conflicts, and political instability. Truly, African leaders bear considerable responsibility for the continent's current predicaments; however, we must also accept the fact that the realities that underlie corruption, poor economic performance, institutional fragmentation, and educational decay result from the nature of the external connection. Indeed, African countries and their leadership have been the victims of superpower rivalry, economic exploitation, military intervention, trade imbalances, and dubious loan practices. Any analysis that focuses on domestic factors as the only causes of educational crisis in Africa is ahistorical.

The current educational crisis in sub-Saharan Africa reflects the critical economic deterioration in Africa. Basically, the incorporation of Africa's weak economy into the global market economy contributes to chaotic educational systems. Since the 1970s, Africa's economic choices have been constrained by the structure of the international economy. At the time of independence, most African states were economically weak due to the international division of global economy. Three and half decades after obtaining independence, most African economies are still characterized by an agrarian economy, the exportation of raw materials, low wages, low savings, low capital accumulation, and a low industrial base. As a result of this weak economic base, African nations have become powerless to compete effectively in the global market. Fluctuations in world prices have had detrimental effects on foreign exchange earnings and hence on the economy. For example, the average decline in terms of trade for sub-Saharan Africa between 1970 and 1979 was 14.5 percent. From 1970 to 1980, all of Africa's principal mineral exports, such as oil, copper, and iron, suffered an annual average decline in nominal price of 18.7 percent. The prices of cocoa and coffee, traditionally two of Africa's most important exports, have been in continual decline since the 1970s. Between 1970 and 1980, many African countries, such as Ethiopia, Somalia, Sierra Leone, and Benin, lost 35 percent of the purchasing power of their exports. Mauritania and Liberia lost 40 percent, while Zaire and Zambia lost more than 50 percent due to worsened terms of trade.31 Since the 1980s, sub-Saharan Africa's terms of trade have declined by 10 percent and, consequently, the region accounts for less than 2 percent of all world trade. Market instability and declines in the terms of trade mean reduction in foreign revenue and reduction in public expenditure on education and other social services. These socioeconomic and political problems have made African nations fragile and powerless, and have inhibited their abilities to provide for the educational needs of the young people.

Decline in agricultural productivity and falling per-capita income in the 1980s did not only mean a decline in national revenue but also a significant reduction in individual incomes, which consequently had adverse effects on the financing of education. With the exception of Nigeria's, Congo's and Gabon's oil economies, sub-Saharan Africa's dominant source of income and employment is agricultural. Shortly after gaining independence in the 1960s, agriculture accounted for over 90 percent of employment and national revenue in most African countries. Currently, agriculture accounts for 72 percent of employment and approximately 40 percent of the value of the continent's exports and 33 percent of its GDP. Due to greater agricultural production in the 1960s, in terms of living standards most Africans were better off then than they are today. However, as a result of the decline in agricultural productivity, per capita food production has declined, food imports have increased by 8 percent per year, while food aid has decreased by 7 percent per annum. Currently, about 100 million Africans, mostly women and children, are malnourished. The decline in agricultural productivity and low prices in the world market have contributed to the reduction in the annual budget allocation for education and other vital social services. For example, as a result of the decline in agricultural productivity, Senegal's real social spending per person fell 48 percent from 1980 to 1985 while Somalia's per capita spending fell by 62 percent from 1980 to 1986. Also, due to the decline in agricultural productivity, the main source of support for both government and individuals, especially to the majority of people in the rural areas, has been reduced significantly. The decline in agricultural productivity as the main source of income has caused hardship for parents unable to bear the financial responsibility of their children's education.

Another major factor in the sub-Saharan Africa educational crisis is population explosion. It is a phenomenon that is having tremendous repercussions on the region's physical resources and on social services such as education, health, and nutrition. The current world population is 5.6 billion, 700 million of which are in Africa. Africa is the region with the fastest rate of population growth, with the population of sub-Saharan Africa doubling since 1965. Between 1985 and 1990, Africa had the highest population growth rate at 3.1 percent, compared with 2.34 percent in South Asia, 2.09 percent in Latin America, 0.23 percent in Europe, 0.90 percent in the United States, and 0.70 percent in Canada. Some African countries have population growth rates even higher than the 3.1 percent average. For example, Malawi, Tanzania, Zambia, Kenya, Côte d'Ivoire, and Nigeria, are growing at about 3.5 percent a year. Every year, Africa's school age population increases by 5 million because more than 50 percent of Africa's population is below the age of 20. Population growth has many advantages when it is related to economic growth. However, rapid population growth without comparable economic growth may result in increased incidents of malnutrition, especially among women and children. Additionally, rapid population growth may lead to more widespread poverty due to the scarcity of gainful employment, to the rise in debt burdens due to increased social spending, to an increase in the number of school-age children, to a rise in the illiteracy rate, and to the degradation of the environment.

The high population growth rate in Africa has caused explosive demands for education at all levels. It has increased the number of school-age children seeking admission to schools with limited resources to absorb them. Consequently, school enrollment rates have stagnated or declined and illiteracy rates have increased. Especially in urban areas—such as Lagos, Nigeria, where over 5 million people reside—population explosion has put major economic pressure on governments. The rise in the school-age population has caused a high demand for education which has drained resources. For example, the implementation of universal primary education was not supported by a strong, stable national income and consequently has caused enormous problems in Nigeria. As a result of the population factor, most African governments can no longer cope with the increasing costs of running schools, hiring qualified teachers, supplying books, and providing instructional materials.

With increasing debt and debt servicing for most African countries, financing education is increasingly difficult. Africa is one of the most indebted continents in the world. The current total debt of Africa as a whole is about $300 billion, with 45 percent of debt servicing.[32] Out of this $300 billion, $130 billion, or 42 percent, of Africa's debt is owed by the North African countries, namely Egypt, Algeria, and Morocco. Sub-Saharan Africa currently owes $170 billion, with $28 billion of that owed to private banks, the majority of them in Europe; the rest is owed to the multilateral institutions such as the World Bank, International Monetary Fund (IMF), and Western governments. African debt is very small by world standards, as Latin America owes three times as much as Africa. The significant difference is the increasing inability of sub-Saharan African countries to service their debts, not to mention their inability to pay the principal loan. For example, Africa's total debt in 1983 was less than that of Brazil alone and only slightly higher than that of Mexico. Nigeria alone currently owes about $45 billion. Adding to the basic complexity of debt, having embarked on heavy borrowing of foreign loans in 1970s, Zaire, under the Mobutu administration, could not give an accurate accounting of how much it owed and to whom.[33] Some African countries that are heavily indebted to the IMF, World Bank, and private international commercial banks include Sudan, Zaire, the Congo, Gabon, Ghana, Nigeria, Côte d'Ivoire, Zambia, Kenya, Tanzania, Cameroon, Madagascar, Guinea, Ethiopia, and Senegal. The average debt service ratio for these countries is more than 35 percent. In 1983, Sudan spent about 150 percent in debt service, Togo 80 percent, and Côte d'Ivoire 40 percent. Arrears in interest payments on Africa's debt to creditors increased from $1 billion in 1982 to $11 billion in 1990. The total foreign aid to the region in 1989 was $21 billion, yet debt servicing alone was $25 billion and the net outflow of capital from Africa was $30 billion between 1983 and 1990. As a consequence of their heavy debts owed to international financial institutions, and their increasing inability to pay, most African states are losing their sovereignty.[34]

Debt crisis has subsequently placed some African governments under the tight control of powerful financial institutions. Many of these African nations are under constant pressure from international financial organizations such as the World Bank and IMF, as well as from many Western governments, to restructure their economies through the Structural Adjustment Program (SAP).[35] The IMF and the World Bank, working through the SAP, have pressured most African states to privatize their economies, devalue local currencies, and cut down on employment spending. In these countries, educational policies, social programs, and foreign trade policies are influenced by the officials of the IMF and the World Bank. These financial institutions sometimes dictate how much money should be spent on education, whether the establishment of additional universities is necessary or not, and whether scholarships and students bursary awards should be awarded. The SAP has influence on government decisions to close down industrial plants, fire or retrench government employees, and devalue local currency. For example, with no discernible success in making the country pay its debt in 1985, the World Bank and IMF took over the Zairian government's key economic positions:

> Since the results of the first two stabilization plans were so meager, the IMF and the

> World Bank decided in 1978 to send their own teams of experts to Zaire to take over key financial positions in the Bank of Zaire, the Finance Ministry, the Custom Office, and Planning.[36]

Many analysts worldwide have interpreted the actions and policies of these powerful international creditors concerning African countries as a recolonization of Africa.

From primary to university levels, debt burden accompanied by SAP has played a major role in Africa's current educational crisis. In keeping with the policies prescribed by the IMF and the World Bank to restructure African education, such pressure on most African governments has led to the deterioration of education in Africa. The implementation of SAP has worsened an already bad situation in some African countries where educational facilities are decaying and where due to inflation the real value of wages can hardly sustain a teacher. Educational crisis in these countries has resulted in malnutrition among school children due to cancellation of government food subsidization. Devaluation of African currencies has pushed the costs of education beyond the reach of an average African by increasing the overall costs of education—nutrition, books, and specifically, the costs of educational equipment. Furthermore, the implementation of the SAP by African governments implies a deep cut in educational budgets, closure of loans and credits to indigent students, reintroduction of school fees, deep cuts in funds to universities, increased inflation, and high rates of unemployment. As a result, the structural adjustment policies have contributed to the inability of the universities to conduct research effectively, to pay professors' salaries, and to equip laboratories and libraries. Many parents have been laid off or retrenched due to the implementation of SAP policies. SAP has created high rates of employment, pushed up inflation rates, and increased the cost of living. Imported educational supplies can no longer be purchased due to inflation and debt service. Consequently, many parents are unable to finance the education of their children. Students, faculty, and many other people concerned about African education have resisted the SAP. The resistance in many cases has led to open confrontations between the masses and the governments implementing SAP policies. Cases of riots precipitated by implementing the IMF prescriptions have been recorded in Zambia, Sudan, Algeria, and Senegal.[37] The food riot in Zambia in 1986 led to several deaths. On March 26, 1990, approximately 127 Ivorian teachers and professors protesting SAP-inspired tax increases were arrested after the government announced a ban on all meetings throughout Côte d'Ivoire.[38] In May 1989, protests and riots against the government's structural adjustment program took place in a number of Nigerian cities. Prompted by food shortages and rising prices, the string of protests was sparked by a university student protest in Benin City, Nigeria, during which at least approximately 22 people were killed by the police.[39] Kenya has recently decided to fight the IMF to regain its sovereignty. In general, SAP has exacted monumental social costs in employment, education, and nutrition. A country's inability to maintain social institutions has direct devastating effects on education.

The end of the cold war has also had adverse effects on educational systems in Africa. As political relations between the East and West improved in the post-cold war era, economic disparities and technological gaps between the North and South seem to have widened. Since the Second World War, much of the economic assistance to Africa has been inspired by the ideological rivalry between the East and West. The Soviet Union used to be a major financial, military, education, and technical donor to sub-Saharan Africa. The Soviet Union provided aid to countries such as Angola, Ethiopia, Mozambique, Zambia, and Sudan in different forms at different times. Thousands of Africans have studied in the Soviet Union. However, the end of East-West ideological struggle had also come to mean reduction in foreign aid to Africa. The Group of 7 (G-7) is moving its resources, investments, and capital to revitalize the economies of the countries in the former Soviet Union, Asia, and the Middle East rather than African nations. Consequently, closure of credit lines and of opportunities for external support to African education has increased. Foreign aid to Africa dropped from $2 to $3 billion in 1982 to $900 million in 1989. The 49 sub-Saharan African nations received $616 million in 1991. Israel with a population of about 4.3 million received more U.S. foreign aid than the more than 550 million people of sub-Saharan Africa. As a result of the decline of foreign assistance to Africa, many African governments had to cut down their education budgets in order to meet other social services to the public.

Implications and Conclusions

What are the implications of the current educational crisis in sub-Saharan Africa and how can this crisis be reversed? Lack of sustainable education systems in Africa in this competitive global system will mean increased illiteracy, increased political instability, population explosion, increased poverty, declines in skilled manpower, lower levels of technology and industrialization, increased human rights abuses, declines in agricultural productivity, heightened civil unrest, and increased tribal conflicts in twenty-first century Africa. All this will further threaten the building of the emerging new world order.

In spite of the numerous problems identified in this study, education analysts believe that prospects for education development in sub-Saharan Africa still exist because the continent holds such wealth of natural resources. What is lacking, and needs immediate attention, however, is effective political leadership for effective educational policies. African governments must renew their commitments to providing qualified teachers and sufficient quality educational facilities and curricular materials and supplies. To reverse the educational crisis, African governments must commit themselves to bettering governance, improving administrative and political structures, supporting democratic institutions and processes, curbing mismanaged economies and wasteful spending, diversifying economies for both domestic and external markets, initiating improvements in certain social conditions that undermine productivity, widespread corruption, asking for debt forgiveness, and slowing down the population growth. Unfortunately, African nations have limited technical and financial resources to tackle all these problems by themselves. African people and governments need financial and technical assistance from foreign donors and organizations to alleviate their educational crisis.

Notes

1. World Bank, *Education in Sub-Saharan Africa: Policies for Adjustment, Revitalization, and Expansion*, Washington, D.C.: World Bank, 1989, p. 12.
2. Julius Ihonvbere, "The State of Academic Freedom in Nigeria." Paper presented at the conference on Africa and Global Human Rights in honor of George Shepherd, Jr., and Edward Hawley. The Radisson Hotel, Denver, Colorado, May 7–9, 1992. p. 30.
3. World Bank, *Education in Sub-Saharan Africa: Policies for Adjustment, Revitalization, and Expansion*, Washington, D.C.: World Bank, 1988, p. 101.
4. World Bank, *Education in Sub-Saharan Africa: Policies for Adjustment, Revitalization, and Expansion*, Washington D.C.: The World Bank, 1988.
5. World Bank, *The African Capacity Building Initiative Toward Improved Policy Analysis and Development Management in Sub-Saharan Africa.* Washington, D.C., World Bank, 1991; For a critique of this study, see C. George Caffentzis, "The World Bank's African Capacity Building Initiative: A Critique. Committee for Academic Freedom in Africa *Newsletter*, New York: Hofstra University: no. 6, Spring 1994, p. 14.
6. "The Education Crisis," *West Africa* (5 September 1988) p. 1622.
7. United Nations Development Programme (UNDP), *Human Development Report 1992*, New York: Oxford University Press, 1992, pp. 56–57.
8. On the impact of "brain drain" in Africa, see World Bank *The African Capacity Building Initiative*, op. cit., Washington D.C.: 1991; p. 12.
9. Ibid., p. 12.
10. Ibid., p. 5.
11. Ibid., p. 5.
12. Stephen D. Younger, *Successful Development in Africa: Case Studies of Projects, Programs, and Policies*, Washington, D.C.: World Bank 1989, p. 138.
13. See Chucks Iloegbunam, "In Deep Crisis," *West Africa* (Dec. 13, 1993, no. 3977), p. 2248.
14. Cafa, "Violations of Academic Freedom in Nigeria," *Committee For Academic Freedom in Africa's Newsletter*, no. 3 (Fall 1992) p. 9.
15. See Chucks Iloegbunam, "In Deep Crisis," *West Africa* (December 13, 1993, no. 3977), p. 2248.
16. "Decay of Universities," *The Nigerian Economist* 4. 15 (29 April, 1991), p. 12; See also M. M. Zaki, "Private Enterprise and Nigerian University Libraries: The Ahmadu Bello University Example," African Research and Documentation: London (No. 59/60), pp. 21–24.
17. Ibid., p. 8.
18. See Baffour Ankomah, "Students in Ferment," *New African* (May 1989) pp. 9–10.

19. Edwin Madunagu, *The Tragedy of the Nigerian Socialist Movement and other Essays* Nigeria: Centaur Press, 1980. pp. 29–30.
20. "Nigeria's Economic Crisis Sparks Violent Protests On Many Campuses," *Chronicle of Higher Education*, 27 May 1992, p. A33.
21. "NASU Strikes Paralyses Activities in Varsities, Polytechnics," *The Guardian* (Lagos) 10 November 1992.
22. Richard Carver, *Africa Report* (July/August 1991).
23. Ihonvbere, op. cit., 1992, p. 16.
24. *New African*, January 1980, p. 28.
25. Cafa, "Violations of Academic Freedom in Nigeria," Committee For Academic Freedom in Africa, (Newsletter) no. 3 (Fall 1992), p. 9.
26. See "What Concerned Nigerians Should Know about the Crisis in Our University System," a newsletter distributed by the Academic Staff Union of Universities, National Secretariat, Nigeria, July 20, 1992.
27. W. Rodney, *How Europe Underdeveloped Africa*, Washington, D.C.: Howard University Press, 1974.
28. L. J. Lewis, *Phelps-Stokes Report on Education in Africa*, London: Oxford University Press, 1962.
29. Fredrick James Clatworthy, *The Formulation of British Colonial Education Policy, 1923–1948*, University of Michigan Comparative Education Dissertation Series, Number 18.
30. World Bank, *Sub-Saharan Africa: From Crisis to Sustainable Growth, A Long Term Perspective Study*. Washington, D.C.: World Bank, 1989, p. xii.
31. John Ravenhill, "Africa's Continuing Crises: The Elusiveness of Development" in John Ravenhill, ed., *Africa in Economic Crisis*, London: Macmillan, 1986, p. 4.
32. Thomas M. Callaghy, "The Political Economy of African Debt: The Case of Zaire," in John Ravenhill, ed., *Africa in Economic Crisis*, London: Macmillan, 1986, p. 317.
33. Ibid, p. 317.
34. Ibid., p. 3089.
35. Sippanonfha Ketudat, "The World Bank and Education: Reflections of a Partner," *Canadian International Education*, 12. 1 (1983), p. 45.
36. Callaghy, op cit., p. 32.
37. J. Loxley, *Debt and Disorder*, Boulder: Westview, 1986.
38. Carver, op cit., pp. 57–59.
39. Ibid., pp. 57–59.

Reform at Mexico's National Autonomous University: Hegemony or Bureaucracy

IMANOL ORDORIKA

Abstract. Mexico's National Autonomous University (UNAM) is the most important higher education institution in this country. Although there seems to be broad consensus on the need for a profound transformation of this University, most attempts in the last 25 years have failed to generate the required reforms. The limitations and obstacles for university reform at UNAM are analyzed in this article. The established power relations and the bureaucratization process are identified as the main political and structural limitations for change. The dominating system at UNAM is analyzed in a historical perspective emphasizing the cultural elements in the conformation of the dominant discourse and alliance. Confrontation and conflict within the University and against external power structures are traced in this historical analysis and exhibited as permanent components in the modern history of UNAM. The existence of a legitimacy crisis in the governance structure of this University is argued in terms of the erosion of the prevailing dominating system, expressed in the open manifestation of inherent contradictions through social conflicts directed against the bureaucracy; the permanent challenge to rules, regulations and established procedures; the lack of academic leadership; and the internal dissent and the deficient articulation within the dominant block. Finally, the building of a new hegemony at UNAM (through a redefinition of the concept of university reform, the reconstruction of the social fabric, the establishment of new constituencies, a rebuilding of collegial relations, and the founding of a new pact with the Mexican State), is shown to be a unique path towards university reform.

Introduction

There seems to be unusual consensus in modern society around the need for reform in universities and institutions of higher education. In a context in which knowledge and technology change with amazing speed, these institutions appear to be conservative and bound to traditions and ineffective practices. Public and private sectors apply much pressure in the direction of financial and administrative change. University authorities blame faculty and students for the immobility of higher education.

This paper argues that the crisis of higher education in Mexico is essentially a consequence of the lack of academic leadership and legitimacy of governing bureaucracies. These authorities have internalized the external demands for change but have been incapable of outlining a reorganization of academic disciplines, a modernization of goals and tasks, and a democratic reform of governance structures. In their eagerness to maintain control over the institutions of higher education, bureaucracies have prevented faculty and students from conceptualizing and putting into practice these kinds of reforms. Bureaucracies have obscured the critical issues of modern university life. They have exercised power in a such a conservative fashion that the present condition of university bureaucracy appears as a clear obstacle for reform in higher education.

This social phenomenon is very evident in the case of Mexico's National Autonomous University (UNAM). The weight of this institution within the country and the magnitude of the bureaucratization process makes its study particularly relevant. The National University is the most important institution of higher education in Mexico.[1] The strong impact of the UNAM on Mexican society is based on its long historical tradition, its moral authority, its prestige, and the presence of its alumni on the most important professional, academic, political and governmental institutions throughout the country for many decades. This University has established the main features of the public higher education system in Mexico. Most of the public universities have attempted to emulate its best attributes and have reproduced its worst characteristics. Although the centrality of the National University has diminished with the expansion of the public system, significant changes at the UNAM deeply affect the rest of the universities and many other institutions in Mexico.

The political nature of university reform and the legitimacy of the transformation process are emphasized throughout this paper. It attempts to expose the myths about the neutrality and the apolitical nature of the University as a mechanism to exclude faculty and students from the process of reform.

This article is part of a broader research on the issues of governance and reform in Mexico's National Autonomous University. The main objective is to identify the causes that explain the lack of structural change at the UNAM, to understand the most important obstacles to transformation, and, by doing so, suggest alternative mechanisms for change.

Why Worry?

Since the beginning of the 1980s the debate over educational issues in Mexico has increased. This is particularly true with regard to public higher education. During the same period of time the discourse has shifted from an emphasis on "educational planning", to the "educational revolution" and presently, to the "modernization of education".

These terms represent the synthesis of diverse educational policies of the Mexican government in different epochs. During the presidency of Luis Echeverria (1970–1976) there were many resources to distribute. The State invested heavily in public higher education with the fundamental purpose of closing the breech between urban middle sectors and the State opened by the 1968 student movement. From 1976 to 1982, during the José López Portillo presidency, an economic crisis required the revision of public expenditures. Investment in public higher education was still large but new requirements were established to rationalize this investment and organize educational institutions. The corresponding official discourse was that of "educational planning". During the presidency of Miguel de la Madrid the financial crisis worsened and structural adjustment policies were adopted. Investment in public education was reduced drastically. This retrenchment was paradoxically called "educational revolution". Carlos Salinas' discourse was centered on the "modernization" of the educational system. As in De la Madrid's period, the main argument was the quest for quality, even at the expense of reducing educational opportunity for many Mexicans. The emphasis was placed on administrative efficiency (Martinez and Ordorika 1993).

In this context, public higher education institutions have been severely judged and questioned. The evaluation is oblivious of the historical contribution of these institutions to national development. The difficult conditions in which they operate are largely ignored when analyzing their overall performance.

Failure To Reform

From the 1970s on, the Mexican government has imposed diverse policy directives upon the National University. These matters have determined the future of this institution in a decisive way. At the beginning of the decade, enrollment expansion and institutional growth, complemented with political control, were the basic requirements. This policy generated an enormous bureaucratization of the University. In the late 1970s, in the midst of a severe economical crisis, the government demanded institutional change, with administrative efficiency as the main objective.

Until now, there has been a refractory attitude towards structural change that can adapt the National University to the contemporary needs of the Mexican society. By structural university reform, I mean one that produces changes to the structure of work and the organization of academic disciplines, and transforms the structure of governance. I am speaking of structural change: organizational (adjustment of educational levels and modalities), government styles, democratization of power, and academic policies. That is, change that deeply alters the traditional relations between members of the university and those of the institution with society.

In the last twenty years, four different University administrations have failed in their intent to transform the UNAM. These attempts have been: the proposal to change the University's General Statute by rector Guillermo Soberón in 1979; rector Octavio Rivero Serrano's "University Reform," in 1983; the modification of the regulations for registration, exams and tuition by rector Jorge Carpizo in 1986–1987; and the unsuccessful venture to raise tuition by rector José Sanikhán in 1992.

In 1979 Guillermo Soberón tried to institutionalize the changes he had generated in the university. These changes can be summarized as the geographic scattering of some university components, increased centralization of decision making, the reduction in the autonomy of faculties and schools within the university, and the subordination of collegial authorities to bureaucratic power.

Soberón stratified the massive institution into two different universities within the UNAM. One would be a small high quality university, with an increasing amount of resources, based on graduate education and research institutes and centers. The other one was to be an enormous, lower quality, resource limited institution concentrated in the baccalarate and undergraduate levels in schools and faculties.

The University Council was set to approve a new General Statute in which these relations would be legalized and a new vision of the University would be sanctioned. Important sectors of the university openly expressed their rejection of this project. APAC, the association of tenured, full-time faculty members strongly opposed most of the articles of the project for a new General Statute. The rector's initiative was stopped by a student movement during the legislation process.

Nevertheless, some of the changes had already been put in place and although they were never legalized they became common practice in the following years. As we will see later, many of the changes put forward by Soberón embodied a partial structural transformation and redefined the internal relations within the university. However, the reform did not address most of the academic concerns and thus failed to reorient the educational performance of UNAM.

In 1982 the Mexican government started to implement structural adjustment policies designed by the IMF and the World Bank.[2] One of the consequences of these policies was the reduction of investment in public education. The pressures on the UNAM were still not very strong. Octavio Rivero Serrano's period as a rector was characterized by its immobility. At the end of his first term as rector, Rivero attempted a process of reform that would guarantee his designation as rector for a second term. The reform was centrally designed and included a long process of legitimation by local and central collegial authorities. Rivero was not reappointed because his administration was characterized as conformist and unwilling to go far enough with the restoration projects of the most conservative sectors of the academic bureaucracy. As a result this reform process was truncated.

In the past decade the Mexican State has gradually abandoned its accumulative and distributive role in the economy. By 1984 the Mexican State was in the midst of a redefinition of its role in the distribution of resources and intervention in society. Social expenditures have been severely cut following the structural adjustment dictates of the IMF and the World Bank (World Bank Report 1990). The Mexican government has increasingly embraced a neo-liberal discourse and practice.

The adoption of neo-liberal policies has generated an enormous scarcity of resources for public higher education. In the UNAM, rector Jorge Carpizo put forward a set of reforms which essentially embodied a retrenchment project argued as a "quest-for-excellence". Beyond the discourse, the project represented a conservative, efficiency-oriented, managerial response to financial scarcity (Cameron 1983). University authorities tried to comply with the new privatizing policies of the Mexican government.

Until this point most reform attempts had been essentially designed and decided in a centralized process controlled by the university administration. Participation by the faculty and students was restricted to a legitimating role with little opportunity to propose initiatives or reverse previously established decisions. I will characterize these as **bureaucratic** attempts to reform.

The 1986–87 student movement generated a strong demand for participation in the process of reform. This was crystallized when the student and faculty demand for a University Congress was reluctantly accepted by the university bureaucracy and the Mexican government.

The only recent participatory experience for University reform, the 1990 University Congress, was frustrated by the Mexican government and the university authorities during the first Sarukhán administration. The Congress was characterized by an intense confrontation between important sectors of faculty and students against the Mexican government and the University authorities.[3] The result was a stalemate on the most important issues, such as finance and governance of higher education. Implementation of the most important agreements that the Congress produced has been blocked by the bureaucracy and after more than two years these have not been put in practice.

I characterize this, and other experiences in which the driving force for transformation has been faculty and/or student social movements and their external alliances as **democratic** reforms.

The latest attempt to produce changes in the institution also took place during the first period of rector Sarukhán in 1992. It is also inscribed in the bureaucratic practice of retrenchment and essentially tried to raise tuition costs transferring the main responsibility of financing public higher education institutions from the State to the students. The attempt was stopped once again by a strong student response.

The Obstacles to Structural Transformation

Identifying the factors that have prevented the transformation of Mexico's National Autonomous University (the UNAM) is the paramount motivation of this paper. The main concern is to understand what are the most important limitations for structural transformation.

Some literature tries to answer this question by establishing that universities are conservative institutions; that faculty possess strong resistance to change; that higher education can only develop gradually; or that the objectives of university reform are excessively ambitious (Cerych 1987). Other authors propose that universities in Latin America have assumed this conservative stereotype when attempting internal changes (Garcia 1982; Levy 1988). Such an attitude contradicts a traditional anti *status quo* external position that frequently permeates this type of institution (Lipset 1975).

For a full understanding of the current problems of the Mexican university it is necessary to realize that the dynamic of the university is determined by internal and external, political and economic factors. The university is part of a social system and there is a permanent tension between the external and the internal. There are very complex interaction mechanisms. These are expressed in diverse spheres and frequently produce flagrant contradictions (Brunner 1985).

The University is part of the power structure of society. Because of this condition, the relations with the government, with diverse groups, and with social actors can be conflictual or complementary. At the internal level, the university is the site of active struggle for institutional control (Muñoz 1989). Problems associated with University governance are necessarily the origin of almost every *campus* conflict, many of which pursue a different distribution of power (Wolff 1970; Becker 1970).[4]

This perspective on universities and the social power structure suggests that "the main obstacles to change are the product of the lack of legitimacy of most of the mechanisms used to orchestrate the reform and/or the incapacity to establish agreements among the diverse political actors in the university scenario" (Muñoz 1990, 58). That is, in a terrain in which most of the initiatives for change are contested, the vertical and centralized procedures used by university authorities to transform the institution are unable to generate the necessary consensus within the university community. At the same time, the authorities have been unwilling to undertake a process of discussion and negotiation with contesting groups to produce a general agreement about university reform.

The main impediments to a structural transformation are therefore political. To understand this situation we have to focus on power relations within the university and the intense and complicated interdependence with the Mexican government. These two matters are interwoven in a complex system of domination. The system itself represents the articulation of relatively heterogeneous political groups within the university and their counterparts and relations in the Federal government. These groups share similar interests and are bounded together by a powerful discourse[5] and a dominating view of the university.

The domination is institutionalized in a powerful bureaucracy. This bureaucracy represents its social base and at the same time is relatively independent from it and, in some occasions, even from the Mexican government.

In summary, the main concern is the issue of change. It is important to look at this problem from a political perspective by analyzing how internal and external power relations have created obstacles to structural transformation at the UNAM. Power relations and struggles within a campus can only be understood when viewed as interwoven with those in the broader society. The internal-external distinction is extremely problematic (Gumport 1993). In this case it is strictly methodological and the focus will be placed on the interactions between these dimensions. These relations are mediated by a dominant alliance. The objective is to understand this social alliance and the way in which it mediates these power relations.

UNAM: Power and Autonomy

Throughout the history of Mexico's National University after the Mexican Revolution the relations between the University and the Mexican State have played a very important role. Taking these relations into account we can roughly and schematically define three periods. From 1917 to 1944 the University assumed a conservative attitude and clashed against the populist policies of the post revolutionary governments. In 1929 the National University was granted autonomy from the government. The independence of the university varied according to the magnitude of the confrontation between this conservative institution and the State. During this epoch the university government shifted frequently from collegial structures to an extreme and almost dictatorial bureaucratic-political system.

The period from 1944 to 1968 is often called the "golden years" of the university. The Mexican government abandoned most of its populist projects and the conservative groups within UNAM closed the gap with the Mexican State. The new pact between government and University was symbolized by the 1944 Organic Law and the construction of the University City in the 1950s. Collegial structures were established but these were severely limited by bureaucratic and political bodies.

The third period goes from 1968 to our days. It is characterized by its conflictual nature. The problematic relations between University and State and the struggles within this higher education institution heavily determine the present situation at UNAM. This paper is focused essentially on the third period.

History of Confrontation

In 1968, during the student movement, the UNAM maintained the highest degree of autonomy in all its history. It was precisely in this confrontation against the government and in the middle of a great social movement that the bureaucratic and collegiate authorities assumed a truly independent attitude towards the State.

The Mexican student movement was militarily destroyed by the government after the killing of hundreds of students in 1968.[6] These events shocked the Mexican society. People within the universities were particularly bewildered by the experience. In the midst of this overwhelming defeat, the students turned their attention, and their action, to the University itself. In the early 1970s students and teachers from several faculties produced some important reforms of local governance structures and procedures, and, to a lesser extent, changes in the curricula. Also as a consequence of the 1968 student movement, teachers and workers in universities began the formation of unions.

These transformations generated strong and permanent conflicts between the government and university community. The State had great interest in controlling these conflicts and overcoming the breach, opened by the student movement, between the government and intellectuals, most of whom resided inside the universities. This interest generated a two-tiered governmental policy towards the UNAM: (a) a very important increase in financing, and (b) the construction of a huge bureaucratic apparatus to control every aspect of university life.

The Conservative Reaction

Another consequence of the 1968 student movement was an extensive debate about the renewal of public higher education. At the end of Javier Barros Sierra's term and during the rectorship of Pablo González Casanova there was an attempt to reexamine traditional values and generate new definitions about the university. During these years (1969–1972) the democratic discourse about the university was emphasized. The importance of the education function and the political autonomy of the university were stressed. The need for an integral university reform that went beyond the inertia of tradition to transform higher education into a motor for political democratization, a socially just economic development, and cultural modernization was promoted strongly by the Barros Sierra, and González Casanova university administrations (Kent 1990). In practical terms these definitions meant an expansion of the higher education system, an increase in academic quality, and the democratization of university life.

The first administrative worker's strike (STEUNAM) and the violent occupation of the rectory building by Castro Bustos and Falcón in 1972[7] hastened González Casanova's resignation, a consequence of Luis Echeverria's government lack of support for the rector of the UNAM.

The unionization process and the progressive trends for reform generated a strong conservative reaction among die-hard power groups within the UNAM. The professional organizations linked to the faculties of medicine, law and engineering, which traditionally controlled the institution, realigned themselves under the leadership of Guillermo Soberón. Rector Soberón represented the conservative and defensive attitude of important sectors of faculty against the unionization process and the politicization of the University. These conservative groups, essentially based on the natural and exact science disciplines, were the internal base for the government's control policy.

The authoritarian process that developed since 1972 consolidated a new social formation that has dominated the UNAM until this moment. This does not mean that the actors are new. Most of the original components of this formation had been part of the university for a long time. Some had direct linkages with the constitutive moments of the modern university (1929 and 1945) through family or political group bonds. As we said before, the schools of medicine, law and engineering provided the broader base of faculty members for the new administration. The relatively new groups in the Coordination of Scientific Research provided the new cohesive element between those traditional parties.

Soberón was the representative of this conservative tendency. He was able to structure a dominant discourse and articulate a broad alliance in the course of the confrontation against SPAUNAM (UNAM's Faculty Union) and STEUNAM (UNAM's Employee and Worker's Union), and the local transformation movements in the faculties of Sciences, Economy, Philosophy, Psychology and Architecture. This discourse stressed the neutral and apolitical nature of the UNAM, the presence of external threats, and the technical nature of university governance.

The most important transformation that concluded in the consolidation of the bureaucracy occurred during the two consecutive administrations of Dr. Guillermo Soberón (from 1973 to 1980) as rector of the UNAM.

Two central elements synthesized Soberón's project for the University. The first one was to guarantee the stability of the institution. The second was to stop the expansion of enrollment and the consequent growth of the UNAM (Kent). The most important problems for the re-establishment of institutional rules were anarchy, unionization, violence, and enrollment expansion (Soberón 1980).

He associated the idea of anarchy to the existence of social and political movements. The unionization process was part of this anarchy. The conflict about labor relations within the university created a "state of crisis in public universities generating lack of stability, and opening the space for issues that have nothing to do with universities or the labor relations within them" (Soberón, 12). A consequence of this anarchy was the eruption of violence on campus as a manifestation of purely criminal actions or the expression of student activism (Soberón).

The other important problem for the new administration was the increasing growth in student enrollment. It was an undesired trend. The Soberonian administration looked forward to stopping this expansion and even to reducing enrollment.

The Stratification of UNAM

The stratification of the UNAM played a very important role in dealing with massive enrollment and in the redefinition of the university elite. The segmentation of the University, into an elite research and graduate studies institution, and a massive preparatory and undergraduate institution within the same University, was done essentially through differentiated investment. The financial resources for research institutes and centers, mainly in the natural sciences area, increased substantially while those of the schools and faculties decreased. The research mission of the UNAM was emphasized in public statements while the teaching goals were placed at a secondary level. The differentiation between teaching and research activities was emphasized. Schools and faculties were discouraged from implementing research activities through lack of investment. Most faculty members in these locations fled towards the institutes or simply abandoned research. At the same time, research institutes and centers established their own graduate programs. In many cases these were parallel to similar graduate programs that existed in the faculties. The first were considered programs of "excellence" and received abundant financial resources. The latter were lower level programs, detached from research activities and with very limited resources.

Beyond the academic implications of this model, we will look at some of the political consequences of this segmentation. The strengthening of the research sector redefined the force correlation within the University elite with the expansion of one of the most conservative sectors at the UNAM. It consolidated Soberón's closest constituency and broadened its political base. This project also had ideological implications. The new social formation was viewed as supported on scientific knowledge and activities. The academic excellence was the foundation of the new governing coalition.

Rollin Kent summarizes the conservative group's worst fears and their project for UNAM. From a Soberonian standpoint, this particular view had

> good motives to think that the university of the 50s and 60s was disappearing as a consequence of the explosive growth of the student population, the strengthening of the left-wing parties and the emergence of the unionization process. These factors seemed to generate a situation in which political agitation would become a permanent feature of university life and therefore a threat to the interests and *modus vivendi* of those university sectors that had flourished in a quickly disappearing context. There were several possible responses towards this situation. The response of Soberonism defined itself by highlighting the deactivation of the political and educational potentiality of the massive zones and by developing the research sector. It was an option that did not perceive the massive university as a cultural challenge, as the requirement to promote educational innovation, it perceived it fundamentally as a challenge in the political sphere (Kent, 66).

The Creation of a Saga or the Selection of Traditions

With this project in mind, and for the purpose of articulating a powerful alliance Soberón recreated the university saga (Clark 1983): He was able to select episodes within the history of the university to establish a dominant tradition (Williams 1977). By reconstructing and reinterpreting the history of the university he established a new legitimacy. These selected traditions articulated in a unique discourse contradictory episodes of the historical development of the UNAM. Most of the views held by Soberón are summarized in his book *La Universidad, ahora* (1983).

The new social alliance was able to present itself as a product of the autonomy movement of 1929 depriving it of original content provided by the antigovernment student struggles that conquered autonomy. Other consequences of this struggle, such as shared governance of students and faculty, were criticized by Soberón. The unresolved demands for democratic election of university officials and against the external intervention of the government in appointing authorities were not compatible with Soberón's ideal University and were therefore forgotten.

The new alliance was viewed also as the incarnation of the Organic Law of 1945 from which it took its legal legitimation. For Soberón, the 1929 autonomy was a "precarious" law because "it gave the President of the Republic the faculty to propose three candidates to the University Council from which it had to appoint the Rector" (Soberón 1983; 107). On the other hand,

> the 1933 Organic Law went beyond by granting total autonomy, nevertheless, it subjected the University and condemned it to indigence, because it determined that it should obtain its own financial resources after an initial ten million pesos handed by the government (p. 107).

For the new Soberonian alliance, the 1945 Organic Law provided the basic ideological foundation of a conservative modernization as opposed to a democratizing transformation of the university as proposed by González Casanova (Kent). From Soberón's standpoint, the essence of the 1945 Organic Law was the differentiation between political and academic issues within the university. In 1945 rector Alfonso Caso insisted that the University had been severely damaged by politics. When proposing the 1945 Organic Law he argued that it withered politics away from the institution by organizing university governance through a combination of legislative and executive authorities whose actions were constrained to the academic realm (Caso 1944).

This discourse served the conservative groups perfectly. The new formation argued that politics had no place in an academic institution. Politics were condemned as a negative and anti-university practice. In reference to university conflicts Soberón wrote:

> It must be understood that even when the cause of a university conflict can be evident, it can never be fully established if there are perverse intentions of political nature or of clear anti-university character behind statements that originally can be judged of a purely academic or administrative nature. On other hand, these polluting factors are attached at the first chance, because everybody wants to 'bring water to his mill.' Do not forget that the UNAM has played and will continue playing a relevant role in the development of Mexico and it constitutes an agent of social mobility; therefore, in every conflict it is said that, in the beginning and later, national or extra national interests that are opposed to the development of the institution can come into the game (p. 106).

Political intentions are therefore perverse and against the nature of the university. This vision provided the new dominant alliance with the perfect excuse to toughen the practice of the bureaucracy in the bargaining processes with diverse internal social actors and justify the repressive attitude during conflicts within the university. At the same time, this discourse excluded most of the members of the university from politics while reserving this arena, at the internal and external levels, for the bureaucracy and the upper echelons of the governing elite.

With this idea of the UNAM as an apolitical institution, the events of 1968 were brushed aside. The democratization processes generated by previous rectors (Barros Sierra and González Casanova) were reversed in the name of academia.

The "menaces" of the "anarchic and anti-academic" consequences of the 1968 were symbolized by the emerging unions. In the presence of this "enemy" the traditional conservative tendencies of the university were able to regroup and acquire a solid identity around these selected, and now dominant, traditions.

The selected traditions, the discourse of apoliticism and neutrality, the response to the external threat, and the technical nature of university governance configured a new ideology within the UNAM. The selection of traditions provided the historical rooting of the new ideological discourse. This ideology provided the new governing alliance with a solid common identity that enhanced its internal articulation. The ideological discourse of the Soberonian coalition played the most important role in the confrontation with the democratic opposition which was unable to put forward a coherent opposing view of the University. The dispute for faculty and public opinion support was essentially a confrontation between this views. The Soberonian ideology was of major importance in the downfall of the democratic opposition. In this process it became a dominating ideology that was consolidated with the ultimate defeat of independent faculty unionization and it was used to solidify the hold of the conservative bureaucracy over the UNAM's political structures.

The Bureaucratization Process

From 1970 to 1980 the bureaucracy expanded rapidly. The growth rate in this sector (239%) was higher than that of students (188%) and faculty (227%) (Kent).[8]

At the same time this bureaucracy diversified in two dimensions: at the level of the academic bureaucracies and at the level of the administrative and political-bureaucratic structures. The first are the structures that directly manage the academic units (programs, departments, schools, faculties and research institutes). They are also the link between these units and the central administration. Rollin Kent argues that "these academic bureaucracies constitute the visible heads of the academic power groups within the university" (p. 98). They emerge from the immediate academic sphere, their formal attributions and their legitimacy are determined by the management of the units themselves.

The creation of new schools, faculties or programs was the source of the expansion of this sector. From 1974 to 1977, the creation of the National Schools of Professional Studies (ENEP's) within the UNAM provided employment for more than 500 officials (deans, academic secretaries, chiefs of division and department, coordinators technical secretaries and administrative officials) (Kent).

> In 1980, 5,170 appointed employees worked at the UNAM. We consider that at least 50% were officials (if for each official there is a secretary or a technical aide). Therefore a labor market for more than 2,000 people, organized in dozens of bureaucratic groups, was formed (p. 101).

These academic bureaucracies are very important political actors in the University as a whole. The academic, administrative and political performance of these groups is heterogeneous within the limits established by the central bureaucracy. The academic bureaucracies are recruiting sources for the central administration. "This link, of political nature, is a strong cohesive element of the whole apparatus" (p. 99).

During this period the political bureaucracy also expands and diversifies at the central level. The University is configured as a system with the stated purpose of acquiring administrative rationality and efficiency. The institution is reorganized into six subsystems (Jimenez Mier y Terán 1983):

- Schools and faculties controlled by the Academic Secretary General.
- Scientific research (natural and exact sciences research institutes and centers) under the Scientific Research Coordinator.
- Humanities research (social sciences and humanities institutes and centers) under the Humanities Coordinator.
- Administrative work under the Administrative Secretary General.
- Legal issues under the General Attorney (of the University).
- Internal and external issues, communication, media, etc. under the Secretary of the Rectorship.

Schools and faculties lost their identities and independence and were gathered in a unique block at the same level of hierarchy as administrative and legal affairs. The legal and political systems (General Attorney and Secretary of the Rectorship) were consolidated. All of these officials and the chairs of several committees are appointed by the rector and depend directly on him (Kent).

At the same time, and in spite of the expansion of the university, the collegial authorities (University and Technical Councils) were not reformed to enhance their representation and functions. These structures were almost reduced to the level of formal legitimators of bureaucratic decisions (Jimenez Mier y Terán).

Bureaucratic growth was the material base for the formation of political clienteles. These constituted a very important element in the solid consensus that rector Guillermo Soberón was able to articulate. At the same time, this process created new channels of political mobility within the University and therefore enhanced and strengthened the career of professional university officials. Rollin Kent argues that the bureaucratic expansion served a cast of officials whose increasingly autonomous interests and performance positioned them above the academic rationale of the University as a whole and the different entities within it (Kent).

Bureaucratization and Political Control

The reaction against the process of unionization and collective bargaining was one of the most important features in consolidating the bureaucratic aspect of governance at the UNAM and the progressive decline of collegiate authority with the reduction of faculty participation in the decision-making processes (Birnbaum in Bensimon 1984).

The task of controlling the University after 1968 enhanced the bureaucratic and political features of governance and administration within the UNAM. The latter was emphasized by the authorities' need to establish powerful coalitions to be able to counteract the action of students, faculty, and manual and administrative workers within the University. After almost a decade of union struggles the defeat of the academic union SPAUNAM after its merge with the staff union STEUNAM into STUNAM in the 1977 strike opened the way for the new governing alliance.

At the structural level the formation was able to consolidate its power. Soberón deprived the collegial authorities of their independence from the bureaucracy. On the basis of the particularities of the process for selecting governing board members (similar to the appointment of supreme court judges in the US), he was able to ensure an overwhelming majority on this board for the next fifteen years. This board selects the directors (deans) for the schools, faculties and research institutes among three candidates proposed by the rector. They in turn represent more than one third of the University Council, who, in turn, appoints the substitutive members of the governing board.

Bureaucratic authorities assumed political power. Collegiate (University council and technical councils) and political authorities (governing board) were thus reduced to a subordinate and legitimizing role. This situation can be illustrated at different levels. On one hand, Soberón strengthened a parallel structure called the Council of Directors composed by the deans of schools, faculties and institutes and the directors of the central administration. This structure is not sanctioned by the Organic Law. It combines authorities selected by the governing board and other directly appointed by the rector. Since deans and directors depend directly from the rector for their selection or reelection he has strong control over this governing structure. The Council of Directors deals with most of the crucial issues for the performance of the UNAM. Some of the decisions made by this body are then turned to the University Council for formal approval.

The University Council has been excluded from decisions like the establishment of enrollment limits. Other issues like university budget and expenditures are decided by the executive authorities and presented to the Council for official sanction. In the last twenty years no University Council has made any change to the budget proposal presented by the rector.

This situation is reproduced at the local level between deans and technical councils. At this site, the decisions about budget and expenditures are of the exclusive competence of the dean in each school or faculty. In the research institutes the collegial authorities, Internal Councils, have no power of decision and are consultation structures for the dean.

Other members of the University and Technical Councils, representatives of students and faculty, are elected by their communities. It has become a tradition that deans and local bureaucracies intervene in this election processes to guarantee that the elected representatives are politically compatible with the local authorities and therefore with the central administration. This complex circle of control is so completed.[9]

University Bureaucracy and the State

As we have seen previously, the new dominant formation at UNAM condemned politics as a anti-university practice. However, the leading bureaucracy was very far from the Weberian ideal of an apolitical specialized administrative corpus. Both the central and the local bureaucracies have been intensely involved in internal and external political processes. At the internal level, in the dispute of power positions, the local groups within the dominant alliance confront each other and generate pressure upon the rector and the governing board for the selection of deans and rector. Confrontation and bargaining processes also take place in the appointment of secretaries and general directors at the central level, or local officials in schools, faculties and institutes.

It has been common practice that external interest groups within the government intervene in these power disputes within the University. If anything, this intervention increased during the Soberón era. After the 1968 events, the University has been seen by the government as a major political problem. The political conditions at the UNAM have been part of most political considerations during the last presidential periods (Luis Echeverría, José López Portillo, Miguel de la Madrid, and Carlos Salinas de Gortari). This situation has strengthened the linkages between internal and external political actors.

Broad sectors of faculty and students still maintained a confrontational attitude against the government. The Soberonian formation was able to generate the idea that the State and the conservative groups in the UNAM had common enemies within the University. The dominant groups abandoned any vestige of their old anti-State tradition and joined the government in a common project for UNAM. The alliance that now dominated the University was able to outline their own conservative view as the only path for the development of this higher education institution. The government adopted that view as its own project for UNAM.

The Soberonian alliance pursued their own academic and political interests. Since the UNAM had reached the political importance of a ministry, the bureaucracy within this institution inserted itself in the political process at the national level. The performance of selected and appointed officials at every level was constrained by their particular political needs within the national political context. Perhaps this situation can be best illustrated by following the political careers of some of the most important officials during the Soberón, Rivero Serrano, and Carpizo administrations.

Our study shows nine important members of the Soberón administration, two from Rivero's period, and three from Jorge Carpizo's rectorship, who occupied high level positions in the Federal Government. This is only a small sample. There are many mid-level officials, general directors, and deans that have also occupied positions in the government after leaving the UNAM. Most of them never go back to their academic positions in the University, if they ever had one before being part of the bureaucracy. The study also shows that most appointed officials are members of the PRI. This suggests that the selection of the UNAM's directors is guided by strong political constraints.

Bureaucracy and Autonomy

The autonomy of the UNAM is granted by the Organic Law. However, it is very evident that the full exercise of autonomy rests fundamentally on two processes which vary according to historical conditions. The first requirement for a real autonomous performance is that university governance relies on the academic community (faculty and students) through collegial structures. On one hand, this guarantees that decision-making is based fundamentally on the internal logic of academic development and the way in which external conditions relate to this logic from the perspective of those involved in academe. On the other hand, in the event of the existence of differences or contradictions between the University and the State, a broad based collegial governance provides internal cohesion that strengthens the bargaining power of the institution.

We have seen that the bureaucratization of UNAM has subordinated the collegial structure and therefore weakened faculty and students participation in decision making. This situation has generated permanent internal conflicts of varying magnitude and importance. The lack of consensus about the

University project opens the door for external intervention and pressures that shift institutional policies to adapt them to each six-year governmental requirement.

The second base for autonomy is the existence of strongly independent executive authorities. Once again this is not the case at UNAM. University bureaucrats are strongly linked to external political groups. Their political strength comes from these external constituencies. Their future careers depend on the bureaucrats' compliance with external designs. All these conditions amount to very little independence of the university bureaucracy from the government.

It is possible to say then that the bureaucratization process of UNAM has weakened the autonomy of the institution towards the Mexican State. During the last twenty years the National University has probably suffered the highest degree of external intervention in its modern history. This intervention takes place in definition of internal policies, the determination of spending patterns for public funding, and the designation of authorities and appointed officials.

Domination Versus Hegemony

Without question, the Soberonian alliance was able to control UNAM and generate some political stability. In the course of the confrontation, Soberón was able to put together transcendental transformations. Since then, the University has remained without considerable change. The social formation that emerged during the Soberón administration has dominated the National University for twenty years. However, the governing elite has been incapable of developing a hegemonic process that can concert the diverse views about the university in a unified effort for reform. Since 1986, even their capacity to control has diminished.

It is possible to analyze this situation in Gramscian terms. Gramsci distinguishes between *intellectual and moral leadership,* and *domination* (Gramsci 1980, 99). On many occasions he also uses the concepts *direct, lead* or *rule* in opposition to that of *domination* (Gramsci 1971, 55*f*). It is said that a group *leads* or *directs* when it is capable of exercising power in a *hegemonic* manner. To do this, the group has to previously establish an "intellectual and moral leadership." Even if the group is firmly in control of power, it must continue to lead (Gramsci 1980).

Since 1973, the Soberonian alliance has been able to dominate but has lacked the capability of leading the institution. In most situations in which domination is exercised without moral and intellectual leadership the domination itself is eventually eroded. The deterioration of the system gives place to a legitimacy crisis.

In the case of UNAM, the legitimacy crisis is expressed in several ways. Some of the most important are: the open manifestation of inherent contradictions through social conflicts directed against the bureaucracy; the permanent challenge to rules; regulations and established procedures; the lack of academic leadership; and the internal dissent and the deficient articulation within the dominant block.

Conclusions

Let us focus on the future of university reform at UNAM. Future transformation attempts make it necessary to look at the relation between confrontation and reform. At the same time it is essential to analyze reform at UNAM as the process of building a new hegemony. With this objective in mind, in this section I shall bring together many elements of the previous analysis and focus on these issues.

As we have seen, the bureaucracy at the UNAM grew in number and strength during the last twenty years. In its drive for political control it displaced faculty members from traditionally academic decisions and activities. The social fabric of the university was dismantled. These actions were undertaken in the midst of an unprecedented period of growth. The required incorporation of new faculty members into the university took place in a completely disorganized academic environment. The academic consequences of this process have been extremely costly to this day.

The bureaucracy at the UNAM has presented itself as an element of continuity. As a receptacle of the essence of the University and a representative of its "best" traditions. As the single path to modernity, that is, the only way to adapt to the new requirements of the environment. Nevertheless, the conflicts and confrontations within the university community and within the bureaucracy have grown in the last ten years. The initiatives for reform have generated intense clashes.

Confrontation and Reform

As Baldridge suggests, from the 1970s up to the present there has been increasing political and economic pressure upon the universities. This is true in the case of the UNAM. Financial constraints have determined the new political demands the government places upon the University. These demands have included the reduction of costs through limitations on student enrollment and by decreasing faculty salaries, the standardization of evaluation processes, and the political control over social actors in the institution.

We must understand that the recent attempts to transform the UNAM have produced the confrontation between two broad directions for reform. On one side, the vague and heterogeneous ideas of broad groups of faculty and students, a set of proposals for democratizing governance, expanding access and guaranteeing the permanence of students in the university. On another, the direction the government has been trying to impose on the university through bureaucratic authorities, which suggests a privatizing, financially efficient set of measures. In Carnoy and Levin's terms "these constituencies can often be viewed as those interested in greater 'equality' versus those interested in greater 'efficiency"' (Carnoy and Levin 1985, 231).

In addition there is also the confrontation between bureaucratic control and democratic participation at the UNAM, and perhaps even more meaningful, the struggle of faculty and students to modify the organization of work and the structure of academic disciplines. These initiatives have encountered a thorough resistance from the bureaucracy.

However, it is necessary to acknowledge that university authorities promote constant bureaucratic adjustments and changes in an attempt to strengthen their overall control over the university. In this situation, the contradiction between the discourse of decentralization and its implementation is very meaningful (Weiler 1990). The main resistance to structural change (in the context of the confrontation of two general views of the university's future) comes from the academic elite and its governing bureaucracy within the UNAM. This group can not evade its commitment to the federal government to apply externally designed reforms, but fear of losing established privileges and control over the university makes the bureaucracy a weak instrument for this purpose.

Paradoxically, the existence of this group has become a liability even for the Mexican government. The government is now interested in certain kinds of reforms through which the elitist interests of bureaucracy can be sacrificed in order to produce the changes demanded by the State from the UNAM.

Reform at UNAM: Building a New Hegemony

We have said that the domination process at UNAM has been unable to generate an academic reform of the University. The difficulty in articulating diverse social actors stems from the lack of hegemony of the governing elite and its representative bureaucracy. We also suggested that after twenty years, even the domination capability of this social alliance has deteriorated. The emergence of new conflicts of students and faculty against the bureaucracy, the challenge to rules and regulations, the confrontations between projects, and the disarticulation of the dominant block are evidence of the existence of a legitimacy crisis. This legitimation crisis can only by solved by the emergence of a new historical block, the product of a new hegemonic process.

The opportunity to overcome this critical situation and advance towards a profound structural reform at the National University requires a redefinition of university governance and consequently the role of bureaucracy as well. The decision making process must be based on representative collegial authorities. Bureaucracy must be reduced in number, importance, and expenditure. It has to be subordinated to the collegial governance structure.

The independence of high university officials relative to the government must be guaranteed by active participation of faculty and students in an academic election process.

Executive authorities must be subordinated to collegial structures.

Due to the State's financial crisis and the pressure of particular economic groups for reductions in public investment it is difficult for public universities to expect increases in federal funding. While maintaining the myth of the neutrality of the university, the bureaucratic response to this problem has been to focus on business as the basic constituency for the university in order to acquire private funding and support for public institutions. Business and the wealthy classes of society have put enormous pressures on this institution for the establishment of new efficiency measures and other forms of privatization. This path can only lead to the disappearance of the University as we know it today.

To be able to maintain and enhance its national and public character, the UNAM must establish new alliances with a different constituencies "whose interests are in equitably expanding public services" (Slaughter 1985, 316).

The reconstruction of the social fabric at the UNAM and the alliance with these new constituencies must be based on a redefinition of the concept of university reform. Up to this point, administrators have understood reform as "structural adaptations to austerity" (Gumport 1993, 8). Their own political welfare and the project for efficiency have been their primary concerns.

The reform of a higher education institution like the UNAM requires a broader perspective. Many issues have to be brought into consideration. The role of higher education in a developing country like Mexico, and the rapidly changing conditions of knowledge, technology and knowledge production have to be analyzed. In today's context, it is important to look at the

> functions and purposes of higher education, including what will constitute legitimate academic knowledge, academic vocations, and knowledge products and whether the commercialization of knowledge for revenue enhancement will be a legitimate direction for higher education in the 21st century (Gumport 1993, 6).

In these terms the relation between the UNAM and the Mexican State must be redefined in a new pact which fully recognizes the autonomy of this University. The responsibilities of the institutions towards society in general have to established.

The Political Nature of Higher Education Reform

Universities have been characterized as complex organizations. Participants are articulated by disciplines and are deeply reflective about the organization of academic work. Therefore, profound structural reform requires ample coincidence among participants. The process of structural change at the university level needs to articulate the visions, projects, and expectations of different social actors within the institution and those of diverse external constituencies. This is essentially a process of hegemony building. The search for internal and external legitimacy, the articulation of adequate constituencies, and the building of hegemony are fundamental elements of university reform which reveal its profound political nature.

We have examined some of the elements of the new hegemonic process at UNAM. Most public higher education institutions in Mexico share the problems of university reform with the National University. Bureaucratic and heavily politicized administrations have attempted transformations which have lacked the required consensus among students and faculty.

Hegemony will be built through the establishment of collegial internal relations within the different sectors of each university, the articulation with new constituencies, and the redefinition of the interrelation with the State. An assessment of the functions and future tasks of public universities will articulate all these relations in the construction of new social formations.

The new hegemonic processes are essentially political. The myth of neutrality and apoliticism must be discarded in order to determine the structure, agenda, size and clientele of public universities (Slaughter). The future of Mexico's National Autonomous University and the Mexican higher education system lies in the deeply interwoven tasks of hegemony building and university reform.

Notes

1. Some figures may illustrate the significance of the UNAM. In 1990 the UNAM had 274,409 students (10,351 graduate, 135,409 undergraduate, 3,681 vocational and 121,812 baccalaureate), 29,085 teachers and researchers and more than 25,000 administrative and manual workers (staff). It had 13 faculties, 4 schools, 5 multi-disciplinary units, 24 research institutes and 13 research centers, and 14 baccalaureate level schools (5 colleges of sciences and humanities and 9 preparatory schools).

   The UNAM has 11.7% of the national enrollment at undergraduate level and 20% at graduate level. Until 1984, this institution alone produced 32.08% of the research in the nation (considering basic research in all areas) with 39.61% in biology, 62.5% in chemistry, 45.27% in mathematics, 75% in earth sciences, 77.27% in astronomy, 33% in communications, electronics and aeronautics, 42.86% in political science, 23.7% in economy, 28.14% in history, 61.11% in philosophy, 57% in information technology, and 33% in sociology as outstanding features (Martínez and Ordorika 1993).
2. After the 1976 devaluation of the Mexican peso and in the midst of a deep economic crisis the concluding Echeverría and emerging López Portillo administrations bargained with the IMF for new credits. These were granted in exchange for a Stabilization Plan designed by the IMF and a compromise by the Mexican government of putting together a Financial Reorganization Plan (Girón, 1984 and 1985). The Stabilization Plan and the Financial Reorganization Plan established that the IMF would scrutinize the Mexican government economic policy very closely during the first three months of the Lopez Portillo administration (January 1st 1977 to December 31st 1979). It also established severe cuts in public expenditures and limits to salary increases (10%) and public job growth (2%) (Girón). The adjustment consequences of these plans were soon put aside with the discovery of new oil fields and the presence of the oil "boom". The Lopez Portillo government increased public expenditure in an attempt to obtain legitimacy for the Mexican State. The heavy reliance on oil trade of the Mexican economy and the new process of indebtment generated a new economic crisis in 1982. On August 13th 1982 the Mexican government declared that it was unable to continue paying its foreign debut which rose to 80,000 million dollars (more than 60,000 million dollars were contracted with 1100 western banks). This situation was extremely risky for these banks and many occidental governments. Mexico was "rescued" by the Reagan administration and the IMF (Girón). The rescue package put together by the IMF and the Swiss International Payment Bank, consisted of a new 1,800 million dollar credit by the latter and 5,000 million dollars delivered by the IMF through a Stabilization Plan. All the private banks which held the Mexican debt granted a ninety day payment postponement. Meanwhile, the Mexican government put together a Plan for Financial Reorganization which was part of the bargain with the IMF (Girón). This Stabilization Plan would guide the Mexican government's economic policy during the first three years of the Miguel de la Madrid administration. The conditions imposed by the IMF upon the Mexican policies were: reorganization of public finances, controlling inflation, reduction of public expenditure, and guaranteeing foreign debt payment (Girón). These changes in economic policies and the requirements of the IMF had an important impact on public expenditure. From 1982 to 1988 there is a very important reduction in federal investment on education as a whole. During this period the federal budget for education decreased in –43.65%. The federal budget for higher education was also reduced strongly from 1982 to 1989. The reduction in this period was greater than that of the total of the education –50/78% (Martinez and Ordorika).
3. The University Congress was composed of 840 delegates. The democratic sectors gathered nearly 80% of the student representatives and 60% of the faculty delegates. This faculty group was very important because it included a vast majority of full time professors and researchers as opposed to the conservative faculty group which was comprised essentially of part-time professors.
4. In Latin America there is a long history of student conflict and activism related to struggles for power within and external to campus. This history was probably inaugurated by the student struggles in Córdoba, Argentina, in 1918. The Córdoba Reform generated a tradition of student movements for shared governance. In Mexico many student uprisings have struggled for access to decision making at the university level. Diverse authors have analyzed the characteristics of student movements in Latin American countries and the USA. For a good study on student movements in Latin America it is important to look at the work of Juan Carlos Portantiero, *Estudiantes y Política en America Latina* (1978). A comparative approach can be found in the work of Philip Altbach. *Student Political Activism* (1989).
5. For the purpose of this work I will take hegemony to signify the process of consensual rule through the articulation of a diversity of social groups and interests in the traditional

Gramscian sense. Ideology will be the ideas and beliefs which constitute the foundation of a hegemonic process. Discourse is the expression of ideology.

6. There are many books about the 1968 student movement and its tragic end. For an accurate chronological and documentary approach, look at *El movimiento estudiantil de Mexico* by Ramón Ramirez (1969). Two excellent testimonial books are *Massacre in Mexico* by Elena Poniatowska (1975), and *Los Dias y los Años* by Luis González de Alba (1971).
7. During three months a small armed group headed by Miguel Castro Bustos and Mario Falcón occupied the rectory building by force. They put forward an ambiguous set of demands including the admission of students from the teaching colleges (escuelas normales) to UNAM. The group used a radical discourse and presented itself as a left-winged revolutionary association. However, it was completely isolated from the student movement and its known political groups. Gonzalez Casanova assumed a hesitant attitude and finally decided to resign when the government failed to support him. Castro Bustos and Falcón were later imprisoned. Years later, Castro Bustos reappeared working for Guillermo Soberón's political group in the state of Guerrero. This is probably a confirmation of the suspected links between Soberón and Miguel Castro Bustos during the rectorship occupation.
8. The book *Modernización conservadora y crisis académica en la UNAM* by Rollin Kent Serna provides a good description and analysis of the bureaucratization process at UNAM from an organizational perspective.
9. For an exhaustive study on the structural and legal characteristics of this governing system look at the book *El Autoritarismo en la UNAM* by Fernando Jimenez Mier y Terán.

References

Becker, H. S. (1970). *Campus Power Struggle.* USA: Transaction Books.

Bensimon, E. M. (1984). 'Selected aspects of governance. An ERIC Review', *Community College Review* 12 (2).

Brunner, J. J. (1985). 'Universidad y Sociedad en America Latina'. Caracas, Venezuela, CRESALC.

Cameron. K. (1983). 'Strategic responses to conditions of decline: Higher education and the private sector', *Journal of Higher Education* (54) No. 4; p. 359–80, Jul–Aug.

Cárdenas, L. (1978) *Palabras Y Documentos Publicos De Lazaro Cardenas.* 1. ed., Mexico: Siglo Veintinuno Editores.

Carnoy, M., and Levin, H. M. (1985). *Schooling and Work in the Democratic State.* 1st. ed., Stanford, California: Stanford University Press.

Caso, A. (1944). *Anteproyecto de Ley Orgánica de la UNAM que el rector presenta a la consideración del Consejo Constituyente Universitario.* México, DF: Imprenta Universitaria, UNAM.

Cerych. L. (1987). 'The Policy Perspective', in Clark, B. (ed.), *Perspectives on Higher Education.* California: University of California Press.

Clark, B. R. (1983). *The Higher Education System: Academic Organization in Cross National Perspective.* Berkeley CA: University of California Press.

García, L. J. (1982). *Universidad y Politica en America Latina.* Deslinde.

Girón, A. (1985). 'La Banca Transnacional y el Petroleo en Mexico'. En Problemas del Desarrollo. No. 60. México, DF. Noviembre–Enero.

Girón, A. (1984). "¿Y el Endeudamiento Externo para Quien?" En Problemas del Desarrollo. No. 58. México, DF. Mayo–Julio.

Gramsci, A. (1980). *Il Resorgimento.* México, DF: Juan Pablos Editores, S. A.

Gramsci, A. (1971). *Selections from the Prison Notebooks.* London: Lawrence & Wishart.

Gumport, P. J. (1993). 'The contested terraine of academic program reduction', *Journal of Higher Education* (May/June).

Jimenez Mier y Teran, F. (1983). 'El Autoritarismo en la UNAM', Ph.D Dissertation, Facultad de Ciencias Politicas y Sociales, UNAM.

Kent Serna, R. (1990). *Modernización conservadora y crisis académica en la UNAM.* Mexico, DF: Nueva Imagen.

Levy, D. C. (1980). University and Government in Mexico. New York, NY: Praeger.

Levy D. C. (1988). *The State and Higher Education in Latin America: private and public patterns.* Connecticut, USA: Yale University Press.

Lipset, S. M. (1975). 'Who is the enemy?,' in Hook, S., Kurtz, P., and Todorovich, M. (eds), *The Idea of a Modern University,* Buffalo, NY: Prometheus Books.

Martínez Della Rocca, S., and Ordorika Sacristán, I. (1993). *UNAM: Espejo del Mejor Mexico Posible: La universidad en el contexto educativo nacional.* Mexico, DF: Editorial ERA.

Muñoz García, H. (1989). *Política y Universidad.* Instituto de Investigaciones Sociales, UNAM.

Muñoz García, H. (1990). 'Gestar una nueva cultura política', *Universidad Futura* 2 (4): 58,59.

Slaughter, S., and Silva, E. T. (1985). 'Towards a political economy of retrenchment: The American public research universities', *The Review of Higher Education* 8 (4): 295–318.

Soberón Acevedo, G. (1980). *Informe del rector, 1973–1980, UNAM.* México, DF: UNAM.

Soberón Acevedo, G., de los Angeles Knochenhauer, M., and Olmedo, C. (1983). *La Universidad, ahora.* México, DF: El Colegio Nacional.

Weiler, H. N. (1990). 'Comparative perspectives on educational decentralization: An exercise in contradiction?', *Educational Evaluation and Policy Analysis* 12 (4 Winter).

Williams, R. (1977). *Marxism and Literature.* New York: Basic Books.

Wolff, R. P. (1970). *The Ideal of the University.* Boston, MA: Beacon Press.

Policies for Higher Education in Latin America: The Context

SIMON SCHWARTZMAN

Abstract. Latin American higher education developed since the nineteenth century from the tensions between the Catholic tradition of Iberian colonization and the enlightenment, rationalistic and predominantly French views present in the independence movements, and embodied in the "Napoleonic" institutions established throughout the region. This article discusses how this system evolved, facing the problems of enlarged enrolment, diversification, and the current problems of reform, as alternatives among the poles of bureaucratic, oligarchic and market mechanisms of coordination.

Latin American higher education has been a topic for research and enquiry for some time now, and we know several important things about it.[1] There has been less success in proposing policies for improvement and change, and less still in the implementation of these policies. This article seeks to provide some reflections on the broader context in which policy proposals have been presented and tried out.

1. History

Latin American universities[2] are said to be Napoleonic, which means to be controlled and strictly supervised by the central government according to uniform, nationwide standards. There is also a clear predominance of public, non-confessional universities, in spite of the strong presence of the Catholic Church, and the fact that the first universities were established by the Spanish crown under the Church's control and supervision. The present institutions, most of them created or profoundly transformed after independence in the early 19th century, were built as a reaction against the colonial heritage, including the church and its universities. They were meant to be part of the effort to transform the old colonies into modern nation-states, with professional elites trained according to the best technical and legal knowledge available at the time, and educated in institutions controlled by the state and freed from the traditional religious thinking.

Intentions not always yield the expected results. In contrast to what happened in Germany, for instance, Latin American universities were extremely slow in opening space for empirical research, that could provide support for technical education in the professional schools; in contrast with Britain, there was no place for general education in the liberal arts tradition, which became restricted to the secondary schools, the last bastion of traditional Catholic education; and, in contrast with France itself, very little was developed which could be compared with elite institutions, where high-level professional education could be protected from the changes and uncertainties of the broader higher education system.

A dominant feature is the weight of the professional schools in law, medicine, engineering, dentistry and a few others. In other societies, these units are often placed outside the main universities, or at least organized independently from the institutions' academic and administrative core, usually more concerned with general education, the humanities and the sciences. Latin American higher education, from its beginnings, was defined almost as a synonym of education for the professions. The centrality of these units has led both to the preservation of some quality (since some of them have good traditions of competent work) and to resistance to innovations that have come from other groups entering the universities and from governments and administrations trying to promote change.

One of the main differences among countries is the presence of European links and, above all, European immigrants in the history of their universities. European links could be established either by Latin American students going to Europe, or by importing European professors and researchers to teach or man local institutions and research centers, with presumably very different outcomes. Places with a strong presence of European immigrants and linkages, such as Buenos Aires and São Paulo, developed very different, and usually better institutions, than those that remained more isolated, such as Mexico or Rio de Janeiro.

Another important difference is the outcome of the Church-State conflict about educational issues, which took place almost everywhere. Mexico and Argentina, with their large, lay national universities, should be seen in contrast with Chile or Colombia, where Catholic and lay institutions were able to survive side by side. Mexico and Argentina also typify the pattern of university systems dominated by a central, national university, in contrast with decentralized systems like Brazil, Colombia and even Chile. These historical differences may help to understand the varying paths taken by each country when faced with the pressures for expansion in the second half of this century. Mexico and Argentina responded by opening up the gates of their national universities, while Brazil and Colombia, and more recently Chile, responded by opening space for the creation of a large number of new, private institutions, Catholic or not.

2. Expansion and change

In all countries, higher education changed very little, if at all, until the sixties and seventies, when they came under irresistible pressures, coming from both internal and external sources, in a context of severe political instability and political authoritarianism.

The more visible and probably less understood of these pressures came from the student movement. Political activism among Latin American students is an ingrained tradition, dating at least from the 19th century law schools, and reaching its first peak with the Cordoba Reform Movement of 1918, that inaugurated the tradition of local autonomy and government through collective bodies of professors, students and alumni. The student movements of the fifties and sixties hoped to change not only the universities, but the whole society, and evolved into a pattern of confrontation between students and governments which degenerated in many cases into terrorism, violent repression from military governments and guerrilla warfare. For the universities, these movements helped to delegitimize whatever academic traditions they had in the past, and made it very difficult for governments to try policies other than those of repression and confrontation.

Another source of pressure came from a young generation of scholars, many of them trained abroad, who pressed for the establishment of research institutes, departments, research money and full-time work in the traditional universities. Their criticism against the old organizational models and institutions coincided with that of the students, which led many of them to similar patterns of political confrontation, repression and exile. In some countries, those who remained were partially absorbed by the professional schools, or in specially created institutes and research centers; in others they went on to organize their own institutions, with local or international money.

Less conspicuous, but probably more fundamental in its consequences, was the large number of women, elder and poorer persons who started to flood the universities, which were until recently all male, elite institutions for the privileged young. These new groups were either absorbed by the traditional universities or incorporated in new, private institutions, or some combination of both; in either case, enrolment grew at extremely high rates.

Fourth, there was the creation of a new professional group that barely existed twenty years ago, the university lecturer. In most countries, the expansion of higher education led to the hiring of a large number of instructors who were different both from the traditional professor (who got his earnings from private practice) and the researcher (who could raise money from research agencies and research contracts). The university lecturer in Latin American universities organized very quickly in strong professional unions, took the torch of political militancy from the students of ten years before (if they were not the same persons!) and put forward an agenda of employment protection, egalitarian treatment and public financing that blocked most attempts at evaluation, differentiation and administrative rationalization that emerged from time to time. A parallel development was the creation of large administrative bureaucracies in universities, with their own unions and political agendas.

And last, but not least, was the anti-intellectual and anti-academic attitudes of so many Latin American governments, military or not. For them, universities were either irrelevant or a source of nuisance and political trouble. The combination of anti-intellectualism and authoritarianism on the government's side and political mobilization and increasing costs in the universities led to the gloomiest period of Latin American university life, from which it is now trying to recover.

The process of expansion was extremely rapid, and ran its course in a few years, after the massive incorporation of women and working students, leaving a host of new problems and situations. Its most immediate consequences was that higher education became very expensive to maintain, not just because of the increased number of students, but mostly because of the growing number of academic and administrative staff, and their ability to organize and press for their demands. In most countries, uniform wage policies were established for the whole public sector, and negotiated directly between government and the teachers' unions, bypassing the universities' internal authorities and even the ministers of education. Governments granted more than they could afford, leaving to inflation the task of reducing payment levels until the next round of negotiations. Other countries let the salary levels in public institutions deteriorate, or never implemented policies of full-time employment for academic staff. Another policy was to restrain expansion in the public system as a whole, with some attempts at compensation through the creation of a few high quality, well protected institutions or the stimulus for the development of the private sector.

3. Ethos

An important consequence of these transformations was the further dilution of the academic ethos that somehow existed in a few leading institutions in most countries. The frailty of academic ethos is not mentioned often as an important problem in higher education, probably because of the difficulties in tackling such a diffuse cultural element. Countries having well established higher education institutions today had in the past social groups with strong commitment and interest in cultural and educational activities, which provided their academic institutions with normative and cultural contents that go a long way towards explaining their vigor. In Latin America, as in other regions where governments imported their educational institutions from abroad, these contents sometimes barely existed, in spite of the large number of laws, norms and regulations placed by the educational authorities on the educational institutions. The study of the history of the social and cultural movements associated with educational institutions is the only way to ascertain the presence of such contents, which do not reveal themselves in the legislation, the course syllabus or the academic credentials of professors. When the contents are weak, empty routines and power plays take precedence (formal titles, pay scales, job tenure, institutional power), and the substance of educational work is threatened.

In the past, universities were privileged places for the children of the elites, and the university professor, even if not an academic, was usually a prestigious member of a liberal profession, and transmitted to his students not only the knowledge, but also the attitudes and values typical of his social standing. Now, the universities became flooded with lower middle class students looking for academic credentials in ill-defined professional fields, women furthering their education without clear professional commitments, teachers with no anchorage in the liberal professions or in scientific communities, large and often ineffectual administrative bureaucracies and, in the private sector, educational entrepreneurs coming from unknown places and selling unrecognizable products to an inexperienced market of education buyers. The overall effect of these transformations is very difficult to assess. In very broad terms, many more people have access to education now, the traditional curricula were opened to new alternatives and experimentation, and in some countries and places, full-time teaching and research were introduced for the first time in higher education. The general feeling, however, is of deterioration and loss of quality, and an idealization of the past.

A fresh perspective into the questions of academic ethos can be obtained through the typology of "cultural biases" proposed by Mary Douglas and developed by Aron Wildavsky and associates.[3] Basically, the idea is to look at culture as functionally related to two main dimensions of the social structure, hierarchy (grid) and group cohesion, or solidarity (group). Applied to the variety of Western academic experiences, Table 1 is obtained.

The main notion to keep in mind is not only that these types are never pure, but that it is precisely the tensions among them that provides the universities with their dynamism. From its origins, the European universities combined elements of strong individualism, corporatist[4] organization and close links with the Church hierarchy. The old universities, however, were something more than channels for the transmission of the teachings of the Church. They were responsible also for the creation of an open space for the development of rational thinking, through the rediscovery of the classic tradition. The universities at the Renaissance developed an international community linked by individuals who travelled among the main cities, spoke a common language, Latin, fought with determination for their ideas, and carved their autonomy regarding the surrounding communities and the Church. Universities where these elements of individualism did not emerge remained simply as branches of religious bureaucracies, and withered away. The Protestant Reform, and later the industrial and bourgeois revolutions, strengthened the individualistic component in the traditional European universities, leading to different accommodations among the religious, political and academic authorities. Spain and Portugal, however, were left out of the three revolutions, which explains why their universities did not follow the same path.

The Napoleonic universities developed in the early 19th century together with the emergence of strongly centralized nation states, which followed, in France, a period of intense revolutionary mobilization centered in the *citoyen* as an individualized subject of the political life, the economy and of reason itself. The German universities developed at the same time, combined with a protestant tradition which placed strong accent on individual achievement and community values, but also in a context of political centralism, in the Prussian state first, and in the Bismarckian regime by the end of the century.

Of the three main European models, England is probably the country where state dominance over the universities was less conspicuous and individualism more stressed in the academic ethos, as another dimension of economic and political liberalism. The French model, however, was the one to be copied in Latin America and in many other countries aspiring to the values of modernization and rationality. What was usually missed, in these adaptations, was the values of individual rationalism and citizenship which were so central to the French revolution, and worked as a counterweight to the constraints of the Napoleonic restoration.

What kept hierarchy and competitive individualism together was the relative isolation of the universities regarding the rest of society, which led to the need to develop protective barriers and a sense of identity and protection

TABLE 1
Cultural Biases in University Systems

	Low Group	*High Group*
High grid	*fatalism*—confessional universities	*hierarchy*—Napoleonic and German universities
Low grid	*individualism*—English and American traditions	*egalitarianism*—corporatist universities

against outside interferences and pressures. In Latin America, first among students, and later among teachers and employees, new forms of egalitarian solidarity came to prevail, geared towards the control of financial, political and institutional power within the universities, and displacing, together with the old hierarchical and individualistic cultures, much of their intellectual, pedagogic and ethical contents.

This brief digression on cultural theory suggests that the traditional models of European universities meet strong cultural barriers in their adaptation to the contemporary world, in Latin America as elsewhere, and points to the profound differences in perspective among those who try to carry on with university reforms today. Neither the pressures to make the universities more business-like, at one extreme, or more democratic and egalitarian, at the other, are likely to assure that the universities will be able to produce and transmit knowledge with the same competence as the best of them did in the past. And since the past will not return, the solution adopted by many countries has been to accept that "university" is too broad a term to encompass things so different, and to move in the direction of highly differentiated systems, which could preserve and strengthen their traditional institutions and groups, while opening the space for new manifestations of mass, technical, specialized, vocational, further and other varieties of higher education.

4. Policy and Governance

The current policy problems for higher education can be summarized in three: given its current size and composition, how can higher education continue to be financed, in a context of dwindling public resources and unrelenting pressures for higher expenditures and increasing costs; how to assure its quality, whatever the meaning of this term; and how it could be geared to fulfil the roles it is expected to play to attend to the economic, social and cultural needs of each country. There are other questions to be addressed in this process: how to distribute the benefits of higher education more equitably, how to correct for regional imbalances, how to make the use of public resources more efficient. These are not just "technical" questions, to be handled by a more or less competent administration. They imply deep differences in values and perceptions, and the way they are handled affects different social groups, and can have costly political implications. To deal with these questions, a host of interest group associations, negotiating arenas and regulatory agencies were established in all countries—teachers' unions, rectors' conferences, educational fora, councils of education at different levels, grant-giving agencies, ministerial departments. Most of the disputes on policies of higher education in the region are not actually about policy alternatives, but about the preliminary question of who is entitled to do what. These disputes have the effect of pre-empting some decisions, and of thwarting the development of managerial competence and administrative skills in agencies submitted to constant political negotiation and bickering.

Besides the policy-setting problems at the national level, the institutions themselves are often unable to pull themselves together to further their own goals. The establishment of stronger central administrations was a trend in all universities which tried to move away from the dominance of the traditional schools and to deal positively with the newcoming actors. Ideally, modernizing administrations should evolve from the reliance on professional schools to the reliance on academic communities, which are the mainstays of modern research universities, and responsible for the "bottom-heaviness" which should be, in Burton Clark's expression, the main feature of academic organizations. The problem for Latin American universities, however, is the weakness of their country's academic communities, and the strength of other sectors. As the administrations freed themselves from the professional oligarchies, they often fell prey to the students', teachers' and employees' unions. In many Latin American universities now the administrative authorities are elected by these groups, sometimes by a one-man-one-vote method, making the administrative seats thoroughly political positions.

This predicament is compounded by ingrained traditions of collective rule. The Cordoba Reform movement of 1918 established the principle of tri-partite government—students, professors and alumni—which in many institutions replaced the traditional professional congregations, and have recently been replaced, again, by assemblies of professors, students and employees. The problem with these collective bodies is not so much their composition, but that they go well beyond what one would expect from legislative bodies. They control the acts of the administration in their minute details, and often at all levels—departments, courses, institutes, schools, universities. Universities' administrators not only have to play politics to be appointed, but have also to play politics to have their acts approved and implemented on a daily basis, making everything slow and complicated.

Governance in private institutions goes often to the other extreme. Central administrators are appointed by the owners (or, in Catholic Universities, by the Church), and usually lack collective bodies to temper and compensate for the top-heaviness that prevails. Sometimes this is a blessing, giving the institutions much more freedom to innovate and to respond to changing conditions and demand of the education market. But, in many countries—like Brazil and Colombia—private institutions cater to the poorer and less demanding social segments, and their freedom of action usually leads to poor products to sell.

No wonder that governance in Latin American academic institutions is so often paralyzed, or unable to put forward policies that go against one actor or another. But the very existence of a plurality of interests and groups opens the space for institutional leadership. In some places more than others, it is possible to find researchers unhappy with their working conditions, students pressing for better education, professionals concerned with their standards, external sources willing to bring support to new projects and initiatives. The art of governance in Latin American universities, as in any institution, is very much the art of finding and keeping good allies. It is also the art of association. Networking of universities is a new and growing phenomenon everywhere, from National Councils of Rectors to continental initiatives like the Interamerican University Organization. Networks move slowly, but can give leverage for local initiatives, and become important channels for information and mutual support.

5. Finance

In the public sector, the problems of financing tend to overwhelm all others. Ministers of education can distribute money to the universities in times of abundance, but can hardly ask them to trim their costs in times of scarcity. Professors' and employees' salaries are usually negotiated directly with the unions, and universities are usually not free to establish their own budgets and pay scales. Large investments are exceptional decisions, made by central authorities sometimes with the support of international agencies. This pattern leaves most of the universities' budgets outside the control of their administration, which can only deal with minor, current expenses.

This traditional pattern of rigidity can be circumvented in many ways, and Brazilian institutions have a large experience of doing so. It is possible to diversify the sources of income. Research money can be obtained from research supporting agencies and through research contracts; university real estate can be sold or rented, and the income invested in financial markets; tuition fees cannot be charged for regular courses in most public universities, but can exist for extension work. Different arrangements can be made to receive and manage this money. Non-profit, private corporations have been organized by universities and units within universities to make contracts, receive and invest money, hire staff and pay additional salaries to professors. Arrangements of this kind can lead to questionable practices, if not properly controlled, but can also provide space for initiatives and creativity that would be routinely stifled by conventional procedures.

Financial and administrative flexibility can also be introduced in more conventional ways in public universities. The three public universities of the state of São Paulo, Brazil, work now with a fixed percentage of the state's tax revenues, and give great flexibility and autonomy to its units and research centers to run their own budgets and revenues with independence, keeping control only of the adherence to the general principles of proper bookkeeping. The example of São Paulo suggests that the rigidity in the administration of resources in many Brazilian public universities—and probably also elsewhere—is often a matter of bureaucratic and administrative conservatism and lack of imagination, more than actual legal limitations.

There is a long tradition in Latin America against giving public money to private institutions, and this was actually forbidden by the 1988 Brazilian constitution. There are, however, loopholes, and there is a large system of student credit provided by public corporations that pays tuition for students in the private sector and amounts to a significant subsidy, given the low interest rates and the high number of forfeits.

Tuition in most public universities in Latin America is tabu. In Chile, however, once this tabu was broken, there was no question of going back to free education for all. In Brazil, the selectiveness of public universities makes the charge of tuition a matter of social justice. Still, there is no hope of making Latin American universities self-supporting. There is so much one could charge for tuition, there is no philanthropic money that could compensate for the lack of public subsidies, and there are no examples in the world of university systems that can function only with the support of students, or with revenues of its research activities and services.

6. Comprehensive Reform

It was typical of some military regimes in Latin America to try out deep changes in their country's higher education systems, very often motivated by short-range—and short sighted—political concerns. They nearly always failed to achieve their main goals, but sometimes introduced changes which proved to be significant and long-lasting. Other reforms were introduced by civilian governments, whether as a reaction against previous military interventions, as in the case of Argentina, or by their own perception of the needs to change.

To take a few examples, Brazil changed its legislation for higher education in 1968, ending the traditional chair system and opening the way for graduate education, the strengthening of academic departments and the creation of research institutes. Colombia followed similar lines. Chile introduced a very ambitious project of regulating higher education through market mechanisms and institutional differentiation in 1981. In Argentina the military stimulated the creation of new universities in the provinces, the expansion of non-university tertiary education and the beginning of a private sector. University autonomy returned with civilian rule in 1984, and the universities went through a "normalization" period aimed at returning to the institutional framework of 1966, which included a policy of open admissions. Mexico began differentiating after 1968, both through provincial institutions and a growing private sector.

The repertoire of reform measures attempted in the last several years is not very large. It is useful to think of them in terms of the typology proposed by Burton Clark for the three main poles of coordination and control in higher education systems, namely the State, the academic oligarchies and the market. One could think of the changes in the last several years as attempts to move the weight of authority among these poles, and it is possible to evaluate the policies and their outcomes in terms of these attempts.

We have seen how Latin American higher education institutions have been from the beginning organized by the state, along with the Napoleonic tradition, and their history until the last decades has been a constant fight with oligarchies for political control. What "state" means has varied in time and space. It can mean the ministry of education, the treasury department, the civil service administration, the military, or even the Congress, while establishing legislation and approving the national budget. The problem with state control is its inability to fine tune its policies. Governments can pass legislation, send troops and cut or grant budgets, but cannot make institutions organized around skills and personal commitment to perform under command.

The term "oligarchy" does not need to have a derogatory meaning. Good universities have been always ruled from inside, and it is not by chance that the issue of academic and administrative autonomy commands so much attention in this field. The academic oligarchies we are talking about, however, can make a great difference. In the past, Latin American higher education institutions were ruled by life-appointed chair holders, the "catedráticos", very often notable men in the liberal professions. They controlled not just their chairs, but also their institutions' academic senates and congregations. Now there are scientists organized around their societies, unionized teachers, unionized employees, liberal professionals and their associations in the schools of medicine, law and engineering, religious congregations running the Catholic universities, the lobby of education entrepreneurs in the non-religious private sector, and even some remnants of the old student movement. "University autonomy" can mean any combination of these groups—in the last several years in Brazil it has meant the election of academic authorities by the equal vote of professors, students and employees (one third each), and it is difficult to imagine which kind of policy could come out of this arrangement.

The flaws of the State and the stalemates of academic oligarchy have led to the search for the third alternative of coordination, the market, with its compelling logic of cost reduction and the stimulation of entrepreneurship. However, market driven educational institutions are not likely to embark on long-term projects of social relevance and quality. There are no examples of countries with good quality higher education institutions based solely or predominantly on market domination, and it is difficult to imagine that they could exist. "Market competition" can mean different things in higher education, from competition for student fees to competition for academic excellence. The prestigious research universities in the United States, with their competition for endowments of philanthropic money and talented professors, are at one extreme; there is a host of institutions working at the other end, however, selling low-quality education for bargain prices, and there are no mechanisms linking one extreme with the other.

7. Conclusions

This broad overview of the context and main policy alternatives for Latin American higher education can give us some clues about why policies so often go wrong. Policy initiatives may fail because they try to shift the coordination and control of higher education systems to one of the three poles of coordination, with exclusion of the others; or because they may favor the "wrong" sector within each pole (say, the military, the more traditional professional associations or the tuition market for low quality education). Even if well chosen, none of these poles, in isolation, can carry on a coherent agenda of educational reform, because of the opposition from the others.

This conclusion is not very surprising, but may be important. Policy-oriented studies often take for granted the existence of a free agent—usually "the government"—which can act as it sees fit, given only the limits of their budgets. Governmental policies are normally the result of different and conflicting forces, and to understand the constant jockeying for who can decide what is often more important than identification and evaluation of policy alternatives. Higher education systems require the presence of checks and balances among government, oligarchies and markets to function properly. In the long run, markets can establish healthy competition and patterns of cost-effectiveness and identify demand; governments can establish long-term goals, grant support and define the relative power of interest groups and oligarchies; and these groups, under appropriate conditions, are the only ones who really can know what higher education institutions are about, and what they can do. Policies that take this complex really into account may stand a chance to succeed.

Notes

1. A very incomplete list of references include, in alphabetical order, José Joaquín Brunner, *Educación Superior en América Latina: Cambios y Desafios*, Santiago de Chile. Fondo de Cultura Económica, 1990; R. Drysdale, *Higher Education in Latin America: Problems, Policies and Institutional Change*, Washington, The World Bank, March 1987; Daniel C. Levy, *Higher Education and the State in Latin America: Private Challenges to Public Dominance*, Chicago University Press, 1986; Juan Carlos Portantiero, *Estudiantes y politicas en America Latina 1918–1938 el proceso de la reforma universitaria*, Colombia, Siglo Veintiuno, 1978; S. Schwartzman, "The Quest for University Research: Policies and Research Organization in Latin America", in B. Wittrock and A. Elzinga, *The University Research System*, Almqvist & Wiksell International, Stockholm, Sweden, 1985; S. Schwartzman, "Latin America: Higher Education in a Lost Decade", *Prospects*, 1992 XXI, 3, 1991, 363–373; Juan Carlos Tedesco. La *Juventud Universitaria en America Latina*, Caracas

CRESALC, 1986; Juan Carlos Tedesco, *Tendencias y Perspectivas en el Desarrollo de la Educacion Superior en la America Latina y el Caribe*, Paris, UNESCO, 1983, 43 pp; Hebe M. C. Vessuri. "The Universities, Scientific Research and the National Interest in Latin America", *Minerva* 21:1, 1–38, 1966; Donald R. Winkler, *Higher Education in Latin America—Issues of Efficiency and Equity*, Washington, The World Bank Discussion Papers No. 77, 1990.

2. The word "university" will be used in this text as a synonym for "higher education" in all institutional and academic forms and varieties. In fact, most countries distinguish between universities and other higher education institutions, but the boundaries tend to be formalistic and to vary from country to country and time to time.
3. Michael Thompson, Richard Ellis and Aaron Wildavsky, *Cultural Theory*, Boulder, Westview Press, 1990.
4. The term "corporatism" has been used in political science to describe the pattern of social and political organization derived from the Medieval guilds, according to which society is divided in distinct corporations defined in functional terms, and coordinated by a central authority. In corporatist societies the corporations, as well defined status groups, take precedence over the individual citizen. From its origins, the Western universities have retained some traits of this corporatist nature. The term is now used in common parlance in many Latin American countries to describe the entrenched defense of vested interests by professional and sectorial groups. For an overview, see James M. Malloy, *Authoritarianism and Corporatism in Latin America*, University of Pittsburgh Press, 1977.

Higher Education and Development: The Experience of Four Newly Industrializing Countries in Asia

Jasbir Sarjit Singh

Since the 1970s a number of economies in Asia have successfully upgraded their industrial base and strengthened their capacity to adopt, adapt and create new technologies. Among these countries, the Republic of Korea, Taiwan and Singapore have already demonstrated significant industrial achievement while Malaysia is pursuing the same path. Commonly referred to as newly industrializing countries (NICs) they possess limited natural resources but have recognized the importance of the knowledge and skills composition of their labour force as the key to their productivity and national development transforming them from agricultural to industrial export economies.

Impressed by the success of the NICs in structural adjustment and industrial development other developing countries look to the NICs for lessons on how to stimulate their growth. The principal concern is with the role of human-resource development, in particular with investment in different levels and types of education as a generator of growth. Investment of scarce resources in higher education proves especially problematic; as the most expensive sector of education it is imperative that the higher-education system produces the right mix of manpower pertinent to national needs. Of special interest to developing countries are the higher-education strategies that have enabled NICs to produce a scientific and technological capacity to support industrialization.

Successful restructuring and development in these countries may be attributed to a number of factors, two of which have a direct bearing upon higher-education institutions: (a) the quantity and quality of scientific and technological manpower, and (b) the research and development environment which enables the achievement and sustainability of indigenous industrial development.

Higher-education institutions play a singularly important role in the training of scientific and technological manpower because they are often the sole suppliers of high-level scientific and technological personnel. Research and development activity, though shared with other research and specialized institutions is a crucial part of higher education as it strengthens and enhances their training capacity. Of central concern to the analysis is the extent to which higher-education systems of NICs provide support to their industrialization policies.

This article will portray higher-education developments in selected NICs—the Republic of Korea, Malaysia, Singapore and Taiwan—to assess their role in each country's progress towards industrialization. It will sketch briefly the nature of industrialization and the degree of structural adjustment achieved. The higher education policies and developments that have helped shape these countries' remarkable industrial growth will be identified and reviewed primarily from the perspective of the

Jasbir Sarjit Singh (Malaysia). Chief Project Officer, Education Programme, Commonwealth Secretariat, London, with responsibility for higher education. Until 1990 she was Professor of sociological studies, Faculty of Education, University of Malaya, where she also served as Dean, Institute of Advanced Studies. Her principal interests in teaching and research are education and social mobility, education, learning orientation and work in developing societies. Author of numerous articles in her fields of competence.

TABLE 1
Contribution to GDP and Employment Distribution, Republic of Korea, Malaysia, Singapore and Taiwan (percentages)

		Contribution to GDP			*Distribution of employed*		
Country	*Year*	*Agri-culture*	*Manufac-turing*	*Services*	*Agri-culture*	*Manufac-turing*	*Services*
Republic of Korea	1970	26.5	22.4	51.1	50.4	14.3	35.3
	1980	14.9	31.0	54.1	34.0	22.5	43.5
	1988	10.5	33.2	56.2	20.7	24.4	50.9
Malaysia	1970	30.8	13.4	41.9	53.5	8.7	35.2
	1980	22.2	20.5	45.1	40.6	15.8	36.7
	1988	21.1	24.4	45.0	31.3	16.6	45.5
Singapore	1970	3.0	20.2	71.5	3.5	22.0	67.5
	1980	1.3	29.1	66.7	1.6	20.1	61.5
	1988	0.4	38.0	61.0	0.4	28.5	62.5
Taiwan	1970	18.0	26.2	47.5	36.7	20.9	35.3
	1985	6.9	35.8	48.2	17.5	33.5	41.1
	1988	6.1	38.1	47.7	13.7	34.5	43.7

Sources: Republic of Korea, 1990; Taiwan, 1990; Singapore, 1971/72, 1986, 1990; Malaysia, 1989.

role of higher education in developing and strengthening their scientific and technological capacity. The experiences of these countries will illustrate higher-education developments which may be vital to the growth and development of NICs.

Structural Adjustment

The NICs' annual growth rate of 6–10 per cent since the 1970s has been paralleled by structural adjustment policies that have sought to reallocate the factors of production to bring about improved products or services. They have replaced agriculture with manufacturing as the key factor in promoting and sustaining economic growth, gradually shifting from import substitution industries to export-oriented and selected high technology heavy industries. To achieve this, the NICs have pursued 'corrective and directive structural adjustment' clearly intended to move away from low-wage, low-productivity and unskilled labour-intensive activities and have created for themselves growth niches which lie in high-technology and high value-added activities. (Chowdhury et al., 1986, p. 61)

Singapore's experience in structural adjustment is quite typical. In its first phase of industrialization, efforts were concentrated on a small number of industries—chemical processing, metal engineering and machinery, heavy engineering and electric and electronic engineering (Lim, 1984, pp. 33, 41). Since 1979, seeking to bring about a second industrial revolution, Singapore has directed its industrial sector towards the production of goods that require more skill, pay higher wages and generate more value added. Recognizing its comparative advantage in promoting knowledge-based industries Singapore set in motion measures to become an international centre for exporting software technology to world markets.

In all the NICs changes in sectoral distribution of the employed labour force as well as broad shifts in sectoral contributions to gross domestic product (GDP) are evident (see Table 1), reflecting the slowing down of agricultural production and expansion in the industry, manufacturing and the service sectors. In the Republic of Korea from 1960 to 1985 agricultural production growth averaged 3 percent and during the 1980s 3.7 percent, but from 1965 to 1980 industry grew by 16.4 and 12.4 percent respectively during the 1980s, while manufacturing recorded a growth of 18.7 percent during the period 1965 to 1980 and 13.5 percent in the 1980s. Singapore experienced a decline in agricultural production during the 1980s (minus 5.1 per cent) while industry and manufacturing showed a marked growth-rate of 11.9 and 13.2 percent respectively from 1965 to 1980 and 4.5 and 4.8 percent respectively in the 1980s. (World Bank, 1990, pp. 180–1).

The adjustment policy has been greatly facilitated by the consciously formulated and far reaching policies for manpower development, education and training (Chowdhury et al., 1986, p. 11). The correspondence between structural adjustment and human-resource development has been evidently directed at obtaining the mix of skills needed to sustain the planned industrialization. As the demand for skills built up, the proportion of enrollments in secondary and higher education increased. To accommodate the demand for technicians and engineers, enrollments in schools, colleges and universities were tilted in favour of science entrants. The outcome is clearly evident: the shape of the educational pyramid in all the countries has been transformed (see Table 2) with clear implications for the qualifications structure of the labour force.

Targeted Higher-Education Priorities

Since the 1970s the NICs have planned for higher education within the framework of national priorities set for the larger education system under the control of the Ministry of Education. Higher education is seen as a vital component of the process of nation-building, expected to bring about socio-economic and political development of the country. As part of the national education system a tight rein has been kept on all developments in higher education. However, as has been argued for the Republic of Korea, despite serious flaws, strains on students and parents, and denial of opportunities for individual personal development, the education system managed to contribute to the country's economic progress. (Selth, 1988, p. 16).

There is evidence of a high degree of coordinated control which is exercised through large subsidies comprising frequently around 95 percent of the development and recurrent costs of these institutions or legislative enactments that have empowered these governments to moderate the expansion and direction of higher education. During the period from the 1960s to the 1980s, the Republic of Korea's five year development plans prompted the government to regulate the establishment of new departments and set student quotas for different universities and disciplines, influencing the curriculum and university appointments (Bom Mo Chung, 1988, p. 52). The government stipulated the number of courses, the combination of subjects to be taken, the bestowing of doctorate degrees and regulation of overseas students (Seith, 1988, p. 11). Malaysian higher education has been closely

TABLE 2
Enrollments in Educational Institutions in the Republic of Korea, Malaysia, Singapore and Taiwan

				Enrollments		
Country	*Population (1988) (millions)*	*GDP(1988) ($)*	*Year*	*Primary (%)*	*Secondary (%)*	*Higher (%)*
Republic of Korea	42.0	3600	1970	73.1	24.3	2.6
			1980	54.2	40.1	5.7
			1988	44.4	42.6	13.0
Malaysia	16.9	1940	1970	75.0	24.3	0.6
			1980	63.8	34.7	1.5
			1988	59.1	37.1	3.8[1]
Singapore	2.6	9070	1970	68.9	28.5	2.6
			1980	58.1	37.4	4.5
			1988	48.2	43.1	8.7
Taiwan	19.9	6302	1970	65.9	29.0	5.1
			1980	57.6	34.9	7.5
			1988	56.9	33.5	9.6

1 Estimate for 1990; Malaysia, 1986, p. 485.

Sources: Republic of Korea, 1990; Taiwan, 1990; Singapore, 1971/72, 1986, 1990; Malaysia, 1989.

TABLE 3
Expansion of Higher Education in Selected NICs, for Both University and College Sectors, 1970–90

	Enrollments						
Country	*1970*	*1975*	*1980*	*Average annual increase 1970–80 (%)*	*1985*	*1990*	*Average annual increase 1970–80 (%)*
Republic of Korea	201,436	297,219	615,452	20.5	1,062,195	1,529,244[1]	14.8
Malaysia	10,995	25,420	32,280	19.4	359,346	75,178[2]	13.3
Singapore	13,683	18,078	22,633	6.2	39,913	50,742[3]	12.4
Taiwan	203,473	289,435	342,528	6.8	428,576	535,064[4]	5.6

1. 1988 data from UNESCO, 1990.
2. 1990 estimate.
3. 1989 data (includes Institute of Education).
4. 1989 data.

Sources:
Republic of Korea: Kim Jong Chul and Hung Sah-Myung, 1984, Table II, p. 7; Kim Shin Bok, Table 1, p. 66; Lee Sungho, 1989. p. 58, Table 2.1.
Malaysia: Malaysia, 1986, p. 264; Malaysia, 1989, p. 95.
Singapore: Singapore, 1971/72; Singapore, 1990a, p. 32.
Taiwan: Taiwan, 1990, pp. 283–4.

guarded by the Ministry of Education as one of the principal actors in national development. The Universities and Colleges Act, 1971, stipulates that no higher-education institution with the status of a university shall be established except in accordance with the provision of this Act (Isahak Haron, 1988, p. 6). The government also exercises full authority over student enrollments, staff appointments, curricula and financing. Consecutive five-year plans have set out targets for readjusting higher education and a strict policy of quotas is adhered to through a central admissions unit. Singapore has closely co-ordinated the development of technical institutes, polytechnics and universities as the producers of the appropriate type and quantity of manpower for the economy. Access to universities and colleges has been prompted by objective criteria and not individual need, and enrolment levels have been pegged to a ten-year manpower plan. The government actively influences career choices and it encourages students to enter fields where there are shortages and stay out of others that have become competitive. Expanding faculties are encouraged with a proper supply of qualified skills (Pang Eng Fong, 1982, p. 157). Taiwan proves no exception in relation to the regulation of access, structure and content of higher education. All decisions, from the appointment of presidents, the establishment of new departments, colleges or universities, the number of students enrolled in a department to the curriculum, the number of teachers per faculty, the teaching load, tuition fees and faculty salaries are approved by the Ministry of Education. (Hsieh, 1989, p. 179). The government has maintained a ratio of 3:7 in favour of vocational schools to keep the level of output at the technician level high. Recent changes to allow more students to move up to comprehensive schools have been influenced not by student or parental pressure but by the concern to upgrade the labour force to meet the demand for high level manpower (Yi-Rong Young, 1991, pp. 6–7).

Investment in Higher Education

Recognizing the higher-education system as the valued producer of high-level manpower NIC governments were willing to invest large amounts in it. In all the NICS the percentage of expenditure on education increased steadily as a part of the GNP, and of higher education as a part of the total education budget. The Republic of Korea's educational expenditure in the 1980s has been 5.5 per cent of GNP of which 30 percent has been allocated to higher education. The government considers that one of its major roles 'is to see to it that the maximally possible, if not sufficient expenditure is secured' (Bom Mo Chung, 1988, p. 53). Malaysia in 1985 was spending 6.9 percent of its GNP on education with 15.6 percent of it on the higher-education budget (compared with 7.1 percent in 1970). Singapore, in 1989/90, similarly spent about 22 percent of its education budget on its universities and polytechnics (Singapore, 1990b, p. 33). At the same time Taiwan's education expenditure has increased from 1.73 percent in 1985 to 5.3 percent of the GNP in 1985 with 20 percent to higher education (Taiwan, 1990, pp. 39, 43).

Higher-Education Structures

The high expenditure is paralleled by increased enrollments (Table 3). Since the 1970s, the NICs have experienced rapid growth in higher education: an annual increase of around 20 percent in Malaysia and the Republic of Korea and 6.2 and 6.8 percent respectively in Singapore and Taiwan between 1970 and 1980; and an annual growth-rate of 14.8 percent in the Republic of Korea, around 13.3 per cent in Malaysia, 12.4 percent in Singapore and 5.6 percent in Taiwan during the 1980s.

The size and structures of the higher-education systems in these countries are varied. Singapore has only had the National University of Singapore, the Nanyang Technological Institute (upgraded to the status of a university in 1991), two polytechnics and the Institute of Education with a total enrollment in 1989 of 50,742, of which 22,094 were in universities, 27,106 in polytechnics and 1,542 in teacher-training colleges (Singapore, 1990b, p. 32). Malaysia has six national universities, one international university, MARA Institute of Technology, Tengku Abdul Rahman College and four polytechnics with an estimated enrolment in 1990 of 75,178. Higher education in the Republic of Korea, begun by American missionaries, underwent rapid reconstruction and expansion following the Korean War designed largely on the United States model. By 1986 there were 111 colleges and universities with an enrolment of 992,233 students, with another 69,962 students in graduate schools but nearly 70 per cent of these institutions are private (Altbach, 1989, p. 16). By 1988 a higher-education enrollment of 1,529,244 was recorded (UNESCO, 1990, pp. 3–356). This represents a third of the college age cohort, but the government is directly involved in only a quarter of the students with less than 2 percent subsidy to private colleges (Bom Mo Chung, 1988, p. 54). In Taiwan by 1989 there were 535,064 students enrolled in 116 higher-education institutions comprising 21 universities, 20 independent colleges and 75 junior colleges.

Despite these differences a number of common features are discernible. The systems that developed in the Republic of Korea and Taiwan more closely resemble the American university system with a range in the quality of institutions and a clear 'social pecking order' (Lee Sungho, 1989, p. 36). There clearly emerged in the Republic of Korea and Taiwan a two-tiered hierarchy with the majority of students aspiring to enter the state financed colleges—placing great pressure on entrance for coveted places. In Malaysia and Singapore the institutions are of more uniform quality, reminiscent of British higher-education institutions. The universities are at the apex with specialized institutes awarding diplomas and certificates.

The NICs provide useful lessons in the structuration of higher education. Recognizing that they cannot take all applicants into a high technology and capital intensive system, the Republic of Korea and Taiwan have evolved a two-tier system, one lower-level, low-cost and localized tier and one high-level specialized tier. They have successfully expanded and diversified their higher-education systems to meet national skills requirements as well as satisfy to some extent the aspirations of the population by providing all who desire access to some level of higher education and avenues to move from one level of higher education to another. Thus, nearly 30 percent of this age cohort have access to higher education. Following the British trend, Malaysia and Singapore have retained a few élitist institutions almost fully subsidized by the government leading to credentials that enable employment in the upper echelons of the occupational structure. A small group of polytechnics and institutions of technology provide training to technicians. However it is unlikely that this can be maintained and the indications are that as the pressure for more higher education builds up in these countries, it is the lower tier that will have to be expanded.

Science and Technology Manpower

The countries under review had inherited an imbalanced development in the levels and type of manpower: over-production of managerial and under-production of para-professional and vocational as well as an oversupply of arts and social science graduates and a shortage of natural science and technical graduates. During the last thirty years the NICs concerned themselves with the task of enlarging their pool of scientific and research personnel; evidence can be adduced from all the countries of the strategies they have pursued to sharpen the focus on science and technology manpower and research (see Table 4).

The government of the Republic of Korea was prompted to control all non-development-related aspects of higher education. The First Five Year Economic Development Plan in 1962 emphasized higher education in the natural sciences and engineering. The government moderately increased the enrollment quotas in science and engineering every year while limiting social science and humanities intakes. In 1967 a Ministry of Science and Technology was created and a series of laws were enacted to promote developments—the Electronics Industrial Promotion Law in 1969 and the Eight-year Development Plan for the Electronics Industry (1969–76), while a number of science-and-technology institutes were established around the country (Sanyal, 1990, p. 20). New departments in social sciences were restricted and research grants were made available more readily to projects with practical application than to basic research. The government exerted considerable effort to encourage students towards vocational and technical schools and colleges. Graduate education which in the past was limited largely to medicine and limited to a few prestigious universities such as Seoul National and Yonsei has been extended to science and engineering and greatly strengthened through the establishment of more graduate schools, in particular the establishment of the Korea Institute of Science and Technology (KAIST) in 1981. Its principal objective is to educate and develop high-calibre and competent manpower in both abstruse theory and practical applications in the field of science and technology and to develop the nation's science and technological potential (Lee Sungho, 1989, pp. 42–3). Enrollment in scientific fields has wavered between 40 and 50 percent during the 1960s and 1970s, though in 1985 it was reported to be only 33.1 percent (UNESCO, 1990). At post-graduate level more than 50 percent have been enrolled in these disciplines; in 1986 there were 12,018 Master's degree students and 3,871 doctoral science-and-engineering students out of a total of 30,265 graduates representing 52.5 percent of the total graduate student population (Lee Sungho, 1989, pp. 39, 59–60).

TABLE 4
Enrollments in Higher-Education Institutions by Field of Study in Selected NICs (percentages in italics)

	1970			*1980*			*1989/90*		
Country	*Arts*	*Science*	*Technical*	*Arts*	*Science*	*Technical*	*Arts*	*Science*	*Technical*
Republic of Korea	115,230	36,422	49,784	312,250	93,566	209,636	1,021,622	218,019	289,603
	57.2	*18.1*	*24.7*	*50.7*	*15.2*	*34.1*	*66.8*	*14.3*	*18.9*
Malaysia	6,245	3,297	1,453	14,790	11,325	6,165	42,500	17,408	15,269
	56.8	*30.0*	*13.2*	*45.8*	*35.1*	*19.1*	*56.5*	*23.2*	*20.3*
Singapore	2,708	541	4,769	6,850	1,630	8,000	13,589	5,209	30,650
	33.7	*6.7*	*59.6*	*41.7*	*9.8*	*48.5*	*27.5*	*10.5*	*62.0*
Taiwan	122,434	31,153	49,886	185,365	41,977	115,186	294,700	60,869	179,495
	60.2	*15.3*	*24.5*	*54.1*	*12.3*	*33.6*	*55.1*	*11.4*	*33.5*

Sources:
Republic of Korea: UNESCO, 1972, p. 384; 1987, pp. 3313; 1990, pp. 3–356.
Malaysia: Malaysia, 1986, p. 264; 1989, pp. 94–95.
Singapore: Singapore, 1971/72, p. 167; data represents students admitted into these disciplines for the year 1970.
Taiwan: Taiwan, 1990, pp. 283–4.

As Singapore's industrialization took off, its education system was also adjusted to produce knowledge-based graduates and technicians for its specific industries. In the 1970s engineering, accounting and business management/administration were given more emphasis in the university sector. As new priority industries required a high level of skills and technology, the Nanyang Technological Institute and the polytechnics produced practice-oriented engineers. The Report of the Economic Committee in 1986 endorsed the assumption that the government should create the infrastructure and environment conducive for science-and-technology development goals for Singapore's high-technology policy which would allow industry to exploit and advance new technologies, develop competence in new technologies and move into high-technology industries which would help Singapore's growth and carried implications for the expansion of programmes to train manpower needed to carry out R&D in industry. At all the institutes of higher education less than 30 percent are in arts and humanities studies. Both at the National University of Singapore and at the Nanyang Technological Institute Master's programmes with specialized focus have increased (Pang and Gopinathan, 1989, p. 140).

Malaysia has gradually shifted from overemphasis on the social sciences and humanities to science and technology, achieving a ratio of three science to two arts students in secondary schools, by deliberately adjusting the admission quotas and concentrating on the development of specialized science-and-technology institutions. In the 1970s from the one comprehensive university, the University of Malaya, Malaysia established a university of science, upgraded the agricultural and technical colleges to universities and began to develop postgraduate courses in science, medicine and engineering. To focus on applied research and courses with developmental bias, the Institute of Advanced Studies was founded in 1980 at the University of Malaya. As a result the share of arts students shrank from 56.8 percent in 1970 to 45.8 percent in 1980, while the proportion of science and engineering students increased from 43.2 to 54.2 percent. Since then the proportion of arts and humanities enrollments has increased but this has been largely in business and accountancy studies.

The importance Taiwan placed on science and technology is apparent from the predominance of technological and engineering colleges and universities established during the 1970s and 1980s, enabling a great push for science and engineering as well as postgraduate education. In 1975 only 47.5 percent of undergraduate degrees and 4 percent of the Master's and doctoral degrees were granted in science and engineering. In 1982 the government launched a special programme to train more graduate students seeking significant expansion of graduate programmes in strategic areas such as information, materials, electronics, automation and biotechnology, increasing faculty and the number of scholarships for students. As a result in 1985 Master's and doctoral graduates in science and engineering increased from 54 percent (in 1980) to 64 percent and from 18 to 48 percent respectively. Since then the level of science and engineering enrolment has tapered off, with about 44 percent of all students in public and private universities and colleges in 1990 enrolled in science-and-technology courses. In the public sector at first-degree level 51 percent were in science and engineering. Science and engineering graduate enrollments now comprise 57 percent of the total graduate population, that is, 60 percent of all Master's and 28 percent of all Ph.D. enrollments were in scientific and technological fields.

Strengthening Engineering and Technological Studies

As industrialization became more prominent the need was not merely for undifferentiated scientific manpower but for specialized engineers rather than natural scientists, and for technicians to support their work. In this respect, a clear relationship is evident in NICs between the proportion of technology students and the level of industrialization (see Table 3). The Republic of Korea, Taiwan, Singapore and, to a lesser extent, Malaysia, concentrated in their prestigious universities on the production of engineers relevant to their targeted industries. The Republic of Korea and Taiwan multiplied their electrical and electronic engineering departments and students, while Singapore concentrated on training specialists in computer hardware and software and in biotechnology. At the same time the higher-education system was diversified, providing opportunities for large numbers to study technology at a lower level, in the two- to five-year junior colleges and polytechnics which enabled their graduates to work at practical levels in industry, while allowing a small proportion to move on to institutes of technology for more specialized studies.

During the 1980s Singapore clearly shifted emphasis in favour of engineering students, with an accelerated output of engineering graduates. Engineering enrollments in higher education in 1980 comprised 8,000 out of a total of 16,480, or 48 percent of tertiary students. By 1989 out of a total of 49,448, 62 percent of all universities and college students were enrolled in engineering. By 1980 Singapore also enrolled 10.2 percent of its students in postgraduate studies which since then have been considerably increased through the establishment of key specialized centres to provide excellent opportunities for postgraduate education: the Institute of Molecular and Cell Biology, Institute of Systems Science and the Centre for Advanced Studies. It has instituted prestigious research awards to draw the best students into postgraduate studies and has targeted 10 percent of its university population to be research students by 1990 (Pang and Gopinathan, 1989, p. 147). It has added prestige to its engineering studies by establishing in 1990 a postgraduate school of engineering 'to strengthen and to give focus to the postgraduate programmes' and to assist the faculty in developing into a centre of excellence for postgraduate training and research in engineering.

The story in the Republic of Korea is somewhat similar. Structural change from light to heavy industry in the 1970s led to an increased demand for engineers and research scientists in the academic system. The primary goal in the 1960s and early 1970s was to produce technicians and engineers who could absorb or initiate foreign technology. The mid-1970s saw a change to capital- and technology-intensive industrial sectors. The new industries needed scientists and research engineers who could promote creative assimilation of foreign technology as well as invention and innovation. The academic system was now required to expand its mission to move away from basic research to expand indigenous sources of scientific and technological creation through promotion of production, assessment and validation of ideas (Lee Sungho, 1989, p. 55).

The influence of the new developments was sharply felt in the electrical and electronics departments whose student numbers increased rapidly to keep pace with developments in these industries which led the industrialization process. The number and variety of courses in electronics leading to Master's and doctoral degrees increased. In the electronic industries courses ranged from semi-conductor and electronic material, digital systems, communications, automatic control and measurement, electronic circuits and systems, and computers. Master's degree students increased from 2,259 to 5,504 and Ph.D. students from 462 to 1,026 during the six-year period from 1985 to 1991. Similarly, the number of electronic departments increased from four in four-year colleges in 1965, to thirty-six in 1975 and 100 in 1988, while in graduate schools the numbers rose from three in 1965 to twenty-one in 1975 and seventy-five in 1986. Enrollments in electronic departments rose in four-year colleges from 279 in 1965 to 6,042 in 1975 and 35,873 in 1984, and the number of graduate students increased from 4 in 1965 to 125 in 1975 and 1,659 in 1984 (Sanyal and Hyun, 1989, pp. 92–102).

Taiwan has a high proportion of engineering students among its science enrollments. The proportion of engineering students has gradually increased from 24.5 percent in 1970 to 33.6 percent in 1980 and throughout the 1980s engineering enrollments comprised around 33 percent of total higher-education enrollments. In comparison pure science enrollments have remained at around 11 percent. By 1989, of the total enrolment in science and engineering, 47.1 percent were enrolled in engineering courses. More importantly in the public sector day session engineering students constituted 56.8 percent of the total science and engineering students.

Compared with the Republic of Korea, Taiwan and Singapore, Malaysia's output of science-and-technology graduates has been slower and the focus has until recently been on the basic science courses—biology, chemistry, physics and mathematics. Between 1981 and 1988, 45 percent of all science students graduated in these fields. Graduates in the applied sciences have remained low at between 2 and 3 percent of all enrollments. Generally, technology-oriented graduates from the engineering faculties accounted for only about 24 percent of the graduates of whom the largest proportion had graduated in civil engineering. The level of enrollments in post-graduate studies by the mid-1980s was still only around 4 percent of total enrollments and there were few graduate centres. In postgraduate studies too, the concentration of science and engineering studies had made little headway accounting for barely 19 percent of the postgraduate population (Singh, 1989, pp. 91, 120–1).

Ensuring Quality

While quantitative expansion provided the basic pool of scientists, technologists and craftsmen for industry, attention was also turned to the type and quality of higher education to produce an élite corpus of science-and-technology manpower. Malaysia and Singapore have maintained a tight grip on access to higher education and especially in the scientific fields—requiring better A-level results to enter science and engineering courses than the arts and humanities. The number of applicants far exceed the places offered allowing only the best to enter these courses. The Republic of Korea and Taiwan followed a more open entry system allowing large numbers to enter the higher-education sector but within that sector a small prestigious, difficult of access, competitive and publicly funded group of Universities emerged that produced the highly skilled manpower needed for research and industry. Both groups of countries were selective and promoted a small élite group of scientific manpower: one through limited entry along the British lines and the other through keenly contested entry into the key institution along American lines.

The experience in the Republic of Korea bears illustration. The harsh Korean education system, which forces students to undergo a rigorous regime to reach the higher levels of education permits only the finest and best qualified to survive (Selth, 1988, p. 17); there is a process of natural attrition that allows only 7–8 percent of those who entered primary school to attain college and university education. Quality has been further augmented by regulating entrants into departments and particularly into the premier institutions. With the top colleges—Seoul National University, Yonsei University and Ewha Women's University—allowed to accept less than a quarter of the entrants into higher-education competition into these institutions became fiercer. The key institutions in the Republic of Korea have been nurtured and given facilities and funds above the others. Their staff have better qualifications, they have more funds, they are encouraged to do research and publish, and are provided with a more conducive research environment. Further improvements were effected during the 1980s through reform of college entrance examinations and entrance to be based on a combination of school record and national achievement tests. A 30 percent larger enrollment than expected to pass was permitted—setting a graduation quota (Park Yungchul, 1983, p. 6). This further placed pressure on the students to perform well while in university or college. They were rewarded in turn with easy access into the key jobs encouraging more to try the difficult route into these institutions.

While the higher-education systems may be viewed as quite contrary to the traditions of freedom of access and scholarship that are extolled in many developed countries they did serve national needs to produce a breed of technologists that were the best within the country.

Research Structures and Environment

As intellectual centres and producers of knowledge universities in the NICs present a paradox: they remain on the periphery of a world system of knowledge; yet within their own countries they represent the most important centres of knowledge and indigenous research geared to national development needs. At one level these researchers and scientists of developing countries are influenced by the knowledge, training, patents, innovations and research agendas generated in the research centres of the industrialized world. Working in small scientific communities and lacking the personnel, equipment or funding to enable them to work independently they orient their research and writing to issues of international concern and for recognition by the international forums. The orientation is reinforced from within their universities where recognition and promotion is accorded to those who meet the international criteria. At another level there is plenty of evidence that they have succeeded in creating an indigenous base and they have demonstrated their faith in their own capacity by committing considerable resources to the development of local research and development. They recognize that locally rooted research and knowledge development will contribute to a mature academic system as well as promote scientific developments to assist local technology for industry and provide the key personnel for further research and industrial development (Altbach, 1989, pp. 4–6).

While the universities are important in the research and development plans of the NICs: the extent to which they are central to the R&D of countries varies. The National University of Singapore plays a central role in the scientific research in the priority areas identified by the Singapore Government and carried out within the university departments or specialized institutions such as the Institute of Systems Science, which concentrates on research related to computer application. With its large number of academic staff and scientific facilities, the National University is the largest scientific agency in the country. It has achieved close collaboration for research and training with local industry (Pang and Gopinathan, 1989, p. 145). Malaysian universities on the other hand have only recently begun to sharpen their focus on scientific research for development purposes. Most of the earlier research in natural products was undertaken by specialized research institutes with the universities playing the role of trainers and teachers of scientific manpower. The development of the specialized science-and-technology universities and the setting up of the Institute of Advanced Studies point to an enhanced role for universities in development-oriented research. With the launch of the Industrial Master Plan, 1986–91, and the identification of research priorities universities are expected to play a greater role in the training of postgraduate researchers, a function that is viable only when it takes place in conjunction with a lively research environment. Nevertheless, the teaching and training function retains importance with universities expected to carry out about 22 percent of the national R&D. The universities are themselves keen to increase this research profile and have specifically directed their research agenda to national priorities. Interdisciplinary and multidisciplinary collaborative research have mushroomed and a number of consultancy agencies within universities have sprung up to undertake research on a scale and range of problems not possible within existing academic structures (Singh, 1989, pp. 87–8).

In the Republic of Korea the private sector with its large industrial corporations plays a significant role in the sponsorship and execution of research. The government has tried to give the universities an important role through the establishment of the Korea Advanced Institute of Science and Technology (KAIST), which is to provide leadership in the training of élite scientists as well as in research. However, support for university research remains low. Research expenditure on university scientists is 15 percent of that of business and industry. The role of universities is perceived largely to train the R&D personnel and to conduct all the basic research (Lee Sungho, 1989, p. 55).

In Taiwan, the universities and the Academia Sinica represent the two agencies involved in scientific research. The universities engage in both applied and basic research but research is limited to the prestigious public institutions. They receive research money from the National Science Council but this is usually inadequate for large-scale efforts (Hsieh, 1989, pp. 189–90). With the establishment of the Science-based Industrial Park, located close to several important universities, more university researchers have become involved with high-technology research (Altbach et al., 1989, p. 25).

All countries have attempted to improve the motivation and the conditions for local research. Research was recognized as a team effort to be effectively carried out in a co-operative effort. If the problems of developing countries were to be advanced, multi-disciplinary teams working in close collaboration were most likely to succeed. Hence we see the setting up of such teams and project groups to carry out research in strategic development areas—marine ecology, agricultural processing, natural disaster mitigation, increasing crop and annual production, and finding alternative uses for traditional products like tin and rubber. All such projects have greatly enhanced the productivity of these countries. In countries where professors' salaries were low, efforts have been made to raise their incomes and status, as in Taiwan where the National Research Council paid supplementary research stipends. Outstanding scientists and their work are given recognition by the instituting of outstanding research awards by the professional bodies and research councils.

Singapore has introduced a package of reforms to make for a more conducive research environment. It has improved staff/student ratios, tripled the research budget, increased the ties with prestigious foreign universities in developed countries, and improved university and industry ties which have benefitted both parties. In particular excellence in research and scholarship has been paraded as an ideal to be upheld. Visiting scholars and advisory panels of outstanding calibre internationally are invited to dialogue with local scholars, advise the government and the Science Council, give directions and often set standards for research. Within the university, research and publication in respected international journals are highly regarded for promotion, and staff are given an orientation and training that leans towards research. To some extent these measures exist in other countries. All vie for international standards while maintaining a local thrust and validity in their research.

Universities clearly play a prominent role in the development of scientific research which provides the stimulus to indigenous development. By stressing research and publications for promotion they have brought scientific research into prominence. Through funding managed by national research councils, governments have managed to orient their research agendas to problems of national priority. Most importantly, universities provide the training for all technologically skilled manpower that flows into industry and other research institutes. They represent in these countries the core of highly skilled manpower to which emerging new functions can be added. Universities fulfil multiple roles in their development which no other institution has the capacity to fulfil.

The Language of Science

The approach the NICs have adopted to the language question in higher education is instructive. All function in the international knowledge and research system by using English, which enables them access to English-language journals and research networks, the largest pool of international scientific knowledge.

In Singapore despite official recognition of four languages—Malay, English, Mandarin and Tamil—English is in effect the only language of post-secondary and higher education. All scientific journals are published in English and the government has adopted a policy of using English to be part of the international economy in trade and scientific knowledge exchange. As such, language is not an issue. A high proportion (close to 50 percent) of the teaching staff at the National University of Singapore are foreign and teaching materials from abroad are commonly used. The other three countries have a more interesting approach to language, with lessons for other developing countries. All have used a foreign language prior to independence, all have an indigenous language as the principal medium of instruction, all have to varying degrees made provision for instruction in and the use of English in higher education and all have made tremendous efforts to develop and adapt their indigenous language capacity and vocabulary for scientific purposes.

Malaysia has gradually changed the medium of instruction from English to Bahasa Malaysia. At present all undergraduate and a high proportion of graduate courses are conducted in Bahasa Malaysia. This has been accompanied by massive efforts to provide textbooks and instructional materials in Bahasa Malaysia, spearheaded by a government-funded agency, Dewan Bahasa dan Pustaka (Language and Literature Agency), which has promoted writing, translation and publication of texts and scholarly journals in Bahasa Malaysia. At the same time, the need for English as a language of international communication and science and technology is recognized and it is a second language for all university students ensuring that they possess at least the capacity to read and understand foreign journals and texts. Over the last few years the requirements for English have been increased and a pass in English made a condition for graduating. A considerable amount of postgraduate teaching, research and writing of theses, which are externally validated, continue to be in English. Many academic staff are competent in English and write both locally and for international publications in English. More than 90 percent of scientific writing is in English—both locally and overseas, compared with 70 percent, which is the norm for all the faculties (Singh, 1989, pp. 130–1).

After their bitter experience with Japan, followed by nationalist governments strongly influenced by the United States, Taiwan and the Republic of Korea made the indigenous languages the principal media of instruction at all levels of the education system while English was adopted for communication with the rest of the world. In the Republic of Korea, most of the journals are published in Korean but Taiwan has promoted a number of scientific journals for international circulation. Both countries provide English for advanced training in science and technology as many of the reference materials are in that language. Professors in the prestigious universities are rewarded by better promotion prospects if they write in English and publish in international journals.

Altbach et al. (1989) conclude that 'all four countries function in an international scientific system dominated by English and all have made adjustments to this fact'. The Republic of Korea has the longest indigenous scientific infrastructure with journals and texts published largely in Korean. In Taiwan, teaching is done in the indigenous language but texts and other materials for advanced work are largely in English. Malaysia has gone a long way to indigenization of teaching but shortages of materials and the need to be part of an international scientific network have prompted a high degree of advanced scientific teaching, research and publication in English. Singapore's scientific teaching and research activities function wholly in English. All depend on the international scientific community for validation of their courses and postgraduate education. All place a value on publications in international journals for promotion. Such a focus keeps the link with English as a language of science and technology and also with the values and concepts of the international scientific community (Altbach et al., 1989, p. 8).

The NICs that have been examined here—the Republic of Korea, Malaysia, Singapore and Taiwan—have over the last two decades achieved quite remarkable industrial growth as a key component of overall national development. All have been imbued with the belief that education is an agent for development and in the absence of many national resources investment in education is of primary importance as the engine for change and progress. They have identified targeted growth areas within industry and manufacturing and structured their education systems to supply the necessary levels of skills for their proper functioning. In particular the higher-education systems have been developed in tandem with their industrialization policies demonstrating many of the characteristics of planned economies, with fixed growth targets and manpower forecasting aligned to intended growth patterns.

The NICs have demonstrated their ability to enforce and implement their plans through legislation and regular development plans. A number of features are pertinent: all the countries at some point in their development adopted specific measures that increased their science-and-technology capacity. Initially science enrollment and subsequently engineering and technology rather than natural science and medical enrollments were given priority; specialized institutes and centres of science and engineering, advanced study and research were established; the areas of study and research were targeted to maximize the heavy investment of scarce resources; postgraduate education was given a boost with the award of research scholarships, establishment of graduate schools in these fields and improved staff/student ratio. The Republic of Korea, Singapore and Taiwan demonstrate these qualities to a higher degree than Malaysia, but the trend in the latter is clearly towards the same pattern. Within their institutions research has gained prestige and is the most highly regarded activity of university staff. Universities are cognizant of this function and the support and environment for research has gradually improved. Mindful of their constituents, university researchers devote considerable time to consultancy and publication locally, but also remain aware of the need to maintain an international profile and standards and keep up their contacts with these research and scientific colleges. They have received encouragement from a large number of measures their institutions have introduced to stimulate and raise the quality of their research. The international dimension has been easy to maintain in these countries because they have retained an international language, in this case English, either as the primary medium of instruction as in Singapore, or as a second language, as in Malaysia, or as the language of scientific research and publication as in the Republic of Korea and Taiwan.

Higher-education systems have been shown to fulfil two essential prerequisites for industrial development. First, higher education has supplied adequate manpower quantity and quality to work at the different levels of the economy. Two clear strata have developed—one high-level scientific and professional layer of top research, managerial and executive positions in industry and a second layer that supplies the practitioners. Secondly, the specialized research institutions and universities have been able to adopt, adapt and improve the technology that has been imported. Considerable effort has been made to use technology for local development and there is evidence of fairly active scientific activity which partly interfaces with the international community but at the same time provides a focus for technology transfer and adaptation for local developmental needs. The success of the NICs in structural adjustment and development draws attention to the role of human-resource development in development. In particular interest is focused on the contribution that higher education may make to this process. Discussions on human-resource-led development present conflicting conclusions about the crucial role of education in the take-off for industrial development. While little conclusive evidence has been adduced by research proving that higher education is a sufficient condition for development, the evidence from the NICs points to the need for higher education as a necessary condition. As has been shown, the NICs have made large investments in higher education and shaped their higher-education systems and institutions to suit their particular needs both quantitatively and qualitatively. The role of higher-education institutions as the principal producers of the scientific and technological know-how and manpower contributing to national goals and development cannot be overlooked.

References and Bibliography

Altbach, P. G., et al. (eds.). 1989. *Scientific Development and Higher Education: The Case of Newly Industrializing Nations*. New York, Praeger.

Bom, Mo Chung. 1988. The Role of Government in Higher Education. Country Report: Korea. In: *The Role of Government in Asian Higher Education Systems: Issues and Prospects*. Hiroshima, Reports from the Fourth International Seminar on Higher Education in Asia, Research Institute for Higher Education, Hiroshima University.

Chowdhury, A.; Kerkpatrick, C. H.; Islam, I. 1986. Structural Adjustment and Human Resources Development in ASEAN. Asian Network of Human Development Planning Institutes Technical Workshop, Bangkok, 16–18 December 1986. ILO-ARTEP.

Hsieh, S. H. 1989. University Education and Research in Taiwan. In: P. G. Altbach, et al. (eds.), *Scientific Development and Higher Education: The Case of Newly Industrializing Nations*, pp. 177–214. New York, Praeger.

Isahak, Haron. 1988. The Role of the Government in Higher Education in Malaysia. *The Role of Government in Asian Higher Education Systems: Issues and Prospects*. Hiroshima, Reports from the Fourth International Seminar on Higher Education in Asia, Research Institute for Higher Education, Hiroshima University.

Kim Jong-Chol; Hong Sah-Myung. 1984. *Higher Education in Korea*. Seoul, Korean Educational Development Institute. (Contract Research Report, 84–1).

Republic of Korea. National Bureau of Statistics, Economic Planning Board. 1990. *Major Statistics of Korean Economy, 1990*. Seoul, National Bureau of Statistics.

Lee Sungho. 1989. Higher Education and Research Environments in Korea. In: P. G. Altbach, et al. (eds.), *Scientific Development and Higher Education: The Case of Newly Industrializing Nations*, pp. 31–82. New York, Praeger.

Lim, David. 1984. *Industrial Restructuring in Singapore*. Bangkok, ILO-ARTEP. (Asian Employment Programme Working Papers.)

Malaysia. 1986. *Fifth Malaysia Plan, 1986–90*. Kuala Lumpur, National Printing Department.

——. 1988. *Third Malaysia Plan*. Kuala Lumpur, National Printing Department.

——. 1989. *Mid-Term Review of the Fifth Malaysia Plan 1986–90*. Kuala Lumpur, National Printing Department.

Pang Eng Fong. 1982. *Education, Manpower and Development in Singapore*. Singapore, Singapore University Press.

Pang Eng Fong; Gopinathan, S. 1989. Public Policy, Research Environment and Higher Education in Singapore. In: P. G. Altbach, et al., (eds.), *Scientific Development and Higher Education: The Case of Newly Industrializing Nations*, pp. 137–76. New York, Praeger.

Park, Yungchul. 1983. *South Korea's Experience with Industrial Adjustment in the 1970s*. Bangkok, ILO-ARTEP. (Asian Employment Programme Working Papers.)

Sanyal, B. C. 1990. *Technological Development and its Implications for Educational Planning*. Paris, International Institute for Educational Planning. (Research Report, 85.)

Sanyal, B. C.; Hyun-Sook Yu. 1989. *Technological Development in the Micro-electronics Industry and its Implications for Educational Planning in the Republic of Korea*. Paris, International Institute for Educational Planning. (HEP Research Report, 72).

Selth, A. 1988. *The Development of Public Education in the Republic of Korea: An Australian Perspective*. Nathan, Queensland, Centre for the Study of Australian-Asian Relations. Division of Asian and International Studies, Nathan, Queensland. Griffith University. (Research Paper, 46.)

Singapore Department of Statistics. 1971/72, 1986, 1990a. *Year Book of Statistics*, Singapore, Department of Statistics.

——. Ministry of Education. 1990b. *Education Statistics Digest, 1990*. Singapore, Ministry of Education.

Singh, J. S. 1989. Scientific Personnel, Research Environment and Higher Education in Malaysia. In: P. G. Altbach, et al., (eds.), *Scientific Development and Higher Education: The Case of Newly Industrializing Nations*, pp. 83–136. New York, Praeger.

Taiwan. Council for Economic Planning and Development. 1990. *Taiwan Statistical Data Book, 1989*. Taiwan, CEPD.

UNESCO. 1972–90. *Statistical Yearbook* (varied years).

World Bank. 1990. *Development Report*. New York, Oxford University Press.

Yi-Rong Young. 1991. Higher Education and National Development in Taiwan. Paper delivered at the 1991 Bristol Conference on Higher Education and Development, Bristol (United Kingdom), 7–9 January.

The Development of Higher Education in Taiwan

WEN-HSING WU*, SHUN-FEN CHEN** AND CHEN-TSOU WU**

Abstract. Taiwan had been ruled by Japan for fifty-one years before the end of World War II. The island's higher education was established during that period, mainly to support Japan's policies of colonization and expansion. When Taiwan was restored to China in 1945, the Japanese system of education was replaced by that of modern China, which followed the American prototype after 1922. American impact on the island's higher education has been substantial since then. However, there are some unique features in Taiwan's higher education. Centralized administration and college entrance examinations are two examples.

The purpose of this article is to examine foreign influence on the development of higher education in Taiwan. The first part discusses the establishment and shaping of higher education in Taiwan under Japanese rule. The second part examines the reform and development of the island's higher education after World War II. The process of transition from the colonial system to the Chinese system before 1949 is first explored. Then, the development of higher education after 1949 is discussed, under the headings of institutional type, entrance examinations, curriculum, study abroad, and so forth. The foreign impact upon the current system and the unique features of this system is presented in the final part of the paper.

Higher Education During the Japanese Occupation Period (1895-1945)

In imperial China, higher learning was offered in the capital, while local regions provided only elementary and secondary education. Although in the last years of the Ching Dynasty, Western-style universities were founded in several cities, there was no institution of higher education in Taiwan before it was ceded to Japan. Therefore in tracing the development of higher education on this island, we must start from the Japanese occupation period.

In the Japanese occupation period, a Western-style system of education was established in Taiwan. Although the colonial government in Taiwan adopted a policy of gradual assimilation, and instruction at each level was in Japanese, ethnic discrimination and separation existed in education for a long time. In the years prior to 1919, the so-called "experimental period" in education, Japanese authorities did not establish a complete system of education in Taiwan.[1] The main educational institutions were common schools (elementary schools), which were set up in order to replace *shu-fang*, the traditional Chinese private schools. There were very few post-primary institutions. Of

* Department of History, National Taiwan Normal University, Taipei, Taiwan, R.O.C.
**Department of Education, National Taiwan Normal University, Taipei, Taiwan, R.O.C.

them only a five-year medical school can be classified as an institution of higher learning.

In the early days of Japanese rule, epidemic diseases were prevalent in Taiwan. The traditional Chinese herb doctors, lacking knowledge in Western medicine, were not able to provide the necessary treatment. At the same time, Japanese doctors trained in Western medical science were insufficient in number. In view of the above facts, the colonial government established a medical training center attached to Taihoku Hospital. Two years later, the center was converted into a medical school for training Taiwanese doctors of Western medicine so as to replace Chinese herb doctors gradually.[2] Although the school encountered problems with the recruitment of students in the beginning, access to it soon became highly competitive. (Less than 10 percent of the applicants were admitted.) There were three reasons for this: first, the medical school was one of only two schools of the highest level in Taiwan which Taiwanese students might attend; second, the colonial government tried very hard to encourage Taiwanese graduates of common schools with outstanding records to take the school's entrance examination; third, physicians usually earned a high income. Consequently, the Taiwanese elite competed for the profession of medicine. Such a trend still prevails today.[3]

Since neither the level of the students it admitted nor the period of study was equivalent to that of the medical schools in Japan, the academic standard of this medical school was lower than its counterparts in the ruling country. In 1918, a one-year Department of Tropical Medicine and a three-year Department of

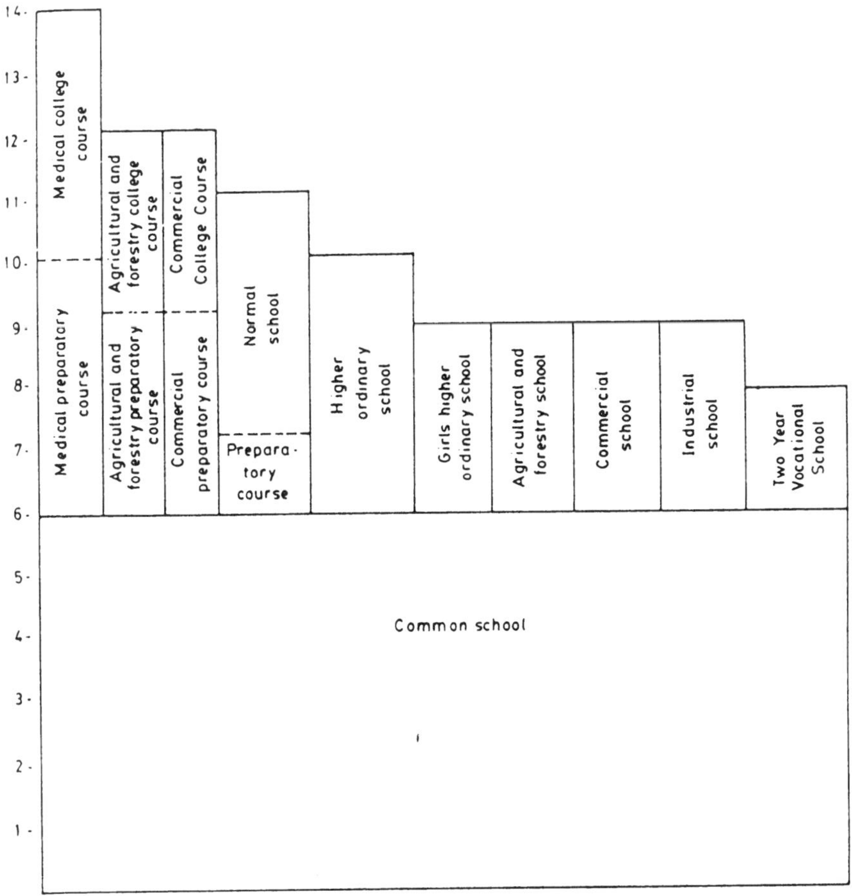

***Fig. 1:* School system as outlined by the 1919 rescript**

Source: E. Patricia Tsurumi, Japanese Colonial Education in Taiwan, 1895–1945. (Cambridge, Massachusetts: Harvard University Press, 1977), p. 85.

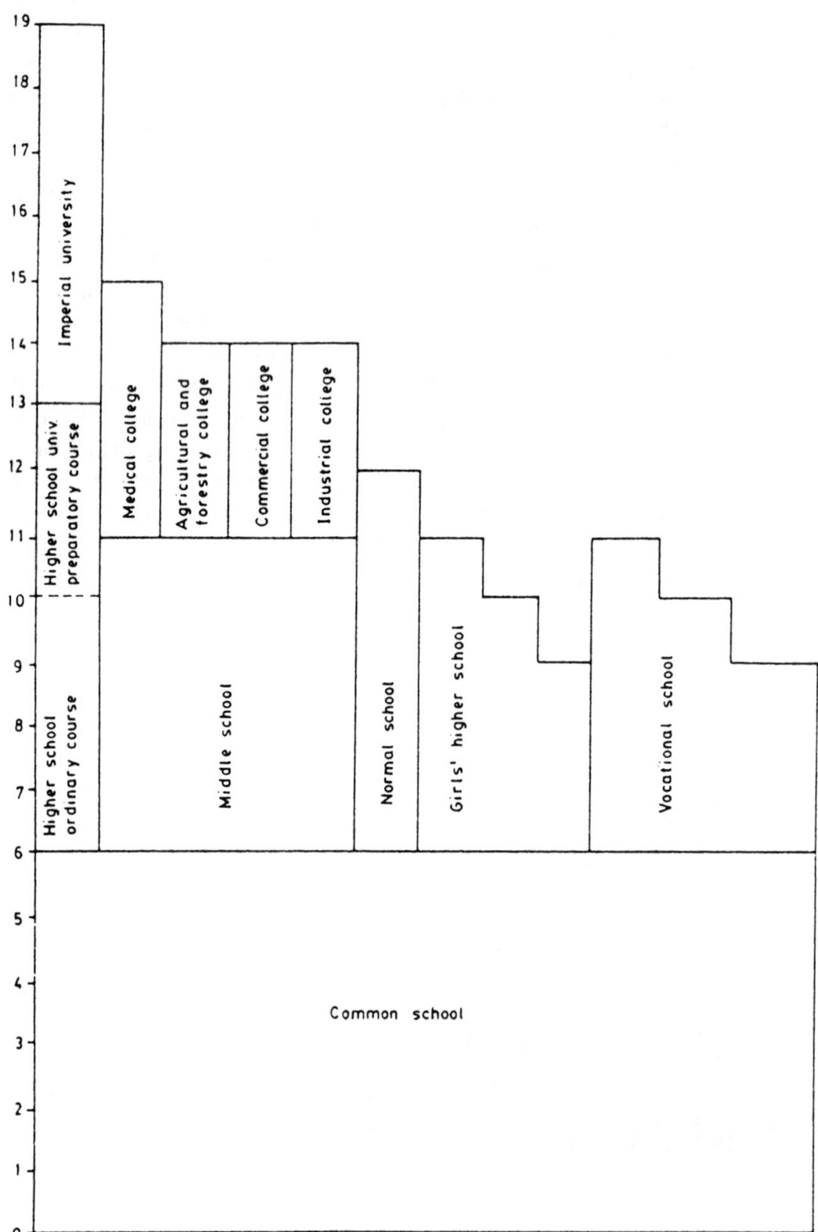

Fig. 2: **School system as outlined by the 1922 rescript**
Source: Taiwan Kyoiku Kai, ed., Taiwan Kyoiku Enkaku Shi.

Research were set up, admitting the school's own graduates. Soon a four-year specialized Department of Medicine was established, admitting graduates of Japanese middle schools. As a result, the medical school became a true institution of higher learning. In the meanwhile, since the usual practice of admitting only Taiwanese students was given up by the medical school, Japanese students choosing to be doctors could pursue studies in Taiwan.[4]

In 1919, an Education Rescript was promulgated in order to fulfill the policy of assimilation, answer the call of Taiwanese for educational reform, and meet the demands of the Island's economy for raising the level of general and technical education.[5] As shown in Figure 1, the institutions of higher education included a six-year agriculture and forestry college, a six-year commercial college, an eight-year medical college, and Taihoku Commercial

College (for Japanese students only). Since these colleges were equivalent to post-primary vocational schools in Japan, and the level of the medical college was also lower than its Japanese counterpart, it was obvious that Taiwanese were discriminated against by the Japanese colonial rulers.[6] It was pointed out that the aim of this system, which emphasized secondary vocational education, was to "integrate Taiwanese into the colonial economy's rapidly growing industrial and commercial sectors" so as to decrease the need for recruiting skilled workers from Japan.[7]

The educational system designed by the 1919 Rescript did not satisfy Taiwanese demands for education. Even some Japanese considered the system inadequate and criticized it. Three years later, in 1922, a new rescript was promulgated, declaring that ethnic discrimination and separation were to be removed for the advancement of "integrated schooling" from secondary level up (except for normal schools). Later a number of post-primary institutions were set up based on the model of Japanese institutions. The educational system outlined by the 1922 Rescript is shown in Figure 2. The institutions of higher education founded after the integration rescript included: Taihoku Higher School, the higher course of which was for university preparation; Taihoku Imperial University, converted from a two-faculty university in 1928 into a comprehensive one in 1943; and a few college admitting middle school graduates with a study period of three to four years, such as: Taihoku Medical College, Taichu Agriculture and Forestry College, Tainan Commercial College, Taihoku Commercial College, Tainan Industrial College, and Private Taihoku Girl's College.

In reality the places offered by these institutions were largely occupied by Japanese students (see Tables 1 and 2). Taiwanese did not enjoy equal educational opportunities. Even Japanese public opinion mentioned this fact

TABLE 1
Number of Taihoku Imperial University Graduates till 1943 by Faculty and Ethnic Group

Ethnic group	*Faculty*			
	Literature & Politics	*Science & Agriculture*	*Medicine*	*Total*
Taiwanese	45 (14%)	37 (11%)	79 (45%)	161 (19%)
Japanese	277 (86%)	303 (89%)	97 (55%)	677 (81%)
Total	322 (100%)	340 (100%)	176 (100%)	838 (100%)

Source: Wu Wen-hsing, A Study of the Taiwanese Elite under Japanese Rule (Ph.D. dissertation, National Taiwan Normal University, 1986), p. 104.

TABLE 2
Number of College Graduates till 1942 by Institution and Ethnic Group

Ethnic group	*Institution*				
	Agr. & Forestry college	*Commercial college*	*Industrial college*	*Medical college*	*Total*
Taiwanese	99 (12%)	425 (21%)	162 (21%)	1661 (74%)	2347 (40%)
Japanese	716 (88%)	1607 (79%)	610 (79%)	598 (26%)	3531 (60%)
Total	815 (100%)	2023 (100%)	772 (100%)	2259 (100%)	5878 (100%)

Source: Wu Wen-hsing, A Study of the Taiwanese Elite under Japanese Rule (Ph.D. dissertation, National Taiwan Normal University, 1986), pp. 101, 105.

and concluded that the so-called "assimilation" actually decreased the opportunities for Taiwanese students to enter institutions of higher education in their homeland.[8] Taiwanese, of course, kept on criticizing this aspect of educational inequality. As shown in Tables 1 and 2, the number of Japanese graduates was much larger than the Taiwanese counterpart except in the field of medicine. It was obvious that the so-called "integrated schooling" was only lip service since 80 percent of the educational opportunities offered by Taiwan's higher learning institutions, except Medical College and Faculty of Medicine, Taihoku Imperial University, were taken by Japanese students. In the whole population of the islanders, the number of Taiwanese college graduates was very small. It was not surprising that many Taiwanese went to Japan to study. (The number of Taiwanese receiving higher learning in Japan amounted to 60,000 before the end of World War II.) Japanese institutions' admittance of Taiwanese students somewhat ameliorated the inadequacy of higher education on the island.[9]

The institutions of higher ameliorated learning in Taiwan established after 1922 were comparable to those in Japan. However, there were some distinguishing features in these institutions. This was because the institutions were mainly founded to serve special purposes. For example, the Medical College focused on the investigation, study, and prevention of tropical diseases. Its teaching faculty involved many distinguished Japanese scholars of medicine. Attracted by the abundance of research materials in Taiwan, they were involved in the study of tropical diseases, such as epidemics, parasites, and so forth. Their efforts finally made the college a research center of tropical medicine. Many of its graduates turned out to be outstanding scholars in that field.[10] Commercial colleges were set up in order to support the expansion of Japanese economic forces in Taiwan, South China, and the South Pacific regions. Therefore, these colleges offered the subject of second language, such as Chinese and Malay, and of area studies on the above regions, in addition to ordinary courses.[11] Taiwan Industrial College was established to meet the demands for developing Taiwan's industry. The three departments it created initially, Mechanics, Electrical Engineering, and Applied Chemistry, were closely related to the needs of Taiwan's industry.[12] Although the level of these colleges was lower than that of universities, journals were published periodically, and a thesis was required for graduation.

The founding of Taihoku Imperial University was significantly due to Japan's ambition for expanding southward. Since Taiwan was considered a good place for conducting area studies on South China and the South Pacific, the university was originally made a research center for such studies. Many distinguished scholars were recruited to the university. The ratio of teachers to students was as high as 3 to 5. More than 100 chairs were created in the university's five faculties with graduate studies offered by each faculty. The total number of volumes in the library amounted to nearly 500,000. In addition, there were three research institutions affiliated with the university. The university usually received government sponsorship and funding for its research.[13] Its research findings were often used by the decision-makers in the colonial government or in Japan, and have been important references for studies on modern Taiwan, south China, and the South Pacific. In short, the most important function of higher education institutions in Taiwan during the Japanese occupation period was to provide research material or high-level manpower needed for Japan's colonial policy, rather than to raise the quality of the people ruled.

Higher Education after World War II (1945 to the Present)

At the end of World War II, Taiwan was restored to China. The restoration meant not only that the territorial sovereignty of Taiwan was given back to China, but that Chinese culture was resumed on the island. Since the Republic of China had its own longstanding educational policies and systems, the reformation of education in Taiwan, after its restoration to China, is distinct from that in new countries just proclaiming independence. For better understanding of higher education in Taiwan after 1945, a brief review is made as follows on the rise of the educational system in modern China.

In the mid-nineteenth century, after being forced to open the country to international contacts by Western powers, the Ching court decided to initiate reforms by introducing Western institutions and ideas. Establishing Western style schools was deemed a necessary step to achieve this goal. In the beginning, the Japanese system of education, which was modeled on that of the European countries, was adopted. Later, in the 1922 educational reform of the Republic, it was replaced by the American prototype.[14] Up to 1949, American influence upon each level of education in the Chinese mainland had been substantial. At the tertiary level, the influence was shown in such aspects as institutional organization, curriculum, graduation requirement, degree structure, and the like. With this short description of Chinese education as a background, we now discuss the development of higher education in Taiwan after World War II, which can further be divided into two stages.

TABLE 3
Number of Tertiary Institutions

Year	*Type of Institutions*		
	Colleges and Universities	*Junior Colleges*	*Total*
1950	4	3	7
1960	15	12	27
1970	22	70	92
1980	26	77	103
1986	28	77	105

Source: Ministry of Education, Educational Statistics of the ROC (Taipei, 1987), pp. 2–5.

TABLE 4
Enrollment at Tertiary Institutions

Year	*Type of Institutions*		
	Colleges and Universities	*Junior Colleges**	*Total*
1950	5,379	1,286	6,665
1960	27,172	7,888	35,060
1970	95,145	55,301	150,446
1980	159,394	105,246	264,640
1986	198,166	147,570	345,736

Source: Ministry of Education, Educational Statistics of the ROC (Taipei, 1987), pp. 18–21.

The Period Immediately after Restoration: 1945–1949

After Taiwan was restored, people on the island began to have full access to the opportunities of education, as provided by the Chinese constitution. In the meanwhile, all the tertiary institutions were reformed according to the model of modern Chinese colleges and universities, which was largely based on the American prototype. The tertiary institutions existing on the island prior to 1943 included one university, one higher school, and four colleges (equivalent to junior colleges today). Immediately after Taiwan was restored to China, these institutions, except for the one which was disbanded, were renamed and reorganized based on the model adopted on the Chinese mainland. Later the higher school was transformed into a teachers college, and the three colleges were upgraded to university level. In addition to the changes in existing institutions, three new junior colleges were founded before the Nationalist government was relocated on the island.[15]

The reform of the existing institutions was enforced step by step. For example, in November 1945, Taihoku Imperial University was renamed National Taiwan University. One of its five faculties, Literature and Politics, was divided into two, and the term "faculty" was substituted by "college", which was used in the Chinese educational system. As a result, the university consisted of six colleges (Arts, Law, Science, Medicine, Agriculture, and Engineering). Many Japanese professors were asked to stay and they taught at the university. It was not until August 1946 that the university was reorganized based on the model of Chinese Universities. Its chair system was replaced by the department. Students took required courses and electives offered by their department, and credits were counted for each course. A study period of 4 years was required for graduation instead of 3 to 6 years as in the Japanese system. In order to retain the virtues of the chair system, a number of institutes were set up in each department. Each institute was headed by a full professor, with a number of junior faculty members working as research associates. In the Department of History, for instance, there were 6 institutes (Sociology, Ethnology, South Pacific History, Chinese History, Japanese History, and European History). The total number of institutes within the University's 24 departments (College of Medicine not included) was 84.[16] The research task of each chair was thus undertaken by the institute. On the other hand, Japanese professors were replaced by Chinese professors gradually so that the research and teaching activities of the university might be continued. In the beginning of 1947, about 20 percent of the university's faculty members (both full-time and part-time) were Japanese.[17] At the end of that year, Japanese professors still constituted 8 percent of the faculty members.[18]

There were some problems with the instructional language at that time. Since Taiwanese did not speak Mandarin, it was difficult for them to understand the lectures of the Chinese professors. To overcome this difficulty, Taiwanese freshmen were required to spend several hours per week learning Mandarin and Chinese Literature. Some of them continued to take Mandarin courses in the second year.

In sum, the process of reform during this short period was gradual and smooth. Most of the institutions existing prior to 1943, after being renamed and reorganized, continued to enroll students. Because of the superior research conditions established during the Japanese occupation period, these institutions have continued to enjoy high prestige in Taiwan.

The Period Following the Relocation of the Chinese Government in Taiwan: 1950 to the Present

In the winter of 1949, when the Chinese communists occupied the whole mainland, the Nationalist government was forced to move to Taiwan. This formerly remote island suddenly became the seat of the central government of the Republic of China. Taiwan began to develop rapidly. At the same time, Chinese educational policy was enforced on the island more thoroughly than in the previous period. Japanese influence thus diminished further.

Economy and Education

The success of Taiwan's economic policy is well known. A peaceful land reform, first enforced on the island in the Spring of 1949, successfully led to prosperity in the rural regions. As advances were made in agriculture, the government focused efforts on the development of industry. The first 4-Year Economic Construction Plan began in 1953.[19] It was not until 1963 that Taiwan shifted from an agricultural economy to an economy with equal emphasis on agriculture and industry.[20] The living standards of the people on the island were significantly raised through economic prosperity.

Education is closely related to Taiwan's widely reported economic growth. Popularizing education at elementary and lower-secondary level was an important government policy of the two decades after 1949. Since the early 1960's efforts have been made to expand education at the upper-secondary level, especially vocational and technical education, in order to meet the demands of economic development.

In addition to economic prosperity, the widespread enthusiasm for schooling also accounts for the rapid growth of education in Taiwan during the past four decades. There is an old Chinese saying "The pursuit of knowledge is superior to all the other occupations." Consequently, the Chinese people usually crave for more education as long as their basic needs for living are satisfied.

Expansion

Along with the relocation of the government, many anti-communist mainlanders, including college professors and students, arrived on the island. The number of college professors and students in Taiwan thus increased rapidly. In addition, some equipment, books, and other college facilities from mainland China were turned over to local colleges and universities. The quality of higher education in Taiwan thus improved significantly within a short period due to the influx of these people and assets, especially in the fields of humanities and social sciences, which were very weak in the Japanese occupation period.[21]

TABLE 5
Proportion of Higher-education Students in Total 18- to 24-year-old Population (unit = %)

	Sex		
Year	*Male*	*Female*	*Total*
1950	NA	NA	NA
1960	4.9	1.3	3.1
1970	10.2	6.4	8.3
1980	11.9	9.1	10.5
1986	15.0	13.3	14.2

Source: Directorate-general of Budget, Accounting and Statistics, Executive Yuan, Statistical Yearbook of the ROC (Taipei, 1987), p. 249.

Higher education expanded most rapidly in the 1960s. This was partly due to the growth at the secondary level. In addition, many five-year junior colleges were set up in the decade in order to cultivate medium-level manpower needed by industry and business. As shown in Tables 3 and 4, the number of tertiary institutions in Taiwan increased 15-times (from 7 in 1950 to 105 in 1986), while student enrollment increased 52-times (from 6,665 in 1950 to 345,736 in 1986).[22] Table 5 indicates that the percentage of the relevant age cohort (18–24 years old) going on to post-secondary education increased from 2.2 in 1957 to 14.2 in 1986. Education at the graduate level developed quickly after 1970. The ratio of graduate students to the number of students at four-year institutions increased from 0.09 percent in 1950 to 6.78 percent in 1986 (see Table 6).

Types of Institutions

The 105 institutions of higher learning presently existing in Taiwan can be divided into two categories: (1) colleges and universities, and (2) junior colleges. The colleges and universities offer four-year undergraduate programs leading to a bachelor's degree. Most of them also offer Master's programs and some doctoral. The second category consists of three types of junior colleges: the two-year junior college admits vocational high school graduates; the three-year junior college admits academic high school graduates; and the five-year junior college admits junior high school graduates. A diploma, not a degree, is awarded upon graduation at any junior college. The status of the above institutions in the educational system is shown in Figure 3.

Among all the tertiary institutions, 7 were originally established in mainland China, then were reopened in Taiwan following 1949.[23] Three were formerly colleges or higher schools set up in Taiwan during the Japanese occupation period, but were reorganized and upgraded after 1945.[24] Only one institution, the National Taiwan University, was in existence prior to 1945. The others were opened after Taiwan was restored to China without any predecessors either in mainland China before 1949 or on the island prior to 1945.

In addition to the 105 traditional institutions, the University of the Air was opened in 1986, drawing upon the experience of the British and Japanese Open Universities. It aims to offer opportunities for higher education through ways other than face-to-face instruction. Due to its non-traditional style, the

TABLE 6
Ratio of Graduate Students to the Enrollment of Four-year Institutions

Year	*Number of graduate students (A)*	*Enrollment of 4-year institutions (B)*	*(A) / (B) %*
1950	5	5,379	0.09
1960	473	27,172	1.61
1970	2,295	95,145	2.43
1980	6,303	159,394	3.95
1986	13,437	198,166	6.78

Source: Ministry of Education, Educational Statistics of the ROC (Taipei, 1987), pp. 18–21.

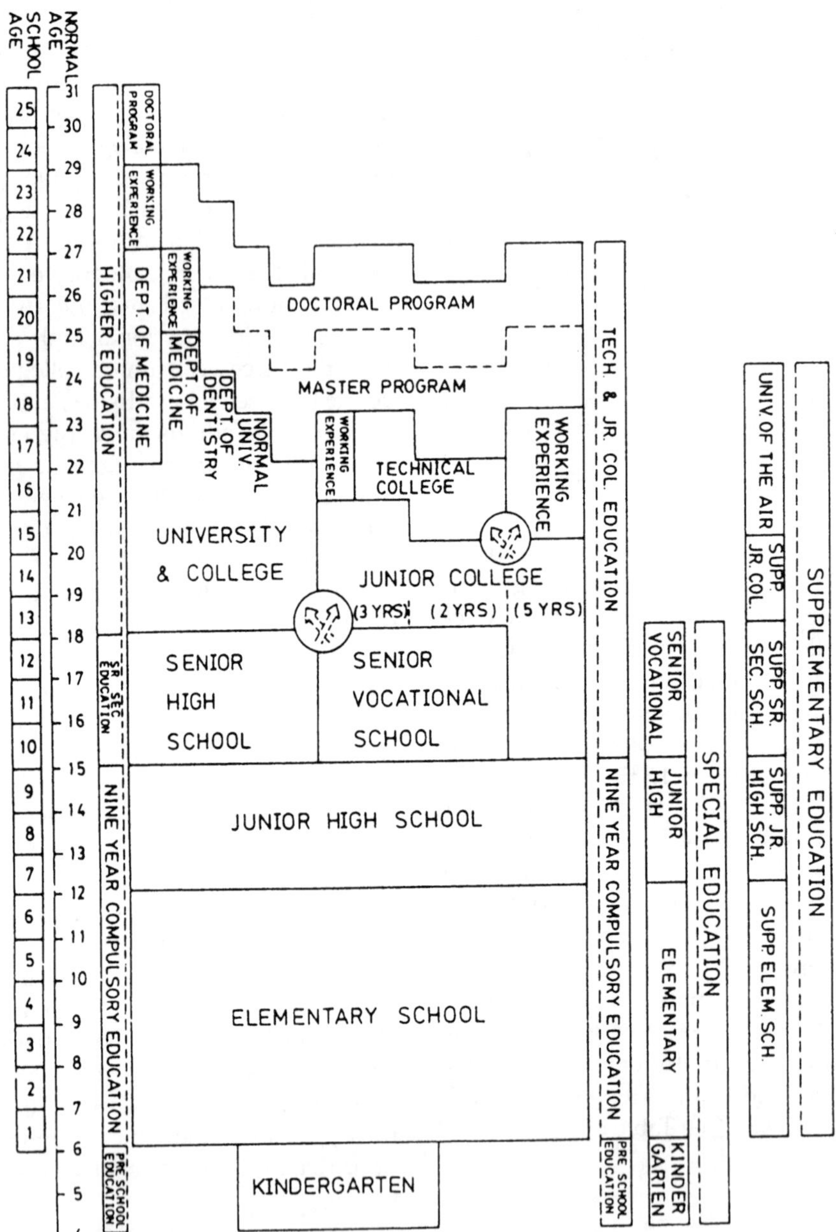

***Fig. 3:* Current educational system in Taiwan, ROC**

Source: Ministry of Education: Educational Statistics of ROC (Taipei, 1987), p. i.

University is classified into the category of supplementary education (adult education), as shown in Figure 1.[25]

The establishment of this University presents a good example of foreign impact upon Taiwan's higher education in recent years. However, the people on Taiwan did revise this foreign model of education according to their own ideas. It was decided that a certain kind of entrance examination needed to be held as a means of screening. (The issue of college entrance examinations will be discussed in the following section.) It was also decided that only a certificate, not a degree, could be awarded to the graduates of this University, since there would be little contact between faculty and students, which would make the education poorer, compared to the traditional college education. In spite of all these restrictions, 20,000 students enrolled in this University in the first year right after its opening, a figure which exceeded the enrollment of any one traditional university in Taiwan at that time.[26] This fact probably indicates that the island's higher education system needs to be expanded further.

Entrance Examinations

It is interesting to note that, although the current tertiary institutions in Taiwan are similar to their American counterparts, the admission policy of Taiwan's colleges is quite different from that of the institutions in America. The students are admitted to the tertiary institutions solely based on their scores on entrance examinations. There are a number of joint entrance examinations given at the tertiary level. Of them, the most competitive one is the Joint Entrance Examination for Colleges and Universities. It was first held in 1954, with around a hundred thousand applicants each year in the last decade. The admission rate is about 30 percent. There are also entrance examinations jointly held by different types of junior colleges. Although there has been prolonged argument over the value of it, the joint entrance examination is still in existence and would probably last for a certain period of time. There are two major reasons for this: first, the examination provides fair competition and excludes any possibility of back door admissions; second, the examination jointly held by similar institutions avoids duplicated admissions.

Fields of Study

Since it is the Ministry of Education that approves the establishment of each institution and decides the enrollment of each department, changes in the ratio of college students enrolled in different fields to the total enrollment usually reflect the direction of government policy. Table 7 shows that the ratio of humanities students increased considerably between 1950 and 1960, but decreased sharply after 1960. In 1986 only 9 percent of the total college students were in the field of humanities. The ratio of engineering students declined first, but increased substantially later. In 1986 it reached as high as 34 percent. The ratio of the social sciences students (mainly business and management) dropped slightly, following a period of rapid growth. In 1986, it was about 31 percent. The ratios of students in other fields either decreased steadily or fluctuated slightly. None of them exceeded 10 percent in 1986. The high proportion of students studying in the fields of engineering and business shows the fact that higher education in Taiwan has been geared to the island's economic development.

Curriculum

As mentioned earlier, after World War II the educational system in Taiwan was reorganized according to the Chinese model. There are three types of courses in Chinese colleges and universities: (1) general courses for all departments, (2) required courses for individual departments, and (3) electives. The first two types of courses are stipulated by the Ministry

TABLE 7
Ratio of College Students in Different Fields to Total Enrollment (unit: %)

Year	*Field*								
	Hmn.	*Educ.*	*Art*	*Law*	*S. Sci.*	*N. Sci.*	*Engr.*	*Med.*	*Agri.*
1950	7	3	1	3	24	7	30	17	7
1960	18	5	3	3	25	9	20	8	9
1970	12	6	3	2	35	7	20	9	6
1980	11	6	3	2	33	6	30	5	4
1986	9	5	2	2	31	6	34	8	3

Source: Ministry of Education, Educational Statistics of the ROC (Taipei, 1958, 1961, 1971, 1981, and 1987).

of Education; only the electives are offered freely by each institution. After being relocated in Taiwan, the government of the Republic of China established its basic policy of preventing the permeation of Communism and preparing for the restoration of the Chinese mainland. College curriculum was then revised to conform to the above policy. In 1950, The Three Principles of the People (later titled The Doctrine of Dr. Sun Yat-Sen) was listed as one of the general courses in all the tertiary institutions. Four years later military training was restored as a college general course with no academic credit. These two courses, created because of the unique condition the country faced, are still required for all the college students.[27]

There are other general courses for college students including Chinese, English, the General History of China, the History of Contemporary China, Physical Education (with no credit), and one of the following alternatives: the Constitution of the Republic of China, International Relationships, Introduction to Philosophy, and Introduction to Law.[28]

College students in Taiwan have been required to take general courses since the higher education system was integrated with that in the Chinese mainland at the end of World War II. The purpose of the requirement is to cultivate all-round persons. However, it has achieved very little. In most institutions students are encouraged to take as many courses in their major fields as possible. As a result, college graduates turn out to be specialists with little knowledge outside their own fields. In view of this fact, in 1983, the Ministry of Education added a new requirement: students in the area of science, engineering, agriculture or medicine must take courses of 4 to 6 credits in the area of humanities, social sciences, or the arts; while students in the area of humanities, law, or business must take courses of 4 to 6 credits in the area of natural science, applied science, or the arts.[29] It was pointed out that such a revision in college curriculum was affected by the renewed interest in general education on American campuses, aroused by the 1978 report on core curriculum issued by Harvard University.[30] However, whether the general education in Taiwan's colleges and universities can be improved by this new requirement or not is still unknown.

In addition to general courses, which must be taken by all the students regardless of their major, the required courses for each department are also stipulated by the Ministry of Education. They are subject to revision every four to six years in order to keep abreast of the world's academic current and to meet the needs of the changing society. In fact the designing and revising of departmental courses are based on the course arrangement in Western universities, especially American institutions, except for the Department of Chinese Literature. The instructional content is largely adopted from Western textbooks. Most departments in the fields of natural science and engineering use textbooks mainly in English while the classroom instruction is in Chinese.

Evaluation of Institutions

In view of the rapid growth in higher education, the Ministry of Education initiated an evaluation of colleges and universities in 1975 as a means of quality control. The idea of the evaluation project came from the accreditation of tertiary institutions in the United States. However, the former aims at analyzing the virtues and defects of each institution's faculty, curriculum, library holdings, and equipment, with no intention to set up a criterion and grant official recognition to those institutions that meet the criterion, as does the American accreditation. This is probably because the founding of each institution, either public or private, must be approved in advance by the Ministry of Education. In other words, the institutions receive governmental recognition once they are set up.

It was found that, in spite of some deficiencies, the evaluation project did help to raise the quality of the island's tertiary institutions.[31] As a result, the Ministry of Education decided to make the project a regular practice, with some revisions made on the evaluation techniques.

Study Abroad

As mentioned earlier, during the Japanese occupation period, the opportunities for Taiwanese youth to receive higher education on the island were limited, and many Taiwanese chose to pursue higher learning in Japan. After World War II, students in Taiwan still wish to study abroad. Students normally go abroad after obtaining the bachelor's degree, and most prefer to study in the United States.

Between 1950 and 1980, of the 63,061 students who were approved to study abroad, only 7,240 returned. The brain drain was as high as 90 percent. However, it decreased to 80 percent between the years 1981 to 1986. It seems that Taiwan's brain drain is slowing down gradually. This could be explained by both the improvement in the domestic conditions of Taiwan and the decrease in the demands for high-level manpower in foreign countries.[32] In addition, the tightening restriction on immigration, especially in the United States, could be another reason. In 1986, 1,583 foreign-educated students returned to Taiwan. Among them 466 were employed by academic institutions (about 30 percent) and others worked for business or the government.

The returned students, with their various advanced degrees, bring back ideas acquired from living abroad. Since Chinese people usually think highly of the returned students, many of them do have the opportunities to exert their influence. For example, in the Ministry of Education, 11 of its 12 Ministers since 1950 have studied abroad (9 were educated in the United States, and 2 in West Germany).[33] The educational policies concerning the University of the Air, the evaluation of higher education, and the general education requirement clearly reflect the Western impact.

At the institutional level, returned students are also influential. Many of them serve as college professors. In 1986, of all the faculty members at the four-year institutions, 28 percent were students returned from the U.S., 5 percent from Europe, and 8 percent from other Asian countries.[34] The ways of teaching and research of the returned scholars are largely based on what they have learned or observed in the foreign countries, especially the U.S.

Conclusion

Historically, the development of higher education in Taiwan can be divided into two periods: (1) the period of Japanese occupation: 1895–1945, and (2) the period after World War II: 1945 to the present.

In Imperial China, higher education was only offered in the capital of the nation, while schools outside the capital were of elementary or secondary level. Toward the end of the nineteenth century, the Ching government began to adopt a Western system of education but no institution of higher education was set up in Taiwan at that time.

After Taiwan was ceded to Japan in 1895, the Japanese system of education was implemented on the island, mainly to support the policies of colonization and expansion. Due to this special purpose, the pattern of higher education in Taiwan was unique, as shown in the limited number of tertiary institutions and their research orientation. In addition, the opportunities of higher learning on the island were insufficient for Taiwanese, since most of the places were taken by the Japanese students.

After World War II Taiwan was restored to China. All but one tertiary institutions on the island were renamed and reorganized. In the first few years following 1945, higher education in Taiwan grew modestly. Only three junior colleges were founded, and the fields of medicine, agriculture, and engineering continued to be dominant in higher education institutions as they were in the pre-War years.

In the winter of 1949, Taiwan became the seat of the Nationalist government. Reconstruction there thus began to speed up. Education at each level has expanded considerably since then. In 1986 the total number of higher education students exceeded 345,000, a figure almost inconceivable four decades ago.

Examining the development of higher education on the island, one can easily find foreign impact, mainly Japanese and American. Taiwan had been ruled by Japan for almost two generations before the end of World War II. It is undeniable that the establishment of tertiary institutions in that period laid the foundation for the development of the island's higher education's later stages. However, the Japanese impact on the current educational system is unsubstantial, since it was weakened intentionally by the government of the Republic of China after 1949. Nevertheless, we can still find some Japanese influence in Taiwan's higher education. First, superior Taiwanese high school graduates still compete for admission to medical colleges, and medicine continues to be a leading field in Taiwan's higher education.

Second, the development in the fields of agriculture and engineering after 1945 is due much to the stress on these fields by the tertiary institutions during the colonial period. Third, the research findings regarding South China and the South Pacific acquired in the Japanese occupation period are still valued by academia.

As soon as Taiwan was restored to China, the Japanese system of education in Taiwan was replaced by that of modern China, which followed the American model after 1922. With respect to higher education, elements such as institutional organization, study period, curriculum, degree structure and graduation requirement are similar to those found in American colleges. American influence can also be inferred by the fact that about 90 percent of the college graduates studying abroad have gone to the United States, and that many students returning from the said country play important roles in various fields related to higher education. The evaluation project on colleges and universities, and the new emphasis on general education are policies reflecting American impact.

However, the island's centralized administration in higher education is contrary to the American system of decentralization. The Ministry of Education in Taipei has the legitimate power in approving the establishment of higher learning institutions, and the addition or deletion of academic programs. It is also the Ministry of Education that determines the student number, tuition rate, and required courses in all the colleges and universities.

Such a centralized administration was established for the purpose of quality control in the late 1920s when Chinese higher education was in a state of chaos. Since centralization has long been a feature of Chinese political administration, governmental intervention in higher education seems tolerable to many people. The ideal of university autonomy has not been fully realized in the island's tertiary institutions. However, urged by many academics, the Ministry of Education is revising the Act of University. It is believed that the highly centralized system will be changed in the near future.

The college entrance examination is another feature in Taiwan's higher education. As there are far more applicants than the places offered by the island's colleges and universities, competition for admission to these institutions is keen. Therefore, the way that colleges select their students usually brings public attention. Since the examination assures fair competition and staves off irregularities, it is considered the most credible approach to judge one's qualification for college admission. Although the examination distorts education at the secondary level, no dramatic change will be made in it in the foreseeable future.

Higher education in Taiwan has grown considerably in the past four decades. In 1986, 14.2 percent of the total 18 to 24-years-old population attend postsecondary education institutions. Applying Martin Trow's concept, Taiwan is progressing toward mass higher education. However, the competition for admission to universities is keen, and it would be desirable to provide more opportunities for higher education to the young people.

Advanced studies at graduate level are also insufficient. As a result, many college graduates have gone abroad for further education. Since many of them chose to stay abroad after completing studies, the rate of brain drain was and still is high. In view of this fact, the government adopted a number of measures, such as development of graduate programs at local institutions, improvement of research facilities, increase of research funds, and so forth, in order to make Taiwan more attractive to highly-trained scholars. Such measures did have some effect, and the rate of brain drain has slowed down gradually in recent years. More efforts need to be done in this respect, so that more students trained by Taiwan's higher education would like to stay and contribute to their society.

Notes

1. Taiwan Kyoiku Kai, ed., *Taiwan Kyoiku Enkaku Shi* [A Record of the Development of Education in Taiwan] (Taihoku, 1939), p. 2.
2. Ibid., pp. 917–918.
3. Wu Wen-hsing. "Jih chu shih chi tai wan she hui ling tao chieh tseng chih yian chiu" [A study of the Taiwanese Elite under Japanese Rule] (Ph.D. diss., National Taiwan Normal University, 1986), pp. 96–98.
4. Taiwan Kyoiku Kai, ed., op. cit., pp. 927–929.
5. Wu Wen-hsing, *Jih chu shih chi tai wan shih fan chiao yu chih yian chin* [Japanese Colonial Normal Education in Taiwan, 1895–1945] (Institute of History, National Taiwan Normal University, 1983), pp. 38–39.

6. Huang Cheng-tsung. "Tai wan chiao yu kai chao lun" [On Taiwan's Educational Reform] *Tai wan ching nian* [Taiwan's Youth] (August, 1921). p. 5; and Wang Min-chuan. "Tai wan chiao yu wen teh kuan chien" [Views on the Problems of Education in Taiwan], *Tat wan ching nian* [Taiwan's Youth] (November, 1921), pp. 32–33.
7. E. Patricia Tsurumi, *Japanese Colonial Education in Taiwan, 1895–1945.* (Cambridge, Massachusetts: Harvard University Press, 1977), p. 88.
8. Yanaihara Tadao, *Yanaihara Tadao zenshu* [Collected Works of Yanaihara Tadao), Vol. 2, (Tokyo, 1963), p. 347.
9. Wu Wen-hsing, "Jih chu shih chi tai wan she hui ling tao chieh tseng chih yian chiu". pp. 115.
10. Oda Toshiro. *Taiwan igaku gojunen* [A Fifty-year History of Medicine in Taiwan] (Tokyo, 1974), pp. 69–70, 105–110, 116–120, 135–137.
11. Taiwan Kyoiku Kai, ed., op. cit., pp. 942–947.
12. Ibid., p. 951.
13. Taihoku Teikoku Daigaku, ed., *Taihoku Teikoku Daigaku Ichiran* [An outline of Taipei Imperial University] (Taihoku, 1943). pp. 42–53; and E. Patricia Tsurumi, op. cit., p. 123.
14. Wu Chen-tsou. *Chung kuo a hsueh chiao yu fa chan shih* [The History of Development of University Education in China] (Taipei: San Ming Book Company, 1982), p. 175.
15. Commission on the Compilation of the Almanac, Ministry of Education, *Ti ssu tsu chung hua min kuo chiao yu nian chian* [The Fourth Almanac of the Education in the Republic of China] (Taipei, Cheng Chung Book Company, 1974), p. 656.
16. *Kuo li tai wan ta hsueh kai kuan* [Catalog of National Taiwan university] (Taipei, 1947), pp. 3–4, 86-93.
17. Ibid., pp. 100–101.
18. *Kuo li tai wan ta hsueh shao kan* [Periodical of National Taiwan University], 5, (December 1, 1947), p. 2.
19. *Li fa yuan kung pao* [Communique of the Legislative Yuan], session 34, no. 1 (October, 1964), p. 144.
20. Ibid., p. 146.
21. Wu Chen-tsou, op. cit. p. 192.
22. When counting the number of higher education students, those who enroll in Grades 1, 2 and 3 at 5-year junior colleges are excluded in this paper since they are not really at the post-secondary level.
23. They are: National Chengchi University, National Tsinghua University, National Chiautung University, National Central University, National Chungshan University, Soochow University, and Fujen University.
24. They are: National Cheng Kung University, National Chungshin University, and National Taiwan Normal University.
25. Ministry of Education, *Educational Statistics of the Republic of China* (Taipei, 1987), p. x.
26. Ibid., pp. 148–155, 199.
27. Department of Higher Education, Ministry of Education. *Ta hsueh pi shiu keh mu piao* [Required Courses for the College] (Taipei, 1983), p. 3.
28. Ibid., p. 1.
29. Ibid., pp. 2–3.
30. Kuo Wen-fan, *Jen wen chu yi te chiao yu hsin nian* [The Educational Beliefs of the Humanism] (Taipei, Wu Nan Publishing Co. Ltd., 1982). p. 49.
31. Lu Mei-yuan. "Wuo kuo ta hsueh chiao yu ping chien chih yian chiu" [A Study on the Evaluation of Higher Education in the Republic of China] (Master thesis, National Taiwan Normal University, 1982), p. 178.
32. Charles H. C. Kao, "Taiwan's Brain Drain," in James Hsiung and others, ed., *Contemporary Republic of China: Taiwan Experience 1950-1980* (New York: American Association for Chinese Studies, 1981). p. 113.
33. For more information about Ministers of Education before 1978, please see Chang Wen-yi. "Chiao yu pu chang kao" [A Study on the Ministers of Education] *Chin Jih Chiao Yu* [Education Today], 34 (June, 1978), pp. 94–106.
34. Data was obtained from Department of Higher Education, Ministry of Education, Republic of China.